Western Society: A Brief History

WESTERN SOCIETY:
A Brief History

John P. McKay
University of Illinois at Urbana-Champaign

Bennett D. Hill
Late of Georgetown University

John Buckler
University of Illinois at Urbana-Champaign

Clare Haru Crowston
University of Illinois at Urbana-Champaign

Merry E. Wiesner-Hanks
University of Wisconsin–Milwaukee

Bedford/St. Martin's

Boston   New York

For Bedford/St. Martin's

Publisher for History: Mary Dougherty
Director of Development for History: Jane Knetzger
Executive Editor for History: Traci Mueller
Senior Production Editor: Rosemary R. Jaffe
Senior Production Supervisor: Joe Ford
Executive Marketing Manager: Jenna Bookin Barry
Associate Editor for History: Lynn Sternberger
Production Assistants: David Ayers and Lidia MacDonald-Carr
Copyeditor: Peggy Flanagan
Text Design: Cia Boynton
Photo Research: Carole Frohlich
Indexer: Jake Kawatski
Cover Design: Donna Lee Dennison
Cover Art: The Fruit Seller by Jan Victors (1620–1676). Oil on canvas, Johnny van Haeften Gallery, London, U.K. The Bridgeman Art Library.
Cartography: Charlotte Miller/GeoNova
Composition: NK Graphics
Printing and Binding: RR Donnelley and Sons

President: Joan E. Feinberg
Editorial Director: Denise B. Wydra
Director of Marketing: Karen R. Soeltz
Director of Editing, Design, and Production: Marcia Cohen
Assistant Director of Editing, Design, and Production: Elise S. Kaiser
Managing Editor: Elizabeth M. Schaaf

Library of Congress Control Number: 2008928070

Manufactured in the United States of America.
4 3 2 1 0 9
f e d c b a

For information, write: Bedford/St. Martin's, 75 Arlington Street, Boston, MA 02116 (617-399-4000)

ISBN-10: 0–312–68299–9 ISBN-13: 978–0–312–68299–6 (combined edition)
ISBN-10: 0–312–68300–6 ISBN-13: 978–0–312–68300–9 (Vol. I)
ISBN-10: 0–312–68301–4 ISBN-13: 978–0–312–68301–6 (Vol. II)

Published and distributed outside North America by:
MACMILLAN PRESS LTD.
Houndmills, Basingstoke, Hampshire RG21 2XS and London
Companies and representatives throughout the world.
ISBN 10: 0–230–59453–0 ISBN 13: 978–0–230–59453–1

Preface

The first edition of *A History of Western Society* grew out of our desire to infuse new life into the study of Western civilization. We knew that historians were using imaginative questions and innovative research to open up vast new areas of historical interest and knowledge. We also recognized that these advances had dramatically affected the subject of European economic, cultural, and, especially, social history, while new scholarship and fresh interpretations were also revitalizing the study of the traditional mainstream of political, diplomatic, and religious developments. Our goal was to write a textbook that reflected these dynamic changes, and we have been gratified by the tremendous response to this book on the part of both instructors and students.

This version of the textbook—*Western Society: A Brief History*—reflects the same goals and approach of its full-length counterpart. But its brevity addresses the needs of a growing number of instructors whose students need a less comprehensive text, either because of increased supplemental reading in the course or because their students benefit from less detail in order to grasp key developments. It also suits courses that cover the entire history of Western civilization in one semester. Finally, its lower price makes it an affordable alternative to larger texts, and the retention of a particularly strong illustration and map program and a full program of pedagogical support make the book a particularly good value.

In developing *Western Society: A Brief History*, we shortened our full-length narrative by thirty percent. We began by judiciously reducing coverage of subjects of secondary importance. We also condensed and combined thematically related sections and aimed throughout the text to tighten our exposition while working hard to retain our topical balance, up-to-date scholarship, and lively, accessible writing style. The result, we believe, is a concise edition that preserves the narrative flow, balance, and power of the full-length work.

Central Themes and Approach

It was our conviction, based on considerable experience introducing large numbers of students to the broad sweep of Western civilization, that a book in which social history was the core element could excite readers and inspire a renewed interest in history. Therefore we incorporated recent research by social historians as we sought to re-create the life of ordinary people in appealing human terms. At the same time, we were determined to give great economic, political, cultural, and intellectual developments the attention they unquestionably deserve. We wanted to give individual readers a balanced, integrated perspective so that they could pursue—on their own or in the classroom—those themes and questions that they found particularly exciting and significant.

In an effort to realize fully the potential of our innovative yet balanced approach, we made many changes, large and small, in the editions that followed the original publication of *A History of Western Society*. In particular, we approached the history of the West as part of the history of the world, devoting more attention throughout the book to Europe's interactions with other cultures and societies. Too, we took advantage of the exciting recent scholarship on women's and gender history to provide even fuller discussion of the role of gender in the shaping of human experience. Producing this briefer edition gave us the opportunity to bring even more clarity and focus to our core themes and approach.

Pedagogy and Features

We know from our own teaching that students need and welcome help in assimilating information and acquiring critical-thinking skills. Thus we retained the class-tested learning and teaching aids of the parent text while adding more such features. Each chapter opens by posing four or five historical questions keyed to its main sections in a clearly defined *chapter preview* that accompanies the chapter introduction. The relevant questions appear at the start of the chapter's main sections, all of which conclude with a *section review* that encapsulates the material presented and provides an answer to the question. Then a carefully crafted *chapter review* at the close of each chapter reprises the chapter questions and summary answers.

In other measures to promote clarity and comprehension, bolded *key terms* in the text are defined in the margin next to their appearance and repeated at the end of the chapter, and confidence-building *phonetic spellings* are located directly after terms that readers are likely to find hard to pronounce. *Chapter chronologies* alert students to the major developments discussed in the chapter and *topic-specific chronologies* appear at key points throughout the book.

We are particularly proud of the illustrative component of our work, its *art and map programs*. Over 340 illustrations, many of them in full color and all contemporaneous with the subject matter—reveal to today's visually attuned students how the past speaks in pictures as well as in words. Recognizing students' difficulties with geography, we also offer over 65 full-color maps and the popular *"Mapping the Past"* chapter feature, which provides questions that encourage students' close investigation of one map in each chapter, often with prompts to compare it to other maps in order to appreciate change over time. Substantive captions for all our illustrations help students to make the most of these informative materials.

We are proud as well of the biographical and primary-source special features that appear in each chapter to spotlight our focus on social history. These were so well received by readers of the full-length edition that we determined to keep them in our concise account.

Each chapter features *"Individuals in Society,"* an illustrated biographical essay of a woman, man, or group intended to extend the chapter narrative while showing students the similarities and differences between these former lives and their own. This special feature evidences our focus on people, both famous and obscure, and we believe that student readers will empathize with these human beings as they themselves seek to define their own identities. Examples include Bithus, a typical Roman soldier (Chapter 6), the German abbess and mystic Hildegard of Bingen (Chapter 10), freed slave and abolitionist Olaudah Equiano (Chapter 19), and Tariq Ramadan, the controversial European-Muslim intellectual (Chapter 31). "Questions for Analysis" guide students' consideration of the historical significance of these figures. For a complete list of the individuals highlighted, see page xxvii.

Each chapter also includes a one- or two-page feature titled *"Listening to the Past,"* chosen to extend and illuminate a major historical issue raised in the chapter through the presentation of a single original source or several voices on the subject. Each "Listening to the Past" selection opens with a problem-setting introduction and closes with "Questions for Analysis" that invite students to evaluate the evidence as historians would. Selected for their interest and importance and carefully fitted into their historical context, these sources, we hope, do indeed allow students to "listen to the past" and to observe how history has been shaped by individual men and women, some of them great aristocrats, others ordinary folk. Sources include Gilgamesh's quest for immortality (Chapter 1), an Arab view of the Crusades (Chapter 9), parliamentary testimony of young British mine workers (Chapter 22), and Simone de Beauvoir's critique of marriage (Chapter 30). A full list of these features appears on page xxvii.

The complete volume presents eight photo essays entitled *"Images in Society."* Each consists of a short narrative with questions, accompanied by several pictures. The goal of the feature is to encourage students to think critically: to view and compare visual illustrations and draw conclusions about the societies and cultures that produced those objects. Thus, in Chapter 1 appears the discovery of the "Iceman," the frozen remains of an unknown herdsman. "The Roman Villa at Chedworth" in Britain mirrors Roman provincial culture (Chapter 6). The essay "From Romanesque to Gothic" treats the architectural shift in medieval church building and aims to show how the Gothic cathedral reflected the ideals and values of medieval society (Chapter 11). "Art in the Reformation" (Chapter 14) examines both the Protestant and Catholic views of religious art. Chapter 17 presents the way monarchs displayed their authority visually in "Absolutist Palace Building." Moving to modern times, the focus in Chapter 19 changes to "London: The Remaking of a Great City," which depicts how Londoners rebuilt their city after a great catastrophe. "Class and Gender Boundaries in Women's Fashion, 1850–1914" studies women's clothing in relationship to women's evolving position in society and gender relations (Chapter 24). Finally, "Pablo Picasso and Modern Art" looks at some of Picasso's greatest paintings to gain insight into his principles and the modernist revolution in art (Chapter 28).

Supplements

To aid in the teaching and learning processes, a wide array of print and electronic supplements for students and instructors accompanies *Western Society: A Brief History*. Some of the materials are available for the first time with our new publisher, Bedford/St. Martin's. For more information on popular value packages and available materials, please visit bedfordstmartins.com/mckaywestbrief/catalog or contact your local Bedford/St. Martin's representative.

For Students

Print Resources

The Bedford Series in History and Culture.   Over 100 titles in this highly praised series combine first-rate scholarship, historical narrative, and important primary documents for undergraduate courses. Each book is brief, inexpensive, and focuses on a specific topic or period. Package discounts are available.

Rand McNally Atlas of Western Civilization.   This collection of over fifty full-color maps highlights social, political, and cross-cultural change and interaction from classical Greece and Rome to the post-industrial Western world. Each map is thoroughly indexed for fast reference.

The Bedford Glossary for European History.   This handy supplement for the survey course gives students historically contextualized definitions for hundreds of terms—from Abbasids to Zionism—that students will encounter in lectures, reading, and exams. Available free when packaged with the text.

Trade Books.   Titles published by sister companies Farrar, Straus and Giroux; Henry Holt and Company; Hill and Wang; Picador; St. Martin's Press; and Palgrave are available at a 50 percent discount when packaged with Bedford/St. Martin's textbooks. For more information, visit bedfordstmartins.com/tradeup.

New Media Resources

WESTERN SOCIETY: A BRIEF HISTORY e-Book.   This electronic version of *Western Society: A Brief History* offers students unmatched value—the complete text of the print book, with easy-to-use highlighting, searching, and note-taking tools, at a significantly reduced price.

Online Study Guide at bedfordstmartins.com/mckaywestbrief.   The popular Online Study Guide for *Western Society: A Brief History* is a free and uniquely personalized learning tool to help students master themes and information presented in the textbook and improve their critical-thinking skills. Assessment quizzes let students evaluate their comprehension, a flashcard activity tests students' knowledge of key terms, and learning objectives help students focus on key points of each chapter. Instructors can monitor students' progress through the online Quiz Gradebook or receive e-mail updates.

Benjamin, A Student's Online Guide to History Reference Sources at bedfordstmartins .com/mckaywestbrief.**   This Web site provides links to history-related databases, indexes, and journals, plus contact information for state, provincial, local, and professional history organizations.

The Bedford Bibliographer at bedfordstmartins.com/mckaywestbrief.**   *The Bedford Bibliographer*, a simple but powerful Web-based tool, assists students with the process of collecting sources and generates bibliographies in four commonly used documentation styles.

The Bedford Research Room at bedfordstmartins.com/mckaywestbrief.**   *The Research Room*, drawn from Mike Palmquist's *The Bedford Researcher*, offers a wealth of resources— including interactive tutorials, research activities, student writing samples, and links to hundreds of other places online—to support students in courses across the disciplines. The site also offers instructors a library of helpful instructional tools.

Diana Hacker's Research and Documentation Online at bedfordstmartins.com/ mckaywestbrief.**   This Web site provides clear advice on how to integrate primary and secondary sources into research papers, how to cite sources correctly, and how to format in MLA, APA, *Chicago*, or CBE style.

The St. Martin's Tutorial on Avoiding Plagiarism at bedfordstmartins.com/ mckaywestbrief.**   This online tutorial reviews the consequences of plagiarism and explains what sources to acknowledge, how to keep good notes, how to organize research, and how to integrate sources appropriately. The tutorial includes exercises to help students practice integrating sources and recognizing acceptable summaries.

For Instructors

Print Resources

Instructor's Resource Manual.   This helpful manual offers both first-time and experienced teachers a wealth of tools for structuring and customizing Western civilization history courses of different sizes. For each chapter in the textbook, the manual includes a set of instructional objectives; a chapter outline; lecture suggestions; suggestions on using primary sources in the classroom; a list of classroom activities; a suggested map activity; an audiovisual bibliography; a list of internet resources; and an annotated list of suggested reading.

New Media Resources

Instructor's Resource CD-ROM. This disc provides instructors with ready-made and customizable PowerPoint multimedia presentations built around chapter outlines, maps, figures, and selected images from the textbook, plus jpeg versions of all maps, figures, and selected images suitable for printing onto transparency acetates. Also included are chapter questions formatted in PowerPoint for use with i>clicker, a classroom response system, as well as outline maps.

Computerized Test Bank. This test bank CD-ROM offers instructors a flexible and powerful tool for test generation and test management. The test bank offers key term identification, essay questions, multiple choice questions with page references and feedback, map questions that refer to maps in the text, and a sample final exam. Instructors can customize quizzes, add or edit both questions and answers, and export questions and answers into a variety of formats, including WebCT and Blackboard.

Book Companion Site at bedfordstmartins.com/mckaywestbrief. The companion Web site gathers all the electronic resources for the text, including the Online Study Guide and related Quiz Gradebook, at a single Web address. Convenient links to PowerPoint chapter outlines and maps, an online version of the Instructor's Resource Manual, the digital libraries at Make History, and PowerPoint chapter questions for i>clicker, a classroom response system, are also available from this site.

Make History at bedfordstmartins.com/mckaywestbrief. Comprising the content of Bedford/St. Martin's acclaimed online libraries—*Map Central*, the Bedford History Image Library, DocLinks, and HistoryLinks—*Make History* provides one-stop access to relevant digital content including maps, images, documents, and Web links. Students and instructors alike can search this free, easy-to-use database by keyword, topic, date, or specific chapter of *Western Society: A Brief History*. Instructors can create collections of content and post their collections to the Web to share with students.

Content for Course Management Systems. A variety of student and instructor resources developed for this textbook are ready to use in course management systems such as WebCT, Blackboard, and other platforms. This e-content includes nearly all of the offerings from the book's Online Study Guide as well as the book's test bank.

Videos and Multimedia. A wide assortment of videos and multimedia CD-ROMs on various topics in European history is available to qualified adopters.

Acknowledgments

It is a pleasure to thank the many instructors who read and critiqued the manuscript for the ninth edition of the parent text, from which this version is derived:

Hugh Agnew, George Washington University
Melanie Bailey, Centenary College of Louisiana
Rachael Ball, Ohio State University
Eugene Boia, Cleveland State University
Robert Brown, State University of New York, Finger Lakes Community College
Richard Eichman, Sauk Valley Community College
David Fisher, Texas Technical University
Wayne Hanley, West Chester University of Pennsylvania
Michael Leggiere, Louisiana State University, Shreveport
John Mauer, Tri-County Technical College
Nick Miller, Boise State University
Wyatt Moulds, Jones County Junior College
Elsa Rapp, Montgomery County Community College
Anne Rodrick, Wofford College
Sonia Sorrell, Pepperdine University
Lee Shai Weissbach, University of Louisville

It is also a pleasure to thank our many editors for their efforts on this edition. To Carol Newman and Rosemary Jaffe, who guided production, and to Tonya Lobato, our development editor, we express our special appreciation. And we thank Carole Frohlich for her contributions in photo research and selection as well as Doug McGetchin of Florida Atlantic University and Cynthia Ward for their editorial contributions.

Many of our colleagues at the University of Illinois and the University of Wisconsin–Milwaukee continue to provide information and stimulation, often without even knowing it. We thank them for it. In addition, John McKay thanks JoAnn McKay for her unfailing support and encouragement. John Buckler thanks Professor Jack Cargill for his advice on topics in Chapter 2. He also thanks Professor Nicholas Yalouris, former General Inspector of Antiquities, for his kind permission to publish the mosaic from Elis, Greece in Chapter 3. He is likewise grateful to Dr. Amy C. Smith, Curator of the Ure Museum of Archaeology of the University of Reading, for her permission to publish the vase also in Chapter 3. His sincerest thanks go also to Professor Paul Cartledge of Clare College, Cambridge University, for his kind permission to publish his photograph of the statue of Leonidas in Chapter 3. Clare Crowston thanks Ali Banihashem, Max Edelson, Tara Fallon, John Lynn, Dana Rabin, and John Randolph. Merry Wiesner-Hanks thanks Jeffrey Merrick, Carlos Galvao-Sobrinho, and Gwynne Kennedy.

Each of us has benefited from the criticism of his or her coauthors, although each of us assumes responsibility for what he or she has written. Originally, John Buckler wrote the first six chapters; Bennett Hill continued the narrative through Chapter 16; and John McKay wrote Chapters 17 through 31. Beginning with the ninth edition of the parent text and continuing with this brief edition, Merry Wiesner-Hanks assumed primary responsibility for Chapters 7 through 14, and Clare Crowston took responsibility for Chapters 15 through 21.

Finally, we continue to welcome the many comments and suggestions that have come from our readers, for they have helped us greatly in this ongoing endeavor.

J. P. M.   J. B.   C. H. C.   M. E. W.

Brief Contents

Contents

12

The Crisis of the Later Middle Ages, 1300–1450
277

13

European Society in the Age of the Renaissance, 1350–1550
307

14

Reformations and Religious Wars, 1500–1600
337

15

European Exploration and Conquest, 1450–1650

370

16

Absolutism and Constitutionalism in Western Europe, ca. 1589–1715

401

30
Cold War Conflicts and Social Transformations, 1945–1985   781

31
Revolution, Rebuilding, and New Challenges: 1985 to the Present   810

Maps, Figures, and Tables

FIGURES

TABLES

Features

About the Authors

John P. McKay Born in St. Louis, John P. McKay received his B.A. from Wesleyan University (1961), his M.A. from the Fletcher School of Law and Diplomacy (1962), and his Ph.D. from the University of California, Berkeley (1968). He began teaching history at the University of Illinois in 1966 and became a Professor there in 1976. John won the Herbert Baxter Adams Prize for his book *Pioneers for Profit: Foreign Entrepreneurship and Russian Industrialization, 1885–1913* (1970). He has also written *Tramways and Trolleys: The Rise of Urban Mass Transport in Europe* (1976) and has translated Jules Michelet's *The People* (1973). His research has been supported by fellowships from the Ford Foundation, the Guggenheim Foundation, the National Endowment for the Humanities, and IREX. He has written well over a hundred articles, book chapters, and reviews, which have appeared in numerous publications, including *The American Historical Review, Business History Review, The Journal of Economic History,* and *Slavic Review.* He contributed extensively to C. Stewart and P. Fritzsche, eds., *Imagining the Twentieth Century* (1997).

Bennett D. Hill A native of Philadelphia, Bennett D. Hill earned an A.B. from Princeton (1956) and advanced degrees from Harvard (A.M., 1958) and Princeton (Ph.D., 1963). He taught history at the University of Illinois, where he was department chair from 1978 to 1981. He published *English Cistercian Monasteries and Their Patrons in the Twelfth Century* (1968), *Church and State in the Middle Ages* (1970), and articles in *Analecta Cisterciensia, The New Catholic Encyclopaedia, The American Benedictine Review,* and *The Dictionary of the Middle Ages.* His reviews appeared in *The American Historical Review, Speculum, The Historian,* the *Journal of World History,* and *Library Journal.* He was one of the contributing editors to *The Encyclopedia of World History* (2001). He was a Fellow of the American Council of Learned Societies and served on the editorial board of *The American Benedictine Review,* on committees of the National Endowment for the Humanities, and as vice president of the American Catholic Historical Association (1995–1996). A Benedictine monk of St. Anselm's Abbey in Washington, D.C., he was also a Visiting Professor at Georgetown University.

John Buckler Born in Louisville, Kentucky, John Buckler received his Ph.D. from Harvard University in 1973. In 1980 Harvard University Press published his *Theban Hegemony, 371–362 B.C.* He published *Philip II and the Sacred War* (Leiden 1989) and also edited *BOIOTIKA: Vorträge vom 5. Internationalen Böotien-Kolloquium* (Munich 1989). In 2003 he published *Aegean Greece in the Fourth Century B.C.* In the following year appeared his editions of W. M. Leake, *Travels in the Morea* (three volumes), and Leake's *Peloponnesiaca.* Cambridge University Press published his *Central Greece and the Politics of Power in the Fourth Century,* edited by Hans Beck, in 2008.

Clare Haru Crowston Born in Cambridge, Massachusetts, and raised in Toronto, Clare Haru Crowston received her B.A. in 1985 from McGill University and her Ph.D. in 1996 from Cornell University. Since 1996, she has taught at the University of Illinois, where she has served as associate chair and Director of Graduate Studies, and is currently Associate Professor of history. She is the author of *Fabricating Women: The Seamstresses of Old Regime France, 1675–1791* (Duke University Press, 2001), which won two awards, the Berkshire Prize and the Hagley Prize. She edited two special issues of the *Journal of Women's History* (vol. 18, nos. 3 and 4) and has published numerous articles and reviews in journals such as *Annales: Histoire, Sciences Sociales, French Historical Studies, Gender and History*, and the *Journal of Economic History*. Her research has been supported with grants from the National Endowment for the Humanities, the Mellon Foundation, and the Bourse Châteaubriand of the French government. She is a past president of the Society for French Historical Studies and a former chair of the Pinkney Prize Committee.

Merry E. Wiesner-Hanks   Having grown up in Minneapolis, Merry E. Wiesner-Hanks received her B.A. from Grinnell College in 1973 (as well as an honorary doctorate some years later), and her Ph.D. from the University of Wisconsin–Madison in 1979. She taught first at Augustana College in Illinois, and since 1985 at the University of Wisconsin–Milwaukee, where she is currently UWM Distinguished Professor in the department of history. She is the co-editor of the *Sixteenth Century Journal* and the author or editor of nineteen books and many articles that have appeared in English, German, Italian, Spanish, and Chinese. These include *Early Modern Europe, 1450–1789* (Cambridge, 2006), *Women and Gender in Early Modern Europe* (Cambridge, 3d ed., 2008), and *Gender in History* (Blackwell, 2001). She currently serves as the Chief Reader for Advanced Placement World History and has also written a number of source books for use in the college classroom, including *Discovering the Western Past* (Houghton Mifflin, 6th ed, 2007) and *Discovering the Global Past* (Houghton Mifflin, 3d. ed., 2006), and a book for young adults, *An Age of Voyages, 1350–1600* (Oxford 2005).

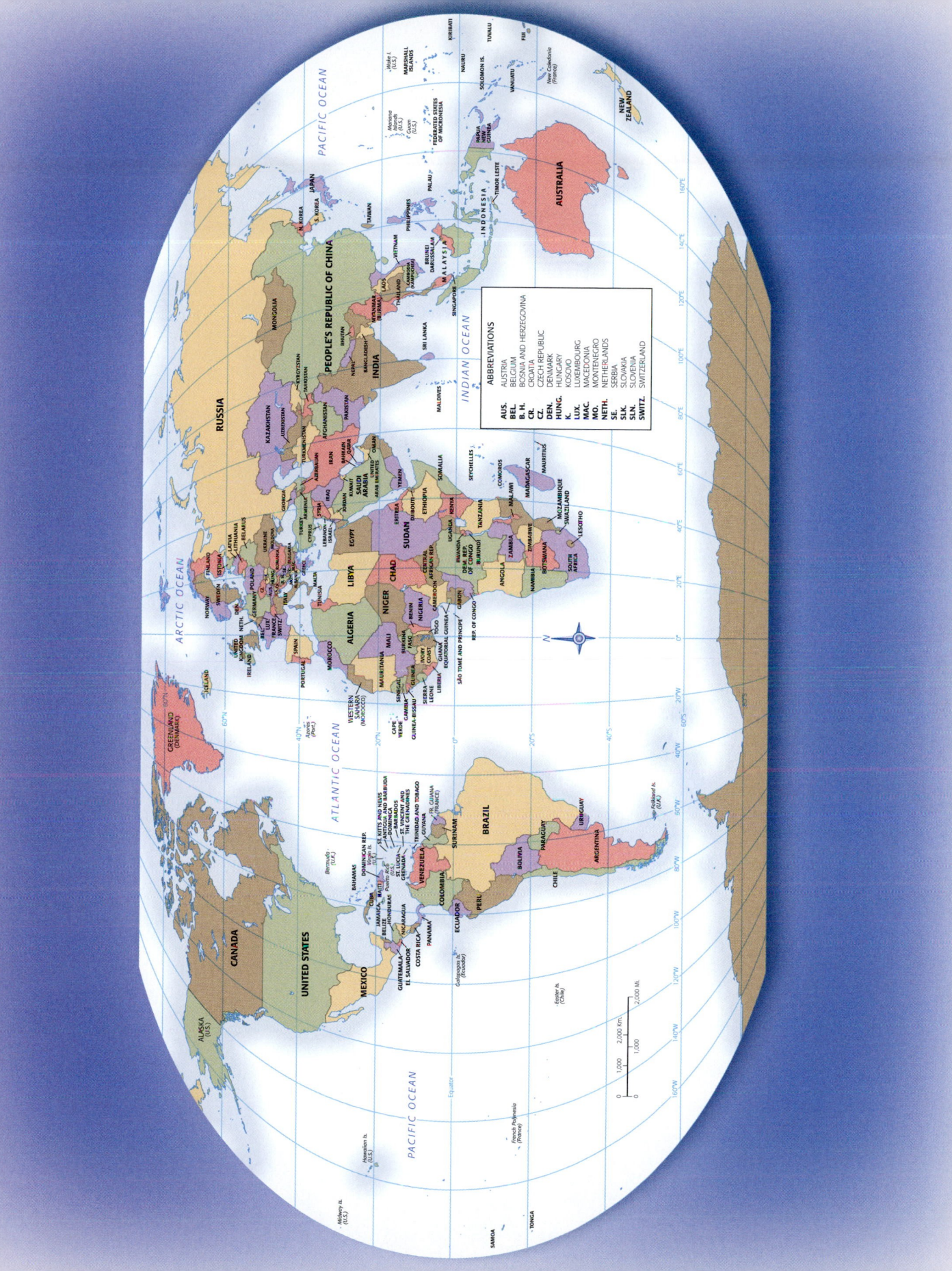

Western Society: A Brief History

CHAPTER 1

Origins

ca. 400,000–1100 B.C.E.

Osiris. Egyptian lord of life and death, powerful and serene, here depicted in his full regalia. (G. Dagli-Orti/The Art Archive)

The civilization and cultures of the modern Western world, like great rivers, have many sources. Peoples in western Europe developed numerous communities uniquely their own but also sharing some common features. They mastered such diverse subjects as astronomy, mathematics, geometry, trigonometry, engineering, religious practices, and social organization. Yet the earliest of these peoples did not record their learning and lore in systems of writing. Their lives and customs are consequently largely lost to us.

Other early peoples confronted many of the same basic challenges as those in Europe. They also made progress, but they took the important step of recording their experiences in writing. The most enduring innovations occurred in the ancient Near East, a region that includes the lands bordering the Mediterranean's eastern shore, the Arabian peninsula, parts of northeastern Africa, and perhaps above all, Mesopotamia, the area of modern Iraq. Fundamental to the development of Western civilization and culture was the invention of writing by the Sumerians, which allowed knowledge of the past to be preserved. It also facilitated the spread and accumulation of learning, science, and literature. Ancient Near Eastern civilizations also produced the first written law codes, as well as religious concepts that still permeate daily life.

From Caves to Towns

How did early peoples evolve from bands of hunter-gatherers to settled farming communities?

Virtually every day brings startling news about the path of human evolution. We now know that by about 400,000 B.C.E. early peoples were making primitive stone tools, which has led historians to refer to this time as the **Paleolithic (pay-lee-oh-LITH-ik) period.** During this period, which lasted until about 7000 B.C.E., people survived as gatherers and hunters, usually dwelling in caves or temporary shelters. These **nomads (NO-madz)** led roaming lives, always in search of new food sources. (See the feature "Images in Society: The Iceman.")

Settled communities began to emerge in the **Neolithic (nee-oh-LITH-ik) period,** usually dated between 7000 and 3000 B.C.E. The term *Neolithic* stems from the new stone tools that came into use at that time. People used these tools to manage crops and animals, leading to fundamental changes in civilization.

Sustained agriculture made possible a stable and secure life. With this settled routine came the evolution of towns and eventually of cities. Neolithic farmers usually raised more food than they could consume, so their surpluses permitted larger, healthier populations. Population growth in turn created an even greater reliance on settled farming, as only systematic agriculture could sustain the increased numbers of people. Since surpluses of food could also be bartered for other commodities, the Neolithic era witnessed the beginnings of the large-scale exchange of goods. Neolithic farmers also improved their tools and agricultural techniques. They domesticated bigger, stronger animals to work for them, invented the plow, and developed new mutations of seeds. By 3000 B.C.E. they had invented the wheel. Agricultural surpluses also made possible the division of labor. It freed some people to become artisans who made tools, pottery vessels, woven baskets, clothing, and jewelry. In short, life became more complex yet also more comfortable for many.

These developments generally led to the further evolution of towns and a whole new way of life. People not necessarily related to one another created rudimentary

Paleolithic period The time between 400,000 and 7000 B.C.E., when early peoples began making primitive stone tools, survived by hunting and gathering, and dwelled in temporary shelters.

nomads Homeless, independent people who lead roaming lives, always in search of pasturage for their flocks.

Neolithic period The period between 7000 and 3000 B.C.E. that serves as the dividing line between anthropology and history; the term itself refers to the new stone tools that came into use at this time.

Stonehenge
Seen in regal isolation, Stonehenge sits among the stars and in April 1997 was along the path of the comet Hale-Bopp. Long before Druids existed, a Neolithic society laboriously built this circle to mark the passing of the seasons. (Jim Burgess)

governments that transcended the family. These governments, led by a recognized central authority, made decisions that channeled the shared wisdom, physical energy, and resources of the whole population toward a common goal. These societies made their decisions according to custom, the generally accepted norms of traditional conduct. Here was the beginning of law. Towns also meant life in individual houses or groups of them, which led to greater personal independence. People erected public buildings and religious monuments, evidence of their growing wealth and communal cooperation. Some of these groups also protected their possessions and themselves by raising walls.

A mute but engaging glimpse of a particular Neolithic society can be seen today in southern England. Between 4700 and 2000 B.C.E. arose the Stonehenge (**STOHN-henj**) people, named after the famous stone circle on Salisbury (**SAWLZ-ber-ee**) Plain. Though named after a single spot, this culture spread throughout Great Britain, Ireland, and Brittany in France. Stonehenge and neighboring sites reveal the existence of prosperous, well-organized, and centrally led communities that were able to pool material and human resources in order to raise the circles. Stonehenge indicates an intellectual world that encompassed astronomy, the environment, and religion. The circle is oriented toward the midwinter sunset and the midsummer sunrise. It thus marked the clocklike celestial change of the seasons. This silent evidence proves the existence of a society prosperous enough to endure over long periods during which lore about heaven and earth could be passed along to successive generations. It also demonstrates that these communities considered themselves members of a wider world that they shared with the deities of nature and the broader universe.

Section Review

- Human communities evolved from bands of hunter-gatherers in the Paleolithic period (until 7000 B.C.E.) to stable farming communities in the Neolithic period (7000–3000 B.C.E.).

- Neolithic innovations included stone tools, the wheel, large-scale exchange of goods, and greater complexity, including division of labor.

- Agricultural surpluses allowed the evolution of towns, government, and law.

- Prosperous, well-organized communities led to the contruction of sophisticated sites such as Stonehenge.

Mesopotamian Civilization

How did the Sumerians create a complex society in the arid climate of Mesopotamia?

The origins of Western civilization are generally traced to an area that is today not seen as part of the West: Mesopotamia (**mes-oh-puh-TAY-mee-uh**), the Greek name for the land between the Euphrates (**you-FRAY-teez**) and Tigris (**TIE-gris**) Rivers. There the arid climate confronted the peoples with the hard problem of farming with scant water supplies. Farmers learned to irrigate their land and later to drain it to prevent the buildup of salt in the soil. **Irrigation** on a large scale, like

irrigation The solution to the problem of arid climates and scant water supplies, a system of watering land and draining to prevent buildup of salt in the soil.

building stone circles in Western Europe, demanded organized group effort. That in turn underscored the need for
strong central authority to direct it. This corporate spirit led
to governments in which individuals subordinated some of
their particular concerns to broader interests. These factors
made urban life possible in a demanding environment. By
about 3000 B.C.E. the Sumerians (SOO-mehr-ee-uhnz),
whose origins are mysterious, established a number of cities
in the southernmost part of Mesopotamia, which became
known as Sumer (see Map 1.1). The fundamental innovation of the Sumerians was the creation of writing, which
evolved from a tool for recording business transactions to the
means of promoting and preserving cultural ideas.

MAPPING THE PAST

MAP 1.1   Spread of Cultures in the Ancient Near East

This map depicts the area of ancient Mesopotamia and Egypt, a region
often called the "cradle of civilization." Map 1.2 on page 14 shows the
balance of power that later extended far beyond the regions depicted
in Map 1.1. **[1]** Does this expansion indicate why Mesopotamia and
Egypt earned the title of "cradle"? **[2]** What geographical features of
this region naturally suggest the direction in which civilization spread?
[3] Why did the first cultures of Mesopotamia spread farther than the
culture of Egypt spread?

CHRONOLOGY

3200 B.C.E.	Development of wheeled transport and invention of cuneiform writing
ca. 3200–2200 B.C.E.	Sumerian and Akkadian domination in Mesopotamia
ca. 3100 B.C.E.	Invention of Egyptian hieroglyphic writing
3100–ca. 1333 B.C.E.	Evolution of Egyptian polytheism and belief in personal immortality
3000–1000 B.C.E.	Origins and development of religion in Mesopotamia
ca. 2700–1000 B.C.E.	Arrival of Indo-European peoples in western Asia and Europe
ca. 2660–1640 B.C.E.	Old and Middle Kingdoms in Egypt
ca. 2600–1200 B.C.E.	Expansion of Mesopotamian trade with neighbors
ca. 2000–1595 B.C.E.	Babylonian empire in Mesopotamia
ca. 1790 B.C.E.	*Epic of Gilgamesh* and Hammurabi's law code
ca. 1600–1200 B.C.E.	Hittite power in Anatolia
ca. 1570–1075 B.C.E.	New Kingdom in Egypt
ca. 1400 B.C.E.	Development of Phoenician alphabet
ca. 1300–1100 B.C.E.	Increased use of iron in western Asia

The Iceman

On September 19, 1991, two German vacationers climbing in the Italian Alps came upon one of the most remarkable finds in European history: a corpse lying face-down and covered in ice (Image 1). They had stumbled on a mystery that still intrigues archaeologists and many others in the scientific world. After chiseling the body out of the ice, various specialists examined the man. Having died 5,300 years ago, he is the earliest and best-preserved corpse from the Neolithic period (Image 2).

The skin of most corpses found in glaciers appears white and waxy, but the skin of the Iceman, as he is generally known, was brown and dry. Forces of nature had so desiccated the body that it became mummified: the body, including the internal organs, was perfectly preserved. The Iceman's less perishable possessions also survived, so scientists were able to examine him almost as though he had died recently.

The Iceman was quite fit, was between twenty-five and thirty-five years of age, and stood about five feet two

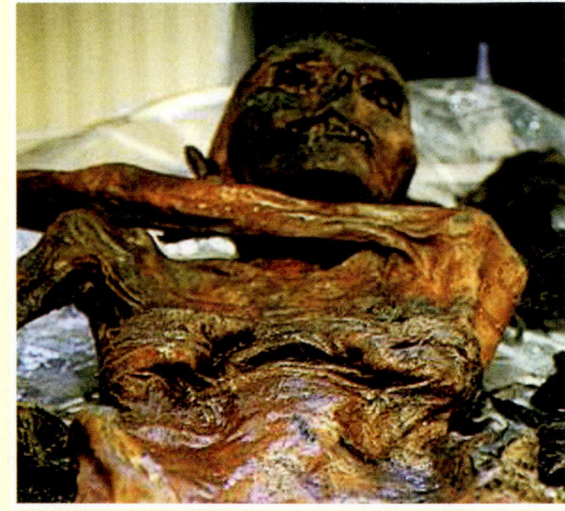

IMAGE 2 The Face of the Iceman   (Rex USA)

inches tall. The bluish tinge of his teeth showed that he had enjoyed a diet of milled grain, perhaps millet—and also showed that he came from an environment where

IMAGE 1 The Discovery of the Iceman   (Paul Hanny)

crops were grown. He wore an unlined robe of animal skins that he had stitched together with careful needle-work, using thread made of grass, which he probably had made for himself. Over his robe he wore a cape of grass, very much like capes worn by shepherds in this region as late as the early twentieth century (even as late as the Second World War German soldiers stuffed straw into their boots to withstand the fierce Russian cold). The Iceman also wore a furry cap.

The equipment discovered with the Iceman demon-strates his mastery of several technologies. He carried a hefty copper ax (a sign of stoneworking), but he seems to have relied chiefly on archery. In his quiver were nu-merous wooden arrow shafts and two finished arrows, all indicating a great deal of knowledge and ingenuity (Im-age 3). The arrows had flint heads (another sign of stoneworking), and feathers were attached with a resin-like glue to the ends of the shafts. These simple facts convey much information about the technological knowledge of this mysterious man. He knew how to work stone, he knew the value of feathers to direct the arrows, and he was fully aware of the basics of ballistics. He chose for his bow the wood of the yew, some of the best wood in central Europe. Yet yew trees do not grow everywhere, so the use of yew wood proves that the Ice-man had thoroughly explored his environment. He car-ried his necessary supplies in a primitive rucksack that he had made.

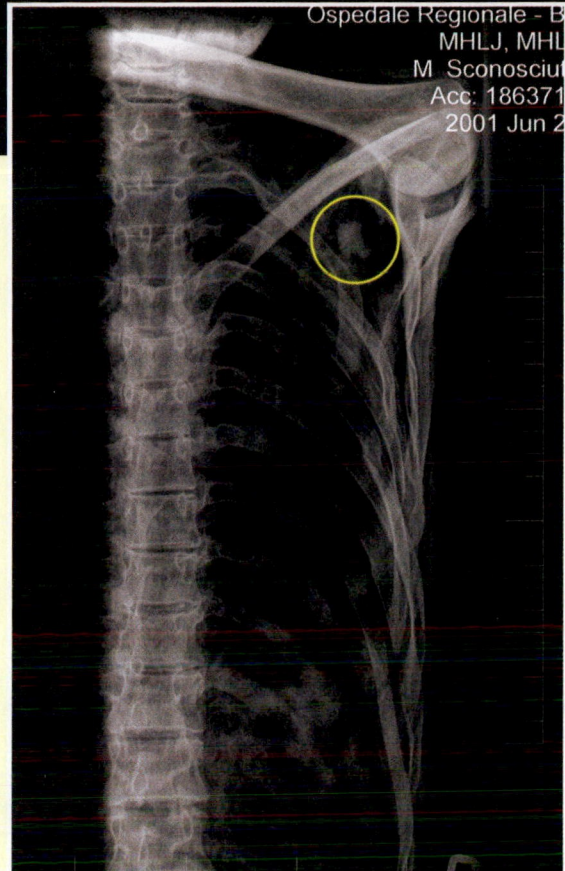

IMAGE 4 X-ray of the Iceman's Shoulder (South Tyrol Museum of Archaeology/AP Images)

One last mystery surrounds the Iceman. When his body was first discovered, scholars assumed that he was a hapless traveler overtaken by a fierce snowstorm. But a recent autopsy found an arrowhead lodged under his left shoulder (Image 4). The Iceman was not alone on his last day. Someone accompanied him, someone who shot him from below and behind. The Iceman is the victim in the first murder mystery of Western history.

Given this information, can you picture the circum-stances of the Iceman's discovery (Image 1)? What was he doing there? From Image 2 can you imagine how nature preserved his remains? From the picture of his arrows (Image 3) can you conclude anything about the Iceman's self-reliance? From Image 4 comes the evi-dence for the cause of his death. Does it necessarily prove that Neolithic society was as violent as ours?

IMAGE 3 The Iceman's Quiver (S.N.S./Sipa Press)

MEANING	PICTOGRAPH	IDEOGRAM	PHONETIC SIGN
A Star			
B Woman			
C Mountain			
D Slave woman			
E Water In			

FIGURE 1.1   Sumerian Writing

(*Source:* From S. N. Kramer, *The Sumerians: Their History, Culture and Character*, 1963. Reprinted by permission of the publisher, the University of Chicago Press.)

cuneiform   Sumerian form of writing (from the Latin term for "wedge-shaped"); used to describe the strokes of the stylus.

The Invention of Writing and the First Schools

The origins of writing probably go back to the ninth millennium B.C.E., when Near Eastern peoples used clay tokens as counters for record keeping. By the fourth millennium people had realized that drawing pictures of the tokens on clay was simpler than making tokens (see Figure 1.1). This breakthrough in turn suggested that more information could be conveyed by adding pictures of still other objects, resulting in a complex system of *pictographs*. These pictographs were the forerunners of a Sumerian form of writing known as **cuneiform** (**kyoo-NEE-uh-form**), from the Latin term for "wedge-shaped," used to describe the strokes of the stylus.

The next step was to simplify the system. Instead of drawing pictures, the scribe made *ideograms*: conventionalized signs that were generally understood to represent ideas. The sign for star could also be used to indicate heaven, sky, or even god. The real breakthrough came when the scribe learned to use signs to represent sounds. For instance, the scribe drew two parallel wavy lines to indicate the word *a* or "water" (line E). Besides water, the word *a* in Sumerian also meant "in." The word *in* expresses a relationship that is very difficult to represent pictorially. Instead of trying to invent a sign to mean "in," some clever scribe used the sign for water because the two words sounded alike. This phonetic use of signs made possible the combining of signs to convey abstract ideas.

The Sumerian system of writing was so complicated that only professional scribes mastered it after many years of study. By 2500 B.C.E. scribal schools flourished throughout Sumer. Most students came from wealthy families and were male. Each school had a master, teachers, and monitors. Discipline was strict, and students were caned for sloppy work and misbehavior. One graduate of a scribal school had few fond memories of the joy of learning:

> *My headmaster read my tablet, said:*
> *"There is something missing," caned me.*
>
> . . . .
>
> *The fellow in charge of silence said:*
> *"Why did you talk without permission," caned me.*
> *The fellow in charge of the assembly said:*
> *"Why did you stand at ease without permission," caned me.*[1]

Although Mesopotamian education was primarily intended to produce scribes for administrative work, schools were also centers of culture and scholarship.

Mesopotamian Thought and Religion

The building of cities, palaces, temples, and canals demanded practical knowledge of geometry and trigonometry. The Mesopotamians made significant advances in mathematics using a numerical system based on units of sixty, ten, and six. They also developed the concept of place value—that the value of a number depends on where it stands in relation to other numbers.

Mesopotamian medicine was a combination of magic, prescriptions, and surgery. Mesopotamians believed that demons and evil spirits caused sickness and that magic spells and prescriptions could drive them out. Over time, some prescriptions were found to work and thus were true medicines. In this slow but empirical fashion medicine grew from superstition to an early form of rational treatment.

The Sumerians originated many religious beliefs, and their successors added to them. The Mesopotamians were **polytheists** (POL-eh-thee-ists), that is, they believed that many gods run the world. However, they did not consider all gods and goddesses equal. Some deities had very important jobs, taking care of music, law, sex, and victory, while others had lesser tasks, overseeing leatherworking and basketweaving.

polytheism The worship of several gods; this was the tradition of Egyptian religion.

Mesopotamian gods were powerful and immortal and could make themselves invisible. Otherwise, Mesopotamian gods and goddesses were very human: they celebrated with food and drink, and they raised families. They enjoyed their own "Garden of Eden," a green and fertile place. They could be irritable, vindictive, and irresponsible. The motives of the gods were not always clear. In times of affliction one could only pray and offer sacrifices to appease them.

Encouraged and directed by the traditional priesthood, which was dedicated to understanding the ways of the gods, the people erected shrines in the center of each city and then built their houses around them. The best way to honor the gods was to make the shrine as grand and as impressive as possible, for gods who had a splendid temple might think twice about sending floods to destroy the city.

Ziggurat
The ziggurat is a stepped tower that dominated the landscape of the Sumerian city. Surrounded by a walled enclosure, it stood as a monument to the gods. Monumental stairs led to the top, where sacrifices were offered for the welfare of the community. (Corbis)

The Mesopotamians had many myths to account for the creation of the universe. According to one Sumerian myth (echoed in Genesis, the first book of the Bible), only the primeval sea existed at first. The sea produced heaven and earth, which were united. Heaven and earth gave birth to Enlil, who separated them and made possible the creation of the other gods. These myths are the earliest known attempts to answer the question "How did it all begin?"

In addition to myths, the Sumerians produced the first epic poem, the *Epic of Gilgamesh* (**GIL-guh-mesh**), which evolved as a reworking of at least five earlier myths. An epic poem is a narration of the achievements, labors, and sometimes the failures of heroes that embodies a people's or a nation's conception of its own past. The Sumerian epic recounts the wanderings of Gilgamesh—the semihistorical king of Uruk (**OO-rook**)—and his companion Enkidu (**EN-kee-doo**). It shows the Sumerians grappling with such enduring questions as life and death, humankind and deity, and immortality. (See the feature "Listening to the Past: A Quest for Immortality" on pages 22–23.)

nobles The top level of Sumerian society; consisted of the king and his family, the chief priests, and high palace officials.

clients Free men and women who were dependent on the nobility; in return for their labor they received small plots of land to work for themselves.

patriarchal Societies in which most power is held by older adult men, especially those from the elite groups.

Sumerian Social and Gender Divisions

Sumerian society was a complex arrangement of freedom and dependence, and its members were divided into four categories: nobles, slaves, clients, and commoners. **Nobles** consisted of the king and his family, the chief priests, and high palace officials. Generally, the king rose to power as a war leader elected by the citizenry; he established a regular army, trained it, and led it into battle. The might of the king and the frequency of warfare quickly made him the supreme figure in the city, and kingship soon became hereditary. The symbol of royal status was the palace, which rivaled the temple in grandeur.

The king and the lesser nobility held extensive tracts of land that were, like the estates of the temple, worked by slaves and clients. Slaves were prisoners of war, convicts, and debtors. While they were subject to whatever treatment their owners might mete out, they could engage in trade, make profits, and even buy their freedom. **Clients** were free men and women who were dependent on the nobility. In return for their labor, the clients received small plots of land to work for themselves. Although this arrangement assured the clients a livelihood, the land they worked remained the possession of the nobility or the temple. Commoners were free and could own land in their own right. Male commoners had a voice in the political affairs of the city and full protection under the law.

Each of these social categories included both men and women, but their experiences were not the same, for Sumerian society made clear distinctions based on gender. Sumerian society—and all Western societies that followed, until very recently—was **patriarchal** (**PAY-tree-AR-kal**), that is, most power was held by older adult men, especially those from the elite groups. Boys became the normal inheritors of family land. Women could sometimes inherit if there were no sons in a family, but they did not gain the political rights that came with land ownership for men.

The states that developed in the ancient Middle East, beginning with Sumer, further heightened gender distinctions. Laws governing sexual relations and marriage practices set up a very unequal relationship between spouses. Women were required to be virgins on marriage and were strictly punished for adultery; sexual relations outside of marriage on the part of husbands were not considered adultery. Religious concepts heightened gender distinctions. In some places heavenly hierarchies came to reflect those on earth, with a single male god, who was viewed as the primary creator of life, dominating the religious pantheon.

Section Review

- Early hunters created a stable life by relying on sustained agriculture that in turn led to the creation of villages and small towns.

- The Mesopotamian civilization of Sumer used irrigation and created a centrally organized urban society.

- Sumerian scribes, trained in schools where they were subject to corporal punishment, used wedge-shaped cuneiform writing to represent words and ideas phonetically.

- Sumerians developed mathematics, medicine, and their polytheistic religion, building temples to appease their hierarchical pantheon.

- The Sumerians produced the first epic poem, the *Epic of Gilgamesh*, about the wanderings of a king and his companion Enkidu.

- Sumerian society was patriarchal and divided between nobles, slaves, clients, and commoners.

The Spread of Mesopotamian Culture

How did the Babylonians unite Mesopotamia politically and culturally and spread that culture to the broader world?

The Sumerians established the basic social, economic, and intellectual patterns of Mesopotamia, but the Semites (**SEH-mites**) played a large part in spreading Sumerian culture far beyond the boundaries of Mesopotamia. The interaction of the Sumerians and Semites, in fact, gives one of the very first glimpses of a phenomenon that can still be seen today. History provides abundant evidence of peoples of different origins coming together, usually on the borders of an established culture. The outcome in these instances was the evolution of a new culture that consisted of two or more old parts. Although the older culture almost invariably looked on the newcomers as inferior, the new just as invariably contributed something valuable to the old. So it was in 2331 B.C.E. The Semitic chieftain Sargon conquered Sumer and created a new empire. The symbol of his triumph was a new capital, the city of Akkad (**AH-kahd**). Sargon, the first "world conqueror," led his armies to the Mediterranean Sea. Although his empire lasted only a few generations, it spread Mesopotamian culture throughout the Fertile Crescent, the belt of rich farmland that extends from Mesopotamia in the east up through Syria in the north and down to Egypt in the west (see Map 1.1).

The Triumph of Babylon

Although the empire of Sargon (**SAHR-gone**) was extensive, it was short-lived. It was left to the Babylonians to unite Mesopotamia politically and culturally. The Babylonians were Amorites (**AM-uh-rites**), a Semitic people who had migrated from Arabia and settled on the site of Babylon along the middle Euphrates, where that river runs close to the Tigris. Babylon enjoyed an excellent geographical position and was ideally suited to be the capital of Mesopotamia. It dominated trade on the Tigris and Euphrates Rivers: all commerce to and from Sumer and Akkad had to pass by its walls. It also looked beyond Mesopotamia. Babylonian merchants followed the Tigris north to Assyria (**uh-SEER-ee-uh**) and Anatolia. The Euphrates led merchants to Syria, Palestine, and the Mediterranean. The city grew to be great because of its commercial importance and soundly based power.

Babylon's king Hammurabi (**ham-moo-RAH-bee**) (r. 1792–1750 B.C.E.) set out to do three things: make Babylon secure, unify Mesopotamia, and win for the Babylonians a place in Mesopotamian civilization. The first two he accomplished by conquering Assyria in the north and Sumer and Akkad in the south. Then he turned to his third goal.

Politically, Hammurabi joined in his kingship the Semitic concept of the tribal chieftain and the Sumerian idea of urban kingship. Culturally, he encouraged the spread of myths that explained how the Babylonian god Marduk (**MAHR-dook**) had been elected king of the gods by the other Mesopotamian deities, thus making Babylon the religious center of Mesopotamia. Through Hammurabi's genius the Babylonians made their own contribution to Mesopotamian culture—a culture vibrant enough to maintain its identity while assimilating new influences. Hammurabi's conquests and the activity of Babylonian merchants spread this enriched culture north to Anatolia and west to Syria and Palestine.

law code A proclamation issued by the Babylonian king Hammurabi to establish law and justice in the language of the land, thereby prompting the welfare of the people; it inflicted harsh punishments, but despite its severity, was pervaded with a spirit of justice and sense of responsibility.

Life Under Hammurabi

One of Hammurabi's most memorable accomplishments was the proclamation of a **law code** that offers a wealth of information about daily life in Mesopotamia. Hammurabi's was not the first law code in Mesopotamia; indeed, the earliest goes back to about 2100 B.C.E. Like earlier lawgivers, Hammurabi proclaimed that he issued his laws on divine authority "to establish law and justice in the language of the land, thereby promoting the welfare of the people."

The Code of Hammurabi has two striking characteristics. First, the law differed according to the social status and gender of the offender. Nobles were not punished as harshly as commoners, nor commoners as harshly as slaves. Certain actions that were crimes for women were not crimes for men. Second, the code demanded that the punishment fit the crime. It called for "an eye for an eye, and a tooth for a tooth," at least among equals. However, a noble who destroyed the eye of a commoner or slave could pay a fine instead of losing his own eye. Otherwise, as long as criminal and victim shared the same social status, the victim could demand exact vengeance.

Hammurabi's code began with legal procedure. There were no public prosecutors or district attorneys, so individuals brought their own complaints before the court. Each side had to produce written documents or witnesses to support its case. For example, in cases of murder, the accuser had to prove the defendant guilty; any accuser who failed to do so was put to death. This strict law was designed to prevent people from lodging groundless charges.

Because farming was essential to Mesopotamian life, Hammurabi's code dealt extensively with agriculture. Farmers who rented land were required to keep the irrigation canals and ditches in good repair. Otherwise the land would be subject to floods and the owners would face crippling losses. Any tenant whose neglect of the canals resulted in damaged crops had to bear all the expense of the lost crops. Those tenants who could not pay the costs were forced into slavery.

Consumer protection is not a modern idea; it goes back to Hammurabi's day. Merchants had to guarantee the quality of their goods and services. A boatman who lost the owner's boat or sank someone else's boat replaced it and its cargo. House builders guaranteed their work with their lives. A merchant who tried to increase the interest rate on a loan forfeited the entire amount.

Hammurabi gave careful attention to marriage and the family. As elsewhere in the Near East, marriage had aspects of a business agreement. The prospective groom or his father offered the prospective bride's father a bridal gift, usually money. If the man and his bridal gift were acceptable, the father provided his daughter with a dowry. After marriage the dowry belonged to the woman (although the husband normally administered it) and was a means of protecting her rights and status. Once the two men agreed on financial matters, they drew up a contract; no marriage was considered legal without one. Fathers often contracted marriages

Law Code of Hammurabi

Hammurabi ordered his code to be inscribed on a stone pillar and set up in public. At the top of the pillar Hammurabi is depicted receiving the scepter of authority from the god Shamash. (Hirmer Verlag München)

while their children were still young, and once contracted, the children were considered to be wed even if they did not yet live together. The husband had virtually absolute power over his household. He could even sell his wife and children into slavery to pay debts. Any son who struck his father could have his hand cut off. A father was free to adopt children and include them in his will. Artisans sometimes adopted children to teach them the family trade.

Law codes, preoccupied as they are with the problems of society, provide a bleak view of things. Other documents give a happier glimpse of life. Although marriage was primarily an arrangement between families, evidence of romantic love survives in Mesopotamian poetry. Countless wills and testaments show that husbands habitually left their estates to their wives, who in turn willed the property to their children. Hammurabi's code restricted married women from commercial pursuits, but financial documents prove that many women engaged in business without hindrance. Some carried on the family business, while others became wealthy landowners in their own right. Mesopotamians found their lives lightened by holidays and religious festivals. Traveling merchants brought news of the outside world and swapped marvelous tales. In all, the Mesopotamians enjoyed a vibrant and creative culture that left its mark on the entire Near East.

Section Review

- The Semitic Amorites of Babylon under King Hammurabi conquered Assyria, Sumer, and Akkad, unifying Mesopotamian civilization on the Tigris and Euphrates Rivers.

- Babylon represented the interaction between the newer Semitic influence and the older Sumerian culture, symbolized in the election of the Babylonian deity Marduk as king of the other Mesopotamian gods.

- The law code of Hammurabi differed according to social status and gender of the offender, and demanded that the punishment fit the crime.

- The strict law code of Hammurabi dealt with agriculture, trade, marriage, and the family.

- In all, Mesopotamians also enjoyed a vibrant culure that celebrated holidays and religious festivals.

Egypt, the Land of the Pharaohs (3100–1200 B.C.E.)

How did Egypt's geography contribute to the rise of a unique culture, and what was the role of the pharoah in this society?

The Greek historian and traveler Herodotus (heh-ROD-uh-tuhs) in the fifth century B.C.E. called Egypt the "gift of the Nile." No other single geographical factor had such a fundamental and profound impact on the shaping of Egyptian life, society, and history as the Nile (see Map 1.2). Unlike the rivers of Mesopotamia, it rarely brought death and destruction by devastating entire cities. The Egyptians never feared the relatively tame Nile in the way the Mesopotamians feared the Tigris. Instead, they sang its praises:

> Hail to thee, O Nile, that issues from the earth and comes to keep Egypt alive! . . .
> He that waters the meadows which Re [Ra] created,
> He that makes to drink the desert . . .
> He who makes barley and brings emmer [wheat] into being . . .
> He who brings grass into being for the cattle . . .
> He who makes every beloved tree to grow . . .
> O Nile, verdant art thou, who makest man and cattle to live.[2]

In the mind of the Egyptians, the Nile was the supreme renewer of the land. Each September the Nile floods its valley, transforming it into a huge area of marsh or lagoon. By the end of November the water retreats, leaving behind a thin covering of fertile mud ready to be planted with crops. Farmers were able to produce an annual agricultural surplus, which in turn sustained a growing and prosperous population. The Nile also unified Egypt. The river was the region's principal highway, promoting communication throughout the valley.

Egypt's natural resources made it nearly self-sufficient. Besides the fertility of its soil, Egypt possessed enormous quantities of stone, which served as the raw material of architecture and sculpture. Abundant clay was available for pottery, as was gold for jewelry and ornaments. The raw materials that Egypt lacked were

MAP 1.2   Ancient Egypt

Geography and natural resources provided Egypt with centuries of peace and abundance.

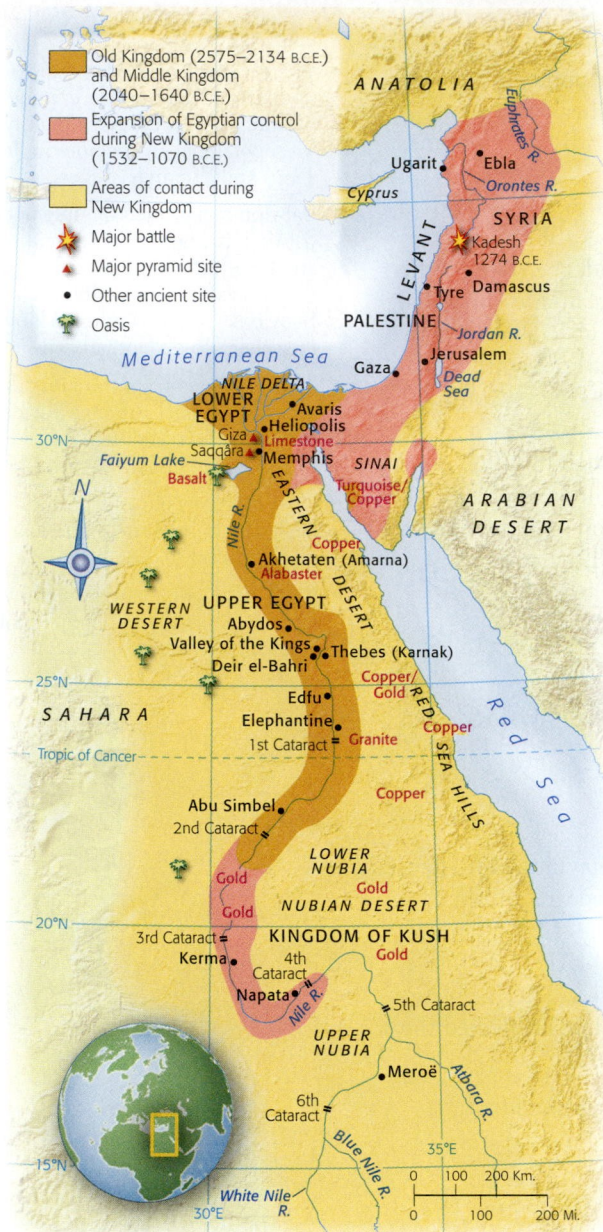

close at hand. The Egyptians could obtain copper from Sinai (**SIGH-nigh**) and timber from Lebanon (**LEB-uh-non**). They had little cause to look to the outside world for their essential needs, a fact that helps explain the insular quality of early Egyptian life.

The God-King of Egypt

The Nile divided ancient Egypt into two entities— Upper Egypt, the upstream valley in the south, and Lower Egypt, the land of the delta where the Nile branches into smaller waterways and then empties into the Mediterranean Sea. The Egyptians told of a great king, Menes (**MEH-neez**), who united Upper and Lower Egypt into a single kingdom around 3100 B.C.E. Thereafter the Egyptians divided their history into dynasties, or families of kings; modern historians organize it into periods (see page 15). The political unification of Egypt ushered in the period known as the Old Kingdom (2660– 2180 B.C.E.), an era remarkable for prosperity, artistic flowering, and the evolution of religious beliefs.

In religion, the Egyptians were polytheists, like the Mesopotamians. They developed complex, often contradictory, ideas of their gods that reflected the world around them. The most powerful of these gods were Amon (**AH-muhn**), a primeval sky-god, and Ra, the sun-god. Amon created the entire cosmos by his thoughts. He caused the Nile to flood and the northern wind to blow. The Egyptians considered Ra (**ra**) the creator of life. He commanded the sky, earth, and underworld. This giver of life could also take it without warning. The obvious similarities between Amon and Ra eventually led the Egyptians to combine them into one god, **Amon-Ra.** Yet the Egyptians never fashioned a formal theology to resolve these differences. Instead they worshiped these gods as different aspects of the same celestial phenomena.

Amon-Ra An Egyptian god, consisting of Amon, a primeval sky-god, and Ra, the sun-god.

Book of the Dead An Egyptian book that preserved their ideas about death and the afterlife; it explains that after death the soul leaves the body to become part of the divine.

The Egyptians likewise developed views of an afterlife that reflected the world around them. The dry air of Egypt preserves much that would decay in other climates. Thus there was a sense of permanence about Egypt: the past was never far from the present. The dependable rhythm of the seasons also shaped the fate of the dead, for, unchanged, they regulated the afterlife, which continued in accordance with the same regularity. The Egyptian **Book of the Dead** explained that the god Osiris (**oh-SIGH-ris**), king of the dead, weighed each person's heart to determine if he or she had lived justly enough to deserve everlasting life. After death the soul left the body to become part of the divine. It entered gladly through the gate of heaven and remained in the presence of Aton (**AHT-on**) (a sun-god) and the stars.

Ra and Horus
The god Ra appears on the left in a form associated with Horus, the falcon-god. The red circle over Ra's head identifies him as the sun-god. In this scene Ra also assumes characteristics of Osiris, god of the underworld. He stands in judgment of the dead woman on the right. She meets the god with respect but without fear, as he will guide her safely to a celestial heaven. (Egyptian Museum, Cairo)

The focal point of religious and political life in the Old Kingdom was the **pharaoh** (**FAY-roh**), who commanded the wealth, resources, and people of all Egypt. The pharaoh's power was such that the Egyptians considered him to be the falcon-god Horus in human form, a living god on earth, who became one with Osiris after death. The queen was associated with the goddess Isis (**EYE-sis**), wife of Osiris, and both the queen and the goddess were viewed as protectors. The pharaoh was not simply the mediator between the gods and the Egyptian people. Above all, he was the power that achieved the integration between gods and human beings, between nature and society, that ensured peace and prosperity for the land of the Nile. The pharaoh was thus a guarantee to his people, a pledge that the gods of Egypt (strikingly unlike those of Mesopotamia) cared for their people.

pharaoh The leader of religious and political life in the Old Kingdom, he commanded the wealth, resources, and people of Egypt.

The pharaoh's surroundings had to be worthy of a god. Just as he occupied a great house in life, so he reposed in a great **pyramid** (**PIR-uh-mid**) after death. The massive tomb contained all the things needed by the pharaoh in his afterlife. The walls of the burial chamber were inscribed with religious texts and spells relating to the pharaoh's journeys after death. After burial the entrance was blocked and concealed to ensure his undisturbed peace. To this day the great

pyramid The burial place of pharaohs, it was a massive tomb that contained all things needed for the afterlife; also symbolized the king's power and his connection with the sun-god.

Periods of Egyptian History

Period	Dates	Significant Events
Archaic	3100–2660 B.C.E.	Unification of Egypt
Old Kingdom	2660–2180 B.C.E.	Construction of the pyramids
First Intermediate	2180–2080 B.C.E.	Political chaos
Middle Kingdom	2080–1640 B.C.E.	Recovery and political stability
Second Intermediate	1640–1570 B.C.E.	Hyksos "invasion"
New Kingdom	1570–1075 B.C.E.	Creation of an Egyptian empire; Akhenaten's religious policy

King Menkaure and Queen
The pharaoh and his wife represent all the magnificence, serenity, and grandeur of Egypt. (Old Kingdom, Dynasty 4, reign of Mycerinus, 2532–2510 B.C.; Greywacke; H x W x D: 54¹¹⁄₁₆ x 22⅜ x 21⁵⁄₁₆ in. (139 x 57 x 54 cm). Harvard University–Museum of Fine Arts Expedition, 11.1738. Museum of Fine Arts, Boston)

pyramids at Giza near Cairo bear silent but magnificent testimony to the god-kings of Egypt.

The Pharaoh's People   Because the common folk stood at the bottom of the social and economic scale, they were always at the mercy of grasping officials. The arrival of the tax collector was never a happy occasion. One Egyptian scribe described the worst that could happen:

> And now the scribe lands on the river-bank and is about to register the harvest-tax. The janitors carry staves and the Nubians rods of palm, and they say, Hand over the corn, though there is none. The cultivator is beaten all over, he is bound and thrown into a well, soused and dipped head downwards. His wife has been bound in his presence and his children are in fetters.[3]

That was an extreme situation. Nonetheless, taxes might amount to 20 percent of the harvest, and tax collection could be brutal.

Egyptian society seems to have been a curious mixture of freedom and constraint. Slavery did not become widespread until the New Kingdom (1570–1075 B.C.E.). There was neither a caste system nor a color bar, and humble people could rise to the highest positions if they possessed talent. On the other hand, most ordinary folk could not easily leave the land of their own free will. Peasants were also subject to forced labor, including work on the pyramids and canals. Young men were drafted into the pharaoh's army, which served both as a fighting force and as a labor corps.

The vision of thousands of people straining to build the pyramids brings to the modern mind a distasteful picture of absolute power. Indeed, the Egyptian view of life and society is alien to those raised with modern concepts of individual freedom and human rights. To ancient Egyptians the pharaoh embodied justice and order—harmony among human beings, nature, and the divine. If the pharaoh was weak or allowed anyone to challenge his unique position, he opened the way to chaos. Twice in Egyptian history the pharaoh failed to maintain rigid centralization. During those two eras, known as the First and Second Intermediate Periods, Egypt was exposed to civil war and invasion. Yet the monarchy survived, and in each period a strong pharaoh arose to crush the rebels or expel the invaders and restore order.

The Hyksos in Egypt (1640–1570 B.C.E.)   While Egyptian civilization flourished behind its bulwark of sand and sea, momentous changes were taking place in the ancient Near East. These changes involved enormous and remarkable movements, especially of peoples who spoke Semitic tongues. The original home of the Semites was perhaps the Arabian peninsula. Some tribes moved into northern Mesopotamia, others into Syria and Palestine, and still others into Egypt. Shortly after 1800 B.C.E. people whom the Egyptians called **Hyksos,** which means "Rulers of the Uplands," began to settle in the Nile Delta. The movements of the Hyksos were part of a larger pattern of migration of peoples during this period. The Hyksos arrived in such numbers that

Hyksos Called Rulers of the Uplands by the Egyptians, these people began to settle in the Nile Delta shortly after 1800 B.C.E.

they were able to take political control, creating a capital city at Avaris in the north-eastern Nile Delta.

Although the Egyptians portrayed the Hyksos as a conquering horde, their entry into the delta was generally peaceful. The Hyksos brought with them the method of making bronze and casting it into tools and weapons. They thereby brought Egypt fully into the **Bronze Age** culture of the Mediterranean world, a culture in which the production and use of bronze implements became basic to society. Bronze tools were sharper and more durable than the copper tools they replaced. The Hyksos' use of bronze armor and weapons revolutionized Egyptian warfare, as did their use of chariots and stronger bows. Yet the newcomers also absorbed Egyptian culture. The Hyksos came to worship Egyptian gods and modeled their monarchy on the pharaonic system.

The New Kingdom: Revival and Empire (1570–1075 B.C.E.)

The pharaohs of the Eighteenth Dynasty arose to challenge the Hyksos. These pharaohs pushed the Hyksos out of the Nile Delta, subdued Nubia in the south, and conquered Palestine and parts of Syria in the northeast. In this way, Egyptian warrior-pharaohs inaugurated the New Kingdom—a period in Egyptian history characterized by enormous wealth and conscious imperialism. During this period, probably for the first time, widespread slavery became a feature of Egyptian life. The pharaoh's armies returned home leading hordes of slaves who constituted a new labor force for imperial building projects.

One pharoah of this period, Akhenaten (ah-keh-NAT-en) (r. 1367–1350 B.C.E.), was more concerned with religion than with conquest. Nefertiti (nef-uhr-TEE-tee), his wife and queen, encouraged his religious bent. (See the feature "Individuals in Society: Nefertiti, the 'Perfect Woman.'") The precise nature of Akhenaten's religious beliefs remains debatable. Most historians, however, agree that Akhenaten and Nefertiti were **monotheists** (mon-oh-THEE-ists); that is, they believed that the sun-god Aton, whom they worshiped, was universal, the only god. They considered all other Egyptian gods and goddesses frauds and disregarded their worship. Yet Akhenaten's monotheism, imposed from above and accompanied by intolerance and persecution, failed to find a place among the people and did not endure beyond his reign.

The Hittites and the End of an Era (ca. 1640–1100 B.C.E.)

How did the Hittites rise to power, and how did they facilitate the exchange of ideas throughout the Near East? How did the Egyptian and Mesopotamian cultures survive the fall of empires?

Like the Mesopotamians and the Egyptians before them, the Hittites (HIT-ites) introduced a new element into the development of the ancient Near East. The Hittites were the first Indo-Europeans to become broadly important throughout the region. The term **Indo-European** refers to a large family of languages that includes English, most of the languages of modern Europe, including Greek and Latin, and languages as far afield as Persian and Sanskrit, spoken in ancient Turkey and India. They left a lasting imprint on the Near East before the empires of the whole region suffered the shock of new peoples and widespread disruption.

Bronze Age The period in which the production and use of bronze implements became basic to society; bronze made farming more efficient and revolutionized warfare.

monotheism The belief in one god; when applied to Egypt it means that only Aton among the traditional Egyptian deities was god.

Indo-European A large family of languages that includes English, most of the languages of modern Europe, Greek, Latin, Persian, and Sanskrit, the sacred tongue of ancient India.

Individuals in Society

Nefertiti, the "Perfect Woman"

Egyptians understood the pharaoh to be the living embodiment of the god Horus, the source of law and morality, and the mediator between gods and humans. His connection with the divine stretched to members of his family, so that his siblings and children were also viewed as in some ways divine. Because of this, a pharaoh often took his sister or half-sister as one of his wives. This concentrated divine blood set the pharaonic family apart from those of other Egyptians (who did not marry close relatives), and allowed the pharaohs to imitate the gods, who in Egyptian mythology often married their siblings. A pharaoh chose one of his wives to be the "Great Royal Wife," or principal queen. Often this was a relative, though sometimes it was one of the foreign princesses who married pharaohs to establish political alliances.

Nefertiti, queen of Egypt (Bildarchiv Preussischer Kulturbesitz/Art Resource, NY)

The familial connection with the divine allowed a handful of women to rule in their own right in Egypt's long history. We know the names of four female pharaohs, the most famous being Hatshepsut (**hat-SHEP-soot**) (ruled 1479–1458 B.C.E.). She was the sister and wife of Thutmose II and, after he died, served as regent for her young stepson Thutmose III, who was actually the son of another woman. Hatshepsut sent trading expeditions and sponsored artists and architects, ushering in a period of artistic creativity and economic prosperity. She built one of the world's great buildings, an elaborate terraced temple at Deir el Bahri, which eventually served as her tomb. Hatshepsut's status as a powerful female ruler was difficult for Egyptians to conceptualize, and she is often depicted in male dress or with a false beard, thus looking more like the male rulers who were the norm. After her death, Thutmose III tried to destroy all evidence that she had ever ruled, smashing statues and scratching her name off inscriptions, perhaps because of personal animosity and perhaps because he wanted to erase the fact that a woman had once been pharaoh. Only within the last decades have historians and archaeologists begun to (literally) piece together her story.

Though female pharaohs were very rare, many royal women had power through their position as "Great Royal Wives." The most famous of these was Nefertiti, the wife of Akhenaten. Her name means "the perfect (or beautiful) woman has come," and inscriptions also give her many other titles. Nefertiti used her position to spread the new religion of the sun-god Aton. Together she and Akhenaten built a new palace at Akhetaten, the present Amarna, away from the old centers of power. There they developed the cult of Aton to the exclusion of the traditional deities. Nearly the only literary survival of their religious belief is the "Hymn to Aton," which declares Aton to be the only god. It describes Nefertiti as "the great royal consort whom he! Akhenaten! Loves, the mistress of the Two Lands! Upper and Lower Egypt!"

Nefertiti is often shown the same size as her husband, and in some inscriptions she is performing religious rituals that would normally have been done only by the pharaoh. The exact details of her power are hard to determine, however. An older theory held that her husband removed her from power, though there is also speculation that she may have ruled secretly in her own right after his death. Her tomb has long since disappeared, though in 2003 an enormous controversy developed over her possible remains. There is no controversy that the bust shown above, now in a Berlin museum, represents Nefertiti, nor that it has become an icon of female beauty since it was first discovered in the early twentieth century.

Questions for Analysis

1. Why might it have been difficult for Egyptians to accept a female ruler?

2. What opportunities do hereditary monarchies such as that of ancient Egypt provide for women? How does this fit with gender hierarchies in which men are understood as superior?

The Coming of the Hittites (ca. 1640–1200 B.C.E.)

During the nineteenth century B.C.E. the native kingdoms in Anatolia engaged in suicidal warfare that left most of the area's once-flourishing towns in ashes and rubble. In this climate of exhaustion the Hittite king, Hattusilis I, led his army to victory against neighboring kingdoms.

The Hittites, like the Egyptians of the New Kingdom, produced an energetic and able line of kings who built a powerful empire. Perhaps their major contribution was the introduction of iron in the form of weapons and tools. Around 1300 B.C.E. the Hittites stopped the Egyptian army of Rameses II at the Battle of Kadesh in Syria. Having fought each other to a standstill, the Hittites and Egyptians first made peace, then an alliance. Alliance was followed by friendship, and friendship by active cooperation between the two greatest powers of the early Near East.

The Hittites and Egyptians next included the Babylonians in their diplomacy. All three empires developed an official etiquette in which they treated one another as "brothers," using this gendered familial term to indicate their connection. These alliances facilitated the exchange of ideas throughout the Near East. Furthermore, the Hittites passed much knowledge and lore from the Near East to the newly arrived Greeks in Europe. The details of Hittite contact with the Greeks are unknown, but enough literary themes and physical objects exist to prove the connection.

Hittite Solar Disc
This cult standard represents Hittite concepts of fertility and prosperity. (A standard is a flag or emblematic object raised on a pole.) The circle surrounding the animals is the sun, beneath which stands a stag flanked by two bulls. Stylized bull's horns spread from the base of the disc. The symbol is also one of might and protection from outside harm. (Museum of Anatolian Civilizations, Ankara)

Sea Peoples Invaders who destroyed the Egyptian empires in the late 13th century; they are otherwise unidentifiable because they went their own ways after their attacks on Egypt.

The Fall of Empires and the Survival of Cultures (ca. 1200 B.C.E.)

The Battle of Kadesh ushered in a period of peace and stability in the Near East that lasted until the thirteenth century B.C.E. Then, however, foreign invaders destroyed both the Hittite and the Egyptian empires. The most famous of these marauders, called the **Sea Peoples** by the Egyptians, launched a series of stunning attacks that brought down the Hittites and drove the Egyptians back to the Nile Delta.

The Egyptians took the lead in the recovery by establishing commercial contact with their new neighbors. With the exchange of goods went ideas. Both sides shared practical concepts of shipbuilding, metal technology, and methods of trade that allowed merchants to transact business over long distances. They began to establish and recognize recently created borders, which helped define them geographically and politically. When the worst was over, the Egyptians made contact with the Semitic peoples of Palestine and Syria, whom they found living in small walled towns. Farther north in the land soon to be named Phoenicia (fi-NEE-sha), they also encountered a people who combined sophisticated seafaring with urban life.

The situation in northern Syria reflected life in the south. Small cities in all these places were mercantile centers, rich not only in manufactured goods, but also in agricultural produce, textiles, and metals. The cities flourished under royal families that shared power and dealt jointly in foreign affairs. These northerners relied heavily on their Mesopotamian heritage. While adopting Babylonian writing to communicate with their more distant neighbors to the east, they also adapted it to write their own north Semitic language. At the same time they welcomed the knowledge of Mesopotamian literature, mathematics, and culture. They worshiped both their own and Mesopotamian deities. Yet the cultural exchange remained a mixture of adoption, adaptation, contrast, and finally balance, as the two cultures came to understand and appreciate each other.

A pattern emerged in Palestine, Syria, and Anatolia. In these areas native cultures established themselves during the prehistoric period. Upon coming into contact with the Egyptian and Mesopotamian civilizations, they adopted many aspects of these cultures, adapting them to their own traditional customs. Yet they also contributed to the advance of Egyptian and Mesopotamian cultures by introducing new technologies and religious ideas. The result was the emergence of a huge group of communities stretching from Egypt in the south to Anatolia in the north and from the Levant in the west to Mesopotamia in the east. Each enjoyed its own individual character, while at the same time sharing many common features with its neighbors.

Section Review

- The iron-wielding Hittites were the first Indo-Europeans to become important in the Near East.

- The Hittites at first fought the Egyptians, such as at the Battle of Kadesh, but then they made peace and included the Babylonians in their fraternal alliance, easing the flow of ideas throughout the three empires and the region.

- The Sea Peoples disturbed this peace, resulting in the downfall of the Hittites and the withdrawal of Egyptians to the Nile Delta.

- The Phoenicians combined sophisticated seafaring with urban life.

- A huge group of communities across the Near East maintained local character while also sharing and helping to develop further common cultural elements from Egypt and Mesopotamia.

Chapter Review

How did early peoples evolve from bands of hunter-gatherers to settled farming communities? (page 3)

For thousands of years Paleolithic peoples moved from place to place in search of food. Only in the Neolithic era—with the invention of new stone tools, a reliance on sustained agriculture, and the domestication of animals—did people begin to live in permanent locations. These villages evolved into towns, where people began to create new social bonds and political organizations. Stonehenge is one example of the collective effort and imagination of a Neolithic community.

Key Terms

Paleolithic period (p. 3)

nomads (p. 3)

Neolithic period (p. 3)

How did the Sumerians create a complex society in the arid climate of Mesopotamia? (page 4)

The earliest area where these developments led to genuine urban societies is Mesopotamia. Here the Sumerians and then other Mesopotamians developed writing, which enabled their culture to be passed on to others. Their religious beliefs reflected a pessimistic view of the world in which the gods could bring destruction without concern for human life. The great Sumerian poem, the *Epic of Gilgamesh*, shows them grappling with questions of life and death that are still of importance today. The beginnings of patriarchy and social class inequalities can also be seen in their culture.

How did the Babylonians unite Mesopotamia politically and culturally and spread that culture to the broader world? (page 11)

The Sumerians established the basic social, economic, and intellectual patterns of Mesopotamia, but the Semites played a large part in spreading Mesopotamian culture to the broader world through both conquest and commercial exchange. First the Akkadians and then the Babylonians came to power in the region. Under Hammurabi, the Babylonians were able to unify Mesopotamia politically and culturally. The law code of Hammurabi illustrates the king's intentions to regulate the lives of his people and promote social harmony.

How did Egypt's geography contribute to the rise of a unique culture, and what was the role of the pharoah in this society? (page 13)

Around the same time in Egypt, the fertile Nile valley and other natural resources contributed to the rise of a wealthy and insular culture. The Egyptians too developed their own writing system and religious beliefs, and they undertook monumental building projects that required sophisticated organizational and intellectual skills. Under the strong central leadership of the pharaoh, Egyptian life was stable and predictable. The Hyksos brought Bronze Age culture to the Egyptians when they settled the Nile Delta.

How did the Hittites rise to power, and how did they facilitate the exchange of ideas throughout the Near East? How did the Egyptian and Mesopotamian cultures survive the fall of empires? (page 17)

Finally, the Hittites, an Indo-European people, entered the Near East from the north. Distant ancestors of the modern folk of Europe and the Americas, the Hittites introduced iron tools and weapons to the region. Along with the Egyptians and then the Babylonians, they developed an alliance that facilitated the exchange of goods and ideas throughout the Near East. Near East peoples received hard knocks from hostile invaders beginning around the thirteenth century B.C.E., but key social, economic, and cultural patterns survived to enrich future generations.

irrigation (p. 4)
cuneiform (p. 8)
polytheism (p. 9)
nobles (p. 10)
clients (p. 10)
patriarchal (p. 10)
law code (p. 12)
Amon-Ra (p. 14)
Book of the Dead (p. 14)
pharaoh (p. 15)
pyramid (p. 15)
Hyksos (p. 16)
Bronze Age (p. 17)
monotheism (p. 17)
Indo-European (p. 17)
Sea Peoples (p. 20)

Notes

1. Quoted in S. N. Kramer, *The Sumerians: Their History, Culture and Character*, 1963. Reprinted by permission of the publisher, the University of Chicago Press. John Buckler is the translator of all uncited quotations from a foreign language in Chapters 1–6.
2. J. B. Pritchard, ed., *Ancient Near Eastern Texts*, 3d ed. (Princeton, N.J.: Princeton University Press, 1969), p. 372. Hereafter called ANET.
3. Quoted in A. H. Gardiner, "Ramesside Texts Relating to the Taxation and Transport of Corn," *Journal of Egyptian Archaeology* 27 (1941): 19–20.

To assess your mastery of this chapter, go to **bedfordstmartins.com/mckaywestbrief**

Listening to the Past

A Quest for Immortality

The human desire to escape death and achieve immortality is one of the oldest wishes of all peoples. The Sumerian Epic of Gilgamesh *is the earliest recorded treatment of this topic. The oldest elements of the epic go back at least to the third millennium B.C.E. According to tradition, Gilgamesh was a king of Uruk whom the Sumerians, Babylonians, and Assyrians considered a hero-king and a god. In the story Gilgamesh and his friend Enkidu set out to attain immortality and join the ranks of the gods. They attempt to do so by performing wondrous feats against fearsome agents of the gods, who are determined to thwart them.*

During their quest Enkidu dies. Gilgamesh, more determined than ever to become immortal, begins seeking anyone who might tell him how to do so. His journey involves the effort not only to escape from death but also to reach an understanding of the meaning of life. Along the way he meets Siduri, the wise and good-natured goddess of wine, who gives him the following advice.

Gilgamesh, where are you hurrying to? You will never find that life for which you are looking. When the gods created man they allotted to him death, but life they retained in their own keeping. As for you, Gilgamesh, fill your belly with good things; day and night, night and day, dance and be merry, feast and rejoice. Let your clothes be fresh, bathe yourself in water, cherish the little child that holds your hand, and make your wife happy in your embrace; for this too is the lot of man.

Ignoring Siduri's advice, Gilgamesh continues his journey, until he finds Utnapishtim [oot-nuh-PISH-tim], a mortal whom the gods so favored that they put him in an eternal paradise. Gilgamesh puts to Utnapishtim the question that is the reason for his quest.

Oh, father Utnapishtim, you who have entered the assembly of the gods, I wish to question you concerning the living and the dead, how shall I find the life for which I am searching?

Utnapishtim said, "There is no permanence. Do we build a house to stand forever, do we seal a contract to hold for all time? Do brothers divide an inheritance to keep forever, does the flood-time of rivers endure? . . . What is there between the master and the servant when both have fulfilled their doom? When the Anunnaki [the gods of the underworld], the judges, come together, and Mammetun [the goddess of fate], the mother of destinies, come together they decree the fates of men. Life and death they allot but the day of death they do not disclose.

Utnapishtim then tells Gilgamesh of a time when gods decided to send a great flood to destroy the Sumerians, who had angered the great god Enlil.

Gilgamesh, from decorative panel of a lyre unearthed at Ur.
(The University Museum, University of Pennsylvania, neg. T4-108)

22

The god Ea, however, intervened and commanded Utnapishtim to build a boat big enough to hold his family, various artisans, and all animals in order to survive the flood that was to come. Enlil was infuriated by the Sumerians' survival, and Ea rebuked him. Then Enlil relented and blessed Utnapishtim with eternal paradise. After telling the story, Utnapishtim foretells Gilgamesh's fate.

O Gilgamesh, this was the meaning of your dream [of immortality]. You were given the kingship, such was your destiny, everlasting life was not your destiny. Because of this do not be sad at heart, do not be grieved or oppressed; he [Enlil] has given you power to bind and to loose, to be the darkness and the light of mankind. He has given you unexampled supremacy over the people, victory in battle from which no fugitive returns, in forays and assaults from which there is no going back. But do not abuse this power, deal justly with your servants in the palace, deal justly before the face of the Sun."

Questions for Analysis

1. What does the *Epic of Gilgamesh* reveal about Sumerian attitudes toward the gods and human beings?

2. At the end of his quest, did Gilgamesh achieve immortality? If so, what was the nature of that immortality?

3. What does the epic tell us about Sumerian views of the nature of human life? Where do human beings fit into the cosmic world?

Source: From *The Epic of Gilgamesh*, translated and with an introduction by N. K. Sanders (Penguin Classics, 1960; Third Edition, 1972). Copyright © N. K. Sanders, 1960, 1964, 1972. Reproduced by permission of Penguin Books Ltd.

CHAPTER 2

Small Kingdoms and Mighty Empires in the Near East

ca. 1100–513 B.C.E.

Chapter Preview

Disruption and Diffusion
How did the Nubians, Kush, and Phoenicians respond to the power vacuum in Egypt and the western Near East?

The Children of Israel
How did the Hebrew state evolve, and what were the unique elements of Hebrew religious thought?

Assyria, the Military Monarchy
What enabled the Assyrians to conquer their neighbors, and how did their aggression finally cause their undoing?

The Empire of the Persian Kings
How did the Persians rise to power and maintain control over their extensive empire? What were the central concepts of their religion, Zoroastrianism?

INDIVIDUALS IN SOCIETY: Wen-Amon

LISTENING TO THE PAST: The Covenant Between Yahweh and the Hebrews

Reconstruction of the "Ishtar Gate," Babylon, early sixth century B.C.E. Located in the Berlin Museum. (Bildarchiv Preussischer Kulturbesitz/Art Resource, NY)

The migratory invasions that brought down the Hittites and stunned the Egyptians in the late thirteenth century B.C. ushered in a new era in the ancient Near East. In the absence of powerful empires, the Phoenicians, Hebrews, and many other peoples carved out small independent kingdoms until the Near East was a patchwork of small states. During this period Hebrew culture and religion evolved under the influence of urbanism, kings, and prophets.

In the ninth century B.C.E. this jumble of small states gave way to an empire that for the first time embraced the entire Near East. Yet the very ferocity of the Assyrian Empire led to its downfall only two hundred years later. In 550 B.C.E. the Persians and Medes (**meeds**), who had migrated into Iran, created a "world empire" stretching from Anatolia in the west to the Indus Valley in the east. For over two hundred years the Persians gave the ancient Near East peace and stability.

Disruption and Diffusion

How did the Nubians, Kush, and Phoenicians respond to the power vacuum in Egypt and the western Near East?

The fall of empires was a time of both massive political disruption and cultural diffusion. In Africa, the decline of Egyptian power energized the kingdoms of Nubia and Kush, who adopted elements of Egyptian culture as they rose to power

Nubian Pyramids
The Nubians adopted many aspects of Egyptian culture and customs. The pyramids shown here are not as magnificent as their Egyptian predecessors, but they served the same purpose of honoring the dead king. Their core was constructed of bricks, which were then covered with stone blocks. At the doors of the pyramids stood monumental gates to the interiors of the tombs. (Michael Yamashita)

Individuals in Society

Wen-Amon

W en-Amon, an official of the temple of Amon-Ra at Karnak in Egypt, personally experienced the weakening of Egypt's power on a trip to Byblos in Phoenicia sometime in the eleventh century B.C.E. His mission was to obtain lumber for Amon-Ra's ceremonial barge. Wen-Amon's detailed account of his experiences comes in the form of an official report to the chief priest of the temple.

The essentials of Egyptian writing: a sheet of papyrus, a stylus or pen, an ink well. (Réunion des Musées Nationaux/Art Resource, NY)

Entrusted with silver to pay for the lumber, Wen-Amon set out on his voyage. He docked at Dor, in modern Israel, which was independent of the pharaoh, but the local prince received him graciously. While his ship was at anchor, one of Wen-Amon's own sailors vanished with the silver. Wen-Amon immediately reported the robbery to the prince and demanded that he investigate the theft. The prince flatly told Wen-Amon that he did not care whether Wen-Amon and the others were important men and that the matter was not his problem. No earlier foreign prince would have dared speak to a high Egyptian official in such terms.

Although rebuffed, Wen-Amon found a ship from Byblos and robbed it of an equivalent amount of silver. When he left Dor and entered the harbor of Byblos, the prince there, who had learned of the theft, ordered him to leave. For twenty-nine days there was an impasse. Finally the two men met and a heated argument ensued. Not until Wen-Amon reminded the prince of the god Amon's power did the prince agree to the sale of the timber.

After the timber was loaded aboard his ship, Wen-Amon saw eleven enemy ships entering the harbor. They anchored, and those in charge reported to the prince of Byblos that they had come for the Egyptians. The prince refused to hand them over, saying that he would never arrest a messenger of Amon-Ra. He agreed, however, to send Wen-Amon away first and allow the enemy ships to pursue the Egyptians. Stormy seas blew the Egyptian ship into Hittite territory. When Wen-Amon landed there, Queen Heteb granted him protection and asylum.

The papyrus breaks off at this point, but it is obvious that Wen-Amon weathered his various storms to return safely to Egypt. The document illustrates the presumption of power by Wen-Amon and his bluster at the lack of respect shown him. It also shows how Egypt's neighbors no longer feared Egyptian power. Finally, it illustrates the impact of Egyptian culture and religion on the peoples living along the coast of the Levant. Although Egyptian political power was in eclipse, its gods were respected.

Questions for Analysis

1. What do Wen-Amon's experiences tell us about political conditions in the eastern Mediterranean?
2. Since Wen-Amon could no longer depend on the majesty of Egypt for respect, how did he fulfill his duty?

in the region. The Phoenicians also thrived with the absence of pressure from the Egyptians and Hittites, using their independence to develop a trade network that spread Mesopotamian culture along the Mediterranean.

The End of Egyptian Power

The long wars against the Sea Peoples impoverished Egypt, weakening its power in the region and at home. The four hundred years of political fragmentation are known as the Third Intermediate Period (eleventh–seventh centuries B.C.E.). (See the feature "Individuals in Society: Wen-Amon.")

In southern Egypt, the pharaoh's decline opened the way to the Nubians, who extended their authority northward throughout the Nile Valley. Nubian kings and aristocrats embraced Egyptian culture wholesale, repeating a Near Eastern phenomenon: new peoples conquered old centers of political and military power but were assimilated into the older culture.

Another independent African state, the kingdom of Kush, grew up during the period of Egyptian weakness. The Kushites worshiped Egyptian gods and used Egyptian hieroglyphs (high-ruh-GLIFS). In the eighth century B.C.E. their king, Piankhy, swept north from their capital at Nepata in the region of modern Sudan, extending his conquests all the way to the Nile Delta. Egypt enjoyed a brief period of peace, but reunification of the realm did not lead to a new Egyptian empire.

The Rise of Phoenicia

The fall of the Hittite Empire and Egypt's collapse created a vacuum of power in the western Near East that allowed for the rise of numerous small states. The Phoenicians, who had long inhabited several cities along the coast of modern Lebanon, used their new freedom to become the seaborne merchants of their broad world. With the Greeks, one of their early customers, they traded their popular purple and blue textiles, from which originated their Greek name, Phoenicians, meaning the "Purple People."

Their growing success inspired new ventures, and the Phoenicians began to manufacture other goods for export, such as metal tools, weapons, and cooking ware. They also expanded their trade routes, first to Egypt, then along the coast of North Africa, eventually to the far western Mediterranean and beyond, to the Atlantic Ocean. Although the Phoenicians did not found colonies, they planted trading posts and small farming communities along the way. Their trading post in Carthage prospered to become a leading city in the western Mediterranean. Through these ventures the Phoenicians peacefully spread Mesopotamian customs to less urbanized peoples.

The Phoenicians' overwhelming cultural achievement was the development of an alphabet: they, unlike other literate peoples, used one letter to designate one sound, a system that vastly simplified writing and reading. The Greeks modified this alphabet and then used it to write their own language.

CHRONOLOGY

ca. 1100–653 B.C.E.	Third Intermediate Period in Egypt
ca. 1100–400 B.C.E.	Era of the prophets in Israel
ca. 1025–925 B.C.E.	United Hebrew kingdom
950–730 B.C.E.	Movement of new peoples into Egypt
ca. 950–500 B.C.E.	Beginning of the Hebrew Bible
ca. 900–612 B.C.E.	Assyrian Empire
ca. 900–550 B.C.E.	Phoenician seafaring and trading in the Mediterranean
ca. 710–550 B.C.E.	Creation of the Persian Empire
ca. 600–500 B.C.E.	Spread of Zoroastrianism
586–538 B.C.E.	Babylonian Captivity of the Hebrews
ca. 550–513 B.C.E.	Expansion of Persian trade from western Asia to India

Section Review

- Long wars against the Sea Peoples impoverished Egypt, leading to the Third Intermediate Period (11th–7th c. B.C.E.) of political fragmentation.

- In southern Egypt the Nubians and the Kushites gained strength as the pharaohs declined.

- In the western Near East the Phoenicians became skilled merchants, manufactured goods for export, and spread their customs peacefully to other peoples.

- The name Phoenician, Greek for the "Purple People," reflected the rich textiles they traded.

- The most remarkable cultural achievement of the Phoenicians was their development of an alphabet using one letter for each sound, vastly simplifying writing.

Phoenician Ships
These small ships seem too frail to breast the waves. Yet Phoenician mariners routinely sailed them, loaded with their cargoes, to the far ports of the Mediterranean. (British Museum/Michael Holford)

The Children of Israel

How did the Hebrew state evolve, and what were the unique elements of Hebrew religious thought?

South of Phoenicia arose a small kingdom, the land of the ancient Israelites or Hebrews. Virtually the only source for much of their history is the Bible, a religious document that contains many myths and legends as well as historical material.

The Evolution of the Jewish State

According to Hebrew tradition, the patriarch Abraham led his people from Mesopotamia in the second millennium B.C.E. Together with other seminomadic peoples, they probably migrated into the Nile Delta seeking good land. According to the Bible the Egyptians enslaved them. One group, however, under the leadership of Moses (**MOH-zis**), left Egypt in what the Hebrews remembered as the Exodus. From Egypt they wandered in the Sinai Peninsula until they settled in Palestine in the thirteenth century B.C.E.

Once in Palestine, the greatest danger to the Hebrews came from the neighboring Philistines (**FIL-uh-steens**), whose superior technology and military organization at first made them invincible. In Saul (ca. 1000 B.C.E.), a farmer of the tribe of Benjamin, the Hebrews found a champion and a spirited leader. In the biblical account Saul led attacks on the Philistines, often without success. Yet in the meantime he established a monarchy over the twelve Hebrew tribes.

Saul's work was carried on by David of Bethlehem, who pushed back the Philistines. To give his kingdom a capital, he captured the city of Jerusalem, which he enlarged, fortified, and made the religious and political center of his realm. His work in consolidating the monarchy and enlarging the kingdom paved the way for his son Solomon.

The Golden Calf

According to the Hebrew Bible, Moses descended from Mount Sinai, where he had received the Ten Commandments, to find the Hebrews worshiping a golden calf, which was against Yahweh's laws. In July 1990 an American archaeological team found this model of a gilded calf inside a pot. The figurine, which dates to about 1550 B.C.E., is strong evidence for the existence of the cult represented by the calf in Palestine. (Courtesy of the Leon Levy Expedition to Ashkelon. Photo: Carl Andrews)

Solomon (ca. 965–925 B.C.E.) applied his energies to creating a nation. He began by dividing the kingdom into twelve territorial districts cutting across the old tribal borders. To bring his kingdom up to the level of its more sophisticated neighbors, he set about a building program that encompassed cities, palaces, fortresses, and roads. The most symbolic of these projects was the Temple of Jerusalem, which became the home of the Ark of the Covenant, the cherished chest that contained the holiest of Hebrew religious articles. The temple in Jerusalem was intended to be the religious heart of the kingdom and the symbol of Hebrew unity.

At Solomon's death, his kingdom broke into two political halves (see Map 2.1). The northern part became Israel, with its capital at Samaria. The southern half was Judah, and Jerusalem remained its center. With political division went a religious rift: Israel, the northern kingdom, established rival sanctuaries for gods other than **Yahweh** (**YAH-way**).

Eventually, the northern kingdom of Israel was wiped out by the Assyrians, but the southern kingdom of Judah survived numerous calamities until the Babylonians crushed it in 587 B.C.E. The survivors were sent into exile in Babylonia, a period commonly known as the **Babylonian Captivity**. In 538 B.C.E. the Persian king Cyrus (**SIGH-russ**) the Great permitted some forty thousand exiles to return to Jerusalem. During and especially after the Babylonian Captivity, the exiles redefined their beliefs and practices and thus established what they believed was the law of Yahweh. Those who lived by these precepts can be called Jews.

Yahweh A god, who in Medieval Latin became Jehovah, that appeared to Moses on Mount Sinai and made a covenant with the Hebrews.

Babylonian Captivity A period of time in 587 B.C.E. when the survivors of a Babylonian attack on the southern kingdom of Judah were sent into exile in Babylonia.

MAP 2.1   Small Kingdoms of the Near East

This map illustrates the political fragmentation of the Near East after the great wave of invasions that occurred during the thirteenth century B.C.E.

Covenant A formal agreement between Yahweh and the Hebrew people that if the Hebrews worshiped Yahweh as their only god, he would consider them his chosen people and protect them from their enemies.

Section Review

- The main source of information for the Hebrews comes from the Bible, a religious document containing myths and legends in addition to history verifiable through other sources.

- King Saul defended the Israelites against the Philistines, and King David founded Jerusalem.

- King Solomon built the Temple of Jerusalem and created a sophisticated nation through an ambitious building program.

- At Solomon's death, the kingdom split into Israel in the north, which the Assyrians wiped out, and Judah in the south.

- The Babylonians crushed Judah in 587 B.C.E., the beginning of the Babylonian Captivity, which lasted until 538 B.C.E.

- Those who followed god Yahweh's law became known as Jews.

- The Hebrews' religion was unique because they knew what Yahweh expected and that if they followed his commandments and lived an ethical life they would be protected.

Elements of Jewish Religion

According to the Bible, the god Yahweh appeared to Moses on Mount Sinai. There Yahweh made a contract with the Hebrews, known as the **Covenant.** If they worshiped Yahweh as their only god, he would consider them his chosen people and protect them from their enemies. As the chosen people, the Hebrews' chief duty was to maintain the worship of Yahweh as he demanded. That worship was embodied in the Ten Commandments, which forbade the Hebrews to steal, murder, lie, or commit adultery. The Covenant was a constant force in Hebrew life (see the feature "Listening to the Past: The Covenant Between Yahweh and the Hebrews" on page 37).

The uniqueness of the Hebrews' religion can be seen by comparing the essence of Hebrew monotheism with the religious outlook of the Mesopotamians. Whereas the Mesopotamians considered their gods capricious, the Hebrews knew what Yahweh expected. The Hebrews believed that their god would protect them and make them prosper if they obeyed his commandments. The Mesopotamians thought human beings insignificant compared to the gods, so insignificant that the gods might even be indifferent to them. The Hebrews, too, considered themselves puny in comparison with Yahweh. Yet they were Yahweh's chosen people, whom he had promised never to abandon. Finally, though the Mesopotamians believed that the gods generally preferred good to evil, their religion did not demand ethical conduct. The Hebrews could please their god only by living up to high moral standards as well as by worshiping him.

Religious leaders were important in Judaism, but not as important as the written texts they interpreted; these texts came to be regarded as the word of Yahweh and thus had a status other writings did not. The most important task for observant Jews was to study religious texts, an activity limited to men until the twentieth century. Women were obliged to provide for men's physical needs so that they could study, which often meant that Jewish women were more active economically than their contemporaries of other religions. Women's religious rituals tended to center on the home, while men's centered on the temple. The reverence for a particular text or group of texts was passed down from Judaism to the other Western monotheistic religions that grew from it, Christianity and Islam.

Assyria, the Military Monarchy

What enabled the Assyrians to conquer their neighbors, and how did their aggression finally cause their undoing?

Small kingdoms like those of the Phoenicians and the Hebrews could exist only in the absence of a major power. The beginning of the ninth century B.C.E. saw the rise of such a power: the Assyrians of northern Mesopotamia, whose chief capital was at Nineveh (**NIN-uh-vuh**) on the Tigris River. The Assyrians were a Semitic-speaking people heavily influenced by the Mesopotamian culture of Babylon to the south. Living in an open, exposed land, the Assyrians experienced frequent and devastating attacks by the tribes to their north and east and by the Babylonians to the south. The constant threat to survival promoted Assyrian political cohesion and military might, and they evolved into one of the most warlike societies in history. Yet they were also a mercantile people who had long pursued commerce with their neighbors to the north and south.

The Power of Assyria

For over two hundred years the Assyrians labored to dominate the Near East. In 859 B.C.E. the new Assyrian king, Shalmaneser (**shal-muh-NEE-zer**), unleashed the first of a long series of attacks on the peoples of Syria and Palestine.

Under the warrior-kings Tiglath-pileser III (**TIG-lath-pih-LEE-zuhr**) (774–727 B.C.E.) and Sargon II (r. 721–705 B.C.E.), the Assyrians stepped up their attacks on Anatolia, Syria, and Palestine. The kingdom of Israel and many other states fell; others, like the kingdom of Judah, became subservient to the warriors from the Tigris. In 717 to 716 B.C.E., Sargon led his army in a sweeping attack along the Philistine coast, where he defeated the pharaoh. Sargon also lashed out at Assyria's traditional enemies to the north and then turned south against a renewed threat in Babylonia. By means of almost constant warfare, Tiglath-pileser III and Sargon II carved out an Assyrian empire that stretched from east and north of the Tigris River to central Egypt (see Map 2.2).

Although it was renowned for gruesome displays of violence, Assyria's success was actually due to its sophisticated military machine. Infantrymen were armed with spears and swords and protected by helmet and armor. Archers charged the enemy on horseback and in chariots. Other heavily armored archers served as a primitive field artillery, sweeping the enemy's walls of defenders so that others could storm the defenses. Slingers also served as artillery in pitched battles.

MAPPING THE PAST

MAP 2.2 The Assyrian and Persian Empires

Compare this map showing the extent of the Assyrian and Persian Empires with Map 2.1 on page 29, which shows the earliest political extent of the Eastern states. **[1]** What do these maps tell us about the growth of political power? **[2]** What new areas have opened to the old cultures? **[3]** What do the two maps suggest about the shift of power and the spread of civilization in the ancient Near East?

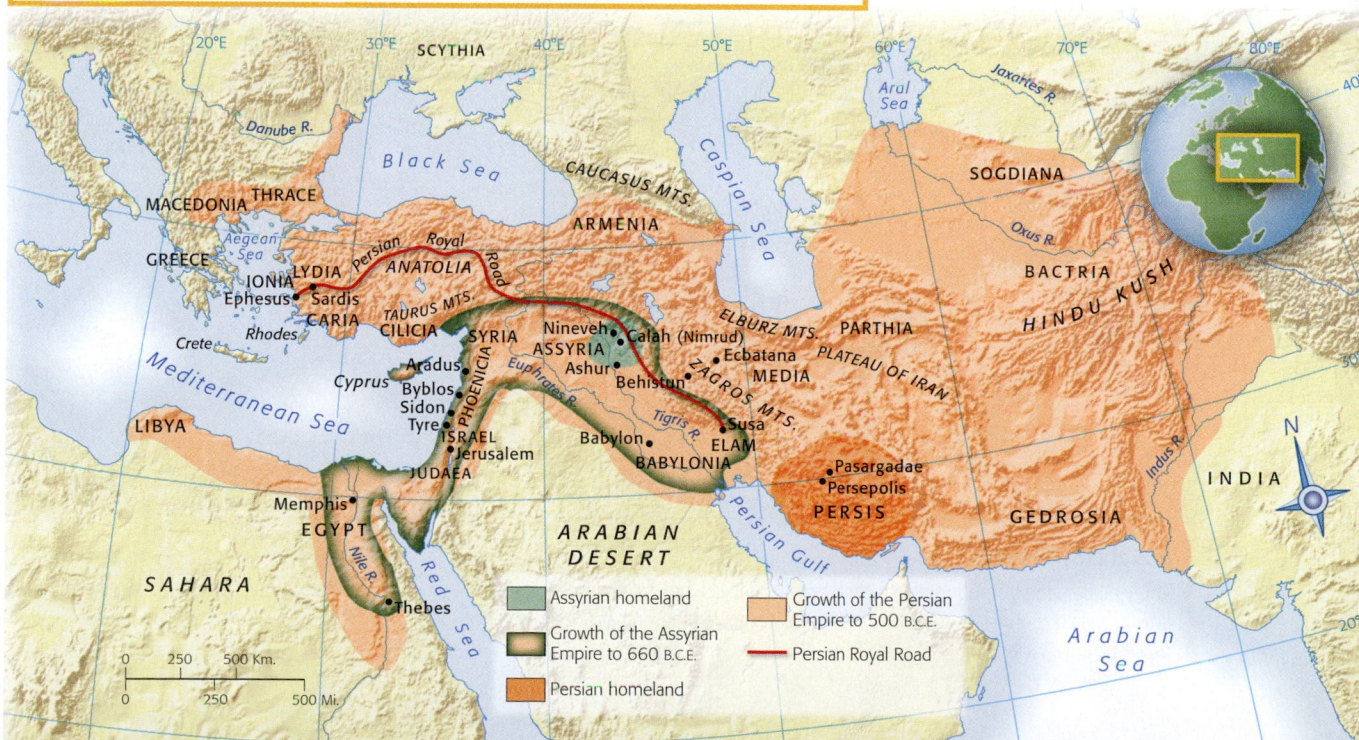

The Assyrians' military genius extended to siege machinery and techniques, including excavation to undermine city walls and battering rams to knock down walls and gates. Never before in the Near East had anyone applied such technical knowledge to warfare. The Assyrians even invented the concept of a corps of engineers, who bridged rivers with pontoons or provided soldiers with inflatable skins for swimming. And the Assyrians knew how to coordinate their efforts, both in open battle and in siege warfare.

Section Review

- Assyrian monarchs Tiglath-pileser III and Sargon II attacked Anatolia, Syria, and Palestine, destroying the Kingdom of Israel and occupying Judah and Egypt.

- Assyria rose to power at the beginning of the 9th c. B.C.E. because of its superior military technology, including heavily armored archers and siege machinery.

- Assyrian artists used a series of pictures to show progression of a story—an idea later adopted by the Persians along with Assyrian military tactics. The Assyrians depicted their military campaigns in continuous friezes and monumental sculpted figures.

- Babylon won independence from Assyria in 626 B.C.E., and the Assyrians disappeared from history until the modern era.

Assyrian Culture

In the seventh century B.C.E. Assyrian power seemed firmly established. Yet the downfall of Assyria was swift and complete. Babylon finally won its independence in 626 B.C.E. and joined forces with a newly aggressive people, the Medes, an Indo-European-speaking folk from Iran. Together the Babylonians and the Medes destroyed the Assyrian Empire in 612 B.C.E., paving the way for the rise of the Persians. The Hebrew prophet Nahum (**NEY-hum**) spoke for many when he asked: "Nineveh is laid waste: who will bemoan her?"[1]

Their cities destroyed and their power shattered, the Assyrians disappeared from history, remembered only as a cruel people of the Old Testament. Two hundred years later, when the Greek adventurer and historian Xenophon (**ZEN-uh-fuhn**) passed by the ruins of Nineveh, he marveled at the extent of the former city but knew nothing of the Assyrians. The glory of their empire was forgotten until modern

Royal Lion Hunt
This wall painting from the seventh century B.C.E. depicts the Assyrian king frightening a lion, a typical representation of the energy and artistic brilliance of Assyrian artists. The lion hunt signified the king as the protector of society, not simply as a sportsman. (Louvre/Réunion des Musées Nationaux/Art Resource, NY)

archaelogy brought the Assyrians out of obscurity. Among the treasures unearthed in recent centuries were monumental sculpted figures—huge winged bulls, human-headed lions, and sphinxes—as well as brilliantly sculpted friezes. Assyrian artists had hit on the idea of portraying a series of episodes in a continuous frieze, so that the viewer could follow the progress of a military campaign from the time the army marched out until the enemy was conquered. These techniques influenced Persian artists, who adapted them to gentler scenes. In fact, many Assyrian innovations, military and political as well as artistic, were taken over by the Persians.

The Empire of the Persian Kings

How did the Persians rise to power and maintain control over their extensive empire? What were the central concepts of their religion, Zoroastrianism?

Like the Hittites before them, the Iranians were Indo-Europeans from central Europe and southern Russia. They migrated into the land known in ancient times as Persia and today as Iran. From Persia would come one of the greatest empires of antiquity, one that encompassed scores of peoples and cultures.

The Land of the Medes and Persians

The Iranians who entered Persia around 1000 B.C.E. were nomads who migrated with their flocks and herds. They were also horse breeders, and the horse gave them a decisive military advantage over the prehistoric peoples of Iran. These centuries of immigration saw constant cultural interchange between conquering newcomers and conquered natives.

Persian Charioteers

Here are two Persians riding in a chariot pulled by four horses. The chariot is simple in construction but elegant in ornamentation. The harness of the horses is worked in elaborate and accurate detail. This chariot was used for ceremonial purposes, not for warfare. (Courtesy of the Trustees of the British Museum)

The Royal Palace at Persepolis
King Darius began and King Xerxes finished building a grand palace worthy of the glory of the Persian Empire. Pictured here is the monumental audience hall, where the king dealt with ministers of state and foreign envoys. (George Holton/Photo Researchers)

Two groups of Iranians gradually began coalescing into larger units: the Persians and the Medes. The Medes united under one king around 710 B.C.E. and then extended their control over the Persians to the south. In 612 B.C.E. they joined the Babylonians to overthrow the Assyrian Empire. With the rise of the Medes, the balance of power in the Near East shifted for the first time east of Mesopotamia.

The Rise of the Persian Empire (550–540 B.C.E.)

In 550 B.C.E. Cyrus the Great (r. 559–530 B.C.E.), king of the Persians and one of the most remarkable statesmen of antiquity, conquered the Medes. Cyrus's conquest of the Medes resulted not in slavery and slaughter but in the union of the Iranian peoples. Having united Iran, Cyrus set out to achieve two goals. First, he wanted to win control of the West and thus of the terminal ports of the great trade routes that crossed Iran and Anatolia. Second, he strove to secure eastern Iran from the pressure of nomadic invaders.

In a series of major campaigns, Cyrus achieved his goals. He swept into Anatolia, easily overthrowing the young kingdom of Lydia (**LID-ee-uh**). His generals subdued the Greek cities along the coast of Anatolia, thus gaining him important ports on the Mediterranean. From Lydia, Cyrus marched to the far eastern corners of Iran and conquered the regions of Parthia (**PAHR-thee-uh**) and Bactria (**BAK-tree-uh**). The Babylonians welcomed him as a liberator when his soldiers moved into their kingdom.

With these victories, Cyrus demonstrated to the world his benevolence as well as his military might. He spared the life of Croesus (**KREE-suhs**), the conquered king of Lydia, to serve him as friend and adviser. He allowed the Greeks to live according to their customs, thus making possible the spread of Greek culture. Cyrus's humanity likewise extended to the Jews, whom he found enslaved in Babylonia. He returned their sacred objects to them and allowed them to return to Jerusalem and rebuild the temple.

Cyrus's successors Darius (**duh-RIE-uhs**) (r. 521–486 B.C.E.) and Xerxes (**ZERK-sees**) (r. 486–464 B.C.E.) rounded out the Persian conquest of the ancient Near East. Within thirty-seven years (550–513 B.C.E.) the Persians transformed themselves from a subject people to the rulers of an empire that included Anatolia, Egypt, Mesopotamia, Iran, and western India. They had created a **world empire** encompassing all the oldest and most honored kingdoms and peoples of the ancient Near East. Never before had this region been united in one such vast political organization (see Map 2.2).

The Persians knew how to preserve the peace. Unlike the Assyrians, they did not resort to royal terrorism to maintain order. Instead, the Persians built an efficient administrative system to govern the empire, based in the capital city of Persepolis (**per-SEP-uh-lis**), near modern Schiras, Iran. From Persepolis they sent directions to the provinces and received reports back from their officials. To do so they maintained a sophisticated system of roads linking the empire. The main highway, the famous **Royal Road,** spanned some 1,677 miles (see Map 2.2). Other roads branched out to link all parts of the empire from the coast of Asia Minor to the valley of the Indus River. This system of communications enabled Persian kings to keep in close touch with their subjects and officials. They were thereby able to make the concepts of right, justice, and good government a practical reality.

world empire All of the oldest and most honored kingdoms and peoples of the ancient Near East that were united under the Persian political organization.

Royal Road The main highway created by the Persians; it spanned 1,677 miles from Greece to Iran.

Zoroastrianism A religion teaching that Ahura Mazda, god of good and light, fought continuously with Ahriman, god of evil and dark, with Ahura Mazda ultimately winning.

Thus Spake Zarathustra

Around 600 B.C.E. a preacher named Zarathustra (**zar-uh-THUH-struh**)—Zoroaster (**zo-ro-ASS-ter**), as he is better known—introduced new spiritual concepts to the people of Iran. Zoroaster taught that life is a constant battleground for the two opposing forces of good and evil. The Iranian god Ahuramazda (**ah-HOOR-uh-MAZZ-duh**) embodied good and truth but was opposed by Ahriman (**AH-ree-mahn**), a hateful spirit who stood for evil and lies. Ahuramazda and Ahriman were locked together in a cosmic battle for the human race, a battle that stretched over thousands of years.

Zoroaster emphasized the individual's responsibility to choose between good and evil. He taught that people possessed the free will to decide between Ahuramazda and Ahriman and that they must rely on their own conscience to guide them through life. Their decisions were crucial, Zoroaster warned, for there would be a time of reckoning. The victorious Ahuramazda, like the Egyptian god Osiris, would preside over a last judgment to determine each person's eternal fate. Those who had lived according to good and truth would enter a divine kingdom. Liars and the wicked, denied this blessed immortality, would be condemned to eternal pain, darkness, and punishment. Thus Zoroaster preached a last judgment that led to a heaven or a hell.

Zoroaster's teachings converted Darius, who did not, however, try to impose them on others. Under the protection of the Persian kings, **Zoroastrianism** (**zo-ro-ASS-tree-uh-niz-uhm**) won converts throughout Iran. It survived the fall of the Persian Empire to influence liberal Judaism, Christianity, and early Islam. Good behavior in the world, even though unrecognized at the time, would receive

Section Review

- Iranians (Medes and Persians) were Indo-European nomads who entered Persia around 1000 B.C.E. and joined the Babylonians to overthrow the Assyrians in 612 B.C.E.

- Cyrus the Great formed the Persian Empire in 550 B.C.E., subduing important Greek port cities on the coast of Anatolia, yet allowing the Greeks to live according to their customs.

- Persian successors Darius and Xerxes built an efficient administrative system that included the Royal Road.

- About 600 B.C.E. a sage named Zarathustra (Zoroaster) taught that a cosmic battle was occurring between the good god Ahuramazda and the evil spirit Ahriman, and individuals would be subjected to eternal heaven or hell through a last judgment by Ahuramazda.

- Darius adopted Zarathustra's religion of Zoroastrianism, and it in turn influenced Judaism, Christianity, and Islam.

ample reward in the hereafter. Evil, no matter how powerful in life, would be punished after death. In some form or another, Zoroastrian concepts still pervade the major religions of the West and every part of the world touched by Islam.

Chapter Review

How did the Nubians, Kush, and Phoenicians respond to the power vacuum in Egypt and the western Near East? (page 25)

During the centuries following the Sea Peoples' invasions, the African kingdoms of the Nubians and the Kush filled the power vacuum in Egypt and adopted elements of Egyptian culture such as hieroglyphs and pyramids. In Anatolia, the Phoenicians in particular took advantage of the fall of the Hittites and the weakness of Egyptian power to spread commodities and ideas through trade.

How did the Hebrew state evolve, and what were the unique elements of Hebrew religious thought? (page 28)

Another group to benefit from the absence of a major power in the region were the Hebrews, who created a small kingdom in Palestine. Their kingdom was short-lived, but their religious beliefs and written codes of law and custom proved to be long lasting. Judaism, their monotheistic religion, continues as a vibrant faith today and was an important source for Christianity and Islam.

What enabled the Assyrians to conquer their neighbors, and how did their aggression finally cause their undoing? (page 30)

In this world rose the Assyrians, another Semitic people who had lived on its periphery. The Assyrians' superior military organization enabled them to conquer many small kingdoms, but they also created many enemies who ultimately joined to defeat them. Assyrian artists, however, were innovators whose ideas were adapted by the Persians.

How did the Persians rise to power and maintain control over their extensive empire? What were the central concepts of their religion, Zoroastrianism? (page 33)

The Persians assimilated the best of the civilizations that they found around them. Through conquest that was mild compared with that of the Assyrians, they broadened the geographical horizons of the ancient world. Their empire looked west to the Greeks and east to the peoples of the Indus Valley, and they gave the Near East a long period of peace. The Persians, whose empire far surpassed the Assyrians', had a farsighted conception of empire. Though as conquerors they willingly used force to accomplish their ends, they preferred to depend on diplomacy to rule. They usually respected their subjects and allowed them to practice their native customs and religions. Thus the Persians gave the Near East both political unity and cultural diversity. Through their religion, Zoroastrianism, they also introduced the concept of life as a battleground between good and evil.

Note

1. Nahum 3:7.

To assess your mastery of this chapter, go to **bedfordstmartins.com/mckaywestbrief**

Key Terms

Yahweh (p. 29)

Babylonian Captivity (p. 29)

Covenant (p. 30)

world empire (p. 35)

Royal Road (p. 35)

Zoroastrianism (p. 35)

Listening to the Past

The Covenant Between Yahweh and the Hebrews

As we mentioned in this chapter, the Hebrew Bible is not a document that we may accept as literal truth, but it does tell us a great deal about the people who created it. From the following passages we may discern what the Hebrews thought about their own past and religion.

The background of the excerpt is a political crisis that has some archaeological support. The king of the Ammonites had threatened to destroy the Hebrews, and word of the threat was sent among the Hebrew tribes. Saul came forth as a leader and rallied the men of Israel and Judah to fight the aggressors, and his army overwhelmed the Ammonites. The elders of the tribes had previously chosen judges to lead the community only in times of crisis. However, the Hebrews demanded that a kingship be established. They turned to Samuel, the last of the judges, who anointed Saul as the first Hebrew king. In this excerpt Samuel reminds the Hebrews of their obligation to honor the Covenant and recognize Yahweh as their true king.

Now therefore behold the king whom you have chosen, and whom you have desired! and behold, the Lord has set a king over you. If you will fear the Lord, and serve him, and obey his voice, and not rebel against the commandment of the Lord, then shall both you and also the king who reigns over you continue following the Lord your God: But if you will not obey the voice of the Lord, but rebel against the commandment of the Lord, then shall the hand of the Lord be against you, as it was against your fathers. Now therefore stand and see this great thing, which the Lord will do before your eyes. Is it not wheat harvest today? I will call to the Lord, and he shall send thunder and rain; that you may perceive and see that your wickedness is great, which you have done in the sight of the Lord, in asking you a king. So Samuel called to the Lord; and the Lord sent thunder and rain that

day: and all the people greatly feared the Lord and Samuel. And all the people said to Samuel, pray for your servants to the Lord your God, so that we will not die: for we have added to all of our sins this evil, to ask us for a king. And Samuel said to the people, Fear not: you have done all this wickedness; yet turn not aside from following the Lord, but serve the Lord with all your heart; And do not turn aside; for then should you go after vain things, which cannot profit nor deliver; for they are vain. For the Lord will not forsake his people for his great name's sake: because it pleases the Lord to make you his people. Moreover, as for me, God forbid that I should sin against the Lord in ceasing to pray for you: but I will teach you the good and the right way: Only fear the Lord, and serve him in truth with all your heart: for consider how great things he has done for you. But if you shall still act wickedly, you will be consumed, both you and your king.

Questions for Analysis

1. What was Samuel's attitude toward kingship?
2. What were the duties of the Hebrews toward Yahweh?
3. Might those duties conflict with those toward the secular king? If so, in what ways, and how might the Hebrews avoid the conflict?

Source: 1 Samuel 11:1–15; 12:1–7, 13–25. Abridged and adapted from *The Holy Bible,* King James Version.

Ark of the Covenant, depicted in a relief from Capernaum Synagogue, second century C.E.
(Ancient Art & Architecture Collection)

CHAPTER 3

Classical Greece

ca. 1650–338 B.C.E.

Chapter Preview

Dionysos at sea. Dionysos here symbolizes the Greek sense of exploration, independence, and love of life. (Bildarchiv Preussischer Kulturbesitz/Art Resource, NY)

The people of ancient Greece developed a culture that fundamentally shaped Western civilization. They were the first to explore most of the questions that continue to concern Western thinkers to this day. Going beyond myth-making, the Greeks strove to understand the world in logical, rational terms. The result was the birth of philosophy and science—subjects that were as important to most Greek thinkers as religion. The concept of politics evolved through Greek philosophy. Greek contributions to the arts and literature were equally profound.

The history of the Greeks is divided into two broad periods: the **Hellenic** (**HELL-len-nic**) **period** (the subject of this chapter), roughly the time between the arrival of the Greeks (approximately 2000 B.C.E.) and the victory over Greece in 338 B.C.E. by Philip of Macedon (**mas-ee-DOHN**); and the **Hellenistic** (**hel-uh-NIS-tik**) **period** (the subject of Chapter 4), the age beginning with the remarkable reign of Philip's son, Alexander the Great (336–323 B.C.E.), and ending with the Roman conquest of the Hellenistic East (200–146 B.C.E.).

Hellenic period The time between the arrival of the Greeks (approximately 2000 B.C.E.) and the victory of Greece in 338 B.C.E. by Philip of Macedon.

Hellenistic period The new culture that arose when Alexander overthrew the Persian Empire and began spreading Hellenism, Greek culture, language, thought, and way of life as far as India. It is called Hellenistic to distinguish it from the Hellenic period.

Hellas: The Land

When the Greeks arrived in Hellas, how did they adapt themselves to their new landscape?

Hellas, as the Greeks still call their land, encompassed the Greek peninsula, the islands of the Aegean (**ah-GEE-uhn**) Sea, and the lands bordering the Aegean, an area known as the **Aegean basin** (see Map 3.1). The Aegean basin included Ionia (**eye-OH-nee-uh**), on the coast of modern Turkey. The Greek peninsula consisted of various regions with distinctive geographical features. In the north and center were Thessaly (**THES-uh-lee**) and Boeotia (**bee-OH-shuh**), regions containing good farmland that helped sustain a strong population capable of fielding a formidable cavalry and infantry. Immediately to the south of Boeotia was Attica (**AT-eh-kah**), an area of thin soil but home to the olive and the vine. Its harbors looked to the Aegean, which invited its inhabitants, the Athenians, to concentrate on maritime commerce. Still farther south was the Peloponnesus (**PELL-eh-puh-neze-us**), a patchwork of high mountains and small plains that divided the area into several regions.

The geographical fragmentation of Greece encouraged political fragmentation. Furthermore, communications were extraordinarily poor. Rocky tracks were far more common than roads, which were seldom paved. These conditions prohibited the growth of a great empire like those of the Near East.

Aegean basin The territory surrounding Greece proper, including the Aegean Sea and Greek islands.

The Minoans and Mycenaeans (ca. 2000–ca. 1100 B.C.E.)

The origins of Greek civilization are complicated, obscure, and diverse. Neolithic peoples had already built prosperous communities in the Aegean, but not until about 2000 B.C.E. did they establish firm contact with one another. By then artisans had discovered how to make bronze, which gave these Stone Age groups more efficient tools and weapons. Some Cretan (**KREE-tan**) farmers and fishermen began to trade their surpluses with their neighbors. The central position of Crete (**kreet**) in the eastern Mediterranean made it a crucial link in this trade. The Cretans voyaged to Egypt, Asia Minor (the lands from the coast of Anatolia to the Euphrates River), other islands, and mainland Greece. They thereby played a vital part in creating an Aegean economy that brought them all into close contact. These favorable circumstances produced the vibrant **Minoan** culture on Crete, named after the mythical King Minos.

Minoan A flourishing and vibrant culture on Crete around 1650 B.C.E., named after King Minos. The symbol of their culture was the palace and its surrounding buildings, the most important one being Cnossus.

THRACE

Byzantium

Sea of Marmara

ANATOLIA

Hebrus R.

Sangarius R.

Hermus R.

Meander R.

LYDIA

Sardis

Smyrna

Ephesus

Miletus

Halicarnassus

Rhodes

Cos

Troy

Hellespont

IONIA

Mycale
479 B.C.E.

Samos

Lesbos

Chios

Nestus R.

Thasos

Lemnos

A e g e a n   S e a

Sea of Crete

35° N

CYCLADES

Naxos

Delos

Andros

Paros

Melos

Crete

Knossos

Gortyn

25° E

Amphipolis

CHALCIDICE

Potidaea

Strymon R.

Mt. Ossa

Mt. Pelion

Artemisium
480 B.C.E.

Euboea

Chalcis

Eretria

Mt. Parnes

Marathon
490 B.C.E.

ATTICA

Axius R.

Pella

MACEDON

Mt. Olympus

Peneus R.

THESSALY

Apidanus R.

Thermopylae
480 B.C.E.

Chaeronea

BOEOTIA

Thebes

Leuctra

Plataea
479 B.C.E.

Eleusis
Athens

Megara

Salamis 480 B.C.E.

Aegina

*Saronic
Gulf*

Mt. Helicon

Delphi

Mt. Parnassus

Gulf of Corinth

Sicyon

Corinth

Nemea

Mycenae

Argos

Epidaurus

Tegea

PINDUS MTS.

AETOLIA

Achelous R.

ACHAEA

Olympia

ELIS

Ellis

ARCADIA

Mantinea

PELOPONNESUS

Sparta

LACONIA

TAYGETOS MTS.

ACARNANIA

Ithaca

Mt. Ithome

MESSENIA

Pylos

Cythera

EPIRUS

Dodona

Aous R.

Corcyra

*I o n i a n
S e a*

20° E

M e d i t e r r a n e a n   S e a

40° N

100 Mi.

100 Km.

50

50

0

0

N

MAP 3.1   Ancient Greece

In antiquity, the home of the Greeks included the islands of the Aegean and the western shore of Asia Minor as well as the Greek peninsula itself.

Ancient Greece

Plains

Major battle of
the Persian Wars

Mountain

Sanctuary

Although the Minoans created a script now called Linear A, very little of it can be read with any certainty. However, archaeology and art offer some glimpses of life on the island. The palace was the political and economic center of its society. About 1650 B.C.E. Crete was dotted with them, but the palace at Cnossus (**NOSS-suhs**) towered above all others in importance. Few specifics are known about Minoan life except that at its head stood a king and his nobles. Minoan society was wealthy and, to judge by the absence of fortifications on the island, relatively peaceful. Minoan artistic remains, including frescoes and figurines, show women as well as men leading religious activities, watching entertainment, and engaging in athletic competitions such as leaping over a bull. We do not know if these represent daily life or mythological scenes, but many scholars see fewer restrictions on women than elsewhere in the ancient world.

Greek-speaking peoples arrived in the peninsula around 2000 B.C.E. They came gradually as individual groups who spoke various dialects of the same language. Despite these dialects, the Greeks considered themselves a related folk. By about 1650 B.C.E. one group had founded a powerful kingdom at Mycenae (**my-SEE-nee**), while others spread elsewhere in Greece. They merged with native inhabitants, and from that union emerged the society that modern scholars call **Mycenaean** (**my-suh-NEE-uhn**), after the most famous site of this new culture.

Early Mycenaean Greeks established cities at Thebes (**theebz**), Athens (**ATH-ins**), and elsewhere. As in Crete, the political unit was the kingdom. The king and his warrior aristocracy stood at the top of society. The seat and symbol of the king's power and wealth was his palace, which was also the economic center of the kingdom. Within its walls royal artisans fashioned jewelry and rich ornaments, made and decorated fine pottery, forged weapons, prepared hides and wool for clothing, and manufactured the other goods needed by the king and his retainers. Palace scribes kept records of taxes and the king's possessions in Greek with a script known as Linear B, which was derived from Minoan Linear A. The Mycenaean economy was marked by an extensive division of labor, all tightly controlled from the palace. At the bottom of the social scale were male and female slaves, who were normally owned by the king and aristocrats but who also worked for ordinary people.

Contacts between the Minoans and Mycenaeans were originally peaceful, and Minoan culture flooded the Greek mainland. But around 1450 B.C.E. the Mycenaeans attacked Crete, destroying many Minoan palaces and taking possession of the grand palace at Cnossus. For about the next fifty years, the Mycenaeans ruled much of the island until a further wave of violence left Cnossus in ashes.

Whatever the explanation of these events, Mycenaean kingdoms in Greece benefited from the fall of Cnossus, quickly expanding commercially throughout the Aegean. Palaces became grander, and citadels were often protected by mammoth stone walls. Prosperity, however, did not bring peace, and between 1300 and 1000 B.C.E. kingdom after kingdom suffered attack and destruction. Although later Greeks accused the Dorians (**DOR-ee-ahns**) of overthrowing the Mycenaean kingdoms, these centers undoubtedly fell because of mutual discord. The fall of the Mycenaean kingdoms ushered in a period of such poverty and disruption that historians usually call it the "Dark Age" of Greece (ca. 1100–800 B.C.E.). Even

ca. 1650–1000 B.C.E.	Arrival of the Mycenaean Greeks in Europe
ca. 1100–800 B.C.E.	Evolution of the polis; Greek migrations within the Aegean basin; poems of Homer and Hesiod
ca. 800–500 B.C.E.	Rise of Sparta and Athens; flowering of lyric poetry
776 B.C.E.	Founding of the Olympic games
ca. 750–550 B.C.E.	Greek colonization of the Mediterranean
ca. 700–500 B.C.E.	Concentration of landed wealth
ca. 640 B.C.E.	Use of coinage in western Asia
ca. 525–362 B.C.E.	Birth and development of tragedy, historical writing, and philosophy; spread of monumental architecture
499–479 B.C.E.	Persian wars
431–404 B.C.E.	Peloponnesian War
404–338 B.C.E.	Spartan and Theban hegemonies; success of Philip of Macedon

Mycenaean A society created from a union between native inhabitants and the powerful group centered at Mycenae; it was named after the most famous site of this new culture.

literacy, which was not widespread in any case, was a casualty of the chaos. None-theless, Greece remained Greek; nothing essential was swept away. Greek religious cults remained vital to the people, and basic elements of social organization continued to function effectively. It was a time of change and challenge, but not of utter collapse.

The disruption of Mycenaean societies caused the widespread movement of Greek peoples. They dispersed beyond mainland Greece farther south to Crete and in greater strength across the Aegean to the shores of Asia Minor. They arrived during a time when traditional states and empires had collapsed. Economic hardship was common, and various groups wandered for years. Yet by the end of the Dark Age, the Greeks had spread their culture throughout the Aegean basin.

Homer, Hesiod, Gods, and Heroes (1100–800 B.C.E.)

The Greeks, unlike the Hebrews, had no sacred book that chronicled their past. Instead they had the poems of Homer and Hesiod (HES-ee-uhd) to describe a legendary Heroic Age when gods and heroes still walked the earth. In terms of pure history these works contain scraps of information about the Bronze Age, much about the early Dark Age, and some about the poets' own era.

Homer's *Iliad* recounts an expedition of Mycenaeans, whom Homer called "Achaeans" (ah-KEY-uhns), to besiege the city of Troy in Asia Minor. The war was incited, as Homer tells it, by the Trojan prince Paris's abduction of the beautiful Helen, wife of a Mycenaean king. The heart of the *Iliad*, however, concerns the quarrel between Agamemnon, leader of the Mycenaean force, and his greatest

The Hellenic Period

Period	Significant Events	Major Writers
Bronze Age	Arrival of the Greeks in Greece	
2000–1100 B.C.E.	Rise and fall of the Mycenaean kingdoms	
Dark Age	Greek migrations within the Aegean basin	Homer
1100–800 B.C.E.	Social and political recovery	Hesiod
	Evolution of the polis	
	Rebirth of literacy	
Archaic Age	Rise of Sparta and Athens	
800–500 B.C.E.	Colonization of the Mediterranean basin	Sappho
	Flowering of lyric poetry	Solon
	Development of philosophy and science in Ionia	Anaximander Heraclitus
Classical Period	Persian wars	Herodotus
500–338 B.C.E.	Growth of the Athenian Empire	Thucydides
	Peloponnesian War	Aeschylus
	Rise of drama and historical writing	Sophocles
	Flowering of Greek philosophy	Euripides
	Spartan and Theban hegemonies	Aristophanes
	Conquest of Greece by Philip of Macedon	Plato Aristotle

warrior Achilles (**uh-KIL-eez**), who refuses to fight when Agamemnon wounds his pride. The *Odyssey* (**OD-uh-see**) narrates Odysseus's (**oh-DIS-ee-uhs**) long journey home from Troy; while quick-witted, his pride is also the source of his misfortunes.

Both of Homer's epics portray engaging but flawed characters who are larger than life and yet typically human. Homer was also strikingly successful in depicting the great gods, who generally sit on Mount Olympus (**oh-LIM-puhs**) and watch the fighting at Troy like spectators at a baseball game, although they sometimes participate in the action. Homer's deities are reminiscent of Mesopotamian gods and goddesses. Hardly a decorous lot, the Olympians are raucous, petty, deceitful, and splendid. In short, they are human.

Hesiod, who lived somewhat later than Homer, made the gods the focus of his epic poem, the *Theogony* (**thee-OG-uh-nee**). Hesiod was influenced by Mesopotamian myths, which the Hittites had adopted and spread to the Aegean. Like the Hebrews, Hesiod envisaged his cosmogony—his account of the way the universe developed—in moral and gendered terms. Originally the primary deity was an earth goddess, Gaia (**GAY-yah**), but through a series of incestuous relationships and generational conflicts, Zeus (zooss) emerged triumphant. He established a moral order with himself at the head, ending the chaotic female-dominated system. In *Theogony* and others of his works, Hesiod attributes all human problems to the first woman, Pandora (**pan-DOHR-uh**), whose curiosity led her to open the container in which pain, war, and other evils had been enclosed.

The Polis

After the Greeks had established the polis, in which they lived their political and social lives, how did they shape it into its several historical forms?

After the upheavals that ended the Mycenaean period and the slow recovery of prosperity during the Dark Age, the Greeks developed the **polis** (**PAU-lis**). The term *polis* is generally interpreted as "city-state," although the word is basically untranslatable. While "city-state" does not capture how integral the countryside was to the community, it is at least a term generally understood and accepted.

The polis was far more than a political institution. Above all it was a community of citizens whose customs comprised the laws of the polis. Even though the physical, religious, and political form of the polis varied from place to place, it was the very badge of Greekness.

Origins of the Polis

Recent archaeological expeditions and careful study have done much to clarify the origins of the polis. Even during the late Mycenaean period, towns had grown up around palaces. These towns and even smaller villages performed basically local functions. The first was to administer the ordinary political affairs of the community. The village also served a religious purpose in that no matter how small, each had its local cult to its own deity. The exchange of daily goods made these towns and villages economically important, if only on a small scale. These settlements also developed a social system that was particularly their own. They likewise had their own views of the social worth and status of their inhabitants and the nature of their public responsibilities. In short, they relied on custom and mutual agreement to direct their ordinary affairs.

polis Generally interpreted as city-state, it was the basic political and institutional unit of Greece.

When fully developed, each polis normally shared a surprisingly large number of features with other poleis. Physically a polis was a society of people who lived in a city (*asty*) and cultivated the surrounding countryside (*chora*). The city's water supply came from public fountains, springs, and cisterns. By the fifth century B.C.E. the city was generally surrounded by a wall. The city contained a point, usually elevated, called the **acropolis** (**ah-KROP-uh-lis**) and a public square or marketplace called the **agora** (**AG-er-uh**). On the acropolis, which in the early period was a place of refuge, stood the temples, altars, public monuments, and various dedications to the gods of the polis. The agora was originally the place where the warrior assembly met, but it became the political center of the polis. In the agora were porticoes, shops, and public buildings and courts.

The countryside was essential to the economy of the polis and provided food to sustain the entire population. But it was also home to sanctuaries for the deities of the polis and the site of important religious rites. The sacred buildings, shrines, and altars were the physical symbols of a polis, uniting country and city dwellers. The religious dedications in them were the possessions not only of the gods but also of the polis, reflecting its power and prestige.

The average polis did not have a standing army. Instead it relied on its citizens for protection. Very rich citizens often served as cavalry, which was, however, never as important as the heavily armed infantry, or **hoplites** (**HOP-lites**). These were the backbone of the army. Hoplites wore metal helmets and body armor, carried heavy, round shields, and armed themselves with spears and swords. They provided their own equipment and were basically amateurs. In some instances the citizens of a polis hired mercenaries to fight their battles. Mercenaries were expensive, untrustworthy, and willing to defect to a higher bidder. Even worse, they sometimes seized control over the polis that had hired them.

acropolis An elevated point within a city on which stood temples, altars, public monuments, and various dedications to the gods of the polis.

agora A public square or marketplace that was a political center of Greece.

hoplites The heavily armed infantry that were the backbone of the Greek army.

monarchy Derived from the Greek for the rule of one man, it was a type of Greek government in which a king represented the community.

tyranny Rule by a tyrant, a man who used his wealth to gain a political following that could take over the existing government.

Governing Structures

Greek city-states had several different types of government. **Monarchy,** rule by a king, was prevalent during the Mycenaean period but afterwards declined. While Sparta (**SPAHR-tuh**) boasted of two kings, they were only part of a more broadly based constitution. During fully developed historical times Greek states were either democracies or oligarchies. Sporadic periods of violent political and social upheaval often led to a third type of government—tyranny. **Tyranny** was rule by one man who had seized power by unconstitutional means, generally by using his wealth to win a political following that toppled the existing legal government.

The Delphic Oracle

The Marmaria, the sanctuary of Athena, is seen here against the backdrop of the mountains that surround the sanctuary of Apollo. Around the oracle clustered many temples to various deities, shrines, and other sacred buildings, all of them in a remote mountainous area especially chosen by Apollo to be his home and the place where he answered the supplications of the faithful. (John Buckler)

Only democracy and oligarchy (**OLL-ih-gahr-key**) played lasting, broad roles in Greek political life, and these two forms flourished across Greece well into later years. In principle, **democracy** meant that all people, without respect to birth or wealth, administered the workings of government. In reality, Greek democracy meant the rule of citizens, not "the people" as a whole, and citizenship was drastically limited. In Athens and in other democracies, only free adult men who had lived in the polis a long time were citizens. Women, foreigners, slaves, and others had no rights. The 10 to 20 percent of the population who were citizens generally shared equally in the determination of policy and the administration of government. Along with military service, citizenship provided men with an opportunity to bond with one another, and it became an important component in Greek ideas of masculinity.

Most Greek states actually preferred oligarchy to democracy as their form of government. **Oligarchy,** which literally means "the rule of the few," was government by a small group of wealthy citizens. Oligarchy generally gave its whole population—leaders and people alike—stable government and freedom to prosper. Men could advance politically by earning enough wealth to qualify for the right to vote for officials and to hold office. Although the wealthy governed the city, they officially endorsed social mobility for capable men and application of the law equally to everyone. Corinthian oligarchs also listened to the will of the citizens, a major factor in their long success.

Oligarchy evolved into federalism first in the region of Boetia, where the oligarchy of Thebes united with neighboring oligarchies to form the "Boeotian Confederacy." **Federalism** in Greece meant a system of government in which individual city-states joined to create one general government. The Boeotian Confederacy of oligarchic city-states proved so successful that elsewhere in Greece other states followed its example. It was particularly popular and widespread later in the Hellenistic period.

democracy A type of Greek government in which all citizens, without regard to birth or wealth, administered the workings of government; it translates as the power of the people.

oligarchy The rule of a few; a type of Greek government in which a small group of wealthy citizens, not necessarily of aristocratic birth, ruled.

federalism One of two political concepts created by Greeks in the fourth century B.C.E. in an attempt to prevent war. It uses the idea that security can be gained through numbers. Greek leagues would band together and marshal their resources to defend themselves from outside interference.

During the classical period (500–338 B.C.E.), however, despite the allure of federalism, the citizens of the vast majority of city-states were determined to remain autonomous. The very integration of the polis proved to be one of its basic weaknesses. The political result, as earlier in Sumer, was almost constant warfare. The polis could dominate, but unlike earlier and later empires, it could not incorporate.

The Archaic Age (800–500 B.C.E.)

What major developments mark the Archaic Greek period in terms of spread of culture and the growth of cities?

The Archaic (**ahr-KAY-ik**) Age was one of the most vibrant periods of Greek history, an era of extraordinary expansion geographically, artistically, and politically. Greeks ventured as far east as the Black Sea and as far west as Spain. With the rebirth of literacy, this period also witnessed a tremendous literary flowering. Politically these were the years when Sparta and Athens—the two poles of the Greek experience—rose to prominence.

Overseas Expansion

During the years 1100–800 B.C.E. the Greeks not only recovered from the breakdown of the Mycenaean world but also grew in wealth and numbers. This new prosperity brought new problems. The increase in population meant that many families had very little land or none at all. Land hunger and the resulting social and political tensions drove many Greek men and women to seek new homes outside of Greece. Other factors, largely intangible, played their part as well: the desire for a new start, a love of excitement and adventure, and natural curiosity about what lay beyond the horizon.

From about 750 to 550 B.C.E., Greeks from the mainland and Asia Minor traveled throughout the Mediterranean and even into the Atlantic Ocean in their quest for new land. They sailed in the greatest numbers to Sicily and southern Italy, where there was ample space for expansion.

Colonization changed the entire Greek world, both at home and abroad. In economic terms it created a much larger market for the exchange of agricultural and manufactured goods. From the east, especially from the northern coast of the Black Sea, came wheat in a volume beyond the capacity of Greek soil. In return flowed Greek wine and olive oil, which could not be produced in the harsher climate of the north. Greek-manufactured goods, notably rich jewelry and fine pottery, circulated from southern Russia to Spain. During this same period the Greeks adopted the custom of minting coins, a custom they apparently imported from Lydia. At first coinage was of little economic importance, and only later did it replace the common practice of barter. In the barter system one person simply exchanges one good for another without the use of money. Thus Greek culture and economics, fertilized by the influences of other societies, spread throughout the Mediterranean basin.

Colonization presented the polis with a huge challenge, for it required organization and planning on an unprecedented scale. The colonizing city, called the **metropolis,** or mother city, first decided where to establish the colony, how to transport colonists to the site, and who would sail. Then the metropolis collected and stored the supplies that the colonists would need both to feed themselves and

metropolis The colonizing or "mother" city, responsible for deciding where to establish the colony.

Mosaic Portrait of Sappho
The Greek letters in the upper left corner identify this idealized portrait as that of Sappho (**SAF-oh**), a poet of the Archaic period. Sappho's verse expressed the intensely personal side of life, including erotic love. She was bisexual, and her name become linked with female homosexual love. The English word *lesbian* is derived from her island home of Lesbos (**LEZ-bos**). (Museum of Sparta/Archaeological Receipts Fund)

to plant their first crop. Once the colonists landed, their leader laid out the new polis, selected the sites of temples and public buildings, and established the government. Then he surrendered power. The colony was thereafter independent of the metropolis. For the Greeks, colonization had two important aspects. First, it demanded that the polis assume a much greater public function than ever before, thus strengthening the city-state's institutional position. Second, colonization spread the polis and its values far beyond the shores of Greece. Even more important, colonization on this scale had a profound impact on the course of Western civilization. It meant that the prevailing culture of the Mediterranean basin would be Greek.

The Growth of Sparta
During the Archaic period the Spartans expanded the boundaries of their polis and made it the leading power in Greece. Like other Greeks, the Spartans faced the problems of overpopulation and land hunger. Unlike other Greeks, the Spartans solved these problems by conquest, not by colonization. To gain more land, the Spartans set out in about 735 B.C.E. to conquer Messenia (**muh-SEE-nee-uh**), a rich, fertile region in the southwestern Peloponnesus. This conflict, the First Messenian War, lasted for twenty years and ended in a Spartan triumph. The Spartans appropriated Messenian land and turned the Messenians into **helots** (**HELL-uts**), or state serfs who worked the land.

| **helots** State serfs who worked the land.

In about 650 B.C.E. Spartan exploitation and oppression of the Messenian helots led to a helot revolt so massive and stubborn that it became known as the Second Messenian War. The Spartan poet Tyrtaeus, a contemporary of these events, vividly portrays the ferocity of the fighting:

For it is a shameful thing indeed
When with the foremost fighters
An elder falling in front of the young men
Lies outstretched,
Having white hair and grey beard,
Breathing forth his stout soul in the dust,
Holding in his hands his genitals
stained with blood.[1]

It took the full might of the Spartan people, aristocrat and commoner alike, to win the Second Messenian War. After the victory non-noblemen, who had done much of the fighting, demanded rights equal to those of the nobility. The agitation of these non-nobles disrupted society until the aristocrats agreed to erase political distinctions among Spartan warriors. An oligarchy of five *ephors* (**EF-fors**), or over-seers, held the real executive power, while two kings and twenty-eight elders delib-erated on foreign and domestic matters.

Every Spartan citizen owed primary allegiance to the polis. Once Spartan boys reached the age of seven, they were enrolled in separate companies with other boys their age. They lived in this **homosocial** (same-sex) setting for much of their lives. They slept outside on reed mats and underwent rugged training until age twenty-four, when they became frontline soldiers. For the rest of their lives, Spar-tan men kept themselves prepared for combat. Their military training never ceased, and the older men were expected to be models of endurance, frugality, and sturdiness to the younger men. In battle Spartans were supposed to stand and die rather than retreat. An anecdote frequently repeated about one Spartan mother sums up Spartan military values. As her son was setting off to battle, the mother handed him his shield and advised him to come back either victorious, carrying the shield, or dead, being carried on it.

In this militaristic atmosphere, citizen women were remarkably free. The Spartan leadership viewed maternal health as important for the bearing of strong children and thus encouraged women to participate in athletics and to eat well. With men in military service most of their lives, citizen women owned property and ran the household; they were not physically restricted or secluded. Marriage often began with a trial marriage period to make sure the couple could have chil-dren, with divorce and remarriage the normal course if they were unsuccessful. Men saw their wives only rarely when they sneaked out of camp, and their most meaningful relations were same-sex ones. Spartan military leaders viewed such relationships as militarily advantageous, judging that men would fight more fiercely in defense of close comrades and lovers. Close links among men thus contributed to Spartan dedication to the state and understanding of civic virtue, which were admired throughout the Greek world.

> **homosocial** Same-sex setting in which Spartan boys lived for much of their lives.

The Evolution of Athens

Like Sparta, Athens faced pressing social and economic problems during the Archaic period, but the Athenian response was far different from that of the Spartans. Instead of creating an oligarchy, the Athenians extended to all citizens the right and duty of governing the polis. Indeed, the Athenian democracy was one of the most thoroughgoing in Greece.

The late seventh century B.C.E. was for Athens a time of turmoil, the causes of which are virtually unknown. In 621 B.C.E. Draco (**DRAY-koh**), an Athenian aristo-crat, doubtless under pressure from the peasants, published the first law code of the Athenian polis. His code was thought harsh, but it nonetheless embodied the ideal that the law belonged to the citizens. Nevertheless, the aristocracy still governed Athens oppressively and by the early sixth century B.C.E. the situation was explosive. The aristocrats owned the best land, met in an assembly to govern the polis, and interpreted the law. Noble landowners were forcing small farmers into economic dependence. Many families were sold into slavery; others were exiled and their land was pledged to the rich.

One person who recognized these problems clearly was the poet Solon (**SOH-luhn**), himself an aristocrat. Solon recited his poems in the Athenian agora, where anyone there could hear his call for justice and fairness and his condemnation of aristocratic greed and dishonesty. The aristocrats realized that Solon was no crazed revolutionary, and the common people trusted him. Around 594 B.C.E. the nobles elected him *archon* (**AHR-kon**), chief magistrate of the Athenian polis, and gave him extraordinary power to reform the state.

Solon immediately freed all people enslaved for debt, recalled all exiles, canceled all debts on land, and made enslavement for debt illegal. Solon allowed even the poorest men into the old aristocratic assembly, where they could take part in the election of magistrates.

Although Solon's reforms solved some immediate problems, they did not bring peace to Athens. Some aristocrats attempted to make themselves tyrants, while others banded together to oppose them. In 546 B.C.E. Pisistratus (**pie-SIS-tra-tus**), an exiled aristocrat, returned to Athens, defeated his opponents, and became tyrant. Pisistratus reduced the power of the aristocracy while supporting the common people. Under his rule Athens prospered, and his building program began to transform the city into one of the splendors of Greece. His reign as tyrant promoted the growth of democratic ideas by arousing rudimentary feelings of equality in many Athenian men.

Democracy took shape in Athens under the leadership of Cleisthenes (**KLAHYS-thuh-neez**), a prominent aristocrat who won the support of lower-status men to emerge triumphant in 508 B.C.E. Cleisthenes created the **deme** (**deem**), a local unit that kept the roll of citizens, or *demos*, within its jurisdiction.

The democracy functioned on the idea that all full citizens were sovereign. Yet not all citizens could take time from work to participate in government. Therefore, they delegated their power to other citizens by creating various offices meant to run the democracy. The most prestigious of them was the board of ten archons who were charged with handling legal and military matters. Six of them oversaw the Athenian legal system. They presided over courts, fixed dates for trials, and ensured that the laws of Athens were consistent. They were all elected for one year. After leaving office they entered the *Areopagus* (**ar-ee-OP-uh-gus**), a select council of ex-archons who handled cases involving homicide, wounding, and arson.

Legislation was in the hands of two bodies, the **boule** (**BOO-lee**), or council, composed of five hundred members, and the **ecclesia** (**ee-KLEE-zhee-uh**), the assembly of all citizens. The boule, separate from the Areopagus, was perhaps the major institution of the democracy. By supervising the various committees of government and proposing bills to the assembly, it guided Athenian political life. It received foreign envoys and forwarded treaties to the assembly for ratification. It oversaw the granting of state contracts and was responsible for receiving many revenues. It held the democracy together. Nonetheless, the ecclesia had the final word. Every citizen could express his opinion on any subject on the agenda, and a simple majority vote was needed to pass or reject a bill.

Athenian democracy was to prove an inspiring ideal in Western civilization. It demonstrated that a large group of people, not just a few, could efficiently run the affairs of state. Because citizens could speak their minds, they did not have to resort

deme A local unit that served as the basis of Cleisthenes' political system.

boule Part of a larger legislative body (with the ecclesia), it is a council composed of five hundred members.

ecclesia An assembly of all citizens that serves as the other legislative body with the boule.

Section Review

- The Greek growth in population and wealth led to overseas colonization throughout the Mediterranean basin.

- The colonizing city, the metropolis, spread Greek culture by determining the sites of colonies.

- Sparta was a militaristic society involved in both the First and Second Messenian wars, making the Messenians into helots (slaves).

- Spartan males lived in a homosocial setting for most of their lives, contributing to their dedication to the state and allowing their women much economic freedom.

- Draco made harsh laws and Solon reformed Athens, leading to tyrannical rule before Cleisthenes established democracy through the *deme*.

- Citizens ruled democratically in Athens through *archons* (legal and military), the *Areopagus* (former archons), the *boule* (council of five hundred), and *ecclesia* (assembly of all citizens).

to rebellion or conspiracy to express their desires. Like all democracies in ancient Greece, however, Athenian democracy was limited. Slaves, women, recent migrants, and foreigners could not be citizens; their opinions about political issues were not taken into account or recorded.

The Classical Period (500–338 B.C.E.)

How did the Greeks develop their literature, philosophy, religion, and art, and how did war affect this intellectual and social process?

In the years 500 to 338 B.C.E., Greek civilization reached its highest peak in politics, thought, and art. In this period the Greeks beat back the armies of the Persian Empire. Then, turning their spears against one another, they destroyed their own political system in a century of warfare. Some thoughtful Greeks felt prompted to record and analyze these momentous events. Herodotus (ca. 485–425 B.C.E.), from Asia Minor, traveled the Greek world to piece together the course of the Persian wars. Although he consulted documents when he could find them, he relied largely on the memories of the participants, making him the first oral historian as well as the "father of history." Next came Thucydides (**thoo-SID-ih-dees**) (ca. 460–ca. 399 B.C.E.), whose account of the Peloponnesian (**PELL-eh-puh-neze-an**) War remains a classic of Western literature. Unlike Herodotus, he was often a participant in the events that he described.

This era also saw the flowering of philosophy, as thinkers in Ionia and on the Greek mainland began to ponder the nature and meaning of the universe and human experience. The Greeks invented drama, and the Athenian tragedians Aeschylus (**ES-kuh-luhs**), Sophocles (**SOF-uh-kleez**), and Euripides (**yoo-RIP-eh-deez**) explored themes that still inspire audiences today. Greek architects reached the zenith of their art and created buildings whose very ruins still inspire awe. Because Greek intellectual and artistic efforts attained their fullest and finest expression in these years, this age is called the "classical period." Few periods in the history of Western society can match it in sheer dynamism and achievement.

Leonidas at Thermopylae
This heroic statue symbolizes the sacrifice of King Leonidas at the battle. Together with his Spartans, the Thespians, and the Thebans, he heroically died to stop the Persians at the pass of Thermopylae. (Professor Paul Cartledge)

The Persian Wars (499–479 B.C.E.)

One of the hallmarks of the classical period was warfare. In 499 B.C.E. the Ionian Greeks, with the feeble help of Athens, rebelled against the Persian Empire. In 490 B.C.E. the Persians struck back at Athens but were beaten off at the Battle of Marathon, on a small plain in Attica. This victory taught the Greeks that they could defeat the Persians and successfully defend their homeland. It also prompted the Persians to try again. In 480 B.C.E. the Persian king Xerxes led a mighty invasion force into Greece. In the face of this emergency, many of the Greeks united and pooled their resources to resist the invaders. The Spartans provided the overall leadership and commanded the Greek armies. The Athenians, led by the wily Themistocles (**thuh-MIS-tuh-kleez**), provided the heart of the naval forces. After an initial defeat at the battle of Thermopylae (**thuhr-MOP-uh-lee**), the Greek military repelled the Persians at sea and on land.

The significance of these Greek victories is nearly incalculable. By defeating the Persians, the Greeks ensured that they would not be taken over by a monarchy, which they increasingly viewed as un-Greek. The decisive victories meant that Greek political forms and intellectual concepts would be handed down to later societies.

<table>
<tr><td>

Growth of the Athenian Empire (478–431 B.C.E.)

</td><td>

The defeat of the Persians created a power vacuum in the Aegean, and the Athenians took advantage of this situation. The Athenians and their allies formed the Delian (**DAY-lee-un**) League, a grand naval alliance

</td></tr>
</table>

aimed at liberating Ionia from Persian rule. Athenians provided most of the warships and crews and determined how many ships or how much money each member of the league should contribute to the allied effort.

Delian League A grand naval alliance aimed at liberating Ionia from Persian rule created by the Athenians and led by Aristides.

The Athenians, supported by the Delian League and led by the young aristocrat Cimon (**SIGH-muhn**), carried the war against Persia. But Athenian success had a sinister side. While the Athenians drove the Persians out of the Aegean, they also became increasingly imperialistic. Athens began reducing its allies to the status of subjects. Tribute was often collected by force, and the Athenians placed the economic resources of the Delian League under tighter and tighter control. Dissident governments were put down, and Athenian ideas of freedom and democracy did not extend to the citizens of other cities.

Athens justified its conduct by its successful leadership. In about 467 B.C.E. Cimon defeated a new and huge Persian force at the Battle of the Eurymedon River in Asia Minor, once again removing the shadow of Persia from the Aegean. But as the threat from Persia waned and the Athenians treated their allies more harshly, major allies such as Thasos (**THAH-saws**) revolted (ca. 465 B.C.E.), requiring the Delian League to use its forces against its own members.

The expansion of Athenian power and the aggressiveness of Athenian rule also alarmed Sparta and its allies. While relations between Athens and Sparta cooled, Pericles (**PER-eh-kleez**) (ca. 494–429 B.C.E.) became the leading statesman in Athens. Like the democracy he led, Pericles, an aristocrat of solid intellectual ability, was aggressive and imperialistic. At last, in 459 B.C.E. Sparta and Athens went to war over conflicts between Athens and some of Sparta's allies. Though the Athenians conquered Boeotia (**bee-OH-shuh**), Megara (**MEG-er-uh**), and Aegina (**ee-JAY-nuh**) in the early stages of the war, they met defeat in Egypt and later in Boeotia. The war ended in 445 B.C.E. with no serious damage to either side and nothing settled. But this war divided the Greek world between the two great powers.

Athens continued its severe policies toward its subject allies and also battled Corinth, one of Sparta's leading supporters (see Map 3.2). Pericles also escalated the tension in the region by excluding Megara from trade with the Athenian empire as punishment for alleged sacrilege. In response the Spartans convened a meeting of their allies, whose complaints of Athenian aggression ended with a demand that Athens be stopped. Reluctantly the Spartans agreed to declare war.

<table>
<tr><td>

The Peloponnesian War (431–404 B.C.E.)

</td><td>

At the outbreak of this conflict, the Peloponnesian War, the Spartan ambassador Melesippus warned the Athenians: "This day will be the beginning of great evil

</td></tr>
</table>

for the Greeks." Indeed, the Peloponnesian War lasted a generation and brought

Athens and allies
Sparta and allies
Neutral Greek states
Persian Empire
⭐ Major battle
🔥 Major siege of city

MAPPING THE PAST

MAP 3.2   The Peloponnesian War

This map shows the alignment of states during the Peloponnesian War. **[1]** What does Map 3.2 tell us about the balance of power during the Peloponnesian War? Which states led the others? **[2]** Are the leading states in Map 3.2 still the leaders in the next century?

in its wake fearful plagues, famine, civil wars, widespread destruction, and huge loss of life.

After a Theban attack on the nearby polis of Plataea (**pluh-TEE-uh**), the Peloponnesian War began in earnest. In the next seven years, the army of Sparta and its Peloponnesian allies invaded Attica five times. The Athenians stood behind their walls, but in 430 B.C.E. the cramped conditions nurtured a plague that killed huge numbers, eventually claiming Pericles himself. (See the feature "Listening to the Past: The Great Plague at Athens, 430 B.C.E." on page 64.) Under a new leader, Cleon (**KLEE-on**), the Athenians counterattacked and defeated the Spartans at Pylos (**PIE-lohs**), yet the Spartans responded by widening the war. Only after ten years of death, destruction, and stalemate did Sparta and Athens agree to the Peace of Nicias (**NISH-ee-uhs**) in 421 B.C.E.

The Peace of Nicias resulted in a cold war. But even cold war can bring horror and misery. Such was the case when in 416 B.C.E. the Athenians sent a fleet to the neutral island of Melos with an ultimatum: the Melians could surrender or perish. The motives of the Athenians were frankly and brutally imperialistic. The Melians resisted. The Athenians conquered them, killed the men of military age, and sold the women and children into slavery.

The cold war grew hotter, thanks to the ambitions of Alcibiades (**al-suh-BAHY-uh-dees**) (ca. 450–404 B.C.E.), an aristocrat, a kinsman of Pericles, and a student of the philosopher Socrates (**SOK-ruh-teez**). Alcibiades convinced the Athenians to attack Syracuse, the leading polis in Sicily. Ultimately the people of Syracuse prevailed, as Thucydides wrote: "[Athenian] infantry, fleet, and everything else were utterly destroyed, and out of many few returned home."[2]

The disaster in Sicily ushered in the final phase of the war, which was marked by three major developments: the renewal of war between Athens and Sparta, Persia's intervention in the war, and the revolt of many Athenian subjects. The year 413 B.C.E. saw Sparta's declaration of war against Athens and widespread revolt within the Athenian Empire. Yet Sparta still lacked a navy, the only instrument that could take advantage of the unrest of Athens's subjects, most of whom lived either on islands or in Ionia. The sly Alcibiades, now working for Sparta, provided a solution: the Persians would build a fleet for Sparta, and Sparta would give Ionia back to Persia. Now equipped with a fleet, the Spartans challenged the Athenians in the Aegean, the result being a long roll of inconclusive naval battles.

The strain of war prompted the Athenians in 407 B.C.E. to recall Alcibiades from exile. He cheerfully double-crossed the Spartans and Persians, but even he could not restore Athenian fortunes. In 405 B.C.E. Athens met its match in the Spartan commander Lysander, who destroyed the last Athenian fleet and blockaded Athens until it was starved into submission. After twenty-seven years the Peloponnesian War was over, and the evils prophesied by the Spartan ambassador Melesippus in 431 B.C.E. had come true.

Athenian Arts in the Age of Pericles

In the last half of the fifth century B.C.E., Pericles turned Athens into the showplace of Greece. He appropriated Delian League funds to pay for a huge building program, planning temples and other buildings to honor Athena (**uh-THEE-nuh**), the patron goddess of the city, and to display to all Greeks the glory of the Athenian polis. The main site of these projects was the acropolis, and the largest monument was the Parthenon (**PAHR-thuh-non**), a temple to Athena.

In many ways the Athenian Acropolis is the epitome of Greek art and its spirit. Although the buildings were dedicated to the gods and most of the sculptures portray gods, these works nonetheless express the Greek fascination with the human form. In the Parthenon sculptures it is visually impossible to distinguish the men and women from the gods and goddesses. The Acropolis also exhibits the rational side of Greek art. Greek artists portrayed action in a balanced and restrained fashion, capturing the noblest aspects of human beings: their reason and dignity.

Other aspects of Athenian cultural life were also rooted in the life of the polis. The development of drama was tied to the religious festivals of the city. The polis sponsored the production of plays and required that wealthy citizens pay the expenses of their production. Many plays were highly controversial, but they were neither suppressed nor censored.

The Athenian dramatists were the first artists in Western society to examine such basic questions as the rights of the individual, the demands of society on the individual, and the nature of good and evil. Conflict is a central element in Athenian drama.

In his trilogy of plays, *The Oresteia* (**ohr-e-STEE-uh**), Aeschylus (525–456 B.C.E.) deals with the themes of betrayal, murder, and reconciliation, urging that

The Acropolis of Athens

These buildings embody the noblest spirit of Greek architecture. From the entrance the visitors walk through the Propylaea, a ceremonial gateway. Ahead opens the grand view of the Parthenon, still noble in ruins. To the left stands another temple, the Erectheum, the whole a monument to Athens itself. (Courtesy, Sotiris Toumbis Editions)

reason and justice be applied to resolve fundamental conflicts. The final play concludes with a prayer that civil dissension never be allowed to destroy the city and that the life of the city be one of harmony and grace.

Sophocles (496–406 B.C.E.) also dealt with matters personal and political. In *Antigone* (an-TIG-uh-nee) he highlights conflicts between divine and human law and comments on the gender order in Greek society. Antigone defies Creon, her uncle and king, to follow divinely established rules and bury her brother against Creon's decree. Creon rages that she is not above the laws he has established, and that if he does not punish her she will be more man than he is. Antigone escapes her punishment by committing suicide.

Perhaps his most famous plays are *Oedipus* (ED-uh-puhs) *the King* and its sequel, *Oedipus at Colonus*. *Oedipus the King* is the tragic story of a man doomed by the gods to kill his father and marry his mother. Try as he might to avoid his fate, Oedipus's every action brings him closer to its fulfillment. When at last he realizes that he has carried out the decree of the gods, Oedipus blinds himself and flees into exile. In *Oedipus at Colonus* Sophocles dramatizes the last days of the broken king, whose patient suffering and piety win him an exalted position. In the end the gods honor him for his virtue. These stories are renowned for their psychological depth and wrenching emotions.

With Euripides (ca. 480–406 B.C.E.), drama entered a new, in many ways more personal, phase. To him the gods were far less important than human beings. The essence of Euripides' tragedy is the flawed character—men and women who bring disaster on themselves and their loved ones because their passions overwhelm reason. Although Euripides' plays were less popular in his lifetime than were those of Aeschylus and Sophocles, his work was to have a significant impact on Roman drama.

Writers of comedy treated the affairs of the polis and its leading politicians bawdily and often coarsely. Even so, their plays also were performed at religious festivals. Best known are the comedies of Aristophanes (**ar-uh-STOFF-uh-neze**) (ca. 445–386 B.C.E.), an ardent lover of his city and a merciless critic of cranks and quacks. He lampooned eminent generals, at times depicting them as morons. He commented snidely on Pericles, poked fun at Socrates, and hooted at Euripides. Through satire, he too commented on human conduct and values.

Woman Grinding Grain
Here a woman takes the grain raised on the family farm and grinds it by hand in a mill. She needed few tools to turn the grain into flour. (National Archaeological Museum, Athens/Archaeological Receipts Fund)

Daily Life in Periclean Athens

The Athenian house was rather simple. It consisted of a series of rooms opening onto a central courtyard that contained the well, an altar, and a washbasin. Larger houses often had a room at the front where the men of the family ate and entertained guests, and a women's quarter at the back. If the family lived in the country, the stalls of the animals faced the courtyard. Country dwellers kept oxen for plowing, pigs for slaughtering, sheep for wool, goats for cheese, and mules and donkeys for transportation. Even in the city chickens and perhaps a goat or two roamed the courtyard together with dogs and cats.

In the city a man might support himself as a craftsman—a potter, bronzesmith, sailmaker, or tanner—or he could contract with the polis to work on public buildings, such as the Parthenon. Certain crafts, including spinning and weaving, were generally done by women. Men and women without skills worked as paid laborers but competed with slaves for work. Slaves were usually foreigners whose native language was not Greek. Citizens and slaves were paid the same amount for their work.

Gender

The social condition of Athenian women has been the subject of much debate. One of the difficulties is the fragmentary nature of the evidence. Women appear frequently in literature and art, often in idealized roles, but seldom in historical contexts of a wider and more realistic nature (see the feature "Individuals in Society: Aspasia"). This is due in part to the fact that most Greek historians of the time recounted primarily the political, diplomatic, and military events of the day, events in which women seldom played a notable part. Yet that does not mean that women were totally invisible in the life of the polis. It indicates instead that ancient sources provide only a glimpse of how women affected the society in which they lived. Athenian men believed that men and women should be segregated and that women should not appear in public, but the reality was less limiting then the ideal.

The status of a free woman of the citizen class was strictly protected by law. Only her children, not those of foreigners or slaves, could be citizens. She was in

Greek Courtship

Here two young lovers embrace. With one arm around his girl and the other holding a wine vessel, he draws his girl nearer. With a smile she seems more interested in her music, for with her right thumb she turns the boy down.   (Erich Lessing/Art Resource, NY)

charge of the household and the family's possessions, yet the law protected her primarily to protect her husband's interests. Raping a free woman was a lesser crime than seducing her, because seduction involved the winning of her affections. This law was concerned not with the husband's feelings but with ensuring that he need not doubt the legitimacy of his children.

A citizen woman's main functions were to have and raise children. Childbirth could be dangerous for both mother and infant, so pregnant women often made sacrifices or visited temples to ask help from the gods. Demeter (**di-MEE-ter**) and Artemis (**AHR-tuh-mis**) were particularly favored. In practical terms, citizen women relied on their friends, relatives, and midwives to assist in the delivery. Greek physicians did not concern themselves with obstetrical care.

Citizen women never appeared in court or in the public political assemblies that were the heart of Athenian democracy, though they did attend public festivals, ceremonies, and funerals. They took part in annual processions to honor the goddess Athena and in harvest festivals honoring the goddess Demeter, who protected the city's crops. In a few cases, women were priestesses in the cults of various goddesses. Priestesses prayed in public on behalf of the city and, like priests, were paid for their services. The most prominent priestess was at Delphi (**DEL-fye**), near Athens, where the god Apollo (**ah-POL-oh**) was understood to give messages about the future. The priestess at the oracle at Delphi interpreted these prophecies, and people came from all over Greece and beyond to hear them.

Greek Religion

Greek religion is extremely difficult for modern people to understand, largely because of the great differences between Greek and modern cultures. In the first place, it is not even easy to talk about "Greek religion," since the Greeks had no uniform faith or creed. Although the Greeks usually worshiped the same deities—Zeus, Hera (**HEER-uh**), Apollo, Athena, and others—the cults of these gods and goddesses varied from polis to polis. The Greeks had no sacred books such as the Bible, and Greek religion was often a matter more of ritual than of belief. Nor did cults impose an ethical code of conduct. Greeks did not have to follow any particular rule of life, practice certain virtues, or even live decent lives in order to participate. Unlike the Egyptians and Hebrews, the Greeks lacked a priesthood as the modern world understands the term. In Greece priests and priestesses existed to care for temples and sacred property and to conduct the proper rituals, but not to make religious rules or doctrines, much less to enforce them. In short, there existed in Greece no central ecclesiastical authority and no organized creed.

The most important members of the Greek pantheon were Zeus, the king of the gods, and his consort, Hera. Although they were the mightiest and most honored of the deities who lived on Mount Olympus, their divine children were closer

Individuals in Society

Aspasia

Aspasia (**a-SPEY-shuh**) was born in the Greek city of Miletus and came to Athens in about 445 B.C.E. She moved in a society in which the greatest glory for women was to be "least talked about by men, either for excellence or blame" (Thucydides 2.46). This ideal became the reality for most Athenian women, whose names and actions never became part of "history." It was not true, however, for Aspasia, who is easily one of the most intriguing women in ancient history. Once in Athens, Aspasia may have become a *hetaira* (**hi-TAHYR-uh**), which literally means "companion." The duties of a hetaira varied. She accompanied men at dinners and drinking parties, where their wives would not have been welcome, and also served as a sexual partner. The major attractions of a successful hetaira included beauty, intelligent conversation, and proper etiquette. In return she was paid for her services. No contemporary sources specifically say that Aspasia was a hetaira, but she may have been.

Contemporary sources do make clear that Aspasia enjoyed a rare opportunity to influence the men who shaped the political life of Athens. The Roman biographer Plutarch reports that she enjoyed the company of the most famous men in Athens. In one of Plato's dialogues, Socrates claims that she taught him the art of public speaking. The story is probably not true, but it points to her public reputation.

Aspasia was introduced to Pericles, who was either already divorced from his wife or divorced her soon afterward. Because Aspasia was not an Athenian citizen, she and Pericles could not marry, but they did have a son, also named Pericles. When Pericles' sons by his wife died in an epidemic, Pericles pressured the Athenian citizenship to let his son by Aspasia become a citizen. Sons of noncitizen women were normally barred from citizenship (a law Pericles himself had introduced), but the law was waived in this case.

Pericles was powerful enough to get his way, though he could not halt criticism and ridicule. Not only had he let himself get attached to a foreign woman, but he was more devoted to her than Athenians felt was appropriate for an adult man. Even Athens's greatest statesman was expected to follow the proper gender order in his personal relationships.

Pericles died shortly after his son became a citizen, and Aspasia disappears from the historical record. We can celebrate her achievements, but we do not know what motivated her. A funeral speech attributed to her is included in one of Plato's dialogues, but whether these were her actual words we will never know.

Idealized portrait of Aspasia. (Alinari/Art Resource, NY)

Questions for Analysis

1. How did Aspasia's position as a foreigner in Athens shape her opportunities?

2. In what ways does her story support and in what ways does it contradict the general picture of gender roles in Athenian society?

Sacrificial Scene

Much of Greek religion was simple and festive, as this scene demonstrates. The participants include women and boys dressed in their finest clothes and crowned with garlands. Musicians add to the festivities. Only the sheep will not enjoy the ceremony. (National Archaeological Museum, Athens/Archaeological Receipts Fund)

to ordinary people. Apollo was especially popular. He represented the epitome of youth, beauty, benevolence, and athletic skill. He was also the god of music and culture and in many ways symbolized the best of Greek culture. His sister Athena, who patronized women's crafts such as weaving, was also a warrior-goddess and had been born from the head of Zeus without a mother. Best known for her cult at Athens, to which she gave her name, she was highly revered throughout Greece, even in Sparta, which eventually became a fierce enemy of Athens. Besides the Olympian gods, each polis had its own minor deities, each with his or her own local cult.

Though Greek religion in general was individual or related to the polis, the Greeks also shared some Pan-Hellenic festivals, the chief of which were held at Olympia in honor of Zeus and at Delphi in honor of Apollo. The festivities at Olympia included the famous athletic contests that have inspired the modern Olympic games. Held every four years, they attracted visitors from all over the Greek world and lasted well into Christian times. The Pythian (**PITH-ee-uhn**) games at Delphi were also held every four years, but these contests included musical and literary contests. Both the Olympic and the Pythian games were unifying factors in Greek life.

The Flowering of Philosophy

The myths and epics of the Mesopotamians are ample testimony that speculation about the origin of the universe and of humans did not begin with the Greeks. The signal achievement of the Greeks was the willingness of some to treat these questions in rational rather than mythological terms. Although Greek philosophy did not fully flower until the classical period, Ionian thinkers had already begun in the Archaic period to ask what the universe was made of. These men are called the

Pre-Socratics, for their work preceded the philosophical revolution begun by the Athenian, Socrates. Though they were keen observers, the Pre-Socratics rarely undertook deliberate experimentation. Instead, they took individual facts and wove them into general theories. Despite appearances, they believed the universe was actually simple and subject to natural laws. Drawing on their observations, they speculated about the basic building blocks of the universe.

The first of the Pre-Socratics, Thales (**THEY-leez**) (ca. 600 B.C.E.), learned mathematics and astronomy from the Babylonians and geometry from the Egyptians. Yet there was an immense and fundamental difference between Near Eastern thought and the philosophy of Thales. The Near Eastern peoples considered such events as eclipses to be evil omens. Thales viewed them as natural phenomena that could be explained in natural terms. In short, he asked why things happened. He believed the basic element of the universe to be water. Although he was wrong, the way in which he had asked the question was momentous: it was the beginning of the scientific method.

Thales' follower Anaximander (**un-nak-suh-MAN-der**) (d. ca. 547 B.C.E.) continued his work. He theorized that the basic element of the universe is the "boundless" or "endless"—something infinite and indestructible. In his view the earth floats in a void, held in balance by its distance from everything else in the universe. Heraclitus (**her-uh-KLAHY-tuhs**) (ca. 500 B.C.E.), however, declared the primal element to be fire. He also declared that the universe was eternal yet changed constantly. An outgrowth of this line of speculation was the theory of Democritus (**di-MOK-reh-tuhs**) (b. ca. 460 B.C.E.) that the universe was made up of invisible, indestructible atoms. The culmination of Pre-Socratic thought was the theory that four simple substances made up the universe: fire, air, earth, and water.

Hippocrates (**hi-POK-ruh-teez**) (second quarter of the fifth century B.C.E.), the father of medicine, contributed ideas about the workings of the body based on empirical knowledge rather than magic. The human body, he declared, contained four humors, or fluids: blood, phlegm, black bile, and yellow bile. In a healthy body the four humors were in perfect balance; too much or too little of any particular humor caused illness.

The teachings of the revolutionary thinker Socrates (ca. 470–399 B.C.E.) are known to us largely through the writings of his student Plato (**PLAY-toh**), whose dialogues show Socrates engaged in probing discourse with others. Socrates' approach was to start with a philosophical problem and to narrow the matter to its essentials. He did so by continuous questioning rather than lecturing, a process known as the Socratic dialogue. Socrates thought that through the pursuit of wisdom, human beings could approach the supreme good and thus find true happiness. Yet in 399 B.C.E. Socrates was brought to trial, convicted, and executed on charges of corrupting the youth of the city and introducing new gods.

A Greek God

Few pieces of Greek art better illustrate the conception of the gods as greatly superior forms of human beings than this magnificent statue, over six feet ten inches in height. Here the god, who may be either Poseidon or Zeus, is portrayed as powerful and perfect but human in form. (National Archaeological Museum, Athens/Archaeological Receipts Fund)

Section Review

- The Greek victories over the Persians at Marathon (490 B.C.E.) and against Xerxes (480 B.C.E.) meant the survival and spread of Greek political and intellectual ideas.

- After driving out the Persians, Athens became increasingly imperialistic, treating their allies harshly, leading to war between Sparta and Athens.

- The Peloponnesian war brought widespread destruction to both Sparta and Athens and was only won when Sparta, with the aid of the Persian navy, finally defeated Athens.

- The Athenian Acropolis exhibited Greek art portraying the noble side of humans and sponsored the production of plays dealing with a variety of themes from drama to comedy and satire.

- Greek women ideally lived a segregated, private life, although some women had important public roles as priestesses, for example at the Delphic oracle.

- Although Greek religion lacked scriptures, ethics, or a priesthood, Greeks worshipped gods and celebrated festivals such as the Olympic games, which unified Greeks culturally.

- Greek philosophers included the Pre-Socratics Thales (water), Anaximander (void), Heraclitus (change), and Democritus (atoms); Hippocrates and his four humors for medicine; and Socrates, Plato, and Aristotle.

Plato (427–347 B.C.E.) carried on his master's search for truth, founding a philosophical school, the Academy. Plato believed that the ideal polis could exist only when its citizens were well educated. He developed the theory that there are two worlds: the impermanent, changing world of appearance that we know through our senses, and the eternal, unchanging realm of "forms" that constitute the essence of true reality. Only the mind can perceive eternal forms. The intellectual journey consists of moving from the realm of appearances to the realm of forms.

Aristotle (**ar-ih-STAH-tahl**) (384–322 B.C.E.) disagreed with Plato's idea of a separate, supernatural reality and believed that genuine knowledge is derived through close examination of the natural world. He believed that the universe operated according to principles and laws that could be discovered through scientific reasoning. Aristotle argued that everything and everyone has an inner potential or purpose that they are meant to fulfill.

The philosophies of Plato and Aristotle both viewed women as inferior beings. Plato associated women with the body and emotions and men with the superior faculties of mind and reason. Aristotle thought that women's primary purpose was to bear children. Athenian philosophers thus reflected the patriarchy of their society, while also pushing beyond the magical thinking of previous generations. Both the breadth of their vision and its limitations are their legacies to Western civilization.

The Final Act (404–338 B.C.E.)

How did the Greek city-states meet political and military challenges, and how did Macedonia become dominant?

The turbulent period from 404 to 338 B.C.E. is sometimes mistakenly seen as a period of failure and decline. It was instead a vibrant era in which Plato and Aristotle thought and wrote, one in which literature, oratory, and historical writing flourished. The architects of the fourth century B.C.E. designed and built some of the finest buildings of the classical period, and engineering made great strides. If the fourth century was a period of decline, this was so only in politics. The Peloponnesian War and its aftermath proved that the polis had reached the limits of its success as an effective political institution. The attempts of various city-states to dominate the others led only to incessant warfare. The polis system was committing suicide.

The Greeks of the fourth century B.C.E. experimented seriously with two political concepts in the hope of preventing war. First was the **Common Peace**, the idea that the states of Greece, whether large or small, should live together in peace and freedom, each enjoying its own laws and customs. In 386 B.C.E. this concept was a vital part of a peace treaty with the Persian Empire, in which the Greeks and Persians pledged themselves to live in harmony.

Federalism, the second concept to become prominent, already had a long history in some parts of Greece (see page 45). Strictly speaking, the new impetus toward federalism was intended more to gain security through numbers than to

Common Peace One of two political concepts created by Greeks in the fourth century B.C.E. in an attempt to prevent war. It was the idea that the states of Greece should live together in peace and freedom, each enjoying its own laws and customs.

prevent war. In the fourth century B.C.E. at least ten other federations of states either came into being or were revitalized. Federalism never led to a United States of Greece, but the concept held great importance not only for fourth-century Greeks but also for the Hellenistic period and beyond. In 1787, when the Founding Fathers met in Philadelphia to frame the Constitution of the United States, they studied Greek federalism very seriously in the hope that the Greek past could help guide the American future.

The Struggle for Hegemony

The chief states, Sparta, Athens, and Thebes, each tried to create a **hegemony** (heh-JEM-uh-nee), that is, a political ascendancy over other states, even though they sometimes paid lip service to the ideals of the Common Peace. In every instance, the ambition, jealousy, pride, and fear of the major powers doomed the effort to achieve genuine peace.

When the Spartans defeated Athens in 404 B.C.E., they used their victory to build an empire instead of ensuring the freedom of all Greeks. Their decision brought the Spartans into conflict with their own allies and with Persia, which now demanded the return of Ionia to its control (see page 39). From 400 to 386 B.C.E. the Spartans fought the Persians for Ionia, a conflict that eventually engulfed Greece itself. After years of stalemate the Spartans made peace with Persia and their Greek enemies. The result was the first formal Common Peace, the King's Peace of 386 B.C.E., which cost Sparta its empire but not its position of ascendancy in Greece.

Not content with Sparta's hegemony of Greece, Agesilaos (ah-gis-il-A-us) betrayed the very concept of the Common Peace to punish cities that had opposed Sparta during the war. He treacherously ordered Thebes to be seized and even condoned an unwarranted and unsuccessful attack on Athens. Agesilaos had gone too far. Even though it appeared that his naked use of force had made Sparta supreme in Greece, his imperialism was soon to lead to Sparta's downfall at the hands of the Thebans, the very people whom he sought to tyrannize.

After routing the once-invincible Spartans from Thebes, the Theban leader Epaminondas (ee-pam-uh-NON-duhs) eliminated Sparta as a major power through a series of invasions. He concluded alliances with many Peloponnesian states but made no effort to dominate them, instead fostering federalism in Greece. He also threw his support behind the Common Peace. Although he made Thebes the leader of Greece from 371 to 362 B.C.E., other city-states and leagues were bound to Thebes only by voluntary alliances. By his insistence on the liberty of the Greeks, Epaminondas, more than any other person in Greek history, successfully blended the three concepts of hegemony, federalism, and the Common Peace. His death at the Battle of Mantinea in 362 B.C.E. put an end to his efforts, but not to these three political ideals.

hegemony A political ascendancy over other states.

Statue of Eirene

The Athenians erected this statue of Eirene (Peace) holding Ploutos (Wealth) in her left arm. Athens had seen only war for some fifty-six years, and the statue celebrated the Common Peace of 375 B.C.E. The bitter irony of this poignant scene is that the treaty lasted scarcely a year. (Glyptothek, Munich/Studio Koppermann)

Philip and the Macedonian Ascendancy

While the Greek states exhausted one another in endless conflicts, a new and unlikely power rose in Macedonia to the north. The land of Macedonia, extensive and generally fertile, nurtured a numerous and hardy population. Yet Macedonia was often internally divided and distracted by foreign opportunists. Nevertheless, under a strong king Macedonia was a power to be reckoned with, and in 359 B.C.E. such a king ascended the throne. Philip II fully understood the strengths and needs of the Macedonians, whose devotion he won virtually on the day that he became king.

The young Philip, already a master of diplomacy and warfare after years spent in Thebes, quickly saw Athens as the principal threat to Macedonia. Once he had secured the borders of Macedonia against barbarian invaders, he launched a series of military operations in the northwestern Aegean. Not only did he win rich territory, but he also slowly pushed the Athenians out of the region. Macedonian warriors gained a reputation for fierceness, as one comic playwright from Athens suggests:

> Do you know that your battle will be with men
> Who dine on sharpened swords,
> And gulp burning firebrands for wine?
> Then immediately after dinner the slave
> Brings us dessert—Cretan arrows
> Or pieces of broken spears.
> We have shields and breastplates for
> Cushions and at our feet slings and arrows,
> And we are crowned with catapults.[3]

These dire predictions and the progress of Philip's military operations at last had their effect. In 338 B.C.E. the armies of Thebes and Athens met Philip's veterans at the Boeotian city of Chaeronea. There on one summer's day Philip's army won a hard-fought victory that gave him command of Greece and put an end to classical Greek freedom. Because the Greeks could not coexist peacefully, they fell to an invader. Yet Philip was wise enough to retain much of what the fourth-century Greeks had achieved. Not opposed to the concepts of peace and federalism, he sponsored a new Common Peace in which all of Greece, except Sparta, was united in one political body under his leadership. Philip thus used the concepts of hegemony, the Common Peace, and federalism as tools of Macedonian domination. The ironic result was the end of the age of classical Greece.

Section Review

- Greeks of the fourth century B.C.E. experimented with the Common Peace and federalism to gain peace and security.
- Sparta, Athens, and Thebes each tried to achieve hegemony (political control) over all of Greece.
- Spartan King Agesilaos used Spartan power to terrorize Athens and Thebes, leading to Sparta's downfall by the Thebans.
- The Theban leader Epaminondas (371–362 B.C.E.) successfully blended hegemony, federalism, and the Common Peace.
- Philip II of Macedon militarily threatened Athens from the north beginning in 359 B.C.E.

Chapter Review

When the Greeks arrived in Hellas, how did they adapt themselves to their new landscape? (page 39)

The Greeks entered a land of mountains and small plains, which led them to establish small communities. Sometimes these small communities were joined together in kingdoms, most prominently the Minoan kingdom on the island of Crete and the Mycenaean kingdom on the mainland. Minoans and Mycenaeans used written records, and the fall of these kingdoms led writing to disappear for centuries, a period known as the Greek Dark Age (1100–800 B.C.E.).

Key Terms
Hellenic period (p. 39)
Hellenistic period (p. 39)
Aegean basin (p. 39)
Minoan (p. 39)

After the Greeks had established the polis, in which they lived their political and social lives, how did they shape it into its several historical forms? (page 43)

Even though kingdoms collapsed, Greek culture continued to spread, and more independent communities were formed. Such a community, called a polis, developed social and political institutions. Some were democracies, in which government was shared among all citizens, which meant adult free men. Other Greeks established smaller governing bodies of citizens, called oligarchs, which directed the political affairs of all.

What major developments mark the Archaic Greek period in terms of spread of culture and the growth of cities? (page 46)

During the Archaic Age (800–500 B.C.E.) Greeks colonized much of the Mediterranean, establishing cities in Asia Minor, southern Italy, Sicily, and southern France. This brought them into contact with many other peoples, and also spread Greek culture widely. During this period Sparta and Athens became the most important poleis.

How did the Greeks develop their literature, philosophy, religion, and art, and how did war affect this intellectual and social process? (page 50)

Sparta and Athens joined together to fight the Persian Empire, but later turned against one another in the Peloponnesian War (431–404 B.C.E.). During this time of warfare, Athenian leaders turned their city into an architectural showplace, supporting the creation of buildings and statues that are still prized. Playwrights presented tragedies and comedies that dealt with basic issues of life. Life for the men in Athens who were citizens revolved around public political assemblies, while for women it revolved around the household. Athenian thinkers regarded women as inferior and did not think they should have a public role. Both women and men took part in ceremonies honoring gods and goddesses, though some men, most prominently the philosophers Plato and Aristotle, developed ideas about the universe and the place of humans in it that did not involve the gods.

How did the Greek city-states meet political and military challenges, and how did Macedonia become dominant? (page 60)

The Greeks destroyed a good deal of their flourishing world in a series of wars. Despite their political advances, they never really learned how to routinely live peacefully with one another. Their disunity allowed for the rise of Macedonia under the leadership of King Philip II, a brilliant military leader.

Mycenaean (p. 41)
polis (p. 43)
acropolis (p. 44)
agora (p. 44)
hoplites (p. 44)
monarchy (p. 44)
tyranny (p. 44)
democracy (p. 45)
oligarchy (p. 45)
federalism (p. 45)
metropolis (p. 46)
helot (p. 47)
homosocial (p. 48)
deme (p. 49)
boule (p. 49)
ecclesia (p. 49)
Delian League (p. 51)
Common Peace (p. 60)
hegemony (p. 61)

Notes

John Buckler is the translator of all uncited quotations from a foreign language in Chapters 1–6.

1. J. M. Edmonds, *Greek Elegy and Iambus* (Cambridge, Mass.: Harvard University Press, 1931), I.70, frag. 10.
2. Thucydides, *History of the Peloponnesian War* 7.87.6.
3. J. M. Edmonds, *The Fragments of Attic Comedy* (Leiden: E. J. Brill, 1971), 2.366–2.369, Mnesimachos frag. 7.

To assess your mastery of this chapter, go to **bedfordstmartins.com/mckaywestbrief**

Listening to the Past

The Great Plague at Athens, 430 B.C.E.

In 430 B.C.E. many of the people of Attica sought refuge in Athens to escape the Spartan invasion. The overcrowding of people, the lack of proper sanitation, and the scarcity of clean water made the population vulnerable to virulent disease, and indeed a severe plague swept the city. The great historian Thucydides lived in Athens at the time and contracted the disease himself. He was one of the fortunate people who survived the ordeal. For most people, however, the disease proved fatal. Thucydides left a vivid description of the nature of the plague and of people's reaction to it.

The most terrible thing of all was the despair into which people fell when they realized that they had caught the plague. Terrible, too, was the sight of people dying like sheep through having caught the disease as a result of nursing others. This indeed caused more deaths than anything else. For when people were afraid to visit the sick, then they died with no one to look after them. Indeed, there were many houses in which all the inhabitants perished through lack of attention. When, on the other hand, they did visit the sick, they lost their own lives, and this was particularly true of those who made it a point of honor to act properly. Such people felt ashamed to think of their own safety and went into their friends' houses at times when even the members of the household were so overwhelmed by the weight of their calamities that they had actually given up the usual practice of making laments for the dead. . . .

A factor that made matters much worse than they were already was the removal of people from the country into the city, and this particularly affected the newcomers. There were no houses for them, and, living as they did during the hot season in badly ventilated huts, they died like flies. The bodies of the dying were heaped one on top of the other, and half-dead creatures could be seen staggering about in the streets or flocking around the fountains in their desire for water.

The catastrophe was so overwhelming that people, not knowing what would happen next to them, became indifferent to every rule of religion and law. Athens owed to the plague the beginnings of a state of unprecedented lawlessness. People now began openly to venture on acts of self-indulgence which before then they used to keep in the dark. Thus they resolved to spend their money quickly and to spend it on pleasure, since money and life alike seemed equally ephemeral. As for what is called honor, no one showed himself willing to abide by its laws, so doubtful was it whether one would survive to enjoy the name for it. It was generally agreed that what was both honorable and valuable was the pleasure of the moment and everything that might conceivably contribute to that pleasure. No fear of god or law of man had a restraining influence. As for the gods, it seemed to be the same thing whether one worshiped them or not, when one saw the good and the bad dying indiscriminately. As for offenses against human law, no one expected to be punished. Instead, everyone felt that already a far heavier sentence had been passed on him and was hanging over him, and that before the time for its execution arrived, it was only natural to get some pleasure out of life.

This, then, was the calamity that fell upon Athens, and the times were hard indeed, with people dying inside the city and the land outside being laid waste.

Questions for Analysis

1. What does this account of the plague say about human nature when put in an extreme crisis?
2. Does popular religion offer any solace during such a catastrophe?
3. How did public laws and customs cope with such a disaster?

Source: From *The History of the Peloponnesian War* by Thucydides, translated by Rex Warner, with an introduction and notes by M. I. Finley (Penguin Classics 1954; Revised edition 1972). Translation copyright © Rex Warner, 1954. Introduction and Appendices copyright © M. I. Finley, 1972. Reproduced by permission of Penguin Books Ltd. and Curtis Brown Group Ltd., London on behalf of the Estate of Rex Warner.

Coin depicting the god Asclepius, represented by a snake, putting an end to urban plague. (Bibliothèque nationale de France)

CHAPTER 4

The Hellenistic World

336–146 B.C.E.

Tetrapylon of Aphrodisias. This monumental gate celebrates the beautiful and rich city of Aphrodisias in modern Turkey. (John Buckler)

Chapter Preview

Alexander and the Great Crusade
Why did Alexander launch his massive attack on the Persian Empire? How extensive were his conquests?

Alexander's Legacy
What happened to Alexander's empire after his death? What was his political and cultural legacy?

The Spread of Hellenism
What effect did Greek migration have on Greek and native peoples?

The Economic Scope of the Hellenistic World
What effects did East-West trade have on ordinary peoples during the Hellenistic period?

Hellenistic Intellectual Advances
What is the intellectual legacy of the Hellenistic period?

INDIVIDUALS IN SOCIETY: Archimedes and the Practical Application of Science

LISTENING TO THE PAST: Alexander and the Brotherhood of Man

65

Two years after his conquest of Greece, Philip of Macedon fell victim to an assassin's dagger. Philip's twenty-year-old son, historically known as Alexander the Great (r. 336–323 B.C.E.), assumed the Macedonian throne. This young man, one of the most remarkable personalities of Western civilization, was to have a profound impact on history. By overthrowing the Persian Empire and by spreading *Hellenism*—Greek culture, language, thought, and way of life—as far as India, Alexander was instrumental in creating a new era, traditionally called **Hellenistic** to distinguish it from the Hellenic. As a result of Alexander's exploits, the individualistic and energetic culture of the Greeks came into intimate contact with the venerable older cultures of the Near East.

Hellenistic The new culture that arose when Alexander overthrew the Persian Empire and began spreading Hellenism, Greek culture, language, thought, and way of life as far as India. It is called Hellenistic to distinguish it from the Hellenic period.

Alexander and the Great Crusade

Why did Alexander launch his massive attack on the Persian Empire? How extensive were his conquests?

In 336 B.C.E. Alexander inherited not only Philip's crown but also his policies. After his victory at Chaeronea (**ker-uh-NEE-uh**), Philip had organized the states of Greece into a huge league under his leadership and announced to the Greeks his plan to lead them and his Macedonians against the Persian Empire. Fully intending to carry out Philip's designs, Alexander proclaimed to the Greek world that the invasion of Persia was to be a great crusade, a mighty act of revenge for the Persian invasion of Greece in 480 B.C.E. It would also be the means by which Alexander would create an empire of his own in the East.

Despite his youth, Alexander was well prepared to lead the attack. Philip had groomed his son to become king and had given him the best education possible.

Alexander at the Battle of Issus

At left, Alexander the Great, bareheaded and wearing a breastplate, charges King Darius of Persia, who is standing in a chariot. The moment marks the turning point of the battle, as Darius turns to flee from the attack. (National Museum, Naples/Alinari/Art Resource, NY)

In 334 B.C.E. Alexander led an army of Macedonians and Greeks into Asia Minor. With him went a staff of philosophers and poets, scientists whose job it was to map the country and study strange animals and plants, and the historian Callisthenes (kuh-LIS-thuh-neez), who was to write an account of the campaign. Alexander intended not only a military campaign but also an expedition of discovery.

In the next three years Alexander won three major battles at the Granicus (gran-UH-kuhs) River, Issus (IS-uhs), and Gaugamela (GAW-guh-mee-luh). As Map 4.1 shows, these battle sites stand almost as road signs marking his march to the East. When Alexander reached Egypt, he quickly seized the land, honored the priestly class, and was proclaimed pharaoh, the legitimate ruler of the country. He next marched to the oasis of Siwah, west of the Nile Valley, to consult the famous oracle of Zeus-Amon. No one will ever know what the priest told him, but henceforth Alexander considered himself the son of Zeus. Next he marched into western Asia, where at Gaugamela he defeated the Persian army. After this victory the principal Persian capital of Persepolis easily fell to him. There he performed a symbolic act of retribution by

CHRONOLOGY

340–262 B.C.E.	Rise of Epicurean and Stoic philosophies
336–24 B.C.E.	Alexander's "Great Crusade"
330–200 B.C.E.	Establishment of new Hellenistic cities
326–146 B.C.E.	Spread of Hellenistic commerce from the western Mediterranean to India
323–301 B.C.E.	Wars of Alexander's successors; establishment of the Hellenistic monarchies
310–212 B.C.E.	Scientific developments in mathematics, astronomy, and physics
305–146 B.C.E.	Growth of mystery religions
301–146 B.C.E.	Flourishing of the Hellenistic monarchies

MAP 4.1 Alexander's Conquests

This map shows the course of Alexander's invasion of the Persian Empire and the speed of his progress. More important than the great success of his military campaigns was his founding of Hellenistic cities in the East.

burning the buildings of Xerxes, the invader of Greece. In 330 B.C.E. he took Ecbatana (**ek-BAT-un-uh**), the last Persian capital, and pursued the Persian king to his death.

The Persian Empire had fallen, and the war of revenge was over, but Alexander had no intention of stopping. He dismissed his Greek troops but permitted many of them to serve on as mercenaries. Alexander then began his personal odyssey. With his Macedonian soldiers and Greek mercenaries, he set out to conquer the rest of Asia. He plunged deeper into the East, into lands completely unknown to the Greek world. It took his soldiers four additional years to conquer Bactria and the easternmost parts of the now-defunct Persian Empire, but still Alexander was determined to continue his march.

In 326 B.C.E. Alexander crossed the Indus River and entered India. There, too, he saw hard fighting, and finally at the Hyphasis (**HIF-ah-sis**) River his troops refused to go farther. Alexander was enraged by the mutiny, for he believed he was near the end of the world. Nonetheless, the army stood firm, and Alexander relented. Still eager to explore the limits of the world, Alexander turned south to the Arabian Sea. Though the tribes in the area did not oppose him, he waged a bloody, ruthless, and unnecessary war against them. After reaching the Arabian Sea and turning west, he led his army through the grim Gedrosian Desert. The army suffered fearfully, and many soldiers died along the way; nonetheless, in 324 B.C.E. Alexander reached his camp at Susa. The great crusade was over, and Alexander himself died the next year in Babylon.

Alexander's Legacy

What happened to Alexander's empire after his death? What was his political and cultural legacy?

Alexander so quickly became a legend during his lifetime that he still seems super-human. That alone makes a reasoned interpretation of him very difficult. Some historians have seen him as a high-minded philosopher, and none can deny that he possessed genuine intellectual gifts. Others, however, have portrayed him as a bloody-minded autocrat, more interested in his own ambition than in any philosophical concept of the common good. Alexander is the perfect example of the need for the historian to use care when interpreting the known facts. (See the feature "Listening to the Past: Alexander and the Brotherhood of Man," on page 84.) What is not disputed is that Alexander was instrumental in changing the face of politics and culture in the eastern Mediterranean. His campaign swept away the Persian Empire, which had ruled for over two hundred years, and opened the East to the tide of Hellenism.

The Political Legacy

In 323 B.C.E. Alexander the Great died at the age of thirty-two. The main question at his death was whether his vast empire could be held together. Although he fathered a successor while in Bactria, his son was an infant at Alexander's death. The child was too young to assume the duties of kingship and was cruelly murdered. That meant that Alexander's empire was a prize for the taking by the strongest of his generals. Within a week of Alexander's death a round of fighting began

MAPPING THE PAST

MAP 4.2   The Hellenistic World

This map depicts the Hellenistic world after Alexander's death. **[1]** What does this map suggest about Alexander's legacy? **[2]** Compare this map to Map 4.1 on page 67, which shows Alexander's conquests. After Alexander's death, were the Macedonians and Greeks able to retain control of all the land he had conquered? **[3]** What does Map 4.2 tell us about the legacy of Alexander's conquests? What does it suggest about the success or failure of Alexander's dreams of conquest?

that was to continue for forty years. No single Macedonian general was able to re-place Alexander as emperor of his entire domain. In effect, the strongest divided it among themselves. By 263 B.C.E. three officers had split the empire into large monarchies (see Map 4.2). Antigonus Gonatas became king of Macedonia and established the Antigonid (**an-TIG-uh-nid**) dynasty, which ruled until the Roman conquest in 168 B.C.E. Ptolemy (**TAWL-uh-mee**) made himself king of Egypt, and his descendants, the Ptolemies, assumed the powers and position of pharaohs. Seleucus (**sih-LOO-sus**), founder of the Seleucid (**sih-LOO-sid**) dynasty, carved out a kingdom that stretched from the coast of Asia Minor to India. In 263 B.C.E. Eumenes (**yoo-MEN-eez**), the Greek ruler of Pergamum (**PUR-guh-mum**), a city in western Asia Minor, won his independence from the Seleucids and created the Pergamene monarchy. Though the Seleucid kings soon lost control of their east-ernmost provinces, Greek influence in this area did not wane. In modern Turke-stan (**tur-kuh-STAN**) and Afghanistan (**af-GAN-uh-stan**) another line of Greek kings established the kingdom of Bactria and even managed to spread their power and culture into northern India.

The political face of Greece itself changed during the Hellenistic period. The day of the polis was over; in its place rose leagues of city-states. The two most powerful and extensive were the Aetolian (ee-TOH-lee-uhn) League in western and central Greece and the Achaean (a-KEY-an) League in the Peloponnesus. Once-powerful city-states like Athens and Sparta sank to the level of third-rate powers.

The political history of the Hellenistic period was dominated by the great monarchies and the Greek leagues. The political fragmentation and incessant warfare that marked the Hellenic period continued on an even wider and larger scale during the Hellenistic period. Never did the Hellenistic world achieve political stability or lasting peace. Hellenistic kings never forgot the vision of Alexander's empire, spanning Europe and Asia, secure under the rule of one man. Try though they did, they were never able to re-create it. In this respect Alexander's legacy fell not to his generals but to the Romans of a later era.

The Cultural Legacy

As Alexander waded ever deeper into the East, distance alone presented him with a serious problem: how was he to retain contact with the Greek world behind him? Communications were vital, for he drew supplies and reinforcements from Greece and Macedonia. His solution was to plant cities and military colonies in strategic places. In these settlements Alexander left Greek mercenaries and Macedonian veterans who were no longer up to active campaigning. Besides keeping the road open to the West, these settlements served the purpose of dominating the countryside around them.

Their military significance apart, Alexander's cities and colonies became powerful instruments in the spread of Hellenism throughout the East. His successors

The Great Altar of Pergamum
A new Hellenistic city needed splendid art and architecture to prove its worth in Greek eyes. The king of Pergamum ordered the construction of this monumental altar, now in Berlin. The scenes depict the mythical victory of the Greek gods over the Giants, who symbolize non-Greeks. The altar served the propaganda purpose of celebrating the victory of Hellenism over the East. (Bildarchiv Preussischer Kulturbesitz/Art Resource, NY)

continued his policy by luring Greek colonists to their realms. For seventy-five years after Alexander's death, Greek immigrants poured into the East. At least 250 new Hellenistic colonies were established. The Mediterranean world had seen no comparable movement of peoples since the Archaic Age (see page 46), when wave after wave of Greeks had turned the Mediterranean basin into a Greek-speaking region.

The overall result of Alexander's settlements and those of his successors was the spread of Hellenism as far east as India. Throughout the Hellenistic period, Greeks and Easterners became familiar with and adapted themselves to each other's customs, religion, and way of life. Although Greek culture did not completely conquer the East, it gave the East a vehicle of expression that linked it to the West. Hellenism became a common bond among the East, peninsular Greece, and the western Mediterranean. This pre-existing cultural bond was later to prove supremely valuable to Rome—itself heavily influenced by Hellenism—in its efforts to impose a comparable political unity on the Western world.

The Spread of Hellenism

What effect did Greek migration have on Greek and native peoples?

When the Greeks and Macedonians entered Asia Minor, Egypt, and the more remote East, they encountered civilizations older than their own. In some ways the Eastern cultures were more advanced than the Greek, in others less so. Thus this third great tide of Greek migration differed from preceding waves, which had spread over land that was uninhabited or inhabited by less-developed peoples.

What did the Hellenistic monarchies offer Greek immigrants politically and materially? More broadly, how did Hellenism and the cultures of the East affect one another? What did the meeting of East and West entail for the history of the world?

Cities and Kingdoms

One of the major developments of these new kingdoms was the resurgence of monarchy, which had many repercussions. For most Greeks, monarchs were something out of the heroic past, something found in Homer's *Iliad* but not in daily life. Furthermore, most Hellenistic kingdoms embraced numerous different peoples who had little in common. Hellenistic kings thus needed a new political concept to unite them. One solution was the creation of a ruler cult that linked the king's authority with that of the gods. Thus, royal power had divine approval and was meant to create a political and religious bond between the kings and their subjects. These deified kings were not considered gods as mighty as Zeus or Apollo, and the new ruler cults probably made little religious impact on those ruled. Nonetheless, the ruler cult was an easily understandable symbol of unity within the kingdom.

Hellenistic kingship was hereditary, which gave women who were members of royal families more power than any women in democracies, in which citizenship was limited to men. Wives of kings and queen mothers had influence over their husbands and sons, and a few women ruled in their own right when there was no male heir.

Hellenistic monarchs continued the policy of establishing cities throughout their kingdoms in order to entice Greeks to immigrate. They gave their cities all

The Main Street of Pergamum

No matter where in old Greece they had come from, all Greeks would immediately feel at home walking along this main street in Pergamum. They would all see familiar sights. To the left is the top of the theater where they could watch the plays of the great dramatists, climb farther to the temple, and admire the fortifications on the right. (Faith Cimok, Turkey)

the external trappings of a polis. Each had an assembly of citizens, a council to prepare legislation, and a board of magistrates to conduct the city's political business. Yet, however similar to the Greek polis they appeared, these cities could not engage in diplomatic dealings, make treaties, pursue their own foreign policy, or wage their own wars. The Greek polis was by definition **sovereign** (SOV-er-in) — an independent, autonomous state run by its citizens, free of any outside power or restraint. Hellenistic kings, however, refused to grant sovereignty to their cities. In effect, these kings willingly built cities but refused to build a polis.

A new Hellenistic city differed from a Greek polis in other ways as well. The Greek polis had one body of law and one set of customs. In the Hellenistic city Greeks represented an elite citizen class. Natives and non-Greek foreigners who lived in Hellenistic cities usually possessed lesser rights than Greeks and often had their own laws. In some instances this disparity spurred natives to assimilate Greek culture in order to rise politically and socially. Yet the Hellenistic city was not homogeneous and could not spark the intensity of feeling that marked the polis.

Though Hellenistic kings never built a true polis, that does not mean that their urban policy failed. Rather, the Hellenistic city was to remain the basic social and political unit throughout the Hellenistic world until the sixth century C.E. Cities were the chief agents of Hellenization, and their influence spread far beyond their walls. These cities formed a broader cultural network in which Greek language, customs, and values flourished. Roman rule in the Hellenistic world would later be based on this urban culture, which facilitated the rise and spread of Christianity. In broad terms, Hellenistic cities were remarkably successful.

sovereign An independent, autonomous state run by its citizens, free of any outside power or restraint.

Men and Women in Hellenistic Monarchies

If the Hellenistic kings failed to satisfy the Greeks' political yearnings, they nonetheless succeeded in giving them unequaled economic and social opportunities. The ruling dynasties of the Hellenistic world were Macedonian, and Greeks filled all important political, military, and diplomatic positions. They constituted an upper class that sustained Hellenism in the East. Besides building Greek cities, Hellenistic kings offered Greeks land and money as lures to further immigration.

The opening of the East offered ambitious Greeks opportunities for well-paying jobs and economic success. Some talented Greek men entered a professional corps of Greek administrators. Greeks and Macedonians also found ready employment in the armies and navies of the Hellenistic monarchies. Greeks were able to dominate other professions as well. The kingdoms and cities recruited Greek writers and artists to create Greek works on Asian soil. Architects, engineers, and skilled craftsmen found their services in great demand because of the building policies of the Hellenistic monarchs.

Increased physical and social mobility benefited some women as well as men. More women learned to read than before, and they engaged in occupations in which literacy was beneficial, including care of the sick. During the Hellenistic period some women took part in commercial transactions. They still lived under legal handicaps; in Egypt, for example, a Greek woman needed a male guardian to buy, sell, or lease land, to borrow money, and to represent her in other transactions. Yet often such a guardian was present only to fulfill the letter of the law. The woman was the real agent and handled the business being transacted.

As long as Greeks continued to replenish their professional ranks, the kingdoms remained strong. In the process they drew an immense amount of talent from the Greek peninsula, draining the vitality of the Greek homeland. However, the Hellenistic monarchies could not keep recruiting Greeks forever, in spite of their wealth and willingness to spend lavishly. In time the huge surge of immigration slowed greatly. Even then the Hellenistic monarchs were reluctant to recruit Easterners to fill posts normally held by Greeks. The result was at first the stagnation of the Hellenistic world and finally, after 202 B.C.E., its collapse in the face of the young and vigorous Roman republic.

Marital Advice

This small terra-cotta sculpture is generally seen as a mother advising her daughter, a new bride. Such intimate scenes of ordinary people were popular in the Hellenistic world, in contrast to the idealized statues of gods and goddesses of the classical period. (British Museum/Michael Holford)

Greeks and Easterners

Because they understood themselves to be "the West," Greeks generally referred to Egypt and what we now call the Near East collectively as "the East." Many historians have continued that usage, seeing the Hellenistic period as a time when Greek and "Eastern" cultures blended to some degree. Eastern civilizations were older than Greek, and the Greeks were a minority outside of Greece. Hellenistic monarchies were remarkably successful in at least partially Hellenizing Easterners and spreading a uniform culture throughout the East, a culture to which Rome eventually fell heir. The prevailing institutions, laws, and language of the East became Greek. Indeed, the Near East had seen nothing comparable since the days when Mesopotamian culture had spread throughout the area.

Yet the spread of Greek culture was wider than it was deep. At best it was a veneer, thicker in some places than in others. Hellenistic kingdoms were never entirely unified in language, customs, and thought. Greek culture took firmest hold along the shores of the Mediterranean, but farther east, in Persia and Bactria, it was less strong. The principal reason for this curious phenomenon is that Greek culture generally did not extend far beyond the reaches of the cities. Many urban residents adopted the aspects of Hellenism that they found useful, but others in the countryside generally did not embrace it wholly.

Cultural Blending

Ptolemy V, a Macedonian by birth and the Hellenistic king of Egypt, dedicated this stone to the Egyptian sacred bull of the Egyptian god Ptah. Nothing here is Greek or Macedonian, a sign that the conquered had, in some religious and ceremonial ways, won over their conquerors. (Egyptian Museum, Cairo)

For non-Greeks the prime advantage of Greek culture was its very pervasiveness. The Greek language became the common speech of Egypt and the Near East. It was also the speech of commerce: anyone who wanted to compete in business had to learn it. As early as the third century B.C.E. some Greek cities were giving citizenship to Hellenized natives.

The vast majority of Hellenized Easterners, however, took only the externals of Greek culture while retaining the essentials of their own ways of life. Though Greeks and Easterners adapted to each other's ways, there was never a true fusion of cultures. Nonetheless, each found useful things in the civilization of the other, and the two fertilized each other. This fertilization, this mingling of Greek and Eastern elements, is what makes Hellenistic culture unique and distinctive.

Hellenism and the Jews

A prime illustration of cultural mingling is the impact of Greek culture on the Jews. At first, Jews in Hellenistic cities were treated as resident aliens. As they grew more numerous, they received permission to form a political corporation, which gave them a great deal of autonomy. They obeyed the king's commands, but there was virtually no royal interference with the Jewish religion. Indeed, the Greeks were typically reluctant to tamper with anyone's religion. Antiochus III (an-TIE-uh-kuhs) (ca. 242–187 B.C.E.), for instance, recognized that most Jews had become loyal subjects, and he went so far as to deny any uninvited foreigner permission to enter the temple at Jerusalem. Only the Seleucid king Antiochus Epiphanes (175–ca. 164 B.C.E.) tried to suppress the Jewish religion in Judaea. He did so not because he hated the Jews (who were a small part of his kingdom), but because he was trying to unify his realm culturally to meet the threat of Rome. To the Jews he extended the same policy that he applied to all subjects. Apart from this instance, Hellenistic Jews suffered no official religious persecution. Some Jews were given the right to become full citizens of Hellenistic cities, but few exercised that right. Citizenship would have allowed them to vote in the assembly and serve as magistrates, but it would also have obliged them to worship the gods of the city—a practice few Jews chose to follow.

Jews living in Hellenistic cities often embraced a good deal of Hellenism. So many Jews learned Greek, especially in Alexandria, that the Old Testament was translated into Greek, and services in the synagogue came to be conducted in Greek. Jews often took Greek names, used Greek political forms, adopted Greek practice by forming their own trade associations, put inscriptions on graves as the Greeks did, and much else. Yet no matter how much of Greek culture or its externals Jews borrowed, they normally remained attached to their religion.

Section Review

- To create unity, Hellenistic kings established remarkably successful cities with the governmental structure of a Greek polis, although they refused to grant them sovereignty and Greeks had more rights than natives and non-Greek foreigners.

- Hellenistic cities formed a broad cultural network upon which the Romans later based their rule.

- The Hellenistic monarchs offered economic and social opportunities to Greeks and benefited women through increased literacy and economic opportunities.

- Greek became the language of commerce in the East, and although a true blending of cultures did not happen, the intermingling of Greek and Eastern cultures makes Hellenistic culture unique.

- Jews in Hellenistic cities generally had religious freedom and many learned Greek but most refused citizenship so they could practice their own religion and not be required to worship the gods of the city.

The Economic Scope of the Hellenistic World

What effects did East-West trade have on ordinary peoples during the Hellenistic period?

Alexander's conquest of the Persian Empire not only changed the political face of the ancient world but also brought the East fully into the sphere of Greek economics. Yet the Hellenistic period did not see a revolution in the way people lived and worked. The material demands of Hellenistic society remained as simple as those of Athenian society in the fifth century B.C.E. Clothes and furniture were essentially unchanged, as were household goods, tools, and jewelry. The real achievement of Alexander and his successors was linking East and West in a broad commercial network. The spread of Greeks throughout the Near East and Egypt created new markets and stimulated trade. The economic unity of the Hellenistic world, like its cultural bonds, would later prove valuable to the Romans.

Alexander's conquest of the Persian Empire had immediate effects on trade. In the Persian capitals Alexander had found vast sums of gold, silver, and other treasure. This wealth financed the building of roads and the development of harbors as well as the creation of new cities. Whole new markets opened to Greek merchants, who eagerly took advantage of the new opportunities. In bazaars, ports, and trading centers Greeks learned of Eastern customs and traditions while spreading knowledge of their own culture.

The Seleucid and Ptolemaic dynasties traded as far afield as India, Arabia, and sub-Saharan Africa. Overland trade with India and Arabia was conducted by caravan and was largely in the hands of Easterners. Once the goods reached the Hellenistic monarchies, Greek merchants took a hand in the trade.

Essential to the caravan trade from the Mediterranean to Afghanistan and India was the southern route through Arabia. The desert of Arabia may seem at first unlikely and inhospitable terrain for a line of commerce, but to the east of it lies the plateau of Iran, from which trade routes stretched to the south and still farther east to China. Commerce from the East arrived at Egypt and the excellent harbors of Palestine, Phoenicia, and Syria. From these ports goods flowed to Greece, Italy, and Spain. The backbone of this caravan trade was the camel, a splendid beast of burden that could endure the harsh heat and aridity of the caravan routes.

Over the caravan routes traveled luxury goods that were light, rare, and expensive. In time these luxury items became more of a necessity than a luxury. In part this development was the result of an increased volume of trade. In the prosperity of the period more people could afford to buy gold, silver,

Harbor and Warehouse at Delos
During the Hellenistic period Delos became a thriving center of trade. Shown here is the row of warehouses at water's edge. From Delos, cargoes were shipped to virtually every part of the Mediterranean. (SuperStock)

Great Silk Road The name of the major route for the silk trade.

ivory, precious stones, spices, and a host of other easily transportable goods. Perhaps the most prominent goods in terms of volume were tea and silk. Indeed, the trade in silk gave the major route its name, the **Great Silk Road.** In return the Greeks and Macedonians sent east manufactured goods, especially metal weapons, cloth, wine, and olive oil. Although these caravan routes can trace their origins to earlier times, they became far more prominent in the Hellenistic period. Business customs developed and became standardized, so that merchants from different nationalities communicated in a way understandable to all of them.

More economically important than this exotic trade were commercial dealings in essential commodities like raw materials, grain, and industrial products. The Hellenistic monarchies usually raised enough grain for their own needs as well as a surplus for export. For the cities of Greece and the Aegean this trade in grain was essential, because many of them could not grow enough. Fortunately for them, abundant wheat supplies were available nearby in Egypt and in the Crimea (**cry-MEE-ah**) in southern Russia.

The Greek cities paid for their grain by exporting olive oil and wine. Another significant commodity was fish, which for export was either salted, pickled, or dried. This trade was doubly important because fish provided poor people with an essential element of their diet. Of raw materials, wood was high in demand.

Most trade in bulk commodities was seaborne, and the Hellenistic merchant ship was the workhorse of the day. The merchant ship had a broad beam and relied on sails for propulsion. It was far more seaworthy than the Hellenistic warship, which was long, narrow, and built for speed. A small crew of experienced sailors could handle the merchant vessel easily. Maritime trade provided opportunities for workers in other industries and trades: sailors, shipbuilders, dockworkers, accountants, teamsters, and pirates. Piracy was always a factor in the Hellenistic world and remained so until Rome extended its power throughout the East.

Throughout the Mediterranean world slaves were almost always in demand as well. Only the Ptolemies discouraged both the trade and slavery itself, and they did so only for economic reasons. Their system had no room for slaves, who would only have competed with free labor. Otherwise slave labor was to be found in the cities and temples of the Hellenistic world, in the factories and fields, and in the homes of wealthier people.

Hellenistic Intellectual Advances

What is the intellectual legacy of the Hellenistic period?

The peoples of the Hellenistic era took the ideas and ideals of the classical Greeks and advanced them to new heights. Their achievements created the intellectual and religious atmosphere that deeply influenced Roman thinking and eventually the religious thought of liberal Judaism and early Christianity. Far from being stagnant, this was a period of vigorous growth, especially in the areas of philosophy, science, and medicine.

Religion in the Hellenistic World

In religion the most significant new ideas were developed outside Greece. At first the Hellenistic period saw the spread of Greek religious cults throughout the Near East and Egypt. When Hellenistic kings founded cities, they also built temples and established new cults and priesthoods for the old Olympian gods.

Greek cults sponsored literary, musical, and athletic contests, which were staged in beautiful surroundings among impressive Greek buildings. On the whole, however, the civic cults were primarily concerned with ritual and neither appealed to religious emotions nor embraced matters such as sin and redemption. Although the new civic cults were lavish in pomp and display, they could not satisfy deep religious feelings or spiritual yearnings. Greeks increasingly sought solace from other sources. Some turned to philosophy as a guide to life, while others turned to superstition, magic, or astrology. Still others might shrug and speak of **Tyche** (TIE-kee), which meant "Fate" or "Chance" or "Doom"—a capricious and sometimes malevolent force.

Beginning in the second century B.C.E., some individuals were increasingly attracted to new **mystery religions,** so called because they featured a body of ritual not to be divulged to anyone not initiated into the cult. These new mystery cults incorporated aspects of both Greek and Eastern religions and had broad appeal for people who yearned for personal immortality. Since the Greeks were already familiar with old mystery cults, such as the Eleusinian (el-yoo-SIN-ee-uhn) mysteries in Attica, the new cults did not strike them as alien. Familiar, too, was the concept of preparation for an initiation. Devotees of the Greek Eleusinian mysteries and other such cults had to prepare themselves mentally and physically before entering the gods' presence. Thus the mystery cults fit well with Greek usage.

The new religions enjoyed one tremendous advantage over the old Greek mystery cults. Whereas old Greek mysteries were tied to particular places, such as Eleusis (ee-LOO-sis), the new religions spread throughout the Hellenistic world.

Tyche Fate or chance or doom; a capricious and sometimes malevolent force.

mystery religions Bodies of ritual not to be divulged to anyone not initiated into the cult. They incorporated aspects of both Greek and Eastern religions and had broad appeal for both Greeks and Easterners who yearned for personal immortality.

Hellenistic Mystery Cult
The scene depicts part of the ritual of initiation into the cult of Dionysus. The young woman here has just completed the ritual. She now dances in joy as the official with the sacred staff looks on. (Scala/Art Resource, NY)

People did not have to undertake long and expensive pilgrimages just to become members of the religion. In that sense the mystery religions came to the people, for temples of the new deities sprang up wherever Greeks lived.

The mystery religions all claimed to save their adherents from the worst that fate could do and promised life for the soul after death. They all had a single concept in common: the belief that by the rites of initiation devotees became united with a god, usually male, who had himself died and risen from the dead. The sacrifice of the god and his victory over death saved the devotee from eternal death. Similarly, all mystery religions demanded a period of preparation in which the convert strove to become holy, that is, to live by the religion's precepts. Once aspirants had prepared themselves, they went through an initiation in which they learned the secrets of the religion. The initiation was usually a ritual of great emotional intensity, symbolizing the entry into a new life.

The mystery religions that took the Hellenistic world by storm were the Egyptian cults of Serapis (**si-REY-pis**) and Isis. Serapis, who was invented by King Ptolemy, was believed to be the judge of souls, who rewarded virtuous and righteous people with eternal life.

The cult of Isis enjoyed even wider appeal than that of Serapis. Isis, wife of Osiris, was believed to have conquered Tyche and promised to save any mortal who came to her. She became the most important goddess of the Hellenistic world, and her worship was very popular among women. Her priests claimed that she had bestowed on humanity the gift of civilization and founded law and literature. She was the goddess of marriage, conception, and childbirth, and like Serapis she promised to save the souls of her believers.

Mystery religions took care of the big things in life, but many people resorted to ordinary magic for daily matters. When a cat walked across their path, they stopped until someone else had passed by them. Or they could throw three rocks across the road. People often purified their houses to protect them from Hecate (**HEK-uh-tee**), a sinister goddess associated with magic and witchcraft. Many people had dreams that only seers and augurs (**AW-gers**) could interpret. Some of these things are familiar today because some old fears are still alive.

Philosophy and the People

During the Hellenistic period, philosophy reached out to touch the lives of more men and women than ever before. Two significant philosophies caught the minds and hearts of contemporary Greeks and some Easterners, as well as some later Romans. The first was **Epicureanism** (**ep-ee-kyoo-REE-uh-niz-uhm**), a practical philosophy of serenity in an often tumultuous world. Epicurus (**ep-ee-KYOOR-uhs**) (340–270 B.C.E.) taught that the principal good of human life is pleasure, which he defined as the absence of pain. He was not advocating drunken revels or sexual dissipation, which he thought actually caused pain. Instead, Epicurus concluded that any violent emotion is undesirable and advocated mild self-discipline. Even poverty he considered good, as long as people had enough food, clothing, and shelter. Epicurus also taught that individuals can most easily attain peace and serenity by ignoring the outside world and looking into their personal feelings and reactions. His followers ignored politics and issues, for they led to tumult, which would disturb the soul.

Opposed to the passivity of the Epicureans, Zeno (**ZEE-noh**) (335–262 B.C.E.), a philosopher from Citium in Cyprus, advanced a different concept of human beings and the universe. Zeno first came to Athens to form his own school, the Stoa, named after the building where he preferred to teach. **Stoicism** (**STOH-uh-siz-uhm**)

Epicureanism A practical philosophy founded by Epicurus, it argued that the principal good of human life is pleasure.

Stoicism The most popular of Hellenistic philosophies, it considered nature an expression of divine will; people could be happy only when living in accordance with nature.

became the most popular Hellenistic philosophy and the one that later captured the mind of Rome. To the Stoics the important question was not whether they achieved anything, but whether they lived virtuous lives. In that way they could triumph over Tyche, for Tyche could destroy achievements but not the nobility of their lives.

Zeno and his followers considered nature an expression of divine will; in their view, people could be happy only when living in accordance with nature. They stressed the unity of man and the universe, stating that all men were brothers and were obliged to help one another. The Stoics' most significant practical achievement was the creation of the concept of **natural law.** The Stoics concluded that as all men were brothers, partook of divine reason, and were in harmony with the universe, one law—a part of the natural order of life—governed them all. The Stoic concept of a universal state governed by natural law is one of the finest heirlooms the Hellenistic world passed on to Rome. The Stoic concept of natural law, of one law for all people, became a valuable tool when the Romans began to deal with many different peoples with different laws. The ideal of the universal state gave the Romans a rationale for extending their empire to the farthest reaches of the world. The obligation of individuals to their fellows served the citizens of the Roman Empire as the philosophical justification for doing their duty. In this respect, too, the real fruit of Hellenism was to ripen only under the cultivation of Rome.

natural law A Stoic concept that as all men were brothers, partook of divine reason, and were in harmony with the universe, one law—a part of the natural order of life—governed them all.

Hellenistic Science

Hellenistic culture achieved its greatest triumphs in the area of science. The most notable of the Hellenistic astronomers was Aristarchus (**ar-uh-STAHR-kuhs**) of Samos (ca. 310–230 B.C.E.), who was educated in Aristotle's school. Aristarchus concluded that the sun is far larger than the earth and that the stars are enormously distant from the earth. He argued against Aristotle's view that the earth was the center of the universe. Instead, Aristarchus propounded the **heliocentric (he-lee-oh-CENT-rik) theory**—that the earth and planets revolve around the sun. His work is all the more impressive because he lacked even a rudimentary telescope. Aristarchus had only the human eye and brain, but they were more than enough.

Unfortunately, Aristarchus's theories did not persuade the ancient world. In the second century C.E. Claudius Ptolemy, a mathematician and astronomer in Alexandria, accepted Aristotle's theory of the earth as the center of the universe, and this view prevailed for fourteen hundred years. Aristarchus's heliocentric theory lay dormant until resurrected in the sixteenth century by the brilliant Polish astronomer Nicolaus Copernicus (**koh-PUR-ni-kuhs**).

In geometry Euclid (**YOO-klid**) (ca. 300 B.C.E.), a mathematician who lived in Alexandria, compiled a valuable textbook of existing knowledge. His book *The Elements of Geometry* has exerted immense influence on Western civilization, for it rapidly became the standard introduction to geometry. Generations of students, from the Hellenistic period to the present, have learned the essentials of geometry from it.

The greatest thinker of the Hellenistic period was Archimedes (**ahr-kuh-MEE-deez**) (ca. 287–212 B.C.E.), a native of Syracuse. (See the feature "Individuals in Society: Archimedes and the Practical Application of Science.") His mathematical research, covering many fields, was his greatest contribution to Western thought. In his book *On Plane Equilibriums* Archimedes dealt for the first time with the basic principles of mechanics, including the principle of the lever. He once said that if he were given a lever and a suitable place to stand, he could move the world. With his treatise *On Floating Bodies* he founded the science of hydrostatics.

heliocentric theory The theory of Aristarchus that the earth and planets revolve around the sun.

Individuals in Society

Archimedes and the Practical Application of Science

Throughout the ages generals have besieged cities to force them to surrender. Between 213 and 211 B.C.E. the Roman general Marcellus laid close siege to the strongly walled city of Syracuse, the home of the scientist Archimedes. Hiero, king of Syracuse and friend of Archimedes, turned to him for help. Archimedes used his knowledge of mechanics to create engines that could fire objects at the enemy.

Archimedes' mill. A slave turns a large cylinder fitted with blades to form a screw that draws water from a well. (Courtesy, Soprintendenza Archeologica di Pompei. Photo: Dr. Penelope M. Allison)

Archimedes, however, began to ply his engines, and shot against the land forces of the attackers all sorts of missiles and immense masses of stones, which came down with incredible din and speed. Nothing whatever could ward off their weight, but they knocked down in heaps those who stood in their way, and threw their ranks into confusion. At the same time huge beams were suddenly projected over the [Roman] ships from the walls [of Syracuse], which sank some of them with great weights plunging down from on high. Others were seized at the prow by iron claws, or beaks like the beaks of cranes, drawn straight up into the air, and then plunged stern first into the depths, or were turned round and round by means of enginery within the city, and dashed upon the steep cliffs that jutted out beneath the wall of the city, with great destruction of the fighting men on board, who perished in the wrecks. Frequently, too, a ship would be lifted out of the water into mid-air, whirled here and there as it hung there, a dreadful spectacle, until its crew had been thrown out and hurled in all directions. Then it would fall empty upon the walls, or slip away from the clutch that had held it.

Then in a council of war the Romans decided to come up under the walls while it was still night. . . . When, therefore, they came under the walls, thinking themselves unnoticed, once more they encountered a great storm of missiles. Huge stones came tumbling down upon them almost perpendicularly, and the wall shot out arrows at them from every point. They therefore retired. And here again, when they were some distance off, missiles darted forth and fell upon them as they were going away, and there was a great slaughter among them. Many of their ships, too, were dashed together, and they could not retaliate in any way upon their foes. For Archimedes had built most of his engines close behind the wall, and the Romans seemed to be fighting against the gods, now that countless mischiefs were poured out upon them from an invisible source.

At last the Romans became so fearful that whenever they saw a bit of rope or a stick of timber projecting a little over the wall. "There it is," they shouted, "Archimedes is training some engine upon us." They then turned their backs and fled. Seeing this, Marcellus desisted from all the fighting and assault, and thenceforth depended on a long siege.

For all his genius, Archimedes did not survive the siege. His deeds of war done, he returned to his thinking and his mathematical problems, even with the siege still in the background. When Syracuse was betrayed to the Romans, soldiers streamed in, spreading slaughter and destruction throughout the city. A Roman soldier came upon Archimedes in his study and killed him outright, thus ending the life of one of the world's greatest thinkers.

Questions for Analysis

1. How did Archimedes' engines repulse the Roman attacks?
2. What effect did his weapons have on the Roman attackers?
3. What is the irony of Archimedes' death?

Source: Reprinted by permission of the publishers and the Trustees of the Loeb Classical Library from *Plutarch: Volume V,* Loeb Classical Library Volume 87, translated by B. Perrin, pp. 475–477, Cambridge, Mass.: Harvard University Press, 1917. The Loeb Classical Library® is a registered trademark of the President and Fellows of Harvard College.

He concluded that whenever a solid floats in a liquid, the weight of the solid is equal to the weight of the liquid displaced. He made his discovery when he stepped into a bath. He noticed that the weight of his body displaced a volume of water equal to it. He immediately ran outside shouting "Eureka, eureka" (I have found it, I have found it).[1]

Archimedes was willing to share his work with others, among them Eratosthenes (**er-uh-TOS-thuh-neez**) (285–ca. 204 B.C.E.), who was librarian of the enormous royal library in Alexandria, Egypt. Eratosthenes used mathematics to further the geographical studies for which he is most famous. He calculated the circumference of the earth geometrically, estimating it as about 24,675 miles. He was not wrong by much: the earth is actually 24,860 miles in circumference. Eratosthenes also concluded that the earth was a spherical globe and that the land was surrounded by ocean.

Using geographical information gained by Alexander the Great's scientists, Eratosthenes tried to fit the East into Greek geographical knowledge. Although for some reason he ignored the western Mediterranean and Europe, he declared that a ship could sail from Spain either around Africa to India or directly westward to India. Not until the great days of Western exploration did sailors such as Vasco da Gama and Magellan actually prove Eratosthenes' theories.

Catapult

This model shows a catapult as its crew would have seen it in action. The arrow was loaded on the long horizontal beam, its point fitting into the housing. There the torsion spring under great pressure released the arrow at the target, which could be some 400 yards away. (Courtesy, Noel Kavan)

For all of its speculation, Hellenistic science made an inestimable, if grim, contribution to practical life. The Greeks and Macedonians applied theories of mechanics to build siege machines, thus revolutionizing the art of warfare. The catapult became the first and most widely used artillery piece. The earliest catapults could shoot only large arrows and small stones. By the time Alexander the Great besieged Tyre in 332 B.C.E., his catapults threw stones big enough to knock down city walls. Generals soon realized that they could also hurl burning bundles over the walls to start fires in the city. To approach enemy town walls safely, engineers built siege towers, large wooden structures that served as artillery platforms, and put them on wheels so that soldiers could roll them up to the wall. Once there, archers stationed on top of them swept the enemy's ramparts with arrows, while other soldiers manning catapults added missile fire. To aid the siege towers, generals added battering rams that brought down large portions of walls. If these new engines made waging war more efficient, they also added to the misery of the people. War was no longer confined to the battlefield and fought between soldiers. It had come to embrace the whole population.

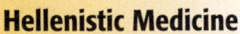

Hellenistic Medicine

The study of medicine flourished during the Hellenistic period, and Hellenistic physicians carried the work of Hippocrates into new areas. Herophilus, who lived in the first half of the third century B.C.E., approached the study of medicine in a systematic, scientific fashion: he dissected dead bodies and measured what he observed. He discovered the nervous system and concluded that two types of

An Unsuccessful Delivery

This funeral stele depicts a mother who has perhaps lost her own life as well as her baby's. Childbirth was the leading cause of death for adult women in antiquity, though funeral steles showing this are quite rare. Another of the few that do show death in childbirth bears the heartbreaking words attributed to the mother by her grieving family: "All my labor could not bring the child forth; he lies in my womb, among the dead." (National Archaeological Museum, Athens/Archaeological Receipts Fund)

Section Review

- Greek religious cults were based on ritual and did not satisfy deeper religious feelings, causing many Greeks to turn to philosophy, astrology, magic, and mystery cults to guide their lives.

- The mystery cults such as the Eleusinian mysteries and the Egyptian cults of Serapis and Isis held broad appeal and promised life after death for those who passed their emotionally intense rituals and adhered to their religious precepts.

- Epicureanism taught individuals to attain peace by seeking pleasure and ignoring the outside world while Stoicism maintained that one achieved happiness by living a dutiful, virtuous life according to universal nature.

- Many significant advances were made in science including the heliocentric theory, geometry, and the basic principles of mechanics, hydrostatics, and using mathematics in geographical studies.

- Advances in science revolutionized warfare with the introduction of the catapult, siege towers, and battering rams.

- The study of medicine led to a greater understanding of the human body through dissection as well as the use of drugs and medicine to treat illnesses, but the popularity of quacks who claimed to cure illness through magic and potions hindered these advances.

nerves, motor and sensory, existed. Herophilus also studied the brain, which he considered the center of intelligence, and discerned the cerebrum (**suh-REE-bruhm**) and cerebellum (**ser-uh-BEL-uhm**). His other work dealt with the liver, lungs, and uterus.

In about 280 B.C.E. Philinus and Serapion, pupils of Herophilus, concentrated on the observation and cure of illnesses rather than focussing on dissection. They also laid heavier stress on the use of drugs and medicine to treat illnesses. Heraclides of Tarentum (**tuh-REN-tuhm**) (perhaps first century B.C.E.) carried on this tradition and discovered the benefits of opium and worked with other drugs that relieved pain.

The Hellenistic world was also plagued by people who claimed to cure illnesses through incantations and magic. Their potions included such concoctions as blood from the ear of an ass mixed with water to cure fever, or the liver of a cat killed when the moon was waning and preserved in salt. Quacks damaged the reputation of dedicated doctors who intelligently tried to heal and alleviate pain. The medical abuses that arose in the Hellenistic period were so flagrant that the Romans, who later entered the Hellenistic world, developed an intense distrust of physicians and also considered the study of Hellenistic medicine beneath the dignity of a Roman. Nonetheless, the work of men like Herophilus and Serapion made valuable contributions to the knowledge of medicine, and the fruits of their work were preserved and handed on to the West.

Chapter Review

Why did Alexander launch his massive attack on the Persian Empire? How extensive were his conquests? (page 66)

Although Alexander may not originally have intended to march all the way to the Indus Valley, he gained so much territory that he saw every reason to continue as far as possible. It was an almost foolhardy adventure, but it permanently changed the face of world history.

What happened to Alexander's empire after his death? What was his political and cultural legacy? (page 68)

Alexander's legacy proved of essential importance to the future of the West. He brought the vital civilization of the Greeks into intimate contact with the older cultures of the East. He and his successors established cities and encouraged a third great wave of Greek migration.

What effect did Greek migration have on Greek and native peoples? (page 71)

In the Aegean and Near East the fusion of Greek and Eastern cultures laid the social, intellectual, and cultural foundations on which the Romans would later build. In the heart of the old Persian empire, Hellenism was only another new influence that was absorbed by older ways of thought and life. Yet overall, in the exchange of ideas and the opportunity for different cultures to learn about one another, a new cosmopolitan society evolved.

What effects did East-West trade have on ordinary peoples during the Hellenistic period? (page 75)

For ordinary men and women, the greatest practical boon of the Hellenistic adventure was economic. Trade connected the world on a routine basis. Economics brought people together just as surely as it brought them goods. By the end of the Hellenistic period, the ancient world had become far broader and more economically intricate than ever before.

What is the intellectual legacy of the Hellenistic period? (page 76)

Hellenistic achievements included intellectual advances as well as trade connections. Mystery religions, such as the worship of the goddess Isis, provided many people with answers to their questions about the meaning of life, while others turned to practical philosophies such as Stoicism for ethical guidance. Mathematicians and scientists developed theoretical knowledge and applied this to practical problems in geography, mechanics, and weaponry. Physicians also approached medicine in a systematic fashion, though many people relied on magic and folk cures for treatment of illness. People of the Hellenistic period not only built on the achievements of their predecessors, but they also produced one of the most creative intellectual eras of classical antiquity.

Key Terms

Hellenistic (p. 66)
sovereign (p. 72)
Great Silk Road (p. 76)
Tyche (p. 77)
mystery religions (p. 77)
Epicureanism (p. 78)
Stoicism (p. 78)
natural law (p. 79)
heliocentric theory (p. 79)

Note

1. Vitruvius, *On Architecture* 9 Preface, 10.

To assess your mastery of this chapter, go to **bedfordstmartins.com/mckaywestbrief**

Listening to the Past

Alexander and the Brotherhood of Man

At one point in his crusade, Alexander found himself confronted with a huge mutiny by his Macedonian veterans. He ordered the most vocal of the rebels to be executed and reminded the others of the glory they had achieved in battle and the shame they would endure at home if they returned as deserters. He then refused to see any of the Macedonians and turned over command of the brigades to the Persians. Alexander's words of reconciliation at the conclusion of this episode have been interpreted as an expression of his desire to establish a "brotherhood of man." Readers can determine for themselves whether Alexander attempted to introduce a new philosophical ideal or whether he harbored his own political motives for political cooperation.

[The Macedonian soldiers] declared they would not retire from the gates either day or night, unless Alexander would take some pity upon them. When he was informed of this, he came out without delay; and seeing them lying on the ground in humble guise, and hearing most of them lamenting with loud voice, tears began to flow also from his own eyes. He made an effort to say something to them, but they continued their importunate entreaties. At length one of them, Callines by name, a man conspicuous both for his age and because he was a captain of the Companion cavalry, spoke as follows, "O king, what grieves the Macedonians is that you have already made some of the Persians kinsmen to yourself, and that Persians are called Alexander's kinsmen, and have the honour of saluting you with a kiss; whereas none of the Macedonians have as yet enjoyed this honour." Then Alexander interrupting him, said, "But all of you without exception I consider my kinsmen, and so from this time I shall call you." When he had

said this, Callines advanced and saluted him with a kiss, and so did all those who wished to salute him. Then they took up their weapons and returned to the camp, shouting and singing a song of thanksgiving. After this Alexander offered sacrifice to the gods to whom it was his custom to sacrifice, and gave a public banquet, over which he himself presided, with the Macedonians sitting around him; and next to them the Persians; after whom came the men of the other nations, preferred in honour for their personal rank or for some meritorious action. The king and his guests drew wine from the same bowl and poured out the same libations, both the Grecian prophets and the Magians commencing the ceremony. He prayed for other blessings, and especially that harmony and community of rule might exist between the Macedonians and Persians.

Questions for Analysis

1. What was the purpose of the banquet?
2. Were all of the guests treated equally?
3. What did Alexander gain from bringing together the Macedonians and Persians?

Source: From *The Greek Historians* by Francis R. B. Godolphin. Copyright © 1942 and renewed 1970 by Random House, Inc. Used by permission of Random House, Inc.

This gilded case for a bow and arrows indicates that Alexander's success came at the price of blood. These vigorous scenes portray more military conflict than philosophical compassion. (Archaeological Museum Salonica/Dagli Orti/The Art Archive)

CHAPTER 5

The Rise of Rome

ca. 750–44 B.C.E.

Chapter Preview

The Roman Forum. (Josephine Powell Photography, Courtesy of Special Collections, Fine Arts Library, Harvard College Library)

Like the Persians under Cyrus and the Greeks under Alexander, the Romans managed to conquer vast territories in less than a century. Their achievement lay in their ability to incorporate conquered peoples into the Roman system. Unlike the Greeks, who refused to share citizenship, the Romans extended their citizenship first to the Italians and later to the peoples of the provinces. With that citizenship went Roman government and law. Rome created a world state that embraced the entire Mediterranean area and extended northward.

Nor was Rome's achievement limited to the ancient world. Rome's law, language, and administrative practices shaped later developments in Europe and beyond. London, Paris, Vienna, and many other modern European cities began as Roman colonies or military camps. When the Founding Fathers created the American republic, they looked to Rome as a model. On the darker side, Napoleon and Mussolini paid their own tribute to Rome by aping its forms. All were acknowledging admiration for the Roman achievement.

Roman history is usually divided into two periods: the republic, the age in which Rome grew from a small city-state to ruler of an empire, and the empire, the period when the republican constitution gave way to constitutional monarchy. The republic is the focus of this chapter.

The Etruscans and Rome

How did the Etruscans shape early Roman history?

While the Greeks pursued their destiny in the East, the Etruscans (**eh-TRUS-kuns**) and Romans entered the peninsula of Italy. The arrival of the Etruscans in the region of Etruria can reasonably be dated to about 750 B.C.E. The Romans settled farther south in Latium. Located at an easy crossing point on the Tiber (**TIE-ber**) River, Rome stood astride the main avenue of communication between northern and southern Italy. Its seven hills were defensive and safe from the floods of the Tiber. (See Map 5.1.)

The Etruscans and the Roman Settlement of Italy (ca. 750–509 B.C.E.)

The Etruscans established permanent settlements that evolved into the first Italian cities, which resembled the Greek city-states in political organization. Their influence spread over the surrounding countryside, which they farmed but also mined, as it contained rich mineral resources. From an early period the Etruscans began to trade natural products, especially iron, with their Greek neighbors on the Mediterranean in exchange for luxury goods. They thereby built a rich cultural life that became the foundation of civilization throughout Italy. In the process they touched a small collection of villages subsequently called Rome.

The Romans had settled in Italy by the eighth century B.C.E. According to one legend, Romulus and Remus founded the city in 753 B.C.E., Romulus making his home on the Palatine Hill, while Remus chose the Aventine (see inset of Map 5.1). Under Etruscan influence the Romans prospered, spreading over all of Rome's seven hills.

From 753 to 509 B.C.E. a line of Etruscan kings ruled the city and introduced many customs. The Romans adopted the Etruscan alphabet, which the Etruscans themselves had adopted from the Greeks. The Romans later handed on this alphabet to medieval Europe and from there to the modern Western world. Even the **toga** (TOH-guh), the white woolen robe worn by citizens, came from the Etruscans.

Under the Etruscans Rome enjoyed contacts with the larger Mediterranean world, while the city continued to grow. In the years 575 to 550 B.C.E. temples and public buildings began to grace the city. The **forum** ceased to be a cemetery and began its history as a public meeting place, similar to the Greek agora. Trade in metalwork became common, and wealthier Romans began to import fine Greek vases. The Etruscans had found Rome a collection of villages and made it a city.

750–31 B.C.E.	Beginning of the economic growth of Rome
750–133 B.C.E.	Traditional founding of Rome; evolution of the Roman state
509–290 B.C.E.	Roman conquest of Italy
499–186 B.C.E.	Introduction of Greek deities
ca. 494–287 B.C.E.	Struggle of the Orders
264–133 B.C.E.	Punic Wars and the conquest of the East
262 B.C.E.	Growth of large estates
239–159 B.C.E.	Rise of Latin Literature
88–31 B.C.E.	Civil war
86–35 B.C.E.	Birth of historical and political writing

The Roman Conquest of Italy (509–290 B.C.E.)

Legend has it that the republic was formed when the son of the Etruscan king raped Lucretia (loo-KREE-shuh), a virtuous Roman woman, and the people rose up in anger. The republic was actually founded in the years after 509, when the Romans fought numerous wars with their neighbors on the Italian peninsula. Not until roughly a century after the founding of the republic did the Romans drive the Etruscans entirely out of Latium (LA-cee-um). Early on, the Romans learned the value of alliances, and the Latin towns around them provided them with a large reservoir of manpower. These alliances involved the Romans in still other wars and took them farther afield in the Italian peninsula.

Around 390 B.C.E. the Romans suffered a major setback when a new people, the Celts—or **Gauls** (gawls), as the Romans called them—swept aside a Roman army and sacked Rome. More intent on loot than on land, they agreed to abandon Rome in return for a thousand pounds of gold. In the century that followed, the Romans rebuilt their city and

toga The white woolen robe worn by citizens.

forum A public meeting place; a development parallel to that of the Greek agora.

Gauls The Celts, people who swept aside a Roman army and sacked Rome around 390 B.C.E.

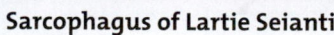

Sarcophagus of Lartie Seianti

The woman portrayed on this lavish sarcophagus is the noble Etruscan Lartie Seianti. Although the sarcophagus is her place of burial, she is portrayed as in life, comfortable and at rest. The influence of Greek art on Etruscan is apparent in almost every feature of the sarcophagus. (Archaeological Museum, Florence/Nimatallah/Art Resource, NY)

recouped their losses. They brought Latium and their Latin allies fully under their control and conquered Etruria. In 343 B.C.E. they grappled with the Samnites in a series of bitter wars for the possession of Campania (kam-PAY-nee-uh) and southern Italy (see Map 5.1). The Samnites were a formidable enemy, but the superior military organization and manpower of the Romans won out in the end. Although Rome had yet to subdue the whole peninsula, for the first time in history it stood unchallenged.

The Romans spread their religious cults, mythology, and drama throughout Italy. They did not force their beliefs on others, but they did welcome their neighbors to religious places of assembly. The Romans and Italians grew closer by the mutual understanding of and participation in religious rites.

With many of their oldest allies, such as the Latin cities, the Romans shared full Roman citizenship. In other instances they granted citizenship without the **franchise,**

franchise The right to vote or hold Roman offices.

MAP 5.1   Italy and the City of Rome

The geographical configuration of the Italian peninsula shows how Rome stood astride north-south communication routes and how the state that united Italy stood poised to move into Sicily and northern Africa.

that is, without the right to vote or hold Roman offices. These allies were subject to Roman taxes and calls for military service but ran their own local affairs. The Latin allies were able to acquire full Roman citizenship by moving to Rome.

The Roman roads, many of which were in use as late as the medieval period, allowed for the flow of communication, trade, and armies from the capital to outlying areas. They were the tangible sinews of unity.

The Roman Republic

What was the nature of the Roman republic?

The Romans summed up their political existence in a single phrase: *senatus populusque Romanum*, "the Roman senate and people." This sentiment reflects the republican ideal of shared government rather than concentrated power within a monarchy. Abbreviated as "SPQR," the letters became a shorthand way of saying "Rome." The beliefs, customs, and laws of the republic—its unwritten constitution—evolved over centuries to meet the demands of the governed.

The Roman State

In the early republic social divisions determined the shape of politics. Political power was in the hands of the aristocracy—the **patricians** (**puh-TREESH-uhns**), who were wealthy landowners. Patrician families formed clans, as did aristocrats in early Greece. Patrician men dominated the affairs of state, provided military leadership in time of war, and monopolized knowledge of law and legal procedure. The common people of Rome, the **plebeians** (**plee-BEE-ahns**), were free citizens with a voice in politics, but they could not hold high political office or marry into patrician families. While some plebeian merchants rivaled the patricians in wealth, most were poor artisans, small farmers, and landless urban dwellers.

The chief magistrates of the republic were the two **consuls**, elected for one-year terms. At first the consulship was open only to patrician men. The consuls commanded the army in battle, administered state business, and supervised financial affairs. When the consuls were away from Rome, *praetors* (**PRAY-ters**) could act in their place. Otherwise, the praetors dealt primarily with the administration of justice.

After the age of overseas conquest, the Romans divided the Mediterranean area into provinces governed by ex-consuls and ex-praetors. Because of their experience in Roman politics, they were well suited to administer the affairs of the provincials and to fit Roman law and custom into new contexts.

Other officials included *quaestors* (**KWEH-ster**), who took charge of the public treasury and prosecuted criminals in the popular courts; *censors*, whose many responsibilities included the supervision of public morals, the power to determine who lawfully could sit in the senate, the registration of citizens, and the leasing of public contracts; and the *aediles* (**AY-dials**), who supervised the streets and markets and presided over public festivals.

Perhaps the greatest institution of the republic was the **senate**, which had originated under the Etruscans as a council of noble elders who advised the king. During the republic the senate advised the consuls and other magistrates. Because the senate sat year after year, while magistrates changed annually, it provided stability and experienced counsel. Technically, the senate could not pass legislation; it could only offer its advice. But increasingly, because of the senate's prestige, its advice came to have the force of law.

patricians The aristocracy; wealthy landowners who held political power.

plebeians The common people of Rome who had few of the patricians' advantages.

consuls The two chief Roman magistrates.

senate Originating under the Etruscans, it was a council of noble elders who advised the king.

natural law A universal law that could be applied to all people and societies.

Struggle of the Orders A great social conflict that developed between patricians and plebeians; the plebeians wanted real political representation and safeguards against patrician domination.

tribunes The people whom plebeians were able to elect; tribunes would in turn protect the plebeians from the arbitrary conduct of patrician magistrates.

paterfamilias A term that means far more than merely father, it indicates the oldest, dominant male of the family, one who held nearly absolute power over the lives of his family as long as he lived.

Section Review

- The Roman political ideal was *"Senatus populusque Romanum"* or *"SPQR"* ("the Roman senate and people"), which meant they valued shared government over a monarchy.

- In the early republic, political power was in the hands of wealthy men—patricians—who were elected for one-year terms as consuls, while the plebeians (the common people) were free but could not hold high office or marry into patrician families.

- The senate advised the consuls and other magistrates, providing stability, and while initially it could not pass legislation, due to its reputation its advice later came to have the force of law.

- The development of Roman law, added to by assemblies and interpreted by praetors, included the adoption of the law of equity and the concept of "natural law," which provided equal justice for all involved.

- The Struggle of the Orders was a conflict between the plebeians and the patricians, during which the plebeians went on strike and won the right to elect their own officials (tribunes), to hold one of the two annual consul positions, and to legal equality.

- The paterfamilias was the male head of the family and held absolute power over the lives of his wife and children as long as he lived.

The Romans created several assemblies, through which men elected magistrates and passed legislation. The *comitia centuriata* (kuh-MISH-ee-uh cent-ur-EE-ah-tah) was a popular assembly organized by *centuries*, which were both military companies and political voting blocs. The patricians possessed the majority of centuries and could easily outvote the plebeians. In 471 B.C.E. plebeian men won the right to meet in an assembly of their own, the *concilium plebis*, and to pass ordinances.

One of the most important achievements of the Romans was their development of a body of law. Roman assemblies added to the law, and praetors interpreted it. The spirit of the law aimed at protecting the property, lives, and reputations of citizens, and redressing wrongs. As the Romans came into more frequent contact with foreigners, the praetors adopted aspects of other legal systems and resorted to the law of equity—what they thought was right and just to all parties. By the time of the late republic, Roman jurists were reaching decisions on the basis of the Stoic concept of **natural law,** a universal law that could be applied to all societies.

Social Conflict in Rome

The inequality between plebeians and patricians led to a conflict known as the **Struggle of the Orders.** Rather than using violence to achieve their goals, the plebeians leveraged their power as a group. The patricians also responded peacefully, ultimately resorting to a practical compromise.

The first showdown between plebeians and patricians came, according to tradition, in 494 B.C.E. To force the patricians to grant concessions, the plebeians literally walked out of Rome and refused to serve in the army. The plebeians' general strike worked, and the patricians made important concessions. They allowed patricians and plebeians to marry one another. They recognized the right of plebeians to elect their own officials, the **tribunes** (trib-YOONS), who could bring plebeian grievances to the senate for resolution. And they gave up their legal monopoly, publishing the law and legal procedures so that plebeians could also argue cases in court.

Further reforms followed after a ten-year battle. Wealthy plebeians wanted the opportunity to provide political leadership for the state. They demanded that the patricians allow them access to all the magistracies of the state. If they could hold the consulship, they could also sit in the senate and advise on policy. They won the right to one of the two annual consul positions. Though decisive, this victory did not automatically end the Struggle of the Orders. That happened only in 287 B.C.E. with the passage of a law that gave the resolutions of the concilium plebis the force of law for patricians and plebeians alike.

The compromise established a new nobility shared by wealthy plebeians and patricians. They were both groups of aristocrats who had simply agreed to share the great offices of power within the republic. This would lead not to major political reform but to an extension of aristocratic rule.

The Struggle of the Orders made all male citizens equal before the law, but a man's independence was limited by the power that the male head of the family, termed the **paterfamilias** (pat-er-fuh-MEE-lee-uhs), had over him. This was also true for all women, who even as adults were always under the legal guardianship of some man. The paterfamilias held nearly absolute power over the lives of his wife and children as long as he lived. He could legally kill his wife for adultery, or divorce her at will. He could kill his children or sell them into slavery. Until the paterfamilias died, his sons could not even own property.

Roman Expansion

How did the Romans take control of the Mediterranean world?

Once the Romans had settled their internal affairs, they turned their attention outward. As seen earlier, they had already come to terms with the Italic peoples in Latium. Only later did Rome achieve primacy over its Latin allies, partly because of successful diplomacy and partly because of overwhelming military power. In 282 B.C.E. Rome expanded even farther in Italy and extended its power across the sea to Sicily, Corsica (**KAWR-si-kuh**), and Sardinia (**sahr-DIN-ee-uh**).

Italy Becomes Roman

In only twenty years, from 282 to 262 B.C.E., the Romans established a string of colonies throughout Italy, some of them populated by Romans and others by Latins. Those living closest to Rome were incorporated into the Roman state. They enjoyed the full franchise and citizenship that the Romans themselves possessed. Those Italians who lived farther afield were bound by treaty with the Romans and were considered allies. Although they received lesser rights of active citizenship, the allies retained their right of local self-government. Through these contacts—social, political, and legal—Rome and the rest of Italy began to share similar views of their common welfare.

Overseas Conquest (282–146 B.C.E.)

In 282 B.C.E., when the Romans had reached southern Italy, they embarked upon a series of wars that left them the rulers of the Mediterranean world (see Map 5.2). These wars became fiercer and were fought on a larger scale than those in Italy. Though the Romans sometimes declared war reluctantly, they nonetheless felt the need to dominate, to eliminate any state that could threaten them. Yet they did not map out grandiose strategies for world conquest but rather responded to situations as they arose.

The Samnite wars had drawn the Romans into the political world of southern Italy. In 282 B.C.E., alarmed by the powerful newcomer, the Greek city of Tarentum (**tuh-REN-tuhm**) in southern Italy called for help from Pyrrhus (**PEER-uhs**), king of Epirus (**eh-PAHY-ruhs**) in western Greece. A relative of Alexander the Great and an excellent general, Pyrrhus won two furious battles but suffered heavy casualties—thus the phrase **Pyrrhic victory** for a victory involving severe losses. Against Pyrrhus's army the Romans threw new legions, and in the end manpower proved decisive. In 275 B.C.E. the Romans drove Pyrrhus from Italy and extended their sway over southern Italy. They then needed to secure the island of Sicily (**SIS-uh-lee**) in order to block the northward expansion of Carthage (**KAHR-thij**).

Pyrrhic victory A phrase for a victory involving severe losses, stemming from the victories of Pyrrhus, which were won despite major casualties.

The Punic Wars and Beyond (264–133 B.C.E.)

By 264 B.C.E. Carthage was the unrivaled power of the western Mediterranean. It had created and defended a mercantile empire that stretched from western Sicily to beyond Gibraltar. The battle for Sicily set the stage for the **First Punic (PYOO-nik) War** between Rome and Carthage, two powers expanding into the same area. The First Punic War lasted for twenty-three years (264–241 B.C.E.). The Romans quickly learned that they could not conquer Sicily

First Punic War A war between Rome and Carthage that lasted 23 years.

North Sea

ATLANTIC OCEAN

BRITAIN

Aral Sea

Caspian Sea

Volga R.

Don R.

Dnieper R.

Baltic Sea

Vistula R.

GERMANY

Elbe R.

Rhine R.

GAUL

BELGICA

Lugdunum (Lyons)

NARBONENSIS

Narbo

Massilia (Marseilles)

ALPS

RAETIA

NORICUM

PANNONIA

ILLYRICUM

CISALPINE GAUL Po R.

Arretium

Lake Trasimene 217 B.C.E.

Rome

Corsica

Capua

Tarentum

ITALY

Cannae 216 B.C.E.

Brundisium

Sardinia

Balearic Is.

New Carthage

Gades

FARTHER SPAIN

Corduba (Córdoba)

NEARER SPAIN

Saguntum

Numantia

Ebro R.

MAURETANIA

NORTH AFRICA

NUMIDIA

Zama 202 B.C.E.

Carthage

AFRICA PROCONSULARIS

SAHARA

Drepana 249 B.C.E.

Sicily

Messana

Syracuse

Malta

Mediterranean Sea

Adriatic Sea

MACEDONIA

Pydna 168 B.C.E.

Cynoscephalae 197 B.C.E.

EPIRUS

Corinth

ACHAEA

Athens

CYRENAICA

Cyrene

Crete

BOSPORAN KINGDOM

DACIA

MOESIA

THRACE

Byzantium

Black Sea

CAUCASUS MTS.

ARMENIA

BITHYNIA and PONTUS

GALATIA

CAPPADOCIA

Pergamum

ASIA

Ephesus

LYCIA

PAMPHYLIA

CILICIA

Tarsus

ANATOLIA

Rhodes

Cyprus

SYRIA

Antioch

Damascus

Jerusalem

JUDAEA

Petra

SINAI

EGYPT

Nile R.

Alexandria

Red Sea

ARABIAN DESERT

PARTHIA

Carrhae 53 B.C.E.

Euphrates R.

Tigris R.

Seleucia

Ctesiphon

Susa

Persian Gulf

Danube R.

Rhône R.

400 Mi.

400 Km.

200

200

0

0

Roman territory in 264 B.C.E.
Roman territory added by 133 B.C.E.
Roman territory added by 44 B.C.E.
Parthian Empire in 44 B.C.E.
Major battle

Map 5.2 Roman Expansion During the Republic

Previous maps have shown that the Greeks and Macedonians concentrated their energies on opening the East. This map indicates that Rome for the first time looked to the West. **[1]** What does this say about the expansion of Roman power in the Mediterranean? **[2]** What does this foreshadow for the subsequent development of Europe?

unless they controlled the sea, and so they built a navy. They fought seven major naval battles with the Carthaginians, won six, and finally wore them down. In 241 B.C.E. the Romans took possession of Sicily, which became their first real province.

The peace treaty between the two powers brought no peace, in part because in 238 B.C.E. the Romans took advantage of Carthaginian weakness to seize the islands of Sardinia and Corsica. Unable to resist the Roman move, Carthage looked to Spain to recoup its fortune. In 237 B.C.E. Hamilcar led an army to Spain in order to turn it into Carthaginian territory. With him he took his nineteen-year-old son, Hannibal, but not before he had led Hannibal to an altar and made him swear forever to be an enemy to Rome. In the following years Hamilcar and his son-in-law Hasdrubal (HAS-droo-buhl) rebuilt Carthaginian power. Rome responded in two ways: first, the Romans made a treaty with Hasdrubal in which the Ebro River of Spain formed the boundary between Carthaginian and Roman interests, and second, the Romans began to extend their own influence in Spain.

In 221 B.C.E. the young Hannibal became Carthaginian commander in Spain. When Hannibal laid siege to Saguntum (suh-GOON-tum), which lay within the sphere of Carthaginian interest, the Romans declared war, claiming that Carthage had attacked a friendly city. So began the **Second Punic War.** In 218 B.C.E. Hannibal struck first by marching more than a thousand miles over the Alps into Italy. Once there, he defeated one Roman army at the Battle of Trebia and later another at the Battle of Lake Trasimene. Hannibal won his greatest victory at the Battle of Cannae (KAN-ee), in which he inflicted some forty thousand casualties on the Romans. He then spread devastation throughout Italy, and a number of cities in central and southern Italy rebelled against Rome. Yet Hannibal failed to crush Rome's iron circle of Latium, Etruria, and Samnium. The wisdom of Rome's political policy of extending citizenship to its allies showed itself in these dark hours. And Rome fought back.

In 210 B.C.E. Rome found its answer to Hannibal in the young commander Scipio, later better known as Scipio Africanus. Scipio copied Hannibal's methods of mobile warfare, streamlining the legions by making their components capable of independent action and introducing new weapons. In the following years, Scipio operated in Spain, which in 207 B.C.E. he wrested from the Carthaginians. Also in 207 B.C.E. the Romans sealed Hannibal's fate in Italy. At the Battle of Metaurus, the Romans destroyed a major Carthaginian army coming to reinforce Hannibal. Scipio then struck directly at Carthage itself, prompting the Carthaginians to recall Hannibal from Italy to defend the homeland.

In 202 B.C.E., near the town of Zama (see Map 5.2), Scipio defeated Hannibal in one of the world's truly decisive battles. Scipio's victory meant that the world of the western Mediterranean would henceforth be Roman. The Second Punic War contained the seeds of still other wars. Unabated fear of Carthage led to the Third

Triumphal Column of Caius Duilius

This curious monument celebrates Rome's naval victory, in the First Punic War. In the battle Caius Duilius (KEY-uhs doo-ILL-ee-us) destroyed fifty Carthaginian ships. He then celebrated his success by erecting this column, which portrays the prows of the enemy ships projecting from the column. (Alinari/Art Resource, NY)

Second Punic War A war fought between Carthage, led by the young Hannibal, and Rome. By the end of the war in 202 B.C.E., Rome was victorious, ensuring that Roman heritage would pass on to the Western world.

Section Review

- Romans established colonies throughout Italy; they incorporated those closest into the Roman state, granting full citizenship, while Italians who lived farther away were considered allies and allowed the right to local self-government.

- The Romans wanted to be free of any state that could threaten them; instead of looking for conquests they acted defensively, such as against Pyrrhus, the Greek king of Epirus, whose army defeated the Romans in several battles, but suffered such losses that the Romans eventually succeeded in driving it out of Italy.

- The First Punic War between Carthage and Rome over control of Sicily became a battle of the sea, which the Romans finally won, gaining Sicily.

- The peace treaty with Carthage did not last and during the Second Punic War, the Carthaginians under Hannibal defeated Rome's legions at Cannae and devastated much of Italy, but were ultimately unable to conquer Rome's power in Latium, Etruria, and Samnium.

- The Roman Scipio Africanus defeated the Carthaginians by attacking Spain and enemy armies in Italy and then Hannibal's army at Zama, while an unnecessary Third Punic War destroyed Carthage and years later Scipio's son Scipio Aemilianus conquered Spain.

- The Romans fought the Macedonians because they had made an alliance with Hannibal and by 133 B.C.E. the Hellenistic kingdoms, Pergamum, and Ptolemaic Egypt fell to Rome.

Punic War, a needless, unjust, and savage conflict that ended in 146 B.C.E. when Scipio Aemilianus (**SKIP-ee-oh AY-mil-ee-an-us**), grandson of Scipio Africanus, destroyed the old hated rival.

During the war with Hannibal, the Romans had invaded Spain, a peninsula rich in material resources and the home of fierce warriors. When the Roman legions tried to reduce the Spanish tribes, they met with bloody and determined resistance. Not until 133 B.C.E., after years of brutal and ruthless warfare, did Scipio Aemilianus finally conquer Spain.

Rome Turns East (211–133 B.C.E.)

During the Second Punic War, King Philip V of Macedonia made an alliance with Hannibal against Rome. Despite the mortal struggle in the West, the Romans found the strength to turn eastward to settle accounts. Their first significant victory against the Macedonians came in 197 B.C.E. Piece by piece the Hellenistic kingdoms and city-states fell to Rome, first Sparta, then the Seleucid kingdom, the Achaean League, the Macedonian kingdom, and finally, in 133 B.C.E., Pergamum and the Ptolemic kingdom of Egypt.

Old Values and Greek Culture

How did Roman society change during the age of expansion?

Rome had conquered the Mediterranean world, but some Romans considered that victory a misfortune. The historian Sallust (86–34 B.C.E.), writing from hindsight, complained that the acquisition of an empire was the beginning of Rome's troubles: "The Romans had easily borne labor, danger, uncertainty, and hardship. To them leisure, riches—otherwise desirable—proved to be burdens and torments. So at first money, then desire for power grew great. These things were a sort of cause of all evils."[1]

Indeed, in the second century B.C.E. the Romans learned that they could not return to what they fondly considered a simple life. They were world rulers. They had to change their institutions, social patterns, and way of thinking to meet the new era. But in the end Rome triumphed here just as it had on the battlefield, for out of the turmoil of change would come the *pax Romana*—"Roman peace."

How did the Romans of the day meet these challenges? How did they lead their lives and cope with these momentous changes? Obviously there are as many answers to these questions as there were Romans. Yet two men represent the major trends of the second century B.C.E. Cato the Elder shared the mentality of those who longed for the good old days and idealized the traditional agrarian way of life. Scipio Aemilianus led those who embraced the new urban life, with its eager acceptance of Greek culture.

Cato and the Traditional Ideal

Marcus Cato (**MAHR-kuhs KAY-toh**) (234–149 B.C.E.) was born a plebeian, but his talent and energy carried him to Rome's highest offices. He created an image of himself as the bearer of "traditional" Roman virtues. His description of his life is partly invented, but its details reflect the way many Romans actually lived.

Because of his political aspirations, Cato often walked to the marketplace of the nearby town and defended anyone who wished his help. He received no fees for these services, but in return Cato's clients gave him their political support or their votes whenever he asked for them. This practice of a patron offering his protection in return for support from a client is know as clientage. The notion of clientage was a particularly Roman custom that helped men of lower social status advance themselves and advance the careers of their patrons.

Cato was married, as were almost all Roman citizens. Grooms were generally somewhat older than their brides, who often married in their early teens. There were two types of marriage in Rome, one of which put the woman under control of her husband's family and one of which kept her under her father's control. Each had advantages and disadvantages for women.

Women could inherit property under Roman law, though they generally received a smaller portion of any family inheritance than their brothers did. A woman's inheritance usually came as a dowry on marriage. By the time of Cato, both men and women could initiate divorce. Women appear to have gained greater control over their dowries, perhaps in response to the fact that Rome's military conquests meant that many husbands were away for long periods of time and women needed some say over family finances.

Until the age of seven, children were under their mother's care. During this time the matron began to educate her daughters in the management of the household. After the age of seven, sons—and in many wealthy households daughters too—began to receive formal education. Formal education for wealthy children

Temple of Mater Matuta

This round temple was dedicated to Mater Matuta (**MAY-ter ma-TWO-tah**), a very old Roman mother goddess. Its shape and architectural ornamentation indicate Hellenistic influence. (Vanni/Art Resource, NY)

was generally in the hands of tutors, who were often Greek slaves. By the late republic, there were also a few schools.

The agricultural year followed the sun and the stars—the farmer's calendar. The main money crops, at least for rich soils, were wheat and flax. Forage crops included clover, vetch, and alfalfa. Prosperous farmers like Cato raised olive trees chiefly for the oil. They also raised grapevines for the production of wine. Cato and his neighbors harvested their cereal crops in summer and their grapes in autumn.

An influx of slaves resulted from Rome's wars and conquests. Races were not enslaved because the Romans thought them inferior. The black African slave was treated no worse—and no better—than the Spaniard. For the talented slave the Romans always held out the hope of eventual freedom. **Manumission**—the freeing of individual slaves by their masters—became so common that it was limited by law.

manumission The freeing of individual slaves by their masters.

For Cato and most other Romans, religion played an important part in life. Originally the Romans thought of the gods as invisible, shapeless natural forces. Only through Etruscan and Greek influence did Roman deities take on human form. Jupiter, the sky-god, and his wife Juno became equivalent to the Greek Zeus and Hera. The gods of the Romans were stern, powerful, and aloof. But as long as the Romans honored the cults of their gods, they could expect divine favor. The shrine of the goddess Vesta (**VES-tuh**), for example, was tended by six so-called vestal virgins, chosen from patrician families. Roman military losses were sometimes blamed on inattention by the vestal virgins, a link between female honor and the Roman state.

Along with the great gods the Romans believed in spirits who haunted fields, forests, crossroads, and even the home itself. Some of these deities were hostile; only magic could ward them off. The spirits of the dead, like ghosts in modern horror films, frequented places where they had lived. They too had to be placated but were ordinarily benign. (See the feature "Listening to the Past: A Magic Charm" on pages 105–106.)

Scipio Aemilianus: Greek Culture and Urban Life

The old-fashioned ideals that Cato represented came into conflict with a new urban culture that reflected Hellenistic influences. The spoils of war went to build baths, theaters, and other places of amusement, and Romans and Italian townspeople began to spend more of their time in leisure pursuits. The poet Horace (**HAWR-iss**)

African Acrobat

Conquest and prosperity brought exotic pleasure to Rome. Every feature of this sculpture is exotic. The young African woman and her daring gymnastic pose would catch anyone's attention. And to add to the spice of her act, she performs using a live crocodile as her platform. Americans would have loved it. (Courtesy of the Trustees of the British Museum)

(64–8 B.C.E.) summed it up well: "Captive Greece captured her rough conqueror and introduced the arts into rustic Latium."

One of the most avid devotees of Hellenism and the new was Scipio Aemilianus, the destroyer of Carthage. Scipio realized that broad and worldly views had to replace the old Roman narrowness. Rome was no longer a small city on the Tiber; it was the capital of the world. Scipio broke with the past in the conduct of his political career, choosing a more personal style of politics, one that reflected his own views and looked unflinchingly at the broader problems that the success of Rome brought to its people. Perhaps more than anyone else of his day, Scipio represented the new Roman—imperial, cultured, and independent.

In his education and interests, too, Scipio broke with the past. As a boy he had received the traditional Roman training in Latin and the law. He mastered the fundamentals of rhetoric and learned how to throw the javelin, fight in armor, and ride a horse. But later Scipio also learned Greek and promoted the spread of Hellenism in Roman society. He became the center of the Scipionic (**SKIP-ee-ohn-ik**) Circle, a small group of Greek and Roman artists, philosophers, historians, and poets. Conservatives like Cato tried to stem the rising tide of Hellenism, but men like Scipio carried the day and helped make the heritage of Greece an abiding factor in Roman life.

The new Hellenism profoundly stimulated the growth and development of Roman art. Soldiers returned from the Hellenistic East with Greek paintings and sculpture to grace Roman temples, public buildings, and private homes. Roman artists copied many aspects of Greek art, but their emphasis on realistic portraiture carried on a native tradition.

Roman Table Manners

This mosaic is a floor that can never be swept clean. It whimsically suggests what a dining room floor looked like after a lavish dinner and also tells something about the menu: a chicken head, a wishbone, and remains of various seafood, vegetables, and fruit are easily recognizable. (Museo Gregoriano Profano, Vatican Museums/Scala/Art Resource, NY)

In literature, the Greek influence was also strong. Fabius Pictor (**FAY-bee-us PIK-ter**) (second half of the third century B.C.E.), a senator, wrote the first history of Rome in Greek. Other Romans translated Greek classics into Latin. Still others, such as the poet Ennius (**EN-ee-us**) (239–169 B.C.E.), the father of Latin poetry, adapted many of Euripides' tragedies for the Roman stage. The Roman dramatist Terence (ca. 195–159 B.C.E.), a member of the Scipionic Circle, wrote comedies of refinement and grace that owed their essentials to Greek models. In contrast, Plautus (**PLAW-tus**) (ca. 254–184 B.C.E.) brought a bawdy humor to his reworkings of Greek plays.

During the second century B.C.E. the Greek custom of bathing also became a Roman passion. Large buildings containing pools and gymnasia went up in great numbers, and the baths became an essential part of the Roman city. They became even more elaborate several centuries later. Architects built intricate systems of aqueducts to supply the bathing establishments with water. Bathing establishments were more than just places to take a bath. They also contained snack bars and halls where people chatted and read and even libraries and lecture halls. The baths were socially important places where men and women went to see and be seen. Social climbers tried to talk to the right people and wangle invitations to dinner; politicians took advantage of the occasion to discuss the affairs of the day; marriages were negotiated by wealthy fathers. Prostitutes added to the attraction of many baths. These women might be slaves, members of the lower classes, or actresses and entertainers who needed more income.

Did Hellenism and new social customs corrupt the Romans? Perhaps the best answer is this: the Roman state and the empire it ruled continued to exist for six more centuries. Rome did not collapse; the state continued to prosper. The golden age of literature was still before it. The high tide of its prosperity still lay in the future.

The Late Republic (133–31 B.C.E.)

What were the main problems and achievements of the late republic?

The wars of conquest created serious problems for the Romans, some of the most pressing of which were political. The republican constitution had suited the needs of a simple city-state but was inadequate to meet the requirements of Rome's new position in international affairs. Officials had to be appointed to govern the provinces and administer the law. These officials and administrative organs had to find places in the constitution. Armies had to be provided for defense, and a system of tax collection had to be created.

Other political problems were equally serious. During the wars Roman generals commanded huge numbers of troops for long periods of time. These men of great power and prestige were on the point of becoming too mighty for the state to control. Although Rome's Italian allies had borne much of the burden of the fighting, they received fewer rewards than did Roman officers and soldiers. Italians began to agitate for full Roman citizenship, including the right to vote. In addition, the armies became weaker as a result of a complex shift in land ownership.

These problems, complex and explosive, largely account for the turmoil of the closing years of the republic. This period produced some of Rome's most famous figures: the Gracchi (**GRAK-hi**), Marius, Sulla (**SUHL-uh**), Cicero, Pompey (**POM-pee**), and Julius Caesar (**JOOL-yuhs SEE-zar**), among others. In one way or another, each of these men attempted to solve Rome's problems. Yet personal ambition often clashed with patriotism to create political tension throughout the period.

Unrest in Rome and Italy

Hannibal's operations and the warfare in Italy had left the countryside a shambles. The prolonged fighting had also drawn untold numbers of Roman and Italian men away from their farms for long periods. The families of these soldiers could not keep the land under full cultivation.

When the legionaries returned to their farms in Italy, they encountered an appalling situation. All too often their farms looked like the farms of people they had conquered. Two courses of action were open to them. They could rebuild as their forefathers had done, or they could take advantage of a new alternative and sell their holdings to wealthy investors who bought up small farms to create huge estates, which the Romans called **latifundia** (**lat-uh-FUHN-dee-uh**).

latifundia Huge Roman estates created by buying up several small farms.

Selling their land appealed to the veterans for a variety of reasons. Many veterans had tasted the rich city life of the Hellenistic states and were reluctant to settle down to a dull life on the farm. Often their farms were so badly damaged that rebuilding hardly seemed worthwhile. Besides, it was hard to make big profits from small farms.

Most veterans migrated to the cities, especially to Rome. Although some found work, most did not. Industry and small manufacturing were generally in the hands of slaves. Even when work was available, slave labor kept the wages of free men low. Instead of a new start, veterans and their families encountered slum conditions.

This trend held ominous consequences for the strength of Rome's armies. The Romans had always believed that only landowners should serve in the army, for only they had something to fight for. Once the war veterans sold their land, they became ineligible for further military service. The landless ex-legionaries wanted a new start, and they were willing to support any leader who would provide it.

One man who recognized the plight of Rome's peasant farmers and urban poor was an aristocrat, Tiberius Gracchus (**tie-BEER-ee-uhs GRAK-uhs**) (163–133 B.C.E.). Appalled by what he saw, Tiberius scolded his countrymen about the legionaries: "[N]ot a man of them has an hereditary altar, not one of all these many Romans an ancestral tomb, but they fight and die to support others in luxury, and though they are styled masters of the world, they have not a single clod of earth that is their own."[2]

After his election as tribune in 133 B.C.E., Tiberius proposed that public land be given to the poor in small lots. Although his reform enjoyed the support of some very distinguished and popular aristocrats, it angered those who had usurped large tracts of public land for their own use. They had no desire to give any of it back, so they bitterly resisted Tiberius's efforts. This was to be expected, yet he made additional problems for himself. He introduced his land bill in the concilium plebis without consulting the senate. When King Attalus III left the kingdom of Pergamum to the Romans in his will, Tiberius had the money appropriated to finance his reforms—another slap at the senate. A large body of senators, led by the *pontifex maximus* (the chief priest), decided to kill Tiberius in cold blood. It was a black day in Roman history. The very people who directed the affairs of state and administered the law had taken the law into their own hands. The death of Tiberius was the beginning of an era of political violence. In the end that violence would bring down the republic.

Although Tiberius was dead, his land bill became law. Furthermore, Tiberius's brother Gaius Gracchus (**GEY-uhs GRAK-uhs**) (153–121 B.C.E.) also became tribune and demanded even more extensive reform than had his brother. To help the urban poor Gaius pushed legislation to provide them with cheap grain for bread. He defended his brother's land law and proposed that Rome send many of its poor and propertyless people out to form colonies in southern Italy. Gaius even went so far as to urge that all Italians be granted full rights of Roman citizenship.

This measure provoked a storm of opposition, and it was not passed in Gaius's lifetime. Had the senate listened to Gaius, it could have prevented a later bloody conflict known as the Social War (91–88 B.C.E.). Yet like his brother Tiberius, Gaius aroused a great deal of personal opposition. To many he seemed too radical; political opponents considered him belligerent and headstrong. When Gaius failed in 121 B.C.E. to win the tribunate for the third time, he feared for his life. In desperation he armed his staunchest supporters, whereupon the senate ordered the consul Opimius to restore order. Opimius did so by having Gaius killed, along with three thousand of his supporters who opposed the senate's order. Once again the cause of reform had met with violence.

The death of Gaius brought little peace, and trouble came from two sources: the outbreak of new wars in the Mediterranean basin and further political unrest in Rome. For five years, the Roman legions made little headway against the rebellious North African kingdom of Jugurtha (**joo-GUR-thuh**). Then in 107 B.C.E. Gaius Marius (**GEY-uhs MAIR-ee-uhs**), an Italian new man (a politician not from the traditional Roman aristocracy), became consul. Marius's values were those of the military camp. He took the unusual but not wholly unprecedented step of recruiting an army by permitting landless men to serve in the legions. In 106 B.C.E. Marius and his new army handily defeated Jugurtha.

An unexpected war broke out in the following year when two groups of German peoples moved into Gaul and later into northern Italy. After the Germans had defeated Roman armies sent to repel them, Marius was again elected consul, even though he was legally ineligible. From 104 to 100 B.C.E. Marius annually held the consulship, putting unprecedented power into a Roman commander's hands.

Before engaging the Germans, Marius encouraged enlistments by promising his volunteers land after the war. Poor and landless veterans flocked to him, and together they conquered the Germans by 101 B.C.E. When Marius proposed a bill to grant land to his veterans, the senate refused to act, in effect turning its back on the soldiers of Rome. It was a disastrous mistake. Henceforth the legionaries expected the commanders—not the senate or the state—to protect their interests.

Another strong general, Sulla, was elected to consul in 88 B.C.E. after putting down the Italian allies in the Social War. While Sulla was away from Rome fighting the last of the rebels, factions agitating on behalf of Marius had him deposed from his consulship. He immediately marched on Rome and restored order, but it was an ominous sign of the deterioration of Roman politics and political ideals. Order restored, Sulla in 88 B.C.E. led an army to Asia Minor where Roman rule was being challenged. In Sulla's absence, rioting and political violence again exploded in Rome. Marius and his supporters marched on Rome and launched a reign of terror.

Although Marius died shortly after his return to power, his supporters continued to hold Rome. Sulla returned in 82 B.C.E., and after a brief but intense civil war, he entered Rome and ordered a ruthless butchery of his opponents. He also proclaimed himself dictator. He launched many political and judicial reforms, including strengthening the senate while weakening the tribunate, and he voluntarily abdicated his dictatorship in 79 B.C.E. Yet Sulla the political reformer proved far less influential than Sulla the successful general and dictator. Civil war was to be the constant lot of Rome for the next fifty years, until the republican constitution gave way to the empire of Augustus (**aw-GUHS-tuhs**) in 27 B.C.E. (See the feature "Individuals in Society: Quintus Sertorius (**KWIN-tuhs ser-TAWR-ee-uhs**).")

One figure who stands apart from the struggles of the late Republic is Cicero (106–43 B.C.E.), a practical politician whose greatest legacy to the Roman world

Individuals in Society

Quintus Sertorius

Quintus Sertorius (126–73 B.C.E.), son of a prominent Italian family, stands as an example of a Roman leader caught up in the political and military upheavals of the day. He became a rebel against Rome while bringing Roman influences to the province of Spain. Sertorius launched his public career in Rome, where he mastered Roman law and became a gifted military officer. When two barbarian tribes invaded Gaul in 105 B.C.E., he fought so effectively that his ability and valor brought him to the attention of senior Roman military commanders. These events honed his martial skills and acquainted him with the new peoples gradually entering western Europe.

Sertorius's success in Gaul led him in 97 B.C.E. to higher command in Spain. From that time until his death, his destiny and Spain's would be intertwined. He, like Marius, Sulla, and other notable men, was swept up in this vast and chaotic episode in republican history. He chose the wrong side and upon defeat fled to Spain, where he worked to establish his own independent authority.

A surprising accident put another tool of authority into Sertorius's hands. As the story goes, one of his soldiers, while hunting, encountered a white fawn and presented it to Sertorius. Sertorius declared that the animal was the gift of Diana whose attributes included the gifts of wisdom and prophecy. This divine endorsement enhanced his authority among the Spaniards.

The Roman civil war soon reached Spain. Sertorius's reputation and exploits persuaded many Spaniards to invite him to lead them against the Romans. As commander, he trained Spanish troups in Roman military tactics. His army's success prompted many Romans to switch sides. Even some senators left Rome to join him. Welcoming them with honor, he got them involved in the civil government that he introduced. Sertorius modeled his Spanish state along Roman civil lines but under his leadership. Spain had never seen so many military, cultural, and civil developments in such a short time.

The Romans to whom he had bestowed a home began to insult, punish, and abuse the Spaniards while doing everything possible to thwart Sertorius's plans. Then they rebelled against him, hoping either to topple him and reign in his place or to return the province to Roman rule. Finally, with a treachery that matched that of the conspirators against Caesar, some Romans who were still considered loyal assassinated Sertorius at a banquet in 73 B.C.E. Roman generals from the East easily took control of Spain.

Death and defeat did not erase Sertorius's achievements in Spain. He introduced the region to Greco-Roman culture. He gave the land and its peoples a civil government that united them. He turned their tribal hordes into an army along Roman lines. He paved the way for peaceful Spanish inclusion into the quickly evolving Roman Empire.

This statue of Quintus Sertorius still bears testimony to Rome's respect for his efforts to unite Romans and Spaniards.
(Courtesy, Luca Bonacina)

Questions for Analysis

1. How did Sertorius create a state in Spain?
2. What was his legacy to Spain, Rome, and Western civilization in general?

and to Western civilization is his mass of political and oratorical writings. Yet Cicero commanded no legions, and only legions commanded respect.

First Triumvirate A political alliance between Caesar, Crassus, and Pompey in which they agreed to advance one another's interests.

Civil War

Sulla's real political heirs were Pompey and Julius Caesar, with at least Caesar realizing that the days of the old republican constitution were numbered. Pompey, a man of boundless ambition, began his career as one of Sulla's lieutenants. After his army put down a rebellion in Spain, he himself threatened to rebel unless the senate allowed him to run for consul. He and another ambitious politician, Crassus (**KRAS-uhs**), pooled political resources, and both won the consulship. They dominated Roman politics until the rise of Julius Caesar, who became consul in 59 B.C.E. Together the three concluded a political alliance, the **First Triumvirate** (**try-UHM-ver-it**), in which they agreed to advance one another's interests.

The man who cast the longest shadow over these troubled years was Julius Caesar (100–44 B.C.E.). Born of a noble family, he received an excellent education, which he furthered by studying in Greece with some of the most eminent teachers of the day. Caesar was a superb orator, and his affable personality and wit made him popular. Caesar launched his military career in Spain, where his courage won the respect and affection of his troops.

In 58 B.C.E. Caesar became governor of Cisalpine Gaul (**sis-AL-pine gawl**), or modern northern Italy. By 50 B.C.E. he had conquered all of Gaul, or modern France. By 49 B.C.E. the First Triumvirate had fallen apart. Crassus had died in battle, and Caesar and Pompey, each suspecting the other of treachery, came to blows. The result was a long and bloody civil war that raged from Spain across northern Africa to Egypt.

Egypt, meanwhile, was embroiled in a battle for control between brother and sister, Ptolemy XIII and Cleopatra (**klee-uh-PA-truh**) VII (69–30 B.C.E.). Cleopatra first allied herself with Pompey but then switched her alliance to Caesar. The two became lovers as well as allies, and she bore him a son. She returned to Rome with Caesar, but was hated by the Roman people as a symbol of the immoral East.

Although Pompey enjoyed the official support of the government, Caesar finally defeated Pompey's forces in 45 B.C.E. He had overthrown the republic and made himself dictator.

Julius Caesar was not merely another victorious general. He was determined to make basic reforms, even at the expense of the old constitution. He extended citizenship to many of the provincials who had supported him. He also founded at least twenty colonies, most of which were located in Gaul, Spain, and North Africa, in part to cope with

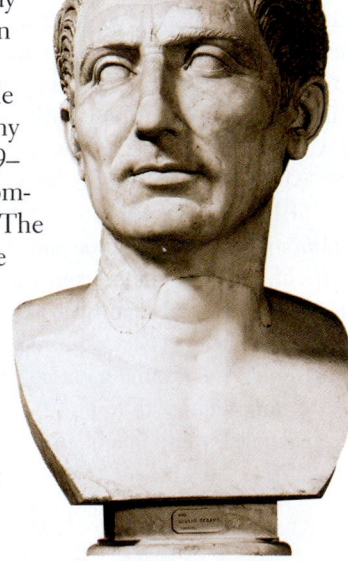

Julius Caesar

In this bust, the sculptor portrays Caesar as a man of power and intensity. It is a study of determination and an excellent example of Roman portraiture. (Museo Archeologico Nazionale Naples/Scala/Art Resource, NY)

Section Review

- The Roman countryside suffered greatly from the prolonged fighting and much of the farmland was in shambles, so returning legionaries often sold their farms to wealthy investors who created huge estates called latifundia.

- Tiberius Gracchus and later his brother Gaius sought land reform for the poor but aristocrats and the senate opposed them vigorously, eventually having them both killed.

- Gaius Marius became consul and gained power by allowing non-landowners into the army and promising them land after the war, but when the senate did not approve this plan, the legionaries turned their allegiance to their commanders, not the senate or state, for protection.

- In the following years, another general, Sulla, was elected consul and fought against Marius for control of Rome, proclaimed himself dictator and introduced many political and judicial reforms before voluntarily abdicating his dictatorship in 79 B.C.E.

- Sulla's political heirs were Pompey, Crassus, and Julius Caesar who formed the First Triumvirate and agreed to help each other, but following Crassus' death Pompey and Caesar suspected each other of treason and fought a bloody civil war.

- Caesar allied with Egypt's Cleopatra, defeating Pompey's forces, and made himself dictator before his assassination, which left his grandnephew Octavian (later called Augustus) and two lieutenants, Marc Antony and Lepidus, to form the Second Triumvirate, avenging Caesar.

- Octavian (Augustus) defeated Antony and Cleopatra in the naval battle of Actium (31 B.C.E.), after which the couple committed suicide, leaving Augustus to rule the entire Roman world.

Rome's burgeoning population. These colonies were important agents in spreading Roman culture in the western Mediterranean.

In 44 B.C.E. a group of conspirators assassinated Caesar and set off another round of civil war. Caesar had named his eighteen-year-old grandnephew, Octavian (ok-TAY-vee-uhn)—or Augustus, as he is better known to history—as his heir. Augustus joined forces with two of Caesar's lieutenants, Marc Antony and Lepidus (LEP-ee-dus), in a pact known as the **Second Triumvirate**, and together they hunted down and defeated Caesar's murderers. In the process, however, Augustus and Antony came into conflict.

In 41 B.C.E. Antony met Cleopatra, who had returned to Egypt after Julius Caesar's assassination. Though Antony was already married to Augustus's sister Octavia, he became Cleopatra's lover. Antony repudiated Octavia, married Cleopatra, and changed his will to favor his children by Cleopatra. Romans turned against Antony as a traitor and a weakling, and in 31 B.C.E. Augustus defeated the army and navy of Cleopatra and Antony at the battle of Actium in Greece. The two committed suicide. This victory put an end to an age of civil war that had lasted since the days of Sulla.

Second Triumvirate A pact between Augustus and two of Caesar's lieutenants, Marc Antony and Lepidus; together they hunted down and defeated Caesar's murderers.

Chapter Review

How did the Etruscans shape early Roman history? (page 86)

The land of Italy proved kinder to the Romans and their neighbors than did the peninsula of Hellas to the Greeks. The newcomers settled comfortably on the seven hills of Rome by the banks of the Tiber River. They came into contact with the Etruscans, who had settled in Italy before their arrival. Separate villages soon merged into one city, creating a single community. Under the governance of the more politically and socially advanced Etruscans, the Romans fully entered the wider world around them.

What was the nature of the Roman republic? (page 89)

Once established, the Romans created an advanced and flexible political constitution of their own. Their society fell into two principal groups: the aristocratic patricians who led the community and the commoners (plebeians) who made up the rest of the citizenry and filled the ranks of the army. The conflict between these two basic social groups resulted in the Struggle of the Orders, which led to greater rights for the plebeians.

How did the Romans take control of the Mediterranean world? (page 91)

From these beginnings the Romans spread their power and influence through the rest of Italy. Beginning as conquerors, the Romans learned to use alliances and political agreements to unite their efforts with those of other Italian communities to create a common policy. They put this association on a formal political basis to create a government shared by Romans and non-Romans. Looking beyond Italy, the Romans fought three hard wars with the Carthaginians, their Punic neighbors in North Africa. In the process they included the Greeks of southern Italy in their growing empire. As these wars spread to western Europe, the Romans won control of Spain and Gaul (modern France). Further warfare next took them eastward into the Hellenistic world. Conquest followed conquest to create the nucleus of the Roman Empire.

Key Terms

toga (p. 87)
forum (p. 87)
Gauls (p. 87)
franchise (p. 88)
patricians (p. 89)
plebeians (p. 89)
consuls (p. 89)
senate (p. 89)
natural law (p. 90)
Struggle of the Orders (p. 90)
tribunes (p. 90)
paterfamilias (p. 90)
Pyrrhic victory (p. 91)
First Punic War (p. 91)
Second Punic War (p. 93)
manumission (p. 96)
latifundia (p. 99)
First Triumvirate (p. 102)
Second Triumvirate (p. 103)

How did Roman society change during the age of expansion? (page 94)

These tumultuous events fundamentally reshaped Roman society. Though some Romans longed for what they saw as simpler times, many were dazzled by Hellenistic sophistication and ways of life. They learned to appreciate the arts and intellectual pursuits of the older Greek and Eastern cultures. They joined fully the broad cultural world of the Mediterranean, all the while making their own contribution.

What were the main problems and achievements of the late republic? (page 98)

In some ways the Romans had moved too far and too fast from their small beginnings. Their empire had become too big for them to manage easily. Their constitution and political institutions could no longer adequately cope with the burdens and pressures that imperial life brought. After a series of bloody civil wars, the general Octavian, soon to be more generally known as Augustus, restored order and forever changed the nature of Roman life and government.

Notes

1. Sallust, *War with Catiline* 10.1–3. John Buckler is the translator of all uncited quotations from a foreign language in Chapters 1–6.
2. Plutarch, *Life of Tiberius Gracchus* 9.5–6.

To assess your mastery of this chapter, go to **bedfordstmartins.com/mckaywestbrief**

Listening to the Past

A Magic Charm

The pursuit of love has one of the oldest histories in the world. When their own efforts failed, lovers of the past might turn to magic to win the hearts of the beloved. The following text of a love charm comes from a papyrus found in Egypt and dates from the period of the Roman Empire. The applicant, in this case a man, asks the spirits of the underworld to assist him.

Take wax [or clay] from a potter's wheel and form two figures, one male and one female. Make the male one look like Ares in arms, holding a sword in his left hand and pointing it at her right collarbone. Her arms must be (tied) behind her back, and she must kneel. Fasten the magical substance on her head or neck. On the figure of the woman you want to attract write as follows. On the head: ISEE IAO ITHI OUNE BRIDO LOTHION NEBOU-TOSOUALETH. On the right ear: OUER MECHAN. On the left: LIBABA OIMATHOTHO. On the face: AMOUNABREO. On the right eye: OROR-MOTHIO AETH. On the right arm: ENE PSA ENESGAPH. On the other: MELCHIOU MELCHIEDA. On the hands: MELCHAMELCHOU AEL. On the breast write the name, on her mother's side, of the woman you want to attract. On the heart: BALAMIN THOOUTH. Under the abdomen: AOBES AOBAR. On her sexual organs: BLICHIANEOI OUOIA. On her buttocks: PISSADARA. On the sole of the right foot: ELO. On the other: ELOAIOE. Take thirteen bronze needles and stick one in the brain and say: "I am piercing your brain, NN." Stick two in the ears, two in the eyes, one in the mouth, two in the midriff, one in the hands, two in the genital organs, two in the soles, saying each time: "I am piercing such and such a member of NN, so that she may remember me, NN alone." Take a lead tablet and write on it the same formula and recite it. Tie the lead leaf [i.e., the lead tablet] to the two creatures with thread from the loom after making three hundred sixty-five knots, saying, as you have learned: "Abrasax, hold her fast." As the sun is setting, you must place it near the tomb of a person who has died an untimely or a violent death, along with the flowers of the season.

The formula to be written and recited: "I am handing over this binding spell to you, gods of the underworld, HYESEMIGADON and KORE PEERSEPH-ONE ERESCHIGAL and ADONIS, the BARBARITHA, chthonic HERMES THOOUTH PHOKENTAZEPSEU AERCHTHATOUMI SONKTAI KALBANACHAMRE and to mighty ANUBIS PSIRINTH who has the keys to the realm of Hades, to gods and daemons of the underworld, to men and women who have died before their time, to young men and women, from year to year, from month to month, from day to day, from hour to hour. I adjure all the daemons in this place to assist this daemon. Arouse yourself for me, whoever you are, male or female, and enter every place, every neighborhood, every house, and attract and bind,

Amulet of Abrasax, the demon with the head of a cock, the body of a Roman soldier, feet of snakes, and whip in the right hand. This amulet protected against other demons. (Kelsey Museum of Archaeology, University of Michigan, KM 26054)

attract NN, daughter of NN, whose magical substance you have. Make NN, daughter of NN be in love with me. Let her not have sexual intercourse with another man, . . . let her not have pleasure with another man, only with me, NN, so that she, NN, is unable to drink or eat, to love, to be strong, to be healthy, to enjoy sleep, NN without me. . . . Yes, drag her, NN, by her hair, by her heart, by her soul to me, NN, every hour of life [or: eternity], night and day, until she comes to me, NN, and let her, NN, remain inseparable from me. Do this, bind her for all the time of my life and force her, NN, to be my, NN, servant, and let her not flutter away from me for even one hour of life [or: eternity]. If you accomplish this for me, I will let you rest at once.

Questions for Analysis

1. How does this magical charm invoke the help of the gods?

2. Does the woman he seeks favor him, or is she reluctant?

3. Is the charm to entice love or to force submission?

Source: Luck, Georg, *Arcana Mundi, Second Edition: Magic and the Occult in the Greek and Roman Worlds: A Collection of Ancient Texts*, pp. 129–131. Copyright © 2006 The Johns Hopkins University Press. Reprinted with permission of The Johns Hopkins University Press.

CHAPTER 6

The Pax Romana

31 B.C.E.–450 C.E.

Hadrian's Wall. (Sandro Vannini/Corbis)

Chapter Preview

Had the Romans conquered the entire Mediterranean world only to turn it into their battlefield? Would they, like the Greeks before them, become their own worst enemies, destroying one another and wasting their strength until they perished? At Julius Caesar's death in 44 B.C.E., it must have seemed so to many. Yet finally, in 31 B.C.E., Augustus restored peace to a tortured world, and with peace came prosperity, new hope, and a new vision of Rome's destiny. The Roman poet Virgil (**VUR-juhl**) expressed this vision most nobly:

> You, Roman, remember—these are your arts:
> To rule nations, and to impose the ways of peace,
> To spare the humble and to wear down the proud.[1]

Augustus created the structure that the modern world calls the "Roman Empire." For the first and second centuries C.E., the lot of the Mediterranean world was the Roman peace—the **pax Romana** (**paks ro-MAN-ah**), a period of security, order, harmony, flourishing culture, and expanding economy and territory. By the third century C.E., Rome and its culture had left an indelible mark on the ages to come.

pax Romana A period during the first and second centuries C.E. of security, order, harmony, flourishing culture, and expanding economy.

Augustus's Settlement (31 B.C.E.–14 C.E.)

How did Augustus transform the Roman Empire?

When Augustus put an end to the civil wars that had raged since 88 B.C.E., he faced monumental problems of reconstruction. The first problem facing him was to rebuild the constitution and the organs of government. Next he had to demobilize much of the army yet maintain enough soldiers to protect the European frontiers. Augustus was highly successful in meeting these challenges. His gift of peace to a war-torn world ushered in the Golden Age of Latin literature.

The Principate and the Restored Republic

In an inscription known as the *Res Gestae* (The Deeds of Augustus), Augustus claimed that he had restored the republic after regaining the peace:

> In my sixth and seventh consulships [28–27 B.C.E.], I had ended the civil war, having obtained through universal consent total control of affairs. I transferred the Republic from my power to the authority of the Roman people and the senate. . . . After that time I stood before all in rank, but I had power no greater than those who were my colleagues in any magistracy.[2]

He took the title of *princeps civitatis* (**prin-SEPS civ-ee-TAT-is**), "First Citizen of the State," a title that carried no power but that indicated that he was the most distinguished of all Roman citizens. Yet despite his claims, Augustus had not restored the republic. He had created a **constitutional monarchy**, something completely new in Roman history. The title **princeps**, "First Citizen," came to mean in Rome, as it does today, "prince" in the sense of a sovereign ruler. The period of the First Citizen came to be known as the **principate**.

Augustus's genius was to gather power while operating within the structure of the republic. As consul he had no more constitutional and legal power than his fellow consul. Yet in addition to the consulship Augustus had many other magistracies, which his fellow consul did not. Constitutionally, his ascendancy within the

constitutional monarchy A monarchy in which the power of the ruler is restricted by the constitution and the laws of the nation.

princeps A title meaning "First Citizen" that later came to mean "prince," in the sense of a sovereign ruler.

principate Position of the emperor resulting fom the combination of his consular and tribunician powers.

state stemmed from the number of magistracies he held and the power granted him by the senate. At first he held the consulship annually; then the senate voted him proconsular power on a regular basis. The senate also voted him the "full power of the tribunes," which gave him the right to call the senate into session, present legislation to the people, and defend their rights. He held either high office or the powers of chief magistrate year in and year out. No other magistrate could do the same. In 12 B.C.E. he became *pontifex maximus* (PAHN-tih-fex MAX-ih-muhs), the chief priest of the state. By assuming this position of great honor, Augustus also became chief religious official.

The main source of Augustus's power was his position as commander of the Roman army. He made a momentous change in the army by turning it into Rome's first permanent, professional force. Soldiers received standard training under career officers who advanced in rank according to experience, ability, and valor. Augustus controlled the deployment of troops and paid their wages, bonuses, and retirement benefits. His title **imperator** (im-puh-RAH-ter), with which Rome customarily honored a general after a major victory, came to mean "emperor" in the modern sense of the term. The army was loyal to the imperator but not necessarily the state.

This arrangement worked well at first, but by the third century C.E. the army would make and break emperors at will. Nonetheless, it is a measure of Augustus's success that his settlement survived as long as it did.

CHRONOLOGY

27 B.C.E.–68 C.E.	Julio-Claudian emperors; expansion into northern and western Europe; growth and stability of trade in the empire
17 B.C.E.–17 C.E.	Flowering of Latin literature
ca. 3 B.C.E.–29 C.E.	Life of Jesus
ca. 30–312 C.E.	Spread of Christianity
41–54 C.E.	Creation of the imperial bureaucracy
60–120 C.E.	Composition of the New Testament
69–96 C.E.	Consolidation of the European frontiers
96–180 C.E.	"Golden age" of prosperity and huge expansion of trade
96–180 C.E.	"Five good emperors"; increasing barbarian menace on the frontiers
193–284 C.E.	Military monarchy; extension of citizenship to all free men
278–337 C.E.	Steady spread of administration, government, and law from Britain to Syria
284–337 C.E.	Inflation and decline of trade and industry; transition to the Middle Ages in the West and the Byzantine Empire in the East
337 C.E.	Baptism of Constantine

Roman Expansion into Northern and Western Europe

Augustus initially used the army to expand the Roman Empire into northern and western Europe (see Map 6.1). First he completed the conquest of Spain. In Gaul, he founded twelve new towns, and the Roman road system linked new settlements with one another and with Italy. But the German frontier, along the Rhine River, was the scene of hard fighting. Roman legions advanced to the Elbe River, and the area north of the Main River and west of the Elbe was on the point of becoming Roman. But in 9 C.E. Augustus's general Varus lost some twenty thousand troops at the Battle of the Teutoburger (two-TO-burg-er) Forest. Thereafter the Rhine remained the Roman frontier.

Meanwhile Roman legions penetrated the area of modern Austria, southern Bavaria, and western Hungary. The regions of modern Serbia, Bulgaria, and Romania fell. Within this area the legionaries built fortified camps linked by roads, and settlements grew up around the camps. Traders began to frequent the frontier and to traffic with the native peoples, who adopted those aspects of Roman culture that fit in with their own way of life. Eventually provincial towns were granted Roman citizenship if they embraced Roman culture and government and were important to the Roman economy. (See the feature "Listening to the Past: Rome Extends Its Citizenship" on pages 131–132.)

On the other hand, the arrival of the Romans often provoked resistance from tribes of peoples who were not Greco-Roman. Romans generally referred to such

imperator A title that usually honored a general after a major victory, it came to mean "emperor."

Augustus as Imperator

Here Augustus, dressed in breastplate and uniform, emphasizes the imperial majesty of Rome and his role as imperator. The figures on his breastplate represent the restoration of peace, one of Augustus's greatest accomplishments and certainly one that he frequently stressed. (Erich Lessing/Art Resource, NY)

barbarians Tribes of people who were not Greco-Roman and who simply wanted to be left alone.

people as **barbarians,** a word derived from a Greek word for those who did not speak Greek. The Romans maintained peaceful relations with the barbarians whenever possible, but their legions remained on the frontier to repel hostile barbarians.

Literary Flowering and Social Changes

Augustus and many of his friends actively encouraged poets and writers, and indeed the period has become known as the golden age of Latin literature. Roman poets and prose writers celebrated the dignity of humanity and the range of its accomplishments. They stressed the physical and emotional joys of a comfortable, peaceful life. Their works were elegant in style and intellectual in conception.

Rome's greatest poet was Virgil (0–19 B.C.E.), a sensitive man who delighted in simple things. Virgil left in his *Georgics* a charming picture of life in the Italian countryside during a period of peace. His masterpiece is the *Aeneid* (**uh-NEE-id**), an epic poem that is the Latin equivalent of the Greek *Iliad* and *Odyssey*. Virgil's account of the founding of Rome and the early years of the city gave final form to the legend of Aeneas, a Trojan hero who escaped to Italy at the fall of Troy. The legend of Aeneas (**ah-NEE-uhs**) was a third story about the founding of Rome, along with those of Romulus and the rape of Lucretia (see page 87). As Virgil told it, Aeneas became the lover of Dido (**DIE-doh**), the widowed queen of Carthage, but left her because his destiny called him to found Rome. She committed suicide, and their relationship eventually became the cause of the Punic Wars. In leaving Dido, an "Eastern" queen, Aeneas put the good of the state ahead of marriage or pleasure; the parallels between this story and the real events involving Antony and Cleopatra were not lost on Virgil's audience. This fit well with Augustus's aims; he had encouraged Virgil to write the *Aeneid* and made sure it was published immediately after Virgil died.

The poet Ovid (**OV-id**) [43 B.C.E.–17? C.E.] shared Virgil's views of the simple pleasures of life and also celebrated the popular culture of the day. In his *Fasti* (**FAS-tee**) (ca. 8 C.E.) he explains the ordinary festivals of the Roman year, and his work offers modern readers a rare glimpse of Roman life and religion.

The historian Livy (**LIV-ee**) (59 B.C.E.–17 C.E.) approved of Augustus's efforts to restore republican virtues. Livy's 142-book history of Rome, titled simply *Ab Urbe Condita (From the Founding of the City)*, began with the legend of Aeneas and ended with the reign of Augustus. His theme of the republic's greatness complemented Augustus's program of restoring the republic.

The poet Horace (65–8 B.C.E.) rose from humble beginnings as the son of an ex-slave to friendship with Augustus. He loved Greek literature and finished his

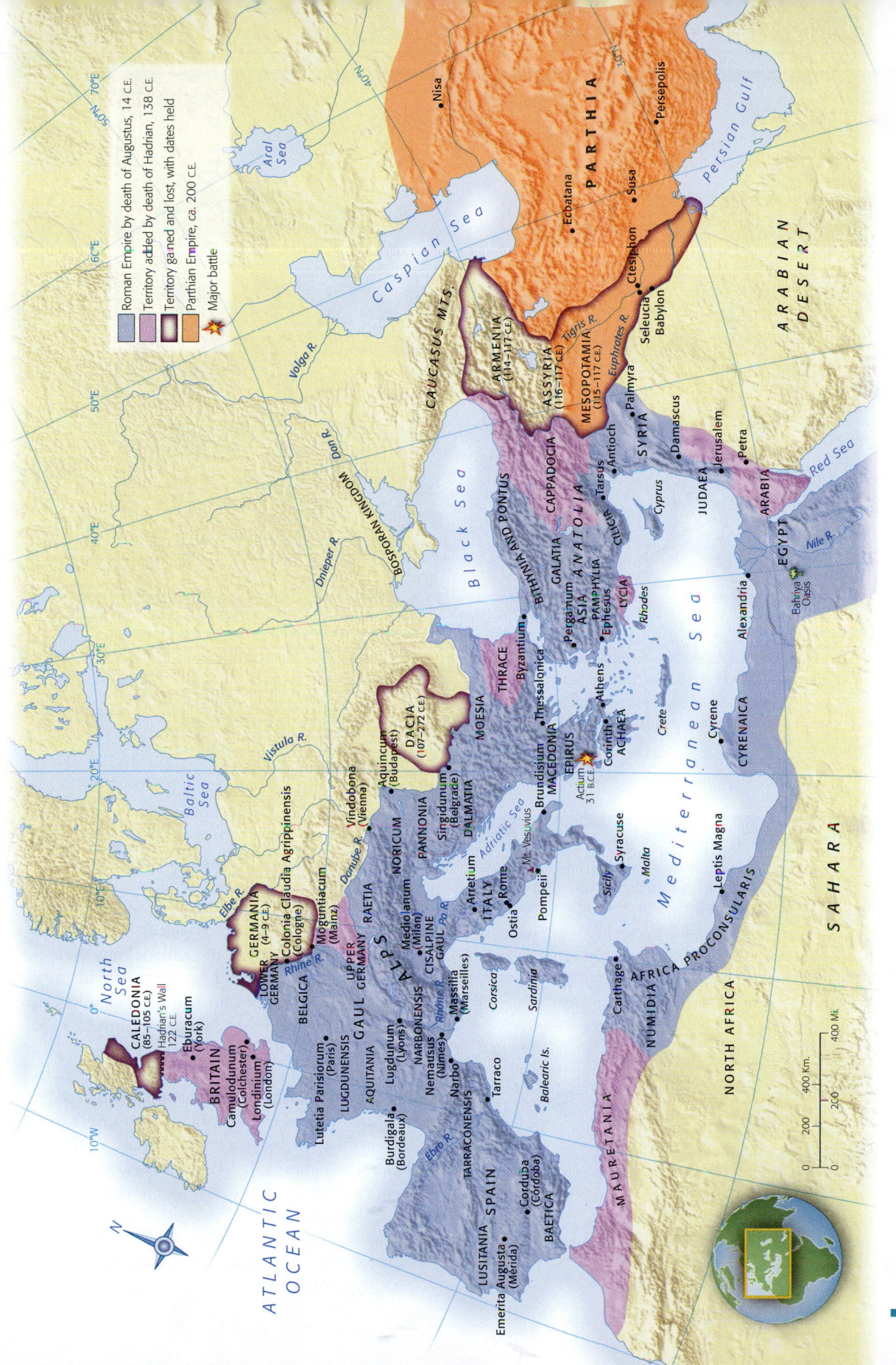

MAP 6.1 **Roman Expansion Under the Empire**

Following Roman expansion during the republic, Augustus added vast tracts of Europe to the Roman Empire, which the emperor Hadrian later enlarged by assuming control over parts of central Europe, the Near East, and North Africa.

Roman Empire by death of Augustus, 14 C.E.

Territory added by death of Hadrian, 138 C.E.

Territory gained and lost, with dates held

Parthian Empire, ca. 200 C.E.

Major battle

Aral Sea

PARTHIA

• Nisa

• Persepolis

Persian Gulf

• Ecbatana

• Susa

Caspian Sea

ARABIAN DESERT

CAUCASUS MTS.

ARMENIA (114–117 C.E.)

ASSYRIA (116–117 C.E.)

MESOPOTAMIA (115–117 C.E.)

Tigris R.

Euphrates R.

Seleucia

Ctesiphon

Babylon

Palmyra •

• Damascus

SYRIA

Antioch •

• Jerusalem

JUDAEA

• Petra

ARABIA

Red Sea

EGYPT

Nile R.

BITHYNIA AND PONTUS

CAPPADOCIA

GALATIA

ASIA ANATOLIA

PAMPHYLIA

Tarsus •

CILICIA

Cyprus

Pergamum •

Ephesus •

LYCIA

Rhodes

Alexandria •

Bahriya Oasis

Black Sea

THRACE

Byzantium •

MOESIA

DACIA (107–272 C.E.)

Aquincum (Budapest) •

Vindobona (Vienna) •

Singidunum (Belgrade) •

PANNONIA

NORICUM

DALMATIA

Danube R.

RAETIA

Mediolanum (Milan) •

Aretium •

Rome •

ITALY

Ostia •

Pompeii •

Mt. Vesuvius

Brundisium •

Thessalonica •

MACEDONIA

EPIRUS

Actium 31 B.C.E.

Corinth •

ACHAEA

Athens •

Crete

Syracuse •

Sicily

Malta

Leptis Magna •

Cyrene •

CYRENAICA

Mediterranean Sea

Adriatic Sea

Carthage •

AFRICA PROCONSULARIS

NUMIDIA

NORTH AFRICA

MAURETANIA

SAHARA

Vistula R.

Baltic Sea

North Sea

CALEDONIA (85–105 C.E.)

Hadrian's Wall 122 C.E.

Eburacum (York) •

BRITAIN

Camulodunum (Colchester) •

Londinium (London) •

Elbe R.

GERMANIA (4–9 C.E.)

Colonia Claudia Agrippinensis (Cologne) •

Moguntiacum (Mainz) •

Rhine R.

LOWER GERMANY

UPPER GERMANY

BELGICA

GAUL

ALPS

Lutetia Parisiorum (Paris) •

LUGDUNENSIS

AQUITANIA

Lugdunum (Lyons) •

CISALPINE GAUL

Nemausus (Nîmes) •

Massilia (Marseilles) •

NARBONENSIS

Narbo •

Burdigala (Bordeaux) •

Rhône R.

Po R.

Ebro R.

Tarraco •

TARRACONENSIS

SPAIN

Corsica

Sardinia

Balearic Is.

Corduba (Córdoba) •

BAETICA

LUSITANIA

Emerita Augusta (Mérida) •

ATLANTIC OCEAN

BOSPORAN KINGDOM

Dnieper R.

Don R.

Volga R.

400 Mi.

400 Km.

0   200   400

0   200

Ara Pacis

This scene from the Ara Pacis, the Altar of Peace erected in Rome by Augustus, celebrates Augustus's restoration of peace and imperial family values. On this side, Mother Earth is depicted with twin babies on her lap, framed by nymphs representing land and sea. The sheep and the cow are both agricultural and sacrificial animals. Other sides of the altar show Romulus and Remus (another set of twins) and Augustus and his wife Livia in traditional Roman clothing. (Scala/Art Resource, NY)

Section Review

- Augustus rebuilt the government to restore the republic and gained power by holding many magistracies and eventually becoming *"pontifex maximus,"* the chief priest of the state and the chief religious official.

- Augustus's real power came as commander of the Roman army, which he controlled as imperator (emperor) and made into a professional organization with standard training wages and advancement opportunities.

- The army completed the conquest of Spain and Gaul but was turned back at the Rhine on the German frontier; next they took Serbia, Bulgaria, and Romania, linking settlements with roads and trading with the natives.

- The golden age of literature celebrated humanity, peace, and comfort as Rome's greatest poet Virgil told the story of the founding of Rome in his epic, the *Aeneid.*

- Augustus promoted marriage and childbearing by releasing women from male guardianship if they gave birth to a certain number of children, by declaring adultery a crime, and by setting up his own family as a model.

- Augustus solved the problem of a legal successor by sharing his powers and wealth with his adopted son, Tiberius; the senate requested that Tiberius be the next ruler of the principate.

education in Athens. After Augustus's victory he returned to Rome and became Virgil's friend. Horace happily turned his pen to celebrating Rome and Augustus.

Concern with morality and traditional Roman virtues was a matter for law as well as literature. Augustus promoted marriage and childbearing through legal changes that released free women and freedwomen (female slaves who had been freed) from male guardianship if they had given birth to a certain number of children. Men and women who were unmarried or had no children were restricted in the inheritance of property. Adultery, defined as sex with a married woman or a woman under male guardianship, was made a crime, not simply the private family matter it had been. In imperial propaganda, Augustus had his own family depicted as a model of traditional morality, with his wife Livia at his side dressed in conservative and somewhat old-fashioned clothing rather than the more daring Greek styles of the time.

The solidity of Augustus's work became obvious at his death in 14 C.E. Since the principate was not technically an office, Augustus could not legally hand it to a successor. Augustus recognized this problem and long before his death had found a way to solve it. He shared his consular and tribunician powers with his adopted son, Tiberius, thus grooming him for the principate. In his will Augustus left most of his vast fortune to Tiberius, and the senate formally requested Tiberius to assume the burdens of the principate. Formalities apart, Augustus had succeeded in creating a dynasty.

The Coming of Christianity

Why did Christianity, originally a minor local religion, sweep across the Roman world to change it fundamentally?

During the reign of the emperor Tiberius (14–37 C.E.), in the Roman province created out of the Jewish kingdom of Judah, Jesus of Nazareth preached, attracted a following, and was executed on the order of the Roman prefect Pontius Pilate. Much contemporary scholarship has attempted to understand who Jesus was and what he meant by his teachings. Views vary widely. Some see him as a visionary and a teacher, others as a magician and a prophet, and still others as a rebel and a revolutionary. The search for the historical Jesus is complicated by many factors. One is the difference between history and faith. History relies on proof for its conclusions; faith depends on belief. Thus, whether Jesus is divine or not is not an issue to be decided by historians. Their role is to understand him in his religious, cultural, social, and historical context.

Unrest in Judaea

The civil wars that destroyed the Roman republic had extended as far as Judaea in the eastern Mediterranean. Jewish leaders took sides in the conflict, and Judaea suffered its share of violence and looting. Although Augustus restored stability, his appointed king for Judaea, Herod (r. 37–4 B.C.E.), was hated by the Jews. Upon Herod's death, the Jews revolted, and Herod's successor waged almost constant war against the rebels. Added to the horrors of this war were years of famine and plague.

Among the Jews two movements spread. First was the rise of the Zealots (**ZEL-uhts**), extremists who fought to rid Judaea of the Romans. The second movement was the growth of militant **apocalypticism**—the belief that the coming of the **Messiah** (**mi-SIGH-uh**) was near. The Messiah would destroy the Roman legions, and all the kingdoms that had ruled Israel, and then inaugurate a period of happiness and plenty for the Jews.

The pagan world of Rome is also part of the story of early Christianity. The term **pagans** (**PAY-gans**) refers to all those who believed in the Greco-Roman gods. Paganism at the time of Jesus' birth can be broadly divided into three spheres: the official state religion of Rome, the traditional Roman cults of hearth and countryside, and the new mystery religions that flowed from the Hellenistic East (see Chapter 4). The mystery religions gave their adherents what neither the state religion nor traditional cults could—the promise of immortality. Yet the mystery religions were by nature exclusive, and none was truly international, open to everyone.

apocalypticism The belief that the coming of the Messiah was near.

Messiah The savior of Israel.

pagans All those who believed in the Greco-Roman gods.

The Life and Teachings of Jesus

Into this climate of Jewish Messianic hope and Roman religious yearning came Jesus of Nazareth (ca. 3 B.C.E.– 29 C.E.). He was raised in Galilee, stronghold of the Zealots. The principal evidence for the life and deeds of Jesus are the four Gospels of the New Testament. These Gospels—the word means "good news"—are records of his teachings and religious doctrines with certain details of his life. The earliest Gospels were written some seventy-five years after his death, and there are discrepancies among the four accounts. These differences indicate that early Christians had a diversity of beliefs about Jesus' nature and purpose. Only slowly, as the Christian church became an institution, were lines drawn more clearly between what was considered correct teaching and what was considered incorrect, or **heresy** (HER-uh-see).

heresy Incorrect teachings within the Christian church.

Despite this diversity, there were certain things about Jesus' teachings that almost all the sources agree on: he preached of a heavenly kingdom, one of eternal happiness in a life after death. His teachings were essentially Jewish. His orthodoxy enabled him to preach in the synagogue and the temple. His major deviation from orthodoxy was his insistence that he taught in his own name, not in the name of Yahweh. Was he then the Messiah? A small band of followers thought so, and Jesus claimed that he was. Yet Jesus had his own conception of the Messiah. He would establish a spiritual kingdom, not an earthly one.

The prefect Pontius Pilate knew little of Jesus' teachings. His concern was maintaining peace and order. The crowds following Jesus at the time of the Passover, a highly emotional time in the Jewish year, alarmed Pilate, who faced a volatile situation. Some Jews believed that Jesus was the long-awaited Messiah, which triggered Roman concerns about rebellion; others hated and feared Jesus and wanted to be rid of him. To avert riot and bloodshed, Pilate condemned Jesus to death and had his soldiers carry out the sentence.

On the third day after Jesus' crucifixion, some of his followers claimed that he had risen from the dead. For the earliest Christians and for generations to come, the resurrection of Jesus became a central element of faith: he had triumphed over death, and his resurrection promised all Christians immortality.

The Spread of Christianity

The memory of Jesus and his teachings survived and flourished. Believers in his divinity met in small assemblies or congregations, often in one another's homes, to discuss the meaning of Jesus' message. These earliest Christians defined their faith to fit the life of Jesus into an orthodox Jewish context. Only later did these congregations evolve into what can be called a church with a formal organization and set of beliefs.

The catalyst in the spread of Jesus' teachings and the formation of the Christian church was Paul of Tarsus, a Hellenized Jew who was comfortable in both the Roman and Jewish worlds. He had begun by persecuting the new sect, but on the road to Damascus he was converted to belief in Jesus. He was the single most important figure responsible for changing Christianity from a Jewish sect into a separate religion. He urged the Jews to include **Gentiles** (JEN-tie-uhls) (non-Jews) in the faith. His was the first universal message of Christianity.

Gentiles A term for non-Jews. Paul helped spread Christianity by not distinguishing between Jews and Gentiles.

Many early Christian converts were women, who seem to have come particularly from the Greco-Roman middle classes. Paul greeted male and female converts by name in his letters and noted that women provided financial support for his activities. Missionaries and others spreading the Christian message worked

The Catacombs of Rome
The early Christians used underground crypts and rock chambers to bury their dead. The bodies were placed in these galleries and then sealed up. The catacombs became places of pilgrimage, and in this way the dead continued to be united with the living. (Catacombe di Priscilla, Rome/Scala/Art Resource, NY)

through families and friendship networks. The growing Christian communities in various cities of the Roman Empire had different ideas about many things, including the proper gender roles for believers. Some communities favored giving women a larger role, while others were more restrictive (see page 120).

Christianity might have remained just another sect had it not reached Rome, the capital of the Western world. Rome proved to be a dramatic step in the spread of Christianity for different reasons. First, Jesus had told his followers to spread his word throughout the world, thus making his teachings universal. The pagan Romans also considered their secular empire universal, and early Christians there combined these two concepts of **universalism.** Secular Rome provided another advantage to Christianity. If all roads led to Rome, they also led outward to the provinces of central and western Europe. The very stability and extent of the Roman Empire enabled early Christians easily to spread their faith southward to Africa and northward into Europe and across the channel to Britain.

The **catacombs,** underground cemeteries for Christian burial, testify to the vitality of the new religion and Rome's toleration of it. Although many people today think of the catacombs as secret meeting places of oppressed Christians, they were actually huge public structures along the Via Appia, one of Rome's proudest lanes. The development of Christian art can be traced on their walls, with pagan and Christian motifs on early tombs, and biblical scenes on later ones.

universalism The result of the combination of the two concepts: first, Jesus told his followers to spread his word throughout the world, thus making his teachings universal, and second, the pagan Romans also considered their secular empire universal.

catacombs Huge public underground cemeteries found along Via Appia in Rome.

The Appeal of Christianity

Christianity offered its adherents the promise of salvation. Christians believed that Jesus had defeated evil and that he would reward his followers with eternal life after death. Christianity also offered the possibility of forgiveness. Human nature was weak, and even the best Christians would fall into sin. But Jesus loved sinners and forgave those who repented.

Christianity was also attractive because it gave the Roman world a cause. Instead of passivity, Christianity stressed the ideal of striving for a goal. By spreading the word of Christ, Christians played their part in God's plan for the triumph of Christianity on earth. The Christian was not discouraged by temporary setbacks, believing Christianity to be invincible.

Christianity also gave its devotees a sense of community. Believers met regularly to celebrate the Eucharist (**YOO-kuh-rist**), the Lord's Supper. Each individual community was in turn a member of a greater community. And that community, according to Christian Scripture, was indestructible, for Jesus had promised, "the gates of hell shall not prevail against it."[3]

Augustus's Successors

How did Augustus's successors build on his foundation to enhance Roman power and stability?

Augustus's success in creating solid political institutions was tested by the dynasty he created, the Julio-Claudians, who schemed against one another trying to win and hold power. This situation allowed a military commander, Vespasian (**ve-SPEY-zhuhn**), to claim the throne and establish a new dynasty, the Flavians. The Flavians were followed by the "Good Emperors," who were successful militarily and politically.

The Julio-Claudians and the Flavians

For fifty years after Augustus's death the dynasty that he established—known as the Julio-Claudians because they were all members of the Julian and Claudian clans—provided the emperors of Rome. Some of the Julio-Claudians, such as Tiberius and Claudius, were sound rulers and able administrators. Others, including Caligula and Nero, were weak and frivolous men. The story of the Julio-Claudians involves adultery, bigamy, murder, incest, sexual promiscuity, forced suicide, and a host of other ills, as emperors and empresses sought to win and hold power. Nonetheless, during their reigns the empire largely prospered.

Augustus's creation of an imperial bodyguard known as the Praetorians (**pray-TOR-ee-ahns**) had repercussions for his successors. In 41 C.E. the Praetorians murdered Caligula and forced the senate to ratify their choice of Claudius as emperor. It was a story repeated frequently. During the first three centuries of the empire, the Praetorian Guard all too often murdered emperors they were supposed to protect and saluted emperors of their own choosing.

Claudius was murdered by his fourth wife to allow her son by a previous marriage, Nero, to become emperor. In 68 C.E. Nero's inept rule led to military rebellion and his suicide, thus opening the way to widespread disruption. In 69 C.E., the "Year of the Four Emperors," four men claimed the position of emperor. Roman armies in Gaul, on the Rhine, and in the East marched on Rome to make their commanders emperor. Vespasian, commander of the eastern armies, emerged triumphant.

Vespasian did not solve the problem of the army in politics. To prevent usurpers from claiming the throne, Vespasian designated his sons Titus and Domitian as his successors. By establishing the Flavian dynasty (named after his clan), Vespasian openly turned the principate into a monarchy. He also expanded the emperor's power by increasing the size of the professional bureaucracy Claudius had created.

Roman History After Augustus

Period	Important Emperors	Significant Events
Julio-Claudians 27 B.C.E.–68 C.E.	Augustus, 27 B.C.E.–14 C.E.	Augustan settlement
	Tiberius, 14–37	Beginning of the principate
	Caligula, 37–41	Birth and death of Jesus
	Claudius, 41–54	Expansion into northern and western Europe
	Nero, 54–68	Creation of the imperial bureaucracy
Year of the Four Emperors 69	Nero	Civil war
	Galba	Major breakdown of the concept of the principate
	Otho	
	Vitellius	
Flavians 69–96	Vespasian, 69–79	Growing trend toward the concept of monarchy
	Titus, 79–81	Defense and further consolidation of the European frontiers
	Domitian, 81–96	
Antonines 96–180	Nerva, 96–98	The "golden age"–the era of the "five good emperors"
	Trajan, 98–117	Economic prosperity
	Hadrian, 117–138	Trade and growth of cities in northern Europe
	Antoninus Pius, 138–161	Beginning of barbarian menace on the frontiers
	Marcus Aurelius, 161–180	
	Commodus, 180–192	
Severi 193–235	Septimius Severus, 193–211	Military monarchy
	Caracalla, 198–217	All free men within the empire given Roman citizenship
	Elagabalus, 218–222	
	Severus Alexander, 222–235	
"Barracks Emperors" 235–284	Twenty-two emperors in forty-nine years	Civil war
		Breakdown of the empire
		Barbarian invasions
		Severe economic decline
Tetrarchy 284–337	Diocletian, 284–305	Political recovery
	Constantine, 306–337	Autocracy
		Legalization of Christianity
		Transition to the Middle Ages in the West
		Birth of the Byzantine Empire in the East

He is also known for sending a Roman army to put down revolts in Judaea, which led to the destruction of Jerusalem and the enslavement of the Jewish survivors.

The Flavians carried on Augustus's work on the frontiers. Domitian, the last of the Flavians, won additional territory in Germany and consolidated it in two new provinces. He defeated barbarian tribes on the Danube (**DAN-yoob**) frontier and strengthened that area as well. Even so, Domitian was one of the most hated of Roman emperors because of his cruelty, and he fell victim to an assassin's dagger.

The Emperor Marcus Aurelius
This equestrian statue, with the emperor greeting his people, represents both the majesty and the peaceful intentions of this emperor and philosopher—one of the five good emperors. Equestrian statues present an image of idealized masculinity, but most portray their subjects as fierce and warlike, not with a hand raised in peace as Marcus Aurelius's hand is here. (Tibor Bognar/Alamy)

Nevertheless, the Flavians had kept the legions in line. Their work paved the way for the Antonine dynasty and the era of the "five good emperors."

The Age of the "Five Good Emperors" (96–180 C.E.)

The **five good emperors**—Nerva, Trajan (**TREY-juhn**), Hadrian (**HEY-dree-uhn**), Antoninus Pius, and Marcus Aurelius—ruled the empire wisely, fairly, and humanely. Yet the nature of their rule was considerably different from what it had been under Augustus.

Augustus had claimed that his influence arose from the collection of offices the senate had bestowed on him and that he was merely the First Citizen. Under the Flavians the principate became a full-blown monarchy, and by the time of the Antonines the principate was an office with definite rights, powers, and prerogatives. While the five good emperors were not power-hungry autocrats, they were absolute kings all the same. They needed vast powers and the help of professional bureaucrats in order to run the empire efficiently. Later rulers would use this same power in a despotic fashion.

The Roman army had also changed since Augustus's time. Under the Flavian emperors the frontiers became firmly fixed, except for a brief period under Trajan, who attempted to expand the empire. No longer a conquering force, the army concentrated on defending what had already been won. Forts and watch stations guarded the borders. Outside the forts the Romans built a system of roads that allowed the forts to be quickly supplied and reinforced in times of trouble. The army had evolved from a mobile unit into a garrison force, with legions guarding specific areas for long periods.

The personnel of the legions was changing, too. Italy could no longer supply all the recruits needed for the army. Increasingly, only the officers came from Italy and from the more Romanized provinces. The legionaries were mostly drawn from the provinces closest to the frontiers. In the third century C.E. this shift would result in an army indifferent to Rome and its traditions. In the age of the five good emperors, however, the army was still a source of economic stability and a Romanizing agent. (See the feature "Individuals in Society: Bithus, a Typical Roman Soldier.")

five good emperors The name for the five emperors who ruled the empire wisely, fairly, and humanely. They created a period of peace and prosperity.

Section Review

- For fifty years after Augustus, the Julio-Claudian dynasty included able rulers, such as Tiberius and Claudius, and inept rulers, such as Caligula and Nero.

- During the Julio-Claudian dynasty, the Praetorians, the imperial bodyguard of Augustus, often murdered emperors and then established successors of their own choosing.

- During the "Year of the Four Emperors" Vespasian finally claimed the throne and openly changed the principate into a monarchy, expanding the emperor's power while his heirs the Flavians continued expansion on the frontiers.

- The "Five Good Emperors" Nerva, Trajan, Hadrian, Antoninus Pius, and Marcus Aurelius ruled fairly but were still kings with vast powers using the aid of professional bureaucrats to rule.

- Under the Flavians, the Roman army changed its role from mobile expansion unit to garrison force, protecting the borders, using forts, and building roads for rapid movement of supplies and reinforcements.

Individuals in Society

Bithus, a Typical Roman Soldier

Few people think of soldiers as missionaries of culture, but they often are. They expose others to their own traditions, habits, and ways of thinking while at the same time they gain an understanding of other cultures that they can bring home. This was true of the soldiers of the Roman Empire. The empire was so vast even by modern standards that soldiers were recruited from all parts of it to serve in distant places. A soldier from Syria might find himself keeping watch on Hadrian's Wall in Britain. He brought with him the ideas and habits of his birthplace and soon realized that others lived life differently. Yet they all lived in the same empire. Despite their ethnic differences, they were united by many commonly shared beliefs and opinions.

Historical records offer us a glimpse into the life of the infantryman Bithus, who was typical of many who served in the legions. Born in Thrace, the region of modern northeastern Greece, his military life took him to Syria, where he spent most of his career. There he met others from as far west as Gaul and Spain, from West Africa, and from the modern Middle East. This experience gave him an idea of the size of the empire. It also taught him about life in other areas.

Unlike many other cohorts who were shifted periodically, Bithus saw service in one theater. While in the army, he raised a family, much like soldiers today. The children of soldiers like Bithus often themselves joined the army, which thereby became a fruitful source of its own recruitment. After twenty-five years of duty, Bithus received his reward on November 7, 88. Upon mustering out of the army he received the grant of Roman citizenship for himself and his family. In his civilian life the veteran enjoyed a social status that granted him honor and privileges accorded only to Romans. From his military records there is no reason to conclude that Bithus had even seen Rome, but because of his service to it, he became as much a Roman as anyone born near the Tiber.

The example of Bithus is important because it is typical of thousands of others who voluntarily supported the empire. In the process they learned about the nature of the empire and something about how it worked. They also exchanged experiences with other soldiers and the local population and this helped shape a sense that the empire was a human as well as a political unit.

Idealized statue of a Roman soldier.
(Deutsches Archaeologisches Institut, Rome)

Questions for Analysis

1. What did Bithus gain from his twenty-five years of service in the Roman army?
2. What effect did soldiers such as Bithus have on the various parts of the Roman Empire where they served, both in their way of seeing new cultures and in their way of sharing new experiences?

Source: Corpus Inscriptionum Latinarum, vol. 16 (Berlin: G. Reimer, 1882), no. 35.

Life in the "Golden Age"

What was life like in the city of Rome in the "golden age," and what was it like in the provinces?

The years of peace and prosperity under the five good emperors are considered by many to represent the "golden age" of Rome. Life in the capital city was significantly different from that in the provinces of northern and western Europe, and the Romans went to no great lengths to spread their culture. Yet roads and secure sea-lanes linked the empire in one vast web, with men and women traveling and migrating more often than they had in earlier eras (see Map 6.2). Through this network of commerce and communication, greater Europe entered the economic and cultural life of the Mediterranean world.

Imperial Rome

Rome was truly an extraordinary city, especially by ancient standards. It was also enormous, with a population somewhere between 500,000 and 750,000. Although it could boast of stately palaces, noble buildings, and beautiful residential areas, most people lived in jerrybuilt apartment houses. Fire and crime were perennial problems, even after Augustus created fire and urban police forces. Streets were narrow and drainage was inadequate. During the republic sanitation had been a common problem. Numerous inscriptions record prohibitions against dumping human refuse and even cadavers on the grounds of sanctuaries and cemeteries. Under the empire this situation improved. By comparison with medieval and early modern European cities, Rome was a healthy enough place to live.

Rome was such a huge city that the surrounding countryside could not feed it. Because of shortages and high prices, the emperor, following republican practice, provided the citizen population with free grain for bread and, later, oil and wine. By feeding the citizenry the emperor prevented bread riots. For those who were not citizens, the emperor provided grain at low prices. By furnishing free bread he eliminated shortages.

The emperor and other wealthy citizens also entertained the Roman populace, often at vast expense. The most popular forms of public entertainment were gladiatorial (**glad-ee-uh-TAWR-ee-uhl**) contests and chariot racing. Many **gladiators** (**glad-ee-ay-TAWRS**) were criminals under a death sentence. These convicts were given no defensive weapons and stood little real chance of survival. Other criminals were sentenced to fight in the arena as fully armed gladiators. Some gladiators were the slaves of gladiatorial trainers; others were prisoners of war. Still others were free men who volunteered for the arena. Even women at times engaged in gladiatorial combat. Some Romans protested gladiatorial fighting, but the emperors recognized the political value of such spectacles, and most Romans appear to have enjoyed them. Christian authors generally opposed gladiatorial and animal combat, but this did not lead to immediate bans.

The Romans were even more addicted to chariot racing than to gladiatorial shows. Under the empire four permanent teams competed against one another. Each had its own color—red, white, green, or blue. Two-horse and four-horse chariots ran a course of seven laps, about five miles. One charioteer, Gaius Appuleius Diocles, raced for twenty-four years. During that time he drove 4,257 starts and won 1,462 of them. His admirers honored him with an inscription that proclaimed him champion of all charioteers.

gladiators Criminals and convicts who were sentenced to be slaughtered in the arena as public entertainment.

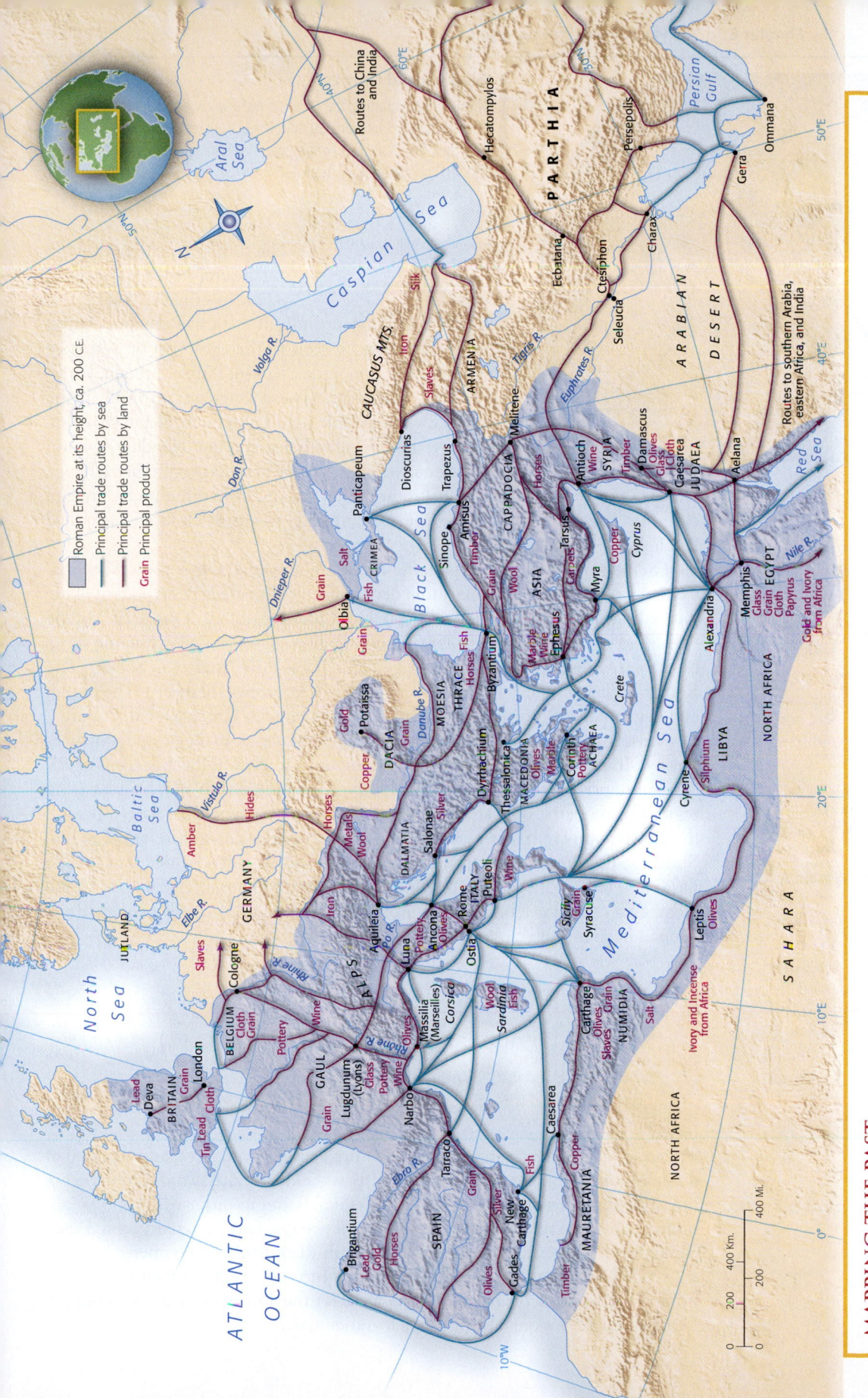

MAPPING THE PAST

MAP 6.2 The Economic Aspect of the Pax Romana

This map gives a good idea of trade routes and the economic expansion of the Roman Empire at its height. Map 11.1 on page 254 is a similar map that shows trade in roughly the same area nearly a millennium later. Examine both maps and answer the following questions: **[1]** To what extent did Roman trade routes influence later European trade routes? **[2]** What similarities and differences do you see in trade in the Mediterranean during these two periods?

Gladiatorial Games

Though hardly games, the contests were vastly popular among the Romans. Gladiators were usually slaves, but successful ones could gain their freedom. The fighting was hard but fair, and the gladiators shown here look equally matched. (Interfoto Pressebildagentur/Alamy)

villa A country estate, which was the primary unit of organized political life.

Rome and the Provinces

The rural population throughout the empire left few records, yet the inscriptions that remain point to a melding of indigenous and Roman cultures. This melding can be seen in the evolution of Romance languages, which include Spanish, Italian, French, Portuguese, and Romanian. These languages evolved in the provinces where people used Latin for legal and state religious purposes, eventually leading to a blending of Latin and their native tongues. The process of cultural exchange was at first more urban than rural, but the importance of cities and towns to the life of the wider countryside ensured that its effects spread far afield.

On the frontiers of the empire, the city was not as central to society. The **villa,** a country estate, was the primary unit of organized political life. This pattern of life differed from that of the Mediterranean, but it prefigured that of the early Middle Ages. The same was true in Britain, where the normal social and economic structures were farms and agricultural villages. (See the feature "Images in Society: The Roman Villa at Chedworth" on pages 124–125.) Very few cities were to be found, and many native Britons were largely unacquainted with Greco-Roman culture.

Across eastern Europe the pattern was much the same. In the Alpine provinces north of Italy, Romans and native Celts came into contact in the cities, but native cultures flourished in the countryside. In Illyria (eh-LEER-ee-uh) and Dalmatia, the regions of modern Albania and the former Yugoslavia (yoo-gah-SLAH-vee-uh), the native population never widely embraced either Roman culture or urban life. Similarly, the Roman soldiers who increasingly settled parts of these lands made little effort to Romanize the natives, and there was less intermarriage than in Celtic areas. To a certain extent, however, Romanization occurred simply because these peoples lived in such close proximity.

Rome in Disarray and Recovery (177–450 C.E.)

What factors led Rome into political and economic chaos, and how and to what extent did it recover?

The long years of peace and prosperity abruptly gave way to a convulsed period of domestic upheaval and foreign invasion. Law yielded to the sword. Only the political mechanisms of the empire—its bureaucrats and its ordinary lower officials, protected by loyal soldiers—staved off internal collapse and foreign invasion. Peace came with the ascension of Diocletian (die-uh-KLEE-shuhn) to emperor in 284.

Once Diocletian had ended the period of turmoil, succeeding emperors confronted the work of repairing the damage. Yet the Roman world, like Humpty Dumpty, could not quite be put back together again.

Civil Wars and Foreign Invasions in the Third Century

After the death of Marcus Aurelius, the last of the five good emperors, misrule by his successors led to a long and intense spasm of fighting. More than twenty different emperors ascended the throne in the forty-nine years between 235 and 284. So many military commanders ruled that the middle of the third century has become known as the age of the **barracks emperors.** The Augustan principate had become a military monarchy, and that monarchy was nakedly autocratic.

Preoccupied with creating and destroying emperors, the army left gaping holes in the border defenses. Taking advantage of the weakness, bands of Goths devastated the Balkans as far south as Greece and down into Asia Minor. The Alamanni (al-uh-MAN-eye), a Germanic people, swept across the Danube. At one point they reached Milan in Italy before being beaten back. Meanwhile, the Franks, still another Germanic folk, invaded eastern and central Gaul and northeastern Spain. Saxons from Scandinavia sailed into the English Channel in search of loot. In the east the Sassanids (suh-SAH-nidz) overran Mesopotamia.

barracks emperors The name of the period in the middle of the third century when many military commanders ruled.

Reconstruction Under Diocletian and Constantine (284–337 C.E.)

At the close of the third century C.E. the emperor Diocletian (r. 284–305) put an end to the period of turmoil. Repairing the damage done in the third century was the major work of the emperor Constantine (r. 306–337) in the fourth. But the price was high.

Under Diocletian, the princeps became *dominus*—"lord." The emperor claimed that he was "the elect of god"—that he ruled because of divine favor. To underline the emperor's exalted position, Diocletian and Constantine adopted the gaudy court ceremonies and trappings of the Persian Empire. People entering the emperor's presence prostrated themselves before him and kissed the hem of his robes.

Diocletian recognized that the empire had become too great for one man to handle and divided it into a western and an eastern half (see Map 6.3). Diocletian assumed direct control of the eastern part; he gave the rule of the western part to a colleague, along with the title **augustus,** which had become synonymous with emperor. Diocletian and his fellow augustus further delegated power by appointing two men to assist them. Each man was given the title of *caesar* to indicate his exalted rank. Although this system is known as the **Tetrarchy** (TEE-trahrk-ee) because four men ruled the empire, Diocletian was clearly the senior partner and final source of authority.

Each half of the empire was further split into two prefectures, each governed by a prefect responsible to an augustus. Diocletian reduced the power of the old provincial governors by dividing

augustus A title that became synonymous with emperor, it was given by Diocletian to a colleague along with the rule of the western part of the empire.

Tetrarchy A system by which four men rule the empire.

Diocletian's Tetrarchy

The emperor Diocletian's attempt to reform the Roman Empire by dividing rule among four men is represented in this piece of sculpture. Here the four tetrarchs demonstrate their solidarity by clasping one another on the shoulder. Nonetheless each man has his other hand on his sword—a gesture that proved prophetic when Diocletian's reign ended and another struggle for power began. (Alinari/Art Resource, NY)

Images in Society

The Roman Villa at Chedworth

On the European borders of the Roman Empire, the villa was often as important as the town. Indeed, villas sometimes assumed many of the functions of towns. They were economic and social centers from which landlords directed the life of the surrounding countryside. The villa at Chedworth in Roman Britain provides an excellent example. The ordinary villa included a large courtyard with barns, gardens, storehouses, and buildings for processing agricultural products and manufacturing goods. The villa also included the comfortable living quarters of the owner and his family. These structures included the usual bedrooms and baths. A small temple or shrine often provided a center for religious devotions. Quarters for servants and slaves were nearby but set apart from the great houses. Equally important were the other buildings that served domestic and light industrial needs. The villa, then, was essentially a small, self-contained community. Yet it was not necessarily isolated. The villa at Chedworth was connected by roads and rivers to other similar neighboring villas. The whole picture depicts a society that, though rural, was nonetheless cultured, comfortable, and in touch with the wider world. A good analogy is the American southern plantation before the Civil War. Like many of these villas, Chedworth survived the demise of the Roman Empire. They all remained to play a crucial role in preserving Greco-Roman civilization in northern Europe.

What did a Roman villa look like, and how can archaeological remains define and explain its functioning? Since few ancient structures remain intact, many must obviously be reconstructed from excavations. Image 1 is the archaeological ground plan of Chedworth. At first it seems to show only a series of foundations. Yet a closer look reveals its design. The large buildings marked 3, 5a, and 5 are the remains of the manorial houses. Rooms 10

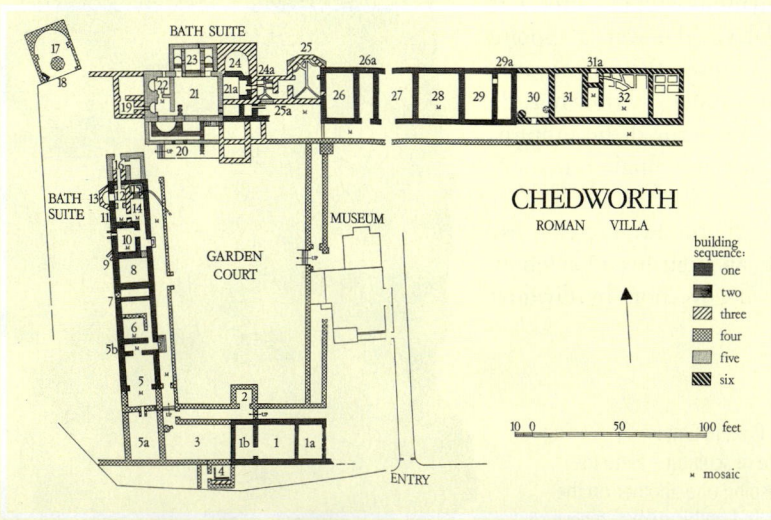

IMAGE 1 Ground Plan of the Roman Villa at Chedworth (From R. Goodburn, *The Roman Villa, Chedworth.* Reproduced with permission.)

IMAGE 2 Archaeological Reconstruction of the Villa (Courtesy, Professor Albert Schachter)

IMAGE 3 Aerial View of Chedworth (Courtesy of West Air Photography)

IMAGE 4 A View of the Site Today (John Buckler)

through 25a are the bath structures. Number 17 is a small temple. Buildings on the northern side, numbers 26–32, were domestic quarters.

Two questions immediately arise. How do we know what these buildings looked like, and how do we know how they functioned? By analyzing the physical remains and the building techniques of the site, archaeologists and architects have made a patient reconstruction of the entire villa (see Image 2). Artifacts found in the structures reveal their functions. The most obvious example is the elaborate bath complex of numbers 19–25a. Image 3 gives an aerial view of the villa, and Image 4 provides an excellent cameo of the western wing of the villa.

From this information can you determine from the ground plan (Image 1) and the reconstruction (Image 2) what the villa actually looked like? From Image 3, an aerial view of Chedworth, together with Images 1 and 2, can you locate the landlord's houses, the temple, and the domestic buildings? Now using these three images, can you identify the buildings in Image 4? Lastly, from this material can you imagine the functions of the villa in its environmental and cultural context?

Legend:
- Prefecture of Gaul
- Prefecture of Italy
- Prefecture of Illyricum
- Prefecture of the East

Line of division between east and west

MAP 6.3   The Roman World Divided

Under Diocletian, the Roman Empire was first divided into a western and an eastern half, a development that foreshadowed the medieval division between the Latin West and the Byzantine East.

dioceses Small administrative units that were governed by a prefect responsible to an augustus.

provinces into smaller units. He organized the prefectures into small administrative units called **dioceses** (DIE-uh-seez), which were in turn subdivided into small provinces. Provincial governors were also deprived of their military power, leaving them only civil and administrative duties.

Diocletian's political reforms were a momentous step. The Tetrarchy soon failed, but his division of the empire into two parts became permanent. Constantine and later emperors tried hard but unsuccessfully to keep the empire together. Throughout the fourth century C.E. the eastern and the western sections drifted apart. In later centuries the western part witnessed the fall of Roman government and the rise of Germanic kingdoms, while the eastern empire evolved into the Byzantine Empire.

Economic, social, and religious problems confronted Diocletian and Constantine. They needed additional revenues to support the army and the imperial court, yet the wars and invasions had struck a serious blow to Roman agriculture. Christianity had become too strong either to ignore or to crush. How Diocletian,

Arch of Constantine
Though standing in stately surroundings, Constantine's arch is decorated with art plundered from the arches of Trajan and Marcus Aurelius. He robbed them rather than decorate his own with the inferior work of his own day. (Michael Reed, photographer/www.mike-reed.com)

Constantine, and their successors responded to these problems influenced later developments.

Inflation and Taxes

The empire was less capable of recovery than in earlier times. Wars and invasions had disrupted normal commerce and the means of production. Mines were exhausted in the attempt to supply much-needed ores, especially gold and silver. In the cities, markets were disrupted, and travel became dangerous. Merchant and artisan families rapidly left devastated regions. The barracks emperors had dealt with economic hardship by cutting the silver content of coins until money was virtually worthless. The immediate result was crippling inflation throughout the empire.

Diocletian's attempt to curb inflation illustrates the methods of absolute monarchy. In a move unprecedented in Roman history, he issued an edict that fixed maximum prices and wages throughout the empire. The emperors dealt with the tax system just as strictly and inflexibly. Taxes became payable in kind, that is, in goods or produce instead of money. All those involved in the growing, preparation, and transportation of food and other essentials were locked into their professions. A baker or shipper could not go into any other business, and his son took up the trade at his death. In this period of severe depression many localities could not pay their taxes. In such cases local tax collectors, who were also locked into service, had to make up the difference from their own funds. This system soon wiped out a whole class of moderately wealthy people.

The Decline of Small Farms

Because of worsening conditions during the third century c.e., many free tenant farmers and their families were killed, fled the land to escape the barbarians, or abandoned farms ravaged in the fighting. Consequently, large tracts of land lay deserted. Great landlords with ample resources began at once to reclaim as much of this land as they could. The huge estates that resulted, called villas, were self-sufficient. Because they often produced more than they consumed, they successfully competed with the declining cities by selling their surplus in the countryside. They became islands of stability in an unsettled world.

The rural residents who remained on the land were exposed to the raids of barbarians or brigands and to the tyranny of imperial officials. In return for the protection and security landlords could offer, the small landholders gave over their lands and their freedom. They could no longer decide to move elsewhere. Henceforth they and their families worked their patrons' land, not their own. Free men and women were becoming what would later be called serfs.

The Acceptance of Christianity

The Roman attitude toward Christianity evolved as well during the period of empire. A splendid analysis of the different phases in the relationship between official Rome and Christianity has come from the eminent Italian scholar Marta Sordi.[4] At first many pagans genuinely misunderstood Christian practices and rites. They thought that such secret rites as the Lord's Supper, at which Christians said that they ate and drank the body and blood of Jesus, were acts of cannibalism. Pagans thought that Christianity was one of the worst of the mystery cults, with immoral and indecent rituals. They also feared that the gods would withdraw their favor from the Roman Empire because of the Christian insistence that the pagan gods either didn't exist or were evil spirits.

There were some cases of pagan persecution of the Christians, including some executions in Rome ordered by the Emperor Nero, but with few exceptions they were local and sporadic in nature. The Christians exaggerated the degree of pagan hostility toward them, and although there were some martyrs, most of the gory stories about the martyrs are fictitious. No constant persecution of Christians occurred.

As time went on, pagan hostility decreased. Pagans realized that Christians were not working to overthrow the state and that Jesus was no rival of Caesar. The emperor Trajan forbade his governors to hunt down Christians. Trajan admitted that he thought Christianity an abomination, but he preferred to leave Christians in peace.

The stress of the third century, however, seemed to some emperors the punishment of the gods. Although the Christians depicted the emperor Diocletian as a fiend, he persecuted them in the hope that gods would restore their blessings on Rome. Yet even these persecutions were never very widespread or long-lived. By the late third century, pagans had become used to Christianity. Constantine recognized Christianity as a legitimate religion and himself died a Christian in 33. Constantine's acceptance of Christianity can be seen as the pagans' alliance with the strongest god of them all.

In time the Christian triumph would be complete. In 380 the emperor Theodosius (**thee-uh-DOH-shee-uhs**) made Christianity the official religion of the Roman Empire. At that point Christians began to persecute the pagans for their beliefs. History had come full circle.

The Construction of Constantinople

The triumph of Christianity was not the only event that made Constantine's reign a turning point in Roman history. Constantine took the bold step of building a new capital for the empire. Constantinople, the New Rome, was constructed on the site of Byzantium, an old Greek city on the Bosporus. Throughout the third century emperors had found Rome and the West hard to defend. The eastern part of the empire was more easily defensible and escaped the worst of the barbarian devastation. It was wealthy and its urban life still vibrant. Moreover, Christianity was more widespread in the East than in the West, and the city of Constantinople was intended to be a Christian center.

From the Classical World to Late Antiquity

The two-faced Roman god Janus, who represented transitions, well symbolizes this period. A great deal of the past remained through these years of change. People still lived under the authority of the emperors and the guidance of Roman law. They communicated with one another as usual, in Latin throughout the West and Greek in the East. Greco-Roman art, architecture, and literature surrounded them.

Yet changes were also under way. Government had evolved from the SPQR of the past to the Christian monarchy of the new age. The empire itself split into East and West, and the latter became the home of barbarians who built a different world on classical foundations. Greek philosophy was replaced by theology, as thinkers tried earnestly to understand Jesus' message.

Through all these changes the lives of ordinary men and women did not change dramatically. They farmed, worked in cities, and hoped for the best for their families. They took new ideas, blended them with old, and created new cultural forms. Gradually the classical world gave way to a vibrant new intellectual, spiritual, and political life.

Section Review

- Following Marcus Aurelius's death, the empire was so preoccupied with military commanders vying for rule that foreign invaders took advantage and swept in on several fronts.

- Diocletian, and later Constantine, ended the turmoil, dividing the empire into a western and eastern half with an augustus and two caesars to rule each half, a system known as the Tetrarchy.

- Because of war, the empire was drained of resources so Diocletian fixed prices and wages and taxes were payable in kind, but this severe system soon wiped out the moderately wealthy.

- As small-scale farming became increasingly dangerous, wealthy landlords bought up the land and offered small tracts of land and protection to the farmers in exchange for their freedom.

- Christians exaggerated stories about martyrs, and although pagans at first misunderstood Christian rites, fearing it was the cause of the empire's troubles, pagans eventually grew used to Christianity and in 380 emperor Theodosius made it the official religion of the Roman Empire.

- Constantine built a new capital, Constantinople, on the site of Byzantium on the Bosporus, intending it to be a Christian center in the wealthier East while abandoning Rome and the western half of the empire to the barbarians.

Chapter Review

How did Augustus transform the Roman Empire? (page 108)

Once Augustus had restored order, he made it endure by remodeling the Roman government. The old constitution of the city-state gave way to the government of an empire. Although Augustus tried to save as much of the old as possible, he necessarily created a virtually new and much expanded system of rule. Furthermore, he made it endure.

Why did Christianity, originally a minor local religion, sweep across the Roman world to change it fundamentally? (page 113)

Christianity triumphed because it offered salvation to all people, men and women, regardless of their nationality, race, or social status.

How did Augustus's successors build on his foundation to enhance Roman power and stability? (page 116)

As life settled down under this calming order, a small event with universal repercussions occurred in remote Judaea. There a young Jew named Jesus taught a new religion,

Key Terms

pax Romana (p. 108)
constitutional monarchy (p. 108)
princeps (p. 108)
principate (p. 108)
imperator (p. 109)
barbarians (p. 110)
apocalypticism (p. 113)
Messiah (p. 113)
pagans (p. 113)
heresy (p. 114)
Gentiles (p. 114)
universalism (p. 115)

(continued)

promising salvation to all who embraced it. Although Roman officials executed him, this new religion did not die. Instead it spread across the East, then to Rome, and by the end of the period throughout the empire.

What was life like in the city of Rome in the "golden age," and what was it like in the provinces? (page 120)

Augustus's success in creating solid political institutions was tested by the dynasty he created, the Julio-Claudians. The fifty years during which they ruled Rome saw emperors and empresses trying to win and hold power through multiple political marriages, murder, and other tactics. In 70 C.E., Vespasian, a military commander, established a new dynasty, the Flavians, who restored some stability in Rome and expanded the empire. The Flavians were followed by a series of effective emperors, later called the "Five Good Emperors," who created a more effective bureaucracy and larger army to govern the huge Roman Empire.

What factors led Rome into political and economic chaos, and how and to what extent did it recover? (page 122)

For many Romans these were rich and happy years. Much of the population enjoyed sufficient leisure time, which many spent pursuing literature and art. Others preferred watching spectacular games including gladiatorial contests and chariot races. In the ever-expanding provinces, Roman and native cultures combined, and products and peoples moved more easily across huge areas.

The good times fell into disarray when a series of weak emperors, many of them backed by soldiers they had commanded, fought for the throne. To worsen matters, barbarians on the frontiers took advantage of these internal troubles to invade, plunder, and destroy. These factors brought Rome near collapse. With the end apparently at hand, two stern and gifted emperors, Diocletian and Constantine, restored order and breathed fresh life into the economic and social order. By the end of this period, Christianity had made such gains that it was recognized as the official religion of the empire. By the end of Constantine's reign the Roman Empire was politically divided and religiously changing. Still, many aspects of Greco-Roman culture remained strong.

catacombs (p. 115)

five good emperors (p. 118)

gladiators (p. 120)

villa (p. 122)

barracks emperors (p. 123)

augustus (p. 123)

Tetrarchy (p. 123)

dioceses (p. 126)

Notes

1. Virgil, *Aeneid* 6.851–6.853. John Buckler is the translator of all uncited quotations from a foreign language in Chapters 1–6.
2. Augustus, *Res Gestae* 6.34.
3. Matthew 16:18.
4. See Marta Sordi, *The Christians and the Roman Empire* (London: Croom Helm, 1986).

To assess your mastery of this chapter, go to **bedfordstmartins.com/mckaywestbrief**

Listening to the Past

Rome Extends Its Citizenship

One of the most dramatic achievements of the pax Romana was the extension of citizenship throughout the Roman Empire. Citizenship gave people advantages in judicial procedures, property transmission, and commercial relations. Male citizens could vote, and both female and male citizens passed citizenship on to their children.

Yet various emperors went even further by viewing Rome not only as a territorial but also as a political concept. In their eyes Rome was a place and an idea. Not every Roman agreed with these cosmopolitan views. The emperor Claudius (r. 41–54) took the first major step in this direction by allowing Romanized Gauls to sit in the senate. He was roundly criticized by some Romans, but in the damaged stone inscription that follows, he presents his own defense.

Surely both my great-uncle, the deified Augustus, and my uncle, Tiberius Caesar, were following a new practice when they desired that all the flowers of the colonies and the municipalities everywhere—that is, the better class and the wealthy men—should sit in this senate house. You ask me: Is not an Italian senator preferable to a provincial? I shall reveal to you in detail my views on this matter when I come to obtain approval for this part of my censorship [a magistracy that determined who was eligible for citizenship and public offices]. But I think that not even provincials ought to be excluded, provided that they can add distinction to this senate house.

Look at that most distinguished and most flourishing colony of Vienna [the modern Vienne in France], how long a time already it is that it has furnished senators to this house! From that colony comes that ornament of the equestrian order—and there are few to equal him—Lucius Vestinus, whom I cherish most intimately and whom at this very time I employ in my affairs. And it is my desire that his children may enjoy the first step in the priesthoods, so as to advance afterwards, as they grow older, to further honors in their rank. . . .

All these distinguished youths whom I gaze upon will no more give us cause for regret if they become senators than does my friend Persicus, a man of most noble ancestry, have cause for regret when he reads among the portraits of his ancestors the name Allobrogicus. But if you agree that these things are so, what more do you want, when I point out to you this single fact, that the territory beyond the boundaries of Narbonese Gaul already sends you senators, since we have men of our order from Lyons and have no cause for regret. It is indeed with hesitation, members of the senate, that I have gone outside the borders of the provinces with which you are accustomed and familiar, but I must now plead openly the cause of Gallia Comata [a region in modern France]. And if anyone, in this connection, has in mind that these people engaged the deified Julius in war for ten years, let him set against that the unshakable loyalty and obedience of a hundred years, tested to the full in many of our crises. When my father Drusus was subduing Germany, it was they who by their tranquility afforded him a safe and securely peaceful rear, even at a time when he had been summoned away to the war from the task of organizing the census which was still new and unaccustomed to the Gauls. How difficult such an operation

Provocatio, the right of appeal, was considered a fundamental element of Roman citizenship. (Courtesy of the Trustees of the British Museum)

is for us at this precise moment we are learning all too well from experience, even though the survey is aimed at nothing more than an official record of our resources. [The rest of the inscription is lost.]

Questions for Analysis

1. What was the basic justification underlying Claudius's decision to allow Gallic nobles to sit in the senate? Did he see them as debasing the quality of the senate?

2. What do his words tell us about the changing nature of the Roman Empire?

Source: Slightly adapted and abbreviated from *Roman Civilization*, 2 volumes, Third Edition. Volume 1 by N. Lewis and M. Reinhold. Copyright © 1966 Columbia University Press. Reprinted with permission of the publisher.

CHAPTER 7

Late Antiquity

350–600

Hagia Sophia (AH-yah SOH-fee-uh) ("Holy Wisdom"), built by the Emperor Justinian in the sixth century, was the largest Christian cathedral in the world for a thousand years. After Constantinople was conquered by the Ottoman Turks in 1453, it became a mosque, and today is a museum. (Editore Sadea Editore)

Chapter Preview

The Byzantine Empire
How was the Byzantine Empire able to survive for so long, and what were its most important achievements?

The Growth of the Christian Church
What factors enabled the Christian church to expand and thrive?

Christian Ideas and Practices
How did Christian thinkers adapt Greco-Roman ideas to Christian theology?

Christian Missionaries and Conversion
What techniques did missionaries develop to convert barbarian peoples to Christianity?

Migrating Peoples
What were some of the causes of the barbarian migrations and how did they affect the regions of Europe?

Barbarian Society
What patterns of social, political, and economic life characterized barbarian society?

INDIVIDUALS IN SOCIETY: Theodora of Constantinople

LISTENING TO THE PAST: The Conversion of Clovis

From the third century onward, the Western Roman Empire slowly disintegrated. The last Roman emperor in the West, Romulus Augustus, was deposed by the Ostrogothic (OS-truh-goth-ic) chieftain Odoacer in 476, but much of the empire had already come under the rule of various barbarian tribes well before this. Scholars have long seen this era as one of the great turning points in Western history, a time when the ancient world was transformed into the very different medieval world. During the past several decades, however, scholars have shifted their focus to continuities as well as changes, and what is now usually termed "late antiquity" has been recognized as a period of creativity and adaptation, not simply of decline and fall.

The two main agents of continuity were the Eastern Roman (or Byzantine) Empire and the Christian church. The Byzantine Empire lasted until 1453, a thousand years longer than the Western Roman Empire, and preserved and transmitted much of ancient law, philosophy, and institutions. Missionaries and church officials spread Christianity within and far beyond the borders of the Roman Empire, transforming a small sect into the most important and wealthiest institution in Europe. The main agents of change in late antiquity were the barbarian groups migrating into the Roman Empire. They brought different social, political, and economic structures with them, but as they encountered Roman culture and became Christian, their own ways of doing things were also transformed.

The Byzantine Empire

How was the Byzantine Empire able to survive for so long, and what were its most important achievements?

Constantine had tried to maintain the unity of the Roman Empire, but during the fifth and sixth centuries the Western and Eastern halves drifted apart. From Constantinople, Eastern Roman emperors worked to hold the empire together and to reconquer at least some of the West from barbarian tribes. Justinian (r. 527–565) waged long wars against the Ostrogoths and temporarily regained Italy and North Africa, but the costs were high. Justinian's wars exhausted the resources of the state, destroyed Italy's economy, and killed a large part of Italy's population. Weakened, Italy fell easily to another Germanic tribe, the Lombards, shortly after Justinian's death. In the late sixth century, the territory of the Western Roman Empire came once again under Germanic sway.

However, the Roman Empire continued in the East. The Eastern Roman or Byzantine Empire (see Map 7.1) preserved the forms, institutions, and traditions of the old Roman Empire, and its people even called themselves Romans. Most important, however, is the role of Byzantium as preserver of the wisdom of the ancient world. Byzantium protected the intellectual heritage of Greco-Roman civilization and then passed it on to the rest of Europe.

Sources of Byzantine Strength

While the Western parts of the Roman Empire gradually succumbed to Germanic invaders, the Eastern Roman or Byzantine Empire survived waves of attacks. In 559 a force of Huns and Slavs reached the gates of Constantinople, and in 583 the Avars (AH-varz), a mounted Mongol people, also threatened the capital. Between 572 and 630 the Sasanid (suh-SAH-nid) Persians put pressure on the Byzantine

Empire, and only two years after the Persians were repelled, Arab forces began their own assaults (see Chapter 8).

Why didn't one or a combination of these enemies capture Constantinople as the Germans had taken Rome? First, the Byzantine Empire enjoyed strong military leadership. General Priskos (d. 612) skillfully led Byzantine armies to a decisive victory over the Avars in 601. Then, after a long war, the emperor Heraclius I (her-uh-KLY-uhs) (r. 610–641) crushed the Persians at Nineveh in Iraq. Second, the capital city was well fortified. Massive triple walls, built by Constantine and Theodosius II (408–450) and kept in good repair, protected Constantinople from sea invasion. Within the walls huge cisterns provided water, and vast gardens and grazing areas supplied vegetables and meat so that the defending people could hold out far longer than the besieging army. Attacking Constantinople by land posed greater geographical and logistical problems than a seventh- or eighth-century army could solve. The site was not absolutely impregnable—as the Venetians demonstrated in 1204 and the Ottoman Turks in 1453 (see pages 211 and 374)—but it was almost so. For centuries, the Byzantine Empire served as a bulwark for the West, protecting it against invasions from the East.

CHRONOLOGY

312	Constantine legalizes Christianity in Roman Empire
340–419	Life of Saint Jerome; creation of the Vulgate
354–430	Life of Saint Augustine
380	Theodosius makes Christianity official religion of Roman Empire
385–461	Life of Saint Patrick
481–511	Reign of Clovis
527–565	Reign of Justinian
529	*The Rule of Saint Benedict*
542–560	"Justinian plague"

MAP 7.1 The Byzantine Empire, ca. 600

The strategic position of Constantinople on the waterway between the Black Sea and the Mediterranean was clear to Constantine when he chose the city as the capital of the Eastern Roman Empire, and it was also clear to later rulers and military leaders. Byzantine territories in Italy were acquired in Emperor Justinian's sixth-century wars and were held for several centuries.

The Law Code of Justinian

Byzantine emperors organized and preserved Roman law, making a lasting contribution to the medieval and modern worlds. Roman law had developed from many sources—decisions by judges, edicts of the emperors, legislation passed by the senate, and the opinions of jurists expert in the theory and practice of law. By the fourth century, it had become a huge, bewildering mass, and its sheer bulk made it almost unusable.

Sweeping and systematic codification took place under the emperor Justinian. He appointed a committee of eminent jurists to sort through and organize the laws. The result was the *Code*, which distilled the legal genius of the Romans into a coherent whole, eliminated outmoded laws and contradictions, and clarified the law itself. Not content with the *Code*, Justinian set about bringing order to the equally huge body of Roman *jurisprudence* (**joor-is-PROOD-ins**), the science or philosophy of law.

During the second and third centuries, the foremost Roman jurists had expressed varied learned opinions on complex legal problems. To harmonize this body of knowledge, Justinian directed his jurists to clear up disputed points and to issue definitive rulings. Accordingly, in 533 his lawyers published the *Digest*, which codified Roman legal thought. Finally, Justinian's lawyers compiled a handbook of civil law, the *Institutes*. These three works—the *Code*, the *Digest*, and the *Institutes*—are the backbone of the *corpus juris civilis* (**KAWR-puhs JOOR-is si-VIL-is**), the "body of civil law," which is the foundation of law for nearly every modern European nation.

Byzantine Intellectual Life

The Byzantines prized education; because of them many masterpieces of ancient Greek literature have survived to influence the intellectual life of the modern world. The literature of the Byzantine Empire was predominately Greek, although Latin was long spoken by top politicians, scholars, and lawyers. Among the large reading public, history was a favorite subject.

Justinian and His Attendants

This mosaic detail is composed of thousands of tiny cubes of colored glass or stone called *tessarae,* which are set in plaster against a blazing golden background. Some attempt has been made at naturalistic portraiture. (Scala/Art Resource, NY)

The most remarkable Byzantine historian was Procopius (ca. 500–ca. 562), who left a rousing account praising Justinian's reconquest of North Africa and Italy. Proof that the wit and venom of ancient Greek and Roman writers lived on in the Byzantine era can be found in Procopius's *Secret History*, a vicious and uproarious attack on Justinian and his wife, the empress Theodora. (See the feature "Individuals in Society: Theodora of Constantinople.")

Although the Byzantines discovered little that was new in mathematics and geometry, they passed Greco-Roman learning on to the Arabs, who made remarkable advances with it. In science, they faithfully learned what the ancients had to teach but made advances only in terms of military applications. For example, the best-known Byzantine scientific discovery was an explosive compound known as "Greek fire" that was heated and propelled by a pump through a bronze tube. As the liquid jet left the tube, it was ignited—somewhat like a modern flamethrower. Greek fire saved Constantinople from Arab assault in 678. In mechanics Byzantine scientists improved and modified artillery and siege machinery.

The Byzantines devoted a great deal of attention to medicine, and the general level of medical competence was far higher in the Byzantine Empire than in western Europe. Yet their physicians could not cope with the terrible disease, often called the "Justinian plague," that swept through the Byzantine Empire and parts of western Europe between 542 and about 560. Probably originating in northwestern India and carried to the Mediterranean region by ships, the disease was similar to modern forms of the bubonic plague. Characterized by high fever, chills, delirium, and enlarged lymph nodes (the buboes that gave bubonic plague its name), or by inflammation of the lungs that caused hemorrhages of black blood, the Justinian plague carried off tens of thousands of people. The epidemic had profound political as well as social consequences. It weakened Justinian's military resources, thus hampering his efforts to restore unity to the Mediterranean world.

By the ninth or tenth century, most major Greek cities had hospitals for the care of the sick. The hospitals might be divided into wards for different illnesses, and hospital staff had surgeons, practitioners, and aides with specialized responsibilities. The imperial Byzantine government bore the costs of these medical facilities.

Section Review

- Germanic invaders overcame the western part of the Roman Empire but the East evaded capture through strong military leadership and a well-fortified capital in Constantinople.

- Emperor Justinian organized the Roman legal system through the *Code* (clarifying the law itself), the *Digest* (codifying Roman legal thought), and the *Institutes* (compiling civil law).

- Theodora, a former actress and dancer, married Justinian and became empress, using her influence to improve the legal status of women and to promote her religious interpretation of Christianity.

- Part villain and part heroine, Theodora manipulated those around her while improving the empire by establishing hospitals, orphanages, and churches.

- The Byzantines made few advances in mathematics and science, but valued education, history, literature, and medicine.

- Procopius was a remarkable historian whose work *Secret History* is a witty and scathing account of the reign of Justinian and Theodora.

The Growth of the Christian Church

What factors enabled the Christian church to expand and thrive?

As the Western Roman Empire disintegrated in the fourth and fifth centuries, the Christian church survived and grew, becoming the most important institution in Europe. The able administrators and highly creative thinkers of the church developed permanent institutions and complex philosophical concepts.

The Church and Its Leaders

Scriptural scholars tell us that the earliest use of the word *church* in the New Testament appears in Saint Paul's Letter to the Christians of Thessalonica (thes-uh-LON-ee-kuh) in northern Greece, written about 51 C.E. *Church* means assembly or congregation (in Greek, *ekklesia*); by *ekklesia* Paul meant the local community of Christian believers. In Paul's later letters the word refers to the entire Mediterranean-wide assembly of Jesus' followers. After the legalization of Christianity by the emperor Constantine (see page 128) and the growth of institutional offices and officials, the word *church* was sometimes applied to those officials—

Individuals in Society

Theodora of Constantinople

The most powerful woman in Byzantine history was the daughter of a bear trainer for the circus. Theodora (ca. 497–548) grew up in what her contemporaries regarded as an undignified and morally suspect atmosphere, and she worked as a dancer and burlesque actress, both dishonorable occupations in the Roman world. Despite her background, she caught the eye of Justinian, who was then a military leader and whose uncle (and adoptive father) Justin had himself risen from obscurity to become the emperor of the Byzantine Empire. Under Justinian's influence, Justin changed the law to allow an actress who had left her disreputable life to marry whom she liked, and Justinian and Theodora married in 525. When Justinian was proclaimed co-emperor with his uncle Justin on April 1, 527, Theodora received the rare title of *augusta*, empress. Thereafter her name was linked with Justinian's in the exercise of imperial power.

The empress Theodora shown with the halo, a symbol of power in Eastern art. (Scala/Art Resource, NY)

Most of our knowledge of Theodora's early life comes from the *Secret History*, a tell-all description of the vices of Justinian and his court, written by Procopius (proh-KOH-pee-uhs) (ca. 550), who was the official court historian and thus spent his days praising those same people. In the *Secret History*, he portrays Theodora and Justinian as demonic, greedy, and vicious, killing courtiers to steal their property. In scene after detailed scene, Procopius portrays Theodora as particularly evil, sexually insatiable, depraved, and cruel, a temptress who used sorcery to attract men, including the hapless Justinian.

In one of his official histories, *The History of the Wars of Justinian*, Procopius presents a very different Theodora. Riots between the supporters of two teams in chariot races—who formed associations somewhat like street gangs and somewhat like political parties—had turned deadly, and Justinian wavered in his handling of the per-

petrators. Both sides turned against the emperor, besieging the palace while Justinian was inside it. Shouting N-I-K-A (victory), the rioters swept through the city, burning and looting, and destroyed half of Constantinople. Justinian's counselors urged flight, but, according to Procopius, Theodora rose and declared:

> For one who has reigned, it is intolerable to be an exile. . . . If you wish, O Emperor, to save yourself, there is no difficulty: we have ample funds and there are the ships. Yet reflect whether, when you have once escaped to a place of security, you will not prefer death to safety. I agree with an old saying that the purple [that is, the color worn only by emperors] is a fair winding sheet to be buried in.

Justinian rallied, had the rioters driven into the hippodrome, and ordered between thirty and thirty-five thousand men and women executed. The revolt was crushed and Justinian's authority restored, an outcome approved by Procopius.

Other sources describe or suggest Theodora's influence on imperial policy. Justinian passed a number of laws that improved the legal status of women, such as allowing women to own property the same way that men could and to be guardians over their own children. He forbade the abandonment of unwanted infants, which happened more often to girls than to boys, as boys were valued more highly. Theodora presided at imperial receptions for Arab sheiks, Persian ambassadors, Germanic princesses from the West, and barbarian chieftains from southern Russia. When Justinian fell ill from the bubonic plague in 532, Theodora took over his duties, banning those who discussed his possible successor. Justinian is reputed to have consulted her every day about all aspects of state policy, including religious policy regarding the doctrinal disputes that continued throughout his reign. Theodora's favored interpretation of Christian doctrine about the nature of Christ was not accepted by the main body of theologians in Constantinople—nor by Justinian—but she urged protection of her fellow believers and in one case hid an aged scholar in the women's quarters of the palace for many years.

Theodora's influence over her husband and her power in the Byzantine state continued until she died, perhaps of cancer, twenty years before Justinian. Her influence may have even continued after death, for Justinian continued to pass reforms favoring women and, at the end of his life, accepted her interpretation of Christian doctrine. Institutions that she established, including hospitals, orphanages, houses for the rehabilitation of prostitutes, and churches, continued to be reminders of her charity and piety.

Theodora has been viewed as a symbol of the manipulation of beauty and cleverness to attain position and power, and also as a strong and capable co-ruler who held the empire together during riots, revolts, and deadly epidemics. Just as Procopius expressed both views, the debate continues today among writers of science fiction and fantasy as well as biographers and historians.

Questions for Analysis

1. How would you assess the complex legacy of Theodora?

2. Since the public and private views of Procopius are so different regarding the empress, should he be trusted at all as a historical source?

much as we use the terms *the college* or *the university* when referring to academic administrators.

In early Christian communities the local people elected their leaders, or bishops. Bishops were responsible for the community's goods and oversaw the distribution of those goods to the poor. They also were responsible for maintaining orthodox (established or correct) doctrine within the community and for preaching. Bishops alone could confirm believers in their faith and ordain men as priests.

The early Christian church benefited from the brilliant administrative abilities of some bishops. Bishop Ambrose, for example, the son of the Roman prefect of Gaul, was a trained lawyer and the governor of a province. He is typical of the Roman aristocrats who held high public office, were converted to Christianity, and subsequently became bishops. Such men later provided social continuity from Roman to Germanic rule. As bishop of Milan, Ambrose himself exercised responsibility in both the business and church affairs of northern Italy.

During the reign of Diocletian (284–305), the Roman Empire had been divided for administrative purposes into geographical units called dioceses. Gradually the church made use of this organizational structure. Christian bishops established their headquarters, or *sees*, in the urban centers of the old Roman dioceses. A bishop's jurisdiction extended throughout the diocese. The center of his authority was his cathedral (from the Latin *cathedra*, meaning "chair"). Thus, church leaders adapted the Roman imperial method of organization for ecclesiastical purposes.

The bishops of Rome—known as "popes," from the Latin word *papa*, meaning "father"—claimed to speak and act as the source of unity for all Christians. They based their claim to be the successors of Saint Peter and heirs to his authority as chief of the apostles on Jesus' words:

> You are Peter, and on this rock I will build my church, and the jaws of death shall not prevail against it. I will entrust to you the keys of the kingdom of heaven. Whatever you declare bound on earth shall be bound in heaven; whatever you declare loosed on earth shall be loosed in heaven.[1]

Petrine Doctrine The statement used by popes, bishops of Rome, based on Jesus' words, to substantiate their claim of being the successors of Saint Peter and heirs to his authority as chief of the apostles.

Theologians call this statement the **Petrine (PEE-tryne) Doctrine.**

After the capital and the emperor moved from Rome to Constantinople (see page 128), the bishop of Rome exercised considerable influence in the West because he had no real competitor there. He became known as the "Patriarch of the West." In the East, the bishops of Antioch, Alexandria, Jerusalem, and Constantinople, because of the special dignity of their sees, also gained the title of patriarch. Their jurisdictions extended over lands adjoining their sees; they consecrated bishops, investigated heresy, and heard judicial appeals.

In the fifth century the bishops of Rome began to stress their supremacy over other Christian communities and to urge other churches to appeal to Rome for the resolution of disputed doctrinal issues. While local churches often exercised their own authority and Rome was not yet as powerful as it would become, these arguments laid the groundwork for later appeals.

The Church and the Roman Emperors

The church benefited considerably from the emperors' support. Constantine had legalized the practice of Christianity in the empire in 312 and encouraged it throughout his reign. He freed the clergy from imperial taxation. At churchmen's request, he helped settle theological disputes and thus preserved doctrinal unity within the church. Constantine generously endowed the building of Christian churches, and one of his gifts—the Lateran (**LAT-er-uhn**) Palace in Rome—remained the official residence of the popes until the fourteenth century. Constantine also declared Sunday a public holiday, a day of rest for the service of God. Because of its favored position in the empire, Christianity slowly became the leading religion (see Map 7.2).

In the fourth century, theological disputes frequently and sharply divided the Christian community. Some disagreements had to do with the nature of Christ. For example, **Arianism** (**AIR-ree-uh-nizm**), which originated with Arius (ca. 250–336), a priest of Alexandria, held that Jesus was created by the will of the Father and thus was not co-eternal with the Father. Arius also reasoned that Jesus the Son must be inferior to God the Father because the Father was incapable of suffering and did not die. Orthodox theologians branded Arius's position a **heresy**—the denial of a basic doctrine of faith.

Arianism enjoyed such popularity and provoked such controversy that Constantine, to whom religious disagreement meant civil disorder, interceded. He summoned church leaders to a council in Nicaea (**neye-SEE-uh**) in Asia Minor and presided over it personally. The council produced the Nicene (**neye-SEEN**) Creed, which defined the orthodox position that Christ is "eternally begotten of

Arianism A theological belief that originated with Arius, a priest of Alexandria, denying that Christ was divine and co-eternal with God the Father.

heresy The denial of a basic doctrine of faith.

MAP 7.2 The Spread of Christianity

Originating in Judaea, the southern part of modern Israel and Jordan, Christianity first spread throughout the Roman world and then beyond it in all directions.

the Father" and of the same substance as the Father. Arius and those who refused to accept the creed were banished, the first case of civil punishment for heresy. This participation of the emperor in a theological dispute within the church paved the way for later emperors to do the same.

In 380 the emperor Theodosius made Christianity the official religion of the empire. Theodosius stripped Roman pagan temples of statues, made the practice of the old Roman state religion a treasonable offense, and persecuted Christians who dissented from orthodox doctrine. Most significant, he allowed the church to establish its own courts and to use its own body of law, called "canon law." These courts, not the Roman government, had jurisdiction over the clergy and ecclesiastical disputes. At the death of Theodosius, the Christian church was considerably independent of the Roman state. The foundation for later growth in church power had been laid.

Later Byzantine emperors continued the pattern of active involvement in church affairs. They appointed the highest officials of the church hierarchy and presided over ecumenical councils, where bishops would gather to make decisions on matters of faith and practice. The emperors also controlled some of the material resources of the church—land, rents, and indebted peasants. On the other hand, the emperors had minimal involvement in church services and rarely tried to impose their views in theological disputes. Greek churchmen vigorously defended the church's independence; some even asserted the superiority of the bishop's authority over the emperor's; and the church possessed such enormous economic wealth and influence over the population that it could block government decisions. The **Orthodox church,** the name generally given to the Eastern Christian church, was less independent of secular control than the Western Christian church, but it was not simply a branch of the Byzantine state.

Orthodox church Eastern orthodox church in the Byzantine empire.

The Development of Christian Monasticism

Christianity began and spread as a city religion. Since the first century, however, some especially pious Christians had felt that the only alternative to the decadence of urban life was complete separation from the world. All-consuming pursuit of material things, sexual promiscuity, and general political corruption disgusted them. They believed that the Christian life as set forth in the Gospel could not be lived in the midst of such immorality. They rejected the values of Roman society and were the first real nonconformists in the church.

This desire to withdraw from ordinary life led to the development of the monastic life. Some scholars believe that the monastic life of extreme material sacrifice appealed to Christians who wanted to make a total response to Christ's teachings; the monks became the new martyrs. Saint Anthony of Egypt (251?–356), the earliest monk for whom there is concrete evidence and the man later considered the father of monasticism, went to Alexandria during the persecutions of the Emperor Diocletian in the hope of gaining martyrdom. Christians believed that monks like the martyrs before them, could speak to God and that their prayers had special influence.

Monasticism began in Egypt in the third century. At first individuals and small groups withdrew from cities and from organized society to seek God through prayer in desert or mountain caves and shelters. Gradually large colonies of monks gathered in the deserts of Upper Egypt. These monks were called hermits, from the Greek word *eremos,* meaning "desert." Many devout women also were attracted to this **eremitical** (**er-uh-MIT-ik-ul**) type of monasticism.

eremitical A form of monasticism that began in Egypt in the third century where individuals and small groups withdrew from cities and organized society to seek God through prayer. The people who lived in caves and sought shelter in the desert and mountains were called hermits, from the Greek word *eremos.*

The Egyptian ascetic Pachomius (**puh-KOH-mee-uhs**) (290–346?) drew thousands of men and women to the monastic life at Tabennisi on the Upper Nile. There were too many for them to live as hermits, and Pachomius organized communities of men and women, creating a second type of monasticism, known as **coenobitic** (**seh-nuh-BIT-ik**) (communal). Saint Basil (329?–379), the scholarly bishop from Asia Minor, encouraged coenobitic monasticism, as he and the church hierarchy thought that communal living provided an environment for training the aspirant in the virtues of charity, poverty, and freedom from self-deception.

coenobitic monasticism Communal living in monasteries, encouraged by Saint Basil and the church because it provided an environment for training the aspirant in the virtues of charity, poverty, and freedom from self-deception.

Western and Eastern Monasticism

In the fourth, fifth, and sixth centuries, information about Egyptian monasticism came to the West, and both men and women sought the monastic life. Because of the difficulties and dangers of living alone in the forests of northern Europe, the eremitical form of monasticism did not take root. Most of the monasticism that developed in Gaul, Italy, Spain, England, and Ireland was coenobitic.

In 529 Benedict of Nursia (480–543), who had experimented with both the eremitical and the communal forms of monastic life, wrote a brief set of regulations for the monks who had gathered around him at Monte Cassino between Rome and Naples. Benedict's guide for monastic life, known as the *Rule of Saint Benedict*, slowly replaced all others. *The Rule of Saint Benedict* came to influence all forms of organized religious life in the Roman church. Men and women who lived in monastic houses all followed sets of rules, first those of Benedict and later those written by other individuals, and because of this came to be called **regular clergy**, from the Latin word *regulus* (rule). Priests and bishops who staffed churches in which people worshiped and who were not cut off from the world were called **secular clergy**. (According to official church doctrine, women are not members of the clergy, but this distinction was not clear to most medieval people.)

regular clergy Men and women who lived in monastic houses and followed sets of rules, first those of Benedict and later those written by other individuals.

secular clergy Priests and bishops who staffed churches where people worshiped and were not cut off from the world.

The Rule of Saint Benedict offered a simple code for ordinary men. It outlined a monastic life of regularity, discipline, and moderation in an atmosphere of silence. Each monk had ample food and adequate sleep. The monk spent part of each day in formal prayer, which Benedict called the *Opus Dei* (Work of God) and Christians later termed the *divine office*, the public prayer of the church. This consisted of chanting psalms and other prayers from the Bible in the part of the monastery church called the "choir." The rest of the day was passed in manual labor, study, and private prayer.

Why did the Benedictine form of monasticism eventually replace other forms of Western monasticism? The monastic life as conceived by Saint Benedict struck a balance between asceticism and activity. It thus provided opportunities for men of entirely different abilities and talents—from mechanics to gardeners to literary scholars. The Benedictine form of religious life also proved congenial to women. Five miles from Monte Cassino at Plombariola, Benedict's twin sister Scholastica (**skoh-LAS-tih-kuh**) (480–543) adapted the *Rule* for use by her community of nuns.

Benedictine monasticism also succeeded partly because it was so materially successful. In the seventh and eighth centuries monasteries pushed back forests and wastelands, drained swamps, and experimented with crop rotation. Benedictine houses made a significant contribution to the agricultural development of Europe. The communal nature of their organization, whereby property was held in common and profits were pooled and reinvested, made this contribution possible.

Finally, monasteries conducted schools for local young people. Some students learned about prescriptions and herbal remedies and went on to provide medical

Section Review

- Early Christian communities elected their leaders, or bishops, who oversaw the doctrine, preaching, and other community functions of their jurisdiction (diocese).

- The bishops of Rome, known as "popes," exercised more and more power, claiming to speak and act as the unitary source of authority for all Christians, while enjoying the benefits of the emperor's support.

- Constantine set up and presided over the council of Nicaea, producing the Nicene Creed, which declared Jesus to be divine and settled a dispute between two Christian factions by banishing anyone who refused to accept it.

- Those who wanted to separate themselves from perceived corruption in society chose one of the two monastic lifestyles: eremitical (isolated) or coenobitic (communal).

- The monk Benedict of Nursia wrote a set of regulations for monks that became favored for both monks (men) and nuns (women) because of its balance between asceticism and activity.

- Monasteries were successful in both the East and West but only the Western monasteries provided schools with educational training for local young people.

treatment in their localities. A few copied manuscripts and wrote books. Local and royal governments drew on the services of the literate men and able administrators the monasteries produced. This was not what Saint Benedict had intended, but perhaps the effectiveness of the institution he designed made it inevitable.

Monasticism in the Greek Orthodox world differed in fundamental ways from the monasticism that evolved in western Europe. First, while *The Rule of Saint Benedict* gradually became the universal guide for all western European monasteries, each individual house in the Byzantine world developed its own set of rules for organization and behavior, including rules about diet, clothing, liturgical functions, commemorative services for benefactors, the training of monks and nuns, and the election of officials. Second, education never became a central feature of the Greek houses. Monks and nuns had to be literate to perform the services of the choir, but no monastery assumed responsibility for the general training of the local young.

There were also similarities between Western and Eastern monasticism. As in the West, Eastern monasteries became wealthy, with fields, pastures, livestock, and buildings. Since bishops and patriarchs of the Greek church were recruited only from the monasteries, Greek houses also exercised cultural influence.

Christian Ideas and Practices

How did Christian thinkers adapt Greco-Roman ideas to Christian theology?

The evolution of Christianity was not simply a matter of institutions such as the papacy and monasteries, but also of ideas. Initially, Christians had believed that the end of the world was near and that they should dissociate themselves from the "filth" of Roman culture. The church father Tertullian (**ter-TUHL-ee-uhn**) (ca. 160–220) claimed: "We have no need for curiosity since Jesus Christ, nor for inquiry since the gospel." Gradually, however, Christians developed a culture of ideas that drew upon classical influences. The distinguished theologian Saint Jerome (340–419) translated the Old and New Testaments from Hebrew and Greek into vernacular Latin; his edition is known as the "Vulgate." The synthesis of Greco-Roman and Christian ideas found greatest expression in the writings of Saint Augustine, whose work had a profound influence on Christian theology.

Christian Notions of Gender and Sexuality

Christian attitudes toward gender and sexuality provide a good example of the ways early Christians both adopted and adapted the views of their contemporary world. In his plan of salvation, Jesus considered women the equal of men. He attributed no disreputable qualities to women and did not refer to them as inferior creatures. On the contrary, women were among his earliest and most faithful converts. He discussed his mission with them (John 4:21–25), and the first persons to whom he revealed himself after his resurrection were women (Matthew 28:9–10).

Women took an active role in the spread of Christianity, preaching, acting as missionaries, being martyred alongside men, and perhaps even baptizing believers. Because early Christians believed that the Second Coming of Christ was imminent, they devoted their energies to their new spiritual family of co-believers. Early Christians often met in people's homes and called one another brother and sister, a metaphorical use of family terms that was new to the Roman Empire.

Some women embraced the ideal of virginity and either singly or in monastic communities declared themselves "virgins in the service of Christ." All this made Christianity seem dangerous to many Romans, especially when becoming Christian actually led some young people to avoid marriage, which was viewed by Romans as the foundation of society and the proper patriarchal order.

Not all Christian teachings about gender were radical, however. In the first century c.e. male church leaders began to place restrictions on female believers. Paul and later writers forbade women to preach, and women were gradually excluded from holding official positions in Christianity other than in women's monasteries. In so limiting the activities of female believers Christianity was following classical Mediterranean culture, just as it patterned its official hierarchy after that of the Roman Empire.

Christian teachings about sexuality also built on classical culture. Many early church leaders, who are often called the church fathers, renounced marriage and sought to live chaste lives not only because they expected the Second Coming imminently, but also because they accepted the hostility toward the body that derived from certain strains of Hellenistic philosophy. Just as spirit was superior to matter, the mind was superior to the body. Though God had clearly sanctioned marriage, celibacy was the highest good. This emphasis on self-denial led to a strong streak of misogyny (hatred of women) in their writings, for they saw women and female sexuality as the chief obstacles to their preferred existence. They also saw intercourse as little more than animal lust, the triumph of the inferior body over the superior mind. Same-sex relations—which were generally acceptable in the Greco-Roman world, especially if they were between socially unequal individuals—were evil. The church fathers' misogyny and hostility toward sexuality had a greater influence on the formation of later attitudes than did the relatively egalitarian actions and words of Jesus.

The Marys at Jesus' Tomb

This late-fourth-century ivory panel tells the story of Mary Magdalene and another Mary who went to Jesus' tomb to anoint the body (Matthew 28:1–7). At the top, guards collapse when an angel descends from Heaven, and at the bottom, the Marys listen to the angel telling them that Jesus had risen. Immediately after this, according to Matthew's Gospel, Jesus appears to the women. Here the artist uses Roman artistic styles to convey Christian subject matter, an example of the assimilation of classical form and Christian teaching. (Castello Sforzesco/Scala/Art Resource, NY)

Saint Augustine on Human Nature, Will, and Sin

The most influential church father in the West was Saint Augustine of Hippo (354–430). Saint Augustine was born into an urban family in what is now Algeria in North Africa. His father, a minor civil servant, was a pagan; his mother, Monica, a devout Christian. It was not until adulthood that he converted to his mother's religion. As bishop of the city of Hippo Regius, he was a renowned preacher, a vigorous defender of orthodox Christianity, and the author of more than ninety-three books and treatises.

Augustine's autobiography, *The Confessions*, is a literary masterpiece. Written in the rhetorical style and language of late Roman antiquity, it marks the synthesis of Greco-Roman forms and Christian thought. *The Confessions* describes Augustine's moral struggle, the conflict between his spiritual aspirations and his sensual self. Many Greek and Roman philosophers had taught that knowledge and virtue are the same: a person who knows what is right will do what is right. Augustine rejected this idea. People do not always act on the basis of rational knowledge.

sacraments Certain rituals defined by the church in which God bestows benefits on the believer through grace.

Section Review

- Christians at first thought the end of the world was near so they should separate themselves from Roman culture, but gradually they developed a culture of ideas that included classical influences.

- Initially, both men and women played important roles, with women preaching and acting as missionaries, but in the first century C.E. male leaders, following classical culture, began to restrict women's participation in official positions.

- Christian teachings on sexuality also adopted ideas from certain strains of Hellenistic philosophy, prescribing celibacy and self-denial as the highest good, leading to misogyny and hostility toward women and same-sex relations.

- Augustine's ideas about sin (the result of will) and grace (the result of God, not humans) became the foundation for Western Christian theology.

- Augustine argued in his work *City of God* that the state is the result of people's will to sin and that the church is responsible for the salvation of all, leading to the church's political view that it was superior to secular authority.

For example, Augustine regarded a life of chastity as the best possible life even before he became a Christian. As he notes in *The Confessions*, as a young man he prayed to God for "chastity and continency" and added "but not yet." His education had not made his will strong enough to avoid temptation; that would come only through God's power and grace.

Augustine's ideas on sin, grace, and redemption became the foundation of all subsequent Western Christian theology, Protestant as well as Catholic. He wrote that the basic or dynamic force in any individual is the will. When Adam ate the fruit forbidden by God in the Garden of Eden (Genesis 3:6), he committed the "original sin" and corrupted the will. Adam's sin was not simply his own, but was passed on to all later humans through sexual intercourse; even infants were tainted. Augustine viewed sexual desire as the result of Adam and Eve's disobedience, linking sexuality even more clearly with sin than had earlier church fathers. Because Adam disobeyed God, all human beings have an innate tendency to sin: their will is weak. But according to Augustine, God restores the strength of the will through grace, which is transmitted in certain rituals that the church defined as **sacraments.** Grace results from God's decisions, not from any merit on the part of the individual.

When the Visigothic (**viz-ee-GOTH-ic**) chieftain Alaric (**AL-er-ik**) conquered Rome in 410, horrified pagans blamed the disaster on the Christians. In response, Augustine wrote *City of God*. This original work contrasts Christianity with the secular society in which it existed. According to Augustine, history is the account of God acting in time. Human history reveals that there are two kinds of people: those who live the life of the flesh in the City of Babylon and those who live the life of the spirit in the City of God. The former will endure eternal hellfire; the latter will enjoy eternal bliss.

Augustine maintained that states came into existence as the result of people's inclination to sin. The state provides the peace, justice, and order that Christians need in order to pursue their pilgrimage to the City of God. The church, while not the equivalent of the City of God, is responsible for the salvation of all—including Christian rulers. Churches later used Augustine's theory to argue their superiority over secular authority. This remained the dominant political theory until the late thirteenth century.

Christian Missionaries and Conversion

What techniques did missionaries develop to convert barbarian peoples to Christianity?

The word *catholic* derives from a Greek word meaning "general," "universal," or "worldwide." Christ had said that his teaching was for all peoples, and Christians sought to make their faith catholic—that is, believed everywhere. This could be accomplished only through missionary activity. As Saint Paul had written to the Christian community at Colossae (**kuh-LOS-ee**) in Asia Minor, "there is no room for distinction between Greek and Jew, between the circumcised or the uncircumcised, or between barbarian or Scythian (**SITH-ee-uhn**), slave and free man. There is only Christ; he is everything and he is in everything."[2] Paul urged Christians to bring the "good news" of Christ to all peoples. The Mediterranean served as the highway over which Christianity spread to the cities of the Roman Empire. From there missionaries took Christian teachings to the countryside, and then to areas beyond the borders of the empire.

Missionaries on the Continent

Among the Germanic tribes of western Europe, religion was not a private or individual matter. It was a social affair, and the religion of the chieftain or king determined the religion of the people. Thus missionaries concentrated their initial efforts not on the people, but on kings or tribal chieftains. According to custom, kings negotiated with all foreign powers, including the gods. Because Christian missionaries represented a "foreign" power (the Christian God), the king dealt with them. Germanic kings accepted Christianity because they believed that the Christian God was more powerful than pagan gods and that the Christian God would deliver victory in battle, or because Christianity taught obedience to (kingly) authority, or because Christian priests possessed knowledge and a charisma that could be associated with kingly power. Kings who converted, such as Ethelbert of Kent and the Frankish chieftain Clovis (**KLOH-vis**), sometimes had Christian wives. Conversion may also have indicated that barbarian kings wanted to enjoy the cultural advantages that Christianity brought, such as literate assistants and an ideological basis for their rule.

In eastern Europe, missionaries traveled far beyond the boundaries of the Byzantine Empire. In 863 the emperor Michael III sent the brothers Cyril (826–869) and Methodius (815–885) (**muh-THOH-dee-uhs**) to preach Christianity in Moravia (a region of the modern central Czech Republic). Other missionaries succeeded in converting the Russians in the tenth century. Cyril invented a Slavic alphabet using Greek characters; this script, called the "Cyrillic (**sih-RIL-ik**) alphabet," is still in use today. Cyrillic script made possible the birth of Russian literature. Similarly, Byzantine art and architecture became the basis and inspiration of Russian forms. The Byzantines were so successful that the Russians claimed to be the successors of the Byzantine Empire. For a time Moscow was even known as the "Third Rome" (the second Rome being Constantinople).

Missionaries in the British Isles

Tradition identifies the conversion of the Celts of Ireland with Saint Patrick (ca. 385–461). After a vision urged him to Christianize Ireland, Patrick studied in Gaul and was consecrated a bishop in 432. He returned to Ireland, where he converted the Irish tribe by tribe, first baptizing the king. By the time of Patrick's death, the majority of the Irish people had received Christian baptism. In his missionary work, Patrick had the strong support of Bridget of Kildare (**kil-DAIR**) (ca. 450–ca. 528), daughter of a wealthy chieftain. Bridget defied parental pressure to marry and became a nun. She and the other nuns at Kildare instructed relatives and friends in basic Christian doctrine, made religious vestments for churches, copied books, taught children, and above all set a religious example by their lives of prayer. In Ireland and later in continental Europe, women shared in the process of conversion.

The Christianization of the English began in 597, when Pope Gregory I (590–604) sent a delegation of monks under the Roman Augustine to Britain. Augustine's approach, like Patrick's, was to concentrate on converting the king. When he succeeded in converting Ethelbert, king of Kent, the baptism of Ethelbert's people took place as a matter of course. Augustine established his headquarters, or see, at Canterbury, the capital of Kent.

Ardagh Silver Chalice

This chalice, crafted about 800 C.E. and used for wine in Christian ceremonies, formed part of the treasure of Ardagh Cathedral in County Limerick, Ireland. Made of several types of metal, it is decorated with Celtic patterns in the same way as Irish manuscripts from this era. Christianity was widespread in Ireland long before anywhere else in northern Europe, and Celtic traditions and practices differed significantly from those of Rome. (National Museum of Ireland)

In the course of the seventh century, two Christian forces competed for the conversion of the pagan Anglo-Saxons: Roman-oriented missionaries traveling north from Canterbury, and Celtic monks from Ireland and northwestern Britain. The Roman and Celtic church organization, types of monastic life, and methods of arriving at the date of the central feast of the Christian calendar (Easter) differed completely. Through the influence of King Oswiu of Northumbria (nawr-THUHM-bree-uh) and the energetic abbess Hilda of Whitby, the Synod (ecclesiastical council) held at Whitby in 664 opted to follow the Roman practices. The conversion of the English and the close attachment of the English church to Rome had far-reaching consequences because Britain later served as a base for the full-scale Christianization of the continent (see Map 7.2).

Conversion and Assimilation

Between the fifth and tenth centuries, the great majority of peoples living on the European continent and the nearby islands were baptized as Christians. When a ruler marched his people to the waters of baptism, though, the work of Christianization had only begun. Baptism meant either sprinkling the head or immersing the body in water. Conversion meant awareness and acceptance of the beliefs of Christianity, including those that seemed strange or radical, such as "love your enemies" or "do good to those that hate you."

How did missionaries and priests get masses of pagan and illiterate peoples to understand and live by Christian ideals and teachings? They did so through preaching, assimilation, and the penitential system. Preaching aimed at presenting the basic teachings of Christianity and strengthening the newly baptized in their faith through stories about the lives of Christ and the saints. But deeply ingrained pagan customs and practices could not be stamped out by words alone or even by imperial edicts. Christian missionaries often pursued a policy of assimila-

Procession to a New Church

In this sixth-century ivory carving, two men in a wagon, accompanied by a procession of people holding candles, carry a relic casket to a church under construction. Workers are putting tiles on the church roof. New churches often received holy items when they were dedicated, and processions were common ways in which people expressed community devotion. (Cathedral Treasury, Trier. Photo: Ann Muenchow)

tion, easing the conversion of pagan men and women by stressing similarities between their customs and beliefs and those of Christianity. In the same way that classically trained scholars such as Jerome and Augustine blended Greco-Roman and Christian ideas, missionaries and converts mixed pagan ideas and practices with Christian ones. Bogs and lakes sacred to Germanic gods became associated with saints, as did various aspects of ordinary life, such as traveling, planting crops, and worrying about a sick child. Aspects of existing mid-winter celebrations, which often centered on the return of the sun as the days became longer, were incorporated into celebrations of Christmas. Spring rituals involving eggs and rabbits (both symbols of fertility) were added to Easter.

Also instrumental in converting pagans was the rite of reconciliation in which the sinner was able to receive God's forgiveness. The penitent knelt individually before the priest, who questioned the penitent about the sins he or she might have committed. A penance such as fasting on bread and water for a period of time or saying specific prayers was imposed as medicine for the soul. The priest and penitent were guided by manuals known as **penitentials** (**pen-uh-TENT-shuls**), which included lists of sins and the appropriate penance. Penitentials gave pagans a sense of expected behavior. The penitential system also encouraged the private examination of conscience and offered relief from the burden of sinful deeds.

Most religious observances continued to be community matters, however, as they had been in the ancient world. People joined with family members, friends, and neighbors to celebrate baptisms and funerals, presided over by a priest. They prayed to saints or to the Virgin Mary to intercede with God, or they simply asked the saints for protection and blessing. The entire village participated in processions marking saints' days or points in the agricultural year, often carrying images of saints or their **relics**—bones, articles of clothing, or other objects associated with the life of a saint—around the houses and fields.

penitentials Manuals for the examination of conscience.

relics Bones, articles of clothing, or other objects associated with the life of a saint.

Section Review

- St. Paul urged Christians to make their faith Catholic, meaning "universal" or "worldwide."

- Christian missionaries spread their faith throughout the Roman Empire and beyond.

- In western Europe missionaries gained influence by converting leaders; in eastern Europe Christianity spread to Moravia and Russia, bringing with it the Cyrillic alphabet and inspiring Russian literature.

- Saint Patrick brought Christianity to Ireland while the nun Bridget of Kildare and other women worked to spread it there.

- Roman and Celtic church organization differed in types of monastic life and dates of the Christian calendar, but after an ecclesiastical council in 664, the British followed the Roman practices, tying the English church to Rome.

- Christian missionaries accomplished conversion of pagans by preaching and by assimilating existing pagan customs.

- The rite of reconciliation forgave individual sins through penance and confession to a priest, yet religion continued to be mostly a community matter.

Migrating Peoples

What were some of the causes of the barbarian migrations and how did they affect the regions of Europe?

The migration of peoples from one area to another has been a dominant and continuing feature of Western history. Mass movements of Europeans occurred in the fourth through sixth centuries, in the ninth and tenth centuries, and in the twelfth and thirteenth centuries. From the sixteenth century to the present, such movements have been almost continuous, involving not just the European continent but the entire world. The causes of early migrations varied and are not thoroughly understood by scholars. But there is no question that the migrations profoundly affected both the regions to which peoples moved and the ones they left behind.

Celts, Germans, and Huns

In surveying the world around them, the ancient Greeks often conceptualized things in dichotomies, or sets of opposites: light/dark, hot/cold, wet/dry, mind/body, male/female, and so on. One of their key dichotomies was Greek/non-Greek, and the Greeks coined the word *barbaros* for those whose native language was not Greek, because they seemed to the Greeks to be speaking nonsense syllables—bar, bar, bar. ("Bar-bar" is the Greek equivalent to "blah-blah" or "yada-yada.") *Barbaros* originally meant simply not speaking Greek, but gradually it also implied unruly, savage, and more primitive than the advanced civilization of Greece. The word brought this meaning with it when it came into Latin and other European languages, with the Romans referring to those who lived beyond the northeastern boundary of Roman territory as **barbarians.** Migrating groups that the Romans labeled as barbarians had pressed along the Rhine-Danube frontier of the Roman Empire since about 150 C.E. (see page 109). In the third and fourth centuries, increasing pressures on the frontiers from the east and north placed greater demands on Roman military manpower, which plague and a declining birthrate had reduced. Therefore, Roman generals recruited barbarian refugees and tribes allied with the Romans to serve in the Roman army, and some rose to the highest ranks.

As Julius Caesar advanced through Gaul between 58 and 50 B.C.E. (see page 102), the largest barbarian groups he encountered were Celts (whom the Romans called Gauls) and Germans. Modern historians have tended to use the terms *German* and *Celt* in a racial sense, but recent research stresses that *Celt* and *German* are linguistic terms, a Celt being a person who spoke a Celtic language, an ancestor of the modern Gaelic or Breton language, and a German one who spoke a Germanic language, an ancestor of modern German, Dutch, Danish, Swedish, or Norwegian.

Celts and Germans were similar to one another in many ways. In the first century C.E., the Celts lived east of the Rhine River in an area bounded by the Main Valley and extending westward to the Somme (**sawm**) River. Germans were more numerous along the North and Baltic Seas. Both Germans and Celts used wheeled plows and a three-field system of crop rotation. Before the introduction of Christianity, both Celtic and Germanic peoples were polytheistic, with hundreds of gods and goddesses with specialized functions whose celebrations were often linked to points in the yearly agricultural cycle. Worship was often outdoors at sacred springs, groves, or lakes.

barbarians A name given by the Romans to all peoples living outside the frontiers of the Roman Empire (except the Persians).

Vandal Landowner

In this mosaic, a Vandal landowner rides out from his Roman-style house. His clothing—Roman short tunic, cloak, and sandals—reflects the way some Celtic and Germanic tribes accepted Roman lifestyles, though his beard is more typical of barbarian men's fashion.
(Courtesy of the Trustees of the British Museum)

The Celts had developed iron manufacturing, using shaft furnaces as sophisticated as those of the Romans to produce iron swords and spears. Celtic priests, called druids (DROO-idz), had legal and educational as well as religious functions, orally passing down laws and traditions from generation to generation. Bards singing poems and ballads also passed down stories of heroes and gods, which were written down much later. Celtic peoples conquered by the Romans often assimilated to Roman ways, adapting the Latin language and other aspects of Roman culture. By the fourth century C.E., under pressure from Germanic groups, the Celts had moved westward, settling in Brittany (modern northwestern France) and throughout the British Isles (England, Wales, Scotland, and Ireland). The Picts of Scotland as well as the Welsh, Britons, and Irish were peoples of Celtic descent. (See Map 7.3.)

MAPPING THE PAST

MAP 7.3   The Barbarian Migrations

This map shows the migrations of various barbarian groups in late antiquity and can be used to answer the following questions: **[1]** The map has no political boundaries. What does this suggest about the impact of barbarian migrations on political structures? **[2]** Human migration is caused by a combination of push factors (circumstances that lead people to leave a place) and pull factors (things that attract people to a new location). Based on the information in this and earlier chapters, what push and pull factors might have shaped the migration patterns you see on the map? **[3]** The movements of barbarian peoples used to be labeled "invasions" and are now usually described as "migrations." How do the dates on the map support the newer understanding of these movements?

The migrations of the Germanic peoples were important in the political and social transformations of late antiquity. Many modern scholars have tried to explain who the Germans were and why they migrated. The present consensus, based on the study of linguistic and archaeological evidence, is that there was not one but rather many Germanic peoples with very different cultural traditions. The largest Germanic tribe, the Goths, was a polyethnic group of about one hundred thousand people, including perhaps fifteen thousand to twenty thousand warriors. The tribe was supplemented by slaves, who, because of their desperate situation under Roman rule, joined the Goths during their migrations.[3]

Why did the Germans migrate? Like the Celts, in part they were pushed by groups living farther eastward, especially by the Huns from central Asia in the fourth and fifth centuries. In part, they were searching for more regular supplies of food, better farmland, and a warmer climate. Conflicts within and among Germanic groups also led to war and disruption, which motivated groups to move. Franks fought Alemanni (**al-uh-MAN-ahy**) in Gaul; Visigoths fought Vandals in the Iberian Peninsula and across North Africa; and Angles and Saxons fought Celtic-speaking Britons in England.

All these factors can be seen in the movement of the Visigoths, one of the Germanic tribes, from an area north of the Black Sea southeastward into the Roman Empire. Pressured by defeat in battle, starvation, and the movement of the Huns, the Visigoths petitioned the emperor Valens to admit them to the empire. Seeing in the hordes of warriors the solution to his manpower problem, Valens agreed. Once the Visigoths were inside the empire, Roman authorities exploited their hunger by forcing them to sell their own people as slaves in exchange for dog flesh: "the going rate was one dog for one Goth." Still, the Visigoths sought peace. Fritigern offered himself as a friend and ally of Rome in exchange for the province of Thrace—land, crops, and livestock. Confident of victory over a considerably smaller army, Valens and his council chose to battle the Visigoths and lost.

Alaric I's invasion of Italy and sack of Rome in 410 represents the culmination of hostility between the Visigoths and the Romans. The Goths burned and looted the city for three days, which caused many Romans to wonder whether God had deserted them. This led the imperial government to pull its troops from the British Isles and many areas north of the Alps, leaving these northern areas more vulnerable and open to migrating groups. A year later Alaric died, and his successor led his people into southwestern Gaul.[4] Establishing their headquarters at Toulouse, they exercised a weak domination over Spain until a Muslim victory at Guadalete in 711 ended Visigothic rule.

One significant factor in Germanic migration was pressure from nomadic steppe peoples from central Asia. This included the Alans, Avars, Bulghars, Khazars, and most prominently the Huns, who attacked the Black Sea area and the Eastern Roman Empire beginning in the fourth century. Under the leadership of their warrior-king Attila, the Huns swept into central Europe in 451, attacking Roman settlements in the Balkans and Germanic settlements along the Danube and Rhine Rivers. After Attila turned his army southward and crossed the Alps into Italy, a papal delegation, including Pope Leo I himself, asked him not to attack Rome. Though papal diplomacy was later credited with stopping the advance of the Huns, a plague that spread among Hunnic troops and their dwindling food supplies were probably much more important. The Huns retreated from Italy, and within a year Attila was dead. Later leaders were not as effective, and the Huns were never again an important factor in European history. Their conquests had slowed down the movements of various Germanic groups, however, allowing barbarian peoples to absorb more of Roman culture as they picked the Western Roman Empire apart.

Germanic Kingdoms

Between 450 and 565, the Germans established a number of kingdoms, but none—other than the Frankish kingdom—lasted very long. The Germanic kingdoms did not have definite geographical boundaries, and their locations are approximate. The Vandals, whose destructive ways are commemorated in the word *vandal*, settled in North Africa. In northern and western Europe in the sixth century, the Burgundians (**ber-GUHN-dee-uhns**) ruled over lands roughly circumscribed by the old Roman army camps at Lyons, Besançon (**buh-zahn-SAWN**), Geneva, and Autun.

In northern Italy the Ostrogothic king Theodoric (r. 471–526) established his residence at Ravenna and gradually won control of all Italy, Sicily, and the territory north and east of the upper Adriatic. Although attached to the customs of his people, Theodoric pursued a policy of assimilation between Germans and Romans. He maintained close relations with the emperor at Constantinople and attracted able scholars such as Cassiodorus (**kas-ee-uh-DAWR-uhs**) (see page 212) to his administration. Theodoric's accomplishments were significant, but his administration fell apart after his death.

The kingdom established by the Franks in the sixth century, in spite of later civil wars, proved to be the most powerful and enduring of all the Germanic kingdoms. In the fourth and fifth centuries, they settled within the empire and allied with the Romans, some attaining high military and civil positions. In the sixth century one group, the Salian (**SAY-lee-uhn**) Franks, issued a law code called the **Salic** (**SAL-ik**) **Law,** the earliest description of Germanic customs. Chlodio (fifth century) is the first member of the Frankish dynasty for whom evidence survives. According to legend, Chlodio's wife went swimming, encountered a sea monster, and conceived Merowig. The Franks believed that Merowig, a man of supernatural origins, founded their ruling dynasty, which was thus called **Merovingian** (**mer-uh-VIN-jee-uhn**).

The reign of Clovis (ca. 481–511) marks the decisive period in the development of the Franks as a unified people. Through military campaigns, Clovis acquired the central provinces of Roman Gaul. Clovis's conversion to Christianity also brought him the crucial support of the papacy and of the bishops of Gaul. (See the feature "Listening to the Past: The Conversion of Clovis" on pages 160–161.) The next two centuries witnessed the steady assimilation of Franks and Gallo-Romans, as many Franks adopted the Latin language and Roman ways, and Gallo-Romans copied Frankish customs and Frankish personal names. These centuries also saw Frankish acquisition of the Burgundian kingdom and of territory held by the Goths in Provence.[5]

Salic Law A law code issued by Salian Franks that provides us with the earliest description of Germanic customs.

Merovingian The Frankish dynasty named after its founder, Merowig, a man of mythical origins.

Anglo-Saxon England

The island of Britain was populated by various Celtic-speaking tribes when it was conquered by Rome during the reign of Claudius. During the first four centuries C.E., it shared fully in the life of the Roman Empire. Towns were planned in the Roman fashion, with temples, public baths, theaters, and amphitheaters. In the countryside large manors controlled the surrounding lands. Roman merchants brought Eastern luxury goods and Eastern religions—including Christianity—into Britain. The Romans suppressed the Celtic chieftains, and a military aristocracy governed. In the course of the second and third centuries, many Celts assimilated to Roman culture, becoming Roman citizens and joining the Roman army.

When imperial troops withdrew from Britain in order to defend Rome from the Visigoths, the Picts from Scotland and the Scots from Ireland invaded British

Celtic territory. According to the eighth-century historian Bede (**beed**) (see page 181), the Celtic king Vortigern invited the Saxons from Denmark to help him against his rivals in Britain. Saxons and other Germanic tribes from modern-day Norway, Sweden, and Denmark turned from assistance to conquest, attacking in a hit-and-run fashion. Their goal was plunder, and at first their invasions led to no permanent settlements. As more Germanic peoples arrived, however, they took over the best lands and eventually conquered most of Britain. Some Britons fled to Wales and the westernmost parts of England, north toward Scotland, and across the English Channel to Brittany. Others remained and eventually intermarried with Germanic peoples.

Historians have labeled the period 500 to 1066, the years of the Norman Conquest, as the "Anglo-Saxon" period, after the two largest Germanic tribes, the Angles and the Saxons. The Germanic tribes destroyed Roman culture in Britain. Christianity disappeared, large urban buildings were allowed to fall apart, and tribal custom superseded Roman law.

Anglo-Saxon England was divided along ethnic and political lines. The Germanic kingdoms in the south, east, and center were opposed by the Britons in the west, who wanted to get rid of the invaders. The Anglo-Saxon kingdoms also fought among themselves, causing boundaries to shift constantly. Finally, in the ninth century, under pressure from the Viking invasions, the Celtic Britons and the Germanic Anglo-Saxons were molded together under the leadership of King Alfred of Wessex (**WES-iks**) (r. 871–899).

The Anglo-Saxon invasion gave rise to a rich body of Celtic mythology, particularly legends about the Celtic King Arthur, who first appeared in Welsh poetry in the sixth century and later in histories, epics, and saints' lives. Most scholars see Arthur as a composite figure who evolved over the centuries in songs and stories. According to these texts, Arthur was the illegitimate son of the king of Britain whose royal parentage was revealed when he successfully drew the invincible sword Excalibur from a stone. Arthur won recognition as king and used Excalibur to win many battles. His quests included a search for the Holy Grail, the dish supposedly used by Jesus at the Last Supper, which was said to have miraculous powers. Arthur held his court at Camelot, where his knights were seated at the Round Table, where all were equal. Those knights included Sir Tristan, Sir Galahad, Sir Percival (Parsifal), and Sir Lancelot; Lancelot's romance with Arthur's wife Guinevere (**GWIN-uh-veer**) led to the end of the Arthurian kingdom. In their earliest form as Welsh poems, the Arthurian legends may represent Celtic hostility to Anglo-Saxon invaders, but they later came to be more important as representations of the ideal of medieval knightly chivalry and as great stories whose retelling has continued to the present.

Section Review

- *"Barbaros,"* the Greek word that is the origin of "barbarian" originally meant not speaking Greek, but later implied savage and primitive.

- Celts and Germans were similar in their polytheism and origins but the Celts moved westward under pressure from Germanic groups.

- Germanic peoples migrated to search for better food and climate and because of conflicts with other groups, such as the Huns.

- The longest-lasting of the Germanic kingdoms was the Frankish kingdom under Clovis, who settled within Roman Gaul and assimilated with the Gallo-Romans.

- The Germanic Anglo-Saxons in Britain destroyed Roman culture as they fought among themselves and with the Britons to the west, before Viking invasions united them under King Alfred.

- Celtic mythology and the legend of King Arthur may represent Celtic hostility toward Anglo-Saxon influence.

Barbarian Society

What patterns of social, political, and economic life characterized barbarian society?

Germanic and Celtic society had originated in the northern parts of central and western Europe and the southern regions of Scandinavia during the Iron Age (800–500 B.C.E.). After Germanic kingdoms replaced the Roman Empire as the primary political structure throughout much of Europe, barbarian customs and traditions formed the basis of European society for centuries.

Runic (ROO-nik) Inscriptions
This eighth-century chest made of whalebone depicts warriors, other human figures, and a horse, with a border of runic letters. This chest tells a story in both pictures and words. The runes are one of the varieties from the British Isles, from a time and place in which the Latin alphabet was known as well. Runes and Latin letters were used side-by-side in some parts of northern Europe for centuries. (Erich Lessing/Art Resource, NY)

runic alphabet Writings that help to give a more accurate picture of barbarian society; the oldest come from shortly after the time of Tacitus.

Kinship, Custom, and Class

Barbarians generally had no notion of the state as we use the term today; they thought in social, not political, terms. The basic social unit was the tribe, a group whose members believed that they were all descended from a common ancestor. Blood united them; kinship protected them. Law was custom—unwritten, preserved in the minds of the elders of the tribe, and handed down by word of mouth from generation to generation. Every tribe had its customs, and every member of the tribe knew what they were. Members were subject to their tribe's customary laws wherever they went, and friendly tribes respected one another's laws.

Barbarian tribes were led by tribal chieftains, who are often called kings, though this implies broader power than they actually had. The chief was the member recognized as the strongest and bravest in battle and was elected from among the male members of the strongest family. He led the tribe in war, settled disputes among its members, conducted negotiations with outside powers, and offered sacrifices to the gods. The period of migrations and conquests of the Western Roman Empire witnessed the strengthening of kingship among tribes.

Closely associated with the king in some southern tribes was the **comitatus**, or "war band." Writing at the end of the first century, Tacitus (**TAS-ee-tuhs**) described the war band as the bravest young men in the tribe. They swore loyalty to the chief, fought with him in battle, and were not supposed to leave the battlefield without him; to do so implied cowardice, disloyalty, and social disgrace. A social egalitarianism existed among members of the war band. The comitatus had importance for the later development of feudalism.

During the migrations of the third and fourth centuries, however, and as a result of constant warfare, the war band was transformed into a system of stratified

comitatus A war band, a group of young men who were closely associated with the king in some southern tribes and who swore loyalty to the chief, fought with him in battle, and were not supposed to leave the battlefield without him.

ranks. During the Ostrogothic conquest of Italy under Theodoric, warrior-nobles also sought to acquire land as both a mark of prestige and a means to power. As land and wealth came into the hands of a small elite class, social inequalities emerged and gradually grew stronger.[6] These inequalities help explain the origins of the European noble class (see pages 234).

Law

Early barbarian tribes had no written laws, but beginning in the late sixth century some tribal chieftains began to collect, write, and publish lists of their customs at the urging of Christian missionaries. The churchmen wanted to understand barbarian ways in order to assimilate the tribes into Christianity. Augustine of Canterbury, for example, persuaded King Ethelbert of Kent to have his folk laws written down; these *Dooms of Ethelbert* date from between 601 and 604, roughly five years after Augustine's arrival in Britain. Moreover, by the sixth century many barbarian kings needed regulations for the Romans under their jurisdiction as well as for their own people.

According to the code of the Salian Franks, every person had a particular monetary value to the tribe. This value was called the **wergeld** (**WUR-gild**), which literally means "man-money" or "money to buy off the spear." Men of fighting age had the highest wergeld, then women of childbearing age, children, and finally the aged. Everyone's value reflected his or her potential military worthiness. If a person accused of a crime agreed to pay the wergeld and if the victim and his or her family accepted the payment, there was peace. If the accused refused to pay the wergeld or if the victim's family refused to accept it, a blood feud ensued. Individuals depended on their kin for protection, and kinship served as a force of social control.

Some codes had specific clauses that protected the virtue of women. For example, the Salic Law of the Franks fined a man the large amount of 15 solidi (**SOL-ih-dee**) if he pressed the hand of a woman, and 35 if he touched her above the elbow. The very high fine of 600 solidi for the murder of a woman of childbearing years—the same value attached to military officers of the king, to priests, and to boys preparing to become warriors—suggests the importance of women in Frankish society, at least for their childbearing capacity.

At first, Romans had been subject to Roman law and Germans to Germanic custom. As German kings accepted Christianity and as Romans and barbarians increasingly intermarried, the distinction between the two laws blurred and, in the course of the seventh and eighth centuries, disappeared. The result would be the new feudal law, to which all who lived in certain areas were subject.

Social and Economic Structures

Barbarian groups usually resided in small villages, and climate and geography determined the basic patterns of agricultural and pastoral life. Many tribes lived in small settlements on the edges of clearings where they raised barley, wheat, oats, peas, and beans. Men and women tilled their fields with simple wooden scratch plows and harvested their grains with small iron sickles. The kernels of grain were eaten as porridge, ground up for flour, or fermented into strong, thick beer; the vast majority of people's caloric intake came from grain in some form.

Within the small villages, there were great differences in wealth and status. Free men and their families constituted the largest class. The number of cattle a man possessed indicated his wealth and determined his social status. Free men also

wergeld Man-money or money to buy off the spear; according to the code of Salian Franks, this is the particular monetary value that every person had in the tribe.

shared in tribal warfare. Slaves (prisoners of war) worked as farm laborers, herdsmen, and household servants.

Did the barbarians produce goods for trade and exchange? Ironworking represented the most advanced craft; much of northern Europe had iron deposits, and the dense forests provided wood for charcoal. Most villages had an oven and smiths who produced agricultural tools and instruments of war—one-edged swords, arrowheads, and shields. In the first two centuries C.E., the quantity and quality of Germanic goods increased dramatically, and the first steel swords were superior to the weapons of Roman troops. These goods were produced for war and for the subsistence economy, not for trade. Goods were also used for gift giving, a major social custom. Gift giving conferred status on the giver, who, in giving, showed his higher (economic) status, cemented friendship, and placed the receiver in his debt.[7] Goods that could not be produced in the village were acquired by raiding and warfare rather than by commercial exchanges.

Barbarian tribes were understood to be made up of kin groups, and those kin groups were made up of families, the basic social unit in barbarian society. Families were responsible for the debts and actions of their members and for keeping the peace in general. Barbarian law codes set strict rules of inheritance based on position in the family and often set aside a portion of land that could not be sold or given away by any family member.

Germanic society was patriarchal: within each household the father had authority over his wife, children, and slaves. Some wealthy and powerful men had more than one wife, a pattern that continued even after they became Christian, but polygamy was not widespread among ordinary people. A woman was considered to be under the legal guardianship of a man, and she had fewer rights to own property than did Roman women in the late Empire. However, once they were widowed (and there must have been many widows in such a violent, warring society), women sometimes assumed their husbands' rights over family property and held the guardianship of their children.

Women found outlets for their talents in monasteries and convents as writers, copyists, artists, embroiderers, teachers, and estate managers. Some houses of religious women, such as Mauberge in northern Francia under Abbess Aldegund (ca. 661), produced important scholarship. The dowry required for entrance to a convent restricted admission as full sisters to upper-class women, but poorer women were taken in as lay sisters. Many women viewed the convent as a place of refuge from family pressures or tribal violence. The sixth-century Queen Radegund, for example, was forced to marry Chlotar I, the murderer of several of her relatives. Radegund later escaped her polygamous union and lived out her life in a convent.

Chapter Review

How was the Byzantine Empire able to survive for so long, and what were its most important achievements? (page 134)

Late antiquity was a period of rupture and transformation, but also of continuities and assimilation. Migrating barbarian groups broke the Western Roman Empire apart, creating much smaller states and more localized economies. As they encountered Roman culture and became Christian, their own ways of doing things were transformed, and the result was a blend of barbarian and Roman culture. In eastern Europe, the

Key Terms

Petrine Doctrine (p. 140)

Arianism (p. 141)

heresy (p. 141)

(continued)

Byzantine Empire thrived throughout late antiquity, maintaining Roman traditions. Throughout Europe, leaders in the Christian Church energetically developed more complex ideas and stronger institutional structures, transforming Christianity into the most powerful agent in the making of Europe. In the east, the Byzantine Empire withstood attacks from Germanic tribes and steppe peoples and remained a state until 1453, a thousand years longer than the Western Roman Empire. Byzantium preserved the philosophical and scientific texts of the ancient world—which later formed the basis for study in science and medicine in both Europe and the Arabic world—and produced a great synthesis of Roman law, the Justinian *Code*, which shapes legal structures in much of Europe and former European colonies to this day.

What factors enabled the Christian church to expand and thrive? (page 137)

Christianity gained the support of the fourth-century emperors and gradually adopted the Roman system of hierarchical organization. The church possessed able administrators and leaders whose skills were tested in the chaotic environment of the end of the Roman Empire in the West. Bishops expanded their activities, and in the fifth century the bishops of Rome began to stress their supremacy over other Christian communities. Monasteries offered opportunities for individuals to develop deeper spiritual devotion and also provided a model of Christian living, a pattern of agricultural development, and a place for education and learning.

How did Christian thinkers adapt Greco-Roman ideas to Christian theology? (page 144)

Christian thinkers reinterpreted the classics in a Christian sense, incorporating elements of Greek and Roman philosophy and of various pagan religious groups into Christian teachings. Prime among these were certain aspects of Greco-Roman notions of gender and sexuality. Most Christian thinkers accepted Greco-Roman ideas that men were superior to women, though they viewed sexuality and the body with greater suspicion than had ancient pagans and developed a strong sense that chastity and an ascetic life were superior to marriage and family life. Of these early thinkers, Augustine of Hippo was the most influential. His ideas about sin, free will, sexuality, and the role of government shaped western European thought from the fifth century on.

What techniques did missionaries develop to convert barbarian peoples to Christianity? (page 146)

Christianity had a dynamic missionary policy, and the church slowly succeeded in assimilating—that is, adapting—barbarian peoples into Christian teaching. Christian missionaries preached the Gospel to Germanic, Celtic, and Slavic peoples, instructed them in the basic tenets of the Christian faith, and used penitentials to give them a sense of expected behavior. Christianity refashioned the Germanic and classical legacies, creating new rituals and practices that were meaningful to people.

What were some of the causes of the barbarian migrations and how did they affect the regions of Europe? (page 149)

The migration of barbarian groups into Europe from the East affected both the regions into which peoples moved and the ones they left behind. Migrations were caused by many factors, including food shortages, disputes among groups, and pressure from outside, and they sometimes involved military actions, though not always. Barbarians are often divided into large linguistic groups, such as the Celtic and Germanic tribes, with ties to other tribes based on kinship and military alliances, not on loyalty to a

Orthodox church (p. 142)

eremitical (p. 142)

coenobitic monasticism (p. 143)

regular clergy (p. 143)

secular clergy (p. 143)

sacraments (p. 146)

penitentials (p. 149)

relics (p. 149)

barbarians (p. 150)

Salic Law (p. 153)

Merovingian (p. 153)

runic alphabet (p. 155)

comitatus (p. 155)

wergeld (p. 156)

particular government. Most barbarian states were weak and short-lived, though that of the Salian Franks was relatively more unified and powerful. Germanic-speaking Angles and Saxons invaded Celtic-speaking England and established a group of small kingdoms that slowly became more unified.

What patterns of social, political, and economic life characterized barbarian society? (page 154)

Though barbarian states were generally feeble politically, barbarian customs and traditions formed the basis of European society for centuries. Barbarian law codes, written down for the first time in the sixth century, set out social and gender distinctions and held the family responsible for the actions of an individual. Most people lived in family groups in villages, where men, women, and children shared in the agricultural labor that sustained society. Christianity and the barbarian states absorbed many aspects of Roman culture, and the Byzantine Empire continued to thrive, but western Europe was very different in 600 from how it had been in 350.

Notes

1. Matthew 16:18–19.
2. Colossians 3:9–11.
3. Wolfram, *History of the Goths* (Berkeley: University of California Press, 1988), pp. 6–10.
4. Ibid., pp. 125–131.
5. E. James, *The Franks* (New York: Basil Blackwell, 1988), pp. 3, 7–10, 58.
6. P. J. Geary, *Before France and Germany: The Creation and Transformation of the Merovingian World* (New York: Oxford University Press, 1988), pp. 108–112.
7. Ibid., p. 50.

To assess your mastery of this chapter, go to **bedfordstmartins.com/mckaywestbrief**

Listening to the Past

The Conversion of Clovis

Modern Christian doctrine holds that conversion is a gradual process of turning toward Jesus and his teachings. But in the early medieval world, conversion was perceived more as a one-time event determined by the tribal chieftain. This selection about the Frankish king Clovis is from The History of the Franks by Gregory, bishop of Tours (ca. 504–594), written about a century after the events it describes.

Queen Clotild continued to pray that her husband might recognize the true God and give up his idol-worship. Nothing could persuade him to accept Christianity. Finally war broke out against the Alamanni and in this conflict he was forced by necessity to accept what he had refused of his own free will. It so turned out that when the two armies met on the battlefield there was a great slaughter and the troops of Clovis were rapidly being annihilated. He raised his eyes to Heaven when he saw this, felt compunction in his heart and was moved to tears. "Jesus Christ," he said, "you who Clotild maintains to be the Son of the living God, you who deign to give help to those in travail and victory to those who trust in you, in faith I beg the glory of your help. If you will give me victory over my enemies, and if I may have evidence to that miraculous power which the people dedicated to your name say that they have experienced, then I will believe in you and I will be baptized in your name. I have called upon my own gods, but, as I see only too clearly, they have no intention of helping me. I therefore cannot believe that they possess any power for they do not come to the assistance of those who trust them. I now call upon you. I want to believe in you, but I must first be saved from my enemies." Even as he said this the Alamanni turned their backs and began to run away. As soon as they saw that their King was killed, they submitted to Clovis. "We beg you," they said, "to put an end to this slaughter. We are prepared to obey you." Clovis stopped the war. He made a speech in which he called for peace. Then he went home. He told the Queen how he had won a victory by calling on the name of Christ. This happened in the fifteenth year of his reign (496).

The Queen then ordered Saint Remigius, Bishop of the town of Rheims (**reemz**), to be summoned in secret. She begged him to impart the

Ninth-century ivory carving showing Clovis being baptized by Saint Remi. (Musée Condé, Chantilly/Laurie Platt Winfrey, Inc.)

160

word of salvation to the King. The Bishop asked Clovis to meet him in private and began to urge him to believe in the true God, Maker of Heaven and earth, and to forsake his idols, which were powerless to help him or anyone else. The King replied: "I have listened to you willingly, holy father. There remains one obstacle. The people under my command will not agree to forsake their gods. I will go and put to them what you have just said to me." He arranged a meeting with his people, but God in his power had preceded him, and before he could say a word all those present shouted in unison: "We will give up worshipping our mortal gods, pious King, and we are prepared to follow the immortal God about whom Remigius preaches." This news was reported to the Bishop. He was greatly pleased and he ordered the baptismal pool to be made ready.

Questions for Analysis

1. According to this account, why did Clovis ultimately accept Christianity?

2. For the Salian Franks, what was the best proof of divine power?

3. On the basis of this selection, do you consider *The History of the Franks* reliable history? Why?

Sources: L. Thorpe, trans., *The History of the Franks by Gregory of Tours* (Harmondsworth, England: Penguin, 1974), p. 159; P. J. Geary, ed., *Readings in Medieval History* (Peterborough, Ontario: Broadview Press, 1991), pp. 165–166.

CHAPTER 8

Europe in the Early Middle Ages

600–1000

Chapter Preview

The Spread of Islam
How did Islam take root in the Middle East and then spread to Europe?

The Frankish Kingdom
How did Frankish rulers govern their kingdoms?

The Empire of Charlemagne
How did Charlemagne gain control of a large part of Europe and how did power become decentralized after his death?

Early Medieval Scholarship and Culture
What were the significant intellectual and cultural changes in Charlemagne's era?

Invasions and Migrations
What effects did the assaults and migrations of the Vikings, Magyars, and Muslims have on the rest of Europe?

INDIVIDUALS IN SOCIETY: Ebo of Reims

LISTENING TO THE PAST: Feudal Homage and Fealty

Garden built by Muslim rulers in Seville, Spain. Tranquil gardens such as this one represented paradise in Islamic culture, perhaps because of the religion's desert origins. (Ric Ergenbright/Corbis)

In the fifteenth century writers and scholars in the growing cities of northern Italy began to think that they were living in a new era, one in which the glories of ancient Greece and Rome were being reborn. What separated their own time from classical antiquity, in their opinion, was a long period of darkness, to which a seventeenth-century professor gave the name "Middle Ages" (*Medium Aevum* in Latin). In this conceptualization, Western history was divided into three periods—ancient, medieval (a word derived from the Latin), and modern.

This three-part schema is still the primary way of organizing Western history. Exactly what marked the dividing lines between these periods was not very clear, however. For a long time the end of the Roman Empire in the West in 476 was seen as the division between the classical period and the Middle Ages, but as we saw in the last chapter, more recent historians have emphasized continuities as well as changes in the fifth and sixth centuries. The transition from ancient to medieval was a slow process, not a single event. The agents in this process included not only the Germanic tribes whose migrations broke the Roman Empire apart but also the new religion of Islam, Slavic and steppe (**step**) peoples in eastern Europe, and Christian officials and missionaries. The period from the end of antiquity to about 1000, conventionally know as the "Early Middle Ages," was a time of disorder and destruction, but also of the creation of a new type of society.

The Spread of Islam

How did Islam take root in the Middle East and then spread to Europe?

In the seventh century C.E. two empires dominated the area today called the Middle East: the Byzantine-Greek-Christian empire and the Sasanian-Persian-Zoroastrian empire. The Arabian peninsula lay between the two.

Around 610 in the Arabian city of Mecca, a merchant called Muhammad began to have religious visions. By the time he died in 632, all Arabia had accepted his creed. A century later his followers controlled Syria, Palestine, Egypt, North Africa, Spain, and part of France. This Arabic expansion profoundly affected the development of Western civilization as well as the history of Africa and Asia.

The Arabs

In Muhammad's time Arabia was inhabited by various tribes, most of them Bedouins (**BED-oo-inz**). These nomadic peoples grazed goats and sheep on the sparse patches of grass that dotted the vast semiarid peninsula. Other Arabs lived in the southern valleys and coastal towns along the Red Sea in Yemen, Mecca, Medina, and the northwestern region called "Hejaz" (**HEE-jaz**). The Hejazi supported themselves by agriculture and trade. Their caravan routes crisscrossed Arabia and carried goods to Byzantium, Persia, and Syria. The Hejazi had wide commercial dealings but avoided cultural contacts with their Jewish, Christian, and Persian neighbors. The wealth produced by their business transactions led to luxurious living in the towns.

Although the nomadic Bedouins condemned the urbanized lifestyle of the Hejazi as immoral and corrupt, Arabs of both types respected one another's local tribal customs. In addition, they had certain religious rules in common. For example, all Arabs kept three months of the year as sacred; during that time fighting stopped so that everyone could attend holy ceremonies in peace. The city of

Kaaba A sanctuary in Mecca where Arabs prayed.

Mecca in what is now Saudi Arabia was the religious center of the Arab world, and fighting was never tolerated there. All Arabs prayed at the **Kaaba** (KAH-buh), the sanctuary in Mecca. Within the Kaaba was a sacred black stone that Arabs revered because they believed it had fallen from heaven.

What eventually molded the diverse Arab tribes into a powerful political and social unity was the religion based on the teachings of Muhammad.

Qur'an The sacred book of Islam.

The Prophet Muhammad

Except for a few vague remarks in the **Qur'an** (kuh-RAHN), the sacred book of Islam, Muhammad (ca. 571–632) left no account of his life. Arab tradition accepts some of the sacred legends that developed about him as historically true, but those legends were not written down until about a century after his death. Orphaned at the age of six, Muhammad was brought up by his grandfather. When he was a young man, he became a merchant in the caravan trade. Later he entered the service of a wealthy widow, and their subsequent marriage brought him financial independence. The Qur'an reveals him to be an extremely devout man, ascetic, self-disciplined, and literate.

Since childhood Muhammad had been subject to seizures during which he lost consciousness and had visions. After 610 these visions apparently became more frequent. Unsure for a time about what he should do, Muhammad discovered his mission after a vision in which the angel Gabriel instructed him to preach.

Muhammad and the Earlier Prophets
Muhammad, with his head surrounded by fire representing religious fervor, leads Abraham, Moses, and Jesus in prayer. Islamic tradition holds that Judaism, Christianity, and Islam all derive from the pure religion of Abraham, but humankind has strayed from that faith. Therefore, Muhammad, as "the seal (last) of the prophets," had to transmit God's revelations to humankind. (Bibliothèque nationale de France)

Muhammad described his visions in a stylized and often rhyming prose and used this literary medium as his *Qur'an*, or "prayer recitation." Muhammad's revelations were written down by his followers during his lifetime and organized into chapters shortly after his death. In 651 Muhammad's third successor as religious leader, Othman, arranged to have an official version published. The Qur'an is regarded by Muslims as the direct words of God to his Prophet Muhammad and is therefore especially revered. (These revelations were in Arabic. When Muslims use translations in other languages, they do so alongside the original Arabic.) At the same time, other sayings and accounts of Muhammad, which gave advice on matters that went beyond the Qur'an, were collected into books termed *hadith* (**hah-DEETH**). Muslim tradition (Sunna) consists of both the Qur'an and the hadith.

Muhammad's visions ordered him to preach a message of a single God and to become God's prophet, which he began to do in his hometown of Mecca. He gathered followers slowly but also provoked a great deal of resistance, and in 622 he migrated with his followers to Medina, an event termed the *hijra* (**HIJ-ruh**) that marks the beginning of the Muslim calendar. At Medina Muhammad was much more successful, gaining converts and working out the basic principles of the faith. In 630 Muhammad returned to Mecca at the head of a large army, and by his death in 632 he had unified most of the Arabian peninsula into a religious/political community of Muslims, a word meaning those who comply with God's will. The religion itself came to be called Islam, which means "submission to God." The Kaaba was rededicated as a Muslim holy place, and Mecca became the most holy city in Islam. According to Muslim tradition, the Kaaba predates the creation of the world and represents the earthly counterpart of God's heavenly throne, to which "pilgrims come dishevelled and dusty on every kind of camel."[1]

CHRONOLOGY

ca. 571–632	Life of the Prophet Muhammad
700	Lindisfarne Gospel produced in Northumbria
711–720	Muslim conquest of Spain
ca. 720	Venerable Bede writes *Ecclesiastical History of the English People*
760s–840s	Carolingian Renaissance
768–814	Reign of Charlemagne
800–900	Free peasants in western Europe increasingly tied to the land as serfs
820	Muslim mathematician al-Khwarizmi writes first treatise on algebra
843	Treaty of Verdun divides Carolingian kingdom
850–1000	Most extensive Viking raids
ca. 900	Establishment of Kievan Rus
950	Muslim Córdoba is Europe's largest and most prosperous city
1001	Establishment of kingdom of Hungary

The Teachings of Islam

Muhammad's religion eventually attracted great numbers of people, partly because of the straightforward nature of its doctrines. The strictly monotheistic theology outlined in the Qur'an has only a few central tenets. Allah, the Arabic word for God, is all-powerful and all-knowing. Muhammad, Allah's prophet, preached his word and carried his message. Muhammad described himself as the successor both of the Jewish patriarch Abraham and of Christ, and he claimed that his teachings replaced theirs. He invited and won converts from Judaism and Christianity.

Because Allah is all-powerful, believers must submit themselves to him. All Muslims have the obligation of the *jihad* (**jee-HAHD**) (literally "self-exertion") to strive or struggle to lead a virtuous life and to spread God's rule and law. In some cases striving was individual against sin; in others it was social and communal and could involve armed conflict, though this was not an essential part of jihad. The Islamic belief of "striving in the path of God" is closely related to the central feature of Muslim doctrine, the coming Day of Judgment. Muslims need not be concerned about *when* judgment will occur, but they must believe with absolute and total conviction that the Day of Judgment *will* come. Consequently, all of a

Muslim's thoughts and actions should be oriented toward the Last Judgment and the rewards of Heaven.

To merit the rewards of heaven, a person must follow the strict code of moral behavior that Muhammad prescribed. The Muslim must recite a profession of faith in God and in Muhammad as God's prophet: "There is no god but God and Muhammad is his prophet." The believer must pray five times a day, fast and pray during the sacred month of Ramadan, and contribute alms to the poor and needy. If possible, the believer must make a pilgrimage to Mecca once during his or her lifetime. According to the Muslim *shari'a* (sha-REE-ah), or sacred law, these five practices—the profession of faith, prayer, fasting, giving alms to the poor, and pilgrimage to Mecca—constitute the **Five Pillars of Islam.**

Five Pillars of Islam The five practices according to the Muslim shari'a, or sacred law, including the profession of faith, prayer, fasting, giving alms to the poor, and a pilgrimage to Mecca.

The Qur'an forbids alcoholic beverages and gambling. It condemns business usury—that is, lending money at interest rates or taking advantage of market demand for products by charging high prices for them. A number of foods, such as pork, are also forbidden, a dietary regulation adopted from the Hebrews.

The Qur'an also sets forth an austere sexual morality. Muslim jurisprudence condemned licentious behavior on the part of men as well as women, which enhanced the status of women in Muslim society. So, too, did Muhammad's opposition to female infanticide. Polygyny, the practice of men having more than one wife, was common in Arab society, but the Qur'an restricted the number of wives to four—or even one, if the man could not treat all fairly. In a military society where there were apt to be many widows, polygyny provided women with a measure of security.

With respect to matters of property, Muslim women were more emancipated than Western women. For example, a Muslim woman retained complete jurisdiction over one-third of her property when she married and could dispose of it in any way she wished. Women in most European countries and the United States did not gain these rights until the nineteenth century.[2]

What did early Muslims think of Jesus? He is described in the Qur'an as a righteous prophet who was born of Mary the Virgin, performed miracles, and continued the work of Abraham and Moses, and he was a sign of the coming Day of Judgment. But Muslims held that Jesus was an apostle only, not God, and that those who called Jesus divine committed blasphemy (showing contempt for God). Muslims esteemed the Judeo-Christian Scriptures as part of God's revelation, although they believed that Christian communities had corrupted the Scriptures and that the Qur'an superseded them. The Christian doctrine of the Trinity—that there is one God in three persons (Father, Son, and Holy Spirit)—conflicts with the Muslim idea of monotheism.[3]

Expansion and Schism

By the time Muhammad died in 632, he had united the nomads of the desert and the merchants of the cities. The doctrines of Islam, instead of the ties of local custom, bound all Arabs. The crescent of Islam, the Muslim symbol, prevailed throughout the Arabian peninsula. During the next century one rich province of the old Roman Empire after another came under Muslim domination—first Syria, then Egypt, and then all of North Africa (see Map 8.1). Long and bitter wars (572–591, 606–630) between the Byzantine and Persian Empires left both so weak and exhausted that they easily fell to Muslim attack. The government headquarters of this vast new empire was established at Damascus in Syria by the ruling Umayyad (oo-MY-ad) family. By the early tenth century a Muslim proverb spoke of the Mediterranean Sea as a Muslim lake, though the Greeks at Constantinople

MAP 8.1 The Islamic World, ca. 900

The rapid expansion of Islam in a relatively short span of time testifies to the Arabs' superior fighting skills, religious zeal, and economic organization as well as to their enemies' weakness.

contested that notion. From the Arabian peninsula, Muslims carried their faith deep into Africa and across Asia all the way to India.

Despite the clarity and unifying force of Muslim doctrine, a schism soon developed within the Islamic faith. Neither the Qur'an nor the hadith gave clear guidance about how successors to Muhammad were to be chosen, but a group of Muhammad's closest followers elected Abu Bakr (a-BOO BAK-uhr), who was a close friend of the Prophet's and a member of a small tribe affiliated with the Prophet's tribe, as **caliph** (KEY-lif, KAL-if), a word meaning successor. This election set a precedent for the ratification of the subsequent patriarchal caliphs, though other Arab tribes unsuccessfully opposed it militarily.

caliph A successor, as chosen by a group of Muhammad's closest followers.

A more serious opposition developed later among supporters of the fourth caliph, Ali. Ali claimed the caliphate because of his blood ties with Muhammad—he was Muhammad's cousin and son-in-law—and because the Prophet had designated him as *imam* (ee-MAHM), or leader. Ali was assassinated shortly after becoming caliph, and some of his supporters began to assert that he should rightly have been the first caliph and that all subsequent caliphs were usurpers. These supporters of Ali—called *Shi'ites* (SHE-ites) or *Shi'a* (SHE-ah) from Arabic terms meaning "supporters" or "partisans" of Ali—saw Ali and subsequent imams as the divinely inspired leaders of the community. The larger body of Muslims who accepted the first elections—called *Sunnis* (SUN-nees), a word derived from *Sunna*, the traditional beliefs and practices of the community—saw the caliphs as political leaders. Since Islam did not have an organized church and priesthood, the caliphs had an additional function of safeguarding and enforcing the religious law (*shari'a*)

Shi'ites Muslims who regard Muhammad's cousin Ali as the rightful successor to the position as caliph.

Sunnis Muslims who regard the succession of leadership through Abu Bakr as legitimate.

with the advice of scholars (*ulama*), particularly the jurists, judges, and scholastics who were knowledgeable about the Qur'an and hadith. Over the centuries, many different kinds of Shi'ites appeared, and enmity between Sunni and Shi'a Muslims sometimes erupted into violence.

Muslim Spain

In Europe, Muslim political and cultural influence was felt most strongly in the Iberian peninsula. In 711 a Muslim force crossed the Strait of Gibraltar and easily defeated the weak Visigothic kingdom. A few Christian princes supported by the Frankish rulers held out in northern mountain fortresses, but the Muslims took over most of Spain. A member of the Umayyad dynasty, Abd al-Rahman (**AHB-d al-ruh-MAHN**) (r. 756–788), established a kingdom in Spain with its capital at Córdoba (**KAWR-doh-buh**).

Throughout the Islamic world, Muslims used the term *al-Andalus* to describe the part of the Iberian Peninsula under Muslim control. The name al-Andalus probably derives from the Arabic for "land of the Vandals," the Germanic people who swept across Spain in the fifth century. In the eighth century, al-Andalus included the entire peninsula from Gibraltar in the south to the Cantabrian Mountains in the north (see Map 8.1). Today we often use the word *Andalusia* (**an-duh-LOO-zhuh**) to refer especially to southern Spain, but eighth-century Christians throughout Europe called the peninsula "Moorish Spain" because the people who invaded and conquered it were Moors—Berbers from northwest Africa. The ethnic term *Moorish* can be misleading, however, because the peninsula was home to sizable numbers of Jews and Christians as well as (Muslim) Moors. In business transactions and in much of daily life, all peoples used the Arabic language. With Muslims, Christians, and Jews trading with and learning from one another and occasionally intermarrying, Moorish Spain and Norman Sicily (see Chapter 9) were the only distinctly pluralistic societies in medieval Europe. Between roughly the eighth and twelfth centuries, Muslims, Christians, and Jews lived close together in Andalusia, and some scholars believe that the early part of this period was an era of remarkable interfaith harmony. Jews in Muslim Spain were generally treated well, and Córdoba became a center of Jewish as well as Muslim learning. Many Christians adopted Arabic patterns of speech and dress, gave up the practice of eating pork, and developed a special appreciation for Arabic music and poetry. Some Christian women of elite status chose the Muslim practice of veiling their faces in public. Records describe Muslim and Christian youths joining in celebrations and merrymaking.

From the sophisticated centers of Muslim culture in Baghdad, Damascus, and Cairo (founded 969), al-Andalus seemed a provincial backwater, a frontier outpost with little significance in the wide context of Islamic civilization. To European peoples, however, Spanish culture was dazzling. For example, the Saxon nun and writer Hroswita of Gandersheim (**GAND-ers-haym**) called the city of Córdoba "the ornament of the world." It became Europe's largest and most prosperous city. With a population of about half a million; with well-paved and well-lighted streets and an abundance of

Harvesting Dates

This detail from an ivory casket given to a Córdoban prince reflects the importance of fruit cultivation in the Muslim-inspired agricultural expansion in southern Europe in the ninth and tenth centuries. (Louvre/Réunion des Musées Nationaux/Art Resource, NY)

fresh water; with 1,000 mosques, 900 public baths, 213,177 houses for ordinary people, and 60,000 mansions for officials and the wealthy; with 80,455 shops and 13,000 weavers producing silks, woolens, and brocades; with 27 free schools and a library containing 400,000 volumes (the largest library in northern Europe, at the Benedictine abbey of St. Gall in Switzerland, had 600 books), Córdoba was indeed an ornament, and the Western world had no comparable urban center. In Spain, as elsewhere in the Arab world, the Muslims had an enormous impact on agricultural development. They began the cultivation of rice, sugar cane, citrus fruits, dates, figs, eggplants, carrots, and, after the eleventh century, cotton. These crops, together with new methods of field irrigation, provided the urban population with food products unknown in the rest of Europe.

In about 950, Caliph Abd al-Rahman III (912–961) of the Umayyad dynasty of Córdoba ruled most of the Iberian Peninsula. Christian Spain consisted of the tiny kingdoms of Castile, León, Catalonia, Aragon, Navarre, and Portugal. However, civil wars among al-Rahman's descendents weakened the caliphate, and the small northern Christian kingdoms expanded southward.

Science and Medicine The Islamic world, both in Spain and elsewhere, profoundly shaped Christian European culture. Toledo, for example, became an important center of learning through which Arab intellectual achievements entered and influenced western Europe. Arabic knowledge of science and mathematics, derived from the Chinese, Greeks, and Hindus, was highly sophisticated. The Muslim mathematician al-Khwarizmi (**al-KHWAHR-iz-mee**) (d. 830) wrote the important treatise *Algebra*, the first work in which the word *algebra* is used mathematically. Al-Khwarizmi adopted the Hindu system of numbers (1, 2, 3, 4), used it in his *Algebra*, and applied mathematics to problems of physics and astronomy. Scholars at Baghdad translated Euclid's *Elements*, the basic text for plane and solid geometry. Muslims also instructed Westerners in the use of the zero, which permitted the execution of complicated problems of multiplication and long division. Use of the zero represented an enormous advance over clumsy Roman numerals. (Since our system of numbers is actually Hindu in origin, the term *Arabic numerals*, coined about 1847, is a misnomer.)

Middle Eastern Arabs translated and codified the scientific and philosophical learning of Greek and Persian antiquity. In the ninth and tenth centuries that knowledge was brought to Spain, where between 1150 and 1250 it was translated into Latin. Europeans' knowledge of Aristotle changed the entire direction of European philosophy and theology (see page 60). Isaac Newton's discoveries in mathematics in the seventeenth century rested on ancient Greek theories translated in Spain.

In the transmission of Greek learning, one Muslim technological accomplishment played a most significant role—paper. Building on techniques invented by the Chinese, Muslims brought their papermaking method to the major hubs of their empire, and it eventually entered Spain. Even before the invention of printing (see page 317), papermaking had a revolutionary impact on the collection and diffusion of knowledge and thus on the transformation of society.[4]

Muslim medical knowledge far surpassed that of the West. By the ninth century Arab physicians had translated most of the treatises of Hippocrates, and later generations made their own advances in the diagnosis and treatment of illnesses and in surgical techniques. Arabic science reached its peak in the physician, philologist, philosopher, poet, and scientist ibn-Sina of Bukhara (980–1037), known in the West as Avicenna. His *al-Qanun* codified all Greco-Arabic medical thought, described the contagious nature of tuberculosis and the spreading of diseases, and listed 760 pharmaceutical drugs.

Unfortunately, many of these treatises came to the West as translations from Greek to Arabic and then to Latin and inevitably lost a great deal in translation. Nevertheless, in the ninth and tenth centuries Arabic knowledge and experience in anatomy and pharmaceutical prescriptions much enriched Western knowledge.

Muslim-Christian Relations

Beyond Andalusian Spain, mutual animosity restricted contact between Muslims and Christians. The Muslim expansion into Christian Europe in the eighth and ninth centuries left a legacy of bitter hostility. Christians felt threatened by a faith that denied the doctrine of the Trinity and Christ's divinity. Europeans' perception of Islam as a menace helped inspire the Crusades of the eleventh through thirteenth centuries (see pages 209–214).

By the thirteenth century Western literature sometimes displayed a sympathetic view of Islam. The Bavarian knight Wolfram von Eschenbach's (**ESH-en-bak**) *Parzival* (**PAHR-tsi-fahl**) and the Englishman William Langland's *Piers the Plowman*—two poems that survive in scores of manuscripts, suggesting that they circulated widely—reveal some broad mindedness and tolerance toward Muslims. Some travelers in the Middle East were impressed by the kindness and generosity of Muslims and with the strictness and devotion with which Muslims observed their faith.[5]

More frequently, however, Christian literature portrayed Muslims as the most dreadful of Europe's enemies, guilty of every kind of crime. In his *Inferno*, the great Florentine poet Dante placed the Muslim philosophers Avicenna (**av-uh-SEN-uh**) and Averroes (**uh-VERR-oh-eez**) with other virtuous "heathens," among them Socrates and Aristotle, in the first circle of hell, where they endured only moderate punishment. Muhammad, however, was consigned to the ninth circle, near Satan himself, where he was condemned as a spreader of discord and scandal.

Muslim views of Christians were also mixed, but here disinterest may have been more common than hostility. Muslim historical writing reflects strong knowledge of European geography but shows an almost total lack of interest in European languages, life, and culture. Commercially, from the Muslim perspective, Europe had very little to offer apart from woolens from the Frisian (**FRIZH-uhn**) Islands in the North Sea and some slaves from central and southeastern Europe.

Animosity began to develop between Muslims and Christians in Spain after the initial period of harmony. Muslim teachers feared that close contact between the two peoples would lead to Muslim contamination and become a threat to the Islamic faith. Christian bishops worried that knowledge of Islam would lead to ignorance of essential Christian doctrines.

Thus, beginning in the late tenth century, Muslim regulations increasingly defined what Christians and Muslims could do. A Christian, however much assimilated, remained an **infidel.** An infidel was an unbeliever, and the word carried a pejorative or disparaging connotation. Such divisions were enhanced in the twelfth century when al-Andalus was taken over by the Almohad dynasty, an extremist group from Morocco that outlawed Judaism and Christianity. When Christian forces conquered Muslim territory in subsequent centuries, Christian rulers regarded their Muslim and Jewish subjects as infidels and enacted similar restrictive measures.

---

infidel An unbeliever, a word carrying a pejorative or disparaging connotation.

Section Review

- Two tribes—the nomadic Bedouins and the city-dwelling Hejaz—respected each other's religious rules, sharing the city of Mecca as the religious center of the Arab world.

- Muhammad founded the religion of Islam, which unified the Arabian peninsula into a political and religious group known as Muslims, based on a belief that he was a prophet of God, and his visions were written down in the Qur'an and other teachings known as the hadith.

- Islam teaches the Five Pillars of Islam: the profession of faith (that there is only one God and Muhammad is his prophet), prayer, fasting, giving alms to the poor, and the pilgrimage to Mecca.

- Islam expanded rapidly, but upon Muhammad's death, a sometimes violent succession dispute developed, the Sunnis accepting an elected line of leadership and the Shi'ites following Muhammad's cousin and son-in-law, Ali.

- The region of Andalusia in the Spanish peninsula enjoyed a unique and peaceful blend of Muslims, Christians, and Jews, with a flourishing capital in Córdoba.

- After a period of peace, discord began to grow between Muslims and Christians when each thought of the other as infidels (unbelievers) who corrupted their respective faiths.

The Frankish Kingdom

How did Frankish rulers govern their kingdoms?

Several centuries before the Muslim conquest of Spain, the Frankish king Clovis converted to Roman Christianity and established a large kingdom in what had been Roman Gaul (see page 153). Though at the time the Frankish kingdom was established it was simply one barbarian kingdom among many, it became the most important state in Europe, expanding to become an empire. Rulers after Clovis used a variety of tactics to enhance their authority and create a stable system.

The Merovingians

Clovis established the Merovingian dynasty, named after a mythical founder Merowig. Before he died, Clovis arranged for his kingdom to be divided among his four sons, a decision that led to civil wars and chronic violence as Clovis's descendants fought among themselves. Still, the royal family and the royal court served as the focus around which conflicts arose, so that the dynasty itself was not threatened.[6]

A Merovingian ruler had multiple sources of income. These included revenues from the royal estates, which were especially large in the north, and the "gifts" of subject peoples, such as plunder and tribute paid by peoples east of the Rhine River. New lands might be conquered and confiscated in order to replenish revenues lost when the ruler endowed land to monasteries or other religious institutions. Fines imposed for criminal offenses and tolls and customs duties on roads, bridges, and waterways (and the goods transported over them) also yielded income. As with the Romans, the minting of coins was a royal monopoly, with drastic penalties for counterfeiting.

The responsibility for collecting royal revenues in a **civitas** (SIV-i-tas)—a city and surrounding territory—fell to a senior official or royal companion known as a **comites** (KOH-meh-tehs). A comites presided over the civitas and was also responsible for hearing lawsuits, enforcing justice, and raising troops. A military leader, known as a *dux* (dooks) or duke, commanded troops from several civitates and was responsible for both defending the kingdom and conquering new lands. The bishop of the civitas also played an important role in the community, and the king depended on him for local information. Merovingian, Carolingian (below), and later medieval rulers traveled constantly to check up on local administrators and peoples. Their hosts were required to provide for the king and his entourage of wives, children, servants, court officials, and warriors and their horses. These visits no doubt strained the local resources.

The court or household of Merovingian kings included scribes who kept records, legal advisors, and treasury agents responsible for aspects of royal finance. These officials could all read and write Latin. Over them all presided the mayor of the palace, the most important secular figure after the king in the kingdom. Usually a leader of one of the great aristocratic families, the mayor also governed in the king's absence.

Kings consulted regularly with the leaders of the aristocracy. This class represented a fusion of Franks and the old Gallo-Roman leadership. Its members possessed landed wealth—villas over which they exercised lordship and dispensed local customary, rather than royal, law—and they often had lavish lifestyles. When

civitas The city and surrounding territory that served as a basis of the administrative system in the Frankish kingdom.

comites A senior official or royal companion later called a count that presided over the civitas.

they were with the king, they constituted the royal court. If the king consulted them and they were in agreement, there was peace. Failure to consult could result in civil war.

The Rise of the Carolingians

From this aristocracy one family gradually emerged to replace the Merovingian dynasty. The rise of the Carolingians—whose name comes from the Latin *Carolus*, or Charles—rests on several factors. First, beginning with Pippin I (d. 640), the head of the Carolingian family acquired and held onto the powerful position of mayor of the palace. Second, a series of advantageous marriage alliances brought the family estates and influence in different parts of the Frankish world. The landed wealth and treasure acquired by Pippin II (d. 714), his son Charles Martel (r. 714–741), and Pippin III (r. 751–768) formed the basis of Carolingian power. Military victories over supporters of the Merovingians ensured their dominance.

Charles Martel's successful wars against the Saxons, Frisians, Alamanni, and Bavarians further enhanced the family's prestige. But it was his victory, in 732, over a Muslim force near Poitiers (**pwa-TYEY**) in central France that was most significant. For Christians, the Frankish victory was one of the great battles of history, halting Muslim expansion in Europe. (Muslims, however, viewed it as a minor skirmish.) Charles Martel and later Carolingians used it to portray themselves as defenders of Christendom against the Muslims.

The battle of Poitiers helped the Carolingians acquire the support of the church, perhaps their most important asset. Charles Martel and Pippin III further strengthened their ties to the church by supporting the work of missionaries who preached Christianity to pagan peoples, along with the Christian duty to obey secular authorities. The most famous of these missionaries was the Englishman Boniface (**BON-uh-feys**) (680–754), who had close ties to the Roman pope. Boniface ordered the oak of Thor, a tree sacred to many pagans, cut down and the wood used to build a church. When the god Thor did not respond by killing Boniface with his lightning bolts, Boniface won many converts.

As mayor of the palace, Charles Martel had exercised the power of king of the Franks. His son Pippin III aspired to have the title as well as its powers. His diplomats were able to convince an embattled Pope Zacharius to rule in his favor in exchange for military support against the Lombards. Chilperic, the last Merovingian ruler, was consigned to a monastery. An assembly of Frankish magnates elected Pippin king, and he was anointed by the missionary Boniface at Soissons.

Saint Boniface

The upper panel of this piece from an early-eleventh-century Fulda Mass book shows the great missionary to Germany baptizing, apparently by full immersion. The lower panel shows his death scene, with the saint protecting himself with a Gospel book. The fluttering robes are similar to those in earlier Anglo-Saxon books, probably modeled on illustrations in books that Boniface brought to Fulda Abbey from England. (Staatsbibliothek Bamberg, Ms. Lit. I, fol. 126v)

When, in 754, Lombard expansion again threatened the papacy, Pope Stephen II journeyed to the Frankish kingdom seeking help. On this occasion, he personally anointed Pippin with the sacred oils and gave him the title "Patrician of the Romans." Pippin promised restitution of the papal lands and later made a gift of estates in central Italy.

Prior to Pippin, only priests and bishops had received anointment. Pippin became the first monarch to be acknowledged as *rex et sacerdos* (**reks et SAK-er-dose**), meaning king and priest. Anointment, rather than royal blood, set the Christian king apart. By having himself anointed, Pippin cleverly eliminated possible threats to the Frankish throne coming from other claimants, and the pope promised him support in the future. When Pippin died, his son Charles succeeded him.

The Empire of Charlemagne

How did Charlemagne gain control of a large part of Europe and how did power become decentralized after his death?

Charles the Great (r. 768–814), generally known by the French version of his name, Charlemagne (**SHAHR-leh-mane**), built on the military and diplomatic foundations of his ancestors and on the administrative machinery of the Merovingian kings. He expanded the Frankish kingdom into what is now Germany and Italy and, late in his long reign, was crowned emperor by the pope.

Charlemagne's Personal Qualities and Marriage Strategies

Charlemagne's secretary and biographer, Einhard, wrote a lengthy idealization of this warrior-ruler. It is the earliest medieval biography of a layman, and historians consider it generally accurate:

> Charles was large and strong, and of lofty stature, though not disproportionately tall . . . the upper part of his head was round, his eyes very large and animated, nose a little long, hair fair, and face laughing and merry. Thus his appearance was always stately and dignified . . . although his neck was thick and somewhat short, and his belly rather prominent; but the symmetry of the rest of his body concealed these defects. His gait was firm, his whole carriage manly and his voice clear, but not so strong as his size led one to expect. His health was excellent, except during the four years preceding his death. . . .[7]

Though crude and brutal, Charlemagne was a man of enormous intelligence. He appreciated good literature, such as Saint Augustine's *City of God*, and Einhard considered him an unusually effective speaker.

The security and continuation of his dynasty and the need for diplomatic alliances governed Charlemagne's complicated marriage pattern. Charlemagne had a total of four legal wives and six concubines, and even after the age of sixty-five he continued to sire children. Though three sons reached adulthood, only one outlived him. Four surviving grandsons ensured perpetuation of the dynasty.

Territorial Expansion

Continuing the expansionist policies of his ancestors, Charlemagne fought more than fifty campaigns and became the greatest warrior of the early Middle Ages. He subdued all of the north of modern France, but his greatest successes were in today's Germany. In the course of a thirty-year war against the Saxons, he added

Section Review

- The Frankish king Clovis, a Roman Christian, established his Merovingian kingdom in what was Roman Gaul; while his four sons fought over it, the dynasty remained.

- Merovingian rulers amassed wealth as they collected revenues, conquered new land, imposed fines and tolls, and minted coins.

- In many Frankish territories, a **comites** (royal official) oversaw cities, a **dux** (duke) commanded the troops, and a bishop relayed local information to the king; the bishop also had religious and community duties.

- The Merovingian king's court included scribes, legal advisors, treasury agents, the mayor of the palace (who was second to the king), and the leaders of the aristocracy.

- Charles Martel, of the aristocratic Carolingian family, gained strength through wealth, advantageous land position, marriage, and most importantly the church; he put his son Pippin on the Frankish throne.

Reliquary Bust of Charlemagne

This splendid twelfth-century gothic idealization portrays the emperor of legend and myth rather than the squat, potbellied ruler described by his contemporary, Einhard. The jeweled helmet or crown is symbolic of Charlemagne's role as defender of church and people. (Photo: Ann Münchow, © Domkapitel Aachen)

most of the northwestern German tribes to the Frankish kingdom. Charlemagne also achieved spectacular results in the south, incorporating Lombardy into the Frankish kingdom. He ended Bavarian independence and defeated the nomadic Avars, opening the Danubian plain for later settlement. He successfully fought the Byzantine Empire for Venetia (excluding the city of Venice itself), Istria, and Dalmatia, and temporarily annexed those areas to his kingdom.

Charlemagne's only defeat came at the hands of the Basques of northwestern Spain, as he was withdrawing after an unsuccessful siege of their territory. Although it was a forbidden topic during Charlemagne's lifetime, the ill-fated expedition inspired the great medieval epic, *The Song of Roland.* Based on legend and written in about 1100 at the beginning of the European crusading movement, the poem portrays the Frankish Count Roland as the ideal chivalric knight and Charlemagne as exercising a sacred kind of kingship. Although many of the epic's details differ from the historical evidence, *The Song of Roland* is important because it reveals the popular image of Charlemagne in later centuries.

By around 805 the Frankish kingdom included all of northwestern Europe except Scandinavia (see Map 8.2). Not since the third century C.E. had any ruler controlled so much of the Western world.

The Government of the Carolingian Empire

Charlemagne ruled a vast rural world dotted with isolated estates and small villages and characterized by constant warfare. According to the chroniclers of the time, only seven years between 714 and 814 were peaceful. Charlemagne's empire was not a state as people today understand that term; it was a collection of peoples and tribes. Apart from a small class of warrior-aristocrats and clergy and a tiny minority of Jews, almost everyone engaged in agriculture. Towns served as the headquarters of bishops, as ecclesiastical centers.

The Carolingian rulers inherited the functions of both the king and the mayor of the palace. The scholar-adviser Alcuin (**AL-kwin**) (see page 183) wrote that "a king should be strong against his enemies, humble to Christians, feared by pagans, loved by the poor and judicious in counsel and maintaining justice."[8] Charlemagne worked to realize that ideal. By military expeditions that brought wealth—lands, booty, slaves, and tribute—and by peaceful travel, personal appearances, and the sheer force of his personality, Charlemagne sought to awe newly conquered peoples and rebellious domestic enemies.

The political power of the Carolingians rested on the cooperation of the dominant social class, the Frankish aristocracy. The lands and booty with which Charles Martel and Charlemagne rewarded their followers in these families enabled the nobles to improve their economic position, but it was only with noble help that the Carolingians were able to wage wars of expansion and suppress rebellions. In short, Carolingian success was a matter of reciprocal help and reward.[9]

For administrative purposes, Charlemagne divided his entire kingdom into *counties* based closely on the old Merovingian civitas (see page 171). Each of the approximately six hundred counties was governed by a count (or in his absence by a viscount) whose responsibilities were similar to those of a Merovingian comites. Counts were at first sent out from the royal court; later a person native to the region was appointed.

MAP 8.2 Charlemagne's Conquests

Though Charlemagne's hold on much of his territory was relatively weak, the size of his empire was not equaled again until the nineteenth-century conquests of Napoleon. (*Source:* Some data from Michael McCormick, *Origins of the European Economy: Communications and Commerce, A.D. 300–900* [Cambridge: Cambridge University Press, 2001], p. 762.)

As a link between local authorities and the central government, Charlemagne appointed officials called **missi dominici** (miss-ee doh-MEH-nee-chee), "agents of the lord king." Each year beginning in 802, two missi (singular: *missus*), usually a count and a bishop or abbot, visited assigned districts to check up on the local counts. They held courts; investigated the district's judicial, financial, and clerical

missi dominici Officials sent by Charlemagne to report on local districts.

activities; and organized commissions to regulate crime, moral conduct, the clergy, education, the poor, and many other matters.

The Imperial Coronation of Charlemagne

In autumn of the year 800, Charlemagne paid a momentous visit to Rome. Einhard gives this account of what happened:

His last journey there [to Rome] was due to another factor, namely that the Romans, having inflicted many injuries on Pope Leo—plucking out his eyes and tearing out his tongue, he had been compelled to beg the assistance of the king. Accordingly, coming to Rome in order that he might set in order those things which had exceedingly disturbed the condition of the Church, he remained there the whole winter. It was at the time that he accepted the name of Emperor and Augustus. At first he was so much opposed to this that he insisted that although that day was a great [Christian] feast, he would not have entered the Church if he had known beforehand the pope's intention. But he bore very patiently the jealousy of the Roman Emperors [that is, the Byzantine rulers] who were indignant when he received these titles. He overcame their arrogant haughtiness with magnanimity.[10]

For centuries scholars have debated the significance of the imperial coronation of Charlemagne. Did Charlemagne plan the ceremony in Saint Peter's on Christmas Day, or did he merely accept the title of emperor? If, as Einhard implies, the coronation displeased Charlemagne, was that because it put the pope in the superior position of conferring power on the emperor? What were Pope Leo's motives in arranging the coronation?

Though final answers will probably never be found, several things seem certain. First, Charlemagne gained the imperial title of Holy Roman emperor and the pope gained a military protector. Charlemagne considered himself a Christian king ruling a Christian people. Through his motto, *Renovatio romani imperi* (Revival of the Roman Empire), Charlemagne was consciously perpetuating old Roman imperial notions while at the same time identifying with the new Rome of the Christian church. Second, later German rulers were eager to gain the imperial title and to associate themselves with the legends of Charlemagne and ancient Rome. Finally, ecclesiastical authorities continually cited the event as proof that the dignity of the imperial crown could be granted only by the pope.

From Baghdad, Harun al Rashid (hah-ROON al-rah-SHEED), caliph of the Abbasid (ah-BASS-id) Empire (786–809), congratulated Charlemagne on his coronation with the gift of an elephant. But although the Muslim caliph recognized Charlemagne as a fellow sovereign, the Greeks regarded the papal acts as rebellious and Charlemagne as a usurper. The imperial coronation thus marks a decisive break between Rome and Constantinople. The coronation of Charlemagne, whether planned by the Carolingian court or by the papacy, was to have a profound effect on the course of German history and on the later history of Europe.

Decentralization and "Feudalism"

Charlemagne left his vast empire to his sole surviving son, Louis the Pious (r. 814–840), who attempted to keep the empire intact. This proved to be impossible. Members of the nobility engaged in plots and open warfare against the emperor, often allying themselves with one of Louis's three sons. (See the feature "Individuals in Society: Ebo of Reims.") In 843, shortly after Louis's death, those sons agreed to the **Treaty of Verdun** (ver-DUHN), which divided the empire into three parts: Charles the Bald received the western part, Lothair the middle part plus the title of emperor, and Louis the eastern part, from which he acquired the title "the German." Though of course no one knew it at the time, this treaty set the pattern for political boundaries in Europe that has been maintained until today. Other than brief periods under Napoleon and Hitler, Europe would never again see as large a unified state as it had under Charlemagne, which is one reason he has become a symbol of European unity in the twenty-first century.

The large-scale division of Charlemagne's empire was accompanied by a decentralization of power at the local level. Civil wars weakened the power and prestige of kings, who could do little about local violence. Likewise, the great invasions of the ninth century, especially the Viking invasions (see page 169), weakened royal authority. The western Frankish kings could do little to halt the invaders, and the local aristocracy had to assume responsibility for defense. Common people turned for protection to the strongest power, the local counts, whom they considered their rightful rulers. Thus, in the ninth and tenth centuries great aristocratic families increased their authority in the regions of their vested interests. They built private castles for defense and to live in, and they governed virtually independent territories in which distant and weak kings could not interfere.

The most powerful nobles were those able to gain the allegiance of warriors, often symbolized in an oath-swearing ceremony of homage and fealty that grew out of earlier Germanic oaths of loyalty. In this ceremony, a warrior (knight) swore his loyalty as a **vassal**—from a Celtic term meaning "servant"—to the more powerful individual, who became his lord. In return for the vassal's loyalty, aid, and military assistance, the lord promised him protection and material support. This support might be a place in the lord's household but was more likely land of the vassal's own, called a **fief** (feef). The fief might contain forests, churches, and towns. The fief theoretically still belonged to the lord, and the vassal only had the use of it. Peasants living on a fief produced the food and other goods necessary to maintain the knight.

Though historians debate this, fiefs appear to have been granted extensively first by Charles Martel and then by his successors, including Charlemagne and his grandsons. These fiefs went to their most powerful nobles, who often took the title of count. As the Carolingians' control of their territories weakened, the practice of granting fiefs moved to the local level, with lay lords, bishops, and abbots granting fiefs as well as kings.

This system, later named **feudalism,** was based on personal ties of loyalty cemented by grants of land rather than on allegiance to an abstract state or governmental system. In some parts of Europe, such as Ireland and the Baltic area, warrior-aristocrats or clan chieftains who controlled relatively small regions were the ultimate political authorities; they generally did not grant fiefs to secure loyalty but relied on strictly personal ties. Thus the word *feudal* does not properly apply to these areas.

Some historians argue, in fact, that the word *feudalism* should not be used at all, as it was unknown in the Middle Ages. In addition, the system that would later be called feudalism changed considerably in form and pattern between the ninth and fifteenth centuries, and differed from place to place. The feudalism of England in 1100, for example, differed greatly from that of France, scarcely fifty miles away, at the same time. The problem is that no one has come up with a better term for this loose arrangement of personal and property ties.

Whether one chooses to use the word *feudalism* or not, this system functioned as a way to organize political authority, particularly because vassals also owed

Treaty of Verdun Treaty signed in 843 by Louis's three sons, dividing the empire into three parts and setting the pattern for political boundaries in Europe that has been maintained until today.

vassal A warrior who swore loyalty to a noble in exchange for protection and support.

fief A piece of land granted by a feudal lord in return for service.

feudalism A political system in which a vassal was promised protection and material support by a lord in return for his loyalty, aid, and military assistance.

Individuals in Society

Ebo of Reims

The term *social mobility* came into broad use only in the twentieth century, but what it signifies—having the opportunity for an upward shift in status within society—is probably as old as organized society itself. "In all ages, service to the state and to men of power has raised some individuals and has enabled them to share in the social prestige that attaches to power."* In the Christian Middle Ages the Catholic Church provided the widest path for social advancement, and the archbishop symbolized political as well as religious prestige. Ebo of Reims (ca. 775–851) represents one such individual.

Emperor Louis the Pious confers with bishops and lay magnates. (Bibliothèque nationale de France)

Ebo's father was a serf freed by Charlemagne; his mother, Himiltruda, was the nurse of Louis the Pious. Ebo's mother probably launched his career, for Ebo was brought up with Louis at the "palace school" at Aachen (**AH-kuhn**), where nobles and others were trained for administrative and judicial service to the emperor. A bond was forged between Ebo and Louis. When Louis became king of Aquitaine, he made Ebo his librarian; when Louis succeeded as emperor in 814, he secured for Ebo the important archiepiscopal see of Reims.

Ebo proved himself a very competent administrator. He began construction of a new cathedral, gaining imperial permission to use the city walls as building blocks. Ebo organized the cathedral chapter—the local clergy who handled routine business of the diocese under the bishop. He reformed the monasteries in his see, ending the diverse forms of religious life by enforcing the *Rule of Saint Benedict* in all houses. Ebo also patronized learning and the arts. He supported the production of manuscripts and the school long associated with the cathedral, and he commissioned the production of a book that bears his name, the *Ebo Gospels*.

Ebo served the emperor as *missus* in his province, where he worked to extend royal authority. Archbishop

Ebo served both church and state when, acting on behalf of Pope Pascal I and Louis the Pious, he led a mission to King Harold of Denmark, whose goal was the conversion of the Danes to Christianity and peaceful relations with the Franks. When Harold and a large Danish entourage visited Louis in 826, the Danes were baptized, and Harold became Louis's vassal.

In 830 Louis was past fifty, an old man by contemporary standards. Louis had three adult sons. Adult sons often posed a test of medieval kingship. Sons wanted power on their own, resented paternal control, and often rebelled. In 833 Archbishop Ebo served as counselor to the sons of Louis the Pious in their plot to remove Louis and replace him with Lothar. Ebo headed a commission of bishops that drew up charges against the emperor, accusing him of failing in his imperial responsibilities, promoting discord among the Frankish people, and tolerating his (second) wife Judith's adultery, thereby bringing moral scandal to the kingdom. Louis was forced to renounce the throne and to do public penance. The charges proved false, and within months Louis regained his throne. A church council deposed Ebo, consigning him to a monastery. When Louis the Pious died, Lothar restored Ebo to Reims, but the pope refused to approve the appointment. Then a dispute with Lothar led Ebo to seek the support of Louis the German, who made him bishop of Hildesheim. Ebo died at Hildesheim.

Why did Ebo betray his boyhood friend and great benefactor? Was he resentful about some real or perceived slight and did he desire revenge? Was he willing to listen to dangerous advice? Did he wish to show himself the equal of any magnate who opposed the emperor? The *Annals of St.-Bertin*, the chief source of information about these events, describes Ebo as ungrateful, disobedient, disloyal, and cruel. What do you think?

Questions for Analysis

1. How does the career of Ebo of Reims illustrate social mobility?

2. What do Ebo's church appointments tell us about the Frankish state? What secular functions did bishops perform?

Sources: R. McKitterick, *The Frankish Kingdoms Under the Carolingians* (New York: Longman, 1983); J. L. Nelson, *Politics and Ritual in Early Medieval Europe* (London: Ronceverte, 1986).

---

* K. Bosl, "On Social Mobility in Medieval Society," in *Early Medieval Society*, ed. S. L. Thrupp (New York: Appleton-Century-Crofts, 1967).

obligations other than military service to the lord. They served as advisers and judges at the lord's court, provided lodging for the lord when he was traveling through their fief, gave him gifts at important family events, and might contribute ransom money if the lord was captured.

Along with granting fiefs to knights, lords gave fiefs to the clergy for spiritual services or promises of allegiance. In addition, the church held pieces of land on its own and granted fiefs to its own knightly vassals. Abbots and abbesses of monasteries, bishops, and archbishops were either lords or vassals in many feudal arrangements.

Women other than abbesses were generally not granted fiefs, but in most parts of Europe they could inherit them if their fathers had no sons. Occasionally, women did go through services swearing homage and fealty and swore to send fighters when the lord demanded them. More commonly, women acted as their husbands' surrogates when the men were away, defending the territory from attack and carrying out his administrative duties.

Feudalism existed at two social levels: at the higher level were the lords of great feudal principalities; below them were their knights, holding fiefs that may have been no larger than a small village with its surrounding land. In fact, some knights were landless and lived in the households of their lords. A wide and deep gap in social standing and political function separated these levels.

Manorialism, Serfdom, and the Slave Trade

The vast majority of people in medieval Europe were peasants who lived in family groups in villages or small towns, raising crops and animals. The village and the land surrounding it were called a *manor*, from the Latin word for "dwelling" or "homestead." Some fiefs might include only one manor, while great lords or kings might have hundreds of manors under their direct control. Residents of manors provided work for their lord in exchange for protection, a system that was later referred to as **manorialism.** Peasants surrendered themselves and their lands to the lord's jurisdiction. The land was returned to them to work, but the peasants became tied to the land by various kinds of payments and services. Like feudalism, manorialism involved an exchange. Because the economic power of the feudal lord and vassal rested on the work of peasants, feudalism and manorialism were inextricably linked.

manorialism A system in which residents of manors provided work for their lord in exchange for protection.

In France, England, Germany, and Italy, local custom determined precisely what services peasants would provide to their lord, but certain practices became common everywhere. The peasant was obliged to give the lord a percentage of the annual harvest, usually in produce, sometimes in cash. The peasant paid a fee to marry someone from outside the lord's estate. To inherit property, the peasant paid a fine, often the best beast the person owned. Above all, the peasant became part of the lord's permanent labor force. With vast stretches of uncultivated virgin land and a tiny labor population, lords encouraged population growth and immigration. The most profitable form of capital was not land but laborers.

In entering into a relationship with a feudal lord, free farmers lost status. Their position became servile, and they became **serfs.** That is, they were bound to the land and could not leave it without the lord's permission. Serfdom was not the same as slavery in that lords did not own the person of the serf, but serfs were subject to the jurisdiction of the lord's court in any dispute over property and in any case of suspected criminal behavior.

serfs Free farmers in the feudal relationship who lost status, therefore becoming servile and bound to the land.

The transition from freedom to serfdom was slow; its speed was closely related to the degree of political order in a given region. In the late eighth century there

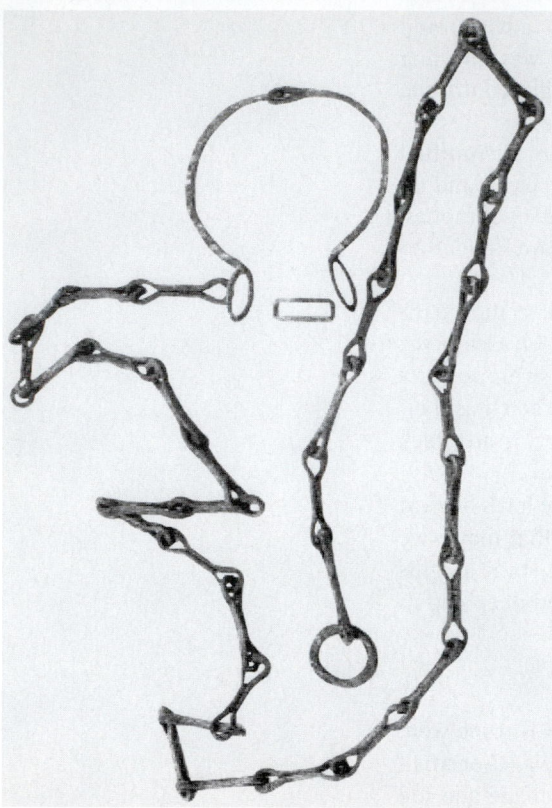

Balkan Neck Shackle (tenth century)

The slave trader restrained the captive by slipping the chain through the loops in the neck collar (*top*), fastening it securely, and then attaching the chain to the captive's limbs. Similar devices for controlling slaves while allowing them to walk were later used in other parts of the world. (The National Museum of History, Sofia, Bulgaria)

were still many free peasants. And within the legal category of serfdom there were many economic levels, ranging from the highly prosperous to the desperately poor. Nevertheless, a social and legal revolution was taking place. By the year 800 perhaps 60 percent of the population of western Europe—completely free a century before—had been reduced to serfdom. The ninth-century Viking assaults on Europe, discussed later in this chapter, created a vast climate of fear and led more people to accept serfdom in exchange for protection.

Persons captured in war often became actual slaves, who were then traded by merchants. Charlemagne's long wars against the Lombards, Avars, Saxons, and other groups produced thousands of prisoners who were exchanged for the Eastern luxury goods that nobles and the clergy desired. When Frankish conquests declined in the tenth century, slave merchants obtained people from the empire's eastern border who spoke Slavic languages; this was the origin of our word *slave*. Slaves sold across the Mediterranean fetched three or four times the amounts brought within the Carolingian Empire, so most slaves were sold to Muslims. For Europeans and Arabs alike, selling captives and other slaves was standard procedure. Christian moralists sometimes complained about the sale of Christians to non-Christians, but they did not object to slavery itself.

In general, the Carolingian period witnessed moderate population growth, as indicated by the steady reduction of forests and wasteland. The highest aristocrats and church officials lived well, with fine clothing and at least a few rooms heated by firewood. Male nobles hunted and managed their estates, while female nobles generally oversaw the education of their children and sometimes inherited and controlled land on their own. Craftsmen and craftswomen on manorial estates manufactured textiles, weapons, glass, and pottery, primarily for local consumption. Sometimes abbeys and manors served as markets; goods were shipped away to towns and fairs for sale; and a good deal of interregional commerce existed. In the towns, which were generally small, artisans and merchants produced and traded luxury goods for noble and clerical patrons. The modest economic expansion benefited townspeople and nobles, but it did not alter the lives of most people very much.

Section Review

- Charlemagne was a brutal but intelligent ruler who fought over fifty military campaigns and used diplomatic alliances so that by 805 the Frankish kingdom extended over all of northwestern Europe except Scandinavia.

- The Carolingian empire was primarily an agricultural society, divided into counties ruled by counts and regulated by missi dominici (agents of the king) who made regular inspection tours.

- The pope gained military protection from Charlemagne by granting him the imperial title Holy Roman Emperor, which the Muslims recognized but the Greeks resented, causing a rift between Rome and Constantinople.

- After Charlemagne's death, his grandsons divided his empire into three parts: Charles the Bald took the west, Lothair the middle with the title of emperor, and Louis the east and the title "the German."

- This division led to decentralization of power as the most powerful nobles gained the support of vassals (warriors) in return for fiefs (land that could contain forests, churches, and towns), in a system known today as feudalism.

- Under feudalism and manorialism, free farmers gained protection but lost ownership of their land and became serfs; in addition, many prisoners of war were sold and traded as slaves.

Early Medieval Scholarship and Culture

What were the significant intellectual and cultural changes in Charlemagne's era?

It is perhaps ironic that Charlemagne's most enduring legacy was the stimulus he gave to scholarship and learning. Barely literate himself, preoccupied with the control of vast territories, much more a warrior than an intellectual, he nevertheless set in motion a cultural revival that had widespread and long-lasting consequences.

Scholarship and Religious Life in Northumbria

The Anglo-Saxon kingdom of Northumbria in medieval England was the original source of the Carolingian intellectual revival. Northumbrian creativity owes a great deal to Saint Benet Biscop (ca. 628–689), who brought manuscripts and other treasures back from Italy. These formed the library on which much later study rested.

Northumbrian monasteries produced scores of books: *missals* (used for the celebration of the Mass), *psalters* (**SAL-ters**) (which contained the 150 psalms and other prayers used by the monks in their devotions), commentaries on the Scriptures, law codes, and collections of letters and sermons. The finest product of Northumbrian art is probably the illuminated manuscript of the Gospel produced at Lindisfarne (**LIN-duhs-farn**) around 700. The incredible expense involved in the publication of such a book—for vellum (calfskin or lambskin specially prepared for writing), coloring, and gold leaf—represents in part an aristocratic display of wealth. The illustrations have a strong Eastern quality, combining the abstract, nonrepresentational style of the Christian Middle East and the narrative (storytelling) approach of classical Roman art. Likewise, the use of geometrical decorative designs shows the influence of Syrian art. Many scribes and artists must have participated in the book's preparation.

In Gaul and Anglo-Saxon England, women shared with men the work of evangelization and the new Christian learning. Kings and nobles, seeking suitable occupations for daughters who did not or would not marry, founded monasteries for nuns, some of which were double monasteries. A **double monastery** housed men and women in two adjoining establishments and was governed by one superior, an *abbess*. Nuns looked after the children given to the monastery as *oblates* (**OB-laytz**) (offerings), the elderly who retired at the monastery, and travelers who needed hospitality. Monks provided protection, since an isolated house of women invited attack in a violent age. Monks also did the heavy work on the land.

Perhaps the most famous abbess of the Anglo-Saxon period was Saint Hilda (614–680). A noblewoman of considerable learning and administrative ability, she ruled the double monastery of Whitby on the Northumbrian coast, advised kings and princes, hosted the famous synod of 664, and encouraged scholars and poets. Several generations after Hilda, Saint Boniface (see page 172) wrote many letters to Whitby and other houses of nuns pleading for copies of books; these letters attest to the nuns' intellectual reputations.[11]

The finest representative of Northumbrian—and indeed all Anglo-Saxon—scholarship is the Venerable Bede (ca. 673–735). When he was seven his parents gave him as an oblate to Benet Biscop's monastery at Wearmouth. Later he was

double monastery A monastery that housed both men and women in two adjoining establishments and was governed by one superior, an abbess.

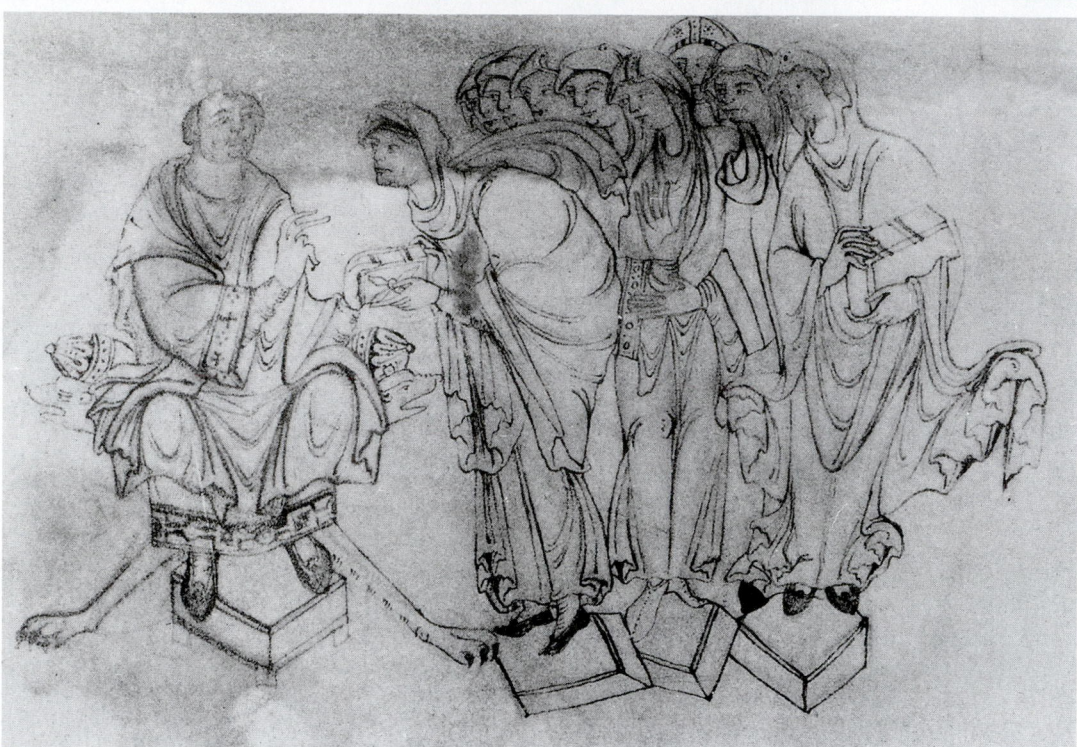

Nuns and Learning

In this tenth-century manuscript, the scholar Saint Aldhelm offers his book *In Praise of Holy Virgins* to a group of nuns, one of whom already holds a book. Early medieval nuns and monks spent much of their time copying manuscripts, preserving much of the learning of the classical world as well as Christian texts. (His Grace the Archbishop of Canterbury and the Trustees of Lambeth Palace Library. MS 200, fol. 68v)

sent to the new monastery at Jarrow five miles away. Surrounded by the books Benet Biscop had brought from Italy, Bede spent the rest of his life there.

Modern scholars praise Bede for his *Ecclesiastical History of the English People* (ca. 720), the chief source of information about early Britain. Bede searched far and wide for his information, discussed the validity of his evidence, compared various sources, and exercised rare critical judgment.

Bede popularized the system of dating events from the birth of Christ, rather than from the foundation of the city of Rome, as the Romans had done, or from the regnal years of kings, as the Germans did. He introduced the term *anno Domini*, "in the year of the Lord," abbreviated A.D. He fitted the entire history of the world into this new dating method. (The reverse dating system of B.C., "before Christ," does not seem to have been widely used before 1700.)

At about the time the monks at Lindisfarne were producing their Gospel book and Bede was writing his *History* at Jarrow, another Northumbrian monk was at work on a nonreligious epic poem that provides considerable information about the society that produced it. In contrast to the works of Bede, which were written in Latin, the poem *Beowulf* (BEY-uh-woolf) was written in the vernacular Anglo-Saxon. Although *Beowulf* is the only native English heroic epic, all the events take place in Denmark and Sweden, suggesting the close relationship between England and the continent in the eighth century. A classic of Western literature, *Beowulf* is the story of the hero's progress from valiant warrior to wise ruler.

Had they remained entirely insular, Northumbrian cultural achievements would have been of slight significance. But an Englishman from Northumbria—Alcuin—played a decisive role in the transmission of English learning to the Carolingian Empire and continental Europe.

The Carolingian Renaissance

In Roman Gaul through the fifth century, the general culture rested on an education that stressed grammar; the works of the Greco-Roman orators, poets, dramatists, and historians; and the legal and medical treatises of the Roman world. Beginning in the seventh and eighth centuries, a new cultural tradition common to Gaul, Italy, the British Isles, and to some extent Spain emerged. This culture was based primarily on Christian sources. Scholars have called this new Christian and ecclesiastical culture, and the educational foundation on which it was based, the "Carolingian Renaissance," because Charlemagne was its major patron.

Charlemagne directed that every monastery in his kingdom "should cultivate learning and educate the monks and secular clergy so that they might have a better understanding of the Christian writings." He also urged the establishment of cathedral and monastic schools where boys might learn to read and to pray properly. Thus the main purpose of this rebirth of learning was to promote an understanding of the Scriptures and of Christian writers.

At his court at Aachen, Charlemagne assembled learned men from all over Europe. The most important scholar and the leader of the palace school was the Northumbrian Alcuin (ca. 735–804). From 781 until his death, Alcuin was the emperor's chief adviser on religious and educational matters. An unusually prolific writer, he prepared some of the emperor's official documents and wrote many moral *exempla*, or "models," that set high standards for royal behavior and constitute a treatise on kingship. Alcuin's letters to Charlemagne set forth political theories on the authority, power, and responsibilities of a Christian ruler.

The scholars at Charlemagne's court also built up libraries, by hand copying books and manuscripts. They used the beautifully clear handwriting known as "caroline minuscule," from which modern Roman type is derived. Unlike the Merovingian majuscule, which had letters of equal size, minuscule had both uppercase and lowercase letters. Caroline minuscule improved the legibility of texts and meant that a sheet of vellum could contain more words and thus be used more efficiently. With the materials at hand, many more manuscripts could be copied. Book production on this scale represents a major manifestation of the revival of learning. Caroline minuscule illustrates the way a seemingly small technological change has broad cultural consequences.

Although scholars worked with Latin, the common people spoke local or vernacular languages. The Bretons, for example, retained their local dialect, and the Saxons and Bavarians could not understand each other. Some scholars believe that

Saint Luke from the Ada Gospels (late eighth to early ninth century)

In this lavishly illuminated painting from a manuscript of the four Gospels of the New Testament, a statuesque Saint Luke sits enthroned, his clothing falling in distinct folds reminiscent of Byzantine art. He is surrounded by an elaborate architectural framework, and above him is a winged ox, the symbol of Luke in early Christian art. The Ada school of painting was attached to the court of Charlemagne and gets its name from Ada, a sister of Charlemagne who commissioned some of the school's work. (Municipal Library, Trier, HS 22fol. 85r)

Latin words and phrases gradually penetrated the various vernacular languages, facilitating communication among diverse peoples.

Once basic literacy was established, monastic and other scholars went on to more difficult work. By the middle years of the ninth century, there was a great outpouring of more sophisticated books. Ecclesiastical writers imbued with the legal ideas of ancient Rome and the theocratic ideals of Saint Augustine instructed the rulers of the West. And it is no accident that medical study in the West began at Salerno in southern Italy in the late ninth century, *after* the Carolingian Renaissance.

Alcuin completed the work of his countryman Boniface—the Christianization of northern Europe. Latin Christian attitudes penetrated deeply into the consciousness of European peoples. By the tenth century the patterns of thought and the lifestyles of educated western Europeans were those of Rome and Latin Christianity.

Invasions and Migrations

What effects did the assaults and migrations of the Vikings, Magyars, and Muslims have on the rest of Europe?

After the Treaty of Verdun (843), continental Europe was fractured politically. All three kingdoms controlled by the sons of Louis the Pious were torn by domestic dissension and disorder. The frontier and coastal defenses erected by Charlemagne and maintained by Louis the Pious were neglected. No European political power was strong enough to put up effective resistance to external attacks. Three groups attacked Europe: Vikings from Scandinavia, representing the final wave of Germanic migrants; Muslims from the Mediterranean; and Magyars forced westward by other peoples (see Map 8.3).

Vikings in Western Europe

From the moors of Scotland to the mountains of Sicily, there arose in the ninth century the prayer, "Save us, O God, from the violence of the Northmen." The Northmen, also known as Vikings, were Germanic peoples from Norway, Sweden, and Denmark who had remained beyond the sway of the Christianizing influences of the Carolingian Empire. Some scholars believe that the name *Viking* derives from the old Norse word *vik*, meaning "creek." A Viking, then, was a pirate who waited in a creek or bay to attack passing vessels.

Viking boats were built for great speed and maneuverability. Propelled either by oars or by sails, deckless, and about sixty-five feet long, a Viking ship could carry between forty and sixty men—enough to harass an isolated monastery or village. These ships, navigated by thoroughly experienced and utterly fearless sailors, moved through the most complicated rivers, estuaries, and waterways in Europe. The Carolingian Empire, with no navy and no notion of the importance of sea power, was helpless. The Vikings moved swiftly, attacked, and escaped to return again.

Scholars disagree about the reasons for Viking attacks and migrations. Recent research asserts that a very unstable Danish kingship and disputes over the succession led to civil war and disorder, which drove warriors abroad in search of booty and supporters. Other writers insist that the Vikings were looking for trade and new commercial contacts. In that case, there were no better targets than the mercantile centers of Francia and Frisia.

Viking attacks were savage. The Vikings burned, looted, and did extensive short-term property damage, but there is little evidence that they caused long-term destruction—perhaps because, arriving in small bands, they lacked the manpower to do so. They seized magnates and high churchmen and held them for ransom; they also demanded tribute from kings. In 844–845 Charles the Bald had to raise seven thousand pounds of silver, and across the English Channel Anglo-Saxon

MAPPING THE PAST

MAP 8.3   Invasions and Migrations of the Ninth Century

This map shows the Viking, Magyar, and Arab invasions and migrations in the ninth century. Compare it with Map 7.3 (page 151) on the barbarian migrations of late antiquity to answer the following questions: **[1]** What similarities do you see in the patterns of migration in these two periods? What significant differences? **[2]** How is Viking expertise in shipbuilding and sailing reflected on this map? Based on the information in Map 7.3, what would you assume about the maritime skills of earlier Germanic tribes?

Animal Headpost from Viking Ship
Skilled woodcarvers produced ornamental headposts for ships, sledges, wagons, and bedsteads. The fearsome quality of many carvings suggests that they were intended to ward off evil spirits and to terrify. (© University Museum of Cultural Heritage, Oslo. Photographer: Eirik Irgens Johnsen)

rulers collected a land tax, the Danegeld, to buy off the Vikings. In the Seine and Loire Valleys the frequent presence of Viking war bands seems to have had economic consequences, stimulating the production of food and wine and possibly the manufacture (for sale) of weapons and the breeding of horses. In the early tenth century Danish Vikings besieged Paris with fleets of more than a hundred highly maneuverable ships, and the Frankish king Charles the Simple bought them off with a large part of northern France. The Vikings established the province of "Northmanland," or Normandy as it was later known, intermarrying with the local population and creating a distinctive Norman culture. From there they sailed around Spain and into the Mediterranean, eventually conquering Sicily from the Muslim Arabs in 1060–1090, while other Normans crossed the English Channel, defeating Anglo-Saxon forces in 1066.

Between 876 and 954 Viking control extended from Dublin across northern Britain to the Vikings' Scandinavian homelands. Norwegian Vikings moved farther west than any Europeans had before, establishing permanent settlements on Iceland and short-lived settlements in Greenland and Newfoundland, in what is now Canada.

In their initial attacks on isolated settlements, the Vikings took *thralls* (slaves) for the markets of Europe, and for trade with the Muslim world. The slave trade represented an important part of Viking commerce. The Icelander Hoskuld Dala-Kolsson paid three marks of silver, three times the price of a common concubine, for a pretty Irish girl; she was one of twelve offered by a Viking trader. No wonder many communities bought peace by paying tribute.

Along with destruction, the Vikings made positive contributions to the areas they settled. They carried their unrivaled knowledge of shipbuilding and seamanship everywhere. The northeastern and central parts of England where the Vikings settled became known as the Danelaw because Danish, not English, law and customs prevailed there. Scholars believe that some legal institutions, such as the ancestor of the modern grand jury, originated in the Danelaw. Thriving centers of Viking trade emerged in England and Ireland.

Slavs and Vikings in Eastern Europe

In antiquity the Slavs lived in central Europe, farming with iron technology, building fortified towns, and worshiping a variety of deities. With the start of the mass migrations of the late Roman Empire, the Slavs moved in different directions and split into what later historians identified as three groups: West, South, and East Slavs.

The group labeled the West Slavs included the Poles, Czechs, Slovaks, and Wends. The South Slavs, comprising peoples who became the Serbs, Croats, Slovenes, Macedonians, and Bosnians, migrated southward into the Balkans. In the seventh century Slavic peoples created the state of Moravia along the banks of the Danube River, and by the tenth century it was Roman Christian. Most of the other West and South Slavs also slowly became Roman Christian. The pattern was similar to that of the Germanic tribes: first the ruler was baptized, and then missionaries preached, built churches, and spread Christian teachings among the common people. The ruler of the Poland was able to convince the pope to establish an independent archbishopric there in 1000, the beginning of a long-lasting connection between Poland and the Roman church. In the Balkans the Serbs accepted Orthodox Christianity, while the Croats became Roman Christian, a division that has had a long impact; it was one of the factors in the civil war in this area in the late twentieth century.

Between the fifth and ninth centuries, the eastern Slavs moved into the practically uninhabited area of present-day European Russia and Ukraine. This enormous area consisted of an immense virgin forest to the north, where most of the eastern Slavs settled, and a vast prairie grassland to the south.

In the ninth century the Vikings appeared in the lands of the eastern Slavs. Called "Varangians" (**va-RAN-gee-anz**) in the old Russian chronicles, their initial raids for plunder gradually turned into trading missions. Moving up and down the rivers, they linked Scandinavia and northern Europe to the Black Sea and to the Byzantine Empire with its capital at Constantinople.

In order to increase and protect their international commerce, the Vikings declared themselves the rulers of the eastern Slavs. According to tradition, the semi-legendary chieftain Ruirik founded a princely dynasty about 860. In any event, the Varangian ruler Oleg (r. 878–912) established his residence at Kiev in modern-day Ukraine. He and his successors ruled over a loosely united confederation of Slavic territories known as Rus with its capital at Kiev until 1054. (The word *Russia* comes from *Rus*, though the origins of *Rus* are hotly debated, with some historians linking it with Swedish words and others with Slavic words.)

The Viking prince and his clansmen quickly became assimilated into the Slavic population, taking local wives and emerging as the noble class. Missionaries of the Byzantine Empire converted the Vikings and local Slavs to Eastern Orthodox Christianity, accelerating the unification of the two groups. Thus the rapidly Slavified Vikings left two important legacies for the future: they created a loose unification of Slavic territories under a single ruling prince and a single ruling dynasty, and they imposed a basic religious unity by accepting Orthodox Christianity (as opposed to Roman Catholicism) for themselves and the eastern Slavs.

Even at its height under Great Prince Iaroslav the Wise (r. 1019–1054), the unity of Kievan Rus was extremely tenuous. Trade, not government, was the main concern of the rulers. Moreover, the Slavified Vikings failed to find a way of peacefully transferring power from one generation to the next. In medieval western Europe, this fundamental problem of government was increasingly resolved by resorting to the principle of **primogeniture** (**pry-muh-JEN-ee-choor**): the king's eldest son received the crown as his rightful inheritance when his father died. Civil war was thus averted; order was preserved. In early Rus, however, there were apparently no fixed rules, and much strife accompanied each succession.

primogeniture A system in which the king's eldest son inherited the crown when his father died.

Possibly to avoid such chaos, Great Prince Iaroslav, before his death in 1054, divided Kievan Rus among his five sons, who in turn divided their properties when they died. Between 1054 and 1237, Kievan Rus disintegrated into more and more competing units, each ruled by a prince claiming to be a descendant of Ruirik.

The princes thought of their land as private property. A given prince owned a certain number of farms or landed estates and had them worked directly by his people, mainly slaves. Outside of these estates, which constituted the princely domain, the prince exercised only limited authority in his principality. Excluding the clergy, two kinds of people lived there: the noble boyars (**BOY-arz**) and the commoner peasants.

The **boyars** were descendants of the original Viking warriors, and they also held their lands as free and clear private property. Although the boyars normally

boyars Descendants of the original Viking warriors, they held their lands as free and clear private property.

fought in princely armies, the customary law declared that they could serve any prince they wished. The ordinary peasants were also truly free. They could move at will wherever opportunities were greatest. In the touching phrase of the times, theirs was "a clean road, without boundaries."[12] In short, fragmented princely power, private property, and personal freedom all went together.

Magyars and Muslims

Groups of central European steppe peoples known as Magyars also raided villages in the late ninth century, taking plunder and captives, and forcing leaders to pay tribute in an effort to prevent further looting and destruction. Moving westward, small bands of Magyars on horseback reached as far as Spain and the Atlantic coast. They subdued northern Italy, compelled Bavaria and Saxony to pay tribute, and even penetrated into the Rhineland and Burgundy. Magyar forces were defeated by a combined army of Frankish and other Germanic troops at the Battle of Lechfeld near Augsburg in southern Germany in 955, and the Magyars settled in the area that is now Hungary in eastern Europe.

Much as Clovis had centuries earlier, the Magyar ruler Géza (**GEE-za**) (r. 970–997), who had been a pagan, decided to become a Roman Christian. This gave him the support of the papacy and offered prospects for alliances with other Roman Christian rulers against the Byzantine Empire, Hungary's southern neighbor. Géza's son Stephen I (r. 997–1038) was officially crowned the king of Hungary by a papal representative on Christmas Day of 1001. He supported the building of churches and monasteries, built up royal power, and encouraged the use of Latin and the Roman alphabet. Hungary's alliance with the papacy shaped the later history of eastern Europe just as Charlemagne's alliance with the papacy shaped western European history. The Hungarians adopted settled agriculture, wrote law codes, and built towns, and Hungary became an important crossroads of trade for German and Muslim merchants.

The ninth century also saw invasions into western Europe from the south. Muslim fleets had attacked Sicily, which was part of the Byzantine Empire, beginning in the seventh century, and by the end of the ninth century they controlled most of the island. The Muslims drove northward and sacked Rome in 846. Expert seamen, they sailed around the Iberian Peninsula from North Africa and captured towns along the Adriatic coast nearly all the way to Venice. They attacked Mediterranean settlements along the coast of Provence and advanced on land as far as the Alps. In the tenth century Frankish, papal, and Byzantine forces were able to retake much territory, though the Muslims continued to hold Sicily. Disputes among the Muslim rulers on the island led one faction to ask the Normans for assistance, and between 1060 and 1090 the Normans gradually conquered all of Sicily.

What was the effect of these invasions on the structure of European society? From the perspective of those living in what had been Charlemagne's empire, Viking, Magyar, and Muslim attacks accelerated the fragmentation of political power. Lords capable of rallying fighting men, supporting them, and putting up resistance to the invaders did so. They also assumed political power in their territories. Weak and defenseless people sought the protection of local strongmen, and free peasants sank to the level of serfs. This period is thus often seen as one of terror and chaos.

People in other parts of Europe might have had a different opinion, however. In Muslim Spain, scholars worked in thriving cities, and new crops such as cotton

Section Review

- Three groups attacked Europe: Vikings from Scandinavia, Muslims from the Mediterranean, and Magyars from the east.

- With Europe fractured politically, the Vikings attacked the Carolingian empire in their highly maneuverable boats in search of booty and new commerce.

- The Vikings spread into what is now Normandy, Sicily, and England, moving north and west, trading in slaves, and displaying their vast maritime and naval skills.

- Vikings also moved eastward into lands populated by Slavic peoples, where they raided, traded, intermarried with Slavic peoples, and eventually assimilated.

- Magyars were central European steppe peoples who moved westward until Franks and Germans defeated them at Lechfeld in 955 in Germany; they settled in Hungary under the rule of Géza, who converted to Roman Christianity, gaining the support of the papacy.

- Muslim fleets attacked Sicily and moved northward as far as the Alps but were only able to hold on to Sicily, which later fell to the Normans.

and sugar enhanced ordinary people's lives. In eastern Europe, states such as Moravia and Hungary became strong kingdoms. A Viking point of view might be the most positive, for by 1100 descendents of the Vikings not only ruled their homelands in Denmark, Norway, and Sweden, but also ruled Normandy, England, Sicily, Iceland, and Kievan Rus, with an outpost in Greenland and occasional voyages to North America.

Chapter Review

How did Islam take root in the Middle East and then spread to Europe? (page 163)

In the seventh century the diverse Arab tribes were transformed into a powerful political and social force by the teachings of the Prophet Muhammad. They conquered much of the Middle East and North Africa, and in the eighth century they crossed into Europe, eventually gaining control of most of the Iberian Peninsula. Muslim-controlled Spain, known as al-Andalus, was the most advanced society in Europe in terms of agriculture, science, and medicine. Some Christian residents assimilated to Muslim practices, but hostility between the two groups was also evident as each increasingly regarded members of the other as infidels.

How did Frankish rulers govern their kingdoms? (page 171)

In western Europe, Frankish rulers of the Merovingian dynasty built on the foundations established by Clovis in the fifth century, dividing their territories into regions and sending out royal officials, later called counts, to administer the regions. Their authority was frequently challenged by civil wars and rebellions by nobles. One of these nobles, Charles Martel, held the important position of mayor of the palace, and in the eighth century he took power and established a new dynasty, the Carolingians. The Carolingians used both military victories and strategic marriage alliances to enhance their authority.

How did Charlemagne gain control of a large part of Europe and how did power become decentralized after his death? (page 173)

Carolingian government reached the peak of its development under Charles Martel's grandson, Charlemagne. Building on the military and diplomatic foundations of his ancestors, Charlemagne waged constant warfare to expand his kingdom, eventually coming to control most of central and western continental Europe except Muslim Spain. Christian missionary activity among the Germanic peoples continued, and strong ties were forged with the Roman papacy, which eventually resulted in Charlemagne's coronation as emperor. After his son's death, Charlemagne's empire was divided between his grandsons in the Treaty of Verdun (843). This division of Charlemagne's empire was accompanied by a decentralization of power at the local level, and a new political form involving mutual obligations, later called "feudalism," developed. The power of the local nobles in the feudal structure rested on landed estates worked by peasants in another system of mutual obligation termed "manorialism." An overwhelmingly agricultural economy supplied food for local needs, but there was some interregional trade in glass, pottery, and woolens and a sizable long-distance trade in slaves.

Key Terms

Kaaba (p. 164)
Qur'an (p. 164)
Five Pillars of Islam (p. 166)
caliph (p. 167)
Shi'ites (p. 167)
Sunnis (p. 167)
infidel (p. 170)
civitas (p. 171)
comites (p. 173)
missi dominici (p. 175)
Treaty of Verdun (p. 177)
vassal (p. 177)
fief (p. 177)
feudalism (p. 177)
manorialism (p. 179)
serfs (p. 179)
double monastery (p. 181)
primogeniture (p. 187)
boyars (p. 187)

What were the significant intellectual and cultural changes in Charlemagne's era? (page 181)

Charlemagne's support of education and learning proved his most enduring legacy. The revival of learning associated with Charlemagne and his court at Aachen, sometimes styled the "Carolingian Renaissance," drew its greatest inspiration from seventh- and eighth-century intellectual developments in the Anglo-Saxon kingdom of Northumbria in northern England. Here women and men in monasteries produced beautiful illustrated texts, and the Venerable Bede popularized the Christian dating system now in use in most of the world. After the Treaty of Verdun, continental Europe was fractured politically, with no European political power strong enough to put up effective resistance to external attack.

What effects did the assaults and migrations of the Vikings, Magyars, and Muslims have on the rest of Europe? (page 184)

Vikings from Scandinavia carried out raids for plunder along the coasts and rivers of western Europe and traveled as far as Iceland, Greenland, and North America. Eventually they settled in England and France, where they established the state of Normandy. In eastern Europe Vikings traded down the rivers as far as Constantinople and formed the state of Kievan Rus, assimilating to Slavic culture and converting to the Orthodox religion. Like the Vikings, the Magyars initially invaded Europe for plunder and then established a permanent state; their ruler Stephen I was crowned as king by a papal representative two hundred years after Charlemagne's coronation. Thus, in both western and eastern Europe, civil rulers and church leaders supported each other's goals and utilized each other's prestige and power, though their alliances and disputes had little effect on the daily life of most people in early medieval Europe.

Notes

1. F. E. Peters, *A Reader on Classical Islam* (Princeton, N.J.: Princeton University Press, 1994), pp. 208–209.
2. J. O'Faolain and L. Martines, eds., *Not in God's Image: Women in History from the Greeks to the Victorians* (New York: Harper & Row, 1973), pp. 108–114.
3. See Jane I. Smith, "Islam and Christendom: Historical, Cultural, and Religious Interaction from the Seventh to the Fifteenth Centuries," in *The Oxford History of Islam*, ed. John L. Esposito (New York: Oxford University Press, 1999), pp. 317–321.
4. J. M. Bloom, *Paper Before Print: The History and Impact of Paper in the Islamic World* (New Haven: Yale University Press, 2001), pp. 9–10, 17, 45, 85–89.
5. JoAnn Hoeppner Moran Cruz, "Western Views of Islam in Medieval Europe," in *Perceptions of Islam*, ed. D. Blanks and M. Frassetto (New York: St. Martin's Press, 1999), pp. 55–81.
6. I. Wood, *The Merovingian Kingdoms, 450–751* (New York: Longman, 1994), p. 101.
7. Einhard, *The Life of Charlemagne*, with a foreword by S. Painter (Ann Arbor: University of Michigan Press, 1960), pp. 50–51.
8. Quoted in R. McKitterick, *The Frankish Kingdoms Under the Carolingians, 751–987* (New York: Longman, 1983), p. 77.
9. See K. F. Werner, "Important Noble Families in the Kingdom of Charlemagne," in *The Medieval Nobility: Studies on the Ruling Class of France and Germany from the Sixth to the Twelfth Century*, ed. and trans. T. Reuter (New York: North-Holland, 1978), pp. 174–184.
10. Quoted in B. D. Hill, ed., *Church and State in the Middle Ages* (New York: John Wiley & Sons, 1970), pp. 46–47.
11. J. Nicholson, "Feminae Glorisae: Women in the Age of Bede," in *Medieval Women*, ed. D. Baker (Oxford: Basil Blackwell, 1978), pp. 15–31, esp. p. 19; and C. Fell, *Women in Anglo-Saxon England and the Impact of 1066* (Bloomington: Indiana University Press, 1984), p. 109.
12. Quoted in R. Pipes, *Russia Under the Old Regime* (New York: Charles Scribner's Sons, 1974), p. 48.

To assess your mastery of this chapter, go to **bedfordstmartins.com/mckaywestbrief**

Listening to the Past

Feudal Homage and Fealty

Feudalism developed in the ninth century during the disintegration of the Carolingian Empire because rulers needed fighting men and officials. A king, lay lord, bishop, or abbot would grant lands or estates to a noble or knight. In turn, the recipient became the vassal of the lord and agreed to perform certain services. In a society that lacked an adequate government bureaucracy, a sophisticated method of taxation, or even the beginnings of national consciousness, personal ties provided some degree of cohesiveness. In the first document, a charter dated 876, the emperor Charles the Bald (r. 843–877), Charlemagne's grandson, grants a benefice, or fief. In the second document, dated 1127, the Flemish notary Galbert of Bruges describes homage and fealty before Count Charles the Good of Flanders (r. 1119–1127). The ceremony consists of three parts: the act of homage; the oath of fealty, intended to reinforce the act; and the investiture (apparently with property). Because all three parts are present, historians consider this evidence of a fully mature feudal system.

In the name of the holy and undivided Trinity. Charles by the mercy of Almighty God august emperor . . . let it be known to all the faithful of the holy church of God and to our now, present and to come, that one of our faithful subjects, by name of Hildebertus, has approached our throne and has beseeched our serenity that through this command of our authority we grant to him for all the days of his life and to his son after him, in right of usufruct and benefice, certain estates which are . . . called Cavaliacus, in the county of Limoges (lee-MOHZH). Giving assent to his prayers for reason of his meritorious service, we have ordered this charter to be written, through which we grant to him the estates already mentioned, in all their entirety, with lands, vineyards, forests, meadows, pastures, and with the men living upon them, so that, without causing any damage through exchanges or diminishing or lessening the land, he for all the days of his life and his son after him, as we have said, may hold and possess them in right of benefice and usufruct. . . .

The hand of God blesses Charles the Bald as he receives the Bible, symbolic of his connection with Israelite kings David and Solomon. (Bibliothèque nationale de France)

191

On Thursday, the seventh of the ides of April [April 7, 1127], acts of homage were again made to the count, which were brought to a conclusion through this method of giving faith and assurance. First, they performed homage in this fashion: the count inquired if [the prospective vassal] wished completely to become his man. He replied, "I do wish it," and with his hands joined and covered by the hands of the count, the two were united by a kiss. Second, he who had done the homage gave faith to the representative of the count in these words: "I promise in my faith that I shall henceforth be faithful to Count William, and I shall fully observe the homage owed him against all men, in good faith and without deceit." Third, he took an oath on the relics of the saints. Then the count, with the rod which he had in his right hand, gave investiture to all those who by this promise had given assurance and due homage to the count, and had taken the oath.

Questions for Analysis

1. Why was the charter drawn up? Why did Charles grant the benefice?

2. Who were the "men living on it," and what economic functions did they perform?

3. What did the joined hands of the prospective vassal and the kiss symbolize?

4. In the oath of fealty, what was meant by the phrase "in my faith"? Why did the vassal swear on relics of the saints?

5. What does this ceremony tell us about the society that used it?

Source: The History of Feudalism by David Herlihy, ed. Copyright © 1970 by David Herlihy. Reprinted by permission of HarperCollins Publishers, Inc.

CHAPTER 9

State and Church in the High Middle Ages

1000–1300

In this thirteenth-century manuscript, knights of King Henry II stab Archbishop Thomas Becket in 1170 in Canterbury Cathedral, a dramatic example of church/state conflict. Becket was soon made a saint, and the spot where the murder occurred became a pilgrimage site; it is still a top tourist destination. (British Library, London)

Chapter Preview

Political Revival
How did medieval rulers create larger and more stable territories?

Law and Justice
How did the administration of law contribute to the development of national states?

The Papacy
How did the papacy attempt to reform the church, and what was the response from other powerful rulers?

The Crusades
How did the motives, course, and consequences of the Crusades reflect and shape developments in Europe?

INDIVIDUALS IN SOCIETY: The Jews of Speyer: A Collective Biography

LISTENING TO THE PAST: An Arab View of the Crusades

Beginning in the last half of the tenth century, the Viking, Muslim, and Magyar invasions that had contributed to the fragmentation of Europe gradually ended. Feudal rulers began to develop new institutions of government that enabled them to assert their power over lesser lords and the general population. Centralized states slowly crystallized, first in western Europe, and then in eastern and northern Europe as well. At the same time, energetic popes built their power within the Western Christian church and asserted their superiority over kings and emperors. A papal call to retake the holy city of Jerusalem led to nearly two centuries of warfare between Christians and Muslims. Christian warriors, clergy, and settlers moved out in all directions from western and central Europe, so that through conquest and colonization border regions were gradually incorporated into a more uniform European culture.

Political Revival

How did medieval rulers create larger and more stable territories?

The eleventh century witnessed the beginnings of new political stability. Rulers in France, England, and Germany worked to reduce private warfare and civil anarchy. Domestic disorder subsided, and external invasions gradually declined. In some parts of Europe, lords in control of large territories began to manipulate feudal institutions to build up their power even further, becoming kings over growing and slowly centralizing states.

As medieval rulers expanded their territories and extended their authority, they developed institutions to rule more effectively, including an enlarged bureaucracy of officials and larger armies. Officials and armies cost money, and rulers in various countries developed slightly different ways of acquiring more revenue and handling financial matters, some more successful than others.

Medieval Origins of the Modern State

Rome's great legacy to Western civilization had been the concepts of the state and the law, but for almost five hundred years after the disintegration of the Roman Empire in the West, the state as a reality did not exist. Political authority was completely decentralized. Power was spread among many lords who gave their localities such protection and security as their strength allowed. There existed many, frequently overlapping layers of authority—earls, counts, barons, knights—between a king and the ordinary people.

In these circumstances, medieval rulers had common goals. The rulers of England, France, and Germany wanted to strengthen and extend royal authority in their territories. They wanted to establish an effective means of communication with all peoples in order to increase public order. They wanted more revenue and efficient bureaucracies. The solutions they found to these problems laid the foundations for modern national states.

The modern state is an organized territory with definite geographical boundaries that are recognized by other states. It has a body of law and jurisdiction over many people. The modern national state counts on the loyalty of its citizens, or at least a majority of them. In return it provides order so that citizens can go about their daily work and other activities. It protects its citizens and their property. The state tries to prevent violence and to apprehend and punish those who commit it.

It supplies a currency or medium of exchange that permits financial and commercial transactions. It conducts relations with foreign governments. To accomplish these minimal functions, the state must have officials, bureaucracies, laws, courts of law, soldiers, information, and money. By the twelfth century medieval kingdoms and some lesser lordships possessed these attributes, at least to the extent that most modern states have them.

England

Before the Viking invasions, England had never been united under a single ruler. The victory of the remarkable Alfred, king of the West Saxons (or Wessex), over the Vikings in 878 inaugurated a great political revival. Alfred and his immediate successors built a system of local defenses and slowly extended royal rule beyond Wessex to other Anglo-Saxon peoples until one law, royal law, took precedence over local custom. England was divided into local units called "shires," or counties, each under the jurisdiction of a shire-reeve (a word that soon evolved into "sheriff") appointed by the king. Sheriffs were unpaid officials from well-off families responsible for collecting taxes, catching and trying criminals, and raising infantry.

936–973	Reign of Otto I in Germany
1059	Lateran Council restricts election of the pope to the College of Cardinals
1066	Norman conquest of England
1073–1085	Gregory VII; strengthening of the papal reform movement
1085–1492	Reconquista; Muslim rulers pushed out of Spain
1095–1291	Crusades
1154–1189	Reign of Henry II in England; revision of legal procedure; beginnings of common law
1180–1223	Reign of Philip II (Philip Augustus); unification efforts in France
1198–1216	Innocent III; height of the medieval papacy
1215	Magna Carta
1230s	Papacy creates the Inquisition
1290	Jews expelled from England
1306	Jews expelled from France

The Bayeux (bay-YUH) Tapestry

William's conquest of England was recorded in thread on a narrative embroidery panel measuring 231 feet by 19 inches. In this scene, two nobles and a bishop acclaim Harold Godwinson as king of England. The nobles hold a sword, symbol of military power, and the bishop holds a stole, symbol of clerical power. Harold himself holds a scepter and an orb, both symbols of royal power. The embroidery provides an important historical source for the clothing, armor, and lifestyles of the Norman and Anglo-Saxon warrior class. It eventually ended up in Bayeux in northern France, where it is displayed in a museum today and is incorrectly called a "tapestry," which is a different kind of needlework. (Tapisserie de Bayeux et avec autorisation spéciale de la Ville de Bayeux)

Domesday Book A surviving record of a general inquiry ordered by William of Normandy; it serves as a source of social and economic information about medieval England.

Exchequer The bureau of finance established by Henry I, becoming the first institution of the governmental bureaucracy of England.

The Viking invasions of England did not end, however, and the island eventually came under Viking rule. The Viking Canute (**kuh-NOOT**) made England the center of his empire while promoting a policy of assimilation and reconciliation between Anglo-Saxons and Vikings. When Canute's heir Edward died childless, there were a number of claimants to the throne of England—the Anglo-Saxon noble Harold Godwinson (ca. 1022–1066), who had been crowned by English nobles, the Norwegian king Harald III (r. 1045–1066), grandson of Canute, and Duke William of Normandy, who was the illegitimate son of Edward's cousin.

In 1066 William invaded England with his Norman vassals, met the exhausted forces of Harold Godwinson, and defeated them—an event now known as the Norman conquest. In both England and Normandy, William the Conqueror limited the power of his noble vassals and church officials and transformed the feudal system into a unified monarchy. In England he replaced Anglo-Saxon sheriffs with Normans. He retained another Anglo-Saxon device, the *writ*, through which the central government communicated with people at the local level, using the local tongue.

In addition to retaining Anglo-Saxon institutions that served his purposes, William also introduced a major innovation, the Norman inquest or general inquiry. William wanted to determine how much wealth there was in his new kingdom, who held what land, and what land had been disputed among his vassals since the Conquest of 1066. Groups of royal officials were sent to every part of the country. The resulting record, called the **Domesday Book** (**DOOMZ-day**) from the Anglo-Saxon word *doom*, meaning "judgment," still survives. It is an invaluable source of social and economic information about medieval England.

The *Domesday Book* provided William and his descendants with information vital for the exploitation and government of the country. Knowing the amount of wealth every area possessed, the king could tax accordingly. Knowing the amount of land his vassals had, he could allot knight service fairly. The book helped English kings regard their country as one unit.

William's son Henry I (r. 1100–1135) established a bureau of finance called the **Exchequer** (**EKS-chek-er**) (for the checkered cloth at which his officials collected and audited royal accounts), which became the first institution of the government bureaucracy of England. In addition to various taxes and annual gifts, Henry's income came from money paid to the crown for settling disputes and as penalties for crimes, as well as money due to Henry in his private position as feudal lord. The latter would include the fee paid by a vassal's son in order to inherit the father's properties and the fee paid by a knight who wished to avoid military service. Henry, like other medieval kings, made no distinction between his private income and state revenues, though the officials of the Exchequer began to keep careful records of the monies paid into and out of the royal treasury.

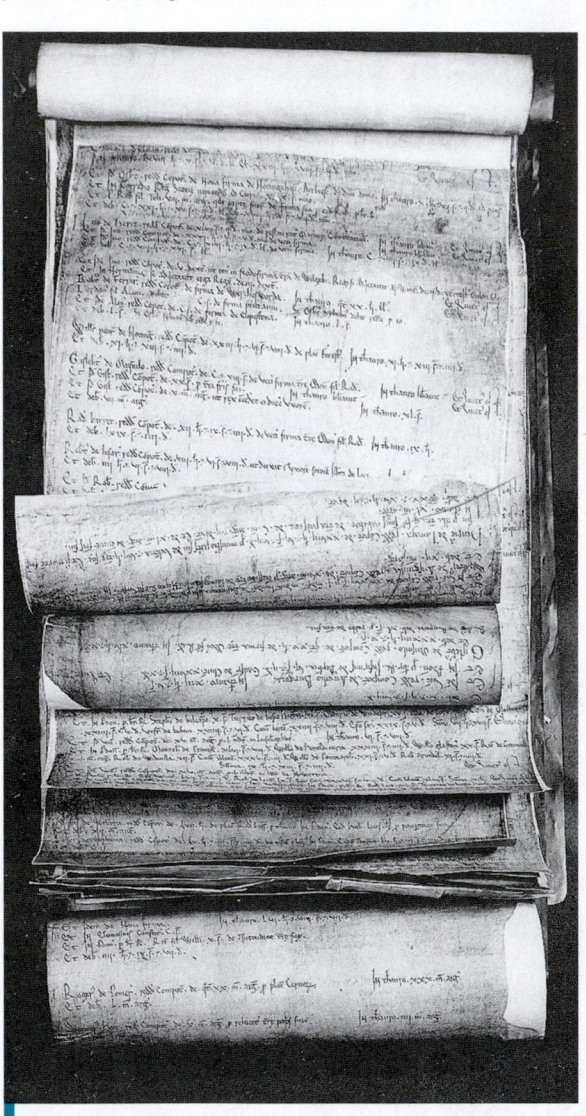

The Pipe Rolls

Twice yearly English medieval sheriffs appeared before the Barons of the Exchequer to account for the monies they had collected from the royal estates and from fines for civil and criminal offenses. Clerks recorded these revenues and royal expenditures on the pipe rolls, whose name derives from the pipelike form of the rolled parchments. A roll exists for 1129–1130, then continuously from 1156 to 1832, representing the largest series of English public records. (Crown copyright material in the Public Record Office is reproduced by permission of the Controller of the Britannic Majesty's Stationery Office [E40 1/1565])

In 1128 William's granddaughter Matilda was married to Geoffrey of Anjou; their son became Henry II of England and inaugurated the Angevin (**AN-juh-vin**) (from Anjou, his father's county) dynasty. Henry inherited the French provinces of Anjou, Normandy, Maine, and Touraine in northwestern France, and then in 1152 he claimed lordship over Aquitaine, Poitou (**pwa-TOO**), and Gascony in southwestern France through his marriage to the great heiress Eleanor of Aquitaine (see Map 9.1). Each of the provinces in Henry's Angevin empire was separate and was only loosely linked to the others by dynastic law and personal oaths. The histories of England and France became closely intertwined, however, leading to disputes and conflicts down to the fifteenth century.

France

France also became increasingly unified in this era. Following the death of the last Carolingian ruler in 987, an assembly of nobles selected Hugh Capet (**ka-PAY**) as his successor. Soon after his own coronation, Hugh crowned his son Robert to ensure the succession and prevent disputes after his death and to weaken the feudal principle of elective kingship. The Capetian kings were weak, but they laid the foundation for later political stability.

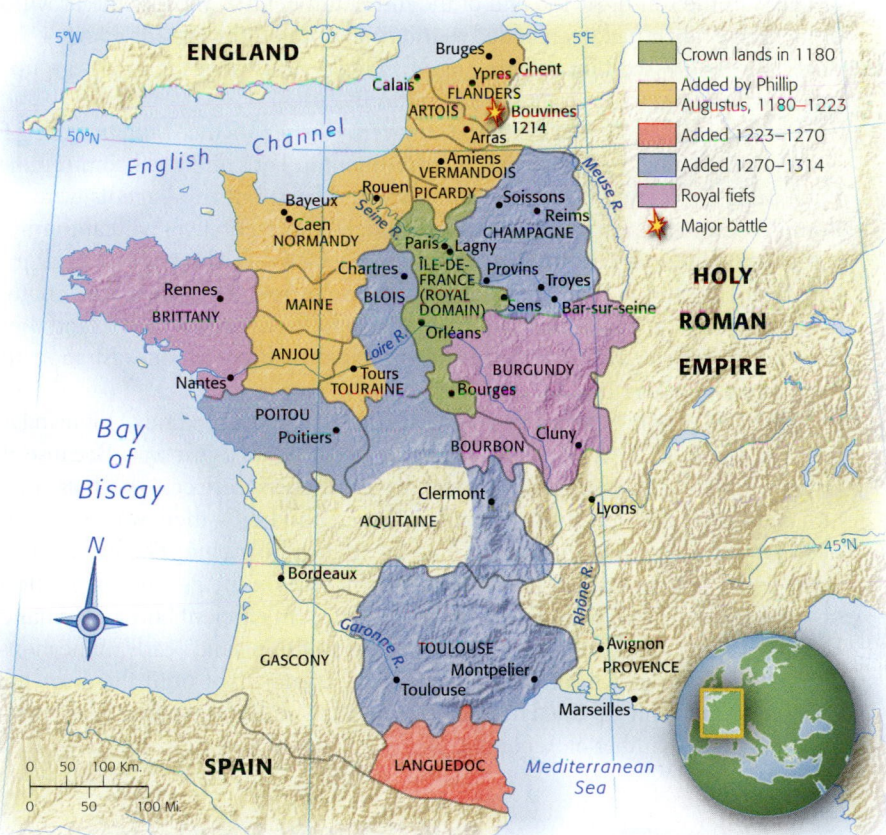

MAP 9.1   The Growth of the Kingdom of France

Some scholars believe that Philip II received the title "Augustus" (from a Latin word meaning "to increase") because he vastly expanded the territories of the kingdom of France. The province of Toulouse (**too-LOOZ**) in the south became part of France as a result of the crusade against the Albigensians (see page 212).

This stability came slowly. In the early twelfth century France still consisted of a number of virtually independent provinces. Each was governed by a local ruler; each had its own laws, customs, coinage, and dialect. Unlike the king of England, the king of France had jurisdiction over a very small area. Chroniclers called King Louis VI (r. 1108–1137) *roi de Saint-Denis* (wah duh san-duh-NEE), king of Saint-Denis, because the territory he controlled was limited to Paris and the Saint-Denis area surrounding the city (see Map 9.1). This region, called the *Île-de-France* (EEL-duh-franz), or royal domain, became the nucleus of the French state. The clear goal of the medieval French king was to increase the royal domain and extend his authority.

The work of unifying France began under Louis VI's grandson Philip II (r. 1180–1223). Rigord, Philip's biographer, gave him the title "Augustus" (from a Latin word meaning "to increase") because he vastly enlarged the territory of the kingdom of France. When King John of England, who was Philip's vassal for the rich province of Normandy, defaulted on his feudal obligation to come to the French court, Philip declared Normandy forfeit to the French crown. He enforced his declaration militarily, and in 1204 Normandy fell to the French. He gained other northern provinces as well, and by the end of his reign Philip was effectively master of northern France.

In the thirteenth century Philip Augustus's descendants acquired important holdings in the south. By the end of the thirteenth century most of the provinces of modern France had been added to the royal domain through diplomacy, marriage, war, and inheritance. The king of France was stronger than any group of nobles who might try to challenge his authority.

Philip Augustus devised a method of governing the provinces and providing for communication between the central government in Paris and local communities. Each province retained its own institutions and laws, but royal agents were sent from Paris into the provinces as the king's official representatives with authority to act for him. These agents were often middle-class lawyers who possessed full judicial, financial, and military jurisdiction in their districts. They were never natives of the provinces to which they were assigned, and they could not own land there. This policy reflected the fundamental principle of French administration that royal interests superseded local interests.

Medieval people believed that a good king lived on the income of his own land and taxed only in time of a grave emergency—that is, a just war. Because the church, and not the state, performed what we call social services—such as education and care of the sick, the aged, and orphaned children—there was no ordinary need for the government to tax. Taxation meant war financing. The French monarchy could not continually justify taxing the people on the grounds of the needs of war. Thus the French kings were slow to develop an efficient bureau of finance. French provincial laws and institutions—in contrast to England's early unification—also retarded the growth of a central financial agency. Not until the fourteenth century, as a result of the Hundred Years' War, did a state financial bureau emerge—the Chamber of Accounts.

Central Europe

In central Europe, the German king Otto I (r. 936–973) defeated many other lords to build up his power. To do this, Otto relied on the church, getting financial support and the bulk of his army from ecclesiastical lands. Otto asserted the right to control ecclesiastical appointments. Before receiving religious consecration and being invested with the staff and ring symbolic of their offices, bishops and abbots had to perform feudal homage for the lands that accompanied the church office. This practice, later known as "lay investiture," created a grave crisis in the eleventh century, as we will see later in this chapter.

Some of our knowledge of Otto derives from *The Deeds of Otto*, a history of his reign in heroic verse written by a nun, Hroswita of Gandersheim (ca. 935–ca. 1003). A learned poet, she also produced six verse plays, and she is considered the first dramatist writing in Europe after the fall of the Roman Empire.

In 955 Otto I inflicted a crushing defeat on the Magyars in the battle of Lech-feld (see page 188), which made Otto a great hero to the Germans. He used this victory to have himself crowned emperor in 962 by the pope in Aachen, which had been the capital of the Carolingian empire. He chose this site to sym-bolize his intention to continue the tradition of Charlemagne and to demonstrate papal support for his rule. It was not exactly clear what Otto was the emperor *of*, however, though by the eleventh century people were increasingly using the term **Holy Roman Empire** to refer to a loose confederation of principalities, duchies (DUTCH-eez), cities, bishoprics, and other types of regional governments stretch-ing from Denmark to Rome and from Burgundy to Poland (see Map 9.2).

Holy Roman Empire The loose confederation of principalities, duchies, cities, bishoprics, and other types of regional governments stretching from Denmark to Rome and from Burgundy to Poland.

MAP 9.2   The Holy Roman Empire and the Kingdom of Sicily, ca. 1200

Frederick Barbarossa greatly expanded the size of the Holy Roman Empire, but it remained a loose collection of various types of governments. The kingdom of Sicily included mainland areas as well as the island in 1200, with an ethnically mixed population ruled by Norman kings.

⭐ Major battle

— Boundary of the Holy Roman Empire

In this large area of central Europe, unified nation-states did not develop until the nineteenth century. The Holy Roman emperors shared power with princes, dukes, archbishops, counts, bishops, abbots, and cities. The office of emperor remained an elected one, though the electors included only seven men—four secular rulers of large territories within the empire and three archbishops.

Through most of the first half of the twelfth century, civil war wracked Germany. When Conrad III died in 1152, the resulting anarchy was so terrible that the electors decided the only alternative to continued chaos was the selection of a strong ruler. They chose Frederick Barbarossa of the house of Hohenstaufen (hoh-uhn-SHTOU-fen) (r. 1152–1190).

Like William the Conqueror in England and Philip in France, Frederick required vassals to take an oath of allegiance to him as emperor and appointed officials to exercise full imperial authority over local communities. He forbade private warfare and established sworn peace associations with the princes of various regions. These peace associations punished those who breached the peace and criminals, with penalties ranging from maiming to execution.

Frederick Barbarossa surrounded himself with men trained in Roman law (see page 203), and he used Roman law to justify his assertion of imperial rights over the towns of northern Italy. Between 1154 and 1188 Frederick made six expeditions into Italy. While he initially made significant conquests in the north, the brutality of his methods provoked revolts, and the Italian cities formed an alliance with the papacy. In 1176 Frederick suffered a defeat at Legnano (see Map 9.2). This battle marked the first time a feudal cavalry of armed knights was decisively defeated by bourgeois (boor-zwah) infantrymen. Frederick was forced to recognize the municipal autonomy of the northern Italian cities.

Sicily

The kingdom of Sicily is a good example of how a strong government could be built on a feudal base by determined rulers. Between 1061 and 1091 a bold Norman knight, Roger de Hauteville, and a small band of mercenaries defeated the Muslims and Greeks who controlled Sicily. Roger then governed a heterogeneous population of Sicilians, Italians, Greeks, Jews, Arabs, and Normans. Roger distributed scattered fiefs to his followers so no vassal would have a centralized power base. He took an inquest of royal property and rights and forbade private warfare. To these Norman practices, Roger fused Arabic and Greek governmental devices. For example, he retained the main financial agency of the previous Muslim rulers, the diwān (di-WAHN), a sophisticated bureau for record keeping and administration.

> **diwān** A sophisticated Muslim bureau for record keeping and administration.

In the multicultural society of medieval Sicily, Muslims and Greeks, as well as Normans, staffed the diwān, as well as the army and judiciary. The diwān kept official documents in Greek, Latin, and Arabic. It supervised the royal estates in Sicily, collected revenues, managed the state monopoly of the sale of salt and lumber, and registered all income to the treasury. With revenues derived from those products, Roger hired mercenaries. He encouraged appeals from local courts to his royal court because such appeals implied respect for his authority.

In 1137 Roger's forces took the city of Naples and much of the surrounding territory in southern Italy. The entire area came to be known as the kingdom of Sicily (or sometimes the kingdom of the Two Sicilies), and was often caught up in conflicts between the pope, the Holy Roman emperor, and the kings of France and Spain over control of Italy.

Roger's grandson Frederick II (r. 1212–1250), who was also the grandson of Frederick Barbarossa of Germany, was crowned king of the Germans at Aachen

(1216) and Holy Roman emperor at Rome (1220). He concentrated his attention on Sicily and showed little interest in the northern part of the Holy Roman Empire. Frederick banned private warfare and placed all castles and towers under royal administration. He also replaced town officials with royal governors and subordinated feudal and ecclesiastical courts to the king's courts. Royal control of the nobility, of the towns, and of the judicial system added up to great centralization, which required a professional bureaucracy and sound state financing.

In 1224 Frederick founded the University of Naples to train officials for his bureaucracy. He too continued the use of Muslim institutions such as the diwān, and he tried to administer justice fairly to all his subjects, declaring, "We cannot in the least permit Jews and Saracens (Muslims) to be defrauded of the power of our protection and to be deprived of all other help, just because the difference of their religious practices makes them hateful to Christians,"[1] implying a degree of toleration exceedingly rare at the time.

Frederick's contemporaries called him the "Wonder of the World." He certainly transformed the kingdom of Sicily. But Sicily required constant attention, and Frederick's absences on crusades and on campaigns in mainland Italy took their toll. Shortly after he died, the unsupervised bureaucracy fell to pieces. The pope, as feudal overlord of Sicily, called in a French prince to rule. Frederick's reign had also weakened imperial power in the German parts of the empire, and in the later Middle Ages lay and ecclesiastical princes held sway in the Holy Roman Empire. Germany and Italy did not become unified states until the nineteenth century.

reconquista The Christian term for the conquest of Muslim territories in the Iberian peninsula by Christian forces.

The Iberian Peninsula

From the eleventh to the thirteenth centuries, power in the Iberian peninsula shifted from Muslim to Christian rulers. Castile, in the north-central part of the peninsula, became the strongest of the growing Christian kingdoms, and Aragon, in the northeast, the second most powerful. In 1085 King Alfonso VI of Castile and León captured Toledo in central Spain. Alfonso VIII (1158–1214), aided by the kings of Aragon, Navarre, and Portugal, crushed the Muslims at Las Navas de Tolosa in 1212, accelerating the Christian push southward. James the Conqueror of Aragon (r. 1213–1276) captured Valencia on the Mediterranean coast in 1233, and three years later Ferdinand of Castile and León captured the great Muslim city Córdoba in the heart of Andalusia. With the fall of Seville in 1248, Christians controlled the entire Iberian Peninsula, save for the small state of Granada (see Map 9.3).

Muslim Spain had had more cities than any other country in Europe, and Christian Spain became highly urbanized. The chief mosques in these cities became cathedrals and Muslim art was destroyed. Victorious Christian rulers expelled the Muslims and recruited immigrants from France and elsewhere in Iberia. The thirteenth century thus witnessed a huge migration of peoples from the north to the depopulated cities of the central and southern parts of the peninsula.

Fourteenth-century clerical propagandists called the movement to expel the Muslims the **reconquista** (reconquest) — a sacred and patriotic crusade to wrest the country from "alien" Muslim hands. This religious myth became part of Spanish political culture and of the

Section Review

- In 1066 William conquered England and transformed the feudal system into a monarchy, introducing the *Domesday Book* to record wealth and land; later bureaucratic innovations included the Exchequer, to audit royal accounts, and the pipe rolls, to audit the sheriffs.

- France became unified and expanded under Phillip II, who governed using royal agents assigned to provinces, giving priority to royal needs over local interests, but the limitation that taxation be used only for wars hindered royal growth.

- The German king Otto I became the Holy Roman Emperor after defeating the Magyars; later, following a series of civil wars in central Europe, Emperor Frederick Barbarossa forbade private warfare and required a sworn peace, using experts in Roman law to extend his dominion over northern Italy.

- In Sicily Roger de Hauteville gained political strength by distributing scattered fiefs to his followers, forbidding private warfare, and using Muslim bookkeeping methods, a policy his grandson Frederick II continued while also founding the University of Naples to train bureaucratic officials.

- The Christian conquest of Spain (the reconquista) linked the peninsula to Christian Europe and the Roman papacy, while introducing new immigrants to replace the expelled Muslims.

MAP 9.3   The Reconquista

The Christian conquest of Muslim Spain was followed by ecclesiastical reorganization, with the establishment of dioceses, monasteries, and the Latin liturgy, which gradually tied the peninsula to the heartland of Christian Europe and to the Roman papacy.   (*Source:* Adapted from David Nicholas, *The Evolution of the Medieval World.* Copyright © 1992. Reprinted by permission of Pearson Education.)

national psychology. As a consequence of the reconquista, the Spanish and Portuguese learned how to administer vast tracts of newly acquired territory. Later, in the sixteenth and seventeenth centuries, they would impose these medieval methods on colonial Mexico, Brazil, Peru, Angola, and the Philippines.

Law and Justice

How did the administration of law contribute to the development of national states?

In the early Middle Ages society perceived of major crimes as acts against an individual, and a major crime was settled when the accused made a cash payment to the victim or his or her kindred. In the High Middle Ages suspects were pursued and punished for acting against the *public* interest. Throughout Europe, however, the form and application of laws depended on local and provincial custom and practice. In the twelfth and thirteenth centuries the law was a hodgepodge of Germanic customs, feudal rights, and provincial practices. Kings in France and

England wanted to blend these elements into a uniform system of rules acceptable and applicable to all of their peoples. Legal developments in continental countries like France were strongly influenced by Roman law, while England slowly built up a unique and unwritten common law.

France and the Holy Roman Empire

The French king Louis IX (r. 1226–1270) was famous in his time for his concern for justice. Each French province, even after being made part of the kingdom of France, retained its unique laws and procedures, but Louis IX created a royal judicial system. He established the Parlement of Paris, a kind of supreme court that welcomed appeals from local administrators and from the courts of feudal lords throughout France. By the very act of appealing the decisions of feudal courts to the Parlement of Paris, French people in far-flung provinces were recognizing the superiority of royal justice.

Louis was the first French monarch to publish laws for the entire kingdom. The Parlement of Paris registered (or announced) these laws, which forbade private warfare, judicial duels, gambling, blaspheming, and prostitution. Louis sought to identify justice with the kingship, and gradually royal justice touched all parts of the kingdom.

In the Holy Roman Empire, justice was administered at two levels. The manorial or seigneurial court, presided over by the lay or ecclesiastical lord, dealt with such common conflicts as damage to crops and fields, trespass, boundary disputes, and debt. The court of high justice, staffed by regional rather than local magistrates, dispensed justice in serious criminal cases involving theft, arson, assault with a weapon, rape, and homicide. The imposition of the death penalty by hanging was the distinctive feature of this court.

The Customs of Aragon

This illumination, imitating the style of Parisian court art, shows King James of Aragon (r. 1213–1276) presiding over a law court. King James—called "the Conqueror" because of his victories over Catalonia, Valencia, and Majorca—ordered several codifications of law. The most important of these, the Customs of Aragon (1247), drew on Roman canonical practice for legal procedures. (Initial N: King James of Aragon Overseeing Court Law of Vidal Mayor, 83.MQ.165, folio 72v. © The J. Paul Getty Museum, Los Angeles)

Henry II and Thomas Becket

Under Henry II (r. 1154–1189) England developed and extended a **common law**, a law that originated in, and was applied by, the king's court and that in the next two or three centuries became common to the entire country. England was unusual in developing one system of royal courts and one secular law. Henry I had occasionally sent out **circuit judges** (royal officials who traveled a given circuit or district) to hear civil and criminal cases. Every year royal judges left London and set up court in the counties. Wherever the king's judges sat, there sat the king's court.

Henry also improved procedure in criminal justice. In 1166 he instructed the sheriffs to summon local **juries** to conduct inquests and draw up lists of known or suspected criminals. These lists, or indictments, sworn to by the juries, were to be presented to the royal judges when they arrived in the community. This accusing jury is the ancestor of the modern grand jury.

Judges determined guilt or innocence in a number of ways. They heard testimony, sought witnesses, and read written evidence. If these were lacking and if a suspect had a bad public reputation, he or she might be submitted to trial by

common law A body of English law that originated in, and was applied by, King Henry II's court and in the next two or three centuries became common to the entire country.

circuit judges Royal officials who traveled a given circuit or district to hear civil and criminal cases.

jury Group of men in medieval England that conducted inquiries into criminal activities, similar to today's grand jury.

ordeal. An accused person could be tried by fire or water. In the latter case, the accused was tied hand and foot and dropped in a lake or river. People believed that water was a pure substance and would reject anything foul or unclean. Thus a person who sank was considered innocent; a person who floated was found guilty. Trial by ordeal was a ritual that appealed to the supernatural for judgment. God determined guilt or innocence, and thus a priest had to be present to bless the water.

Henry II disliked ordeal, and it was used less during his reign than it was on the continent. Gradually, in the course of the thirteenth century, the king's judges adopted the practice of calling on twelve people (other than the accusing jury) to consider the question of innocence or guilt. This became the jury of trial, but it was very slowly accepted because medieval people had more confidence in the judgment of God than in the judgment of twelve ordinary people.

One aspect of Henry's judicial reforms encountered stiff resistance from an unexpected source: the friend and former chief adviser whom Henry had made archbishop of Canterbury—Thomas Becket. In 1164 Henry II insisted that everyone, including clerics, be subject to the royal courts. Becket vigorously protested that church law required clerics to be subject to church courts. The disagreement between Henry II and Becket dragged on for years. Late in December 1170, in a fit of rage, Henry expressed the wish that Becket be destroyed. Four knights took the king at his word. They rode to Canterbury Cathedral and, as the archbishop was leaving evening services, slashed off the crown of his head and scattered his brains on the pavement.

What Thomas Becket could not achieve in life, he gained in death. The assassination of an archbishop turned public opinion in England and throughout western Europe against the king. Miracles were recorded at Becket's tomb; Becket was made a saint; and in a short time Canterbury Cathedral became a major pilgrimage and tourist site. Henry had to back down. He did public penance for the murder and gave up his attempts to bring clerics under the authority of the royal court.

Thieves Plunder Saint Edmund's Chapel

This eleventh-century painting shows thieves searching for jewelry and rich burial fabrics and even pulling the iron nails out of the wooden structure. They are also trying to dig up the coffin of Saint Edmund, the king of East Anglia (r. 841–869), who was defeated in battle and executed by Danish invaders and whose bones could be sold as relics. Crime and violence preoccupied secular and religious authorities alike. (Pierpont Morgan Library/Art Resource, NY)

King John and Magna Carta

Henry II's sons Richard I, known as Lion-Hearted (r. 1189–1199), and John (r. 1199–1216) lacked their father's interest in the work of government. Richard looked on England as a source of revenue for his military enterprises. Soon after his accession, he departed on crusade to the Holy Land. During his reign he spent only six months in England, and the government was run by ministers trained under Henry II.

John's basic problems were financial. King John inherited a heavy debt from his father and brother, and his efforts to squeeze money from knights, widows, and merchants created an atmosphere of resentment. In July 1214 John's cavalry suffered a severe defeat at the hands of Philip Augustus of France at Bouvines in Flanders. This battle ended English hopes for the recovery of territories from France and also strengthened the opposition to John. His ineptitude as a soldier in a society that idealized military glory was the final straw. Rebellion begun by northern barons eventually grew to involve many key members of the English nobility. After lengthy negotiations, John met the barons in 1215 at Runnymede and was forced to approve the peace treaty called **Magna Carta**, "Magna" (great or large) because it was so long and detailed.

For contemporaries, Magna Carta was intended to redress the grievances that particular groups—the barons, the clergy, the merchants of London—had against King John. Charters were not unusual: many kings and lords at the time issued them and then sometimes revoked them, as John did almost immediately. This revocation was largely ignored, however, and every English king until 1485 re-issued Magna Carta as evidence of his promise to observe the law. Thus, this charter alone acquired enduring importance. It came to signify the principle that everyone, including the king and the government, must obey the law.

In the later Middle Ages references to Magna Carta underlined the old Augustinian theory that a government, to be legitimate, must promote law, order, and justice. An English king may not disregard or arbitrarily suspend the law to suit his convenience. The Magna Carta also contains the germ of the idea of "due process of law," meaning that a person has the right to be heard and defended in court and is entitled to the protection of the law. Because later generations referred to Magna Carta as a written statement of English liberties, it gradually came to have an almost sacred importance as a guarantee of law and justice.

The Papacy

How did the papacy attempt to reform the church, and what was the response from other powerful rulers?

Kings and emperors were not the only rulers consolidating their power in the High Middle Ages. Under the leadership of a series of reforming popes in the eleventh century, the church tried to assert control over the clergy and regain its spiritual and political strength. Church control had diminished during the ninth and tenth centuries when kings and feudal lords chose the priests and bishops in their territories, granting them fiefs and expecting loyalty and service in return. Church offices from village priest to pope brought with them the right to collect taxes and fees and often the profits from land under the officeholder's control. They were thus sometimes sold outright—a practice called **simony** (SY-muh-nee), after Simon Magus, a New Testament figure who wanted to buy his way into heaven. Not surprisingly, clergy at all levels who had bought their positions or had been granted them for political reasons were rarely effective moral or spiritual guides. Nonetheless, the popes' efforts to reform their institution were sometimes challenged by medieval kings.

The Gregorian Reforms

The papal reform movement of the eleventh century is frequently called the Gregorian reform movement, after Pope Gregory VII (1073–1085), its most prominent advocate. Serious efforts at reform actually began somewhat earlier, under Pope Leo IX (1049–1054).

During the ninth and tenth centuries the papacy provided little leadership to the Christian peoples of western Europe. Popes were appointed to advance the political ambitions of their families—the great aristocratic families of Rome—and not because of special spiritual qualifications. A combination of political machinations and sexual immorality damaged the papacy's moral prestige.

Magna Carta A long and detailed peace treaty intended to redress the grievances that particular groups had against King John.

simony The sale of church offices.

At the local parish level, there were many married priests. Taking Christ as the model for the priestly life, the Roman church had always encouraged clerical celibacy, and celibacy had been an obligation for ordination since the fourth century. But in the tenth and eleventh centuries probably a majority of European priests were married or living with women, and in some cases they were handing down church positions and property to their children.

Pope Leo and his successors believed that lay control was largely responsible for the church's problems, so they proclaimed the church independent from secular rulers. The Lateran Council of 1059 decreed that the authority and power to elect the pope rested solely in the **college of cardinals,** a special group of priests from the major churches in and around Rome. The college retains that power today. In the Middle Ages the college of cardinals numbered around twenty-five or thirty, most of them from Italy. In 1586 the figure was set at seventy, though today it is much larger, with cardinals from around the world. When the office of pope was vacant, the cardinals were responsible for governing the church.

While reform began long before Gregory's pontificate and continued after it, Gregory VII was the first pope to emphasize the *political* authority of the papacy. His belief that kings had failed to promote reform in the church prompted him to claim an active role in the politics of Western Christendom. He believed that the pope, as the successor of Saint Peter, was the vicar of God on earth and that papal orders were the orders of God. Gregory was particularly opposed to **lay investiture**—the selection and appointment of church officials by secular authority, often symbolized by laymen giving bishops and abbots their symbols of office, such as a staff and ring. In February 1075 Pope Gregory held a council at Rome that decreed that clerics who accepted investiture from laymen were to be deposed, and laymen

college of cardinals A special group of high clergy that has the authority and power to elect the pope and who otherwise are responsible for governing the church when the office of the pope is vacant.

lay investiture The selection and appointment of church officials by secular authority.

Emperor Otto III Handing a Staff to Archbishop Adalbert of Prague (tenth century)
The staff, or crozier (KROH-zher), symbolized a bishop's spiritual authority. Receiving the staff from the emperor gave the appearance that the bishop gained his spiritual rights from the secular power. Pope Gregory VII vigorously objected to this practice. (Bildarchiv Marburg/Art Resource, NY)

who invested clerics were to be *excommunicated* (cut off from the sacraments and all Christian worship).

The church's penalty of **excommunication** relied for its effectiveness on public opinion. Gregory believed that the strong support he enjoyed for his *moral* reforms would carry over to his political ones; he thought that excommunication would compel rulers to abide by his changes. Immediately, however, Henry IV in the Holy Roman Empire, William the Conqueror in England (see page 196), and Philip I in France protested. Gregory's reforms would deprive them not only of church income but also of the right to choose which monks and clerics would help them administer their kingdoms. The tension between the papacy and the monarchy would have a major impact on both institutions and on society.

Meanwhile, the Gregorian reform movement built a strict hierarchical church structure with bishops and ordained priests higher in status than nuns, who could not be ordained. Church councils in the eleventh and twelfth centuries forbade monks and nuns to sing church services together and ordered priests to limit their visits to convents, heightening the sense that contact with nuns should be viewed with suspicion and avoided when possible. Church reformers put a greater emphasis on clerical celibacy and chastity. As part of these measures, Pope Boniface VIII's papal decree of 1298, *Periculoso*, ordered all female religious persons to be strictly **cloistered.** This meant that the nuns were to remain permanently inside the walls of the convent and that visits with those from outside the house, including family members, would be limited. *Periculoso* was not enforced everywhere, but it did mean that convents became more cut off from medieval society. People also gave more donations to male monastic houses where monks who had been ordained as priests could say memorial masses, and fewer to women's houses, many of which became impoverished.

Emperor versus Pope

The strongest reaction to Gregory's moves came from the Holy Roman Empire. Pope Gregory accused Henry of lack of respect for the papacy and insisted that disobedience to the pope was disobedience to God. Henry argued that Gregory's type of reform undermined royal authority and that the pope "was determined to rob me of my soul and my kingdom or die in the attempt."[2]

Within the empire, those who had the most to gain from the dispute quickly took advantage of it. In January 1076 many of the German bishops who had been invested by Henry withdrew their allegiance from the pope. Gregory replied by excommunicating them and suspending Henry from the emperorship. The lay nobility delighted in the bind the emperor had been put in: with Henry IV excommunicated and cast outside the Christian fold, they did not have to obey him and could advance their own interests. Powerful nobles invited the pope to come to Germany to settle their dispute with Henry. Gregory hastened to support them. The Christmas season of 1076 witnessed an ironic situation in Germany: the clergy supported the emperor, while the great nobility favored the pope.

Henry outwitted the pope. Crossing the Alps in January 1077, he approached the castle of Countess Matilda of Tuscany, where the pope was staying. According to legend, Henry stood for three days in the snow seeking forgiveness. As a priest, Pope Gregory was obliged to grant absolution and to readmit the emperor to the Christian community. When the sentence of excommunication was lifted, Henry regained the emperorship and authority over his rebellious subjects. Some historians claim that this incident marked the peak of papal power because the most powerful ruler in Europe, the emperor, had bowed before the pope.

---

excommunication A penalty used by the Catholic Church that meant being cut off from the sacraments and all Christian worship.

cloistered Cut off from the outside world.

Countess Matilda

A staunch supporter of the reforming ideals of the papacy, Countess Matilda (ca. 1046–1115) planned this dramatic meeting at her castle at Canossa in the Apennines (**AP-uh-nines**). The arrangement of the figures—King Henry kneeling, Abbot Hugh of Cluny lecturing, and Matilda persuading—suggests contemporary understanding of the scene in which Henry received absolution. Matilda's vast estates in northern Italy and her political contacts in Rome made her a person of considerable influence in the late eleventh century. (Biblioteca Apostolica Vaticana)

The battle between the pope and the emperor raged on, however. In 1080 Gregory VII again excommunicated and deposed the emperor. In return, Henry invaded Italy, captured Rome, and controlled the city when Gregory died in 1085. But Henry won no lasting victory. Gregory's successors encouraged Henry's sons to revolt against their father. With lay investiture the ostensible issue, the conflict between the papacy and the successors of Henry IV continued into the twelfth century.

Finally, in 1122 at a conference held at Worms, the issue was settled by compromise. Bishops were to be chosen according to canon law—that is, by the clergy—in the presence of the emperor or his delegate. The emperor surrendered the right of investing bishops with the ring and staff. But since lay rulers were permitted to be present at ecclesiastical elections and to accept or refuse feudal homage from the new prelates, they still possessed an effective veto over ecclesiastical appointments. Papal power was enhanced, but neither side won a clear victory.

The long controversy had tremendous social and political consequences in Germany. The lengthy struggle between papacy and emperor allowed emerging noble dynasties to enhance their position. To control their lands, the great lords built castles, symbolizing their increased power and growing independence. (In no European country do more castles survive today.) The German high aristocracy subordinated the knights, enhanced restrictions on peasants, and compelled Henry IV and Henry V to surrender certain rights and privileges. When the papal-imperial conflict ended in 1122, the nobility held the balance of power in Germany, and later German kings, such as Frederick Barbarossa (see page 200), would fail in their efforts to strengthen the monarchy against the princely families. For these reasons, particularism, localism, and feudal independence characterized the Holy Roman Empire in the High Middle Ages. The investiture controversy had a catastrophic effect there.

Innocent III and His Successors

The most powerful pope in history was Innocent III (1198–1216). During his pontificate the church in Rome declared itself to be supreme, united, and "catholic" (worldwide), responsible for the earthly well-being and eternal salvation of all citizens of **Christendom** (the Christian world). Innocent pushed the kings of France, Portugal, and England to do his will, compelling King Philip Augustus of France to take back his wife, Ingeborg of Denmark. He forced King John of England to accept as archbishop of Canterbury a man John did not want.

Innocent called the fourth Lateran Council in 1215, which affirmed the idea that ordained priests had the power to transform bread and wine during church ceremonies into the body and blood of Christ (a change termed "transubstantiation"). This power was possessed by no other group in society, not even kings. According to papal doctrine, priests now had the power to mediate for everyone with God, which set the spiritual hierarchy of the church above the secular hierarchies

Christendom The term used by early medieval writers to refer to the realm of Christianity.

of kings and other rulers. The council also affirmed that Christians should confess their sins to a priest at least once a year and ordered Jews and Muslims to wear special clothing that set them apart from Christians (see page 252).

Some of Innocent III's successors abused their prerogatives to such an extent that their moral impact was seriously weakened. Even worse, Innocent IV (1243–1254) used secular weapons, including military force, to maintain his leadership. These popes badly damaged papal prestige and influence. By the early fourteenth century cries for reform would be heard once again.

The Crusades

How did the motives, course, and consequences of the Crusades reflect and shape developments in Europe?

The **Crusades** of the eleventh and twelfth centuries were wars sponsored by the papacy for the recovery of the holy city of Jerusalem from the Muslim Turks. The word *crusade* was not actually used at the time and did not appear in English until the late sixteenth century. It means literally "taking the cross," from the cross that soldiers sewed on their garments as a Christian symbol. At the time, people going off to fight simply said they were taking "the way of the cross" or "the road to Jerusalem."

Though the reconquista in Spain (see page 201) did not directly inspire the Crusades to the Middle East, the pope did sponsor groups of soldiers in the Spanish campaign as well as in the Norman campaign against the Muslims in Sicily. In both campaigns Pope Gregory VII asserted that any land conquered from the Muslims belonged to the papacy because it had been a territory held by infidels. Thus these earlier wars set a pattern for the centuries-long Crusades.

Background

The Roman papacy had been involved in the bitter struggle over church reform and lay investiture with the German emperors. If the pope could muster a large army against the enemies of Christianity, his claim to be leader of Christian society in the West would be strengthened. Moreover, in 1054 a serious theological disagreement had split the Greek church of Byzantium and the Roman church of the West. The pope and the patriarch of Constantinople excommunicated each other and declared the beliefs of the other to be anathema (**uh-NATH-uh-muh**), that is, totally unacceptable for Christians. The pope believed that a crusade would lead to strong Roman influence in Greek territories and eventually the reunion of the two churches.

In 1071 Turkish soldiers defeated a Greek army at Manzikert in eastern Anatolia and occupied much of Asia Minor (see Map 9.4). The emperor at Constantinople appealed to the West for support. Shortly afterward the holy city of Jerusalem fell to the Turks. Pilgrimages to holy places in the Middle East became very dangerous, and the papacy claimed to be outraged that the holy city was in the hands of unbelievers. Because the Muslims had held Palestine since the eighth century, the papacy actually feared that the Seljuk (**SEL-jook**) Turks would be less accommodating to Christian pilgrims than the previous Muslim rulers had been.

In 1095 Pope Urban II called for a great Christian holy war against the infidels. He urged Christian knights who had been fighting one another to direct their energies against the true enemies of God, the Muslims. Urban proclaimed an

Section Review

- Pope Leo proclaimed the church independent of secular rulers in a papal reform movement, an effort to restore morality to the church by establishing papal election by the college of cardinals; Gregory VII continued this emphasis on the political authority of the church.

- Gregory's reforms also enforced the church penalty of excommunication, and established a strict hierarchical structure with bishops and ordained priests higher than nuns, who could not be ordained.

- Within the empire, Pope Gregory VII excommunicated Emperor Henry IV over the investiture (appointment) of bishops until Henry backed down; the great nobles in Germany sided with the Pope and the clergy supported the emperor.

- The controversy ended with a compromise in which the clergy chose bishops in the presence of the emperor, but the long struggle over this issue had brought increased power to the German nobility.

- Pope Innocent III was the most powerful pope in history, forcing kings to do his will, setting up practices elevating the church above the state and using military force to maintain his leadership.

Crusades Holy wars sponsored by the papacy for the recovery of the Holy Land from the Muslims from the late eleventh to the late thirteenth century.

MAPPING THE PAST

Map 9.4   The Routes of the Crusades

This map shows the many different routes that Western Christians took over the centuries to reach Jerusalem. Use it and the information in the text to answer the following questions: **[1]** How were the results of the various Crusades shaped by the routes that the Crusaders took? **[2]** How did the routes offer opportunities for profit for Venetian and other Italian merchants? **[3]** Why might the Byzantines have worried about the Crusaders even before the Fourth Crusade?

Map legend:
- First Crusade, 1096–1099
- Second Crusade, 1147–1149
- Third Crusade, 1189–1192
- Fourth Crusade, 1202–1204
- Crusade of Frederick II, 1228–1229
- Crusades of Louis IX, 1248–1254 and 1270
- Crusader kingdoms in the East
- Major battle

---

indulgence Remission of the temporal penalties imposed by the church for sin.

indulgence, or a waiver from having to do penance for sin, to those who would fight for and regain the holy city of Jerusalem.

Thousands of people of all classes joined the crusade. Although most of the Crusaders were French, pilgrims from many regions streamed southward from the Rhineland, through Germany and the Balkans. Of all of the developments of the High Middle Ages, none better reveals Europeans' religious and emotional fervor and the influence of the reformed papacy than the extraordinary outpouring of support for the First Crusade.

Motives and Course of the Crusades

Many Crusaders were inspired by the possibility of foreign adventure as well as by religious fervor. Kings, who were trying to establish order and build states, saw the Crusades as an opportunity to get rid of troublemaking knights. Land-hungry younger sons seized upon the chance to acquire fiefs in the Middle East.

The First Crusade was successful, mostly because of the dynamic enthusiasm of the participants. The Crusaders had little more than religious zeal. They knew nothing about the geography or climate of the Middle East. Although there were several counts with military experience among the host, the Crusaders could never agree on a leader. Lines of supply were never set up. Starvation and disease wracked the army. Nevertheless, convinced that "God wills it," the war cry of the Crusaders, the army pressed on, defeating the Turks in several land battles and besieging a few larger towns. (See the feature "Listening to the Past: An Arab View of the Crusades" on pages 218–219.) Finally in 1099, after a three-year trek, they reached Jerusalem, and after a month-long siege they penetrated the city, where they slaughtered the Muslim defenders as well as civilian women and children.

With Jerusalem taken, many Crusaders set off for home again. Only the appearance of Egyptian troops convinced them that they needed to stay, and slowly institutions were set up to rule territories and the Muslim population. Four small "Crusader states"—Jerusalem, Edessa, Tripoli, and Antioch (**AN-tee-ok**)—were established; castles and fortified towns were built to defend against Muslim reconquest (see Map 9.4). Reinforcements arrived in the form of pilgrims and fighters from Europe, so that there was constant coming and going by land and more often by sea after the Crusaders conquered port cities such as Acre. Between 1096 and 1270 the crusading ideal was expressed in eight papally approved expeditions to the East, though none after the First Crusade accomplished very much. Despite this lack of success, for roughly two hundred years members of noble families in Europe went nearly every generation.

Women from all walks of life participated in the Crusades. In war zones some women concealed their sex by donning chain mail and helmets and fought with the knights. Others joined in the besieging of towns and castles. They assisted in filling the moats surrounding fortified places with earth so that ladders and war engines could be brought close. More typically, women provided water to fighting men, a service not to be underestimated in the hot, dry climate of the Middle East. They worked as washerwomen, foraged for food, and provided sexual services. There were many more European men than women, however, so there was a fair amount of intermarriage or at least sexual relations between Christian men and Muslim women.

The Muslim states in the Middle East were politically fragmented when the Crusaders first came, and it took about a century for them to reorganize. They did so dramatically under Saladin (Salah al-Din) (**SAL-uh-din**), who unified Egypt and Syria, and in 1187 the Muslims retook Jerusalem. Christians immediately attempted to take it back in what was later called the Third Crusade (1189–1192). Frederick Barbarossa of the Holy Roman Empire, Richard the Lion-Hearted of England, and Philip Augustus of France participated, and the Third Crusade was better financed than previous ones. But disputes among the leaders and strategic problems prevented any lasting results. The Crusaders were not successful in retaking Jerusalem, but they did keep their hold on port towns, and Saladin allowed pilgrims safe passage to Jerusalem. He also made an agreement with Christian rulers for keeping the peace. From that point on, the Crusader states were more important economically than politically or religiously, giving Italian and French merchants direct access to Eastern products such as perfumes and silk.

In 1202 Innocent III sent out preachers who called on Christian knights to retake Jerusalem. Those who responded—in what would become the Fourth Crusade—decided that going by sea would be better than going by land, and they stopped in Constantinople for supplies. The supplies never materialized, and in 1204 the Crusaders decided to capture and sack Constantinople instead, destroying its magnificent library and shipping gold, silver, and relics home. The Byzantine Empire, as a political unit, never recovered from this destruction. Although the Crusader Baldwin IX of Flanders was chosen emperor, the empire splintered into three parts and soon consisted of little more than the city of Constantinople.

Moreover, the assault by one Christian people on another—even though one of the goals of the Crusades was reunion of the Greek and Latin churches—made the split between the churches permanent. It also helped discredit the entire crusading movement.

In the late thirteenth century Turkish armies gradually conquered all other Muslim rulers and then turned against the Crusader states. In 1291 the last Crusader stronghold, the port of Acre, fell in a battle that was just as bloody as the first battle for Jerusalem two centuries earlier. Knights then needed a new battlefield for military actions, which some found in Spain, where the rulers of Aragon and Castile continued fighting Muslims until 1492.

Crusades Within Europe and the Expansion of Christendom

Crusades were also mounted against groups within Europe that were perceived as threats. In 1208 Pope Innocent III proclaimed a crusade against a group in southern France known either as the Cathars (from the Greek *katharos*, meaning "pure") or as the **Albigensians** (al-bi-JEN-see-uhns) (from the town of Albi in southern France). The Albigensians asserted that the material world was created not by the good God of the New Testament, but by a different evil God of the Old Testament. The good God had created spiritual things, and the evil God or the Devil had created material things; in this dualistic understanding, the soul was good and the body evil. Forces of good and evil battled constantly, and leading a perfect life meant being stripped of all physical and material things. To free oneself from the power of evil, a person had to lead a life of extreme asceticism. Albigensians were divided into the "perfect," who followed the principles strictly, and the "believers," who led ordinary lives until their deaths, when they repented and were saved. They used the teachings of Jesus about the evils of material goods to call for the church to give up its property, rejected the authority of the pope and the sacraments of the church, and began setting up their own bishoprics.

The Albigensians won many adherents in southern France. Faced with widespread defection, Pope Innocent III proclaimed a crusade against them. Fearing that religious division would lead to civil disorder, the French monarchy joined the crusade against the Albigensians. The French inflicted a savage defeat on the Albigensians in 1213. After more years of fighting, the leaders agreed to terms of peace, which left the French monarchy the primary beneficiary.

The end of the war did not mean an end to Albigensianism, but the papacy decided to combat heresy through education and individual punishment. The pope founded the University of Toulouse, which he hoped would promote knowledge of correct belief. In the 1230s and 1240s the papacy established the papal **Inquisition,** sending out inquisitors with the power to seek out suspected heretics, question them in private without revealing who had denounced them, and sentence them to punishments ranging from penance to life imprisonment. Heretics who did not repent were handed over to the secular government to be burned, and their property was confiscated. These measures were very successful, and the last Albigensian leaders were burned in the 1320s, though their beliefs did not die out completely.

Fearful of encirclement by imperial territories, the popes also promoted crusades against Emperor Frederick II in 1227 and 1239. This use of force backfired, damaging papal credibility as the sponsor of peace.

Along with the papal Inquisition, the Crusades also inspired the establishment of new religious orders. For example, the Knights Templars, founded in 1118 with

Albigensians A heretical sect that rejected orthodox doctrine on the relationship of God and man, the sacraments, and clerical hierarchy.

Inquisition Court established by the papacy with power to investigate and try individuals for heresy and other religious crimes.

the strong backing of Saint Bernard of Clairvaux (**klar-VOW**) (see page 239), combined the monastic ideals of obedience and self-denial with the crusading practice of military aggression. Another order, the Teutonic (**too-TON-ik**) Knights, waged wars against the pagan Prussians in the Baltic region. After 1230, and from a base in Poland, they established a new territory, Christian Prussia, and gradually the entire eastern shore of the Baltic Sea came under their hegemony. Military orders served to unify Christian Europe.

Christianity also spread into northern and eastern Europe by more peaceful means. Latin Christian influences entered Scandinavian and Baltic regions primarily through the appointment of bishops and the establishment of dioceses. This took place in Denmark in the tenth and eleventh centuries, and the institutional church spread rather quickly due to the support offered by the strong throne. Dioceses were established in Norway and Sweden in the eleventh century, and in 1164 Uppsala, long the center of the pagan cults of Odin and Thor, became a Catholic archdiocese, though pagan and Christian practices existed side-by-side for centuries in more remote parts of Scandinavia.

Otto I (see page 198) planted a string of dioceses along his northern and eastern frontiers, hoping to pacify the newly conquered Slavs in eastern Europe. Frequent Slavic revolts illustrate the people's resentment of German lords and clerics and indicate that the church did not easily penetrate the region. In the same way that French knights had been used to crush the Albigensians, German nobles built castles and ruthlessly crushed revolts. The church also moved into central Europe, first in Bohemia in the tenth century and from there into Poland and Hungary in the eleventh. In the twelfth and thirteenth centuries, thousands of settlers poured into eastern Europe. New immigrants were German in descent, name, language, and law. Hundreds of small market towns populated by these newcomers supplied the needs of the rural countryside. Larger towns such as Cracow and Riga engaged in long-distance trade and gradually grew into large urban centers.

Consequences of the Crusades

The Crusades provided the means for what one scholar has called "the aristocratic diaspora," the movement of knights from their homes in France to areas then on the frontiers of Christian Europe.[3] Wars of foreign conquest had occurred before the Crusades, as the Norman Conquest of England in 1066 illustrates (see page 196), but for many knights migration began with the taking of the cross. Restless, ambitious knights, many of them younger sons with no prospects, left on crusade to the Holy Land, and some of them were able to carve out lordships in Palestine, Syria, and Greece. Along the Syrian and Palestinian coasts, the Crusaders set up a string of feudal states that managed to survive for about two centuries before the Muslims reconquered them; many of the castles they built still stand today.

The Crusades introduced some Europeans to Eastern luxury goods, but their immediate cultural impact on the West remains debatable. Strong economic and intellectual ties with the East had already been developed by the late eleventh century. The Crusades were a boon to Italian merchants, who profited from outfitting military expeditions, the opening of new trade routes, and the establishment of trading communities in the Crusader states. After those kingdoms collapsed, Muslim rulers still encouraged trade with European businessmen. Commerce with the West benefited both Muslims and Europeans, and it continued to flourish.

The Crusades proved to be a disaster for Jewish-Christian relations. In the eleventh century Jews played a major role in the international trade between the Muslim Middle East and the West. Jews also lent money to peasants, townspeople, and nobles. When the First Crusade was launched, many poor knights had to borrow from Jews to equip themselves for the expedition. Debt bred resentment.

The experience of the Rhenish Jews during the First Crusade (see the feature "Individuals in Society: The Jews of Speyer: A Collective Biography") was not unusual; later Crusades brought similar violence against Jewish communities. In addition to resenting Jewish business competition, Christians harbored the belief that Jews engaged in the ritual murder of Christians to use their blood in religious rituals. These accusations, termed the "blood libel," were condemned by Christian rulers and higher church officials, but were often spread through sermons preached by local priests. They also charged Jews with being "Christ killers" and of using the communion host for diabolical counter-rituals. Such accusations led to the killing of Jewish families and sometimes entire Jewish communities, sometimes by burning people alive in the synagogue or Jewish section of town.

Legal restrictions on Jews gradually increased. Jews were forbidden to have Christian servants or employees, to hold public office, to appear in public on Christian holy days, or to enter Christian parts of town without a badge marking them as Jews. Jews were prohibited from engaging in any trade with Christians except money-lending—which only fueled popular resentment—and in 1275 King Edward I of England prohibited that as well. In 1290 he expelled the Jews from England in return for a large parliamentary grant; it would be four centuries before they would be allowed back in. King Philip the Fair of France followed Edward's example in 1306, and many Jews went to the area of southern France known as Provence, which was not yet part of the French kingdom. In July 1315 the king's need for revenue led him to readmit the Jews to France in return for a huge lump sum and for an annual financial subsidy, but the returning Jews faced hostility and increasing pressure to convert.

The Crusades also left an inheritance of deep bitterness in Christian-Muslim relations. Each side dehumanized the other, viewing those who followed the other religion as unbelievers. Whereas Europeans perceived the Crusades as sacred religious movements, Muslims saw them as expansionist and imperialistic. The ideal of a sacred mission to conquer or convert Muslim peoples entered Europeans' consciousness and became a continuing goal. When in 1492 Christopher Columbus sailed west, hoping to reach India, he used the language of the Crusades in his diaries, which shows that he was preoccupied with the conquest of Jerusalem (see Chapter 15). Columbus wanted to establish a Christian base in India from which a new crusade against Islam could be launched.

The battles in the High Middle Ages between popes and kings, between Christians and Muslims, and between Christians and pagans were signs of how deeply Christianity had replaced tribal, political, and ethnic structures as the essence of Western culture. Christian Europeans identified themselves first and foremost as citizens of "Christendom," or even described themselves as belonging to "the Christian race."[4] Whether Europeans were Christian in their observance of the Gospels remains another matter.

Section Review

- In 1095 Pope Urban II offered an indulgence, or sin waiver, to any who would fight in a great crusade against "God's enemy" the Muslims, and thousands joined in.

- Jews who had moved into Speyer at the invitation of the bishop lived separately but were resented by Christians as economic competition and they became the victims of vicious attacks by Crusaders and burghers.

- The First Crusade was successful mostly due to religious enthusiasm, not skill, but the Crusaders pressed on, taking Jerusalem, slaughtering Muslims, and fortifying towns to prevent recapture.

- Saladin helped the Muslims reorganize and take back Jerusalem, but the Crusaders held the port towns; the Third Crusade failed and the Fourth Crusade never made it to the Holy Land, instead sacking Constantinople, splintering the Byzantine Empire.

- The papacy sent Crusaders against other groups within western Europe, such as the Albigensians, using inquisitors (the Inquisition) to seek out and punish heretics.

- The Crusades left deep animosity between Jews and Christians as well as between Muslims and Christians and contributed to Christianity's replacing tribal, political, or ethnic affiliation as the basis for Western culture.

Individuals in Society

The Jews of Speyer: A Collective Biography

In the winter of 1095–1096 news of Pope Urban II's call for a crusade spread. In the spring of 1096 the Jews of northern France, fearing that a crusade would arouse anti-Semitic hostility, sent a circular letter to the Rhineland's Jewish community seeking its prayers. Jewish leaders in Mainz responded, "All the (Jewish) communities have decreed a fast. . . . May God save us and save you from all distress and hardship. We are deeply fearful for you. We, however, have less reason to fear (for ourselves), for we have heard not even a rumor of the crusade."* Ironically, French Jewry survived almost unscathed, while the Rhenish Jewry suffered frightfully.

Beginning in the late tenth century Jews trickled into Speyer (**SHPAHY-uhr**)—partly through Jewish perception of opportunity and partly because of the direct invitation of the bishop of Speyer. The bishop's charter meant that Jews could openly practice their religion, could not be assaulted, and could buy and sell goods. But they could not proselytize their faith, as Christians could. Jews also extended credit on a small scale and, in an expanding economy with many coins circulating, determined the relative value of currencies. Unlike their Christian counterparts, many Jewish women were literate and acted as moneylenders. Jews also worked as skilled masons, carpenters, and jewelers. As the bishop had promised, the Jews of Speyer lived apart from Christians in a walled enclave where they exercised autonomy: they maintained law and order, raised taxes, and provided religious, social, and educational services for their community. (This organization lasted in Germany until the nineteenth century.) Jewish immigration to Speyer accelerated; everyday relations between Jews and Christians were peaceful.

But Christians resented Jews as newcomers, outsiders, and aliens; for enjoying the special protection of the bishop; and for providing economic competition. Anti-Semitic ideology had received enormous impetus from the virulent anti-Semitic writings of Christian apologists in the first six centuries C.E. Jews, they argued, were *deicides* (**DAY-ah-sides**) (Christ killers); worse, Jews could understand the truth of Christianity but deliberately rejected it; thus they were inhuman. By the late eleventh century anti-Semitism was an old and deeply rooted element in Western society.

Late in April 1096 Emich of Leisingen, a petty lord from the Rhineland who had the reputation of being a lawless thug, approached Speyer with a large band of Crusaders. Joined by a mob of burghers, they planned to surprise the Jews in their synagogue on Saturday morning, May 3, but the Jews prayed early and left before the attackers arrived. Furious, the mob randomly murdered eleven Jews. The bishop took the entire Jewish community into his castle, arrested some of the burghers, and cut off their hands. News of these events raced up the Rhine to Worms, creating confusion in the Jewish community. Some took refuge with Christian friends; others sought the bishop's protection.

A combination of Crusaders and burghers killed a large number of Jews, looted and burned synagogues, and desecrated the Torah and other books. Proceeding on to the old and prosperous city of Mainz, Crusaders continued attacking Jews. Facing overwhelming odds, eleven hundred Jews killed their families and themselves. Crusaders and burghers vented their hatred by inflicting barbaric tortures on the wounded and dying. The Jews were never passive; everywhere they resisted. If the Crusades had begun as opposition to Islam, after 1096 that hostility extended to all those who Christians saw as enemies of society, including heretics, Jews, and lepers. But Jews continued to move to the Rhineland and to make important economic and intellectual contributions. Crusader-burgher attacks served as harbingers of events to come in the later Middle Ages and well into modern times.

An engraving (18th century) of the mass suicide of the Jews of Worms in 1096, when they were overwhelmed by Crusaders (with shields). (Bildarchiv Preussischer Kulturbesitz/Art Resource, NY)

Questions for Analysis

1. How do you explain Christian attacks on the Jews of Speyer? Were they defenses of faith?
2. How did Christian views of the Jews as outsiders contribute to these events? Can you think of more recent examples of similar developments?

*Quoted in R. Chazan, *In the Year 1096: The First Crusade and the Jews* (Philadelphia: Jewish Publication Society, 1996), p. 28.

Chapter Review

How did medieval rulers create larger and more stable territories? (page 194)

The end of the great invasions signaled the beginning of profound changes in European society. As domestic disorder slowly subsided, feudal rulers began to develop new institutions of government that enabled them to assert their power over lesser lords and the general population. Centralized states slowly crystallized, first in England and France, where rulers such as William the Conqueror and Philip Augustus manipulated feudal institutions to build up their power. In central Europe the German king Otto had himself declared emperor and tried to follow a similar path, but unified nation-states did not develop until the nineteenth century. Emperors instead shared power with princes, dukes, archbishops, counts, bishops, abbots, and cities. In the Iberian peninsula Christian rulers of small states slowly expanded their territories, taking over land from Muslim rulers in the reconquista.

How did the administration of law contribute to the development of national states? (page 202)

As medieval rulers expanded territories and extended authority, they required more officials, larger armies, and more money with which to pay for them. They developed different sorts of financial institutions to provide taxes and other income. The most effective financial bureaucracies were those developed in England, including a bureau of finance called the Exchequer, and in Sicily, where Norman rulers retained the main financial agency that had been created by their Muslim predecessors. By contrast, the rulers of France and other continental states continued to rely primarily on the income from their own property to support their military endeavors, so their financial institutions were less sophisticated.

How did the papacy attempt to reform the church, and what was the response from other powerful rulers? (page 205)

In the twelfth and thirteenth centuries rulers in Europe sought to transform a hodge-podge of oral and written customs and rules into a uniform system of laws acceptable and applicable to all their peoples. In England such changes caused conflict with church officials, personified in the dispute between King Henry II and Thomas Becket, the archbishop of Canterbury. Fiscal and legal measures by Henry's son John led to opposition from the high nobles of England, who forced him to sign Magna Carta, agreeing to promise to observe the law. Magna Carta had little immediate impact, but it came to signify the principle that everyone, including the king and the government, must obey the law. At the same time that kings were creating more centralized realms, energetic popes built up their power within the Western Christian church and asserted their superiority over kings and emperors. The Gregorian reform movement led to a grave conflict with kings over lay investiture. The papacy achieved a technical success on the religious issue, but in Germany the greatly increased power of the nobility, at the expense of the emperor, represents the significant social consequence. Having put its own house in order, the Roman papacy built the first strong government bureaucracy in the twelfth and thirteenth centuries. In the High Middle Ages, the church exercised general leadership of European society.

Key Terms

Domesday Book (p. 196)
Exchequer (p. 196)
Holy Roman Empire (p. 199)
diwān (p. 200)
reconquista (p. 201)
common law (p. 203)
circuit judges (p. 203)
jury (p. 203)
Magna Carta (p. 205)
simony (p. 205)
college of cardinals (p. 206)
lay investiture (p. 206)
excommunication (p. 207)
cloistered (p. 207)
Christendom (p. 208)
Crusades (p. 209)
indulgence (p. 210)
Albigensians (p. 212)
Inquisition (p. 212)

How did the motives, course, and consequences of the Crusades reflect and
shape developments in Europe? (page 209)

A papal call to retake the holy city of Jerusalem led to the Crusades, nearly two centuries of warfare between Christians and Muslims. The enormous popular response to
papal calls for crusading reveals the influence of the reformed papacy and a new sense
that war against the church's enemies was a duty of nobles. The Crusades were initially
successful, and small Christian states were established in the Middle East. These did
not last very long, however, and other effects of the Crusades were disastrous. Jewish
communities in Europe were regularly attacked; relations between the Western and
Eastern Christian churches were poisoned by the Crusaders' attack on Constantinople; and Christian-Muslim relations became more uniformly hostile than they had
been earlier.

Notes

1. J. Johns, *Arabic Administration in Norman Sicily: The Royal Diwān* (New York: Cambridge
   University Press, 2002), p. 293.
2. I. S. Robinson, *The Papacy, 1073–1198: Continuity and Innovation* (New York: Cambridge
   University Press, 1990), p. 403.
3. Bartlett, *The Making of Europe: Conquest, Colonization and Cultural Change, 950–1350*
   (Princeton, N.J.: Princeton University Press, 1993), p. 24.
4. Ibid., pp. 250–255.

To assess your mastery of this chapter, go to **bedfordstmartins.com/mckaywestbrief**

Listening to the Past

An Arab View of the Crusades

To medieval Christians the Crusades were papally approved military expeditions for the recovery of the Holy Land; to the Arabs these campaigns were "Frankish wars" or "Frankish invasions" for the acquisition of territory. The Arab perspective is illustrated in a history of the First Crusade by Ibn Al-Athir (1160–1223). Al-Athir, a native of Mosul in northern Mesopotamia (modern Iraq), relied on Arab sources for the events he described. Here is his account of the Crusaders' capture of Antioch in Syria.

The power of the Franks first became apparent when in the year 478/1085–86* they invaded the territories of Islam and took Toledo and other parts of Andalusia. Then in 484/1091 they attacked and conquered the island of Sicily and turned their attention to the African coast. Certain of their conquests there were won back again but they had other successes, as you will see.

In 490/1097 the Franks attacked Syria.... When Yaghi Siyan, the ruler of Antioch, heard of their approach, he was not sure how the Christian people of the city would react, so he made the Muslims go outside the city on their own to dig trenches, and the next day sent the Christians out alone to continue the task. When they were ready to return home at the end of the day he refused to allow them. "Antioch is yours," he said, "but you will have to leave it to me until I see what happens between us and the Franks." "Who will protect our children and our wives?" they said. "I shall look after them for you." So they resigned themselves to their fate, and lived in the Frankish camp for nine months, while the city was under siege.

Yaghi Siyan showed unparalleled courage and wisdom, strength and judgment. If all the Franks who died had survived they would have overrun all the lands of Islam. He protected the families of the Christians in Antioch and would not allow a hair of their heads to be touched.

After the siege had been going on for a long time the Franks made a deal with . . . a cuirass [armor]-maker called Ruzbih whom they bribed with a fortune in money and lands. He worked in the tower that stood over the riverbed, where the

Miniature showing heavily armored knights fighting Muslims.
(Bibliothèque nationale de France)

*Muslims traditionally date events from Muhammad's hegira, or emigration, to Medina, which occurred in 622 according to the Christian calendar.

river flowed out of the city into the valley. The Franks sealed their pact with the cuirass-maker, God damn him! and made their way to the watergate. They opened it and entered the city. Another gang of them climbed the tower with their ropes. At dawn, when more than 500 of them were in the city and the defenders were worn out after the night watch, they sounded their trumpets. . . . Panic seized Yaghi Siyan and he opened the city gates and fled in terror, with an escort of thirty pages. His army commander arrived, but when he discovered on enquiry that Yaghi Siyan had fled, he made his escape by another gate. This was of great help to the Franks, for if he had stood firm for an hour, they would have been wiped out. They entered the city by the gates and sacked it, slaughtering all the Muslims they found there. This happened in jumada I (491/April/May 1098). . . .

It was the discord between the Muslim princes . . . that enabled the Franks to overrun the country.

Questions for Analysis

1. From the Arab perspective, when did the Crusades begin?
2. Why did Antioch fall to the Crusaders?
3. The use of dialogue in historical narrative is a very old device dating from the Greek historian Thucydides (fifth century B.C.E.). Assess the value of Ibn Al-Athir's dialogues for the modern historian.

Sources: P. J. Geary, ed., *Readings in Medieval History* (Peterborough, Ontario: Broadview Press, 1991), pp. 443–444; E. J. Costello, trans., *Arab Historians of the Crusades* (Berkeley and Los Angeles: University of California Press, 1969).

CHAPTER 10

The Changing Life of the People in the High Middle Ages

In these scenes from a German manuscript, *Speculum Virginum,* ca. 1190, the artist shows men, women, and children harvesting, raking, sowing, and digging. All residents in a village engaged in agricultural tasks. (Rheinisches Landesmuseum, Bonn)

Chapter Preview

Village Life
What was life like for the rural common people of medieval Europe?

Popular Religion
How did religious practices and attitudes permeate everyday life?

Nobles
How were the lives of nobles different from the lives of common people?

Monasteries and Convents
What roles did the men and women affiliated with religious orders play in medieval society?

INDIVIDUALS IN SOCIETY: Hildegard of Bingen

LISTENING TO THE PAST: The Pilgrim's Guide to Santiago de Compostela

I n a text produced at the court of Anglo-Saxon king Alfred, Christian society is described as composed of three **orders**: those who pray, those who fight, and those who work. This image of society became popular in the High Middle Ages, especially among people who were worried about the changes they saw around them. They asserted that the three orders had been established by God and that every person had been assigned a fixed place in the social order.

This tripartite model does not fully describe medieval society, however. There were degrees of wealth and status within each group. The model does not take townspeople and the emerging commercial classes (see pages 246–259) into consideration. It completely excludes those who were not Christian, such as Jews, Muslims, and pagans. Those who used the model, generally bishops and other church officials, ignored the fact that each of these groups was made up of both women and men; they spoke only of warriors, monks, and farmers. Despite—or perhaps because of—these limitations, the model of the three orders was a powerful mental construct. We can use it to organize our investigation of life in the High Middle Ages, though we can broaden our categories to include groups and issues that medieval authors did not.

orders Divisions of society in the High Middle Ages, including those who pray, those who fight, and those who work.

Village Life

What was life like for the rural common people of medieval Europe?

The evolution of localized feudal systems into more centralized states had relatively little impact on the daily lives of peasants except when it involved warfare. While only nobles fought, their battles often destroyed the houses, barns, and fields of ordinary people, who might also be killed either directly or as a result of the famine and disease that often accompanied war. People might seek protection in the local castle during times of warfare, but typically they worked and lived without paying much attention to the political developments under way there.

This lack of attention went in the other direction as well. Since villagers did not perform what were considered "noble" deeds, the aristocratic monks and clerics who wrote the records that serve as historical sources did not spend time or precious writing materials on them. When common people were mentioned, it was usually with contempt or in terms of the services and obligations they owed. Usually—but not always. In the early twelfth century Honorius (**hoh-NAWR-ee-uhs**), a monk and teacher at the monastery of Autun, wrote: "What do you say about the agricultural classes? Most of them will be saved because they live simply and feed God's people by means of their sweat."[1]

The Three Orders of Society (fourteenth century)

This book illustration shows the most common image of medieval society: those who fight, those who pray, and those who work. The group of clergy shown here includes a veiled nun; nuns were technically not members of the clergy, but most people considered them as such. (Copyright Royal Library of Belgium)

Slavery, Serfdom, and Upward Mobility

Medieval theologians lumped everyone who worked the land into the category of "those who work," but in fact there were many levels of peasants, ranging from complete slaves to free and very rich farmers. The High Middle Ages was a period of considerable fluidity with significant social mobility.

The number of slaves who worked the land declined steadily in the High Middle Ages. Most rural people in western Europe during this period were serfs rather than slaves, though the distinction between slave and serf was not always clear. Both lacked freedom—the power to do as they wished—and both were subject to the arbitrary will of one person, the lord. Unlike a slave, however, a serf could not be bought and sold like an animal.

People's legal status was based on memory and traditions, not on written documents. The serf was required to perform labor services on the lord's land, usually three days a week except during the planting or harvest seasons, when it was more. Serfs frequently had to pay arbitrary levies. When a man married, he had to pay his lord a fee. When he died, his son or heir had to pay an inheritance tax to inherit his parcels of land. The precise amounts of tax paid to the lord on these important occasions depended on local custom and tradition. A free person had to pay rent to the lord but could move and live as he or she wished.

Serfdom was a hereditary condition. A person born a serf was likely to die a serf, though many serfs did secure their freedom. More than anything else, the economic revival that began in the eleventh century (see pages 255–259) advanced the cause of freedom for serfs. The revival saw the rise of towns, increased land productivity, the growth of long-distance trade, and the development of a money economy. With the advent of a money economy, serfs could save money and, through a third-person intermediary, use it to buy their freedom. Many energetic and hard-working serfs acquired their freedom through this method of manumission in the High Middle Ages.

Another opportunity for increased personal freedom came when lords organized groups of villagers to cut down forests or fill in swamps and marshes between villages to make more land available for farming. In some parts of Europe, peasants migrated to these new areas. The thirteenth century witnessed German peasant migrations into Brandenburg, Pomerania, Prussia, and the Baltic States, with Germans establishing new villages between existing Slavic villages or pushing the Slavs eastward. In the Iberian peninsula, Christian villagers followed after the Christian armies that were gaining areas from Muslims. In Scandinavia, farms were established in areas that had previously been used to harvest furs or lumber. This type of agricultural advancement frequently improved the peasants' social and legal condition. A serf could clear a patch of fen or forestland, make it productive, and, through prudent saving, buy more land and eventually purchase freedom.

Peasants who remained in the villages of their birth often benefited because landlords, threatened with the loss of serfs, relaxed ancient obligations and duties. While it would be unwise to exaggerate the social impact of the settling of new territories, frontier lands in the Middle Ages did provide opportunities for upward mobility.

The Manor

In the High Middle Ages most European peasants, free and unfree, lived in family groups in small villages. One or more villages, and the land surrounding them, made up a manor, controlled by a noble or a church official such as a bishop, abbot, or abbess. Sometimes a single village would be divided among several lords into small manors, for manors varied from several thousand to as few as one hundred acres. The manor was the basic unit of medieval rural organization and the center of rural life. All other generalizations about manors and manorial life have to be limited by variations in the quality of the soil, local climatic conditions, and methods of cultivation. The arable land of the manor was divided into two sections. The *demesne* (di-MAIN), or home farm, was cultivated for the lord. The other part was held by the peasantry. Usually the peasants' portion was larger and was held on condition that they cultivate the lord's demesne. All of the arable land, both the lord's and the peasants', was divided into strips that were scattered throughout the manor. If one strip yielded little, other strips (with better soil) might be more bountiful. All peasants cooperated in the cultivation of the land, working it as a group. This meant that all shared in any disaster as well as in any large harvest.

The peasants' work was typically divided according to gender. Men were responsible for clearing new land, plowing, and the care of large animals, and women were responsible for the care of small animals, spinning, and food preparation. Both sexes harvested and planted, though often there were gender-specific tasks within each of these major undertakings. Women and men worked in the vineyards and in the harvest and preparation of crops needed by the textile industry—flax and plants used for dyeing cloth. In fishing communities wives and daughters dried and salted fish for later use, while husbands and sons went out in boats.

In western and central Europe, villages were generally made up of small houses for individual families, with one married couple, their children (including stepchildren), and perhaps one or two other relatives—a grandmother, a cousin whose parents had died, an unmarried sister or brother of one of the spouses. The household thus contained primarily a **nuclear family** and some households contained only an unmarried person, a widow, or several unmarried people living together. Villages themselves were also *nucleated*—that is, the houses were clumped together, with the fields stretching out beyond the group of houses. In southern and eastern Europe, extended families were more likely to live in the same household or very near to one another. Father and son, or two married brothers, might share a house with the families of both, forming what demographers call a *stem*, or complex household.

A manor usually held pasture or meadowland for the grazing of cattle, sheep, and sometimes goats. Often the manor had some forestland as well. Forests were the source of wood for building and for fuel, resin for lighting, ash for candles, ash and lime for fertilizers and all sorts of sterilizing products, and bark for the manufacture of rope. From the forests came wood for the construction of barrels, vats, and all sorts of storage containers. Last but hardly least, the forests were used for feeding pigs, cattle, and domestic animals on nuts, roots, and wild berries. If the manor was intersected by a river, it had a welcome source of fish and eels.

The medieval village had no police as we know them, so villagers who saw a crime or infraction were expected to chase

909	Abbey of Cluny established
1050–1300	Steady rise in population
1080–1180	Period of milder climate
1098–1179	Life of Hildegard of Bingen
Early 1100s	Production of iron increases greatly
1100–1200	Rapid expansion of the Cistercian Order
1200	Notion of chivalry begins to develop
1215	Fourth Lateran Council accepts seven sacraments

nuclear family Family group consisting of parents and their children, but no other relatives.

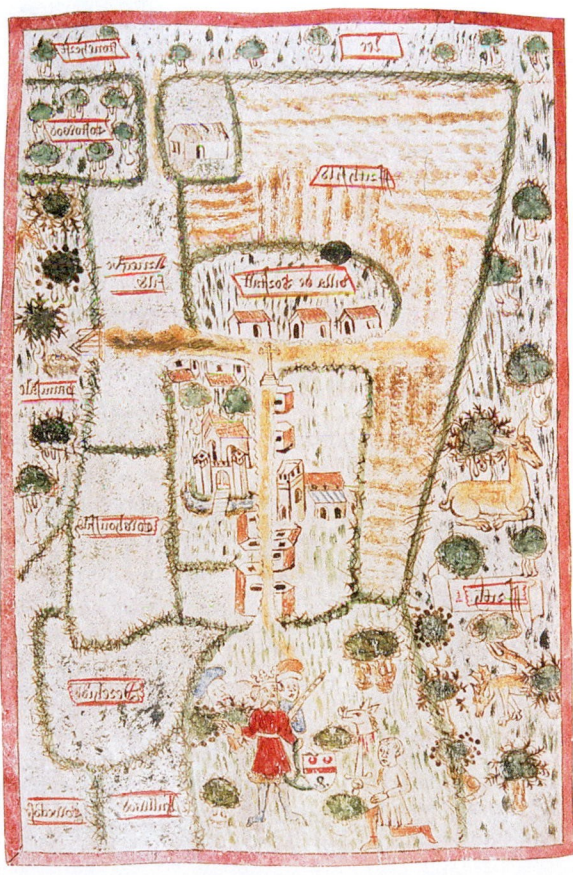

Boarstall Manor, Buckinghamshire

In 1440 Edmund Rede, lord of this estate, had a map made showing his ancestor receiving the title from King Edward I (*lower field*). Note the manor house, church, and peasants' cottages along the central road. In the common fields, divided by hedges, peasants cultivated on a three-year rotation cycle: winter wheat, spring oats, a year fallow. Peasants' pigs grazed freely in the woods, indicated by trees. We don't know whether peasants were allowed to hunt the deer. (Buckinghamshire Record Office, Aylesbury)

the perpetrator and yell to others to join in what was termed *raising the hue and cry*. Villages in many parts of Europe also developed institutions of self-government to handle issues such as crop rotation, and they chose additional officials such as constables and ale-tasters without the lord's interference. We do not know how these officials were chosen or elected in many cases, but we do know that they were always adult men and were generally heads of households. Women had no official voice in running the village, nor did slaves or servants (female or male), who often worked for and lived with wealthier village families. Women did buy, sell, and hold land independently and, especially as widows, headed households; when they did they were required to pay all rents and taxes. In areas of Europe where men were gone fishing or foresting for long periods of time, or where men left seasonally or more permanently in search of work elsewhere, women made decisions about the way village affairs were to be run, though they did not set up formal institutions to do this.

Manors do not represent the only form of medieval rural economy. In parts of Germany and the Netherlands, and in much of southern France, free independent farmers owned land outright, free of rents and services. These farms tended to be small and were surrounded by large estates that gradually swallowed them up. In Scandinavia the soil was so poor and the climate so harsh that people tended to live on widely scattered farms rather than in villages, but they still lived in relatively small family groups.

open-field system System in which the arable land of a manor was divided into two or three fields without hedges or fences to mark the individual holdings of the lord, serfs, and freemen.

Agricultural Methods and Improvements

Medieval farmers employed what historians term the **open-field system,** a pattern that differs sharply from modern farming practices. In the open-field system, the arable land of a manor was divided into two or three fields without hedges or fences to mark the individual holdings of the lord, serfs, and freemen. The village as a whole decided what would be planted in each field, rotating the crops according to tradition and need. Some fields would be planted in crops such as wheat, rye, peas, or barley for human consumption, some in oats or other crops for both animals and humans, and some would be left unworked or *fallow* to allow the soil to rejuvenate. The exact pattern of this rotation varied by location, but in most areas with open-field agriculture the holdings farmed by any one family did not consist of a whole field but, instead, of strips in many fields.

The milder climate of the Mediterranean area allowed for more frequent planting and a greater range of agricultural products; families tended to farm individual square plots rather than long strips. Milder climate also meant that more work (and play) could take place outdoors, which may have somewhat alleviated crowding in households with many family members.

While not approaching the temperatures of the Mediterrarean area, England, France, and Germany experienced exceptionally clement weather in the tenth and eleventh centuries. Meteorologists believe that a slow but steady retreat of polar ice occurred between the ninth and eleventh centuries. The mild winters and dry summers associated with this warming trend helped to increase agricultural output throughout Europe.

The tenth and eleventh centuries also witnessed a number of agricultural improvements, especially in the development of mechanisms that replaced or aided human labor. Water mills were one important part of this. In the ancient world, slaves ground the grain for bread; as slavery was replaced by serfdom, grinding became a woman's task. Water mills replaced human energy and increased productivity. A water mill unearthed near Monte Cassino in Italy could grind about

Windmill

The mill was constructed on a pivot so that it could turn in the direction of the wind. Used primarily to grind grain, as shown here with a man carrying a sack of grain to be ground into flour, windmills were also used to process cloth, brew beer, drive saws, and provide power for iron forges. (Bodleian Library, University of Oxford, MS Bodl. 264, fol. 81r)

1.5 tons of grain in ten hours, a quantity that would formerly have required the exertions of forty people.

Cloth production in medieval Europe grew because of water power. Women freed from the task of grinding grain could spend more time spinning yarn—the bottleneck in cloth production, as each weaver needed at least six spinners. Water mills were also well suited to the process known as *fulling*—scouring, cleansing, and thickening cloth—enabling men and women to full cloth at a much faster rate.

Next, medieval engineers harnessed wind power. Many windmills were erected in the flat areas of northern Europe, including Holland, that lacked fast-flowing streams.

In the early twelfth century the production of iron increased greatly. Iron was first used in agriculture for plowshares (the part of the plow that cuts the furrow and grinds up the earth), and then for pitchforks, spades, and axes. Harrows—cultivating instruments with heavy teeth that broke up and smoothed the soil—began to have iron instead of wooden teeth.

Plows and harrows were increasingly drawn by horses rather than oxen. The development of the padded horse collar that rested on the horse's shoulders and was attached to the load by shafts led to dramatic improvements. The horse collar meant that the animal could put its entire weight into the task of pulling. The use of horses spread in the twelfth century because horses' greater speed brought greater efficiency to farming and reduced the amount of human labor involved. Oxen were still used in areas where the soil was heavy and muddy.

The thirteenth century witnessed a tremendous spurt in the use of horses to haul carts to market. Consequently, goods reached market faster, and the number of markets to which the peasant had access increased. Peasants not only sold products, but also bought them as their opportunities for spending on at least a few nonagricultural goods multiplied.

By twenty-first-century standards, medieval agricultural yields were very low, but there was striking improvement over time. Increased agricultural output had a profound impact on society, improving Europeans' health, commerce, industry, and general lifestyle. A better diet had an enormous impact on women's lives: it meant increased body fat, which increased fertility; also, more iron in the diet meant that women were less anemic and less subject to opportunistic diseases. Some researchers believe that it was during the High Middle Ages that Western women began to outlive men. Improved opportunities also encouraged people to marry somewhat earlier, which meant larger families and further population growth.

Households, Work, and Food

Life for most people in medieval Europe meant country life. Most people rarely traveled more than twenty-five miles beyond their villages. Everyone's world was small, narrow, and provincial in the original sense of the word: limited by the boundaries of the province. This way of life did not have entirely unfortunate results. People had a strong sense of family and the certainty of its support and help in time of trouble. They had a sense of place, and pride in that place was reflected in adornment of the village church.

Life on the manor may have been stable, but it was dull. Medieval men and women often sought escape in heavy drinking. English judicial records of the thirteenth century reveal a surprisingly large number of "accidental" deaths. Strong, robust, commonsensible people do not ordinarily fall on their knives and stab themselves, or slip out of boats and drown, or get lost in the woods on a winter's night, or fall from horses and get trampled. The victims were probably drunk. Many of these accidents occurred, as the court records say, "coming from an ale." Brawls and violent fights were frequent at taverns.

The size and quality of peasants' houses varied according to their relative prosperity, and that prosperity usually depended on the amount of land held. Poorer

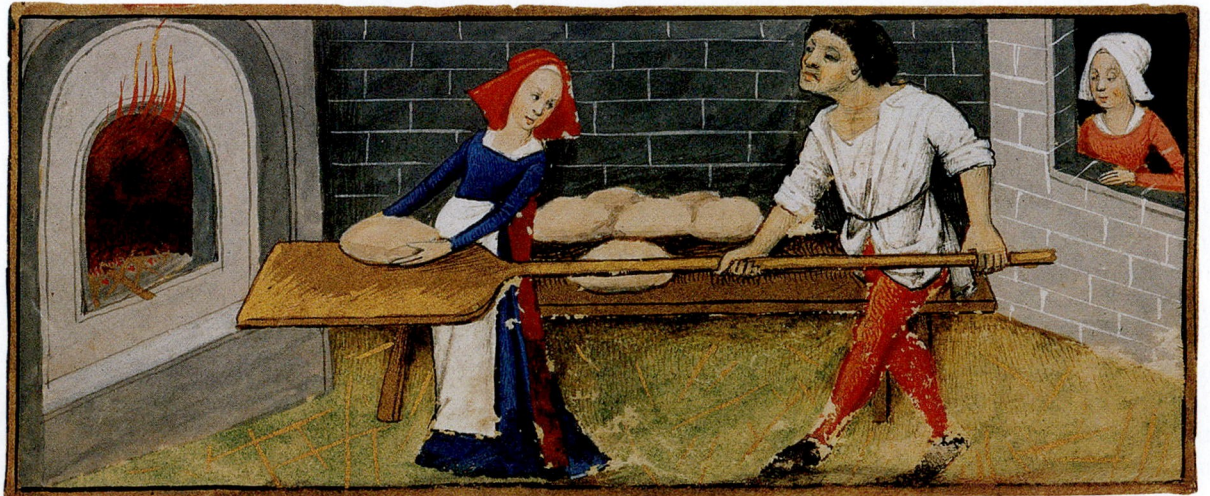

Baking Bread

Bread and beer or ale were the main manorial products for local consumption. While women dominated the making of ale and beer, men and women cooperated in the making and baking of bread—the staple of the diet. Most people did not have ovens in their own homes because of the danger of fire, but instead used the communal manorial oven, which, like a modern pizza oven, could bake several loaves at once. (Bibliothèque nationale de France)

peasants lived in windowless one-room cottages built of wood and clay or wattle (poles interwoven with branches or reeds) and thatched with straw. Prosperous peasants added rooms, and some wealthy peasants in the early fourteenth century had two-story houses with separate bedrooms for parents and children. For most people, however, living space—especially living space close enough to a fire to feel some warmth in cold weather—was cramped, dark, smoky, and smelly, with animals and people both sharing tight quarters, sometimes with each other.

Every house had a small garden and an outbuilding. Onions, garlic, turnips, and carrots were grown and stored through the winter in the main room of the dwelling or in the shed attached to it. Cabbage was shredded and salted for storage. Chickens and eggs were highly valued in the prudently managed household. Animals were too valuable to be used for food on a regular basis, but weaker animals were often slaughtered in the fall so that they did not need to be fed through the winter, and their meat was salted and eaten on great feast days such as Christmas and Easter. The rest of the household's needs—cloth, metal, leather goods, additional food, and copious quantities of ale—was purchased from village market stalls.

Health Care

Scholars are only beginning to explore questions of medieval health care, and there are still many aspects of public health that we know little about. The steady rise in population between the mid-eleventh and fourteenth centuries, usually attributed to warmer climate, increased food supply, and a reduction of violence with growing political stability, may also be ascribed partly to better health care. A recent study of skeletal remains in the village of Brandes in Burgundy showed that peasants enjoyed very good health: they were well built and had excellent teeth, and their bones revealed no signs of chronic disease. Obviously we cannot generalize about the health of all people on the basis of evidence from one village, but such research indicates that medieval adults were tough.

What care existed for the sick? As in the past, the sick everywhere depended above all on the private nursing care of relatives and friends. Beginning in the twelfth century in the British Isles, however, the royal family, the clergy, noble men and women, and newly rich merchants also established institutions to care for the sick or for those who for some reason could not take care of themselves. Within city walls they built hospitals, which were not hospitals in the modern sense, but rather places where those with chronic diseases that were not contagious, poor expectant mothers, the handicapped, people recovering from injuries, foundling children, and mentally retarded or psychologically disturbed children or adults went for care. Outside city walls they built leprosariums or small hospices for people with leprosy and other contagious diseases.

Such institutions might be staffed by members of religious orders, people who had less formally devoted themselves to lives of service, laymen and laywomen who were paid for their work, or a combination of the three. In the twelfth century medical personnel at hospitals were trained on the job, but by the thirteenth century some had been trained in faculties of medicine at Europe's new universities (see page 259). Outside of hospitals, people suffering from wounds, skin diseases, or broken bones turned to barber-surgeons who were trained in an apprenticeship system. For other internal ailments people used apothecaries—also trained through an apprenticeship system—to suggest and mix drugs, which combined herbs, salts, metals, and more fanciful ingredients such as "dragon's blood."

People also relied on men and women who had no official training at all, but who had learned healing techniques from their parents or other older people.

Monastic Entrance

In a world with few career opportunities for "superfluous children," monasteries served a valuable social function. Because a dowry was expected, monastic life was generally limited to the children of the affluent. Here a father—advising his son to be obedient and holding a bag of money for the monastery—hands his son over to the abbot. The boy does not look enthusiastic.
(The J. Paul Getty Museum, Los Angeles. Unknown illuminator, Initial Q: An Abbot Receiving a Child Decretum, ca. 1170–1180 [83.MQ.163.fol.63])

Their treatments were often mixtures of herbal remedies, sayings, specific foods, prayers, amulets, and ritual healing activities. Such combinations were also what people prescribed for themselves, for most treatment of illness was handled by home remedies handed down orally or perhaps through a cherished handwritten family herbal, cookbook, or household guide.

Childbirth and Child Abandonment

The most dangerous period of life for any person, peasant or noble, was infancy and early childhood. In normal years perhaps as many as one-third of all children died before age five, and in years with plagues, droughts, or famines this share climbed to more than half. Children often died from accidents as well as from malnutrition and illness, wandering into cooking fires, drowning in potholes in the road, or getting in the way of horses or cattle. Reaching adulthood meant that people had survived the most dangerous part of their lives, and many lived well into their fifties and sixties.

Childbirth was dangerous for mothers as well as for infants. Though mortality statistics are difficult to determine, every woman would have known someone who died in childbirth, and most would have seen such a death. Women developed prayers, rituals, and special sayings to ensure safe and speedy childbirth. Village women helped one another through childbirth, and women who were more capable acquired specialized midwifery skills. In larger towns and cities, such women gradually developed into professional midwives who were paid for their services and who trained younger women as apprentices, just as barber-surgeons and apothecaries trained their male apprentices. For most women, however, childbirth was handled by female friends and family, not by professionals.

The abandonment of infant children seems to have been the most favored form of family limitation and was widely practiced throughout the Middle Ages. Parents or guardians left children somewhere, sold them, or legally gave authority to some other person or institution. Sometimes parents believed that someone of greater means or status might find

Section Review

- The incidence of slavery was decreasing, as most of the slaves became serfs, an inherited condition, buying their freedom by saving money or migrating to new areas.

- The manor was the basic form of rural medieval life and contained land for the lord (the demesne) and additional land for the peasants, who farmed as a group, with separate jobs for men and women.

- In agriculture, production gradually increased as villages rotated crops in an open-field system, and improvements—such as water and windmills for grinding grain and processing cloth; the use of iron implements such as plows, pitchforks, and spades; and the increased use of horses—resulted in healthier lifestyles. Most people lived in the country in small, dark, smoky, smelly houses, often sharing space with animals, growing goods in small gardens, and purchasing things they could not produce at the market. The lifestyle was often dull, and heavy drinking was a common problem.

- Health care for most people was handled through home remedies given by friends and relatives, but a few hospitals and hospices provided care, and physicians, apothecaries, and barber-surgeons offered a variety of treatments to those who could afford them.

- Childbirth was dangerous for mothers and infants, and infancy and early childhood were the most dangerous times of life, as many children died from illness, famine, accidents, or abandonment, which was a common practice.

the child and bring it up in better circumstances than the natal parents could provide.

Disappointment in the sex of the child or its physical weakness or deformity might have also led parents to abandon it. Among Christians, superfluous children could be given to monasteries as **oblates**. The word *oblate* derives from the Latin *oblatio*, meaning "offering." Boys and girls were given to monasteries or convents as permanent gifts. But oblation also served social and economic functions. The monastery nurtured and educated the child in a familial atmosphere, and it provided career opportunities for the mature monk or nun whatever his or her origins. Oblation has justifiably been described as "in many ways the most humane form of abandonment ever devised in the West."[2] The abandonment of children remained socially acceptable, and church and state authorities never legislated against it.

oblates Children who were given to monasteries as offerings or permanent gifts.

Popular Religion

How did religious practices and attitudes permeate everyday life?

Apart from the land, the weather, and local legal and social conditions, religion had the greatest impact on the daily lives of ordinary people in the High Middle Ages. Religious practices varied widely from country to country and even from province to province. But nowhere was religion a one-hour-a-week affair. Most people in medieval Europe were Christian, but there were small Jewish communities scattered in many parts of Europe and Muslims in the Iberian peninsula, Sicily, other Mediterranean islands, and southeastern Europe.

Village Churches and Christian Symbols

For Christians the village church was the center of community life—social, political, and economic, as well as religious—with the parish priest in charge of a host of activities. Although church law placed the priest under the bishop's authority, the manorial lord appointed him and financed any education in Latin, Scriptures, and liturgy that he might receive. Parish priests were peasants and often were poor. Since they often worked in the fields with the people, they understood the people's labor, needs, and frustrations. The parish priest was also responsible for the upkeep of the church and for taking the lead in providing aid to the poorest of the village.

The center of the Christian religious life was the Mass, the re-enactment of Christ's sacrifice on the cross. Every Sunday and on holy days, the villagers stood at Mass or squatted on the floor (there were no chairs), breaking the painful routine of work. The feasts that accompanied baptisms, weddings, funerals, and other celebrations were commonly held in the churchyard. Medieval drama originated in the church. Mystery plays, based on biblical episodes, were performed first in the sanctuary, then on the church porch, which was often in front of the west door, and then at stations around the town.

From the church porch the priest read orders and messages from royal and ecclesiastical authorities to his parishioners. The west front of the church, with its scenes of the Last Judgment, was the background against which royal judges traveling on circuit disposed of civil and criminal cases. In busy mercantile centers such as London, business agreements and commercial exchanges were made in the aisles of the church itself, as at Saint Paul's.

Popular religion consisted largely of rituals heavy with symbolism. Before slicing a loaf of bread, the pious woman tapped the sign of the cross on it with her knife. Before planting, the village priest customarily went out and sprinkled the fields with water, symbolizing refreshment and life. Everyone participated in village processions. The entire calendar was designed with reference to Christmas, Easter, and Pentecost, events in the life of Jesus and his disciples. The varying colors of the vestments the priests wore at Mass gave villagers a sense of the changing seasons of the church's liturgical year. The signs and symbols of Christianity were visible everywhere.

saints Individuals thought to have lived particularly holy lives and regarded as having the power to work miracles.

Saints and Sacraments

Along with days marking events in the life of Jesus, the Christian calendar was filled with saints' days. **Saints** were individuals who had lived particularly holy lives and were honored locally or more widely for their connection with the divine. The cult of the saints, which developed in a rural and uneducated environment, represents a central feature of popular culture in the Middle Ages. People believed that the saints possessed supernatural powers that enabled them to perform miracles, and the saint became the special property of the locality in which his or her relics rested. Relics such as bones, articles of clothing, the saint's tears, saliva, and even the dust from the saint's tomb were enclosed in the church altar. In return for the saint's healing and support, peasants would offer the saint prayers, loyalty, and gifts. (See the feature "Listening to the Past: The Pilgrim's Guide to Santiago de Compostela" on pages 244–245.)

In the later Middle Ages popular hagiographies (**hag-ee-OG-ruh-fees**) (biographies of saints based on myths, legends, and popular stories) attributed specialized functions to the saints. Saint Elmo (ca. 300), who supposedly had preached unharmed during a thunder and lightning storm, became the patron of sailors. Saint Agatha (third century), whose breasts were torn with shears because she rejected the attentions of a powerful suitor, became the patron of wet nurses, women with breast difficulties, and bell ringers (because of the resemblance of breasts to bells).

Along with the veneration of saints, a new religious understanding developed in the High Middle Ages. Twelfth-century theologians expanded on Saint Augustine's understanding of sacraments—outward and visible signs regarded as instituted by Christ to give grace—and created an entire sacramental system. Only a priest could dispense a sacrament (except when someone was in danger of death), and the list of seven sacraments (baptism, penance, the Eucharist, confirmation, matrimony, ordination, anointment of the dying) was formally accepted by the Fourth Lateran Council in 1215.

Medieval Christians believed that these seven sacraments brought grace, the divine assistance or help needed to lead a good Christian life and to merit salvation. At the center of the sacramental system stood the Eucharist, the small piece of bread that through the words of priestly consecration at the Mass became the living body of Christ and, when worthily consumed, became a channel of Christ's grace. The ritual of consecration, repeated at every altar of Christendom,

The Eucharist

The Fourth Lateran Council of 1215 encouraged all Christians to receive the Eucharist at least once a year after confession and penance. Here a priest places the consecrated bread, called a *host,* on people's tongues. (Biblioteca Apostolica Vaticana)

became a unifying symbol in a complex world. The sacramental system, however, did not replace strong devotion to the saints.

Beliefs

Peasants had a strong sense of the presence of God. They believed that God rewarded the virtuous with peace, health, and material prosperity and punished sinners with disease, poor harvests, and war. Sin was caused by the Devil, who lurked everywhere and constantly incited people to evil deeds. Sin frequently took place in the dark. Thus evil and the Devil were connected in the peasant's mind with darkness or blackness. In some medieval literature, the Devil is portrayed as black, an identification that has had a profound and sorry impact on Western racial attitudes.

In the eleventh century theologians began to emphasize Mary's spiritual motherhood of all Christians. The huge outpouring of popular devotions to Mary concentrated on her special relationship to Christ as all-powerful intercessor with him. The most famous prayer, "Salve Regina," perfectly expresses medieval people's confidence in Mary, their advocate with Christ:

> Hail, holy Queen, Mother of Mercy! Our life, our sweetness, and our hope. To thee we cry, poor banished children of Eve; to thee we send up our sighs, mourning and weeping in this valley of tears. Turn, then, most gracious advocate, thy merciful eyes upon us; and after this our exile show us the blessed fruit of thy womb, Jesus. O merciful, O loving, O sweet Virgin Mary!

The Mass was in Latin, but the priest delivered sermons in the vernacular. However, a common complaint was that priests did a poor job of preaching the Gospel. Nevertheless, people grasped the meaning of biblical stories and church doctrines from the paintings on the church walls or, in wealthy parishes, the scenes in stained-glass windows. Illiterate and uneducated, they certainly could not reason out the increasingly sophisticated propositions of clever theologians. Still, scriptural references and proverbs dotted everyone's language. The English *good-bye*, the French *adieu*, and the Spanish *adios* all derive from words meaning "God be with you." Christianity was the foundation of the common people's culture for most Europeans.

Muslims and Jews

The interpenetration of Christian ceremonies and daily life for most Europeans meant that those who did not participate or who had different religious rituals were clearly marked as outsiders. This included Muslims in the Iberian peninsula, where Christian rulers were establishing kingdoms in territory won through the *reconquista* (see page 201). Islam was outlawed in their territories, and some of the Muslims left Spain, leaving room for new settlers from elsewhere in Christian Europe. Other Muslims converted. In more isolated villages, people simply continued their Muslim rituals and practices, including abstaining from pork, reciting verses from the Qur'an, praying at specified times of the day, and observing Muslim holy days, though they might hide this from the local priest or visiting church or government officials.

Islam was geographically limited in medieval Europe, but by the late tenth century Jews could be found in many areas, often brought in from other parts of Europe as clients of rulers because of their skills as merchants. There were Jewish communities in Italian cities and in the cities along the Rhine such as Cologne,

Worms, Speyer, and Mainz. Jews migrated from there to England and France, where they generally lived in the growing towns, often separate from the larger Christian community.

Jewish dietary laws require meat to be handled in a specific way, so Jews had their own butchers; there were Jewish artisans in many other trades as well, though Jews were forbidden to join Christian guilds. Jews held weekly religious services on Saturday, the Sabbath holy day of rest, and celebrated an annual cycle of holidays, including the High Holidays of Rosh Hashanah and Yom Kippur in the fall and Passover in the spring. Each of these holidays involved special prayers, services, and often foods, and many of them commemorated specific events from Jewish history, including various times when Jews had been rescued from captivity.

The Crusades brought violence against Jews in many cities (see pages 209–214), and restrictions on Jews increased in much of Europe. When Jews were expelled from England and later from France, many of them went to Muslim and Christian areas of the Iberian peninsula. The rulers of both faiths initially welcomed them, though restrictions and violence gradually became more common there as well. Jews continued to live in the independent cities of the Holy Roman Empire and Italy, and some migrated eastward into new towns that were being established in Slavic areas.

Marriage and Children

In the Middle Ages, every major life transition was marked by a ceremony. The sacrament of marriage was followed by a wedding party that often included secular rituals. Some rituals symbolized the "proper" hierarchical relations between the spouses—such as placing the husband's shoe on the bedstead over the couple, symbolizing his authority—or worked to ensure the couple's fertility—such as untying all the knots in the household, for tying knots was one way that people reputed to have magical powers bound up the reproductive power of a man. All this came together in what was often the final event of a wedding, the priest blessing the couple in their marriage bed, often with family and friends standing around or banging on pans, yelling, or otherwise making as much noise as possible. The friends and family members had generally been part of the discussions, negotiations, and activities leading up to the marriage; marriage united two families and was far too important to leave up to two young people alone.

The involvement of family and friends in choosing one's spouse might lead to conflict, but more often the wishes of the young people and their parents, kin, and community were quite similar; all hoped for marriages that provided economic security, honorable standing, and a good number of healthy children. The best marriages offered companionship, emotional support, and even love, but these were understood to grow out of the marriage, not necessarily precede it. Breaking up a marriage meant breaking up the basic production and consumption unit, which was a very serious matter, so marital dissolution by any means other than the death of one spouse was rare.

Most brides hoped to be pregnant soon after their wedding, and if the rituals during the wedding had not been effective in bringing this about, there were other avenues to try. Christian women hoping for children said special prayers to the Virgin Mary or her mother Anne; wore amulets of amber, bone, or mistletoe, thought to increase fertility; repeated charms and verses they had learned from other women; or, in desperate cases, went on pilgrimages to make special supplications. Muslim and Jewish women wore small cases with sacred verses or asked for blessings from religious leaders. Women continued these prayers and rituals through pregnancy and childbirth, often combining religious traditions with folk beliefs handed down orally.

Religious ceremonies also welcomed children into the community. Among Christian families, infants were baptized soon after they were born, for without the sacrament of baptism they could not enter heaven. Thus midwives who delivered children who looked especially weak and sickly often baptized them in an emergency service. In normal baptisms, the women who had assisted the mother in the birth often carried the baby to church, where carefully chosen godparents vowed their support. Godparents were often close friends or relatives, but parents might also choose prominent villagers or even the local lord in the hope that he might later look favorably on the child and provide for it in some way.

Within Judaism, a boy was circumcised and given his name in a ceremony when he was in his eighth day of life. This *brit milah*, or "covenant of circumcision," was viewed as a reminder of the covenant between God and Abraham described in Hebrew Scripture. Muslims also circumcised boys in a special ritual, though the timing varied from a few days after birth to adolescence.

Death and the Afterlife

Death was similarly marked by religious ceremonies. Christians called for a priest to perform the sacrament of extreme unction when they thought the hour of death was near. The priest brought a number of objects and substances regarded as having power over death and the sin related to it. Holy water, holy oil, and a censer with incense all connected to rites that purified and blessed the dying. Lighted candles drove back the darkness both figuratively and literally. A crucifix served to remind the dying of Christ's own agony and the promise of salvation. Most important, the priest gave the dying person a last communion host.

Once the person had died, the body was washed and dressed in special clothing or a sack of plain cloth and buried within a day or two. Family and friends joined in a funeral procession, again with candles, holy water, incense, and a crucifix and marked by the ringing of church bells; sometimes extra women were hired so that the mourning and wailing were especially loud. The procession carried the body into the church, where there were psalms, prayers, and a funeral Mass, and then to a consecrated space for burial, the wealthy sometimes inside the church—in the walls, under the floor, or under the building itself in a crypt—but most often in the churchyard or a cemetery close by. Standing at the graveside, the priest asked for God's grace on the soul of the deceased and also asked that soul to "rest in peace."

This final request was made not only for the benefit of the dead, but also for that of the living. The souls of the dead were widely believed to return to earth: mothers who had died in childbed might come back seeking to take their children with them; executed criminals to gain revenge on those who had brought them to justice (for this reason they were buried at crossroads, permanently under the sign of the cross, or under the gallows itself); everyday people came seeking help from surviving family members in achieving their final salvation.

Jewish Cemetery
Tomb in Worms of a thirteenth-century German Jewish rabbi who was imprisoned by the emperor and died in prison. Jewish and Christian cemeteries were separated in medieval Europe, with Christian cemeteries generally next to churches and Jewish ones often outside town walls. (Erich Lessing/Art Resource, NY)

purgatory A place where souls on their way to heaven went after death to make amends for their earthly sins.

Section Review

- The village church was the center of life for the people, with priest-led Masses, feasts, dramas, and sometimes business exchanges, all of which provided distractions from daily toil.

- Medieval people worshiped saints, offering them prayers and gifts, and believed that the sacraments brought divine help and salvation.

- Peasants believed that God rewarded the just and punished evildoers, that sin was from the Devil, and that Christianity was the basis for common people's lives.

- Christians treated Muslims and Jews as outsiders, so Muslims practiced in secret while Jews lived with many restrictions and often experienced violence.

- Marriage was a celebration involving both families and divorce was a rarity. Couples welcomed children, Christians baptizing them soon after birth, while Jewish and Muslim parents circumcised their infant sons.

- After Christians died, rituals and symbols were thought to help them move through purgatory; Muslims fasted and said special prayers, and Jews observed specific mourning rites.

Priests were hired to say memorial masses on anniversaries of family deaths, especially one week, one month, and one year afterward; large churches had a number of side altars so that many masses could be going on at one time.

Learned theologians sometimes denied that souls actually returned, and during the twelfth century they increasingly emphasized the idea of **purgatory**, a place where souls on their way to heaven went after death to make amends for their earthly sins. (Those on their way to hell went straight there.) Souls safely in purgatory did not wander the earth, but they could still benefit from earthly activities; memorial masses, prayers, and donations made in their names could shorten their time in purgatory and hasten their way to heaven. So could indulgences, documents bearing the pope's name that released the souls from purgatory. (Indulgences, it was believed, also relieved the living of penalties imposed by the priest in confession for serious sins.) Indulgences could be secured for a small fee, and people came to believe that indulgences and pilgrimages to the shrines of saints could ensure a place in heaven for their deceased relatives (and also, perhaps, for themselves). Thus the bodies of the dead on earth and their souls in purgatory both required things from the living, for death did not sever family obligations and connections.

The living also had obligations to the dead among Muslims and Jews. In both groups, deceased people were to be buried quickly, and special prayers were to be said by mourners and family members. Muslims fasted on behalf of the dead and maintained a brief period of official mourning. The Qur'an promises an eternal paradise with flowing rivers to "those who believe and do good deeds" (Qur'an, 4:57) and a hell of eternal torment to those who do not.

Jews observed specified periods of mourning during which the normal activities of daily life were curtailed. Every day for eleven months after a death and every year after that on the anniversary of the death, a son of the deceased was to recite Kaddish, a special prayer of praise and glorification of God. Judaism emphasized this life more than an afterlife, so beliefs about what happens to the soul after death were more varied; the very righteous might go directly to a place of spiritual reward, but most souls went first to a place of punishment and purification generally referred to as *Gehinnom*. After a period that did not exceed twelve months, the soul ascended to the world to come. Those who were completely wicked during their lifetime might simply go out of existence or continue in an eternal state of remorse.

Nobles

How were the lives of nobles different from the lives of common people?

nobility A small group of people at the top of the medieval social structure, whose official role was fighting.

The **nobility**, though a small fraction of the total population, strongly influenced all aspects of medieval culture—political, economic, religious, educational, and artistic. Despite political, scientific, and industrial revolutions, the nobility continued to hold real political and social power in Europe into the nineteenth century. In order to account for this continuing influence, it is important to understand the development of the nobility in the High Middle Ages.

Origins and Status of the Nobility

In the early Middle Ages noble status was generally limited to very few families who were either descended from officials at the Carolingian court or leading families among Germanic tribes. Beginning in the eleventh century, knights in the service of higher nobles or kings began to claim noble status. The noble class grew larger and more diverse, ranging from poor knights who held tiny pieces of land (or sometimes none at all) to dukes and counts with vast territories.

Originally, most knights focused solely on military skills, but gradually a different ideal of knighthood emerged, usually termed **chivalry** (SHIV-uhl-ree). Chivalry was a code of conduct originally devised by the clergy to transform the crude and brutal behavior of the knightly class. It may have originated in oaths administered to Crusaders in which fighting was declared to have a sacred purpose and knights vowed loyalty to the church as well as to their lords. Other qualities gradually became part of chivalry: bravery, generosity, honor, graciousness, mercy, and eventually gallantry toward women. The chivalric ideal—and it was an ideal, not a standard pattern of behavior—created a new standard of masculinity for nobles, in which loyalty and honor remained the most important qualities, but graceful dancing and intelligent conversation were not considered unmanly.

chivalry Code of conduct originally devised by the clergy to transform the crude and brutal behavior of the knightly class.

Childhood

For children of aristocratic birth, the years from infancy to around the age of seven or eight were primarily years of play. Infants had rattles, as the twelfth-century monk Guibert of Nogent reports, and young children had special toys.

At about the age of seven, a boy of the noble class who was not intended for the church was placed in the household of one of his father's friends or relatives. There he became a servant to the lord and received formal training in arms. He was expected to serve the lord at the table, to assist him as a private valet, and, as he gained experience, to care for the lord's horses and equipment.

Training was in the arts of war. The boy learned to ride and to manage a horse. He had to acquire skill in wielding a sword, which sometimes weighed as much as twenty-five pounds. He had to be able to hurl a lance, shoot with a bow and arrow, and care for armor and other equipment. Increasingly, in the eleventh and twelfth centuries, noble youths learned to read and write some Latin. Still, on thousands of charters from that period, nobles signed with a cross (+) or some other mark. Literacy among the nobility became more common in the thirteenth century. Formal training was concluded around the age of twenty-one with the ceremony of knighthood. The custom of knighting, though never universal, seems to have been widespread in France and England but not in Germany.

Noble girls were also trained in preparation for their future tasks. They were often taught to read the local language and perhaps some Latin and to write and do enough arithmetic to keep household accounts. They also learned music, dancing, and embroidery and how to ride and hunt, both common noble pursuits. Much of this took place in the girl's own home, but, like boys, noble girls were often sent to the homes of relatives or higher nobles to act as servants or ladies in waiting. While her brothers cared for armor and horses, a noble girl looked after clothing and household goods and learned how to run a household. She often

Saint Maurice

Certain individuals were held up to young men as models of ideal chivalry. One of these was Saint Maurice (d. 287), a soldier apparently executed by the Romans for refusing to renounce his Christian faith. He first emerges in the Carolingian period, and later he was held up as a model knight and declared a patron of the Holy Roman Empire and protector of the imperial (German) army in wars against the pagan Slavs. Until 1240 he was portrayed as a white man, but after that he was usually represented as a black man, as in this sandstone statue from Magdeburg Cathedral (ca. 1250). We have no idea why this change happened. Who commissioned this statue? Who carved it? Did an actual person serve as the model, and if so what was he doing in Magdeburg? (Image of the Black Project, Harvard University/Hickey-Robertson, Houston)

learned from experience that she could expect to spend weeks, months, or even years running a castle and a manor on her own while her future husband was away fighting.

Youth and Marriage

The ceremony of knighthood was one of the most important in a man's life, but knighthood did not necessarily mean adulthood, power, and responsibility. Sons were completely dependent on their fathers for support. A young man remained a youth until he was in a financial position to marry—that is, until his father died. That might not happen until he was in his late thirties, and marriage at forty was not uncommon. Increasingly, families adopted primogeniture, with property passing to the oldest son. Younger sons might be forced into the clergy or simply forbidden to marry. One factor—the inheritance of land and the division of properties—determined the lifestyles of the aristocratic nobility. The result was tension, frustration, and sometimes violence.

Once knighted, the young man traveled for two to three years. His father selected a group of friends to accompany, guide, and protect him. The band's chief pursuit was fighting. They meddled in local conflicts, sometimes departed on crusades, hunted, and did the tournament circuit. The **tournament**, in which a number of men competed from horseback (in contrast to the **joust**, which involved only two competitors), gave the young knight experience in pitched battle. Since the horses and equipment of the vanquished were forfeited to the victors, the knight could also gain a reputation and a profit. Young knights took great delight in spending money on horses, armor, gambling, drinking, and women. Everywhere they went, they stirred up trouble, for chivalric ideals of honorable valor and gallant masculinity rarely served as a check on actual behavior.

tournament An arena for knights to compete on horseback giving them valuable experience in pitched battle.

joust A competition between two knights on horseback.

Parents often wanted to settle daughters' futures as soon as possible. Men tended to prefer young brides. A woman in her late twenties or thirties would have fewer years of married fertility, limiting the number of children she could produce and thus threatening the family's continuation. Therefore, aristocratic girls in the High Middle Ages were married at around the age of sixteen, often to much older men. In the early Middle Ages the custom was for the groom to present a dowry to the bride and her family, but by the late twelfth century the process was reversed because men were in greater demand. Thereafter, the sizes of dowries offered by brides and their families rose higher and higher. Families engaged in complicated marriage strategies to balance the money they paid out to marry off daughters with the money they received in marrying off sons.

When society included so many married young women and unmarried young men, sexual tensions also arose. The young male noble, unable to marry for a long time, could satisfy his lust with peasant girls or prostitutes. But what was a young woman unhappily married to a much older man to do? Medieval literature is filled with stories of young bachelors in love with young married women and of cuckolded husbands who are not able to see what is going on in their households. Scholars disagree, however, about whether this reflected social realities or was simply wishful thinking.

Power and Responsibility

A male member of the nobility became an adult when he came into the possession of his property. He then acquired vast authority over lands and people. With it went responsibility. In the words of Honorius of Autun:

Soldiers: You are the arm of the Church, because you should defend it against its enemies. Your duty is to aid the oppressed, to restrain yourself from rapine and fornication, to repress those who impugn the Church with evil acts, and to resist those who are rebels against priests. Performing such a service, you will obtain the most splendid of benefices from the greatest of Kings.[3]

The responsibilities of a nobleman in the High Middle Ages depended on the size and extent of his estates, the number of dependents, and his position in his territory relative to others of his class and to the king. As a vassal, he was required to fight for his lord or for the king when called on to do so. By the mid-twelfth century this service was limited to forty days a year in most parts of western Europe. The noble was obliged to attend his lord's court on important occasions when the lord wanted to put on great displays, such as at Easter, Pentecost, and Christmas. When the lord knighted his eldest son or married off his eldest daughter, he called his vassals to his court. The vassals were expected to attend and to present a contribution known as a "gracious aid."

Until the late thirteenth century, when royal authority intervened, a noble in France or England had great power over those on his estates. He maintained order among them and dispensed justice to them. Holding the manorial court, which punished criminal acts and settled disputes, was one of his gravest obligations. The quality of justice varied widely: some lords were vicious tyrants who exploited and persecuted their peasants; others were reasonable and evenhanded. In any case, the quality of life on the manor and its productivity were related in no small way to the temperament and decency of the lord—and his lady.

Women played a large and important role in the functioning of the estate. They were responsible for the practical management of the household's "inner economy"—cooking, brewing, spinning, weaving, caring for yard animals. When the lord was away for long periods, the women frequently managed the herds, barns, granaries, and outlying fields as well. Often the responsibilities of the estate fell to them permanently, as the number of men slain in medieval warfare ran high.

Throughout the High Middle Ages, fighting remained the dominant feature of the noble lifestyle. The church's preaching and condemnations reduced but did not stop violence. Lateness of inheritance, depriving nobles of constructive outlets for their energy, together with the military ethos of their culture, encouraged petty warfare and disorder. The nobility thus represented a constant source of trouble for the monarchy. In the thirteenth century kings drew on the financial support of the middle classes to build the administrative machinery that gradually laid the foundations of strong royal government. The Crusades relieved the rulers of France, England, and the German Empire of some of their most dangerous elements. Complete royal control of the nobility, however, came only in modern times.

Elephant Ivory Mirror Case

The mirror case, forerunner of the modern woman's compact, protected a polished metal disk used by wealthy ladies as a looking glass. In this mid-fourteenth-century case, the French artist created a chivalric hunting scene. An aristocratic couple on horseback, holding falcons and accompanied by attendants, is portrayed in a forested landscape that is held in an eight-lobed frame with lions around the disk. Amazingly, the diameter of the case is less than four inches. Elephant ivory came from sub-Saharan Africa via the Mediterranean trade. (The Metropolitan Museum of Art, Gift of George M. Blumenthal, 1941 [41.100.160]. Photograph © 1995 The Metropolitan Museum of Art)

Section Review

- Originally, nobility was restricted to a few high aristocrats such as dukes and counts, but then it expanded to include knights, who aspired to follow the chivalric code of conduct with loyalty and honor, their most important virtues.

- Boys of the noble class began training for knighthood at about age seven, when they became pages to knights, managing their horses and acting as valets or servants, while girls received domestic training.

- The young noblemen were eligible to become full-fledged knights by age twenty-one, while daughters married starting around age sixteen, often paying dowries to the groom's family.

- Noble sons could not marry or inherit property until the death of their father, so they often had many years to travel, participate in tournaments, and cause trouble before they could settle down.

- A nobleman's power and responsibility were determined by the size of his estate, where he maintained order and dispensed justice to his peasants when he was not away fighting.

Monasteries and Convents

What roles did the men and women affiliated with religious orders play in medieval society?

Priests, bishops, monks, and nuns played significant roles in medieval society, both as individuals and as members of institutions. In the previous chapter we traced the evolution of the papacy and the church hierarchy in the High Middle Ages; here we focus on monks, nuns, and others who lived in religious houses.

In the fifth century Saints Benedict and Scholastica had written rules (*regulus* in Latin) for the men and women living in monasteries and convents (see page 148), who were known as regular clergy. In the early Middle Ages many religious houses followed the Benedictine Rule, while others developed their own patterns. In the High Middle Ages this diversity became more formalized, and **religious orders,** groups of monastic houses following a particular rule, were established. Historians term the foundation, strengthening, and reform of religious orders in the High Middle Ages the "monastic revival." They link it with the simultaneous expansion of papal power (see pages 205–209), because many of the same individuals were important in both.

Medieval people believed that monks and nuns performed an important social service — prayer. In the Middle Ages prayer was looked on as a vital service, as crucial as the labor of peasants and the military might of nobles. Just as the knights protected and defended society with the sword and the peasants provided sustenance through their toil, so the monks and nuns worked to secure God's blessing for society with their prayers and chants.

religious orders Groups of monastic houses following a particular rule.

Monastic Revival

In the early Middle Ages the best Benedictine monasteries had been centers of learning, copying and preserving manuscripts, maintaining schools, and setting high standards of monastic observance. Charlemagne had encouraged and supported these monastic activities, and the collapse of the Carolingian Empire had disastrous effects.

The Viking, Magyar, and Muslim invaders attacked and ransacked many monasteries across Europe. Some communities fled and dispersed. In the period of political disorder that followed the disintegration of the Carolingian Empire, many religious houses fell under the control and domination of local lords. Powerful laymen appointed themselves or their relatives as abbots, took the lands and goods of monasteries, and spent monastic revenues. The level of spiritual observance and intellectual activity in monasteries and convents declined.

The secular powers who selected church officials compelled them to become their vassals. Abbots, bishops, and archbishops thus had military responsibilities that required them to fight with their lords, or at least to send contingents of soldiers when called on to do so. As feudal lords themselves, ecclesiastical officials also had judicial authority over knights and peasants on their lands. The conflict between a prelate's religious duties on the one hand and his judicial and military obligations on the other posed a serious dilemma.

An opportunity for reform came in 909, when William the Pious, duke of Aquitaine, established the abbey of Cluny in Burgundy. Duke William declared that the monastery was to be free from any feudal responsibilities to him or any other lord, its members subordinate only to the pope.

The monastery at Cluny came to exert vast religious influence. The first two abbots of Cluny, Berno (910–927) and Odo (927–942), followed the Benedictine Rule closely and set very high standards of religious behavior. Cluny gradually came to stand for clerical celibacy and the suppression of simony (the sale of church offices). In the eleventh century Cluny was fortunate in having a series of highly able abbots who ruled for a long time. In a disorderly world, the monastery gradually came to represent stability. Therefore, laypersons placed lands under its custody and monastic priories (a priory is a religious house, usually smaller in number than an abbey, governed by a prior or prioress) under its jurisdiction for reform. Benefactors wanted to be associated with Cluniac piety, and monasteries under Cluny's jurisdiction enjoyed special protection, at least theoretically, from violence. In this way, hundreds of monasteries, primarily in France and Spain, came under Cluny's authority.

Deeply impressed laypeople showered gifts on monasteries with good reputations, such as Cluny and its many daughter houses. But as the monasteries became richer, the lifestyle of the monks grew increasingly luxurious. Monastic observance and spiritual fervor declined. Soon fresh demands for reform were heard, and the result was the founding of new religious orders in the late eleventh and early twelfth centuries.

The Cistercians (**si-STUR-shuhns**), because of their phenomenal expansion and the great economic, political, and spiritual influence they exerted, are the best representatives of the new reforming spirit. In 1098 a group of monks left the rich abbey of Molesmes in Burgundy and founded a new house in the swampy forest of Cîteaux (**sit-OH**). They planned to avoid all involvement with secular feudal society. They decided to accept only uncultivated lands far from regular habitation. They intended to refuse all gifts of mills, serfs, tithes, and ovens—the traditional manorial sources of income. The early Cistercians (the word is derived from *Cîteaux*) determined to avoid elaborate liturgy and ceremony and to keep their chant simple. Finally, they refused to allow the presence of powerful laypeople in their monasteries because such influence was usually harmful to careful observance.

The first monks at Cîteaux experienced sickness, a dearth of recruits, and terrible privations. But their obvious sincerity and high ideals eventually attracted attention. In 1112 a twenty-three-year-old nobleman called Bernard joined the community at Cîteaux, together with some of his brothers and other noblemen. Three years later Bernard was appointed founding abbot of Clairvaux (**klare-VOH**) in Champagne. From this position he conducted a vast correspondence, attacked the theological views of Peter Abelard (see page 261), intervened in the disputed papal election of 1130, drafted a constitution for the Knights Templars, and preached the Second Crusade. This reforming movement gained impetus. Cîteaux founded 525 new monasteries in the course of the twelfth century, and its influence on European society was profound. In England Saint Gilbert (1085?–1189) organized a community of nuns at Sempringham that followed the more rigorous Cistercian Rule "as far as the weakness of their sex allowed," as Gilbert put it. This convent established several daughter houses, and Gilbert asked the

Monastery of Saint Martin de Canigou
The Benedictine monastery of Saint Martin de Canigou was constructed in 1009 in the eastern Pyrenees (PIR-uh-neez) by a nobleman from one of the small Christian kingdoms in northern Spain. Like hundreds of other monasteries, it came under the influence of the abbey of Cluny (KLOO-nee). With its thick walls and strategic position, it served as a Christian defensive fortress against the Muslims in battles of the reconquista. (Editions Gaud)

Cistercians to take them all on as official female branches. They refused, saying that they did not want the burden of overseeing women, setting a pattern for other men's religious orders.

Unavoidably, however, Cistercian success brought wealth, and wealth brought power. By the later twelfth century economic prosperity and political power had begun to compromise the original Cistercian ideals.

Life in Convents and Monasteries

Throughout the Middle Ages social class also defined the kinds of religious life open to women. Kings and nobles usually established convents for their daughters, sisters, aunts, or aging mothers. Entrance was restricted to women of the founder's class. Like monks, many nuns came into the convent as children, and very often sisters, cousins, aunts, and nieces could all be found in the same place. Thus, though nuns were to some degree cut off from their families because they were cloistered, family relationships were maintained within the convent.

The office of **abbess** or **prioress** was the most powerful position a woman could hold in medieval society (see the feature "Individuals in Society: Hildegard of Bingen"). Abbesses were part of the feudal structure in the same way that bishops and abbots were, with manors under their financial and legal control. They appointed tax collectors, bailiffs, judges, and often priests in the territory under their control; some abbesses in the Holy Roman Empire even had the right to name bishops and send representatives to the imperial assemblies. Abbesses also opened and supported hospitals, orphanages, and schools; they hired builders, sculptors, and painters to construct and decorate residences and churches.

Monasteries for men were headed by an **abbot** or **prior,** who was generally a member of a noble family, often a younger brother in a family with several sons. The main body of monks, known as *choir monks*, were aristocrats and did not till the land themselves. In each house one monk, the *cellarer*, or general financial manager, was responsible for supervising the peasants or lay brothers who did the agricultural labor. **Lay brothers** were generally peasants and had simpler religious and intellectual obligations than did the choir monks. In women's houses, a nun acted as cellarer and was in charge of **lay sisters** who did the actual physical work. The *novice master* or *novice mistress* was responsible for the training of recruits, instructing them in the *Rule*, the chant, the Scriptures, and the history and traditions of the house. The efficient operation of a monastic house also required the services of cooks, laundresses, gardeners, seamstresses, mechanics, blacksmiths, pharmacists, and others whose essential work has left, unfortunately, no written trace.

The pattern of life within individual monasteries varied widely from house to house and from region to region. One central activity, however, was performed everywhere. Daily life centered on the *liturgy* or *Divine Office*, psalms and other prayers prescribed by Saint Benedict that monks and nuns prayed seven times a day and once during the night. Prayers were offered for peace, rain, good harvests, the civil authorities, the monks' families, and their benefactors. Monastic patrons in turn lavished gifts on the monasteries, which often became very wealthy.

Monks and nuns also performed social services. Monasteries often ran schools that gave primary education to young boys, while convents took in girls. Abbeys like Saint Albans, situated north of London on a busy thoroughfare, served as hotels and resting places for travelers. Monasteries frequently operated "hospitals" and leprosaria, which provided care and attention to the sick, the aged, and the afflicted—primitive care, it is true, but often all that was available. Monastaries and convents also fed the poor; at the French abbey of Saint-Requier in the eleventh

---

abbess/prioress Head of convent for women, usually a nun of considerable social standing.

abbot/prior Head of a monastery for men, who was generally a member of a noble family.

lay brothers/lay sisters Peasants who did the agricultural labor for the monastery since choir monks were aristocrats and therefore could not till the land themselves.

Individuals in Society

Hildegard of Bingen

The tenth child of a lesser noble family, Hildegard (1098–1179) (HIL-duh-gahrd), was given as an oblate to an abbey in the Rhineland when she was eight years old; there she learned Latin and received a good education. She spent most of her life in various women's religious communities, two of which she founded herself. When she was a child, she began having mystical visions, often of light in the sky, but told few people about them. In middle age, however, her visions became more dramatic: "And it came to pass . . . when I was 42 years and 7 months old, that the heavens were opened and a blinding light of exceptional brilliance flowed through my entire brain. And so it kindled my whole heart and breast like a flame, not burning but warming . . . and suddenly I understood of the meaning of expositions of the books."* She wanted the church to approve of her visions and wrote first to Saint Bernard of Clairvaux, who answered her briefly and dismissively, and then to Pope Eugenius, who encouraged her to write them down. Her first work was *Scivias* (Know the Ways of the Lord), a record of her mystical visions that incorporates vast theological learning.

Obviously possessed of leadership and administrative talents, Hildegard left her abbey in 1147 to found the convent of Rupertsberg near Bingen. There she produced *Physica* (On the Physical Elements) and *Causa et Curae* (Causes and Cures), scientific works on the curative properties of natural elements, poems, a mystery play, and several more works of mysticism. She carried on a huge correspondence with scholars, prelates, and ordinary people. When she was over fifty she left her community to preach to audiences of clergy and laity, and she was the only woman of her time whose opinions on religious matters were considered authoritative by the church.

* From *Scivias*, trans. Mother Columba Hart and Jane Bishop, *The Classics of Western Spirituality* (New York/Mahwah: Paulist Press, 1990).

Hildegard's visions have been explored by theologians and also by neurologists, who judge that they may have originated in migraine headaches, as she reported many of the same phenomena that migraine sufferers do: auras of light around objects, areas of blindness, feelings of intense doubt and intense euphoria. The interpretations that she developed come from her theological insight and learning, however, not illness. That same insight also emerged in her music, which is what she is best known for today. Eighty of her compositions survive—a huge number for a medieval composer—most of them written to be sung by the nuns in her convent, so they have strong lines for female voices.

In one of her visions, Hildegard saw the metaphorical figure Synagogue as a very tall woman who holds in her arms Moses with the stone tablets of the Ten Commandments. (Reinisches Bildarchiv, Koln, RBA-13 328)

Questions for Analysis

1. Why do you think Hildegard might have kept her visions secret? Why do you think she sought church approval for them?

2. In what ways might Hildegard's vision of Synagogue have been shaped by her own experiences? How does this vision compare with other ideas about the Jews that you have read about in this chapter?

Section Review

- In the High Middle Ages, monasteries and convents became affiliated with certain religious orders, which set the pattern of life for the men and women who lived in these religious houses.

- Monasteries gained wealth through donations, which often led to a decline in spiritual ideals; this in turn led to reform movements that sought to return the monasteries to stricter standards of poverty and separation from society.

- Convents were home to many women and were led by an abbess or prioress, one of the few positions of power for women in this age.

- Daily life in a convent or monastery centered on prayers said seven times a day or more, and on performing social services such as running schools and hospitals and feeding the poor.

- Hildegard of Bingen, the nun believed to have mystical powers, wrote books and composed music, becoming a woman of influence with a large following.

century, for example, 110 persons were given food daily. In short, monasteries and convents performed a variety of social services in an age when there was no "state" and no conception of social welfare as a public responsibility.

The agricultural recession of the fourteenth century (see pages 278–280) forced the lay nobility to reduce their endowment of monasteries. This development, combined with internal mismanagement, compelled many houses to restrict the number of recruits so that they could live within their incomes. Since the nobility continued to send their children to monasteries, there was no shortage of applicants for the limited number of places. Widespread relaxation in the observance of the Benedictine Rule and the weakening of community life, however, meant that the atmosphere in many monasteries resembled that of a comfortable and secure rooming house rather than an austere religious establishment.

Chapter Review

What was life like for the rural common people of medieval Europe? (page 221)

Generalizations about peasant life in the High Middle Ages must always be qualified according to manorial customs, the weather and geography, and the personalities of local lords. Everywhere, however, the performance of agricultural services and the payment of rents preoccupied peasants, with men, women, and children all working the land. Though peasants led hard lives, the reclamation of wastelands and forestlands, migration to frontier territory, or manumission offered means of social mobility. The warmer climate of the High Middle Ages and technological improvements such as water mills and horse-drawn plows increased the available food supply, though the mainstay of the peasant diet was still coarse bread. Death in childbirth of both infant and mother was a common occurrence, though there were some improvements in health care through the opening of hospitals.

How did religious practices and attitudes permeate everyday life? (page 229)

Religion provided strong emotional and spiritual solace for the majority of Europeans who were Christians as well as for Muslims and Jews. Within Christianity, the village church was the center of community life, where people attended services, honored the saints, and experienced the sacraments. People also carried out rituals full of religious meaning in their daily lives, and every major life transition—childbirth, weddings, death—was marked by a ceremony that included religious elements. This was true for Muslims and Jews as well as Christians, but the centrality of Christian ceremonies for most people meant that Muslims and Jews were increasingly marked as outsiders, and Christian persecution of Jews increased in the late eleventh century.

How were the lives of nobles different from the lives of common people? (page 234)

Nobles were a tiny fraction of the total population, but they exerted great power over all aspects of life. Aristocratic values and attitudes, often described as chivalry, shaded

Key Terms

orders (p. 221)

nuclear family (p. 223)

open-field system (p. 224)

oblates (p. 229)

saints (p. 230)

purgatory (p. 234)

nobility (p. 234)

chivalry (p. 235)

tournament (p. 236)

joust (p. 236)

religious orders (p. 238)

abbess/prioress (p. 240)

abbot/prior (p. 240)

lay brothers/lay sisters (p. 241)

all aspects of medieval culture. By 1100 the knightly class was united in its ability to fight on horseback, its insistence that each member was descended from a valorous ancestor, its privileges, and its position at the top of the social hierarchy. Noble children were trained for their later roles in life, with boys trained for war and women for marriage and running estates. Noblemen often devoted considerable time to fighting, and intergenerational squabbles were common. Yet noblemen, and sometimes noblewomen, also had heavy judicial, political, and economic responsibilities.

What roles did the men and women affiliated with religious orders play in medieval society? (page 238)

Monks and nuns exercised a profound influence on medieval society. In their prayers, monks and nuns battled for the Lord, just as the chivalrous knights did on the battlefield. In their chants and rich ceremonials and in their architecture and literary productions, monasteries and convents inspired Christian peoples. In the tenth century, under the leadership of the Abbey of Cluny, many monasteries shook off the dominance of local lords and became independent institutions. Cluny's success led people to donate land and goods, and it became wealthier, leading those who sought a more rigorous life to found a new religious order, the Cistercians. Monks and nuns were generally members of the upper classes and spent much of their days in group prayer and other religious activities, while lay brothers and sisters worked the lands owned by the monastery. Monasteries were an important part of the economy of medieval Europe, though sometimes the inhabitants lived beyond their means, which was also true of nobles and people who lived in Europe's growing towns.

Notes

1. Honorius of Autun, "Elucidarium sive Dialogus de Summa Totius Christianae Theologiae," in *Patrologia Latina*, ed. J. P. Migne (Paris: Garnier Brothers, 1854), vol. 172, col. 1149.
2. S. R. Scargill Bird, ed., *Custumals of Battle Abbey in the Reigns of Edward I and Edward II* (London: Camden Society, 1887), pp. 238–239.
3. Honorius of Autun, "Elucidarium sive Dialogus," vol. 172, col. 1148.

To assess your mastery of this chapter, go to **bedfordstmartins.com/mckaywestbrief**

Listening to the Past

The Pilgrim's Guide to Santiago de Compostela

Making pilgrimages to the shrines of holy persons is a common practice in many religions. Christian shrines often contained a body understood to be that of a saint or objects that had been in physical contact with the saint; thus believers perceived shrines as places where Heaven and earth met. A visit to a shrine and veneration of the saint's relics, Christians believed, would lead to the saint's intercession with God. After Jerusalem and Rome, the shrine of Saint James (Sant'Iago in Spanish) at Compostela in the Iberian peninsula became the most famous in the Christian world. Saint James was one of the twelve apostles and was said to have carried Christianity to Spain. Santiago de Compostela was situated in the kingdom of Galicia, close to the west coast of Spain.

In the twelfth century an unknown French author put together a sort of guidebook for the streams of pilgrims who travelled to Santiago from all over Europe. This excerpt from the Pilgrim's Guide details the characteristics of people one would meet on the way.

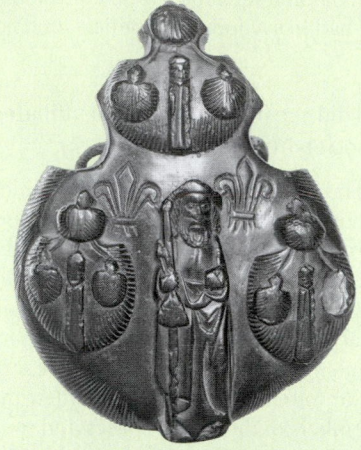

Pilgrims' badge from Santiago de Compostela. Enterprising smiths began making metal badges for pilgrims to buy as proof of their journey and evidence of their piety. The scallop shell became particularly associated with St. James and eventually with pilgrimages in general. Pilgrims who had visited many shrines would clink from the badges worn on their hats or capes, sometimes becoming objects of satire just as tourists laden with souvenirs are today. (Institut Amatller d'Art Hispanic)

After this valley is found the land of Navarre [**nuh-VAHR**], which abounds in bread and wine, milk and cattle. The Navarrese and Basques [**baskz**] are held to be exactly alike in their food, their clothing and their language, but the Basques are held to be of whiter complexion than the Navarrese. The Navarrese wear short black garments extending just down to the knee, like the Scots, and they wear sandals which they call *lavarcas* made of raw hide with the hair on and are bound around the foot with thongs, covering only the soles of the feet and leaving the upper foot bare. In truth, they wear black woollen hooded and fringed capes, reaching to their elbows, which they call *saias*. These people, in truth, are repulsively dressed, and they eat and drink repulsively. For in fact all those who dwell in the household of a Navarrese, servant as well as master, maid as well as mistress, are accustomed to eat all

Pilgrims' routes: monasteries in Cluny, Vézelay (vay-zuh-LAY), Saint-Gilles, and Moissac served as inns for pilgrims.

244

their food mixed together from one pot, not with spoons but with their own hands, and they drink with one cup. If you saw them eat you would think them dogs or pigs. If you heard them speak, you would be reminded of the barking of dogs. For their speech is utterly barbarous. . . .

This is a barbarous race unlike all other races in customs and in character, full of malice, swarthy in color, evil of face, depraved, perverse, perfidious, empty of faith and corrupt, libidinous, drunken, experienced in all violence, ferocious and wild, dishonest and reprobate, impious and harsh, cruel and contentious, unversed in anything good, well-trained in all vices and iniquities, like the Geats and Saracens in malice. . . .

However, they are considered good on the battlefield, bad at assaulting fortresses, regular in giving tithes, accustomed to making offerings for altars. For, each day, when the Navarrese goes to church, he makes God an offering of bread or wine or wheat or some other substance. . . .

Then comes Galicia [**guh-LISH-ee-uh**] . . . this is wooded and has rivers and is well-provided with meadows and excellent orchards, with equally good fruits and very clear springs; there are few cities, towns or cornfields. It is short of wheaten bread and wine, bountiful in rye bread and cider, well-stocked with cattle and horses, milk and honey, ocean fish both gigantic and small, and wealthy in gold, silver, fabrics, and furs of forest animals and other riches, as well as Saracen treasures. The Galicians, in truth, more than all the other uncultivated Spanish peoples, are those who most closely resemble our French race by their manners, but they are alleged to be irascible and very litigious. . . .

Questions for Analysis

1. How would you evaluate the author's opinion of the people of Navarre? of Galicia? How do these people compare with his own countrymen, the French?

2. Pilgrimages were in many ways the precursors of modern tourism. How would you compare the two in terms of economic effects and the expectations of the travelers?

Sources: From *The Pilgrim's Guide to Santiago de Compostela*, critical edition and annotated translation by Paula Gerson, Jeanne Krochalis, Annie Shaver-Crandell, and Alison Stones. Reprinted by permission of the authors. Data for map from Jonathan Sumption, *Pilgrimage: An Image of Medieval Religion* (Totowa, N.J.: Rowman and Littlefield, 1975).

CHAPTER 11

The Creativity and Challenges of Medieval Cities

Chapter Preview

Towns and Economic Revival
How did medieval cities originate, and what impact did they have on the economy and on culture?

Medieval Universities
How did universities evolve, and what needs of medieval society did they serve?

Arts and Architecture
How did the arts and architecture express the ideals, attitudes, and interests of medieval people?

Cities and the Church
Why did towns become the center of religious heresy, and what was the church's response?

INDIVIDUALS IN SOCIETY: Francesco Datini

IMAGES IN SOCIETY: From Romanesque to Gothic

LISTENING TO THE PAST: Courtly Love

This manuscript illumination shows a street scene of a medieval town, with a barber, cloth merchants, and an apothecary all offering their wares and services on the ground floor of their household-workshops. (Snark/Art Resource, NY)

The High Middle Ages witnessed some of the most remarkable achievements in the entire history of Western society. Europeans displayed tremendous creativity and vitality in many facets of culture. Relative security and an increasing food supply allowed for the growth and development of towns and a revival of long-distance trade. The university, a new—and very long-lasting—type of educational institution came into being, providing advanced training in theology, medicine, and law. Traditions and values were spread orally through stories and songs, some of which were written down as part of the development of vernacular literature. Gothic cathedrals manifested medieval people's deep Christian faith and their pride in their own cities, though the cities were also home to heretical movements that challenged church power.

Towns and Economic Revival

How did medieval cities originate, and what impact did they have on the economy and on culture?

The rise of towns and the growth of a new business and commercial class was a central part of Europe's recovery after the disorders of the tenth century. The growth of towns was made possible by some of the changes we have already traced: a rise in population; increased agricultural output, which provided an adequate food supply for new town dwellers; and a minimum of peace and political stability, which allowed merchants to transport and sell goods. The development of towns was to lay the foundations for Europe's transformation, centuries later, from a rural agricultural society into an urban industrial society—a change with global implications. In their backgrounds and abilities, townspeople represented diversity and change. Their occupations and their preoccupations were different from those of the feudal nobility and the laboring peasantry.

The Rise of Towns

Early medieval society was agricultural and rural. The emergence of a new class that was neither of these constituted a social revolution. Most of the members of the new class—artisans and merchants—came from the peasantry. The landless younger sons of large families were driven away by land shortage. Some were forced by war and famine to seek new possibilities. As in central Europe and Spain after the reconquista (see page 201), others were immigrants colonizing newly conquered lands. And some were unusually enterprising and adventurous, curious, and willing to take a chance.

Medieval towns began in many different ways. Some were fortifications erected during the ninth-century Viking invasions. Such towns were at first places of defense into which farmers from the surrounding countryside moved when their area was attacked. Later, merchants were attracted to the fortifications because they had something to sell and wanted to be where the customers were. They settled just outside the walls, in the *faubourgs* (**foh-BOORS**) or *suburbs*—both of which mean "outside" or "in the shelter of the walls." Other towns grew up around great cathedrals and monasteries whose schools drew students—potential customers—from far and wide. Many other towns grew from the sites of earlier Roman army camps. The restoration of order and political stability promoted rebirth and new development in these locations.

Carcassonne (kar-ka-SAWN)
This town in Languedoc (southern France) originated in pre-Roman times. Its thick double walls are an excellent example of the fortified medieval town. (Guido Alberto Rossi/TIPS Images)

Whether evolving from a newly fortified place or an old Roman army camp, from a cathedral site, a river junction, or a place where several overland routes met, medieval towns had a few common characteristics. Walls enclosed the town. (The terms *burgher* (**BUR-ger**) and *bourgeois* derive from the Old English and Old German words *burg, burgh, borg,* and *borough* for "a walled or fortified place." Thus a burgher or bourgeois was originally a person who lived or worked inside the walls.) The town had a marketplace. It often had a mint for the coining of money and a court to settle disputes.

As population increased, towns rebuilt their walls, expanding the living space to accommodate growing numbers. Through an archaeological investigation of the amount of land gradually enclosed by walls, historians have extrapolated rough estimates of medieval towns' populations. For example, the walled area of the German city of Cologne equaled 100 hectares in the tenth century (1 hectare = 2.471 acres), about 320 hectares in the twelfth, and 397 hectares in the fourteenth century. In the late twelfth century Cologne's population was at least 32,000; in the mid-fourteenth century it was perhaps 40,000. The concentration of the textile industry in the Low Countries brought into being the most populous cluster of cities in western Europe: Ghent, Bruges, Tournai, and Brussels. Venice, Florence, and Paris, each with about 110,000 people, and Milan with possibly 200,000, led all Europe in population.

Town Liberties and Merchant Guilds

The history of towns in the eleventh through thirteenth centuries consists largely of merchants' efforts to acquire liberties. In the Middle Ages *liberties* meant special privileges. **Town liberties** included the privilege of living and trading on the lord's land. The most important privilege a medieval townsperson could gain was

town liberties Privileges that included living and trading on the lord's land and, most importantly, personal freedom.

personal freedom. It gradually developed that an individual who lived in a town for a year and a day, and was accepted by the townspeople, was free of servile obligations and status. More than anything else, perhaps, the freedom that came with residence in a town contributed to the emancipation of the serfs in the High Middle Ages. Merchants joined together to form a **merchant guild** that prohibited nonmembers from trading in the town, and they often made up the earliest town government, serving as mayors and members of the city council, so that a town's economic policies were determined by its merchants' self-interest.

By the late eleventh century, especially in the towns of the Low Countries and northern Italy, the leaders of the merchant guilds were rich and powerful. They constituted an oligarchy in their towns, controlling economic life and bargaining with kings and lords for political independence. Full rights of self-government included the right to hold a town court that alone could judge members of the town, the right to select the mayor and other municipal officials, and the right to tax residents.

A charter that King Henry II of England granted to the merchants of Lincoln around 1157 nicely illustrates the town's rights. The quoted passages clearly suggest that the merchant guild had been the governing body in the city for almost a century and that anyone who lived in Lincoln for a year and a day was considered free:

> *Henry, by the grace of God, etc. . . . Know that I have granted to my citizens of Lincoln all their liberties and customs and laws which they had in the time of Edward [King Edward the Confessor] and William and Henry, kings of England. And I have granted them their gild-merchant, comprising men of the city and other merchants of the shire, as well and freely as they had it in the time of our aforesaid predecessors. . . . And all the men who live within the four divisions of the city and attend the market, shall stand in relation to gelds [taxes] and customs and the assizes [ordinances or laws] of the city as well as ever they stood in the time of Edward, William and Henry, kings of England. I also confirm to them that if anyone has lived in Lincoln for a year and a day without dispute from any claimant, and has paid the city taxes, and if the citizens can show by the laws and customs of the city that the claimant has remained in England during that period and has made no claim, then let the defendant remain in peace in my city of Lincoln as my citizen, without [having to defend his] right.*[1]

Feudal lords were reluctant to grant towns self-government, fearing loss of authority and revenue if they gave the merchant guilds full independence. When burghers bargained for a town's political independence, however, they offered sizable amounts of ready cash and sometimes promised payments for years to come. Consequently, feudal lords ultimately agreed to the burghers' requests.

Craft Guilds

While most towns were initially established as trading centers, they quickly became centers of production as well. Peasants left their villages—either with their lord's approval or without it—and moved to towns, providing both workers and customers. Some of them began to specialize in certain types of food and clothing production; others purchased and butchered cattle to sell meat and leather; others

merchant guild A band of merchants prohibiting nonmembers from trading in the town, and often serving as the earliest town government.

made metal arms, armor, and tableware. Wealthy merchants then bought these products for their own use, or they exported the finished products to other areas; certain cities became known for their fine fabrics, their reliable arms and armor, or their elegant gold and silver work.

Like merchants, producers recognized that organizing would bring benefits, and beginning in the twelfth century in many cities they developed **craft guilds.** These guilds set quality standards for their particular product, and they regulated the size of workshops, the training period, and the conduct of members. In most cities individual guilds, such as those of shoemakers or blacksmiths, achieved a monopoly in the production of one particular product, forbidding nonmembers to work. The craft guild then chose some of its members to act as inspectors and set up a court to hear disputes between members, though the city court remained the final arbiter.

Each guild set the pattern by which members were trained. A person who wanted to become a shoemaker, for instance, spent four to seven years as an apprentice, then at least that long as a journeyman, working in the shop of a master dyer, after which the person could theoretically make a "masterpiece." If the masterpiece—in the case of a shoemaker, of course, the masterpiece was a pair of shoes—was approved by the other master shoemakers and if they thought the market in their town was large enough to support another shoemaker, the person could then become a master and start a shop. Though the time required as an apprentice and as a journeyman varied slightly from guild to guild, all guilds fol-

craft guild A band of producers that regulated most aspects of production.

Spanish Apothecary

Town life meant variety—of peoples and products. Within the town walls, a Spanish pharmacist, seated outside his shop, describes the merits of his goods to a crowd of Christians and Muslims. (From the Cantigas of Alfonso X, ca. 1283. El Escorial/Laurie Platt Winfrey, Inc.)

lowed this same three-stage process. Guilds limited the amount of raw materials each master could have and the size of the workshop, thus assuring each master that his household-workshop would be able to support itself.

Many guilds required that masters be married, as they recognized the vital role of the master's wife. She assisted in running the shop, often selling the goods her husband had produced. Their children, both male and female, also worked alongside the apprentices and journeymen. The sons were sometimes formally apprenticed, but the daughters were generally not because many guilds limited formal membership to males. Most guilds did allow a master's widow to continue operating a shop for a set period of time after her husband's death, for they recognized that she had the necessary skills and experience. Such widows paid all guild dues, but they were not considered full members and could not vote or hold office in the guilds. The fact that women were not formally guild members did not mean that they did not work in guild shops, however, for alongside the master's wife and daughters female domestic servants often performed the lesser-skilled tasks. In addition, there were a few all-female guilds in several European cities, particularly in Cologne and Paris, in which girls were formally apprenticed in the same way boys were in regular craft guilds.

Both craft and merchant guilds provided their members with protection and social support. They took care of elderly masters who could no longer work, and they often supported masters' widows and orphans. They maintained an altar at a city church and provided for the funerals of members and baptisms of their children. Guild members marched together in city parades and reinforced their feelings of solidarity with one another by special ceremonies and distinctive dress.

City Life

Most streets in a medieval town were marketplaces as much as passages for transit. At the main marketplace just inside the city gates, poor people selling soap, candles, wooden dishes, and similar cheap products stood next to farmers from the surrounding countryside with eggs, chickens, or vegetables, people selling firewood or mushrooms they had gathered, and pawnbrokers selling used clothing and household goods. Because there was no way to preserve food easily, people—usually female family members or servants—had to shop every day, and the market was where they met their neighbors, exchanged information, and talked over recent events.

In some respects the entire city was a marketplace. A window or door in a craftsman's home opened onto the street and displayed the finished product made within to attract passersby. The family lived above the business on the second or third floor. As the business and the family expanded, additional stories were added.

Second and third stories were built jutting out over the ground floor and thus over the street. Since the streets were narrow to begin with, houses lacked fresh air and light. Initially, houses were made of wood and thatched with straw. Fire was a constant danger; because houses were built so close to one another, fires spread rapidly. Municipal governments consequently urged construction in stone or brick.

Most medieval cities developed with little town planning. As the population increased, space became more and more limited. Air and water pollution presented serious problems. Many families raised pigs for household consumption in sties next to the house. Horses and oxen, the chief means of transportation and power, dropped tons of dung on the streets every year. It was universal practice in the early towns to dump household waste, both animal and human, into the road in front of one's house. The stench must have been abominable.

People of all sorts, from beggars to fabulously wealthy merchants, regularly rubbed shoulders in the narrow streets and alleys of crowded medieval cities. This interaction did not mean that people were unaware of social differences, however, for clothing was a clear marker of social standing and sometimes of occupation. Monks, nuns, and friars wore black, white, or grey woolen clothing that marked them as members of a particular religious order, while priests and bishops wore layers of specialized clothing, especially when they were officiating at religious services. Military men and servants who lived in noble households wore dress with distinctive colors known as **livery** (**LIV-uh-ree**). Wealthier urban residents wore bright colors, imported silk or fine woolen fabrics, and fancy headgear, while poorer ones wore darker clothing made of rough linen or linen and wool blends. When universities developed in European cities, students wore clothing and headgear that marked their status. University graduates—lawyers, physicians, and university professors—often wore dark robes, trimmed with fur if they could afford it; the robes worn in contemporary academic ceremonies are descended from this medieval dress.

livery Dress of distinctive colors worn by military men and servants who lived in noble households.

In the later Middle Ages many cities attempted to make clothing distinctions a matter of law as well as of habit. They passed **sumptuary laws** that regulated the value of clothing and jewelry that people of different social groups could wear. Only members of high social groups could wear velvet, satin, pearls, or fur, for example, or have clothing embroidered with gold thread or dyed in colors that were especially expensive to produce, such as the purple dye that came from mollusk shells. Along with enforcing social differences, sumptuary laws also attempted to impose moral standards by prohibiting plunging necklines on women or doublets that were too short on men and to protect local industries by restricting the use of imported fabrics or other materials. Some of these laws marked certain individuals as members of groups not fully acceptable in urban society—prostitutes might be required to wear red or yellow bands on their clothes that were supposed to represent the flames of hell, and Jews to wear yellow circles or stars to distinguish them from their Christian neighbors. (Many Jewish communities also developed their own sumptuary laws prohibiting extravagant or ostentatious dress.) In some cities, sumptuary laws were expanded to include restrictions on expenditures for parties and family celebrations, again set by social class. Weddings for members of the nobility or the urban elite could include imported wine, fancy food, musicians, and hundreds of guests, while those for the children of artisans could serve only local beer to several dozen guests.

sumptuary laws Laws that regulated the value and style of clothing that various social groups could wear, and the amount they could spend on family celebrations.

Servants and the Poor

Many urban households hired domestic servants, with a less wealthy household employing one woman who assisted in all aspects of running the household and a wealthier one employing a large staff of male and female servants with specific duties. In Italian cities, household servants included slaves, usually young women brought in from areas outside of western Christianity, such as the Balkans. (Like Islam, Christianity favored slaves who were not believers.)

Along with permanent servants, many households hired additional workers to do specific tasks—laundering clothing and household linens, caring for children or invalids, repairing houses and walls, and carrying messages or packages around the city or the surrounding countryside. In contrast to rural peasants, who raised most of their own food, urban workers bought all their food, so they felt any increase in the price of ale or bread immediately. Their wages were generally low, and children from such families sought work at very young ages.

In cities with extensive cloth production, such as Florence or the towns of Flanders, the urban poor included workers who were paid by the piece. If prices dipped, merchants simply did not pay workers, who were left with thread or unfinished cloth that they technically did not own, and who had no wages with which to buy food.

The possibilities for legitimate employment were often very limited, and illegal activities offered another way for people to support themselves. They stole merchandise from houses, wagons, and storage facilities, fencing it to local pawnbrokers or taking it to the next town to sell. They stole goods or money directly from people, cutting the strings of their bags or purses. They sold sex for money— what later came to be called prostitution—standing on street corners or moving into houses that by the fifteenth century became official city brothels (see page 298). They made and sold mixtures of herbs and drugs offering to heal all sorts of ailments, perhaps combining this with a puppet show, trained animals, magic tricks, or music to draw customers. Or they did all these things, and also worked as laundresses, day laborers, porters, peddlers, or street vendors when they could. Cities also drew in orphans, blind people, and the elderly, who resorted to begging for food and money.

The Revival of Long-Distance Trade

The growth of towns went hand in hand with a remarkable revival of trade as artisans and craftsmen manufactured goods for local and foreign consumption (see Map 11.1). Most trade centered in towns and was controlled by professional traders. Long-distance trade was risky and required large investments of capital. Shipwrecks were common. Pirates infested the sea-lanes, and robbers and thieves roamed virtually all of the land routes. Since the risks were so great, merchants preferred to share them. A group of people would thus pool their capital to finance an expedition to a distant place. When the ship or caravan returned and the goods brought back were sold, the investors would share the profits. If disaster struck the caravan, an investor's loss was limited to the amount of that individual's investment.

Which towns took the lead in medieval "international" trade? In the late eleventh century the Italian cities, especially Venice, led the West in trade in general and completely dominated trade with the East. Lombard and Tuscan merchants exchanged those goods at the town markets and regional fairs of France, Flanders, and England. (Fairs were periodic gatherings that attracted buyers, sellers, and goods from all over Europe.) The towns of Bruges (**BROOGH**), Ghent, and Ypres (**EE-pruh**) in Flanders were also leaders in long-distance trade, and built up a vast industry in the manufacture of cloth.

Two circumstances help explain the lead Venice and the Flemish towns gained in long-distance trade. Both enjoyed a high degree of peace and political stability. Geographical factors were equally, if not more, important. Venice was ideally located at the northwestern end of the Adriatic Sea, with easy access to the transalpine land routes as well as the Adriatic and Mediterranean sea-lanes. The markets of North Africa, Byzantium, and Russia and the great fairs of Ghent in Flanders and Champagne in France provided commercial opportunities that Venice quickly seized. The geographical situation of Flanders also offered unusual possibilities: just across the channel from England, Flanders had easy access to English wool. Indeed, Flanders and England developed a very close economic relationship.

Wool was the cornerstone of the English medieval economy. Population growth in the twelfth century and the success of the Flemish and Italian textile industries created foreign demand for English wool. The production of English

Legend

- Textile and manufacturing areas
- Northern sea routes
- Venetian sea routes
- Genoese sea routes
- Other sea routes
- Overland routes

Aral Sea

Caspian Sea

Baghdad

Slave market

Rostov

Fish
Sea of Azov

Black Sea

Saffa

Sinope

Trebizond

Fruits+foodstuffs

Sivas

Ankara   Cotton Carpets+rugs

Antioch

Opium

Smyrna   Fruits+foodstuffs

Slave market

Damascus   Precious woods

Tripoli
Beirut   Iron Glassware
Sidon
Tyre   Horses

Silk Paper

Cairo   Slave market
Alexandria   Cotton
    Indigo
    Cotton

Jerusalem

Slaves

Constantinople

Cyprus

Rhodes

Crete

Aegean Sea

Olives

Wine

Raisins

Currants

Mediterranean Sea

Wool

Fish

Furs   Flax
Honey
Novgorod   Furs

Moscow   Furs

Pitch

Hemp

Wax

Flax

Reval

Riga

Flax

Königsberg

Warsaw

Kiev

Slave market

Wheat

Skins+hides

Horses

Silver

Belgrade

Silver

Ragusa

Horses

Adriatic Sea

Slaves

Olives

Wine

Taranto

Olives

Messina

Sicily   Olives
    Wine

Syracuse

Tripoli   Gold
Slave market   Slaves

Fish

Gotland

Baltic Sea

Fish

Fish

Grain   Pitch
Tar
Breslau   Iron
Kraków   Silver
Grain   Iron

Danzig

Stockholm

Copenhagen

Copper

Oslo

Fish

Grain

Bergen

Fish

Fish

Pitch

Lübeck

Hamburg   Flax
Bremen   Hemp
Amsterdam

Hemp
Frankfurt
Magdeburg   Salt
Leipzig
Prague   Iron   Paper
Nuremberg   Silver
Augsburg   Salt
Wine   Mfd. wares
    Glass
Cologne   Wine Copper   Venice
Strasbourg   Wheat Silver   Bologna   Artwares
    Salt   Geneva   Milan   Florence
Basel   Mfd. wares   Genoa
    Wine   Pisa
    Mfd. wares   Timber
Avignon   Wine   Pitch
Lyons   Marseilles
Wool   *Corsica*   Silver

North Sea

Durham

York   Wool

Lead   Iron

Edinburgh
Carlisle   Lead
Chester   Tin
Bristol   Iron
Southampton   Iron
    Fish   Salt
Rennes   Flax
Nantes   Wine Wheat
    Salt

London
Brussels
Bruges   Paper
Calais
Rouen
Paris   Iron
Orléans
Tours
Limoges   Wine
Bordeaux   Wine
Clermont   Wool
Bayonne   Iron
Toulouse

Ireland

ATLANTIC OCEAN

Bay of Biscay

Fruits+foodstuffs

León   Copper
Santiago   Leather
Fruits+foodstuffs   Metalwares
Wine   Paper   Valencia
Lisbon   Toledo   Horses
    Córdoba   Cartagena
Cork Cotton   Olives   Granada   Almeira
Seville   Silk   Ceuta   Olives
    Slave market

Balearic Is.

Barcelona

Sardinia

Dates

Algiers   Slave market
    Olives

Tunis   Fish

Skins+hides

Naples   Cotton
Rome   Wine
    Olives

Wool

Gold
Slaves

Wool

Slaves
Gold

Gold
Slaves

N

200 Mi.

400 Km.

200

200

0

0

MAPPING THE PAST

MAP 11.1   Trade and Manufacturing in Medieval Europe

The development of towns and the reinvigoration of trade were directly related in medieval Europe. Using both of the maps in this chapter and the information in your text, answer the following questions: **[1]** What part of Europe had the highest density of towns? Why? **[2]** Which towns were the largest and most important centers of long-distance trade (see p. 253)? **[3]** What role did textile and other sorts of manufacturing play in the growth of towns? **[4]** Does the development of towns seem more closely related to that of universities, monastery schools, or cathedral schools? Why?

---

wool stimulated Flemish manufacturing, and the expansion of the Flemish cloth industry in turn spurred the production of English wool. The availability of raw wool also encouraged the development of domestic cloth manufacture in England.

Business Procedures   The growth of a money economy made possible the steadily expanding volume of international trade in the High Middle Ages. Beginning in the 1160s the opening of new silver mines in Germany, Bohemia, northern Italy, northern France, and western England led to the minting and circulation of vast quantities of silver coins. Demand for sugar (to replace honey), pepper, cloves, and Asian spices to season a bland diet; for fine wines from the Rhineland, Burgundy, and Bordeaux; for luxury woolens from Flanders and Tuscany; for furs from Ireland and Russia; for brocades and tapestries from Flanders and silks from Constantinople and even China; for household furnishings such as silver plate—not to mention the desire for products associated with a military aristocracy such as swords and armor—surged markedly.

To meet the greater volume, the work of merchants became specialized. Three separate types of merchants emerged: the sedentary merchant who ran the "home office," financing and organizing the firm's entire export-import trade; the carriers who transported goods by land and sea; and the company agents living abroad who, on the advice of the home office, looked after sales and procurements.

Business procedures changed radically. Commercial correspondence proliferated and regular courier service among commercial cities began. Commercial accounting became more complex when firms had to deal with shareholders, manufacturers, customers, branch offices, employees, and competing firms. Tolls on roads became high enough to finance what has been called a "road revolution," involving new surfaces, bridges, new passes through the Alps, and new inns and hospices for travelers. The growth of mutual confidence among merchants facilitated the growth of sales on credit.

In all these transformations, merchants of the Italian cities led the way. (See the feature "Individuals in Society: Francesco Datini.") They formalized their agreements with new types of contracts, including permanent partnerships termed *compagnie* (**kahm-pa-NYEE**) (literally "bread together," that is, sharing bread, and the root of the English word *company*). Many of these compagnie began as agreements between brothers or other relatives and in-laws, but quickly grew to include people who were not family members. In addition, they began to involve individuals—including a few women—who invested only their money, leaving the actual running of the business to the active partners.

Individuals in Society

Francesco Datini

In 1348, when he was a young teenager, Francesco Datini (1335–1410) lost his father, his mother, a brother, and a sister to the Black Death epidemic that swept through Europe (see pages 280–285). Leaving his hometown of Prato in northern Italy, he apprenticed himself to merchants in nearby Florence for several years to learn accounting and other business skills. At fifteen, he moved to the city of Avignon (**ah-vee-NYON**) in southern France. The popes were living in Avignon instead of Rome, and the city offered many opportunities for an energetic and enterprising young man. Datini first became involved in the weapons trade, which offered steady profits, and then handled spices, wool and silk cloth, and jewels. He was very successful, and when he was thirty-one he married the young daughter of another merchant in an elaborate wedding that was the talk of Avignon.

Statue of Franceso Datini outside the city hall in Prato. (© Peter Horree/Alamy)

In 1378 the papacy returned to Italy, and Datini soon followed, setting up trading companies in Prato, Pisa, Florence, and eventually other cities as well. He focused on cloth and leather and sought to control the trade in products used for preparation as well, especially the rare dyes that created the brilliant colors favored by wealthy noblemen and townspeople. He eventually had offices all over Europe and became one of the richest men of his day, opening a mercantile bank and a company that produced cloth, as well as his many branch offices.

Datini was more successful than most, but what makes him particularly stand out was his record-keeping. He kept careful account books and ledgers, all of them headed by the phrase "in the name of God and profit." He wrote to the managers of each of his offices every week, providing them with careful advice and blunt criticism: "You cannot see a crow in a bowl of milk." Taking on the son of a friend as an employee, he wrote to

the young man: "Do your duty well, and you will acquire honor and profit, and you can count on me as if I were your own father. But if you do not, then do not count on me; it will be as if I had never known you."

When Datini was away from home, which was often, he wrote to his wife every day, and she sometimes responded in ways that were less deferential than we might expect of a woman who was many years younger. "I think it is not necessary," she wrote at one point, "to send me a message every Wednesday to say that you will be here on Sunday, for it seems to me that on every Friday you change your mind."

Datini's obsessive record-keeping lasted beyond his death, for someone put all of his records—hundreds of ledgers and contracts, eleven thousand business letters, and over a hundred thousand personal letters—in sacks in his opulent house in Prato, where they were found in the nineteenth century. They provide a detailed picture of medieval business practices and also reveal much about Datini as a person. Ambitious, calculating, luxury-loving, and a workaholic, Datini seems similar to a modern CEO. Like many of today's self-made super-rich people, at the end of his life Datini began to think a bit more about God and less about profit. In his will, he set up a foundation for the poor in Prato and a home for orphans in Florence, both of which are still in operation. In 1967 scholars established an institute for economic history in Prato, naming it in Datini's honor; the institute now manages the collection of Datini documents and gathers other relevant materials in its archives.

Questions for Analysis

1. How would you evaluate Datini's motto: as an honest statement of his aims, a hypocritical justification of greed, a blend of both, or something else?
2. Changes in business procedures in the Middle Ages have been described as a "commercial revolution." Do Datini's activities support this assessment? Why?

Source: Iris Origo, *The Merchant of Prato: Francesco di Marco Datini, 1335–1410* (New York: Alfred A. Knopf Inc., 1957).

The ventures of the German Hanseatic League also illustrate these new business procedures. The **Hanseatic (han-see-AT-ik) League** was a mercantile association of towns. Initially the towns of Lübeck and Hamburg wanted mutual security, exclusive trading rights, and, where possible, a monopoly. During the next century, perhaps two hundred cities from Holland to Poland joined the league, but Lübeck always remained the dominant member. From the thirteenth to the sixteenth centuries, the Hanseatic League controlled the trade of northern Europe (see Map 11.1). In the fourteenth century the Hanseatics branched out into southern Germany and Italy by land and into French, Spanish, and Portuguese ports by sea.

At cities such as Bruges and London, Hanseatic merchants secured special trading concessions exempting them from all tolls and allowing them to trade at local fairs. Hanseatic merchants established foreign trading centers, called "factories," the most famous of which was the London Steelyard, a walled community with warehouses, offices, a church, and residential quarters for company representatives. By the late thirteenth century Hanseatic merchants had developed an important business technique, the business register. Merchants publicly recorded their debts and contracts and received a league guarantee for them.

The dramatic increase in trade ran into two serious difficulties in medieval Europe. One was the problem of money. Despite investment in mining operations to increase the production of metals, the amount of gold, silver, and copper available for coins was simply not adequate for the increased flow of commerce. Merchants developed paper letters of exchange, in which coins or goods in one location were exchanged for a sealed letter (much like a modern deposit statement), which could be used in place of metal coinage elsewhere. This made the long, slow, and very dangerous shipment of coins unnecessary. Begun in the late twelfth century, the bill of exchange was the normal method of making commercial payments by the early fourteenth century among the cities of western Europe, and it proved to be a decisive factor in the later development of credit and commerce in northern Europe.

The second problem was a moral and theological one. Church doctrine frowned on lending money at interest, termed **usury (YOO-zhuh-ree)**. This restriction on Christians is one reason why Jews were frequently the moneylenders in early medieval society; it was one of the few occupations not forbidden them by Christian authorities. As money lending became more important to commercial ventures, the church relaxed its position. It declared that some interest was legitimate as a payment for the risk the investor was taking, and that only interest above a certain level would be considered usury. (This definition of usury has continued; modern governments generally set limits on the rate legitimate businesses may charge for loaning money.) The church itself then got into the money-lending business, opening pawnshops in cities and declaring that the shops were benefiting the poor by charging a lower rate of interest than that available from secular moneylenders. In rural areas, Cistercian monasteries loaned money at interest.

The stigma attached to lending money was in many ways attached to all the activities of a medieval merchant. Medieval people were uneasy about a person making a profit merely from the investment of money rather than labor, skill, and time. Merchants themselves shared these ideas to some degree, so they gave generous donations to the church and to charities. They also took pains not to flaunt their wealth through flashy dress and homes. By the end of the Middle Ages, society had begun to accept the role of the merchant.

Hanseatic League A mercantile association of towns that allowed for mutual protection and security.

usury Lending money at interest.

commercial revolution The transformation of the European economy as a result of changes in business procedures and growth in trade.

mercantile capitalism Capitalism primarily involving trade rather than production.

The Commercial Revolution

Changes in business procedures, combined with the growth in trade, led to a transformation of the European economy, often called the **commercial revolution** by historians, who see it as the beginning of the modern capitalist economy. Though you may be most familiar with using *revolution* to describe a violent political rebellion such as the American Revolution or the French Revolution, the word is also used more broadly to describe economic and intellectual changes such as the Industrial Revolution and the scientific revolution. These do not necessarily involve violence and may last much longer than political revolutions. What makes them revolutions is the extent of their effects on society. In calling this transformation the "commercial revolution," historians point not only to an increase in the sheer volume of trade and in the complexity and sophistication of business procedures, but also to the new attitude toward business and making money. Some even detect a "capitalist spirit" in which making a profit is regarded as a good thing in itself, regardless of the uses to which that profit is put.

Part of this capitalist spirit was a new attitude toward time. Country people needed only approximate times—dawn, noon, sunset—for their work. Monasteries needed much more precise times to call monks together for the recitation of the Divine Office. In the early Middle Ages monks used a combination of hourglasses, sundials, and water-clocks to determine the time, and then rang bells by hand. About 1280 new types of mechanical mechanisms seem to have been devised in which weights replaced falling water and bells were rung automatically. Records begin to use the word *clock* (from the Latin word for bell) for these machines, which sometimes figured the movement of astronomical bodies as well as the hours. The merchants who ran city councils quickly saw clocks as both useful and a symbol of their prosperity. Beautiful and elaborate mechanical clocks, usually installed on the cathedral or town church, were in general use in Italy by the 1320s, in Germany by the 1330s, in England by the 1370s, and in France by the 1380s. Buying and selling goods had initiated city people into the practice of quantification, and clocks contributed to the development of a mentality that conceived of the universe in quantitative terms.

Capitalism in the Middle Ages primarily involved trade rather than production, so it is termed **mercantile capitalism.** In a few places, such as Florence, cloth production was organized along capitalist lines, with a cloth merchant owning the raw materials, the finished product, and sometimes the tools, and with workers paid simply for their labor. Most production in the Middle Ages was carried out by craft guilds or by people working on their own, however.

Mechanical Clock

Slowly falling weights provide the force that pushes the hand on the face of this large, twenty-four-hour clock. Accurate time was important to monks such as the one seated here, although this clock appears to be in a public place, not a monastery, a reflection of the increasing importance of time-keeping to many social groups. (Bibliothèque royale Albert 1er, Brussels)

The commercial revolution created a great deal of new wealth, which did not escape the attention of kings and other rulers. Wealth could be taxed, and through taxation kings could create strong and centralized states. In the years to come, alliances with the middle classes enabled kings to defeat feudal powers and aristocratic interests and to build the states that came to be called "modern." The commercial revolution also provided the opportunity for thousands of serfs to improve their social position. The slow but steady transformation of European society from almost completely rural and isolated to relatively more sophisticated constituted the greatest effect of the commercial revolution that began in the eleventh century.

Even so, merchants and business people did not run medieval communities other than in central and northern Italy and in the county of Flanders. Most towns remained small, and urban residents were never more than 10 percent of the population. The castle, the manorial village, and the monastery dominated the landscape. The feudal nobility and churchmen determined the preponderant social attitudes, values, and patterns of thought and behavior. The commercial changes of the eleventh through thirteenth centuries did, however, lay the economic foundations for the development of urban life and culture.

Section Review

- Merchant guilds were organized groups of merchants within a town, controlling the economic life and working to gain political independence for their town in order to have their own court, mayor, officials, and taxes.
- Craft guilds developed in each trade, allowing members to set quality standards, open shops, offer apprenticeships, and provide care and protection to members and their families.
- Towns built up with little planning, resulting in crowded, unsanitary conditions where all members of society intermingled, while laws regulated what clothes you could wear, depending on your social class, profession, or ethnic group.
- Wealthy households hired servants, and poor people were paid by the day for their labor, but since wages were low, they sometimes also engaged in theft, begging, and prostitution.
- Trade offered the possibility of great wealth, but it was risky, making merchants frequently vulnerable to robbers and pirates.
- The largest trade centers were in Venice and the Flemish towns, where merchants specialized and formed more formalized partnerships called companies.
- Increased trade spurred a commercial revolution and the beginnings of modern capitalism as merchants developed new business procedures, paper letters of exchange to substitute for metal coins, and a new attitude toward wealth and time.

Medieval Universities

How did universities evolve, and what needs of medieval society did they serve?

Just as the first strong secular states emerged in the thirteenth century, so did the first universities. This was no coincidence. The new bureaucratic states and the church needed educated administrators, and universities were a response to this need. The word *university* derives from the Latin *universitas* (oo-nee-VERS-ee-tas), meaning "corporation" or "guild." Medieval universities were educational guilds that produced educated and trained individuals, and they continue to influence institutionalized learning in the Western world.

Origins

In the early Middle Ages, outside of the aristocratic court or the monastery, anyone who received an education got it from a priest. Priests taught the rudiments of reading and writing as well as the Latin words of the Mass. Few boys acquired elementary literacy, however, and peasant girls did not obtain even that. The peasant father who wished to send his son to school had to secure the permission of his lord. Because the lord stood to lose the services of educated peasants, he limited the number of serfs sent to school.

Since the time of the Carolingian Empire, monasteries and cathedral schools had offered most of the available formal instruction, which focused on the Scriptures and the writings of the church fathers. Monasteries were unwilling to accept

■	University
✝	Monastery school
🏰	Cathedral school

MAP 11.2 Intellectual Centers of Medieval Europe

Universities provided more sophisticated instruction than did monastery and cathedral schools. What other factors distinguished the three kinds of intellectual centers?

large numbers of noisy lay students. In contrast, schools attached to cathedrals and run by the bishop and his clergy were frequently situated in bustling cities, and in the eleventh century in Italian cities like Bologna (**boe-LOAN-yuh**), wealthy businessmen had established municipal schools. In the course of the twelfth century, cathedral schools in France and municipal schools in Italy developed into educational institutions that attracted students from a wide area (see Map 11.2). These schools were called *studium generale* ("general center of study") or *universitas magistrorum et scholarium* ("universal society of teachers and students"), the origin of the English word *university*. The first European universities appeared in Italy in Bologna and Salerno.

The growth of the University of Bologna coincided with a revival of interest in Roman law during the investiture controversy. The study of Roman law as embodied in the Justinian *Code* had never completely died out in the West, but in the late eleventh century a complete manuscript of the *Code* was discovered in a library in Pisa. This discovery led scholars in nearby Bologna, beginning with Irnerius (ca. 1055–ca. 1130) (**er-NEHR-ee-us**), to study and teach Roman law intently again. His fame attracted students from all over Europe. Irnerius not only explained the Roman law of the Justinian *Code*, but he also applied it to difficult practical situations.

At Salerno in southern Italy interest in medicine had persisted for centuries. Medical practitioners—mostly men, but apparently also a few women—received training first through apprenticeship and then in an organized medical school. Individuals associated with Salerno, such as Constantine the African (fl. 1065–1085)—who was a convert from Islam and later a Benedictine monk—began to translate medical works out of Arabic. These translations included writings by the ancient Greek physicians and Muslim medical writers. Students of medicine poured into Salerno and soon attracted royal attention. In 1140, when King Roger II of Sicily took the practice of medicine under royal control, his ordinance stated:

> Who, from now on, wishes to practice medicine, has to present himself before our officials and examiners, in order to pass their judgment. Should he be bold enough to disregard this, he will be punished by imprisonment and confiscation of his entire property. In this way we are taking care that our subjects are not endangered by the inexperience of the physicians.[2]

In the first decades of the twelfth century, students converged on Paris. They crowded into the cathedral school of Notre Dame (**noh-truh DAHM**) and spilled over into the area later called the "Latin Quarter"—whose name reflects either the Italian origin of many of the students attracted to Paris by the surge of interest in the classics, logic, and theology, or the Latin language spoken in the area. The cathedral school's international reputation drew scholars from all over Europe to Paris.

Abelard and Heloise

One of the young men drawn to Paris was Peter Abelard (**AB-uh-lahrd**) (1079–1142), the son of a minor Breton knight. He was fascinated by logic, which he believed could be used to solve most problems. He had a brilliant mind and, though orthodox in his philosophical teaching, appeared to challenge ecclesiastical authorities. His book *Sic et Non* (**seek et nohn**) (Yes and No) was a list of apparently contradictory propositions drawn from the Bible and the writings of the church fathers. One such proposition, for example, stated that sin is pleasing to God and is not pleasing to God. Abelard used a method of systematic doubting in his writing and teaching. As he put it in the preface to *Sic et Non*, "By doubting we come to questioning, and by questioning we perceive the truth." While other scholars merely asserted theological principles, Abelard discussed and analyzed them. Through reasoning he even tried to describe the attributes of the three persons of the Trinity, the central mystery of the Christian faith. Abelard was severely censured by a church council, but his cleverness, boldness, and imagination made him a highly popular figure among students.

In a supposedly autobiographical statement, *A History of My Calamities*, Abelard described his academic career and his private life. He was hired by one of the

Law Lecture at Bologna

This beautifully carved marble sculpture, with the fluid drapery characteristic of late Gothic style, suggests the students' intellectual intensity. Medieval students often varied widely in age; here some have moustaches and some look like adolescents. (Museo Civico, Bologna/Scala/Art Resource, NY)

cathedral priests, Fulbert, to tutor his clever niece Heloise. The relationship between teacher and pupil passed beyond the intellectual. She became pregnant, and Fulbert pressured the couple to marry. Abelard insisted that the union be kept secret for the sake of his career, an arrangement Heloise much resented. Distrusting Abelard, Fulbert hired men to castrate him. Wounded in spirit as well as body, Abelard persuaded Heloise to enter a convent. He entered a monastery, and their baby, baptized Astrolabe (**AS-truh-layb**) for a recent Muslim navigational invention, was adopted by her family. The lovers were later buried together in a cemetery in Paris. Some scholars consider *A History of My Calamities* the most famous autobiography of the twelfth century, a fine example of the new self-awareness of the period's rebirth of learning. Other scholars believe the entire *History* a forgery, the source of a romantic legend with no basis in historical fact.[3]

Instruction and Curriculum

The influx of students eager for learning, together with dedicated and imaginative teachers, created the atmosphere in which universities grew. In northern Europe—at Paris and later at Oxford and Cambridge in England—associations or guilds of professors organized universities. They established the curriculum, set the length of time for study, and determined the form and content of examinations. By the end of the fifteenth century there were at least eighty universities in Europe. Some universities also offered younger students training in the liberal arts that could serve as a foundation for more specialized study in all areas.

Universities were all-male communities. The few women trained at Salerno during its early years of development were the last women in Europe to receive formal university training in any subject until the nineteenth century, although a handful of professor's daughters in one or two places were reputed to have listened to lectures from behind a curtain. (Most European universities did not admit or grant degrees to women until after World War I.) Though university classes were not especially expensive, the many years that university required meant that the sons of peasants or artisans could rarely attend, unless they could find wealthy patrons who would pay their expenses while they studied. Most students were the sons of urban merchants or lower-level nobles, especially the younger sons who would not inherit family lands.

University faculties grouped themselves according to academic disciplines — law, medicine, arts, and theology. The professors (a term first used in the fourteenth century) were known as "schoolmen" or **Scholastics.** They developed a method of thinking, reasoning, and writing in which questions were raised and authorities cited on both sides of the question. The goal of the Scholastic method was to arrive at definitive answers and to provide a rational explanation for what was believed on faith. Schoolmen held that reason and faith constituted two harmonious realms whose truths complemented each other.

> **Scholastics** University professors who developed a method of thinking, reasoning, and writing in which questions were raised and authorities cited on both sides of the question.

The Scholastic approach rested on the recovery of classical philosophical texts. Ancient Greek and Arabic texts had entered Europe in the early twelfth century. Knowledge of Aristotle and other Greek philosophers came to Paris and Oxford by way of Islamic intellectual centers at Baghdad, Córdoba, and Toledo. These texts, which formed the basis of Western philosophical and theological speculation, were not the only Islamic gifts. The major contribution of Arabic culture to the new currents of Western thought rested in the stimulus Arabic philosophers and commentators gave to Europeans' reflection on the Greek texts. Aristotle had stressed the importance of the direct observation of nature, as well as the principles that theory must follow fact and that knowledge of a thing requires an explanation of its causes. The schoolmen reinterpreted Aristotelian texts in a Christian sense. But in their exploration of the natural world, they did not precisely follow Aristotle's axioms. Medieval scientists argued from authority, such as the Bible, the Justinian *Code*, or an ancient scientific treatise, rather than from direct observation and experimentation as modern scientists do. Thus the conclusions of medieval scientists were often wrong. Nevertheless, natural science gradually emerged as a discipline distinct from philosophy, and Scholastics laid the foundations for later scientific work.

At all universities the standard method of teaching was the *lecture* — that is, a reading. The syllabus consisted of a core of ancient texts. The professor read a passage from the Bible, the Justinian *Code*, or one of Aristotle's treatises. He then explained and interpreted the passage; his interpretation was called a *gloss*. Texts and glosses were sometimes collected and reproduced as textbooks. For example, the Italian Peter Lombard (d. 1160), a professor at Paris, wrote what became the standard textbook in theology, *Sententiae* (sen-TEN-shee-uh) (The Sentences), a compilation of basic theological principles.

Examinations were given after three, four, or five years of study, when the student applied for a degree. The professors determined the amount of material students had to know for each degree, and students frequently insisted that the professors specify precisely what that material was. Examinations were oral and very difficult. If the candidate passed, he was awarded a license to teach, which was the earliest form of academic degree. Initially these licenses granted the title of *master* or *doctor*, still in use today and both derived from Latin words meaning "teach." Bachelor's degrees came later. Most students, however, did not become teachers. They staffed the expanding diocesan, royal, and papal administrations.

Jewish scholars as well as Christian ones produced elaborate commentaries on law and religious tradition. Medieval universities were closed to Jews, but in some cities in the eleventh century special rabbinic academies opened that concentrated particularly on the study of the Talmud, a compilation of legal arguments, proverbs, sayings, and folklore that had been produced in the fifth century in Babylon (present-day Iraq). The Talmud was written in Aramaic, so that simply learning to read it required years of study, and medieval scholars began to produce commentaries on the Talmud to help facilitate this. The most famous of these was that of Rabbi Solomon bar Isaac, known as Rashi (1040–1105), who lived in Troyes, a city in France. Men seeking to become rabbis—highly respected figures within the Jewish community with authority over economic and social as well as religious matters—spent long periods of time studying the Talmud, which served as the basis for their legal decisions in all areas of life.

summa Reference books created by Scholastics on the topics of law, philosophy, vegetation, animal life, and theology.

Thomas Aquinas and the Teaching of Theology

Thirteenth-century Scholastics devoted an enormous amount of time to collecting and organizing knowledge on all topics. These collections were published as **summa** (SOOM-uh), or reference books. There were summa on law, philosophy, vegetation, animal life, and theology. Saint Thomas Aquinas (1225–1274), a professor at Paris, produced the most famous collection, the *Summa Theologica*, which deals with a vast number of theological questions.

Aquinas drew an important distinction between faith and reason. He maintained that, although reason can demonstrate many basic Christian principles such as the existence of God, other fundamental teachings such as the Trinity and original sin cannot be proved by logic. That reason cannot establish them does not, however, mean they are contrary to reason. Rather, people understand such doctrines through revelation embodied in Scripture. Scripture cannot contradict reason, nor reason Scripture:

> *The light of faith that is freely infused into us does not destroy the light of natural knowledge [reason] implanted in us naturally. For although the natural light of the human mind is insufficient to show us these things made manifest by faith, it is nevertheless impossible that these things which the divine principle gives us by faith are contrary to these implanted in us by nature [reason]. Indeed, were that the case, one or the other would have to be false, and, since both are given to us by God, God would have to be the author of untruth, which is impossible. . . . [I]t is impossible that those things which are of philosophy can be contrary to those things which are of faith.*[4]

Aquinas also investigated the branch of philosophy called *epistemology* (ee-pis-tuh-MOL-uh-jee), which is concerned with how a person knows something. Aquinas stated that one knows, first, through sensory perception of the physical world—seeing, hearing, touching, and so on. He maintained that there can be nothing in the mind that is not first in the senses. Second, knowledge comes through reason, the mind exercising its natural abilities. Aquinas stressed the power of human reason to know, even to know God. His five proofs for God's existence exemplify the Scholastic method of knowing. His work later became the fundamental text of Roman Catholic doctrine.

Section Review

- Universities became the primary centers of advanced learning, providing educated administrators for church and state.

- Peter Abelard was a brilliant scholar whose writings on logic fascinated students though they displeased the church; his autobiography describing his love affair with equally brilliant Heloise was widely read.

- Universities were all-male and grouped by disciplines such as law, medicine, the arts, and theology, each having their own distinct curriculum; upon graduation, students earned a license to teach. The scholastic method of teaching posed questions and then discussed both sides of the issue to provide a rational answer, combining lectures with readings, many of which became textbooks.

- Saint Thomas Aquinas was a professor whose works dealt with theological questions depicting the difference between faith and reason.

Arts and Architecture

How did the arts and architecture express the ideals, attitudes, and interests of medieval people?

The High Middle Ages saw the creation of new types of literature, architecture, and music. Technological advances in such areas as papermaking and stone masonry made innovations possible, but so did the growing wealth and sophistication of patrons. Artists and artisans flourished in the more secure environment of the High Middle Ages, producing works that celebrated the glories of love, war, and God.

Vernacular Literature and Entertainment

Latin was the language used in university education, scholarly writing, and works of literature; in short, it was the language of high culture. In contrast to Roman times, however, by the High Middle Ages no one spoke Latin as his or her original mother tongue. The barbarian invasions, the mixture of peoples, and evolution over time had resulted in a variety of local **dialects** that blended words and linguistic forms in various ways. These dialects were specific to one region, and as kings increased the size of their holdings they often ruled people who spoke many different dialects. In the early Middle Ages almost all written works continued to be in Latin, but in the High Middle Ages some authors began to write in their local dialect, that is, in the everyday language of their region, which linguistic historians call the vernacular. This new **vernacular literature** gradually transformed some local dialects into literary languages, such as French, German, Italian, and English, while other dialects remained (and remain to this day) simply means of oral communication. Most people in the High Middle Ages could no more read vernacular literature than they could read Latin, however, so oral transmission continued to be the most important way information was conveyed and traditions passed down.

By the thirteenth century, however, techniques of making paper from old linen cloth and rags began to spread from Spain, where they had been developed by the Arabs, providing a much cheaper material on which to write. People started to write down things that were more mundane and less serious—personal letters, lists, poems, songs, recipes, rules, instructions—in various vernacular dialects, using spellings that were often personal and idiosyncratic. The writings included fables, legends, stories, and myths that had circulated orally for generations, and slowly a body of written vernacular literature developed. Stories and songs in the vernacular were performed and composed at the courts of nobles and rulers. In Germany and most of northern Europe, they favored stories and songs recounting the great deeds of warrior heroes, such as the knight Roland who fought against the Muslims and Hildebrand who fought the Huns. These epics, known as *chansons de geste* (**SHAN-suhn duh jest**) ("songs of great deeds"), celebrate violence, slaughter, revenge, and physical power. In southern Europe, especially in the area of southern France known as Provence, poets who called themselves **troubadours** (**TROO-bah-door**) wrote and sang lyric verses celebrating love, desire, beauty, and gallantry. (See the feature "Listening to the Past: Courtly Love" on pages 275–276.) A troubadour was a poet who wrote lyric verse in Provençal (**proh-vuhn-SAHL**), the regional spoken language of southern France, and sang it at one of the noble courts. Troubadours included a few women, called *trobairitz*, most of whose exact identities are not known.

dialect A regional variety of a language, with differences in vocabulary, grammar, and pronunciation.

vernacular literature Writings in the author's local dialect, that is, in the everyday language of the region.

troubadours Poets who wrote and sang lyric verses celebrating love, desire, beauty, and gallantry.

Eleanor of Aquitaine may have taken troubadour poetry from France to England when she married Henry II. Since the songs of the troubadours were widely imitated in Italy, England, and Germany, they spurred the development of vernacular literature there as well. The romantic motifs of the troubadours also influenced the northern French *trouvères* (**troo-VAIR**), who wrote adventure-romances in the form of epic poems in a language we call Old French, the ancestor of modern French. At the court of his patron, Marie of Champagne, Chrétien de Troyes (**krey-TYEN duh trwah**) (ca. 1135–ca. 1190) used the legends of the fifth-century British king Arthur (see page 154) as the basis for innovative tales of battle and forbidden love. His most popular story is that of the noble Lancelot, whose love for Guinevere, the wife of King Arthur, his lord, became physical as well as spiritual. Most of the troubadours and trouvères came from and wrote for the aristocratic classes, and their poetry suggests the interests and values of noble culture. Their influence eventually extended to all social groups, however, for people who could not read heard the poems and stories from people who could, so that what had originally come from oral culture was recycled back into it every generation.

Drama, derived from the church's liturgy, emerged as a distinct art form during the High Middle Ages. Plays based on biblical themes and on the lives of the saints were performed in the towns. *Mystery* plays were financed and performed by "misteries," members of the craft guilds, and *miracle* plays were acted by amateurs or professional actors, not guild members.. By combining comical farce based on ordinary life with serious religious scenes, plays gave ordinary people an opportunity to identify with religious figures and think about the mysteries of their faith.

Games and sports were common forms of entertainment and relaxation. There were games akin to modern football, rugby, and soccer in which balls were kicked and thrown, wrestling matches, and dog fights. People played card and board games of all types, gambling on these and on games with dice. Dancing was part of religious and family celebrations.

Churches and Cathedrals

The visual arts, especially architecture, flourished as expressions of religious ideas as well. Tens of thousands of churches, chapels, abbeys, and, most spectacularly, **cathedrals** were built in the twelfth and thirteenth centuries. (A cathedral is the church of a bishop and the administrative headquarters of a diocese, a church district headed by a bishop. The word comes from the Greek word *kathedra*, meaning seat, because the bishop's throne, a symbol of the office, is located in the cathedral.)

Most of the churches in the early Middle Ages had been built primarily of wood, which meant they were very susceptible to fire. They were often small, with a flat roof, in a rectangular or slightly cross-shaped form called a *basilica* (**buh-SIL-eh-kuh**), based on earlier Roman public buildings. With the end of the Viking and Magyar invasions and the increasing political stability of the eleventh century, bishops and abbots supported the construction of larger and more fire-resistant churches made almost completely out of stone. These were based on the basilican style, but features were added that made the cross shape more pronounced. As the size of the church grew horizontally, it also grew vertically. Builders adapted Roman-style rounded barrel vaults made of stone for the ceiling; this use of Roman forms led this style to be labeled **Romanesque.**

The next architectural style was **Gothic,** so named by a later scholar who incorrectly attributed the style to Gothic tribes. In Gothic churches the solid stone barrel-vaulted roof was replaced by a roof made of stone ribs with plaster in be-

cathedral The church of a bishop and the administrative headquarters of a diocese.

Romanesque An architectural style, with rounded arches and small windows.

Gothic An architectural style typified by pointed arches and large, stained glass windows.

tween. This made the ceiling much lighter, so that the side pillars and walls did not need to carry so much weight. Solid walls could be replaced by windows, which let in great amounts of light. (See the feature "Images in Society: From Romanesque to Gothic.")

Begun in the Île-de-France, Gothic architecture spread throughout France with the expansion of royal power. From France the new style spread to England, Germany, Italy, Spain, and eastern Europe. In those countries, the Gothic style competed with strong indigenous architectural traditions and thus underwent transformations that changed it to fit local usage. French master masons (MAY-sens) were soon invited to design and supervise the construction of churches in other parts of Europe.

master mason Man in charge of the design and construction of cathedrals and other major buildings.

Extraordinary amounts of money were needed to build these houses of worship. Consider, for example, the expense and labor involved in quarrying and transporting the stone alone. More stone was quarried for churches in medieval France than had been mined in ancient Egypt, where the Great Pyramid alone consumed 40.5 million cubic feet of stone.

Money was not the only need. A great number of artisans had to be assembled: quarrymen, sculptors, stonecutters, masons, mortar makers, carpenters, blacksmiths, glassmakers, roofers. Each master craftsman had apprentices, and unskilled laborers had to be recruited for the heavy work. The construction of a large cathedral was rarely completed in a lifetime; many were never finished at all. Because generation after generation added to the building, many Gothic churches show the architectural influences of two or even three centuries. (These variations in style were one of the aspects of Gothic buildings hated by later Renaissance architects, who regarded unity of style as essential in an attractive building.)

Bishops and abbots sketched out what they wanted and set general guidelines, but they left practical needs and aesthetic considerations to the master mason. He held overall responsibility for supervision of the project. (Medieval chroniclers applied the term *architect* to the abbots and bishops who commissioned the projects or the lay patrons who financed them, not to the draftsmen who designed them.) **Master masons** were paid higher wages than other masons; their contracts usually ran for several years, and great care was taken in their selection. Being neither gentlemen, clerics, nor laborers, master masons fit uneasily into the social hierarchy.

Since cathedrals were symbols of civic pride, towns competed to build the largest and most splendid church. In northern France in the late twelfth and early thirteenth centuries, cathedrals grew progressively taller. In 1163 the citizens of Paris began Notre Dame Cathedral, planning it to reach the height of 114 feet. When reconstruction on Chartres Cathedral was begun in 1194, it was to be 119 feet. Many cathedrals well over 100 feet tall were built as each bishop and town sought to outdo the neighbors. Medieval people built cathedrals to glorify God—and if mortals were impressed, all the better.

Tree of Jesse

In Christian symbolism, a tree stands for either life or death. Glassmakers depicted the ancestors of Christ as a tree's branches, based on the prophecy of Isaiah (11:1–2)—"a shoot shall sprout from the stump of Jesse, and from his roots a bud shall blossom, the spirit of the Lord shall rest upon him"—and the genealogy of Jesus in Matthew (1:1–16). In this stained glass from the west façade of Chartres Cathedral (ca. 1150–1170), Jesse, David, and Solomon are shown from bottom to top; a fourth panel (not shown) depicts Mary holding the Christ child. (© Clive Hicks)

Images in Society

From Romanesque to Gothic

The word *church* has several meanings: assembly, congregation, sect. The Greek term from which it is derived means "a thing belonging to the Lord," and this concept was applied to the building where a congregation assembled. In the Middle Ages people understood the church building to be "the house of God and the gate to Heaven"; it served as an image or representation of supernatural reality (Heaven). A church symbolized faith. Christians revealed and exercised faith; they communicated with God through prayer—that is, by raising their minds and hearts to God. The church building seemed the ideal place for prayer: communal prayer built faith, and faith encouraged prayer.

Architecture became the dominant art form of the Middle Ages. Nineteenth-century architectural historians coined the term *Romanesque*, meaning "in the Roman manner," to describe church architecture in most of Europe between the tenth and twelfth centuries. The main features of the Romanesque style—solid walls, rounded arches, and masonry vaults—had been the characteristics of large Roman buildings. With the massive barrel vaulting of the roof, heavy walls were required to carry the weight (see Image 1). Romanesque churches had a massive quality, reflecting the increasing political and economic stability of the period and suggesting that they were places of refuge and security in times of attack. A Romanesque church was a "fortress of God."

Gothic churches, by contrast, were walls of light. Visitors and worshipers approached the west end of the building, noticing the carved statues in the *tympanum* (**TIM-puh-nuhm**) (space above the portal, or door), perhaps awestruck by the lancets and rose window over the portal. Inside, a long row of columns directed their gaze down the *nave* (center aisle), and they proceeded to the *transept* (cross aisle), which separated the sanctuary and the choir (reserved for the clergy) from the body

IMAGE 1   Saint-Savin-sur-Gartempe (Romanesque), Early Twelfth Century. (Editions Gaud)

of the church (the laypeople's area). See Image 2. So that the flow of pilgrims would not disturb the clergy in their chants, *ambulatories* (walkways) were constructed around the sanctuary. Off the ambulatories, radiating chapels surrounded the *apse* (**aps**), the semicircular domed projection at the east end of the building. Apsidal chapels, each dedicated to and containing the relics of a particular saint, were visible from the exterior, as were the *flying buttresses* that supported the outward thrusts of the interior vaults. Above the apse and the

IMAGE 2 Amiens Cathedral, Mid-Thirteenth Century. (Editions Gaud)

west, south, and north portals, circular windows emerged from the radiating stone tracery in the form of roses.

Compare the interior of the abbey church of Saint-Savin-sur-Gartempe (Image 1), a Romanesque church

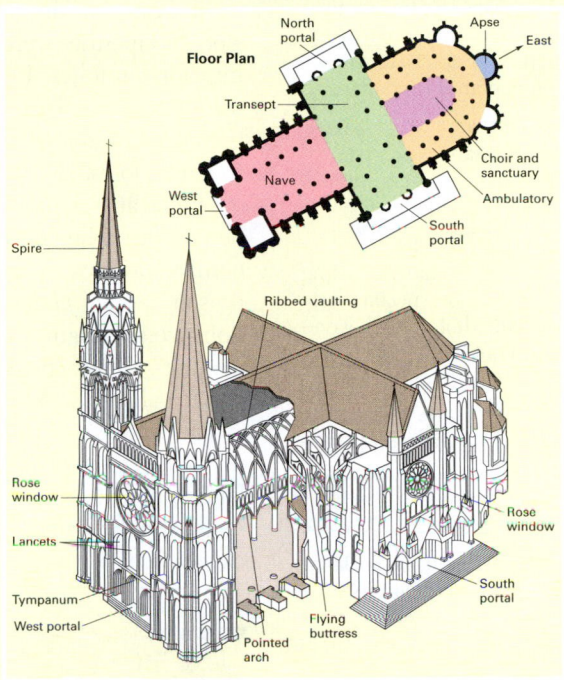

IMAGE 4 Elements of a Gothic Church (Chartres Cathedral).

built in about 1100 in Poitou (**pwa-TOO**), France, and the interior of Amiens (**AM-ee-uhnz**) Cathedral (Image 2), a Gothic church built from 1220 to 1288. What are the most striking differences? What developments made the changes from Romanesque to Gothic structurally possible?

Architecture reveals the interests and values of a society, its goals and aspirations. What does Sainte-Chapelle (Image 4), built by King Louis IX of France to house relics—the crown of thorns placed on Jesus' head before the Crucifixion, a nail from the Crucifixion, a fragment of Jesus' cross—tell us about the values and aspirations of thirteenth-century French society?

A Gothic church represents more than a house of prayer or worship. Medieval people did not compartmentalize the various aspects of their lives as modern people tend to do. What civic, social, economic, and political functions did a church building serve?

IMAGE 3 Sainte-Chapelle, Paris, Mid-Thirteenth Century. (Scala/Art Resource, NY)

Section Review

- All the arts, including literature, architecture, and music, flourished in the High Middle Ages through technological advances, increased wealth, and a more stable society.

- Latin was the language of high culture and education, but with advances in papermaking, a cheaper writing material was available, and literature from oral transmissions was written down gradually in vernacular or local dialects.

- Troubadours and female trobairitz were poets who wrote and sang lyric verse and provided a form of entertainment to the aristocratic classes along with dramas, games, and sports.

- Architecture provides the longest-lasting form of medieval art, most spectacularly in Romanesque cathedrals, which were massive "fortresses of God," and in Gothic cathedrals, which had many windows and were full of light.

- Cathedrals required huge amounts of money, skilled workers, and many years to complete, and were built to glorify God and to impress people.

- Stained glass windows along with elaborate tapestries were a focal point in Gothic churches, reflecting everyday life and scripture to enhance religious life and teachings.

Stained glass beautifully reflects the creative energy of the High Middle Ages. It is both an integral part of Gothic architecture and a distinct form of painting. As Gothic churches became more skeletal and had more windows, stained glass replaced manuscript illumination as the leading form of painting. At Chartres the craft and merchant guilds—drapers, furriers, haberdashers, tanners, butchers, bakers, fishmongers, and wine merchants—donated money and are memorialized in stained-glass windows. Thousands of scenes in the cathedral celebrate nature, country life, and the activities of ordinary people.

Tapestry making also came into its own in the fourteenth century. Heavy woolen tapestries were first made in the monasteries and convents as wall hangings for churches. Because they could be moved and lent an atmosphere of warmth, they replaced mural paintings. Early tapestries depicted religious scenes, but later hangings produced for the knightly class bore secular designs, especially romantic forests and hunting spectacles.

Once at least part of a Gothic cathedral had been built, the building began to be used for religious services. The Mass and other services became increasingly complex to fit with their new surroundings. Originally, services were chanted in unison, termed *plainsong* or *Gregorian chant*, but by the eleventh century additional voices singing on different pitches were added to create *polyphony* (**puh-LIF-uh-nee**). Certain parts of the service were broken off into stand-alone polyphonic pieces called *motets*, a style that composers soon adapted to secular music as well as ecclesiastical. Church leaders sometimes fumed that motets and polyphony made the text impossible to understand—Pope John XXII called this style an "avalanche of notes" in 1324—but, along with incense, candles, stained-glass windows, and the building itself, music made any service in a Gothic cathedral a rich experience.

Cities and the Church

Why did towns become the center of religious heresy, and what was the church's response?

The soaring towers of Gothic cathedrals were visible symbols of the Christian faith and civic pride of medieval urban residents, but many city people also felt that the church did not meet their spiritual needs. The bishops, usually drawn from the feudal nobility, did not understand urban culture and were suspicious of it. Christian theology, formulated for an earlier rural age, did not address the problems of the more sophisticated mercantile society. The new monastic orders of the twelfth century, such as the Cistercians, situated in remote, isolated areas had little relevance to the towns. Townspeople wanted a pious clergy capable of preaching the Gospel, and they disapproved of clerical ignorance and luxurious living. Critical of the clergy, neglected, and spiritually unfulfilled, townspeople turned to heretical sects.

Heretical Groups

Ironically, the eleventh-century Gregorian reform movement, which had worked to purify the church of disorder, led to some twelfth- and thirteenth-century heretical movements. Papal efforts to improve the sexual morality of the clergy, for example, had largely succeeded. When Gregory VII forbade married priests to celebrate church ceremonies, he expected public opinion to force priests to put aside their wives and concubines. But Gregory did not foresee the consequences of this order. Laypersons assumed they could, and indeed should, remove priests for any type of immorality or for not living according to standards that the parishioners judged appropriate.

In northern Italian towns, Arnold of Brescia (**BREH-shee-uh**), a vigorous advocate of strict clerical poverty, denounced clerical wealth. In France, Peter Waldo, a rich merchant of Lyons, gave his money to the poor and preached that only prayers, not sacraments, were needed for salvation. The **Waldensians** (**wawl-DEN-see-uhnz**)—as Peter's followers were called—bitterly attacked the sacraments and church hierarchy, and they carried these ideas across Europe. As we saw in Chapter 9, the Albigensians asserted that the material world was evil and that religious leaders should be those who rejected worldly things, not the wealthy bishops or the papacy (see page 212).

Waldensians The followers of Peter Waldo, a French merchant who gave his money to the poor and preached that only prayers were needed for salvation.

The Friars

In its continuing struggle against heresy, the church gained the support of two remarkable men, Saint Dominic (**DOM-uh-nik**) and Saint Francis, and of the orders they founded. Born in Castile, a province of Spain famous for its zealous Christianity, Domingo de Gúzman (1170?–1221) received a sound education and was ordained a priest. In 1206 he accompanied his bishop on an unsuccessful mission to win back the Albigensian heretics of Languedoc in France. Determined to succeed through ardent preaching, Dominic subsequently returned to France with a few followers. In 1216 the group—officially known as the "Preaching Friars" though often called **Dominicans** (**DOM-mihn-uh-kuns**)—won papal recognition as a new religious order.

Francesco di Bernardone (1181–1226), son of a wealthy Italian cloth merchant, was particularly inspired by two biblical texts: "If you seek perfection, go, sell your possessions, and give to the poor. You will have treasure in heaven. Afterward, come back and follow me." (Matthew 19:21); and Jesus' advice to his disciples as they went out to preach, "Take nothing for the journey, neither walking staff nor travelling bag, nor bread, nor money" (Luke 9:3). Francis's asceticism did not emphasize withdrawal from the world, but joyful devotion; in contrast to the Albigensians, who saw the material world as evil, Francis saw all creation as God-given and good. He wrote hymns to natural objects such as "brother moon" and was widely reported to perform miracles involving animals.

The simplicity, humility, and joyful devotion with which Francis carried out his mission soon attracted companions. Although he resisted pressure to establish an order, his followers became so numerous that he was obliged to develop some formal structure. In 1221 the papacy approved the "Rule of the Little Brothers of Saint Francis," as the **Franciscans** (**fran-SIS-kenz**) were known.

Dominicans The followers of Dominic, officially known as the "Preaching Friars."

The new Dominican and Franciscan orders differed significantly from older monastic orders such as the Benedictines and the Cistercians. First, the Dominicans and Franciscans were **friars,** not monks. Their lives and work focused on the cities and university towns, the busy centers of commercial and intellectual life, not the secluded and cloistered world of monks. They thought that *more* contact with ordinary Christians, not less, was a better spiritual path.

Second, the friars stressed apostolic poverty, a life based on the Gospel's teachings, in which they would own no property and depend on Christian people for their material needs. Hence they were called **mendicants** or mendicant orders, that is, begging friars. Benedictine and Cistercian abbeys, on the other hand, held land—not infrequently great tracts of land. Finally, the friars usually drew their

Franciscans The followers of Francis and his mission of simplicity, humility, and joyful devotion.

friars Men belonging to certain religious orders who did not live in monasteries but out in the world.

mendicants Begging friars.

members largely from the burgher class, from small property owners and shop-keepers. The monastic orders, by contrast, gathered their members (at least until the thirteenth century) overwhelmingly from the nobility.

The friars represented a response to the spiritual and intellectual needs of the thirteenth century. The Dominicans preferred that their friars be university graduates in order to better preach to a sophisticated urban society. The Dominicans soon held professorial chairs at leading universities, and they count Thomas Aquinas, probably the greatest medieval philosopher in Europe, as their most famous member. The Franciscans followed suit at the universities and also produced intellectual leaders. Women sought to develop similar orders devoted to active service out in the world. Clare of Assisi (1193–1253) sought to live in poverty and became a follower of Francis, who established a place for her to live in a nearby church. She was joined by other women, and they attempted to establish a rule for life in their community that would follow Francis's ideals of absolute poverty and allow them to serve the poor. Her rule was accepted by the papacy only after many decades, and then only because she agreed that the order, called the **Poor Clares,** would be enclosed.

Poor Clares A women's order established by Clare of Assisi, in devotion to active service out in the world.

In the growing cities of Europe, especially in the Netherlands, groups of women seeking to live a religious life came together as what later came to be known as **Beguines** (bih-GEENS). (The origins of the word are debated.) They lived communally in small houses called *beguinages*, combining a life of prayer with service to the needy. In a few cities these beguinages grew quite large, eventually incorporating churches and other buildings as well as housing for several hundred women. Beguine spirituality emphasized direct personal communication with God, sometimes through mystical experiences, rather than through the intercession of a saint or official church rituals. Many Beguines were also devoted to the church's sacraments, however, especially the Eucharist, and initially some church officials gave guarded approval of the movement. By the fourteenth century, however, they were declared heretical and much of their property was confiscated, for church officials were clearly uncomfortable with women who were neither married nor cloistered nuns.

Beguines Groups of women seeking to live a religious life in the growing cities of Europe.

The Friars and Papal Power

Beginning in 1233 the papacy used the friars to staff its new ecclesiastical court, the Inquisition (see page 212). Popes selected the friars to direct the Inquisition because bishops proved unreliable and because special theological training was needed. *Inquisition* means "investigation," and the Franciscans and Dominicans developed ex-

Saint Dominic and the Inquisition

The fifteenth-century court painter to the Spanish rulers Ferdinand and Isabella, Pedro Berruguete here portrays an event from the life of Saint Dominic: Dominic presides at the trial of Count Raymond of Toulouse, who had supported the Albigensian heretics. Raymond, helmeted and on horseback, repented and was pardoned; his companions, who would not repent, were burned. Smoke from the fire has put one of the judges to sleep, and other officials, impervious to the human tragedy, chat among themselves. (Museo del Prado, Madrid/Institut Amatller d'Art Hispanic)

pert methods of rooting out unorthodox thought. Ironically, within a hundred years of Francis's death one of the Inquisition's targets was the Spiritual Franciscans, a breakaway group that wanted to follow Francis's original ideals of poverty and denied the pope's right to countermand that ideal.

Modern Americans consider the procedures of the Inquisition exceedingly unjust, and there was substantial criticism of it in the Middle Ages. The accused did not learn the evidence against them or see their accusers; they were subjected to lengthy interrogations often designed to trap them; and torture could be used to extract confessions. Medieval people, however, believed that heretics destroyed the souls of their neighbors. By attacking religion, it was also thought, heretics destroyed the very bonds of society. By the mid-thirteenth century secular governments steadily pressed for social conformity, and they had the resources to search out and punish heretics. So successful was the Inquisition as a tool of royal power that within a century heresy had been virtually extinguished.

Popes and kings jointly supported the Inquisition, but in the late thirteenth century the papacy came into a violent dispute with several of Europe's leading rulers. Pope Boniface VIII (1294–1303), arguing from precedent, insisted that King Edward I of England and Philip the Fair of France obtain his consent for taxes they had imposed on the clergy. Edward immediately denied the clergy the protection of the law, and Philip halted the shipment of all ecclesiastical revenue to Rome. Boniface had to back down.

The battle for power between the papacy and the French monarchy became a bitter war of propaganda. Finally, in 1302, in a letter titled **Unam Sanctam** (because its opening sentence spoke of one holy Catholic Church), Boniface insisted that all Christians—including kings—were subject to the pope. Philip maintained that he was completely sovereign in his kingdom and responsible to God alone. French mercenary troops assaulted and arrested the aged pope at Anagni in Italy. Although Boniface was soon freed, he died shortly afterward. The confrontation at Anagni foreshadowed serious difficulties in the Christian church, but religious struggle was only one of the crises that would face Western society in the fourteenth century.

Section Review

- People increasingly turned to heretical sects to meet their spiritual needs as traditional Christianity lost touch with laypeople.
- The Dominican and Franciscan friars sought to counteract heresy through vigorous preaching, services to laypeople, and devotion to poverty; they lived out in the world instead of in cloistered monasteries.
- The Beguines were groups of women who came together to live a life of prayer and service to the needy; though the church initially approved of them, it later declared them heretical.
- The Inquisition, the church's response to heresy, had the support of both popes and kings even though it used cruel and unjust methods to seek out and punish heretics.
- The struggle for power between the papacy and the monarchy was an ongoing problem.

Unam Sanctam An official letter issued by Pope Boniface VIII claiming that all Christians were subject to the pope.

Chapter Review

How did medieval cities originate, and what impact did they have on the economy and on culture? (page 247)

Medieval cities—whether beginning around the sites of cathedrals, fortifications, or market towns—recruited people from the countryside with the promise of greater freedom and new possibilities. Cities provided economic opportunity, which, together with the revival of long-distance trade and a new capitalistic spirit, led to greater wealth, a higher standard of living, and upward social mobility for many people. Merchants and artisans formed guilds to protect their means of livelihood. Not everyone in medieval cities shared in the prosperity, however; many residents lived hand-to-mouth on low wages.

How did universities evolve, and what needs of medieval society did they serve? (page 259)

The towns that became centers of trade and production in the High Middle Ages developed into cultural and intellectual centers. Trade brought in new ideas as well as

Key Terms

town liberties (p. 248)
merchant guild (p. 249)
craft guild (p. 250)
livery (p. 252)
sumptuary laws (p. 252)
Hanseatic League (p. 257)
usury (p. 257)
commercial revolution (p. 258)
mercantile capitalism (p. 258)
Scholastics (p. 263)

(continued)

merchandise, and in many cities a new type of educational institution—the university— emerged from cathedral and municipal schools. Universities developed theological, legal, and medical courses of study based on classical models and provided trained officials for the new government bureaucracies. University-trained professionals joined merchants and guild masters as well-off members of the urban elite, heading large households staffed with servants and charging high prices for their services.

How did the arts and architecture express the ideals, attitudes, and interests of medieval people? (page 265)

University education was in Latin and was limited to men, but the High Middle Ages also saw the creation of new types of vernacular literature. Poems, songs, and stories, written down in local dialects, celebrated things of concern to ordinary people. In this, the troubadours of southern France led the way, using Arabic models to create romantic stories of heterosexual love. The ability to read the vernacular was still limited, however, so oral transmission continued as the most important way that information was conveyed and traditions passed down. The oral culture of medieval cities included plays with religious themes and also games, songs, and dancing.

Economic growth meant that merchants, nobles, and guild masters had disposable income they could spend on artistic products and more elaborate consumer goods. They supported the building of churches and cathedrals as visible symbols of their Christian faith and their civic pride; cathedrals in particular grew larger and more sumptuous, with high towers, stained-glass windows, and multiple altars. The sturdy Romanesque style was replaced by the soaring Gothic, in which sophisticated building techniques allowed windows to grow ever taller and wider. Cathedrals were places for socializing as well as worship, and increasingly complex music added to the experience.

Why did towns become the center of religious heresy, and what was the church's response? (page 270)

Town residents demonstrated their deep religious faith in the construction of Gothic cathedrals, but many urban people thought that the church did not fulfill their spiritual needs. They turned instead to heresies, many of which taught that the church had grown too powerful and wealthy. Combating heresy became a principal task of new types of religious orders, most prominently the Dominicans and Franciscans, who preached, ministered to city dwellers, and also staffed the papal Inquisition, a special court designed to root out heresy. These efforts were largely successful, and the church continued to exercise leadership of Christian society in the High Middle Ages, though the clash between the papacy and the kings of France and England at the end of the thirteenth century seriously challenged papal power.

summa (p. 264)

dialect (p. 264)

vernacular literature (p. 265)

troubadours (p. 265)

cathedral (p. 266)

Romanesque (p. 266)

Gothic (p. 266)

master masons (p. 267)

Waldensians (p. 271)

Dominicans (p. 271)

Franciscans (p. 271)

friars (p. 271)

mendicants (p. 271)

Poor Clares (p. 272)

Beguines (p. 272)

Unam Sanctam (p. 273)

Notes

1. D. C. Douglas and G. W. Greenaway, *English Historical Documents*, vol. 2, pp. 969–970.
2. Quoted in H. E. Sigerist, *Civilization and Disease* (Chicago: University of Chicago Press, 1943), p. 102.
3. See John F. Benton, "Fraud, Fiction and Borrowing in the Correspondence of Abelard and Heloise," in *Culture, Power and Personality in Medieval France*, ed. T. N. Bisson (London and Rio Grande: The Hambledon Press, 1991), pp. 417–449, esp. pp. 430–443, which convincingly demonstrate that "the most personal parts of the correspondence are not genuine" and that the letters were probably written in the later thirteenth century; and the same scholar's "The Correspondence of Abelard and Heloise," in the same volume, pp. 487–512.
4. Quoted in J. H. Mundy, *Europe in the High Middle Ages, 1150–1309* (New York: Basic Books, 1973), pp. 474–475.

To assess your mastery of this chapter, go to **bedfordstmartins.com/mckaywestbrief**

Listening to the Past

Courtly Love

Whether female or male, the troubadour poets celebrated *fin'amor*, a Provençal word for the pure or perfect love knight was supposed to feel for his lady, which has in English come to be called chivalry or "courtly love." In courtly love lyrics, the writer praises his or her love object, idealizing the beloved and promising loyalty and great deeds. Most of these songs are written by, or from the perspective of, a male lover who is socially beneath his female beloved; her higher status makes her unattainable, so the lover's devotion can remain chaste and pure, rewarded by her handkerchief, or perhaps a kiss, but nothing more. The noblemen and noblewomen who listened to these songs viewed such love as ennobling, and some authors even wrote courtly love lyrics directed to the Virgin Mary, the ultimate unattainable woman.

Scholars generally agree that poetry praising perfect love originated in the Muslim culture of the Iberian Peninsula, where heterosexual romantic love had long been the subject of poems and songs. Southern France was a border area where Christian and Muslim culture mixed; Spanish Muslim poets sang at the courts of Christian nobles, and Provençal poets picked up their romantic themes.

It is very difficult to know whether courtly love literature influenced the treatment of real women to any great extent—peasant women were certainly no less in danger of rape from knightly armies in the thirteenth century than they had been in the tenth—but it did introduce an ideal of heterosexual romance into Western literature that had not been there in the classical or early medieval period. The following excerpt is from a poem written by Arnaut Daniel, a thirteenth-century troubadour. Not much is known about him, but the songs that have survived capture courtly love conventions perfectly.

In this fourteenth-century painting, a lady puts the helmet on her beloved knight. (akg-images)

I only know the grief that comes to me,
to my love-ridden heart, out of over-loving,
since my will is so firm and whole
that it never parted or grew distant from her
whom I craved at first sight, and afterwards:
and now, in her absence, I tell her burning words;
then, when I see her, I don't know, so much I have
    to, what to say.

To the sight of other women I am blind, deaf to
    hearing them
since her only I see, and hear and heed,
and in that I am surely not a false slanderer,
since heart desires her more than mouth may say;
wherever I may roam through fields and valleys,
    plains and mountains
I shan't find in a single person all those qualities
which God wanted to select and place in her.

I have been in many a good court,
but here by her I find much more to praise:
measure and wit and other good virtues,
beauty and youth, worthy deeds and fair disport;
so well kindness taught and instructed her
that it has rooted every ill manner out of her:
I don't think she lacks anything good. . . .

Far fewer poems by female troubadours (trobairitz) have survived than by male, but those that have
express strong physical and emotional feelings. The

following excerpt is from the twelfth-century Countess of Dia.

> I've suffered great distress
> From a knight whom I once owned.
> Now, for all time, be it known:
> I loved him—yes, to excess.
> His jilting I've regretted,
> Yet his love I never really returned.
> Now for my sin I can only burn:
> Dressed, or in my bed . . .
>
> Lovely lover, gracious, kind,
> When will I overcome your fight?
> O if I could lie with you one night!
> Feel those loving lips on mine!
> Listen, one thing sets me afire:
> Here in my husband's place I want you,
> If you'll just keep your promise true:
> Give me everything I desire.

Questions for Analysis

1. Both of these songs focus on a beloved who does not return the lover's affection. What similarities and differences do you see in them?

2. How does courtly love reinforce other aspects of medieval society? Are there aspects of medieval society it contradicts?

3. Can you find examples from current popular music that parallel the sentiments expressed in these two songs?

Sources: First poem: Leonardo Malcovati, *Prosody in England and Elsewhere: A Comparative Approach* (London: Gival Press, 2006), and online at http://www.trobar.org/troubadours/; second poem: quoted in J. J. Wilhelm, ed., *Lyrics of the Middle Ages: An Anthology* (New York: Garland Publishers, 1993), pp. 83–84.

CHAPTER 12

The Crisis of the Later Middle Ages

1300–1450

In this lavishly illustrated French chronicle, Wat Tyler, the leader of the English Peasant's Revolt, is stabbed during a meeting with the king. Tyler died soon afterward, and the revolt was ruthlessly crushed. (Bibliothèque nationale de France)

Chapter Preview

Prelude to Disaster
What were the demographic, social, and economic consequences of climate change?

The Black Death
How did the spread of the plague shape European society?

The Hundred Years' War
What were the causes of the Hundred Years' War, and how did the war affect European politics, economics, and cultural life?

Challenges to the Church
What were the causes of the Great Schism, and how did church leaders, intellectuals, and ordinary people respond?

Economic and Social Change
How did economic and social tensions contribute to revolts, crime, violence, and a growing sense of ethnic and national distinctions?

INDIVIDUALS IN SOCIETY: Jan Hus

LISTENING TO THE PAST: Christine de Pizan

During the later Middle Ages the last book of the New Testament, the Book of Revelation, inspired thousands of sermons and hundreds of religious tracts. The Book of Revelation deals with visions of the end of the world, with disease, war, famine, and death. It is no wonder this part of the Bible was so popular. Between 1300 and 1450 Europeans experienced a frightful series of shocks: climate change, economic dislocation, plague, war, social upheaval, and increased crime and violence. Death and preoccupation with death make the fourteenth century one of the most wrenching periods of Western civilization. Yet, in spite of the pessimism and crises, important institutions and cultural forms, including representative assemblies and national literatures, emerged. Even institutions that experienced severe crisis, such as the Christian church, saw new types of vitality.

Prelude to Disaster

What were the demographic, social, and economic consequences of climate change?

In the first half of the fourteenth century, Europe experienced a series of climate changes that led to lower levels of food production, which had dramatic and disastrous ripple effects. Political leaders attempted to find solutions, but were unable to deal with the economic and social problems that resulted.

The period from about 1000 to about 1300 saw a warmer than usual climate in Europe, which underlay all the changes and vitality of the High Middle Ages. About 1300 the climate changed, becoming colder and wetter. Historical geographers refer to the period from 1300 to 1450 as a "little ice age."

An unusual number of storms brought torrential rains, ruining the wheat, oat, and hay crops on which people and animals almost everywhere depended. Since long-distance transportation of food was expensive and difficult, most urban areas depended for bread and meat on areas no more than a day's journey away. Poor harvests—and one in four was likely to be poor—led to scarcity and starvation. Almost all of northern Europe suffered a **"Great Famine"** in the years 1315–1322, which contemporaries interpreted as a recurrence of the biblical "seven lean years" (Genesis 42). Even in non-famine years, the cost of grain, livestock, and dairy products rose sharply.

Great Famine A terrible famine that hit much of Europe after a period of climate change (1315–1322).

Reduced caloric intake meant increased susceptibility to disease, especially for infants, children, and the elderly. Workers on reduced diets had less energy, which in turn meant lower productivity, lower output, and higher grain prices.

Hardly had western Europe begun to recover from this disaster when another struck: an epidemic of typhoid fever carried away thousands. Then in 1318 disease hit cattle and sheep, drastically reducing the herds and flocks. Another bad harvest in 1321 brought famine and death.

The catastrophes of the fourteenth century had grave social consequences. In parts of the Low Countries and in the Scottish-English borderlands, entire villages were abandoned. In Flanders and East Anglia (eastern England), some peasants were forced to mortgage, sublease, or sell their holdings to richer farmers in order to buy food. Throughout the affected areas, young men and women sought work in the towns. Overall, the population declined because of the deaths caused by famine and disease; postponement of marriages may have also played a part.

Meanwhile, the international character of trade and commerce meant that a disaster in one country had serious implications elsewhere. For example, the infection that attacked English sheep in 1318 caused a sharp decline in wool exports in the following years. Without wool, Flemish weavers could not work, and thousands were laid off. Without woolen cloth, the businesses of Flemish, Hanseatic, and Italian merchants suffered. Unemployment encouraged people to turn to crime.

As the subsistence crisis deepened, popular discontent and paranoia increased. In France, starving people focused their anger on the rich, speculators, and the Jews, who were targeted as creditors fleecing the poor through pawnbroking. (Expelled from France in 1306, Jews were readmitted in 1315 and were granted the privilege of lending at high interest rates.) Rumors spread of a plot by Jews and their agents, the lepers, to kill Christians by poisoning the wells. Based on "evidence" collected by torture, many lepers and Jews were killed, beaten, or hit with heavy fines.

Government responses to these crises were ineffectual. The three sons of Philip the Fair who sat on the French throne between 1314 and 1328 condemned speculators, who held stocks of grain back until conditions were desperate and prices high; forbade the sale of grain abroad; and published legislation prohibiting fishing with traps that took large catches. These measures had few positive results.

CHRONOLOGY

1309–1376	Babylonian Captivity; papacy in Avignon
1310–1320	Dante, *Divine Comedy*
1315–1322	Famine in northern Europe
1324	Marsiglio of Padua, *Defensor Pacis*
1337–1453	Hundred Years' War
1348	Black Death arrives in mainland Europe
1358	Jacquerie peasant uprising in France
1378–1417	Great Schism
1381	Peasants' Revolt in England
1387–1400	Chaucer, *Canterbury Tales*
1405	Christine de Pizan, *The Treasure of the City of Ladies*
1415	English smash the French at Agincourt
1429	French victory at Orléans; Charles VII crowned king
1431	Joan of Arc declared a heretic and burned at the stake

Death from Famine

In this fifteenth-century painting, dead bodies lie in the middle of a path, while a funeral procession at the right includes a man with an adult's coffin and a woman with the coffin of an infant under her arm. People did not simply allow the dead to lie in the street in medieval Europe, though during famines and epidemics it was sometimes difficult to maintain normal burial procedures. (Erich Lessing/Art Resource, NY)

Black Death Bubonic plague that first struck Europe in 1347 and was spread mainly by rats and fleas. In less virulent forms, the disease reappeared many times until 1721.

In England, Edward I's incompetent son, Edward II (r. 1307–1327), also condemned speculators, after his attempts to set price controls on livestock and ale proved futile. He did try to buy grain abroad, but little was available: yields in the Baltic were low; the French crown, as we have seen, forbade exports; and the grain shipped from northern Spain was grabbed by pirates. Such grain as reached southern English ports was stolen by looters and sold on the black market. The Crown's efforts at famine relief failed.

The Black Death

How did the spread of the plague shape European society?

Royal attempts to provide food from abroad were unsuccessful, but they indicate the extent of long-distance shipping by the beginning of the fourteenth century. In 1291 Genoese (**JEN-oh-eez**) sailors had opened the Strait of Gibraltar to Italian shipping by defeating the Moroccans. Then, shortly after 1300, important advances were made in the design of Italian merchant ships. A square rig was added to the mainmast, and ships began to carry three masts instead of just one. Additional sails better utilized wind power to propel the ship. The improved design meant that cargo could now move quickly and regularly across great distances. So, however, could disease pathogens carried by the vermin that stowed away on these vessels. The most frightful of these diseases first emerged in western Europe in 1347 and was later called the **Black Death.** (Sometime in the fifteenth century, the Latin phrase *atra mors*, meaning "dreadful death," was translated as "black death," and the phrase stuck.)

Spread of the Disease

Most historians and almost all microbiologists identify the disease that spread in the fourteenth century as the bubonic (**byoo-BON-ik**) plague, caused by the bacillus *Yersinia pestis*. The disease normally afflicts rats. Fleas living on the infected rats drink their blood; the bacteria that cause the plague multiply in the flea's gut; and the flea passes them on to the next rat it bites by throwing up into the bite. Usually the disease is limited to rats and other rodents, but at certain points in history—perhaps when most rats have been killed off—the fleas have jumped from their rodent hosts to humans and other animals.

The classic symptom of the bubonic plague was a growth the size of a nut or an apple in the armpit, in the groin, or on the neck. This was the boil, or *bubo*, that gave the disease its name and caused agonizing pain. If the bubo was lanced and the pus thoroughly drained, the victim had a chance of recovery. The next stage was the appearance of black spots or blotches caused by bleeding under the skin. Finally, the victim began to cough violently and spit blood. This stage, indicating the presence of millions of bacilli in the bloodstream, signaled the end, and death followed in two or three days.

Plague symptoms were first described in 1331 in southwestern China, part of the Mongol Empire. Plague-infested rats accompanied Mongol armies and merchant caravans carrying silk, spices, and gold across central Asia in the 1330s. Then they stowed away on ships, carrying the disease to the ports of the Black Sea by the 1340s. Later stories told of more dramatic means of spreading the disease as well, reporting that Mongol armies besieging the city of Kaffa on the shores of the Black Sea catapulted plague-infected corpses over the walls to infect those inside.

The city's residents dumped the corpses into the sea as fast as they could, but they were already infected.

In October 1347 Genoese ships brought the plague from Kaffa to Messina, from which it spread across Sicily. Venice and Genoa were hit in January 1348, and from the port of Pisa (**PEE-zuh**) the disease spread south to Rome and east to Florence and all of Tuscany. By late spring southern Germany was attacked. Frightened French authorities chased a galley bearing the disease away from the port of Marseilles, but not before plague had infected the city, from which it spread to Languedoc (**lahng-DAWK**) and Spain. In June 1348 two ships entered the Bristol Channel and introduced it into England. All Europe felt the scourge of this horrible disease (see Map 12.1).

Although urban authorities from London to Paris to Rome had begun to try to achieve a primitive level of sanitation by the fourteenth century, urban conditions remained ideal for the spread of disease. Narrow streets filled with refuse and human excrement were as much cesspools as thoroughfares. Dead animals and sore-covered beggars greeted the traveler. Houses whose upper stories projected over

MAPPING THE PAST

MAP 12.1   The Course of the Black Death in Fourteenth-Century Europe

Use the map and the information in the text to answer the following questions: **[1]** How did the expansion of trade that resulted from the commercial revolution contribute to the spread of the Black Death? **[2]** When did the plague reach Paris? Why do you think it got to Paris before it spread to the rest of northern France or to southern Germany? **[3]** Which cities were spared? What might account for this? **[4]** Which regions were spared? Would the reasons for this be the same as those for cities, or might other causes have been operating in rural areas?

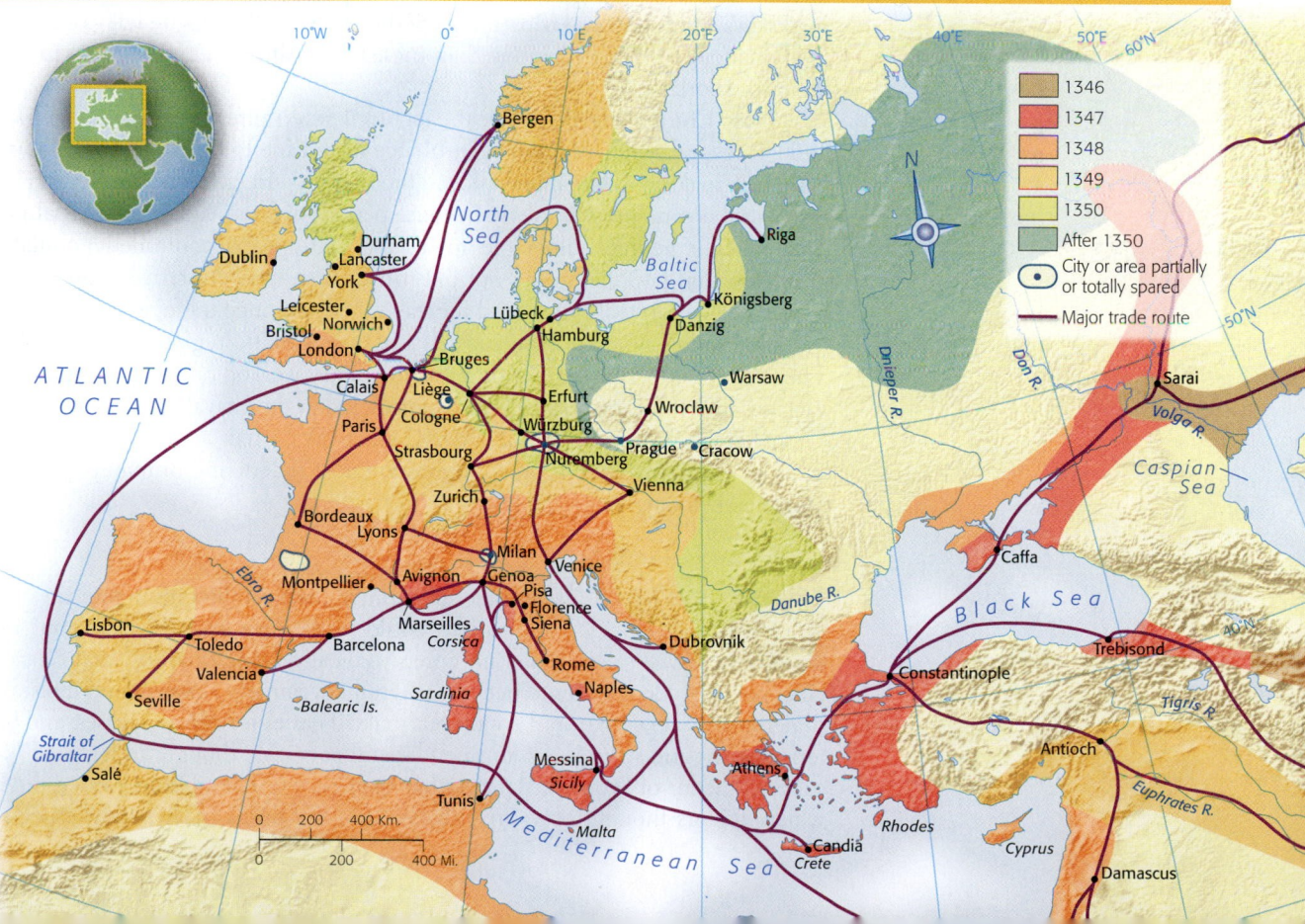

the lower ones blocked light and air. And extreme overcrowding was commonplace. When all members of an aristocratic family lived and slept in one room, it should not be surprising that six or eight persons in a middle-class or poor household slept in one bed—if they had one. Closeness, after all, provided warmth. Houses were beginning to be constructed of brick, but many wood, clay, and mud houses remained. A determined rat had little trouble entering such a house.

Standards of personal hygiene remained frightfully low. Fleas and body lice were universal afflictions: everyone from peasants to archbishops had them. One more bite did not cause much alarm. But if that nibble came from a bacillus-bearing flea, an entire household or area was doomed.

Mortality rates cannot be specified because population figures for the period before the arrival of the plague do not exist for most countries and cities. Of a total English population of perhaps 4.2 million, probably 1.4 million died of the Black Death in its several visits. Densely populated Italian cities endured incredible losses. Florence lost between one-half and two-thirds of its population when the plague visited in 1348. The most widely accepted estimate for western Europe is that the plague killed about one-third of the population in the first wave of infection.

Nor did central and eastern Europe escape the ravages of the disease. One chronicler records that, in the summer and autumn of 1349, between five hundred and six hundred died every day in Vienna. Styria, in what today is central Austria, was very hard hit, with cattle straying unattended in the fields.

As the Black Death took its toll on the German Empire, waves of emigrants fled to Poland, Bohemia, and Hungary. The situation there was better, though disease was not completely absent. The plague seems to have entered Poland through the Baltic seaports and spread from there. Still, population losses were lower than elsewhere in Europe. The plague spread from Poland to Russia, reaching Pskov, Novgorod, and Moscow. In Serbia, though, the plague left vast tracts of land unattended, which prompted an increase in Albanian immigration to meet the labor shortage.

Across Europe the Black Death recurred intermittently from the 1360s to 1400. It reappeared with reduced virulence from time to time over the following centuries, making its last appearance in the French port city of Marseilles in 1721. Survivors became more prudent. Because periods of famine had caused malnutrition, making people vulnerable to disease, Europeans controlled population growth so that population did not outstrip food supply. Western Europeans improved navigation techniques and increased long-distance trade, which permitted the importation of grain from sparsely populated Baltic regions (see page 281). They strictly enforced quarantine measures. They worked on the development of vaccines. But it was only in 1947, six centuries after the arrival of the plague in the West, that the American microbiologist Selman Waksman discovered an effective vaccine, streptomycin. Plague continues to infect rodent and human populations sporadically today.

Care

Fourteenth-century medical literature indicates that physicians could sometimes ease the pain, but they had no cure. Medical doctors observed that crowded cities had high death rates, especially when the weather was warm and moist. We understand that warm, moist conditions make it easier for germs, viruses, and bacteria to grow and spread, but fourteenth-century people thought in terms of "poisons" in the air or "corrupted air" rather than germs. The poisons caused illness, which doctors thought of as an imbalance in the fluids in the body, especially blood. Certain symptoms of the plague, especially bleeding and vomiting, were believed to be the body's natural reaction to too much fluid. Doctors frequently prescribed bloodletting—that is, taking blood from the body by applying leeches or making small cuts in veins—as standard treatment.

If the plague came from poisoned air, people reasoned, then strong-smelling herbs or other substances held in front of the nose or burned as incense might stop it. Perhaps loud sounds like ringing church bells or firing the newly invented cannon might help. Medicines made from plants that were bumpy or that oozed liquid might work, keeping the more dangerous swelling and oozing of the plague away. Magical letter and number combinations, called *cryptograms*, were especially popular in Muslim areas. They were often the first letters of words in prayers or religious sayings, and they gave people a sense of order when faced with the randomness with which the plague seemed to strike.

Wealthier people often fled cities for the countryside, though sometimes this simply spread the plague faster. Some cities tried shutting their gates to prevent infected people and animals from coming in, which worked in a few cities. They also walled up houses in which there was plague, trying to isolate those who were sick from those who were still healthy. Along with looking for medical causes and cures, people also searched for scapegoats, and savage cruelty sometimes resulted. Many people believed that the Jews had poisoned the wells of Christian communities and thereby infected the drinking water. This charge led to the murder of thousands of Jews across Europe.

Patients in a Hospital Ward, Fifteenth Century

In the thirteenth century, merchants donated some of their fortunes to establish hospitals, which filled past capacity when the plague struck. The practice of putting two or more adults in the same bed, as shown here, contributed to the spread of the disease. At the Hôtel-Dieu (**oh-tel-DEW**) in Paris, nurses complained of being forced to put eight to ten children in a single bed in which a patient had recently died. (Giraudon/The Bridgeman Art Library)

Many people did not see the plague as a medical issue, but instead interpreted it as the result of something within themselves. God must be punishing them for terrible sins, they thought, so the best remedies were religious ones: asking for forgiveness, prayer, trust in God, making donations to churches, and trying to live better lives. In Muslim areas, religious leaders urged virtuous living in the face of death: give to the poor, reconcile with your enemies, free your slaves, and say a proper goodbye to your friends and family.

Social, Economic, and Cultural Consequences

It is noteworthy that, in an age of mounting criticism of clerical wealth (see page 291), the behavior of the clergy during the plague was often exemplary. Priests, monks, and nuns cared for the sick and buried the dead. In places like Venice, from which even physicians fled, priests remained to give what ministrations they could. Consequently, their mortality rate was phenomenally high. The German clergy especially suffered a severe decline in personnel in the years after 1350.

Economic historians and demographers sharply dispute the impact of the plague on the economy in the late fourteenth century. The traditional view that the plague had a disastrous effect has been greatly modified. The clearest evidence comes from England, where by the early fifteenth century most landlords enjoyed the highest revenues of the medieval period. Why? The answer appears to lie in the fact that England and many parts of Europe suffered from overpopulation in the early fourteenth century. Population losses caused by the Black Death led to increased productivity by restoring a more efficient balance between labor, land, and capital.

What impact did visits of the plague have on urban populations? The rich evidence from a census of the city of Florence and its surrounding territory taken between 1427 and 1430 is fascinating. The region had suffered repeated epidemics since 1347. The census showed a high proportion of people who were age sixty or older, suggesting that the plague took the young rather than the mature. The high mortality rate of adults between the ages of twenty and fifty-nine led Florentine guilds to recruit many new members. It appears that economic organizations tried to keep their numbers constant, even though the size of the population, and its pool of potential guild members, was shrinking. Moreover, in contrast to the pre-1348 period, many new members of the guilds were not related to existing members. Thus the post-plague years represent an age of "new men."

The Black Death brought on a general European inflation. High mortality produced a fall in production, shortages of goods, and a general rise in prices. The price of wheat in most of Europe increased, as did the costs of meat, sausage, and cheese. This inflation continued to the end of the fourteenth century. But labor shortages meant that workers could demand better wages, and the broad mass of people enjoyed a higher standard of living. The greater demand for labor also meant greater mobility for peasants in rural areas and for industrial workers in the towns and cities.

The psychological consequences of the plague were profound. Imagine an entire society in the grip of the belief that it was at the mercy of a frightful affliction about which nothing could be done. It is not surprising that some sought release in wild living, while others turned to the severest forms of asceticism and frenzied religious fervor. Some extremists joined groups of **flagellants** (**FLAJ-eh-lents**), who whipped and scourged themselves as penance for their and society's sins in the belief that the Black Death was God's punishment for humanity's wickedness.

flagellants People who believed that the plague was God's punishment for sin and sought to do penance by flagellating (whipping) themselves.

Flagellants

In this manuscript illumination from 1349, shirtless flagellants scourge themselves with whips as they walk through the streets of the Flemish city of Tournai. The text notes that they are asking for God's grace to return to the city after it had been struck with the "most grave" illness. (Ann Ronan Picture Library, London/HIP/Art Resource, NY)

Groups of flagellants traveled from town to town, often provoking hysteria against Jews and growing into unruly mobs. Officials worried that they would provoke violence and riots, and ordered groups to disband or forbade them to enter cities.

Elaborate funeral services, which had provided comfort to the mourners as well as tribute to the dead, were abandoned in favor of hasty burials, sometimes in mass graves. Hospitality to travelers was replaced with hostility and suspicion, and European port cities began quarantining arriving ships to determine whether passengers brought the plague.

Popular endowments of educational institutions multiplied. The years of the Black Death witnessed the foundation of new colleges at old universities and of entirely new universities. The foundation charters specifically mention the shortage of priests and the decay of learning. Whereas universities such as those at Bologna and Paris had international student bodies, new institutions established in the wake of the Black Death had more national or local constituencies. Thus the international character of medieval culture weakened, paving the way for schism (**SKIZ-uhm**) in the Catholic Church even before the Reformation.

The literature and art of the fourteenth century reveal a terribly morbid concern with death. One highly popular artistic motif, the Dance of Death, depicted a dancing skeleton leading away a living person.

Section Review

- Improvements in ship design meant food and goods could now travel long distances, but rodents and fleas carrying the Black Death (bubonic plague) could also travel on these ships.

- The Black Death first appeared in China and then spread via Mongol armies and merchant caravans to ships across the Black Sea, Sicily, and into all of Europe.

- Crowded living conditions, poor sanitation, and low levels of personal hygiene helped the disease to spread, causing widespread population losses.

- Various attempted cures included bloodletting, herbal concoctions, quarantines, religious fervor to appease God, and victimizing Jews suspected of poisoning Christian wells.

- The population decrease meant new guild members, high inflation rates, and shortages of goods, but labor shortages resulted in better wages and greater mobility.

- New universities and colleges arose to resupply the shortage of priests and the learned, but the fear of outsiders who might bring the plague led to more national and local student bodies, weakening international bonds.

The Hundred Years' War

What were the causes of the Hundred Years' War, and how did the war affect European politics, economics, and cultural life?

The plague ravaged populations in Asia, North Africa, and Europe; in western Europe a long international war added further death and destruction. England and France had engaged in sporadic military hostilities from the time of the Norman Conquest in 1066, and in the middle of the fourteenth century these became more intense. From 1337 to 1453, the two countries intermittently fought one another in what was the longest war in European history, ultimately dubbed the Hundred Years' War though it actually lasted 116 years.

Causes

The Hundred Years' War had both distant and immediate causes. The distant cause was that in 1259, France and England had signed the Treaty of Paris, in which the English king agreed to become—for himself and his successors—vassal of the French crown for the duchy of Aquitaine (**AK-wi-tain**). The English claimed Aquitaine as an ancient inheritance. French policy, however, was strongly expansionist, and the French kings resolved to absorb the duchy into the kingdom of France so Aquitaine became disputed territory.

The immediate cause of the war was a dispute over who would inherit the French throne after Charles IV of France, the last surviving son of Philip the Fair, died childless in 1328. With him ended the Capetian (**kuh-PEE-shuhn**) dynasty of France. Charles IV did have a sister, however—Isabella—and her son was Edward III, king of England. An assembly of French barons, meaning to exclude Isabella and Edward from the French throne, proclaimed that "no woman nor her son could succeed to the [French] monarchy." The barons passed the crown to Philip VI of Valois (r. 1328–1350), a nephew of Philip the Fair.

In 1329 Edward III paid homage to Philip VI for Aquitaine. In 1337 Philip, eager to exercise full French jurisdiction in Aquitaine, confiscated the duchy. Edward III interpreted this action as a gross violation of the treaty of 1259 and as a cause for war. Moreover, Edward argued, as the eldest directly surviving male descendant of Philip the Fair, he

English Merchants in Flanders

In this 1387 illustration, an English merchant requests concessions from the count of Flanders to trade English wool at a favorable price. Flanders was officially on the French side during the Hundred Years' War, but Flemish cities depended heavily on English wool for their textile manufacturing. Hence the count of Flanders agreed to the establishment of the Merchant Staple, an English trading company with a monopoly on trade in wool.

(Copyright © British Library Board)

deserved the title of king of France. Edward III's dynastic argument upset the feudal order in France: to increase their independent power, French vassals of Philip VI used the excuse that they had to transfer their loyalty to a more legitimate overlord, Edward III. One reason the war lasted so long was that it became a French civil war, with some French barons supporting English monarchs in order to thwart the centralizing goals of the French crown.

The Popular Response

The governments of both England and France manipulated public opinion to support the war. The English public was convinced that the war was waged for one reason: to secure for King Edward the French crown he had been unjustly denied. Edward III issued letters to the sheriffs describing the evil deeds of the French in graphic terms and listing royal needs. Kings in both countries instructed the clergy to deliver sermons filled with patriotic sentiment. Philip VI sent agents to warn communities about the dangers of invasion and to stress the French crown's revenue needs to meet the attack. The English were led to believe that King Philip intended "to have seized and slaughtered the entire realm of England." Both sides developed a deep hatred of the other.

Most important of all, the Hundred Years' War was popular because it presented unusual opportunities for wealth and advancement. Poor knights and knights who were unemployed were promised regular wages. Criminals who enlisted were granted pardons. The great nobles expected to be rewarded with estates. Royal exhortations to the troops before battles repeatedly stressed that, if victorious, the men might keep whatever they seized. The French chronicler Jean Froissart (FROI-sahrt) wrote that, at the time of Edward III's expedition of 1359, men of all ranks flocked to the English king's banner. Some came to acquire honor, but many came "to loot and pillage the fair and plenteous land of France."[1]

The Course of the War to 1419

The war was fought almost entirely in France and the Low Countries (see Map 12.2). It consisted mainly of a series of random sieges and cavalry raids. In 1335 the French began ravaging the countryside in Aquitaine, sacking and burning coastal towns in southern England, and supporting Scottish incursions into northern England. Such tactics lent weight to Edward III's propaganda campaign. In fact, royal propaganda on both sides fostered a kind of early nationalism.

During the war's early stages, England was highly successful. At Crécy (KRES-ee) in northern France in 1346, English longbowmen scored a great victory over French knights and crossbowmen. Although the aim of the longbow was not very accurate, it allowed for rapid reloading, and an English archer could send off three arrows to the French crossbowman's one. The result was a blinding shower of arrows that unhorsed the French knights and caused mass confusion. The ring of cannon—probably the first use of artillery in the West—created further panic. Thereupon the English horsemen charged and butchered the French.

This was not war according to the chivalric rules that Edward III would have preferred. Nevertheless, his son, Edward the Black Prince, used the same tactics ten years later to smash the French at Poitiers, where he captured the French king and held him for ransom. Again, at **Agincourt** (AJ-in-kawrt) near Arras (AR-uhs) in 1415, the chivalric English soldier-king Henry V (r. 1413–1422) gained the field over vastly superior numbers. Henry followed up his triumph at Agincourt with the reconquest of Normandy. By 1419 the English had advanced to the walls

Agincourt The location near Arras in Flanders where an English victory in 1415 led to the reconquest of Normandy.

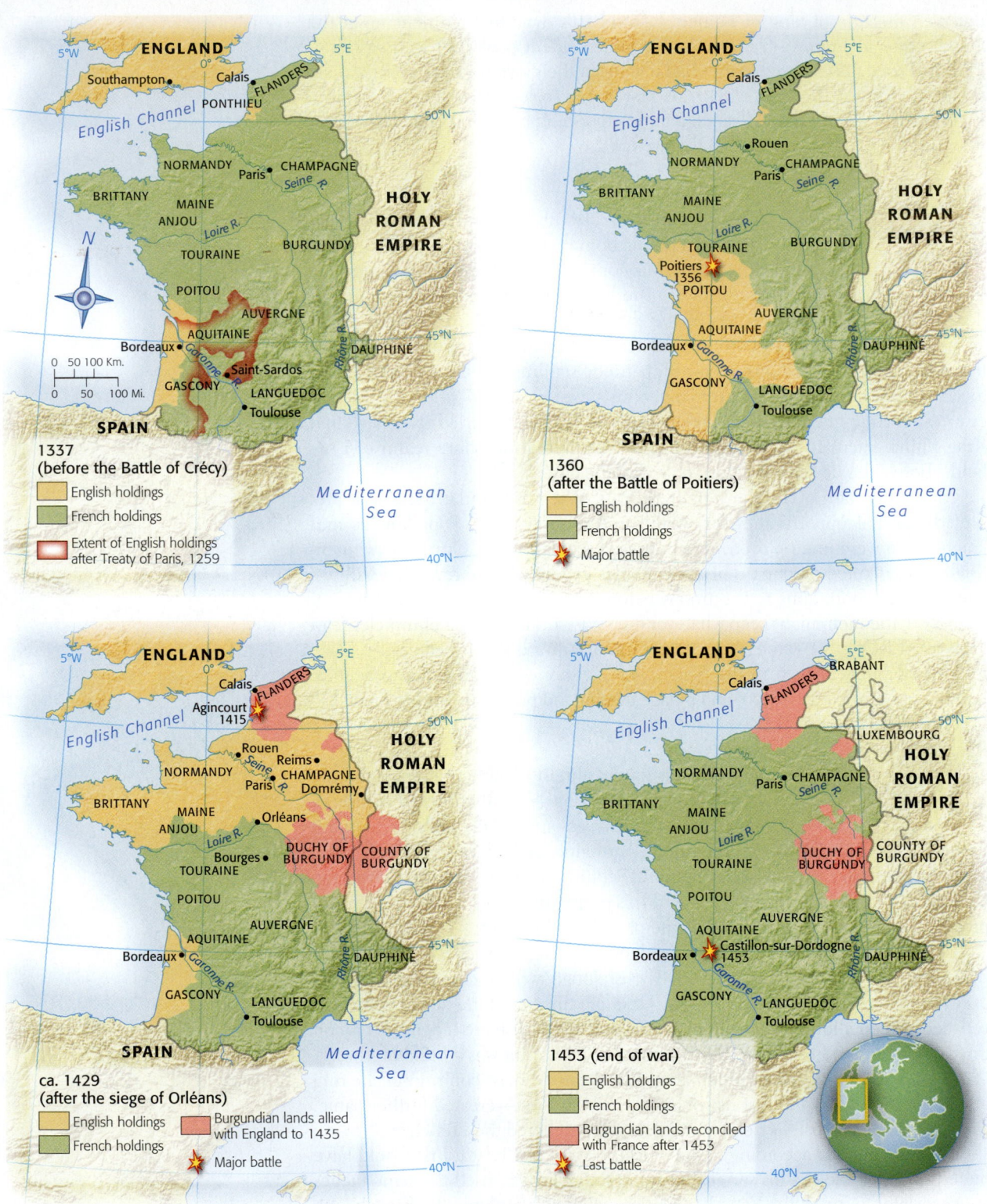

MAP 12.2 English Holdings in France During the Hundred Years' War

The year 1429 marked the greatest extent of English holdings in France.

of Paris (see Map 12.2). But the French cause was not lost. Though England had scored the initial victories, France won the war.

Joan of Arc and France's Victory

The ultimate French success rests heavily on the actions of an obscure French peasant girl, Joan of Arc, whose vision and work revived French fortunes and led to victory. A great deal of pious and popular legend surrounds Joan the Maid because of her peculiar appearance on the scene, her astonishing success, her martyrdom, and her canonization by the Catholic Church. The historical fact is that she saved the French monarchy, which was the embodiment of France.

Born in 1412 to well-to-do peasants in the village of Domrémy in Champagne, Joan of Arc grew up in a religious household. During adolescence she began to hear voices, which she later said belonged to Saint Michael, Saint Catherine, and Saint Margaret. In 1428 these voices spoke to her with great urgency, telling her that the dauphin (**DAW-fin**) (the uncrowned King Charles VII) had to be crowned and the English expelled from France. Joan went to the French court, persuaded the king to reject the rumor that he was illegitimate, and secured his support for her relief of the besieged city of Orléans (**AWR-lee-uhn**).

Joan arrived before Orléans on April 28, 1429. Seventeen years old, she knew little of warfare and believed that if she could keep the French troops from swearing and frequenting brothels, victory would be theirs. On May 8 the English, weakened by disease and lack of supplies, withdrew from Orléans. Ten days later Charles VII was crowned king at Reims. These two events marked the turning point in the war.

Joan's presence at Orléans, her strong belief in her mission, and the fact that she was wounded enhanced her reputation and strengthened the morale of the army. In 1430 England's allies, the Burgundians, captured Joan and sold her to the English. When the English handed her over to the ecclesiastical authorities for trial, the French court did not intervene. In 1431 the court condemned her as a heretic—her claim of direct inspiration from God, thereby denying the authority of church officials, constituted heresy—and burned her at the stake. The relief of Orléans stimulated French pride and rallied French resources. As the war dragged on, demands for an end increased in England. The clergy and intellectuals pressed for peace. Parliamentary opposition to additional war grants stiffened. Slowly the French reconquered Normandy and, finally, ejected the English from Aquitaine. At the war's end in 1453, only the town of Calais (**KAL-lay**) remained in English hands.

Costs and Consequences

In France thousands of soldiers and civilians had been slaughtered and hundreds of thousands of acres of rich farmland were ruined, leaving the rural economy of many parts of France a shambles. The war had disrupted trade and the great fairs, resulting in the drastic reduction of French participation in international commerce.

The war had wreaked havoc in England as well, even though only the southern coastal ports saw battle. England spent the huge sum of over £5 million on the war effort, and despite the money raised by some victories, the net result was an enormous financial loss. The government attempted to finance the war by raising taxes on the wool crop, which priced wool out of the export market. In addition, the social order was disrupted as the knights who ordinarily served as sheriffs, coroners, jurymen, and justices of the peace were abroad. The war stimulated technological experimentation, especially with artillery. Cannon revolutionized warfare, making the stone castle no longer impregnable. Because only central governments, not private nobles, could afford cannon, they strengthened the military power of national states.

The long war also had a profound impact on the political and cultural lives of the two countries. Most notably, it stimulated the development of the English Parliament. Between 1250 and 1450, **representative assemblies** flourished in many European countries. In the English Parliament, German diets, and Spanish cortes, deliberative practices developed that laid the foundations for the representative institutions of modern liberal-democratic nations. While representative assemblies declined in most countries after the fifteenth century, the English Parliament endured. Edward III's constant need for money to pay for the war compelled him to summon not only the great barons and bishops, but knights of the shires and burgesses from the towns as well. Parliament met in thirty-seven of the fifty years of Edward's reign.[2]

The frequency of the meetings is significant. Representative assemblies were becoming a habit. Knights and wealthy urban residents—or the "Commons," as they came to be called—recognized their mutual interests and began to meet apart from the great lords. The Commons gradually realized that they held the country's purse strings, and a parliamentary statute of 1341 required that all nonfeudal levies have parliamentary approval. By signing the law, Edward III acknowledged that the king of England could not tax without Parliament's consent. During the course of the war, money grants were increasingly tied to royal redress of grievances: to raise money, the government had to correct the wrongs its subjects protested.

In England, theoretical consent to taxation and legislation was given in one assembly for the entire country. France had no such single assembly; instead, there were many regional or provincial assemblies. Why did a national representative assembly fail to develop in France? Linguistic, geographical, economic, legal, and political differences were very strong. People tended to think of themselves as Breton, Norman, Burgundian, or whatever, rather than French. Provincial assemblies, highly jealous of their independence, did not want a national assembly. The costs of sending delegates to it would be high, and the result was likely to be increased taxation. In addition, the initiative for convening assemblies rested with the king. But some monarchs lacked the power to call such an assembly, and others, including Charles VI, found the idea of representative assemblies thoroughly distasteful.

In both countries, however, the war did promote the growth of **nationalism**—the feeling of unity and identity that binds together a people. After victories, each country experienced a surge of pride in its military strength. Just as English patriotism ran strong after Crécy and Poitiers, so French national confidence rose after Orléans. French national feeling demanded the expulsion of the enemy not merely from Normandy and Aquitaine but from all French soil. Perhaps no one expressed this national consciousness better than Joan of Arc when she exulted that the enemy had been "driven out of *France.*"

---

representative assemblies
Deliberative meetings of lords and wealthy urban residents that flourished in many European countries between 1250 and 1450 and were the precursors to the English Parliament, German diets, and Spanish cortes.

nationalism A sense of unity among a people living in a particular area, based on language, shared customs, and culture, and often accompanied by hostility to outsiders.

Section Review

- Animosity arose between England and France involving the duchy of Aquitaine and the question of succession to the French Capetian dynasty in 1328; the resulting standoff led to the Hundred Years' War.

- Even though each side feared invasion and slaughter, they each believed their cause was just and many benefited from the war, gaining land, regular wages, or simply the spoils of looting and pillaging.

- The combatants fought most of the war in France, the English gaining an early lead using sieges and raids with longbow and cannon fire and advancing all the way to Paris, but eventually the French won.

- Joan of Arc saved the French monarchy and contributed to ending the war, but the English burned her at the stake as a heretic for claiming a direct connection with God.

- Economic costs of the war were high in both countries, with farms ruined and trade disrupted, but this period saw the beginning of the English parliament and the growth of nationalism and pride in both France and England.

Challenges to the Church

What were the causes of the Great Schism, and how did church leaders, intellectuals, and ordinary people respond?

In times of crisis or disaster, people of all faiths have sought the consolation of religion. While local clergy eased the suffering of many, a dispute over who was the legitimate pope weakened the church as an institution. New ideas about church government took root.

The Babylonian Captivity and Great Schism

In order to control the church and its policies, Philip the Fair of France pressured Pope Clement V to settle permanently in Avignon in southeastern France, where the popes already had their summer residence (see Map 11.2). Clement, critically ill with cancer, lacked the will to resist Philip. The popes lived in Avignon from 1309 to 1376, a period in church history often called the **Babylonian Captivity** (referring to the seventy years the ancient Hebrews were held captive in Mesopotamian Babylon).

The Babylonian Captivity badly damaged papal prestige. The Avignon papacy reformed its financial administration and centralized its government. But the seven popes at Avignon concentrated on bureaucratic matters to the exclusion of spiritual objectives. Though some of the popes led austere lives, the general atmosphere was one of luxury and extravagance. The leadership of the church was cut off from its historic roots and the source of its ancient authority, the city of Rome. In 1377 Pope Gregory XI brought the papal court back to Rome. Unfortunately, he died shortly after the return. At Gregory's death, Roman citizens demanded an Italian pope who would remain in Rome. Between the time of Gregory's death and the opening of the conclave, great pressure was put on the cardinals to elect an Italian. At the time, none of them protested this pressure, and they chose a distinguished administrator, the archbishop of Bari, Bartolomeo Prignano, who took the name Urban VI.

Urban VI (1378–1389) had excellent intentions for church reform, but he went about this in a tactless and bullheaded manner. He attacked clerical luxury, denouncing individual cardinals by name, and even threatened to excommunicate certain cardinals.

The cardinals slipped away from Rome and met at Anagni. They declared Urban's election invalid because it had come about under threats from the Roman mob, and they asserted that Urban himself was excommunicated. The cardinals then elected Cardinal Robert of Geneva, the cousin of King Charles V of France, as pope. Cardinal Robert took the name Clement VII. There were thus two popes—Urban at Rome and Clement VII (1378–1394), who set himself up at Avignon in opposition to Urban. So began the **Great Schism,** which divided Western Christendom until 1417.

The powers of Europe aligned themselves with Urban or Clement along strictly political lines. France naturally recognized the French pope, Clement. England, France's historic enemy, recognized the Italian pope, Urban. Scotland, whose attacks on England were subsidized by France, followed the French and supported Clement. Aragon, Castile, and Portugal hesitated before deciding for Clement at Avignon. The German emperor, who bore ancient hostility to France,

Babylonian Captivity The period from 1309 to 1376 when the popes resided in Avignon, rather than in Rome. The phrase refers to the seventy years when the Hebrews were held captive in Babylon.

Great Schism The division, or split, in church leadership (1378–1417) when there were two, then three, popes.

recognized Urban. At first the Italian city-states recognized Urban; when he alienated them, they opted for Clement.

John of Spoleto, a professor at the law school at Bologna, eloquently summed up intellectual opinion of the schism, or division: "The longer this schism lasts, the more it appears to be costing, and the more harm it does; scandal, massacres, ruination, agitations, troubles and disturbances."[3] The common people, wracked by inflation, wars, and plague, were thoroughly confused about which pope was legitimate. The schism weakened the religious faith of many Christians and brought church leadership into serious disrepute. The schism also brought to the fore conciliar ideas about church government.

The Conciliar Movement

Theories about the nature of the Christian church and its government originated in the very early church, but the years of the Great Schism witnessed their maturity.

conciliarists People who believed that the authority in the Roman church should rest in a general council composed of clergy, theologians, and laypeople, rather than in the pope alone.

Conciliarists believed that reform of the church could best be achieved through periodic assemblies, or general councils, representing all the Christian people. While acknowledging that the pope was head of the church, conciliarists favored a balanced or constitutional form of church government, with papal authority shared with a general council, in contrast to the monarchical one that prevailed.

The intellectual roots of the conciliar movement can be traced to the rector Marsiglio of Padua a half century earlier. In his *Defensor Pacis* (The Defender of the Peace), Marsiglio argued against the medieval idea of a society governed by both church and state, with church supreme. Instead, Marsiglio claimed, the state was the great unifying power in society and the church should be subordinate to it. Church leadership should rest in a general council, made up of laymen as well as priests, and superior to the pope. Marsiglio was excommunicated for these radical ideas and his work was condemned.

The English scholar and theologian John Wyclif (**WIK-lif**) (ca. 1330–1384) went even further than Marsiglio of Padua in his argument against medieval church structure. Wyclif wrote that Scripture alone should be the standard of Christian belief and practice, and papal claims of temporal power had no foundation in the Scriptures. He urged that the church be stripped of its property. He wanted Christians to read the Bible for themselves, and produced the first complete translation of the Bible into English.

Wyclif has been hailed as the precursor of the Reformation of the sixteenth century. Although his ideas were condemned by church leaders, they were spread by humble clerics and enjoyed great popularity in the early fifteenth century. His followers, known as Lollards, spread his ideas and

Spoon with Fox Preaching to Geese (southern Netherlands, ca. 1430)

Taking as his text a contemporary proverb, "When the fox preaches, beware your geese," the artist shows, in the bowl of a spoon, a fox dressed as a monk or friar, preaching with three dead geese in his hood, while another fox grabs one of the congregation. The preaching fox reads from a scroll bearing the word *pax* (peace), implying the perceived hypocrisy of the clergy. The object suggests the widespread criticism of churchmen in the later Middle Ages. (Painted enamel and gilding on silver; 17.6 x 4.9 x 2.6 cm, Museum of Fine Arts, Boston, Helen and Alice Colburn Fund, 51.2472)

made many copies of his Bible. Lollard teaching allowed women to preach, and they played a significant role in the movement. After Anne, sister of Wenceslaus (**WEN-sis-laws**), king of Germany and Bohemia, married Richard II of England, members of her household carried Lollard books back to Bohemia.

In response to continued calls throughout Europe for a council, the cardinals of Rome and Avignon summoned a council at Pisa in 1409. That gathering of prelates and theologians deposed both popes and selected another. Neither the Avignon pope nor the Roman pope would resign, however, and the appalling result was the creation of a threefold schism.

Finally, under pressure from the German emperor Sigismund (**SEE-gis-muhnd**), a great council met at the imperial city of Constance (**KON-stuhns**) (1414–1418). It had three objectives: to end the schism, to reform the church "in head and members" (from top to bottom), and to wipe out heresy. The council condemned the Czech reformer Jan Hus (**yahn HOOS**) (see the feature "Individuals in Society: Jan Hus"), and he was burned at the stake. The council eventually deposed both the Roman pope and the successor of the pope chosen at Pisa, and it isolated the Avignon antipope. A conclave elected a new leader, the Roman cardinal Colonna, who took the name Martin V (1417–1431).

Martin proceeded to dissolve the council. Nothing was done about reform. In the later fifteenth century the papacy concentrated on Italian problems to the exclusion of universal Christian interests. Though the church was reunited, the spiritual mystique of the clergy had weakened, and lay people were not willing to rely on the clergy or church hierarchy for their salvation. Pious men and women increasingly formed **confraternities** (**kon-fruh-TUR-nih-teez**), voluntary groups of lay people designed to express devotion through prayer, charitable giving, and devotional activities.

Economic and Social Change

How did economic and social tensions contribute to revolts, crime, violence, and a growing sense of ethnic and national distinctions?

In the fourteenth century economic and political difficulties, disease, and war profoundly affected the lives of European peoples. Decades of slaughter and destruction, punctuated by the decimating visits of the Black Death, made a grave economic situation virtually disastrous. In many parts of France and the Low Countries, fields lay in ruin or untilled for lack of labor power. In England, as taxes increased, criticisms of government policy and mismanagement multiplied. Crime and new forms of business organization aggravated economic troubles, and throughout Europe the frustrations of the common people erupted into widespread revolts.

Peasant Revolts

Nobles and clergy lived on the produce of peasant labor, thinking little of adding taxes to the burden of peasant life. While peasants had endured centuries of exploitation, the difficult conditions of the fourteenth and fifteenth centuries spurred a wave of **peasant revolts** across Europe. Peasants were sometimes joined by their urban counterparts on the social ladder, resulting in a wider revolution of poor against rich.

The first large-scale rebellion was in Flanders in the 1320s. In order to satisfy peace agreements, Flemish peasants were forced to pay taxes to the French, who

---

confraternities Voluntary lay groups organized by occupation, devotional preference, neighborhood, or charitable activity.

Section Review

- The so-called Babylonian Captivity was a period when the popes resided in Avignon instead of Rome, worked on bureaucratic reforms, lived in luxury, and lost their focus on spiritual objectives.

- The papacy relocated to Rome under Pope Gregory, but his death saw the beginning of the Great Schism (1378–1417) when two popes, Urban VI and Clement VII, competed to be the true pope.

- Conciliarists Rector Marsiglio, who advocated a general council to share power with the pope, and John Wyclif, who wrote that scripture was the basis of religion and translated the first Bible into English, both argued against medieval church structure.

- A third council (Pisa, 1409) calling for an end to the schism only resulted in a tri-fold schism, which ended when a fourth council at Constance (1414–1418) finally united the church, but the church's reputation was damaged and the faithful began to meet in small groups for devotional services.

- The priest Jan Hus denounced church abuses and papal authority, and when the church burned him at the stake in 1415, despite a promise of safe conduct, the nobility publicly made their first protest to ecclesiastical authority.

peasant revolts Revolts by peasants in the fourteenth and fifteenth centuries, often caused by social and economic conditions.

Individuals in Society

Jan Hus

In May 1990 the Czech Republic's parliament declared July 6, the date of Jan Hus's execution in 1415, a Czech national holiday. The son of free farmers, Hus (ca. 1369–1415) was born in Husinec in southern Bohemia, an area of heavy German settlement, and grew up conscious of the ethnic differences between Czechs and Germans. Most of his professors at Charles University in Prague were Germans. In 1396 he received a master's degree, and just before his ordination as a priest in 1400 he wrote that he would not be a "clerical careerist," implying that ambition for church offices motivated many of his peers.

The execution of Jan Hus. (University of Prague/The Art Archive)

The young priest lectured at the university and preached at the private Bethlehem Chapel. During his twelve years there Hus preached only in Czech. He denounced superstition, the sale of indulgences, and other abuses, but his remarks were thoroughly orthodox. He attracted attention among artisans and the small Czech middle class, but not Germans. His austere life and lack of ambition enhanced his reputation.

Around 1400 Czech students returning from study at Oxford introduced into Bohemia the reforming ideas of the English theologian John Wyclif. When German professors condemned Wyclif's ideas as heretical, Hus and the Czechs argued "academic freedom," the right to read and teach Wyclif's works regardless of their particular merits. When popular demonstrations against ecclesiastical abuses and German influence at the university erupted, King Vaclav (**vah-SLAV**) IV (1378–1419) placed control of the university in Czech hands. Hus was elected rector, the top administrative official.

The people of Prague, with perhaps the largest urban population in central Europe, 40 percent of it living below the poverty line and entirely dependent on casual labor, found Hus's denunciations of an overendowed church appealing. Hus considered the issues theological; his listeners saw them as socioeconomic.

Church officials in Prague were split about Hus's ideas, and popular unrest grew. The king forced Hus to leave the city, but he continued to preach and write. He disputed papal authority, denounced abuses, and argued that everyone should receive both bread and wine in the Eucharist (**YOO-kuh-rist**). (By this time, in standard Western Christian practice, the laity received only the bread; the priest received the wine *for* the laity, a mark of his distinctiveness.) Hus also defended transubstantiation (see page 341); insisted that church authority rested on Scripture, conscience, and tradition (in contrast to sixteenth-century Protestant reformers, who placed authority in Scripture alone); and made it clear that he had no intention of leaving the church or inciting a popular movement.

In 1413 the emperor Sigismund urged the calling of a general council to end the schism. Hus was invited, and, given the emperor's safe conduct (protection from attack or arrest), agreed to go. What he found was an atmosphere of inquisition. The safe conduct was disregarded, and Hus was arrested. Under questioning about his acceptance of Wyclif's ideas, Hus repeatedly replied, "I have not held; I do not hold." Council members were more interested in proving Hus a Wyclite than in his responses. They took away his priesthood, banned his teachings, burned his books, and burned Hus himself at the stake. He then belonged to the ages.

The ages have made good use of him. His death aggravated the divisions between the bishops at Constance and the Czech clerics and people. In September 1415, 452 nobles from all parts of Bohemia signed a letter saying that Hus had been unjustly executed and rejecting council rulings. This event marks the first time that an ecclesiastical decision was publicly defied. Revolution swept through Bohemia, with Hussites—Czech nobles and people—insisting on clerical poverty and both the bread and wine at the Eucharist, and with German citizens remaining loyal to the Roman church. In the sixteenth century reformers hailed Hus as the forerunner of Protestantism. In the eighteenth century Enlightenment philosophes evoked Hus as a defender of freedom of expression. In the nineteenth century central European nationalists used Hus's name to defend national sentiment against Habsburg rule. And in the twentieth century Hus's name was used against German fascist and Russian communist tyranny.

Questions for Analysis

1. Since Jan Hus lived and died insisting that his religious teaching was thoroughly orthodox, why has he been hailed as a reformer?

2. What political and cultural interests did the martyred Hus serve?

claimed fiscal rights over the county of Flanders. Monasteries also pressed peasants for additional money, above their customary tithes. In retaliation, peasants burned and pillaged castles and aristocratic country houses. A French army crushed peasant forces, and savage repression and the confiscation of peasant property followed in the 1330s.

In 1358, when French taxation for the Hundred Years' War fell heavily on the poor, the frustrations of the French peasantry exploded in a massive uprising called the **Jacquerie** (**zhahk-REE**), after a mythical agricultural laborer, Jacques Bonhomme (Good Fellow). Peasants blamed the nobility for oppressive taxes, for the criminal brigandage of the countryside, for losses on the battlefield, and for the general misery. Crowds swept through the countryside, slashing the throats of nobles, burning their castles, raping their wives and daughters, and killing or maiming their horses and cattle. Artisans, small merchants, and parish priests joined the peasants. Urban and rural groups committed terrible destruction, and for several weeks the nobles were on the defensive. Then the upper class united to repress the revolt with merciless ferocity. Thousands of the "Jacques," innocent as well as guilty, were cut down. That forcible suppression of social rebellion, without any effort to alleviate its underlying causes, served to drive protest underground.

The Peasants' Revolt in England in 1381 involved thousands of people. Its causes were complex and varied from place to place. In general, though, the thirteenth century had witnessed the steady commutation of labor services for cash rents, and the Black Death had drastically cut the labor supply. As a result, peasants demanded higher wages and fewer manorial obligations. Their lords countered with a law freezing wages and binding workers to their manors. Unable to climb higher, the peasants sought release for their economic frustrations in revolt. Economic grievances combined with other factors. The south of England, where the revolt broke out, had been subjected to destructive French raids. The English government did little to protect the south, and villagers grew increasingly frightened and insecure. Moreover, decades of aristocratic violence against the weak peasantry had bred hostility and bitterness. Social and religious agitation by the popular preacher John Ball fanned the embers of discontent. Ball's famous couplet "When Adam delved and Eve span; Who was then the gentleman?" reflected real revolutionary sentiment.

The English revolt was ignited by the reimposition of a head tax on all adult males. Despite widespread opposition to the tax in 1380, the royal council ordered the sheriffs to collect it again in 1381 on penalty of a huge fine. Beginning with assaults on the tax collectors, the uprising in England followed a course similar to that of the Jacquerie in France. Castles and manors were sacked. Manorial records were destroyed. Many nobles, including the archbishop of Canterbury (**KAN-ter-ber-ee**), who had ordered the collection of the tax, were murdered.

The center of the revolt lay in the highly populated and economically advanced south and east, but sections of the north and the Midlands also witnessed rebellions. Violence took different forms in different places. Urban discontent merged with rural violence. In English towns where skilled Flemish craftsmen were employed, fear of competition led to their being attacked and murdered. Apprentices and journeymen, frustrated because the highest positions in the guilds were closed to them, rioted.

The boy-king Richard II (r. 1377–1399) met the leaders of the revolt, agreed to charters ensuring peasants' freedom, tricked them with false promises, and then crushed the uprising with terrible ferocity. The nobility tried to restore ancient duties of serfdom, but nearly a century of freedom had elapsed, and the

Jacquerie A massive uprising by French peasants in 1358 protesting heavy taxation.

commutation of manorial services continued. Rural serfdom disappeared in England by 1550.

Urban Conflicts

In Flanders, France, and England, peasant revolts often blended with conflicts involving workers in cities. Unrest also occurred in Italian, Spanish, and German cities.

These revolts typically flared up in urban centers where the conditions of work were changing for many people. In the thirteenth century craft guilds had organized the production of most goods, with masters, journeymen, and apprentices working side by side. In the fourteenth century a new system evolved to make products on a larger scale. Capitalist investors hired many households, with each household performing only one step of the process. Initially these investors were wealthy bankers and merchants, but eventually shop masters embraced the system. This promoted a greater division within guilds between wealthier masters and the poorer masters and journeymen they hired. Some masters became so wealthy that they no longer had to work in a shop themselves, nor did their wives and family members, though they still generally belonged to the craft guild.

While capitalism provided opportunities for some artisans to become investors and entrepreneurs, especially in cloth production, for many it led to a decrease in income and status. Guilds often responded to competition by limiting membership to existing guild families, which meant that journeymen who were not master's sons or who could not find a master's widow or daughter to marry could never become masters themselves. They remained journeymen their entire lives, losing their sense of solidarity with the masters of their craft. Resentment led to rebellion over economic issues.

Urban uprisings were also sparked by issues involving honor, such as employers' requiring workers to do tasks they regarded as beneath them. As their actual status and economic prospects declined and their work became basically wage labor, journeymen and poorer masters emphasized skill and honor as qualities that set them apart from less-skilled workers.

Guilds increasingly came to view the honor of their work as tied to an all-male workplace. When urban economies were expanding in the High Middle Ages, the master's wife and daughters worked alongside him, and female domestic servants also carried out productive tasks. (See the feature "Listening to the Past: Christine de Pizan" on pages 305–306.) Masters' widows ran shops after the death of their husbands. But in the fourteenth century, a woman's right to work slowly eroded. First, masters' widows were limited in the amount of time they could keep operating a shop or were prohibited from hiring journeymen; then female domestic servants were excluded from any productive tasks; then the number of daughters a master craftsman could employ was limited. When women were allowed to work, it was viewed as a substitute for charity.

Sex in the City

Peasant and urban revolts and riots had clear economic bases, but some historians have suggested that late medieval marital patterns may have also played a role in unrest. In northwestern Europe, people believed that couples should be economically independent before they married, so both spouses spent long periods as servants or workers in other households saving money and learning skills, or they waited until their own parents had died and the family property was distributed.

The most unusual feature of this pattern was the late age of marriage for women. Women entered marriage as adults and took charge of running a household immediately. They were thus not as dependent on their husbands or their mothers-in-law as were women who married at younger ages. They had fewer pregnancies than women who married earlier, though not necessarily fewer surviving children.

Men of all social groups were older when they married. In general, men were in their middle or late twenties at first marriage, with wealthier urban merchants often much older. Journeymen and apprentices were often explicitly prohibited from marrying, as were the students at universities, as they were understood to be in "minor orders" and thus like clergy, even if they were not intending on careers in the church.

The prohibitions on marriage for certain groups of men and the late age of marriage for most men meant that cities and villages were filled with large numbers of young adult men with no family responsibilities who often formed the core of riots and unrest. Not surprisingly, this situation also contributed to a steady market for sexual services outside of marriage, what in later centuries was termed prostitution. Research on the southern French province of Languedoc in the fourteenth and fifteenth centuries has revealed the establishment of legal houses of prostitution in many cities. Municipal authorities set up houses or red-light districts either outside the city walls or away from respectable neighborhoods. For example, authorities in Montpellier set aside Hot Street for prostitution, required public women to live there, and forbade anyone to molest them. Prostitution thus passed from being a private concern to a social matter requiring public supervision. The towns of Languedoc were not unique. Public authorities in Amiens, Dijon, Paris, Venice, Genoa, London, Florence, Rome, most of the larger German towns, and the English port of Sandwich set up brothels.

Visiting brothels was associated with achieving manhood in the eyes of young men, though for the women themselves their activities were work. Indeed, in some cases the women had no choice, for they had been traded to the brothel manager by their parents or other people in payment for debt, or had quickly become indebted to him (or, more rarely, her) for the clothes and other finery regarded as essential to their occupation. Poor women—and men—also sold sex illegally outside of city brothels, combining this with other sorts of part-time work such as laundering or sewing. Prostitution was an urban phenomenon because only populous towns had large numbers of unmarried young men, communities of transient merchants, and a culture accustomed to a cash exchange.

Though selling sex for money was legal in the Middle Ages, the position of women who did so was always marginal. In the late fifteenth century cities began to limit brothel residents' freedom of movement and choice of clothing, requiring them to wear distinctive head coverings or bands on their clothing so that they would not be mistaken for "honorable" women. The cities also began to impose harsher penalties on women who did not live in the designated house or section of town. A few prostitutes did earn enough to donate money to charity or buy property, but most were very poor.

Along with buying sex, young men also took it by force. Unmarried women often found it difficult to avoid sexual contact. Many of them worked as domestic servants, where their employers or employers' sons or male relatives could easily coerce them, or they worked in proximity to men. Notions of female honor kept upper-class women secluded in their homes, particularly in southern and eastern Europe, but there was little attempt anywhere to keep female servants or day laborers from the risk of seduction or rape. Rape was a capital crime in many parts of Europe, but the actual sentences handed out were more likely to be fines and brief

Prostitute Invites a Traveling Merchant
Poverty drove women into prostitution, which, though denounced by moralists, was accepted as a normal part of the medieval social fabric. In the cities and larger towns where prostitution flourished, public officials passed laws requiring prostitutes to wear a special mark on their clothing, regulated hours of business, forbade women to drag men into their houses, and denied business to women with the "burning sickness," gonorrhea. (Bodleian Library, Oxford, MS. Bodl. 264, fol. 245V)

imprisonment, with the severity of the sentence dependent on the social status of the victim and the perpetrator.

Same-sex relations—what in the late nineteenth century would be termed "homosexuality"—were another feature of medieval urban life (and of village life, though there are very few sources relating to sexual relations of any type in the rural context). Same-sex relations were of relatively little concern to church or state authorities in the early Middle Ages, but this attitude changed beginning in the late twelfth century. By 1300 most areas had defined such actions as "crimes against nature." Same-sex relations, usually termed "sodomy," became a capital crime in most of Europe, with adult offenders threatened with execution by fire. The Italian cities of Venice, Florence, and Lucca created special courts to deal with sodomy, which saw thousands of investigations.

Sodomy was not a marginal practice, which may account for the fact that, despite harsh laws and special courts, actual executions for sodomy were rare. Same-sex relations often developed within the context of all-male environments, such as the army, the craft shop, and the artistic workshop, and were part of the collective male experience. Homoerotic relationships played important roles in defining stages of life, expressing distinctions of status, and shaping masculine gender identity. Same-sex relations involving women almost never came to the attention of legal authorities, so it is difficult to find out how common they were. However, female-female desire was expressed in songs, plays, and stories, as was male-male desire, offering evidence of the way people understood same-sex relations.

Fur-Collar Crime

The Hundred Years' War had provided employment and opportunity for thousands of idle and fortune-seeking knights. But during periods of truce and after the war finally ended, many nobles once again had little to do. Inflation hurt them. Although many were living on fixed incomes, their chivalric code demanded lavish generosity and an aristocratic lifestyle. Many nobles turned to crime as a way of raising money. The fourteenth and fifteenth centuries witnessed a great deal of "fur-collar crime," so called for the miniver fur nobles alone were allowed to wear on their collars.

Groups of noble brigands roamed the English countryside stealing from both rich and poor. Operating like modern urban racketeers, knightly gangs demanded that peasants pay "protection money" or else have their hovels burned and their fields destroyed. They seized wealthy travelers and held them for ransom.

When accused of wrongdoing, fur-collar criminals intimidated witnesses, threatened jurors, and used "pull" or cash to bribe judges. As a fourteenth-century English judge wrote to a young nobleman, "For the love of your father I have hindered charges being brought against you and have prevented execution of indictment actually made."[4] Criminal activity by nobles continued decade after decade because governments were too weak to stop it.

The ballads of Robin Hood, a collection of folk legends from late medieval England, describe the adventures of the outlaw hero and his merry men as they avenge the common people against fur-collar criminals—grasping landlords, wicked sheriffs, and mercenary churchmen. Robin Hood was a popular figure because he symbolized the deep resentment of aristocratic corruption and abuse; he represented the struggle against tyranny and oppression.

Ethnic Tensions and Restrictions

Large numbers of people in the twelfth and thirteenth centuries migrated from one part of Europe to another: the English into Scotland and Ireland; Germans, French, and Flemings into Poland, Bohemia, and Hungary; the French into Spain. The colonization of frontier regions meant that peoples of different ethnic backgrounds lived side by side. Everywhere in Europe, towns recruited people from the countryside (see page 249). In frontier regions, townspeople were usually long-distance immigrants and, in eastern Europe, Ireland, and Scotland, ethnically different from the surrounding rural population. In eastern Europe, German was the language of the towns; in Irish towns, French, the tongue of Norman or English settlers, predominated.

In the early periods of conquest and colonization, and in all regions with extensive migrations, a legal dualism existed: native peoples remained subject to their traditional laws; newcomers brought and were subject to the laws of the countries from which they came. On the Prussian and Polish frontier, for example, the law was that "men who come there . . . should be judged on account of any crime or contract engaged in there according to Polish custom if they are Poles and according to German custom if they are Germans."[5] Likewise, the conquered Muslim subjects of Christian kings in Spain had the right to be judged under Muslim law by Muslim judges.

The great exception to this broad pattern was Ireland. From the start, the English practiced an extreme form of discrimination toward the native Irish. The English distinguished between the free and the unfree, and the entire Irish population, simply by the fact of Irish birth, was unfree. When an English legal structure was established, the Irish were denied access to the common-law courts. In civil (property) disputes, an English defendant need not respond to his Irish plaintiff; no Irish person could make a will. In criminal procedures, the murder of an Irishman was not considered a felony. Other than in Ireland, although native peoples commonly held humbler positions, both immigrant and native townspeople prospered during the expanding economy of the thirteenth century. But when economic recession hit during the fourteenth century, ethnic tensions multiplied.

The later Middle Ages witnessed a movement away from legal pluralism or dualism and toward legal homogeneity and an emphasis on blood descent. The dominant ethnic group in an area tried to bar the other from positions of church leadership and guild membership. Marriage laws were instituted that attempted to maintain ethnic purity and some church leaders actively promoted ethnic discrimination.

The most extensive attempt to prevent intermarriage and protect ethnic purity is embodied in Ireland's **Statute of Kilkenny** (**kil-KEN-ee**) (1366), which states that "there were to be no marriages between those of immigrant and native stock; that the English inhabitants of Ireland must employ the English language and bear English names; that they must ride in the English way (i.e., with saddles) and have English apparel; that no Irishmen were to be granted ecclesiastical benefices or admitted to monasteries in the English parts of Ireland. . . ."[6]

Late medieval chroniclers used words such as *gens* (**zhahn**) (race or clan) and *natio* (**NAHT-ee-oh**) (species, stock, or kind) to refer to different groups. They held that peoples differed according to language, traditions, customs, and laws. None of these were unchangeable, however, and commentators increasingly also described ethnic differences in terms of "blood"—"German blood," "English blood," and so on—which made ethnicity heritable. Religious beliefs also came to be conceptualized as blood, with people regarded as having Jewish blood, Muslim blood, or Christian blood. The most dramatic expression of this was in Spain, where "purity of the blood"—having no Muslim or Jewish ancestors—became an obsession. Blood was also used as a way to talk about social differences, especially for nobles. Just as Irish and English were prohibited from marrying each other, those of "noble blood" were prohibited from marrying commoners in many parts of Europe. As Europeans increasingly came into contact with people from Africa and Asia, and particularly as they developed colonial empires, these notions of blood also became a way of conceptualizing racial categories (see page 325).

> **Statute of Kilkenny** Laws issued in 1366 that discriminated against the Irish, forbidding marriage between the English and the Irish, requiring the use of the English language, and denying the Irish access to ecclesiastical offices.

Literacy and Vernacular Literature

The development of ethnic identities had many negative consequences, but a more positive effect was the increasing use of the vernacular. Two masterpieces of European culture, Dante's (**DAHN-tay**) *Divine Comedy* (1310–1320) and Chaucer's (**CHAW-ser**) *Canterbury Tales* (1387–1400), illustrate a sophisticated use of the rhythms and rhymes of the vernacular.

Dante Alighieri (**ah-lee-ghee-AIR-ee**) (1265–1321) called his work a "comedy" because he wrote it in Italian and in a different style from the "tragic" Latin; a later generation added the adjective *divine*, referring both to its sacred subject and to Dante's artistry. The *Divine Comedy* is an epic poem of one hundred cantos (verses) each of whose three equal parts (1 + 33 + 33 + 33) describes one of the realms of the next world: Hell, Purgatory, and Paradise. The Roman poet Virgil, representing reason, leads Dante through Hell, where Dante observes the torments of the damned and denounces the disorders of his own time, especially ecclesiastical ambition and corruption. Passing up into Purgatory, Virgil shows the poet how souls are purified of their disordered inclinations. From Purgatory, Beatrice (**BEE-uh-triss**), a woman Dante once loved and the symbol of divine revelation in the poem, leads him to Paradise. In Paradise, home of the angels and saints, Saint Bernard —representing mystic contemplation—leads Dante to the Virgin Mary. Through her intercession, he at last attains a vision of God.

The *Divine Comedy* portrays contemporary and historical figures, comments on secular and ecclesiastical affairs, and draws on Scholastic philosophy. Within the framework of a symbolic pilgrimage to the City of God, the *Divine Comedy* embodies the psychological tensions of the age. A profoundly Christian poem, it also contains bitter criticism of some church authorities. In its symmetrical structure and use of figures from the ancient world, such as Virgil, the poem perpetuates the classical tradition, but as the first major work of literature in the Italian vernacular, it is distinctly modern.

Geoffrey Chaucer (1342–1400) was an official in the administrations of the English kings Edward III and Richard II and wrote poetry as an avocation. Chaucer's *Canterbury Tales* is a collection of stories in lengthy rhymed narrative. On a pilgrimage to the shrine of Saint Thomas Becket at Canterbury (see page 203), thirty people of various social backgrounds tell tales. For example, the gross Miller tells a vulgar story about a deceived husband; the earthy Wife of Bath, who has buried five husbands, sketches a fable about the selection of a spouse; and the elegant Prioress, who violates her vows by wearing jewelry, delivers a homily on the Virgin. In depicting the interests and behavior of all types of people, Chaucer presents a rich panorama of English social life in the fourteenth century. Like the *Divine Comedy*, the *Canterbury Tales* reflects the cultural tensions of the times. Ostensibly Christian, many of the pilgrims are also materialistic, sensual, and worldly, suggesting the ambivalence of the broader society's concern for the next world and frank enjoyment of this one.

Beginning in the fourteenth century, a variety of evidence attests to the increasing literacy of laypeople. Wills and inventories reveal that many people, not just nobles, possessed books—mainly devotional, but also romances, manuals on manners and etiquette, histories, and sometimes legal and philosophical texts. In England the number of schools in the diocese of York quadrupled between 1350 and 1500. Information from Flemish and German towns is similar: children were sent to schools and were taught the fundamentals of reading, writing, and arithme-

Schoolmaster and Schoolmistress Teaching

Ambrosius Holbein (HOHL-bine), elder brother of the more famous Hans Holbein, produced this signboard for the Swiss educator Myconius; it is an excellent example of what we would call commercial art—art used to advertise, in this case Myconius's profession. The German script above promised that all who enrolled, girls and boys, would learn to read and write. Most schools were for boys only, but a few offered instruction for girls as well. By modern standards the classroom seems bleak: the windows have glass panes but they don't admit much light, and the schoolmaster is prepared to use the sticks if the boy makes a mistake. (Kunstmuseum Basel, Acc. No. 311/Martin Buhler, photographer)

tic. Laymen increasingly served as managers or stewards of estates and as clerks to guilds and town governments; such positions obviously required that they be able to keep administrative and financial records.

The penetration of laymen into the higher positions of governmental administration, long the preserve of clerics, also illustrates rising lay literacy. With growing frequency, the upper classes sent their daughters to convent schools, where, in addition to instruction in singing, religion, needlework, deportment, and household management, girls gained the rudiments of reading and sometimes writing.

The spread of literacy represents a response to the needs of an increasingly complex society. Trade, commerce, and expanding government bureaucracies required more and more literate people. Late medieval culture remained an oral culture in which most people received information by word of mouth. But by the mid-fifteenth century, even before the printing press was turning out large quantities of reading materials, the evolution toward a literary culture was already perceptible.

Section Review

- Peasant revolts due to increased taxes, economic frustration, and fear, resulted in widespread violence and destruction, leading to a backlash of repression by the nobility.
- Urban conflict occurred as capitalism magnified the disparity between rich and poor and caused limits on entry into guilds and on women's right to work in guild shops.
- Poor women were forced into prostitution in urban centers, and homosexuality and rape were common.
- After the Hundred Years' War, unemployed young nobles, called fur-collar criminals, roamed the countryside, stealing and causing trouble.
- The large migrations of different ethnicities brought with them the laws of their countries of origin, except in Ireland, where English law discriminated against the Irish.
- Ethnic identities increased the use of vernacular language, and great works of literature such as Dante's *Divine Comedy* and Chaucer's *Canterbury Tales* reflected the tensions of the era.
- With the advancements in trade, commerce, and government, literacy increased and more books became available.

Chapter Review

What were the demographic, social, and economic consequences of climate change? (page 278)

The crises of the fourteenth and fifteenth centuries were acids that burned deeply into the fabric of traditional medieval society. Bad weather brought poor harvests, which contributed to widespread famine and disease and an international economic depression. Political leaders attempted to find solutions, but were unable to deal with the economic and social problems that resulted.

How did the spread of the plague shape European society? (page 280)

In 1348 a new disease, most likely the bubonic plague, came to mainland Europe, carried from the Black Sea by ships. It spread quickly by land and sea and within two years may have killed as much as one-third of the European population. Contemporary medical explanations for the plague linked it to poisoned air or water, and treatments were ineffective. Many people regarded the plague as a divine punishment and sought remedies in religious practices such as prayer, pilgrimages, or donations to churches. Population losses caused by the Black Death led to inflation but in the long run may have contributed to more opportunities for the peasants and urban workers who survived the disease.

What were the causes of the Hundred Years' War, and how did the war affect European politics, economics, and cultural life? (page 286)

The miseries of the plague were enhanced in England and France by the Hundred Years' War, which was fought intermittently in France from 1337 to 1453. The war began as a dispute over the succession to the French crown, and royal propaganda on both sides fostered a kind of early nationalism. The English won most of the battles

Key Terms

Great Famine (p. 278)
Black Death (p. 280)
flagellants (p. 284)
Agincourt (p. 287)
representative assemblies (p. 290)
nationalism (p. 290)
Babylonian Captivity (p. 291)
Great Schism (p. 291)
conciliarists (p. 292)
confraternities (p. 293)
peasant revolts (p. 293)
Jacquerie (p. 296)
Statute of Kilkenny (p. 301)

and in 1419 advanced to the walls of Paris. The appearance of Joan of Arc rallied the French cause, and French troops eventually pushed English forces out of all of France except the port of Calais. The war served as a catalyst for the development of representative government in England. In France, on the other hand, the war stiffened opposition to national assemblies.

What were the causes of the Great Schism, and how did church leaders, intellectuals, and ordinary people respond? (page 291)

Religious beliefs offered people solace through these difficult times, but the Western Christian church was going through a particularly difficult period in the fourteenth and early fifteenth centuries. The papacy moved to Avignon in France, where it was dominated by the French monarchy. This led eventually to some cardinals electing a second, Roman pope, a division in the church called the Great Schism. The Avignon papacy and the Great Schism weakened the prestige of the church and people's faith in papal authority. The conciliar movement, by denying the church's universal sovereignty, strengthened the claims of secular governments to jurisdiction over all their peoples. As members of the clergy challenged the power of the pope, laypeople challenged the authority of the church itself. Women and men increasingly relied on direct approaches to God, often through mystical encounters, rather than on the institutional church. Some, including John Wyclif and Jan Hus, questioned basic church doctrines.

How did economic and social tensions contribute to revolts, crime, violence, and a growing sense of ethnic and national distinctions? (page 293)

The plague and the war both led to higher taxes and economic dislocations, which sparked peasant revolts in Flanders, France, and England. Peasant revolts often blended with conflicts involving workers in cities, where working conditions were changing to create a greater gap between wealthy merchant-producers and poor workers. Unrest in the countryside and cities may have been further exacerbated by marriage patterns that left large numbers of young men unmarried and rootless. The pattern of late marriage for men contributed to a growth in prostitution, which was an accepted feature of medieval urban society. Along with peasant revolts and urban crime and unrest, violence perpetrated by nobles was a common part of late medieval life. The economic and demographic crises of the fourteenth century also contributed to increasing ethnic tensions in the many parts of Europe where migration had brought different population groups together. A growing sense of ethnic and national identity led to restrictions and occasionally to violence, but also to the increasing use of vernacular languages for works of literature. The increasing number of schools that led to the growth of lay literacy represents another positive achievement of the later Middle Ages.

Notes

1. Quoted in J. Barnie, *War in Medieval English Society: Social Values and the Hundred Years' War* (Ithaca, N.Y.: Cornell University Press, 1974), p. 34.
2. See G. O. Sayles, *The King's Parliament of England* (New York: W. W. Norton, 1974), app., pp. 137–141.
3. Quoted in J. H. Smith, *The Great Schism, 1378: The Disintegration of the Medieval Papacy* (New York: Weybright & Talley, 1970), p. 15.
4. Quoted in B. A. Hanawalt, "Fur Collar Crime: The Pattern of Crime Among the Fourteenth-Century English Nobility," *Journal of Social History* 8 (Spring 1975): p. 7.
5. Quoted in R. Bartlett, *The Making of Europe: Conquest, Colonization and Cultural Change, 950–1350* (Princeton, N.J.: Princeton University Press, 1993), p. 205.
6. Quoted ibid., p. 239.

To assess your mastery of this chapter, go to **bedfordstmartins.com/mckaywestbrief**

Listening to the Past

Christine de Pizan

Christine de Pizan (**duh PEE-zahn**) *(1364?–1430; earlier spelled "Pisan") was the well-educated daughter and wife of men who held positions at the court of the king of France. Widowed at twenty-five, Christine decided to support her family through writing. She began to write prose works and poetry, sending them to wealthy individuals in the hope of receiving their support. Her efforts resulted in commissions to write specific works, including a biography of the French king Charles V and a book of military tactics. She became the first woman in Europe to make her living as a writer, a difficult profession for anyone in this era before the printing press.*

Among Christine's many works were several in which she considered women's nature and proper role in society, which had been a topic of debate since ancient times. The following selection is from The Treasure of the City of Ladies *(1405, also called* The Book of Three Virtues*), which provides moral suggestions and practical advice on behavior and household management. Most of the book is directed toward princesses and court ladies (who would have been able to read it), but she also includes shorter sections for the wives of merchants and artisans, serving-women, female peasants, and even prostitutes. This is her advice to the wives of artisans, whose husbands were generally members of urban craft guilds.*

All wives of artisans should be very painstaking and diligent if they wish to have the necessities of life. They should encourage their husbands or their workmen to get to work early in the morning and work until late, for mark our words, there is no trade so good that if you neglect your work you will not have difficulty putting bread on the table. And besides encouraging the others, the wife herself should be involved in the work to the extent that she knows all about it, so that she may know how to oversee his workers if her husband is absent, and to reprove them if they do not do well. She ought to oversee them to keep them from idleness, for through careless workers the master is sometimes ruined. And when customers come to her husband and try to drive a hard bargain, she ought to warn him solicitously to take care that he does not make a bad deal. She should advise him to be chary of giving too much credit if he does not know precisely where and to whom it is going, for in this way many come to poverty, although sometimes the greed to earn more or to accept a tempting proposition makes them do it.

In addition, she ought to keep her husband's love as much as she can, to this end: that he will stay at home more willingly and that he may not have any reason to join the foolish crowds of other young men in taverns and indulge in unnecessary

Several manuscripts of Christine's works included illustrations showing her writing, which would have increased their appeal to the wealthy individuals who purchased them. (Copyright © British Library Board)

and extravagant expense, as many tradesmen do, especially in Paris. By treating him kindly she should protect him as well as she can from this. It is said that three things drive a man from his home: a quarrelsome wife, a smoking fireplace and a leaking roof. She too ought to stay at home gladly and not go every day traipsing hither and yon gossiping with the neighbours and visiting her chums to find out what everyone is doing. That is done by slovenly housewives roaming about the town in groups. Nor should she go off on these pilgrimages got up for no good reason and involving a lot of needless expense. Furthermore, she ought to remind her husband that they should live so frugally that their expenditure does not exceed their income, so that at the end of the year they do not find themselves in debt.

Questions

1. How would you describe Christine's view of the ideal artisan's wife?

2. The regulations of craft guilds often required that masters who ran workshops be married. What evidence does Christine's advice provide for why guilds would have stipulated this?

3. How are economic and moral virtues linked for Christine?

Source: Christine de Pisan, *The Treasure of the City of Ladies,* translated with an introduction by Sarah Lawson (Penguin Classics, 1985). Translation copyright © Sarah Lawson, 1985. Reproduced by permission of Penguin Books Ltd. For more on Christine, see: C. C. Willard, *Christine de Pisan: Her Life and Works* (1984), and S. Bell, *The Lost Tapestries of the City of Ladies: Christine de Pizan's Renaissance Legacy* (2004).

CHAPTER 13

European Society in the Age of the Renaissance

1350–1550

Michelangelo's frescoes in the Sistine Chapel in the Vatican, commissioned by the pope. The huge ceiling includes biblical scenes, and the far wall, painted much later, shows a dramatic and violent Last Judgment. (Vatican Museum)

Chapter Preview

Economic and Political Developments
What economic and political developments in Italy provided the setting for the Renaissance?

Intellectual Change
What were the key ideas of the Renaissance, and how were they different for men and women and for southern and northern Europeans?

Art and the Artist
How did changes in art both reflect and shape new ideas?

Social Hierarchies
What were the key social hierarchies in Renaissance Europe, and how did ideas about hierarchy shape people's lives?

Politics and the State in the Renaissance (ca. 1450–1521)
How did the nation-states of western Europe evolve in this period?

INDIVIDUALS IN SOCIETY: Leonardo da Vinci

LISTENING TO THE PAST: An Age of Gold

W hile the Four Horsemen of the Apocalypse seemed to be carrying war, plague, famine, and death across northern Europe, a new culture was emerging in southern Europe. The fourteenth century witnessed the beginnings of remarkable changes in many aspects of Italian intellectual, artistic, and cultural life. Artists and writers thought that they were living in a new golden age, but not until the sixteenth century was this change given the label we use today—the **Renaissance,** from the French version of a word meaning rebirth.

The word *Renaissance* was first used by the artist and art historian Giorgio Vasari (**vuh-ZAHR-ee**) (1511–1574) to describe the art of "rare men of genius," such as his contemporary, Michelangelo (**my-kuhl-AN-juh-low**). Through their works, Vasari judged, the glory of the classical past had been reborn—or perhaps even surpassed—after centuries of darkness. Vasari used *Renaissance* to describe painting, sculpture, and architecture, what he termed the "Major Arts." Gradually, however, the word was used to refer to many aspects of life at this time, first in Italy and then in the rest of Europe. This new attitude had a slow diffusion out of Italy, with the result that the Renaissance "happened" at different times in different parts of Europe: Italian art of the fourteenth through the early sixteenth centuries is described as "Renaissance," and so is English literature of the late sixteenth century, including Shakespeare's plays and poetry.

Although Vasari viewed the Renaissance as a sharp break with the Middle Ages, some contemporary historians have chosen to view the Renaissance as a bridge between the medieval and modern eras because it corresponded chronologically with the late medieval period and because there were many continuities along with the changes. Others have questioned whether the word *Renaissance* should be used at all to describe an era in which many social groups saw decline rather than advance. These debates remind us that these labels—medieval, Renaissance, modern—while offering a useful framework for viewing various periods, are also laden with value judgments.

Renaissance A French word, translated from the Italian *rinascita,* first used by art historian and critic Giorgio Vasari (1511–1574), meaning rebirth of the culture of classical antiquity; English-speaking students adopted the French term.

Economic and Political Developments

What economic and political developments in Italy provided the setting for the Renaissance?

The cultural achievements of the Renaissance rest on the economic and political developments of earlier centuries. Economic growth laid the material basis for the Italian Renaissance, and ambitious merchants gained political power to match their economic power. They then used their money and power to buy luxuries and hire talent.

Commercial Developments

Scholars tend to agree that the first artistic and literary manifestations of the Italian Renaissance appeared in Florence, which possessed enormous wealth because Florentine merchants and bankers had acquired control of papal banking toward the end of the thirteenth century. From their position as tax collectors for the papacy, Florentine mercantile families began to dominate European banking on both sides of the Alps, setting up offices in major European and North African cities. The profits from loans, investments, and money exchanges that poured back to Florence were pumped into urban industries. Such profits contributed to the city's economic vitality and allowed banking families to control the city's politics and culture.

By the first quarter of the fourteenth century, the economic foundations of Florence were so strong that even severe crises could not destroy the city. In 1344 King Edward III of England repudiated his huge debts to Florentine bankers and forced some of them into bankruptcy. Florence suffered frightfully from the Black Death, losing at least half its population. Serious labor unrest shook the political establishment. Nevertheless, the basic Florentine economic structure remained stable.

Communes and Republics

The northern Italian cities were **communes,** sworn associations of free men seeking complete political and economic independence from local nobles. The merchant guilds that formed the communes built and maintained the city walls, regulated trade, raised taxes, and kept civil order. The local nobles frequently moved into the cities, marrying into rich commercial families and starting their own businesses. This merger of the northern Italian feudal nobility and the commercial elite created a powerful oligarchy that ruled the city and surrounding countryside. Yet because of rivalries among different powerful families, Italian communes were often politically unstable.

Unrest coming from below exacerbated the instability. Merchant elites made citizenship in the communes dependent on a property qualification, years of residence within the city, and social connections. Only a tiny percentage of the male population possessed these qualifications and thus could hold office in the commune's political councils. The common people, called the **popolo,** were disenfranchised and heavily taxed, and they bitterly resented their exclusion from power. Throughout most of the thirteenth century, in city after city, the popolo used armed force and violence to take over the city governments. Republican governments—in which political power theoretically resides in the people and is exercised by their chosen representatives—were established in Bologna, Siena, Parma, Florence, Genoa, and other cities. The victory of the popolo proved temporary, however, because they could not establish civil order within their cities. Merchant oligarchies

communes Associations of merchants in Italian cities such as Milan, Florence, Genoa, and Pisa who sought political and economic independence from local nobles; members of communes wanted self-government.

popolo Disenfranchised, common people in Italian cities who resented their exclusion from power.

A Bank Scene, Florence

Originally a "bank" was just a counter; moneychangers who sat behind the counter became "bankers," exchanging different currencies and holding deposits for merchants and business-people. In this scene from fifteenth-century Florence, the bank is covered with an imported Ottoman geometric rug, one of many imported luxury items handled by Florentine merchants. (Prato, San Francesco/Scala/Art Resource, NY)

condottieri Military leaders in Italian city-states who often took over political control as well.

signori Government by one-man rule in Italian cities such as Milan, in which the ruler handed power down to his son.

courts Magnificent households and palaces where the signori and the most powerful merchant oligarchs required political business to be conducted.

patrons Patrician merchants and bankers, popes and princes, who supported the arts as a means of glorifying themselves and their families.

reasserted their power and sometimes brought in powerful military leaders to establish order. These military leaders, called **condottieri** (kawn-duh-TYAIR-ey) (singular, condottiero), had their own mercenary armies, and in many cities they took over political power as well.

Many cities in Italy became **signori** (see-YOHR- ee), in which one man ruled and handed down the right to rule to his son. Some signori (the word is plural in Italian and is used both for persons and forms of government) kept the institutions of communal government in place, but these had no actual power.

In the fifteenth century the signori in many cities and the most powerful merchant oligarchs in others transformed their households into **courts.** They built magnificent palaces in the centers of cities and required all political business to be done there. They became **patrons** of the arts, hiring architects to design and build these palaces, artists to fill them with paintings and sculptures, and musicians and composers to fill them with music. They supported writers and philosophers, flaunting their patronage of learning and the arts. They used ceremonies connected with family births, baptisms, marriages, funerals, or triumphant entrances into the city as occasions for magnificent pageantry and elaborate ritual. Courtly culture afforded signori and oligarchs the opportunity to display and assert their wealth and power. The courts of the rulers of Milan, Florence, and other cities were models for those developed later by rulers of nation-states.

The Balance of Power Among the Italian City-States

In the fifteenth century five powers dominated the Italian peninsula: Venice, Milan, Florence, the Papal States, and the kingdom of Naples (see Map 13.1). Venice, with its enormous trade empire ranked as an international power. Though Venice was a republic in name, an oligarchy of merchant aristocrats actually ran the city. Milan was also called a republic, but the condottieri turned signori of the Sforza (SFAWRT-suh) family ruled harshly and dominated the smaller cities of the north. Likewise, in Florence the form of government was republican, with authority vested in several councils of state. In reality, between 1434 and 1494, power in Florence was held by the great Medici (MED-ih-chee) banking family. Though not public officers, Cosimo (1434–1464) and Lorenzo (1469–1492) ruled from behind the scenes. In central Italy Pope Alexander VI (1492–1503), aided militarily and politically by his son Cesare Borgia (CHE-zah-reh BAWR-zhuh), reasserted papal authority in the papal lands. South of the Papal States, the kingdom of Naples was under the control of Aragon.

The major Italian city-states controlled the smaller ones, such as Siena, Mantua, Ferrara, and Modena, and competed furiously among themselves for territory. The large cities used diplomacy, spies, paid informers, and any other available means to get information that could be used to advance their ambitions. While the states of northern Europe were moving toward centralization and consolidation, the world of Italian politics resembled a jungle where the powerful dominated the weak.

In one significant respect, however, the Italian city-states anticipated future relations among competing European states after 1500. Whenever one Italian state appeared to gain a predominant position within the peninsula, other states combined to establish a *balance of power* against the major threat. In the formation of these alliances, Renaissance Italians invented the machinery of modern diplomacy: permanent embassies with resident ambassadors in capitals where political relations and commercial ties needed continual monitoring. The resident ambassador was one of the great achievements of the Italian Renaissance.

MAP 13.1   The Italian City-States, ca. 1494
In the fifteenth century the Italian city-states represented great wealth and cultural sophistication. The political divisions of the peninsula invited foreign intervention.

At the end of the fifteenth century Venice, Florence, Milan, and the papacy possessed great wealth and represented high cultural achievement. Wealthy and divided, however, they were also an inviting target for invasion. When Florence and Naples entered into an agreement to acquire Milanese territories, Milan called on France for support.

The invasion of Italy in 1494 by the French king Charles VIII (r. 1483–1498) inaugurated a new period in Italian and European power politics. Italy became the focus of international ambitions and the battleground of foreign armies, particularly those of France and the Holy Roman Empire in a series of conflicts called the Habsburg-Valois (**HABZ-berg VAL-wah**) Wars (named for the German and

humanism The new philosophy that emphasized the critical study of Latin and Greek literature with the goal of understanding human nature.

individualism A basic feature of the Italian Renaissance that stressed personality, uniqueness, genius, and self-consciousness.

French dynasties). The Italian cities suffered severely from continual warfare, especially in the frightful sack of Rome in 1527 by imperial forces under the emperor Charles V. Thus the failure of the city-states to form some federal system, to consolidate, or at least to establish a common foreign policy led to centuries of subjection by outside invaders. Italy was not to achieve unification until 1870.

Intellectual Change

What were the key ideas of the Renaissance, and how were they different for men and women and for southern and northern Europeans?

The Renaissance was characterized by self-conscious awareness among fourteenth- and fifteenth-century Italians that they were living in a new era. The realization that something new and unique was happening first came to writers in the fourteenth century, especially to the poet and humanist Francesco Petrarch (**PEE-trahrk**) (1304–1374). Petrarch thought that he was living at the start of a new age, a period of light following a long night of Gothic gloom. For Petrarch, the Germanic migrations had caused a sharp cultural break with the glories of Rome and inaugurated what he called the "Dark Ages." Along with many of his contemporaries, Petrarch believed that he was witnessing a new golden age of intellectual achievement.

Humanism

Petrarch and other poets, writers, and artists showed a deep interest in the ancient past, in both the physical remains of the Roman Empire and classical Latin texts. The study of Latin classics became known as the *studia humanitates*, usually translated as "liberal studies" or the "liberal arts." Like all programs of study, the liberal arts contained an implicit philosophy, which was generally known as **humanism.** Humanism emphasized human beings, their achievements, interests, and capabilities. Whereas medieval writers looked to the classics to reveal God, Renaissance humanists studied the classics to understand human nature.

Renaissance humanists retained a Christian perspective, however: men (and women, though to a lesser degree) were made in the image and likeness of God. For example, in a remarkable essay, *On the Dignity of Man* (1486), the Florentine writer Giovanni Pico della Mirandola (1463–1494) stressed that man possesses great dignity because he was made as Adam in the image of God before the Fall and as Christ after the Resurrection. According to Pico, man's place in the universe is somewhere between the beasts and the angels, but because of the divine image planted in him, there are no limits to what he can accomplish. Humanists generally rejected classical ideas that were opposed to Christianity, or they sought through reinterpretation an underlying harmony between the pagan and secular and the Christian faith.

Interest in human achievement led humanists to emphasize the importance of the individual. Groups such as families, guilds, and religious organizations continued to provide strong support for the individual and to exercise great social influence. Yet in the Renaissance, artists and intellectuals, unlike their counterparts in the Middle Ages, prized their own uniqueness. This attitude of **individualism** stressed the full development of one's special capabilities and talents. The idea of the "genius" who transcends traditions and rules is believed to have originated in this period. Thirst for fame and the quest for glory drove Italian creativity. (See the feature "Individuals in Society: Leonardo da Vinci.")

Individuals in Society

Leonardo da Vinci

What makes a genius? An infinite capacity for taking pains? A deep curiosity about an extensive variety of subjects? A divine spark as manifested by talents that far exceed the norm? Or is it just "one percent inspiration and ninety-nine percent perspiration," as Thomas Edison said? To most observers, Leonardo da Vinci was one of the greatest geniuses in the history of the Western world. In fact, Leonardo was one of the individuals that the Renaissance label "genius" was designed to describe: a special kind of human being with exceptional creative powers.

Leonardo (who, despite the title of a recent bestseller and movie, is always called by his first name) was born in Vinci, near Florence, the illegitimate son of Caterina, a local peasant girl, and Ser Piero da Vinci, a notary public. Caterina later married another native of Vinci. When Ser Piero's marriage to Donna Albrussia produced no children, he and his wife took in Leonardo. Ser Piero secured Leonardo's apprenticeship with the painter and sculptor Andrea del Verrocchio in Florence. In 1472, when Leonardo was just twenty years old, he was listed as a master in Florence's "Company of Artists."

Leonardo's most famous portrait, *Mona Lisa*, shows a woman with an enigmatic smile that Giorgio Vasari described as "so pleasing that it seemed divine rather than human." The portrait, probably of the young wife of a rich Florentine merchant (her exact identity is hotly debated), may actually be the best-known painting in the history of art. One of its competitors in that designation would be another work of Leonardo's, *The Last Supper*, which has been called "the most revered painting in the world."

Leonardo's reputation as a genius does not rest simply on his paintings, however, which are actually few in number, but rather on the breadth of his abilities and interests. In these, he is often understood to be the first "Renaissance man," a phrase we still use for a multi-talented individual. He wanted to reproduce what the eye can see, and he drew everything he saw around him, including executed criminals hanging on gallows as well as the beauties of nature. Trying to understand how the human body worked, Leonardo studied live and dead bodies, doing autopsies and dissections to investigate muscles and circulation. He carefully analyzed the effects of light, using his analysis to paint strong contrasts of light and shadow, and he experimented with perspective.

Leonardo used his drawings as the basis for his paintings and also as a tool of scientific investigation. He drew plans for hundreds of inventions, many of which would become reality centuries later, such as the helicopter, tank, machine gun, and parachute. He was hired by one of the powerful new rulers in Italy, Duke Ludovico Sforza of Milan, to design practical things that the duke needed, including weapons, fortresses, and water systems, as well as to produce works of art. Leonardo left Milan when Sforza was overthrown in war and spent the last years of his life painting, drawing, and designing for the pope and the French king.

Leonardo experimented with new materials for painting and sculpture, some of which worked and some of which did not. The experimental method he used to paint *The Last Supper* caused the picture to deteriorate rapidly, and it began to flake off the wall as soon as it was finished. Leonardo actually regarded it as never quite completed, for he could not find a model for the face of Christ that would evoke the spiritual depth he felt it deserved. His gigantic equestrian statue in honor of Ludovico's father, Duke Francesco Sforza, was never made. The clay model collapsed, and only notes survived. He planned to write books on many subjects but never finished any of them, leaving only notebooks. Leonardo once said that "a painter is not admirable unless he is universal." The patrons who supported him—and he was supported very well—perhaps wished that his inspirations would have been a bit less universal in scope, or at least accompanied by more perspiration.

Leonardo da Vinci, *Lady with an Ermine*. The enigmatic smile and smoky quality of this portrait can be found in many of Leonardo's works. (Czartoryski Museum, Krakow/The Bridgeman Art Library)

Questions for Analysis

1. In what ways do the notion of a "genius" and of a "Renaissance man" support one another? In what ways do they contradict one another? Which seems a better description of Leonardo?

2. Has the idea of artistic genius changed since the Renaissance? How?

Sources: Giorgio Vasari, *Lives of the Artists*, vol. 1, trans. G. Bull (London: Penguin Books, 1965); S. B. Nuland, *Leonardo da Vinci* (New York: Lipper/Viking, 2000).

Education

One of the central preoccupations of the humanists was education and moral behavior. Humanists poured out treatises, often in the form of letters, on the structure and goals of education and the training of rulers. They taught that a life active in the world should be the aim of all educated individuals and that education was not simply for private or religious purposes, but benefited the public good.

Humanists put their ideas into practice. They opened schools and academies in Italian cities and courts in which pupils began with Latin grammar and rhetoric, went on to study Roman history and political philosophy, and then learned Greek in order to study Greek literature and philosophy. These classics, humanists taught, would provide models of how to write clearly, argue effectively, and speak persuasively, important skills for future diplomats, lawyers, military leaders, businessmen, and politicians. Gradually, humanist education became the basis for intermediate and advanced education for a large share of the males of the middle and upper classes.

Humanists were ambivalent about education for women. While they saw the value of exposing women to classical models of moral behavior and reasoning, they also thought that a program of study that emphasized eloquence and action was not proper for women, whose sphere was private and domestic. Humanists never established schools for girls, though a few women of very high social status did gain a humanist education from private tutors. The ideal Renaissance woman looked a great deal more like her medieval counterpart than did the Renaissance man.

The Prince A treatise by Machiavelli on ways to gain, keep, and expand power; because of its subsequent impact it is probably the most important literary work of the Renaissance.

No book on education had broader influence than Baldassare Castiglione's (ball-duh-SAH-ree kah-stee-lee-OW-nee) *The Courtier* (1528). This treatise sought to train, discipline, and fashion the young man into the courtly ideal, the gentleman. According to Castiglione, who himself was a courtier serving several different rulers, the educated man of the upper class should have a broad background in many academic subjects, and his spiritual and physical as well as intellectual capabilities should be trained. Castiglione envisioned a man who could compose a sonnet, wrestle, sing a song and accompany himself on an instrument, ride expertly, solve difficult mathematical problems, and, above all, speak and write eloquently. Castiglione also included discussion of the perfect court lady, who, like the courtier, was to be well educated and able to play a musical instrument, to paint, and to dance. Physical beauty, delicacy, affability, and modesty were also important qualities for court ladies.

Political Thought

No Renaissance book on any topic has been more widely read than the short political treatise *The Prince* by Niccolò Machiavelli (NICK-oh-loh mak-ee-uh-VEL-ee) (1469–1527). The subject of *The Prince* (1513) is

Raphael: Portrait of Castiglione

In this portrait by Raphael, the most sought-after portrait painter of the Renaissance, Castiglione is shown dressed exactly as he advised courtiers to dress, in elegant, but subdued clothing that would enhance the splendor of the court, but never outshine the ruler. (Scala/Art Resource, NY)

political power: how the ruler should gain, maintain, and increase it. Its hero is Cesare Borgia, who ruthlessly conquered the Papal States and exacted total obedience from them (see page 310). As a good humanist, Machiavelli explores the problems of human nature and concludes that human beings are selfish and out to advance their own interests. This pessimistic view of humanity led him to maintain that the prince might have to manipulate the people in any way he finds necessary:

> For a man who, in all respects, will carry out only his professions of good, will be apt to be ruined amongst so many who are evil. A prince therefore who desires to maintain himself must learn to be not always good, but to be so or not as necessity may require.[1]

The prince should combine the cunning of a fox with the ferocity of a lion to achieve his goals. Asking rhetorically whether it is better for a ruler to be loved or feared, Machiavelli writes, "It will naturally be answered that it would be desirable to be both the one and the other; but as it is difficult to be both at the same time, it is much more safe to be feared than to be loved, when you have to choose between the two."[2]

Unlike medieval political theorists, Machiavelli maintained that the ruler should be concerned with the way things actually are rather than aiming for an ethical ideal. The sole test of a "good" government is whether it is effective, whether the ruler increases his power. Machiavelli did not advocate amoral behavior, but he believed that political action cannot be restricted by moral considerations. Nevertheless, on the basis of a crude interpretation of *The Prince*, the word *Machiavellian* entered the language as a synonym for the politically devious, corrupt, and crafty, indicating actions in which the end justifies the means. The ultimate significance of Machiavelli rests on two ideas: first, that one permanent social order reflecting God's will cannot be established, and second, that politics has its own laws, based on expediency, not morality.

Secular Spirit

Machiavelli's *The Prince* is often seen as a prime example of another aspect of the Renaissance, secularism. Secularism involves a basic concern with the material world instead of with the eternal world of spirit. A secular way of thinking tends to find the ultimate explanation of everything and the final end of human beings within the limits of what the senses can discover. Even though medieval business people ruthlessly pursued profits and medieval monks fought fiercely over property, the dominant ideals focused on the otherworldly, on life after death. Renaissance people often had strong and deep spiritual interests, but in their increasingly secular society, attention was concentrated on the here and now. Wealth allowed greater material pleasures, a more comfortable life, and the leisure time to appreciate and patronize the arts. The rich, social-climbing residents of Venice, Florence, Genoa, and Rome came to see life more as an opportunity to be enjoyed than as a painful pilgrimage to the City of God.

In *On Pleasure*, humanist Lorenzo Valla (**VAHL-lah**) (1406–1457) defends the pleasures of the senses as the highest good. Scholars praise Valla as a father of modern historical criticism. His study *On the False Donation of Constantine* (1444) demonstrates by careful textual examination that an anonymous eighth-century document supposedly giving the papacy jurisdiction over vast territories in western Europe was a forgery. Medieval people had accepted the Donation of Constantine as a reality, and the proof that it was an invention weakened the foundations of

secularism A way of thinking that tends to find the ultimate explanation of everything and the final end of human beings in what reason and the senses can discover, rather than in any spiritual or transcendental belief.

Bennozzo Gozzoli: Procession of the Magi, 1461
This segment of a huge fresco covering three walls of a chapel in the Medici Palace in Florence shows members of the Medici family and other contemporary individuals in a procession accompanying the biblical three wise men as they brought gifts to the infant Jesus. Reflecting the self-confidence of his patrons, Gozzoli places the elderly Cosimo and Piero at the head of the procession, accompanied by their grooms. (Scala/Art Resource, NY)

papal claims to temporal authority. Lorenzo Valla's work exemplifies the application of critical scholarship to old and almost sacred writings as well as the new secular spirit of the Renaissance.

The tales in *The Decameron* (1350–1353), by the Florentine Giovanni Boccaccio (**jo-VAH-nee boh-KAH-chee-oh**) (1313–1375), which describe ambitious merchants, lecherous friars, and cuckolded husbands, portray a frankly acquisitive, sensual, and worldly society. Although Boccaccio's figures were stock literary characters, *The Decameron* contains none of the "contempt of the world" theme so pervasive in medieval literature. Renaissance writers justified the accumulation and enjoyment of wealth with references to ancient authors.

Nor did church leaders do much to combat the new secular spirit. In the fifteenth and early sixteenth centuries, the papal court and the households of the cardinals were just as worldly as those of great urban patricians. Of course, most of the popes and higher church officials had come from the bourgeois aristocracy. Renaissance popes beautified the city of Rome, patronized artists and men of letters, and expended enormous enthusiasm and huge sums of money. Pope Julius II (1503–1513) tore down the old Saint Peter's Basilica and began work on the present structure in 1506. Michelangelo's dome for Saint Peter's is still considered his greatest architectural work.

Despite their interest in secular matters, however, few people (including Machiavelli) questioned the basic tenets of the Christian religion. The thousands of pious paintings, sculptures, processions, and pilgrimages of the Renaissance period prove that strong religious feeling persisted.

Christian Humanism

In the last quarter of the fifteenth century, students from the Low Countries, France, Germany, and England flocked to Italy, imbibed the "new learning," and carried it back to their own countries. Northern humanists, often called **Christian humanists**, interpreted Italian ideas about and attitudes toward classical antiquity, individualism, and humanism in terms of their own traditions. They developed a program for broad social reform based on Christian ideals.

Christian humanists were interested in an ethical way of life. To achieve it, they believed that the best elements of classical and Christian cultures should be combined. For example, the classical ideals of calmness, stoical patience, and

Christian humanists Northern humanists who interpreted Italian ideas about and attitudes toward classical antiquity, individualism, and humanism in terms of their own traditions.

broad-mindedness should be joined in human conduct with the Christian virtues of love, faith, and hope. Northern humanists also stressed the use of reason, rather than acceptance of dogma, as the foundation for an ethical way of life. They believed that, although human nature had been corrupted by sin, it was fundamentally good and capable of improvement through education.

The Englishman Thomas More (1478–1535) envisioned a society that would bring out this inherent goodness in his revolutionary book *Utopia* (1516). *Utopia*, whose title means both "a good place" and "nowhere," describes an ideal community on an island somewhere off the mainland of the New World. All children receive a good education, primarily in the Greco-Roman classics, and learning does not cease with maturity, for the goal of all education is to develop rational faculties. Adults divide their days between manual labor or business pursuits and intellectual activities. Because profits from business and property are held in common, there is absolute social equality. Citizens of Utopia lead an ideal, nearly perfect existence because they live by reason; their institutions are perfect.

Contrary to the long-prevailing view that vice and violence existed because people were basically corrupt, More maintained that acquisitiveness and private property promoted all sorts of vices and civil disorders. Since society protected private property, society's flawed institutions were responsible for corruption and war. According to More, the key to improvement and reform of the individual was reform of the social institutions that molded the individual. His ideas were profoundly original in the sixteenth century.

Better known by contemporaries than Thomas More was the Dutch humanist Desiderius Erasmus (**dez-ih-DARE-ee-us uh-RAZ-muhs**) (1466?–1536) of Rotterdam. His fame rested largely on his exceptional knowledge of Greek and the Bible. Erasmus's long list of publications includes *The Education of a Christian Prince* (1504), a book combining idealistic and practical suggestions for the formation of a ruler's character through the careful study of Plutarch, Aristotle, Cicero, and Plato; *The Praise of Folly* (1509), a satire of worldly wisdom and a plea for the simple and spontaneous Christian faith of children; and, most important, a critical edition of the Greek New Testament (1516). In the preface to the New Testament, Erasmus explained the purpose of his great work:

> I wish that even the weakest woman should read the Gospel—should read the epistles of Paul. And I wish these were translated into all languages, so that they might be read and understood, not only by Scots and Irishmen, but also by Turks and Saracens.[3]

Two fundamental themes run through all of Erasmus's work. First, education is the means to reform, the key to moral and intellectual improvement. The core of education ought to be study of the Bible and the classics. (See the feature "Listening to the Past: An Age of Gold" on pages 335–336.) Second, the essence of Erasmus's thought is, in his own phrase, "the philosophy of Christ." By this Erasmus meant that Christianity is an inner attitude of the heart or spirit. Christianity is not formalism, special ceremonies, or law; Christianity is Christ—his life and what he said and did, not what theologians have written.

The Printed Word

The fourteenth-century humanist Petrarch and the sixteenth-century humanist Erasmus had similar ideas about many things, but the immediate impact of their ideas was very different because of one thing: the printing press with movable metal type. The ideas of Petrarch were spread slowly from person to person by

The Print Shop

This sixteenth-century engraving captures the busy world of a print shop. On the left, men set pieces of type, and an individual wearing glasses checks a copy. At the rear, another applies ink to the type, while a man carries in fresh paper on his head. At the right, the master printer operates the press, while a boy removes the printed pages and sets them to dry. The well-dressed figure in the right foreground may be the patron checking to see whether his job is done. (Giraudon/Art Resource, NY)

hand copying. The ideas of Erasmus were spread quickly through print, in which hundreds or thousands of identical copies could be made in a short time. Print shops were gathering places for those interested in new ideas. Though printers were trained through apprenticeships just like blacksmiths or butchers, they had connections to the world of politics, art, and scholarship that other craftsmen did not.

Printing with movable metal type developed in Germany in the middle of the fifteenth century as a combination of existing technologies. Several metalsmiths, most prominently Johan Gutenberg, recognized that the metal stamps used to mark signs on jewelry could be covered with ink and used to mark symbols onto a surface, in the same way that other craftsmen were using carved wood stamps to print books. (This woodblock printing technique originated in China and Korea centuries earlier.) Gutenberg and his assistants made stamps—later called *type*—for every letter of the alphabet and built racks that held the type in rows. This type could be rearranged for every page and so used over and over. The printing revolution was also enabled by the ready availability of paper, which was also made using techniques that had originated in China.

Gutenberg's invention involved no special secret technology or materials, and he was not the only one to recognize the huge market for books. Other craftsmen made their own type, built their own presses, and bought their own paper, setting themselves up in business (see Map 13.2). Historians estimate that somewhere between 8 million and 20 million books were printed in this manner in Europe before 1500, many more than the number of books produced in all of Western history up to that point.

The effects of the invention of movable-type printing were not felt overnight. Nevertheless, within a half century of the publication of Gutenberg's Bible of 1456, movable type had brought about radical changes. Printing transformed both the private and the public lives of Europeans. It gave hundreds or even thousands of people identical books, so that they could more easily discuss the ideas that the

MAPPING THE PAST

MAP 13.2 The Growth of Printing in Europe

The speed with which artisans spread printing technology across Europe provides strong evidence for the existing market in reading material. Presses in the Ottoman Empire were first established by Jewish immigrants who printed works in Hebrew, Greek, and Spanish. Use this map and those in other chapters to answer the following questions: **[1]** What part of Europe had the greatest number of printing presses by 1550? Why might this be? **[2]** Printing was developed in response to a market for reading materials. Use Maps 11.1 and 11.2 (pages 254 and 260) to help explain why printing spread the way it did. **[3]** Many historians also see printing as an important factor in the spread of the Protestant Reformation. Use Map 14.2 (page 358) to test this assertion.

books contained with one another in person or through letters. Printed materials reached an invisible public, allowing silent individuals to join causes and groups of individuals widely separated by geography to form a common identity; this new group consciousness could compete with older, localized loyalties.

Government and church leaders both used and worried about printing. They printed laws, declarations of war, battle accounts, and propaganda, and they also attempted to censor books and authors whose ideas they thought were wrong. Officials developed lists of prohibited books and authors, enforcing their prohibitions by confiscating books, arresting printers and booksellers, or destroying the presses of printers who disobeyed. None of this was very effective, and books were printed secretly, with fake title pages, authors, and places of publication, and smuggled all over Europe.

Printing also stimulated the literacy of laypeople and eventually came to have a deep effect on their private lives. Although most of the earliest books and pamphlets dealt with religious subjects, printers produced anything that would sell. They printed professional reference sets for lawyers, doctors, and students, and historical romances, biographies, and how-to manuals for the general public. They discovered that illustrations increased a book's sales, so they published both history and pornography full of woodcuts and engravings. Single-page broadsides and flysheets allowed great public events and "wonders" such as comets or two-headed calves to be experienced vicariously by a stay-at-home readership. Since books and other printed materials were read aloud to illiterate listeners, print bridged the gap between the written and oral cultures.

Art and the Artist

How did changes in art both reflect and shape new ideas?

No feature of the Renaissance evokes greater admiration than its artistic masterpieces. The 1400s (*quattrocento*) and 1500s (*cinquecento*) bore witness to dazzling creativity in painting, architecture, and sculpture. In all the arts, the city of Florence led the way. But Florence was not the only artistic center, for Rome and Venice also became important, and northern Europeans perfected their own styles.

Art and Power

In early Renaissance Italy, powerful urban groups commissioned works of art. The Florentine cloth merchants, for example, delegated Filippo Brunelleschi (Fill-EEP-oh broon-el-ES-kee) to build the magnificent dome on the cathedral of Florence and selected Lorenzo Ghiberti (law-REN-tsow gee-BER-tee) to design the bronze doors of the Baptistery. These works represented the merchants' dominant influence in the community.

Increasingly in the later fifteenth century, individuals and oligarchs, rather than corporate groups, sponsored works of art. Patrician merchants and bankers and popes and princes spent vast sums on the arts as a means of glorifying themselves and their families. Patrons varied in their level of involvement as a work progressed; some simply ordered a specific subject or scene, while others oversaw the work of the artist or architect very closely, suggesting themes and styles and demanding changes while the work was in progress.

In addition to power, art reveals changing patterns of consumption in Renaissance Italy. In the rural world of the Middle Ages, society had been organized for war and men of wealth spent their money on military gear. As Italian nobles settled in towns (see page 248), they adjusted to an urban culture. Rather than employing knights for warfare, cities hired mercenaries. Expenditure on military hardware declined. For the rich merchant or the noble recently arrived from the countryside, a grand urban palace represented the greatest outlay of cash. Wealthy individuals and families ordered gold dishes, embroidered tablecloths, wall tapestries, paintings on canvas (an innovation), and sculptural decorations to adorn their homes. By the late sixteenth century the Strozzi banking family of Florence spent more on household goods than on anything else except food; the value of those furnishings was three times that of their silver and jewelry.

After the palace itself, the private chapel within the palace symbolized the largest expenditure for the wealthy of the sixteenth century. Decorated with religious scenes and equipped with ecclesiastical furniture, the chapel served as the center of the household's religious life and its cult of remembrance of the dead.

Subjects and Style

The content and style of Renaissance art were often different from those of the Middle Ages. The individual portrait emerged as a distinct artistic genre. In the fifteenth century members of the newly rich middle class often had themselves painted in scenes of romantic chivalry or courtly society. Rather than reflecting a spiritual ideal, as medieval painting and sculpture tended to do, Renaissance portraits showed human ideals, often portrayed in a more realistic style. The Florentine painter Giotto (**JAW-toh**) (1276–1337) led the way in the use of realism; his treatment of the human body and face replaced the formal stiffness and artificiality that had long characterized representation of the human body. Piero della Francesca (1420–1492) and Andrea Mantegna (1430/31–1506) seem to have pioneered *perspective* in painting, the linear representation of distance and space on a flat surface. The sculptor Donatello (1386–1466) revived the classical figure, with its balance and self-awareness. In architecture, Filippo Brunelleschi (1377–1446) looked to the classical past for inspiration, designing a hospital for orphans and

Botticelli: Primavera, or Spring (ca. 1482)
Venus, the Roman goddess of love, is flanked on her left by Flora, goddess of flowers and fertility, and on her right by the Three Graces, goddesses of banquets, dance, and social occasions. Above, Venus's son Cupid, the god of love, shoots darts of desire, while at the far right the wind god Zephyrus chases the nymph Chloris. Botticelli captured the ideal for female beauty in the Renaissance: slender, with pale skin, a high forehead, red-blond hair, and sloping shoulders. (Digital image © The Museum of Modern Art/Licensed by Scala/Art Resource, NY)

Rogier van der Weyden: Deposition

Taking as his subject the suffering and death of Jesus, a popular theme of Netherlandish piety, van der Weyden describes (in an inverted T) Christ's descent from the cross, surrounded by nine sorrowing figures. An appreciation of human anatomy, the rich fabrics of the clothes, and the pierced and bloody hands of Jesus were all intended to touch the viewers' emotions. (Museo del Prado/Scala/Art Resource, NY)

foundlings in which all proportions—of the windows, height, floor plan, and covered walkway with a series of rounded arches—were carefully thought out to achieve a sense of balance and harmony. As the fifteenth century advanced, classical themes and motifs, such as the lives and loves of pagan gods and goddesses, figured increasingly in painting and sculpture. Religious topics, such as the Annunciation of the Virgin and the Nativity, remained popular among both patrons and artists, but frequently the patron had himself and his family portrayed in the scene.

Art produced in northern Europe in the fourteenth and fifteenth centuries tended to be more religious in orientation than that produced in Italy. Some Flemish painters, notably Rogier van der Weyden (1399/1400–1464) and Jan van Eyck (1366–1441), were considered the artistic equals of Italian painters and were much admired in Italy. Van Eyck, one of the earliest artists to use oil-based paints successfully, shows the Flemish love for detail in paintings such as *Ghent Altarpiece* and the portrait *Giovanni Arnolfini and His Bride*; the effect is great realism and remarkable attention to human personality. Northern architecture was little influenced by the classical revival so obvious in Renaissance Italy.

In the fifteenth century the center of the new art shifted to Rome, where wealthy cardinals and popes wanted visual expression of the church's and their own families' power and piety. Michelangelo, a Florentine who had spent his young adulthood at the court of Lorenzo de' Medici, went to Rome in about 1500 and began the series of statues, paintings, and architectural projects from which he gained an international reputation: the Pieta, Moses, the redesigning of the Capitoline Hill in central Rome, and, most famously, the ceiling and altar wall of the Sistine Chapel. Pope Julius II, who commissioned the Sistine Chapel, demanded that Michelangelo work as fast as he could and frequently visited the artist at his work with suggestions and criticisms. Michelangelo complained in person and by letter about the pope's meddling, but his reputation did not match the power of the pope, and he kept working.

Raphael Sanzio (rah-fahy-EL) (1483–1520), another Florentine, got the commission for frescoes in the papal apartments, and in his relatively short life he painted hundreds of portraits and devotional images, becoming the most sought-after artist in Europe. Raphael also oversaw a large workshop with many collaborators and apprentices—who assisted on the less difficult sections of some paintings—and wrote treatises on his philosophy of art in which he emphasized the importance of imitating nature and developing an orderly sequence of design and proportion.

Venice became another artistic center in the sixteenth century. Titian (TISH-uhn) (1490–1576) produced portraits, religious subjects, and mythological scenes, developing techniques of painting in oil without doing elaborate drawings first, which speeded up the process and pleased patrons eager to display their acquisition. Titian and other sixteenth-century painters developed an artistic style known in English as "mannerism" (from *maniera* or "style" in Italian) in which artists sometimes distorted figures, exaggerated musculature, and heightened color to express emotion and drama more intently. (This is the style in which Michelangelo painted the Last Judgment in the Sistine Chapel, shown in the frontispiece to this chapter.)

Whether in Italy or northern Europe, most Renaissance artists trained in the workshops of older artists; Botticelli, Raphael, Titian, and at times even Michelangelo were known for their large, well-run, and prolific workshops. Though they might be "men of genius," artists were still expected to be well trained in proper artistic techniques and stylistic conventions, for the notion that artistic genius could show up in the work of an untrained artist did not emerge until the twentieth century. Beginning artists spent years copying drawings and paintings, learning how to prepare paint and other artistic materials, and, by the sixteenth century, reading books about design and composition. Younger artists gathered together in the evenings for further drawing practice; by the later sixteenth century some of these informal groups had turned into more formal artistic "academies," the first of which was begun in 1563 in Florence by Vasari under the patronage of the Medicis.

The types of art in which more women were active, such as textiles, needlework, and painting on porcelain, were not regarded as "major arts," but only as "minor" or "decorative" arts. Like painting, embroidery changed in the Renaissance to become more classical in its subject matter, naturalistic, and visually complex. Embroiderers were not trained to view their work as products of individual genius, however, so they rarely included their names on their works, and there is no way to discover who they were.

Several women did become well known as painters in their day. Stylistically, their works are different from one another, but their careers show many similarities. The majority of female painters were the daughters of painters or of minor noblemen with ties to artistic circles. Many were eldest daughters or came from families in which there were no sons, so their fathers took unusual interest in their

Artemisia Gentileschi: Esther Before Ahasuerus (ca. 1630)

In this oil painting, Gentileschi (**jen-tee-LES-kee**) shows an Old Testament scene of the Jewish woman Esther who saved her people from being killed by her husband, King Ahasuerus. This deliverance is celebrated in the Jewish holiday of Purim. Both figures are in the elaborate dress worn in Renaissance courts. Typical of a female painter, Artemisia Gentileschi was trained by her father. She mastered the dramatic style favored in the early seventeenth century and became known especially for her portraits of strong biblical and mythological heroines.

(Image copyright © The Metropolitan Museum of Art/Art Resource, NY)

Section Review

- Individuals and oligarchs spent elaborate sums on works of art to display their wealth and power.

- Art began to be more realistic and show human ideals, often portraying individuals or families.

- Rome and Venice gained international fame as art centers, producing artists such as Michelangelo, Raphael Sanzio, and the "mannerism" painter, Titian.

- Leonardo da Vinci epitomized the "Renaissance man" as a painter, scientist, and inventor.

- Young artists became apprentices, creating formal groups called "academies" that excluded women.

careers. Many women began their careers before they were twenty and produced far fewer paintings after they married, or stopped painting entirely. Women were not allowed to study the male nude, which was viewed as essential if one wanted to paint large history paintings with many figures. Women could also not learn the technique of fresco, in which colors are applied directly to wet plaster walls, because such works had to be done out in public, which was judged inappropriate for women. Joining a group of male artists for informal practice was also seen as improper, and the artistic academies that were established were for men only. Like universities, humanist academies, and most craft guild shops, artistic workshops were male-only settings in which men of different ages came together for training and created bonds of friendship, influence, patronage, and sometimes intimacy.

Women were not alone in being excluded from the institutions of Renaissance culture. Though a few "rare men of genius" such as Leonardo or Michelangelo emerged from artisanal backgrounds, most scholars and artists came from families with at least some money. Renaissance culture did not influence the lives of most people in cities and did not affect life in the villages at all. A small, highly educated minority of literary humanists and artists created the culture of and for an exclusive elite. The Renaissance maintained, or indeed enhanced, a gulf between the learned minority and the uneducated multitude that has survived for many centuries.

Social Hierarchies

What were the key social hierarchies in Renaissance Europe, and how did ideas about hierarchy shape people's lives?

The division between educated and uneducated people was only one of many social hierarchies evident in the Renaissance. Every society has social hierarchies; in ancient Rome, for example, there were patricians and plebeians (see page 89).

Such hierarchies are to some degree descriptions of social reality, but they are also idealizations—that is, they describe how people *imagined* their society to be, without all the messy reality of social-climbing plebeians or groups that did not fit the standard categories. Social hierarchies in the Renaissance built on those of the Middle Ages but also developed new features that contributed to modern social hierarchies.

Race

Renaissance people did not use the word *race* the way we do, but often used "race," "people," and "nation" interchangeably for ethnic, national, and religious groups—the French race, the Jewish nation, the Irish people, and so on. They did make distinctions based on skin color that provide some of the background for later conceptualizations of race, but these distinctions were interwoven with other characteristics when people thought about human differences.

Ever since the time of the Roman republic, a few black Africans had lived in western Europe. They had come, along with white slaves, as the spoils of war. Even after the collapse of the Roman Empire, Muslim and Christian merchants continued to import them. Unstable political conditions in many parts of Africa enabled enterprising merchants to seize people and sell them into slavery. Local authorities afforded them no protection. Long tradition, moreover, sanctioned the practice of slavery. The evidence of medieval art attests to the continued presence of Africans in Europe throughout the Middle Ages and to Europeans' awareness of them.

Beginning in the fifteenth century sizable numbers of black slaves entered Europe. Portuguese sailors brought perhaps a thousand Africans a year to the markets of Seville, Barcelona, Marseilles (**mahr-SAY**), and Genoa. In the late fifteenth century this flow increased, with thousands of people leaving the west African coast. By 1530 between four thousand and five thousand were being sold to the Portuguese each year. By the mid-sixteenth century blacks, slave and free,

Carpaccio: Black Laborers on the Venetian Docks (detail)

Enslaved and free blacks, besides working as gondoliers on the Venetian canals, served on the docks: here, seven black men careen—clean, caulk, and repair—a ship. Carpaccio's (**kahr-PAH-choh**) reputation as one of Venice's outstanding painters rests on his eye for details of everyday life. (Gallerie dell'Accademia, Venice/Scala/Art Resource, NY)

constituted about 10 percent of the population of the Portuguese cities of Lisbon and Évora and roughly 3 percent of the Portuguese population. In the Iberian peninsula, African slaves intermingled with the people they lived among and sometimes intermarried. Cities such as Lisbon had significant numbers of people of mixed African and European descent.

Although blacks were concentrated in the Iberian Peninsula, there must have been some Africans in northern Europe as well. In the 1580s, for example, Queen Elizabeth I of England complained that there were too many "blackamoores" competing with needy English people for places as domestic servants.[4] Black servants were much sought after; the medieval interest in curiosities, the exotic, and the marvelous continued in the Renaissance. Italian aristocrats had their portraits painted with their black pageboys to indicate their wealth (see the illustration on page 316, in which Gozzoli's depiction of Cosimo de' Medici shows him with a black groom). Blacks were so greatly in demand at the Renaissance courts of northern Italy, in fact, that the Venetians defied papal threats of excommunication to secure them. In 1491 Isabella of Este, duchess of Mantua, instructed her agent to secure a black girl between four and eight years old, "shapely and as black as possible." The duchess saw the child as a source of entertainment: "We shall make her very happy and shall have great fun with her." She hoped the girl would become "the best buffoon in the world,"[5] as the cruel ancient practice of a noble household's retaining a professional "fool" for the family's amusement persisted through the Renaissance—and down to the twentieth century. Tradition, stretching back at least as far as the thirteenth century, connected blacks with music and dance. In Renaissance Spain and Italy, blacks performed as dancers, as actors and actresses in courtly dramas, and as musicians, sometimes making up full orchestras.

Africans were not simply amusements at court. In Portugal, Spain, and Italy, slaves supplemented the labor force in virtually all occupations—as servants, agricultural laborers, craftsmen, and as seamen on ships going to Lisbon and Africa. Agriculture in Europe did not involve large plantations, so large-scale agricultural slavery did not develop there; African slaves formed the primary work force on the sugar plantations set up by Europeans on the Atlantic islands in the late fifteenth century, however (see page 386).

Until the voyages down the African coast in the late fifteenth century, Europeans had little concrete knowledge of Africans and their cultures. They perceived Africa as a remote place, the home of strange people isolated by heresy and Islam from superior European civilization. Africans' contact, even as slaves, with Christian Europeans could only "improve" the blacks, they thought. The expanding slave trade only reinforced negative preconceptions about the inferiority of black Africans.

Class

The notion of class—working class, middle class, upper class—did not exist in the Renaissance. By the thirteenth century, however, and even more so by the fifteenth, the idea of a changeable hierarchy based on wealth, what would later come to be termed "social class," was emerging alongside the medieval concept of orders (see page 221). This was particularly true in towns. Most residents of towns were technically members of the "third estate," that is "those who work" rather than "those who fight" and "those who pray." However, this group now included wealthy merchants who oversaw vast trading empires and lived in splendor that rivaled the richest nobles. As we saw earlier, in many cities these merchants had

Italian City Scene

In this detail from a fresco by the Italian painter Lorenzo Lotto, the artist captures the mixing of social groups in a Renaissance Italian city. The crowd of men in the right foreground includes wealthy merchants in elaborate hats and colorful coats. Two mercenary soldiers (carrying a sword and a pike), probably in hire to a condottiero, wear short doublets and tight hose stylishly slit to reveal colored undergarments, while boys play with toy weapons at their feet. Clothing like that of the soldiers, which emphasized the masculine form, was frequently the target of sumptuary laws both for its expense and its "indecency." At the left, women sell vegetables and bread, which would have been a common sight at any city marketplace. (Scala/Art Resource, NY)

gained political power to match their economic might, becoming merchant oligarchs who ruled through city councils.

The development of a hierarchy of wealth did not mean an end to the hierarchy of orders, however, and even poorer nobility still had higher status. If this had not been the case, wealthy Italian merchants would not have bothered to buy noble titles and country villas as they began doing in the fifteenth century, nor would wealthy English or Spanish merchants have been eager to marry their daughters and sons into often impoverished noble families. The nobility maintained its status in most parts of Europe not by maintaining rigid boundaries, but by taking in and integrating the new social elite of wealth.

Along with being tied to the hierarchy of orders, social status was also linked with considerations of honor. Among the nobility, for example, certain weapons and battle tactics were favored because they were viewed as more honorable. Among urban dwellers, certain occupations, such as city executioner or manager of the municipal brothel, might be well paid but were understood to be "dishonorable" and so of low status.

Gender

Renaissance people would not have understood the word *gender* to refer to categories of people, but they would have easily grasped the concept. Toward the end of the fourteenth century, learned men (and a few women) began what was termed the **"debate about women"** (*querelle des femmes*), a debate about women's character and nature that would last for centuries. Misogynist (mi-SOJ-uh-nist) critiques of women from both clerical and secular authors denounced females as devious, domineering, and demanding. In answer, several authors compiled long lists of famous and praiseworthy women exemplary for their loyalty, bravery, and morality. Christine de Pizan was among those writers who were not only interested in defending women, but also in exploring the reasons behind women's secondary status—that is, why the great philosophers, statesmen, and poets had generally been men. In this they were anticipating recent discussions about the "social construction of gender" by six hundred years. (See the feature "Listening to the Past: Christine de Pizan" in Chapter 12 on pages 305–306.)

debate about women Debate among writers and thinkers about women's qualities and proper role in society.

With the development of the printing press, popular interest in the debate about women grew, and works were translated, reprinted, and shared around Europe. Prints that juxtaposed female virtues and vices were also very popular, with the virtuous women depicted as those of the classical or biblical past and the vice-ridden dressed in contemporary clothes. The favorite metaphor for the virtuous wife was either the snail or the tortoise, both animals that never leave their "houses" and are totally silent, although such images were never as widespread as those depicting wives beating their husbands or hiding their lovers from them.

Beginning in the sixteenth century, the debate about women also became one about female rulers, sparked primarily by dynastic accidents in many countries, including Spain, England, France, and Scotland, which led to women serving as advisers to child kings or ruling in their own right (see pages 330 and 353). The questions were vigorously and at times viciously disputed. They directly concerned the social construction of gender: could a woman's being born into a royal family and educated to rule allow her to overcome the limitations of her sex? Should it? Or stated another way: which was (or should be) the stronger determinant of character and social role, gender or rank? There were no successful rebellions against female rulers simply because they were women, but in part this was because female rulers, especially Queen Elizabeth I of England, emphasized qualities regarded as masculine—physical bravery, stamina, wisdom, duty—whenever they appeared in public.

Ideas about women's and men's proper roles determined the actions of ordinary men and women even more forcefully. The dominant notion of the "true" man was that of the married head of household, so men whose class and age would have normally conferred political power but who remained unmarried did not participate to the same level as their married brothers. Unmarried men in Venice, for example, could not be part of the ruling council. Women were also understood as "married or to be married," even if the actual marriage patterns in Europe left many women (and men) unmarried until quite late in life (see page 298). This meant that women's work was not viewed as supporting a family—even if it did—and was valued less than men's. If they worked for wages, and many women did, women earned about half to two-thirds of what men did even for the same work. Of all the ways in which Renaissance society was hierarchically arranged—class, age, level of education, rank, race, occupation—gender was regarded as the most "natural" and therefore the most important to defend.

Section Review

- Social hierarchies of the Renaissance were based on how people imagined their societies to be, not on how society actually worked.

- Black Africans first came to Europe in Roman times as spoils of war, but were not present in great numbers until the Renaissance and the onset of the slave trade.

- Free and enslaved blacks worked in all occupations, but the wealthy sought them as exotic household novelties.

- The nobility maintained its status by integrating the newly economically and politically powerful merchant class.

- Female rulers maintained their power by assuming masculine qualities but debates emerged about women's secondary status.

Politics and the State in the Renaissance (ca. 1450–1521)

How did the nation-states of western Europe evolve in this period?

The High Middle Ages had witnessed the origins of many of the basic institutions of the modern state. Sheriffs, inquests, juries, circuit judges, professional bureaucracies, and representative assemblies all trace their origins to the twelfth and thirteenth centuries. The linchpin for the development of states, however, was strong monarchy, and during the period of the Hundred Years' War, no ruler in western Europe was able to provide effective leadership. The resurgent power of feudal nobilities weakened the centralizing work begun earlier.

Beginning in the fifteenth century, rulers utilized aggressive methods to rebuild their governments. First in Italy, then in France, England, and Spain, rulers began the work of reducing violence, curbing unruly nobles, and establishing domestic order. They emphasized royal majesty and royal sovereignty and insisted on the respect and loyalty of all subjects.

France

The Hundred Years' War left France drastically depopulated, commercially ruined, and agriculturally weak. Nonetheless, the ruler whom Joan of Arc had seen crowned at Reims, Charles VII (r. 1422–1461), revived the monarchy and France. He seemed an unlikely person to do so. Frail, indecisive, and burdened with questions about his paternity (his father had been deranged; his mother, notoriously promiscuous), Charles VII nevertheless began France's long recovery.

Charles reconciled the Burgundians and Armagnacs (**ahr-muhn-YAKZ**), who had been waging civil war for thirty years. By 1453 French armies had expelled the English from French soil except in Calais. Charles reorganized the royal council, giving increased influence to middle-class men, and strengthened royal finances through such taxes as the *gabelle* (**guh-BEL**) (on salt) and the *taille* (**teyl**) (land tax). These taxes remained the Crown's chief sources of income until the Revolution of 1789.

By establishing regular companies of cavalry and archers—recruited, paid, and inspected by the state—Charles created the first permanent royal army. His son Louis XI (r. 1461–1483), called the "Spider King" because of his treacherous character, improved upon Charles's army and used it to stop aristocratic brigandage and to curb urban independence. The army was also employed in 1477, when Louis conquered Burgundy upon the death of its ruler Charles the Bold. Three years later, the extinction of the house of Anjou (**AN-joo**) brought Louis the counties of Anjou, Bar, Maine, and Provence.

Two further developments strengthened the French monarchy. The marriage of Louis XII (r. 1498–1515) and Anne of Brittany added the large western duchy of Brittany to the state. Then the French king Francis I and Pope Leo X reached a mutually satisfactory agreement about church and state powers in 1516. The new treaty, the Concordat of Bologna, approved the pope's right to receive the first year's income of new bishops and abbots. In return, Leo X recognized the French ruler's right to select French bishops and abbots. French kings thereafter effectively controlled the appointment and thus the policies of church officials in the kingdom.

England

English society suffered severely from the disorders of the fifteenth century. The aristocracy dominated the government of Henry IV (r. 1399–1413) and indulged in mischievous violence at the local level. Population, decimated by the Black Death, continued to decline. Between 1455 and 1471 adherents of the ducal houses of York and Lancaster waged civil war, commonly called the **Wars of the Roses** because the symbol of the Yorkists was a white rose and that of the Lancastrians a red one. The chronic disorder hurt trade, agriculture, and domestic industry. Under the pious but mentally disturbed Henry VI (r. 1422–1461), the authority of the monarchy sank lower than it had been in centuries.

The Yorkist Edward IV (r. 1461–1483) began establishing domestic tranquility. He succeeded in defeating the Lancastrian forces and after 1471 began to reconstruct the monarchy. Edward, his brother Richard III (r. 1483–1485), and Henry VII (r. 1485–1509) of the Welsh house of Tudor worked to restore royal

Wars of the Roses Civil war in England over who would become the next king.

prestige, to crush the power of the nobility, and to establish order and law at the local level. All three rulers used methods that Machiavelli himself would have praised—ruthlessness, efficiency, and secrecy.

Edward IV and subsequently the Tudors, excepting Henry VIII, conducted foreign policy on the basis of diplomacy, avoiding expensive wars. Thus the English monarchy did not depend on Parliament for money, and the Crown undercut that source of aristocratic influence.

Henry VII did summon several meetings of Parliament in the early years of his reign, primarily to confirm laws, but the center of royal authority was the **royal council,** which governed at the national level. There Henry VII revealed his distrust of the nobility: though not completely excluded, very few great lords were among the king's closest advisers. Regular representatives on the council numbered between twelve and fifteen men, and while many gained high ecclesiastical rank, their origins were in the lesser landowning class, and their education was in law. They were, in a sense, middle class.

The royal council handled any business the king put before it—executive, legislative, and judicial. For example, the council conducted negotiations with foreign governments and secured international recognition of the Tudor dynasty through the marriage in 1501 of Henry VII's eldest son Arthur to Catherine of Aragon, the daughter of Ferdinand and Isabella of Spain. The council dealt with real or potential aristocratic threats through a judicial offshoot, the **court of Star Chamber,** so called because of the stars painted on the ceiling of the room. The court applied principles of Roman law, and its methods were sometimes terrifying: accused persons were not entitled to see evidence against them; sessions were secret; torture could be applied to extract confessions; and juries were not called. These procedures ran directly counter to English common-law precedents, but they effectively reduced aristocratic troublemaking. Because the government halted the long period of anarchy, it won the key support of the merchant and agricultural upper middle class.

Secretive, cautious, and thrifty, Henry VII rebuilt the monarchy. He encouraged the cloth industry and built up the English merchant marine. English exports of wool and the royal export tax on that wool steadily increased. Henry crushed an invasion from Ireland and secured peace with Scotland through the marriage of his daughter Margaret to the Scottish king. When Henry VII died in 1509, he left a country at peace both domestically and internationally, a substantially augmented treasury, and the dignity and role of the royal majesty much enhanced.

royal council The body of men who represented the center of royal authority; Renaissance princes tended to prefer middle-class councilors to noble ones.

court of Star Chamber A division of the English royal council, a court that used Roman legal procedures to curb real or potential threats from the nobility, so named because of the stars painted on the ceiling of the chamber in which the court sat.

Spain

While England and France laid the foundations of unified nation-states during the Renaissance, Spain remained a conglomerate of independent kingdoms. By the middle of the fifteenth century, the kingdoms of Castile and Aragon dominated the weaker Navarre, Portugal, and Granada, and the Iberian Peninsula, with the exception of Granada, had been won for Christianity. But even the wedding in 1469 of the dynamic and aggressive Isabella of Castile and the crafty and persistent Ferdinand of Aragon did not bring about administrative unity. Rather, their marriage constituted a dynastic union of two royal houses, not the political union of two peoples. Although Ferdinand and Isabella (r. 1474–1516) pursued a common foreign policy, until about 1700 Spain existed as a loose confederation of separate kingdoms, each maintaining its own *cortes* (parliament), laws, courts, and systems of coinage and taxation. Ferdinand and Isabella were able to exert their authority in ways similar to the rulers of France and England, however. They curbed aristocratic power by excluding aristocrats and great territorial magnates from the royal council, which had full executive, judicial, and legislative powers under the monarchy. Instead they appointed only people of middle-class background to the council. The council and various government boards recruited men trained in Roman law, which exalted the power of the Crown. They also secured from the Spanish pope Alexander VI the right to appoint bishops in Spain and in the Hispanic territories in America, enabling them to establish the equivalent of a national church. And with the revenues from ecclesiastical estates, they were able to expand their territories to include the remaining land held by Arabs in southern Spain. The victorious entry of Ferdinand and Isabella into Granada on January 6, 1492, signaled the conclusion of the reconquista (see Map 9.3 on page 202). Granada in the south was incorporated into the Spanish kingdom, and in 1512 Ferdinand conquered Navarre in the north.

There still remained a sizable and, in the view of the majority of the Spanish people, potentially dangerous minority, the Jews. When the kings of France and England had expelled the Jews from their kingdoms (see page 214), many had sought refuge in Spain. During the long centuries of the reconquista, Christian kings had renewed Jewish rights and privileges; in fact, Jewish industry, intelligence, and money had supported royal power. While Christians of all classes borrowed from Jewish moneylenders and while all who could afford them sought Jewish physicians, a strong undercurrent of resentment of Jewish influence and wealth festered.

In the fourteenth century anti-Semitism in Spain was aggravated by fiery anti-Jewish preaching, by economic dislocation, and by the search for a scapegoat during the Black Death. Anti-Semitic pogroms swept the towns of Spain; one scholar estimates that 40 percent of the Jewish population was killed or forced to convert.[6] Those converted were called *conversos* (**kon-VER-sowz**) or **New Christians**. Conversos were often well educated and held prominent positions in government, the church, medicine, law, and business. Numbering perhaps two hundred thousand in a total Spanish population of about 7.5 million, New Christians and Jews exercised influence disproportionate to their numbers.

New Christians A term applied to Jews who accepted Christianity, but since many were from families who had become Christian centuries earlier, the word *new* is not accurate.

Such successes bred resentment. Aristocratic grandees resented their financial dependence; the poor hated the converso tax collectors; and churchmen doubted the sincerity of their conversions. Queen Isabella shared these suspicions, and she and Ferdinand received permission from Pope Sixtus IV to establish an Inquisition to "search out and punish converts from Judaism who had transgressed against Christianity by secretly adhering to Jewish beliefs and performing rites of the Jews."[7] Investigations and trials began immediately, as officials of the Inquisition looked for conversos who showed any sign of incomplete conversion, such as not eating pork.

Recent scholarship has carefully analyzed documents of the Inquisition. Most conversos identified themselves as sincere Christians; many came from families that had received baptism generations before. In response, officials of the Inquisition developed a new type of anti-Semitism. A person's status as a Jew, they argued, could not be changed by religious conversion, but was in their blood and was heritable, so Jews could never be true Christians. In what were known as "purity of the blood" laws, having pure Christian blood became a requirement for noble status. Ideas about Jews developed in Spain were important components in European concepts of race, and discussions of "Jewish blood" later expanded into notions of the "Jewish race."

Felipe Bigarny: Ferdinand and Isabella

In these wooden sculptures, the Burgundian artist Felipe Bigarny portrays Ferdinand and Isabella as paragons of Christian piety, kneeling at prayer. Ferdinand is shown in armor, a symbol of his military accomplishments and masculinity. Isabella wears a simple white head-covering rather than something more elaborate to indicate her modesty, a key virtue for women, though her actions and writings indicate that she was more determined and forceful than Ferdinand.
(Capilla Real, Granada/Laurie Platt Winfrey, Inc.)

Section Review

- Charles VII reorganized France by creating the first permanent royal army, with later kings adding strength by coming to terms with the pope over church and state power.

- The Wars of the Roses in England damaged English trade, agriculture, and industry.

- Edward VII strengthened the monarchy and brought domestic and international peace.

- Ferdinand and Isabella in Spain decreased aristocratic power, strengthened the monarchy, and gained favor with the pope to expand their territories.

- The financial success of the Spanish Jews who converted to Christianity for protection against anti-Semitism incurred jealousy, so Ferdinand and Isabella ordered an Inquisition to eliminate these Jews, leading to the notion that being Jewish was by "blood," so a Jew could never truly convert to Christianity.

Shortly after the conquest of Granada, Isabella and Ferdinand issued an edict expelling all practicing Jews from Spain. Of the community of perhaps 200,000 Jews, 150,000 fled. Absolute religious orthodoxy and purity of blood ("untainted" by Jews or Muslims) served as the theoretical foundation of the Spanish national state.

The diplomacy of the Catholic rulers of Spain achieved a success they never anticipated. In 1496 Ferdinand and Isabella married their second daughter Joanna, heiress to Castile, to the archduke Philip, heir to the Burgundian Netherlands and the Holy Roman Empire. Philip and Joanna's son, Charles V (r. 1519–1556) thus succeeded to a vast patrimony. When Charles's son Philip II joined Portugal to the Spanish crown in 1580, the Iberian Peninsula was at last politically united.

Chapter Review

What economic and political developments in Italy provided the setting for the Renaissance? (page 308)

The Italian Renaissance rested on the phenomenal economic growth of the High Middle Ages. In the period from about 1050 to 1300, a new economy emerged based on Venetian and Genoese shipping and long-distance trade and on Florentine banking. These commercial activities, combined with the struggle of urban communes for political independence from surrounding feudal lords, led to the appearance of a new ruling group in Italian cities—merchant oligarchs. Unrest in some cities led to their being taken over by single rulers, but however Italian cities were governed, they jockeyed for power with one another and prevented the establishment of a single Italian nation-state.

What were the key ideas of the Renaissance, and how were they different for men and women and for southern and northern Europeans? (page 312)

The Renaissance was characterized by self-conscious awareness among fourteenth- and fifteenth-century Italians, particularly scholars and writers known as humanists, that they were living in a new era. Key to this attitude was a serious interest in the Latin classics, a belief in individual potential, and a more secular attitude toward life. All these are evident in political theory developed during the Renaissance, particularly that of Machiavelli. Humanists opened schools for boys and young men to train them for an active life of public service, but they had doubts about whether humanist education was appropriate for women. As humanism spread to northern Europe, religious concerns became more pronounced, and Christian humanists set out plans for the reform of church and society. Their ideas were spread to a much wider audience than those of early humanists because of the development of the printing press with movable metal type, which revolutionized communication.

How did changes in art both reflect and shape new ideas? (page 320)

Interest in the classical past and in the individual also shaped Renaissance art in terms of style and subject matter. Painting became more naturalistic, and the individual portrait emerged as a distinct artistic genre. Wealthy merchants, cultured rulers, and powerful popes all hired painters, sculptors, and architects to design and ornament public and private buildings. Art in Italy became more secular and classical, while that in northern Europe retained a more religious tone. Artists began to understand themselves as having a special creative genius, though they continued to produce works on order for patrons, who often determined the content and form.

What were the key social hierarchies in Renaissance Europe, and how did ideas about hierarchy shape people's lives? (page 324)

Social hierarchies in the Renaissance built on those of the Middle Ages, but new features also developed that contributed to the modern social hierarchies of race, class, and gender. Black Africans entered Europe in sizable numbers for the first time since the collapse of the Roman Empire, and Europeans fit them into changing understandings of ethnicity and race. The medieval hierarchy of orders based on function in society intermingled with a new hierarchy based on wealth, with new types of elites becoming more powerful. The Renaissance debate about women led many to discuss

Key Terms

Renaissance (p. 308)
communes (p. 309)
popolo (p. 309)
condottieri (p. 310)
signori (p. 310)
courts (p. 310)
patrons (p. 310)
humanism (p. 312)
individualism (p. 312)
The Prince (p. 314)
secularism (p. 315)
Christian humanists (p. 316)
debate about women (p. 327)
Wars of the Roses (p. 329)
royal council (p. 330)
court of Star Chamber (p. 330)
New Christians (p. 331)

women's nature and proper role in society, a discussion sharpened by the presence of a number of ruling queens in this era.

How did the nation-states of western Europe evolve in this period? (page 328)

With taxes provided by business people, kings in western Europe established greater peace and order, both essential for trade. Feudal monarchies gradually evolved in the direction of nation-states. In Spain, France, and England, rulers also emphasized royal dignity and authority, and they utilized Machiavellian ideas to ensure the preservation and continuation of their governments. Like the merchant oligarchs and signori of Italian city-states, Renaissance monarchs manipulated culture to enhance their power.

Notes

1. C. E. Detmold, trans., *The Historical, Political and Diplomatic Writings of Niccolò Machiavelli* (Boston: J. R. Osgood, 1882), pp. 51–52.
2. Ibid., pp. 54–55.
3. Quoted in F. Seebohm, *The Oxford Reformers* (London: J. M. Dent & Sons, 1867), p. 256.
4. J. Hale, *The Civilization of Europe in the Renaissance* (New York: Atheneum, 1994), p. 44.
5. Quoted in J. Devisse and M. Mollat, *The Image of the Black in Western Art*, vol. 2, trans. W. G. Ryan (New York: William Morrow, 1979), pt. 2, pp. 187–188.
6. See B. F. Reilly, *The Medieval Spains* (New York: Cambridge University Press, 1993), pp. 198–203.
7. B. Netanyahu, *The Origins of the Inquisition in Fifteenth Century Spain* (New York: Random House, 1995), p. 921.

To assess your mastery of this chapter, go to **bedfordstmartins.com/mckaywestbrief**

Listening to the Past

An Age of Gold

As the foremost scholar of the early sixteenth century and a writer with international contacts, Desiderius Erasmus (1466?–1536) maintained a vast correspondence. In the following letter to Wolfgang Capito (1478?–1541), a German scholar and professor of theology at the University of Basel, he explains his belief that Europe was entering a golden age. The letter also reflects the spiritual ideals of northern European humanists.

To Capito

It is no part of my nature, most learned Wolfgang, to be excessively fond of life; whether it is that I have, to my own mind, lived nearly long enough, having entered my fifty-first year, or that I see nothing in this life so splendid or delightful that it should be desired by one who is convinced by the Christian faith that a happier life awaits those who in this world earnestly attach themselves to piety. But at the present moment I could almost wish to be young again, for no other reason but this, that I anticipate the near approach of a golden age, so clearly do we see the minds of princes, as if changed by inspiration, devoting all their energies to the pursuit of peace. The chief movers in this matter are Pope Leo and Francis, King of France.

There is nothing this king does not do or does not suffer in his desire to avert war and consolidate peace . . . and exhibiting in this, as in everything else, a magnanimous and truly royal character. Therefore, when I see that the highest sovereigns of Europe—Francis of France, Charles the King Catholic, Henry [VIII] of England, and the Emperor Maximilian—have set all their warlike preparations aside and established peace upon solid and, as I trust, adamantine foundations, I am led to a confident hope that not only morality and Christian piety, but also a genuine and purer literature, may come to renewed life or greater splendour; especially as this object is pursued with equal zeal in various regions of the world. . . . To the piety of these princes it is due, that we see everywhere, as if

Hans Holbein the Younger, *Erasmus* (ca. 1521). Holbein persuaded his close friend Erasmus to sit for this portrait and portrayed him at his characteristic work, writing. (Louvre/Scala/Art Resource, NY)

upon a given signal, men of genius are arising and conspiring together to restore the best literature.

Polite letters, which were almost extinct, are now cultivated and embraced by Scots, by Danes, and by Irishmen. Medicine has a host of champions. . . . The Imperial Law is restored at Paris by William Budé, in Germany by Udalric Zasy; and mathematics at Basel by Henry of Glaris. In the theological sphere there was no little to be done, because this science has been hitherto mainly professed by those who are most pertinacious in their abhorrence of the better literature,* and are the more successful in defending their own ignorance as they do it under pretext of piety, the unlearned

---

* Latin, Greek, and Hebrew.

vulgar being induced to believe that violence is offered to religion if anyone begins an assault upon their barbarism. . . . But even here I am confident of success if the knowledge of the three languages continues to be received in schools, as it has now begun. . . .

But one doubt still possesses my mind. I am afraid that, under cover of a revival of ancient literature, paganism may attempt to rear its head—as there are some among Christians that acknowledge Christ in name but breathe inwardly a heathen spirit—or, on the other hand, that the restoration of Hebrew learning may give occasion to a revival of Judaism. This would be a plague as much opposed to the doctrine of Christ as anything that could

happen. . . . I know that your sincere piety will have regard to nothing but Christ, to whom all your studies are devoted. . . .

Questions for Analysis

1. What does Erasmus mean by a "golden age"?

2. Do education and learning ensure improvement in the human condition, in his opinion? Do you agree?

3. What would you say are the essential differences between Erasmus's educational goals and those of modern society?

Source: Epistles 522 and 530, from *The Epistles of Erasmus*, trans. F. M. Nichols (London: Longmans, Green & Co., 1901).

CHAPTER 14

Reformations and Religious Wars

1500–1600

Giorgio Vasari: *Massacre of Coligny and the Huguenots* (1573). This fresco shows the Saint Bartholomew's Day massacre in Paris, one of many bloody events in the religious wars that accompanied the Reformation. (Vatican Palace/Scala/Art Resource, NY)

Chapter Preview

The Early Reformation
What were the central ideas of the reformers, and why were they appealing to different social groups?

The Reformation and German Politics
How did the political situation in Germany shape the course of the Reformation?

The Spread of the Protestant Reformation
How did Protestant ideas and institutions spread beyond German-speaking lands?

The Catholic Reformation
How did the Catholic Church respond to the new religious situation?

Religious Violence
What were the causes and consequences of religious violence, including riots, wars, and witch hunts?

INDIVIDUALS IN SOCIETY: Teresa of Ávila

IMAGES IN SOCIETY: Art in the Reformation

LISTENING TO THE PAST: Martin Luther, *On Christian Liberty*

In 1500 there was one Christian church in western Europe to which all Christians at least nominally belonged. Fifty years later there were many, as a result of a religious reform movement that gained wide acceptance and caused Christianity to break into many divisions.

Along with the Renaissance, the Reformation is often seen as a key element in the creation of the "modern" world. This radical change contained many elements of continuity, however. Sixteenth-century reformers looked back to the early Christian church for their inspiration, and many of their reforming ideas had been advocated for centuries.

The Early Reformation

What were the central ideas of the reformers, and why were they appealing to different social groups?

Calls for reform in the church came from many quarters in early-sixteenth-century Europe—from educated laypeople such as Christian humanists and urban residents, from villagers and artisans, and from church officials themselves. This dissatisfaction helps explain why the ideas of Martin Luther, an obscure professor from a new and not very prestigious German university, found a ready audience. Within a decade of his first publishing his ideas (using the new technology of the printing press), much of central Europe and Scandinavia had broken with the Catholic Church and even more radical concepts of the Christian message were being developed and linked to calls for social change.

The Christian Church in the Early Sixteenth Century

Sixteenth-century Europeans of all social classes devoted an enormous amount of their time and income to religious causes and foundations. Despite—or perhaps because of—the depth of their piety, many people were also highly critical of the Roman Catholic Church and its clergy. The papal conflict with the German emperor Frederick II in the thirteenth century, followed by the Babylonian Captivity and then the Great Schism, badly damaged the prestige of church leaders. Humanists denounced corruption in the church. In *The Praise of Folly*, Erasmus condemned the superstitions of the parish clergy and the excessive rituals of the monks. Many ordinary people agreed. Court records, bishop's visitations of parishes, and even popular songs and printed images show widespread **anticlericalism,** or opposition to the clergy.

In the early sixteenth century critics of the church concentrated their attacks on three disorders—clerical immorality, clerical ignorance, and clerical pluralism, with the related problem of absenteeism. Charges of clerical immorality were aimed at a number of priests who were drunkards, neglected the rule of celibacy, gambled, or indulged in fancy dress. Charges of clerical ignorance applied to barely literate priests who delivered sermons of poor quality and who were obviously ignorant of the Latin words of the Mass.

In regard to absenteeism and **pluralism,** many clerics, especially higher ecclesiastics, held several *benefices* (**BEN-ah-fiss-es**) (or offices) simultaneously but seldom visited the benefices, let alone performed the spiritual responsibilities those offices entailed. Instead, they collected revenues from all of them and hired a poor priest, paying him just a fraction of the income to fulfill the spiritual duties of a

anticlericalism Opposition to the clergy.

pluralism The clerical practice of holding more than one church benefice (or office) at the same time and enjoying the income from each.

particular local church. Many Italian officials in the papal curia held benefices in England, Spain, and Germany. Revenues from those countries paid the Italian priests' salaries, provoking not only charges of absenteeism but also nationalistic resentment.

There was also local resentment of clerical privileges and immunities. Priests, monks, and nuns were exempt from civic responsibilities, such as defending the city and paying taxes. Yet religious orders frequently held large amounts of urban property, in some cities as much as one-third. City governments were increasingly determined to integrate the clergy into civic life. This brought city leaders into opposition with bishops and the papacy, which for centuries had stressed the independence of the church from lay control and the distinction between members of the clergy and laypeople.

Martin Luther

By itself, widespread criticism of the church did not lead to the dramatic changes of the sixteenth century. Those resulted from the personal religious struggle of a German university professor, Martin Luther (1483–1546), who was also a priest. Martin Luther was born at Eisleben in Saxony. At considerable sacrifice, his father sent him to school and then to the University of Erfurt, where he earned a master's degree with distinction. Luther was to proceed to the study of law and a legal career, which for centuries had been the stepping-stone to public office and material success. Instead, however, a sense of religious calling led him to join the Augustinian friars, an order whose members often preached, taught, and assisted the poor. Luther was ordained a priest in 1507 and after additional study earned a doctorate of theology. From 1512 until his death in 1546, he served as professor of the Scriptures at the new University of Wittenberg. Throughout his life, he frequently cited his professorship as justification for his reforming work.

Martin Luther was a very conscientious friar. His scrupulous observance of the religious routine, frequent confessions, and fasting, however, gave him only temporary relief from anxieties about sin and his ability to meet God's demands. Through his study of Saint Paul's letters in the New Testament, he gradually arrived at a new understanding of Christian doctrine. His understanding is often summarized as "faith alone, grace alone, Scripture alone." He believed that salvation and justification come through faith. Faith is a free gift of God, not the result of human effort. God's word is revealed only in Scripture, not in the traditions of the church.

At the same time that Luther was engaged in scholarly reflections and professorial lecturing, Pope Leo X authorized the sale of a special St. Peter's indulgence to finance his building plans in Rome. An **indulgence** was a document, signed by the pope or another church official, that substituted for penance. The archbishop who controlled the area in which Wittenberg was located, Albert of Mainz, was an enthusiastic promoter of this indulgence sale. He received a share of the profits in order to pay off a debt from a wealthy banking family, a debt he had incurred in order to purchase a papal dispensation allowing him to become the bishop of

CHRONOLOGY

1477	Union of Burgundian and Habsburg dynasties
1517	Martin Luther, "Ninety-five Theses on the Power of Indulgences"
1521	Diet of Worms
1521–1559	Habsburg-Valois Wars
1525	Peasants' War in Germany
1526	Turkish victory at Mohács, which allows spread of Protestantism in Hungary
1536	John Calvin, *The Institutes of the Christian Religion*
1540	Papal approval of Society of Jesus (Jesuits)
1542	Sacred Congregation of the Holy Office and Roman Inquisition
1545–1563	Council of Trent
1555	Peace of Augsburg, official recognition of Lutheranism
1558–1603	Reign of Elizabeth in England
1560–1660	Height of the European witch hunt
1568–1578	Civil war in the Netherlands
1572	Saint Bartholomew's Day massacre
1598	Edict of Nantes

indulgence A papal statement (a document addressed to an individual) granting remission of priest-imposed penalty for sin (no one knew what penalty God would impose after death). Popular belief, however, held that an indulgence secured complete remission of all penalties for sin, before and after death.

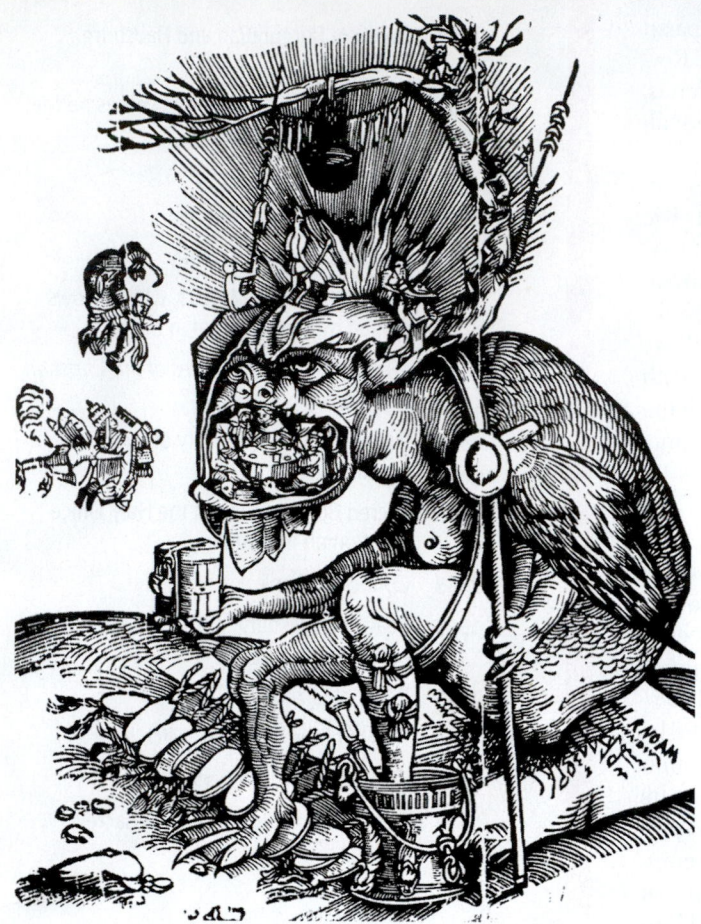

The Folly of Indulgences

In this woodcut from the early Reformation, the church's sale of indulgences is viciously satirized. With one claw in holy water, another resting on the coins paid for indulgences, and a third stretched out for offerings, the church, in the form of a rapacious bird, writes out an indulgence with excrement. The creature's head and gaping mouth represent Hell, with foolish Christians inside, others being cooked in a pot above, and a demon delivering the pope in a three-tiered crown and holding the keys to Heaven, a symbol of papal authority. Illustrations such as this, often printed as single-sheet broadsides and sold very cheaply, clearly conveyed criticism of the church to people who could not read. (Kunstsammlungen der Veste Coburg)

several other territories as well. Albert's indulgence sale, run by a Dominican friar who mounted an advertising blitz, promised that the purchase of indulgences would bring full forgiveness for one's own sins or release from purgatory for a loved one. One of the slogans—"As soon as coin in coffer rings, the soul from purgatory springs"—brought phenomenal success.

Luther was severely troubled that many people believed they had no further need for repentance once they had purchased indulgences. He wrote a letter to Archbishop Albert on the subject and enclosed in Latin his "Ninety-five Theses on the Power of Indulgences." His argument was that indulgences undermined the seriousness of the sacrament of penance, competed with the preaching of the Gospel, and downplayed the importance of charity in Christian life. After Luther's death, biographies reported that the theses were also posted on the door of the church at Wittenberg Castle on October 31, 1517. Such an act would have been very strange—they were in Latin and written for those learned in theology, not for normal churchgoers—but it has become a standard part of Luther lore. In any case, Luther intended the theses for academic debate, but by December 1517 they had been translated into German and were read throughout the Holy Roman Empire.

Luther was ordered to come to Rome, which he was able to avoid because of the political situation in the empire, but he did engage in formal scholarly debate with a representative of the church, Johann Eck, at Leipzig in 1519. He denied both the authority of the pope and the infallibility of a general council. The Council of Constance, he said, had erred when it had condemned Jan Hus (see page 294).

The papacy responded with a letter condemning some of Luther's propositions, ordering that his books be burned, and giving him two months to recant or be excommunicated. Luther retaliated by publicly burning the letter. By January 3, 1521, when the excommunication was supposed to become final, the controversy involved more than theological issues. The papal legate wrote, "All Germany is in revolution. Nine-tenths shout 'Luther' as their war cry; and the other tenth cares nothing about Luther, and cries 'Death to the court of Rome.'"[1] In this highly charged atmosphere, the twenty-one-year-old emperor Charles V held his first diet (assembly of the Estates of the empire) in the German city of Worms. Charles summoned Luther to appear before the **Diet of Worms.** When ordered to recant, Luther replied in language that rang all over Europe:

> *Unless I am convinced by the evidence of Scripture or by plain reason—for I do not accept the authority of the Pope or the councils alone, since it is established that they have often erred and contradicted themselves—I am bound by the Scriptures I have cited and my conscience is captive to the Word of God. I cannot and will not recant anything, for it is neither safe nor right to go against conscience. God help me. Amen.[2]*

Protestant Thought

As he developed his ideas, Luther gathered followers, who came to be called Protestants. The word **Protestant** derives from the protest drawn up by a small group of reforming German princes at the Diet of Speyer in 1529. The princes "protested" the decisions of the Catholic majority. At first Protestant meant "Lutheran," but with the appearance of many protesting sects, it became a general term applied to all non-Catholic western European Christians.

The most important early reformer other than Luther was the Swiss humanist, priest, and admirer of Erasmus, Ulrich Zwingli (**ZWING-glee**) (1484–1531). Zwingli announced in 1519 that he would preach not from the church's prescribed readings but, relying on Erasmus's New Testament, go right through the New Testament "from A to Z," that is, from Matthew to Revelation. Zwingli was convinced that Christian life rested on the Scriptures, which were the pure words of God and the sole basis of religious truth. He went on to attack indulgences, the Mass, the institution of monasticism, and clerical celibacy. In his gradual reform of the church in Zurich, he had the strong support of the city authorities, who had long resented the privileges of the clergy.

Luther, Zwingli, and other Protestants agreed on many things. First, how is a person to be saved? Traditional Catholic teaching held that salvation is achieved by both faith and good works. Protestants held that salvation comes by faith alone, irrespective of good works or the sacraments. God, not people, initiates salvation. (See the feature "Listening to the Past: Martin Luther, *On Christian Liberty*" on pages 368–369.) Second, where does religious authority reside? Christian doctrine had long maintained that authority rests both in the Bible and in the traditional teaching of the church. For Protestants, authority rested in the Bible alone. For a doctrine or issue to be valid, it had to have a scriptural basis. Because of this, most Protestants rejected Catholic teachings about the sacraments (see page 368), holding that only baptism and the Eucharist have scriptural support. Third, what is the church? Protestants held that the church is a spiritual *priesthood of all believers*, an invisible fellowship not fixed in any place or person, which differed markedly from the Roman Catholic practice of a clerical, hierarchical institution headed by the pope in Rome. Fourth, what is the highest form of Christian life? The medieval church had stressed the superiority of the monastic and religious life over the secular. Luther disagreed and argued that every person should serve God in his or her individual calling.

Protestants did not agree on everything. One important area of dispute was the ritual of the Eucharist (also called communion, or the Lord's Supper). Catholicism holds the dogma of **transubstantiation:** by the consecrating words of the priest during the Mass, the bread and wine become the actual body and blood of Christ, who is then fully present in the bread and wine. In opposition, Luther believed that Christ is really present in the consecrated bread and wine, but this is

Diet of Worms An assembly held by Charles V (1521) in the German city of Worms where Luther defended his doctrines before the emperor, refusing to recant.

Protestant The name originally given to Lutherans, after a group of reforming princes protested decisions of the Catholic princes at the Diet of Speyer (1529); as other reforming groups appeared, the term came to mean all non-Catholic western Christian groups.

transubstantiation Catholic doctrine of the Eucharist, that when the bread and wine are consecrated by the priest at Mass, they are transformed into the actual body and blood of Christ.

Lucas Cranach the Elder: The Ten Commandments, 1516
Cranach, who was the court painter for the Elector of Saxony from 1505 to 1553, painted this giant illustration of the Ten Commandments (more than 5 feet by 11 feet) for the city hall in Wittenberg just at the point when Luther was beginning to question Catholic doctrine. Cranach became an early supporter of Luther, and many of his later works depict the reformer and his ideas. This close association, and the fact that the painting captures the Protestant emphasis on biblical texts very well, led it to be moved to the Luther House in Wittenberg, the largest museum of the Protestant Reformation in the world. Paintings were used by both Protestants and Catholics to teach religious ideas.   (Lutherhalle, Wittenberg/The Bridgeman Art Library)

the result of God's mystery, not the actions of a priest. Zwingli understood the Lord's Supper as a *memorial*, in which Christ was present in spirit among the faithful, but not in the bread and wine. The Colloquy of Marburg, summoned in 1529 to unite Protestants, failed to resolve these differences, though Protestants reached agreement on almost everything else.

The Appeal of Protestant Ideas

Pulpits and printing presses spread Luther's message all over Germany. By the time of his death, people of all social classes had become Lutheran. What was the immense appeal of Luther's religious ideas and those of other Protestants?

Educated people and humanists were much attracted by Luther's ideas. He advocated a simpler personal religion based on faith, a return to the spirit of the early church, the centrality of the Scriptures in the liturgy and in Christian life, and the abolition of elaborate ceremonies—precisely the reforms the Christian humanists had been calling for. His insistence that everyone should read and reflect on the Scriptures attracted the literate and thoughtful middle classes partly because Luther appealed to their intelligence. This included many priests and monks, who became clergy in the new Protestant churches. Luther's ideas also appealed to townspeople who envied the church's wealth and resented paying for it. After Zurich became Protestant, the city council taxed the clergy and placed them under the jurisdiction of civil courts.

Scholars in many disciplines have attributed Luther's fame and success to the invention of the printing press, which rapidly reproduced and made known his ideas. Many printed works included woodcuts and other illustrations, so that even those who could not read could grasp the main ideas. (See the feature "Images in Society: Art in the Reformation" on pages 344–345.) Equally important was Luther's incredible skill with language, as seen in his two catechisms (1529), compendiums of basic religious knowledge. Hymns such as "A Mighty Fortress Is Our God" (which Luther wrote) were also important means of conveying central points of doctrine. Luther's linguistic skill, together with his translation of the New Testament into German in 1523, led to the acceptance of his dialect of German as the standard version of the German language.

Both Luther and Zwingli recognized that if reforms were going to be permanent, political authorities as well as concerned individuals and religious leaders would have to accept them. Zwingli worked closely with the city council of Zurich, and in other cities and towns of Switzerland and south Germany city councils similarly took the lead. They appointed pastors that they knew had accepted Protestant ideas, required them to swear an oath of loyalty to the council, and oversaw their preaching and teaching.

Luther lived in a territory ruled by a noble—the Elector of Saxony—and he also worked closely with political authorities, viewing them as fully justified in asserting control over the church in their territories. Indeed, he demanded that German rulers reform the papacy and ecclesiastical institutions, and he instructed all Christians to obey their secular rulers, whom he saw as divinely ordained to maintain order. Individuals may have been convinced of the truth of Protestant teachings by hearing sermons, listening to hymns, or reading pamphlets, but a territory became Protestant when its ruler, whether a noble or a city council, brought in a reformer or two to reeducate the territory's clergy, sponsored public sermons, and confiscated church property. This happened in many of the states of the empire during the 1520s and then moved beyond the empire to Denmark-Norway and Sweden.

The Radical Reformation

Some individuals and groups rejected the idea that church and state needed to be united, and sought to create a voluntary community of believers as they understood it to have existed in New Testament times. In terms of theology and spiritual practices, these individuals and groups varied widely, though they are generally termed "radicals" for their insistence on a more extensive break with the past. Some adopted the baptism of believers—for which they were given the title of "Anabaptists" or rebaptizers by their enemies—while others saw all outward sacraments or rituals as misguided. Some groups attempted communal ownership of property, living very simply and rejecting anything they thought unbiblical. Some reacted harshly to members who deviated, but others argued for complete religious toleration and individualism.

Religious radicals were met with fanatical hatred and bitter persecution. Protestants and Catholics alike saw—quite correctly—that the radicals' call for the separation of church and state would lead ultimately to the secularization of society. In Saxony, in Strasbourg, and in the Swiss cities, radicals were either banished or cruelly executed by burning, beating, or drowning. Their community spirit and the edifying example of their lives, however, contributed to the survival of radical ideas. Later, the Quakers, with their gentle pacifism; the Baptists, with their emphasis on inner spiritual light; the Congregationalists, with their democratic church organization; and in 1787 the authors of the U.S. Constitution, with their opposition to the "establishment of religion" (state churches), would all trace their origins, in part, to the radicals of the sixteenth century.

Images in Society

Art in the Reformation

In the Reformation era, controversy raged over the purpose and function of art. Protestants and Catholics disagreed, and Protestant groups disagreed with one another. The Bible specifically prohibits making images of anything "in the heavens above or the earth below or the waters beneath the earth" (Exodus 20:4–6 and Deuteronomy 5:8–10). Based on this, some Protestant leaders, including Ulrich Zwingli, stressed that "the Word of God" should be the only instrument used in the work of evangelization. Martin Luther disagreed, saying he was not "of the opinion that the Gospel should blight and destroy all the arts." Luther believed that painting and sculpture had value in spreading the Gospel message because "children and simple folk are more apt to retain the divine stories when taught by pictures and parables than merely by words or instruction." Similar debates involved music, with Luther supporting and even writing hymns, and Swiss Protestants removing organs from their churches.

Lucas Cranach the Elder (1472–1553), a close friend of Luther's, is the finest representative of Protestant Reformation artists. He and Luther collaborated on the production of woodcuts and paintings, such as *The Ten Commandments* (see page 342), that spread the new evangelical theology. Each square in Cranach's painting represents one of the Ten Commandments.

Lucas Cranach the Younger (1515–1586) continued his father's work of spreading Luther's message. His woodcut *The True and False Churches* (Image 1) contains blatant and more subtle messages. At the center Luther stands in a pulpit, preaching the word of God from an open Bible. At the right, a flaming open mouth symbolizing the jaws of Hell engulfs the pope, cardinals, and friars, one kind of "false church." The scene at the left actually suggests another kind of "false church," however. Cranach shows a crucified Christ emerging out of the "lamb of God" on the altar as people are receiving communion. This image represents the Lutheran understanding of the Lord's Supper, in which Christ is really present in the bread and wine, in contrast to other Protestants who saw the ceremony as a memorial (see page 342). The woodcut thus could be understood on different levels by different viewers, which is true of much effective religious art.

For John Calvin, the utter transcendence of God made impossible any attempt to bring God down to human level through visual portraiture; to domesticate or to humanize God would deprive him of his glory. In houses of worship Calvin emphasized the centrality of the divine word, allowing wall inscriptions from the Bible. In later life, Calvin tolerated narrative biblical scenes as long as they did not include pictures of God or Jesus Christ. In the Netherlands, which adopted a Calvinist version of Protestantism, many formerly Catholic churches were stripped of all statues, images, and decoration and were redesigned with a stark, bare simplicity that mirrored the Calvinist ideal. Notice the interior of the church of Saint Bavo in Haarlem (Image 2).

IMAGE 1 Lucas Cranach the Younger: The True and False Churches (Staatliche Kunstsammlungen Dresden)

IMAGE 2 Church of Saint Bavo, Haarlem (Pieter Jansz. Saenredam, S. Bavo in Haarlem. John G. Johnson Collection, Philadelphia Museum of Art)

IMAGE 3 Jesuit Priest Distributing Holy Pictures (From Pierre Chenu, *The Reformation* [New York: St. Martin's Press, 1986])

The Catholic Church officially addressed the subject of art at the Council of Trent in December 1563. The church declared that honor and veneration should be given to likenesses of Christ, the Virgin Mary, and the saints; that images would remind people of the saints' virtues, which should be imitated; and that pictorial art would promote piety and the love of God. Examine the painting *Jesuit Priest Distributing Holy Pictures* (Image 3). Such pictures and images of saints were often given to children to help educate them on matters of doctrine. How do these pictures serve the same function as the Protestant *Ten Commandments* shown on page 342?

Both Protestants and Catholics used religious art for propaganda purposes, to oppose religious heterodoxy, and to arouse piety in laypeople. Catholic Reformation art came into full flowering with the style later known as baroque (**buh-ROKE**) (see page 415). Baroque art originated in Rome and reflected the dynamic and proselytizing spirit of the Counter-Reformation. The church encouraged artists to appeal to the senses, to touch the souls and kindle the faith of ordinary people while proclaiming the power and confidence of the reformed Catholic Church.

In addition to this underlying religious emotionalism, the baroque drew from the Catholic Reformation a sense of drama, motion, and ceaseless striving. The interior of the Jesuit church of Jesus—the Gesù (**JAY-soo**)—combined all these characteristics in its lavish, shimmering, wildly active decorations and frescoes

(Image 4). This triumphant, elaborate, and flamboyant church celebrates both the Catholic baroque and Rome as the artistic capital of Europe. How would you compare the Gesù with the Saint Bavo church (Image 2)?

IMAGE 4 Ceiling of the Gesù (Scala/Art Resource, NY)

The German Peasants' War

In the early sixteenth century the economic condition of the peasantry varied from place to place but was generally worse than it had been in the fifteenth century and was deteriorating. Crop failures in 1523 and 1524 aggravated an explosive situation. Nobles had aggrieved peasants by seizing village common lands, imposing new rents and requiring additional services, and by taking the peasants' best horses or cows in payment for death duties. The peasants made demands that they believed conformed to the Scriptures, and they cited Luther as a theologian who could prove that they did.

Luther wanted to prevent rebellion. Initially he sided with the peasants, blasting the lords for robbing their subjects. But when rebellion broke out, the peasants who expected Luther's support were soon disillusioned. Freedom for Luther meant independence from the authority of the Roman church; it did *not* mean opposition to legally established secular powers. Firmly convinced that rebellion would hasten the end of civilized society, he wrote the tract *Against the Murderous, Thieving Hordes of the Peasants*: "Let everyone who can smite, slay, and stab [the peasants], secretly and openly, remembering that nothing can be more poisonous, hurtful or devilish than a rebel."[3] The nobility ferociously crushed the revolt. Historians estimate that more than seventy-five thousand peasants were killed in 1525.

The German Peasants' War of 1525 greatly strengthened the authority of lay rulers. Not surprisingly, the Reformation lost much of its popular appeal after 1525, though peasants and urban rebels sometimes found a place for their social and religious ideas in radical groups. Peasants' economic conditions did moderately improve, however. For example, in many parts of Germany, enclosed fields, meadows, and forests were returned to common use.

The Reformation and Marriage

Luther and Zwingli both believed that a priest or nun's vows of celibacy went against human nature and God's commandments. Luther married a former nun, Katharina von Bora (1499–1532), and Zwingli married a Zurich widow, Anna Reinhart (1491–1538). Both women quickly had several children. Most other Protestant reformers also married, and their wives had to create a new and respectable role for themselves—pastor's wife—to overcome being viewed as simply a new type of priest's concubine. They were living demonstrations of their husband's convictions about the superiority of marriage to celibacy, and they were expected to be models of wifely obedience and Christian charity.

Protestants did not break with medieval scholastic theologians in their idea that women were to be subject to men. Women were advised to be cheerful rather than grudging in their obedience, for in doing so they demonstrated their willingness to follow God's plan. Men were urged to treat their wives kindly and considerately, but also to enforce their authority, through physical coercion if necessary. Both continental and English marriage manuals use the metaphor of breaking a horse for teaching a wife obedience, though laws did set limits on the husband's power to do so. A few women took Luther's idea about the priesthood of all believers to heart and wrote religious pamphlets and hymns, but no sixteenth-century Protestants officially allowed women to hold positions of religious authority. Monarchs such as Elizabeth I of England and female territorial rulers of the states of the Holy Roman Empire did determine religious policies, however.

Catholics viewed marriage as a sacramental union that, if validly entered into, could not be dissolved. Protestants saw marriage as a contract in which each part-

Lucas Cranach the Elder: Martin Luther and Katharina von Bora
Cranach painted this double marriage portrait to celebrate Luther's wedding in 1525 to Katharina von Bora, a former nun. The artist was one of the witnesses at the wedding and, in fact, had presented Luther's marriage proposal to Katharina. Using a go-between for proposals was very common, as was having a double wedding portrait painted. This particular couple quickly became a model of the ideal marriage, and many churches wanted their portraits. More than sixty similar paintings, with slight variations, were produced by Cranach's workshop and hung in churches and wealthy homes.
(Uffizi, Florence/Scala/Art Resource, NY)

ner promised the other support, companionship, and the sharing of mutual goods. Because, in Protestant eyes, marriage was created by God as a remedy for human weakness, marriages in which spouses did not comfort or support one another physically, materially, or emotionally endangered their own souls and the surrounding community. The only solution might be divorce and remarriage, which most Protestants came to allow, although divorce remained rare everywhere in Europe as marriage was such an important social and economic institution.

The Reformation generally brought the closing of monasteries and convents, and marriage became virtually the only occupation for upper-class Protestant women. Women in some convents recognized this and fought the Reformation, or argued that they could still be pious Protestants within convent walls. Most nuns left, however, and we do not know what happened to them. The Protestant emphasis on marriage made unmarried women (and men) suspect, for they did not belong to the type of household regarded as the cornerstone of a proper, godly society.

Section Review

- Many people were discontented with the Catholic Church and charged that the clergy were immoral, uneducated, and concerned more with wealth than fulfilling their spiritual duties.

- Martin Luther was a priest and theology professor who initially wanted to reform abuses in the Catholic Church, but came to break with the church; leading a movement later termed the Protestant Reformation.

- Both Luther and the Swiss reformer Ulrich Zwingli advocated that salvation was from God, that the Scripture and not the popes held all truth, that the church was what the people believed and not a physical place, and opposed the hierarchy of the priests over believers.

- Disputes arose over the proper role of the arts in religion, with Luther allowing music, painting, and sculpture, while Zwingli and the stricter Calvinists banned religious images.

- The printing press greatly boosted the spread of Protestant ideas and both Luther and Zwingli targeted political rulers to ensure the success of their reforms.

- Radical groups such as the Anabaptists, wanting communal living and complete separation of church and state, experienced harsh persecution, although their ideas survived.

- German peasants lost interest in the Reformation when Luther failed to back their demands for better conditions and the nobility viciously crushed their rebellion during the German Peasants' War of 1525.

- Protestants thought celibacy was against human nature and God and allowed church leaders to marry, but still believed women were inferior to men.

The Reformation and German Politics

How did the political situation in Germany shape the course of the Reformation?

Criticism of the church was widespread in Europe in the early sixteenth century, and calls for reform came from many areas. Yet such movements could be more easily squelched by the strong central governments of Spain, France, and England. The Holy Roman Empire, in contrast, included hundreds of largely independent states. Against this background of decentralization and strong local power, Martin Luther had launched a movement to reform the church. Two years after Luther published the "Ninety-five Theses," the electors chose as emperor a nineteen-year-old Habsburg prince who ruled as Charles V. The course of the Reformation was shaped by this election and by the political relationships surrounding it.

The Rise of the Habsburg Dynasty

War and diplomacy were important ways that states increased their power in sixteenth-century Europe, but so was marriage. The benefits of an advantageous marriage stretched across generations, a process that can be seen most dramatically with the Habsburgs. The Holy Roman emperor Frederick III, a Habsburg who was the ruler of most of Austria, acquired only a small amount of territory—but a great deal of money—with his marriage to Princess Eleonore of Portugal in 1452. He arranged for his son Maximilian to marry Europe's most prominent heiress, Mary of Burgundy, in 1477; she inherited the Netherlands, Luxembourg, and the County of Burgundy in what is now eastern France. Through this union with the rich and powerful duchy of Burgundy, the Austrian house of Habsburg, already the strongest ruling family in the empire, became an international power. The marriage of Maximilian and Mary angered the French, however, who considered Burgundy French territory, and inaugurated centuries of conflict between the Austrian house of Habsburg and the kings of France.

Maximilian learned the lesson of marital politics well, marrying his son and daughter to the children of Ferdinand and Isabella, the rulers of Spain, much of southern Italy, and eventually the Spanish New World empire. His grandson Charles V (1500–1558) fell heir to a vast and incredibly diverse collection of states and peoples, each governed in a different manner and held together only by the person of the emperor (see Map 14.1 on page 349). Charles's Italian adviser, the grand chancellor Gattinara, told the young ruler, "God has set you on the path toward world monarchy." Charles not only believed this but also was convinced that it was his duty to maintain the political and religious unity of Western Christendom.

The Political Impact of the Protestant Reformation

In the sixteenth century the practice of religion remained a public matter. Rulers determined the official form of religious practice in his (or occasionally her) jurisdiction. Almost everyone believed that the presence of a faith different from that of the majority represented a political threat to the security of the state. Few believed in religious liberty.

Luther's ideas appealed to German rulers for a variety of reasons. Though Germany was not a nation, people did have an understanding of being German because of their language and traditions. Luther frequently used the phrase "we

MAP 14.1 The Global Empire of Charles V

Charles V exercised theoretical jurisdiction over more European territory than anyone since Charlemagne. He also claimed authority over large parts of North and South America, though actual Spanish control was weak in much of this area.

NORTH AND SOUTH AMERICA

Spanish holdings, 1550

Lands inherited by Charles V
Lands gained by Charles V, 1519–1556
States favorable to Charles V
Enemies of Charles V
Boundary of the Holy Roman Empire

OTTOMAN EMPIRE

NORTH AFRICA

Germans" in his attacks on the papacy. Luther's appeal to national feeling influenced many rulers otherwise confused by or indifferent to the complexities of the religious issues. Some German rulers were sincerely attracted to Lutheran ideas, but material considerations swayed many others to embrace the new faith. The rejection of Roman Catholicism and adoption of Protestantism would mean the legal confiscation of lush farmlands, rich monasteries, and wealthy shrines. Thus many political authorities in the empire used the religious issue to extend their financial and political power and to enhance their independence from the emperor.

Charles V was a vigorous defender of Catholicism, however, so it is not surprising that the Reformation led to religious wars. The first battleground was Switzerland, which was officially part of the Holy Roman Empire, though it was really a loose confederation of thirteen largely autonomous territories called "cantons." Some cantons remained Catholic, and some became Protestant, and in the late 1520s the two sides went to war. Zwingli was killed on the battlefield in 1531, and both sides quickly decided that a treaty was preferable to further fighting. The treaty basically allowed each canton to determine its own religion and ordered each side to give up its foreign alliances, a policy of neutrality that has been characteristic of modern Switzerland.

Trying to halt the spread of religious division, Charles V called an Imperial Diet in 1530, to meet at Augsburg. The Lutherans developed a statement of faith, later called the Augsburg Confession, and the Protestant princes presented this to the emperor. (The Augsburg Confession remained an authoritative statement of belief for many Lutheran churches for centuries.) Charles refused to accept it and ordered all Protestants to return to the Catholic Church and give up any confiscated church property. This demand backfired, and Protestant territories in the empire—mostly northern German principalities and southern German cities—formed a military alliance. The emperor could not respond militarily, as he was in the midst of a series of wars with the French: the Habsburg-Valois wars, fought in Italy along the eastern and southern borders of France and eventually in Germany. The Ottoman Turks had also taken much of Hungary and in 1529 were besieging Vienna.

The 1530s and early 1540s saw complicated political maneuvering among many of the powers of Europe. Various attempts were made to heal the religious split with a church council, but intransigence on both sides made it increasingly clear that this would not be possible and that war was inevitable. Charles V realized that he was fighting not only for religious unity, but also for a more unified state, against territorial rulers who wanted to maintain their independence. He was thus defending both church and empire.

Fighting began in 1546, and initially the emperor was very successful. This success alarmed both France and the pope, however, who did not want Charles to become even more powerful. The pope withdrew papal troops, and the Catholic king of France sent money and troops to the Lutheran princes. Finally, in 1555 Charles agreed to the Peace of Augsburg, which, in accepting the status quo, officially recognized Lutheranism. The political authority in each territory was permitted to decide whether the territory would be Catholic or Lutheran. Most of northern and central Germany became Lutheran, while the south remained Roman Catholic. There was no freedom of religion, however. Princes or town councils established state churches to which all subjects of the area had to belong. Dissidents had to convert or leave.

The Peace of Augsburg ended religious war in Germany for many decades. His hope of uniting his empire under a single church dashed, Charles V abdicated in 1556, transferring power over his Spanish and Netherlandish holdings to his son Philip and his imperial power to his brother Ferdinand.

The Spread of the Protestant Reformation

How did Protestant ideas and institutions spread beyond German-speaking lands?

States within the Holy Roman Empire and the kingdom of Denmark-Norway were the earliest territories to accept the Protestant Reformation, but by the later 1520s religious change came to England, France, and eastern Europe. In all of these areas, a second generation of reformers built on Lutheran and Zwinglian ideas to develop their own theology and plans for institutional change. The most important of the second-generation reformers was John Calvin, whose ideas would profoundly influence the social thought and attitudes of European and English-speaking peoples all over the world, especially in Canada and the United States.

The Reformation in England and Ireland

As on the continent, the Reformation in England had economic as well as religious causes. However, the impetus for England's break with Rome was the ruler's desire for a new wife.

King Henry VIII (r. 1509–1547) was married to Catherine of Aragon, the daughter of Ferdinand and Isabella and widow of his older brother Arthur. Marriage to a brother's widow went against canon law, and Henry had been required to obtain a special papal dispensation to marry Catherine. The marriage had produced only one living heir, a daughter, Mary. By 1527 Henry decided that God was showing his displeasure with the marriage by denying him a son, and he appealed to the pope to have the marriage annulled. He was also in love with a court lady-in-waiting, Anne Boleyn, and assumed that she would give him the son he wanted. Normally an annulment would not have been a problem, but the troops of Emperor Charles V were in Rome at that point, and Pope Clement VII was essentially their prisoner. Charles V was the nephew of Catherine of Aragon and thus was vigorously opposed to an annulment, which would have declared his aunt a fornicator and his cousin Mary a bastard. The pope stalled.

Since Rome appeared to be thwarting Henry's matrimonial plans, he decided to remove the English church from papal jurisdiction. Henry used Parliament to legalize the Reformation in England and to make himself the supreme head of the Church of England. Some opposed the king and were beheaded, among them Thomas More, the king's chancellor and author of *Utopia* (see page 317). When Anne Boleyn failed twice to produce a male child, Henry VIII charged her with adulterous incest and in 1536 had her beheaded. His third wife, Jane Seymour, gave Henry the desired son, Edward, but she died in childbirth. Henry went on to three more wives. Between 1535 and 1539, under the influence of his chief minister, Thomas Cromwell, Henry decided to dissolve the English monasteries because he wanted their wealth. The king ended nine hundred years of English monastic life, dispersing the monks and nuns and confiscating their lands. Hundreds of properties were sold to the middle and upper classes and the proceeds enriched the Exchequer. The dissolution of the monasteries did not achieve a more equitable distribution of land and wealth. Rather, the redistribution of land strengthened the upper classes and tied them to the Tudor dynasty.

Henry's motives combined personal, political, social, and economic elements. Theologically, he retained such traditional Catholic practices and doctrines as confession, clerical celibacy, and transubstantiation. Meanwhile, Protestant literature

Allegory of the Tudor Dynasty

The unknown creator of this work intended to glorify the virtues of the Protestant succession; the painting has no historical reality. Enthroned Henry VIII (r. 1509–1547) hands the sword of justice to his Protestant son Edward VI (r. 1547–1553). The Catholic Queen Mary (r. 1553–1558) and her husband Philip of Spain are followed by Mars, god of war, signifying violence and civil disorder. At right the figures of Peace and Plenty accompany the Protestant Elizabeth I (r. 1558–1603), symbolizing England's happy fate under her rule. (Yale Center for British Art, Paul Mellon Collection/The Bridgeman Art Library)

circulated, and Henry approved the selection of men of Protestant sympathies as tutors for his son.

Most clergy and officials accepted Henry's moves, but all did not quietly acquiesce. In 1536 popular opposition in the north to the religious changes led to the Pilgrimage of Grace, a massive multiclass rebellion that proved the largest in English history. The "pilgrims" accepted a truce, but their leaders were arrested, tried, and executed. Recent scholarship points out that people rarely "converted" from Catholicism to Protestantism overnight. People responded to an action of the crown that was played out in their own neighborhood—the closing of a monastery, the ending of masses for the dead—with a combination of resistance, acceptance, and collaboration.

Loyalty to the Catholic Church was particularly strong in Ireland. Ireland had been claimed by English kings since the twelfth century, but in reality the English had firm control of only the area around Dublin, known as the Pale. In 1536, on orders from London, the Irish parliament, which represented only the English landlords and the people of the Pale, approved the English laws severing the church from Rome. The Church of Ireland was established on the English pattern, and the (English) ruling class adopted the new reformed faith. Most of the Irish people remained Roman Catholic, thus adding religious antagonism to the ethnic hostility that had been a feature of English policy toward Ireland for centuries (see page 300). Irish armed opposition to the Reformation led to harsh repression by the English. Catholic property was confiscated and sold, and the profits were shipped to England. With the Roman church driven underground, Catholic clergy acted as national as well as religious leaders.

The nationalization of the church and the dissolution of the monasteries led to important changes in government administration in both England and Ireland. Vast tracts of formerly monastic land came temporarily under the Crown's jurisdiction, and new bureaucratic machinery had to be developed to manage those properties. Cromwell reformed and centralized the king's household, the council, the secretariats, and the Exchequer. New departments of state were set up. Surplus funds from all departments went into a liquid fund to be applied to areas where there were deficits. This balancing resulted in greater efficiency and economy. Henry VIII's reign saw the growth of the modern centralized bureaucratic state.

In the short reign of Henry's sickly son, Edward VI (r. 1547–1553), strongly Protestant ideas exerted a significant influence on the religious life of the country. Archbishop Thomas Cranmer simplified the liturgy, invited Protestant theologians to England, and prepared the first *Book of Common Prayer* (1549). In stately and dignified English, the *Book of Common Prayer* included, together with the Psalter, the order for all services of the Church of England.

The equally brief reign of Mary Tudor (r. 1553–1558) witnessed a sharp move back to Catholicism. The devoutly Catholic daughter of Catherine of Aragon, Mary rescinded the Reformation legislation of her father's reign and restored Roman Catholicism. Mary's marriage to her cousin Philip of Spain, son of the emperor Charles V, proved highly unpopular in England, and her execution of several hundred Protestants further alienated her subjects. During her reign, many Protestants fled to the continent. Mary's death raised to the throne her sister Elizabeth (r. 1558–1603) and inaugurated the beginnings of religious stability.

Elizabeth, Henry's daughter with Anne Boleyn, had been raised a Protestant, but at the start of her reign sharp differences existed in England. On the one hand, Catholics wanted a Roman Catholic ruler. On the other hand, a vocal number of returning exiles wanted all Catholic elements in the Church of England eliminated. The latter, because they wanted to "purify" the church, were called "Puritans."

Shrewdly, Elizabeth chose a middle course between Catholic and Puritan extremes. She referred to herself as the "supreme governor of the Church of England," which allowed Catholics to remain loyal to her without denying the pope. She required her subjects to attend church or risk a fine, but did not interfere with their privately held beliefs. The Anglican Church, as the Church of England was called, moved in a moderately Protestant direction. Services were conducted in English, monasteries were not re-established, and clergymen were (grudgingly) allowed to marry. But the episcopate was not abolished, and the bishops remained as church officials, and church services were quite traditional.

Elizabeth's reign was threatened by European powers attempting to re-establish Catholicism. In 1586 Elizabeth's cousin and heir to the crown, Mary, Queen of Scots, became implicated in a plot to assassinate Elizabeth. Hoping to reunite England with Catholic Europe through Mary, Philip of Spain (Philip II) gave the conspiracy his full backing. When the English executed Mary, the Catholic pope urged Philip to retaliate.

Philip prepared a vast fleet to sail from Lisbon to Flanders, where a large army of Spanish troops were stationed, and then escort barges carrying the troops across the English Channel. On May 9, 1588, *la felicissima armada* — "the most fortunate fleet," as it was ironically called in official documents — sailed from Lisbon harbor composed of more than 130 vessels. The **Spanish Armada** met an English

Book of Common Prayer The official (parliament-approved) prayer book of the Church of England, containing the prayers for all services, the forms for administration of the sacraments, and a manual for the ordination of deacons, priests, and bishops.

Spanish Armada The fleet sent by Philip II of Spain in 1588 against England as a religious crusade against Protestantism. Weather and the English fleet defeated it.

fleet in the channel before it reached Flanders. The English ships were smaller, faster, and more maneuverable, and many of them had greater firing power than their Spanish counterparts. A combination of storms and squalls, spoiled food and rank water, inadequate Spanish ammunition, and, to a lesser extent, English fire ships that caused the Spanish to scatter, gave England the victory. On the journey home many Spanish ships went down around Ireland; perhaps 65 managed to reach home ports.

The battle in the English Channel has frequently been described as one of the decisive battles in world history. In fact, it had mixed consequences. Spain soon rebuilt its navy, and after 1588 the quality of the Spanish fleet improved. The war between England and Spain dragged on for years. Yet the defeat of the Spanish Armada prevented Philip II from reimposing Catholicism on England by force. In England the victory contributed to a David and Goliath legend that enhanced English national sentiment.

Calvinism

In 1509, while Luther was preparing for a doctorate at Wittenberg, John Calvin (1509–1564) was born in Noyon in northwestern France. As a young man he studied law, which had a decisive impact on his mind and later his thought. In 1533 he experienced a religious crisis, as a result of which he converted to Protestantism.

Calvin believed that God had specifically selected him to reform the church. Accordingly, he accepted an invitation to assist in the reformation of the city of Geneva. There, beginning in 1541, Calvin worked assiduously to establish a Christian society ruled by God through civil magistrates and reformed ministers. Geneva, "a city that was a church," became the model of a Christian community for sixteenth-century Protestant reformers.

The Institutes of the Christian Religion Calvin's formulation of Christian doctrine, which became a systematic theology for Protestantism.

To understand Calvin's Geneva, it is necessary to understand Calvin's ideas. These he embodied in *The Institutes of the Christian Religion*, first published in 1536 and definitively issued in 1559. The cornerstone of Calvin's theology was his belief in the absolute sovereignty and omnipotence of God and the total weakness of humanity. Before the infinite power of God, he asserted, men and women are as insignificant as grains of sand.

Calvin did not ascribe free will to human beings because that would detract from the sovereignty of God. Men and women cannot actively work to achieve salvation; rather, God in his infinite wisdom decided at the beginning of time who would be saved and who damned. This viewpoint constitutes the theological principle called **predestination.**

predestination The teaching that God has determined the salvation or damnation of individuals based on His will and purpose, not on their merit of works.

Many people consider the doctrine of predestination, which dates back to Saint Augustine and Saint Paul, to be a pessimistic view of the nature of God. But "this terrible decree," as even Calvin called it, did not lead to pessimism or fatalism. Rather, the Calvinist believed in the redemptive work of Christ and was confident that God had elected (saved) him or her. Predestination served as an energizing dynamic, forcing a person to undergo hardships in the constant struggle against evil.

Calvin aroused Genevans to a high standard of morality. He had two remarkable assets: complete mastery of the Scriptures and exceptional eloquence. In the reformation of the city, the Genevan Consistory also exercised a powerful role. This body of laymen and pastors was assembled "to keep watch over every man's life [and] to admonish amiably those whom they see leading a disorderly life."[4]

Although all municipal governments in early modern Europe regulated citizens' conduct, none did so with the severity of Geneva's Consistory under Calvin's leadership. Absence from sermons, criticism of ministers, dancing, card playing, family quarrels, and heavy drinking were all investigated and punished by the Consistory. Serious crimes and heresy were handled by the civil authorities, which, with the Consistory's approval, sometimes used torture to extract confessions. Between 1542 and 1546 alone seventy-six persons were banished from Geneva and fifty-eight executed for heresy, adultery, blasphemy, and witchcraft. Among them was the Spanish humanist Michael Servetus, who was burned at the stake for denying the scriptural basis for the Trinity, rejecting child baptism, and insisting that a person under twenty cannot commit a mortal sin. This last idea was considered especially dangerous to public morality.

Religious refugees from France, England, Spain, Scotland, and Italy visited Calvin's Geneva. Subsequently, the Reformed church of Calvin served as the model for the Presbyterian church in Scotland, the Huguenot church in France, and the Puritan churches in England and New England.

Calvinism became the compelling force in international Protestantism. The Calvinist ethic of the "calling" dignified all work with a religious aspect. Hard work, well done, was pleasing to God. This doctrine encouraged an aggressive, vigorous activism. These factors, together with the social and economic applications of Calvin's theology, made Calvinism the most dynamic force in sixteenth- and seventeenth-century Protestantism.

Young John Calvin

Even in youth, Calvin's face showed the strength and determination that were later to characterize his religious zeal. (Bibliothèque de Genève, Département Iconographique)

The Establishment of the Church of Scotland

Calvinism found a ready audience in Scotland, where the Scottish nobles supported reform. One man, John Knox (1505?–1572), dominated the reform movement, which led to the establishment of a state church.

Knox was determined to structure the Scottish church after the model of Geneva, where he had studied and worked with Calvin. The Presbyterian Church of Scotland was strictly Calvinist in doctrine, adopted a simple and dignified service of worship, and laid great emphasis on preaching. Its name describes its governance by *presbyters*, or ministers, instead of bishops. Knox's *Book of Common Order* (1564) became the liturgical directory for the church.

The Reformation in Eastern Europe

While political and economic issues determined the course of the Reformation in western and northern Europe, ethnic factors often proved decisive in eastern Europe, where people of diverse backgrounds had settled in the later Middle Ages.

In Bohemia in the fifteenth century, a Czech majority was ruled by Germans. Most Czechs had adopted the ideas of Jan Hus, and the emperor had been forced to recognize a separate Hussite church. Yet Lutheranism appealed to Germans in Bohemia in the 1520s and 1530s, and the nobility embraced Lutheranism in opposition to the Catholic Habsburgs. The forces of the Catholic Reformation (see page 357) promoted a Catholic spiritual revival in Bohemia, and some areas reconverted. This complicated situation would be one of the causes of the Thirty Years' War (see pages 435–437).

By 1500 Poland and the Grand Duchy of Lithuania were jointly governed by king, senate, and diet (parliament), but the two territories retained separate officials, judicial systems, armies, and forms of citizenship. The combined realms covered about 440,150 square miles, making Poland-Lithuania the largest European polity. A population of only about 7.5 million people was very thinly scattered over that land.

The population of Poland-Lithuania was also very diverse; Germans, Italians, Tartars, and Jews lived with Poles and Lithuanians. Such peoples had come as merchants, invited by medieval rulers because of their wealth or to make agricultural improvements. Each group spoke its native language, though all educated people spoke Latin. Luther's ideas took root in Germanized towns but were opposed by King Sigismund I (r. 1506-1548) as well as by ordinary Poles who held strong anti-German feeling. The Reformed tradition of John Calvin, with its stress on the power of church elders, appealed to the Polish nobility, however. The fact that Calvinism originated in France, not in Germany, also made it more attractive than Lutheranism. But doctrinal differences among Calvinists, Lutherans, and other groups prevented united opposition to Catholicism, and a Counter-Reformation gained momentum. By 1650, due to the efforts of Stanislaus Hosius (1505–1579) and those of the Jesuits (see page 359), the identification of Poland and Roman Catholicism was well established.

Hungary's experience with the Reformation was even more complex. Lutheranism was spread by Hungarian students who had studied at Wittenberg, but the Catholic hierarchy and Hungarian magnates threatened to execute all Lutherans. However, a military event on August 26, 1526, had profound consequences for both the Hungarian state and the Protestant Reformation there. On the plain of Mohács in southern Hungary, the Ottoman sultan Suleiman the Magnificent (see page 439) inflicted a crushing defeat on the Hungarians, killing King Louis II, many of the magnates, and more than sixteen thousand ordinary soldiers. The Hungarian kingdom was then divided into three parts: the Ottoman Turks absorbed the great plains, including the capital, Buda; the Habsburgs ruled the north and west; and Ottoman-supported Janos Zapolya held eastern Hungary and Transylvania.

The Turks were indifferent to the religious conflicts of the infidels. Many Magyar (Hungarian) magnates accepted Lutheranism; Lutheran schools and parishes headed by men educated at Wittenberg multiplied; and peasants welcomed the new faith. The majority of people were Protestant until the late seventeenth century, when Hungarian nobles recognized Habsburg (Catholic) rule and Ottoman Turkish withdrawal in 1699 led to Catholic restoration.

Section Review

- John Calvin and others who developed their own theology led the spread of the Protestant Reformation beyond Germany to England, France, and eastern Europe.

- In England, King Henry VIII broke with Rome over his desire to divorce his wife Catherine of Aragon, using Parliament to legalize the Reformation and make himself the head of the Church of England.

- Following Henry's death, England returned to Catholicism briefly while his daughter Mary was queen, then adopted moderate Protestantism under his daughter Elizabeth.

- In Geneva, John Calvin emphasized the absolute power of God and demanded high standards of morality; Calvinism encouraged hard work and dynamic activism.

- Calvinism was the model for the Presbyterian Church of Scotland established by John Knox who advocated a simple service, an emphasis on preaching, and governance by ministers instead of bishops.

The Catholic Reformation

How did the Catholic Church respond to the new religious situation?

Between 1517 and 1547 Protestantism made remarkable advances. Nevertheless, the Roman Catholic Church made a significant comeback. After about 1540 no new large areas of Europe, other than the Netherlands, accepted Protestant beliefs (see Map 14.2). Many historians see the developments within the Catholic Church after the Protestant Reformation as two interrelated movements, one a drive for internal reform linked to earlier reform efforts, and the other a Counter-Reformation that opposed Protestants intellectually, politically, militarily, and institutionally. In both movements, the papacy, new religious orders, and the Council of Trent that met from 1545 to 1563 were important agents.

The Reformed Papacy Renaissance popes and advisers were not blind to the need for church reforms, but they resisted calls for a general council representing the entire church, fearing loss of power, revenue, and prestige. This changed beginning with Pope Paul III (1534–1549), and the papal court became the center of the reform movement rather than its chief opponent. The lives of the pope and his reform-minded cardinals, abbots, and bishops were models of decorum and piety.

In 1542 Pope Paul III established the Sacred Congregation of the **Holy Office,** with jurisdiction over the Roman Inquisition, a powerful instrument of the Catholic Reformation. The Inquisition was a committee of six cardinals with judicial authority over all Catholics and the power to arrest, imprison, and execute. Within the Papal States, the Inquisition effectively destroyed heresy (and some heretics).

> **Holy Office** The official Roman Catholic agency founded in 1542 to combat international doctrinal heresy and to promote sound doctrine on faith and morals.

The Council of Trent Pope Paul III also called an ecumenical council, which met intermittently from 1545 to 1563 at Trent, an imperial city close to Italy. It was called not only to reform the church but also to secure reconciliation with the Protestants. Lutherans and Calvinists were invited to participate, but their insistence that the Scriptures be the sole basis for discussion made reconciliation impossible.

Nonetheless, the decrees of the Council of Trent laid a solid basis for the spiritual renewal of the Catholic Church. It gave equal validity to the Scriptures and to tradition as sources of religious truth and authority. It reaffirmed the seven sacraments and the traditional Catholic teaching on transubstantiation. It tackled the disciplinary matters that had disillusioned the faithful, requiring bishops to reside in their own dioceses, suppressing pluralism and simony, and forbidding the sale of indulgences. Clerics who kept concubines were to give them up. In a highly original decree, the council required every diocese to establish a seminary for the education and training of the clergy. Seminary professors were to determine whether candidates for ordination had *vocations,* genuine callings to the priesthood. This was a novel idea, since from the time of the early church, parents had determined their sons' (and daughters') religious careers. Finally, great emphasis was laid on preaching and instructing the laity, especially the uneducated.

One decision had especially important social consequences for laypeople. The Council of Trent stipulated that for a marriage to be valid, consent (the essence of marriage) as given in the vows had to be made publicly before witnesses, one of

Predominant religion in 1555

- Lutheran
- Calvinist (Reformed)
- Church of England
- Roman Catholic
- Orthodox
- Muslim
- Spread of Calvinism
- Huguenot center
- Ottoman Empire, 1566

400 Mi.

400 Km.

200

200

0

0

N

Black Sea

Mediterranean Sea

Adriatic Sea

Baltic Sea

North Sea

ATLANTIC OCEAN

OTTOMAN EMPIRE

BESSARABIA

MOLDAVIA

WALLACHIA

Danube R.

TRANSYLVANIA

BULGARIA

SERBIA

GREECE

HUNGARY

Belgrade

Buda
Pest

LITHUANIA

PRUSSIA

POLAND

Warsaw

Riga

Helsinki

SWEDEN

Stockholm

NORWAY
1536/1607

Bergen

DENMARK

Copenhagen

BRANDENBURG

SAXONY

Hamburg

Wittenberg
Martin Luther

Birthplace of
Martin Luther,
1483–1546

Eisleben

Leipzig

Erfurt

Prague

Jan Hus,
1369–1415

BOHEMIA

MORAVIA

AUSTRIA

Vienna

Munich

Augsburg

Nuremberg

HOLY ROMAN
EMPIRE

Stuttgart

Speyer

Marburg

Worms

Birthplace of
John Calvin,
1509–1564

Edict of Worms,
1521

Münster

Amsterdam

NETHERLANDS

Antwerp

Brussels

Noyon

Paris

Strasbourg

Basel

Zurich

Ulrich Zwingli,
1484–1531

Geneva
John Calvin

Avignon

Marseilles

Council of Trent,
1545–1563

Trent

Venice

Milan

Pavia

Genoa

Pisa

Florence

ITALY

Rome
Roman Inquisition
established, 1542

Naples

Bari

Corsica

Sardinia

Sicily

SCOTLAND
1560

Edinburgh
John Knox,
1505–1572

Penetration of Calvinism
to England after 1558

ENGLAND 1536

Oxford
John Wyclif,
1320–1384

London

Plymouth

IRELAND

Dublin

FRANCE

Rennes

Orléans

Nantes

Edict of Nantes,
1598

La Rochelle

Bordeaux

Toulouse

Loyola
Birthplace of
Ignatius Loyola,
1491–1556

SPAIN

Madrid

Toledo

Seville

Granada

Valencia

Barcelona

Balearic Is.

PORTUGAL

Lisbon

TUNIS

ALGIERS

OTTOMAN EMPIRE

MOROCCO

60°N

50°N

40°N

30°E

20°E

10°E

0°

10°W

MAPPING THE PAST

MAP 14.2   Religious Divisions in Europe

The Reformations shattered the religious unity of Western Christendom. The situation was even more complicated than a map of this scale can show. Many cities within the Holy Roman Empire, for example, accepted a different faith than the surrounding countryside; Augsburg, Basel, and Strasbourg were all Protestant, though surrounded by territory ruled by Catholic nobles. Use the map and the information in the book to answer the following questions: **[1]** Why was the Holy Roman Empire the first arena of religious conflict in sixteenth-century Europe? **[2]** Are there similarities in regions where a particular branch of the Christian faith was maintained or took root? **[3]** To what degree can nonreligious factors be used as an explanation for the religious divisions in sixteenth-century Europe?

whom had to be the parish priest. Trent thereby ended the widespread practice of secret marriages in Catholic countries. The decrees of the Council of Trent laid a solid basis for the spiritual renewal of the church. For four centuries the doctrinal and disciplinary legislation of Trent served as the basis for Roman Catholic faith, organization, and practice.

New Religious Orders

The establishment of new religious orders within the church reveals a central feature of the Catholic Reformation. Most of these new orders developed in response to one crying need: to raise the moral and intellectual level of the clergy and people. (See the feature "Individuals in Society: Teresa of Ávila.") Education was a major goal of the two most famous orders.

The Ursuline order of nuns, founded by Angela Merici (1474–1540), attained enormous prestige for the education of women. The daughter of a country gentleman, Angela Merici worked for many years among the poor, sick, and uneducated around her native Brescia in northern Italy. In 1535 she established the first women's religious order concentrating exclusively on teaching young girls, with the goal of re-Christianizing society by training future wives and mothers. After receiving papal approval in 1565, the Ursulines rapidly spread to France and the New World.

The Society of Jesus, or **Jesuits,** founded by Ignatius Loyola (1491–1556), played a powerful international role in strengthening Catholicism in Europe and spreading the faith around the world. While recuperating from a severe battle wound in his legs, Loyola studied a life of Christ and other religious books and decided to give up his military career and become a soldier of Christ. The first Jesuits, whom Loyola recruited primarily from the wealthy merchant and professional classes, saw the Reformation as a pastoral problem, its causes and cures related not to doctrinal issues but to people's spiritual condition. Reform of the church, as Luther and Calvin understood that term, played no role in the future the Jesuits planned for themselves. Their goal was "to help souls."

The Society of Jesus developed into a highly centralized, tightly knit organization. In addition to the traditional vows of poverty, chastity, and obedience, professed members vowed to go anywhere the pope said they were needed. They attracted many recruits and achieved phenomenal success for the papacy and the reformed Catholic Church, carrying Christianity to India and Japan before 1550 and to Brazil, North America, and the Congo in the seventeenth century. Within Europe the Jesuits brought southern Germany and much of eastern Europe back

Jesuits Members of the Society of Jesus, founded by Ignatius Loyola and approved by the papacy in 1540, whose goal was the spread of the Roman Catholic faith through humanistic schools and missionary activity.

Section Review

- The Council at Trent (1545–1563) failed to reconcile Protestants and Catholics but succeeded in renewing the spirituality of the Catholic Church.

- The reforms of Trent included establishing seminaries to train young clergy, determining "callings" or church vocations, and reforming marriage laws, which ended secret marriages.

- The mystical Carmelite nun Teresa of Ávila reformed her order, stressing poverty, enclosure, obedience, and social equality.

- The Ursuline nuns were the first order solely dedicated to the education of young women.

- The Jesuits contributed to the spread of Catholicism and strengthened the papacy by travelling throughout much of the world preaching and teaching.

Individuals in Society

Teresa of Ávila

Her family derived from Toledo, center of the Moorish, Jewish, and Christian cultures in medieval Spain. Her grandfather, Juan Sanchez, made a fortune in the cloth trade. A "New Christian" (see pages 330–332), he was accused of secretly practicing Judaism. Although he endured the humiliation of a public repentance, he moved his family south to Ávila. Beginning again, he recouped his wealth and, aspiring to the prestige of an "Old Christian," bought noble status. Juan's son Alzonzo Sanchez de Cepeda married a woman of thoroughly Christian background, giving his family an aura of impeccable orthodoxy. The third of their nine children, Teresa, became a saint and in 1970 was the first woman declared a Doctor of the Church, a title given to a theologian of outstanding merit.

Seventeenth-century cloisonné enamelwork illustrating Teresa of Ávila's famous vision of an angel piercing her heart. (By gracious permission of Catherine Hamilton Kappauf)

At age twenty, inspired more by the fear of Hell than the love of God, Teresa (1515–1582) entered the Carmelite Convent of the Incarnation in Ávila. Most of the nuns were daughters of Ávila's leading citizens; they had entered the convent because of a family decision about which daughters would marry and which would become nuns. Their lives were much like those of female family members outside the convent walls, with good food, comfortable surroundings, and frequent visits from family and friends. Teresa was frequently ill, but she lived quietly in the convent for many years. In her late thirties, she began to read devotional literature intensely and had profound mystical experiences—visions and voices in which Christ chastised her for her frivolous life and friends. She described one such experience in 1560:

It pleased the Lord that I should see an angel. . . . Short, and very beautiful, his face was so aflame that he appeared to be one of the highest types of angels. . . . In his hands I saw a long golden spear and at the end of an iron tip I seemed to see a point of fire. With this he seemed to pierce my heart several times so that it penetrated to my entrails. When he drew it out . . . he left me completely afire with the great love of God.*

Teresa responded with a new sense of purpose: although she encountered stiff opposition, she resolved to found a reformed house. Four basic principles were to guide the new convent. First, poverty was to be fully observed, symbolized by the nuns' being barefoot, hence *discalced.* Charity and the nuns' own work must support the community. Second, the convent must keep strict enclosure; the visits of powerful benefactors with material demands were forbidden. Third, Teresa intended an egalitarian atmosphere in which class distinctions were forbidden. She had always rejected the emphasis on "purity of blood," a distinctive and racist feature of Spanish society that was especially out of place in the cloister. All sisters, including those of aristocratic background, must share the manual chores. Finally, like Ignatius Loyola and the Jesuits, Teresa placed great emphasis on obedience, especially to one's confessor.

Between 1562 and Teresa's death in 1582, she founded or reformed fourteen other houses of nuns, traveling widely to do so. Though Teresa did not advocate institutionalized roles for women outside the convent, she did chafe at the restrictions placed on her because of her sex, and she thought of the new religious houses she founded as answers to the Protestant takeover of Catholic churches elsewhere in Europe. From her brother, who had obtained wealth in the Spanish colonies, Teresa learned about conditions in Peru and instructed her nuns "to pray unceasingly for the missionaries working among the heathens." Through prayer, Teresa wrote, her nuns could share in the exciting tasks of evangelization and missionary work otherwise closed to women. Her books, along with her five hundred extant letters, show her as a practical and down-to-earth woman as well as a mystic and a creative theologian.

Questions for Analysis

1. How did sixteenth-century convent life reflect the values of Spanish society?
2. How is the life of Teresa of Ávila typical of developments in the Catholic Reformation? How is her life unusual?

* *The Autobiography of St. Teresa of Ávila*, trans. and ed. E. A. Peers (New York: Doubleday, 1960, pp. 273–274).

to Catholicism. Jesuit schools adopted the modern humanist curricula and methods, educating the sons of the nobility as well as the poor. As confessors and spiritual directors to kings, Jesuits exerted great political influence.

Religious Violence

What were the causes and consequences of religious violence, including riots, wars, and witch hunts?

In 1559 France and Spain signed the Treaty of Cateau-Cambrésis (**cah-toh-kam-BRIE-sees**), which ended the long conflict known as the Habsburg-Valois Wars. Spain was the victor. France, exhausted by the struggle, had to acknowledge Spanish dominance in Italy, where much of the fighting had taken place. However, over the next century religious differences led to riots, civil wars, and international conflicts. Especially in France and the Netherlands, Protestants and Catholics used violent actions as well as preaching and teaching against each other, for each side regarded the other as a poison in the community that would provoke the wrath of God. Catholics continued to believe that Calvinists and Lutherans could be reconverted; Protestants persisted in thinking that the Roman church should be destroyed. Catholics and Protestants alike feared people of other faiths, who they often saw as agents of Satan. Even more, they feared those who were explicitly identified with Satan: witches living in their midst. This era was the time of the most virulent witch persecutions in European history, as both Protestants and Catholics tried to make their cities and states more godly.

French Religious Wars

The costs of the Habsburg-Valois Wars, waged intermittently through the first half of the sixteenth century, forced the French to increase taxes and borrow heavily. King Francis I (r. 1515–1547) also tried two new devices to raise revenue: the sale of public offices and a treaty with the papacy. The former proved to be only a temporary source of money: once a man bought an office he and his heirs were exempt from taxation. But the latter, known as the Concordat of Bologna (see page 329), gave the French crown the right to appoint all French bishops and abbots, ensuring a rich supplement of money and offices. Because French rulers possessed control over appointments and had a vested financial interest in Catholicism, they had no need to revolt against Rome.

Significant numbers of those ruled, however, were attracted to the "reformed religion," as Calvinism was called. Initially, Calvinism drew converts from among reform-minded members of the Catholic clergy, the industrious middle classes, and artisan groups. Most French Calvinists (called **Huguenots**) lived in major cities, such as Paris, Lyons, and Rouen. When Henry II died in 1559, perhaps one-tenth of the population had become Calvinist.

The feebleness of the French monarchy was the seed from which the weeds of civil violence sprang. The three weak sons of Henry II who occupied the throne could not provide the necessary leadership, and they were often dominated by their mother, Catherine de' Medici. The French nobility took advantage of this monarchical weakness. Just as German princes in the Holy Roman Empire had adopted Lutheranism as a means of opposition to Emperor Charles V, so French nobles frequently adopted the reformed religion as a religious cloak for their independence. Armed clashes between Catholic royalist lords and Calvinist

Huguenots Originally a pejorative term for French Calvinists, later the official title for members of this group.

antimonarchical lords occurred in many parts of France. Both Calvinists and Catholics believed that the others' books, services, and ministers polluted the community. Preachers incited violence, and religious ceremonies such as baptisms, marriages, and funerals triggered it.

Calvinist teachings called the power of sacred images into question, and mobs in many cities took down and smashed statues, stained-glass windows, and paintings. Though it was often inspired by fiery Protestant sermons, this **iconoclasm** is an example of men and women carrying out the Reformation themselves, rethinking the church's system of meaning and the relationship between the unseen and the seen. Catholic mobs responded by defending images, and crowds on both sides killed their opponents, often in gruesome ways.

A savage Catholic attack on Calvinists in Paris on August 24, 1572 (Saint Bartholomew's Day), followed the usual pattern. The occasion was the marriage ceremony of the king's sister Margaret of Valois to the Protestant Henry of Navarre, which was intended to help reconcile Catholics and Huguenots. Instead, Huguenot wedding guests in Paris were massacred, and other Protestants were slaughtered by mobs. Religious violence spread to the provinces, where thousands were killed. This **Saint Bartholomew's Day massacre** led to a civil war that dragged on for fifteen years. Agriculture in many areas was destroyed; commercial life declined severely; and starvation and death haunted the land.

What ultimately saved France was a small group of moderates of both faiths, called **politiques**, who believed that only the restoration of strong monarchy could reverse the trend toward collapse. The politiques also favored accepting the Huguenots as an officially recognized and organized pressure group. The death of Catherine de' Medici, followed by the assassination of King Henry III, paved the way for the accession of Henry of Navarre (the unfortunate bridegroom of the St. Bartholomew's Day massacre), a politique who became Henry IV (r. 1589–1610).

Henry's willingness to sacrifice religious principles to political necessity saved France. He converted to Catholicism but also issued the **Edict of Nantes**, which granted liberty of conscience and liberty of public worship to Huguenots in 150 fortified towns. The reign of Henry IV and the Edict of Nantes prepared the way for French absolutism in the seventeenth century by helping restore internal peace in France.

The Netherlands Under Charles V

In the Netherlands, what began as a movement for the reformation of the church developed into a struggle for Dutch independence. Emperor Charles V had inherited the seventeen provinces that compose present-day Belgium and the Netherlands (see page 348). Each was self-governing and enjoyed the right to make its own laws and collect its own taxes. They were united politically only in recognition of a common ruler, the emperor. The cities of the Netherlands made their living by trade and industry.

In the Low Countries as elsewhere, corruption in the Roman church and the critical spirit of the Renaissance provoked pressure for reform, and Lutheran ideas took root. Charles V had grown up in the Netherlands, however, and he was able to limit their impact. But Charles V abdicated in 1556 and transferred power over the Netherlands to his son Philip, who had grown up in Spain. Protestant ideas spread.

By the 1560s Protestants in the Netherlands were primarily Calvinists. Calvinism's intellectual seriousness, moral gravity, and emphasis on any form of labor well done appealed to middle-class merchants and financiers and working-class

iconoclasm Ridicule and destruction of religious images.

Saint Bartholomew's Day massacre Massacre of thousands of Protestants in Paris and other cities by Catholics, beginning on Saint Bartholomew's Day (August 24) 1572.

politiques Moderates of both religious faiths who held that only a strong monarchy could save France from total collapse.

Edict of Nantes A document issued by Henry IV of France in 1598, granting liberty of conscience and of public worship to Calvinists in 150 towns; it helped restore peace in France.

Iconoclasm in the Netherlands

Calvinist men and women break stained-glass windows, remove statues, and carry off devotional altarpieces. Iconoclasm, or the destruction of religious images, is often described as a "riot," but here the participants seem very purposeful. Calvinist Protestants regarded pictures and statues as sacrilegious and saw removing them as a way to purify the church. (The Fotomas Index/The Bridgeman Art Library)

people. Whereas Lutherans taught respect for the powers that be, Calvinism tended to encourage opposition to "illegal" civil authorities.

In the 1560s Spanish authorities attempted to suppress Calvinist worship and raised taxes, which sparked riots. Thirty churches in Antwerp were sacked and the religious images in them destroyed in a wave of iconoclasm. From Antwerp the destruction spread. Philip II sent twenty thousand Spanish troops under the duke of Alva to pacify the Low Countries. Alva interpreted "pacification" to mean the ruthless extermination of religious and political dissidents. On top of the Inquisition, he opened his own tribunal, soon called the "Council of Blood." On March 3, 1568, fifteen hundred men were executed.

For ten years, civil war raged in the Netherlands between Catholics and Protestants and between the seventeen provinces and Spain. Eventually the ten southern provinces, the Spanish Netherlands (the future Belgium), came under the control of the Spanish Habsburg forces. The seven northern provinces, led by Holland, formed the **Union of Utrecht** and in 1581 declared their independence from Spain. The north was Protestant; the south remained Catholic. Philip did not accept this, and war continued. England was even drawn into the conflict, supplying money and troops to the northern United Provinces. (Spain launched an unsuccessful invasion of England in response; see pages 353–354.) Hostilities ended in 1609 when Spain agreed to a truce that recognized the independence of the United Provinces.

Union of Utrecht The alliance of seven northern provinces (led by Holland) that declared its independence from Spain and formed the United Provinces of the Netherlands.

The Great European Witch Hunt

The relationship between the Reformation and the upsurge in trials for witchcraft that occurred at roughly the same time is complex. Increasing persecution for witchcraft actually began before the Reformation in the 1480s, but it became especially common about 1560. Religious reformers' extreme notions of the Devil's powers and the insecurity created by the religious wars contributed to this increase. Both Protestants and Catholics tried and executed witches, with church officials and secular authorities acting together.

The heightened sense of God's power and divine wrath in the Reformation era was an important factor in the witch hunts, but other factors were also significant. One of these was a change in the idea of what a witch was. Nearly all premodern societies believe in witchcraft and make some attempts to control witches, who are

Hans Baldung Grien: Witches' Sabbat (1510)
In this woodcut, Grien combines learned and popular beliefs about witches: they traveled at night, met at sabbats (or assemblies), feasted on infants (in dish held high), concocted strange potions, and had animal "familiars" that were really demons (here, a cat). Grien also highlights the sexual nature of witchcraft by portraying the women naked and showing them with goats, which were common symbols of sexuality. (Germanisches Nationalmuseum Nürnberg)

understood to be people who use magical forces. In the later Middle Ages, however, many educated Christian theologians, canon lawyers, and officials added a demonological component to this notion of what a witch was. For them, the essence of witchcraft was making a pact with the Devil that required the witch to do the Devil's bidding. Witches were no longer simply people who used magical power to get what they wanted, but rather people used by the Devil to do what *he* wanted. Some demonological theorists also claimed that witches were organized in an international conspiracy to overthrow Christianity. Witchcraft was thus spiritualized, and witches became the ultimate heretics, enemies of God.

Trials involving this new notion of witchcraft as diabolical heresy began in Switzerland and southern Germany in the late fifteenth century, became less numerous in the early decades of the Reformation when Protestants and Catholics were busy fighting each other, and then picked up again in about 1560. Scholars estimate that during the sixteenth and seventeenth centuries somewhere between 100,000 and 200,000 people were officially tried for witchcraft and between 40,000 and 60,000 were executed. While the trials were secret, executions were not, and the lists of charges were read out for all to hear.

Though the gender balance varied widely in different parts of Europe, between 75 and 85 percent of those tried and executed were women. Ideas about women, and the roles women actually played in society, were thus important factors shaping the witch hunts. Some demonologists expressed virulent **misogyny**, or hatred of women, and particularly emphasized women's powerful sexual desire, which could be satisfied only by a demonic lover. Most people viewed women as weaker and so more likely to give in to any kind of offer by the Devil, including better food or nicer clothing. Women were associated with nature, disorder, and the body, all of which were linked with the demonic.

Most witch trials began with a single accusation in a village or town. Individuals accused someone they knew of using magic to spoil food, make children ill, kill animals, raise a hailstorm, or do other types of harm. Tensions within families, households, and neighborhoods often played a role in these accusations. Women number very prominently among accusers and witnesses as well as among those accused of witchcraft because the actions witches were initially charged with, such as harming children or curdling milk, were generally part of women's sphere. A woman also gained economic and social security by conforming to the standard of the good wife and mother and by confronting women who deviated from it.

misogyny Hatred of women.

Once a charge was made, judges began to question other neighbors and acquaintances, building up a list of suspicious incidents that might have taken place over decades. Historians have pointed out that one of the reasons those accused of witchcraft were often older was that it took years to build up a reputation as a witch. At this point, the suspect was brought in for questioning by legal authorities. Judges and inquisitors sought the exact details of a witch's demonic contacts, including sexual ones. Suspects were generally stripped and shaved in a search for a "witch's mark," or "pricked" to find a spot insensitive to pain, and then tortured.

Once the initial suspect had been questioned, and particularly if he or she had been tortured, the people who had been implicated were brought in for questioning. This might lead to a small hunt, involving from five to ten victims, and it sometimes grew into a much larger hunt, what historians have called a "witch panic." Panics were most common in the part of Europe that saw the most witch accusations in general—the Holy Roman Empire, Switzerland, and parts of France. Most of this area consisted of very small governmental units, which were jealous of each other and after the Reformation were divided by religion. The rulers of these small territories often felt more threatened than did the monarchs of western Europe, and they saw persecuting witches as a way to demonstrate their piety and concern for order.

Sometimes witch panics were the result of legal authorities' rounding up a group of suspects together. Such panics often occurred after some type of climatic disaster, such as an unusually cold and wet summer, and they came in waves. In large-scale panics a wider variety of suspects were taken in—wealthier people, children, a greater proportion of men. Mass panics tended to end when it became clear to legal authorities, or to the community itself, that the people being questioned or executed were not what they understood witches to be, or that the scope of accusations was beyond belief. Some from their community might be in league with Satan, they thought, but not this type of person and not as many as this.

Similar skepticism led to the gradual end of witch hunts in Europe. Even in the sixteenth century a few individuals questioned whether witches could ever do harm, make a pact with the Devil, or engage in the wild activities attributed to them. Doubts about whether secret denunciations were valid or torture would ever yield a truthful confession gradually spread among the same type of religious and legal authorities who had so vigorously persecuted witches. Prosecutions for witchcraft became less common and were gradually outlawed. The last official execution for witchcraft in England was in 1682, though the last one in the Holy Roman Empire was not until 1775.

Section Review

- The religious differences between Catholics and Protestants led to conflict and violence, each side viewing the other as wrong.

- The French Calvinist Huguenots clashed with the Catholic majority in bloody riots and massacres, ending only when moderates of both faiths aided in securing official recognition for the minority.

- Protestant ideas spread to the Netherlands, where civil war raged for years between the Dutch and Spain, ending when Spain recognized the independence of the United Provinces.

- Witch hunts intensified with the belief that witches did the bidding of the Devil, and all were in danger of experiencing God's wrath as a result of their acts.

- Witch hunts began with an accusation (usually of a woman), then an investigation, often under torture, and sometimes grew to a "witch panic" involving more people, until the whole witch hunt movement gradually faded with the growth of scepticism.

Chapter Review

What were the central ideas of the reformers, and why were they appealing to different social groups? (page 338)

The Catholic Church in the early sixteenth century had serious problems, and many individuals and groups had long called for reform. This background of discontent helps explain why Martin Luther's ideas found such a ready audience. Luther and other Protestants developed a new understanding of Christian doctrine that emphasized faith, the power of God's grace, and the centrality of the Bible. Protestant ideas were attractive to educated people and urban residents, and they spread rapidly through preaching, hymns, and the printing press. By 1530 many parts of the Holy Roman

Key Terms

anticlericalism (p. 338)

pluralism (p. 338)

indulgence (p. 339)

Diet of Worms (p. 341)

(continued)

Empire and Scandinavia had broken with the Catholic Church. Some reformers developed more radical ideas about infant baptism, the ownership of property, and separation between church and state. Both Protestants and Catholics regarded these as dangerous, and radicals were banished or executed. The German Peasants' War, in which Luther's ideas were linked to calls for social and economic reform, was similarly put down harshly. The Protestant reformers did not break with medieval ideas about the proper gender hierarchy, though they did elevate the status of marriage and viewed orderly households as the key building blocks of society.

How did the political situation in Germany shape the course of the Reformation? (page 348)

The progress of the Reformation was shaped by the political situation in the Holy Roman Empire. The Habsburg emperor, Charles V, ruled almost half of Europe along with Spain's overseas colonies. Within the empire his authority was limited, however, and local princes, nobles, and cities actually held most power. This decentralization allowed the Reformation to spread. Charles remained firmly Catholic, and in the 1530s religious wars began in Germany. These were brought to an end with the Peace of Augsburg in 1555, which allowed rulers in each territory to choose whether their territory would be Catholic or Lutheran.

How did Protestant ideas and institutions spread beyond German-speaking lands? (page 351)

In England, Henry VIII's desire for a son who would succeed to his throne triggered the break with Rome, and a Protestant church was established. Protestant ideas also spread into France and eastern Europe. In all these areas, a second generation of reformers built on Lutheran and Zwinglian ideas to develop their own theology and plans for institutional change. The most important of the second-generation reformers was John Calvin, whose ideas would come to shape Christianity over a much wider area than did Luther's.

How did the Catholic Church respond to the new religious situation? (page 357)

The Roman Catholic Church responded slowly to the Protestant challenge, but by the 1530s the papacy was leading a movement for reform within the church instead of blocking it. Catholic doctrine was reaffirmed at the Council of Trent, and reform measures such as the opening of seminaries for priests and a ban on holding multiple church offices were introduced. New religious orders such as the Jesuits and the Ursulines spread Catholic ideas through teaching, and in the case of the Jesuits through missionary work.

What were the causes and consequences of religious violence, including riots, wars, and witch hunts? (page 361)

Religious differences led to riots, civil wars, and international conflicts in the later sixteenth century. In France and the Netherlands, Calvinist Protestants and Catholics used violent actions against one another, and religious differences mixed with political and economic grievances. Long civil wars resulted, which in the case of the Netherlands became an international conflict. War ended in France with the Edict of Nantes in which Protestants were given some civil rights, and in the Netherlands with a division of the country into a Protestant north and Catholic south. The era of religious wars was also the time of the most extensive witch persecutions in European history, as

Protestant (p. 341)
transubstantiation (p. 341)
Book of Common Prayer (p. 353)
Spanish Armada (p. 353)
The Institutes of the Christian Religion (p. 354)
predestination (p. 354)
Holy Office (p. 357)
Jesuits (p. 359)
Huguenots (p. 361)
iconoclasm (p. 362)
Saint Bartholomew's Day massacre (p. 362)
politiques (p. 362)
Edict of Nantes (p. 362)
Union of Utrecht (p. 363)
misogyny (p. 364)

both Protestants and Catholics tried to rid their cities and states of people they regarded as linked to the Devil.

Notes

1. Quoted in O. Chadwick, *The Reformation* (Baltimore: Penguin Books, 1976), p. 55.
2. Quoted in E. H. Harbison, *The Age of Reformation* (Ithaca, N.Y.: Cornell University Press, 1963), p. 52.
3. Quoted in S. E. Ozment, *The Age of Reform, 1250–1550: An Intellectual and Religious History of Late Medieval and Reformation Europe* (New Haven, Conn.: Yale University Press, 1980), p. 284.
4. E. W. Monter, *Calvin's Geneva* (New York: John Wiley & Sons, 1967), p. 137.

To assess your mastery of this chapter, go to **bedfordstmartins.com/mckaywestbrief**

Listening to the Past

Martin Luther, *On Christian Liberty*

The idea of liberty or freedom has played a powerful role in the history of Western society and culture, but the meaning and understanding of liberty has undergone continual change and interpretation. In the Roman world, where slavery was a basic institution, liberty meant the condition of being a free man, independent of obligations to a master. In the Middle Ages possessing liberty meant having special privileges or rights that other persons or institutions did not have.

The idea of liberty also has a religious dimension, and the reformer Martin Luther formulated a classic interpretation of liberty in his treatise On Christian Liberty *(sometimes translated* On the Freedom of a Christian*). Luther writes that Christians were freed from sin and death through Christ, not through their own actions.*

On effective preaching, especially to the uneducated, Luther urged the minister "to keep it simple for the simple." (Church of St. Marien, Wittenberg/The Bridgeman Art Library)

A Christian man is the most free lord of all, and subject to none; a Christian man is the most dutiful servant of all, and subject to everyone.

Although these statements appear contradictory, yet, when they are found to agree together, they will do excellently for my purpose. They are both the statements of Paul himself, who says, "Though I be free from all men, yet have I made myself a servant unto all" (I Cor. 9:19), and "Owe no man anything but to love one another" (Rom. 13:8). Now love is by its own nature dutiful and obedient to the beloved object. Thus even Christ, though Lord of all things, was yet made of a woman; made under the law; at once free and a servant; at once in the form of God and in the form of a servant.

Let us examine the subject on a deeper and less simple principle. Man is composed of a twofold nature, a spiritual and a bodily. As regards the spiritual nature, which they name the soul, he is called the spiritual, inward, new man; as regards the bodily nature, which they name the flesh, he is called the fleshly, outward, old man. The Apostle speaks of this: "Though our outward man perish, yet the inward man is renewed day by day" (II Cor. 4:16). The result of this diversity is that in the Scriptures opposing statements are made concerning the same man, the fact being that in the same man these two men are opposed to one another; the flesh lusting against the spirit, and the spirit against the flesh (Gal. 5:17).

We first approach the subject of the inward man, that we may see by what means a man becomes justified, free, and a true Christian; that is, a spiritual, new, and inward man. It is certain that absolutely none among outward things, under whatever name they may be reckoned, has any influence in producing Christian righteousness or liberty, nor, on the other hand, unrighteousness or slavery. This can be shown by an easy argument.

What can it profit to the soul that the body should be in good condition, free, and full of life, that it should eat, drink, and act according to its pleasure, when even the most impious slaves of every kind of vice are prosperous in these matters? Again, what harm can ill health, bondage, hunger, thirst, or any other outward evil, do to the soul, when even the most pious of men, and the freest in the purity of their conscience, are harassed by these things? Neither of these states of things has to do with the liberty or the slavery of the soul.

... [A]nd since it [faith] alone justifies, it is evident that by no outward work or labour can the inward man be at all justified, made free, and saved; and that no works whatever have any relation to him. ... Therefore the first care of every Christian ought to be to lay aside all reliance on works, and strengthen his faith alone more and more, and by it grow in knowledge, not of works, but of Christ Jesus, who has suffered and risen again for him, as Peter teaches (I Peter 5).

Questions for Analysis

1. What did Luther mean by liberty?
2. What aspects of Luther's message might especially appeal to the poor and powerless?

Source: Luther's Primary Works, ed. H. Wace and C. A. Buchheim (London: Holder and Stoughton, 1896). Reprinted in *The Portable Renaissance Reader*, ed. James Bruce Ross and Mary Martin McLaughlin (New York: Penguin Books, 1981), pp. 721–726.

CHAPTER 15

European Exploration and Conquest

1450–1650

Chapter Preview

World Contacts Before Columbus
What was the Afro-Eurasian trading world before Columbus?

The European Voyages of Discovery
How and why did Europeans undertake ambitious voyages of expansion that would usher in a new era of global contact?

Europe and the World After Columbus
What effect did overseas expansion have on the conquered societies, on enslaved Africans, and on world trade?

Changing Attitudes and Beliefs
How did culture and art in this period respond to social and cultural transformation?

INDIVIDUALS IN SOCIETY: Juan de Pareja

LISTENING TO THE PAST: Columbus Describes His First Voyage

A detail from an early-seventeenth-century Flemish painting depicting maps, illustrated travel books, a globe, a compass, and an astrolabe. (Reproduced by courtesy of the Trustees, The National Gallery, London)

Prior to 1400 Europeans were relatively marginal players in a centuries-old trading system that linked Africa, Asia, and Europe. Elite classes everywhere prized Chinese porcelains and silks, while wealthy members of the Celestial Kingdom, as China called itself, wanted ivory and black slaves from East Africa, and exotic goods and peacocks from India. African people wanted textiles from India and cowrie shells from the Maldive Islands. Europeans craved spices and silks, but they had few desirable goods to offer their trading partners.

The European search for better access to Southeast Asian trade led to a new overseas empire in the Indian Ocean and the accidental discovery of the Western Hemisphere. Within a short time, South and North America had joined a worldwide web. Europeans came to dominate trading networks and political empires of truly global proportions. The era of "globalization" had begun.

Global contacts created new forms of cultural exchange, assimilation, conversion, and resistance. Europeans sought to impose their cultural values on the people they encountered and struggled to comprehend the peoples and societies they found. New forms of racial prejudice emerged in this period, but so did new openness and curiosity about different ways of life. Together with the developments of the Renaissance and the Reformation, the Age of Discovery laid the foundations for the modern world as we know it today.

World Contacts Before Columbus

What was the Afro-Eurasian trading world before Columbus?

Columbus did not sail west on a whim. To understand his and other Europeans' explorations, we must first understand late medieval trade networks. Historians now recognize important ties between Europe and other parts of the world prior to Columbus's voyages, arguing that a type of "world economy" linked the products and people of Europe, Asia, and Africa in the fifteenth century. The West was not the dominant player in 1492, and the European voyages derived from the possibilities and constraints of this system.

The Trade World of the Indian Ocean

The center of the pre-Columbian world trade network was the Indian Ocean. Its location made it a crossroads for commercial and cultural exchange between China (always the biggest market for Southeast Asian goods), India, the Middle East, Africa, and Europe. From the seventh through the thirteenth centuries, the volume of this trade steadily increased. After a period of decline resulting from the Black Death, demand for Southeast Asian goods accelerated once more in the late fourteenth century.

Merchants congregated in a series of multicultural, cosmopolitan port cities strung around the Indian Ocean. Most of these cities had some form of autonomous self-government. Mutual self-interest had largely limited violence and attempts to monopolize trade. As one historian stated, "before the arrival of the Portuguese . . . in 1498 there had been no organised attempt by any political power to control the sea-lanes and the long-distance trade of Asia. . . . The Indian Ocean as a whole and its different seas were not dominated by any particular nations or empires."[1]

The most developed area of this commercial web lay to the east on the South China Sea. In the fifteenth century the port of Malacca (**muh-LAH-kuh**) became a great commercial entrepôt (**ON-truh-poh**), to which goods were shipped for temporary storage while awaiting redistribution to other places. To Malacca came Chinese porcelains, silks, and camphor (used in the manufacture of many medications, including those to reduce fevers); pepper, cloves, nutmeg, and raw materials such as sappanwood and sandalwood from the Moluccas; sugar from the Philippines; and Indian printed cotton and woven tapestries, copper weapons, incense, dyes, and opium.

The Mongol emperors opened the doors of China to the West, encouraging European traders like Marco Polo to do business there. Marco Polo's tales of his travels from 1271 to 1295 and his encounter with the Great Khan fueled Western fantasies about the exotic Orient. Unbeknownst to the West, the Mongols fell to the new Ming Dynasty in 1368. During the Ming Dynasty (1368–1644), China entered a period of agricultural and commercial expansion, population growth, and urbanization. Historians agree that it had the most advanced economy in the world and played a key role in the fifteenth-century revival of Indian Ocean trade.

China also took the lead in naval expeditions, sending Admiral Zheng He's fleet of 317 ships far along the trade web, voyaging as far west as Egypt. Court

The Port of Banten in Western Java
Influenced by Muslim traders and emerging in the early sixteenth century as a Muslim kingdom, Banten evolved into a thriving entrepôt. The city stood on the trade route to China and, as this Dutch engraving suggests, in the seventeenth century the Dutch East India Company used Banten as an important collection point for spices purchased for sale in Europe. (Archives Charmet/The Bridgeman Art Library)

conflicts and the need to defend against renewed Mongol encroachment led to the abandonment of the expeditions and ship-building after the deaths of Zheng He and the emperor. Despite the Chinese decision not to pursue overseas voyages, trade continued in the South China Sea.

Another center of trade in the Indian Ocean was India, the crucial link between the Persian Gulf and the Southeast Asian and East Asian trade networks. The need for stopovers along the sea voyage led to the development of trading posts along the southern coast of the subcontinent, and these trading posts evolved into thriving commercial centers. India itself was an important contributor of goods to the world trading system. Most of the world's pepper was grown in India, and Indian cotton and silk textiles were highly prized.

Africa

Africa also played an important role in the world trade system before Columbus. Around 1450 Africa had a few large and developed empires along with hundreds of smaller polities. Cairo, the capital of the powerful Mameluke (**MAM-look**) Egyptian empire, was a hub for Indian Ocean trade goods. Sharing in the newfound Red Sea prosperity was the African highland state of Ethiopia, which in 1270 saw the rise of a new dynasty claiming descent from the biblical King Solomon and the Queen of Sheba. Trading hubs flourished as well on the east coast of Africa, where Swahili-speaking city-states were peopled by confident and urbane merchants known for their prosperity and culture.

Another important African contribution to world trade was gold. In the fifteenth century most of the gold that reached Europe came from Sudan in West Africa and from the Akan (**AH-kahn**) peoples living near present-day Ghana (**GAH-nuh**). Transported across the Sahara by Arab and African traders on camels, the gold was sold in the ports of North Africa. Other trading routes led to the Egyptian cities of Alexandria and Cairo, where the Venetians held commercial privileges.

Nations in the inland savannah that sat astride the north-south caravan routes grew wealthy from this trade. In the mid-thirteenth century Sundiata Keita (**soon-JAH-tuh KEY-tah**) founded the powerful kingdom of Mali. His famous successor, Mansa Musa, reportedly discussed sending vessels to explore the Atlantic Ocean, which suggests that not only the Europeans envisaged westward naval exploration. By the time the Portuguese arrived, however, the Malian empire was fading, to be replaced by the Songhay (**song-GAH-ee**), who themselves fell to Moroccan invasion at the end of the sixteenth century. The Portuguese diversion of gold away from the trans-Sahara routes weakened this area politically and economically.

Gold was one important object of trade; slaves were another. Slavery was practiced in Africa, as virtually everywhere else in the world, before the arrival of Europeans. Arabic and African merchants took West African slaves to the Mediterranean to be sold in European, Egyptian, or Middle Eastern markets and also brought eastern Europeans—a major element of European slavery—to West Africa as slaves. In addition, Indian and Arabic merchants traded slaves in the coastal regions of East Africa. European contact would revolutionize the magnitude and character of African slavery (see page 389).

Africa—or legends about Africa—played an important role in Europeans' imagination of the outside world. They long cherished the belief in a Christian nation in Africa ruled by a mythical king, Prester John, thought to be a descendant of one of the three kings who visited Jesus after his birth.

The Ottoman and Persian Empires

The Middle East was crucial to the late medieval world trade system, serving as an intermediary for trade from all points of the compass. In addition, the Middle East was an important supplier of goods for foreign exchange, especially silk and cotton. Two great rival empires, the Persian Safavids (sah-FAH-vidz) and the Turkish Ottomans, dominated this region. Persian merchants could be found in trading communities as far away as the Indian Ocean. Persia was also a major producer and exporter of silk. Although both were Muslim states, the Persians' Shi'ite faith clashed with the Ottomans' adherence to Sunnism. Economically, the two competed for control over western trade routes to the East. Under a succession of brilliant military leaders, however, the Ottomans were ultimately able to monopolize these routes.

Under Sultan Mohammed II (r. 1451–1481), the Ottomans captured Europe's largest city, Constantinople, in May 1453. Renamed Istanbul, the city became the capital of the Ottoman Empire. The emperor Suleiman I (SOO-lay-man) (1494–1566) completed the conquest of Anatolia in 1461 and pressed northwest into the Balkans. By the early sixteenth century the Ottomans controlled the sea trade on the eastern Mediterranean. Steadily expanding, they conquered Syria, Palestine, Egypt, and the rest of North Africa. They worked westward into Europe, gathering parts of the Hungarian kingdom. Their advance was halted by Habsburg forces, and Vienna stood as the westward limit of their expansion into Europe.

Turkish expansion badly frightened Europeans. Ottoman armies seemed nearly invincible and the empire's desire for expansion limitless. In France in the sixteenth century, twice as many books were printed about the Turkish threat as about the American discoveries. The strength of the Ottomans helps explain some of the missionary fervor Christians brought to new territories. It also raised economic concerns. With trade routes to the east in the hands of the Ottomans, Europeans were convinced that they needed new trade routes.

The Taking of Constantinople by the Turks
The Ottoman conquest of the capital of the Byzantine Empire in 1453 sent waves of shock and despair through Europe. Capitalizing on the city's strategic and commercial importance, the Ottomans made it the center of their empire. (Bibliothèque nationale de France)

Genoese and Venetian Middlemen

Europe was the western terminus of the world trading system. In the late Middle Ages, the Italian city-states of Venice and Genoa controlled the European luxury trade with the East.

In 1304, Venice etablished formal relations with the sultan of Mameluke Egypt, opening offices in Cairo, the gateway to Asian trade. The city's merchants specialized in expensive luxury goods like spices, silks, and carpets. They did not, as later Europeans did, explore new routes to get to the sources of supply of these goods. Instead, they obtained them from middlemen in the Eastern Mediterranean or Asia Minor. A little went a long way. Venetians purchased no more than 500 tons of spices a year around 1400, but with a profit of about 40 percent.

The Venetians exchanged Eastern luxury goods for European products they could trade abroad, including Spanish and English wool, German metal goods, Flemish textiles, and silk cloth made in their own manufactures with imported raw materials. The demand for such goods in the East, however, was low. To make up the difference, the Venetians earned currency in the shipping industry and through trade in firearms and slaves, mostly Christians taken from the Balkans. At least half of what they traded with the East took the form of precious metal, much of it acquired in Egypt and North Africa. When the Portuguese arrived in Asia, they found Venetian coins everywhere.

Venice's ancient rival was Genoa. In the wake of the Crusades, Genoa dominated the northern route to Asia through the Black Sea. Expansion in the thirteenth and fourteenth centuries took the Genoese as far as Persia and the Far East. In 1291 they sponsored an expedition by the Vivaldi brothers into the Atlantic in search of "parts of India." The ships were lost, and their exact destination and motivations remain unknown. However, the voyage underlines the long history of Genoese aspirations for Atlantic exploration.

In the fifteenth century Genoa made a bold change of direction. With Venice claiming victory over the spice trade, the Genoese shifted focus from trade to finance and from the Black Sea to the western Mediterranean. Given its location on the northwestern coast of Italy, Genoa had always been active in the western Mediterranean, trading with North African ports, southern France, Spain, and even England and Flanders through the Strait of Gibraltar. When new voyages took place in the western Atlantic, Genoese merchants, navigators, and financiers provided their skills to the Iberian monarchs, whose own subjects had much less commercial experience. The Genoese, for example, ran many of the sugar plantations established on the Atlantic islands colonized by the Portuguese. From their settlement in Seville, Genoese merchants financed Spanish colonization of the New World and conducted profitable trade with its colonies.

After the loss of the Black Sea—and thus the source of slaves—to the Ottomans, the Genoese sought new supplies of slaves in the West, taking the Guanches (indigenous peoples from the Canary Islands), Muslim prisoners and Jewish refugees from Spain, and by the early 1500s both black and Berber Africans. With the growth of Spanish colonies in the New World, Genoese and Venetian merchants became important players in the Atlantic slave trade.

Italian experience in colonial administration, slaving, and international trade and finance served as crucial models for the Iberian states as they pushed European expansion to new heights. Mariners, merchants, and financiers from Venice and Genoa—most notably Christopher Columbus—played a crucial role in bringing the fruits of this experience to the Iberian peninsula.

The European Voyages of Discovery

How and why did Europeans undertake ambitious voyages of expansion that would usher in a new era of global contact?

As we have seen, Europe was by no means isolated before the voyages of exploration and the "discovery" of the New World. But because they did not produce many products desired by Eastern elites, Europeans were relatively modest players

Section Review

- The pre-Columbian trading world centered on the cosmopolitan port cities of the Indian Ocean, which conducted brisk commerce with China and India.
- Africa was a center of world trade in gold and slaves and its east coast city-states played an important role in Indian Ocean trade.
- The rival Ottoman and Persian empires were intermediaries for trade between east and west; Ottoman expansion badly frightened Europeans and closed trading opportunities in the Eastern Mediterranean.
- In the late Middle Ages, Venice and Genoa controlled European luxury trade with the east, losing prominence with the rise of the Ottomans.
- Italian mariners and merchants drew on their long trading experience to assist and finance Spanish and Portuguese voyages, colonization, and slave-trading in the New World.

in the Afro-Eurasian trading world. Yet the demand for Eastern goods grew as the population recovered from the Black Death, and Europeans sought an expanded role. New European players entered the scene, eager to undo Italian and Ottoman dominance of trade with the East. A century after the plague, Iberian explorers began the overseas voyages that helped create the modern world, with staggering consequences for their own continent and the rest of the planet.

Causes of European Expansion

European expansion had multiple causes. By the middle of the fifteenth century, the European market was eager for luxury goods from the East and for spices in particular. These spices not only added flavor to the monotonous European diet, but they also served as perfumes, medicines, and dyes. Apart from a desire for trade goods, religious fervor was another important catalyst for expansion. The passion and energy ignited by the Iberian reconquista encouraged the Portuguese and Spanish to continue the Christian crusade. Since organized Muslim polities such as the Ottoman Empire were too strong to defeat, Iberians turned their attention to non-Christian peoples elsewhere.

Individual explorers combined these motivations in unique ways. Christopher Columbus was a devout Christian who was increasingly haunted by messianic obsessions in the last years of his life. As Bartholomew Diaz put it, his own motives were "to serve God and His Majesty, to give light to those who were in darkness and to grow rich as all men desire to do." When Vasco da Gama reached the port of Calicut, India, in 1498 and a native asked what the Portuguese wanted, he replied, "Christians and spices."[2] The bluntest of the Spanish conquistadors, Hernando Cortés, announced as he prepared to conquer Mexico, "I have come to win gold, not to plow the fields like a peasant."[3]

Eagerness for exploration could be heightened by a lack of opportunity at home. After the reconquista, young men of the Spanish upper classes found their economic and political opportunities greatly limited. The ambitious turned to the Americas to seek their fortunes.[4] A desire for glory and the urge to explore motivated many as well. Whatever the reasons, the voyages were made possible by the growth of government power. Individuals did not possess the massive sums needed to explore mysterious oceans and control remote continents. The Spanish monarchy was stronger than before and in a position to support foreign ventures. In Portugal explorers looked to Prince Henry the Navigator (1394–1460) for financial support and encouragement. Like voyagers, monarchs shared a mix of motivations, from desire to please God to desire to win glory and profit from trade.

Ordinary sailors were ill paid, and life at sea meant danger, overcrowding, unbearable stench, and hunger. For months at a time, 100 to 120 people lived and worked in a space of between 150 and 180 square meters. Horses, cows, pigs, chickens, rats, and lice accompanied them on the voyages. As one scholar concluded, "traveling on a ship must have been one of the most uncomfortable and oppressive experiences in the world."[5]

Why did men choose to join these miserable crews? They did so to escape poverty at home, to continue a family trade, to win a few crumbs of the great riches of empire, or to find a better life as illegal immigrants in the colonies. Moreover, many orphans and poor boys were placed on board as young pages and had little say in the decision. Women also paid a price for the voyages of exploration. Left alone for months or years at a time, and frequently widowed, sailors' wives struggled to feed their families. The widow of a sailor lost on Magellan's 1519 voyage had to wait until 1547 to collect her husband's salary from the Crown.[6]

The people who stayed at home had a powerful impact on the process. Court coteries and factions influenced a monarch's decisions and could lavishly reward individuals or cut them out of the spoils of empire. Then there was the public: the small number of people who could read were a rapt audience for tales of fantastic places and unknown peoples. Scholars have frequently described the European discoveries as a manifestation of Renaissance curiosity about the physical universe — the desire to know more about the geography and peoples of the world. Fernández de Oviedo's (oh-VYE-do) *General History of the Indies* (1547), a detailed eyewitness account of plants, animals, and peoples, was widely read. Indeed, the elite's desire for the exotic goods brought by overseas trade helped stimulate the whole process of expansion.

Technological Stimuli to Exploration

Technological developments in shipbuilding, weaponry, and navigation provided another impetus for European expansion. Since ancient times, most seagoing vessels had been narrow, open boats called *galleys*, propelled largely by slaves or convicts manning the oars. Though well suited to the placid waters of the Mediterranean, galleys could not withstand the rough winds and uncharted shoals of the Atlantic. The need for sturdier craft, as well as population losses caused by the Black Death, forced the development of a new style of ship that would not require much manpower to sail.

In the course of the fifteenth century, the Portuguese developed the **caravel,** a small, light, three-masted sailing ship. Though somewhat slower than the galley, the caravel held more cargo. Its triangular lateen sails and sternpost rudder also made the caravel a much more maneuverable vessel. When fitted with cannon, it could dominate larger vessels.

Great strides in cartography and navigational aids were also made during this period. Around 1410 Arab scholars reintroduced Europeans to **Ptolemy's *Geography*.** Written in the second century C.E. by a Hellenized Egyptian, the work synthesized the geographical knowledge of the classical world. It also treated the idea of latitude and longitude that, when plotted using an astrolabe, allowed mariners to map their location. The magnetic compass also enabled sailors to determine their direction and position at sea. Although it showed the world as round, Ptolemy's work also contained crucial errors. Unaware of the Americas, he showed the world as much smaller than it is, so that Asia appeared not very distant from Europe to the west. Based on this work, cartographers fashioned new maps that combined classical knowledge with the latest information from mariners. First the Genoese and Venetians, and then the Portuguese and Spanish, took the lead in these advances.[7]

Much of the new technology that Europeans used on their voyages was borrowed from the East. For example, gunpowder, the compass, and the sternpost rudder were all Chinese inventions. The lateen sail, which allowed European ships to tack against the wind, was a product of the Indian Ocean trade world and was brought to the

General History of the Indies A fifty-volume first-hand description of the natural plants, animals, and peoples of Spanish America. Its author, Fernández de Oviedo, was a former colonial administrator who was named Historian of the Indies by the King of Spain in 1532.

caravel A small, maneuverable, three-mast sailing ship developed by the Portuguese in the fifteenth century. The caravel gave the Portuguese a distinct advantage in exploration and trade.

Ptolemy's *Geography* A second century C.E. work that synthesized the classical knowledge of geography and treated the concepts of longitude and latitude. The work was reintroduced to Europeans in 1410 by Arab scholars and provided a template for later geographical scholarship.

Nocturnal

An instrument for determining the hour of night at sea by finding the progress of certain stars around the polestar (center aperture). (National Maritime Museum, London)

Mediterranean on Arab ships. Navigational aids, such as the astrolabe, were also acquired from others, and advances in cartography drew on the rich tradition of Judeo-Arabic mathematical and astronomical learning in Iberia.

The Portuguese Overseas Empire

At the end of the fourteenth century Portugal was a small and poor nation on the margins of European life whose principal activities were fishing and subsistence farming. It would have been hard for a European to predict Portugal's phenomenal success overseas in the next two centuries. Yet Portugal had a long history of seafaring and navigation. Blocked from access to western Europe by Spain, the Portuguese turned to the Atlantic and North Africa, whose waters they knew better than other Europeans. Nature favored the Portuguese: winds blowing along their coast offered passage to Africa, its Atlantic islands, and, ultimately, Brazil.

In the early phases of Portuguese exploration, Prince Henry, a younger son of the king, played a leading role. A nineteenth-century scholar dubbed Henry "the Navigator" because of his support for the study of geography and navigation and for the annual expeditions he sponsored down the western coast of Africa. Although he never personally participated in voyages of exploration, Henry's involvement ensured that Portugal did not abandon the effort despite early disappointments.

The objectives of Portuguese policy included aristocratic desires for martial glory, the historic Iberian crusade to Christianize Muslims, and the quest to find gold, slaves, an overseas route to the spice markets of India, and the mythical king Prester John. Portugal's conquest of Ceuta, an Arab city in northern Morocco, in 1415 marked the beginning of European exploration and control of overseas territory. In the 1420s, under Henry's direction, the Portuguese began to settle the Atlantic islands of Madeira (ca. 1420) and the Azores (1427). In 1443 the Portuguese founded their first African commercial settlement at Arguim in present-day Mauritania (mawr-ee-TAY-nee-uh). By the time of Henry's death in 1460, his support for exploration was vindicated by thriving sugar plantations on the Atlantic islands and new access to gold.

Under King John II (r. 1481–1495) the Portuguese established trading posts and forts on the gold-rich Guinea coast and penetrated into the African continent all the way to Timbuktu (see Map 15.1). Portuguese ships transported gold to Lisbon, and by 1500 Portugal controlled the flow of African gold to Europe. The golden century of Portuguese prosperity had begun.

Still the Portuguese pushed farther south down the west coast of Africa. In 1487 Bartholomew Diaz rounded the Cape of Good Hope at the southern tip, but storms and a threatened mutiny forced him to turn back. On a later expedition in

MAPPING THE PAST

MAP 15.1   Overseas Exploration and Conquest, Fifteenth and Sixteenth Centuries

The voyages of discovery marked a dramatic new phase in the centuries-old migrations of European peoples. This map depicts the voyages of Ferdinand Magellan, Christopher Columbus, and Vasco da Gama. **[1]** What was the contemporary significance of each of these voyages? **[2]** Was the importance of the voyages primarily economic, political, or cultural? **[3]** Which voyage had the most impact, and why?

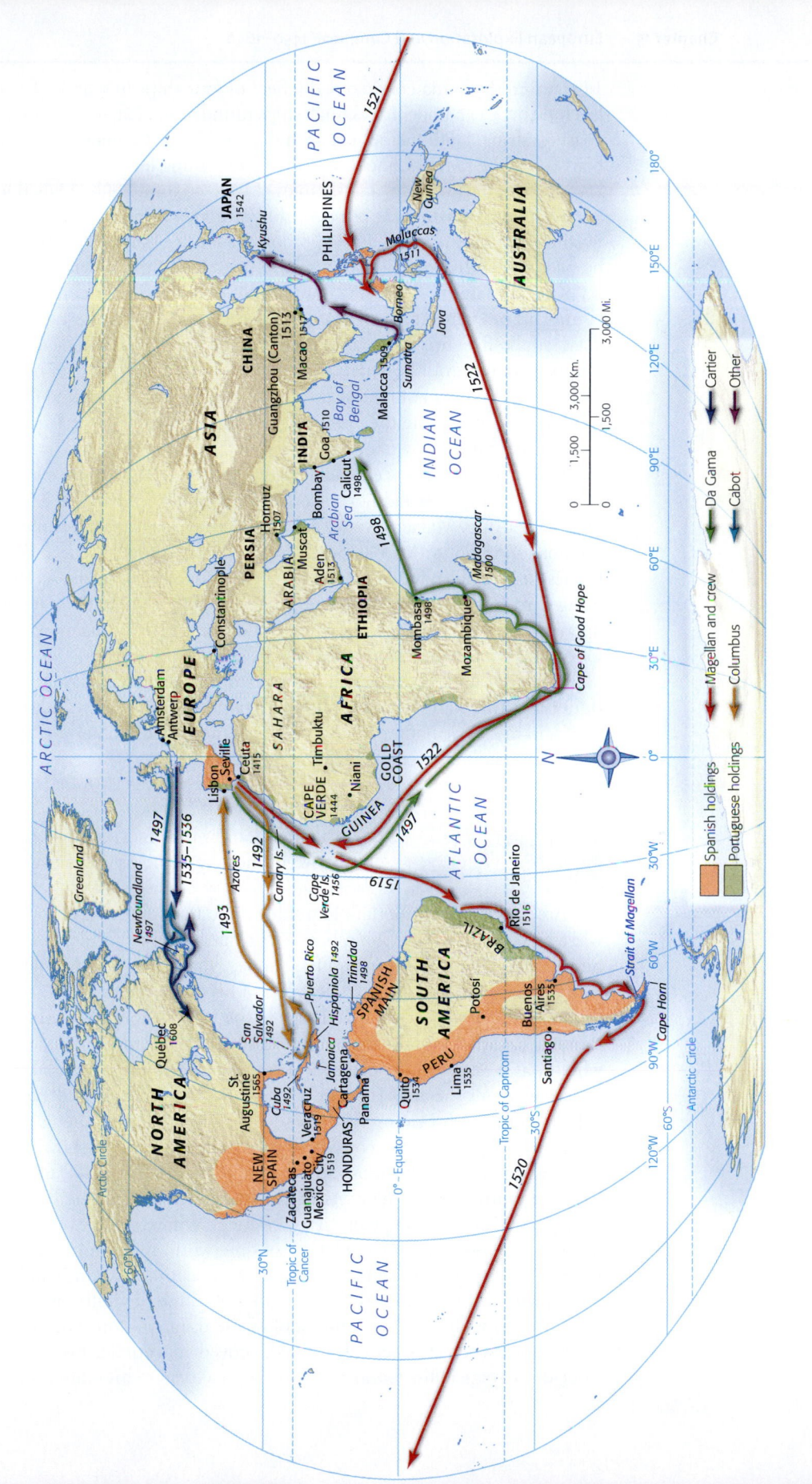

PACIFIC OCEAN

JAPAN 1542

PHILIPPINES

Moluccas 1511

New Guinea

AUSTRALIA

CHINA

Guangzhou (Canton) 1513
Macao 1517

Borneo

Java

Sumatra

Malacca 1509

Bay of Bengal

INDIAN OCEAN

1522

ASIA

INDIA

Goa 1510
Bombay
Calicut 1498

Arabian Sea

1498

Hormuz 1507
Muscat
Aden 1513

Madagascar 1500

PERSIA

ARABIA

ETHIOPIA

Mombasa 1498
Mozambique

Cape of Good Hope

Constantinople

EUROPE

AFRICA

SAHARA

Amsterdam
Antwerp

Lisbon
Seville
Ceuta 1415

CAPE VERDE 1444
Timbuktu
Niani

GUINEA

GOLD COAST

1522

1497

ATLANTIC OCEAN

1519

ARCTIC OCEAN

Greenland

Newfoundland 1497

1497

1535–1536

Azores

1492

Canary Is.

Cape Verde Is. 1456

1493

NORTH AMERICA

Québec 1608

St. Augustine 1565

San Salvador 1492

Cuba 1492

Puerto Rico 1492
Hispaniola 1492

Jamaica

Trinidad 1498

SPANISH MAIN

NEW SPAIN

Zacatecas
Guanajuato
Mexico City 1519

HONDURAS
Veracruz 1519

Cartagena
Panama

SOUTH AMERICA

BRAZIL

Rio de Janeiro 1516

Quito 1534

PERU

Lima 1535

Potosí

Buenos Aires 1535

Santiago

Strait of Magellan

Cape Horn

1520

1520

Tropic of Cancer

Equator

Tropic of Capricorn

Antarctic Circle

Arctic Circle

PACIFIC OCEAN

N

3,000 Mi.

3,000 Km.

1,500

1,500

0

0

Da Gama
Cabot

Cartier
Other

Magellan and crew
Columbus

Spanish holdings
Portuguese holdings

1497 Vasco da Gama commanded a fleet of four ships in search of a sea route to the Indian Ocean trade. Da Gama's ships rounded the Cape and sailed up the east coast of Africa. With the help of an Indian guide, da Gama sailed across the Arabian Sea to the port of Calicut in India. Overcoming local hostility, he returned to Lisbon loaded with spices and samples of Indian cloth. He had failed to forge any trading alliances with local powers, and Portuguese arrogance ensured the future hostility of Muslim merchants who dominated the trading system. Nonetheless, he had proved the possibility of lucrative trade with the East via the Cape route.

King Manuel (r. 1495–1521) promptly dispatched thirteen ships under the command of Pedro Alvares Cabral, assisted by Diaz, to set up trading posts in India. Half the fleet was lost on the return voyage, but the six spice-laden vessels that dropped anchor in Lisbon harbor in July 1501 more than paid for the entire expedition. Thereafter, a Portuguese convoy set out for passage around the Cape every March. Lisbon became the entrance port for Asian goods into Europe—but this was not accomplished without a fight.

As we have seen, port city-states had controlled the rich spice trade of the Indian Ocean, and they did not surrender it willingly. Portuguese cannons blasted open the ports of Malacca, Calicut, Ormuz, and Goa, the vital centers of Muslim domination of South Asian trade. This bombardment laid the foundation for Portuguese imperialism in the sixteenth and seventeenth centuries—a strange way to bring Christianity to "those who were in darkness." As one scholar wrote about the opening of China to the West, "while Buddha came to China on white elephants, Christ was borne on cannon balls."[8]

In March 1493, between the voyages of Diaz and da Gama, Spanish ships under a triumphant Genoese mariner named Christopher Columbus (1451–1506), in the service of the Spanish crown, entered Lisbon harbor. Spain also had begun the quest for an empire.

The Problem of Christopher Columbus   Christopher Columbus is a controversial figure in history—glorified by some as the brave discoverer of America, vilified by others as a cruel exploiter of Native Americans. It is important to put him into the context of his own time. First, what kind of man was Columbus, and what forces or influences shaped him? Second, in sailing westward from Europe, what were his goals? Third, did he achieve his goals, and what did he make of his discoveries?

In his dream of a westward passage to the Indies, Columbus embodied a longstanding Genoese ambition to circumvent Venetian domination of eastward trade, which was now being claimed by the Portuguese. Columbus was also very knowledgeable about the sea. He had worked as a mapmaker, and he was familiar with such fifteenth-century Portuguese navigational developments as *portolans*—written descriptions of the courses along which ships sailed, showing bays, coves, capes, and ports, and the distances between these places—and the use of the compass as a nautical instrument. As he implied in his *Journal*, he had acquired not only theoretical but also practical experience: "I have spent twenty-three years at sea and have not left it for any length of time worth mentioning, and I have seen everything from east to west [meaning he had been to England] and I have been to Guinea [north and west Africa]."[9] Although some of Columbus's geographical information, such as his measurement of the distance from Portugal to Japan as 2,760 miles when it is actually 12,000, proved inaccurate, his successful thirty-three-day voyage to the Caribbean owed a great deal to his seamanship.

Columbus was also a deeply religious man. He had witnessed the Spanish reconquest of Granada and shared fully in the religious and nationalistic fervor surrounding that event. Like the Spanish rulers and most Europeans of his age, Columbus understood Christianity as a missionary religion that should be carried to places where it did not exist. He viewed himself as a divine agent: "God made me the messenger of the new heaven and the new earth of which he spoke in the Apocalypse of St. John . . . and he showed me the post where to find it."[10]

What was the object of this first voyage? Columbus wanted to find a direct ocean trading route to Asia. Rejected by the Portuguese in 1483 and by Ferdinand and Isabella of Spain in 1486, the project finally won the backing of the Spanish monarchy in 1492. Inspired by the stories of Marco Polo, Columbus dreamed of reaching the court of the Mongol emperor, the Great Khan (not realizing that the Ming Dynasty had overthrown the Mongols in 1368). Based on Ptolemy's *Geography* and other texts, he expected to pass the islands of Japan and then land on the east coast of China.

How did Columbus interpret what he had found, and in his mind did he achieve what he had set out to do? He landed in the Bahamas, which he christened San Salvador, on October 12. Columbus believed he had found some small islands off the east coast of Cipangu (Japan). On encountering natives of the islands, he gave them some beads and "many other trifles of small value," pronouncing them delighted with these gifts and eager to trade. In a letter he wrote to Ferdinand and Isabella on his return to Spain, Columbus described the natives as handsome, peaceful, and primitive people whose body painting reminded him of the Canary Islands natives. He concluded that they would make good slaves and could quickly be converted to Christianity. (See the feature "Listening to the Past: Columbus Describes His First Voyage" on pages 398–399.)

Columbus received reassuring reports—via hand gestures and mime—of the presence of gold and of a great king in the vicinity. From San Salvador, Columbus sailed southwest, believing that this course would take him to Japan or the coast of China. He landed on Cuba on October 28. Deciding that he must be on the mainland near the coastal city of Quinsay (Hangzhou) (hahng-jo), he sent a small embassy inland with letters from Ferdinand and Isabella and instructions to locate the grand city. The expedition included an Arabic-speaking member to serve as interpreter with the khan.

The landing party, however, found only small villages. Confronted with this disappointment, Columbus apparently gave up on his aim to meet the Great Khan. Instead, he focused on trying to find gold or other valuables among the peoples he had discovered. In January, confident that gold would later be found, he headed back to Spain. News of his voyage spread rapidly across Europe.[11]

Over the next decades, the Spanish confirmed Columbus's change of course by adopting the model of conquest and colonization they had already introduced

The Portuguese Fleet Embarked for the Indies
This image shows a Portuguese trading fleet in the late fifteenth century, bound for the riches of the Indies. Between 1500 and 1635, over nine hundred ships sailed from Portugal to ports on the Indian Ocean, in annual fleets composed of five to ten ships. (British Museum/HarperCollins Publishers/The Art Archive)

in the Canary Islands rather than one of exchange with equals (as envisaged for the Mongol khan). On his second voyage, Columbus forcibly subjugated the island of Hispaniola, enslaved its indigenous peoples, and laid the basis for a system of land grants tied to their labor service. Columbus himself, however, had little interest in or capacity for governing. Revolt soon broke out against him and his brother on Hispaniola. A royal expedition sent to investigate returned the brothers to Spain in chains. Columbus was quickly cleared of wrongdoing, but he did not recover his authority over the territories. Instead, they came under royal control.

Columbus was very much a man of his times. To the end of his life in 1506, he believed that he had found small islands off the coast of Asia. He never realized the scope of his achievement: to have found a vast continent unknown to Europeans, except for a fleeting Viking presence centuries earlier. He could not know that the scale of his discoveries would revolutionize world power, raising issues of trade, settlement, government bureaucracy, and the rights of native and African peoples.

Later Explorers

The Florentine navigator Amerigo Vespucci (**ve-SPOO-chee**) (1454–1512) realized what Columbus had not. Writing about his discoveries on the coast of modern-day Venezuela, Vespucci stated: "Those new regions which we found and explored with the fleet . . . we may rightly call a New World." This letter, titled *Mundus Novus* (The New World), was the first document to describe America as a continent separate from Asia. In recognition of Amerigo's bold claim, the continent was named for him. (When later cartographers realized that Columbus had made the discovery first, it was too late to change the maps.)

To settle competing claims to the Atlantic discoveries, Spain and Portugal turned to Pope Alexander VI. The **Treaty of Tordesillas** (**tor-duh-SEE-yuhs**) (1494) gave Spain everything to the west of an imaginary line drawn down the Atlantic and Portugal everything to the east. This arbitrary division worked in Portugal's favor when in 1500 an expedition led by Pedro Alvares Cabral landed on the coast of Brazil, which Cabral claimed as Portuguese territory. The country's name derives from the brazilwood trees found there, an important source of red dye.

The search for profits determined the direction of Spanish exploration and expansion into South America. When it became apparent that the Portuguese were reaping enormous riches in Asian trade while the Caribbean yield of gold was insubstantial, new routes to the East and new sources of gold and silver were sought. In 1519 the Spanish ruler Charles V commissioned the Portuguese mariner Ferdinand Magellan (1480–1521) to find a direct route to the spices of the Moluccas off the southeast coast of Asia. Magellan sailed southwest across the Atlantic to Brazil, and after a long search along the coast he located the treacherous straits that now bear his name (see Map 15.1). The new ocean he sailed into after a rough passage through the straits seemed so peaceful that Magellan dubbed it the Pacific. He was soon to realize his mistake. His fleet sailed north up the west coast of South America and then headed west into the immense expanse of the Pacific toward the Malay Archipelago. (Some of these islands were conquered in the 1560s and named the "Philippines" for Philip II of Spain.)

Terrible storms, disease, starvation, and violence haunted the expedition. Magellan had set out with a fleet of five ships and around 270 men. Sailors on two of the ships attempted mutiny on the South American coast; one ship was lost, and another ship deserted and returned to Spain before even traversing the straits. The trip across the Pacific took ninety-eight days, and the men survived on rats and sawdust. Magellan himself was killed in a skirmish in the Philippines. The expedi-

Treaty of Tordesillas The 1494 agreement giving Spain everything to the west of an imaginary line drawn down the Atlantic and giving Portugal everything to the east.

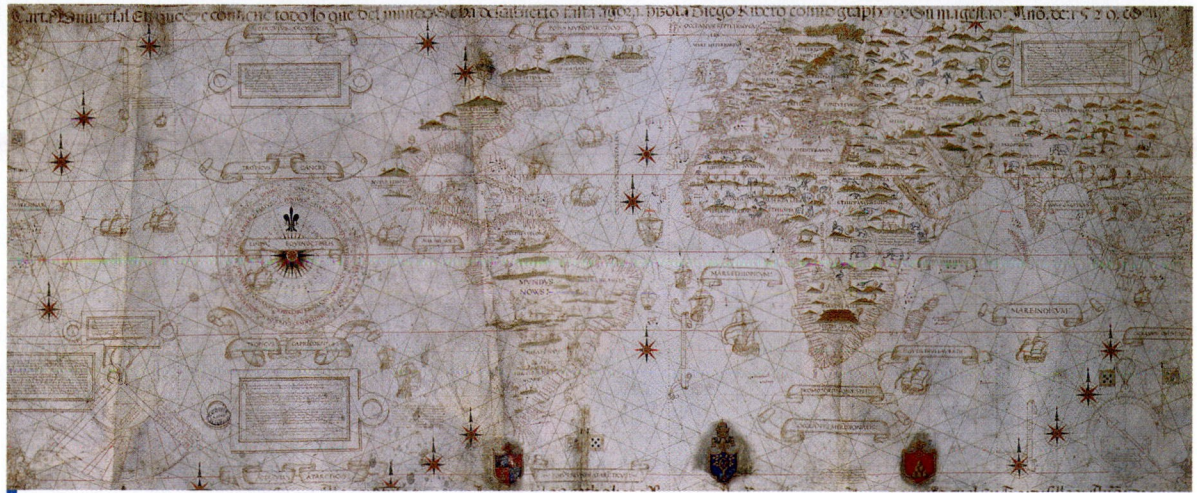

World Map of Diogo Ribeiro, 1529
This map integrates the wealth of new information provided by European explorers in the decades after Columbus's 1492 voyage. Working on commission for the Spanish king Charles V, the mapmaker has incorporated new details on Africa, South America, India, the Malay Archipelago, and China. Note the inaccuracy in his placement of the Moluccas or Spice Islands, which are much too far east. This "mistake" was intended to serve Spain's interests in trade negotiations with the Portuguese. (Biblioteca Apostolica Vaticana)

tion had enough survivors to man only two ships, and one of them was captured by the Portuguese. One ship with eighteen men returned to Spain from the east by way of the Indian Ocean, the Cape of Good Hope, and the Atlantic in 1522. The voyage had taken almost exactly three years.

Despite the losses, this voyage revolutionized Europeans' understanding of the world by demonstrating the vastness of the Pacific. The earth was clearly much larger than Columbus had believed. The voyage actually made a small profit in spices, but Magellan had proved the westward passage to the Indies to be too long and dangerous for commercial purposes. Spain abandoned the attempt to oust Portugal from the Eastern spice trade and concentrated on exploiting her New World territories.

The English and French also set sail across the Atlantic during the early days of exploration. In 1497 John Cabot, a Genoese merchant living in London, aimed for Brazil but discovered Newfoundland. The next year he returned and explored the New England coast, perhaps going as far south as Delaware. Since these expeditions found no spices or gold, Henry VII lost interest in exploration. Between 1534 and 1541 Frenchman Jacques Cartier made several voyages and explored the St. Lawrence region of Canada. The first permanent French settlement, at Quebec, was founded in 1608.

New World Conquest

In 1519, the year Magellan departed on his worldwide expedition, a brash and determined Spanish **conquistador** (**kon-KEY-stuh-dor**) ("conqueror") named Hernando Cortés (1485–1547) crossed from Hispaniola in the West Indies to mainland Mexico in search of gold. Accompanied by six hundred men, seventeen horses, and ten cannon, Cortés was to launch the conquest of Aztec Mexico.

Cortés landed at Vera Cruz in February 1519. From there he led a march to Tenochtitlán (**teh-noch-tit-LAN**) (now Mexico City), capital of the sophisticated

conquistador Spanish for "conqueror," the term refers to Spanish soldier-explorers, such as Hernando Cortés and Francisco Pizarro, who sought to conquer the New World for the Spanish crown.

Aztec Empire A Native American civilization that possessed advanced mathematical, astronomical, and engineering technology. Its capital, Tenochtitlán (now the site of Mexico City), was larger than any contemporary European city. Conquered by Cortés in 1520.

Aztec Empire ruled by Montezuma II (r. 1502–1520). Larger than any European city of the time, the capital was the heart of a civilization with advanced mathematics, astronomy, and engineering, with a complex social system, and with oral poetry and historical traditions.

The Spaniards arrived in the capital when the Aztecs were preoccupied with harvesting their crops. According to a later Spanish account, the timing was ideal. A series of natural phenomena, signs, and portents seemed to augur disaster for the Aztecs. A comet was seen in daytime, and two temples were suddenly destroyed, one by lightning unaccompanied by thunder. These and other apparently inexplicable events had an unnerving and demoralizing effect on Montezuma.

Even more important was the empire's internal weakness. The Aztec state religion, the sacred cult of Huitzilopochtli (**wheat-zeel-oh-POSHT-lee**), necessitated constant warfare against neighboring peoples to secure captives for religious sacrifice and laborers for agricultural and infrastructural work. When Cortés landed, recently defeated tribes were not yet fully integrated into the empire. Increases in tribute provoked revolt, which led to reconquest, retribution, and demands for higher tribute, which in turn sparked greater resentment and fresh revolt. When the Spaniards appeared, the Totonac people greeted them as liberators, and other subject peoples joined them against the Aztecs.[12]

Montezuma himself refrained from attacking the Spaniards as they advanced toward his capital and welcomed Cortés and his men into Tenochtitlán. Historians have often condemned the Aztec ruler for vacillation and weakness. But he relied on the advice of his state council, itself divided, and on the dubious loyalty of tributary communities. When Cortés—with incredible boldness—took Montezuma hostage, the emperor's influence over his people crumbled.

Doña Marina Translating for Hernando Cortés During His Meeting with Montezuma

In April of 1519 Doña Marina (or La Malinche as she is known in Mexico) was among twenty women given to the Spanish as slaves. Fluent in Nahuatl (**NAH-what-el**) and Yucatec (**YOO-kuh-tek**) Mayan (spoken by a Spanish priest accompanying Cortés), she acted as an interpreter and diplomatic guide for the Spanish. She had a close personal relationship with Cortés and bore his son Don Martín Cortés in 1522. Doña Marina has been seen as a traitor to her people, as a victim of Spanish conquest, and as the founder of the Mexican people. She highlights the complex interaction between native peoples and the Spanish and the particular role women often played as cultural mediators between the two sides. (The Granger Collection, New York)

Later, in retaliation for a revolt by the entire population of Tenochtitlán that killed many Spaniards, Montezuma was executed. Afterwards, the Spaniards escaped from the city and defeated the Aztec army at Otumba near Lake Texcoco. On August 13, 1520, the last Aztec emperor surrendered to the Spanish.

More amazing than the defeat of the Aztecs was the fall of the remote **Inca Empire** perched at 9,800 to 13,000 feet above sea level. (The word *Inca* refers both to the people who lived in the valleys of the Andes Mountains in present-day Peru and to their ruler.) The borders of this vast and sophisticated empire were well fortified, but the Inca neither expected foreign invaders nor knew of the fate of the Aztec empire to the north. The imperial government, based in the capital city of Cuzco (**KOOS-koh**), commanded loyalty from the people, but at the time of the Spanish invasion it had been embroiled in a civil war over succession. The Inca Huascar (WAHS-kahr) had been fighting his half-brother Atahualpa (**ah-tah-WAHL-pa**) for five years over the crown.

Francisco Pizarro (ca. 1475–1541), a conquistador of modest Spanish origins, landed on the northern coast of Peru on May 13, 1532, the very day Atahualpa won the decisive battle. The Spaniard soon learned about the war and its outcome. As Pizarro advanced across the steep Andes toward Cuzco, Atahualpa was proceeding to the capital for his coronation. Like Montezuma in Mexico, Atahualpa was kept fully informed of the Spaniards' movements and accepted Pizarro's invitation to meet in the provincial town of Cajamarca. Intending to extend a peaceful welcome to the newcomers, Atahualpa and his followers were unarmed. The Spaniards captured him and collected an enormous ransom in gold. Instead of freeing the new emperor, however, they executed him in 1533 on trumped-up charges.

Decades of violence ensued, marked by Incan resistance and internal struggles among Spanish forces for the spoils of empire. By the 1570s the Spanish crown had succeeded in imposing control. With Spanish conquest, a new chapter opened in European relations with the New World.

Europe and the World After Columbus

What effect did overseas expansion have on the conquered societies, on enslaved Africans, and on world trade?

Europeans had maintained commercial relations with Asia and sub-Saharan Africa since Roman times. In the Carolingian era the slave trade had linked northern Europe and the Islamic Middle East. The High Middle Ages had witnessed a great expansion of trade with Africa and Asia. But with the American discoveries, for the first time commercial and other relations became worldwide, involving all the continents except Australia. European involvement in the Americas led to the acceleration of global contacts. In time, these contacts had a profound influence on European society and culture.

Spanish Settlement and Indigenous Population Decline

In the sixteenth century perhaps two hundred thousand Spaniards immigrated to the New World. Mostly ex-soldiers and adventurers unable to find employment in Spain, they came for profits. After assisting in the conquest of the Aztecs and the subjugation of the Incas, these men carved out vast estates in temperate grazing areas and imported Spanish sheep, cattle, and horses

Inca Empire The vast and sophisticated Peruvian empire, centered at the capital city of Cusco, that was at its peak from 1438 until 1532.

for the kinds of ranching with which they were familiar. In coastal tropical areas unsuited for grazing the Spanish erected huge plantations to supply sugar for the European market. Around 1550 silver was discovered in present-day Bolivia and Mexico. How were the cattle ranches, sugar plantations, and silver mines to be worked? The conquistadors first turned to the Amerindians.

The Spanish quickly established the **encomienda system** (in-co-mee-EN-dah), in which the Crown granted the conquerors the right to employ groups of Amerindians as agricultural or mining laborers or as tribute payers. Theoretically, the Spanish were forbidden to enslave the natives; in actuality, the encomiendas were a legalized form of slavery. Laboring in the blistering heat of tropical cane fields or in the dark, dank, and dangerous mines, the Amerindians died in staggering numbers.

Students of the history of medicine have suggested another crucial explanation for indigenous population losses: disease. Having little or no resistance to diseases brought from the Old World, the inhabitants of the highlands of Mexico and Peru, especially, fell victim to smallpox, typhus, influenza, and other diseases. According to one expert, smallpox caused "in all likelihood the most severe single loss of aboriginal population that ever occurred."[13] (The old belief that syphilis was a New World disease imported to Europe by Columbus's sailors has been discredited by the discovery of pre-Columbian skeletons in Europe bearing signs of the disease.)

Although disease was a leading cause of death, there were many others, including malnutrition and starvation as people were forced to neglect their own fields. Many indigenous peoples also died through outright violence.[14] According to the Franciscan missionary Bartolomé de Las Casas (1474–1566), the Spanish maliciously murdered thousands:

> To these quiet Lambs . . . came the Spaniards like most c(r)uel Tygres, Wolves and Lions, enrag'd with a sharp and tedious hunger; for these forty years past, minding nothing else but the slaughter of these unfortunate wretches, whom with divers kinds of torments neither seen nor heard of before, they have so cruelly and inhumanely butchered, that of three millions of people which Hispaniola itself did contain, there are left remaining alive scarce three hundred persons.[15]

Las Casas's remarks concentrate on the Caribbean islands, but the death rate elsewhere was also overwhelming. The Franciscan, Dominican, and Jesuit missionaries who accompanied the conquistadors and settlers played an important role in converting the Amerindians to Christianity, teaching them European methods of agriculture, and inculcating loyalty to the Spanish crown. In terms of numbers of people baptized, missionaries enjoyed phenomenal success, though the depth of the Amerindians' understanding of Christianity remains debatable. Missionaries, especially Las Casas, asserted that the Amerindians had human rights, and through Las Casas's persistent pressure the emperor Charles V abolished the worst abuses of the encomienda system in 1531.

For colonial administrators the main problem posed by the astronomically high death rate was the loss of a subjugated labor force. As early as 1511 King Ferdinand of Spain observed that the Amerindians seemed to be "very frail" and that "one black could do the work of four Indians."[16] Thus was born an absurd myth and the new tragedy of the Atlantic slave trade.

Sugar and Slavery

Throughout the Middle Ages slavery was deeply entrenched in the Mediterranean. The bubonic plague, famines, and other epidemics created a severe shortage of agricultural and domestic workers throughout Europe, encouraging Italian

---

encomienda system The Spanish system whereby the Crown granted the conquerors the right to employ groups of Amerindians in a town or area as agricultural or mining laborers or as tribute payers; it was a disguised form of slavery.

A New World Sugar Refinery, Brazil
Sugar, a luxury in great demand in Europe, was the most important and most profitable plantation crop in the New World. This image shows the processing and refinement of sugar on a Brazilian plantation. Sugar cane was grown, harvested, and processed by African slaves who labored under brutal and ruthless conditions to generate enormous profits for plantation owners. (The Bridgeman Art Library/ Getty Images)

merchants to buy slaves from the Black Sea region and the Balkans. Renaissance merchants continued the slave trade despite papal threats of excommunication. The Genoese set up colonial stations in the Crimea and along the Black Sea, and according to an international authority on slavery, these outposts were "virtual laboratories" for the development of slave plantation agriculture in the New World.[17] This form of slavery had nothing to do with race; almost all slaves were white. How, then, did black African slavery enter the European picture and take root in South and then North America?

In 1453 the Ottoman capture of Constantinople halted the flow of white slaves. Mediterranean Europe, cut off from its traditional source of slaves, then turned to sub-Saharan Africa, which had a long history of slave trading. (See the feature "Individuals in Society: Juan de Pareja.")

Native to the South Pacific, sugar was taken in ancient times to India, where farmers learned to preserve cane juice as granules that could be stored and shipped. From there, sugar cane growing traveled to China and the Mediterranean, where islands like Crete, Sicily, and Cyprus had the necessary warm and wet climate. When Genoese and other Italians colonized the Canary Islands and the Portuguese settled on the Madeira Islands, sugar plantations came to the Atlantic. In this stage of European expansion, "the history of slavery became inextricably tied up with the history of sugar."[18] Originally sugar was an expensive luxury that only the very affluent could afford, but population increases and monetary expansion in the fifteenth century led to an increasing demand for it.

Resourceful Italians provided the capital, cane, and technology for sugar cultivation on plantations in southern Portugal, Madeira, and the Canary Islands.

Individuals in Society

Juan de Pareja (pa-REH-ha)

A marginal person is one who lives outside the mainstream of the dominant society, who is not fully assimilated into or accepted by that society. Apart from revealing little-known aspects of past cultures, marginalized people teach us much about the values and ideals of the dominant society. Such a person was the Spanish religious and portrait painter Juan de Pareja.

Pareja was born in Antequera, an agricultural region and the old center of Muslim culture near Seville in southern Spain. Of his parents we know nothing. Because a rare surviving document calls him a "mulatto," one of his parents must have been white and the other must have had some African blood. In 1630 Pareja applied to the mayor of Seville for permission to travel to Madrid to visit his brother and "to perfect his art." The document lists his occupation as "a painter in Seville." Since it mentions no other name, it is reasonable to assume that Pareja arrived in Madrid a free man. Sometime between 1630 and 1648, however, he came into the possession of the artist Diego Velázquez (1599–1660); Pareja became a slave.

Velázquez, Juan de Pareja (1650). (The Metropolitan Museum of Art, Fletcher Fund, Rogers Fund, and Bequest of Miss Adelaide Milton de Groot (1876–1967), by exchange, supplemented by gifts from friends of the Museum, 1971. [1971.86]. Photograph © 1986 The Metropolitan Museum of Art)

During the long wars of the reconquista, Muslims and Christians captured each other in battle and used the defeated as slaves. The fifteenth and sixteenth centuries had seen a steady flow of sub-Saharan Africans into the Iberian Peninsula. Thus early modern Spain was a slaveholding society.

How did Velázquez acquire Pareja? By purchase? As a gift? Had Pareja fallen into debt or committed some crime and thereby lost his freedom? We do not know. Velázquez, the greatest Spanish painter of the seventeenth century, had a large studio with many assistants. Pareja was set to grinding powders to make colors and to preparing canvases. He must have demonstrated ability because, when Velázquez went to Rome in 1648, he chose Pareja to accompany him.

In 1650, as practice for a portrait of Pope Innocent X, Velázquez painted Pareja. That same year, Velázquez signed the document that gave Pareja his freedom, to become effective in 1654. Pareja lived out the rest of his life as an independent painter.

What does the public career of this seventeenth-century marginal person tell us about the man and his world? Pareja's career suggests that a person of talent and ability could rise in Spanish society despite the social and religious barriers that existed at the time. Jonathan Brown, the leading authority on Velázquez, describes Pareja's appearance in Velázquez's portrait as "self-confident." A more enthusiastic student writes, "The man was technically a slave. . . . However, we can see from Velázquez's painting that the two were undeniably equals. That steady look of self-controlled power can even make us wonder which of the two had a higher opinion of himself."

Questions for Analysis

1. Since slavery was an established institution in Spain, speculate on Velázquez's possible reasons for giving Pareja his freedom.

2. What issues of cultural diversity might Pareja have faced in seventeenth-century Spain?

Sources: Jonathan Brown, *Velázquez: Painter and Courtier* (New Haven, Conn.: Yale University Press, 1986); *Grove Dictionary of Art* (New York: Macmillan, 2000); Sister Wendy Beckett, *Sister Wendy's American Collection* (New York: Harper Collins Publishers, 2000), p. 15.

Meanwhile, in the period 1490 to 1530, Portuguese traders brought between three hundred and two thousand black slaves to Lisbon each year (see Map 15.2), where they performed most of the manual labor and constituted 10 percent of the city's population. From there slaves were transported to the sugar plantations of Madeira, the Azores, and the Cape Verde Islands. Sugar and these small Atlantic island colonies gave New World slavery its distinctive shape. Columbus himself, who spent a decade in Madeira, brought sugar plants on his voyages to "the Indies."

In Africa, where slavery was entrenched (as it was in the Islamic world, southern Europe, and China), African kings and dealers sold black slaves to European merchants who participated in the transatlantic trade. The Portuguese brought the first slaves to Brazil; by 1600 four thousand were being imported annually. After its founding in 1621, the Dutch West India Company, with the full support of the government of the United Provinces, transported thousands of Africans to Brazil and the Caribbean, mostly to work on sugar plantations. In the late seventeenth century, with the chartering of the Royal African Company, the English got involved. In total, scholars estimate that European traders from all these nations brought over eleven million African slaves to the West Indies and North America, with the peak of the trade occuring in the eighteenth century.

European sailors found the Atlantic passage cramped and uncomfortable, but conditions for African slaves were lethal. Before 1700, when slavers decided it was better business to improve conditions, some 20 percent of slaves died on the voyage.[19] The most common cause of death was from dysentery induced by poor-quality food and water, intense crowding, and lack of sanitation. Men were often kept in irons during the passage, while women and girls were fair game for sailors. To increase profits, slave traders packed several hundred captives on each ship. One slaver explained that he removed his boots before entering the slave hold because he had to crawl over their packed bodies.[20]

By 1790 there were 757,181 blacks in a total U.S. population of 3,929,625. In Brazil during the same decade, blacks numbered about 2 million in a total population of 3.25 million. African slaves ultimately worked in an infinite variety of occupations: as miners, soldiers, sailors, servants, and artisans and in the production of cotton, rum, indigo, tobacco, wheat and corn. Sugar remained a predominant slave-produced crop, leading to boycotts by European abolitionists in the late eighteenth century.

The Columbian Exchange

The Age of Discovery led to the migration of peoples, which in turn led to an exchange of fauna and flora — of animals, plants, and disease, a complex process known as the **Columbian exchange.** Spanish and Portuguese immigrants to the Americas wanted the diet with which they were familiar, so they searched for climatic zones favorable to those crops. Everywhere they settled they brought and raised wheat — in the highlands of Mexico, the Rio de la Plata, New Granada (in northern South America), and Chile. By 1535 Mexico was exporting wheat. Grapes did well in parts of Peru and Chile. It took the Spanish longer to discover areas where suitable soil and adequate rainfall would nourish olive trees, but by the 1560s the coastal valleys of Peru and Chile were dotted with olive groves. Columbus had brought sugar plants on his second voyage; Spaniards also introduced rice and bananas from the Canary Islands, and the Portuguese carried these items to Brazil. Not all plants arrived intentionally. In clumps of mud on shoes and in the folds of textiles came the seeds of immigrant grasses.

Columbian exchange The exchange of animals, plants, and diseases between the Old and the New Worlds.

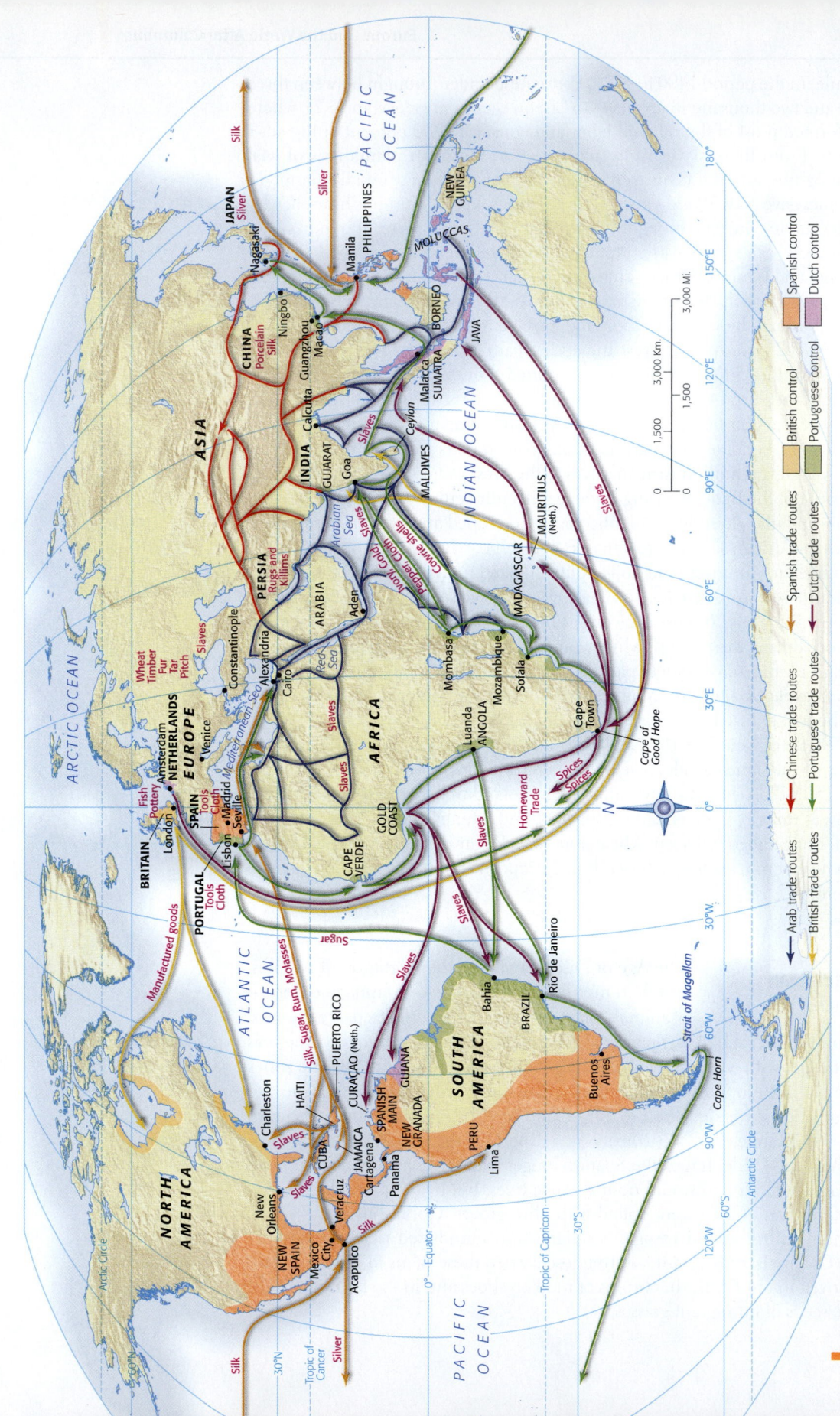

MAP 15.2 Seaborne Trading Empires in the Sixteenth and Seventeenth Centuries

By the mid-seventeenth century, trade linked all parts of the world. Notice that trade in slaves was not confined to the Atlantic but involved almost all parts of the world.

Legend:

British control
Portuguese control
Spanish control
Dutch control

Arab trade routes
British trade routes
Chinese trade routes
Portuguese trade routes
Spanish trade routes
Dutch trade routes

Scale: 0 1,500 3,000 Km. / 0 1,500 3,000 Mi.

Apart from wild turkeys and game, Native Americans had no animals for food; apart from alpacas and llamas, they had no animals for travel or to use as beasts of burden. On his second voyage in 1493 Columbus introduced horses, cattle, sheep, dogs, pigs, chickens, and goats. The multiplication of these animals proved spectacular. The horse enabled the Spanish conquerors and the Amerindians to travel faster and farther and to transport heavy loads.

The Spanish and Portuguese returned to Europe with maize (corn), white potatoes, and many varieties of beans, squash, pumpkins, avocados, and tomatoes. Because maize grows in climates too dry for rice and too wet for wheat, gives a high yield per unit of land, and has a short growing season, it proved an especially important crop for Europeans. So too did the nutritious white potato, which slowly spread from west to east—to Ireland, England, and France in the seventeenth century; and to Germany, Poland, Hungary, and Russia in the eighteenth. Ironically, the white potato reached New England from old England in 1718.

Colonial Administration

Columbus, Cortés, and Pizarro had claimed the lands they had "discovered" for the Spanish crown. How were these lands governed? In the sixteenth century the Crown divided its New World territories into four **viceroyalties** or administrative divisions: New Spain, which consisted of Mexico, Central America, and present-day California, Arizona, New Mexico, and Texas, with the capital at Mexico City; Peru, originally all the lands in continental South America, later reduced to the territory of modern Peru, Chile, Bolivia, and Ecuador, with the viceregal seat at Lima; New Granada, including present-day Venezuela, Colombia, Panama, and, after 1739, Ecuador, with Bogotá as its administrative center; and La Plata, consisting of Argentina, Uruguay, and Paraguay, with Buenos Aires as the capital.

> **viceroyalties** The name for the four administrative units of Spanish possessions in the Americas: New Spain, Peru, New Granada, and La Plata.

Within each territory, the viceroy, or imperial governor, exercised broad military and civil authority as the direct representative of the sovereign in Madrid. The viceroy presided over the *audiencia* (**ow-dee-ENS-ee-ah**), a board of twelve to fifteen judges that served as his advisory council and the highest judicial body. The reform-minded Spanish king Charles III (r. 1759–1788) introduced the system of *intendants*, pioneered by the Bourbon kings of France, to the New World territories. These royal officials possessed broad military, administrative, and financial authority within their *intendancies* and were responsible not to the viceroy but to the monarchy in Madrid.

> **audiencia** Presided over by the viceroy, the twelve to fifteen judges who served as an advisory council and as the highest judicial body.

The Portuguese governed their colony of Brazil in a similar manner. After the union of the crowns of Portugal and Spain in 1580, Spanish administrative forms were introduced. Local officials called *corregidores* (**kuh-REG-i-dawr-eez**) held judicial and military powers. Mercantilist policies placed severe restrictions on Brazilian industries that might compete with those of Portugal. In the seventeenth century the use of black slave labor made possible the cultivation of coffee and cotton, and in the eighteenth century Brazil produced around one-tenth of the world's sugar. The unique feature of colonial Brazil's culture and society was its thoroughgoing intermixture of Indians, whites, and blacks.

Silver and the Economic Effects of Spain's Discoveries

The sixteenth century has often been called Spain's golden century, but silver mined in the Americas was the true source of Spain's incredible wealth. In 1545, at an altitude of fifteen thousand feet, the Spanish discovered an incredible source of silver at Potosí (**poh-toh-SEE**) (in present-day Bolivia) in territory conquered from the Inca Empire. The frigid place where nothing grew had been unsettled. A half-century later, 160,000 people lived there, making it about the size of the city of London. In the second half of the sixteenth century Potosí yielded perhaps 60 percent of all the silver mined in the world. From Potosí and the mines at Zacatecas (**sah-kah-TE-kahs**) and Guanajuato (**gwah-nah-HWAH-taw**) in Mexico, huge quantities of precious metals poured forth, destined for the port of Seville in Spain.

The mining of gold and silver became the most important industry in the colonies. The Crown claimed the **quinto**, one-fifth of all precious metals mined in South America. Gold and silver yielded the Spanish monarchy 25 percent of its total income.

In many ways, it was not Spain but China that controlled the world trade in silver. The Chinese demanded silver for its products and for the payment of imperial taxes. China was thus the main buyer of world silver, serving as a "sink" for half the world's production. The silver market drove world trade, with the Americas and Japan being mainstays on the supply side and China dominating the demand side.

quinto One-fifth of all precious metals mined in the Americas that the Crown claimed as its own.

The Birth of the Global Economy

With the Europeans' discovery of the Americas and their exploration of the Pacific, the entire world was linked for the first time in history by seaborne trade. That trade brought into being three successive commercial empires: the Portuguese, the Spanish, and the Dutch.

The Portuguese were the first worldwide traders, and Portuguese was the language of the Asian maritime trade. In the sixteenth century they controlled the sea route to India (see Map 15.2). From their fortified bases at Goa on the Arabian Sea and at Malacca on the Malay Peninsula, ships carried goods to the Portuguese settlement at Macao in the South China Sea. From Macao Portuguese ships loaded with Chinese silks and porcelains sailed to the Japanese port of Nagasaki and to the Philippine port of Manila, where Chinese goods were exchanged for Spanish (that is, Latin American) silver. Throughout Asia the Portuguese traded in slaves—black Africans, Chinese, and Japanese. The Portuguese exported to India horses from Mesopotamia and copper from Arabia; from India they exported hawks and peacocks for the Chinese and Japanese markets. Back to Portugal they brought Asian spices that had been purchased with textiles produced in India and with gold and ivory from East Africa. They also shipped back sugar from their colony in Brazil, produced by African slaves whom they had transported across the Atlantic.

Chinese Porcelain

This porcelain from a seventeenth-century Chinese ship's cargo, recovered from the sea, was intended for European luxury markets. (Christie's Images)

Spanish possessions in the New World constituted basically a land empire, and in the sixteenth century the Spaniards devised a method of governing that empire (see page 391). But across the Pacific the Spaniards also built a seaborne empire centered at Manila in the Philippines, which had been "discovered" by Ferdinand Magellan in 1521 and later conquered by the Spanish navigator Miguel Lopez de Legazpi. The city of Manila served as the transpacific bridge between Spanish America and the extreme Eastern trade. In Manila, Spanish traders used silver from American mines to purchase Chinese silk for European markets. The European demand for silk was so huge that in 1597, for example, 12 million pesos of silver, almost the total value of the transatlantic trade, moved from Acapulco to Manila (see Map 15.2). After about 1640 the Spanish silk trade declined because it could not compete with Dutch imports.

In the latter half of the seventeenth century the worldwide Dutch seaborne trade predominated. The Dutch Empire was built on spices. In 1599 a Dutch fleet returned to Amsterdam carrying 600,000 pounds of pepper and 250,000 pounds of cloves and nutmeg. Those who had invested in the expedition received a 100 percent profit. The voyage led to the establishment in 1602 of the Dutch East India Company, founded with the stated intention of capturing the spice trade from the Portuguese.

The Dutch fleet, sailing from the Cape of Good Hope in Africa and avoiding the Portuguese forts in India, steered directly for the Sunda Strait in Indonesia (see Map 15.2). The Dutch wanted direct access to and control of the Indonesian sources of spices. In return for assisting Indonesian princes in local squabbles and disputes with the Portuguese, the Dutch won broad commercial concessions. Through agreements, seizures, and outright war, they gained control of the western access to the Indonesian archipelago. Gradually, they acquired political domination over the archipelago itself. The Dutch managed to expel the Portuguese from Ceylon and other East Indian islands. By 1650 the Dutch West India Company had successfully intruded on the Spanish possessions in the Americas, in the process gaining control of much of the African and American trade.

Changing Attitudes and Beliefs

How did culture and art in this period respond to social and cultural transformation?

The age of overseas expansion was characterized by an extraordinary degree of intellectual and artistic ferment. This effervescence can be seen in the development of the essay as a distinct literary genre, in other prose, in poetry, in drama, in art, and in music. In many ways, literature, the visual arts, music, and the drama of the period mirrored the social and cultural conditions that gave rise to them. An important theme running through the culture of this time was the encounter with radically new places and peoples.

New Ideas About Race

Ancient Greeks and Romans were in close contact with Africa and they also practiced slavery, but they did not associate one with the other. Slavery, which was endemic in the ancient world, stemmed from either capture in war or debt. Although generations could be born in captivity, no particular ethnic or racial associations were involved. How did slavery come to be so closely associated with race in the Age of Discovery?

Settlers brought to the Americas the racial attitudes they had absorbed in Europe. In the sixteenth and seventeenth centuries in England, for example, slavers' accounts of their travels depicted Africans as savages because of their eating habits, morals, clothing, and social customs; as barbarians because of their language and methods of war; and as heathens because they were not Christian (nearly the

Section Review

- The Spanish set up the encomienda system of labor, forcing the Amerindians to work in plantations, causing great suffering from malnutrition, disease, and violence that killed large numbers.

- Europeans originally turned to Africa for slaves as Europe had a labor shortage and a diminishing supply of white slaves in the Mediterranean.

- The plantation model of slavery developed for sugar production on Atlantic islands was brought to the New World, along with great numbers of African slaves; the history of sugar and slavery were inextricably linked.

- The Columbian Exchange included the plants, animals, and diseases that accompanied people as they migrated to the New World and those they took back with them.

- The Spanish set up viceroys, or governors, to rule their new territories with military and civic authority.

- The majority of silver mined in Bolivia and Mexico was traded to China for luxury goods desired by Europeans.

- Europeans established trade routes that linked the world by sea for the first time, giving birth to a global economy.

identical language with which the English described the Irish—see page 301). Africans were believed to possess a potent sexuality; African women were considered sexually aggressive, with a "temper hot and lascivious."[21] Medieval Arabs had also depicted Africans as primitive people ideally suited to enslavement.

The racial biases that the Portuguese, Spanish, Dutch, and English brought to the New World also derived from Christian theological speculation. As Europeans turned to Africa for new sources of slaves, they used ideas about Africans' primitiveness and barbarity to defend slavery and even argue that enslavement benefited Africans by bringing the light of Christianity to heathen peoples. Thus, the institution of slavery contributed to the dissemination of more rigid notions of racial inferiority. From rather vague assumptions and prejudices, Europeans developed more elaborate ideological notions of racial superiority and inferiority to safeguard the ever-increasing profits gained from plantation slavery.

Michel de Montaigne and Cultural Curiosity

Racism was not the only possible reaction to the new worlds emerging in the sixteenth century. Decades of religious fanaticism, bringing civil anarchy and war, led both Catholics and Protestants to doubt that any one faith contained absolute truth. Added to these doubts was the discovery of peoples in the New World who had radically different ways of life. These shocks helped produce ideas of skepticism and cultural relativism in the sixteenth and seventeenth centuries. Skepticism is a school of thought founded on doubt that total certainty or definitive knowledge is ever attainable. The skeptic is cautious and critical and suspends judgment. Cultural relativism suggests that one culture is not necessarily superior to another, just different. Both notions found expression in the work of Frenchman Michel de Montaigne (1533–1592) (duh mon-TEN).

Montaigne developed a new literary genre, the essay—from the French *essayer*, meaning "to test or try"—to express his thoughts and ideas. Montaigne's *Essays* provides insight into the mind of a remarkably civilized man. From the ancient authors, especially the Roman Stoic Seneca, Montaigne acquired a sense of calm, patience, tolerance, and broad-mindedness.

Montaigne's essay "On Cannibals" reveals the impact of overseas discoveries on one European's consciousness. His tolerant mind rejected the notion that one culture is superior to another:

> I long had a man in my house that lived ten or twelve years in the New World, discovered in these latter days, and in that part of it where Villegaignon landed [Brazil]. . . .
>   I find that there is nothing barbarous and savage in [that] nation, . . . excepting, that every one gives the title of barbarism to everything that is not in use in his own country. As, indeed, we have no other level of truth and reason, than the example and idea of the opinions and customs of the place wherein we live.[22]

In his own time and throughout the seventeenth century, few would have agreed with Montaigne. The publication of his ideas, however, anticipated a basic shift in attitudes. Montaigne inaugurated an era of doubt. "Wonder," he said, "is the foundation of all philosophy, research is the means of all learning, and ignorance is the end."[23]

Elizabethan and Jacobean Literature

In addition to the essay as a literary genre, the period fostered remarkable creativity in other branches of literature. England—especially in the latter part of Elizabeth's reign and in the first years of her successor, James I (r. 1603–1625)—witnessed remarkable literary expression. The terms *Elizabethan* and *Jacobean* (referring to the reign of James) are used to designate the English music, poetry, prose, and drama of this period.

The undisputed master of this period is the dramatist William Shakespeare, whose genius lay in the originality of his characterizations, the diversity of his plots, his understanding of human psychology, and his unexcelled gift for language. Shakespeare was a Renaissance man in his deep appreciation of classical culture, individualism, and humanism. Such plays as *Julius Caesar, Pericles,* and *Antony and Cleopatra* deal with classical subjects and figures. Several of his comedies have Italian Renaissance settings. The nine history plays, including *Richard II, Richard III,* and *Henry IV,* express English national consciousness. Shakespeare's later tragedies, including *Hamlet, Othello,* and *Macbeth,* explore an enormous range of human problems and are open to an almost infinite variety of interpretations.

Another great masterpiece of the Jacobean period was the Authorized Bible. So called because it was produced under the royal sponsorship of James I (it had no official ecclesiastical endorsement), the Authorized Bible represented the Anglican and Puritan desire to encourage laypeople to read the Scriptures. It quickly achieved great popularity and displaced all earlier versions. British settlers carried this Bible to the North American colonies, where it became known as the King James Bible.

Section Review

- A flowering of artistic expression in poetry, prose, drama, art, and music accompanied the age of overseas expansion.

- Europeans developed prejudicial racial attitudes from Christian theology and beliefs about the alleged primitiveness and barbarity of Africans that they used to justify slavery.

- The Frenchman Michel de Montaigne discussed skepticism, the philosophy based on doubt that absolute certainty or definitive knowledge is ever attainable, and cultural relativism, which suggests that one culture is not necessarily superior to another.

- The dramatic works of William Shakespeare during the reign of Elizabeth crowned a period of remarkable creativity in English music, poetry, prose, and drama, that later saw the creation of another masterpiece—the King James Bible.

Chapter Review

What was the Afro-Eurasian trading world before Columbus? (page 371)

Prior to Columbus's voyages, well-developed trade routes linked the peoples and products of Africa, Asia, and Europe. The Indian Ocean was the center of the Afro-Eurasian trade world, ringed by cosmopolitan commercial cities such as Mombasa, Malacca, and Macao. Venetian and Genoese merchants brought sophisticated luxury goods, like silks and spices, into western Europe from the East. Overall, though, Europeans played a minor role in the Afro-Eurasian trading world, since they did not produce many products desired by Eastern elites.

How and why did Europeans undertake ambitious voyages of expansion that would usher in a new era of global contact? (page 375)

In the sixteenth and seventeenth centuries Europeans gained access to large parts of the globe for the first time. European peoples had the intellectual curiosity, driving ambition, religious zeal, and material incentive to challenge their marginal role in the pre-existing trade world. The revived monarchies of the sixteenth century now possessed sufficient resources to back ambitious seafarers like Christopher Columbus and Vasco da Gama. Exploration and exploitation contributed to a more sophisticated standard of living, in the form of spices and Asian luxury goods.

Key Terms

General History of the Indies (p. 377)

caravel (p. 377)

Ptolemy's *Geography* (p. 377)

Treaty of Tordesillas (p. 382)

conquistador (p. 383)

Aztec Empire (p. 384)

Inca Empire (p. 385)

encomienda system (p. 386)

Columbian exchange (p. 389)

viceroyalties (p. 391)

audiencia (p. 391)

quinto (p. 392)

What effect did overseas expansion have on the conquered societies, on enslaved Africans, and on world trade? (page 385)

Other consequences of European expansion had global proportions. Indian Ocean trade, long dominated by Muslim merchants operating from autonomous city-ports, increasingly fell under the control of Portuguese merchants sponsored by their Crown. Later these would shift to the Dutch East India Company. In the New World, Europeans discovered territories wholly unknown to them and forcibly established new colonies. The resulting Columbian exchange contributed to the decimation of native populations by disease and fostered the exchange of a myriad of plant, animal, and viral species. The slave trade took on new proportions of scale and intensity, as many millions of Africans were transported to labor in horrific conditions in the mines and plantations of the New World.

How did culture and art in this period respond to social and cultural transformation? (page 393)

Cultural attitudes were challenged as well. While most Europeans did not question the superiority of Western traditions and beliefs, new currents of religious skepticism and new ideas about race were harbingers of developments to come. The essays of Montaigne, the plays of Shakespeare, and the King James Bible remain classic achievements of the Western cultural heritage. They both reflected dominant cultural values and projected new ideas into the future.

Notes

1. K. N. Chaudhuri, *Trade and Civilisation in the Indian Ocean: An Economic History from the Rise of Islam to 1750* (Cambridge: Cambridge University Press, 1985), p. 14.
2. Quoted in C. M. Cipolla, *Guns, Sails, and Empires: Technological Innovation and the Early Phases of European Expansion, 1400–1700* (New York: Minerva Press, 1965), p. 132.
3. Quoted in F. H. Littell, *The Macmillan Atlas: History of Christianity* (New York: Macmillan, 1976), p. 75.
4. See C. R. Phillips, *Ciudad Real, 1500–1750: Growth, Crisis, and Readjustment in the Spanish Economy* (Cambridge, Mass.: Harvard University Press, 1979), pp. 103–104, 115.
5. Pablo E. Pérez-Mallaína, *Spain's Men of the Sea: Daily Life on the Indies Fleet in the Sixteenth Century* (Baltimore: Johns Hopkins University Press, 1998), p. 133.
6. Ibid., p. 19.
7. G. V. Scammell, *The World Encompassed: The First European Maritime Empires, c. 800-1650* (Berkeley: University of California Press, 1981), p. 207.
8. Quoted in Cipolla, *Guns, Sails, and Empires*, pp. 115–116.
9. Quoted in F. Maddison, "Tradition and Innovation: Columbus' First Voyage and Portuguese Navigation in the Fifteenth Century," in *Circa 1492: Art in the Age of Exploration*, ed. J. A. Levenson (Washington, D.C.: National Gallery of Art, 1991), p. 69.
10. Quoted in R. L. Kagan, "The Spain of Ferdinand and Isabella," in *Circa 1492: Art in the Age of Exploration*, ed. J. A. Levenson (Washington, D.C.: National Gallery of Art, 1991), p. 60.
11. Peter Hulme, *Colonial Encounters: Europe and the Native Caribbean, 1492–1797* (London and New York: Methuan, 1986). 22–31.
12. G. W. Conrad and A. A. Demarest, *Religion and Empire: The Dynamics of Aztec and Inca Expansionism* (New York: Cambridge University Press, 1993), pp. 67–69.
13. Quoted in Crosby, *The Columbian Exchange: Biological and Cultural Consequences of 1492* (Westport, Conn.: Greenwood, 1972), p. 39.
14. Ibid., pp. 35–59.
15. Quoted in C. Gibson, ed., *The Black Legend: Anti-Spanish Attitudes in the Old World and the New* (New York: Knopf, 1971), pp. 74–75.
16. Quoted in L. B. Rout, Jr., *The African Experience in Spanish America* (New York: Cambridge University Press, 1976), p. 23.
17. C. Verlinden, *The Beginnings of Modern Colonization*, trans. Y. Freccero (Ithaca, N.Y.: Cornell University Press, 1970), pp. 5–6, 80–97.

18. This section leans heavily on D. B. Davis, *Slavery and Human Progress* (New York: Oxford University Press, 1984), pp. 54–62; the quotation is on p. 58.
19. Herbert S. Klein, "Profits and the Causes of Mortality," in David Northrup, ed., *The Atlantic Slave Trade* (Lexington, Mass.: D. C. Heath and Co., 1994), p. 116.
20. Malcolm Cowley and Daniel P. Mannix, "The Middle Passage," in David Northrup, ed., *The Atlantic Slave Trade* (Lexington, Mass.: D. C. Heath and Co., 1994), p. 101.
21. Quoted in D .P. Mannix, with M. Cowley, *Black Cargoes: A History of the Atlantic Slave Trade* (New York: Viking Press, 1968), p. 19.
22. C. Cotton, trans., *The Essays of Michel de Montaigne* (New York: A. L. Burt, 1893), pp. 207, 210.
23. Ibid., p. 523.

To assess your mastery of this chapter, go to **bedfordstmartins.com/mckaywestbrief**

Listening to the Past

Columbus Describes His First Voyage

On his return voyage to Spain in January 1493, Christopher Columbus composed a letter intended for wide circulation and had copies of it sent ahead to Isabella and Ferdinand and others when the ship docked at Lisbon. Because the letter sums up Columbus's understanding of his achievements, it is considered the most important document of his first voyage. Remember that his knowledge of Asia rested heavily on Marco Polo's Travels, *published around 1298.*

Christopher Columbus, by Ridolpho Ghirlandio. Friend of Raphael and teacher of Michelangelo, Ghirlandio (1483–1561) enjoyed distinction as a portrait painter, and so we can assume that this is a good likeness of the older Columbus. (Scala/Art Resource, NY)

Since I know that you will be pleased at the great success with which the Lord has crowned my voyage, I write to inform you how in thirty-three days I crossed from the Canary Islands to the Indies, with the fleet which our most illustrious sovereigns gave me. I found very many islands with large populations and took possession of them all for their Highnesses; this I did by proclamation and unfurled the royal standard. No opposition was offered.

I named the first island that I found "San Salvador," in honour of our Lord and Saviour who has granted me this miracle. . . . When I reached Cuba, I followed its north coast westwards, and found it so extensive that I thought this must be the mainland, the province of Cathay.* . . . From there I saw another island eighteen leagues eastwards which I then named "Hispaniola."†

Hispaniola is a wonder. The mountains and hills, the plains and meadow lands are both fertile and beautiful. They are most suitable for planting crops and for raising cattle of all kinds, and there are good sites for building towns and villages. The harbours are incredibly fine and there are many great rivers with broad channels and the majority contain gold.‡ The trees, fruits and plants are very different from those of Cuba. In Hispaniola there are many spices and large mines of gold and other metals. . . .§

I hoped to win them to the love and service of their Highnesses and of the whole Spanish nation and to persuade them to collect and give us of the things which they possessed in abundance and which we needed. They have no religion and are not idolaters; but all believe that power and goodness dwell in the sky and they are firmly convinced that I have come from the sky with these ships and people. In this belief they gave me a good reception everywhere, once they had overcome their fear; and this is not because they are stupid—far from it, they are men of great intelligence, for they navigate

---

* Cathay is the old name for China. In the log-book and later in this letter Columbus accepts the native story that Cuba is an island that they can circumnavigate in something more than twenty-one days, yet he insists here and later, during the second voyage, that it is in fact part of the Asiatic mainland.
† Hispaniola is the second largest island of the West Indies; Haiti occupies the western third of the island, the Dominican Republic the rest.

‡ This did not prove to be true.
§ These statements are also inaccurate.

all those seas, and give a marvellously good account of everything—but because they have never before seen men clothed or ships like these. . . .

In conclusion, to speak only of the results of this very hasty voyage, their Highnesses can see that I will give them as much gold as they require, if they will render me some very slight assistance; also I will give them all the spices and cotton they want. . . . I will also bring them as much aloes as they ask and as many slaves, who will be taken from the idolaters. I believe also that I have found rhubarb and cinnamon and there will be countless other things in addition. . . .

So all Christendom will be delighted that our Redeemer has given victory to our most illustrious King and Queen and their renowned kingdoms, in this great matter. They should hold great celebrations and render solemn thanks to the Holy Trinity with many solemn prayers, for the great triumph which they will have, by the conversion of so many peoples to our holy faith and for the temporal benefits which will follow, for not only Spain, but all Christendom will receive encouragement and profit.

This is a brief account of the facts. Written in the caravel off the Canary Islands.‖
15 February 1493

At your orders
THE ADMIRAL

Questions for Analysis

1. How did Columbus explain the success of his voyage?
2. What was Columbus's view of the Native Americans he met?
3. Evaluate his statements that the Caribbean islands possessed gold, cotton, and spices.
4. Why did Columbus cling to the idea that he had reached Asia?

Source: From *The Four Voyages of Christopher Columbus,* edited and translated by J. M. Cohen (Penguin Classics, 1969). Copyright © J. M. Cohen, 1969. Reproduced by permission of Penguin Books, Ltd.

‖ Actually, Columbus was off Santa Maria in the Azores.

CHAPTER 16

Absolutism and Constitutionalism in Western Europe

ca. 1589–1715

Hyacinthe Rigaud, *Louis XIV, King of France and Navarre* (1701). Louis XIV is surrounded by the symbols of his power: the sword of justice, the scepter of power, and the crown. The vigor and strength of the king's stocking-covered legs contrast with the age and wisdom of his lined face. (Scala/Art Resource, NY)

Chapter Preview

Seventeenth-Century Crisis and Rebuilding
What were the common crises and achievements of seventeenth-century states?

Absolutism in France and Spain
To what extent did French and Spanish monarchs succeed in creating absolute monarchies?

The Culture of Absolutism
What cultural forms flourished under absolutist governments?

Constitutionalism
What is constitutionalism, and how did this form of government emerge in England and the Dutch Republic?

INDIVIDUALS IN SOCIETY: Glückel of Hameln

LISTENING TO THE PAST: The Court at Versailles

The seventeenth century was a period of crisis and transformation. Agricultural and manufacturing slumps meant that many people struggled to feed themselves and their families. After a long period of growth in the sixteenth century, population rates stagnated or even fell. Religious and dynastic conflicts led to almost constant war, visiting violence and destruction on ordinary people.

The demands of war reshaped European states. Armies grew larger than they had been since the time of the Roman Empire. To pay for these armies, governments greatly increased taxes. They also created new bureaucracies to collect the taxes and to foster economic activity that might increase state revenue. Despite numerous obstacles, European states succeeded in gathering more power during this period. What one historian described as the long European "struggle for stability" that originated with the Reformation in the early sixteenth century was largely resolved by 1680.[1]

Important differences existed, however, in terms of *which* authority within the state possessed sovereignty—the Crown or privileged groups. Between roughly 1589 and 1715 two basic patterns of government emerged in Europe: absolute monarchy and the constitutional state. Almost all subsequent European governments have been modeled on one of these patterns.

Seventeenth-Century Crisis and Rebuilding

What were the common crises and achievements of seventeenth-century states?

Historians often refer to the seventeenth century as an "age of crisis." After the economic and demographic growth of the sixteenth century, Europe faltered into stagnation and retrenchment. This was partially due to climate changes beyond anyone's control, but it also resulted from the bitterness of religious divides, the increased pressures exerted by governments, and the violence and dislocation of war. Overburdened peasants and city dwellers took action to defend themselves, sometimes profiting from elite conflicts to obtain redress of their grievances. In the long run, however, governments proved increasingly able to impose their will on the populace. This period witnessed a spectacular growth in army size as well as new forms of taxation, government bureaucracies, and increased state sovereignty.

Economic and Demographic Crisis

In the seventeenth century the vast majority of western Europeans lived in villages centered on a church and a manor. A small number of peasants in each village owned enough land to feed themselves and the livestock necessary to work their land. These independent farmers were leaders of the peasant village. They employed the landless poor, rented out livestock and tools, and served as agents for the noble lord. Below them were small landowners and tenant farmers who did not have enough land to be self-sufficient. These families sold their best produce on the market to earn cash for taxes, rent, and food. At the bottom were the rural proletariat who worked as dependent laborers and servants.

Rich or poor, bread was the primary element of the diet. Peasants paid stiff fees to the local miller for grinding grain into flour and sometimes to the lord for the right to bake bread in his oven. Bread was most often accompanied with a soup made of roots, herbs, beans, and perhaps a small piece of salt pork. One of the biggest annual festivals in the rural village was the killing of the family pig. The whole family gathered to help, sharing a rare abundance of meat with neighbors and carefully salting the extra and putting down the lard.

Rural society lived on the edge of subsistence. Because of the crude technology and low crop yield, peasants were constantly threatened by scarcity and famine. In the seventeenth century a period of colder and wetter climate, dubbed by historians as a "little ice age," meant a shorter farming season. A bad harvest created dearth; a series of bad harvests could lead to famine. Recurrent famines significantly reduced the population of early modern Europe. Most people did not die of outright starvation, but rather of diseases brought on by malnutrition and exhaustion. Facilitated by the weakened population, outbreaks of bubonic plague continued in Europe until the 1720s.

Industry also suffered. While the evidence does not permit broad generalizations, it appears that the output of woolen textiles, one of the most important European manufactures, declined sharply in the first half of the seventeenth century. Food prices were high, wages stagnated, and unemployment soared. This economic crisis was not universal: it struck various regions at different times and to different degrees. In the middle decades of the century, Spain, France, Germany, and England all experienced great economic difficulties; but these years were the golden age of the Netherlands.

The urban poor and peasants were the hardest hit. When the price of bread rose beyond their capacity to pay, they frequently took action. In towns they invaded the bakers' shop to seize bread and resell it at a "just price." In rural areas they attacked convoys taking grain away to the cities and also redistributed it. Women often led these actions, since their role as mothers gave them some impunity in authorities' eyes. Historians have labeled this vision of a world in which community needs predominate over competition and profit a **moral economy.**

1589–1610	Henry IV in France
1598	Edict of Nantes
1602	Dutch East India Company founded
1605–1715	Food riots common across Europe
1618–1648	Thirty Years' War
1635	Birth of French Academy
1640–1680	Golden age of Dutch art (Vermeer, Van Steen, Rembrandt)
1642–1649	English civil war ends with execution of Charles I
1643–1715	Louis XIV in France
1648–1653	The Fronde
1653–1658	Military rule in England under Oliver Cromwell
1659	Treaty of the Pyrenees marks end of Spanish imperial dominance
1660	Restoration of English monarchy under Charles II
1665–1683	Jean-Baptiste Colbert applies mercantilism to France
1685	Edict of Nantes revoked
1688–1689	Glorious Revolution in England
1701–1713	War of the Spanish Succession
1713	Peace of Utrecht

moral economy A historian's term for an economic perspective in which the needs of a community take precedence over competition and profit.

Seventeenth-Century State-Building: Common Obstacles and Achievements

In this context of economic and demographic depression, monarchs began to make new demands on their people. Traditionally, historians have distinguished sharply between the "absolutist" governments of France, Spain, Central Europe, and Russia and the constitutional monarchies of England and the Dutch Republic. Whereas absolutist monarchs gathered all power under their personal control, constitutional monarchs were obliged to respect laws passed by representative institutions. More recently, historians have emphasized commonalities among these powers. Despite their political differences, absolutist and constitutional monarchs shared common projects of protecting and expanding their frontiers, raising new taxes, and consolidating state control.

Rulers who wished to increase their authority encountered formidable obstacles. Some obstacles were purely material. Without paved roads, telephones, or

An English Food Riot

Nothing infuriated ordinary women and men more than the idea that merchants and landowners were withholding grain from the market in order to push high prices even higher. In this cartoon an angry crowd hands out rough justice to a rich farmer accused of hoarding. (Courtesy of the Trustees of the British Museum)

other modern technology, it took weeks to convey orders from the central government to the provinces. Rulers also suffered from a lack of information about their realms, due to the limited size of their bureaucracies. Without accurate knowledge of the number of inhabitants and the wealth they possessed, it was impossible to police and tax the population effectively. Cultural and linguistic differences presented their own obstacles. In some kingdoms the people spoke a language different from the Crown's, diminishing their willingness to obey its commands.

Local power structures presented another serious obstacle to a monarch's attempts to centralize power. Across Europe, nobles retained great legal, military, political, and financial powers, in addition to their traditional social prestige. Moreover, the church, legislative corps, town councils, guilds, and other bodies had acquired autonomy during the course of the Middle Ages. In some countries whole provinces held separate privileges granted when they became part of the kingdom.

While some monarchs succeeded in breaking the power of these institutions and others were forced to concede political power to elected representatives, the situation was nuanced. Absolutist monarchs did not crush the power of nobles and other groups but rather had to compromise with them. Louis XIV, the model of absolutist power, succeeded because he co-opted and convinced nobles. And in England and the Netherlands constitutional government did not mean democracy, the rule of the people.

Both absolutist and constitutional monarchs were able to overcome obstacles and achieve new levels of central control. They exercised greater power in four areas in particular: greater taxation, growth in armed forces, larger and more efficient bureaucracies, and the increased ability to compel obedience from their subjects. Over time, centralized power added up to something close to **sovereignty**. A state may be termed sovereign when it possesses a monopoly over the instruments of justice and the use of force within clearly defined boundaries. In a sovereign state, no system of courts, such as ecclesiastical tribunals, competes with state courts in the dispensation of justice; and private armies, such as those of feudal lords, present no threat to central authority because the state's army is stronger. State law touches all persons in the country. While seventeenth-century states did not acquire total sovereignty, they made important strides toward that goal.

sovereignty The supreme authority in a political community; a modern state is said to be sovereign when it controls the instruments of justice (the courts) and the use of force (military and police powers) within geographical boundaries recognized by other states.

Popular Political Action

In the seventeenth century bread riots turned into **popular revolts** in England, France, Spain, Portugal, and Italy.[2] In 1640 Philip IV of Spain faced revolt on three fronts simultaneously: Catalonia, the economic center of his realm; Portugal; and the northern provinces of the Netherlands. In 1647 the city of Palermo, in Spanish-occupied Sicily, exploded in protest over food shortages caused by a series of bad harvests. The city government responded by subsidizing the price of bread, but Madrid ordered an end to subsidies. Local women led a bread riot, shouting, "Long live the king and down with the taxes and the bad government!" Apart from affordable food, rebels demanded the suppression of extraordinary taxes, participation in municipal government, and the end to noble tax exemptions. Lacking unity and strong leadership, the revolt was squelched.[3] The Spanish were equally successful in the Netherlands, at first; by the early 1570s, however, a new wave of revolt broke out, resulting in the independent Dutch Republic (see page 424).

In France, uprisings became "a distinctive feature of life"[4] in the cities, where resentment at taxes fostered violence. Major insurrections occurred at Dijon in 1630 and 1668, at Bordeaux (**bor-DOH**) in 1635 and 1675, at Montpellier in 1645, at Lyons from 1667 through 1668 and again in 1692, and at Amiens in 1685, 1695, 1704, and 1711. All were characterized by deep popular anger, a vocabulary of violence, and what a recent historian calls "the culture of retribution"—that is, the punishment of royal "outsiders," officials who attempted to announce or collect taxes.[5] Royal officials were sometimes seized, beaten, and hacked to death. The limitations of royal authority gave some leverage to rebels. Royal edicts were sometimes suspended, prisoners released, and discussions initiated. By the end of the seventeenth century, this leverage had largely disappeared. Municipal governments were better integrated into the national structure, and local authorities had prompt military support from the central government. People who publicly opposed royal policies and taxes received swift and severe punishment.[6]

popular revolts Uprisings that were extremely common in the seventeenth century across Europe, due to the increasing pressures of taxation and warfare.

Section Review

- Rural society was dependent on crops, especially grain, so when a period of colder weather came, crop yields fell, bringing famine, malnutrition, and disease.
- Economic crisis hit the urban poor and peasants hardest and often led to "moral economy" tactics: when bread prices were too high, the peasants seized the grain or bread to resell or redistribute at "just" prices.
- Absolutist monarchs had full personal control, while constitutional monarchs followed laws representative institutions passed.
- In the seventeenth century, both absolutist and constitutional monarchs confronted—and partially overcame—limitations on their sovereignty, produced by poor infrastructure, weak bureaucracies, cultural differences, and local power structures.
- Popular revolts arose as peasants protested food shortages and tax increases, but the rise of central authority by the end of the period allowed governments to repress them severely.

Absolutism in France and Spain

To what extent did French and Spanish monarchs succeed in creating absolute monarchies?

In the Middle Ages monarchs were said to rule "by the grace of God." Law was given by God; kings discovered or "found" the law and acknowledged that they must respect and obey it. In the seventeenth century absolutist state, kings amplified these claims, asserting that, because they were chosen by God, they were responsible to God alone. They claimed exclusive power to make and enforce laws, denying any other institution or group the authority to check their power.

Philosophers and theologians supported the kings' position with arguments for the necessity of absolute power for the public good. In *Leviathan* (li-VYE-uh-thuhn) (1651), the English philosopher Thomas Hobbes argued that any limits on or divisions of government power would lead only to paralysis or civil war. At the court of Louis XIV the French theologian Bossuet (baw-SWAY) proclaimed that without "absolute authority the king could neither do good nor repress evil."

The Foundations of Absolutism: Henry IV, Sully, and Richelieu

Louis XIV's absolutism had long roots. In 1589 his grandfather Henry IV (r. 1589–1610), the founder of the Bourbon dynasty, acquired a devastated country. As we saw in Chapter 14, civil wars between Protestants and Catholics wracked France in the last decades of the sixteenth century. Catastrophically poor harvests meant that peasants across France lived on the verge of starvation. Commercial activity had fallen to one-third its 1580 level. Nobles, officials, merchants, and peasants wanted peace, order, and stability. "Henri le Grand" (Henry the Great), as the king was called, promised "a chicken in every pot" and inaugurated a remarkable recovery. He was beloved because of the belief that he cared about the people; his was the only royal statue the Paris crowd did not tear down two hundred years later in the French Revolution.

Aside from a short war in 1601, Henry kept France at peace. He had converted to Catholicism but also issued the Edict of Nantes (see page 362), allowing Protestants the right to worship in 150 traditionally Protestant towns throughout France. Along with his able chief minister, the Protestant Maximilien de Béthune (mak-suh-MIL-yuhn duh bay-TOON), duke of Sully, Henry IV laid the foundations for the growth of state power. He sharply lowered direct taxes on the overburdened peasants and focused instead on increasing income from indirect taxes on salt, sales, and transit. He also instituted an annual fee on royal officials to guarantee heredity in their offices. (Although effective at the time, the long-term effect of this tax was to reduce royal control over officeholders.)

Alongside fiscal reform, Henry sponsored new industries and trade and improved the infrastructure of the country, building new roads, bridges, and canals to repair the ravages of years of civil war. In only twelve years he significantly raised royal revenues and restored public order.[7] Yet despite his efforts at peace, Henry was murdered in 1610 by François Ravaillac, a Catholic zealot, setting off a national crisis.

After the death of Henry IV his wife, the queen-regent Marie de' Medici (MED-ih-chee), headed the government for the child-king Louis XIII (r. 1610–1643). In 1624 Marie de' Medici secured the appointment of Armand Jean du Plessis—Cardinal Richelieu (ree-shuh-LYOO) (1585–1642)—to the council of ministers. Richelieu's maneuvers would allow the monarchy to maintain power within Europe and within its own borders despite the turmoil of the Thirty Years' War (see pages 435–436).

Richelieu's goal was to subordinate competing groups and institutions to the French monarchy. The nobility constituted the foremost threat. Nobles sat in royal councils, ran the army, controlled large provinces of France, and were immune from direct taxation. Richelieu sought to curb their power. In 1624 he succeeded in reshuffling the royal council, eliminating nobles who were potential power brokers and dominating the council as its president. In 1628 he became the first minister of the French crown.

Cardinal Richelieu's political genius is best reflected in the administrative system he established to strengthen royal control. He extended the use of **intendants,** commissioners for each of France's thirty-two districts who were appointed directly by the monarch, to whom they were solely responsible. Intendants could not be natives of the districts where they held authority; thus they had no vested interest in their localities. They recruited men for the army, supervised the collection of taxes, presided over the administration of local law, checked up on the local nobility, and regulated economic activities—commerce, trade, the guilds, marketplaces in their districts. They were to use their power for three related purposes: to inform the central government about their districts, to enforce royal orders, and to undermine the influence of the regional nobility. As the intendants' power increased under Richelieu, so did the power of the centralized French state.

Under Richelieu the French monarchy also reasserted the principle of one people united by one faith. In 1627 Louis XIII decided to end Protestant military and political independence because, he said, it constituted "a state within a state." According to Louis, Huguenots were politically disobedient because they did not allow Catholics to worship in their cities.[8] Attention focused on La Rochelle, fourth largest of the French Atlantic ports and a major commercial center with strong ties to the northern Protestant states of Holland and England. Louis personally supervised the siege of La Rochelle. After the city fell in October 1628, its municipal government was suppressed and its walled fortifications were destroyed. Although Protestants retained the right of public worship, the king reinstated the Catholic liturgy, and Cardinal Richelieu himself celebrated the first Mass. The fall of La Rochelle weakened the influence of aristocratic Huguenots and was one step in the removal of Protestantism as a strong force in French life. Richelieu did not aim to wipe out Protestantism in the rest of Europe, however. His main foreign policy goal was to destroy the Catholic Habsburgs' grip on territories that surrounded France. Consequently, Richelieu supported the Habsburgs' enemies, including Protestants. In 1631 he signed a treaty with the Lutheran king Gustavus Adolphus promising French support against the Habsburgs in what has been called the Swedish phase of the Thirty Years' War (see page 436). French influence became an important factor in the political future of the German Empire. Richelieu acquired for France extensive rights in Alsace in the east and Arras in the north.

In building the French state, Richelieu knew that his approach sometimes seemed to contradict traditional Christian teaching. As a priest and bishop, how did he justify his policies? He developed his own *raison d'état* (reason of state): "Where the interests of the state are concerned, God absolves actions which, if privately committed, would be a crime."[9] Richelieu's successor as chief minister for the next boy-king, Louis XIV, was Cardinal Jules Mazarin (1602–1661). Along with the regent, Queen Mother Anne of Austria, Mazarin continued Richelieu's centralizing policies. His struggle to increase royal revenues to meet the costs of war with Spain led to the uprisings of 1648–1653 known as the **Fronde.** A *frondeur* was originally a street urchin who threw mud at the passing carriages of the rich, but the word came to be applied to the many individuals and groups who opposed the policies of the government. The most influential of these groups were the robe nobility—court judges—and the sword nobility—the aristocracy—both of whom resented growing centralized control. During the first of several riots, the queen mother fled Paris with Louis XIV. As the rebellion continued, civil order broke down completely. In 1651 Anne's regency ended with the declaration of Louis as king in his own right. Much of the rebellion died away, and its leaders came to terms with the government.

intendants   Royal commissioners. Appointed by and answering directly to the monarch, they were key elements in Richelieu's plan to centralize the French state.

Fronde   A series of violent uprisings during the minority of Louis XIV triggered by oppressive taxation and growing royal authority; the last attempt of the French nobility to resist the king by arms.

The conflicts of the Fronde had significant results for the future. The twin evils of noble factionalism and popular riots left the French wishing for peace and for a strong monarch to re-impose order. This was the legacy that Louis XIV inherited when he assumed personal rule in 1661. Humiliated by his flight from Paris, he was determined to avoid any recurrence of rebellion.

Louis XIV and Absolutism

The reign of Louis XIV (r. 1643–1715) was the longest in European history, and the French monarchy reached the peak of absolutist development. In the magnificence of his court and the brilliance of the culture that he presided over, the "Sun King" dominated his age.

Religion, Anne, and Mazarin all taught Louis the doctrine of the **divine right of kings**: God had established kings as his rulers on earth, and they were answerable ultimately to God alone. Though kings were divinely anointed and shared in the sacred nature of divinity, they could not simply do as they pleased. They had to obey God's laws and rule for the good of the people.

Louis worked very hard at the business of governing. He ruled his realm through several councils of state, and insisted on taking a personal role in many of the councils' decisions. He selected councilors from the recently ennobled or the upper middle class because he wanted "people to know by the rank of the men who served him that he had no intention of sharing power with them."[10] Despite increasing financial problems, Louis never called a meeting of the Estates General. The nobility therefore had no means of united expression or action. Nor did Louis have a first minister; he kept himself free from worry about the inordinate power of a Richelieu. Louis also used spying and terror—a secret police force, a system of informers, and the practice of opening private letters—to eliminate potential threats.

Religion was also a tool of national unity under Louis. In 1685 he revoked the Edict of Nantes, by which his grandfather Henry IV had granted liberty of conscience to French Huguenots. The new law ordered the destruction of Huguenot churches, the closing of schools, the Catholic baptism of Huguenots, and the exile of Huguenot pastors who refused to renounce their faith. The result was the departure of some of his most loyal and industrially skilled subjects.

Richelieu had already deprived French Calvinists of political rights and many had converted to Catholicism. Why, then, did Louis XIV undertake such an apparently unnecessary, cruel, and self-destructive measure? First, Louis considered religion primarily a political question. Although he was personally tolerant, he hated division within the realm and insisted that religious unity was essential to his royal dignity and to the security of the state. Second, aristocrats had long petitioned Louis to crack down on Protestants. His decision to do so won him enormous praise.

Louis's personal hold on power, his exclusion of great nobles from his councils, and his ruthless pursuit of religious unity persuaded many earlier historians that his reign witnessed the creation of an **absolute monarchy.** Louis supposedly crushed the political pretensions of the nobility, leaving them with social grandeur and court posing but no real power. A later generation of historians has revised that view, showing the multiple constraints on Louis's power and his need to cooperate with the nobles. Louis may have declared his absolute power, but in practice he governed through collaboration with nobles, who maintained tremendous prestige and authority in their ancestral lands. Scholars also underline the traditional nature of Louis's motivations. Like his predecessors, Louis XIV sought to enhance

divine right of kings The belief that God had established kings as his rulers on earth and that they were answerable ultimately to God alone.

absolute monarchy A form of government in which sovereignty is vested in a single person, the king or queen; absolute monarchs in the sixteenth and seventeenth centuries based their authority on the theory of the divine right of kings.

Rubens: The Death of Henri IV and The Proclamation of the Regency (1622–1625)

In 1622 the regent Marie de' Medici commissioned Peter Paul Rubens to paint a cycle of paintings depicting her life. This one portrays two distinct moments: the assassination of Henry IV (shown on the left ascending to Heaven), and Marie's subsequent proclamation as regent. The other twenty-three canvasses in the cycle similarly glorify Marie, a tricky undertaking given her unhappy marriage to Henry IV and her tumultuous relationship with her son Louis XIII, who removed her from the regency in 1617. As in this image, Rubens frequently resorted to allegory and classical imagery to elevate the events of Marie's life. (Réunion des Musées Nationaux/ Art Resource, NY)

the glory of his dynasty and his country, mostly through war. The creation of a new state apparatus was a means to that goal, not an end in itself.

Financial and Economic Management Under Louis XIV: Colbert

France's ability to build armies and fight wars depended on a strong economy. The king named Jean-Baptiste Colbert (1619–1683), the son of a wealthy merchant-financier of Reims, as controller general of finances. Colbert came to manage the entire royal administration and proved himself a financial genius. His central principle was that the wealth and the economy of France should serve the state. He did not invent the system called "mercantilism," but he rigorously applied it to France.

Mercantilism is a collection of governmental policies for the regulation of economic activities, especially commercial activities, by and for the state. In seventeenth- and eighteenth-century economic theory, a nation's international power was thought to be based on its wealth, specifically its gold supply. Because resources were limited, mercantilist theory held, state intervention was needed to secure the largest part of a limited resource. To accumulate gold, a country always had to sell more goods abroad than it bought. Colbert thus insisted that France should be self-sufficient, able to produce within its borders everything French subjects needed. Consequently, the outflow of gold would be halted; debtor states would pay in bullion; unemployment and poverty would greatly diminish; and with the wealth of the nation increased, its power and prestige would be enhanced.

mercantilism A system of economic regulations aimed at increasing the power of the state.

Colbert supported old industries and created new ones so that France would be self-sufficient. He focused especially on textiles, the most important sector of the economy, reinforcing the system of state inspection and regulation and forming guilds. Colbert encouraged foreign craftsmen to immigrate to France by giving them special privileges, and he worked to bring more female workers into the labor force. To encourage the people to buy French goods, he abolished many domestic tariffs and raised tariffs on foreign products. One of Colbert's most ambitious projects was the creation of a merchant marine to transport French goods. In 1661 France possessed 18 unseaworthy vessels; by 1681 it had 276 working ships manned by trained sailors. In 1664 Colbert founded the Company of the East Indies with (unfulfilled) hopes of competing with the Dutch for Asian trade.

Colbert also hoped to make Canada—rich in untapped minerals and some of the best agricultural land in the world—part of a vast French empire. He sent four thousand peasants from western France to the province of Quebec. (In 1608, one year after the English arrived at Jamestown, Virginia, Sully had established the city of Quebec, which became the capital of French Canada.) Subsequently, the Jesuit Jacques Marquette and the merchant Louis Joliet sailed down the Mississippi River and claimed possession of the land on both sides as far south as present-day Arkansas. In 1684 the French explorer Robert La Salle continued down the Mississippi to its mouth and claimed vast territories and the rich delta for Louis XIV. The area was called, naturally, "Louisiana."

During Colbert's tenure as controller general, Louis was able to pursue his goals without massive tax increases and without creating a stream of new offices. Colbert managed to raise revenues significantly by cracking down on inefficiences and corruption in the tax collection system. The constant pressure of warfare after Colbert's death, however, undid many of his economic achievements.

Louis XIV's Wars

Louis XIV wrote that "the character of a conqueror is regarded as the noblest and highest of titles." In pursuit of the title of conqueror, he kept France at war for thirty-three of the fifty-four years of his personal rule. In 1666 Louis appointed François le Tellier (later, marquis de Louvois) as secretary of state for war. Under the king's watchful eye, Louvois created a professional army that was modern in the sense that the French state, rather than private nobles, employed the soldiers. Louvois utilized several methods in recruiting troops: dragooning, in which press gangs seized men off the streets; conscription; and, after 1688, lottery. With these techniques, the French army grew from roughly 125,000 men in the Thirty Years' War (1618–1648) to 250,000 during the Dutch War (1672–1678) and 340,000 during the War of the League of Augsburg (1688–1697).[11] Uniforms and weapons were standardized and rational systems of training and promotion devised. Many historians believe that the new loyalty, professionalism, and size of the French army is the best case for the success of absolutism under Louis XIV. Whatever his compromises elsewhere, the French monarch had firm control of his armed forces. As in so many other matters, Louis's model was followed across Europe.

Louis's supreme goal was to expand France to what he considered its "natural" borders and to secure those lands from any threat of invasion. His armies managed to expand French borders to include important commercial centers in the Spanish Netherlands and Flanders, as well as all of Franche-Comté between 1667 and 1678. In 1681 Louis seized the city of Strasbourg, and three years later he sent armies into the province of Lorraine. At that moment the king seemed invincible.

In fact, Louis had reached the limit of his expansion. The wars of the 1680s and 1690s brought no additional territories.

Louis understood his wars largely as defensive undertakings, but his neighbors naturally viewed French expansion with great alarm. Louis's wars inspired the formation of Europe-wide coalitions against him. As a result, he was obliged to support a huge army in several different theaters of war. This task placed unbearable strains on French resources, especially given the inequitable system of taxation.

Colbert's successors as minister of finance resorted to the devaluation of the currency and the old device of selling offices and tax exemptions. They also created new direct taxes in 1695 and 1710, which nobles and clergymen had to pay for the first time. In exchange for this money, the king reaffirmed the traditional social hierarchies by granting honors, pensions, and titles to the nobility. Commoners had to pay the new taxes as well as the old ones.

A series of bad harvests between 1688 and 1694 added social to fiscal catastrophe. The price of wheat skyrocketed. The result was widespread starvation, and in many provinces the death rate rose to several times the normal figure. Parish registers reveal that France buried at least one-tenth of its population in those years, perhaps 2 million in 1693 and 1694 alone. Rising grain prices, new taxes for war, a slump in manufacturing, and the constant nuisance of pillaging troops all meant great suffering for the French people. France wanted peace at any price and won a respite for five years, which was shattered by the War of the Spanish Succession (1701–1713).

In 1700 the childless Spanish king Charles II (r. 1665–1700) died, opening a struggle for control of Spain and its colonies. His will bequeathed the Spanish crown and its empire to Philip of Anjou, Louis XIV's grandson (Louis's wife, Maria-Theresa, had been Charles's sister). This testament violated a prior treaty by which the European powers had agreed to divide the Spanish possessions between the king of France and the Holy Roman emperor, both brothers-in-law of Charles II. Claiming that he was following both Spanish and French national interests, Louis broke with the treaty and accepted the will.

In 1701 the English, Dutch, Austrians, and Prussians formed the Grand Alliance against Louis XIV. The allied powers united to prevent France from becoming too strong in Europe and to check France's expanding commercial power in North America, Asia, and Africa. The war dragged on until 1713. The **Peace of Utrecht,** which ended the war, applied the principle of partition. Louis's grandson Philip remained the first Bourbon king of Spain on the understanding that the French and Spanish crowns would never be united. France surrendered Newfoundland, Nova Scotia, and the Hudson Bay territory to England, which also acquired Gibraltar, Minorca, and control of the African slave trade from Spain. The Dutch gained little because Austria received the former Spanish Netherlands (see Map 16.1).

Peace of Utrecht A series of treaties, from 1713 to 1715, that ended the War of the Spanish Succession, ended French expansion in Europe, and marked the rise of the British Empire.

The Peace of Utrecht had important international consequences. It represented the balance-of-power principle in operation, setting limits on the extent to which any one power—in this case, France—could expand. The treaty completed the decline of Spain as a great power. It vastly expanded the British Empire, and it gave European powers experience in international cooperation. The Peace of Utrecht also marked the end of French expansion. Thirty-five years of war had brought rights to all of Alsace and the gain of important cities in the north such as Lille, as well as Strasbourg. But at what price? In 1714 an exhausted France hovered on the brink of bankruptcy. It is no wonder that when Louis XIV died on September 1, 1715, many subjects felt as much relief as they did sorrow.

Legend

- French Bourbon lands
- Spanish Bourbon lands
- Austrian Habsburg lands
- Prussian lands
- Great Britain
- Boundary of the Holy Roman Empire
- Russian Empire
- Russian gains, by 1725
- Ottoman Empire, 1722

RUSSIAN EMPIRE

• Moscow

• Smolensk

• St. Petersburg

INGRIA

ESTONIA

LIVONIA

• Riga

LITHUANIA

POLAND

• Warsaw

EAST PRUSSIA

S W E D E N

Baltic Sea

Vistula R.

PRUSSIA

BRANDENBURG

• Berlin

SAXONY

SILESIA

Oder R.

BOHEMIA

Elbe R.

KINGDOM OF DENMARK

DENMARK

• Oslo

NORWAY

HANOVER

HOLY ROMAN EMPIRE

PALATINATE

Rhine R.

BAVARIA

Danube R.

AUSTRIA

• Vienna

UKRAINE

Dnieper R.

Dnieper R.

Dniester R.

Don R.

CRIMEA

Black Sea

MOLDAVIA

TRANSYLVANIA

WALLACHIA

Danube R.

BULGARIA

HUNGARY

• Buda

• Pest

SLAVONIA

CROATIA

BOSNIA

SERBIA

• Belgrade

HERZEGOVINA

MONTENEGRO

ALBANIA

REPUBLIC OF VENICE

Adriatic Sea

O T T O M A N   E M P I R E

• Constantinople

Aegean Sea

GREECE

North Sea

UNITED NETHERLANDS

• Utrecht

LORRAINE

• Strasbourg

SWITZERLAND

SAVOY

MILAN

MODENA

GENOA

Po R.

TUSCANY

PAPAL STATES

• Rome

KINGDOM OF NAPLES

• Naples

Corsica (Genoa)

Sardinia (Austria)

Sicily (Savoy)

Mediterranean Sea

GREAT BRITAIN

SCOTLAND

• Edinburgh

ENGLAND

• London

Thames R.

IRELAND

• Dublin

FRANCE

• Paris

Seine R.

Loire R.

Rhône R.

Garonne R.

• Toulouse

• Marseilles

Minorca (Gr. Br.)

Balearic Is.

CATALONIA

Ebro R.

SPAIN

• Madrid

Duero R.

Tagus R.

GIBRALTAR (Gr. Br.)

PORTUGAL

• Lisbon

ATLANTIC OCEAN

50 N

60 N

40 E

30 E

20 E

10 E

0

10 W

N

300 Mi.

300 Km.

150

150

0

0

MAPPING THE PAST

MAP 16.1   Europe in 1715

The series of treaties commonly called the Peace of Utrecht (April 1713–November 1715) ended the War of the Spanish Succession and redrew the map of Europe. A French Bourbon king succeeded to the Spanish throne. France surrendered to Austria the Spanish Netherlands (later Belgium), then in French hands, and France recognized the Hohenzollern (**HOH-uhn-zol-urn**) rulers of Prussia. Spain ceded Gibraltar to Great Britain, for which it has been a strategic naval station ever since. Spain also granted to Britain the *asiento*, the contract for supplying African slaves to America. **[1]** Identify the areas on the map that changed hands as a result of the Peace of Utrecht. How did these changes affect the balance of power in Europe? **[2]** How and why did so many European countries possess scattered or discontiguous territories? What does this suggest about European politics in this period? **[3]** Does this map suggest potential for future conflict?

The Decline of Absolutist Spain in the Seventeenth Century

As French power was growing, Spanish power was diminishing. By the early seventeenth century the seeds of disaster were sprouting. Between 1610 and 1650 Spanish trade with the colonies fell 60 percent, due to competition from local industries in the colonies and from Dutch and English traders. At the same time, the native Indians and African slaves who toiled in the South American silver mines suffered frightful epidemics of disease. Ultimately, the lodes started to run dry, and the quantity of metal produced steadily declined after 1620.

In Madrid, however, royal expenditures constantly exceeded income. To meet mountainous state debt and declining revenues, the Crown repeatedly devalued the coinage and declared bankruptcy. In 1596, 1607, 1627, 1647, and 1680, Spanish kings found no solution to the problem of an empty treasury other than to cancel the national debt. Given the frequency of cancellation, national credit plummeted.

Seventeenth-century Spain was the victim of its past. It could not forget the grandeur of the sixteenth century and respond to changing circumstances. Although Spain lacked the finances to fight expensive wars, the imperial tradition demanded the revival of war with the Dutch at the expiration of a twelve-year truce in 1622 and a long war with France over Mantua (1628–1659). Spain thus became embroiled in the Thirty Years' War. These conflicts, on top of an empty treasury, brought disaster.

In 1640 Spain faced serious revolts in Catalonia and Portugal. The Portuguese succeeded in regaining independence from Habsburg rule under their new king, John IV (r. 1640–1656). In 1643 the French inflicted a crushing defeat on a Spanish army at Rocroi in what is now Belgium. By the Treaty of the Pyrenees of 1659, which ended the French-Spanish conflict, Spain was compelled to surrender extensive territories to France. This treaty marked the decline of Spain as a great military power.

Spain's decline can also be traced to a failure to invest in productive enterprises. In contrast to the other countries of western Europe, Spain had only a tiny middle class. Public opinion, taking its cue from the aristocracy, condemned moneymaking as vulgar and undignified. Thousands entered economically unproductive professions: there were said to be nine thousand monasteries in the province of Castile alone. Some three hundred thousand people who had once been Muslims were expelled by Philip III in 1609, significantly reducing the pool

Peeter Snayers: Spanish Troops (detail)
The long wars that Spain fought over Dutch independence, in support of Habsburg interests in Germany, and against France left the country militarily exhausted and financially drained by the mid-1600s. Here, Spanish troops—thin, emaciated, and probably unpaid—straggle away from battle. (Museo Nacional del Prado, Madrid. Photo: José Baztan y Alberto Otero)

of skilled workers and merchants. Those working in the textile industry were forced out of business when the flood of gold and silver produced severe inflation, pushing their production costs to the point where they could not compete in colonial and international markets. Other businessmen found so many obstacles in the way of profitable enterprise that they simply gave up.[12] Spanish aristocrats, attempting to maintain an extravagant lifestyle they could no longer afford, increased the rents on their estates. High rents and heavy taxes in turn drove the peasants from the land. Agricultural production suffered, and peasants departed for the large cities, where they swelled the ranks of unemployed beggars.

Spanish leaders seemed to lack the will to reform. If one can discern personality from pictures, the portraits of Philip III (r. 1598–1622), Philip IV (r. 1622–1665), and Charles II (r. 1665–1700) hanging in the Prado, the Spanish national museum in Madrid, reflect the increasing weakness of the dynasty. Pessimism and fatalism permeated national life. In the reign of Philip IV, a royal council was appointed to plan the construction of a canal linking the Tagus and Manzanares Rivers in Spain. After interminable debate, the committee decided that "if God had intended the rivers to be navigable, He would have made them so." Spain ignored new scientific methods because they came from heretical nations, Holland and England.

In the brilliant novel **Don Quixote** (dohn kee-HOH-tee), Spanish writer Miguel de Cervantes (1547–1616) produced one of the great masterpieces of world literature. The main character, Don Quixote, lives in a world of dreams, traveling about the countryside seeking military glory. From the title of the book, the English language has borrowed the word *quixotic*. Meaning "idealistic but

Don Quixote A novel authored by Miguel de Cervantes that is perhaps the greatest work of Spanish literature. It is a survey of the entire fabric of Spanish society that can be read on several levels: as a burlesque of chivalric romances and as an exploration of conflicting views (idealistic vs. realistic) of life and of the world.

impractical," the term characterizes seventeenth-century Spain. As a leading scholar has written, "The Spaniard convinced himself that reality was what he felt, believed, imagined. He filled the world with heroic reverberations. Don Quixote was born and grew."[13]

The Culture of Absolutism

What cultural forms flourished under absolutist governments?

Under absolutist monarchs, culture became an instrument of state power. The **baroque style** in art and music flourished in Spain, Italy, and Central Europe. Baroque masters like Rubens painted portraits celebrating the glory of European monarchs. Architecture became an important tool for the French monarch Louis XIV, who made the magnificent palace of Versailles (vehr-SIGH) the center of his kingdom, inspiring imitators across Europe (see Chapter 17). Even language reflected the growing power of the French crown. Within France Richelieu established an academy to oversee French literature and language. Outside its borders French became the common language of the European elite.

Baroque Art and Music

Rome and the revitalized Catholic church of the later sixteenth century played an important role in the early development of the baroque. As we have seen (pages 539–540), the papacy and the Jesuits encouraged the growth of an intensely emotional, exuberant art aimed at kindling the faith of ordinary churchgoers. In addition to this underlying religious emotionalism, the baroque drew its sense of drama, motion, and ceaseless striving from the art and architecture of the Catholic Reformation. Yet baroque art was more than just "Catholic art" in the seventeenth century and the first half of the eighteenth. True, neither Protestant England nor the Netherlands ever came fully under the spell of the baroque, but neither did Catholic France. And Protestants accounted for some of the finest examples of baroque style, especially in music. The baroque style spread partly because its tension and bombast spoke to an agitated age that was experiencing great violence and controversy in politics and religion.

In painting, the baroque reached maturity early with the painter Peter Paul Rubens (1577–1640). Rubens studied the masters of the High Renaissance such as Michelangelo but developed his own style, which was characterized by animated figures, melodramatic contrasts, and monumental size. Rubens excelled in glorifying monarchs such as Queen Mother Marie de' Medici of France (see the painting on page 409). He was also a devout Catholic; nearly half of his pictures treat Christian subjects. Yet one of Rubens's trademarks was fleshy, sensual nudes who populate his canvases as Roman goddesses, water nymphs, and remarkably voluptuous saints and angels.

In music, the baroque style reached its culmination almost a century later in the dynamic, soaring lines of Johann Sebastian Bach (1685–1750), an organist and choirmaster of several Lutheran churches across Germany. Bach's organ music combined the baroque spirit of invention, tension, and emotion in both secular concertos and sublime religious cantatas. Unlike Rubens, Bach was not fully appreciated in his lifetime, but since the early nineteenth century his reputation has grown steadily.

Section Review

- Henry IV of France restored order and prosperity but his premature death left queen-regent Marie de' Medici and Cardinal Richelieu to rule for the boy Louis XIII; Richelieu led France into the Thirty Years' War and continued Henry IV's work of increasing the power of the centralized state.

- After the death of Louis XIII, Cardinal Mazarin and the regent, Queen Mother Anne of Austria, ruled for the boy-king Louis XIV; the Fronde uprisings during this time protested growing royal power and war-related tax increases.

- The "Sun King" Louis XIV created an "absolute monarchy," ruling according to the doctrine of the "divine right of kings" in which a king answered to God alone.

- Jean-Baptiste Colbert, Louis XIV's brilliant finance minister, adopted mercantilist policies intended to foster economic self-sufficiency so that everything French subjects needed would be produced internally—therefore halting the external flow of gold and increasing the wealth of the nation.

- Louis XIV built a large, loyal, professional army that expanded French borders but required expensive maintenance, taxing French resources.

- The Peace of Utrecht ended the War of the Spanish Succession and redrew the map of Europe, marking the end of French expansion, an increase in the British Empire, and the decline of Spain.

- Spain's power declined due to a loss of trade with the colonies, diminished production of South American silver, bankruptcy from fighting wars, a failure to invest in productive enterprises, the deportation of formerly Muslim workers, and high rents and heavy taxes that drove peasants from the land.

baroque style An intensely emotional and exuberant style of art, practiced by artists such as Rubens and associated with the late-sixteenth-century Catholic Reformation; in music, it reached maturity almost a century later with the compositions of Bach.

Juan de Pareja: The Calling of Saint Matthew
Using rich but subdued colors, Pareja depicts the biblical text (Mark 2:13–17), with Jesus in traditional first-century dress and the other figures, arranged around a table covered with an oriental carpet, in seventeenth-century apparel. Matthew, at Jesus's right hand, seems surprised by the "call." Pareja, following a long tradition, includes himself (*standing, far left*).
(Museo Nacional del Prado, Madrid/The Bridgeman Art Library)

Court Culture

In 1682 Louis formally established his court at Versailles, which became the center of the kingdom: a model of rational order and the perfect symbol of the king's power. The art and architecture of Versailles were tools of Louis's policy, used to overawe his subjects and foreign visitors. The Russian tsar Peter the Great imitated Versailles in the construction of his palace, Peterhof, as did the Prussian emperor Frederick the Great in his palace at Potsdam outside Berlin and the Habsburgs at Schonbrunn outside Vienna. (See the feature "Images in Society: Absolutist Palace Building" on pages 440–441.)

The palace was the summit of political, social, and cultural life. The king required all great nobles to spend at least part of the year in attendance on him at Versailles. Between three thousand and ten thousand people occupied the palace each day. Given the demand for space, even high nobles had to make do with cramped and uncomfortable living quarters. The palace gardens, and the palace itself on some occasions, were open to the public, allowing even local peasants a glimpse of their sovereign. More than a royal residence or administrative center, Versailles was a mirror of French greatness to the world.

Much has been made of the "domestication" of the nobility at Versailles. Nobles had to follow a tortuous system of court etiquette, and they vied for the honor of serving the monarch, with the highest in rank claiming the privilege to hand the king his shirt when he dressed. These rituals were far from meaningless or trivial. The king controlled immense resources and privileges; access to him meant favored treatment for pensions, military and religious posts, honorary titles, and a host of other benefits. Courtiers sought these rewards for themselves and for their family members and followers. As in ancient Rome, a patronage system—in which higher-ranked individuals protected lower-ranked ones in return for loyalty and services—dominated political life. Patronage flowed from the court to the provinces; it was the mechanism through which Louis gained cooperation from social elites.

Although they were denied public offices and posts, women played a central role in the patronage system. At court, the king's wife, mistresses, and other female relatives used their high rank to establish their own patronage relations. They recommended individuals for honors, advocated policy decisions, and brokered alliances between noble factions. Noblewomen played a similar role, bringing their family connections to marriage to form powerful social networks. Onlookers sometimes resented the influence of powerful women at court. The Duke of Saint-Simon said of Madame de Maintenon, Louis XIV's mistress and secret second wife:

> The power of Madame de Maintenon was, as may be imagined, immense. She had everybody in her hands, from the highest and most favored ministers to the meanest subject of the realm. Many people have been ruined by her, without having been able to discover the author of the ruin, search as they might.

French Classicism

To this day, culture is a central element of French national pride and identity. French emphasis on culture dates back to Cardinal Richelieu, whose efforts at state centralization embraced cultural activities. In 1635 he gave official recognition to a group of scholars interested in grammar and rhetoric. Thus was born the French Academy, which prepared a dictionary to standardize the French language; the dictionary was completed in 1694 and has been updated in many successive editions. The Academy survives today as a prestigious society and retains authority over correct usage in the French language.

Scholars characterize the art and literature of the age of Louis XIV as **French classicism.** By this they mean that the artists and writers of the late seventeenth century imitated the subject matter and style of classical antiquity, that their work resembled that of Renaissance Italy, and that French art possessed the classical qualities of discipline, balance, and restraint. This was a movement away from the perceived excesses of baroque style.

French classicism A style of French art, architecture, and literature (ca. 1600–1750), based on admiration and imitation of Greek and Roman models but with greater exuberance and complexity.

Louis XIV was an enthusiastic patron of the arts. Music and theater frequently served as backdrops for court ceremonials. Louis favored Jean-Baptiste Lully (1632–1687), whose orchestral works combined lively animation with the restrained austerity typical of French classicism. Louis also supported François Couperin (1668–1733), whose harpsichord and organ works possessed the regal grandeur the king loved, and Marc-Antoine Charpentier (1634–1704), whose solemn religious music entertained him at meals.

Louis XIV loved the stage, and in the plays of Molière (**mohl-YAIR**) (1622–1673) and Racine (ra-SEEN) (1639–1699) his court witnessed the finest achievements in the history of the French theater. As playwright, stage manager, director, and actor, Molière (born Jean-Baptiste Poquelin) produced comedies that exposed the hypocrisies and follies of polite society through brilliant caricature. *Tartuffe* (**tahr-TOOF**) satirized the religious hypocrite; his plays *Le Bourgeois Gentilhomme* (The Bourgeois Gentleman) and *Les Précieuses ridicules* (The Pretentious Young Ladies) mocked the social pretensions of the bourgeoisie, stopping short of criticizing the high nobility.

Section Review

- The baroque style, practiced by artists such as Rubens, was intensely emotional and exuberant; it was particularly associated with the late sixteenth century Catholic Reformation, but appeared in both religious and secular themes and in Protestant artists.

- Baroque composers such as Bach combined invention, tension, and emotion in their music, much of which was organ music played in church.

- The palace at Versailles was the showpiece and center of the French kingdom, crowded with nobles vying for the king's favor and patronage

- French classicism, a movement reviving classical antiquity in art and literature, was popular during the reign of Louis XIV; theater also gained popularity with playwrights such as the comic Molière and the tragedian Racine.

- The French language was adopted by elites across Europe for diplomacy, scholarship, and polite conversation.

constitutionalism A form of government in which power is limited by law and balanced between the authority and power of the government on the one hand, and the rights and liberties of the subject or citizen on the other hand.

Molière's contemporary Jean Racine based his tragic dramas on Greek and Roman legends. His persistent theme was the conflict of good and evil. Several plays—*Andromaque* (ahn-dro-MAK), *Bérénice* (bear-ay-NEES), *Iphigénie* (if-ee-jay-NEE), and *Phèdre* (FAY-druh)—bear the names of women and deal with the power of female passion. For simplicity of language, symmetrical structure, and calm restraint, the plays of Racine represent the finest examples of French classicism.

Louis XIV's reign inaugurated the use of French as the language of polite society, international diplomacy, and, gradually, scholarship and learning. The royal courts of Sweden, Russia, Poland, and Germany all spoke French. France inspired a cosmopolitan European culture in the late seventeenth century, which looked to Versailles as its center.

Constitutionalism

What is constitutionalism, and how did this form of government emerge in England and the Dutch Republic?

While France and later Prussia, Russia, and Austria (see Chapter 17) developed the absolutist state, England and Holland evolved toward **constitutionalism**, which is the limitation of government by law. Constitutionalism also implies a balance between the authority and power of the government, on the one hand, and the rights and liberties of the subjects, on the other.

A nation's constitution may be written or unwritten. It may be embodied in one basic document, occasionally revised by amendment, like the Constitution of the United States. Or it may be only partly formalized and include parliamentary statutes, judicial decisions, and a body of traditional procedures and practices, like the English and Dutch constitutions. Whether written or unwritten, a constitution gets its binding force from the government's acknowledgment that it must respect that constitution—that is, that the state must govern according to the laws.

Absolutist Claims in England (1603–1649)

In 1588 Queen Elizabeth I of England exercised very great personal power; by 1689 the English monarchy was severely circumscribed. Change in England was anything but orderly. Seventeenth-century England executed one king and experienced a bloody civil war; experimented with military dictatorship, then restored the son of the murdered king; and finally, after a bloodless revolution, established constitutional monarchy. Political stability came only in the 1690s. After such a violent and tumultuous century, how did England produce a constitutional monarchy?

A rare and politically astute female monarch, Elizabeth was able to maintain control over her realm in part by refusing to marry and submit to a husband. The problem with this strategy was that it left the queen with no immediate heir to continue her legacy.

In 1603 Elizabeth's Scottish cousin James Stuart succeeded her as James I (r. 1603–1625). King James was well educated and had thirty-five years' experience as king of Scotland. But he was not as interested in displaying the majesty of monarchy as Elizabeth had been. Urged to wave at the crowds who waited to greet their new ruler, James complained that he was tired and threatened to drop his breeches "so they can cheer at my arse." Moreover, in contrast to Elizabeth, James was a poor judge of character, and in a society already hostile to the Scots, James's

Scottish accent was a disadvantage.[14] James's greatest problem, however, stemmed from his belief that a monarch has a divine (or God-given) right to his authority and is responsible only to God. James went so far as to lecture the House of Commons: "There are no privileges and immunities which can stand against a divinely appointed King." This notion, implying total royal jurisdiction over the liberties, persons, and properties of English men and women, formed the basis of the Stuart concept of absolutism. Such a view ran directly counter to the long-standing English idea that a person's property could not be taken away without due process of law. James's expression of such views before the English House of Commons was a grave political mistake, especially given the royal debt that he had inherited from Elizabeth. The House of Commons guarded the state's pocketbook.

In England, unlike France, there was no social stigma attached to paying taxes. Members of the wealthy House of Commons were willing to assess and pay taxes to ease the royal debt provided they had some say in the formulation of state policies. James I and his son Charles I, however, considered such ambitions intolerable and a threat to their divine-right prerogative. Consequently, at every Parliament between 1603 and 1640, bitter squabbles erupted between the Crown and the articulate and legally minded Commons. Charles I's attempt to govern without Parliament (1629–1640) and to finance his government by arbitrary nonparliamentary levies brought the country to a crisis.

<table>
<tr><td>**Religious Divides**</td><td>Religious issues also embittered relations between the king and the House of Commons. In the early seventeenth century increasing numbers of English people</td></tr>
</table>

felt dissatisfied with the Church of England established by Henry VIII and reformed by Elizabeth. Many **Puritans** believed that the Reformation had not gone far enough. They wanted to "purify" the Anglican church of Roman Catholic elements—elaborate vestments and ceremonials, bishops, and even the giving and wearing of wedding rings.

It is difficult to establish what proportion of the English population was Puritan. According to present scholarly consensus, the dominant religious groups in the early seventeenth century were Calvinist; their more zealous members were Puritans. It also seems clear that many English people were attracted by Calvinism's emphasis on hard work, sobriety, thrift, competition, and postponement of pleasure. These values, which have frequently been called the "Protestant ethic" or "capitalist ethic," fit in precisely with the economic approaches and practices of many successful business people and farmers. While it is hazardous to identify capitalism with Protestantism—there were many successful Catholic capitalists, for example—the "Protestant virtues" represented the prevailing values of members of the House of Commons.

Puritans wanted to abolish bishops in the Church of England, and when James I said, "No bishop, no king," he meant that the bishops were among the chief supporters of the throne. Under Charles I, people believed that the country was being led back to Roman Catholicism. Not only did he marry a French Catholic princess, but he also supported the policies of the Archbishop of Canterbury William Laud (1573–1645), who tried to impose elaborate ritual on all churches.

In 1637 Laud attempted to impose two new elements on church organization in Scotland: a new prayer book, modeled on the Anglican *Book of Common Prayer,* and bishoprics, which the Presbyterian Scots firmly rejected. The Scots therefore revolted. To finance an army to put down the Scots, King Charles was compelled to summon Parliament in November 1640.

Puritans Members of a sixteenth- and seventeenth-century reform movement within the Church of England that advocated "purifying" it of Roman Catholic elements, such as bishops, elaborate ceremonials, and the wedding ring.

a Confectioner | a Smith | a Sho-maker | a Taylor
a Sadler | a Porter | a Box-maker | a Sope-boyler
a Glover | a meal-man | a Chiik en-man | a Button-maker

Puritan Occupations

These twelve engravings depict typical Puritan occupations and show that the Puritans came primarily from the artisan and lower middle classes. The governing classes and peasants adhered to the traditions of the Church of England. (Visual Connection Archive)

Charles I was an intelligent man, but contemporaries found him deceitful and treacherous. After quarreling with Parliament over his right to collect customs duties on wine and wool and over what the Commons perceived as religious innovations, Charles had dissolved Parliament in 1629. From 1629 to 1640, he ruled without Parliament, financing his government through extraordinary stopgap levies considered illegal by most English people. For example, the king revived a medieval law requiring coastal districts to help pay the cost of ships for defense, but he levied the tax, called "ship money," on inland as well as coastal counties. Most members of Parliament believed that such taxation without out consent amounted to despotism. Consequently, they were not willing to trust the king with an army. Moreover, many supported the Scots' resistance to Charles's religious innovations and had little wish for military action against them. Accordingly, this Parliament, called the "Long Parliament" because it sat from 1640 to 1660, enacted legislation that limited the power of the monarch and made arbitrary government impossible.

In 1641 the Commons passed the Triennial Act, which compelled the king to summon Parliament every three years. The Commons impeached Archbishop Laud and then went further and threatened to abolish bishops. King Charles, fearful of a Scottish invasion—the original reason for summoning Parliament—accepted these measures. Understanding and peace were not achieved, however, partly because radical members of the Commons pushed increasingly revolutionary propositions, and partly because Charles maneuvered to rescind those he had already approved.

The next act in the conflict was precipitated by the outbreak of rebellion in Ireland, where English governors and landlords had long exploited the people. In 1641 the Catholic gentry of Ireland led an uprising in response to a feared invasion by anti-Catholic forces of the British Long Parliament.

Without an army, Charles I could neither come to terms with the Scots nor respond to the Irish rebellion. After a failed attempt to arrest parliamentary leaders who remained unwilling to grant him an army, Charles left London for the north of England. There, he recruited an army drawn from the nobility and its cavalry staff, the rural gentry, and mercenaries. The parliamentary army was composed of the militia of the city of London, country squires with business connections, and men with a firm belief in the spiritual duty of serving.

The English civil war (1642–1649) pitted the power of the king against that of the Parliament. After three years of fighting, Parliament's **New Model Army** defeated the king's armies at the battles of Naseby and Langport in the summer of 1645. Charles, though, refused to concede defeat and accept restrictions on royal authority and church reform. Both sides jockeyed for position, waiting for a decisive event. This arrived in the form of the army under the leadership of Oliver Cromwell, a member of the House of Commons. In 1647 Cromwell's forces captured the king and dismissed members of the Parliament who opposed his actions. In 1649 the remaining representatives, known as the "Rump Parliament," put Charles on trial for high treason, a severe blow to the theory of divine-right monarchy. Charles was found guilty and beheaded on January 30, 1649, an act that sent shock waves around Europe.

New Model Army The parliamentary army, under the command of Oliver Cromwell, that fought the army of Charles I in the English civil war.

Puritanical Absolutism in England: Cromwell and the Protectorate

With the execution of Charles, kingship was abolished. A *commonwealth*, or republican government, was proclaimed. Theoretically, legislative power rested in the surviving members of Parliament, and executive power was lodged in a council of state. In fact, the army that had defeated the king controlled the government, and Oliver Cromwell controlled the army. Though called the **Protectorate,** the rule of Cromwell (1653–1658) constituted military dictatorship.

The army prepared a constitution, the Instrument of Government (1653), that invested executive power in a lord protector (Cromwell) and a council of state. The instrument provided for triennial parliaments and gave Parliament the sole power to raise taxes. But after repeated disputes, Cromwell dismissed Parliament in 1655 and the instrument was never formally endorsed. Cromwell continued the standing army and proclaimed quasi-martial law. He divided England into twelve military districts, each governed by a major general. Reflecting Puritan ideas of morality, Cromwell's state forbade sports, kept the theaters closed, and rigorously censored the press.

On the issue of religion, Cromwell favored some degree of toleration, and the Instrument of Government gave all Christians except Roman Catholics the right to practice their faith. Cromwell had long associated Catholicism in Ireland with sedition and heresy. In September of the year that his army came to power, it crushed a rebellion at Drogheda and massacred the garrison. Another massacre followed in October. These brutal acts left a legacy of Irish hatred for England. After Cromwell's departure for England, the atrocities worsened. The English banned Catholicism in Ireland, executed priests, and confiscated land from Catholics for English and Scottish settlers.

Cromwell adopted mercantilist policies similar to those of absolutist France. He enforced a Navigation Act (1651) requiring that English goods be transported on English ships. The Navigation Act was a great boost to the development of an English merchant marine and brought about a short but successful war with the commercially threatened Dutch. Cromwell also welcomed the immigration of Jews because of their skills, and they began to return to England after four centuries of absence.

The Protectorate collapsed when Cromwell died in 1658 and his ineffectual son, Richard, succeeded him. Having lost support of the army, Richard was forced to abdicate. Fed up with military rule, the English longed for a return to civilian government and, with it, common law and social stability. By 1660 they were ready to restore the monarchy.

Protectorate The military dictatorship established by Oliver Cromwell following the execution of Charles I in 1649.

Cartoon of 1649: "The Royall Oake of Brittayne"

Chopping down this tree signifies the end of royal authority, stability, Magna Carta (see page 205), and the rule of law. As pigs graze (representing the unconcerned common people), being fattened for slaughter, Oliver Cromwell, with his feet in Hell, quotes Scripture. This is a royalist view of the collapse of Charles I's government and the rule of Cromwell. (Courtesy of the Trustees of the British Museum)

Test Act Written in 1673, this act stated that those who refused to receive the Eucharist of the Church of England could not vote, hold public office, preach, teach, attend the universities, or even assemble for meetings.

The Restoration of the English Monarchy

The Restoration of 1660 brought Charles II (r. 1660–1685) to the throne at the invitation of a special session of Parliament called for that purpose. He was the eldest son of Charles I and had been living on the European continent. Both houses of Parliament were also restored, together with the established Anglican church, the courts of law, and the system of local government through justices of the peace. The Restoration failed to resolve two serious problems, however. What was to be the attitude of the state toward Puritans, Catholics, and dissenters from the established church? And what was to be the relationship between the king and Parliament?

Charles II, an easygoing and sensual man, was not interested in imposing religious uniformity on the English, but members of Parliament were. They enacted the **Test Act** of 1673 against those who refused to receive the Eucharist of the Church of England, denying them the right to vote, hold public office, preach, teach, attend the universities, or even assemble for meetings. But these restrictions could not be enforced. When the Quaker William Penn held a meeting of his Friends and was arrested, the jury refused to convict him.

In politics Charles II was determined "not to set out in his travels again," which meant that he intended to avoid exile by working well with Parliament. Therefore he appointed a council of five men to serve both as his major advisers and as members of Parliament, thus acting as liaison agents between the executive and the legislature. This body—known as the "Cabal" from the names of its five members (Clifford, Arlington, Buckingham, Ashley-Cooper, and Lauderdale)—was an ancestor of the later cabinet system. It gradually came to be accepted that the Cabal was answerable in Parliament for the decisions of the king. This development gave rise to the concept of ministerial responsibility: royal ministers must answer to the Commons.

Harmony between the Crown and Parliament was upset in 1670, however. When Parliament did not grant Charles an adequate income, he entered into a secret agreement with his cousin Louis XIV. The French king would give Charles two hundred thousand pounds annually, and in return Charles would relax the laws against Catholics, gradually re-Catholicize England, support French policy against the Dutch, and convert to Catholicism himself. When the details of this treaty leaked out, a great wave of anti-Catholic fear swept England. This fear was compounded by a crucial fact: with no legitimate heir, Charles would be succeeded by his Catholic brother, James, duke of York. A combination of hatred for French absolutism and hostility to Catholicism produced virtual hysteria. The Commons passed an exclusion bill denying the succession to a Roman Catholic, but Charles quickly dissolved Parliament, and the bill never became law.

When James II (r. 1685–1688) succeeded his brother, the worst English anti-Catholic fears, already aroused by Louis XIV's revocation of the Edict of Nantes, were realized. In violation of the Test Act, James appointed Roman Catholics to positions in the army, the universities, and local government. When these actions were challenged in the courts, the judges, whom James had appointed, decided for the king. The king was suspending the law at will and appeared to be reviving the absolutism of his father and grandfather. He went further. Attempting to broaden his base of support with Protestant dissenters and nonconformists, James issued a declaration of indulgence granting religious freedom to all.

Two events gave the signals for revolution. First, seven bishops of the Church of England were imprisoned in the Tower of London for protesting the declaration of indulgence but were subsequently acquitted amid great public enthusiasm. Second, in June 1688 James's second wife produced a male heir. The fear of a Roman Catholic dynasty supported by France and ruling outside the law prompted a group of eminent persons to offer the English throne to James's Protestant daughter Mary and her Dutch husband, Prince William of Orange. In December 1688 James II, his queen, and their infant son fled to France and became pensioners of Louis XIV. Early in 1689 William and Mary were crowned king and queen of England.

The Triumph of England's Parliament: Constitutional Monarchy and Cabinet Government

The English call the events of 1688 and 1689 the "Glorious Revolution" because it replaced one king with another with a minimum of bloodshed. It also represented the destruction, once and for all, of the idea of divine-right monarchy. William and Mary accepted the English throne from Parliament and in so doing explicitly recognized the supremacy of Parliament. The revolution of 1688 established the principle that sovereignty, the ultimate power in the state, was divided between king and Parliament and that the king ruled with the consent of the governed.

The men who brought about the revolution quickly framed their intentions in the Bill of Rights, the cornerstone of the modern British constitution. The principles of the Bill of Rights were formulated in direct response to Stuart absolutism. Law was to be made in Parliament; once made, it could not be suspended by the Crown. Parliament had to be called at least once every three years. Both elections to and debate in Parliament were to be free in the sense that the Crown was not to interfere in them (this aspect of the bill was widely disregarded in the eighteenth century). The independence of the judiciary was established, and there was to be no standing army in peacetime. And while Protestants could possess arms, the feared Catholic minority could not. Additional legislation granted freedom of worship to Protestant dissenters and nonconformists and required that the English monarch always be Protestant.

Second Treatise of Civil Government
A work of political philosophy published by John Locke in 1690 that argued government's only purpose was to defend the natural rights of life, liberty, and property. A justification of the Glorious Revolution of 1688 to 1689.

The Glorious Revolution and the concept of representative government found its best defense in political philosopher John Locke's **Second Treatise of Civil Government** (1690). Locke (1632–1704) maintained that a government that oversteps its proper function—protecting the natural rights of life, liberty, and property—becomes a tyranny. By "natural" rights Locke meant rights basic to all men because all have the ability to reason. Under a tyrannical government, the people have the natural right to rebellion. Such rebellion can be avoided if the government carefully respects the rights of citizens and if people zealously defend their liberty. Locke linked economic liberty and private property with political freedom. On the basis of this link, he justified limiting the vote to property owners.

The events of 1688 and 1689 did not constitute a *democratic* revolution. The revolution placed sovereignty in Parliament, and Parliament represented the upper classes. The great majority of English people acquired no say in their government. The English revolution established a constitutional monarchy; it also inaugurated an age of aristocratic government that lasted at least until 1832 and in many ways until 1928, when women received full voting rights.

The Dutch Republic in the Seventeenth Century

In the late sixteenth century the seven northern provinces of the Netherlands fought for and won their independence from Spain. The independence of the Republic of the United Provinces of the Netherlands was recognized in 1648, in the treaty that ended the Thirty Years' War. The seventeenth century witnessed an unparalleled flowering of Dutch scientific, artistic, and literary achievement. In this period, often called the "golden age of the Netherlands," Dutch ideas and attitudes played a profound role in shaping a new and modern worldview. At the same time, the United Provinces was another model of the development of the modern constitutional state.

States General The national assembly of the United Provinces of the Netherlands; because many issues had to be refereed back to the provinces, the United Provinces was a confederation, or weak union of strong states.

stadtholder The chief executive officer in each province of the United Provinces; in the seventeenth century these positions were often held by the princes of the House of Orange.

The government of the United Provinces had none of the standard categories of seventeenth-century political organization. The Dutch were not monarchical but rather fiercely republican. Within each province, an oligarchy of wealthy merchants and financiers called "regents" handled domestic affairs in the local Estates (assemblies). The provincial Estates held virtually all the power. A federal assembly, or **States General,** handled matters of foreign affairs, such as war. But the States General did not possess sovereign authority; all issues had to be referred back to the local Estates for approval. In each province, the Estate appointed an executive officer, known as the **stadtholder** (STAT-hohl-der), who carried out ceremonial functions and was responsible for military defense. Although in theory freely chosen by the Estates and answerable to them, in practice the Princes of Orange were almost always chosen as stadtholders. Tensions persisted between supporters of the staunchly republican Estates and those of the aristocratic House of Orange. Holland, which had the largest navy and the most wealth, dominated the seven provinces of the republic and the States General.

The political success of the Dutch rested on the phenomenal commercial prosperity of the Netherlands. The moral and ethical bases of that commercial wealth were thrift, frugality, and religious toleration. As long as business people conducted their religion in private, the government did not interfere with them. Although there is scattered evidence of anti-Semitism, Jews enjoyed a level of acceptance and assimilation in Dutch business and general culture unique in early modern Europe. (See the feature "Individuals in Society: Glückel of Hameln.") For example, Benedict Spinoza (1632–1677), a descendant of Spanish Jews who fled the Inquisition, passed his entire life in Amsterdam, supporting himself as a

Individuals in Society

Glückel of Hameln

In 1690 a Jewish widow in the small German town of Hameln* in Lower Saxony sat down to write her autobiography. She wanted to distract her mind from the terrible grief she felt over the death of her husband and to provide her twelve children with a record "so you will know from what sort of people you have sprung, lest today or tomorrow your beloved children or grandchildren came and know naught of their family." Out of her pain and heightened consciousness, Glückel (1646–1724) produced an invaluable source for scholars.

She was born in Hamburg two years before the end of the Thirty Years' War. In 1649 the merchants of Hamburg expelled the Jews, who moved to nearby Altona, then under Danish rule. When the Swedes overran Altona (1657–1658), the Jews returned to Hamburg "purely at the mercy of the Town Council." Glückel's narrative proceeds against a background of the constant harassment to which Jews were subjected—special papers, permits, bribes—and in Hameln she wrote, "And so it has been to this day and, I fear, will continue in like fashion."

When Glückel was "barely twelve," her father betrothed her to Chayim Hameln (HI-um HAH-muhln). She married at age fourteen. She describes him as "the perfect pattern of the pious Jew," a man who stopped his work every day for study and prayer, fasted, and was scrupulously honest in his business dealings. Only a few years older than Glückel, Chayim earned his living dealing in precious metals and in making small loans on pledges (articles held on security). This work required his constant travel to larger cities, markets, and fairs, often in bad weather, always over dangerous roads. Chayim consulted his wife about all his business dealings. As he lay dying, a friend asked if he had any last wishes. "None," he replied. "My wife knows everything. She shall do as she has always done." For thirty years Glückel had been his friend, full business partner, and wife. They had thirteen children, twelve of whom survived their father, eight then unmarried. As Chayim had foretold, Glückel succeeded in launching the boys in careers and in providing dowries for the girls.

Glückel's world was her family, the Jewish community of Hameln, and the Jewish communities into which her children married. Social and business activities took her to Amsterdam, Baiersdorf, Bamberg, Berlin, Cleves, Danzig, Metz, and Vienna, so her world was not narrow or provincial. She took great pride that Prince Frederick of Cleves, later the king of Prussia, danced at the wedding of her eldest daughter. The rising prosperity of Chayim's businesses allowed the couple to maintain up to six servants.

Glückel was deeply religious, and her culture was steeped in Jewish literature, legends, and mystical and secular works. Above all, she relied on the Bible. Her language, heavily sprinkled with scriptural references, testifies to a rare familiarity with the basic book of Western civilization. The Scriptures were her consolation, the source of her great strength in a hostile world.

Gentleness and deep mutual devotion seem to pervade Rembrandt's *The Jewish Bride*. (Rijksmuseum-Stichting Amsterdam)

Students who would learn about business practices, the importance of the dowry in marriage, childbirth, the ceremony of bris, birthrates, family celebrations, and even the meaning of life can gain a good deal from the memoirs of this extraordinary woman who was, in the words of one of her descendants, the poet Heinrich Heine, "the gift of a world to me."

Questions for Analysis

1. Consider the ways in which Glückel of Hameln was both an ordinary and an extraordinary woman of her times. Would you call her a marginal or a central person in her society?

2. How was Glückel's life affected by the broad events and issues of the seventeenth century?

Source: The Memoirs of Glückel of Hameln (New York: Schocken Books, 1977).

---

* A town immortalized by the Brothers Grimm. In 1284 the town contracted with the Pied Piper to rid it of rats and mice; he lured them away by playing his flute. When the citizens refused to pay, he charmed away their children in revenge.

Jan Steen: The Christening Feast

As the mother, surrounded by midwives, rests in bed *(rear left)* and the father proudly displays the swaddled child, thirteen other people, united by gestures and gazes, prepare the celebratory meal. Very prolific, Steen was a master of warm-hearted domestic scenes. In contrast to the order and cleanliness of many seventeenth-century Dutch genre paintings, Steen's more disorderly portrayals gave rise to the epithet "a Jan Steen household," meaning an untidy house. (Wallace Collection, London/The Bridgeman Art Library)

lens grinder while producing important philosophical treatises. In the Dutch Republic, toleration paid off: it attracted a great deal of foreign capital and investment. People of all races and creeds traded in Amsterdam, at whose docks on the Amstel River five thousand ships were berthed.

The Dutch came to dominate the shipping business by putting profits from their original industry—herring fishing—into shipbuilding. They boasted the lowest shipping rates and largest merchant marine in Europe. Their shipping power allowed them to control the Baltic grain trade, buying entire crops in Poland, eastern Prussia, and Swedish Pomerania. Because the Dutch dealt in bulk, nobody could undersell them. Foreign merchants coming to Amsterdam could buy anything from precision lenses for the microscope (recently invented by Dutchman Anton van Leeuwenhoek) to muskets for an army of five thousand. Although Dutch cities became famous for their exports—diamonds and linens from Haarlem, pottery from Delft—Dutch wealth depended less on exports than on transport.

Dutch East India Company A joint stock company chartered by the States General of the Netherlands to expand trade and promote relations between the Dutch government and its colonial ventures. It established a colony at the Cape of Good Hope (1652), and in the 1630s it paid a return of 35 percent on investments.

In 1602 leaders of the Estate of Holland formed the **Dutch East India Company,** a joint stock company. The investors each received a percentage of the profits proportional to the amount of money they had put in. Within half a century the Dutch East India Company had cut heavily into Portuguese trading in East Asia. The Dutch seized the Cape of Good Hope, Ceylon, and Malacca and established trading posts in each place. In the 1630s the Dutch East India Company was paying its investors about a 35 percent annual return on their investments. The Dutch West India Company, founded in 1621, traded extensively with Latin America and Africa (see Map 16.2). Ultimately both companies would move beyond trading to imperialist exploitation.

Trade and commerce brought the Dutch the highest standard of living in Europe, and perhaps in the world. Salaries were high for all workers except women, but even women's wages were high when compared with those of women in other parts of Europe. All classes of society, including unskilled laborers, ate well. Massive granaries held surplus supplies so that the price of bread remained low. A higher percentage of the worker's income could therefore be spent on fish, cheese, butter, vegetables, and even meat. A scholar has described the Netherlands as "an island of plenty in a sea of want." Consequently, the Netherlands experienced very few of the food riots that characterized the rest of Europe.[15] The Dutch republic was not a federation but a confederation—that is, a weak union of strong provinces. Wealthy and lacking a monarch, the provinces were a temptation to other European powers. Nonetheless, the Dutch resisted the long Spanish effort at reconquest and withstood both French and English attacks in the second half of the century. They were severely weakened, however, by the long War of the Spanish Succession, which was a costly drain on Dutch labor and financial resources. The peace signed in 1713 to end the war brought the republic few gains to compensate for its expenses and marked the beginning of Dutch economic decline.

Section Review

- In England, King James I's belief that he was subject only to God led to tension with the House of Commons as he tried to govern without Parliament.

- Financial and religious disputes between King Charles I and the House of Commons led to civil war, and even though the king allied himself with northern nobles, Parliament won out, tried Charles for treason, and beheaded him in 1649.

- After Charles's death, Cromwell came to power, proclaiming a commonwealth that was actually a military dictatorship, holding Puritanical ideals of morality, earning the ire of the Irish by outlawing Catholicism in Ireland, but also boosting the English sea trade and allowing Jewish immigration.

- After Cromwell's death, the 1660 Restoration brought Charles to the throne, who alienated the English by favoring Catholics; Protestant fears intensified when the Catholic James II succeeded his brother, ending in the Glorious Revolution of 1688, whereby James was exiled to France while his Protestant daughter Mary and her Dutch husband William of Orange were crowned as the monarchs.

- The government of William and Mary was a constitutional monarchy that provided freedom of religion, but economic and political liberty came only with property ownership, so the masses still had no political rights.

- The Dutch republic in the seventeenth century found political success and prosperity by providing religious tolerance, attracting foreign capital, and promoting trade.

MAP 16.2 Seventeenth-Century Dutch Commerce

Dutch wealth rested on commerce, and commerce depended on the huge Dutch merchant marine, manned by perhaps forty-eight thousand sailors. The fleet carried goods from all parts of the globe to the port of Amsterdam.

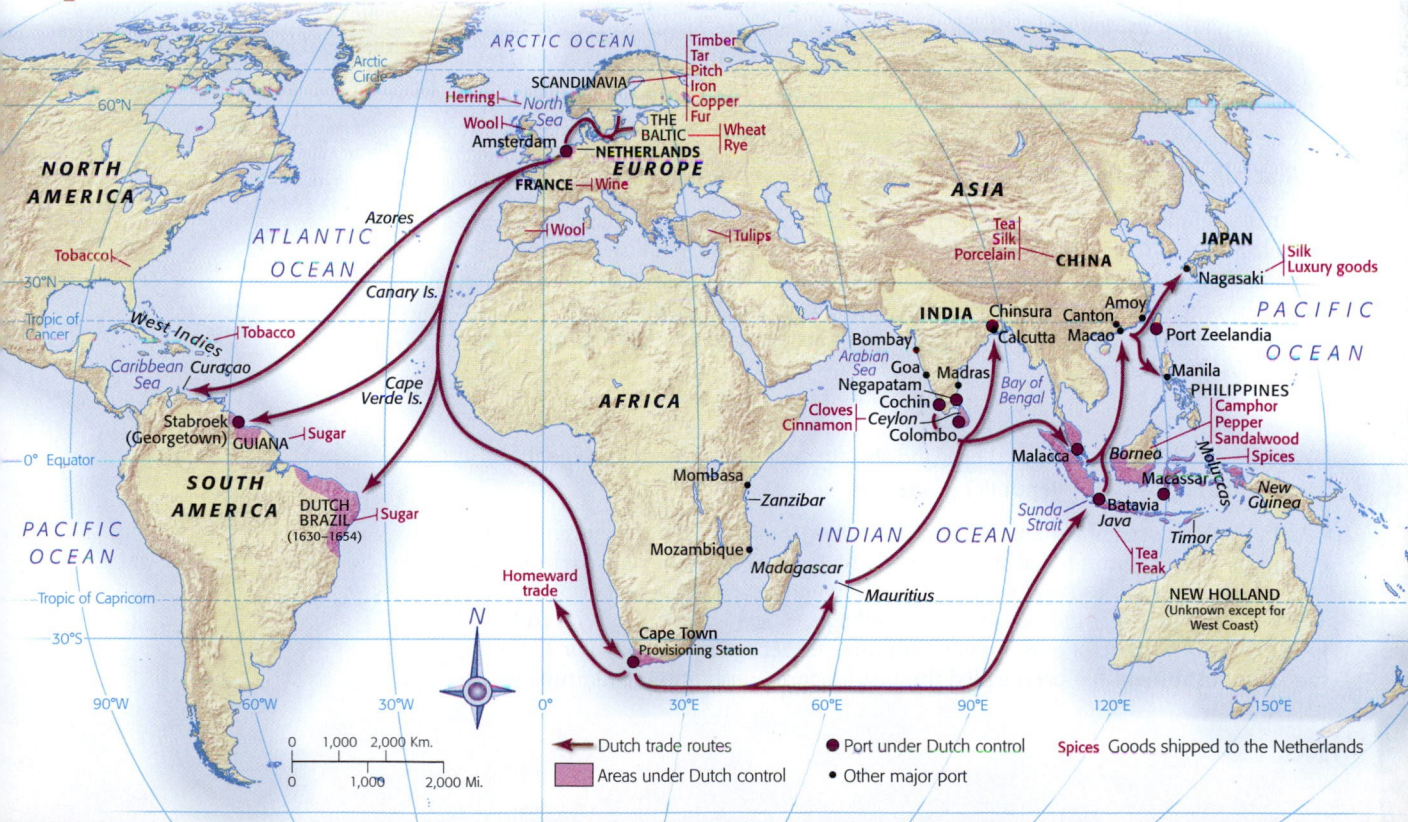

Chapter Review

What were the common crises and achievements of seventeenth-century states? (page 402)

Most parts of Europe experienced the seventeenth century as a period of severe economic, social, and military crisis. Across the continent, rulers faced popular rebellions from their desperate subjects, who were pushed to the brink by poor harvests, high taxes, and decades of war. Many forces, including powerful noblemen, the church, and regional and local loyalties, constrained the state's authority. Despite these obstacles, most European states emerged from the seventeenth century with increased powers and more centralized control. Whether they ruled through monarchical fiat or parliamentary negotiation, European governments strengthened their bureaucracies, raised more taxes, and significantly expanded their armies.

According to Thomas Hobbes, the central drive in every human is "a perpetual and restless desire of Power, after Power, that ceaseth only in Death." The seventeenth century solved the problem of sovereign power in two fundamental ways: absolutism and constitutionalism.

To what extent did French and Spanish monarchs succeed in creating absolute monarchies? (page 405)

Under Louis XIV France witnessed the high point of absolutist ambition in western Europe. The king saw himself as the representative of God on earth, and it has been said that "to the seventeenth century imagination God was a sort of image of Louis XIV."[16] Under Louis's rule, France developed a centralized bureaucracy, a professional army, and a state-directed economy, all of which he personally supervised.

Despite his claims to absolute power, Louis XIV ruled, in practice, by securing the collaboration of high nobles. In exchange for confirmation of their ancient privileges, the nobles were willing to cooperate with the expansion of state power. This was a common pattern in attempts at absolutism across Europe. In Spain, where monarchs made similar claims to absolute power, the seventeenth century witnessed economic catastrophe and a decline in royal capacities.

What cultural forms flourished under absolutist governments? (page 415)

France's dominant political role in Europe elevated its cultural influence as well. French became the common language of the European elite, as all heads turned to Versailles and the radiant aristocratic culture emanating from it. Within France, the Bourbon monarchy pursued culture as one more aspect of absolutist policy, creating cultural academies, sponsoring playwrights and musicians, and repressing Protestantism with a bloody hand.

What is constitutionalism, and how did this form of government emerge in England and the Dutch Republic? (page 418)

As Louis XIV personified absolutist ambitions, so Stuart England exemplified the evolution of the constitutional state. The conflicts between Parliament and the first two Stuart rulers, James I and Charles I, tested where sovereign power would reside. The resulting civil war did not solve the problem. The Instrument of Government provided for a balance of government authority and recognition of popular rights; as such, the Instrument has been called the first modern constitution. Unfortunately, it

Key Terms

moral economy (p. 403)

sovereignty (p. 405)

popular revolts (p. 405)

intendants (p. 407)

Fronde (p. 407)

divine right of kings (p. 408)

absolute monarchy (p. 408)

mercantilism (p. 409)

Peace of Utrecht (p. 411)

Don Quixote (p. 414)

baroque style (p. 415)

French classicism (p. 417)

constitutionalism (p. 418)

Puritans (p. 419)

New Model Army (p. 421)

Protectorate (p. 421)

Test Act (p. 422)

Second Treatise of Civil Government (p. 424)

States General (p. 424)

stadtholder (p. 424)

Dutch East India Company (p. 426)

did not survive the Protectorate. James II's absolutist tendencies brought on the Glorious Revolution of 1688 and 1689, and the people who made that revolution settled three basic issues: sovereign power was divided between king and Parliament, with Parliament enjoying the greater share; government was to be based on the rule of law; and the liberties of English people were made explicit in written form in the Bill of Rights.

Having won independence from Spain, the United Provinces of the Netherlands provided another model of constitutional government, one dominated by wealthy urban merchants rather than the landed gentry who controlled the English system. The federal constitution of the Netherlands invested power in the Estates General, but diluted their authority by giving veto power to provincial assemblies. Dominated by Holland, the Netherlands provided a shining example of industriousness, prosperity, and relative tolerance for the rest of Europe.

Notes

1. The classic study is by Theodore K. Rabb, *The Struggle for Stability in Early Modern Europe* (Oxford: Oxford University Press, 1975).
2. G. Parker and L. M. Smith, "Introduction," and N. Steensgaard, "The Seventeenth Century Crisis," in *The General Crisis of the Seventeenth Century*, ed. G. Parker and L. M. Smith (London: Routledge & Kegan Paul, 1985), pp. 1–53, esp. p. 12.
3. H. G. Koenigsberger, "The Revolt of Palermo in 1647," *Cambridge Historical Journal* 8 (1944–1946): 129–144.
4. See W. Beik, *Urban Protest in Seventeenth-Century France: The Culture of Retribution* (New York: Cambridge University Press, 1997), p. 1.
5. Ibid.
6. See ibid., chaps. 1, 2, 3, and 11.
7. Ibid., pp. 22–26.
8. See M. Turchetti, "The Edict of Nantes," in *The Oxford Encyclopedia of the Reformation*, ed. H. J. Hillerbrand, vol. 3 (New York: Oxford University Press, 1996), pp. 126–128.
9. Quoted in J. H. Elliott, *Richelieu and Olivares* (Cambridge: Cambridge University Press, 1984), p. 135; and in W. F. Church, *Richelieu and Reason of State* (Princeton, N.J.: Princeton University Press, 1972), p. 507.
10. Quoted in J. Wolf, *Louis XIV* (New York: W. W. Norton, 1968), p. 146.
11. John A. Lynn, "Recalculating French Army Growth," in *The Military Revolution Debate: Readings on the Military Transformation of Early Modern Europe*, ed. Clifford J. Rogers (Boulder, Colo.: Westview Press, 1995), p. 125.
12. J. H. Elliott, *Imperial Spain, 1469–1716* (New York: Mentor Books, 1963), pp. 306–308.
13. B. Bennassar, *The Spanish Character: Attitudes and Mentalities from the Sixteenth to the Nineteenth Century*, trans. B. Keen (Berkeley: University of California Press, 1979), p. 125.
14. For a revisionist interpretation, see J. Wormald, "James VI and I: Two Kings or One?" *History* 62 (June 1983): 187–209.
15. S. Schama, *The Embarrassment of Riches: An Interpretation of Dutch Culture in the Golden Age* (New York: Alfred A. Knopf, 1987), pp. 165–170; quotation is on p. 167.
16. C. J. Friedrich and C. Blitzer, *The Age of Power* (Ithaca, N.Y.: Cornell University Press, 1957), p. 112.

To assess your mastery of this chapter, go to **bedfordstmartins.com/mckaywestbrief**

Listening to the Past

The Court at Versailles

Although the Duc de Saint-Simon (1675–1755) was a soldier, courtier, and diplomat, his enduring reputation rests on The Memoirs (1788), *his eyewitness account of the personality and court of Louis XIV. A nobleman of extremely high status, Saint-Simon resented Louis's high-handed treatment of the ancient nobility and his promotion of newer nobles and the bourgeoisie. The Memoirs, excerpted here, remains a monument of French literature and an indispensable historical source, partly for its portrait of the court at Versailles.*

Very early in the reign of Louis XIV the Court was removed from Paris, never to return. The troubles of the minority had given him a dislike to that city; his enforced and surreptitious flight from it still rankled in his memory; he did not consider himself safe there, and thought cabals would be more easily detected if the Court was in the country, where the movements and temporary absences of any of its members would be more easily noticed. . . . No doubt that he was also influenced by the feeling that he would be regarded with greater awe and veneration when no longer exposed every day to the gaze of the multitude.

He availed himself of the frequent festivities at Versailles, and his excursions to other places, as a means of making the courtiers assiduous in their attendance and anxious to please him; for he nominated beforehand those who were to take part in them, and could thus gratify some and inflict a snub on others. He was conscious that the substantial favours he had to bestow were not nearly sufficient to produce a continual effect; he had therefore to invent imaginary ones, and no one was so clever in devising petty distinctions and preferences which aroused jealousy and emulation. . . .

Not only did he expect all persons of distinction to be in continual attendance at Court, but he was quick to notice the absence of those of inferior degree; at his *lever* (**LEV-ay**) [formal rising from bed in the morning], his *coucher* (**KOO-shay**) [preparations for going to bed], his meals, in the gardens of Versailles (the only place where the courtiers in general were allowed to follow him), he used to cast his eyes to right and left; nothing escaped him, he saw everybody. If any one habitually living at Court absented himself he insisted on knowing the reason; those who came there only for flying visits had also to give a satisfactory explanation; any one who seldom or never appeared there was certain to incur his displeasure. If asked to bestow a favour on

Louis XIV was extremely proud of the gardens at Versailles and personally led ambassadors and other highly ranked visitors on tours of the extensive palace grounds. (Erich Lessing/Art Resource, NY)

such persons he would reply haughtily: "I do not know him"; of such as rarely presented themselves he would say, "He is a man I never see"; and from these judgements there was no appeal.

He loved splendour, magnificence, and profusion in all things, and encouraged similar tastes in his Court; to spend money freely on equipages [horse carriages] and buildings, on feasting and at cards, was a sure way to gain his favour, perhaps to obtain the honour of a word from him. Motives of policy had something to do with this; by making expensive habits the fashion, and, for people in a certain position, a necessity, he compelled his courtiers to live beyond their income, and gradually reduced them to depend on his bounty for the means of subsistence. This was a plague which, once introduced, became a scourge to the whole country, for it did not take long to spread to Paris, and thence to the armies and the provinces; so that a man of any position is now estimated entirely according to his expenditure on his table and other luxuries. This folly, sustained by pride and ostenta-tion, has already produced widespread confusion; it threatens to end in nothing short of ruin and a general overthrow.

Questions for Analysis

1. What was the role of etiquette and ceremony at the court of Versailles? How could Louis XIV use them in everyday life at court to influence and control nobles?

2. How important do you think Louis's individual character and personality were to his style of governing? What challenges might this present to his successors?

3. Consider the role of ceremony in some modern governments, such as the U.S. government. How does it compare to Louis XIV's use of ceremony as portrayed by Saint-Simon?

4. Do you think Saint-Simon is an objective and trustworthy recorder of life at court? Why?

Source: "The Court at Versailles" from *The Memoirs of the Duke de Saint Simon,* ed. F. Arkwright (New York: Brentano's, n.d.), Vol. V, pp. 271–274, 276–278.

CHAPTER 17

Absolutism in Central and Eastern Europe

to 1740

Chapter Preview

Warfare and Social Change in Central and Eastern Europe
What social and economic changes affected central and eastern Europe from 1400 to 1650?

The Rise of Austria and Prussia
How did the rulers of Austria and Prussia manage to build powerful absolute monarchies?

The Development of Russia and the Ottoman Empire
What were the distinctive features of Russian and Ottoman absolutism in this period?

INDIVIDUALS IN SOCIETY: Hürrem

IMAGES IN SOCIETY: Absolutist Palace Building

LISTENING TO THE PAST: A Foreign Traveler in Russia

Peter the Great's magnificent new crown, created for his joint coronation in 1682 with his half-brother Ivan. (State Museum of the Kremlin, Moscow)

The crises of the seventeenth century—religious division, economic depression, and war—were not limited to western Europe. Central and eastern Europe experienced even more catastrophic dislocation, with German lands serving as the battleground of the Thirty Years' War and borders constantly vulnerable to attack from the east. In Prussia and Habsburg Austria absolutist states emerged in the aftermath of this conflict.

Russia and the Ottoman Turks also developed absolutist governments. These empires seemed foreign and exotic to western Europeans, who saw them as the antithesis of their political, religious, and cultural values. To Western eyes, their own monarchs respected law—either divine or constitutional—while Eastern despots ruled with an iron fist. In this view, the Ottoman Muslim state was home to fanaticism and heresy, and even Russian Orthodoxy had rituals and traditions, if not core beliefs, that differed sharply from either Catholicism or Protestantism. Beneath the surface, however, these Eastern governments shared many similarities with Western ones.

The most successful Eastern empires lasted until 1918, far longer than monarchical rule endured in France, the model of absolutism under Louis XIV. Eastern monarchs had a powerful impact on architecture and the arts, encouraging new monumental construction to reflect their glory. Questions about the relationship between East and West remain potent today, as evidenced by the debate surrounding Turkey's bid for membership in the European Union.

Warfare and Social Change in Central and Eastern Europe

What social and economic changes affected central and eastern Europe from 1400 to 1650?

When absolute monarchy emerged in the seventeenth century, it built on social and economic foundations laid between roughly 1400 and 1650. In those years the elites of eastern Europe rolled back the gains made by the peasantry during the High Middle Ages and reimposed a harsh serfdom on the rural masses. The nobility also reduced the importance of the towns and the middle classes. This process differed from developments in western Europe, where peasants won greater freedom and the urban middle class continued its rise. The Thirty Years' War represented the culmination of these changes. Decades of war in central Europe led to depopulation and economic depression, which allowed lords to impose everharsher controls on the peasantry.

The Consolidation of Serfdom

The period from 1050 to 1300 was a time of general economic expansion in eastern Europe characterized by the growth of trade, towns, and population. The rulers of eastern Europe attracted settlers to the frontier beyond the Elbe River with economic and legal incentives and the offer of greater personal freedom. These benefits were also gradually extended to the local Slavic populations, even those of central Russia. Thus, by 1300 **serfdom** had all but disappeared in eastern Europe.

After the Black Death (1348), however, as Europe's population and economy declined grievously, lords sought to solve their economic problems by more heavily

serfdom A system used by nobles and rulers in which peasants were bound to the land they worked and to the lords they served.

Estonia in the 1660s

The Estonians were conquered by German military nobility in the Middle Ages and reduced to serfdom. The German-speaking nobles ruled the Estonian peasants with an iron hand, and Peter the Great reaffirmed their domination when Russia annexed Estonia (see Map 17.3 on page 445). (Mansell Collection/Time Life Pictures/Getty Images)

exploiting the peasantry. This reaction generally failed in the West, where by 1500 almost all peasants were free or had their serf obligations greatly reduced. East of the Elbe, however, the landlords won. They pushed for laws restricting or eliminating the peasants' right to move wherever they wished. They also took more of their peasants' land and imposed heavier labor obligations. Instead of being independent farmers paying freely negotiated rents, peasants became forced laborers on the lords' estates. By the early 1500s, lords in many territories could command their peasants to work without pay as many as six days a week. The peasants had no recourse through the courts to fight these injustices. The local lord was also the prosecutor, judge, and jailer.

Between 1500 and 1650 the social, legal, and economic conditions of peasants in eastern Europe continued to decline, and free peasants became serfs. Polish nobles gained complete control over their peasants in 1574, after which they could legally inflict the death penalty whenever they wished. In Prussia in 1653 peasants were assumed to be tied to their lords in hereditary subjugation—bound to their lords and the land from one generation to the next. In Russia a peasant's right to move from an estate was permanently abolished in 1603. In 1649 the tsar lifted the nine-year time limit on the recovery of runaways and eliminated all limits on lords' authority over their peasants.

Political factors were crucial to the re-emergence of serfdom in eastern Europe. In the late Middle Ages central and eastern Europe experienced innumerable wars and general political chaos, which allowed noble landlords to increase their power. There were, for example, many disputed royal successions, so that weak kings were forced to grant political favors to win the nobility's support. Thus while strong monarchs and effective central government were rising in Spain, France, and England, kings were generally losing power in the East and could not resist the demands of lords regarding peasants.

Moreover, most Eastern monarchs did not oppose the growth of serfdom. The typical king was only first among noble equals. He, too, wanted to squeeze his peasants. The Western concept of sovereignty, as embodied in a king who protected the interests of all his people, was not well developed in eastern Europe before 1650.

Not only the peasants suffered. Also with the approval of kings, landlords systematically undermined the medieval privileges of the towns and the power of the urban classes. Instead of selling products to local merchants, landlords sold directly to foreigners. For example, Dutch ships sailed up the rivers of Poland and eastern Germany to the loading docks of the great estates, completely bypassing the local towns. Moreover, "town air" no longer "made people free," for the Eastern towns had lost their medieval right of refuge and were now compelled to return runaways to their lords. The population of the towns and the importance of the urban middle classes declined greatly.

The Thirty Years' War

The Holy Roman Empire was a confederation of hundreds of principalities, independent cities, duchies, and other polities loosely united under an elected emperor. An uneasy truce had prevailed in the Holy Roman Empire since the Peace of Augsburg (**AWGZ-burg**) of 1555 (see page 350). According to the settlement, the faith of the prince determined the religion of his subjects. Later in the century, however, Catholics and Lutherans grew alarmed as the faiths of various areas shifted. Calvinists and Jesuits had converted some Lutheran princes; Lutherans had acquired Catholic bishoprics. Lutheran princes felt compelled to form the Protestant Union (1608), and Catholics retaliated with the Catholic League (1609). Each alliance was determined that the other should make no religious or territorial advance. Dynastic interests were also involved; the Spanish Habsburgs strongly supported the goals of their Austrian relatives—the unity of the empire and the preservation of Catholicism within it.

The immediate catalyst of violence was the closure of some Protestant churches by Ferdinand of Styria, the new Catholic king in Bohemia (**boh-HEE-mee-uh**) in 1617. On May 23, 1618, Protestants hurled two of Ferdinand's officials from a castle window in Prague. They fell seventy feet but survived: Catholics claimed that angels had caught them; Protestants said that the officials had fallen on a heap of soft horse manure. Called the "defenestration of Prague," this event marked the beginning of the Thirty Years' War (1618–1648).

The war is traditionally divided into four phases. The first, or Bohemian, phase (1618–1625) was characterized by civil war in Bohemia between the Catholic League, led by Ferdinand, and the Protestant Union, headed by Frederick, the elector of the Palatinate of the Rhine, one of the states of the Holy Roman Empire. The Protestant Union fought for religious liberty and independence from Habsburg rule. In 1620 Catholic forces defeated Frederick at the Battle of the White Mountain.

The second, or Danish, phase of the war (1625–1629)—so called because of the leadership of the Protestant king Christian IV of Denmark (r. 1588–1648)—witnessed additional Catholic victories. The Catholic imperial army led by Albert of Wallenstein swept through Silesia, north to the Baltic, and east into Pomerania, scoring smashing victories. Wallenstein, an unscrupulous opportunist who used his vast riches to build an army loyal only to himself, seemed more interested in carving out his own empire than in aiding the Catholic cause. He quarreled with the Catholic League, and soon the Catholic forces were divided. Religion was eclipsed as a basic issue of the war.

Habsburg power peaked in 1629. The emperor issued the Edict of Restitution, whereby all Catholic properties lost to Protestantism since 1552 were restored, and only Catholics and Lutherans were allowed to practice their faiths. When Wallenstein began ruthless enforcement, Protestants throughout Europe feared the collapse of the balance of power in north-central Europe.

CHRONOLOGY

ca. 1400–1650	Re-emergence of serfdom in eastern Europe
1462–1505	Reign of Ivan III in Russia
1533–1584	Reign of Ivan the Terrible in Russia
1618–1648	Thirty Years' War
1620	Habsburgs crush Protestantism in Bohemia
1620–1740	Growth of absolutism in Austria and Prussia
1640–1688	Reign of Frederick William in Prussia
1652	Nikon reforms Russian Orthodox Church
1670–1671	Cossack revolt led by Razin
ca. 1680–1750	Construction of palaces by absolutist rulers
1683–1718	Habsburgs defend Vienna; win war with Ottoman Turks
1702	Peter the Great founds St. Petersburg
1713–1740	Growth of Prussian military

The third, or Swedish, phase of the war (1630–1635) began with the arrival in Germany of the Swedish king Gustavus Adolphus (goo-STAV-us ah-DOLF-us) (r. 1594–1632). The ablest administrator of his day and a devout Lutheran, he intervened to support the empire's oppressed Protestants. The French chief minister, Cardinal Richelieu, subsidized the Swedes, hoping to weaken Habsburg power in Europe. Gustavus Adolphus won two important battles but was fatally wounded in combat. The Swedish victories ended the Habsburg ambition to unite the German states under imperial authority.

The last, or French, phase of the war (1635–1648) was prompted by Richelieu's concern that the Habsburgs would regain their strength after the death of Gustavus Adolphus. Richelieu declared war on Spain and sent military as well as financial assistance to the Swedes and the Protestant princes fighting in Germany. The war dragged on. The French, Dutch, and Swedes, supported by Scots, Finns, and German mercenaries, burned, looted, and destroyed German agriculture and commerce. Finally, in October 1648 peace was achieved.

Peace of Westphalia A series of treaties that concluded the Thirty Years' War, recognized the sovereign authority of over three hundred German princes, acknowledged the independence of the United Provinces, made Calvinism a permissible creed within Germany, and reduced the role of the Roman Catholic Church in European politics.

Consequences of the Thirty Years' War

The 1648 **Peace of Westphalia** (west-FEY-lee-uh) that ended the Thirty Years' War marked a turning point in European history. Conflicts fought over religious faith ended. The treaties recognized the sovereign, independent authority of more than three hundred German princes (see Map 17.1). Since the time of Holy Roman Emperor Frederick II (1194–1250), Germany had followed a pattern of state-building different from that of France and England: the emperor shared authority with the princes. After the Peace of Westphalia, the emperor's power continued to be severely limited, and the Holy Roman Empire remained a loosely knit federation.

The peace agreement acknowledged the independence of the United Provinces of the Netherlands. France acquired the province of Alsace along with the advantages of the weakened status of the empire. Sweden received a large cash indemnity and jurisdiction over German territories along the Baltic Sea, leaving it as a major threat to the future kingdom of Brandenburg-Prussia (BRAN-duhn-burg PRUHSH-uh). The papacy lost the right to participate in central European religious affairs and the Augsburg agreement of 1555 became permanent, adding Calvinism to Catholicism and Lutheranism as legally permissible creeds. The north German states remained Protestant; the south German states, Catholic.

The Thirty Years' War was probably the most destructive event for the central European economy and society prior to the twentieth century. Perhaps one-third of urban residents and two-fifths of the rural population died. Entire areas were depopulated by warfare, by the flight of refugees, and by disease. The trade of southern German cities such as Augsburg, already hard hit by the shift in transportation routes from the Mediterranean to the Atlantic, was virtually destroyed. All of Europe was experiencing severe inflation due to the influx of Spanish silver, but the destruction of land and foodstuffs made the price rise worse in central Europe than anywhere else. Agricultural areas suffered catastrophically. Many small farmers lacked the revenue to rework their holdings and had to become day laborers. In parts of central Europe, especially in areas east of the Elbe River, loss of land contributed to the consolidation of serfdom.[1]

Some people prospered, however. Nobles and landlords who controlled agricultural estates profited from rising food prices. They bought or seized the land of failed small farmers and then demanded more unpaid labor on those enlarged estates. Surpluses in wheat and timber were sold to foreign merchants, who exported them to the growing cities of the West.

Section Review

- The great decline in population and economy from the Black Death (1348), as well as many wars and political instability, led eastern European landlords to reimpose harsh serfdom on peasants and undermine the privileges of urban dwellers, a tactic that failed in western Europe, where by 1500 most peasants were free.

- Conflict between Lutheran and Catholic princes within the Holy Roman Empire broke the peace of Augsburg (1555), resulting in the outbreak of the Thirty Years' War (1618–1648).

- The Thirty Years' War erupted in Prague in 1618 and continued through four phases: Bohemian, Danish, Swedish, and French.

- Consequences of the Thirty Years' War included an end to conflicts over religious faith, legal inclusion of Calvinism, greater independence of princes in the Holy Roman Empire, severe inflation, the loss of small farms, and the destruction of a third of the population.

North Sea

NORWAY

SWEDEN

FINLAND

SCOTLAND

Edinburgh

ESTONIA

LIVONIA

RUSSIA

IRELAND

Dublin

North
Sea

DENMARK

Copenhagen

Baltic
Sea

Vilna

ENGLAND

Danzig

PRUSSIA

POLAND-
LITHUANIA

London

UNITED
PROVINCES

Amsterdam

Magdeburg

Berlin

Warsaw

ATLANTIC

OCEAN

Antwerp

Essen

Cologne

SAXONY

SILESIA

SPANISH
NETHERLANDS

Rhine R.

Prague

Vistula R.

Dnieper R.

Seine R.

Paris

LOWER
PALATINATE

UPPER
PALATINATE

BOHEMIA

MORAVIA

Nantes

Metz

Loire R.

FRANCE

BAVARIA

Augsburg

Vienna

AUSTRIA

MOLDAVIA

JEDISAN

FRANCHE-
COMTÉ

Salzburg

Zurich

TYROL

STYRIA

Buda

Pest

TRANSYLVANIA

BESSARABIA

Geneva

SWITZERLAND

Trent

CARINTHIA

HUNGARY

Rhône R.

SAVOY

CARNIOLA

SLAVONIA

Black Sea

PIEDMONT

MILAN

Venice

CROATIA

Belgrade

WALLACHIA

Danube R.

GENOA

REPUBLIC OF VENICE

BOSNIA

SERBIA

SPAIN

TUSCANY

PAPAL
STATES

Adriatic Sea

HERZEGOVINA

Ebro R.

Corsica
(to Genoa)

MONTENEGRO

BULGARIA

Constantinople

Tagus R.

Rome

Balearic Is.

Sardinia

NAPLES

Naples

OTTOMAN EMPIRE

Mediterranean Sea

N

Palermo

Sicily

Aegean Sea

GREECE

Athens

Crete
(to Rep. Of Venice)

Inset map:

North
Sea

SWEDEN

JUTLAND

Copenhagen

DENMARK

Baltic
Sea

55°N

SCHLESWIG

WISMAR

POMERANIA

Lübeck

Hamburg

BREMEN

MECKLENBURG

VERDEN

Elbe R.

BRANDENBURG

10°E

15°E

Legend:

- Austrian Habsburg lands
- Spanish Habsburg lands
- Other German states
- Swedish lands by 1648
- Ottoman Empire and tributary states
- Boundary of the Holy Roman Empire

0   150   300 Km.

0   150   300 Mi.

MAP 17.1   Europe After the Thirty Years' War

Which country emerged from the Thirty Years' War as the strongest European power? What dynastic house was that country's major rival in the early modern period?

The Rise of Austria and Prussia

How did the rulers of Austria and Prussia manage to build powerful absolute monarchies?

The monarchs of central and eastern Europe gradually gained political power in three key areas. First, they imposed permanent taxes without consent. Second, they maintained permanent standing armies to police the country and fight abroad. Third, they conducted relations with other states as they pleased. They were able to gain these powers by allowing the nobles greater control over serfs and by providing protection from outside invaders.

As with all general historical developments, there were important variations on the absolutist theme in eastern Europe. Royal absolutism in Prussia was stronger and more effective than in Austria. This would give Prussia a thin edge in the struggle for power in east-central Europe in the eighteenth century. Prussian-style absolutism had great long-term political significance, for it was a rising Prussia that unified the German people in the nineteenth century and imposed on them a militaristic stamp.

The Austrian Habsburgs

Like all of central Europe, the Habsburgs emerged from the Thirty Years' War impoverished and exhausted. Their efforts to destroy Protestantism in the German lands and to turn the weak Holy Roman Empire into a real state had failed. Although the Habsburgs remained the hereditary emperors, real power lay in the hands of a bewildering variety of separate political jurisdictions, including independent cities, small principalities, medium-sized states such as Bavaria and Saxony, and some of the territories of Prussia and the Habsburgs.

Defeat in central Europe encouraged the Habsburgs to turn away from a quest for imperial dominance and to focus inward and eastward in an attempt to unify their diverse holdings. If they could not impose Catholicism in the empire, at least they could do so in their own domains.

The Habsburg victory over Bohemia during the Thirty Years' War was an important step in this direction. The victorious king, Ferdinand II (r. 1619–1637), had drastically reduced the power of the **Bohemian Estates,** which was the largely Protestant representative assembly. He also confiscated the landholdings of many Protestant nobles and gave them to a few loyal Catholic nobles and to the foreign aristocratic mercenaries who led his armies. After 1650 a large portion of the Bohemian nobility was of recent origin and owed everything to the Habsburgs.

Bohemian Estates The largely Protestant representative body of the different estates in Bohemia. Significantly reduced in power by Ferdinand II.

With the help of this new nobility, the Habsburgs established direct rule over Bohemia. The condition of the enserfed peasantry worsened substantially: three days per week of unpaid labor—the *robot*—became the norm, and a quarter of the serfs worked for their lords every day but Sundays and religious holidays. Protestantism was also stamped out. The reorganization of Bohemia was a giant step toward creating absolutist rule. As in France in the same years, the pursuit of religious unity was an essential element of absolutism.

Ferdinand III (r. 1637–1657) continued to build state power. He centralized the government in the hereditary German-speaking provinces, which formed the core Habsburg holdings. For the first time, a permanent standing army was ready to put down any internal opposition.

Austrian Rule in Hungary

The Habsburg monarchy then turned east toward the plains of Hungary, which had been divided between the Ottomans and the Habsburgs in the early sixteenth century (see page 356). Between 1683 and 1699 the Habsburgs pushed the Ottomans from most of Hungary and Transylvania. The recovery of all of the former kingdom of Hungary was completed in 1718.

The Hungarian nobility, despite its reduced strength, effectively thwarted the full development of Habsburg absolutism. Throughout the seventeenth century Hungarian nobles—the most numerous in Europe—rose in revolt against attempts to impose absolute rule. They never triumphed decisively, but neither were they crushed the way the Czech nobility had been in 1620.

The Hungarians resisted because many of them remained Protestants, especially in areas formerly ruled by the Turks. In some of these regions, the Ottomans acted as military allies to the nobles, against the Habsburgs. Finally, the Hungarian nobility, and even part of the peasantry, became attached to a national ideal long before most of the other peoples of eastern Europe. Hungarian nobles were determined to maintain as much independence and local control as possible. In 1703, with the Habsburgs bogged down in the War of the Spanish Succession (see page 411), the Hungarians rose in one last patriotic rebellion under Prince Francis Rákóczy.

Rákóczy and his forces were eventually defeated, but the Habsburgs had to accept a compromise. Charles VI (r. 1711–1740) restored many of the traditional privileges of the aristocracy in return for Hungarian acceptance of hereditary Habsburg rule. Thus Hungary, unlike Austria and Bohemia, was never fully integrated into a centralized, absolute Habsburg state.

Despite checks on their ambitions in Hungary, the Habsburgs made significant achievements in state-building overall by forging consensus with the church and the nobility. A sense of common identity and loyalty to the monarchy grew among elites in Habsburg lands, even to a certain extent in Hungary. The best evidence for this consensus is the spectacular sums approved by the Estates for the growth of the army. German became the language of the common culture and zealous Catholicism also helped fuse a collective identity. Vienna became the political and cultural center of the empire. By 1700 it was a thriving city with a population of one hundred thousand, with its own version of Versailles, the royal palace of Schönbrunn. (**SHUN-broon**) (See the feature "Images in Society: Absolutist Palace Building" on pages 440–441.)

Prussia in the Seventeenth Century

In the fifteenth and sixteenth centuries, the Hohenzollern family had ruled parts of eastern Germany as the imperial electors of Brandenburg and the dukes of Prussia, but they had little real power. The **elector of Brandenburg** had the right to help choose the Holy Roman emperor, which bestowed prestige, but the elector had no military strength of his own. Nothing suggested that the Hohenzollern family and its territories would come to play as important a role in European affairs as they did.

The elector of Brandenburg was a helpless spectator in the Thirty Years' War, his territories alternately ravaged by Swedish and Habsburg armies. Yet foreign armies also dramatically weakened the political power of the Estates, which helped the elector Frederick William (r. 1640–1688) make significant progress toward royal absolutism. This constitutional struggle was the most crucial in Prussian history until that of the 1860s.

elector of Brandenburg One of the electors of the Holy Roman Empire, with the right to help choose the emperor, hereditarily held by the Hohenzollern family. Frederick William, "the Great Elector," was able to use and expand the office, ultimately resulting in the consolidation of the Prussian state under his successors.

Images in Society

Absolutist Palace Building

By 1700 palace building had become a veritable obsession for the rulers of central and eastern Europe. Their dramatic palaces symbolized the age of absolutist power, just as soaring Gothic cathedrals had expressed the idealized spirit of the High Middle Ages. With its classically harmonious, symmetrical, and geometric design, Versailles, shown in Image 1, served as the model for the wave of palace building that began in the last decade of the seventeenth century.

Located ten miles southwest of Paris, Versailles began as a modest hunting lodge built by Louis XIII in 1623. His son, Louis XIV, loved the site so much that he spent decades enlarging and decorating the original chateau. Between 1668 and 1670, his architect Louis Le Vau (**LOO-ee luh VOH**) enveloped the old building within a much larger second structure that still exists today. In 1682 the new palace became the official residence of the Sun King and his court, although construction continued until 1710, when the royal chapel was completed. At any one time, several thousand people lived in the bustling and crowded palace. The awesome splendor of the eighty-yard Hall of Mirrors, replete with floor to ceiling mirrors and ceiling murals illustrating the king's triumphs, contrasted with the strong odors from the courtiers who commonly relieved themselves in discreet corners. Royal palaces like Versailles were intended to overawe the people and proclaim their owners' authority and power.

In 1693 Charles XI of Sweden, having reduced the power of the aristocracy, ordered the construction of his Royal Palace, which dominates the center of Stockholm to this day. Another such palace was Schönbrunn, an enormous Viennese Versailles begun in 1695 by Emperor Leopold to celebrate Austrian military victories and Habsburg might. Image 2 shows architect Joseph Bernhard Fischer von Erlach's ambitious plan for

IMAGE 1 Pierre-Denis Martin: View of the Chateau de Versailles, 1722 (Châteaux de Versailles et de Trianon, Versailles/Réunion des Musées Nationaux/Art Resource, NY)

Schönbrunn palace. Erlach's plan emphasizes the palace's vast size and its role as a site for military demonstrations. Ultimately financial constraints resulted in a more modest building.

Petty German princes contributed mightily to the palace-building mania. Frederick the Great of Prussia noted that every descendant of a princely family "imagines himself to be something like Louis XIV. He builds his Versailles, has his mistresses, and maintains his army."* The elector-archbishop of Mainz, the ruling prince of that city, confessed apologetically that "building is a craze which costs much, but every fool likes his own hat."†

In central and eastern Europe, the favorite noble servants of royalty became extremely rich and powerful,

* Quoted in R. Ergang, *The Potsdam Fuhrer: Frederick William I, Father of Prussian Militarism* (New York: Octagon Books, 1972), p. 13.
† Quoted in J. Summerson, in *The Eighteenth Century: Europe in the Age of Enlightenment*, ed. A. Cobban (New York: McGraw-Hill, 1969), p. 80.

IMAGE 2 Project for the Palace at Schönbrunn (ca. 1700) (Austrian National Library, Vienna)

IMAGE 3 Prince Eugene's Summer Palace, Vienna (Erich Lessing/Art Resource, NY)

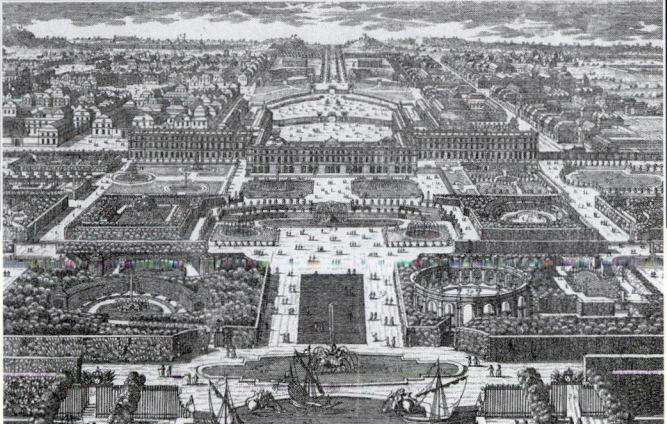

IMAGE 4 View of the Petit Parc at Versailles from the Canal (Bibliothèque nationale de France)

and they too built grandiose palaces in the capital cities. These palaces were in part an extension of the monarch, for they surpassed the buildings of less-favored nobles and showed all the high road to fame and fortune. Take, for example, the palaces of Prince Eugene of Savoy, a French nobleman who became Austria's most famous military hero. It was Eugene who led the Austrian army, smashed the Turks, fought Louis XIV to a standstill, and generally guided the triumph of absolutism in Austria. Rewarded with great wealth by his grateful king, Eugene called on the leading architects of the day, J. B. Fischer von Erlach and Johann Lukas von Hildebrandt, to consecrate his glory in stone and fresco. Fischer built Eugene's Winter (or Town) Palace in Vienna, and he and Hildebrandt collaborated on the prince's Summer Palace on the city's outskirts, shown in Image 3. The

prince's summer residence featured two baroque gems, the Lower Belvedere and the lovely Upper Belvedere, completed in 1722 and shown here. The building's interior is equally stunning, with crouching giants serving as pillars and a magnificent great staircase.

Palace gardens were an extension of the architecture. The rational orderliness and symmetry of a garden showed that the ruler's force extended even to nature, which offered its subjugated pleasures to the delight of sovereign and courtiers. The terraces and waterworks of these gardens served as showcases for the latest techniques in military and civil engineering. Exotic plants and elaborate designs testified to the sovereign's global trading networks and elevated taste.

The gardens at Versailles, shown in Image 4, exemplify absolutist palace gardens. In the foreground of this image we see a mock naval campaign being enacted on the canal for the edification of courtiers. For diplomatic occasions, Louis XIV himself wrote lengthy guides for viewing the gardens of Versailles. Modern visitors can still follow his itineraries. The themes of the sculptures in the Versailles gardens also hailed Louis's power, with images of Apollo, the sun god, and Neptune, the sea god, making frequent appearances.

Compare the image of Prince Eugene's summer palace with the plans for Schönbrunn and the palace of Versailles. What did concrete objects and the manipulation of space accomplish for these rulers that mere words could not? What disadvantages might stem from using architecture in this way? Is the use of space and monumental construction still a political tool in today's world?

When he came to power in 1640, the twenty-year-old Frederick William, later known as the "Great Elector," was determined to unify his three provinces and enlarge them by diplomacy and war. These provinces were Brandenburg; Prussia, inherited in 1618; and scattered holdings along the Rhine, inherited in 1614 (see Map 17.2). Each was inhabited by German-speaking people, but each had its own Estates. Although the Estates had not met regularly during the chaotic Thirty Years' War, taxes could not be levied without their consent. The Estates of Brandenburg and Prussia were dominated by the nobility and the landowning classes, known as the **Junkers** (YOONG-kuhrs).

To pay for the permanent standing army he first established in 1660, Frederick William forced the Estates to accept the introduction of permanent taxation without consent. The Estates' power declined rapidly thereafter, for the Great Elector had both financial independence and superior force. The state's total revenue tripled during his reign, and the size of the army leaped by ten. In 1688 a population of one million was supporting a peacetime standing army of thirty thousand.

Two factors were central to the Great Elector's triumph. First, as in the formation of every absolutist state, war was a decisive factor. The ongoing struggle between Sweden and Poland for control of the Baltic after 1648 and the wars of Louis XIV in western Europe created an atmosphere of permanent crisis. The nomadic Tatars (TAY-terz) of the Crimea in southern Russia swept through Prussia in the winter of 1656–1657, killing and carrying off thousands as slaves. This invasion softened up the Estates and strengthened the urgency of the Great Elector's demands for more military funding.

Second, the nobility proved willing to accept Frederick William's new claims in exchange for reconfirmation of their own privileges, including authority over

Junkers The nobility of Brandenburg and Prussia. Reluctant allies of Frederick William in his consolidation of the Prussian state.

MAP 17.2   The Growth of Austria and Brandenburg-Prussia to 1748

Austria expanded to the southwest into Hungary and Transylvania at the expense of the Ottoman Empire. It was unable to hold the rich German province of Silesia, however, which was conquered by Brandenburg-Prussia.

the serfs. The Junkers chose not to join representatives of the towns in a common front against the elector. Instead, they accepted new taxes that fell primarily on towns. The elector used naked force to break the liberties of the towns; the main leader of urban opposition in the key city of Königsberg (**KUHN-nigz-burg**), for example, was arrested and imprisoned for life without trial.

Like Louis XIV, the Great Elector built his absolutist state in collaboration with traditional elites, reaffirming their privileges in return for loyal service and revenue. He also created a larger centralized government bureaucracy to oversee his realm and to collect the new taxes. Pre-existing representative institutions were bypassed. The Diet of Brandenburg did not meet again after 1652. In 1701 the elector's son, Frederick I (1701–1713), received the elevated title of king of Prussia (instead of elector) as a reward for aiding the Holy Roman emperor in the War of the Spanish Succession.

The Consolidation of Prussian Absolutism

Frederick William I, "the Soldiers' King" (r. 1713–1740), completed his grandfather's work. He created a strong centralized bureaucracy and eliminated the last traces of parliamentary estates and local self-government. He truly established Prussian absolutism and transformed Prussia into a military state. King Frederick William was intensely attached to military life. He always wore an army uniform, and he lived the highly disciplined life of the professional soldier. He began his work by five or six in the morning; at ten he almost always went to the parade ground to drill or inspect his troops. Years later he summed up his life's philosophy in his instructions to his son: "A formidable army and a war chest large enough to make this army mobile in times of need can create great respect for you in the world, so that you can speak a word like the other powers."[2]

The king's power grab brought him into considerable conflict with the Junkers. In his early years he even threatened to destroy them; yet, in the end, the Prussian nobility was not destroyed but enlisted—into the army. Responding to a combination of threats and opportunities, the Junkers became the officer caste. A new compromise was worked out whereby the proud nobility imperiously commanded the peasantry in the army as well as on the estates.

Through penny-pinching and hard work, Frederick William achieved results. Prussia, twelfth in Europe in population, had the fourth largest army by 1740. Moreover, soldier for soldier, the Prussian army was the best in Europe, astonishing foreign observers with its precision, skill, and discipline. For the next two hundred years Prussia and then Prussianized Germany would win many crucial military battles.

Frederick William and his ministers also built an exceptionally honest and conscientious bureaucracy to administer the country and foster economic

A Prussian Giant Grenadier
Frederick William I wanted tall, handsome soldiers. He dressed them in tight bright uniforms to distinguish them from the peasant population from which most soldiers came. He also ordered several portraits of his favorites from his court painter, J. C. Merk. Grenadiers (**gren-AH-deers**) wore the miter cap instead of an ordinary hat so that they could hurl their heavy grenades unimpeded by a broad brim. (The Royal Collection © 2008, Her Majesty Queen Elizabeth II)

- In the aftermath of the Thirty Years' War, monarchs of central and eastern Europe gained new power through increased taxation, the creation of permanent standing armies, and exercising a free hand in foreign policy.

- The Austrian Habsburgs gained control over Bohemia by reducing the power of the Estates and creating a new and loyal nobility, but were less successful in Hungary, where they were forced to compromise with a fiercely independent Protestant nobility.

- In Prussia, the elector of Brandenburg, Frederick William Hohenzollern, the "Great Elector," set out to unify his provinces under absolutist rule by restoring privileges to the Junker nobility and by using the threat of war to build the best army in Europe.

- His grandson, King Frederick William I, transformed Prussia into a military state, centralized government, eliminated parliament and local self-government, and incorporated the nobility within his army to enforce obedience.

- Palace building modeled on Versailles near Paris and Schönbrunn in Vienna spread through central and eastern Europe, as princes competed for power and aristocrats showcased the riches won through service to the monarchy.

Mongol Yoke The two-hundred-year rule of the Mongol khan over the former territories of Kievan Rus'; this period is considered a prelude to the rise of absolutist Russia.

development. And like the miser he was known to be, the king loved his "blue boys" so much that he hated to "spend" them. This most militaristic of kings was, paradoxically, almost always at peace.

Nevertheless, Prussians paid a heavy and lasting price for the obsessions of their royal drillmaster. Civil society became rigid and highly disciplined, and Prussia became the "Sparta of the North"; unquestioning obedience was the highest virtue. As a Prussian minister later summed up: "To keep quiet is the first civic duty."[3] Thus the policies of Frederick William I combined with harsh peasant bondage and Junker tyranny to lay the foundations for a highly militaristic country.

The Development of Russia and the Ottoman Empire

What were the distinctive features of Russian and Ottoman absolutism in this period?

A favorite parlor game of nineteenth-century intellectuals was debating whether Russia was a Western (European) or non-Western (Asian) society. This question was particularly fascinating because it was unanswerable. To this day, Russia differs from the West in some fundamental ways, though its history has paralleled that of the West in other aspects.

There was no question in the mind of Europeans, however, that the Ottomans were outsiders. Even absolutist rulers disdained Ottoman sultans as cruel and tyrannical despots. Despite stereotypes, the Ottomans were in many ways more tolerant than Westerners, providing protection and security to other religions while steadfastly maintaining their Muslim faith. The Ottoman state combined the Byzantine heritage of the territory they conquered with Persian and Arab traditions. Flexibility and openness to other ideas and practices were sources of strength for the empire.

The Mongol Yoke and the Rise of Moscow

In the thirteenth century the Kievan principality (see page 445) was conquered by the Mongols, a group of nomadic tribes from present-day Mongolia who had come together under Chinggis Khan (1162–1227). At its height, the Mongol empire stretched from Korea to eastern Europe, and the portion that encompassed Russia was known as the Golden Horde. The two-hundred-year period of rule under the Mongol khan (king), known as the **Mongol Yoke**, set the stage for the rise of absolutist Russia.

The Mongols forced the Slavic princes to submit to their rule and to give them tribute and slaves. Although the Mongols conquered, they were quite willing to use local princes as obedient servants and tax collectors. Thus, they did not abolish the title of "great prince," bestowing it instead on the prince who served them best and paid them most handsomely. Beginning with Alexander Nevsky in 1252, the princes of Moscow became particularly adept at serving the Mongols. They loyally put down popular uprisings and collected the khan's taxes. As reward, the princes of Moscow emerged as hereditary great princes. Eventually the Muscovite princes were able to destroy the other princes who were their rivals for power. Ivan III (r. 1462–1505) consolidated power around Moscow and won Novgorod (**NOV-guh-rod**), almost reaching the Baltic Sea (see Map 17.3).

By 1480 Ivan III felt strong enough to stop acknowledging the khan as his supreme ruler and cease tribute payments to the Mongols. To legitimize their new

Principality of Moscow, ca. 1300

Acquisitions by Ivan III's accession (1462)

Acquisitions under Ivan III (1462–1505)

Acquisitions by death of Ivan the Terrible (1584)

Acquisitions by Peter the Great's accession (1689)

Acquisitions under Peter the Great (1689–1725)

★ Major battle

MAPPING THE PAST

MAP 17.3   The Expansion of Russia to 1725

After the disintegration of the Kievan (**KEE-ef-ahn**) state and the Mongol conquest, the princes of Moscow and their descendants gradually extended their rule over an enormous territory. **[1]** Compare this map with Map 17.4, which shows Ottoman expansion from 1300. What explains the fantastic success of both the Russians and the Ottomans in expanding their territories? Why was the sixteenth century such an important period for expansion? **[2]** How do you explain the geographic direction that expansion followed in each case? **[3]** What happened after the periods shown on these maps? Did the territorial development of the two states diverge from each other or follow the same trajectory?

authority, the princes of Moscow drew on two sources of authority. First, they declared themselves *autocrats*, meaning that, like the khans, they were the sole source of power. Yet also like the khans, they needed the cooperation of the local elites. The highest-ranking nobles, or **boyars,** enabled the tsars to rule with an extremely limited government apparatus. In addition to political authority, Moscow also took over Mongol tribute relations and borrowed institutions such as the tax system, postal routes, and the census.

boyars The highest-ranking nobles in Russia.

The second source of legitimacy lay in Moscow's claim to the political and religious inheritance of the Byzantine Empire. After the fall of Constantinople (**kon-stan-tun-OH-puhl**) to the Turks in 1453, the princes of Moscow saw themselves as the heirs of both the caesars and Orthodox Christianity, the one true faith. The title **tsar,** first taken by Ivan IV in 1547, is a contraction of *caesar*. All the other kings of Europe were heretics; only the Russians were rightful and holy rulers. The idea was promoted by Orthodox churchmen, who spoke of "holy Russia" as the "Third Rome." Ivan's marriage to the daughter of the last Byzantine emperor further enhanced the aura of Moscow's imperial inheritance.

tsar A title first taken by Ivan IV, it is a contraction of the word *caesar*.

Tsar and People to 1689

Developments in Russia took a chaotic turn with the reign of Ivan IV (r. 1533–1584), the famous "Ivan the Terrible," who ascended to the throne at age three. His mother died, possibly poisoned, when he was eight, leaving Ivan to suffer insults and neglect from the boyars at court. At age sixteen he suddenly pushed aside his hated advisers, and in an awe-inspiring ceremony, complete with gold coins pouring down on his head, Ivan majestically crowned himself, taking the august title of tsar for the first time.

Ivan's reign was characterized by endless wars and violent purges. He was successful in defeating the remnants of Mongol power, adding vast new territories to the realm and laying the foundations for the huge, multiethnic Russian empire. He engaged in a much longer struggle against the large Polish-Lithuanian state, without success. After the sudden death of his beloved wife Anastasia [of the Romanov (**ROH-muh-nawf**) family], the increasingly demented Ivan jailed and executed any he suspected of opposing him. Many were intimates of the court from the leading boyar families, and their families, friends, servants, and peasants were also executed. Their large estates were broken up, with some of the land added to the tsar's domain and the rest given to the lower **service nobility,** a group of newly made nobles who served in the tsar's army.

service nobility A newly emerging class of nobles who held some of the tsar's land on the explicit condition that they serve in the tsar's army.

Ivan also took strides toward making all commoners servants of the tsar. As the service nobles demanded more from those peasants who survived the wars and persecutions, growing numbers fled toward wild, recently conquered territories to the east and south. There they joined free groups and outlaw armies known as **Cossacks** (**KOS-akz**) and maintained a precarious independence. The solution to the problem of peasant flight was to tie peasants ever more firmly to the land and to the noble landholders, who in turn served the tsar.

Cossacks Free groups and outlaw armies living on the steppes bordering Russia, whose numbers were increased by runaway peasants during the time of Ivan the Terrible.

Simultaneously, urban traders and artisans were also bound to their towns and jobs so that the tsar could tax them more heavily. Ivan assumed that the tsar owned Russia's trade and industry, just as he owned all the land. The urban classes had no security in their work or property, and even the wealthiest merchants were dependent agents of the tsar. These restrictions checked the growth of the Russian middle classes and stood in sharp contrast to developments in western Europe, where the middle classes were gaining security in their private property.

Saint Basil's Cathedral, Moscow

With its sloping roofs and colorful onion-shaped domes, Saint Basil's is a striking example of powerful Byzantine influences on Russian culture. According to tradition, an enchanted Ivan the Terrible blinded the cathedral's architects to ensure that they would never duplicate their fantastic achievement, which still dazzles the beholder in today's Red Square. (George Holton/Photo Researchers)

After the death of Ivan and his successor, Russia entered a chaotic period known as the "Time of Troubles" (1598–1618). While Ivan's relatives struggled for power, the Cossacks and peasants rebelled against nobles and officials, demanding fairer treatment. This social explosion from below brought the nobles, big and small, together. They crushed the Cossack rebellion at the gates of Moscow and elected Ivan's sixteen-year-old grandnephew, Michael Romanov, the new hereditary tsar (r. 1613–1645). Michael's election was represented as a restoration of tsarist autocracy. (See the feature "Listening to the Past: A Foreign Traveler in Russia" on pages 456–457.)

Although the new tsar successfully reconsolidated central authority, social and religious uprisings continued through the seventeenth century. One of the largest rebellions was led by the Cossack Stenka Razin, who attracted a great army of urban poor and peasants, killing landlords and government officials, and proclaiming freedom from oppression. Eventually this rebellion was defeated.

Despite the turbulence of the period, the Romanov tsars made several important achievements during the second half of the seventeenth century. After a long war, Russia gained a large mass of Ukraine from weak and decentralized Poland in 1667 (see Map 17.3) and completed the conquest of Siberia by the end of the century. Territorial expansion was accompanied by growth of the bureaucracy and the army. Foreign experts were employed to help build and reform the Russian army. The great profits from Siberia's natural resources, especially furs, funded the Romanov's bid for great power status.

The Reforms of Peter the Great

Heir to the first efforts at state-building, Peter the Great (r. 1682–1725) embarked on a tremendous campaign to accelerate and complete these processes. A giant for his time, at six feet seven inches, and possessing enormous energy and willpower, Peter was determined to build and improve the army. He was equally determined to continue the tsarist tradition of territorial expansion. After 1689 Peter ruled independently for thirty-six years, only one of which was peaceful.

Fascinated by weapons and foreign technology, the tsar led a group of two hundred fifty Russian officials and young nobles on an eighteen-month tour of western European capitals. Traveling unofficially to avoid lengthy diplomatic ceremonies, Peter worked with his hands at various crafts and met with foreign kings and experts. He was particularly impressed with the growing power of the Dutch and the English, and he considered how Russia could profit from their example.

Returning to Russia, Peter entered into a secret alliance with Denmark and Poland to wage a sudden war of aggression against Sweden, with the goal of securing access to the Baltic Sea and opportunities for westward expansion. Peter and his allies believed that their combined forces could win easy victories because Sweden was in the hands of a new and inexperienced king.

Eighteen-year-old Charles XII of Sweden (1697–1718) surprised Peter. He defeated Denmark quickly in 1700, then turned on Russia. In a blinding snowstorm, his well-trained professional army attacked and routed unsuspecting Russians besieging the Swedish fortress of Narva (**NAHR-vuh**) on the Baltic coast. Peter and the survivors fled in panic to Moscow. It was, for the Russians, a grim beginning to the long and brutal Great Northern War, which lasted from 1700 to 1721.

Suffering defeat and faced with a military crisis, Peter responded with measures designed to increase state power, strengthen his armies, and gain victory. He required every nobleman, great or small, to serve in the army or in the civil administration—for life. Since a more modern army and government required skilled technicians and experts, Peter created schools and universities to produce them. One of his most hated reforms was requiring a five-year education away from home for every young nobleman. Peter established an interlocking military-

Gustaf Cederstrom: The Swedish Victory at Narva (1701)

This poignant re-creation focuses on the contrast between the Swedish officers in handsome dress uniforms and the battered Russian soldiers laying down their standards in surrender. Charles XII of Sweden scored brilliant, rapid-fire victories over Denmark, Saxony, and Russia, but he failed to make peace with Peter while he was ahead and eventually lost Sweden's holdings on the Baltic coast. (The National Museum of Fine Arts, Stockholm)

civilian bureaucracy with fourteen ranks, and he decreed that all had to start at the bottom and work toward the top. Some people of non-noble origins rose to high positions in this embryonic meritocracy. Drawing on his experience abroad, Peter searched out talented foreigners and placed them in his service. These measures gradually combined to make the army and government more powerful and efficient.

Peter also greatly increased the service requirements of commoners. In the wake of the Narva disaster, he established a regular standing army of more than two hundred thousand peasant-soldiers commanded by officers from the nobility. In addition, special forces of Cossacks and foreigners numbered more than one hundred thousand. Taxes on peasants increased threefold during Peter's reign. Serfs were arbitrarily assigned to work in the growing number of factories and mines that supplied the military.

Peter's new war machine was able to crush the small army of Sweden in Ukraine at Poltava (**pol-TAH-vah**) in 1709, one of the most significant battles in Russian history. Russia's victory was conclusive in 1721, and Estonia and present-day Latvia (see Map 17.3) came under Russian rule for the first time. The cost was high—warfare consumed eighty to eighty-five percent of all revenues. But Russia became the dominant power in the Baltic and very much a European Great Power.

After his victory at Poltava, Peter channeled enormous resources into building a new Western-style capital on the Baltic to rival the great cities of Europe. Originally a desolate and swampy Swedish outpost, the magnificent city of St. Petersburg was designed to reflect modern urban planning, with wide, straight avenues; buildings set in a uniform line; and large parks.

Peter the Great dictated that all in society realize his vision. Just as the government drafted the peasants for the armies, so it drafted twenty-five thousand to forty thousand men each summer to labor in St. Petersburg without pay. Many peasant construction workers died from hunger, sickness, and accidents. Nobles were ordered to build costly stone houses and palaces in St. Petersburg and to live in them most of the year. Merchants and artisans were also commanded to settle and build in the new capital. These nobles and merchants were then required to pay for the city's infrastructure. The building of St. Petersburg was, in truth, an enormous direct tax levied on the wealthy, with the peasantry forced to do the manual labor.

There were other important consequences of Peter's reign. For Peter, modernization meant Westernization, and both Westerners and Western ideas flowed into Russia for the first time. He required nobles to shave their heavy beards and wear Western clothing, previously banned in Russia. He required them to attend parties where young men and women would mix together and freely choose their own spouses. He forced a warrior elite to accept administrative service as an honorable occupation. From these efforts a new class of Western-oriented Russians began to emerge.

At the same time, vast numbers of Russians hated Peter's massive changes. For nobles, one of Peter's most detested reforms was the imposition of unigeniture—inheritance of land by one son alone—cutting daughters and other sons from

Peter the Great in 1723

This compelling portrait by Grigory Musikiysky captures the strength and determination of the warrior tsar after more than three decades of personal rule. In his hand Peter holds the scepter, symbol of royal sovereignty, and across his breastplate is draped an ermine fur, a mark of honor. In the background are the battleships of Russia's new Baltic fleet and the famous St. Peter and St. Paul Fortress that Peter built in St. Petersburg. (Kremlin Museums, Moscow/The Bridgeman Art Library)

family property. For peasants, the reign of the reforming tsar saw a significant increase in the bonds of serfdom. The gulf between the enserfed peasantry and the educated nobility increased, even though all were caught up in the tsar's demands.

Thus Peter built on the service obligations of old Muscovy (**MUHS-kuh-vee**). His monarchical absolutism was the culmination of the long development of a unique Russian civilization. Yet the creation of a more modern army and state introduced much that was new and Western to Russia. This development paved the way for Russia to move somewhat closer to the European mainstream in its thought and institutions during the Enlightenment, especially under Catherine the Great.

The Growth of the Ottoman Empire

Most Christian Europeans perceived the Ottomans as the antithesis of their own values and traditions and viewed the empire as driven by an insatiable lust for warfare and conquest. In their view the fall of Constantinople was a catastrophe and the taking of the Balkans a despotic imprisonment of those territories. From the perspective of the Ottomans, the world looked very different. The siege of Constantinople liberated a glorious city from its long decline under the Byzantines. Rather than being a despoiled captive, the Balkans became a haven for refugees fleeing the growing intolerance of Western Christian powers. The Ottoman Empire provided Jews, Muslims, and even some Christians safety from the Inquisition and religious war.

The Ottomans came out of Central Asia as conquering warriors, settled in Anatolia (present-day Turkey), and, at their peak in the mid-sixteenth century, they ruled one of the most powerful empires in the world. Their possessions stretched from western Persia across North Africa and into the heart of central Europe (see Map 17.4).

When the Ottomans captured Constantinople in 1453 they fulfilled a long-held Islamic dream. Under Suleiman the Magnificent (r. 1520–1566), they made great inroads into eastern Europe, capturing Bosnia, Croatia, Romania, Ukraine, and part of Hungary at the battle of Mohács in 1526. For the next hundred and fifty years, the Ottomans ruled the many different ethnic groups living in southeastern Europe and the eastern Mediterranean. In 1529 their European expansion was halted with a failed siege of the Habsburg capital, Vienna. The Ottoman loss at the battle of Lepanto (**leh-PAN-toh**) in 1571, against the Christian Holy League, confirmed the limits of their ambitions in Europe.

The Ottoman Empire was originally built on a unique model of state and society. There was an almost complete absence of private landed property. Agricultural land was the personal hereditary property of the **sultan** (**SUHL-tun**), and peasants paid taxes to use the land. There was therefore no security of landholding and no hereditary nobility.

The Ottomans also employed a distinctive form of government administration. The top ranks of the bureaucracy were staffed by the sultan's slave corps. Because Muslim law prohibited enslaving other Muslims, the sultan's agents purchased slaves along the borders of the empire. Within the realm, the sultan levied a "tax" of one thousand to three thousand male children on the conquered Christian populations in the Balkans every year. Young slaves were raised in Turkey as Muslims and were trained to fight and to administer. The most talented rose to the top of the bureaucracy, where they might acquire wealth and power; the less fortunate formed the brave and skillful core of the sultan's army, the **janissary** (**JAN-uh-ser-ee**) corps. These highly organized and efficient troops gave the Ottomans a formidable advantage in war with western Europeans. By 1683, service in the janissary

sultan The ruler of the Ottoman Empire; he owned all the agricultural land of the empire and was served by an army and bureaucracy composed of highly trained slaves.

janissary corps The core of the sultan's army, composed of conscripts from non-Muslim parts of the empire until 1683.

corps had become so prestigious that the sultan ceased recruitment by force and it became a volunteer force open to Christians and Muslims.

The Ottomans divided their subjects into religious communities, and each *millet*, or "nation," enjoyed autonomous self-government under its religious leaders. (The Ottoman Empire recognized Orthodox Christians, Jews, Armenian Christians, and Muslims as distinct millets.) The **millet** (**MIL-it**) **system** created a powerful bond between the Ottoman ruling class and the different religious leaders, who supported the sultan's rule in return for extensive authority over their own communities. Each millet collected taxes for the state, regulated group behavior, and maintained law courts, schools, synagogues, and hospitals for its people.

After 1453 Constantinople—renamed Istanbul (**is-tahn-BOOL**)—became the capital of the empire. The "old palace" was for the sultan's female family members, who lived in isolation under the care of eunuchs. The newly constructed Topkapi palace was where officials worked and young slaves trained for future administrative or military careers. To prevent wives from bringing foreign influence

millet system A system used by the Ottomans whereby subjects were divided into religious communities with each millet (nation) enjoying autonomous self-government under its religious leaders.

MAP 17.4   The Ottoman Empire at Its Height, 1566

The Ottomans, like their great rivals the Habsburgs, rose to rule a vast dynastic empire encompassing many different peoples and ethnic groups. The army and the bureaucracy served to unite the disparate territories into a single state under an absolutist ruler.

The Sultan's Harem at Topkapi Palace, Istanbul
Sultan Suleiman I created separate quarters at the Topkapi Palace for his wife Hürrem and her ladies-in-waiting. His successors transferred all of their wives, concubines, and female family members to the harem (**HAIR-uhm**) at Topkapi, carefully situated out of sight of the staterooms and courtyards where public affairs took place. The harem was the object of intense curiosity and fascination in the West. (Vanni/Art Resource, NY)

into government—a constant concern in the West—sultans procreated only with their concubines and not with official wives. They also adopted a policy of allowing each concubine to produce only one male heir. At a young age, each son went to govern a province of the empire under his mother's supervision. These practices were intended to stabilize power and prevent a recurrence of the civil wars of the late fourteenth and early fifteenth centuries.

Sultan Suleiman undid these policies when he boldly married his concubine and had several children with her. He established a wing in the Topkapi palace for his own female family members and his brothers' families. Starting with Suleiman, imperial wives begin to take on more power. Marriages were arranged between sultans' daughters and high-ranking servants, creating powerful new members of the imperial household. Over time, the sultan's exclusive authority waned in favor of a more bureaucratic administration. These changes brought the Ottoman court closer to the European model of factionalism, intrigue, and informal female power. (See the feature "Individuals in Society: Hürrem.")

The Ottoman Empire experienced the same economic and social crises that affected the rest of Europe in this period. In the 1580s and 1590s rebellions broke out among many different groups in the vast empire: frustrated students, underpaid janissaries, and ambitious provincial governors. Revolts continued during the seventeenth century as the janissaries formed alliances with court factions that resulted in the overthrow or execution of several Ottoman sultans.

In the late seventeenth century the Ottomans succeeded in marshaling their forces for one last attack on the Habsburgs, and a huge Turkish army laid siege to Vienna in 1683. Not only did they fail to hold the city, but their retreat became a rout. As Russian and Venetian allies attacked on

Section Review

- The Mongols under Chinggis Khan added the Kievan principality in Russia to the Mongol Empire stretching from Korea to Eastern Europe, ruling the area as the Golden Horde for the next two hundred years through the Russian princes, who collected taxes and maintained order.

- By 1480 the prince of Moscow, Ivan III, defied the khan (Mongol ruler) and seized power to begin the dynasty of the tsars.

- The reign of Ivan IV "the Terrible" featured constant war, violent purges, peasant and outlaw army (Cossack) uprisings, and the addition of vast new territories.

- Following Ivan's death, a period of chaos known as the "Time of Troubles" (1598–1618) ensued, ending with the coronation of Ivan's grandnephew, Michael, the first Romanov tsar.

- Despite ongoing rebellions, the seventeenth-century Romanov tsars succeeded in consolidating royal authority, increasing the bureaucracy and army, and acquiring Siberia and parts of Ukraine.

- Peter the Great (r. 1682–1725) transformed Russian society and the Russian landscape by drafting citizens for military or civil service, enabling him to create a powerful war machine, enlarge the empire, and build the modern, Westernized capital city of St. Petersburg on Baltic coastal land conquered from Sweden.

- Despite Christian stereotypes, the Ottoman empire was tolerant of religious diversity and protected Jews and other religious refugees.

- The Ottomans captured Constantinople in 1453 and renamed it Istanbul, then conquered much of southeastern Europe until their expansion was halted with the failed siege of Vienna in 1529.

- Highly trained slaves staffed the elite of the sultan's administration and army; while the millet system allowed autonomous self-government to religious minority groups; all land in the empire belonged to the sultan.

- Starting with Sultan Suleiman, wives began to exercise more power and the sultan's exclusive authority gave way to more bureaucratic administration.

Individuals in Society

Hürrem

In Muslim culture *harem* means a sacred place or a sanctuary, which is forbidden to profane outsiders. The term was applied to the part of the household occupied by women and children and forbidden to men outside the family. The most famous member of the Ottoman sultan's harem was Hürrem, wife of Suleiman the Magnificent.

Hürrem (1505?–1558) came to the harem as a slave-concubine. Like many of the sultan's concubines, Hürrem was of foreign birth. Tradition holds that she was born Aleksandra Lisowska in what was then the kingdom of Poland and today is Ukraine. She was captured during a Tartar raid and enslaved. Between 1517 and 1520, when she was about fifteen years old, she entered the imperial harem. Venetian ambassadors' reports insist that she was not outstandingly beautiful but was possessed of wonderful grace, charm, and good humor. These qualities gained her the Turkish nickname Hürrem, or "joyful one." After her arrival in the harem, Hürrem quickly became the imperial favorite.

Suleiman's love for Hürrem led him to break all precedents for the role of a concubine, including the rule that concubines must cease having children once they gave birth to a male heir. By 1531 Hürrem had given birth to one daughter and five sons. In 1533 or 1534 Suleiman entered formal marriage with his consort—an unprecedented honor for a concubine. He reportedly gave his exclusive attention to his wife and also defied convention by allowing Hürrem to remain in the palace throughout her life instead of accompanying her son to a provincial governorship as other concubines had done.

Contemporaries were shocked by Hürrem's influence over the sultan and resentful of the apparent role she played in politics and diplomacy. The Venetian ambassador Bassano wrote that "the Janissaries and the entire court hate her and her children likewise, but because the Sultan loves her, no one dares to speak."* She was suspected of using witchcraft to control the sultan and accused of ordering the death of the sultan's first-born son (with another mother) in 1553. These stories were based on court gossip and rumor. The correspondence between Suleiman and Hürrem, unavailable until the nineteenth century, along with Suleiman's own diaries, confirms her status as the sultan's most trusted confidant and adviser. During his frequent absences, the pair exchanged passionate love letters. Hürrem included information about the political situation and warnings about any potential uprisings. She also intervened in affairs between the empire and her former home. She wrote to Polish king Sigismund Augustus and seems to have helped Poland attain its privileged diplomatic status.

Hürrem and her ladies in the harem.
(Bibliothèque nationale de France)

She brought a particularly feminine touch to diplomatic relations, sending the Persian shah and the Polish king personally embroidered articles.

Hürrem used her enormous pension to contribute a mosque, two schools, a hospital, a fountain, and two public baths to Istanbul. In Jerusalem, Mecca, and Istanbul, she provided soup kitchens and hospices for pilgrims and the poor. She died in 1558. When her husband died in 1566, their son Selim II (r. 1566–1574) inherited the throne.

Drawing from reports of contemporary Western observers, historians depicted Hürrem as a manipulative and power-hungry social climber. They saw her career as the beginning of a "sultanate of women" in which strong imperial leadership gave way to court intrigue and dissipation. More recent historians have emphasized the intelligence and courage Hürrem demonstrated in navigating the ruthlessly competitive world of the harem.

Hürrem's journey from Ukrainian maiden to harem slave girl to sultan's wife captured enormous

* Cited in Galina Yermolenko, "Roxolana: The Greatest Empresse of the East," in *The Muslim World* 95, 2 (2005).

public attention. She is the subject of numerous paintings, plays, and novels as well as an opera, a ballet, and a symphony by the composer Haydn. Interest in and suspicion of Hürrem continues. In 2003 a Turkish miniseries once more depicted her as a scheming intriguer.

Questions for Analysis

1. Compare Hürrem to other powerful early modern women such as Isabella of Castile, Elizabeth I of England, and Catherine de' Medici of France.

2. What can an exceptional woman like Hürrem reveal about the broader political and social world in which she lived?

Source: Leslie P. Pierce, *The Imperial Harem: Women and Sovereignty in the Ottoman Empire* (New York: Oxford University Press, 1993).

other fronts, the Habsburgs conquered almost all of Hungary and Transylvania by 1699 (see Map 17.4). The Habsburgs completed their victory in 1718, with the Treaty of Passarowitz. From this point on, a weakened Ottoman empire ceased to pose a threat to Western Europe.

Chapter Review

What social and economic changes affected central and eastern Europe from 1400 to 1650? (page 433)

From about 1400 to 1650 social and economic developments in eastern Europe diverged from those in western Europe. In the East, after enjoying relative freedom in the Middle Ages, peasants and townspeople lost freedom and fell under the economic, social, and legal authority of the nobles, who increased their power and prestige.

How did the rulers of Austria and Prussia manage to build powerful absolute monarchies? (page 438)

Within this framework of resurgent serfdom and entrenched nobility, Austrian and Prussian monarchs fashioned absolutist states in the seventeenth and early eighteenth centuries. These monarchs won absolutist control over standing armies, taxation, and representative bodies, but they did not question underlying social and economic relationships. Indeed, they enhanced the privileges of the nobles, who filled enlarged armies and growing state bureaucracies. In exchange for entrenched privileges over their peasants, nobles thus cooperated with the growth of state power.

Triumphant absolutism interacted spectacularly with the arts. Central and eastern European rulers built grandiose palaces, and even whole cities, like Saint Petersburg, to glorify their power and majesty.

What were the distinctive features of Russian and Ottoman absolutism in this period? (page 444)

In Russia the social and economic trends were similar, but the timing of political absolutism was different. Mongol conquest and rule were a crucial experience, and a harsh indigenous tsarist autocracy was firmly in place by the reign of Ivan the Terrible in the sixteenth century. More than a century later Peter the Great succeeded in modernizing Russia's traditional absolutism by reforming the army and the bureaucracy. Farther to the east, the Ottoman sultans developed a distinctive political and economic system in which all land theoretically belonged to the sultan, who was served by a slave corps of administrators and soldiers. The Ottoman Empire was relatively tolerant on religious matters and served as a haven for Jews and other marginalized religious groups.

Key Terms

serfdom (p. 433)
hereditary subjugation (p. 434)
Peace of Westphalia (p. 436)
Bohemian Estates (p. 438)
elector of Brandenburg (p. 439)
Junkers (p. 442)
Mongol Yoke (p. 444)
boyars (p. 446)
tsar (p. 446)
service nobility (p. 446)
Cossacks (p. 446)
sultan (p. 450)
millet system (p. 451)
janissary corps (p. 453)

Notes

1. H. Kamen, "The Economic and Social Consequences of the Thirty Years' War," *Past and Present* 39 (April 1968): 44–61.
2. H. Rosenberg, *Bureaucracy, Aristocracy, and Autocracy: The Prussian Experience, 1660–1815* (Boston: Beacon Press, 1966), p. 43.
3. Quoted in Rosenberg, *Bureaucracy, Aristocracy, and Autocracy*, p. 40.

To assess your mastery of this chapter, go to **bedfordstmartins.com/mckaywestbrief**

Listening to the Past

A Foreign Traveler in Russia

*Seventeenth-century Russia remained a remote and mysterious land for western and even central Europeans, who had few direct contacts with the tsar's dominion. Knowledge of Russia came mainly from occasional travelers who had visited Muscovy and sometimes wrote accounts of what they saw. The most famous of these accounts—*Travels in Muscovy*—was by the German Adam Olearius (ca. 1599–1671), who was sent to Moscow by the duke of Holstein on three diplomatic missions in the 1630s. Published in German in 1647 and soon translated into several languages (but not Russian), Olearius's unflattering study played a major role in shaping European ideas about Russia.*

The government of the Russians is what political theorists call a "dominating and despotic monarchy," where the sovereign, that is, the tsar or the grand prince who has obtained the crown by right of succession, rules the entire land alone, and all the people are his subjects, and where the nobles and princes no less than the common folk—townspeople and peasants—are his serfs and slaves, whom he rules and treats as a master treats his servants. . . .

If the Russians be considered in respect to their character, customs, and way of life, they are justly to be counted among the barbarians. . . . The vice of drunkenness is so common in this nation, among people of every station, clergy and laity, high and low, men and women, old and young, that when they are seen now and then lying about in the streets, wallowing in the mud, no attention is paid to it, as something habitual. If a cart driver comes upon such a drunken pig whom he happens to know, he shoves him onto his cart and drives him home, where he is paid his fare. No one ever refuses an opportunity to drink and to get drunk, at any time and in any place, and usually it is done with vodka. . . .

The Russians being naturally tough and born, as it were, for slavery, they must be kept under a harsh and strict yoke and must be driven to do their work with clubs and whips, which they suffer without impatience, because such is their station, and they are accustomed to it. Young and half-grown fellows sometimes come together on certain days and train themselves in fisticuffs, to accustom themselves to receiving blows, and, since habit is second nature, this makes blows given as punishment easier to bear. Each and all, they are slaves and serfs. . . .

Although the Russians, especially the common populace, living as slaves under a harsh yoke, can bear and endure a great deal out of love for their masters, yet if the pressure is beyond measure, then it can be said of them: "Patience, often wounded, finally turned into fury." A dangerous indignation

The brutality of serfdom is shown in this illustration from Olearius's *Travels in Muscovy.* (University of Illinois Library, Champaign)

results, turned not so much against their sovereign as against the lower authorities, especially if the people have been much oppressed by them and by their supporters and have not been protected by the higher authorities. And once they are aroused and enraged, it is not easy to appease them. Then, disregarding all dangers that may ensue, they resort to every kind of violence and behave like madmen. . . . They own little; most of them have no feather beds; they lie on cushions, straw, mats, or their clothes; they sleep on benches and, in winter, like the non-Germans [natives] in Livonia, upon the oven, which serves them for cooking and is flat on the top; here husband, wife, children, servants, and maids huddle together. In some houses in the countryside we saw chickens and pigs under the benches and the ovens.

Questions for Analysis

1. In what ways were all social groups in Russia similar, according to Olearius?

2. How did Olearius characterize the Russians in general? What supporting evidence did he offer for his judgment?

3. Does Olearius's account help explain Stenka Razin's rebellion? In what ways?

4. On the basis of these representative passages, why do you think Olearius's book was so popular and influential in central and western Europe?

Source: G. Vernadsky and R. T. Fisher, Jr., eds., *A Source Book for Russian History from Early Times to 1917*, 3 vols., vol. 1, pp. 249–251. Copyright © 1972. Reprinted by permission of the publisher, Yale University Press.

CHAPTER 18

Toward a New Worldview

1540–1789

Chapter Preview

Voltaire, the renowned Enlightenment thinker, leans forward on the left to exchange ideas and witty conversation with Frederick the Great, king of Prussia. (Bildarchiv Preussischer Kulturbesitz/Art Resource, NY)

The intellectual developments of the seventeenth and eighteenth centuries created the modern worldview that the West continues to hold—and debate—to this day. In the seventeenth century fundamentally new ways of understanding the natural world emerged. In the nineteenth century scholars hailed these achievements as a "scientific revolution" that produced modern science as we know it. The new science created in the seventeenth century entailed the search for precise knowledge of the physical world based on the union of experimental observations with sophisticated mathematics.

In the eighteenth century philosophers extended the use of reason from the study of nature to the study of human society. They sought to bring the light of reason to bear on the darkness of prejudice, outmoded traditions, and ignorance. Self-proclaimed members of an "Enlightenment" movement, they wished to bring the same progress to human affairs as their predecessors had brought to the understanding of the natural world. While the scientific revolution ushered in modern science, the Enlightenment created concepts of human rights, equality, progress, universalism, and tolerance that still guide Western societies today.

While many view the scientific revolution and the Enlightenment as bedrocks of the achievement of Western civilization, others have seen a darker side. For these critics, the mastery over nature permitted by the scientific revolution now threatens to overwhelm the earth's fragile equilibrium, and the belief in the universal application of "reason" can lead to arrogance and intolerance, particularly intolerance of other people's spiritual values. Such vivid debate about the legacy of these intellectual and cultural developments testifies to their continuing importance in today's world.

The Scientific Revolution

What was revolutionary in the new attitudes toward the natural world?

The emergence of modern science was a development of tremendous long-term significance. A noted historian has said that the scientific revolution was "the real origin both of the modern world and the modern mentality."[1] With the scientific revolution Western society began to acquire its most distinctive traits.

Scientific Thought in 1500

Since developments in astronomy and physics were at the heart of the scientific revolution, one must begin with the traditional European conception of the universe. The practitioners of the scientific revolution did not consider their field *science* but rather **natural philosophy** and their intention was philosophical: to ask fundamental questions about the nature of the universe, its purpose, and how it functioned. In the early 1500s natural philosophy was still based primarily on the ideas of Aristotle, the great Greek philosopher of the fourth century B.C.E. Medieval theologians such as Thomas Aquinas brought Aristotelian philosophy into harmony with Christian doctrines. According to the revised Aristotelian view, a motionless earth was fixed at the center of the universe. Around it moved ten separate transparent crystal spheres. In the first eight spheres were embedded, in turn, the moon, the sun, the five known planets, and the fixed stars. Then followed two spheres added during the Middle Ages to account for slight changes in the positions of the stars over the centuries. Beyond the tenth sphere was Heaven, with the

natural philosophy An early modern term for the study of the nature of the universe, its purpose, and how it functioned; it encompassed what we would call today "science."

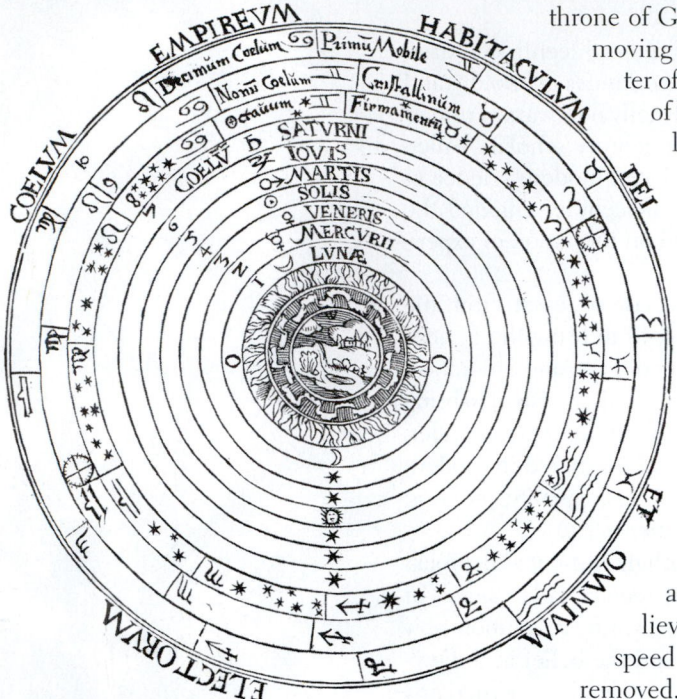

throne of God and the souls of the saved. Angels kept the spheres moving in perfect circles. Thus human beings were at the center of the universe and were the critical link in a "great chain of being" that stretched from the throne of God to the lowliest insect on earth.

Aristotle's views, suitably revised by medieval philosophers, also dominated thinking about physics and motion on earth. Aristotle had distinguished sharply between the world of the celestial spheres and that of the earth. The celestial spheres consisted of a perfect, incorruptible "quintessence," or fifth essence. The earth was composed of four imperfect, changeable elements. The "light" elements (air and fire) naturally moved upward, while the "heavy" elements (water and earth) naturally moved downward. These natural directions of motion did not always prevail, however, for elements were often mixed together and could be affected by an outside force such as a human being. Aristotle and his followers also believed that a uniform force moved an object at a constant speed and that the object would stop as soon as that force was removed.

The Aristotelian Universe as Imagined in the Sixteenth Century

A round earth is at the center, surrounded by spheres of water, air, and fire. Beyond this small nucleus, the moon, the sun, and the five planets were imbedded in their own rotating crystal spheres, with the stars sharing the surface of one enormous sphere. Beyond, the heavens were composed of unchanging ether. (Image Select/Art Resource, NY)

Copernican hypothesis The idea that the sun, not the earth, was the center of the universe; this had tremendous scientific and religious implications.

The Copernican Hypothesis

The first great departure from the medieval system came from Nicolaus Copernicus (koh-PUR-ni-kuhs) (1473–1543). As a young man Copernicus studied church law and astronomy in various European universities. He saw how professional astronomers still depended for their most accurate calculations on the second century B.C.E. work of Ptolemy. Copernicus felt that Ptolemy's cumbersome and occasionally inaccurate rules detracted from the majesty of a perfect Creator. He preferred an old Greek idea being discussed in Renaissance Italy: that the sun, rather than the earth, was at the center of the universe. Finishing his university studies and returning to a church position in East Prussia, Copernicus worked on his hypothesis from 1506 to 1530. Never questioning the Aristotelian belief in crystal spheres or the idea that circular motion was most perfect and divine, Copernicus theorized that the stars and planets, including the earth, revolved around a fixed sun. Yet fearing the ridicule of other astronomers, Copernicus did not publish his *On the Revolutions of the Heavenly Spheres* until 1543, the year of his death.

The **Copernican hypothesis** brought sharp attacks from religious leaders, especially Protestants, who objected to the idea that the earth moved but the sun did not. Martin Luther noted that the theory was counter to the Bible: "as the Holy Scripture tells us, so did Joshua bid the sun stand still and not the earth."[2] John Calvin also condemned Copernicus. Catholic reaction was milder at first. The Catholic Church had never held to literal interpretations of the Bible, and not until 1616 did it officially declare the Copernican hypothesis false.

This slow reaction also reflected the slow progress of Copernicus's theory for many years. Other events were almost as influential in creating doubts about traditional astronomical ideas. In 1572 a new star appeared and shone very brightly for almost two years. The new star, which was actually a distant exploding star, made an enormous impression on people. It seemed to contradict the idea that the heavenly spheres were unchanging and therefore perfect. In 1577 a new comet suddenly moved through the sky, cutting a straight path across the supposedly impenetrable crystal spheres. It was time, as a typical scientific writer put it, for "the radical renovation of astronomy."[3]

From Brahe to Galileo

One astronomer who agreed was Tycho Brahe (**TEE-koh BRAH-hee**) (1546–1601). Born into a prominent Danish noble family, Brahe was an imposing man who had lost a piece of his nose in a duel and replaced it with a special bridge of gold and silver alloy. He established himself as Europe's leading astronomer with his detailed observations of the new star of 1572. For twenty years he meticulously observed the stars and planets with the naked eye in the most sophisticated observatory of his day. His limited understanding of mathematics prevented him, however, from making much sense out of his mass of data. Part Ptolemaic, part Copernican, he believed that all the planets except the earth revolved around the sun and that the entire group of sun and planets revolved in turn around the earth-moon system.

It was left to Brahe's assistant, Johannes Kepler (**YO-han-nis KEP-ler**) (1571–1630), to rework Brahe's mountain of observations. A brilliant mathematician, Kepler would eventually move beyond his early belief that the universe was built on mystical mathematical relationships and a musical harmony of the heavenly bodies.

Kepler formulated three famous laws of planetary motion. First, building on Copernican theory, he demonstrated in 1609 that the orbits of the planets around the sun are elliptical rather than circular. Second, he demonstrated that the planets do not move at a uniform speed in their orbits. Third, in 1619 he showed that the time a planet takes to make its complete orbit is precisely related to its distance from the sun. Kepler's contribution was monumental. Whereas Copernicus had speculated, Kepler proved mathematically the precise relations of a sun-centered (solar) system. His work demolished the old system of Aristotle and Ptolemy, and in his third law he came close to formulating the idea of universal gravitation.

While Kepler was unraveling planetary motion, a young Florentine named Galileo Galilei (**gal-uh-LAY-oh gal-uh-LAY-ee**) (1564–1642) was challenging all the old ideas about motion. Like Kepler and so many early scientists, Galileo was a poor nobleman first marked for a religious career. Instead, his fascination with mathematics led to a professorship in which he examined motion and mechanics in a new way. Indeed, his great achievement was the elaboration and consolidation of the **experimental method.** That is, rather than speculate about what might or should happen, Galileo conducted controlled experiments to find out what actually *did* happen.

In some of these experiments Galileo measured the movement of a rolling ball across a surface that he constructed, repeating the action again and again to verify his results. In his famous acceleration experiment, he showed that a uniform force—in this case, gravity—produced a uniform acceleration. Through another experiment, he formulated the **law of inertia** (**in-UR-shuh**). Rest was not the

experimental method The approach, first developed by Galileo, that the proper way to explore the workings of the universe was through repeatable experiments rather than speculation.

law of inertia A law formulated by Galileo that stated that rest was not the natural state of an object. Rather, an object continues in motion forever unless stopped by some external force.

Galileo's Paintings of the Moon

When Galileo published the results of his telescopic observations of the moon, he added these paintings to illustrate the marvels he had seen. Galileo made two telescopes, which are shown here. The larger one magnifies fourteen times, the smaller one twenty times. (Biblioteca Nazionale Centrale, Florence/Art Resource, NY; Museum of Science, Florence/Art Resource, NY)

natural state of objects. Rather, an object continues in motion forever unless stopped by some external force. Aristotelian physics was in shambles.

In the tradition of Brahe, Galileo also applied the experimental method to astronomy. On hearing details about the invention of the telescope in Holland, Galileo made one for himself and trained it on the heavens. He wrote in 1610 in *Siderus Nuncius*:

> By the aid of a telescope anyone may behold [the Milky Way] in a manner which so distinctly appeals to the senses that all the disputes which have tormented philosophers through so many ages are exploded by the irrefutable evidence of our eyes, and we are freed from wordy disputes upon the subject. For the galaxy is nothing else but a mass of innumerable stars planted together in clusters.[4]

Reading these famous lines, one feels a crucial corner in Western civilization being turned. No longer should one rely on established authority. A new method of learning and investigating was being developed, one that proved capable of great extension. A historian investigating documents of the past, for example, is not so different from a Galileo studying stars and rolling balls.

Galileo was employed in Florence by the Medici grand dukes of Tuscany, and his work eventually aroused the ire of some theologians. The issue was presented in 1624 to Pope Urban VIII, who permitted Galileo to write about different possible systems of the world as long as he did not presume to judge which one actually existed. After the publication in Italian of his widely read *Dialogue on the Two Chief Systems of the World* in 1632, which openly lampooned the traditional views of Aristotle and Ptolemy and defended those of Copernicus, Galileo was tried for heresy by the papal Inquisition. Imprisoned and threatened with torture, the aging Galileo recanted, "renouncing and cursing" his Copernican errors.

Newton's Synthesis

The accomplishments of Kepler, Galileo, and other scientists had taken effect by about 1640. The old astronomy and physics were in ruins, and several fundamental breakthroughs had been made. But the new findings failed to explain what forces controlled the movement of the planets and objects on Earth. That challenge was taken up by the English scientist Isaac Newton (1642–1727).

Newton was born into the lower English gentry and he attended Cambridge University. A genius who spectacularly united the experimental and theoretical-mathematical sides of modern science, Newton was far from being the perfect rationalist eulogized by later centuries. Like many other practitioners of the new science, Newton was both intensely religious and fascinated by alchemy.

He arrived at some of his most basic ideas about physics in 1666 at age twenty-four but was unable to prove them mathematically. In 1684, after years of studying optics, Newton returned to physics for eighteen extraordinarily intensive months. The result was his towering accomplishment, a single explanatory system that could integrate the astronomy of Copernicus, as corrected by Kepler's laws, with the physics of Galileo and his predecessors. Newton did this by means of a set of mathematical laws that explain motion and mechanics. These laws of dynamics are complex, and it took scientists and engineers two hundred years to work out all their implications. Nevertheless, the key feature of the Newtonian synthesis was the **law of universal gravitation.** According to this law, every body in the universe attracts every other body in the universe in a precise mathematical relationship, whereby the force of attraction is proportional to the quantity of matter of the objects and inversely proportional to the square of the distance between them. The whole universe—from Kepler's elliptical orbits to Galileo's rolling balls—was unified in one majestic system. Newton's synthesis prevailed until the twentieth century.

law of universal gravitation Newton's law that every body in the universe attracts every other body in the universe in a precise mathematical relationship, whereby the force of attraction is proportional to the quantity of matter of the objects and inversely proportional to the square of the distance between them.

Causes of the Scientific Revolution

The scientific revolution drew on long-term developments in European culture. The first was the development of the medieval university. By the fourteenth and fifteenth centuries leading universities had evolved to include professorships of mathematics, astronomy, and physics (natural philosophy) within their faculties of philosophy. Although the prestige of the new fields was low, critical thinking was now applied to scientific problems by a permanent community of scholars. And an outlet existed for the talents of a Galileo or a Newton: all the great pathfinders either studied or taught at universities.

Second, the Renaissance also stimulated scientific progress. The recovery of ancient texts showed that classical mathematicians had their differences; Europeans were thus forced to try to resolve these ancient controversies by means of their own efforts. Renaissance patrons played a role in funding scientific investigations as well as artistic projects, as the Medicis of Florence did for Galileo.

The navigational problems of long sea voyages in the age of overseas expansion were a third factor in the scientific revolution. As early as 1484 the king of Portugal appointed a commission of mathematicians to perfect tables to help seamen find their latitude. Navigational problems were also critical in the development of many new scientific instruments, such as the telescope, barometer, thermometer, pendulum clock, microscope, and air pump. Better instruments, which permitted more accurate observations, often led to important new knowledge. Galileo with his telescope was by no means unique.

The fourth factor in the scientific revolution was the development of better ways of obtaining knowledge about the world. Two important thinkers, Francis

Bacon (1561–1626) and René Descartes (**dey-KAHRT**) (1596–1650) were influential in describing and advocating for improved scientific methods, based on experimentation and mathematical reasoning.

The English politician and writer Francis Bacon was the greatest early propagandist for the new scientific method. Bacon argued that the researcher who wants to learn more about leaves or rocks should not speculate about the subject but should rather collect a multitude of specimens and then compare and analyze them. General principles will then emerge. Bacon's contribution was to formalize the empirical method, which had already been used by Brahe and Galileo, into the general theory of inductive reasoning known as **empiricism.**

empiricism A theory of inductive reasoning that calls for acquiring evidence through observation and experimentation rather than reason and speculation.

The French philosopher René Descartes was a true genius who made his first great discovery in mathematics. As a twenty-three-year-old soldier serving in the Thirty Years' War, he experienced a life-changing intellectual vision on a single night in 1619. Descartes saw that there was a perfect correspondence between geometry and algebra and that geometrical, spatial figures could be expressed as algebraic equations and vice versa. A major step forward in the history of mathematics, Descartes's discovery of analytic geometry provided scientists with an important new tool.

Descartes's greatest achievement was to develop his initial vision into a whole philosophy of knowledge and science. He decided it was necessary to doubt everything that could reasonably be doubted and then, as in geometry, to use deductive reasoning from self-evident principles to ascertain scientific laws. Descartes's reasoning ultimately reduced all substances to "matter" and "mind"—that is, to the physical and the spiritual. His view of the world as consisting of two fundamental entities is known as **Cartesian** (**kahr-TEE-zhuhn**) **dualism.** Descartes was a profoundly original and extremely influential thinker.

Cartesian dualism Descartes's view that all of reality could ultimately be reduced to mind and matter.

Bacon's inductive experimentalism and Descartes's deductive, mathematical reasoning are combined in the modern scientific method, which began to crystallize in the late seventeenth century. Neither man's extreme approach was sufficient by itself. Bacon's inability to appreciate the importance of mathematics and his obsession with practical results clearly showed the limitations of antitheoretical empiricism. Likewise, some of Descartes's positions—he believed, for example, that it was possible to deduce the whole science of medicine from first principles—demonstrated the inadequacy of rigid, dogmatic rationalism. Thus the modern scientific method has joined precise observations and experimentalism with the search for general laws that may be expressed in rigorously logical, mathematical language.

Science and Society

The rise of modern science had many consequences, some of which are still unfolding. First, it went hand in hand with the rise of a new and expanding social group—the international **scientific community.** Members of this community were linked together by common interests and shared values as well as by journals and the learned scientific societies founded in many countries in the later seventeenth and the eighteenth centuries. Their personal success depended on making new discoveries, and science became competitive. Second, as governments intervened to support and sometimes direct research, the new scientific community became closely tied to the state and its agendas. National academies of science were created under state sponsorship in London in 1662, Paris in 1666, Berlin in 1700, and later across Europe. At the same time, scientists developed a critical attitude toward established authority that would inspire thinkers to question traditions in other domains as well.

scientific community The international social group that expanded with the rise of modern science; its members were linked together by common interests and shared values as well as by journals and the learned scientific societies founded in many countries in the later seventeenth and eighteenth centuries.

Metamorphoses of the Caterpillar and Moth

Maria Sibylla Merian (1647–1717), the stepdaughter of a Dutch painter, became a celebrated scientific illustrator in her own right. Her finely observed pictures of insects in the South American colony of Surinam introduced many new species, shown in their various stages of development. For Merian, science was intimately tied with art: she not only painted but also bred caterpillars and performed experiments on them. Her two-year stay in Surinam, accompanied by a teenaged daughter, was a daring feat for a seventeenth-century woman. (Bildarchiv Preussischer Kulturbesitz/Art Resource, NY)

Some things did not change in the scientific revolution. Scholars have recently analyzed representations of femininity and masculinity in the scientific revolution and have noted that nature was often depicted as a female, whose veil of secrecy needed to be stripped away and penetrated by male experts. (At the same time, the Americas were similarly depicted as a female terrain whose potentially fertile lands needed to be controlled and impregnated by male colonists.) New "rational" methods for approaching nature did not question traditional inequalities between the sexes—and may have worsened them in some ways. Women were largely shut out of the academies and then refused membership into scientific communities because they lacked academic credentials. (This continued for a long time. Marie Curie, the first person to win two Nobel prizes, was rejected by the French Academy of Science in 1911 because she was a woman.[5])

There were, however, a number of noteworthy exceptions. In Italy, universities and academies did offer posts to women, attracting some foreigners spurned by their own countries. Women were allowed to work as makers of wax anatomical models and as botanical and zoological illustrators. Women were also very much involved in informal scientific communities, attending salons, participating in scientific experiments, and writing learned treatises. Some female intellectuals were recognized as full-fledged members of the philosophical dialogue. In England, Margaret Cavendish, Anne Conway, and Mary Astell all contributed to debates about Descartes's mind-body dualism, among other issues. Descartes himself conducted an intellectual correspondence with the princess Elizabeth of Bohemia, of whom he stated: "I attach more weight to her judgement than to those messieurs the Doctors, who take for a rule of truth the opinions of Aristotle rather than the evidence of reason."[6]

The scientific revolution had few consequences for economic life and the living standards of the masses until the late eighteenth century. True, improvements in the techniques of navigation facilitated overseas trade and helped enrich states and merchant companies. But science had relatively few practical economic applications. Thus the scientific revolution of the seventeenth century was first and foremost an intellectual revolution. For more than a hundred years its greatest impact was on how people thought and believed.

Section Review

- Natural philosophy was based on Aristotle's ideas: the earth was the center of the universe, heaven was perfect, and the earth's four elements (air, fire, water, earth) were imperfect and changeable.

- The Copernican hypothesis stated that the sun, not the earth, was fixed and the planets and stars revolved around it—an idea the church rejected.

- Tycho Brahe, an astronomer, took detailed observations of the planets from which his assistant, Johannes Kepler, a mathematician, was able to determine and prove planetary motion, while Galileo Galilei developed the experimental method, using controlled experiments to verify results.

- Newton used a set of mathematical laws that explain motion and mechanics to synthesize his law of universal gravitation, which unified the universe into one magnificent system.

- The scientific revolution was a product of the medieval university, Renaissance funding, the need for navigational instruments, and the scientific method of experimentation and mathematical reasoning.

- The scientific revolution was an intellectual revolution, fostering international scientific communities and critical thinking in many fields beyond science.

The Enlightenment

How did the new worldview affect the way people thought about society and human relations?

Enlightenment The intellectual and cultural movement of the late seventeenth and eighteenth centuries that introduced a new worldview that has played a large role in shaping the modern mind. The three central concepts of the Enlightenment were the use of reason, the scientific method, and progress.

rationalism A secular, critical way of thinking in which nothing was to be accepted on faith, and everything was to be submitted to reason.

The scientific revolution was the single most important factor in the creation of the new worldview of the eighteenth-century **Enlightenment.** This worldview, which has played a large role in shaping the modern mind, grew out of a rich mix of diverse and often conflicting ideas. Despite the diversity, three central concepts stand at the core of Enlightenment thinking. The most important and original idea was that the methods of natural science could and should be used to examine and understand all aspects of life. This was what intellectuals meant by *reason*, a favorite word of Enlightenment thinkers. Nothing was to be accepted on faith. Everything was to be submitted to **rationalism,** a secular, critical way of thinking. A second important Enlightenment concept was that the scientific method was capable of discovering the laws of human society as well as those of nature. Thus was social science born. Its birth led to the third key idea, that of progress. Armed with the proper method of discovering the laws of human existence, Enlightenment thinkers believed, it was at least possible for human beings to create better societies and better people. Their belief was strengthened by some modest improvements in economic and social life during the eighteenth century.

The Emergence of the Enlightenment

Loosely united by certain key ideas, the European Enlightenment was a broad intellectual and cultural movement that gained strength gradually and did not reach its maturity until about 1750. Yet it was the generation that came of age between the publication of Newton's *Principia* (**prin-SIP-ee-uh, prin-KIP-ee-uh**) in 1687 and the death of Louis XIV in 1715 that tied the crucial knot between the scientific revolution and a new outlook on life. Talented writers of that generation popularized hard-to-understand scientific achievements for the educated elite.

A new generation came to believe that the human mind is capable of making great progress. Medieval and Reformation thinkers had been concerned primarily with sin and salvation. The humanists of the Renaissance had emphasized worldly matters, but their inspiration was the wisdom of the past. Enlightenment thinkers came to believe that, at least in science and mathematics, their era had gone far beyond antiquity. Progress, at least intellectual progress, was very possible.

The excitement of the scientific revolution also generated doubt and uncertainty, contributing to a widespread crisis in late seventeenth-century European thought. In the wake of the devastation wrought by the Thirty Years' War, some people asked whether ideological conformity in religious matters was really necessary. Others skeptically asked if religious truth could ever be known with absolute certainty and concluded that it could not. This was a new development because many seventeenth-century scientists, Catholic and Protestant, believed that their work exalted God and helped explain his creation to fellow believers.

The most famous of these skeptics was Pierre Bayle (1647–1706), a French Huguenot who despised Louis XIV and found refuge in the Netherlands. Bayle critically examined the religious beliefs and persecutions of the past in his *Historical and Critical Dictionary* (1697). Demonstrating that human beliefs had been extremely varied and very often mistaken, he concluded that nothing can ever be known beyond all doubt, a view known as **skepticism.** A very influential text, his

skepticism The belief that nothing can ever be known beyond all doubt and that humanity's best hope was open-minded toleration.

Popularizing Science

The frontispiece illustration of *Conversations on the Plurality of Worlds* by Bernard de Fontenelle (1657–1757) invites a nonscientific audience to share the pleasures of astronomy with an elegant lady and an entertaining teacher. The drawing shows the planets revolving around the sun. (By permission of the Syndics of Cambridge University Library)

Dictionary was reprinted frequently in the Netherlands and in England and was found in more private libraries of eighteenth-century France than any other book.

The rapidly growing travel literature on non-European lands and cultures was another cause of uncertainty. In the wake of the great discoveries, Europeans were learning that the peoples of China, India, Africa, and the Americas all had their own very different beliefs and customs. Europeans shaved their faces and let their hair grow. Turks shaved their heads and let their beards grow. In Europe a man bowed before a woman to show respect. In Siam a man turned his back on a woman when he met her because it was disrespectful to look directly at her. Countless similar examples discussed in the travel accounts helped change the perspective of educated Europeans. They began to look at truth and morality in relative, rather than absolute, terms. If anything was possible, who could say what was right or wrong?

An additional cause and manifestation of European intellectual turmoil was John Locke's epochal *Essay Concerning Human Understanding* (1690). Locke's essay brilliantly set forth a new theory about how human beings learn and form their ideas, rejecting Descartes's view that all people are born with certain basic ideas and ways of thinking. Locke insisted that all ideas are derived from experience. The human mind at birth is like a blank tablet, or **tabula rasa** (TAB-yuh-luh RAH-suh), on which the environment writes the individual's understanding and beliefs. Human development is therefore determined by education and social institutions, for good or for evil. Locke's *Essay Concerning Human Understanding* passed through many editions and translations. Along with Newton's *Principia*, it was one of the dominant intellectual inspirations of the Enlightenment.

tabula rasa A blank tablet, incorporated into Locke's belief that all ideas are derived from experience, and that the human mind at birth is like a blank tablet on which the environment writes the individual's understanding and beliefs.

The Philosophes and the Public

By the time Louis XIV died in 1715, many of the ideas that would soon coalesce into the new worldview had been assembled. Yet Christian Europe was still strongly attached to its traditional beliefs, as witnessed by the powerful revival of religious orthodoxy in the first half of the eighteenth century (see pages 526–530). By the outbreak of the American Revolution in 1775, however, a large portion of western Europe's educated elite had embraced many of the new ideas. This acceptance was the work of the **philosophes** (FIL-uh-sawfz), a group of influential intellectuals who proudly proclaimed that they, at long last, were bringing the light of knowledge to their ignorant fellow creatures.

Philosophe is the French word for "philosopher," and it was in France that the Enlightenment reached its highest development. There were at least three reasons for this. First, French was the international language of the educated classes in the

philosophes Intellectuals in France who proclaimed that they were bringing the light of knowledge to their fellow creatures in the Age of Enlightenment.

eighteenth century, and France was still the wealthiest and most populous country in Europe. Second, although French intellectuals were not free to openly criticize either church or state, they were not as strongly restrained as intellectuals in eastern and east-central Europe. Philosophes like the baron de Montesquieu (**MON-tuh-skyoo**) (1689–1755) used satire and double meanings to spread their message to the public. Third, the French philosophes made it their goal to reach a larger audience of elites, many of whom were joined together in the eighteenth-century concept of the "republic of letters"—an imaginary, transnational realm of the well-educated.

The influence of writers like Montesquieu on the enlightened public can be seen in the results of his political writing. Disturbed by the growth in royal absolutism under Louis XIV and inspired by the example of the physical sciences, Montesquieu set out to apply the critical method to the problem of government. *The Spirit of Laws* (1748) was a complex comparative study of republics, monarchies, and despotisms—a great pioneering inquiry in the emerging social sciences.

Showing that forms of government were shaped by history, geography, and customs, Montesquieu focused on the conditions that would promote liberty and prevent tyranny. He argued for a **separation of powers,** with political power divided and shared by a variety of classes and legal estates holding unequal rights and privileges. Admiring greatly the English balance of power among the king, the houses of Parliament, and the independent courts, Montesquieu believed that in France the thirteen high courts—the *parlements*—were frontline defenders of liberty against royal despotism. Apprehensive about the uneducated poor, Montesquieu was clearly no democrat, but his theory of separation of powers had a great impact on the constitutions of the young United States in 1789 and of France in 1791.

The most famous and in many ways most representative philosophe was François Marie Arouet, who was known by the pen name Voltaire (**vohl-TAIR**) (1694–1778). In his long career, this son of a comfortable middle-class family wrote more than seventy witty volumes, hobnobbed with kings and queens, and died a millionaire because of shrewd business speculations. His early career, however, was turbulent, and he was arrested on two occasions for insulting noblemen. Voltaire moved to England for three years in order to avoid a longer prison term in France, and there he came to share Montesquieu's enthusiasm for English institutions.

Returning to France and soon threatened again with prison in Paris, Voltaire had the great fortune of meeting Gabrielle-Emilie Le Tonnelier de Breteuil, marquise du Châtelet (**SHA-tuh-lay**) (1706–1749), an intellectually gifted woman from the high aristocracy with a passion for science. Inviting Voltaire to live in her country house at Cirey in Lorraine and becoming his long-time companion (under the eyes of her tolerant husband), Madame du Châtelet studied physics and mathematics and published scientific articles and translations.

Excluded from the Royal Academy of Sciences because of her gender, Madame du Châtelet depended on private tutors for instruction and became uncertain of her ability to make important scientific discoveries. She therefore concentrated on spreading the ideas of others, and her translation—with an accompanying commentary—of Newton's *Principia* into French for the first (and only) time was her greatest work. But she, who had patiently explained Newton's complex mathematical proofs to Europe's foremost philosophe, had no doubt that women's limited scientific contributions in the past were due to limited and unequal education. She once wrote that if she were a ruler "I would reform an abuse which cuts off, so to speak, half the human race. I would make women participate in all the rights of humankind, and above all in those of the intellect."[7]

separation of powers The idea, developed by the philosophe Montesquieu, that despotism could be avoided when political power was divided and shared by a variety of classes and legal estates holding unequal rights and privileges.

While living at Cirey, Voltaire wrote various works praising England and popularizing English scientific progress. Newton, he wrote, was history's greatest man, for he had used his genius for the benefit of humanity. "It is," wrote Voltaire, "the man who sways our minds by the prevalence of reason and the native force of truth, not they who reduce mankind to a state of slavery by force and downright violence . . . that claims our reverence and admiration."[8] In the true style of the Enlightenment, Voltaire mixed the glorification of science and reason with an appeal for better individuals and institutions.

Yet like almost all of the philosophes, Voltaire was a reformer, not a revolutionary, in social and political matters. He pessimistically concluded that the best one could hope for in the way of government was a good monarch, since human beings "are very rarely worthy to govern themselves." Nor did he believe in social and economic equality in human affairs. The idea of making servants equal to their masters was "absurd and impossible." The only realizable equality, Voltaire thought, was that "by which the citizen only depends on the laws which protect the freedom of the feeble against the ambitions of the strong."[9]

Voltaire's philosophical and religious positions were much more radical. In the tradition of Bayle, his voluminous writings challenged, often indirectly, the Catholic Church and Christian theology at almost every point. Voltaire clearly believed in God, but his was a distant, deistic God, the great Clockmaker who built an orderly universe and then stepped aside and let it run. Above all, Voltaire and most of the philosophes hated all forms of religious intolerance, which they believed often led to fanaticism and savage, inhuman action. Simple piety and human kindness—as embodied in Christ's great commandments to "love God and your neighbor as yourself"—were religion enough, as may be seen in Voltaire's famous essay on religion. (See the feature "Listening to the Past: Voltaire on Religion" on pages 482–483.)

The ultimate strength of the French philosophes lay in their number, dedication, and organization. The philosophes felt keenly that they were engaged in a common undertaking that transcended individuals. Their greatest and most representative intellectual achievement was, quite fittingly, a group effort—the seventeen-volume *Encyclopedia: The Rational Dictionary of the Sciences, the Arts, and the Crafts*, edited by Denis Diderot (**duh-nee DEE-duh-roe**) (1713–1784) and Jean le Rond d'Alembert (**al-em-BAHR**) (1717–1783). From different circles and with different interests, the two men set out to find coauthors who would examine the rapidly expanding whole of human knowledge. Even more fundamentally, they set out to teach people how to think critically and objectively about all matters. As Diderot said, he wanted the *Encyclopedia* to "change the general way of thinking."[10]

Not every article was daring or original, but the overall effect was little short of revolutionary. Science and the industrial arts were exalted, religion and immortality questioned. Intolerance, legal injustice, and out-of-date social institutions were openly criticized. The encyclopedists were convinced that greater knowledge would result in greater human happiness, for knowledge was useful and made possible economic, social, and political progress. The *Encyclopedia* was widely read,

Madame du Châtelet

The marquise du Châtelet was fascinated by the new world system of Isaac Newton. She helped spread Newton's ideas in France by translating his *Principia* and by influencing Voltaire, her companion for fifteen years until her death. (Giraudon/Art Resource, NY)

especially in less-expensive reprint editions published in Switzerland, and it was extremely influential in France and throughout western Europe as well. It summed up the new worldview of the Enlightenment.

Urban Culture and the Public Sphere

Enlightenment ideas did not float on air. A series of new institutions and practices emerged in the late seventeenth and eighteenth centuries to facilitate their spread. First, the European production and consumption of books grew significantly in the eighteenth century. Moreover, the types of books people read changed dramatically. The proportion of religious and devotional books published in Paris declined after 1750; history and law held constant; the arts and sciences surged.

Reading more books on many more subjects, the educated public in France and throughout Europe increasingly approached reading in a new way. The result was what some scholars have called a **"reading revolution."** The old style of reading in Europe had been centered on a core of sacred texts that inspired reverence and taught earthly duty and obedience to God. Reading had been patriarchal and communal, with the father of the family slowly reading the text aloud and the audience savoring each word. Now reading involved a broader field of books that constantly changed. Reading became individual and silent, and texts could be

reading revolution The transition in Europe from a society where literacy consisted of patriarchal and communal reading of religious texts to a society where literacy was commonplace and reading material was broad and diverse.

Selling Books, Promoting Ideas
This appealing bookshop with its intriguing ads for the latest works offers to put customers "Under the Protection of Minerva," the Roman goddess of wisdom. Large packets of books sit ready for shipment to foreign countries. Book consumption surged in the eighteenth century. (Musée des Beaux-Arts, Dijon/Art Resource, NY)

questioned. Subtle but profound, the reading revolution ushered in new ways of relating to the written word.

Conversation, discussion, and debate also played a critical role in the Enlightenment. Paris set the example, and other French and European cities followed. In Paris a number of talented, wealthy women presided over regular social gatherings in their elegant private drawing rooms, or **salons.** There they encouraged the exchange of witty, uncensored observations on literature, science, and philosophy. Talented hostesses, or *salonnières* (sal-lon-ee-AIRZ), mediated the public's freewheeling examination of Enlightenment thought. As one philosophe described his Enlightenment hostess and her salon:

> **salons** Regular social gatherings held by talented and rich Parisian women in their homes, where philosophes and their followers met to discuss literature, science, and philosophy.

> *She could unite the different types, even the most antagonistic, sustaining the conversation by a well-aimed phrase, animating and guiding it at will. . . . Politics, religion, philosophy, news: nothing was excluded. Her circle met daily from five to nine. There one found men of all ranks in the State, the Church, and the Court, soldiers and foreigners, and the leading writers of the day.[11]*

As this passage suggests, the salons created a cultural realm free from religious dogma and political censorship. There a diverse but educated public could debate issues and form its own ideas. Through their invitation lists, salon hostesses brought together members of the intellectual, economic, and social elites. In such an atmosphere, the philosophes, the French nobility, and the prosperous middle classes intermingled and influenced one another. Thinking critically about almost any question became fashionable and flourished alongside hopes for human progress through greater knowledge and enlightened public opinion.

Enlightenment Culture
An actor performs the first reading of a new play by Voltaire at the salon of Madame Geoffrin. Voltaire, then in exile, is represented by a bust statue. (Réunion des Musées Nationaux/Art Resource, NY)

rococo A popular style in Europe in the eighteenth century, known for its soft pastels, ornate interiors, sentimental portraits, and starry-eyed lovers protected by hovering cupids.

Elite women also exercised an unprecedented feminine influence on artistic taste. Soft pastels, ornate interiors, sentimental portraits, and starry-eyed lovers protected by hovering cupids were all hallmarks of the style they favored. This style, known as **rococo** (ruh-KOH-koh), was popular throughout Europe in the eighteenth century. It has been argued that feminine influence in the drawing room went hand in hand with the emergence of polite society and the general attempt to civilize a rough military nobility. Similarly, some philosophes championed greater rights and expanded education for women, claiming that the position and treatment of women were the best indicators of a society's level of civilization and decency.[12] To be sure, for these male philosophes greater rights for women did not mean equal rights, and the philosophes were not particularly disturbed by the fact that elite women remained legally subordinate to men in economic and political affairs. Elite women lacked many rights, but so did most men.

While membership at the salons was restricted to the well-born, the well-connected, and the exceptionally talented, a number of institutions emerged for the rest of society. Lending libraries served an important function for people who could not afford to buy their own books. The coffeehouses that first appeared in the late seventeenth century became meccas of philosophical discussion. In addition to these institutions, book clubs, Masonic lodges, and journals all played roles in the creation of a new **public sphere** that celebrated open debate informed by critical reason. The public sphere was an idealized space where members of society came together as individuals to discuss issues relevant to the society, economics, and politics of the day.

public sphere An idealized intellectual space that emerged in Europe during the Enlightenment, where members of society came together as individuals to discuss issues relevant to the society, economics, and politics of the day.

What of the common people? Did they participate in the Enlightenment? Enlightenment philosophes did not direct their message to peasants or urban laborers. They believed that the masses had no time or talent for philosophical speculation and that elevating them would be a long, slow, potentially dangerous process. Deluded by superstitions and driven by violent passions, they thought, the people were like little children in need of firm parental guidance. French philosophe d'Alembert characteristically made a sharp distinction between "the truly enlightened public" and "the blind and noisy multitude."[13]

There is some evidence, however, that the people were not immune to the words of the philosophes. At a time of rising literacy, book prices were dropping in cities and towns, and many philosophical ideas were popularized in cheap pamphlets. Moreover, even illiterate people had access to written material, through the practice of public reading. Although they were barred from salons and academies, ordinary people were not immune to the new ideas in circulation.

Late Enlightenment

After about 1770 a number of thinkers and writers began to attack the Enlightenment's faith in reason, progress, and moderation. The most famous of these was the Swiss Jean-Jacques Rousseau (1712–1778), the son of a poor watchmaker who made his way into the world of Paris salons through his brilliant intellect. Appealing but neurotic, Rousseau came to believe that his philosophe friends and the women of the Parisian salons were plotting against him. In the mid-1750s he broke with them, living thereafter as a lonely outsider with his uneducated common-law wife and going in his own highly original direction.

Like other Enlightenment thinkers, Rousseau was passionately committed to individual freedom. Unlike them, however, he attacked rationalism and civilization as destroying, rather than liberating, the individual. Warm, spontaneous feeling had to complement and correct cold intellect. Moreover, the basic goodness of the individual and the unspoiled child had to be protected from the cruel refinements of civilization. Rousseau's ideals greatly influenced the early romantic movement (see pages 517–518), which rebelled against the culture of the Enlightenment in the late eighteenth century.

Reconfirming Montesquieu's critique of women's influence in public affairs, Rousseau called for a rigid division of gender roles. According to Rousseau, women and men were radically different beings. Destined by nature to assume a passive role in sexual relations, women should also be passive in social life. Women's passion for fashion, attending salons, and pulling the strings of power was unnatural and had a corrupting effect on both politics and society. Rousseau thus rejected the sophisticated way of life of Parisian elite women. These views contributed to calls for privileged women to abandon their stylish corsets and to breast-feed their children.

Rousseau's contribution to political theory in *The Social Contract* (1762) was equally significant. His contribution was based on two fundamental concepts: the general will and popular sovereignty. According to Rousseau, the **general will** is sacred and absolute, reflecting the common interests of all the people, who have displaced the monarch as the holder of sovereign power. The general will is not necessarily the will of the majority, however. At times the general will may be the authentic, long-term needs of the people as correctly interpreted by a farseeing minority. (The concept has since been used by many dictators who have claimed that they, rather than some momentary majority of the voters, represent the general will.)

As the reading public developed, it joined forces with the philosophes to call for the autonomy of the printed word. Immanuel Kant (1724–1804), a professor in East Prussia and the greatest German philosopher of his day, posed the question of the age when he published a pamphlet in 1784 entitled *What Is Enlightenment?* Kant answered, "*Sapere Aude!* (**SAP-eh-ray OW-day**) [dare to know] Have courage to use your own understanding!—that is the motto of enlightenment." He argued that if serious thinkers were granted the freedom to exercise their reason publicly in print, enlightenment would almost surely follow. Kant was no revolutionary; he also insisted that in their private lives, individuals must obey all laws, no matter how unreasonable, and should be punished for "impertinent" criticism. Kant thus tried to reconcile absolute monarchical authority with a critical public sphere. This balancing act characterized experiments with "enlightened absolutism" in the eighteenth century.

general will Rousseau's concept that the common interest of all the people is sacred and absolute, and is not necessarily reflected by the will of the majority but by the interpretation of a farseeing minority.

Race and the Enlightenment

In recent years, historians have found in the scientific revolution and the Enlightenment a crucial turning point in European ideas about race. A primary catalyst for new ideas about race was the urge to classify nature, unleashed by the scientific revolution's insistence on careful empirical observation. In *The System of Nature* (1735) Swedish botanist Carl von Linné argued that nature was organized into a God-given hierarchy. As scientists developed more elaborate taxonomies of plant and animal species, they also began to classify humans into hierarchically ordered "races" and to investigate the origins of race. The Comte de Buffon (**komt duh buh-FAWN**) argued that humans originated with one species that then developed into distinct races due largely to climatic conditions. According to Immanuel Kant, there were four human races, each of which had derived from an original race of "white brunette" people.

Using the word *race* to designate biologically distinct groups of humans, akin to distinct animal species, was new. Previously, Europeans grouped other peoples

- The Enlightenment brought together the scientific revolution and a new worldview that believed that the human mind is capable of progress.

- The Enlightenment reached its peak in France with the philosophes, including Voltaire, who mixed science and reason with an appeal for improving humans and institutions, and ultimately in the group work of the *Encyclopedia*, which taught critical thinking in an effort to make possible economic, social, and political progress.

- Enlightenment ideas spread through the reading revolution and from conversations and debate by the educated public in salons, which were free from religious and political censorship.

- Salons, book clubs, lodges, journals, and libraries created a new "public sphere" where intellectuals could debate and reason, but did not include the lower classes, who received second-hand influence from these ideas.

- Some thinkers began to critique the Enlightenment's faith in reason; Rousseau, for example, argued for a rigid division of gender roles and for balancing cold intellect with warm, spontaneous feeling.

- Some Europeans used science to create racial hierarchies to defend slavery and colonial domination of "naturally inferior" races as well as to enforce social inequalities between men and women.

enlightened absolutism Term coined by historians to describe the rule of eighteenth-century monarchs who, without renouncing their own absolute authority, adopted Enlightenment ideals of rationalism, progress, and tolerance.

into "nations" based on their historical, political, and cultural affiliations, rather than on supposedly innate physical differences. Unsurprisingly, when European thinkers drew up a hierarchical classification of human species, their own "race" was placed at the top. Europeans had long believed they were culturally superior to "barbaric" peoples in Africa and, since 1492, the New World. Now emerging ideas about racial difference taught them they were biologically superior as well.

These ideas did not go unchallenged. James Beattie responded directly to claims of white superiority by pointing out that Europeans had started out as savage as nonwhites and that many non-European peoples in the Americas, Asia, and Africa had achieved high levels of civilization.

Scholars are only at the beginning of efforts to understand links between Enlightenment ideas about race and its notions of equality, progress, and reason. There are clear parallels, though, between the use of science to propagate racial hierarchies and its use to defend social inequalities between men and women. As Rousseau used women's "natural" passivity to argue for their passive role in society, so others used non-Europeans' "natural" inferiority to defend slavery and colonial domination. The new powers of science and reason were thus marshaled to imbue traditional stereotypes with the force of natural law.

The Enlightenment and Absolutism

What impact did this new way of thinking have on political developments and monarchical absolutism?

How did the Enlightenment influence political developments? To this important question there is no easy answer. Most Enlightenment thinkers outside of England and the Netherlands believed that political change could best come from above—from the ruler—rather than from below, especially in central and eastern Europe. It was necessary to educate and "enlighten" the monarch, who could then make good laws and promote human happiness.

Many government officials were attracted to and interested in philosophical ideas. They were among the best-educated members of society, and their daily involvement in complex affairs of state made them naturally interested in ideas for improving or reforming human society. Encouraged and instructed by these officials, some absolutist rulers of the later eighteenth century tried to govern in an "enlightened" manner. Yet the actual programs and accomplishments of these rulers varied greatly. It is necessary to examine the evolution of monarchical absolutism at close range before trying to judge the Enlightenment's effect and the meaning of what historians have often called the **enlightened absolutism** of the later eighteenth century.

Enlightenment teachings inspired European rulers in small as well as large states in the second half of the eighteenth century. Absolutist princes and monarchs in several west German and Italian states, as well as in Scandinavia, Spain, and Portugal, proclaimed themselves more enlightened. A few smaller states were actually the most successful in making reforms, perhaps because their rulers were not overwhelmed by the size and complexity of their realms. Denmark, for example, carried out extensive and progressive land reform in the 1780s that practically abolished serfdom and gave Danish peasants secure tenure on their farms. Yet by far the most influential of the new-style monarchs were in Prussia, Russia, and Austria, and they deserve primary attention.

Frederick the Great of Prussia

Frederick II (r. 1740–1786), commonly known as Frederick the Great, built masterfully on the work of his father, Frederick William I (see page 443). Although in his youth he embraced culture and literature rather than the crude life of the barracks, by the time he came to the throne Frederick was determined to use the splendid army that his father had left him.

Therefore, when Maria Theresa of Austria inherited the Habsburg dominions upon the death of her father Charles VI, Frederick pounced. He invaded her rich, mainly German province of Silesia (si-LEE-zhuh) in violation of the Pragmatic Sanction that had guaranteed her succession. In 1742, as other greedy powers were falling on her lands in the general European War of the Austrian Succession (1740–1748), Maria Theresa was forced to cede almost all of Silesia to Prussia (see Map 17.2 on page 442). In one stroke Prussia had doubled its population to six million people. Now Prussia unquestionably towered above all the other German states and stood as a European Great Power.

Though successful in 1742, Frederick had to spend much of his reign fighting against great odds to save Prussia from total destruction. When the ongoing competition between Britain and France for colonial empire brought another great conflict in 1756 (see page 497), Maria Theresa fashioned an aggressive alliance with the leaders of France and Russia. During the Seven Years' War (1756–1763), the aim of the alliance was to conquer Prussia and divide up its territory. Despite invasions from all sides, Frederick fought on with stoic courage. In the end he was miraculously saved: Peter III came to the Russian throne in 1762 and called off the attack against Frederick, whom he greatly admired.

The terrible struggle of the Seven Years' War tempered Frederick's interest in territorial expansion and brought him to consider how more humane policies for his subjects might also strengthen the state. Thus Frederick went beyond a superficial commitment to Enlightenment culture for himself and his circle. He tolerantly allowed his subjects to believe as they wished in religious and philosophical matters. He promoted the advancement of knowledge, improving his country's schools and permitting scholars to publish their findings. Moreover, Frederick tried to improve the lives of his subjects more directly. As he wrote his friend Voltaire, "I must enlighten my people, cultivate their manners and morals, and make them as happy as human beings can be, or as happy as the means at my disposal permit."

The legal system and the bureaucracy were Frederick's primary tools. Prussia's laws were simplified, torture of prisoners was abolished, and judges decided cases quickly and impartially. Prussian officials became famous for their hard work and honesty. After the Seven Years' War ended in 1763, Frederick's government energetically promoted the reconstruction of agriculture and industry in his war-torn country. Frederick himself set a good example. He worked hard and lived modestly, claiming that he was "only the first servant of the state." Thus Frederick justified monarchy in terms of practical results and said nothing of the divine right of kings.

Frederick's dedication to high-minded government went only so far, however. While he condemned serfdom in the abstract, he accepted it in practice and did not even free the serfs on his own estates. He accepted and extended the privileges of the nobility, who remained the backbone of the army and the entire Prussian state.

Nor did Frederick listen to thinkers like Moses Mendelssohn (MEN-dul-suhn) (1729–1786), who urged that Jews be given freedom and civil rights. (See the feature "Individuals in Society: Moses Mendelssohn and the Jewish Enlightenment.") The vast majority of Jews were confined to tiny, overcrowded ghettos, were

Individuals in Society

Moses Mendelssohn and the Jewish Enlightenment

In 1743 a small, humpbacked Jewish boy with a stammer left his poor parents in Dessau (**DES-ow**) in central Germany and walked eighty miles to Berlin, the capital of Frederick the Great's Prussia. According to one story, when the boy reached the Rosenthaler (**ROH-zuhn-taw-ler**) Gate, the only one through which Jews could pass, he told the inquiring watchman that his name was Moses and that he had come to Berlin "to learn." The watchman laughed and waved him through. "Go Moses, the sea has opened before you."* Embracing the Enlightenment and seeking a revitalization of Jewish religious thought, Moses Mendelssohn did point his people in a new and uncharted direction.

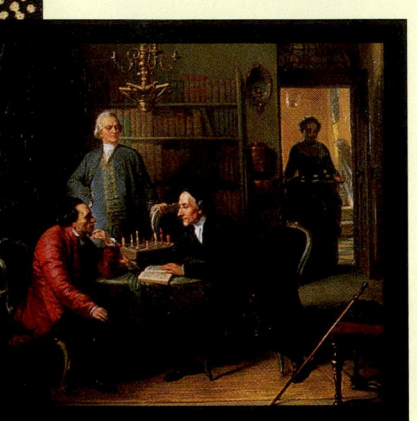

Lavater *(right)* attempts to convert Mendelssohn, in a painting by Moritz Oppenheim of an imaginary encounter. (Collection of the Judah L. Magnes Museum, Berkeley)

In Berlin, the young Mendelssohn turned to a learned rabbi he had previously known in Dessau, studied Jewish law, and eked out a living copying Hebrew manuscripts in a beautiful hand. But he was soon fascinated by an intellectual world that had been closed to him in the Dessau ghetto. There, like most Jews throughout central Europe, he had spoken Yiddish—a mixture of German, Polish, and Hebrew. Now, working mainly on his own, he mastered German; learned Latin, Greek, French, and English; and studied mathematics and Enlightenment philosophy. Word of his exceptional abilities spread in Berlin's Jewish community (1,500 of the city's 100,000 inhabitants). He began tutoring the children of a wealthy Jewish silk merchant, and he soon became the merchant's clerk and later his partner. But his great passion remained the life of the mind and the spirit, which he avidly pursued in his off hours.

Gentle and unassuming in his personal life, Mendelssohn was a bold thinker. Reading eagerly in Western philosophy since antiquity, he was, as a pious Jew, soon convinced that Enlightenment teachings need not be opposed to Jewish thought and religion. Indeed, he concluded that reason could complement and strengthen religion, although each would retain its integrity as a separate sphere.† Developing his idea in his first great work, "On the Immortality of the Soul" (1767), Mendelssohn used the neutral setting of a philosophical dialogue between Socrates and his followers in ancient Greece to argue that the human soul lived forever. In refusing to bring religion and critical thinking into conflict, he was strongly influenced by contemporary German philosophers who argued similarly on behalf of Christianity. He reflected the way the German Enlightenment generally supported established religion, in contrast to the French Enlightenment, which attacked it. This was the most important difference in Enlightenment thinking between the two countries.

Mendelssohn's treatise on the human soul captivated the educated German public, which marveled that a Jew could have written a philosophical masterpiece. In the excitement, a Christian zealot named Lavater challenged Mendelssohn in a pamphlet to accept Christianity or to demonstrate how the Christian faith was not "reasonable." Replying politely but passionately, the Jewish philosopher affirmed that all his studies had only strengthened him in the faith of his fathers, although he certainly did not seek to convert anyone not born into Judaism. Rather, he urged toleration in religious matters. He spoke up courageously for his fellow Jews and decried the oppression they endured, and he continued to do so for the rest of his life.

Orthodox Jew and German philosophe, Moses Mendelssohn serenely combined two very different worlds. He built a bridge from the ghetto to the dominant culture over which many Jews would pass, including his novelist daughter Dorothea and his famous grandson, the composer Felix Mendelssohn.

Questions for Analysis

1. How did Mendelssohn seek to influence Jewish religious thought in his time?
2. How do Mendelssohn's ideas compare with those of the French Enlightenment?

---

* H. Kupferberg, *The Mendelssohns: Three Generations of Genius* (New York: Charles Scribner's Sons, 1972), p. 3.

† D. Sorkin, *Moses Mendelssohn and the Religious Enlightenment* (Berkeley: University of California Press, 1996), pp. 8 ff.

excluded by law from most business and professional activities, and could be ordered out of the kingdom at a moment's notice.

Catherine the Great of Russia

Catherine the Great of Russia (r. 1762–1796) was one of the most remarkable rulers of her age, and the French philosophes adored her. Catherine was a German princess from Anhalt-Zerbst (**AHN-hahlt ZEHR-bst**), a totally insignificant principality sandwiched between Prussia and Saxony. Her father commanded a regiment of the Prussian army, but her mother was related to the Romanovs of Russia, and that proved to be Catherine's chance.

At the age of fifteen she was married to the heir to the Russian throne. When her husband Peter III came to power in 1762, his decision to withdraw Russian troops from the coalition against Prussia alienated the army. At the end of six months Catherine and her conspirators deposed Peter III in a palace revolution, and the Orlov brothers murdered him. The German princess became empress of Russia.

Catherine had drunk deeply at the Enlightenment well. Never questioning the common assumption that absolute monarchy was the best form of government, she set out to rule in an enlightened manner. She had three main goals. First, she worked hard to continue Peter the Great's effort to bring the culture of western Europe to backward Russia. To do so, she imported Western architects,

Catherine the Great as Equestrian and Miniature of Count Grigory Grigoryevich Orlov

Catherine conspired with her lover Count Orlov to overthrow her husband Peter III and became empress of Russia. Strongly influenced by the Enlightenment, she cultivated the French philosophes and instituted moderate reforms, only to reverse them in the aftermath of Pugachev's rebellion. This equestrian portrait now hangs above her throne in the palace throne room. (left: Musée des Beaux-Arts, Chartres/The Bridgeman Art Library; right: State Hermitage Museum, St. Petersburg)

sculptors, musicians, and intellectuals. She bought masterpieces of Western art in wholesale lots and patronized the philosophes. An enthusiastic letter writer, she corresponded extensively with Voltaire and praised him as the "champion of the human race." When the French government banned the *Encyclopedia*, she offered to publish it in St. Petersburg, and she sent money to Diderot when he needed it. With these and countless similar actions, Catherine won good press in the West for herself and for her country. Moreover, this intellectual ruler, who wrote plays and loved good talk, set the tone for the entire Russian nobility. Peter the Great westernized Russian armies, but it was Catherine who Westernized the imagination of the Russian nobility.

Catherine's second goal was domestic reform, and she began her reign with sincere and ambitious projects. Better laws were a major concern. In 1767 she appointed a special legislative commission to prepare a new law code. No new unified code was ever produced, but Catherine did restrict the practice of torture and allowed limited religious toleration. She also tried to improve education and strengthen local government. The philosophes applauded these measures and hoped more would follow.

Such was not the case. In 1773 a common Cossack soldier named Emelian Pugachev (**PEW-gah-chev**) sparked a gigantic uprising of serfs, very much as Stenka Razin had done a century earlier (see page 447). Proclaiming himself the true tsar, Pugachev issued "decrees" abolishing serfdom, taxes, and army service. Thousands joined his cause, slaughtering landlords and officials over a vast area of southwestern Russia. Pugachev's untrained forces eventually proved no match for Catherine's noble-led regular army. Betrayed by his own company, Pugachev was captured and savagely executed.

Pugachev's rebellion put an end to any intentions Catherine might have had about reforming the system. The peasants were clearly dangerous, and her empire rested on the support of the nobility. After 1775 Catherine gave the nobles absolute control of their serfs. She extended serfdom into new areas, such as Ukraine. In 1785 she formalized the nobility's privileged position, freeing nobles forever from taxes and state service. Under Catherine the Russian nobility attained its most exalted position, and serfdom entered its most oppressive phase.

Catherine's third goal was territorial expansion, and in this respect she was extremely successful. Her armies subjugated the last descendants of the Mongols and the Crimean Tartars, and began the conquest of the Caucasus (**KAW-kuh-suhs**). Her greatest coup by far was the partition of Poland (see Map 18.1). When, between 1768 and 1772, Catherine's armies scored unprecedented victories against the Turks and thereby threatened to disturb the balance of power between Russia and Austria in eastern Europe, Frederick of Prussia obligingly came forward with a deal. He proposed that Turkey be let off easily and that Prussia, Austria, and Russia each compensate itself by taking a gigantic slice of the weakly ruled Polish territory. Catherine jumped at the chance. The first partition of Poland took place in 1772. Two more partitions, in 1793 and 1795, gave all three powers more Polish territory, and the ancient republic of Poland vanished from the map.

The Austrian Habsburgs

In Austria two talented rulers did manage to introduce major reforms, although traditional power politics was more important than Enlightenment teachings. One was the empress Maria Theresa (1740–1780), a remarkable but old-fashioned absolutist. The other was her son, Joseph II (r. 1780–1790), a fascinating individual.

MAPPING THE PAST

MAP 18.1   The Partition of Poland and Russia's Expansion, 1772–1795

By 1700 Poland had become a weak and decentralized republic with an elected king. All important decisions continued to require the unanimous agreement of all nobles elected to the Polish Diet, which meant that nothing could ever be done to strengthen the state. In 1772 war threatened between Russia and Austria over Russian gains from the Ottoman Empire. To satisfy desires for expansion without fighting, Prussia's Frederick the Great proposed that parts of Poland be divided among Austria, Prussia, and Russia. In 1793 and 1795 the three powers partitioned the remainder of the country. **[1]** Why was Poland vulnerable to partition in the latter half of the eighteenth century? What does it say about European politics at the time that a country could simply cease to exist on the map? Could that happen today? **[2]** Of the three powers that divided the kingdom of Poland, which benefited the most? How did the partition affect the geographical boundaries of each state, and what was the significance? **[3]** Which border with the former Poland remained unchanged? Why do you think this was the case?

For an earlier generation of historians, he was the "revolutionary emperor," a tragic hero whose lofty reforms were undone by the landowning nobility he dared to challenge. More recent scholarship has revised this romantic interpretation and has stressed how Joseph II continued the state-building work of his mother.

Emerging from the long War of the Austrian Succession in 1748 with the serious loss of Silesia, Maria Theresa and her closest ministers were determined to introduce reforms that would make the state stronger and more efficient. Three aspects of these reforms were most important. First, Maria Theresa introduced measures aimed at limiting the papacy's political influence in her realm. Second,

Section Review

- Frederick the Great of Prussia struggled militarily during the Seven Years' War but also promoted Enlightenment policies to improve the lives of his subjects.

- Moses Mendelssohn, an orthodox Jew and German philosophe who believed reason and religion could strengthen each other, promoted religious toleration and received the admiration of the educated German public.

- Catherine the Great of Russia enjoyed Enlightenment ideas and hosted Western intellectuals and artists while attempting domestic reform, but after a peasant-led revolt, instead increased the power of the nobility.

- Catherine focused on territorial expansion, defeating the Turks and accepting the division of Polish territory between Russia, Austria, and Prussia.

- Maria Theresa enacted Enlightenment policies to limit papal influence, strengthen bureaucracy, and improve conditions for the peasants.

- Her son Joseph II went further and abolished serfdom in favor of cash payments, but both the nobles and the peasants rejected his reforms and his brother and successor Leopold II re-established serfdom.

a whole series of administrative reforms strengthened the central bureaucracy, smoothed out some provincial differences, and revamped the tax system, taxing even the lands of nobles without special exemptions. Third, the government sought to improve the lot of the agricultural population, cautiously reducing the power of lords over their hereditary serfs and their partially free peasant tenants.

Coregent with his mother from 1765 onward and a strong supporter of change, Joseph II moved forward rapidly when he came to the throne in 1780. Most notably, Joseph abolished serfdom in 1781, and in 1789 he decreed that all peasant labor obligations be converted into cash payments. This measure was violently rejected not only by the nobility but also by the peasants it was intended to help, because they lacked the necessary cash. When a disillusioned Joseph died prematurely at forty-nine, the entire Habsburg empire was in turmoil. His brother Leopold II (r. 1790–1792) canceled Joseph's radical edicts in order to re-establish order. Peasants once again were required to do forced labor for their lords.

The eastern European absolutists of the later eighteenth century combined old-fashioned state-building with the culture and critical thinking of the Enlightenment. In doing so, they succeeded in expanding the role of the state in the life of society. They perfected bureaucratic machines that were to prove surprisingly adaptive and capable of enduring into the twentieth century. Their failure to implement policies we would recognize as humane and enlightened—such as abolishing serfdom—may reveal inherent limitations in Enlightenment thinking about equality and social justice, rather than in their execution of an Enlightenment program. The fact that leading philosophes supported rather than criticized Eastern rulers' policies suggests some of the blinders of the era.

Chapter Review

| What was revolutionary in the new attitudes toward the natural world? (page 459)

| Decisive breakthroughs in astronomy and physics in the seventeenth century demolished the imposing medieval synthesis of Aristotelian philosophy and Christian theology. These developments had only limited practical consequences at the time, but the impact of new scientific knowledge on intellectual life was enormous. The emergence of modern science was a distinctive characteristic of Western civilization and became a key element of Western identity. During the eighteenth century scientific thought fostered new ideas about racial differences and provided justifications for belief in Western superiority.

| How did the new worldview affect the way people thought about society and human relations? (page 466)

| Interpreting scientific findings and Newtonian laws in a manner that was both anti-tradition and antireligion, Enlightenment philosophes extolled the superiority of rational, critical thinking. This new method, they believed, promised not just increased knowledge but even the discovery of the fundamental laws of human society. Although

Key Terms

natural philosophy (p. 459)

Copernican hypothesis (p. 460)

experimental method (p. 461)

law of inertia (p. 461)

law of universal gravitation (p. 463)

empiricism (p. 464)

Cartesian dualism (p. 464)

scientific community (p. 464)

Enlightenment (p. 466)

rationalism (p. 466)

skepticism (p. 466)

tabula rasa (p. 467)

they reached different conclusions when they turned to social and political realities, they did stimulate absolute monarchs to apply reason to statecraft and the search for useful reforms. Above all, the philosophes succeeded in shaping an emerging public opinion and spreading their radically new worldview.

| philosophes (p. 467) |
| separation of powers (p. 468) |
| reading revolution (p. 470) |
| salons (p. 471) |
| rococo (p. 472) |
| public sphere (p. 472) |
| general will (p. 473) |
| enlightened absolutism (p. 474) |

What impact did this new way of thinking have on political developments and monarchical absolutism? (page 474)

The ideas of the Enlightenment were an inspiration for monarchs, particularly absolutist rulers in central and eastern Europe who saw in them important tools for reforming and rationalizing their governments. Their primary goal was to strengthen their states and increase the efficiency of their bureaucracies and armies. Enlightened absolutists believed that these reforms would ultimately improve the lot of ordinary people, but this was not their chief concern. With few exceptions, they did not question the institution of serfdom. The fact that leading philosophes supported rather than criticized Eastern rulers' policies suggests some of the limitations of the era.

Notes

1. H. Butterfield, *The Origins of Modern Science* (New York: Macmillan, 1951), p. viii.
2. Quoted in A. G. R. Smith, *Science and Society in the Sixteenth and Seventeenth Centuries* (New York: Harcourt Brace Jovanovich, 1972), p. 97.
3. Quoted in Butterfield, *The Origins of Modern Science*, p. 47.
4. Ibid., p. 120.
5. L. Schiebinger, *The Mind Has No Sex? Women in the Origins of Modern Science* (Cambridge, Mass.: Harvard University Press, 1989), p. 2.
6. Jacqueline Broad, *Women Philosophers of the Seventeenth Century* (Cambridge: Cambridge University Press, 2003), p. 17.
7. Schiebinger, *The Mind Has No Sex?* p. 64.
8. Quoted in L. M. Marsak, ed., *The Enlightenment* (New York: John Wiley & Sons, 1972), p. 56.
9. Quoted in G. L. Mosse et al., eds., *Europe in Review* (Chicago: Rand McNally, 1964), p. 156.
10. Quoted in P. Gay, "The Unity of the Enlightenment," *History* 3 (1960): 25.
11. Quoted in G. P. Gooch, *Catherine the Great and Other Studies* (Hamden, Conn.: Archon Books, 1966), p. 149.
12. See E. Fox-Genovese, "Women in the Enlightenment," in *Becoming Visible: Women in European History*, 2d ed., ed. R. Bridenthal, C. Koonz, and S. Stuard (Boston: Houghton Mifflin, 1987), esp. pp. 252–259, 263–265.
13. Jean Le Rond d'Alembert, *Eloges lus dans les séances publiques de l'Académie française* (Paris, 1779), p. ix, quoted in Mona Ozouf, "'Public Opinion' at the End of the Old Regime," *The Journal of Modern History* 60, Supplement: *Rethinking French Politics in 1788* (September 1988), p. S9.

To assess your mastery of this chapter, go to **bedfordstmartins.com/mckaywestbrief**

Listening to the Past

Voltaire on Religion

Voltaire was the most renowned and probably the most influential of the French philosophes. His biting satirical novel Candide *(1759) is still widely assigned in college courses, and his witty yet serious* Philosophical Dictionary *remains a source of pleasure and stimulation. The Dictionary consists of a series of essays on topics ranging from Adam to Zoroaster, from certainty to circumcision. The following passage is taken from the essay on religion. In it Voltaire describes being deep in meditation when a genie transported him to a desert filled with the bones of those who had been killed because of their religious practices or beliefs. The genie then led him to the "heroes of humanity, who tried to banish violence and plunder from the world."*

An impish Voltaire, by the French sculptor Houdon. (Courtesy of Board of Trustees of the Victoria & Albert Museum)

[At last] I saw a man with a gentle, simple face, who seemed to me to be about thirty-five years old. From afar he looked with compassion upon those piles of whitened bones, through which I had been led to reach the sage's dwelling place. I was astonished to find his feet swollen and bleeding, his hands likewise, his side pierced, and his ribs laid bare by the cut of the lash. "Good God!" I said to him, "is it possible for a just man, a sage, to be in this state? I have just seen one who was treated in a very hateful way, but there is no comparison between his torture and yours. Wicked priests and wicked judges poisoned him; is it by priests and judges that you were so cruelly assassinated?"

With great courtesy he answered, "Yes."

"And who were these monsters?"

"They were hypocrites."

"Ah! that says everything; I understand by that one word that they would have condemned you to the cruelest punishment. Had you then proved to them, as Socrates did, that the Moon was not a goddess, and that Mercury was not a god?"

"No, it was not a question of planets. My countrymen did not even know what a planet was; they were all arrant ignoramuses. Their superstitions were quite different from those of the Greeks."

"Then you wanted to teach them a new religion?"

"Not at all; I told them simply: 'Love God with all your heart and your neighbor as yourself, for that is the whole of mankind's duty.' Judge yourself if this precept is not as old as the universe; judge yourself if I brought them a new religion." . . .

"But did you say nothing, do nothing that could serve them as a pretext?"

"To the wicked everything serves as pretext."

"Did you not say once that you were come not to bring peace, but a sword?"

"It was a scribe's error; I told them that I brought peace and not a sword. I never wrote anything; what I said can have been changed without evil intention."

"You did not then contribute in any way by your teaching, either badly reported or badly interpreted, to those frightful piles of bones which I saw on my way to consult with you?"

"I have only looked with horror upon those who have made themselves guilty of all these murders."

. . . [Finally] I asked him to tell me in what true religion consisted.

"Have I not already told you? Love God and your neighbor as yourself."

"Is it necessary for me to take sides either for the Greek Orthodox Church or the Roman Catholic?"

"When I was in the world I never made any difference between the Jew and the Samaritan."

"Well, if that is so, I take you for my only master." Then he made a sign with his head that filled me with peace. The vision disappeared, and I was left with a clear conscience.

Questions for Analysis

1. Who is the man that Voltaire meets in this passage? Why did the writer decide to leave this person unnamed?

2. What is Voltaire's message?

3. If a person today thought and wrote like Voltaire, would that person be called a defender or a destroyer of Christianity? Why?

Source: F. M. Arouet de Voltaire, *Oeuvres complètes*, vol. 8, trans. J. McKay (Paris: Firmin-Didot, 1875), pp. 188–190.

CHAPTER 19

The Expansion of Europe in the Eighteenth Century

Chapter Preview

Agriculture and the Land
What were the causes and effects of the agricultural revolution, and what nations led the way in these developments?

The Beginning of the Population Explosion
Why did European population rise dramatically in the eighteenth century?

Cottage Industry and Urban Guilds
What is cottage industry, and how did it contribute to Europe's economic and social transformation?

Building the Global Economy
How did colonial markets boost Europe's economic and social development, and what conflicts and adversity did world trade entail?

INDIVIDUALS IN SOCIETY: Olaudah Equiano

IMAGES IN SOCIETY: London: The Remaking of a Great City

LISTENING TO THE PAST: The Debate over the Guilds

The East India Dock, London (detail), by Samuel Scott, a painting infused with the spirit of maritime expansion. (© Board of Trustees of the Victoria & Albert Museum)

The world of absolutism and aristocracy, a combination of raw power and elegant refinement, was a world apart from that of the common people. For most people in the eighteenth century, life remained a struggle with poverty and uncertainty, with the landlord and the tax collector. In 1700 peasants on the land and artisans in their shops lived little better than their ancestors had in the Middle Ages. Only in science and thought, and there only among intellectual elites and their followers, had Western society succeeded in going beyond the great achievements of the High Middle Ages, achievements that in turn owed much to Greece and Rome.

Everyday life was a struggle because European societies still could not produce very much by modern standards. Ordinary men and women might work like their beasts in the fields, but there was seldom enough good food, warm clothing, and decent housing. Life went on; history went on. The wars of religion ravaged Germany in the seventeenth century; Russia rose to become a Great Power; the state of Poland disappeared; monarchs and nobles continually jockeyed for power and wealth. In 1700 the idea of progress, of substantial and ongoing improvement in the lives of great numbers of people, was still the dream of a small elite in fashionable salons.

Yet the economic basis of European life was beginning to change. In the course of the eighteenth century the European economy emerged from the long crisis of the seventeenth century, responded to challenges, and began to expand once again. Population resumed its growth, while colonial empires developed and colonial elites prospered. Some areas were more fortunate than others. The rising Atlantic powers—Holland, France, and above all England—and their colonies led the way. The expansion of agriculture, industry, trade, and population marked the beginning of a surge comparable to that of the eleventh- and twelfth-century springtime of European civilization. But this time, broadly based expansion was not cut short. This time the response to new challenges led toward one of the most influential developments in human history, the Industrial Revolution, considered in Chapter 22.

Agriculture and the Land

What were the causes and effects of the agricultural revolution, and what nations led the way in these developments?

At the end of the seventeenth century the economy of Europe was agrarian. With the possible exception of Holland, at least 80 percent of the people of all western European countries drew their livelihoods from agriculture. In eastern Europe the percentage was considerably higher. Yet even in a rich agricultural region such as the Po Valley in northern Italy, every bushel of wheat sown yielded on average only five or six bushels of grain at harvest. By modern standards output was distressingly low.

In most regions of Europe in the sixteenth and seventeenth centuries, climatic conditions produced poor or disastrous harvests every eight or nine years. Unbalanced and inadequate food in famine years made people extremely susceptible to illnesses such as influenza and smallpox. In famine years the number of deaths soared far above normal. A third of a village's population might disappear in a year or two. But new developments in agricultural technology and methods gradually brought an end to the ravages of hunger in western Europe.

The Agricultural Revolution

One way for European peasants to improve their difficult position was to take land from those who owned it but did no labor. Yet the social and political conditions that sustained the ruling elites were ancient and deeply rooted, and powerful forces stood ready to crush protest. Only with the coming of the French Revolution were European peasants, mainly in France, able to improve their position by means of radical mass action.

Technological progress offered another possibility. If peasants (and their noble landlords) could eliminate the need to leave part of the land fallow, or unplanted, in order to restore fertility to the soil, they could greatly increase the land under cultivation. So remarkable were the possibilities and the results that historians have often spoken of the progressive elimination of the fallow, which occurred gradually throughout Europe from the mid-seventeenth century on, as an **agricultural revolution.** This revolution, which took longer than historians used to believe, was a great milestone in human development.

Because grain crops exhaust the soil and make fallowing necessary, the secret to eliminating the fallow lies in alternating grain with nitrogen-storing crops. The most important of these soil-reviving crops are peas and beans, root crops such as turnips and potatoes, and clovers and grasses. As the eighteenth century went on, the number of crops that were systematically rotated grew. New patterns of organization allowed some farmers to develop increasingly sophisticated patterns of **crop rotation** to suit different kinds of soils. For example, farmers in French Flanders near Lille in the late eighteenth century used a ten-year rotation, alternating a number of grain, root, and hay crops in a given field on a ten-year schedule. Continual experimentation led to more scientific farming.

Improvements in farming had multiple effects. The new crops made ideal feed for animals, and because peasants and larger farmers had more fodder, hay, and root crops for the winter months, they could build up their herds of cattle and sheep. More animals meant more meat and better diets. More animals also meant more manure for fertilizer and therefore more grain for bread and porridge.

Advocates of the new crop rotations, who included an emerging group of experimental scientists, some government officials, and a few big landowners, believed that new methods were scarcely possible within the traditional framework of open fields and common rights. A farmer who wanted to experiment with new methods would have to get all the landholders in a village to agree to the plan. Advocates of improvement argued that innovating agriculturalists needed to enclose and consolidate their scattered holdings into compact, fenced-in fields in order to farm more effectively. In doing so, the innovators also needed to enclose their individual shares of the natural pasture, the common. According to proponents of this movement, known as **enclosure,**

agricultural revolution The period in Europe from the mid-seventeenth century on, during which great agricultural progress was made and the fallow was gradually eliminated.

crop rotation The system by which farmers rotated the types of crops grown in each field so as to replenish the soil of its natural resources.

enclosure The movement to fence in fields in order to farm more effectively.

Enclosure in Streatley, Berkshire County, England

This map shows the results of enclosure in early-nineteenth-century Streatley, a village ten miles west of Reading on the River Thames. The area marked in yellow was the enclosed territory, appropriated mostly by a few large landowners and the city of Reading. The legend provides a detailed list of land ownership, including references to "old inclosures." (Courtesy, Berkshire Record Office, Ref # Streatley (1817), MRI 256)

a revolution in village life and organization was the necessary price of technical progress.

That price seemed too high to many poor rural people who had small, inadequate holdings or very little land at all. Traditional rights were precious to these poor peasants. They used commonly held pastureland to graze livestock, and marsh or moor lands outside the village as a source for firewood, berries, and other foraged goods that could make the difference between survival and famine in harsh times. Thus when the small landholders and the village poor could effectively oppose the enclosure of the open fields and the common lands, they did so. Moreover, in many countries they found allies among the larger, predominately noble landowners who were also wary of enclosure because it required large investments and posed risks for them as well.

The old system of unenclosed fields and the new system of continuous rotation coexisted in Europe for a long time. Open fields could be found in much of France and Germany in the early years of the nineteenth century because peasants there had successfully opposed efforts to introduce the new techniques in the late eighteenth century. Until the end of the eighteenth century, the new system was extensively adopted only in the Low Countries and England.

CHRONOLOGY

ca. 1650–1790	Growth of Atlantic economy
ca. 1650–1850	Agricultural improvement and revolution
1651–1663	British Navigation Acts
1652–1674	Anglo-Dutch wars; rise of British mercantilism
ca. 1690–1790	Enlightenment
1700–1790	Height of Atlantic slave trade; expansion of rural industry in Europe
1701–1713	War of the Spanish Succession
1701–1763	Mercantilist wars of empire
1720–1722	Last of bubonic plague in Europe
1720–1789	Growth of European population
1740–1748	War of the Austrian Succession
1750–1790	Rise of economic liberalism
1756–1763	Seven Years' War
1759	Fall of Quebec
1760–1815	Height of parliamentary enclosure in England
1776	Smith, *Wealth of Nations*
1807	British slave trade abolished

The Leadership of the Low Countries and England

The new methods of the agricultural revolution originated in the Low Countries. One reason for early Dutch leadership in farming was that the area was one of the most densely populated in Europe. The Dutch were forced at an early date to seek maximum yields from their land and to increase the cultivated area through the steady draining of marshes and swamps. As the urban population of Amsterdam grew with its rise as an international trading hub, Dutch peasants found a huge market for their surplus crops. Each agricultural region specialized in what it did best. Thus the Low Countries became "the Mecca of foreign agricultural experts who came . . . to see Flemish agriculture with their own eyes, to write about it and to propagate its methods in their home lands."[1]

The English were the best students. In the first half of the seventeenth century Dutch experts made a great contribution to draining the extensive marshes, or fens, of wet and rainy England. Swampy wilderness was converted into thousands of acres of some of the most fertile land in England.

Jethro Tull (1674–1741), part crank and part genius, was an important English innovator. A true son of the early Enlightenment, Tull adopted a critical attitude toward accepted ideas about farming and tried to develop better methods through empirical research. He was especially enthusiastic about using horses, rather than slower-moving oxen, for plowing. He also advocated sowing seed with drilling equipment rather than scattering it by hand. Drilling distributed seed in an even manner and at the proper depth. Selective breeding of ordinary livestock was another marked improvement over the haphazard old pattern.

By the mid-eighteenth century English agriculture was in the process of a long but radical transformation. The eventual result was that by 1870 English farmers

proletarianization The transformation of large numbers of small peasant farmers into landless rural wage earners.

Section Review

- European economies were agrarian; low crop yields in years of poor climate resulted in famine, disease, and death.

- The agricultural revolution involved the gradual elimination of the practice of leaving land fallow and the development of crop rotation patterns that allowed crops to restore nutrients to the soil.

- Enclosure meant fencing in fields to farm more effectively, but most peasants opposed it and only the Low Countries and England used it extensively.

- Enclosure and the new methods of farming increased production but led to an estate agricultural system and proletarianization, changing peasant farmers into landless laborers.

were producing 300 percent more food than they had produced in 1700, although the number of people working the land had increased by only 14 percent. This great surge of agricultural production provided food for England's rapidly growing urban population. Growth in production was achieved in part by land enclosures. About half the farmland in England was enclosed through private initiatives prior to 1700; in the eighteenth century, a series of acts of Parliament enclosed most of the remaining common land.

The eighteenth-century enclosure movement marked the completion of two major historical developments in England—the rise of market-oriented estate agriculture and the emergence of a landless rural proletariat. By 1815 a tiny minority of wealthy English (and Scottish) landowners held most of the land and pursued profits aggressively, leasing their holdings to middle-sized farmers, who relied on landless laborers for their workforce. These landless laborers usually worked from dawn to dusk, six days a week, all year long. Moreover, landless laborers had lost that bit of independence and self-respect that common rights had provided and were completely dependent on cash wages. In no other European country had this **proletarianization** (proh-le-TAIR-ee-uh-nize-ay-shun)—this transformation of large numbers of small peasant farmers into landless rural wage earners—gone so far. And England's village poor found the cost of change heavy and unjust.

The Beginning of the Population Explosion

Why did European population rise dramatically in the eighteenth century?

Another factor that affected the existing order of life and forced economic changes in the eighteenth century was the beginning of the "population explosion." Explosive growth continued in Europe until the twentieth century, by which time it was affecting non-Western areas of the globe. What were the causes of this new population growth?

A common misperception holds that the population of Europe was always rising quickly. On the contrary, until 1700 the total population of Europe grew slowly much of the time, and it followed an irregular cyclical pattern (see Figure 19.1). The population dipped after 1350 as a result of the Black Death and, after recovering, population growth slowed and dipped again in the seventeenth century. Famine, epidemic disease, and war ravaged Europe during that century, as we have seen. There were, of course, some exceptions. Areas such as Russia and colonial New England, where there was a great deal of frontier to be settled, experienced population growth.

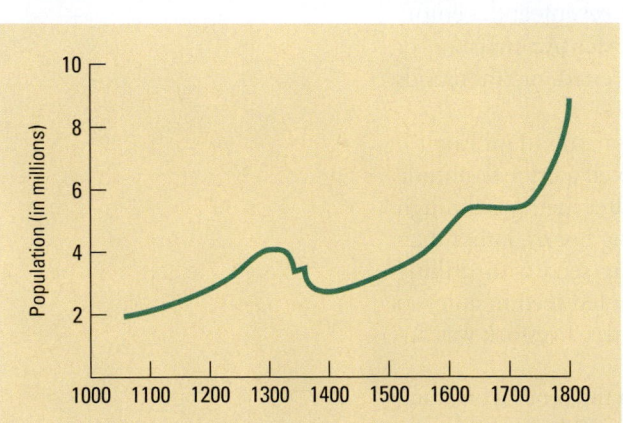

FIGURE 19.1 The Growth of Population in England, 1000–1800

England is a good example of both the uneven increase of European population before 1700 and the third great surge of growth, which began in the eighteenth century. (*Source:* "Long-Term Population Trends in England and Wales, 1000–1800," from E. A. Wrigley, *Population and History.* Copyright © 1969. Reprinted by permission of the author.)

In the eighteenth century the population of Europe began to grow markedly. This increase in numbers occurred in all areas of Europe, western and eastern, northern and southern, dynamic and stagnant. Growth was especially dramatic after about 1750 (see Figure 19.2).

What caused this population growth? In some areas women had more babies than before because new opportunities for employment in rural industry allowed them to marry at an earlier age. But the basic cause for Europe as a whole was a decline in mortality—fewer deaths.

The bubonic plague mysteriously disappeared. Following the Black Death in the fourteenth century, plagues had remained part of the European experience, striking again and again with savage force, particularly in towns. As late as 1720 a ship from Syria and the Levant brought the disease to Marseilles, killing up to one hundred thousand in the city and surrounding region. By 1722 the epidemic had passed, and that was the last time plague fell on western and central Europe. Exactly why plague disappeared is unknown. Stricter measures of quarantine in Mediterranean ports and along the Austrian border with Turkey helped by carefully isolating human carriers of plague. Chance and plain good luck were probably just as important.

Advances in medical knowledge did not contribute much to reducing the death rate in the eighteenth century. The most important advance in preventive medicine in this period was inoculation against smallpox, and this great improvement was long confined mainly to England, probably doing little to reduce deaths throughout Europe until the latter part of the century. However, improvements in the water supply and sewerage, which were frequently promoted by strong absolutist monarchies, resulted in somewhat better public health and helped reduce such diseases as typhoid and typhus in some urban areas of western Europe. Improvements in water supply and the drainage of swamps also reduced Europe's large insect population. Flies and mosquitoes played a major role in spreading diseases, especially those striking children and young adults. Thus early public health measures helped the decline in mortality that began with the disappearance of plague and continued into the early nineteenth century.

Human beings also became more successful in their efforts to safeguard the supply of food. The eighteenth century was a time of considerable canal and road building in western Europe. These advances in transportation, which were also among the more positive aspects of strong absolutist states, lessened the impact of local crop failure and famine. Emergency supplies could be brought in, and localized starvation became less frequent. Wars became more gentlemanly and less destructive than in the seventeenth century and spread fewer epidemics. New foods, particularly the potato from South America, were introduced. In short, population grew in the eighteenth century primarily because years of abnormal death rates were less catastrophic. Famines, epidemics, and wars continued to occur, but their severity moderated.

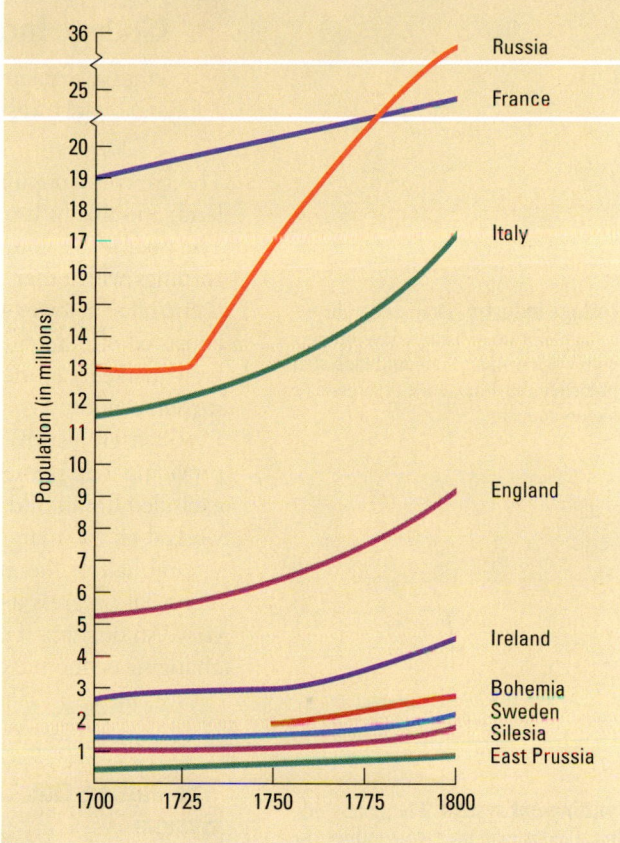

FIGURE 19.2   The Increase of Population in Europe in the Eighteenth Century

France's large population continued to support French political and intellectual leadership. Russia emerged as Europe's most populous state because natural increase was complemented by growth from territorial expansion.

Section Review

- The European population fell in the seventeenth century from famine, disease, and war, but in the eighteenth century it began to grow steadily, primarily due to a decline in mortality.

- The disappearance of epidemic disease and improvements in water supply and sewerage contributed to improved public health.

- Swamp drainage decreased the insect population and thus the diseases they caused; improved methods of food storage and transportation as well as less destructive warfare meant fewer deaths.

Cottage Industry and Urban Guilds

What is cottage industry, and how did it contribute to Europe's economic and social transformation?

cottage industry Domestic industry; a stage of rural industrial development with wage workers and hand tools that preceded the emergence of large-scale factory industry.

The growth of population increased the number of rural workers with little or no land, and this in turn contributed to the development of industry in rural areas. The poor in the countryside increasingly needed to supplement their agricultural earnings with other types of work, and urban capitalists were eager to employ them, often at lower wages than urban workers were paid. **Cottage industry,** which consisted of manufacturing with hand tools in peasant cottages and work sheds, grew markedly in the eighteenth century and became a crucial feature of the European economy.

Craft guilds (**gildz**) continued to dominate production in towns and cities, providing their masters with economic privileges as well as a social identity. Those excluded from guild membership—women, day laborers, Jews, and foreigners—worked on the margins of the urban economy. Critics attacked the guilds in the second half of the eighteenth century as outmoded institutions that obstructed technical progress and innovation. Until recently, most historians repeated that view. An ongoing reassessment of guilds now emphasizes their ability to adapt to changing economic circumstances.

putting-out system The system of rural industry in the eighteenth century in which a merchant loaned raw materials to cottage workers who processed them and returned the finished products to the merchant.

The Putting-Out System

Cottage industry was often organized through the **putting-out system.** The two main participants in the putting-out system were the merchant capitalist and the rural worker. The merchant loaned, or "put out," raw materials to cottage workers who processed the raw materials in their own homes and returned the finished products to the merchant. There were many variations on this basic relationship. Sometimes rural workers bought their own raw materials and worked as independent producers before they sold to the merchant. Sometimes whole families were involved in domestic industry; at other times the tasks were closely associated with one gender. Sometimes several workers toiled together to perform a complicated process in a workshop outside the home.

As industries grew in scale and complexity, production was often broken into many stages. For example, a merchant would provide raw wool to one group of workers for spinning into thread. He would then pass the thread to another group of workers to be bleached, to another for dying, and to another for weaving into cloth. The merchant paid outworkers by the piece and proceeded to sell the finished product to regional, national, or international markets.

The putting-out system grew because it had competitive advantages. Labor costs were cheaper in the countryside, where underemployed peasants were willing to work for less than their guild counterparts. Because they did not operate within guild guidelines, merchants and workers were able to experiment with procedures as they saw fit. While the goods that non-guild workers produced were not of exceptional quality, they were acceptable for everyday use. Textiles; all manner of knives, forks, and housewares; buttons and gloves; and clocks could be produced quite satisfactorily in the countryside.

Rural manufacturing did not spread across Europe at an even rate. It developed most successfully in England, particularly for the spinning and weaving of woolen cloth. By 1500 half of England's textiles were being produced in the countryside. By 1700 English industry was generally more rural than urban and heavily reliant on the putting-out system. Most continental countries, with the exception of Flanders and the Netherlands, developed rural industry more slowly. The latter part of the eighteenth century witnessed a remarkable expansion of rural industry in certain densely populated regions of continental Europe (see Map 19.1).

The Textile Industry

Until the nineteenth century, the industry that employed the most people in Europe was textiles. The making of linen, woolen, and eventually cotton cloth was the typical activity of cottage workers engaged in the putting-out system. A look inside the cottage of the English weaver illustrates a way of life as well as an economic system.

MAPPING THE PAST

MAP 19.1   Industry and Population in Eighteenth-Century Europe

The growth of cottage manufacturing in rural areas helped country people increase their income and contributed to population growth. The putting-out system began in England, and much of the work was in the textile industry. Cottage industry was also strong in the Low Countries—modern-day Belgium and Holland. **[1]** What types of textiles were produced in Europe? How would you account for the distribution of each type of cloth across Europe? **[2]** What was the relationship between population density and the growth of textile production? Was this a fixed or variable relationship? What geographic characteristics seem to have played a role in encouraging this industry? **[3]** Did metal production draw on different demographic and geographic conditions? Why do you think this was the case?

The Weaver's Repose
This painting by Decker Cornelis Gerritz (1594–1637) captures the pleasure of release from long hours of toil in cottage industry. The loom realistically dominates the cramped living space and the family's modest possessions. (Musées Royaux des Beaux-Arts, Brussels. Copyright A.C.I.)

The rural worker lived in a small cottage with tiny windows and little space. Indeed, the worker's cottage was often a single room that served as workshop, kitchen, and bedroom. There were only a few pieces of furniture, of which the weaver's loom was by far the largest and most important.

Handloom weaving was a family enterprise. All members of the family helped in the work, so that "every person from seven to eighty (who retained their sight and who could move their hands) could earn their bread," as one eighteenth-century English observer put it.[2] Operating the loom was considered a man's job, reserved for the male head of the family. Women and children worked at auxiliary tasks, such as winding threads on bobbins and mounting the threads on the frame.

There was always a serious imbalance in textile manufacture before mechanization: the work of four or five spinners was needed to keep one weaver steadily employed. Since the weaver's family usually could not produce enough thread, alternate sources of labor were needed. Merchants turned to the wives and daughters of agricultural workers, who took on spinning work in their spare time. Many widows and single women also became "spinsters," so many in fact that the word became a synonym for an unmarried woman. (In other parts of Europe, such as the Rhineland, spinning employed whole families and was not reserved for women.) As the industry expanded and merchants covered ever greater distances in search of workers, they sometimes turned to local shopkeepers to manage the spinners in their villages.

Conditions were particularly hard for female workers. While men could earn decent wages through long hours of arduous labor, women's wages were always terribly low. In the Yorkshire wool industry, a male wool comber earned a good wage of twelve shillings or more a week, while a spinner could hope for only three-and-a-half shillings.[3] A single or widowed spinner faced a desperate struggle against poverty. Any period of illness or unemployment could spell disaster for her and any dependent children.

Relations between workers and employers were often marked by sharp conflict. There were constant disputes over the weights of materials and the quality of finished work. Moreover, the pace of work depended on the agricultural calendar. In spring and late summer, planting and haymaking occupied all hands in the rural village, leading to shortages in the supply of thread. Merchants, whose livelihood depended on their ability to meet orders on time, bitterly resented their lack of control over rural labor. They accused workers—especially female spinners—of laziness, intemperance, and immorality. If workers failed to produce enough thread, they reasoned, it must be because their wages were too high and they had little incentive to work. Merchants thus insisted on maintaining the lowest possible wages to force the "idle" poor into productive labor. They also successfully lobbied for new police powers over workers. Imprisonment and public whipping became common punishments for pilfering small amounts of yarn or cloth. For poor workers, their right to hold onto the bits and pieces left over in the production process was akin to the traditional peasant right of gleaning in common lands.

Urban Guilds

The high point of the **guild system** in most of Europe occurred in the seventeenth and eighteenth centuries, rather than in the High Middle Ages as previously believed. Guilds grew in number in cities and towns across Europe during this period. In Louis XIV's France, for example, finance minister Jean-Baptiste Colbert revived the urban guilds and used them to encourage high-quality production and to collect taxes. The number of guilds in the city of Paris grew from 60 in 1672 to 129 in 1691.

Guild masters occupied the summit of the world of work. Each guild received a detailed set of privileges from the Crown, including exclusive rights to produce and sell certain goods, access to restricted markets in raw materials, and the rights to train apprentices, hire workers, and open shops. Any individual who violated these monopolies could be prosecuted. Guilds also served social and religious functions, providing a locus of sociability and group identity to the urban middle class.

To ensure that there was enough work to go around, guilds jealously restricted their membership to local men who were good Christians, had several years of work experience, paid stiff membership fees, and completed a masterpiece. They also favored family connections. A master's sons enjoyed automatic access to their father's guild, while outsiders were often barred from entering. In the 1720s, Parisian guild masters numbered only about thirty-five thousand in a population of five hundred thousand. Most men and women worked in non-guild trades, as domestic servants, as manual laborers, and as vendors of food and other small goods.

Critics of guilds in France derided them as outmoded and exclusionary institutions that obstructed technical innovation and progress. Indeed, French guilds were abolished by the Revolution of the late eighteenth century. (See the feature "Listening to the Past: The Debate over the Guilds" on pages 508–509.) Many historians have repeated that charge. More recent scholarship, however, has emphasized the flexibility and adaptability of the guild system and its vitality through the eighteenth century. Guild masters adopted new technologies and found creative ways to circumvent impractical rules. For many merchants and artisans, economic regulation did not hinder commerce but instead fostered the confidence necessary to stimulate it. In an economy where buyers' and sellers' access to information was so limited, regulation helped each side trust in the other's good faith.

During the eighteenth century some guilds grew more accessible to women. This was particularly the case in dressmaking; given the great increase in textile production, more hands were needed to fashion clothing for urban elites. In 1675 Colbert granted seamstresses a new all-female guild in Paris, and soon seamstresses joined tailors' guilds in parts of France, England, and the Netherlands. In the late seventeenth century new vocational training programs were established for poor girls in many European cities, mostly in needlework. There is also evidence that

guild system The organization of artisanal production into trade-based associations, or guilds, each of which received a monopoly over their trade and the right to train apprentices and hire workers; the system was abolished in France in 1791 but persisted into the nineteenth century in other parts of Europe.

The Linen Industry in Ireland
Many steps went into making textiles. Here the women are beating away the woody part of the flax plant so that the man can comb out the soft part. The combed fibers will then be spun into thread and woven into cloth by this family enterprise. The increased labor of women and girls in the late seventeenth century helped produce an "industrious revolution." (Victoria and Albert Museum London/Eileen Tweedy/The Art Archive)

industrious revolution The shift that occurred as families in northwestern Europe worked harder and longer hours and focused on earning wages instead of producing goods for household consumption, especially among women and children; this reduced families' economic self-sufficiency but increased their ability to purchase consumer goods.

more women were hired as skilled workers by male guilds, often in defiance of official statutes.

While many artisans welcomed the economic liberalization that followed the French Revolution, some continued to espouse the ideals of the guilds. Because they had always been semi-clandestine, journeymen's associations frequently survived into the nineteenth century. They espoused the values of hand craftsmanship and limited competition, in contrast to the proletarianization and loss of skills endured in mechanized production. Nevertheless, by the middle of the nineteenth century economic deregulation was championed by most European governments and elites.

The Industrious Revolution

One scholar has used the term **industrious revolution** to describe the social and economic changes taking place in Europe in the late seventeenth and early eighteenth centuries.[4] This occurred as households in northwestern Europe reduced leisure time, stepped up the pace of work, and, most importantly, redirected the labor of women and children away from the production of goods for household consumption and toward wage work. By working harder and increasing the number of wageworkers, households could purchase more goods, even in a time of stagnant or falling real wages.

New sources and patterns of labor established important foundations for the Industrial Revolution of the late eighteenth and nineteenth centuries. They created households in which all members worked for wages rather than in a united family business and in which consumption relied on market-produced rather than homemade goods. It was not until the mid-nineteenth century, with rising industrial wages, that a new model emerged in which the male "breadwinner" was expected to earn enough to support the whole family and women and children were relegated back to the domestic sphere. With 77 percent of U.S. women between ages twenty-five and fifty-four in the workforce in the year 2000, today's world is experiencing a sec-

Section Review

- The increase of landless rural workers led to cottage industries where peasants manufactured products in their homes for urban capitalists.

- Urban merchants "put out" raw materials, which the cottage industry workers processed and returned to the merchants, who then sold the finished product.

- The textile industry employed the most people in Europe and was typically a family enterprise: the men wove while women and children spun the wool and did other tasks; wages were low and working conditions hard.

- Urban guild masters were at the top of the work world, enjoying exclusive rights to sell and produce some goods while the guilds served a social and religious function to their members.

- The "industrious revolution" describes a shift whereby families in northwestern Europe worked harder and longer hours and focused on earning wages instead of producing goods for household consumption, especially among women and children; this reduced their economic self-sufficiency but increased their ability to purchase consumer goods.

ond industrious revolution in a similar climate of stagnant wages and increased demand for consumer goods.

Building the Global Economy

How did colonial markets boost Europe's economic and social development, and what conflicts and adversity did world trade entail?

In addition to agricultural improvement, a decline in mortality, and growing cottage industry, the expansion of Europe in the eighteenth century was characterized by the growth of world trade. Spain and Portugal revitalized their empires and began drawing more wealth from renewed development. Yet once again the countries of northwestern Europe—the Netherlands, France, and above all Great Britain—benefited most. Great Britain, which was formed in 1707 by the union of England and Scotland into a single kingdom, gradually became the leading maritime power. Thus the British played the critical role in building a fairly unified Atlantic economy that provided remarkable opportunities for them and their colonists. They also conducted ruthless competition with France and the Netherlands for trade and territory in Asia.

Mercantilism and Colonial Wars

Britain's commercial leadership in the eighteenth century had its origins in the mercantilism of the seventeenth century (see page 409). Mercantilism aimed particularly at creating a favorable balance of foreign trade in order to increase a country's stock of gold. A country's gold holdings served as an all-important treasure chest that could be opened periodically to pay for war in a violent age.

Beginning with Oliver Cromwell in 1651, the English government enacted a series of laws designed to build English power and wealth under the mercantile system. Known as the **Navigation Acts,** these laws controlled the import of goods to Britain and British colonies. The most significant of these acts required the colonists to ship their products on British (or American) ships and to buy almost all European goods from Britain. It was believed that these economic regulations would help British merchants and workers as well as colonial plantation owners and farmers; and the emerging British Empire would develop a shipping industry with a large number of experienced seamen who could serve when necessary in the Royal Navy.

The Navigation Acts were a form of economic warfare. Their initial target was the Dutch, who were far ahead of the English in shipping and foreign trade in the mid-seventeenth century (see page 426). In conjunction with three Anglo-Dutch wars between 1652 and 1674, the Navigation Acts seriously damaged Dutch shipping and commerce. The British seized the thriving Dutch colony of New Amsterdam in 1664 and renamed it "New York." By the late seventeenth century the Netherlands was falling behind England in shipping, trade, and colonies.

Thereafter France stood clearly as England's most serious rival in the competition for overseas empire. Rich in natural resources, with a population three or four times that of England, and allied with Spain, continental Europe's leading military power was already building a powerful fleet and a worldwide system of rigidly monopolized colonial trade. Thus from 1701 to 1763 Britain and France were locked in a series of wars to decide, in part, which nation would become the leading maritime power and claim the profits of Europe's overseas expansion (see Map 19.2).

Navigation Acts A series of English laws that controlled the import of goods to Britain and British colonies.

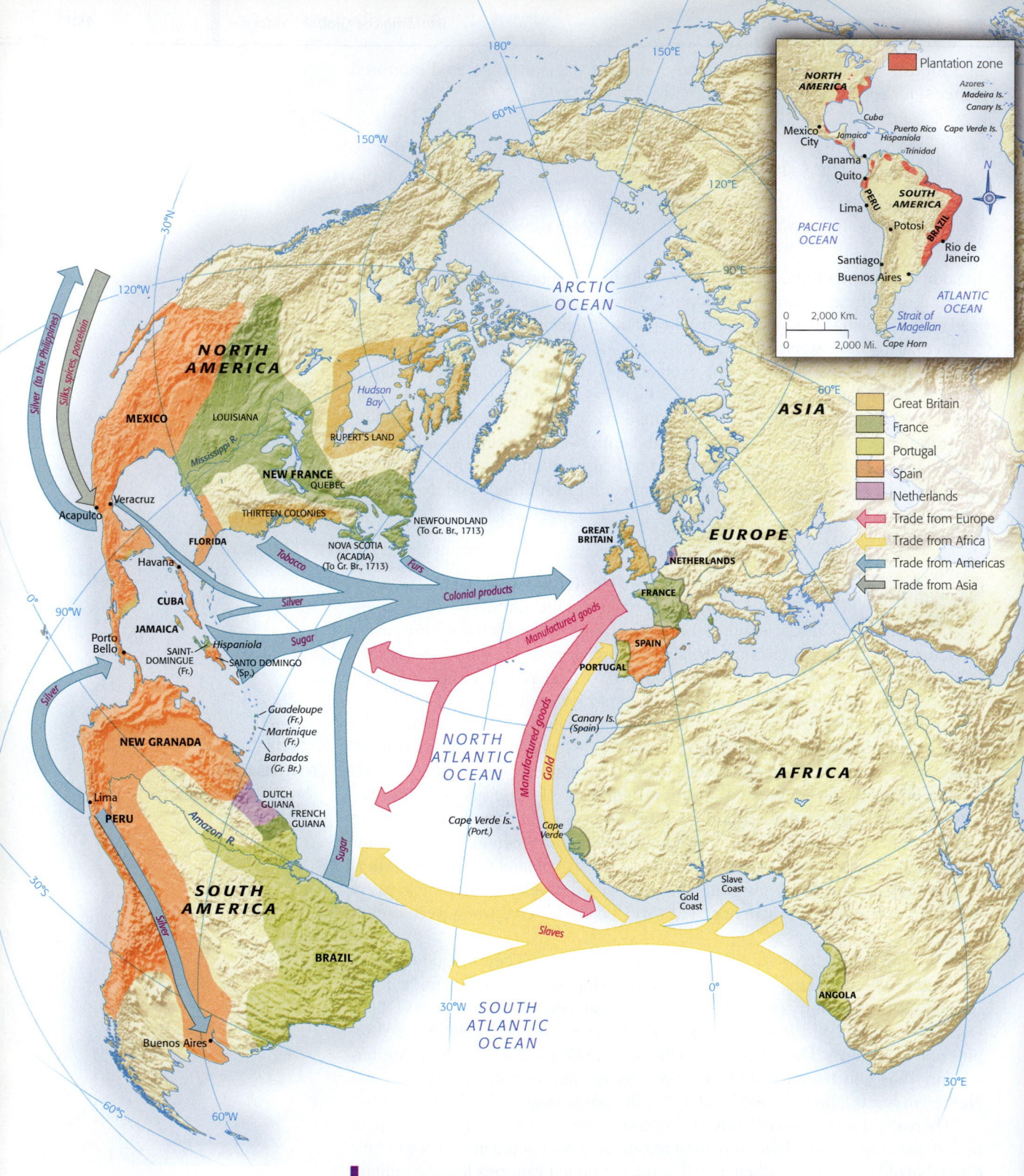

MAP 19.2   The Atlantic Economy in 1701

The growth of trade encouraged both economic development and military conflict in the Atlantic basin. Four continents were linked together by the exchange of goods and slaves.

The first round was the War of the Spanish Succession (see page 411), which started when Louis XIV of France accepted the Spanish crown willed to his grandson. Besides upsetting the continental balance of power, a union of France and Spain threatened to encircle and destroy the British colonies in North America (see Map 19.2). Defeated by a great coalition of states after twelve years of fighting, Louis XIV was forced in the Peace of Utrecht (**YOO-trekt**) (1713) to cede Newfoundland, Nova Scotia, and the Hudson Bay territory to Britain. Spain was compelled to give Britain control of its West African slave trade—the so-called *asiento* (**a-SYEN-toh**)—and to let Britain send one ship of merchandise into the Spanish colonies annually through Porto Bello on the Isthmus of Panama. France was still a mighty competitor, however. The War of the Austrian Succession (1740–1748) over Maria Theresa's Austrian empire (see page 475) brought France and England back into conflict. But the Seven Years' War (1756–1763) marked the decisive round in the Franco-British competition for colonial empire.

The fighting began in North America. The population of New France was centered in Quebec and along the St. Lawrence River, but French soldiers and Canadian fur traders had also built forts and trading posts along the Great Lakes, through the Ohio country, and down the Mississippi to New Orleans. Allied with many Native American tribes, the French built more forts in 1753 in what is now western Pennsylvania to protect their claims. The following year a Virginia force attacked a small group of French soldiers, and soon the war to conquer Canada was on.

French and Canadian forces under the experienced marquis de Montcalm fought well and scored major victories until 1758. Then, led by their new chief minister, William Pitt, the British diverted men and money from the war in Europe and used their superior sea power to destroy the French fleet and choke off French commerce around the world. In 1759 a combined British naval and land force defeated Montcalm's army in a dramatic battle that sealed the fate of France in North America.

British victory on all colonial fronts was ratified in the **Treaty of Paris** (1763), ending the Seven Years' War in Europe and the colonies. Canada and all French territory east of the Mississippi River passed to Britain, and France ceded Louisiana to Spain as compensation for Spain's loss of Florida to Britain. France also gave up most of its holdings in India, opening the way to British dominance on the subcontinent. By 1763 Britain had realized its goal of monopolizing a vast trading and colonial empire.

Treaty of Paris The treaty that ended the Seven Years' War in Europe and the colonies in 1763 and ratified British victory on all colonial fronts.

In the eighteenth century, stimulated by trade and empire building, London grew into the West's largest and richest city. (See the feature "Images in Society: London: The Remaking of a Great City" on pages 498–499.) Above all, the rapidly growing and increasingly wealthy agricultural populations of the mainland colonies of North America provided an expanding market for English manufactured goods. Foreign trade became the bread and butter of some industries; for example, by 1750 half the nails made in England were going to the colonies. Thus, the mercantilist system achieved remarkable success for England in the eighteenth century, and by the 1770s England stood on the threshold of the epoch-making industrial changes that are described in Chapter 22.

Despite their losses, the French still profited enormously from colonial trade. The colonies of Saint Domingue (**san do-MANG**) (modern-day Haiti) and Martinique and Guadeloupe (which remain French departments today) provided immense fortunes in sugar and coffee plantations and slave trading during the second half of the eighteenth century. By 1789 the population of Saint Domingue included five hundred thousand slaves whose labor had allowed the colony to

Images in Society

London: The Remaking of a Great City

The imperial capital and intercontinental trade center of London dominated Britain and astonished the visitor. Equal in population to Paris with four hundred thousand inhabitants in 1650, the super city of the West grew to nine hundred thousand in 1801, while second-place Paris had six hundred thousand. And as London grew, its citizens created a new urban landscape and style of living.

Image 1 shows the "true profile" of London and its built environment as viewed from the south before the Great Fire of 1666, which raged for four days and destroyed about 80 percent of the old, predominately wooden central city. With the River Thames flowing eastward toward the sea, one sees from left to right pre-fire St. Paul's Cathedral, London Bridge crowded with houses, ships at the wharves, and the medieval Tower of London. Clearly visible in the distance are the open fields of the large estates surrounding London, while beyond the view on the left are the royal palace and adjacent government buildings. Also missing is the famous London smog, the combination of fog and smoke from coal-burning fireplaces that already polluted the metropolis. How would you characterize pre-fire London?

Reconstruction proceeded quickly after the Great Fire so that people could regain shelter and employment. Brick construction was made mandatory to prevent fire, but only a few streets were straightened or widened. Thus social classes remained packed together in the rebuilt city. The rich merchant family in a first-class city residence (Image 2), built in the 1670s and still standing in 1939, shared a tiny courtyard and constantly rubbed shoulders with poor and middling people in everyday life.

As London rebuilt and kept growing, big noble landowners followed two earlier examples and sought to increase their incomes by setting up residential developments on their estates west of the city. A landowner would lay out a square with streets and building lots, which he or she would lease to speculative builders who put up fine houses for sale or rent. Soho Square, first laid out in the 1670s and shown in Image 3 as it appeared in 1731, was fairly typical. The spacious square with its gated park is

IMAGE 1 London Before the Great Fire (Hulton Archive/Getty Images)

IMAGE 2 Merchant Family's Residence (built 1670–1680)
(English Heritage/NMR)

IMAGE 3 Soho Square, 1731 (Private Collection/The Stapleton Collection/The Bridgeman Art Library)

surrounded by three-story row houses set on deep, narrow lots. Set in the country but close to the city, a square like Soho was a kind of elegant "village" with restrictive building codes that catered to aristocrats, officials, and successful professionals who were served by artisans and shopkeepers living in alleys and side streets. Do you see a difference between the houses on the square and on the street behind? How would you compare Soho Square with the hills in the distance and with the old London of Images 1 and 2? The classy, new area, known as the West End, contrasted sharply with the shoddy rentals and makeshift shacks of laborers and sailors in the mushrooming East End, which artists rarely painted. Thus residential segregation by income level increased substantially in eighteenth-century London.

As the suburban villages grew and gradually merged together, the West End increasingly attracted the well-to-do from all over England. Rural landowners and provincial notables came for the social season from October to May. Operating out of comfortable second homes purchased or rented in the West End, they played the national market

IMAGE 4 Bloomsbury Square, 1787 (HarperCollins Publishers/The Art Archive)

for mortgages, marriages, and recreation. Image 4, showing classy Bloomsbury Square in 1787 and the original country mansion of the enterprising noble developer, provides a glimpse into this well-born culture. How does Image 4 complement Image 3? What message is the artist conveying with the milkmaid and her cows? Some historians believe that London's West End was an important social innovation. Reconsidering these images, do you agree?

become the world's leading producer of coffee and sugar. It was the most profitable plantation colony in the New World and the one that consumed the greatest number of slaves.[5] The wealth generated from colonial trade fostered the confidence of the merchant classes in Paris, Bordeaux, and other large cities, and merchants soon joined other elite groups clamoring for more political responsibility.

The third major player in the Atlantic economy, Spain, saw its colonial fortunes improve during the eighteenth century. Not only did it gain Louisiana from France in 1763, but its influence expanded westward all the way to northern California through the efforts of Spanish missionaries and ranchers. Its mercantilist goals were boosted by a recovery in silver production, which had dropped significantly in the seventeenth century.

Silver mining also stimulated food production for the mining camps, and wealthy Spanish landowners developed a system of **debt peonage** (PEE-uh-nij) to keep indigenous workers on their estates. Under this system, which was similar to serfdom, a planter or rancher would keep workers in perpetual debt bondage by advancing them food, shelter, and a little money.

The profits from mining and agriculture gave the **Creoles** (KREE-ohlz)—people of Spanish blood born in America—the means to purchase more and more European luxuries and manufactured goods. A class of wealthy Creole merchants

debt peonage   A system that allowed a planter or rancher to keep his workers or slaves in perpetual debt bondage by periodically advancing food, shelter, and a little money; it was a form of serfdom.

Creoles   People of Spanish blood born in America.

mestizo   Spanish term for a person of mixed racial origins, especially Native American and European.

Forming the Mexican People

It was not uncommon for Creole men in Latin America to take Indian wives, with the result that roughly 30 percent of the population was racially mixed by the end of the colonial period. This painting, by an unknown eighteenth-century artist, shows the union of a Spanish man and a Native American woman that has produced a racially mixed **mestizo** (mess-TEE-zoh) child on the left, and a group that features a mestizo woman and a Spaniard with their little daughter on the right. Paintings such as this reflect contemporary fascination with the spectrum of racial difference produced in the colonies. (Private Collection, Mexico)

arose to handle this flourishing trade, which often relied on smuggled goods from Great Britain. The Creoles strove to become a genuine European aristocracy and looked upon the agents sent by Spain as meddlesome rivals.

The Atlantic Slave Trade

As Britain built its empire in North America, it secured an important outlet for surplus population, so that migration abroad limited poverty at home. The settlers also benefited, for they enjoyed privileged access to virtually free and unlimited land. And unlike the great majority of European peasants, American farmers kept most of what they produced. Indeed, on the eve of the American Revolution white men and women in the mainland British colonies had one of the highest living standards in the world.[6] Cheap land and the tremendous demand for scarce labor also fostered the growth of slavery in the British colonies. The Spanish and the Portuguese had first brought African slaves to the Americas in the sixteenth century. In the seventeenth century the Dutch aggressively followed their example and transported thousands of Africans first to Brazil and then to the Caribbean to work on highly profitable sugar plantations. The English established their own Caribbean sugar plantations, and, in the eighteenth century, tobacco planters in Virginia and Maryland embarked on plantation agriculture using slave labor.

Taken to the Americas in chains, Africans made a decisive contribution to the development of the Atlantic economy. Above all, the labor of enslaved Africans made possible large-scale production of valuable commodities for sale in Europe. Indeed, an important recent study concludes that in the years from 1761 to 1800 Africans and their descendants in Brazil, Spanish America, the Caribbean, and Britain's mainland slave colonies accounted for more than *four-fifths* of all the commodities produced in the Americas for sale in the Atlantic economy.[7] It was this flood of ever-cheaper sugar, coffee, tobacco, rice, and (in the nineteenth century) cotton that generated hard cash in the Americas—cash that paid for manufactured goods and services from Britain and Europe as well as for more slaves from Africa.

The forced migration of millions of Africans—cruel, unjust, and tragic—remained a key element in the Atlantic system and western European economic expansion throughout the eighteenth century. Indeed, the brutal **Atlantic slave trade** intensified dramatically after 1700 and especially after 1750. According to one authoritative estimate, European traders purchased and shipped over six million African slaves across the Atlantic between 1701 and 1800, fully 52 percent of the estimated total of almost 12 million Africans transported between 1450 and 1900.[8] In 1790, when the U.S. population was approaching 4 million, slaves accounted for almost 20 percent of the total.

Intensification of the slave trade resulted in fundamental changes in its organization. After 1700, as Britain became the undisputed leader in the slave trade, European governments and ship captains cut back on fighting among themselves and concentrated on commerce. They generally adopted the shore method of trading, which was less expensive than maintaining fortified trading posts. Thus European ships sent boats ashore or invited African dealers to bring traders and slaves out to their ships. This method allowed ships to move easily along the coast from market to market and to depart more quickly for the Americas.

Some African merchants and rulers who controlled exports profited from the greater demand for slaves, and some Africans secured foreign products that they found appealing because of price or quality. But generally such economic returns did not spread very far, and the negative consequences of the expanding slave trade

Atlantic slave trade The forced migration of Africans across the Atlantic for slave labor on plantations and in other industries; although many European countries participated, its peak was among the English in the eighteenth century and ultimately the trade involved almost twelve million Africans.

Slaves Harvesting Sugar Cane

In this 1828 print a long line of hard-working slaves systematically harvests the ripe cane on the island of Antigua, while on the right more slaves load cut cane into wagons for refining at the plantation's central crushing mill. The manager on horseback may be ordering the overseer to quicken the work pace, always brutal and unrelenting at harvest time. Slave labor made high-intensity capitalist production of sugar possible in the Americas. (John Carter Brown Library at Brown University)

predominated. Wars between Africans to obtain salable captives increased, and leaders purchased more arms and bought relatively fewer textiles and consumer goods. And while the population of Europe (and Asia) grew substantially in the eighteenth century, that of Africa stagnated or possibly declined.

Slaves were typically captives who had been taken in battles between African states, but as demand grew, slave dealers tried new approaches. Kidnappers seized and enslaved men and women like Olaudah Equiano (oh-LAU-duh ay-kwee-AHN-oh) and his sister, whose tragic separation, exile, and exploitation personified the full horror of the Atlantic slave trade. (See the feature "Individuals in Society: Olaudah Equiano.") Another approach was for African rulers to change the punishment for misdemeanors from fines to enslavement in order to generate more captives for sale.

Most Europeans did not personally witness the horrors of the slave trade between Africa and the Americas, and until 1700, and perhaps even 1750, they considered the African slave trade a legitimate business. But as details of the plight of slaves became known, a campaign to abolish slavery developed in Britain. Between 1788 and 1792, according to some recent scholarship, the abolition campaign grew into the first peaceful mass political movement based on the mobilization of public opinion in British history. British women played a critical role in this mass movement, denouncing the immorality of human bondage and stressing the cruel and sadistic treatment of female slaves and slave families. These attacks put the defenders of slavery on the defensive. In 1807 Parliament abolished the British

Individuals in Society

Olaudah Equiano

The slave trade was a mass migration involving millions of human beings. It was also the sum of individual lives spent partly or entirely in slavery. Although most of those lives remain hidden to us, Olaudah Equiano (1745–1797) is an important exception.

Equiano was born in Benin (modern Nigeria) of Ibo ethnicity. His father, one of the village elders (or chieftains), presided over a large household that included "many slaves," prisoners captured in local wars. All people, slave and free, shared in the cultivation of family lands. One day, when all the adults were in the fields, two strange men and a woman broke into the family compound, kidnapped the eleven-year-old boy and his sister, tied them up, and dragged them into the woods. Brother and sister were separated, and Olaudah was sold several times to various dealers before reaching the coast. As it took six months to walk there, his home must have been far inland.

The slave ship and the strange appearance of the white crew terrified the boy. Much worse was the long voyage from Benin to Barbados in the Caribbean, as Equiano later recounted. "The stench of the [ship's] hold . . . became absolutely pestilential . . . [and] brought on a sickness among the slaves, of which many died. . . . The shrieks of the women and the groans of the dying rendered the whole a scene of horror almost inconceivable." Placed on deck with the sick and dying, Equiano saw two and then three of his "enchained countrymen" escape somehow through the nettings and jump into the sea, "preferring death to such a life of misery."*

Equiano's new owner, an officer in the Royal Navy, took him to England and saw that the lad received some education. Engaged in bloody action in Europe for almost four years as a captain's boy in the Seven Years' War, Equiano hoped that his loyal service and Christian baptism would help secure his freedom. He also knew that slavery was generally illegal in England. But his master deceived him. Docking in London, he and his accomplices forced a protesting and heartbroken Equiano onto a ship bound for the Caribbean.

There he was sold to Robert King, a Quaker merchant from Philadelphia who dealt in sugar and rum.

Equiano developed his mathematical skills, worked hard to please as a clerk in King's warehouse, and became first mate on one of King's ships. Allowed to trade on the side for his own profit, Equiano amassed capital, repaid King his original purchase price, and received his deed of manumission at the age of twenty-one. King urged his talented former slave to stay on as a business partner, but Equiano hated the limitations and dangers of black freedom in the colonies— he was almost kidnapped back into slavery while loading a ship in Georgia—and could think only of England. Settling in London, Equiano studied, worked as a hairdresser, and went to sea periodically as a merchant seaman. He developed his ardent Christian faith and became a leading member of London's sizable black community.

Olaudah Equiano, in an engraving from his autobiography. (National Portrait Gallery, Smithsonian Institution/Art Resource, NY)

Equiano loathed the brutal slavery and the vicious exploitation that he saw in the West Indies and Britain's mainland colonies. A complex and sophisticated man, he also respected the integrity of Robert King and admired British navigational and industrial technologies. He encountered white oppressors and made white friends. He once described himself as "almost an Englishman." In the 1780s he joined with white and black activists in the antislavery campaign and wrote *The Interesting Narrative of the Life of Olaudah Equiano Written by Himself*, a well-documented autobiographical indictment of slavery. Above all, he urged Christians to live by the principles they professed and to treat Africans equally as free human beings and children of God. With the success of his widely read book, he carried his message to large audiences across Britain and Ireland and inspired the growing movement to abolish slavery.

Questions for Analysis

1. What aspects of Olaudah Equiano's life as a slave were typical? What aspects were atypical?

2. Describe Equiano's culture and personality. What aspects are most striking? Why?

---

* Olaudah Equiano, *The Interesting Narrative of the Life of Olaudah Equiano Written by Himself*, ed. with an introduction by Robert J. Allison (Boston: Bedford Books, 1995), pp. 56–57. Recent scholarship has re-examined Equiano's life and thrown some details of his identity into question.

slave trade, although slavery continued in British colonies and the Americas for years.

Trade and Empire in Asia

As the Atlantic economy took shape, Europeans continued to vie for dominance in the Asian trade. The Dutch, who had dominated as a supplier of Asian goods to Europeans in the seventeenth century, failed to diversify to meet changing consumption patterns. Spices continued to comprise much of its shipping, despite their declining importance in the European diet. Fierce competition from its main rival, the English East India Company (est. 1600), also severely undercut Dutch trade.

Britain initially struggled for a foothold in Asia. With the Dutch monopolizing the Indian Ocean, the British focused on India, where they were minor players throughout the seventeenth century. The English East India Company relied on trade concessions from the powerful Mughal emperor, who granted only piecemeal access to the subcontinent. Finally, in 1716 the Mughals conceded empire-

The British in India (ca. 1785)
This Indian miniature shows (*center*) the wife of a British officer attended by many Indian servants. A British merchant (*left*) awaits her attention. The picture reflects the luxurious lifestyle of the British elite in India; many returned home with colossal fortunes. (Scala/Art Resource, NY)

wide trading privileges. To further their economic interests, British company agents increasingly intervened in local affairs and made alliances or waged war against Indian princes. However, they faced competition from France, which also had company agents and troops stationed on the subcontinent. Forces from the two sides clashed in the 1740s.

With the Treaty of Paris that ended the Seven Years' War in 1763 (page 497), France lost its possessions in India. British ascendancy in India subsequently accelerated. In 1764 English East India Company forces defeated the Mughal emperor, leaving him on the throne as a ruler in title only. Robert Clive a company agent who had led its forces in battle, became the first British governor general of Bengal, in northeast India, with direct authority over the province. By the early 1800s the British had overcome vigorous Indian resistance to gain economic and political dominance of much of the subcontinent, and India was lauded as the "jewel" in the British Empire in the nineteenth century.

Adam Smith and Economic Liberalism

Although mercantilist policies strengthened European colonial empires in the eighteenth century, a strong reaction against mercantilism ultimately set in. Creole merchants chafed at regulations imposed from Madrid, while English merchants complained loudly about the trade monopoly enjoyed by the British East India Company. These independent merchants led the call for "free trade," borrowing from the ideas of Scottish Enlightenment philosopher Adam Smith (1723–1790), whose *Inquiry into the Nature and Causes of the Wealth of Nations* (1776) established the basis for modern economics.

Smith described eighteenth-century mercantilism as a combination of stifling government regulations and unfair privileges for state-approved monopolies and government favorites. Far preferable was free competition, which would best protect consumers from price gouging and give all citizens a fair and equal right to do what they did best. Fearful of political oppression, Smith argued that government should limit itself to "only three duties": it should provide a defense against foreign invasion, maintain civil order with courts and police protection, and sponsor certain indispensable public works and institutions that could never adequately profit private investors. He believed that the pursuit of self-interest in a competitive market would be sufficient to improve the living conditions of citizens.

In the nineteenth and twentieth centuries Smith was often seen as an advocate of unbridled capitalism, but his ideas were considerably more complex. In his own mind, Smith spoke for truth, not for special interests. Unlike many disgruntled merchant capitalists, he applauded the modest rise in real wages of British workers in the eighteenth century and went on to say that "No society can surely be flourishing and happy, of which the far greater part of the members are poor and miserable." He also deplored the deadening effects of the division of labor and called for government intervention to raise workers' living standards.

Smith's provocative work had a great international impact, going through eight editions in English and being translated into several languages within twenty years. It quickly emerged as the classic argument for **economic liberalism.**

economic liberalism Based on the writings of Adam Smith, a belief in free trade and competition. Smith argued that the invisible hand of free competition would benefit all individuals, rich and poor.

Section Review

- Britain imposed a form of economic warfare with the Navigation Acts, which required the transportation of British products on British ships.

- England went through a series of wars with the Dutch and then the French in the struggle for maritime supremacy and although Britain gained a trading monopoly and colonial empire, France and Spain continued to profit from their own colonial trade.

- The Atlantic slave trade grew enormously as colonial plantations used slaves to produce commodities for sale in Europe and although public outcry at its horrors led the British to end their involvement in the trade in 1807, slavery itself continued in the Americas and the British colonies.

- The Great Fire of 1666 destroyed much of London; reconstruction kept the social classes mixed in the old city but new suburbs created segregation by income level.

- The British East India Company vied with the French and the Dutch for trading dominance in Asia and emerged as dominant rulers within the Indian subcontinent.

- Adam Smith's writings gained international fame, promoting free trade in a competitive market, an arrangement he thought would protect consumers and benefit all citizens.

Chapter Review

What were the causes and effects of the agricultural revolution, and what nations led the way in these developments? (page 485)

While the European educated elite was developing a new view of the world in the eighteenth century, Europe as a whole was experiencing a gradual but far-reaching expansion. As agriculture began showing signs of modest improvement across the continent, first the Low Countries and then England launched changes that gradually revolutionized it. New crops and intensified crop rotation created new food sources for both people and livestock. Enclosure of common land allowed landowners to reap the fruits of agricultural innovation at the cost of excluding poor peasants from their traditional access to the land. The gap between wealthy landowner and landless poor stretched wider in this period.

Why did European population rise dramatically in the eighteenth century? (page 488)

For reasons historians do not yet understand, the recurring curse of bubonic plague disappeared. Less vulnerable to food shortages and free from the plague, the populations of all European countries grew significantly. During the eighteenth century the European population recovered from the stagnation and losses of the previous century to reach unprecedented new levels.

What is cottage industry, and how did it contribute to Europe's economic and social transformation? (page 490)

Population increases encouraged the growth of wage labor, cottage industry, and merchant capitalism. To escape the constraints of urban guilds, merchants transported production to the countryside. Peasant households set up industrial production within their cottages, allocating family members' labor during the slack seasons of agriculture or, in some cases, abandoning farming altogether for a new life of weaving or spinning. The spread of cottage industry was one sign of an "industrious revolution" that helped pave the path of the Industrial Revolution of the late eighteenth century. Women's labor was crucial to the spread of cottage industry and the renewed vitality of the urban trades.

How did colonial markets boost Europe's economic and social development, and what conflicts and adversity did world trade entail? (page 495)

The products of peasant industry were exported across Europe and even across the world. During the eighteenth century Europeans continued their overseas expansion, fighting for empire and profit and, in particular, consolidating their hold on the Americas. A revived Spain and its Latin American colonies participated fully in this expansion. As in agriculture and cottage industry, however, England and its empire proved most successful. The English concentrated much of the growing Atlantic trade in their hands, a development that challenged and enriched English industry and intensified interest in new methods of production and in an emerging economic liberalism. Thus, by the 1770s England was approaching an economic breakthrough as fully significant as the great political upheaval destined to develop shortly in neighboring France.

Key Terms

agricultural revolution (p. 486)

crop rotation (p. 486)

enclosure (p. 486)

proletarianization (p. 488)

cottage industry (p. 490)

putting-out system (p. 490)

guild system (p. 493)

industrious revolution (p. 494)

Navigation Acts (p. 495)

Treaty of Paris (p. 497)

debt peonage (p. 500)

Creoles (p. 500)

mestizo (p. 500)

Atlantic slave trade (p. 501)

economic liberalism (p. 505)

Notes

1. B. H. Slicher van Bath, *The Agrarian History of Western Europe, A.D. 500–1850* (New York: St. Martin's Press, 1963), p. 240.
2. Quoted in I. Pinchbeck, *Women Workers and the Industrial Revolution, 1750–1850* (New York: F. S. Crofts, 1930), p. 113.
3. Richard J. Soderlund, "'Intended as a Terror to the Idle and Profligate': Embezzlement and the Origins of Policing in the Yorkshire Worsted Industry, c. 1750–1777," *Journal of Social History* 31 (Spring 1998): 658.
4. Ibid. In addition, Jan de Vries, "The Industrious Revolution and the Industrious Revolution," *The Journal of Economic History* 54, 2 (June 1994): 249–270, discusses the second industrious revolution of the second half of the twentieth century.
5. Laurent Dubois and John D. Garrigus, *Slave Revolution in the Caribbean, 1789–1904* (New York: Palgrave, 2006), p. 8.
6. G. Taylor, "America's Growth Before 1840," *Journal of Economic History* 24 (December 1970): 427–444.
7. J. Inikori, *Africans and the Industrial Revolution in England: A Study in International Trade and Economic Development* (Cambridge: Cambridge University Press, 2002), pp. 481–482.
8. P. E. Lovejoy, *Transformations in Slavery: A History of Slavery in Africa* (Cambridge: Cambridge University Press, 1983), p. 19.

To assess your mastery of this chapter, go to **bedfordstmartins.com/mckaywestbrief**

Listening to the Past

The Debate over the Guilds

Guilds, also known as trade corporations, claimed that their rules guaranteed fair wages, high-quality goods, and community values. However, both French philosophes and enlightened government officials increasingly disagreed. The following excerpt, from a 1776 law abolishing French guilds by the reform minister Jacques Turgot (tur-GOH), is an important example of the liberal critique in action. A vociferous response from the guilds led to the law's repeal only six months later. New guild regulations responded to some of the critiques, for example by allowing women to join all guilds. In 1791 French revolutionaries definitively abolished the guild system.

A German brush maker and guild member shows a customer his wares. (The Fotomas Index/The Bridgeman Art Library)

Edict Abolishing the Guilds in France

In nearly all the towns of our Kingdom the practice of different arts and crafts is concentrated in the hands of a small number of masters, united in a corporation, who alone have the exclusive right to manufacture and sell particular articles; so that those of our subjects who, through wish or necessity intend to practise in these fields, must have attained the mastership, to which they are admitted only after very long tests which are as difficult as they are useless, and after having satisfied rules or manifold exactions, which absorb part of the funds they need to set up in business or even to exist. . . .

God, in giving man needs, by making work necessary, has made the right to work a universal prerogative, and this is the first, the most sacred and the most indefeasible of all rights.

We regard it as one of the first duties of our law, and one of the acts most worthy of our charity, to free our subjects from all attacks against the inalienable right of mankind. Consequently, we wish to abolish these arbitrary institutions, which do not allow the poor man to earn his living; which reject a sex whose weakness has given it more needs and fewer resources, and which seem, in condemning it to an inevitable misery, to support seduction and debauchery; which destroy emulation and industry and nullify the talents of those whose circumstances have excluded them from membership of a corporation; which deprive the State and the arts of all the knowledge brought to them by foreigners; which retard the progress of these arts through the innumerable difficulties encountered by inventors with whom different corporations dispute the right to exploit their discoveries . . . which, by the huge expenses artisans are obliged to sustain to obtain the right to work, by their various exactions and frequent fines for alleged illegalities, by all kinds of expenditure, waste and interminable law suits, resulting from the respective claims of all these corporations on the extent of their exclusive privileges, burden industry with an oppressive tax, which bears heavily on the people, and is without benefit to the State; which finally, by the facility they provide for members of corporations to combine to force the poorest members to submit to the laws of the rich, become an instrument of privilege and encourage developments, the effect of which is to raise above their natural level the price of those goods which are most essential for the people.

Questions for Analysis

1. How did Turgot justify the abolition of French guilds? Do you think his reasons are valid? How might the guilds respond?

2. Do guilds—and modern-day unions—help or hurt workers? Defend your position.

Source: S. Pollard and C. Holmes, eds., *Documents of European Economic History*, Volume One: *The Process of Industrialization, 1750–1870*, 1968, pp. 53–56.

CHAPTER 20

The Changing Life of the People

Chapter Preview

A quack doctor uses a snake and a dog to sell a miraculous cure-all in an Italian village market, in a painting (detail) by Michele Graneri (1736–1778). (Dagli Orti Private Collection/The Art Archive)

The discussion of agriculture and industry in the previous chapter showed the common people at work, straining to make ends meet within the larger context of population growth, gradual economic expansion, and ferocious political competition. The world of work was embedded in a rich complex of family organization, community practices, everyday experiences, and collective attitudes.

In recent years, historians have intensively studied all these aspects of popular life. The challenge has been formidable because regional variations abounded and the common people left few written records. Yet imaginative research has resulted in major findings and much greater knowledge. It is now possible to follow the common people into their homes, workshops, churches, and taverns and to ask, "What were the everyday experiences of ordinary people?"

Marriage and the Family

What changes occurred in marriage and the family in the course of the eighteenth century?

The basic unit of social organization is the family. Within the structure of the family human beings love, mate, and reproduce. It is primarily the family that teaches the child, imparting values and customs that condition an individual's behavior for a lifetime. The family is also an institution woven into the web of history. It evolves and changes, assuming different forms in different times and places.

Late Marriage and Nuclear Families

In the previous chapter, we noted the common misconception that populations of the past always grew quickly. Another popular error is that before the modern era people married at a young age and settled in large multigenerational households. In recent years historians have used previously neglected parish registers of births, deaths, and marriages to uncover details of European family life before the nineteenth century. It is now clear that the extended, three-generation family was a rarity in western and central Europe by 1700. Indeed, the extended family may never have been common in Europe, although it is hard to know about the early Middle Ages because very few records survive. When young European couples married, they normally established their own households and lived apart from their parents. If a three-generation household came into existence, it was usually because a widowed parent moved into the home of a married child.

Moreover, most people did not marry young in the seventeenth and eighteenth centuries. The average person who was neither rich nor aristocratic married surprisingly late, many years after reaching adulthood and beginning to work. In one well-studied, apparently typical English village in the seventeenth and eighteenth centuries, both men and women married for the first time at an average age of twenty-seven or older. A similar pattern existed in eighteenth-century France, where women married around age twenty-five and men around age twenty-seven. A substantial portion of men and women never married at all. The custom of late marriage combined with a nuclear-family household distinguished European society from other areas of the world.

Why was marriage delayed? The main reason was that couples normally did not marry until they could support themselves economically. Peasants often needed to wait until the father's death to inherit land and marry. In the towns, men and women worked to accumulate enough savings to start a small business and establish a household. In some areas couples needed the legal permission or tacit approval of the local lord or landowner in order to marry. Austria and Germany had legal restrictions on marriage, and well into the nineteenth century poor couples had particular difficulty securing the approval of local officials. This pattern helped society maintain some kind of balance between the number of people and the available economic resources.

Work Away from Home

Many young people worked within their families until they could start their own households. Boys plowed and wove; girls spun and tended the cows. Others left home to work elsewhere. In the towns a lad would begin apprenticeship around age fifteen and finish in his late teens or early twenties. During that time he would not be permitted to marry. In most trades he earned little and worked hard, but if he was lucky, he might eventually be admitted to a guild. Many poor families could not afford apprenticeship, and their sons drifted from one tough job to another: hired hand for a small farmer, wage laborer on a new road, carrier of water in a nearby town. They were always subject to economic fluctuations, and unemployment was a constant threat.

Many girls also left their families to work in adolescence. Some apprenticed to mistresses in traditionally female occupations, becoming seamstresses, linen drapers, or midwives. As the demand for skilled labor grew, even male guildsmen hired girls and women, despite guild restrictions.

Service in another family's household, though, was by far the most common job for girls, and even middle-class families often sent their daughters into service. The legions of young servant girls worked hard but had little independence. Sometimes the employer paid the girl's wages directly to her parents. Constantly under the eye of her mistress, the servant girl had many tasks—cleaning, shopping, cooking, caring for the baby. Court records are full of servant girls' complaints of physical mistreatment by their mistresses. There were many like the fifteen-year-old English girl in the early eighteenth century who told the judge that her mistress had not only called her "very opprobrious names, as Bitch, Whore and the like," but also "beat her without provocation and beyond measure."[1]

Male apprentices told similar tales of verbal and physical abuse at their masters' hands. Boys were far less vulnerable, though, to the sexual harassment and assault that threatened female servants. In theory, domestic service offered a young girl protection and security in a new family. But in practice

Boucher: The Pretty Cook

Increased migration to urban areas in the eighteenth century contributed to a loosening of traditional morals and soaring illegitimacy rates. Young women who worked as servants or shop girls could not be supervised as closely as those who lived at home. The themes of seduction, fallen virtue, and familial conflict were popular in eighteenth-century art, such as this painting by François Boucher (**frahn-SWA boo-SHEY**) (1703–1770), master of the rococo. (Réunion des Musées Nationaux/Art Resource, NY)

she was often the easy prey of a lecherous master or his sons or friends. If the girl became pregnant, she could be quickly fired and thrown out in disgrace to make her own way, which often led to a life of prostitution and petty thievery. "What are we?" exclaimed a bitter Parisian prostitute. "Most of us are unfortunate women, without origins, without education, servants and maids for the most part."[2]

Prostitutes encountered increasingly harsh and repressive laws in the sixteenth and early seventeenth centuries, as officials across Europe began to close licensed brothels and declare prostitution illegal. Despite this repression, prostitution flourished in European cities and towns in the eighteenth century. Most prostitutes were working women who turned to the sex trade when confronted with unemployment or seasonal shortages of work. Farther up the social scale were courtesans whose wealthy protectors provided apartments, servants, beautiful clothing, and cash allowances. As she aged, such a woman could descend once more to streetwalking.

1717	Elementary school attendance mandatory in Prussia
1720–1780	Government-run foundling homes established
1740–1780	Reign of Maria Theresa in Austria
1740–1786	Reign of Frederick the Great in Prussia
1750–1790	Wesley preaches revival in England
1750–1850	Illegitimacy explosion
1757	Madame du Coudray, *Manual on the Art of Childbirth*
1762	Rousseau advocates more attentive child care in *Emile*
1763	Louis XV orders Jesuits out of France
1796	Jenner performs first smallpox vaccination

Premarital Sex and Community Controls

Did late marriage in preindustrial Europe go hand in hand with many illegitimate children? For most of western and central Europe until at least 1750, the answer is no. English parish registers seldom listed more than one illegitimate child out of every twenty children baptized. Some French parishes in the seventeenth century had extraordinarily low rates of illegitimacy, with less than 1 percent of the babies born out of wedlock. Illegitimate babies were apparently a rarity, at least as far as the official church records are concerned. This does not mean that premarital intercourse was unusual, however. A significant number of women were pregnant on their wedding day.

The combination of very low rates of illegitimate births with large numbers of pregnant brides reflects the powerful **community controls** of the traditional village, particularly the open-field village, with its pattern of cooperation and common action. No doubt many couples were already betrothed, or at least "going steady," before they entered into intimate relationships, and pregnancy simply set the marriage date once and for all. But if a couple wavered about marriage, they could expect to be pressured by irate parents, anxious village elders, indignant priests, and stern landlords. The prospect of an unwed (and therefore poor) mother was seen as a grave threat to the economic, social, and moral stability of the closely knit community.

Community controls extended to domestic disputes and marital scandals as well. The people in peasant communities gave such affairs loud and unfavorable publicity either at the time of the event or during the Carnival season (see page 530). The young men of the village would typically gang up on the person they wanted to punish and force him or her to sit astride a donkey facing backward and holding up the donkey's tail. They would parade the overly brutal spouse-beating husband (or wife), or the couple whose adultery had been discovered, all around the village, loudly proclaiming the offender's misdeeds with scorn and ridicule. The donkey ride and other colorful humiliations ranging from rotten vegetables splattered on the doorstep to obscene and insulting midnight serenades were common punishments throughout much of Europe. They epitomized the community's far-reaching effort to police personal behavior and maintain community standards.

community controls A pattern of cooperation and common action that was mobilized by perceived threats to the economic, social, and moral stability of the closely knit community.

New Patterns of Marriage and Illegitimacy

In the second half of the eighteenth century, the pattern of few births out of wedlock began to break down. The number of illegitimate births soared between about 1750 and 1850 as much of Europe experienced an **illegitimacy explosion.** In Frankfurt, Germany, for example, illegitimate births rose steadily from about 2 percent of all births in the early 1700s to a peak of about 25 percent around 1850. In Bordeaux, France, 36 percent of all babies were being born out of wedlock by 1840. Small towns and villages experienced less startling climbs, but between 1750 and 1850 increases from a range of 1 to 3 percent initially to 10 to 20 percent were commonplace. Fewer young people were abstaining from premarital intercourse, and, more important, fewer young men were marrying the women they got pregnant. Thus a profound sexual and cultural transformation took place.

Historians are still debating the meaning of this transformation, but one trend seems to explain the rise of illegitimate births in urban areas. The needs of a growing population sent many young villagers to towns and cities in search of employment. Most young women in urban areas found work only as servants or textile workers. Poorly paid and with little possibility of truly independent lives, they looked to marriage for security. But without the social controls of village life, their courtships could lead to illegitimate children rather than marriage. Because the lives of their partners were also insecure, many men hesitated to take on the financial burden of a wife and child. Thus the romantic aspirations of many young people were frustrated by low wages, inequality, and changing economic and social conditions. Old patterns of marriage and family were breaking down. Only in the late nineteenth century would more stable patterns reappear.

The pattern of late marriage also eroded in some areas in the second half of the eighteenth century. First, the growth of cottage industry created new opportunities for earning a living, opportunities not tied to the land. Cottage workers married at a younger age because they did not have to wait to inherit a farm. A scrap of

illegitimacy explosion The sharp increase in out-of-wedlock births that occurred in Europe between 1750 and 1850, caused by urbanization, unemployment, and the breakdown of community controls.

David Allan: The Penny Wedding (1795)

The spirited merrymaking of a peasant wedding was a popular theme of European artists. In rural Scotland "penny weddings" like this one were common: guests provided cash gifts; any money left after paying for the wedding went to the newlyweds to help them get started. Dancing, feasting, and drinking characterized these community parties, which led the Presbyterian church to oppose them and hasten their decline. (National Galleries of Scotland)

ground for a garden and a cottage for the loom and spinning wheel could be quite enough for a modest living. Couples married not only at an earlier age but also for different reasons. Nothing could be so businesslike as peasant marriages that were often dictated by the needs of the couples' families. After 1750, however, courtship became more extensive and freer as cottage industry grew. It was easier to yield to the attraction of the opposite sex and fall in love. Members of the older generation were often highly critical of the lack of responsibility they saw in the union of "people with only two spinning wheels and not even a bed." But such scolding did not stop cottage workers from marrying for love rather than for economic considerations as they blazed a path that factory workers would follow in the nineteenth century. Ironically, therefore, both the rise of illegitimate births and the new tendencies toward earlier marriage reflect a weakening of parental and communities' control over young people.

Children and Education

What was life like for children, and how did attitudes toward childhood evolve?

In the traditional framework of agrarian Europe, women married late but then began bearing children rapidly. If a woman married before she was thirty, and if both she and her husband lived to fifty, she would most likely give birth to six or more children. The newborn child entered a dangerous world. Newborns were vulnerable to infectious diseases of the chest and stomach, and many babies died of dehydration brought about by bad bouts of ordinary diarrhea. Of those who survived infancy, many more died in childhood. Even in rich families little could be done for an ailing child. Childbirth could also be dangerous. Women who bore six children faced a cumulative risk of dying in childbirth of 5 to 10 percent, a thousand times as great as the risk in Europe today.[3]

Schools and formal education played only a modest role in the lives of ordinary children, and many boys and many more girls never learned to read. Nevertheless, basic literacy was growing among the popular classes, whose reading habits have been intensively studied in recent years. Attempting to peer into the collective attitudes of the common people and compare them with those of the book-hungry cultivated public, historians have produced some fascinating insights.

Child Care and Nursing

In the countryside, women of the lower classes generally breast-fed their infants for two years or more. Breast-feeding decreases the likelihood of pregnancy for the average woman by delaying the resumption of ovulation. By nursing their babies, women limited their fertility and spaced their children from two to three years apart. If a newborn baby died, nursing stopped, and a new life could be created. Nursing also saved lives: the breast-fed infant received precious immunity-producing substances with its mother's milk and was more likely to survive than when it was given other food.

Women of the aristocracy and upper middle class seldom nursed their own children. The upper-class woman felt that breast-feeding was crude and undignified. Instead, she hired a live-in wet nurse to suckle her child (which usually meant sending the nurse's own infant away to be nursed). Urban mothers of more modest means also relied on wet nurses to free them for full-time work. Unable to afford

Section Review

- Most European couples married after reaching adulthood when they could support themselves in a nuclear family that lived separate from the parents.

- Young men worked at home, were apprenticed, or worked as hired labor until they could marry; women often worked as servants, and conditions for both sexes were harsh.

- Low illegitimate birth rates most likely indicate the amount of pressure a village had on individuals and families, enforcing marriage for pregnancy and openly ridiculing domestic violence or adultery.

- The second half of the eighteenth century brought a steep rise in the number of illegitimate births, a result of young women and men working in urban areas where relationships led to pregnancy but not marriage; on the other hand, the age of marriage fell as cottage industry workers were able to support themselves sooner.

Arrival of the Wet Nurses
Wet-nursing was big business in eighteenth-century France, particularly in Paris and the north. Here, rural wet nurses bring their charges back to the city to be reunited with their families after around two years of care. These children were lucky survivors of a system that produced high mortality rates. (Réunion des Musées Nationaux/Art Resource, NY)

wet-nursing A widespread and flourishing business in the eighteenth century in which women would breast-feed other women's babies for money.

live-in wet nurses, they often turned to the cheaper services of women in the countryside. Rural **wet-nursing** was a widespread business in the eighteenth century, conducted within the framework of the putting-out system. The traffic was in babies rather than in yarn or cloth, and two or three years often passed before the wet-nurse worker in the countryside finished her task. The wet nurse generally had little contact with the family that hired her, and she was expected to privilege the newcomer at the expense of her own nursing child.

Reliance on wet nurses contributed to high levels of infant mortality. A study of parish registers in northern France during the late seventeenth and early eighteenth centuries reveals that 35 percent of babies died before their first birthdays, and another 20 percent before age ten.[4] In England, where more mothers nursed, only some 30 percent of children did not reach their tenth birthdays. Frenchwomen also gave birth to more children since nursing tends to slow down the return of fertility after childbirth.

In the second half of the eighteenth century critics mounted a harsh attack against wet-nursing. Upper-class women responded positively to the new mindset, but poor urban women who depended on jobs where nursing was not possible continued to rely on wet nurses. Not until the late-nineteenth-century introduction of sterilized cows' milk and artificial nipples did wet-nursing cease as a practice.

Foundlings and Infanticide

The young woman who could not provide for a child had few choices, especially if she had no prospect of marriage. Abortions were illegal, dangerous, and apparently rare. In desperation, some women, particularly in the countryside, hid unwanted pregnancies, delivered in secret, and smothered their newborn infants. If discovered, **infanticide** (**in-fAN-tuh-side**) was punishable by death.

Women in cities could leave their infants at foundling homes, which multiplied in the eighteenth century. In eighteenth-century England, for example, the government acted on a petition calling for a foundling hospital "to prevent the frequent murders of poor, miserable infants at birth" and "to suppress the inhuman custom of exposing newborn children to perish in the streets." As the number of homes increased, the number of foundlings being cared for surged. By the end of the century European foundling hospitals were admitting annually about one hundred thousand abandoned children, nearly all of them infants. While most of the children were the offspring of unwed mothers, others were the offspring of married couples, for whom an additional mouth to feed often meant tragedy.

Great numbers of babies entered foundling homes, but few left. Even in the best of these homes, 50 percent of the babies normally died within a year. In the worst, fully 90 percent did not survive.[5] They succumbed to long journeys over rough roads, intentional and unintentional neglect by their wet nurses, and customary childhood illnesses. So great were the losses that some contemporaries called the foundling hospitals "legalized infanticide."

infanticide The willful destruction of a newborn infant.

Attitudes Toward Children

What were the typical circumstances of children's lives? The topic of parental attitudes toward children in the early modern period remains controversial. Some scholars have claimed that parents did not risk forming emotional attachments to young children because of high mortality rates. With a reasonable expectation that a child might die, some scholars believe, parents maintained an attitude of indifference, if not downright negligence.

The French essayist, Michel de Montaigne (**mon-TAIN**), exemplifies this attitude. He wrote: "I cannot abide that passion for caressing new-born children, which have neither mental activities nor recognisable bodily shape by which to make themselves loveable and I have never willingly suffered them to be fed in my presence."[6]

In contrast to this harsh picture, however, historians have drawn ample evidence from diaries, letters, and family portraits that many parents did cherish their children and suffered greatly when they died. The English poet Ben Jonson wrote movingly of the death of his seven-year-old son Benjamin:

On My First Son
Farewell, thou child of my right hand, and joy;
My sin was too much hope of thee, loved boy.
Seven years thou wert lent to me, and I thee pay,
Exacted by thy fate, on the just day.

In a society characterized by violence and brutality, discipline of children was often severe. The novelist Daniel Defoe (**duh-FOH**) (1659–1731), who was always delighted when he saw young children working hard in cottage industry, coined the axiom "Spare the rod and spoil the child." He meant it. So did Susannah Wesley (1669–1742), mother of John Wesley, the founder of Methodism. According to her, the first task of a parent toward her children was "to conquer the will, and bring them to an obedient temper." She reported that her babies were "taught to fear the rod, and to cry softly; by which means they escaped the abundance of correction they might otherwise have had, and that most odious noise of the crying of children was rarely heard in the house."[7]

The Enlightenment produced an enthusiastic new discourse about childhood and child rearing. Starting around 1760, critics called for greater tenderness toward children and proposed imaginative new teaching methods. They objected to the practices of swaddling babies, using rigid whale-boned corsets to "straighten them out," and dressing children in miniature versions of adult clothing. Instead parents were urged to dress their children in simpler and more comfortable clothing to allow freedom of movement. For Enlightenment critics, the best hopes for creating a new society, untrammeled by the prejudices of the past, lay in a radical revision of child-rearing techniques according to "natural" laws.

One of the century's most influential works on child rearing was Jean-Jacques Rousseau's (zhahn-zhock roo-SOE) *Emile*, which fervently advocated breast-feeding and natural dress. Rousseau argued that boys' education should include plenty of fresh air and exercise and that they should be taught practical craft skills in addition to book learning. Reacting to what he perceived as the vanity and frivolity of upper-class Parisian women, Rousseau insisted girls' education focus on their future domestic responsibilities. For Rousseau, women's "nature" destined them solely for a life of marriage and child rearing. The ideas of Rousseau and other reformers were enthusiastically adopted by elite women, who did not adopt universal nursing but did at least begin to supervise their wet nurses more carefully.

For all his influence, Rousseau also reveals the occasional hypocrisy of Enlightenment thinkers. With regard to the child-rearing techniques he believed would create a better society, Rousseau had extremely high expectations; when it came to the five children he fathered with his common-law wife, however, he abandoned them all in foundling hospitals despite their mother's protests. None are known to have survived. For Rousseau, the idea of creating a natural man was more important than raising real children.

Schools and Popular Literature

The availability of formal education outside the home increased during the eighteenth century. Prussia led the way in the development of universal education, inspired by the Protestant idea that every believer should be able to read the Bible and by the new idea of a population capable of effectively serving the state. As early as 1717 Prussia made attendance at elementary schools compulsory, and more Protestant German states, such as Saxony and Württemberg (WUR-tuhm-burg), followed during the eighteenth century. In Scotland the focus on Bible study led to the creation of parish schools for all children, and in England "charity schools" were established for the poor. In Catholic France, some Christian schools were established to teach the catechism and prayers as well as reading and writing, and the Catholic Habsburg state went even further, promoting elementary education enthusiastically in the eighteenth century. Thus some elementary education was becoming a reality, and schools were of growing significance in the life of the child.

The result of these efforts was a remarkable growth in basic literacy between 1600 and 1800. Whereas in 1600 only one male in six was barely literate in France and Scotland, and one in four in England, by 1800 almost nine out of ten Scottish males, two out of three French males, and more than half of English males were literate. In all three countries, the bulk of the jump occurred in the eighteenth century. Women were also increasingly literate, although they lagged behind men.

Raoux: Young Woman Reading a Letter

Literacy rates for men and women rose substantially during the eighteenth century. The novel also emerged as a new literary genre in this period. With its focus on emotions, love, and family melodrama, the novel was seen as a particularly feminine genre, and it allowed women writers more access to publication. Writing and reading letters were also associated with women. Some contemporaries worried that women's growing access to reading and writing would excite their imagination and desires, leading to moral dissolution. (Réunion des Musées Nationaux/Art Resource, NY)

The growth in literacy promoted a growth in reading, and historians have carefully examined what the common people read in an attempt to discern what they were thinking. While the Bible remained the overwhelming favorite, especially in Protestant countries, short pamphlets known as chapbooks were the staple of popular literature. Printed on the cheapest paper available, many chapbooks dealt with religious subjects. They featured Bible stories, prayers, devotions, and the lives of saints and exemplary Christians. Promising happiness after death, devotional literature was also intensely practical. It gave the believer moral teachings and a confidence in God that helped in daily living.

Entertaining, often humorous stories formed a second element of popular literature. Fairy tales, medieval romances, true crime stories, and fantastic adventures were some of the delights that filled the peddler's pack as he approached a village. These tales presented a world of danger and magic, of supernatural powers, fairy godmothers, and evil trolls. The significance of these entertaining stories for the peasant reader is debated. Many scholars see them reflecting a desire for pure escapism and a temporary flight from harsh everyday reality. Others see the tales reflecting ancient folk wisdom and counseling prudence in a world full of danger and injustice, where wolves dress up like grandmothers and eat Little Red Riding Hoods.

Finally, some popular literature was highly practical, dealing with rural crafts, household repairs, useful plants, and similar matters. Much lore was stored in almanacs, where calendars listing secular, religious, and astrological events were mixed with agricultural schedules, arcane facts, and jokes. The almanac was universal, was not controversial, and was highly appreciated even by many in the comfortable classes. "Anyone who could would read an almanac."[8] In this way, elites still shared some elements of a common culture with the masses.

While the vast majority of ordinary people did not read the great works of the Enlightenment, that does not mean they were immune to its ideas. Urban working people were exposed to new ideas through public conversation and cheap publications that helped translate Enlightenment critiques into ordinary language. Servants who had overheard the discussions of their educated employers might disseminate new ideas on trips back to their villages.

Section Review

- Lower-class rural women generally breast-fed their infants, while urban and upper-class women most often hired a wet nurse, typically a rural woman, to suckle their infants.

- An unwanted pregnancy brought social and economic disaster, causing some women to turn to infanticide; in response, Europeans set up foundling hospitals that took in large numbers of infants, but few left, as infant death rates were high.

- The Enlightenment brought calls for a new tenderness and freedom for children; among the most influential was Rousseau's plea for boys to get exercise and practical life skills along with book learning and for girls to learn appropriate domestic skills.

- A growing number of schools contributed to increased literacy, and reading rates rose with the introduction of popular and devotional literature, novels, fairy tales, and books on practical subjects such as the almanac. The Bible and Bible stories remained favorite reading material.

Food, Medicine, and New Consumption Habits

How did new patterns of consumption and changing medical care affect people's lives?

One of the most important developments in European society in the eighteenth century was the emergence of a fledgling consumer culture. Much of the expansion took place in the upper and upper-middle classes, but a boom in cheap reproductions of luxury items also permitted people of modest means to purchase more objects. From food to ribbons and from coal stoves to umbrellas, the material world of city dwellers grew richer and more diverse. These developments created new expectations for comfort and hygiene in daily life. Medical practitioners greatly increased in number, although their techniques did not differ much from those of previous generations.

The possibility of picking and choosing among a new variety of consumer goods and provisioners encouraged the development of new notions of individuality and self-expression. A shop girl could stand out from her peers by her choice of a striped jacket, a colored parasol, or simply a new ribbon for her hair. New attitudes about privacy and intimate life also emerged. Whereas families previously shared common living spaces, in the eighteenth century they erected new partitions within their homes to create private nooks. Alongside an upturn in economic production, this "consumer revolution," as it has been called, dramatically changed European life in the eighteenth century. As in other developments, England led the way.

Diets and Nutrition

At the beginning of the eighteenth century, ordinary men and women depended on grain as fully as they had in the past. Brown bread and gruel remained the mainstays of people's diets, and while they did eat vegetables, their choices were typically limited to peas, beans, cabbage, carrots, and wild greens. Patterns of food consumption changed markedly as the century progressed. There was a general growth of market gardening, and a greater variety of vegetables appeared in towns and cities. This was particularly the case in the Low Countries and England, which pioneered new methods of farming.

The Columbian exchange of foods was also responsible for dietary changes. Originating in the Americas—along with corn, squash, tomatoes, and many other useful plants—the humble potato provided an excellent new food source for Europeans. Containing a good supply of carbohydrates, calories, and vitamins A and C, the potato offset the lack of vitamins from green vegetables in the poor person's diet, and it provided a much higher caloric yield than grain for a given piece of land. After initial resistance, the potato became an important dietary supplement in much of Europe by the end of the century. In the course of the eighteenth century the large towns and cities of maritime Europe also began to receive semitropical fruits, such as oranges and lemons, from Portugal and the West Indies, but they remained expensive.

The most remarkable dietary change in the eighteenth century was in the consumption of sugar and tea. No other commodities grew so quickly in consumption. Previously expensive and rare luxury items, they became dietary staples for people of all social classes. This was possible because of the steady drop in prices created by the expansion of colonial production and slave labor. Other colonial

Royal Interest in the Potato
Frederick the Great of Prussia, shown here supervising cultivation of the potato, used his influence and position to promote the new food on his estates and throughout Prussia. Peasants could grow potatoes with the simplest hand tools, but it was backbreaking labor, as this painting by R. Warthmüller suggests. (Private Collection, Hamburg/akg-images)

goods also became important items of daily consumption in this period, including coffee, tobacco, and chocolate.

Part of the motivation for consuming these products was a desire to emulate the habits of "respectable" people. The accelerating pace of work in the eighteenth century also seems to have created new needs for stimulants among working people. (See the feature "Listening to the Past: A Day in the Life of Paris" on pages 533–534.) Whereas the gentry took tea as a leisurely and genteel ritual, the lower classes usually drank tea at work. With the widespread adoption of these products (which turned out to be mildly to extremely addictive), working people in Europe became increasingly dependent on faraway colonial economies. Their understanding of daily necessities and how to procure those necessities shifted definitively, linking them into a globalized capitalism far beyond their ability to shape or control.

Toward a Consumer Society

Along with foodstuffs, all manner of other goods increased in variety and number in the eighteenth century. This proliferation led to a growth in consumption and new attitudes toward consumer goods so wide-ranging that some historians have referred to an eighteenth-century **"consumer revolution."** The long-term result of this revolution was the birth of a new type of society, in which people had greater access to finished goods and derived their self-identity as much from their consuming practices as from their working lives and place in the production process. The full emergence of a consumer society did not take place until much later, but its roots lie in the developments of the eighteenth century.

consumer revolution The growth in consumption and new attitudes toward consumer goods as a result of an increase in quantity and variety of foodstuffs and other goods in the eighteenth century.

Increased demand for consumer goods was not merely an innate response to increased supply. Eighteenth-century merchants cleverly pioneered new techniques to incite demand: they initiated marketing campaigns, opened fancy boutiques with large windows, and advertised the patronage of royal princes and princesses. By diversifying their product lines and greatly accelerating the turnover of styles, they seized the reins of fashion from the courtiers who had earlier controlled it. Instead of setting new styles, duchesses and marquises now bowed to the dictates of fashion merchants. Fashion also extended beyond court circles to touch many more items and social groups.

Clothing was one of the chief indicators of nascent consumerism. The wiles of entrepreneurs made fashionable clothing seem more desirable, while legions of women entering the textile and needle trades made it ever cheaper. As a result, eighteenth-century western Europe witnessed a dramatic rise in the consumption of clothing, particularly in large cities. One historian has documented an enormous growth in the size and value of Parisians' wardrobes from 1700 to 1789, as well as a new level of diversity in garments and accessories, colors, and fabrics. Colonial economies played an important role, supplying new materials, such as cotton and vegetable dyes, at low cost. Cheaper copies of elite styles made it possible for working people to aspire to follow fashion for the first time.[9]

Women were typically more interested in acquiring a fashionable wardrobe than were their husbands, brothers, and fathers. This was true across the social spectrum; in ribbons, shoes, gloves, and lace, French working women reaped in the consumer revolution what they had sewn in the industrious revolution (see pages 494–495). There were also new gender distinctions in dress. Previously, noblemen vied with women in the magnificence and ostentation of their dress; by the end of the eighteenth century men had begun to don early versions of the plain dark suit that remains standard male formalwear in the West. This was one

The Fashion Merchant's Shop
Shopping in fancy boutiques became a favorite leisure pastime of the rich in the eighteenth century. Whereas shops had previously been dark, cramped spaces, now they were filled with light from large plate-glass windows, staffed by finely dressed attendants, and equipped with chairs and large mirrors for a comfortable shopping experience. Fashion merchants (or milliners) sold hats, shawls, parasols, and an infinite variety of accessories and decorations. (Courtesy, University of Illinois Library)

more aspect of the increasingly rigid distinction drawn between appropriate male and female behavior.

The consumer revolution extended into the home as well. In 1700 a meal might be served in a common dish, with each person dipping his or her spoon into the pot. By the end of the eighteenth century even humble households contained a much greater variety of cutlery and dishes, making it possible for each person to eat from his or her own plate. More books and prints, which also proliferated at lower prices, decorated the walls. Improvements in glass-making provided more transparent glass, which allowed daylight to penetrate into gloomy rooms. Cold and smoky hearths were increasingly replaced by more efficient and cleaner coal stoves, which also eliminated the backache of cooking over an open fire. People began to assign specific functions to rooms, moving away from the practice of using the same room for sleeping, receiving guests, and working. Inner walls or screens were added to create these specific areas along with greater privacy. Rooms became warmer, better lit, more comfortable, and more personalized.

The scope of the new consumer economy should not be exaggerated. These developments were concentrated in large cities in northwestern Europe and in North America. Even in these centers the elite benefited the most from new modes of life. This was not yet the society of mass consumption that emerged toward the end of the nineteenth century with the full expansion of the Industrial Revolution. The eighteenth century did, however, lay the foundations for one of the most distinctive features of modern Western life: societies based on the consumption of goods and services obtained through the market in which individuals form their identities and self-worth through the goods they consume.

Medical Practitioners

With these advances in daily life, how did the care of sickness, pain, and disease evolve? Medical science continued to struggle in vain against these scourges. Yet the Enlightenment's focus on research and experimentation, along with a remarkable rise in the number of medical practitioners, laid the foundation for significant breakthroughs in the middle and late nineteenth century.

Care of the sick in the eighteenth century was the domain of several competing groups: faith healers, apothecaries (or pharmacists), physicians, surgeons, and midwives. Both men and women were prominent in the healing arts, as had been the case since the Middle Ages. But by 1700 the range of medical activities open to women was severely restricted because women were generally denied admission to medical colleges and lacked the diplomas necessary to practice. In the course of the eighteenth century, the position of women as midwives and healers further eroded.

Faith healers remained active. They and their patients believed that demons and evil spirits caused disease by lodging in the body and that the proper treatment was to exorcise, or drive out, the offending devil. This demonic view of disease was strongest in the countryside, where popular belief placed great faith in the healing power of religious relics, prayer, and the laying on of hands.

In the larger towns and cities, apothecaries sold a vast number of herbs, drugs, and patent medicines for every conceivable "temperament and distemper." Their prescriptions were incredibly complex—a hundred or more drugs might be included in a single prescription—and often very expensive. Like all varieties of medical practitioners, apothecaries advertised their wares, their high-class customers, and their miraculous cures in newspapers and commercial circulars. Medicine, like food and fashionable clothing, thus joined the era's new commercial culture.

Physicians, who were invariably men, were apprenticed in their teens to practicing physicians for several years of on-the-job training. This training was then
rounded out with hospital work or some university courses. Because such prolonged training was expensive, physicians came mainly from prosperous families,
and they usually concentrated on urban patients from similar social backgrounds.
They had little contact with urban workers and less with peasants. While physicians in the eighteenth century were increasingly willing to experiment with new
methods, they continued to practice the medieval cures of blood-letting and purging of the bowels.

Surgeons, in contrast to physicians, made considerable medical and social
progress in the eighteenth century. Long considered to be ordinary male artisans
comparable to butchers and barbers, surgeons began studying anatomy seriously
and improved their art. They learned to perform amputations when faced with
severely wounded limbs, but they labored in the face of incredible difficulties.
Almost all operations were performed without painkillers, for the anesthesias of
the day were hard to control and were believed too dangerous for general use.
Many patients died from the agony and shock of such operations. Surgery was also
performed in utterly unsanitary conditions, for there was no knowledge of bacteri-
ology and the nature of infection. The simplest wound treated by a surgeon could
fester and lead to death.

Midwives continued to deliver the overwhelming majority of babies throughout the eighteenth century. Trained initially by another woman practitioner—and
regulated by a guild in many cities—the midwife primarily assisted in labor and delivering babies but also handled other medical issues specific to women and infants. In France one enterprising Parisian midwife secured royal financing for
her campaign to teach better birthing techniques to village midwives, which reinforced the position of women practitioners. (See the feature "Individuals in Society: Madame du Coudray, the Nation's Midwife.") However, their profession came
under attack by surgeon-physicians, who used their monopoly over the new instrument of the forceps to seek lucrative new business. While midwives generally lost
no more babies than did male doctors, the doctors persuaded growing numbers of
wealthy women of the superiority of their services.

Experimentation and the intensified search for solutions to human problems
led to some real advances in medicine after 1750. The eighteenth century's greatest medical triumph was the conquest of smallpox. With the progressive decline of
bubonic plague, smallpox became the most terrible of the infectious diseases, and
it is estimated that 60 million Europeans died of it in the eighteenth century. Fully
80 percent of the population was stricken at some point in life.

The first step in the conquest of this killer in Europe came in the early eighteenth century. Lady Mary Wortley Montagu (**MON-tuh-gyoo**) brought the practice of **smallpox inoculation** to England from the Muslim lands of western Asia
where she had lived as the wife of the British ambassador. But inoculation with the
pus of a smallpox victim was risky because about one person in fifty died from it.
In addition, people who had been inoculated were infectious and often spread
the disease.

While the practice of inoculation with the smallpox virus was refined over the
century, the crucial breakthrough was made by Edward Jenner (1749–1823), a
talented country doctor. His starting point was the countryside belief that dairy
maids who had contracted cowpox did not get smallpox. Cowpox produces sores
that resemble those of smallpox, but the disease is mild and is not contagious. For
eighteen years Jenner practiced a kind of Baconian science, carefully collecting
data. Finally, in 1796 he performed his first vaccination on a young boy using

smallpox inoculation The practice
of vaccinating people with cowpox so
that they would not come down with
smallpox.

Individuals in Society

Madame du Coudray, the Nation's Midwife

In 1751 a highly esteemed Parisian midwife left the capital for a market town in central France. Having accepted an invitation to instruct local women in the skills of childbirth, Madame Angelique Marguerite Le Boursier du Coudray (**kood-RAY**) soon demonstrated a marvelous ability to teach students and win their respect. The thirty-six-year-old midwife found her mission: she would become the nation's midwife.

For eight years Madame du Coudray taught young women from the impoverished villages of Auvergne (**oh-VAIRN**). In doing so, she entered into the world of unschooled midwives who typically were solid matrons with several children who relied on traditional birthing practices and folk superstitions. Trained in Paris through a rigorous three-year apprenticeship and imbued with an Enlightenment faith in the power of knowledge, du Coudray had little sympathy for these village midwives. Many peasant mothers told her about their difficult deliveries and their many uterine "infirmities," which they attributed to "the ignorance of the women to whom they had recourse, or to that of some inexperienced village [male] surgeons."* Du Coudray agreed. Botched deliveries by incompetents resulted in horrible deformities and unnecessary deaths.

Determined to raise standards, Madame du Coudray saw that her unlettered pupils learned through the senses, not through books. Thus she made, possibly for the first time in history, a life-sized obstetrical model—a "machine"—out of fabric and stuffing for use in her classes. "I had . . . the students maneuver in front of me on a machine . . . which represented the pelvis of a woman, the womb, its opening, its ligaments, the conduit called the vagina, the bladder, and *rectum intestine*. I added an [artificial] child of natural size, whose joints were flexible enough to be able to be put in different positions." Now du Coudray could demonstrate the problems of childbirth, and each student could practice on the model in the "lab session."

As her reputation grew, Madame du Coudray sought to reach a national audience. In 1757 she published the first of several editions of her *Manual on the Art of Childbirth*. Handsomely and effectively illustrated (see the image below), the *Manual* incorporated her hands-on teaching method and served as a text and reference for students and graduates. In 1759 the government authorized Madame du Coudray to carry her instruction "throughout the realm" and promised financial support. Her reception was not always warm, for she was a self-assured and demanding woman who could anger old midwives, male surgeons, and skeptical officials. But aided by servants, a niece, and her husband, this inspired and indefatigable woman took her course from town to town until her retirement in 1784. Typically her students were young peasant women on tiny stipends who came into town from surrounding villages for two to three months of instruction. Classes met

Plate from Madame du Coudray's manual, illustrating "another incorrect method of delivery." (Rare Books Division, Countway [Francis A.] Library of Medicine)

mornings and afternoons six days a week, with ample time to practice on the mannequin (**MAN-uh-kin**). After a recuperative break, Madame du Coudray and her entourage moved on.

Teaching thousands of fledgling midwives, Madame du Coudray may well have contributed to the decline in infant mortality and to the increase in population occurring in France in the eighteenth century—an increase she and her royal supporters fervently desired. Certainly she spread better knowledge about childbirth from the educated elite to the common people.

Questions for Analysis

1. How do you account for Madame du Coudray's remarkable success?
2. Does Madame du Coudray's career reflect tensions between educated elites and the common people? If so, how?

* Quotes are from Nina Gelbart, *The King's Midwife: A History and Mystery of Madame du Coudray* (Berkeley: University of California Press, 1998), pp. 60–61. This definitive biography is excellent.

Section Review

- Potatoes and new vegetables from the colonies added to the diet as did sugar and tea; their falling prices helped them become staples for all social classes.

- Increased availability of finished goods and new techniques for marketing them helped produce a consumer revolution in some parts of Europe, especially among women, thus marking the first step toward a society in which people derive self-identity from the possessions they consume.

- Eighteenth-century medical practitioners included countryside faith healers, apothecaries selling a wide range of advertised treatments, physicians and surgeons who worked primarily with the wealthy and were almost all men, and midwives who assisted women in birthing and faced new competition from male doctors.

- Madame du Coudray was a French midwife who brought her training and knowledge of childbirth to the masses by holding classes and offering hands-on training.

- The biggest breakthrough in medicine was the smallpox inoculation, which William Jenner perfected using cowpox to vaccinate people.

matter taken from a milkmaid with cowpox. After performing more successful vaccinations, Jenner published his findings in 1798. The new method of treatment spread rapidly, and smallpox soon declined to the point of disappearance in Europe and then throughout the world.

Religion and Popular Culture

What were the patterns of popular religion and culture, and how did they interact with the worldview of the educated public and the Enlightenment?

Though the critical spirit of the Enlightenment made great inroads in the eighteenth century, the majority of ordinary men and women, especially those in rural areas, remained committed Christians. Religious faith promised salvation and eternal life, and it gave comfort and courage in the face of sorrow and death. Religion also remained strong because it was usually embedded in local traditions, everyday social experience, and popular culture.

Yet the popular religion of the European village was everywhere enmeshed in a larger world of church hierarchies and state power. These powerful outside forces sought to regulate religious life at the local level. Their efforts created tensions that helped set the scene for a vigorous religious revival in Germany and England. Similar tensions arose in Catholic countries, where powerful elites criticized and attacked popular religious practices that their increasingly rationalistic minds deemed foolish and superstitious.

The Institutional Church

As in the Middle Ages, the local parish church remained the focal point of religious devotion and community cohesion. Congregations gossiped and swapped stories after services, and neighbors came together in church for baptisms, marriages, funerals, and special events. Priests and parsons kept the community records of births, deaths, and marriages, distributed charity, looked after orphans, and provided primary education to the common people. Thus the parish church was woven into the very fabric of community life.

While the parish church remained central to the community, it was also subject to greater control from the state. In Protestant areas, princes and monarchs headed the official church, and they regulated their "territorial churches" strictly, selecting personnel and imposing detailed rules. By the eighteenth century, the radical ideas of the Reformation had resulted in another version of church bureaucracy. Catholic monarchs in this period also took greater control of religious matters in their kingdoms, weakening papal authority. Spain, a deeply Catholic country with devout rulers, took firm control of ecclesiastical appointments. Papal proclamations could not even be read in Spanish churches without prior approval from the government. Spain also asserted state control over the Spanish Inquisition, which pursued heresy as an independent agency under Rome's direction and went far toward creating a "national" Catholic Church, as France had done earlier.

A more striking indication of state power and papal weakness was the fate of the Society of Jesus, or Jesuits. The well-educated Jesuits were extraordinary teachers, missionaries, and agents of the papacy. In many Catholic countries, they exercised tremendous political influence, holding high government positions and educating the nobility in their colleges. Yet by playing politics so effectively, the

Jesuits eventually elicited a broad coalition of enemies. Bitter controversies led Louis XV to order the Jesuits out of France in 1763 and to confiscate their property. France and Spain then pressured Rome to dissolve the Jesuits completely. In 1773 a reluctant pope caved in, although the order was revived after the French Revolution.

Some Catholic rulers also believed that the clergy in monasteries and convents should make a more practical contribution to social and religious life. Austria, a leader in controlling the church (see page 479) and promoting primary education, showed how far the process could go. Maria Theresa began by sharply restricting entry into "unproductive" orders. In his Edict on Idle Institutions, her successor Joseph II abolished contemplative orders, henceforth permitting only orders that were engaged in teaching, nursing, or other practical work. The state also expropriated the dissolved monasteries and used their wealth for charitable purposes and higher salaries for ordinary priests. These measures recalled the radical transformation of the Protestant Reformation.

Protestant Revival

By the late seventeenth century the vast reforms of the Reformation were complete and routinized in most Protestant churches. Indeed, many official Protestant churches had settled into a smug complacency. In the Reformation heartland, one concerned German minister wrote that the Lutheran church "had become paralyzed in forms of dead doctrinal conformity" and badly needed a return to its original inspiration.[10] His voice was one of many that prepared and then guided a powerful Protestant revival that succeeded because it answered the intense but increasingly unsatisfied needs of common people.

The Protestant revival began in Germany. It was known as **Pietism** (PIE-uh-tiz-um), and three aspects helped explain its powerful appeal. First, Pietism called for a warm, emotional religion that everyone could experience. Enthusiasm—in prayer, in worship, in preaching, in life itself—was the key concept. "Just as a drunkard becomes full of wine, so must the congregation become filled with spirit," declared one exuberant writer. Another said simply, "The heart must burn."[11]

Second, Pietism reasserted the earlier radical stress on the priesthood of all believers, thereby reducing the gulf between official clergy and Lutheran laity. Bible reading and study were enthusiastically extended to all classes, and this provided a powerful spur for popular education as well as individual religious development (see page 518). Finally, Pietists believed in the practical power of Christian rebirth in everyday affairs. Reborn Christians were expected to lead good, moral lives and to come from all social classes.

Pietism had a major impact on John Wesley (1703–1791), who served as the catalyst for popular religious revival in England. As a teaching fellow at Oxford University, Wesley organized a Holy Club for similarly minded students, who were soon known contemptuously as **Methodists** because they were so methodical in their devotion. Yet like the young Luther, Wesley remained intensely troubled about his own salvation even after his ordination as an Anglican priest in 1728.

Wesley's anxieties related to grave problems of the faith in England. The government shamelessly used the Church of England to provide favorites with high-paying jobs. Building of churches practically stopped while the population grew, and in many parishes there was a shortage of pews. Churches were customarily locked on weekdays. Services and sermons had settled into an uninspiring routine. Moreover, Enlightenment skepticism was making inroads among the educated classes, and deism was becoming popular. Some bishops and church leaders

Pietism The name for the Protestant revival that began in Germany; it stressed enthusiasm, the priesthood of all believers, and the practical power of Christian rebirth in everyday affairs.

Methodists The name given to a Protestant religious group started by John Wesley, so named because of their methodical devotion.

Hogarth's Satirical View of the Church
William Hogarth (1697–1764) was one of the foremost satirical artists of his day. This image mocks a London Methodist meeting, where the congregation swoons in enthusiasm over the preacher's sermon. The woman in the foreground giving birth to rabbits refers to a hoax perpetrated in 1726 by a servant named Mary Tofts; the credulousness of those who believed Tofts is likened to that of the Methodist congregation. (HIP/Art Resource, NY)

seemed to believe that doctrines such as the Virgin Birth were little more than elegant superstitions.

Spiritual counseling from a sympathetic Pietist minister from Germany prepared Wesley for a mystical, emotional "conversion" in 1738. He described this critical turning point in his *Journal*:

> In the evening I went to a [Christian] society in Aldersgate Street where one was reading Luther's preface to the Epistle to the Romans. About a quarter before nine, while he was describing the change which God works in the heart through faith in Christ, I felt my heart strangely warmed. I felt I did trust in Christ, Christ alone for salvation; and an assurance was given me that he had taken away my sins, even mine, and saved me from the law of sin and death.[12]

Wesley took the good news of salvation to the people, traveling some 225,000 miles by horseback and preaching more than forty thousand sermons in fifty years. Crowds assembled in open fields to hear him speak. Of critical importance was Wesley's rejection of Calvinist predestination—the doctrine of salvation granted to only a select few. Instead, he preached that *all* men and women who earnestly sought salvation might be saved. It was a message of hope and joy, of free will and universal salvation.

Wesley's ministry won converts, formed Methodist cells, and eventually resulted in a new denomination. And as Wesley had been inspired by the Pietist revival in Germany, so evangelicals in the Church of England and the old dissenting groups now followed Wesley's example, giving impetus to an even broader awakening among the lower classes. In Protestant countries, religion remained a vital force in the lives of the people.

Jansenism A form of Catholic revival that originated with the Flemish theologian, Cornelius Jansen, emphasizing the heavy weight of original sin and accepting the doctrine of predestination, rejected as heresy by the official church.

Catholic Piety

Catholicism had its own version of the Pietist revivals that shook Protestant Europe. **Jansenism** (JAN-suh-niz-uhm) has been described by one historian as the "illegitimate off-spring of the Protestant Reformation and the Catholic Counter-Reformation."[13] It originated with the Flemish theologian Cornelius Jansen (1585–1638), who called for a return to the austere early Christianity of Saint Augustine. In contrast to the worldly Jesuits, Jansen emphasized the heavy weight of original sin and accepted the doctrine of predestination.

Although outlawed by papal and royal edicts as Calvinist heresy, Jansenism attracted Catholic followers eager for religious renewal, particularly in France.

Many members of elite French society, especially judicial nobles and some parish priests, became known for their Jansenist piety and spiritual devotion. Such stern religious values encouraged the judiciary's increasing opposition to the monarchy in the second half of the eighteenth century. Among the poor, a different strain of Jansenism took hold. Prayer meetings brought men and women together in ecstatic worship, and some participants fell into convulsions and spoke in tongues.

Jansenism was an urban phenomenon. In the countryside, many peasants in Catholic countries held religious beliefs that were marginal to the Christian faith altogether, often of obscure or even pagan origin. On the Feast of Saint Anthony, for example, priests were expected to bless salt and bread for farm animals to protect them from disease. One saint's relics could help cure a child of fear, and there were healing springs for many ailments. The ordinary person combined strong Christian faith with a wealth of time-honored superstitions.

Inspired initially by the fervor of the Catholic Counter- Reformation and then to some extent by the critical rationalism of the Enlightenment, parish priests and Catholic hierarchies sought increasingly to "purify" popular religious practice. French priests particularly denounced the "various remnants of paganism" found in popular bonfire ceremonies during Lent, in which young men, "yelling and screaming like madmen," tried to jump over the bonfires in order to help the crops

Procession of Nuns at Port-Royal des Champs

The convent of Port-Royal, located twenty miles southwest of Paris, was a center of Jansenist activity throughout the seventeenth century. Angered by the nuns' defiance, Louis XIV ordered them forcibly relocated in 1709. To generate support, the artist Magdelaine Horthemels painted a series of images depicting the pious and placid religious life at the convent. The convent was nonetheless destroyed by Louis's forces in 1710. This image is one of many copies of Horthemels' work made by Jansenists in the eighteenth century. (Réunion des Musées Nationaux/ Art Resource, NY)

grow and protect themselves from illness. One priest saw rational Christians regressing into pagan animals—"the triumph of Hell and the shame of Christianity."[14]

In contrast with Protestant reformers, many Catholic priests and hierarchies preferred a compromise between theological purity and the people's piety. Thus, the severity of the attack on popular Catholicism varied widely by country and region. Where authorities pursued purification vigorously, as in Austria under Joseph II, pious peasants saw only an incomprehensible attack on the true faith and drew back in anger.

Carnival The pre-Lent festival of reveling and excess in Catholic and Mediterranean Europe.

blood sports Spectator sports involving torture and forced combat of animals, such as bullbaiting and cockfighting.

Leisure and Recreation

The combination of religious celebration and popular recreation was most strikingly displayed at **Carnival,** a time of reveling in Catholic and Mediterranean Europe. Carnival preceded Lent—the forty days of fasting and penitence before Easter—and for a few exceptional days in February or March, a wild release of drinking, masquerading, and dancing reigned. Moreover, a combination of plays, processions, and rowdy spectacles turned the established order upside down. Peasants dressed up as nobles and men as women, and rich masters waited on their servants at the table. This annual holiday gave people a much-appreciated chance to release their pent-up frustrations and aggressions before life returned to the usual pattern of hierarchy and hard work.

Despite the spread of literacy, the culture of the common people was largely oral rather than written. In the cold, dark winter months, families gathered around the fireplace to talk, sing, tell stories, do craftwork, and keep warm. In some parts of Europe, women would gather together in groups in someone's cottage to chat, sew, spin, and laugh. Sometimes a few young men would be invited so that the daughters (and mothers) could size up potential suitors in a supervised atmosphere. A favorite recreation of men was drinking and talking with buddies in public places, and it was a sorry village that had no tavern.

Towns and cities offered a wide range of amusements. Many of these had to be paid for because the eighteenth century saw a sharp increase in the commercialization of leisure-time activities. Urban fairs featured prepared foods, acrobats, freak shows, open-air performances, optical illusions, and the like. Such entertainments attracted a variety of social classes. So did the growing number of commercial, profit-oriented spectator sports. These ranged from traveling circuses and horse races to boxing matches and bullfights. Modern sports heroes, such as brain-bashing heavyweight champions and haughty matadors, made their appearance on the historical scene.

Blood sports, such as bullbaiting and cockfighting, remained popular with the masses. In bullbaiting, the bull, usually staked on a chain in the courtyard of an inn, was attacked by ferocious dogs for the amusement of the innkeeper's clients. Eventually the maimed and tortured animal was slaughtered by a butcher and sold as meat. In cockfighting two roosters, carefully trained by their owners and armed with razor-sharp steel spurs, slashed and clawed each other in a small ring until the victor won—and the loser died. An added attraction of cockfighting was that the screaming spectators could bet on the lightning-fast combat and its uncertain outcome.

In trying to place the vibrant popular culture of the common people in broad perspective, historians have stressed the growing criticism levied against it by the educated elites in the second half of the eighteenth century. These elites, who had previously shared the popular enthusiasm for religious festivals, Carnival, drinking in taverns, blood sports, and the like, now tended to see these activities as superstition, sin, disorder, and vulgarity.[15] The resulting attack on popular culture, which

Section Review

- The local parish was still the center of community life but increasingly the state exerted more control and, in Catholic areas, weakened papal authority.

- Protestant revival was known as Pietism and became popular because it included emotion and enthusiasm, enforced the priesthood of all believers, and promoted morality for all social classes.

- John Wesley, frustrated with uninspiring services and routines, attracted followers, later called Methodists, with his message of universal salvation, hope, and joy.

- In Catholic countries, especially France, Jansenism gained a hold in the cities and focused on a return to piety and on a belief in original sin and predestination, while in the countryside a combination of Christian and pagan beliefs was common.

- For recreation people got together to tell stories, drink in taverns, watch sporting events, attend an urban fair, or celebrate, dance, and let loose during Carnival—all pastimes increasingly frowned upon as sinful by educated elites.

had its more distant origins in the Protestant clergy's efforts to eliminate frivolity and superstition, was intensified as an educated public embraced the critical worldview of the Enlightenment.

Chapter Review

| What changes occurred in marriage and the family in the course of the eighteenth century? (page 511)

In the current generation, imaginative research has greatly increased our understanding of ordinary life and social patterns of the past. In the eighteenth century the life of the people remained primarily rural and oriented toward the local community. Tradition, routine, and well-established codes of behavior framed much of the everyday experience. Thus, just as the three-field agricultural cycle and its pattern of communal rights had determined traditional patterns of grain production, so did community values in the countryside strongly encourage a late marriage age and a low rate of illegitimate births. Yet powerful forces also worked for change. Many changes came from outside and above, from the aggressive capitalists, educated elites, and government officials. Closely knit villages began to lose control over families and marital practices, as can be seen in the earlier marriages of cottage workers and in the beginning of the explosion in illegitimate births.

| What was life like for children, and how did attitudes toward childhood evolve? (page 515)

Infancy and childhood were highly vulnerable stages of life. In some parts of Europe fewer than half of all children reached the age of ten. Infant mortality was high in areas like France, in which wet-nursing was commonly practiced. Treatment of children could be harsh in an early modern society that was characterized by much higher levels of violence and brutality than Western societies today. The second half of the eighteenth century witnessed a new concern with methods of child raising inspired by Enlightenment efforts to reform human society. Schools for non-elite children spread across Europe, leading to a growth in literacy rates.

| How did new patterns of consumption and changing medical care affect people's lives? (page 520)

The urban populace benefited from the surge in agricultural and industrial production. People found a greater variety of food products at the market, including new stimulants produced in the colonies that soon became staples of elite and popular consumption. Within homes, standards of comfort and hygiene increased, and the emerging consumer society offered new possibilities for self-expression and individuality. Medical techniques continued to follow traditional patterns, but the number of practitioners grew, and great strides were made against smallpox.

| What were the patterns of popular religion and culture, and how did they interact with the worldview of the educated public and the Enlightenment? (page 526)

Patterns of recreation and leisure, from churchgoing and religious festivals to sewing and drinking in groups within an oral culture, reflected and reinforced community ties

Key Terms

community controls (p. 513)
illegitimacy explosion (p. 514)
wet-nursing (p. 516)
infanticide (p. 517)
consumer revolution (p. 521)
smallpox inoculation (p. 524)
Pietism (p. 527)
Methodists (p. 527)
Jansenism (p. 528)
Carnival (p. 530)
blood sports (p. 530)

and values. Many long-standing beliefs and practices remained strong forces and sustained continuity in popular life. A wave of religious revival counteracted the secular tendencies of the Enlightenment, ensuring that religion continued to have a strong hold over the popular classes. The next great wave of change would be inaugurated by revolution in politics.

Notes

1. Quoted in J. M. Beattie, "The Criminality of Women in Eighteenth-Century England," *Journal of Social History* 8 (Summer 1975): 86.
2. Quoted in R. Cobb, *The Police and the People: French Popular Protest, 1789–1820* (Oxford: Clarendon Press, 1970), p. 238.
3. Pier Paolo Viazzo, "Mortality, Fertility, and Family," in *Family Life in Early Modern Times, 1500–1789*, ed. David I. Kertzer and Marzio Barbagli (New Haven: Yale University Press, 2001), p. 180.
4. Robert Woods, "Did Montaigne Love His Children? Demography and the Hypothesis of Parental Indifference," *Journal of Interdisciplinary History* 33, 3 (2003): 426.
5. Alysa Levene, "The Estimation of Mortality at the London Foundling Hospital, 1741–99," *Population Studies* 59, 1 (2005): 87–97.
6. Cited in Woods, "Did Montaigne Love His Children?," p. 421.
7. Ibid., pp. 13, 16.
8. E. Kennedy, *A Cultural History of the French Revolution* (New Haven: Yale University Press, 1989), p. 47.
9. Daniel Roche, *The Culture of Clothing: Dress and Fashion in the Ancien Regime*. Translated by Jean Birrell (Cambridge: Cambridge University Press, 1996).
10. Quoted in K. Pinson, *Pietism as a Factor in the Rise of German Nationalism* (New York: Columbia University Press, 1934), p. 13.
11. Ibid., pp. 43–44.
12. Quoted in S. Andrews, *Methodism and Society* (London: Longmans, Green, 1970), p. 327.
13. Dale Van Kley, "The Rejuvenation and Rejection of Jansenism in History and Historiography," *French Historical Studies* 29 (Fall 2006): 649–684.
14. Quoted in T. Tackett, *Priest and Parish in Eighteenth-Century France* (Princeton, N.J.: Princeton University Press, 1977), p. 214.
15. Woloch, *Eighteenth-Century Europe*, pp. 220–221; see also pp. 214–220 for this section.

To assess your mastery of this chapter, go to **bedfordstmartins.com/mckaywestbrief**

Listening to the Past

A Day in the Life of Paris

Louis-Sébastien Mercier (1740–1814) was the best chronicler of everyday life in eighteenth-century Paris. His masterpiece was the Tableau de Paris (1781–1788), a multi-volume work composed of 1,049 chapters that covered subjects ranging from convents to cafés, bankruptcy to booksellers, the latest fashions to royal laws. He aimed to convey the infinite diversity of people, places, and things he saw around him, and in so doing he left future generations a precious record of the changing dynamics of Parisian society in the second half of the eighteenth century.

Mercier was born in 1740 to a weapons-maker father and a mother similarly descended from the respectable artisan classes. Neither rich nor poor, the family enjoyed a comfortable lifestyle without luxury. This middling position ideally suited Mercier for observing the extremes of wealth and poverty around him. Although these volumes contain many wonderful glimpses of daily life, they should not be taken for an objective account. Mercier brought his own moral and political sensibilities, influenced by Jean-Jacques Rousseau, to the task.

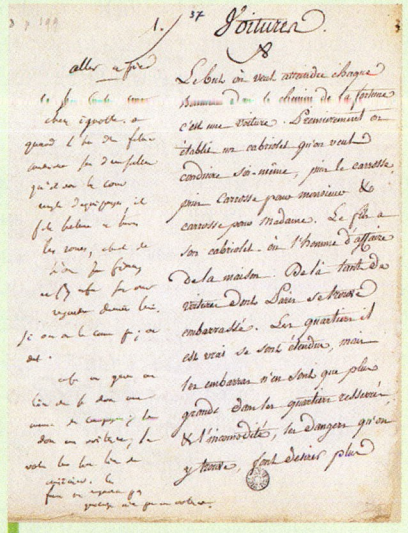

A page from Mercier's original manuscript.
(Bibliothèque nationale de France)

At one in the morning six thousand peasants arrive, bringing the town's provision of vegetables and fruits and flowers, and make straight for the Halles;* their beasts have come eighteen leagues perhaps, and are weary. As for the market itself, it never sleeps. Morpheus never shakes his poppy-seed there. Perpetual noise, perpetual motion, the curtain never rings down on the enormous stage; first come the fishmongers, and after these the egg-dealers, and after these the retail buyers; for the Halles keep all the other markets of Paris going; they are the warehouses whence these draw their supplies. The food of the whole city is shifted and sorted in high-piled baskets; you may see eggs, pyramids of eggs, moved here and there, up steps and down, in and out of the throngs, miraculous; not one is ever broken. . . .

This impenetrable din contrasts oddly with the sleeping streets, for at that hour none but thieves and poets are awake.

* The city's central wholesale food market.

Twice a week, at six, those distributors of the staff of life, the bakers of Gonesse,† bring in an enormous quantity of loaves to the town, and may take none back through the barriers. And at this same hour workmen take up their tools, and trudge off to their day's labour. Coffee with milk is, unbelievably, the favoured drink among these stalwarts nowadays.

At street-corners, where the pale light from a street lamp falls, the coffee women stand, carrying their tin urns on their backs; they sell their coffee in earthenware cups, two sous a cup, one penny, and not too well sugared at that; but our workmen find it very much to their taste. . . .

So coffee-drinking has become a habit, and one so deep-rooted that the working classes will start the day on nothing else. It is not costly, and has more flavour to it, and more nourishment too, than anything else they can afford to drink; so they consume immense quantities, and say that if a man can only have coffee for breakfast it will keep him going till nightfall. They take only two meals in the

† A suburb of Paris, famous for the excellent bread baked there.

twenty-four hours; that at midday and the evening snack of supper, what they call the *persillade*. . . .

If the sybarites of Paris, those who like to lie abed till noon, had their way, there would be no smiths in the city, no horses shod, and no pots and pans mended; all such noise would be banished without the walls. . . .

Their complaint is well founded; but if their remedy were followed, and carried to extremes, there would be no hats made in Paris, because of the stink of the felt; no leather tanned, no varnish nor perfume made for the same reason, although they themselves make use of these commodities. . . . Privilege would allow no shop-windows, but only porticoes to shelter carriages; would strew straw in the streets from midnight till midday, when Privilege does the world the honor of waking . . . for only Privilege may be privileged to fill the streets with the clatter of wheels and hoofs and to keep others from sleeping.

Questions for Analysis

1. What different social groups does Mercier describe in Paris? On what basis does he categorize people?

2. What is Mercier's attitude toward the poor and the rich? Does he approve or disapprove of Parisian society as he describes it?

Source: From *Panorama of Paris: Selections from "Le Tableau de Paris,"* Louis Sebastien Mercier, based on the translation by Helen Simpson, edited and with a new preface and translations by Jeremy D. Popkin. Copyright © 1999 The Pennsylvania State University. Reprinted by permission of Penn State Press.

In this painting by the female artist Nanine Vallain, the figure of Liberty bears a copy of the Declaration of the Rights of Man in one hand and a pike to defend them in the other. The painting hung in the Jacobin Club until its fall from power. (Musée de la Revolution Française, Vizille/The Bridgeman Art Library)

CHAPTER 21

The Revolution in Politics

1775–1815

Chapter Preview

Background to Revolution
What social, political, and economic factors formed the background to the French Revolution?

Revolution in Metropole and Colony (1789–1791)
What were the immediate events that sparked the Revolution, and how did they result in the formation of a constitutional monarchy in France? How did the ideals and events of the early Revolution raise new aspirations in the colonies?

World War and Republican France (1791–1799)
How and why did the Revolution take a radical turn at home and in the colonies?

The Napoleonic Era (1799–1815)
Why did Napoleon Bonaparte assume control of France, and what factors led to his downfall? How did the new republic of Haiti gain independence from France?

INDIVIDUALS IN SOCIETY: Toussaint L'Ouverture

LISTENING TO THE PAST: Revolution and Women's Rights

535

The last years of the eighteenth century were a time of great upheaval. A series of revolutions and revolutionary wars challenged the old order of monarchs and aristocrats. The ideas of freedom and equality, ideas that continue to shape the world, flourished and spread. The revolutionary era began in North America in 1775. Then in 1789 France, the most influential country in Europe, became the leading revolutionary nation. It established first a constitutional monarchy, then a radical republic, and finally a new empire under Napoleon. Inspired by both the ideals of the Revolution and internal colonial conditions, the slaves of Saint-Domingue rose up in 1791. Their rebellion led to the creation of the new independent nation of Haiti in 1805.

The armies of France violently exported revolution beyond the nation's borders in an effort to establish new governments throughout much of Europe. The world of modern domestic and international politics was born.

Background to Revolution

What social, political, and economic factors formed the background to the French Revolution?

The origins of the French Revolution have been one of the most debated topics in history. In order to understand the path to revolution, numerous interrelated factors must be taken into account. These include deep social changes in France, a long-term political crisis that eroded monarchical legitimacy, the impact of new political ideas derived from the Enlightenment, the emergence of a "public sphere" in which such opinions were formed and shared, and, perhaps most importantly, a financial crisis created by France's participation in expensive overseas wars.

estates The three legal categories, or orders, of France's inhabitants: the clergy, the nobility, and everyone else.

Legal Orders and Social Change

As in the Middle Ages, France's 25 million inhabitants were still legally divided into three orders, or **estates**—the clergy, the nobility, and everyone else. As the nation's first estate, the clergy numbered about one hundred thousand and had important privileges, including exemption from regular taxes and the ability to tax landowners. The second estate consisted of some four hundred thousand nobles who owned about 25 percent of the land in France outright. The nobility also enjoyed special privileges associated with their exalted social position, including lighter taxes, exclusive hunting and fishing rights, monopolies on bread baking and wine pressing equipment, and the right to wear swords. The third estate was a conglomeration of very different social groups—prosperous merchants, lawyers, and officials along with

A FAUT ESPERER Q'EU JEU LA FINIRA BEN TOT.

The Three Estates

In this political cartoon from 1789 a peasant of the third estate struggles under the crushing burden of a happy clergyman and a plumed nobleman. The caption—"Let's hope this game ends soon"—sets forth a program of reform that any peasant could understand. (Réunion des Musées Nationaux/Art Resource, NY)

poorer peasants, urban artisans, and unskilled day laborers—united only by their shared legal status as distinct from the nobility and clergy.

In discussing the origins of the French Revolution, historians long focused on growing tensions between the nobility and the comfortable members of the third estate, the *bourgeoisie* (**boor-zwah-ZEE**) or upper middle class. In this formulation, the French bourgeoisie eventually rose up to lead the entire third estate in a great social revolution that destroyed feudal privileges and established a capitalist order based on individualism and a market economy.

In recent years, a flood of new research has challenged these accepted views. Above all, revisionist historians have questioned the existence of growing social conflict between a progressive capitalistic bourgeoisie and a reactionary feudal nobility in eighteenth-century France. Instead, they see both bourgeoisie and nobility as highly fragmented, riddled with internal rivalries. The sword nobility, for example, who descended from the oldest noble families, was separated by differences in wealth, education, and worldview from the newer and less prestigious robe nobility, who acquired noble titles through service in the royal administration and judiciary. Differences within the bourgeoisie—between wealthy financiers and local lawyers, for example—were no less profound. Rather than standing as unified blocs against each other, nobility and bourgeoisie formed two parallel social ladders increasingly linked together at the top by wealth, marriage, and Enlightenment culture.

Revisionist historians note that the nobility and the bourgeoisie were not really at odds in the economic sphere. Investment in land and government service were the preferred activities of both groups, and the ideal of the merchant capitalist was to gain enough wealth to retire from trade, purchase an estate, and live nobly as a large landowner. Indeed, wealthy members of the third estate could even move into the second estate by serving the government and purchasing noble positions. At the same time, wealthy nobles often acted as aggressive capitalists, investing especially in mining, metallurgy, and foreign trade. In addition, until the revolution actually began, key sections of the nobility were liberal and generally joined the bourgeoisie in opposition to the government.

Revisionists have clearly shaken the belief that the bourgeoisie and the nobility were inevitably locked in growing conflict before the Revolution. Yet they also make clear that the Old Regime had ceased to correspond with social reality by the 1780s. Legally, society was still based on rigid orders inherited from the Middle Ages. In reality, France had already moved far toward being a society based on wealth and education in which an emerging elite that included both aristocratic and bourgeois notables was frustrated by a bureaucratic monarchy that continued to claim the right to absolute power.

The Crisis of Political Legitimacy

Overlaying these social changes was a century-long political and fiscal struggle between the monarchy and its opponents that was primarily enacted in the law courts. When Louis XIV died, his successor Louis XV (r. 1715–1774) was only five years

CHRONOLOGY

1775–1783	American Revolution
1786–1789	Financial crisis in France
1789	Feudalism abolished in France; ratification of U.S. Constitution; storming of the Bastille
1789–1799	French Revolution
1790	Burke, *Reflections on the Revolution in France*
1791	Slave insurrection in Saint-Domingue
1792	Wollstonecraft, *A Vindication of the Rights of Woman*
1793	Execution of Louis XVI
1793–1794	Economic controls to help poor in France; Robespierre's Reign of Terror
1794	Robespierre deposed and executed
1794–1799	Thermidorian reaction
1799–1815	Napoleonic era
1804	Haitian republic declares independence
1812	Napoleon invades Russia
1814–1815	Napoleon defeated and exiled

old. The high courts of France—the *parlements*—regained the ancient right to evaluate royal decrees publicly in writing before they were registered and given the force of law. The parlements used this power to prevent the king from imposing taxes after the War of the Austrian Succession, and then the Seven Years' War plunged France into a fiscal crisis. During the latter crisis, the Parlement of Paris asserted that it was acting as the representative of the entire nation when it checked the king's power to levy taxes.

After years of attempting to compromise with the parlements, Louis XV roused himself for a determined defense of his absolutist inheritance. His appointee as chancellor, René de Maupeou (maw-POO), abolished the existing parlements, exiled the vociferous members of the Parlement of Paris to the provinces, and began to tax the privileged groups. Public opinion as a whole sided with the old parlements, however, and there was widespread criticism of "royal despotism." The king also came under attack for sexual scandals and lost the sacred aura of God's anointed on earth.

desacralization The stripping away of the sacred aura of the king as God's anointed on earth.

Despite this progressive **desacralization** (dee-SAY-kruh-lie-ZAY-shun) of the monarchy, its power was still great enough to ride over the opposition, and Louis XV would probably have prevailed if he had lived to a ripe old age, but he died in 1774. The new king, Louis XVI (r. 1774–1792), was a shy twenty-year-old with good intentions. Taking the throne, he is reported to have said, "What I should like most is to be loved."[1] The eager-to-please monarch yielded in the face of vehement opposition from France's educated elite. He dismissed chancellor Maupeou and repudiated the strong-willed minister's work. Louis also waffled on the economy, dismissing controller general Turgot when his attempts to liberalize the economy drew fire. A weakened but unreformed monarchy now faced a judicial opposition that claimed to speak for the entire French nation. Increasingly locked in stalemate, the country was drifting toward renewed financial crisis and political upheaval.

The Impact of the American Revolution

Coinciding with the first years of Louis XVI's reign, the American Revolution had an enormous impact on France both in practical and ideological terms. French expenses to support the colonists bankrupted the Crown, while the ideals of liberty and equality provided heady inspiration for political reform.

Like the French Revolution some years later, the American Revolution had its immediate origins in struggles over increased taxes. The high cost of the Seven Years' War—fought with little financial contribution from the colonies—doubled the British national debt. When the government tried to recoup some of the losses in increased taxes on the colonies in 1765, the colonists reacted with anger.

The key questions were political rather than economic. To what extent could the home government assert its power while limiting the authority of colonial legislatures and their elected representatives? Accordingly, who should represent the colonies, and who had the right to make laws for Americans? The British government replied that Americans were represented in Parliament, albeit indirectly (like most British people themselves), and that the absolute supremacy of Parliament throughout the empire could not be questioned. Many Americans felt otherwise.

A series of disputes between the American colonies and the British government ultimately led to open rebellion. The uncompromising attitude of the British government and its use of German mercenaries dissolved loyalties to the home country and rivalries among the separate colonies. On July 4, 1776, an assembly of colonists adopted the Declaration of Independence. Written by Thomas Jefferson, it boldly listed the tyrannical acts committed by George III (r. 1760–1820) and confidently proclaimed the sovereignty of the American states. It also universalized the traditional rights of English people, stating that "all men are created equal. . . . They are endowed by their Creator with certain unalienable rights. . . . Among these are life, liberty, and the pursuit of happiness."

On the international scene, the French wanted revenge for the humiliating defeats of the Seven Years' War. They sympathized with the rebels and supplied guns and gunpowder from the beginning. By 1777 French volunteers were arriving in Virginia, and a dashing young nobleman, the marquis de Lafayette (1757–1834), quickly became one of Washington's most trusted generals. In 1778 the French government offered a formal alliance to the American ambassador in Paris, Benjamin Franklin, and in 1779 and 1780 the Spanish and Dutch declared war on Britain. Catherine the Great of Russia helped organize the League of Armed Neutrality in order to protect neutral shipping rights, which Britain refused to recognize.

Thus by 1780 Great Britain was engaged in an imperial war against most of Europe as well as against the thirteen colonies. In these circumstances, and in the face of severe reverses, a new British government offered peace on extremely generous terms. By the Treaty of Paris of 1783, Britain recognized the independence of the thirteen colonies and ceded all its territory between the Allegheny Mountains and the Mississippi River to the Americans. Out of the bitter rivalries of the Old World, the Americans snatched dominion over a vast territory.

Europeans who dreamed of a new era were fascinated by the political lessons of the American Revolution. The Americans had begun with a revolutionary defense against tyrannical oppression, and they had been victorious. They had then shown how rational beings could assemble together to exercise sovereignty and write a new social contract. All this gave greater reality to the concepts of individual liberty and representative government and reinforced one of the primary ideas of the Enlightenment: that a better world was possible.

No country felt the consequences of the American Revolution more directly than France. Hundreds of French officers served in America and were inspired by the experience, the marquis de Lafayette chief among them. French intellectuals and publicists engaged in passionate analysis of the new federal Constitution (1789) as well as the constitutions of the various states of the new United States. Perhaps more importantly, the expenses of supporting the revolutionary forces provided the last nail in the coffin for the French treasury.

Financial Crisis

The French Revolution thus had its immediate origins in the king's financial difficulties. Thwarted by the Parlement of Paris in its efforts to raise revenues by reforming the tax system, the government was forced to finance all of its enormous expenditures during the American war with borrowed money. As a result, the national debt and the annual budget deficit soared.

By the 1780s, fully 50 percent of France's annual budget went for interest payments on the debt. Another 25 percent went to maintain the military, while 6 percent was absorbed by the king and his court at Versailles. Less than 20 percent of the entire national budget was available for the productive functions of the state, such as transportation and general administration. This was an impossible financial situation.

Louis XVI's minister of finance revived old proposals to impose a general tax on all landed property as well as to form provincial assemblies to help administer

Assembly of Notables A group of important noblemen and high-ranking clergy called by Louis XVI to impose a general tax, but who ended up opposing it.

Section Review

- French society had three social orders or estates: the clergy, nobility, and everyone else, including the bourgeoisie or upper middle class that was increasingly frustrated with the monarchy's right to absolute power.

- The monarchy and the high courts, the parlements, were at odds over financial and political power; Louis XV's attempt to rein in the parlements failed as Louis XVI restored them to power.

- The French supported the American Revolution with money, volunteers, and arms; the rebels in turn inspired the French by their ability to oppose the British and create their own sovereign nation.

- The royal government, indebted from the American war, attempted to raise taxes, but parlement thwarted it, so finally Louis XVI called for a session of the Estates General.

Estates General A legislative body in pre-revolutionary France made up of representatives of each of the three classes, or estates; it was called into session in 1789 for the first time since 1614.

the tax, and he convinced the king to call an **Assembly of Notables** to gain support for the idea. The notables, who were mainly important noblemen and high-ranking clergy, opposed the new tax. In exchange for their support, they demanded that control over all government spending be given to the provincial assemblies. When the government refused, the notables responded that such sweeping tax changes required the approval of the Estates General, the representative body of all three estates, which had not met since 1614.

Facing imminent bankruptcy, the king tried to reassert his authority. He dismissed the notables and established new taxes by decree. In stirring language, the judges of the Parlement of Paris promptly declared the royal initiative null and void. When the king tried to exile the judges, a tremendous wave of protest swept the country. Frightened investors also refused to advance more loans to the state. Finally, in July 1788, Louis XVI bowed to public opinion and called for a spring session of the Estates General.

Revolution in Metropole and Colony (1789–1791)

What were the immediate events that sparked the Revolution, and how did they result in the formation of a constitutional monarchy in France? How did the ideals and events of the early Revolution raise new aspirations in the colonies?

Although inspired by the ideals of the American Revolution, the French Revolution did not mirror the American example. It was more radical and more complex, more influential and more controversial, more loved and more hated. For Europeans and most of the rest of the world, it was the great revolution of the eighteenth century, *the* revolution that opened the modern era in politics. In turn, the slave insurrection in Saint-Domingue—which ultimately resulted in the second independent republic of the Americas—inspired liberation movements across the world.

The Formation of the National Assembly

Once Louis had agreed to hold the **Estates General,** following precedent, he set elections for the three orders. Elected officials from the noble order were primarily conservatives from the provinces, but fully one-third of the nobility's representatives were liberals committed to major changes. The third estate elected lawyers and government officials to represent them, with few delegates representing business or the working poor.

As at previous meetings of the Estates General, local assemblies were to prepare a list of grievances for their representatives to bring to the next electoral level. The petitions for change coming from the three estates showed a surprising degree of consensus. There was general agreement that royal absolutism should give way to a constitutional monarchy in which laws and taxes would require the consent of the Estates General in regular meetings. All agreed that individual liberties would have to be guaranteed by law and that economic regulations should be loosened. The striking similarities in the grievance petitions of the clergy, nobility, and third estate reflected a shared commitment to a basic reform platform among the educated elite.

Yet an increasingly bitter quarrel undermined this consensus during the intense electoral campaign: *how* would the Estates General vote, and precisely *who* would lead in the political reorganization that was generally desired? The Estates

General of 1614 had sat as three separate houses. Each house held one vote, despite the fact that the third estate represented the majority population of France. Given the close ties between them, the nobility and clergy would control all decisions. As soon as the estates were called, the aristocratic Parlement of Paris ruled that the Estates General should once again sit separately. In response to protests from some reform-minded critics, the government agreed that the third estate should have as many delegates as the clergy and the nobility combined but then rendered this act meaningless by upholding voting by separate order.

In May 1789 the twelve hundred delegates of the three estates paraded in medieval pageantry through the streets of Versailles to an opening session resplendent with feudal magnificence. The estates were almost immediately deadlocked. Delegates of the third estate refused to transact any business until the king ordered the clergy and nobility to sit with them in a single body. Finally, after a six-week war of nerves, a few parish priests began to go over to the third estate, which on June 17 voted to call itself the **National Assembly.** On June 20 the delegates of the third estate, excluded from their hall because of "repairs," moved to a large indoor tennis court. There they swore the famous Oath of the Tennis Court, pledging not to disband until they had written a new constitution.

National Assembly The first French revolutionary legislature; a constituent assembly made up of primarily of representatives of the third estate and a few nobles and clergy who joined them, in session from 1789 to 1791.

The king's response was ambivalent. On June 23 he made a conciliatory speech urging reforms to a joint session, and four days later he ordered the three estates to meet together. At the same time, the vacillating and indecisive monarch apparently followed the advice of relatives and court nobles who urged him to dissolve the Estates General by force. Belatedly asserting his "divine right" to rule, the king called an army of eighteen thousand troops toward Versailles, and on July 11 he dismissed his finance minister and his other more liberal ministers.

The Revolt of the Poor and the Oppressed

While delegates of the third estate pressed for political rights, economic hardship gripped the common people. A poor grain harvest in 1788 caused the price of bread to soar, unleashing a classic economic depression of the preindustrial age. With food so expensive and with so much uncertainty, the demand for manufactured goods collapsed. Thousands of artisans and small traders were thrown out of work. By the end of 1789 almost half of the French people would be in need of relief. One person in eight was a pauper living in extreme want. In Paris perhaps 150,000 of the city's 600,000 people were without work in July 1789.

Against this background of poverty and ongoing political crisis, the people of Paris entered decisively onto the revolutionary stage. They believed in a general, though ill-defined, way that the economic distress had human causes. They believed that they should have steady work and enough bread at fair prices to survive. Specifically, they feared that the dismissal of the king's moderate finance minister would put them at the mercy of aristocratic landowners and grain speculators. Rumors that the king's troops would sack the city began to fill the air. Angry crowds formed, and passionate voices urged action. On July 13 the people began to seize arms for the defense of the city as the king's armies moved toward Paris, and on July 14 several hundred people marched to the Bastille (**bass-TEE**) to search for weapons and gunpowder.

The Bastille, once a medieval fortress, was a royal prison guarded by eighty retired soldiers and thirty Swiss mercenaries. The governor of the fortress-prison refused to hand over the powder, panicked, and ordered his men to resist, killing ninety-eight people attempting to enter. Cannon were brought to batter the main gate, and fighting continued until the prison surrendered. The governor of the prison was later hacked to death, and his head was stuck on a pike and paraded through the streets. The next day a committee of citizens appointed the marquis de Lafayette commander of the city's armed forces. Paris was lost to the king, who was forced to recall the finance minister and disperse his troops. The popular uprising had broken the power monopoly of the royal army and thereby saved the National Assembly.

As the delegates resumed their inconclusive debates at Versailles, the countryside sent them a radical and unmistakable message. Throughout France peasants began to rise in insurrection against their lords, ransacking manor houses and burning feudal documents that recorded their obligations. In some areas peasants reinstated traditional village practices, undoing recent enclosures and reoccupying old common lands. They seized forests, and taxes went unpaid. Fear of vagabonds and outlaws—called the **Great Fear** by contemporaries—seized the countryside and fanned the flames of rebellion. The long-suffering peasants were doing their best to free themselves from manorial rights and exploitation. In the end, they were successful. On the night of August 4, 1789, the delegates at Versailles agreed to abolish all the old noble privileges—peasant serfdom where it still existed, exclusive hunting rights, fees for justice, village monopolies, and a host of other dues. Thus the French peasantry, which already owned about 30 percent of all the land, achieved an unprecedented victory in the early days of revolutionary upheaval. Henceforth, French peasants would seek mainly to protect and consolidate their triumph. As the Great Fear subsided in the countryside, they became a force for order and stability.

Great Fear In the summer of 1789, the fear of vagabonds and outlaws that seized the French countryside and fanned the flames of revolution.

A Limited Monarchy

The National Assembly moved forward. On August 27, 1789, it issued the Declaration of the Rights of Man and of the Citizen, which stated, "Men are born and remain free and equal in rights." The declaration also maintained that mankind's natural rights are "liberty, property, security, and resistance to oppression" and that "every man is presumed innocent until he is proven guilty." As for law, "it is an expression of the general will; all citizens have the right to concur personally or through their representatives in its formation. . . . Free expression of thoughts and opinions is one of the most precious rights of mankind: every citizen may therefore speak, write, and publish freely." In short, this clarion call of the liberal revolutionary ideal guaranteed equality before the law, representative government for a sovereign people, and individual freedom. This revolutionary credo, only two pages long, was disseminated throughout France and Europe and around the world.

Moving beyond general principles to draft a constitution proved difficult. The questions of how much power the king should retain and whether he could permanently veto legislation led to another deadlock. Once again the decisive answer came from the poor—in this instance, the poor women of Paris.

Women customarily bought the food and managed the poor family's slender resources. The economic crisis worsened after the fall of the Bastille, as aristocrats fled the country and the luxury market collapsed. Foreign markets also shrunk in the aftermath of the crisis, and unemployment grew. In addition, household managers could no longer look to the church for grants of food and money.

On October 5 some seven thousand desperate women marched the twelve miles from Paris to Versailles to demand action. This great crowd invaded the Assembly, "armed with scythes, sticks and pikes." One tough old woman defiantly shouted into the debate, "Who's that talking down there? Make the chatterbox

a Versaille a Versaille. du 5 Octobre 1789.

The Women of Paris March to Versailles

On October 5, 1789, a large group of Parisian market women marched to Versailles to protest the price of bread. For the people of Paris, the king was the baker of last resort, responsible for feeding his people during times of scarcity. The crowd forced the royal family to return with them and to live in Paris, rather than remain isolated from their subjects at court. (Erich Lessing/Art Resource, NY)

shut up. That's not the point: the point is that we want bread."[2] Hers was the genuine voice of the people, essential to any understanding of the French Revolution.

The women invaded the royal apartments, slaughtered some of the royal bodyguards, and furiously searched for the queen, Marie Antoinette (**ann-twah-NET**), who was widely despised for her frivolous and supposedly immoral behavior. "We are going to cut off her head, tear out her heart, fry her liver, and that won't be the end of it," they shouted, surging through the palace in a frenzy. It seems likely that only the intervention of Lafayette and the National Guard saved the royal family. But the only way to calm the disorder was for the king to live in Paris, as the crowd demanded.

The National Assembly followed the king to Paris, and the next two years, until September 1791, saw the consolidation of the liberal revolution. Under middle-class leadership, the National Assembly abolished the French nobility as a legal order and pushed forward with the creation of a **constitutional monarchy**, which Louis XVI reluctantly agreed to accept in July 1790. In the final constitution, the king remained the head of state, but all lawmaking power was placed in the hands of the National Assembly, elected by the economic upper half of French males. New laws broadened women's rights to seek divorce, to inherit property, and to obtain financial support for illegitimate children from fathers, but women were not allowed to hold political office or even vote. The men of the National Assembly believed that civic virtue would be restored if women focused on child rearing and domestic duties.

The National Assembly replaced the complicated patchwork of historic provinces with eighty-three departments of approximately equal size. The jumble of weights and measures that varied from province to province was reformed, leading

constitutional monarchy A form of government in which the king retains his position as head of state, while the authority to tax and make new laws resides in an elected body.

to the introduction of the metric system in 1793. Monopolies, guilds, and workers' associations were prohibited, and barriers to trade within France were abolished in the name of economic liberty. Thus the National Assembly applied the critical spirit of the Enlightenment in a thorough reform of France's laws and institutions.

The Assembly also imposed a radical reorganization on the country's religious life. It granted religious freedom to the small minority of French Jews and Protestants. Of greater impact, it then nationalized the Catholic Church's property and abolished monasteries as useless relics of a distant past. The government used all former church property as collateral to guarantee a new paper currency, the *assignats* (**AS-ig-nat**), and then sold the property in an attempt to put the state's finances on a solid footing. Although the church's land was sold in large blocks, peasants eventually purchased much when it was subdivided. These purchases strengthened their attachment to the new revolutionary order in the countryside.

Imbued with the rationalism and skepticism of the eighteenth-century philosophes, many delegates distrusted popular piety and "superstitious religion." Thus they established a national church, with priests chosen by voters. The National Assembly then forced the Catholic clergy to take a loyalty oath to the new government. The pope formally condemned this attempt to subjugate the church, and only half the priests of France swore the oath. Many sincere Christians, especially those in the countryside, were upset by these changes in the religious order. The attempt to remake the Catholic Church, like the Assembly's abolition of guilds and workers' associations, sharpened the conflict between the educated classes and the common people that had been emerging in the eighteenth century.

Revolutionary Aspirations in Saint-Domingue

The French Revolution radically transformed not only the territorial nation of France but its overseas colonies as well. On the eve of the Revolution, Saint-Domingue—the most profitable of all Caribbean colonies—was even more rife with social tensions than France itself. The island was composed of a variety of social groups who resented and mistrusted one another. The European population included French colonial officials, wealthy plantation owners and merchants, and poor immigrants. Greatly outnumbering the white population were the colony's five hundred thousand slaves, along with a sizable population of free people of African and mixed African European descent. This last group referred to themselves as "free coloreds" or **free people of color.**

free people of color Sizable population of free people of African and mixed African-European descent living in the French isles of the Caribbean.

The political and intellectual turmoil of the 1780s, with its growing rhetoric of liberty, equality, and fraternity, raised new challenges and possibilities for each of these groups. For slaves, news of abolitionist movements in France, and the royal government's own attempts to rein in the worst abuses of slavery, led to hopes that the mother country might grant them freedom. Free people of color found in such rhetoric the principles on which to base a defense of their legal and political rights. They looked to political reforms in Paris as a means of gaining political enfranchisement and regaining legal rights that had been rescinded by colonial administrators. The white elite looked to revolutionary ideals of representative government for the chance to gain control of their own affairs, as had the American colonists before them. The meeting of the Estates General and the Declaration of the Rights of Man and of the Citizen raised these conflicting colonial aspirations to new levels.

The National Assembly, however, frustrated the hopes of all these groups. It ruled that each colony would draft its own constitution, with free rein over decisions on slavery and the enfranchisement of free people of color. After dealing this blow to the aspirations of slaves and free coloreds, the committee also reaffirmed French monopolies over colonial trade, thereby angering planters as well.

Following a failed revolt in Saint-Domingue led by Vincent Ogé (**oh-ZHAY**), a free man of color, the National Assembly attempted a compromise. It granted political rights to free people of color born to two free parents who possessed sufficient property. When news of this legislation arrived in Saint-Domingue, the white elite was furious and the colonial governor refused to enact it. Violence now erupted between groups of whites and free coloreds in parts of the colony. The liberal revolution had failed to satisfy the contradictory ambitions in the colonies.

World War and Republican France (1791–1799)

How and why did the Revolution take a radical turn at home and in the colonies?

When Louis XVI accepted the final version of the National Assembly's constitution in September 1791, a young and still obscure provincial lawyer and delegate named Maximilien Robespierre (**ROBES-pee-air**) (1758–1794) concluded, "The Revolution is over." Robespierre was both right and wrong. He was right in the sense that the most constructive and lasting reforms were in place. Nothing substantial in the way of liberty and fundamental reform would be gained in the next generation. He was wrong in the sense that a much more radical stage lay ahead. New heroes and new ideologies were to emerge in revolutionary wars and international conflict in which Robespierre himself would play a central role.

Foreign Reactions and the Beginning of War

The outbreak and progress of revolution in France produced great excitement and a sharp division of opinion in Europe and the United States. Liberals and radicals saw a mighty triumph of liberty over despotism. In Great Britain especially, they hoped that the French example would lead to a fundamental reordering of Parliament, which was in the hands of the aristocracy and a few wealthy merchants. After the French Revolution began, conservative leaders such as Edmund Burke (1729–1797) were deeply troubled by the aroused spirit of reform. In 1790 Burke published *Reflections on the Revolution in France,* one of the great defenses of European conservatism. He defended inherited privileges in general and those of the English monarchy and aristocracy. He glorified the unrepresentative Parliament and predicted that thoroughgoing reform like that occurring in France would lead only to chaos and tyranny. Burke's work sparked much debate.

One passionate rebuttal came from a young writer in London, Mary Wollstonecraft (**WOOL-stuhn-kraft**) (1759–1797). Incensed by Burke's book, Wollstonecraft immediately wrote a blistering, widely read attack, *A Vindication of the Rights of Man* (1790). Then she made a daring intellectual leap, developing for the first time the logical implications of natural-law philosophy in her masterpiece, *A Vindication of the Rights of Woman* (1792). To fulfill the still-unrealized potential of the French Revolution and to eliminate the sexual inequality she had felt so keenly, she demanded that

> the Rights of Women be respected . . . [and] JUSTICE for one-half of the human race. . . . It is time to effect a revolution in female manners, time to restore to them

their lost dignity, and make them, as part of the human species, labor, by reforming themselves, to reform the world.

Setting high standards for women—"I wish to persuade women to endeavor to acquire strength, both of mind and body"[3]—Wollstonecraft broke with those who had a low opinion of women's intellectual potential. She advocated rigorous co-education, which would make women better wives and mothers, good citizens, and economically independent. Women could manage businesses and enter politics if only men would give them the chance. Wollstonecraft's analysis testified to the power of the Revolution to excite and inspire outside of France. Paralleling ideas put forth independently in France by Olympe de Gouges (**oh-LIMP duh GOOJ**) (1748–1793), a self-taught writer and woman of the people (see the feature "Listening to the Past: Revolution and Women's Rights" on pages 563–564), Wollstonecraft's work marked the birth of the modern women's movement for equal rights, and it was ultimately very influential.

The kings and nobles of continental Europe, who had at first welcomed the revolution in France as weakening a competing monarchy, realized that their power was also threatened. In June 1791, Louis XVI and Marie Antoinette were arrested and returned to Paris after trying unsuccessfully to slip out of France. The shock of this arrest led the monarchs of Austria and Prussia to issue the Declaration of Pillnitz in August 1791. This carefully worded statement declared their willingness to intervene in France in certain circumstances and was expected to have a sobering effect on revolutionary France without causing war.

But the crowned heads of Europe misjudged the revolutionary spirit in France. The representative body that convened in October 1791 had completely new delegates and a different character. The great majority of the legislators were still prosperous, well-educated middle-class men, but they were younger and less cautious than their predecessors. Many of the deputies belonged to a political club called the **Jacobin** (**JAK-uh-bin**) **club,** after the name of the former monastery in which they held their meetings. Such clubs had proliferated in Parisian neighborhoods since the beginning of the Revolution, drawing men and women to debate the burning political questions of the day.

Jacobin club A political club in Revolutionary France whose members were radical republicans.

The new representatives to the Assembly whipped themselves into a patriotic fury against the Declaration of Pillnitz. If the kings of Europe were attempting to incite a war against France, then "we will incite a war of people against kings. . . . Ten million Frenchmen, kindled by the fire of liberty, armed with the sword, with reason, with eloquence would be able to change the face of the world and make the tyrants tremble on their thrones."[4] In April 1792 France declared war on Francis II, the Habsburg monarch.

France's crusade against tyranny went poorly at first. Prussian forces joined Austria against the French, who broke and fled at their first military encounter with this First Coalition. The road to Paris lay open, and it is possible that only conflict between the Eastern monarchs over the division of Poland saved France from defeat.

The Assembly declared the country in danger, and volunteers rallied to the capital. In this supercharged wartime atmosphere, rumors of treason by the king and queen spread in Paris. On August 10, 1792, a revolutionary crowd attacked the royal palace at the Tuileries (**TWEE-luh-reez**), while the king and his family fled for their lives to the nearby Legislative Assembly. Rather than offering refuge, the Assembly suspended the king from all his functions, imprisoned him, and called for a new National Convention to be elected by universal male suffrage. Monarchy in France was on its deathbed, mortally wounded by war and popular upheaval.

The Second Revolution

The fall of the monarchy marked a rapid radicalization of the Revolution, a phase that historians often call the **second revolution.** Louis's imprisonment was followed by the September Massacres. Wild stories that imprisoned counter-revolutionary aristocrats and priests were plotting with the allied invaders seized the city. As a result, angry crowds invaded the prisons of Paris and slaughtered half the men and women they found. In late September 1792 the new, popularly elected National Convention proclaimed France a republic.

The republic sought to create a new popular culture, fashioning compelling symbols that broke with the past and glorified the new order. Its new revolutionary calendar eliminated saints' days and renamed the days and the months after the seasons of the year, while also adding secular holidays designed to instill a love of nation. These secular celebrations were less successful in villages, where Catholicism was stronger.

All the members of the National Convention were republicans, and at the beginning almost all belonged to the Jacobin club of Paris. But the Jacobins themselves were increasingly divided into two bitterly competitive groups—the **Girondists (juh-RON-dists)**, named after a department in southwestern France that was home to several of their leaders, and **the Mountain,** led by Robespierre and another young lawyer, Georges Jacques Danton. The Mountain was so called because its members sat on the uppermost benches on the left side of the assembly hall. A majority of the indecisive Convention members, seated in the "Plain" below, floated back and forth between the rival factions.

This division emerged clearly after the National Convention overwhelmingly convicted Louis XVI of treason. The Girondists accepted his guilt but did not wish to put the king to death. By a narrow majority, the Mountain carried the day, and Louis was executed on January 21, 1793, on the newly invented guillotine. Both the Girondists and the Mountain were determined to continue the "war against tyranny." The Prussians had been stopped at the Battle of Valmy on September 20, 1792, one day before the republic was proclaimed. French armies then invaded Savoy and captured Nice, moved into the German Rhineland, and by November 1792 were occupying the entire Austrian Netherlands (modern Belgium). Everywhere they went French armies of occupation chased the princes, abolished feudalism, and "liberated" the people.

But the French armies also lived off the land, requisitioning food and supplies and plundering local treasures. The liberators looked increasingly like foreign invaders. International tensions mounted. In February 1793 the National Convention, at war with Austria and Prussia, declared war on Britain, Holland, and Spain as well. Republican France was now at war with almost all of Europe, a great war that would last almost without interruption until 1815.

Groups within France added to the turmoil. Peasants in western France revolted against being drafted into the army, and devout Catholics, royalists, and foreign agents encouraged their rebellion. In Paris the National Convention was locked in a life-and-death political struggle between the Mountain and the more moderate Girondists. With the middle-class delegates so bitterly divided, the laboring poor of Paris emerged as the decisive political factor. The laboring poor and the petty traders were often known as the **sans-culottes (sanz-koo-LOT)**, "without breeches," because their men wore trousers instead of the knee breeches of the aristocracy and the solid middle class. They demanded radical political action to guarantee them their daily bread. The Mountain joined with sans-culottes activists in the city government to engineer a popular uprising that forced the Convention to arrest thirty-one Girondist deputies for treason on June 2. All power passed to the Mountain.

second revolution From 1792 to 1795, the second phase of the French Revolution during which the fall of the French monarchy introduced a rapid radicalization of politics.

Girondists A group contesting control of the National Convention in France, named after a department in southwestern France.

the Mountain The radical faction of the National Convention led by Robespierre and Danton, so called because its members sat in the uppermost benches of the assembly hall.

sans-culottes The name for the laboring poor of Paris, so called because the men wore trousers instead of the knee breeches of the aristocracy and middle class; it came to refer to the militant radicals of the city.

Contrasting Visions of the Sans-Culottes
The woman on the left, with her playful cat and calm simplicity, suggests how the French sans-culottes saw themselves as democrats and virtuous citizens. The ferocious sans-culotte harpy on the right, a creation of wartime England's vivid counter-revolutionary imagination, screams for more blood, more death: "I am the Goddess of Liberty! Long live the guillotine!"
(Bibliothèque nationale de France)

The Convention also formed the Committee of Public Safety to deal with the threats from within and outside France. The committee, which Robespierre came to lead, was given dictatorial power to deal with the national emergency. Moderates in leading provincial cities, such as Lyons and Marseilles, revolted and demanded a decentralized government. The peasant revolt also spread, and the republic's armies were driven back on all fronts. By July 1793 only the areas around Paris and on the eastern frontier were firmly held by the central government. Defeat seemed imminent.

Total War and the Terror

A year later, in July 1794, the Austrian Netherlands and the Rhineland were once again in the hands of conquering French armies, and the First Coalition was falling apart. This remarkable change of fortune was due to the revolutionary government's success in harnessing, for perhaps the first time in history, the explosive forces of a planned economy, revolutionary terror, and modern nationalism in a total war effort.

Robespierre and the Committee of Public Safety first collaborated with the fiercely patriotic sans-culottes to establish a **planned economy** with egalitarian social overtones. Rather than let supply and demand determine prices, the government set maximum allowable prices for key products. Though the state was too weak to enforce all its price regulations, it did fix the price of bread in Paris at levels the poor could afford. Rationing was introduced, and bakers were permitted

planned economy In response to inflation and high unemployment, Robespierre and the government set maximum prices for products, rather than relying on supply and demand.

The French Revolution

May 5, 1789	Estates General convene at Versailles.
June 17, 1789	Third estate declares itself the National Assembly.
June 20, 1789	Oath of the Tennis Court is sworn.
July 14, 1789	Storming of the Bastille occurs.
July–August 1789	Great Fear ravages the countryside.
August 4, 1789	National Assembly abolishes feudal privileges.
August 27, 1789	National Assembly issues Declaration of the Rights of Man.
October 5, 1789	Women march on Versailles and force royal family to return to Paris.
November 1789	National Assembly confiscates church lands.
July 1790	Civil Constitution of the Clergy establishes a national church.
	Louis XVI reluctantly agrees to accept a constitutional monarchy.
June 1791	Royal family is arrested while attempting to flee France.
August 1791	Austria and Prussia issue the Declaration of Pillnitz.
	Slave insurrections break out in Saint-Domingue.
April 1792	France declares war on Austria.
August 1792	Parisian mob attacks the palace and takes Louis XVI prisoner.
September 1792	September Massacres occur.
	National Convention declares France a republic and abolishes monarchy.
January 1793	Louis XVI is executed.
February 1793	France declares war on Britain, Holland, and Spain.
	Revolts take place in some provincial cities.
	Slavery abolished in French colonies.
March 1793	Bitter struggle occurs in the National Convention between Girondists and the Mountain.
April–June 1793	Robespierre and the Mountain organize the Committee of Public Safety and arrest Girondist leaders.
September 1793	Price controls are instituted to aid the sans-culottes and mobilize the war effort.
	British troops invade Saint-Domingue.
1793–1794	Reign of Terror darkens Paris and the provinces.
February 1794	National Convention abolishes slavery in all French territories.
Spring 1794	French armies are victorious on all fronts.
July 1794	Robespierre is executed.
	Thermidorian reaction begins.
1795–1799	Directory rules.
1795	Economic controls are abolished, and suppression of the sans-culottes begins.
	Toussaint L'Ouverture named brigadier general.
1797	Napoleon defeats Austrian armies in Italy and returns triumphant to Paris.
1798	Austria, Great Britain, and Russia form the Second Coalition against France.
1799	Napoleon overthrows the Directory and seizes power.

to make only the "bread of equality"—a brown bread made of a mixture of all available flours. White bread and pastries were outlawed as luxuries. The poor of Paris may not have eaten well, but at least they ate.

They also worked, mainly to produce arms and munitions for the war effort. The government told craftsmen what to produce, nationalized many small workshops, and requisitioned raw materials and grain. The second revolution and the ascendancy of the sans-culottes had produced an embryonic emergency socialism, which thoroughly frightened Europe's propertied classes and had great influence on the subsequent development of socialist ideology.

Second, while radical economic measures supplied the poor with bread and the armies with weapons, the **Reign of Terror** (1793–1794) used revolutionary terror to solidify the home front. Special revolutionary courts responsible only to Robespierre's Committee of Public Safety tried rebels and "enemies of the nation" for political crimes. Some forty thousand French men and women were executed or died in prison. Another three hundred thousand suspects were arrested.

The third and perhaps most decisive element in the French republic's victory over the First Coalition was its ability to draw on the explosive power of patriotic dedication to a national state and a national mission. An essential part of modern **nationalism,** this commitment was something new in history. With a common language and a common tradition newly reinforced by the ideas of popular sovereignty and democracy, large numbers of French people were stirred by a common loyalty. They developed an intense emotional commitment to the defense of the nation and saw the war as a life-and-death struggle between good and evil.

The fervor of nationalism, combined with the all-out mobilization of resources, made the French army unstoppable. After August 1793 all unmarried young men were subject to the draft, resulting in the largest fighting force in the history of European warfare. Recent research concludes that the French armed forces outnumbered their enemies almost four to one.[5] French generals used mass assaults at bayonet point to overwhelm the enemy. "No maneuvering, nothing elaborate," declared the fearless General Hoche. "Just cold steel, passion and patriotism."[6] By spring 1794 French armies were victorious on all fronts. The republic was saved.

Reign of Terror The period from 1793 to 1794, during which Robespierre used revolutionary terror to solidify the home front of France, resulting in the death of some 40,000 French men and women.

nationalism Patriotic dedication to a national state and mission; it was a decisive element in the French republic's victory.

Revolution in Saint-Domingue

The second stage of revolution in Saint-Domingue also resulted from decisive action from below. In August 1791 groups of slaves organized a revolt that spread across much of the northern plain. By the end of August the uprising was "10,000 strong, divided into 3 armies, of whom 700 or 800 are on horseback, and tolerably well-armed."[7] During the next month slaves attacked and destroyed hundreds of sugar and coffee plantations.

On April 4, 1792, as war loomed with the European states, the National Assembly issued a new decree enfranchising all free blacks and free people of color. The Assembly hoped this measure would win the loyalty of free blacks and their aid in defeating the slave rebellion.

Less than two years later, on February 4, 1794, slavery was abolished in the entire French Caribbean, and in 1795 the former slaves won full political rights. The National Convention was forced to make these concessions when Saint-Domingue came under siege from Spanish and British troops hoping to capture the profitable colony. With the former slaves and free colored forces on their side, the French gradually regained control of the island in 1796.

The key leader in the French victory was General Toussaint L'Ouverture (**too-SAN loo-ver-CHORE**) (1743–1803). (See the feature "Individuals in Society: Toussaint L'Ouverture.") L'Ouverture was then named commander of the western province of Saint-Domingue. The increasingly conservative nature of the French government, however, threatened to undo the gains made by former slaves and free people of color. As exiled planters gained a stronger voice in French policy-making, L'Ouverture and other local leaders grew ever more wary of what the future might hold.

The Thermidorian Reaction and the Directory (1794–1799)

With the French army victorious, Robespierre and the Committee of Public Safety relaxed the emergency economic controls, but they extended the political Reign of Terror. In March 1794, to the horror of many sans-culottes, Robespierre wiped out many of his critics. Two weeks later, Robespierre sent many of his long-standing collaborators, including the famous orator Danton, up the steps to the guillotine. A strange assortment of radicals and moderates in the Convention, knowing that they might be next, organized a conspiracy. They howled down Robespierre when he tried to speak to the National Convention on 9 Thermidor (July 27, 1794). The next day it was Robespierre's turn to be shaved by the revolutionary razor.

As Robespierre's closest supporters followed their leader to the guillotine, France unexpectedly experienced a thorough reaction to the despotism of the Reign of Terror. In a general way, this **Thermidorian (thur-mi-DAWR-ee-uhn) reaction** recalled the early days of the Revolution. The middle-class lawyers and professionals who had led the liberal revolution of 1789 reasserted their authority, drawing support from their own class, the provincial cities, and the better-off peasants. The National Convention abolished many economic controls, let prices rise sharply, and severely restricted the local political organizations in which the sans-culottes had their strength.

Thermidorian reaction The period after the execution of Robespierre in 1794; it was a reaction to the violence of the Reign of Terror.

The collapse of economic controls, coupled with runaway inflation, hit the working poor very hard. After the Convention used the army to suppress the sans culottes' protests, the urban poor lost their revolutionary fervor. Excluded and disillusioned, they would have little interest in and influence on politics until 1830. The poor of the countryside turned toward religion as a relief from earthly cares. Rural women, especially, brought back the Catholic Church and the open worship of God as the government began to soften its antireligious revolutionary stance.

As for the middle-class members of the National Convention, in 1795 they wrote yet another constitution that they believed would guarantee their economic position and political supremacy. As in previous elections, the mass of the population voted only for electors, whose number was cut back to men of substantial means. Electors then elected

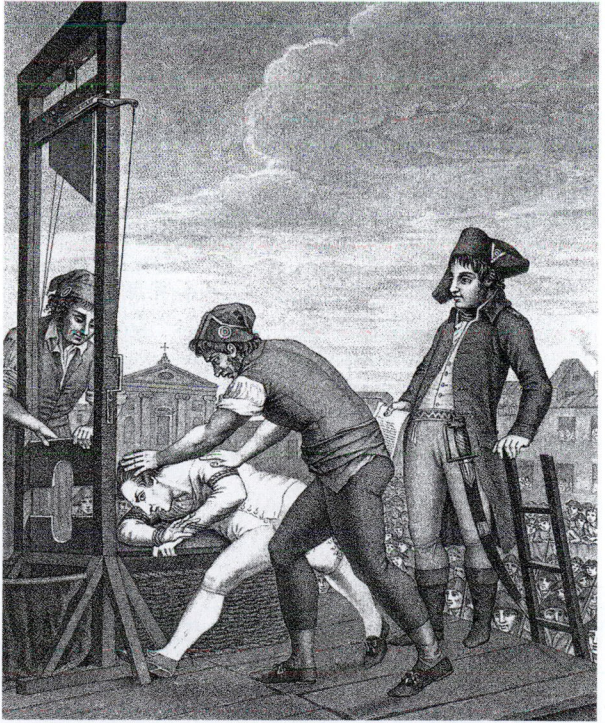

The Execution of Robespierre

The guillotine was painted red and was completely wooden except for the heavy iron blade. Large crowds witnessed the executions in a majestic public square in central Paris, then known as the Place de la Revolution and now called the Place de la Concorde (Harmony Square).
(Snark/Art Resource, NY)

- The revolution in France brought mixed reactions elsewhere, from Edmund Burke's book defending conservatism to Mary Wollstonecraft's passionate plea to eliminate sexual inequality.

- The monarchs of Austria and Prussia responded to the arrest of the royal family with the Declaration of Pillnitz, inciting such anger that the National Assembly, led by members of the Jacobin political club, declared war on the Habsburg monarch and then suspended the king from all his functions.

- The National Convention declared France a republic, executed the king in 1793, and sought to create a new republican, secular culture.

- The National Convention faced division between the moderate Girondists and the radical Mountain as French armies battled Prussian and Austrian forces, ending up at war against most of Europe.

- Robespierre and the Committee of Public Safety established a planned economy, fixed the price of bread, provided work to aid the war effort, initiated the Reign of Terror, and worked to promote a strong sense of nationalism, all of which helped to save the republic, though at the cost of many lives.

- In the Caribbean island of Saint-Domingue (today's Haiti), slaves revolted and, under the pressure of war, the French government first enfranchised free people of color, then abolished slavery and extended political rights to former slaves.

- Under the leadership of Toussaint L'Ouverture, a former slave, French forces in Saint-Domingue defeated Spanish and British invaders.

- The Thermidorian Reaction led to the execution of Robespierre, a new National Convention, the end of economic controls, a new constitution, the establishment of the Directory, and a coup d'état by Napoleon.

the members of a reorganized legislative assembly as well as key officials throughout France. The new assembly also chose a five-man executive—the Directory.

The Directory continued to support French military expansion abroad. War was no longer so much a crusade as a means to meet ever-present, ever-unsolved economic problems. Large, victorious French armies reduced unemployment at home and were able to live off the territories they conquered and plundered.

The unprincipled action of the Directory reinforced widespread disgust with war and starvation. This general dissatisfaction revealed itself clearly in the national elections of 1797, which returned a large number of conservative and even monarchist deputies who favored peace at almost any price. The members of the Directory, fearing for their skins, used the army to nullify the elections and began to govern dictatorially. Two years later Napoleon Bonaparte (nuh-POH-lee-uhn BOH-nuh-pahrt) ended the Directory in a coup d'état (koo day-TA) and substituted a strong dictatorship for a weak one. The effort to establish stable representative government had failed.

The Napoleonic Era (1799–1815)

Why did Napoleon Bonaparte assume control of France, and what factors led to his downfall? How did the new republic of Haiti gain independence from France?

For almost fifteen years, from 1799 to 1814, France was in the hands of a keen-minded military dictator of exceptional ability. One of history's most fascinating leaders, Napoleon Bonaparte (1769–1821) realized the need to put an end to civil strife in France in order to create unity and consolidate his rule. And he did. But Napoleon saw himself as a man of destiny, and the glory of war and the dream of universal empire proved irresistible. For years he spiraled from victory to victory, but in the end he was destroyed by a mighty coalition united in fear of his restless ambition.

Napoleon's Rule of France

In 1799 when he seized power, young General Napoleon Bonaparte was a national hero. Born in Corsica into an impoverished noble family in 1769, Napoleon left home and became a lieutenant in the French artillery in 1785. After a brief and unsuccessful adventure fighting for Corsican independence in 1789, he returned to France as a French patriot and a dedicated revolutionary. Rising rapidly in the new army, Napoleon was placed in command of French forces in Italy and won brilliant victories there in 1796 and 1797. His next campaign, in Egypt, was a failure, but Napoleon returned to France before the fiasco was generally known, and his reputation remained intact.

Napoleon soon learned that some prominent members of the legislature were plotting against the Directory. The dissatisfaction of these plotters stemmed not so much from the fact that the Directory was a dictatorship as from the fact that it was a weak dictatorship. Ten years of upheaval and uncertainty had convinced these disillusioned revolutionaries that a strong military ruler was needed to restore order. Thus the conspirators and Napoleon organized a takeover. On November 9, 1799, they ousted the Directors, and the following day soldiers disbanded the legislature at bayonet point. Napoleon was named first consul of the republic, and a new constitution consolidating his position was overwhelmingly approved in a

The Napoleonic Era

November 1799	Napoleon overthrows the Directory.
December 1799	French voters overwhelmingly approve Napoleon's new constitution.
1800	Napoleon founds the Bank of France.
1801	France defeats Austria and acquires Italian and German territories in the Treaty of Lunéville.
	Napoleon signs the Concordat with the pope.
1802	France signs the Treaty of Amiens with Britain.
	French forces arrive in Saint-Domingue.
April 1803	Toussaint L'Ouverture dies in France.
January 1804	Jean Jacques Dessalines declares Haitian independence.
March 1804	Napoleonic Code comes into force.
December 1804	Napoleon crowns himself emperor.
May 1805	First Haitian constitution promulgated.
October 1805	Britain defeats the French and Spanish fleet at the Battle of Trafalgar.
December 1805	Napoleon defeats Austria and Russia at the Battle of Austerlitz.
1807	Napoleon redraws the map of Europe in the treaties of Tilsit.
1810	The Grand Empire is at its height.
June 1812	Napoleon invades Russia with 600,000 men.
Fall–Winter 1812	Napoleon makes a disastrous retreat from Russia.
March 1814	Russia, Prussia, Austria, and Britain sign the Treaty of Chaumont, pledging alliance to defeat Napoleon.
April 1814	Napoleon abdicates and is exiled to Elba.
February–June 1815	Napoleon escapes from Elba and rules France until he is defeated at the Battle of Waterloo.

plebiscite in December 1799. Republican appearances were maintained, but Napoleon was already the real ruler of France.

The essence of Napoleon's domestic policy was to use his great and highly personal powers to maintain order and end civil strife. He did so by working out unwritten agreements with powerful groups in France whereby the groups received favors in return for loyal service. Napoleon's bargain with the solid middle class was codified in the famous Civil Code of 1804, which reasserted two of the fundamental principles of the liberal and essentially moderate revolution of 1789: equality of all male citizens before the law and absolute security of wealth and private property. Napoleon and the leading bankers of Paris established the privately owned Bank of France, which loyally served the interests of both the state and the financial oligarchy. Peasants were also appeased when Napoleon defended the gains in land and status they had claimed during the revolution.

At the same time Napoleon perfected a thoroughly centralized state. As recent scholarship shows, Napoleon consolidated his rule by recruiting disillusioned revolutionaries for the network of ministers, prefects, and centrally appointed mayors that depended on him and came to serve him well. Only former revolutionaries who leaned too far to the left or to the right were pushed to the sidelines.[8] Nor were members of the old nobility slighted. In 1800 and again in 1802 Napoleon granted amnesty to one hundred thousand émigrés on the condition that they return to France and take a loyalty oath. Members of this returning elite soon ably occupied many high posts in the expanding centralized state. Napoleon also created a new imperial nobility in order to reward his most talented generals and officials.

Napoleon applied his diplomatic skills to healing the Catholic Church in France so that it could serve as a bulwark of order and social peace. After arduous negotiations, Napoleon and Pope Pius VII (1800–1823) signed the Concordat (kon-KAWR-dat) of 1801. The pope gained the precious right for French Catholics to practice their religion freely, but Napoleon gained political power: his government now nominated bishops, paid the clergy, and exerted great influence over the church in France.

The domestic reforms of Napoleon's early years were his greatest achievement. Much of his legal and administrative reorganization has survived in France to this day. More generally, Napoleon's domestic initiatives gave the great majority of French people a welcome sense of stability and national unity.

Order and unity had a price: Napoleon's authoritarian rule. Women, who had often participated in revolutionary politics, lost many of the gains they had made in the 1790s. Under the law of the new Napoleonic Code, women were dependents of either their fathers or their husbands, and they could not make contracts or even have bank accounts in their own names. Indeed, Napoleon and his advisers aimed at re-establishing a family monarchy, where the power of the husband and father was as absolute over the wife and the children as that of Napoleon was over his subjects.

Free speech and freedom of the press were continually violated. By 1811 only four newspapers were left, and they were little more than organs of government propaganda. The occasional elections were a farce. Later laws prescribed harsh penalties for political offenses, and people were watched carefully under an efficient spy system. People suspected of subversive activities were arbitrarily detained, placed under house arrest, or consigned to insane asylums. After 1810 political suspects were held in state prisons, as they had been during the Terror. There were about twenty-five hundred such political prisoners in 1814.

Napoleon's Expansion in Europe

Napoleon was above all a military man, and a great one. After coming to power in 1799 he sent peace feelers to Austria and Great Britain, the two remaining members of the Second Coalition that had been formed against France in 1798. When these overtures were rejected, French armies led by Napoleon decisively defeated the Austrians. In the Treaty of Lunéville (1801), Austria accepted the loss of almost all its Italian possessions, and German territory on the west bank of the Rhine was incorporated into France. The British agreed to the Treaty of Amiens in 1802, allowing France to remain in control of Holland, the Austrian Netherlands, the west bank of the Rhine, and most of the Italian peninsula. The Treaty of Amiens was clearly a diplomatic triumph for Napoleon, and peace with honor and profit increased his popularity at home.

In 1802 Napoleon was secure but driven to expand his power. Aggressively redrawing the map of Germany so as to weaken Austria and encourage the secondary states of southwestern Germany to side with France, Napoleon tried to restrict

The Coronation of Napoleon, 1804 (detail)
In this grandiose painting by Jacques-Louis David, Napoleon prepares to crown his wife, Josephine, in an elaborate ceremony in Notre Dame Cathedral. Napoleon, the ultimate upstart, also crowned himself. Pope Pius VII, seated glumly behind the emperor, is reduced to being a spectator. (Louvre/Réunion des Musées Nationaux/Art Resource, NY)

British trade with all of Europe. He then plotted to attack Great Britain, but his Mediterranean fleet was virtually annihilated by Lord Nelson at the Battle of Trafalgar on October 21, 1805. Invasion of England was henceforth impossible. Renewed fighting had its advantages, however, for the first consul used the wartime atmosphere to have himself proclaimed emperor in late 1804.

Austria, Russia, and Sweden joined with Britain to form the Third Coalition against France shortly before the Battle of Trafalgar. Actions such as Napoleon's assumption of the Italian crown had convinced both Alexander I of Russia and Francis II of Austria that Napoleon was a threat to their interests and to the European balance of power. Yet the Austrians and the Russians were no match for Napoleon, who scored a brilliant victory over them at the Battle of Austerlitz (**AW-ster-lits**) in December 1805. Alexander I decided to pull back, and Austria accepted large territorial losses in return for peace as the Third Coalition collapsed.

Napoleon then proceeded to reorganize the German states to his liking. In 1806 he abolished many of the tiny German states as well as the ancient Holy Roman Empire and established by decree the German Confederation of the Rhine, a union of fifteen German states minus Austria, Prussia, and Saxony. Naming himself "protector" of the confederation, Napoleon firmly controlled western Germany.

Napoleon's intervention in German affairs alarmed the Prussians, who mobilized their armies after more than a decade of peace with France. Napoleon attacked and won two more brilliant victories in October 1806 at Jena (**YEY-nah**) and Auerstädt (**OW-er-stat**), where the Prussians were outnumbered two to one.

The war with Prussia, now joined by Russia, continued into the following spring. After Napoleon's larger armies won another victory, Alexander I of Russia was ready to negotiate the peace. In the subsequent treaties of Tilsit, Prussia lost half of its population, while Russia accepted Napoleon's reorganization of western and central Europe and promised to enforce Napoleon's economic blockade against British goods.

The War of Haitian Independence

With Toussaint L'Ouverture acting increasingly as an independent ruler of the western province of Saint-Domingue, another general, André Rigaud, set up his own government in the southern peninsula, which had long been more isolated from France than the rest of the colony. Civil war broke out between the two sides in 1799, when L'Ouverture's forces, led by his lieutenant Jean Jacques Dessalines (dey-sa-LEEN), invaded the south. Victory over Rigaud gave Toussaint control of the entire colony. (See the feature "Individuals in Society: Toussaint L'Ouverture.")

L'Ouverture's victory was soon challenged, however, by Napoleon's arrival in power. Napoleon intended to reinvigorate the Caribbean plantation economy as a basis for expanding French power. He ordered his brother-in-law General Charles-Victor-Emmanuel Leclerc to crush the new regime.

In 1802 Leclerc landed in Saint-Domingue. Although Toussaint L'Ouverture cooperated with the French and turned his army over to them, he was arrested and deported to France, along with his family, where he died in 1803. Jean Jacques Dessalines united the resistance under his command and led it to a crushing victory over the French forces. Of the fifty-eight thousand French soldiers, fifty thousand were lost in combat and to disease. On January 1, 1804, Dessalines formally declared the independence of Saint-Domingue and the creation of the new sovereign nation of Haiti, the name used by the pre-Columbian inhabitants of the island. (France's other Caribbean colonies were not granted independence. Slavery was re-established and remained in force until 1848.)

Haiti, the second independent state in the Americas and the first in Latin America, was thus born from the first successful large-scale slave revolt in history. Fearing the spread of slave rebellion to the United States, President Thomas Jefferson refused to recognize Haiti. Both the American and the French Revolutions thus exposed their limits by acting to protect economic interests at the expense of revolutionary ideals of freedom and equality. Yet, Haitian independence had fundamental repercussions for world history. As one recent historian of the Haitian revolution commented:

> The slave insurrection of Saint-Domingue led to the expansion of citizenship beyond racial barriers despite the massive political and economic investment in the slave system at the time. If we live in a world in which democracy is meant to exclude no one, it is in no small part because of the actions of those slaves in Saint-Domingue who insisted that human rights were theirs too.[9]

The Grand Empire and Its End

Napoleon resigned himself to the loss of Saint-Domingue, but he still maintained imperial ambitions in Europe. Increasingly, he saw himself as the emperor of Europe and not just of France. The so-called **Grand Empire** he built had three parts. The core, or first part, was an ever-expanding France, which by 1810 included Belgium, Holland, parts of northern Italy, and much German territory on the east bank of the Rhine. Beyond French borders Napoleon established the

Grand Empire Napoleon's name for the European empire over which he intended to rule. This Grand Empire would consist of France, a number of lesser dependent states ruled by his relations, and several major allied states (Austria, Prussia, and Russia).

Individuals in Society

Toussaint L'Ouverture

Little is known of the early life of the brilliant military and political leader Toussaint L'Ouverture. He was born in 1743 on a plantation outside Le Cap owned by the Count de Bréda (**bree-DAH**). According to tradition, Toussaint was the eldest son of a captured African prince from modern-day Benin. Toussaint Bréda, as he was then called, occupied a privileged position among slaves. Instead of performing backbreaking labor in the fields, he served his master as a coachman and livestock keeper. During the 1770s, after being freed, he leased his own small coffee plantation, worked by slaves. A devout Catholic who led a frugal and ascetic life, L'Ouverture impressed others with his enormous physical energy, intellectual acumen, and air of mystery.

Toussaint L'Ouverture entered history in 1791 when he joined the slave uprisings that swept Saint-Domingue. (At some point he took on the cryptic *nom de guerre* "l'ouverture" meaning "the opening.") Toussaint rose to prominence among rebel slaves allied with Spain and by early 1794 controlled his own army. In 1794 he defected to the French side and led his troops to a series of victories against the Spanish. In 1795 France's National Convention promoted L'Ouverture to brigadier general.

Over the next three years L'Ouverture successively eliminated rivals for authority on the island. First he freed himself of the French commissioners sent to govern the colony. With a firm grip on power in the northern province, Toussaint defeated General André Rigaud in 1800 to gain control in the south. His army then marched on the capital of Spanish Santo Domingo on the eastern half of the island, meeting little resistance. The entire island of Hispaniola was now under his command.

With control of Saint-Domingue in his hands, L'Ouverture was confronted with the challenge of building a postemancipation society, the first of its kind. The task was made even more difficult by the chaos wreaked by war, the destruction of plantations, and bitter social and racial tensions. For L'Ouverture the most pressing concern was to re-establish the plantation economy.

Without revenue to pay his army, the gains of the rebellion could be lost. He therefore encouraged white planters to return and reclaim their property. He also adopted harsh policies toward former slaves, forcing them back to their plantations and restricting their ability to acquire land. When they resisted, he sent troops across the island to enforce submission.

In 1801 L'Ouverture convened a colonial assembly to draft a new constitution that reaffirmed his draconian labor policies. The constitution named L'Ouverture governor for life, leaving Saint-Domingue as a colony in name alone. When news of the constitution arrived in France, an angry Napoleon dispatched General Leclerc (**luh-CLAIR**) to re-establish French control. In June 1802 Leclerc's forces arrested L'Ouverture and took him to France. He was jailed at Fort de Joux (**for duh ZHOO**) in the Jura Mountains near the Swiss border, where he died of pneumonia on April 7, 1803. It was left to his lieutenant, Jean Jacques Dessalines, to win independence for the new Haitian nation.

Equestrian portrait of Toussaint L'Ouverture. (Réunion des Musées Nationaux/Art Resource, NY)

Questions for Analysis

1. Toussaint L'Ouverture was both slave and slave owner. How did each experience shape his life and actions?

2. Despite their differences, what did Toussaint L'Ouverture and Napoleon Bonaparte have in common? Why did they share a common fate?

second part: a number of dependent satellite kingdoms, on the thrones of which he placed (and replaced) the members of his large family. The third part comprised the independent but allied states of Austria, Prussia, and Russia. After 1806 both satellites and allies were expected to support Napoleon's continental system and to cease trade with Britain.

The impact of the Grand Empire on the peoples of Europe was considerable. In the areas incorporated into France and in the satellites (see Map 21.1), feudal dues and serfdom had been abolished. Some of the peasants and middle class benefited from these reforms. Yet Napoleon had to put the prosperity and special interests of France first in order to safeguard his power base. Levying heavy taxes in money and men for his armies, he came to be regarded more as a conquering tyrant than as an enlightened liberator. Thus French rule encouraged the growth of reactive nationalism, for individuals in different lands developed patriotic feelings for their own lands in opposition to Napoleon's imperialism.

The first great revolt occurred in Spain. In 1808 a coalition of Catholics, monarchists, and patriots rebelled against Napoleon's attempts to make Spain a French satellite with a Bonaparte as its king. French armies occupied Madrid, but the foes of Napoleon fled to the hills and waged uncompromising guerrilla warfare. Spain was a clear warning: resistance to French imperialism was growing.

Yet Napoleon pushed on, determined to hold his complex and far-flung empire together. In 1810, when the Grand Empire was at its height, Britain still remained at war with France, helping the guerrillas in Spain and Portugal. The continental system, organized to exclude British goods from the continent and force that "nation of shopkeepers" to its knees, was a failure. Instead, it was France that suffered from Britain's counter-blockade, which created hard times for French artisans and the middle class. Perhaps looking for a scapegoat, Napoleon turned on Alexander I of Russia, who in 1811 openly repudiated Napoleon's war of prohibitions against British goods.

Napoleon's invasion of Russia began in June 1812 with a force that eventually numbered 600,000, probably the largest force yet assembled in a single army. Only one-third of this Great Army was French, however; nationals of all the satellites and allies were drafted into the operation. Originally planning to winter in the Russian city of Smolensk (smoh-LENSK) if Alexander did not sue for peace, Napoleon reached Smolensk and recklessly pressed on toward Moscow. The great Battle of Borodino that followed was a draw, and the Russians retreated in good order. Alexander ordered the evacuation of Moscow, which then burned in part, and he refused to negotiate. Finally, after five weeks in the abandoned city, Napoleon ordered a retreat. That retreat was one of the greatest military disasters in history. The Russian army, the Russian winter, and starvation cut Napoleon's army to pieces.

MAPPING THE PAST

MAP 21.1   Napoleonic Europe in 1810

Only Great Britain remained at war with Napoleon at the height of the Grand Empire. Many British goods were smuggled through Helgoland, a tiny but strategic British possession off the German coast. Compare this map with Map 16.1, which shows the division of Europe in 1715. **[1]** How had the balance of power shifted in Europe from 1715 to 1810? What changed, and what remained the same? **[2]** Why did Napoleon succeed in achieving vast territorial gains where Louis XIV did not? **[3]** In comparing Map 16.1 with this map, what was the impact of Napoleon's wars on Germany and the Italian peninsula? What significance do you think this had for these regions in the nineteenth century?

French empire
Dependent states
Allied with Napoleon
At war with Napoleon
⭐ **Major battle**

400 Mi.
400 Km.
200
200
0

N
50 N

GREAT BRITAIN

London

ATLANTIC
OCEAN

North
Sea

KINGDOM
OF NORWAY
AND
DENMARK

Copenhagen

Stockholm

Baltic
Sea

60 N

St. Petersburg

Moscow

Smolensk

Borodino
1812

Kiev

RUSSIAN EMPIRE

KINGDOM
OF
SWEDEN

SWEDISH
POMERANIA

Königsberg
Danzig

Tilsit
Friedland
1807

Neman R.

GRAND DUCHY
OF WARSAW

PRUSSIA

Berlin

SAXONY

Elbe R.

Lübeck
Hamburg
Bremen

WESTPHALIA

Jena 1806

Auerstädt
1806

CONFEDERATION
OF THE RHINE

Rhine R.

Brussels
Waterloo
1815

Paris

Amiens

Lunéville

FRANCE

WÜRTEMBERG
BADEN
Zurich
SWITZERLAND

BAVARIA

Marengo
1800

Milan
Genoa

KINGDOM
OF
ITALY

Corsica

Elba

Sardinia

Marseilles

Rome

Naples

KINGDOM
OF NAPLES

Palermo

KINGDOM OF
SICILY

Malta (Gr. Br.)

Mediterranean
Sea

Austerlitz
1805
Wagram
1804

Vienna

AUSTRIAN EMPIRE

Buda
Pest

Pressburg

ILLYRIAN PROVINCES

Danube R.

OTTOMAN

EMPIRE

Constantinople

Black Sea

Athens

Ionian Is.
(Gr. Br.)

30 E

20 E

10 E

0

SPAIN

Madrid

PORTUGAL

Lisbon

GIBRALTAR (Gr. Br.)

Trafalgar
1805

10 W

Section Review

- Napoleon brought about civil order by offering favors for loyal service, letting the poor keep land, appointing disillusioned revolutionaries and amnestied nobles to government posts, and exercising the power to nominate clergy to posts in exchange for granting religious freedom for Catholics.

- Civil liberties and freedoms for women suffered under Napoleon's authoritarian rule.

- Napoleon defeated the Austrians, proclaimed himself emperor, defeated Prussia and Russia at Austerlitz and then abolished the Holy Roman Empire by creating the German Confederation of the Rhine, and gained Russia's support in a blockade against the British, who had thwarted him at Trafalgar.

- Civil war in Saint-Domingue ended with victory for Toussaint L'Ouverture, who allowed white planters to return, forced former slaves to return to their plantations, and named himself governor for life, but Napoleonic forces captured him and deported him to France.

- The resistance led by Dessalines crushed the French and Saint-Domingue became the sovereign nation of Haiti.

- Napoleon's Grand Empire faced a Spanish revolt supported by the British, a failed French coalition invasion of Russia, and a Europe united against France.

- Napoleon abdicated and was exiled to the island of Elba, but he escaped and after the Hundred Days the allies defeated him at Waterloo; the French restored the Bourbon dynasty under Louis XVIII.

When the frozen remnants staggered into Poland and Prussia in December, 370,000 men had died and another 200,000 had been taken prisoner.[10]

Leaving his troops to their fate, Napoleon raced to Paris to raise yet another army. Austria and Prussia deserted Napoleon and joined Russia and Great Britain in the Treaty of Chaumont in March 1814, by which the four powers pledged allegiance to defeat the French emperor. All across Europe patriots called for a "war of liberation" against Napoleon's oppression. Less than a month later, on April 4, 1814, a defeated Napoleon abdicated his throne. After this unconditional abdication, the victorious allies granted Napoleon the island of Elba off the coast of Italy as his own tiny state. Napoleon was even allowed to keep his imperial title, and France was required to pay him a yearly income of 2 million francs.

The allies also agreed to the restoration of the Bourbon dynasty under Louis XVIII (r. 1814–1824) and promised to treat France with leniency in a peace settlement. The new monarch tried to consolidate support among the people by issuing the Constitutional Charter, which accepted many of France's revolutionary changes and guaranteed civil liberties.

Yet Louis XVIII—old, ugly, and crippled by gout—totally lacked the glory and magic of Napoleon. Hearing of political unrest in France and diplomatic tensions in Vienna, Napoleon staged a daring escape from Elba in February 1815. Landing in France, he issued appeals for support and marched on Paris with a small band of followers. French officers and soldiers who had fought so long for their emperor responded to the call. Louis XVIII fled, and once more Napoleon took command. But Napoleon's gamble was a desperate long shot, for the allies were united against him. At the end of a frantic period known as the Hundred Days, they crushed his forces at Waterloo on June 18, 1815, and imprisoned him on the rocky island of St. Helena, far off the western coast of Africa.

Louis XVIII returned again and recommenced his reign. The allies now dealt more harshly with the apparently incorrigible French. As for Napoleon, he took revenge by writing his memoirs, skillfully nurturing the myth that he had been Europe's revolutionary liberator, a romantic hero whose lofty work had been undone by oppressive reactionaries. An era had ended.

Chapter Review

What social, political, and economic factors formed the background to the French Revolution? (page 536)

The French Revolution was forged by multiple and complex factors. Whereas an earlier generation of historians was convinced that the origins of the Revolution lay in class struggle between the entrenched nobility and the rising bourgeoisie, it is now clear that many other factors were involved. Certainly, French society had undergone significant transformations during the eighteenth century, which dissolved many economic and social differences among elites without removing the legal distinction between them. These changes were accompanied by political struggles between the monarchy and its officers, particularly in the high law courts. Emerging public opinion focused on the shortcomings of monarchical rule, and a rising torrent of political theory, cheap pamphlets, gossip, and innuendo offered scathing and even pornographic

Key Terms

estates (p. 536)

desacralization (p. 538)

Assembly of Notables (p. 540)

Estates General (p. 540)

National Assembly (p. 541)

Great Fear (p. 542)

constitutional monarchy (p. 543)

depictions of the king and his court. With their sacred royal aura severely tarnished, Louis XV and his successor Louis XVI found themselves unable to respond to the financial crises generated by French involvement in the Seven Years' War and the American Revolution. Louis XVI's half-hearted efforts to redress the situation were quickly overwhelmed by elite and popular demands for fundamental reform.

> **What were the immediate events that sparked the Revolution, and how did they result in the formation of a constitutional monarchy in France? How did the ideals and events of the early Revolution raise new aspirations in the colonies? (page 540)**

Forced to call a meeting of the Estates General for the first time in almost two centuries, Louis XVI fell back on the traditional formula of one vote for each of the three orders of society. Debate over the composition of the assembly called forth a bold new paradigm: that the Third Estate in itself constituted the French nation. By 1791 the National Assembly had eliminated Old Regime privileges and had established a constitutional monarchy. Talk in France of liberty, equality, and fraternity raised new and contradictory aspirations in the colony of Saint-Domingue. White planters lobbied for increased colonial autonomy; free people of color sought the return of legal equality; slaves of African birth or descent took direct action on revolutionary ideals by rising in rebellion against their masters.

> **How and why did the Revolution take a radical turn at home and in the colonies? (page 545)**

With the execution of the royal couple and the declaration of terror as the order of the day, the French Revolution took an increasingly radical turn from the end of 1792. Popular fears of counter-revolutionary conspiracy combined with the outbreak of war against a mighty alliance of European monarchs convinced many that the Revolution was vulnerable and must be defended against its multiple enemies. In a spiraling cycle of accusations and executions, the Jacobins eliminated their political opponents and then factions within their own party. The Directory government that took power after the fall of Robespierre restored political equilibrium at the cost of the radical platform of social equality he had pursued.

> **Why did Napoleon Bonaparte assume control of France, and what factors led to his downfall? How did the new republic of Haiti gain independence from France? (page 552)**

Wearied by the weaknesses of the Directory, a group of conspirators gave Napoleon Bonaparte control of France. His brilliant reputation as a military leader and his charisma and determination made him seem ideal to lead France to victory over its enemies. As is so often the case in history, Napoleon's relentless ambitions ultimately led to his downfall. His story is paralleled by that of Toussaint L'Ouverture, another soldier who emerged to the political limelight from the chaos of revolution only to endure exile and defeat. Unlike Napoleon, L'Ouverture's cause ultimately prevailed. After his exile, war between the French forces and the armies he had led and inspired led to French defeat and independence for Saint-Domingue.

As complex as its origins are the legacies of the French Revolution. These included liberalism, assertive nationalism, radical democratic republicanism, embryonic socialism, self-conscious conservatism, abolitionism, decolonization, and movements for racial and sexual equality. The Revolution also left a rich and turbulent history of electoral competition, legislative assemblies, and even mass politics. Thus the French Revolution and conflicting interpretations of its significance presented a whole range

free people of color (p. 544)
Jacobin club (p. 546)
second revolution (p. 547)
Girondists (p. 547)
the Mountain (p. 547)
sans-culottes (p. 547)
planned economy (p. 548)
Reign of Terror (p. 550)
nationalism (p. 550)
Thermidorian reaction (p. 551)
Grand Empire (p. 556)

of political options and alternative visions of the future. For this reason, it was truly the revolution in modern European politics.

Notes

1. Quoted in G. Wright, *France in Modern Times*, 4th ed. (New York: W. W. Norton, 1987), p. 34.
2. G. Pernoud and S. Flaisser, eds., *The French Revolution* (Greenwich, Conn.: Fawcett, 1960), p. 61.
3. Quotations from Wollstonecraft are drawn from E. W. Sunstein, *A Different Face: The Life of Mary Wollstonecraft* (New York: Harper & Row, 1975), pp. 208, 211; and H. R. James, *Mary Wollstonecraft: A Sketch* (London: Oxford University Press, 1932), pp. 60, 62, 69.
4. Quoted in L. Gershoy, *The Era of the French Revolution, 1789–1799* (New York: Van Nostrand, 1957), p. 150.
5. T. Blanning, *The French Revolutionary Wars, 1787–1802* (London: Arnold, 1996), pp. 116–128.
6. Quoted ibid., p. 123.
7. Quoted in Laurent Dubois, *Avengers of the New World: The Story of the Haitian Revolution* (Cambridge: Harvard University Press, 2004), p. 97.
8. I. Woloch, *Napoleon and His Collaborators: The Making of a Dictatorship* (New York: W. W. Norton, 2001), pp. 36–65.
9. Ibid., p. 3.
10. D. Sutherland, *France, 1789–1815: Revolution and Counterrevolution* (New York: Oxford University Press, 1986), p. 420.

To assess your mastery of this chapter, go to **bedfordstmartins.com/mckaywestbrief**

Listening to the Past

Revolution and Women's Rights

The 1789 Declaration of the Rights of Man was a revolutionary call for legal equality, representative government, and individual freedom that excluded women from its manifesto. Among those who saw the contradiction in granting supposedly universal rights to only half the population was Marie Gouze (1748–1793), known to history as Olympe de Gouges. The daughter of a provincial butcher and peddler, she pursued a literary career in Paris after the death of her husband. De Gouges's great work was her Declaration of the Rights of Woman *(1791). Excerpted here, it called on males to end their oppression of women and to give women equal rights. A radical on women's issues, de Gouges sympathized with the monarchy and criticized Robespierre in print. Convicted of sedition, she was guillotined in November 1793.*

Olympe de Gouges in 1784; aquatint by Madame Aubry (1748–1793). (Musée de la Ville de Paris, Musée Carnavalet, Paris, France/The Bridgeman Art Library)

. . . Man, are you capable of being just? . . . Tell me, what gives you sovereign empire to oppress my sex? Your strength? Your talents? Observe the Creator in his wisdom . . . and give me, if you dare, an example of this tyrannical empire. Go back to animals, consult the elements, study plants . . . and distinguish, if you can, the sexes in the administration of nature. Everywhere you will find them mingled; everywhere they cooperate in harmonious togetherness in this immortal masterpiece.

Man alone has raised his exceptional circumstances to a principle. . . . [H]e wants to command as a despot a sex which is in full possession of its intellectual faculties; he pretends to enjoy the Revolution and to claim his rights to equality in order to say nothing more about it. . . . Mothers, daughters, sisters and representatives of the nation demand to be constituted into a national assembly. Believing that ignorance, omission, or scorn for the rights of woman are the only causes of public misfortunes and of the corruption of governments, [the women] have resolved to set forth in a solemn declaration the natural, inalienable, and sacred rights of woman. . . .

I. Woman is born free and lives equal to man in her rights. Social distinctions can be based only on the common utility.

II. The purpose of any political association is the conservation of the natural and imprescriptible rights of woman and man; these rights are liberty, property, security, and especially resistance to oppression.

III. The principle of all sovereignty rests essentially with the nation, which is nothing but the union of woman and man. . . .

IV. Liberty and justice consist of restoring all that belongs to others; thus, the only limits on the exercise of the natural rights of woman are perpetual male tyranny; these limits are to be reformed by the laws of nature and reason.

V. Laws of nature and reason proscribe all acts harmful to society. . . .

VI. The law must be the expression of the general will; all female and male citizens must contribute either personally or through their representatives to its formation; it must be the same for all: male and female citizens, being equal in the eyes of the law, must be equally admitted to all honors, positions, and public employment according to their capacity and without other distinctions besides those of their virtues and talents. . . .

IX. Once any woman is declared guilty, complete rigor is [to be] exercised by the law.

X. No one is to be disquieted for his very basic opinions; woman has the right to mount the scaffold; she must equally have the right to mount the rostrum, provided that her demonstrations do not disturb the legally established public order.

XI. The free communication of thoughts and opinions is one of the most precious rights of woman, since that liberty assures the recognition of children by their fathers. Any female citizen thus may say freely, I am the mother of a child which belongs to you, without being forced by a barbarous prejudice to hide the truth. . . .

XIII. For the support of the public force and the expenses of administration, the contributions of woman and man are equal; she shares all the duties . . . and all the painful tasks; therefore, she must have the same share in the distribution of positions, employment, offices, honors, and jobs. . . .

XVI. No society has a constitution without the guarantee of rights and the separation of powers; the constitution is null if the majority of individuals comprising the nation have not cooperated in drafting it.

XVII. Property belongs to both sexes whether united or separate; for each it is an inviolable and sacred right. . . .

Questions for Analysis

1. On what basis did de Gouges argue for gender equality? Did she believe in natural law?

2. What consequences did "scorn for the rights of woman" have for France, according to de Gouges?

3. Did de Gouges stress political rights at the expense of social and economic rights? If so, why?

Source: Olympe de Gouges, "Declaration of the Rights of Woman," from *Women in Revolutionary Paris, 1789–1795: Selected Documents Translated with Notes and Commentary.* Translated with notes and commentary by Darline Gay Levy, Harriet Branson Applewhite, and Mary Durham Johnson. Copyright © 1979 Board of Trustees. Used with permission of the editors and the University of Illinois Press.

CHAPTER 22

The Revolution in Energy and Industry

ca. 1780–1860

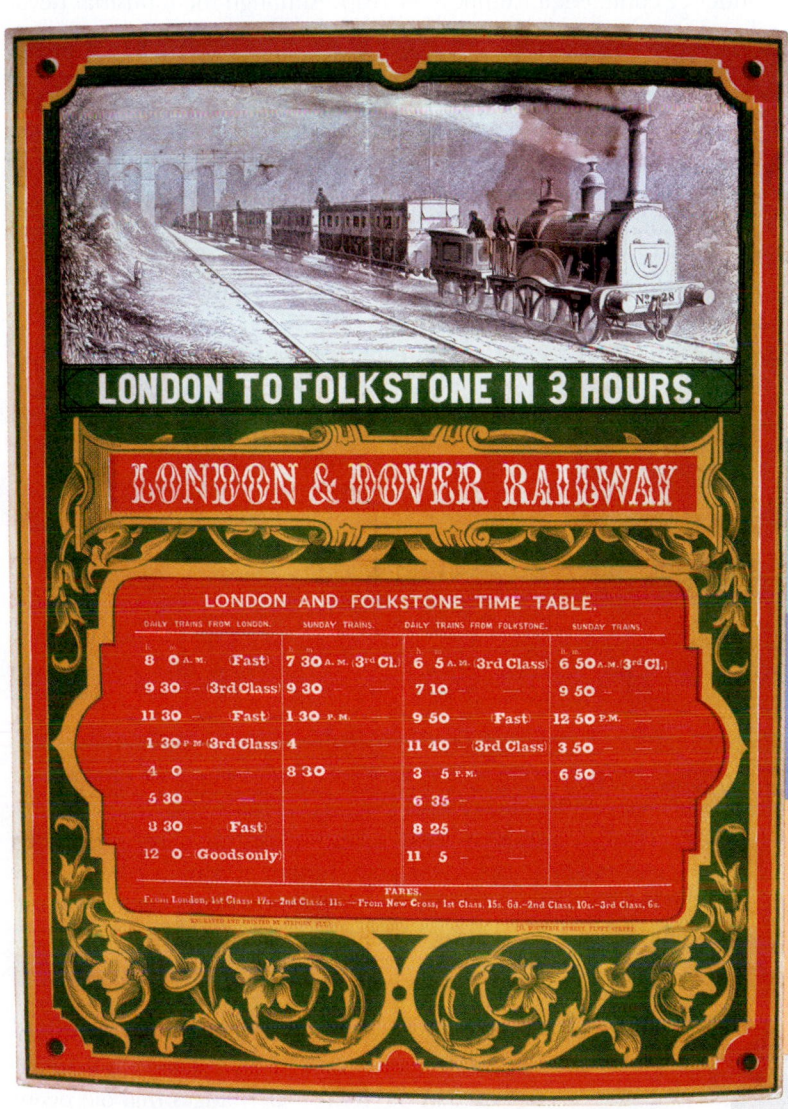

LONDON TO FOLKSTONE IN 3 HOURS.

LONDON & DOVER RAILWAY

LONDON AND FOLKSTONE TIME TABLE.

DAILY TRAINS FROM LONDON.	SUNDAY TRAINS.	DAILY TRAINS FROM FOLKSTONE.	SUNDAY TRAINS.
8 0 A.M. (Fast)	7 30 A.M. (3rd Cl.)	6 5 A.M. (3rd Class)	6 50 A.M. (3rd Cl.)
9 30 — (3rd Class)	9 30 —	7 10 —	9 50 —
11 30 — (Fast)	1 30 P.M.	9 50 — (Fast)	12 50 P.M.
1 30 P.M. (3rd Class)	4 —	11 40 — (3rd Class)	3 50 —
4 0 — —	8 30 —	3 5 P.M. —	6 50 —
5 30 — —		6 35 —	
8 30 — (Fast)		8 25 —	
12 0 (Goods only)		11 5 —	

FARES.
From London, 1st Class 17s.—2nd Class 11s.—From New Cross, 1st Class 15s. 6d.—2nd Class, 10s.—3rd Class, 6s.

A colorful timetable poster lists the trains from London to Folkstone, the English Channel's gateway port to the European continent, and proudly proclaims the speed of the journey. (Private Collection/The Bridgeman Art Library)

Chapter Preview

The Industrial Revolution in Britain
What were the origins of the Industrial Revolution in Britain, and how did it develop between 1780 and 1850?

Industrialization in Continental Europe
How after 1815 did continental countries respond to the challenge of industrialization?

Relations Between Capital and Labor
How did the Industrial Revolution affect social classes, the standard of living, and patterns of work? What measures were taken to improve the conditions of workers?

INDIVIDUALS IN SOCIETY: The Strutt Family

LISTENING TO THE PAST: Testimony Concerning Young Mine Workers

While the revolution in France was opening a new political era, another revolution was beginning to transform economic and social life. This was the Industrial Revolution, which began in Great Britain around the 1780s and started to influence continental Europe after 1815. Although the Industrial Revolution was less dramatic than the French Revolution, it brought about numerous radical changes. Quite possibly only the development of agriculture during Neolithic times had a comparable impact and significance.

The Industrial Revolution profoundly modified much of human experience. It changed patterns of work, transformed the social class structure, and eventually even altered the international balance of political power. The Industrial Revolution also helped ordinary people gain a higher standard of living as the widespread poverty of the preindustrial world was gradually reduced.

Unfortunately, the improvement in the European standard of living was quite limited until about 1850 for at least two reasons. First, even in Britain, only a few key industries experienced a technological revolution, holding down the increase in total production. Second, Europe's population continued to grow rapidly, leaving most individuals poorer and making the wrenching transformation all the more difficult.

The Industrial Revolution in Britain

What were the origins of the Industrial Revolution in Britain, and how did it develop between 1780 and 1850?

The Industrial Revolution began in Great Britain, that historic union of England, Scotland, and Wales. It was something new in history, and it was quite unplanned. With no models to copy and no idea of what to expect, Britain had to pioneer not only in industrial technology but also in social relations and urban living. Between 1793 and 1815, these formidable tasks were complicated by almost constant war with France. As the trailblazer in economic development—while France was undergoing political change—Britain must command special attention.

Eighteenth-Century Origins

Although many aspects of the British Industrial Revolution are still matters for scholarly debate, it is generally agreed that the industrial changes that did occur grew out of a long process of development. First, the British economy was expanding both domestically and abroad. The North American colonial empire that Britain aggressively built, augmented by a strong position in Latin America and in the African slave trade, provided a growing market for British manufactured goods. Within Britain, goods flowed easily between markets along miles of navigable water. Beginning in the 1770s, a canal-building boom greatly enhanced this natural transportation advantage. Rivers and canals also provided easy movement of England's and Wales's enormous deposits of iron and coal, raw materials that would be critical to Europe's early industrial age.

Second, improved agricultural methods played a central role in bringing about the Industrial Revolution in Britain. The result, especially before 1760, was a period of bountiful crops and low food prices that freed up the family budget for other purchases.

Third, Britain had other assets that helped give rise to industrial leadership. Unlike eighteenth-century France, Britain had an effective central bank and well-developed credit markets. The monarchy and the aristocratic oligarchy, which had jointly ruled the country since 1688, provided stable and predictable government. At the same time, the government let the domestic economy operate with few controls, encouraging personal initiative, technical change, and a free market. Finally, Britain had long had a large class of hired agricultural laborers who were relatively mobile—compared to village-bound peasants in France and western Germany, for example—and along with cottage workers they formed a potential industrial labor force for capitalist entrepreneurs.

All these factors combined to initiate the **Industrial Revolution,** a term first coined by awed contemporaries in the 1830s to describe the burst of major inventions and technical changes they had witnessed in certain industries. This technical revolution went hand in hand with an impressive quickening in the annual rate of industrial growth in Britain. The decisive quickening of growth probably came in the 1780s, after the American War of Independence and just before the French Revolution.

The Industrial Revolution was, however, a longer process than the political revolutions that began around the same time. It was not complete in Britain until 1850 at the earliest, and it had no real impact on continental countries until after 1815.

Industrial Revolution A term first coined by awed contemporaries in the 1830s to describe the burst of major inventions and technical changes they had witnessed in certain industries.

The First Factories

The first decisive breakthrough of the Industrial Revolution was the creation of large factories for the British cotton textile industry in the 1770s and 1780s. Technological innovations in the manufacture of cotton cloth led to a new system of production and social relationships. Since no other industry experienced such a rapid or complete transformation before 1830, these trailblazing developments deserve special consideration.

Although the putting-out system of merchant capitalism (see page 490) was expanding all across Europe in the eighteenth century, this pattern of rural industry was most fully developed in Britain. There, as demand for product grew, the system's limitations began to outweigh its advantages for the first time. This was especially true in the British textile industry after about 1760.

A constant shortage of thread in the textile industry prompted many a tinkering worker to come up with a better spinning wheel; James Hargreaves succeeded with his cotton-spinning jenny about 1765. At almost the same moment, Richard Arkwright invented (or possibly pirated) another kind of spinning machine, the water frame. These breakthroughs produced an explosion in the infant cotton textile industry in the 1780s, and by 1790 the new machines were producing ten times as much cotton yarn as had been made in 1770.

Hargreaves's **spinning jenny** was simple, inexpensive, and could be hand-operated by a single person. Arkwright's **water frame,** however, quickly acquired a capacity of several hundred spindles and demanded much more power—waterpower. The water frame thus required large specialized mills, factories that

spinning jenny A spinning machine created by James Hargreaves in 1765 that used six to twenty-four spindles mounted on a sliding carriage to spin a fine thread.

water frame A spinning machine created by Richard Arkwright that had a capacity of several hundred spindles and used water power; it therefore required a larger and more specialized mill but the thread it spun was thicker; generally the thread was then spun on a spinning jenny to achieve the desired thickness.

Woman Working a Hargreaves Spinning Jenny
The loose cotton strands on the slanted bobbins passed up to the sliding carriage and then on to the spindles in back for fine spinning. The worker, almost always a woman, regulated the sliding carriage with one hand, and with the other she turned the crank on the wheel to supply power. By 1783 one woman could spin by hand a hundred threads at a time on an improved model. (Mary Evans Picture Library)

employed as many as one thousand workers from the very beginning. The water frame could spin only coarse, strong thread, which was then put out for respinning on hand-powered cottage jennies. Around 1790 an alternative technique invented by Samuel Crompton also began to require more power than the human arm could supply. After that time, all cotton spinning was gradually concentrated in factories.

The first consequences of these revolutionary developments were generally beneficial to Westerners. Millions of poor people, who had earlier worn nothing underneath their coarse, filthy outer garments, could afford the comfort and cleanliness of cotton slips and underpants as well as cotton dresses and shirts.

Families using cotton in cottage industry were freed from their constant search for thread, which could now be spun in the cottage on the jenny or obtained from a nearby factory. The wages of weavers rose markedly until about 1792. They were known to walk proudly through the streets with 5-pound notes stuck in their hatbands, and they dressed like the middle class. As a result, large numbers of agricultural laborers became hand-loom weavers, while mechanics and capitalists sought to invent a power loom to save on labor costs. This Edmund Cartwright achieved in 1785. But the power looms of the factories worked poorly at first, and hand-loom weavers continued to receive good wages until at least 1800.

Most people preferred to work in their cottages rather than in early factories, so factory owners often turned to children who had been abandoned by their parents and put in the care of local parishes. Apprenticed as young as five or six years of age, boy and girl workers were forced by law to labor for their "masters" for as many as fourteen years. Housed, fed, and locked up nightly in factory dormitories, the young workers received little or no pay. Hours were appalling—commonly thirteen or fourteen hours a day, six days a week. Harsh physical punishment maintained discipline. To be sure, poor children typically worked long hours outside the home for brutal masters, but this was exploitation on a truly unprecedented scale. This exploitation ultimately sparked an increase in humanitarian attitudes toward child laborers in the early nineteenth century.

The Steam Engine Breakthrough

In order to grow, the cotton textile industry needed a more expandable source of power than rivers and streams. The iron industry was also stagnating because of its dependence on processed wood (charcoal), which was in ever shorter supply as forests were depleted. The shortage of energy had become particularly severe in Britain by the eighteenth century. As this early energy crisis grew worse, Britain looked toward its abundant and widely scattered reserves of coal as an alternative to its vanishing wood. Coal was first used in Britain in the late Middle Ages as a source of heat. By 1640 most homes in London were heated with it, and it also provided heat for making beer, glass, soap, and other products. The breakthrough came when industrialists began to use coal to produce mechanical energy and to power machinery.

As more coal was produced, mines were dug deeper and deeper and were constantly filling with water. Mechanical pumps, usually powered by animals walking in circles at the surface, had to be installed. At one mine, fully five hundred horses were used in pumping. Such power was expensive and bothersome. In an attempt to overcome these disadvantages, Thomas Savery in 1698 and Thomas Newcomen in 1705 invented the first primitive **steam engines.** Both engines were extremely inefficient. Both burned coal to produce steam, which was then used to operate a pump. However, by the early 1770s, many of the Savery engines and hundreds of the Newcomen engines were operating successfully, though inefficiently, in English and Scottish mines.

In 1763, a gifted young Scot named James Watt (1736–1819) was called on to repair a Newcomen engine. Watt saw that the Newcomen engine's waste of energy could be reduced by adding a separate condenser. This splendid invention, patented in 1769, greatly increased the efficiency of the steam engine.

To invent something in a laboratory is one thing; to make it a practical success is quite another. Watt needed skilled workers, precision parts, and capital, and the relatively advanced nature of the British economy proved essential. A partnership with a wealthy English toymaker provided risk capital and a manufacturing plant. In the craft tradition of locksmiths, tinsmiths, and millwrights, Watt found skilled mechanics who could install, regulate, and repair his sophisticated engines. From ingenious manufacturers such as the cannonmaker John Wilkinson, Watt was gradually able to purchase precision parts. In more than twenty years of constant effort, Watt made many further improvements. By the late 1780s, the steam engine had become a practical and commercial success in Britain.

The steam engine of Watt and his followers was the Industrial Revolution's most fundamental advance in technology. For the first time in history, humanity had, at least for a few generations, almost unlimited power at its disposal. For the first time, inventors and engineers could devise and implement all kinds of power

steam engines A breakthrough invention by Thomas Savery in 1698 and Thomas Newcomen in 1705 that burned coal to produce steam, which was then used to operate a pump; although inefficient they were used successfully in English and Scottish mines.

The Saltash Bridge
Railroad construction presented innumerable challenges, such as the building of bridges to span rivers and gorges. Civil engineers responded with impressive feats, and their profession bounded ahead. This painting portrays the inauguration of I. K. Brunel's Saltash Bridge, where the railroad crosses the Tamar River into Cornwall in southwest England. The high spans allow large ships to pass underneath. (Elton Collection, Ironbridge Gorge Museum Trust)

equipment to aid people in their work. For the first time, abundance was at least a possibility for ordinary men and women.

The steam engine was quickly put to use in several industries in Britain. It drained mines and made possible the production of ever more coal to feed steam engines elsewhere. The steam-power plant began to replace waterpower in the cotton-spinning mills during the 1780s, contributing greatly to that industry's phenomenal rise. Steam took the place of waterpower in flour mills, in the malt mills used in breweries, in the flint mills supplying the china industry, and in the sugar mills of the West Indies colonies. It was put to use in the British iron industry, which grew from producing 17,000 tons in 1740 to 3 million tons in 1844. Once scarce and expensive, iron became the cheap, basic, indispensable building block of the economy.

The Coming of the Railroads

As industry grew, so did the need to transport large quantities of goods over long distances. Overland shipment of freight, relying solely on horsepower, was still quite limited and frightfully expensive; shippers used rivers and canals for heavy freight whenever possible. It was logical, therefore, that inventors would try to use steam power for transportation.

As early as 1800, an American ran a "steamer on wheels" through city streets. Other experiments followed. In the 1820s, English engineers created steam cars capable of carrying fourteen passengers at ten miles an hour—as fast as the mail coach. But the noisy, heavy steam automobiles frightened passing horses and damaged themselves as well as the roads with their vibrations. For the rest of the century, horses continued to reign on highways and city streets.

The coal industry had long been using plank roads and rails to move coal wagons within mines and at the surface. Rails reduced friction and allowed a horse or a human being to pull a heavier load. Thus once a rail capable of supporting a heavy locomotive was developed in 1816, all sorts of experiments with steam engines on rails went forward. In 1830 George Stephenson's **Rocket** sped down the track of the just-completed Liverpool and Manchester Railway at sixteen miles per hour. This was the world's first important railroad, fittingly steaming in the heart of industrial England. The line from Liverpool to Manchester was a financial as well as a technical success, and many private companies were organized to build more rail lines. Within twenty years, they had completed the main trunk lines of Great Britain. Other countries were quick to follow.

Rocket The name given to George Stephenson's effective locomotive that was first tested in 1830 on the Liverpool and Manchester Railway at 16 miles per hour.

The economic consequences of the railroad were tremendous. As the barrier of high transportation costs was lowered, markets became larger and even nationwide. Larger markets encouraged larger factories with more sophisticated machinery in a growing number of industries. Such factories could make goods more cheaply and gradually subjected most cottage workers and many urban artisans to severe competitive pressures.

In all countries, the construction of railroads required a large number of laborers. Many landless farm laborers and poor peasants, long accustomed to leaving their villages for temporary employment, went to build railroads. By the time the work was finished, urban life seemed more appealing. By the time they sent for their wives and sweethearts to join them, they had become urban workers.

The railroad, with trains reaching speeds of fifty miles per hour by 1850, gave the entire society a new sense of power and speed. Painters such as Joseph M. W. Turner (1775–1851), succeeded in expressing this sense of power and awe. So did the massive new train stations, the cathedrals of the industrial age. Leading railway engineers such as Isambard Kingdom Brunel (**IZ-uhm-bahrd broo-NEL**) and Thomas Brassey, whose tunnels pierced mountains and whose bridges spanned valleys, became public idols—the astronauts of their day. Everyday speech absorbed the images of railroading. After you got up a "full head of steam," you "highballed" along. And if you didn't "go off the track," you might "toot your own whistle." The railroad fired the imagination.

Industry and Population

In 1851 London was the site of a famous industrial fair. This Great Exhibition was held in the newly built **Crystal Palace,** an architectural masterpiece made entirely of glass and iron, both of which were now cheap and abundant. For the millions who visited, one fact stood out: the little island of Britain was the "workshop of the world." It alone produced two-thirds of the world's coal and more than one-half of its iron and cotton cloth. More generally, it has been carefully estimated that in 1860 Britain produced a truly remarkable 20 percent of the entire world's output of industrial goods, whereas it had produced only about 2 percent of the world total in 1750.[1] Experiencing revolutionary industrial change, Britain became the first industrial nation (see Map 22.1).

Crystal Palace The location of the Great Exposition in 1851 in London, an architectural masterpiece made entirely of glass and iron, both of which were now cheap and abundant.

MAP 22.1 The Industrial Revolution in England, ca. 1850

Industry concentrated in the rapidly growing cities of the north and the Midlands, where rich coal and iron deposits were in close proximity.

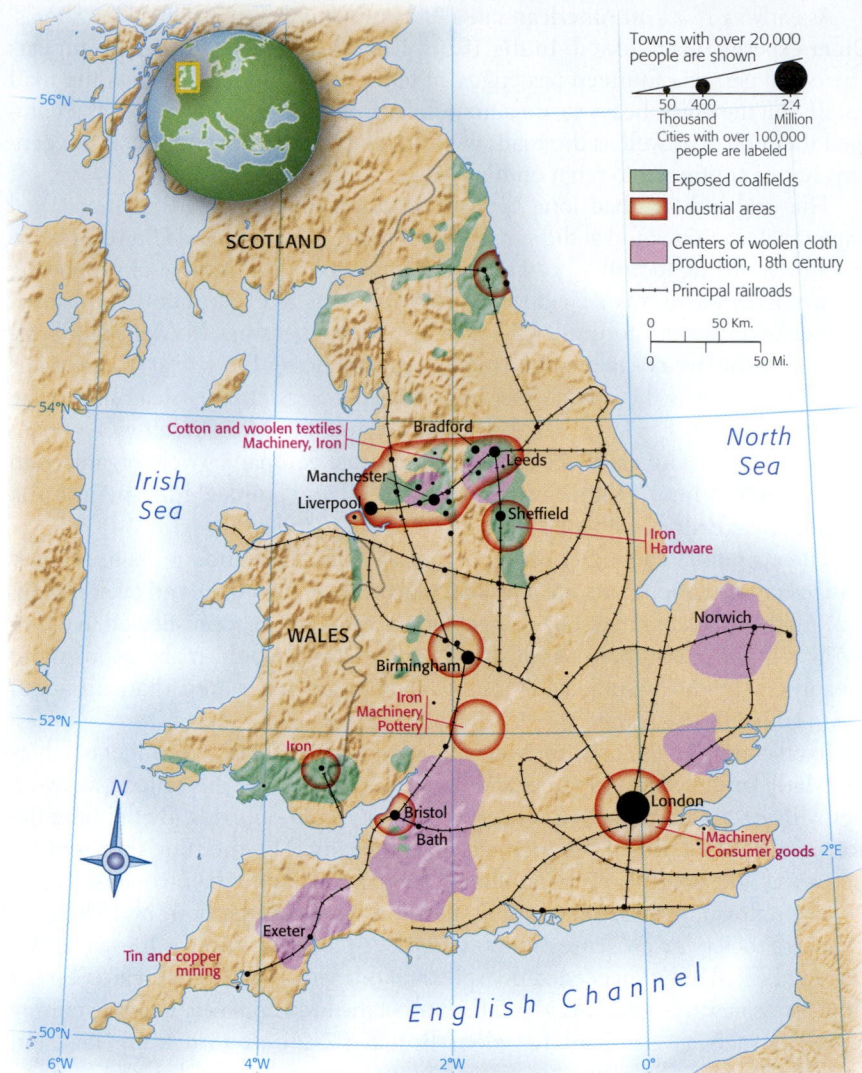

Towns with over 20,000 people are shown

50   400   2.4
Thousand   Million
Cities with over 100,000 people are labeled

Exposed coalfields

Industrial areas

Centers of woolen cloth production, 18th century

Principal railroads

0   50 Km.
0   50 Mi.

SCOTLAND

Irish Sea

North Sea

Cotton and woolen textiles Machinery, Iron

Bradford

Leeds

Manchester

Liverpool

Sheffield

Iron Hardware

WALES

Norwich

Birmingham

Iron Machinery Pottery

Iron

Bristol

Bath

London

Machinery Consumer goods

Exeter

Tin and copper mining

English Channel

Section Review

- The causes of the Industrial Revolution included an expanding British economy, improved agricultural methods, effective banking and credit markets, stable government, a relatively free market, and a mobile labor force.

- The invention of the spinning jenny and then the water frame revolutionized the cotton textile industry, increasing wages for weavers, but requiring large factories where owners apprenticed young children who worked long hours under harsh conditions.

- The invention of—and subsequent improvements to—the steam engine was the catalyst to the industrial revolution, replacing water power in the production of coal, flour, malt, sugar, flint, and, most importantly, iron.

- The steam engine was a financial and technical success, lowering transportation costs, enlarging consumer markets and factories, lowering prices, increasing employment, and expanding urbanization.

- At the same time that Britain's industry was booming, the population was growing rapidly as well, providing more workers for the labor force.

At the same time that Britain's gross national product (GNP) was skyrocketing, its population was exploding as well. Although the question is still debated, many economic historians now believe that rapid population growth in Great Britain was not harmful because it facilitated industrial expansion. More people meant a more mobile labor force, with a wealth of young workers in need of employment and ready to go where the jobs were.

Contemporaries were much less optimistic. In his famous and influential *Essay on the Principle of Population* (1798), Thomas Malthus (1766–1834) argued that population would always tend to grow faster than the food supply. In Malthus's opinion, the only hope of warding off such "positive checks" to population growth as war, famine, and disease was "prudential restraint." That is, young men and women had to limit the growth of population by the old tried-and-true means of marrying late in life. While Malthus and his followers were proved wrong in the long term, until the 1820s, or even the 1840s, contemporary observers might reasonably have concluded that the economy and the total population were racing neck and neck, with the outcome very much in doubt.

Industrialization in Continental Europe

How after 1815 did continental countries respond to the challenge of industrialization?

The new technologies developed in the British Industrial Revolution were adopted by business in continental Europe to a considerable but variable degree and at different rates of change. Continental Europe faced a number of challenges in attempting to develop new industries, but all European states (as well as the United States, Canada, and Japan) managed to raise per capita industrial levels in the nineteenth century.

The Challenge of Industrialization

In 1750 all the countries of Europe were fairly close together on a per capita level of industrialization—that is, according to how much industrial product was produced, on average, for each person in a year. But Britain had opened up a noticeable lead over all continental countries by 1800, and that gap progressively widened as the British Industrial Revolution accelerated to 1830 and reached full maturity by 1860. The British level of per capita industrialization was twice the French level in 1830, for example, and more than three times the French level in 1860. All other large countries (except the United States) had fallen even farther behind Britain than France had at both dates.

Posing the greatest obstacle to European expansion was the political and social turmoil caused by the French Revolution and its aftermath. On the continent, the upheavals that began with the French Revolution disrupted trade, created runaway inflation, and fostered social anxiety. War severed normal communications between Britain and the continent, severely handicapping continental efforts to use new British machinery and technology. Moreover, the years from 1789 to 1815 were, even for those of the privileged French economic classes, who received special favors from Napoleon after 1800, a time of "national catastrophe"—in the graphic words of a famous French scholar.[2] Thus France and the rest of Europe were further behind Britain in 1815 than in 1789.

This widening gap made it more difficult, if not impossible, for other countries to follow the British pattern in energy and industry after peace was restored in 1815. Above all, in the newly mechanized industries, British goods were being produced very economically, and these goods had come to dominate world markets completely while the continental states were absorbed in war between 1792 and 1815. In addition, British technology had become so advanced and complicated that very few engineers or skilled technicians outside England understood it. Moreover, the technology of steam power had grown much more expensive. It involved large investments in the iron and coal industries and, after 1830, required the existence of railroads, which were very costly. Continental business people had great difficulty finding the large sums of money the new methods demanded, and there was a shortage of laborers accustomed to working in factories. All these disadvantages slowed the spread of modern industry (see Map 22.2).

After 1815, however, when continental countries began to face up to the British challenge, they had at least three important advantages over non-Western countries. First, most continental countries had a rich tradition of putting-out enterprise, merchant capitalists, and skilled urban artisans. Second, continental capitalists were able to "borrow" knowledgeable engineers and skilled factory

MAPPING THE PAST

Map 22.2   Continental Industrialization, ca. 1850

Although continental countries were beginning to make progress by 1850, they still lagged far behind Britain. For example, continental railroad building was still in an early stage, whereas the British rail system was essentially complete (review Map 22.1, page 572). Coal played a critical role in nineteenth-century industrialization both as a power source for steam engines and as a raw material for making iron and steel. **[1]** Locate the major exposed (that is, known) coal deposits in 1850. Which countries and areas appear rich in coal resources, and which appear poor? Is there a difference between northern and southern Europe? **[2]** What is the relationship between known coal deposits and emerging industrial areas?

workers from England, even though English laws tried to prevent the export of talent and equipment. English entrepreneurs also set up their own factories in Europe, some producing the machinery needed for other industries. Third, continental countries were independent of foreign control and could act in their own self-interest to foster industry.

tariff protection A government's way of supporting and aiding their own economy by laying high taxes on the cheaper, imported goods of another country, as when France responded to cheaper British goods flooding their country by imposing high tariffs on British imports.

Government Support and Corporate Banking

Continental governments played an important role in helping business people develop new industries. These governments fashioned economic policies to serve their own interests; **tariff protection** was one such policy.

For example, after Napoleon's wars ended in 1815, France was suddenly flooded with cheaper and better British goods. The French government responded by laying high tariffs on many British imports in order to protect the French economy. The governments of German states formed a customs union or Zollverein (**TSOLL-feh-rine**), allowing goods to move between the German member states without tariffs, while erecting a single uniform tariff against other nations. Without such protections, the German writer Friedrich List (1789–1846) argued, Britain could "make the rest of the world, like the Hindus, its serfs in all industrial and commercial relations."

After 1815 continental governments bore the cost of building roads and canals to improve transportation. They also bore to a significant extent the cost of building railroads. Belgium led the way in the 1830s and 1840s. In an effort to tie the newly independent nation together, the Belgian government decided to construct a state-owned system that helped make the country an early industrial leader. Several of the smaller German states also built state systems.

The Prussian government provided another kind of invaluable support for the construction of a national rail system. It guaranteed that the state treasury would pay the interest and principal on railroad bonds if the closely regulated private companies in Prussia were unable to do so. Thus railroad investors in Prussia ran little risk, and capital was quickly raised.

In France the state shouldered all the expense of acquiring and laying roadbed, including bridges and tunnels. Finished roadbed was leased to a carefully supervised private company, which usually benefited from a state guarantee of its

A German Ironworks, 1845

This big business enterprise, the Borsig ironworks in Berlin, mastered the new British method of smelting iron ore with coke. Germany, and especially the state of Prussia, was well endowed with both iron and coal, and the rapid exploitation of these resources after 1840 transformed a poor agricultural country into an industrial powerhouse. (akg-images)

debts. In short, governments helped pay for railroads, the all-important leading sector in continental industrialization.

Finally, banks, like governments, also played a larger and more creative role on the continent than in Britain. Previously, banks in Europe had generally avoided industrial investment as being too risky because the partners in these private banks risked losing their entire personal fortunes if an investment failed. In the 1830s, two important Belgian banks pioneered in a new direction. They received permission from the growth-oriented government to establish themselves as corporations enjoying limited liability. That is, a stockholder could lose only his or her original investment in the bank's common stock and could not be assessed for any additional losses. Publicizing the risk-reducing advantage of limited liability, these Belgian banks were able to attract many shareholders, large and small. They mobilized impressive resources for investment in big companies, became industrial banks, and successfully promoted industrial development.

Similar corporate banks became important in France and Germany in the 1850s and 1860s. Usually working in collaboration with governments, they established and developed many railroads and many companies working in heavy industry, which were increasingly organized as limited liability corporations.

The combined efforts of skilled workers, entrepreneurs, governments, and industrial banks meshed successfully between 1850 and the financial crash of 1873. This was a period of unprecedented economic growth on the continent. In Belgium, Germany, and France, key indicators of modern industrial development—such as railway mileage, iron and coal production, and steam-engine capacity—increased at average annual rates of 5 to 10 percent. As a result, rail networks were completed in western and much of central Europe, and the leading continental countries mastered the industrial technologies that had first been developed in Great Britain. In the early 1870s, Britain was still Europe's most industrial nation, but a select handful of countries were closing the gap that had been opened up by the Industrial Revolution.

Europe's continent-wide increases stood in stark contrast to the large and tragic decreases that occurred at the same time in many non-Western countries, most notably in China and India. European countries industrialized to a greater or lesser extent even as most of the non-Western world *de*-industrialized. Thus differential rates of wealth- and power-creating industrial development, which heightened disparities within Europe, also greatly magnified existing inequalities between Europe and the rest of the world. We shall return to this momentous change in world economic relationships in Chapter 26.

Section Review

- The countries of Europe faced a great challenge to keep up with Britain's industry and were hindered by disruptions caused by war and by the lack of skilled engineers, railroads, funding, and laborers accustomed to factory work.

- Continental governments paved the way for industry in their own countries by imposing tariffs on foreign goods and by encouraging and financing railroad-building.

- Banks mobilized funding for investments by offering limited liability, causing a rapid rise in economic growth across Europe, the completion of rail networks, and the adaptation of new industrial technologies.

Relations Between Capital and Labor

How did the Industrial Revolution affect social classes, the standard of living, and patterns of work? What measures were taken to improve the conditions of workers?

Industrial development brought new social relations and intensified long-standing problems between capital and labor in both urban workshops and cottage industry. A new group of factory owners and industrial capitalists arose. These men and women and their families strengthened the wealth and size of the middle class, which had previously been made up mainly of merchants and professional people. The nineteenth century became the golden age of the middle class. Modern industry also created a much larger group, the factory workers. For the first time, large numbers of men, women, and children came together under one roof to work with complicated machinery for a single owner or a few partners in large companies.

The growth of new occupational groups in industry stimulated new thinking about social relations. Often combined with reflections on the French Revolution, this thinking led to the development of a new overarching interpretation—a new paradigm—regarding social relationships (see Chapter 23). Briefly, this paradigm argued, with considerable success, that individuals were members of economically determined classes, which had conflicting interests. Accordingly, the comfortable, well-educated "public" of the eighteenth century came increasingly to see itself as the backbone of the middle class (or the middle classes), and the "people" gradually transformed themselves into the modern working class (or working classes). And if the new class interpretation was more of a deceptive simplification than a fundamental truth for some critics, it appealed to many because it seemed to explain what was happening. Therefore, conflicting classes existed, in part, because many individuals came to believe they existed and they developed an appropriate sense of class feeling—what Marxists call **class-consciousness.**

class-consciousness A sense of class differentiation that existed, in part, because many individuals came to believe that conflicting classes existed.

The New Class of Factory Owners

Early industrialists operated in a highly competitive economic system, and success and large profits were by no means certain. Manufacturers waged a constant battle to cut their production costs while also investing profits back into the business for new and better machinery. "Dragged on by the frenzy of this terrible life," according to one of the dismayed critics, the struggling manufacturer had "no time for niceties. He must conquer or die, make a fortune or drown himself."[3]

Most early industrialists drew upon their families and friends for labor and capital, but they came from a variety of backgrounds. Many were from well-established merchant families, which provided a rich network of contacts and support. Others were of modest means, especially in the early days. Artisans and skilled workers of exceptional ability had unparalleled opportunities. Members of ethnic and religious groups who had been discriminated against in the traditional occupations controlled by the landed aristocracy jumped at the new chances and often helped each other. Scots, Quakers, and other Protestant dissenters were tremendously important in Britain; Protestants and Jews dominated banking in Catholic France. Many of the industrialists were newly rich, and, not surprisingly, they were very proud and self-satisfied.

As factories and firms grew larger, opportunities declined, at least in well-developed industries. It became considerably harder for a gifted but poor young mechanic to start a small enterprise and end up as a wealthy manufacturer. Formal education (for males) became more important as a means of success and advancement, and at the advanced level it was very expensive. In Britain by 1830 and in France and Germany by 1860, leading industrialists were more likely to have inherited their well-established enterprises, and they were financially much more secure than their struggling fathers and mothers had been. They also had a greater sense of class-consciousness, fully aware that ongoing industrial development had widened the gap between themselves and their workers.

The wives and daughters of successful businessmen also found fewer opportunities for active participation in Europe's increasingly complex business world. Rather than contributing as vital partners in a family-owned enterprise, as so many middle-class women such as Elizabeth Strutt had done (see the feature "Individuals in Society: The Strutt Family"), these women were increasingly valued for their ladylike gentility. By 1850 some influential women writers and most businessmen

Individuals in Society

The Strutt Family

For centuries economic life in Europe revolved around hundreds of thousands of small family enterprises. These family enterprises worked farms, crafted products, and traded goods. They built and operated the firms and factories of the early industrial era, with the notable exceptions of the capital-hungry railroads and a few big banks. Indeed, until late in the nineteenth century, close-knit family groups continued to control most successful businesses, including those organized as corporations.

Jedediah Strutt (ca. 1790), by Joseph Wright of Derby. (Derby Museum & Art Gallery/The Bridgeman Art Library)

One successful and fairly well-documented family enterprise began with the marriage of Jedediah Strutt (1726–1797) and Elizabeth Woollat (1729–1774) in Derbyshire in northern England in 1755. The son of a farmer, Jedediah fell in love with Elizabeth when he lodged with her parents. Both young people grew up in the close-knit dissenting Protestant community, which did not accept the doctrines of the state-sponsored Church of England, and the well-educated Elizabeth worked in a local school for dissenters and then for a dissenter minister in London.

Aided by Elizabeth, who was "obviously a very capable woman" and who supplied some of the drive her husband had previously lacked, Jedediah embarked on a new career.* He invented a machine to make handsome, neat-fitting ribbed silk stockings, which had previously been made by hand. He secured a patent, despite strong opposition from competitors, and went into production. Elizabeth helped constantly in the enterprise, which was nothing less than an informal partnership between husband and wife.†

In 1757, for example, when Jedediah was fighting to uphold his patent in the local court, Elizabeth left her son of nine months and journeyed to London to seek a badly needed loan from her former employer. She also canvassed her London relatives and dissenter friends for orders for stockings and looked for sales agents and sources of capital. Elizabeth's letters reveal a detailed knowledge of ribbed stockings and the prices and quality of different kinds of thread. The family biographers conclude that her husband "owed much of his success to her energy and counsel." Elizabeth was always "active in the business—a partner in herself."‡ Despite the invaluable business contribution of wives like Elizabeth, the legal rights and consequences of partnership were denied to married women in Britain and Europe in the eighteenth and nineteenth centuries.

The Strutt enterprise grew and gradually prospered, but it always retained its family character. The firm built a large silk mill and then went into cotton spinning in partnership with Richard Arkwright, the inventor of the water frame (see page 567). The brothers of both Jedediah and Elizabeth worked for the firm, and their eldest daughter worked long hours in the warehouse. Bearing three sons, Elizabeth fulfilled yet another vital task because the typical family firm looked to its own members for managers and continued success. All three sons entered the business and became cotton textile magnates. Elizabeth never saw these triumphs. The loyal and talented wife in the family partnership died suddenly at age forty-five while in London with Jedediah on a business trip.

Questions for Analysis

1. How and why did the Strutts succeed?
2. What does Elizabeth's life tell us about the role of British women in the early Industrial Revolution?

---

* R. Fitton and A. Wadsworth, *The Strutts and the Arkwrights, 1758–1830: A Study of the Early Factory System* (Manchester, England: Manchester University Press, 1958), p. 23.
† See the excellent discussion by C. Hall, "Strains in the 'Firm of Wife, Children and Friends'? Middle-Class Women and Employment in Early Nineteenth-Century England," in P. Hudson and W. Lee, eds., *Women's Work and the Family Economy in Historical Perspective* (Manchester, England: Manchester University Press, 1990), pp. 106–132.
‡ Fitton and Wadsworth, *The Strutts*, pp. 110–111.

assumed that middle-class wives and daughters should steer clear of undignified work in offices and factories. Rather, a middle-class lady should protect and enhance her femininity. She should concentrate on her proper role as wife and mother, preferably in an elegant residential area far removed from ruthless commerce and the volatile working class.

The New Factory Workers

The social consequences of the Industrial Revolution have long been hotly debated. The condition of British workers during the transformation has always generated the most controversy among historians because Britain was the first country to industrialize and because the social consequences seemed harshest there. Before 1850 other countries had not proceeded very far with industrialization, and almost everyone agrees that the economic conditions of European workers improved after 1850. Thus the experience of British workers to about 1850 deserves special attention. (Industrial growth also promoted rapid urbanization, with its own awesome problems, as will be shown in Chapter 24.)

From the beginning, the Industrial Revolution in Britain had its critics. Among the first were the romantic poets. William Blake (1757–1827) called the early factories "satanic mills" and protested against the hard life of the London poor. William Wordsworth (1770–1850) lamented the destruction of the rural way of life and the pollution of the land and water. Some handicraft workers—notably the **Luddites** (**LUD-eytes**), who attacked whole factories in northern England in 1812 and after—smashed the new machines, which they believed were putting them out of work. Doctors and reformers wrote eloquently of problems in the factories and new towns.

Was the new poverty of industrial workers worse than the old poverty of cottage workers and agricultural laborers? Friedrich Engels (**ENG-guhlz**) (1820–1895), the future revolutionary and colleague of Karl Marx, charged that it was. After studying conditions in northern England, this young middle-class German issued a blistering indictment of the middle classes in *The Condition of the Working Class in England.* "At the bar of world opinion," he wrote, "I charge the English middle classes with mass murder, wholesale robbery, and all the other crimes in the calendar." Engels's extremely influential charge of middle-class exploitation and increasing worker poverty was embellished by Marx and later socialists.

Meanwhile, other observers believed that conditions were improving for the working people. Andrew Ure (**yoo-RAY**) wrote in 1835 in his study of the cotton industry that conditions in most factories were not harsh and were even quite good. Edwin Chadwick, a conscientious government official well acquainted with the problems of the working population, concluded that the "whole mass of the laboring community" was increasingly able "to buy more of the necessities and minor luxuries of life."[4] Nevertheless, if all the contemporary assessments had been counted up, those who thought conditions were getting worse for working people would probably have been the majority.

In an attempt to go beyond the contradictory judgments of contemporaries, some historians have looked at different kinds of sources. The most recent studies also confirm the view that the early years of the Industrial Revolution were hard ones for British workers. There was little or no increase in the purchasing power of the average British worker from about 1780 to about 1820. The years from 1792 to 1815, a period of almost constant warfare with France, were particularly difficult. Food prices rose faster than wages, and the living conditions of the laboring poor declined. Only after 1820, and especially after 1840, did real wages rise substantially,

Luddites Handicraft workers who attacked whole factories in northern England in 1812 and after, smashing the new machines that they believed were putting them out of work.

so that the average worker earned and consumed roughly 50 percent more in real terms in 1850 than in 1770.[5] In short, there was considerable economic improvement for workers throughout Great Britain by 1850, but that improvement was hard won and slow in coming.

This important conclusion must be qualified, however. The hours in the average workweek increased, as some economic historians now believe it had been increasing in parts of northern Europe since the seventeenth century. Thus, to a large extent, workers earned more simply because they worked more. Indeed, significant recent research shows that in England nonagricultural workers labored about 250 days per year in 1760 as opposed to 300 days per year in 1830, while the normal workday remained an exhausting eleven hours throughout the entire period.[6]

Another way to consider the workers' standard of living is to look at the goods that they purchased. Again the evidence is somewhat contradictory. Speaking generally, workers ate somewhat more food of higher nutritional quality as the Industrial Revolution progressed, except during wartime. Diets became more varied; people ate more potatoes, dairy products, fruits, and vegetables. Clothing improved, but housing for working people probably deteriorated somewhat. In short, per capita use of specific goods supports the position that the standard of living of the working classes rose, at least moderately, after the long wars with France.

Conditions of Work

What about working conditions? Did workers eventually earn more only at the cost of working longer and harder? Were workers exploited harshly by the new factory owners?

The first factories were cotton mills, which began functioning along rivers and streams in the 1770s. Cottage workers, accustomed to the putting-out system, were reluctant to work in the new factories even when they received relatively good wages because factory work was unappealing. In the factory, workers had to keep up with the machine and follow its tempo. They had to show up every day and work long, monotonous hours. Factory workers had to adjust their daily lives to the shrill call of the factory whistle.

Cottage workers were not used to that kind of schedule. All members of the family worked hard and long, but in spurts, setting their own pace. They could interrupt their work when they wanted to. Women and children could break up their long hours of spinning with other tasks. On Saturday afternoon the head of the family delivered the week's work to the merchant manufacturer and got paid. Saturday night was a time of relaxation and drinking, especially for the men. Recovering from his hangover on Tuesday, the weaver bent to his task on Wednesday and then worked frantically to meet his deadline on Saturday. Like some students today, he might "pull an all-nighter" on Thursday or Friday in order to get his work finished.

Also, early factories resembled English poorhouses, where totally destitute people went to live at public expense. Some poorhouses were industrial prisons, where the inmates had to work in order to receive their food and lodging. The similarity between large brick factories and large stone poorhouses increased the cottage workers' aversion to factories.

By 1790 the factory system was gaining greater acceptance. Many more factories were being built, mainly in urban areas, where they could use steam power rather than waterpower and attract a workforce more easily than in the countryside. The need for workers was great, especially when the practice of using abandoned and orphaned children was outlawed by Parliament in 1802. Indeed, people came from near and far to work in the cities, both as factory workers and as laborers, builders, and domestic servants. Yet as they took these new jobs, working people did not simply give in to a system of labor that had formerly repelled them. Rather, they helped modify the system by carrying over old, familiar working traditions.

For one thing, they often came to the mills and the mines as family units. This was how they had worked on farms and in the putting-out system. The mill or mine owner bargained with the head of the family and paid him or her for the work of the whole family. In the cotton mills, children worked for their mothers or fathers, collecting scraps and "piecing" broken threads together. In the mines, children sorted coal and worked the ventilation equipment. Their mothers hauled coal in the tunnels below the surface, while their fathers hewed with pick and shovel at the face of the seam.

The preservation of the family as an economic unit in the factories from the 1790s on made the new surroundings more tolerable, and parents felt that their children were still under their control when they worked side by side. Adult workers were not particularly interested in limiting the minimum working age or hours of their children as long as family members worked together. Only when technical changes threatened to place control and discipline in the hands of impersonal managers and overseers did adult workers protest against inhuman conditions in the name of their children.

Some enlightened employers and social reformers in Parliament worked to change this practice, arguing that more humane standards were necessary. For example, Robert Owen (1771–1858), a very successful manufacturer in Scotland, testified in 1816 before an investigating committee on the basis of his experience. He stated that "very strong facts" demonstrated that employing children under ten years of age as factory workers was "injurious to the children, and not beneficial to the proprietors."[7] Workers also provided graphic testimony at such hearings as the reformers pressed Parliament to pass corrective laws. They scored some important successes.

Their most significant early accomplishment was the **Factory Act of 1833.** It limited the factory workday for children between nine and thirteen to eight hours and that of adolescents between fourteen and eighteen to twelve hours, although the act made no effort to regulate the hours of work for children at home or in small businesses. Children under nine were to be enrolled in the elementary schools that factory owners were required to establish. The employment of children declined rapidly. Thus the Factory Act broke the pattern of whole families working together in the factory because efficiency required standardized shifts for all workers.

Ties of blood and kinship were important in other ways in Great Britain in the formative years between about 1790 and 1840. Many manufacturers and builders hired subcontractors, who in turn hired the work crews. The subcontractor might be as harsh as the greediest capitalist, but the relationship between subcontractor and work crew was close and personal because many of his hires were friends and relatives. This kind of personal relationship had traditionally existed in cottage industry and in urban crafts, and it was more acceptable to many workers than impersonal factory discipline.

Ties of kinship were particularly important for newcomers, who often traveled great distances to find work. Many urban workers in Great Britain were from Ireland. Forced out of rural Ireland by population growth and deteriorating economic conditions from 1817 on, Irish in search of jobs could not be choosy; they took what they could get. As early as 1824, most of the workers in the Glasgow cotton

Factory Act of 1833 This act limited the factory workday for children between nine and thirteen to eight hours and that of adolescents between fourteen and eighteen to twelve hours.

mills were Irish; in 1851 one-sixth of the population of Liverpool was Irish. Like many other immigrant groups held together by ethnic and religious ties, the Irish worked together, formed their own neighborhoods, and not only survived but also thrived.

Changes in the Division of Labor by Gender

The era of the Industrial Revolution witnessed major changes in the gender division of labor. In preindustrial Europe most people generally worked in family units. By tradition, certain jobs were defined by gender—women and girls for milking and spinning, men and boys for plowing and weaving—but many tasks might go to either sex. Family employment carried over into early factories and subcontracting, but it collapsed as child labor was restricted and new attitudes emerged. A different sexual division of labor gradually arose to take its place. The man emerged as the family's primary wage earner, while the woman found only limited job opportunities. Generally denied good jobs at good wages in the growing urban economy, women were expected to concentrate on unpaid housework, child care, and craftwork at home.

This new pattern of **separate spheres** had several aspects. First, all studies agree that married women from the working classes were much less likely to work full-time for wages outside the house after the first child arrived, although they often

separate spheres A rigid gender division of labor with the wife as mother and homemaker and the husband as wage earner.

Workers at a Large Cotton Mill

This 1833 engraving shows adult women operating power looms under the supervision of a male foreman, and it accurately reflects both the decline of family employment and the emergence of a gender-based division of labor in many English factories. The jungle of belts and shafts connecting the noisy looms to the giant steam engine on the ground floor created a constant din. (Time Life Pictures/Getty Images)

earned small amounts doing putting-out handicrafts at home and taking in boarders. Second, when married women did work for wages outside the house, they usually came from the poorest families, where the husbands were poorly paid, sick, unemployed, or missing. Third, these poor married (or widowed) women were joined by legions of young unmarried women, who worked full-time but only in certain jobs. Fourth, all women were generally confined to low-paying, dead-end jobs. Virtually no occupation open to women paid a wage sufficient for a person to live independently. Men predominated in the better-paying, more promising employments. Evolving gradually, but largely in place by 1850, the new sexual division of labor in Britain constituted a major development in the history of women and of the family.

If the reorganization of paid work along gender lines is widely recognized, there is no agreement on its causes. One school of scholars sees little connection with industrialization and finds the answer in the deeply ingrained sexist attitudes of a "patriarchal tradition," which predated the economic transformation. These scholars stress the role of male-dominated craft unions in denying working women access to good jobs and relegating them to unpaid housework. Other scholars, stressing that the gender roles of women and men can vary enormously with time and culture, look more to a combination of economic and biological factors in order to explain the emergence of a sex-segregated division of labor.

Three ideas stand out in this more recent interpretation. First, relentless factory discipline conflicted with child care in a way that labor on the farm or in the cottage had not. A woman operating earsplitting spinning machinery could mind a child of seven or eight working beside her (until such work was outlawed), but she could no longer pace herself through pregnancy or breast-feed her baby on the job. One mother of four, in describing her past experience of working in the mines, provided a real insight into why many women accepted the emerging gender division of labor:

> While working in the pit I was worth to my [miner] husband seven shillings a week, out of which we had to pay 2½ shillings to a woman for looking after the younger children. I used to take them to her house at 4 o'clock in the morning, out of their own beds, to put them into hers. Then there was one shilling a week for washing; besides, there was mending to pay for, and other things. The house was not guided. The other children broke things; they did not go to school when they were sent; they would be playing about, and get ill-used by other children, and their clothes torn. Then when I came home in the evening, everything was to do after the day's labor, and I was so tired I had no heart for it; no fire lit, nothing cooked, no water fetched, the house dirty, and nothing comfortable for my husband. It is all far better now, and I wouldn't go down again.[8]

Second, running a household in conditions of primitive urban poverty was an extremely demanding job in its own right. There were no supermarkets or public transportation. Everything had to be done on foot, with children in tow. Yet another brutal job outside the house—a "second shift"—had limited appeal for the average married woman. Thus women might well have accepted the emerging division of labor as the best available strategy for family survival in the industrializing society.[9]

Third, why were the women who did work for wages outside the home confined to certain "women's jobs"? No doubt the desire of males to monopolize the best opportunities and hold women down provides part of the answer. Yet as some feminist scholars have argued, sex-segregated employment was also a collective response to the new industrial system, where young people mingled without parental supervision. Continuing to mix after work, they were "more likely to form liaisons, initiate courtships, and respond to advances."[10] Such intimacy also led to more unplanned pregnancies and fueled the illegitimacy explosion that had begun in the late eighteenth century and that gathered force until at least 1850 (see pages 514–515). Thus segregation of jobs by gender was partly an effort by older people to help control the sexuality of working-class youths. The **Mines Act of 1842,** for example, prohibited underground work for all women as well as for boys under ten.

Mines Act of 1842 This act prohibited underground work for all women as well as for boys under ten.

The Early Labor Movement in Britain

Many kinds of employment changed slowly during and after the Industrial Revolution in Great Britain. In 1850 more British people still worked on farms than in any other occupation. The second-largest occupation was domestic service, with more than one million household servants, 90 percent of whom were women. Thus many old, familiar jobs outside industry lived on and provided alternatives for individual workers. This helped ease the transition to industrial civilization.

Within industry itself, the pattern of artisans working with hand tools in small shops remained unchanged in many trades, even as some others were revolutionized by technological change. For example, as in the case of cotton and coal, the British iron industry was completely dominated by large-scale capitalist firms by 1850. Many large ironworks had more than one thousand people on their payrolls. Yet the firms that fashioned iron into small metal goods, such as tools, tableware, and toys, employed on average fewer than ten wage workers, who used time-honored handicraft skills. Only gradually after 1850 did some owners find ways to reorganize some handicraft industries with new machines and new patterns of work. The survival of small workshops gave many workers an alternative to factory employment.

Combination Acts Passed in 1799, these acts outlawed unions and strikes. They were repealed by Parliament in 1824.

Working-class solidarity and class-consciousness developed in small workshops as well as in large factories. In the northern factory districts, where thousands of "hired hands" looked across at a tiny minority of managers and owners, anticapitalist sentiments were frequent by the 1820s. Commenting in 1825 on a strike in the woolen center of Bradford and the support it had gathered from other regions, one paper claimed with pride that "it is all the workers of England against a few masters of Bradford."[11] Modern technology had created a few versus a many.

As in France during the French Revolution, the British government attacked monopolies, guilds, and workers combinations in the name of economic freedom, adding to the ill will between classes. In 1799 Parliament passed the **Combination Acts,** which outlawed unions and strikes. In 1813 and 1814, Parliament repealed an old law regulating the wages of artisans and the conditions of apprenticeship. As a result of

THE WORKSHOP

Celebrating Skilled Labor

This handsome engraving embellished the membership certificate of the British carpenters union, one of the leading "new model unions" that represented skilled workers effectively after 1850. The upper panel shows carpenters building the scaffolding for a great arch; the lower panel captures the spirit of a busy workshop. (E & E Image Library/Art Resource, NY)

these and other measures, certain skilled artisan workers, such as bootmakers and high-quality tailors, found aggressive capitalists ignoring traditional work rules and flooding their trades with unorganized women workers and children to beat down wages.

The liberal capitalist attack on artisan guilds and work rules was bitterly resented by many craftworkers, who subsequently played an important part in gradually building a modern labor movement to improve working conditions and to serve worker needs. The Combination Acts were widely disregarded by workers. Printers, papermakers, carpenters, tailors, and other such craftsmen continued to take collective action, and societies of skilled factory workers also organized unions. They were not afraid to strike; there was, for example, a general strike of adult cotton spinners in Manchester in 1810. In the face of widespread union activity, Parliament repealed the Combination Acts in 1824, and unions were tolerated, though not fully accepted, after 1825.

The next stage in the development of the British trade-union movement was the attempt to create a single large national union. This effort was led not so much by working people as by social reformers such as Robert Owen, a self-made cotton manufacturer. In 1834 Owen organized one of the largest and most visionary of the early national unions, the **Grand National Consolidated Trades Union.** When this and other grandiose schemes collapsed, the British labor movement moved once again after 1851 in the direction of craft unions. The most famous of these "new model unions" was the Amalgamated Society of Engineers, which represented skilled machinists. These unions won real benefits for members and became an accepted part of the industrial scene.

British workers also engaged in direct political activity in defense of their own interests. After the collapse of Owen's national trade union, many working people went into the Chartist movement, which sought political democracy. The key Chartist demand—that all men be given the right to vote—became the great hope of millions. Workers were also active in campaigns to limit the workday in factories to ten hours and to permit duty-free importation of wheat into Great Britain to secure cheap bread. Thus working people developed a sense of their own identity and played an active role in shaping the new industrial system. They were neither helpless victims nor passive beneficiaries.

Grand National Consolidated Trades Union Organized by Robert Owen in 1834, this was one of the largest and most visionary early national unions.

Section Review

- Early industrialists worked hard to establish their factories, but the next generation inherited already prosperous businesses so they had a new class-consciousness, prizing their wealth and role in society.

- Conditions for factory workers improved over time but were harsh, with long hours and low wages; although clothing and diets improved, housing conditions did not.

- Critics of the harsh new conditions included William Blake and Friedrich Engels, while apologists such as Andrew Ure depicted conditions in optimistic terms.

- Factories often employed whole families until the Factory Act of 1833 limited the number of hours children and adolescents could work and required children under age nine to attend school.

- The division of labor between men and women emerged, with men the primary wage earners while married women were confined to the home and unmarried women to low-paying jobs.

- Farmers, domestic service, and small artisans coexisted with industry and formed the working class, organizing unions and taking collective action against capitalists to improve working conditions, wages, and democratic political rights, such as in the Chartist movement.

Chapter Review

What were the origins of the Industrial Revolution in Britain, and how did it develop between 1780 and 1850? (page 566)

Western society's industrial breakthrough grew out of a long process of economic and social change in which the rise of capitalism, overseas expansion, and the growth of rural industry stood out as critical preparatory developments. Eventually taking the lead in all of these developments, and also profiting from stable government, abundant natural resources, and a flexible labor force, Britain experienced between the 1780s and the 1850s an epoch-making transformation, one that is still aptly termed the Industrial Revolution.

Key Terms
Industrial Revolution (p. 567)
spinning jenny (p. 567)
water frame (p. 567)
steam engines (p. 569)

(continued)

How after 1815 did continental countries respond to the challenge of industrialization? (page 573)

Building on technical breakthroughs, power-driven equipment, and large-scale enterprise, the Industrial Revolution in England greatly increased output in certain radically altered industries, stimulated the large handicraft and commercial sectors, and speeded up overall economic growth. By 1850 the level of British per capita industrial production was surpassing continental levels by a growing margin, and Britain savored a near monopoly in world markets for mass-produced goods.

Continental countries inevitably took rather different paths to the urban industrial society. They relied more on handicraft production in both towns and villages. Only in the 1840s did railroad construction begin to create the strong demand for iron, coal, and railway equipment that speeded up the process of industrialization in the 1850s and 1860s.

How did the Industrial Revolution affect social classes, the standard of living, and patterns of work? What measures were taken to improve the conditions of workers? (page 576)

The rise of modern industry had a profound impact on people and their lives. In the early stages, Britain again led the way, experiencing in a striking manner the long-term social changes accompanying the economic transformation. Factory discipline and Britain's stern capitalist economy weighed heavily on working people, who, however, actively fashioned their destinies and refused to be passive victims. Improvements in the standard of living came slowly, but they were substantial by 1850. The era of industrialization fostered new attitudes toward child labor, encouraged protective factory legislation, and called forth a new sense of class feeling and an assertive labor movement. It also promoted a more rigid division of roles and responsibilities within the family that was detrimental to women, another gradual but profound change of revolutionary proportions.

Notes

1. P. Bairoch, "International Industrialization Levels from 1750 to 1980," *Journal of European Economic History* 11 (Spring 1982): 269–333.
2. M. Lévy-Leboyer, *Les banques européennes et l'industrialisation dans la première moitié du XIXe siècle* (Paris: Presses Universitaires de France, 1964), p. 29.
3. J. Michelet, *The People*, trans. with an introduction by J. P. McKay (Urbana: University of Illinois Press, 1973; original publication, 1846), p. 64.
4. Quoted in W. A. Hayek, ed., *Capitalism and the Historians* (Chicago: University of Chicago Press, 1954), p. 126.
5. N. Crafts, *British Economic Growth During the Industrial Revolution* (Oxford University Press, 1985), p. 95.
6. H-J. Voth, *Time and Work in England, 1750–1830* (Oxford: Oxford University Press, 2000), pp. 268–270; also pp. 118–133.
7. Quoted in E. R. Pike, *"Hard Times": Human Documents of the Industrial Revolution* (New York: Praeger, 1966), p. 109.
8. Ibid., *"Hard Times,"* p. 208.
9. See especially J. Brenner and M. Rama, "Rethinking Women's Oppression," *New Left Review* 144 (March–April 1984): 33–71, and sources cited there.
10. J. Humphries, ". . . 'The Most Free from Objection' . . . : The Sexual Division of Labor and Women's Work in Nineteenth-Century England," *Journal of Economic History* 47 (December 1987): 948.
11. Quoted in D. Geary, ed., *Labour and Socialist Movements in Europe Before 1914* (Oxford: Berg, 1989), p. 29.

To assess your mastery of this chapter, go to **bedfordstmartins.com/mckaywestbrief**

Listening to the Past

Testimony Concerning Young Mine Workers

The use of child labor in British industrialization quickly attracted the attention of humanitarians and social reformers. This interest led to investigations by parliamentary commissions, which resulted in laws limiting the hours and the ages of children working in large factories. Designed to build a case for remedial legislation, parliamentary inquiries gave large numbers of workers a rare chance to speak directly to contemporaries and to historians.

The moving passages that follow are taken from testimony gathered in 1841 and 1842 by the Ashley Mines Commission. Interviewing employers and many male and female workers, the commissioners focused on the physical condition of the youth and on the sexual behavior of workers far underground. The subsequent Mines Act of 1842 sought to reduce immoral behavior and sexual bullying by prohibiting underground work for all women (and for boys younger than ten).

Mr. Payne, coal master:

That children are employed generally at nine years old in the coal pits and sometimes at eight. In fact, the smaller the vein of coal is in height, the younger and smaller are the children required; the work occupies from six to seven hours per day in the pits; they are not ill-used or worked beyond their strength; a good deal of depravity exists but they are certainly not worse in morals than in other branches of the Sheffield trade, but upon the whole superior; the morals of this district are materially improving; Mr. Bruce, the clergyman, has been zealous and active in endeavoring to ameliorate their moral and religious education. . . .

Patience Kershaw, hurrier, aged 17:

My father has been dead about a year; my mother is living and has ten children, five lads and five lasses; the oldest is about thirty, the youngest is four; three lasses go to mill; all the lads are colliers, two getters and three hurriers [workers who move coal wagons underground]; one lives at home and does nothing; mother does nought but look after home.

All my sisters have been hurriers, but three went to the mill. Alice went because her legs swelled from hurrying in cold water when she was hot. I never went to day-school; I go to Sunday-school, but I cannot read or write; I go to pit at five o'clock in the morning and come out at five in the evening; I get my breakfast of porridge and milk first; I take my dinner with me, a cake, and eat it as I go; I do not stop or rest any time for the purpose; I get nothing else until I get home, and then have potatoes and meat, not every day meat. I hurry in the clothes I have now got on, trousers and ragged jacket; the bald place upon my head is made by thrusting the

This illustration of a girl dragging a coal wagon was one of several that shocked public opinion and contributed to the Mines Act of 1842. (The British Library)

corves [coal wagons]; my legs have never swelled, but sisters' did when they went to mill; I hurry the corves a mile and more under ground and back; they weigh 300; I hurry 11 a day; I wear a belt and chain at the workings to get the corves out; the putters [miners] that I work for are *naked* except their caps; they pull off all their clothes; I see them at work when I go up; sometimes they beat me, if I am not quick enough, with their hands; they strike me upon my back; the boys take liberties with me, sometimes, they pull me about; I am the only girl in the pit; there are about 20 boys and 15 men; all the men are naked; I would rather work in mill than in coal-pit.

Questions for Analysis

1. To what extent is the testimony of Patience Kershaw in harmony with that of Payne?

2. Describe Kershaw's work. What do you think of her work? Why?

3. The witnesses were responding to questions from middle-class commissioners. What did the commissioners seem interested in? Why?

Source: From *Voices of the Industrial Revolution*, edited by J. Bowditch and C. Ramsland. Copyright © 1961. Reprinted by permission of University of Michigan Press.

CHAPTER 23

Ideologies and Upheavals

1815–1850

Revolutionaries in Transylvania. Ana Ipatescu, of the first group of revolutionaries in Transylvania against Russia, 1848. (National Historical Museum, Bucharest/The Art Archive)

Chapter Preview

The Peace Settlement
How did the victorious allies fashion a general peace settlement, and how did Metternich uphold a conservative European order?

Radical Ideas and Early Socialism
What were the basic tenets of liberalism, nationalism, and socialism, and what groups were most attracted to these ideologies?

The Romantic Movement
What were the characteristics of the romantic movement, and who were some of the great romantic artists?

Reforms and Revolutions
How after 1815 did liberal, national, and socialist forces challenge conservatism in Greece, Great Britain, and France?

The Revolutions of 1848
Why in 1848 did revolution triumph briefly throughout most of Europe, and why did it fail almost completely?

INDIVIDUALS IN SOCIETY: Jules Michelet

LISTENING TO THE PAST: Speaking for the Czech Nation

The momentous economic and political transformation of modern times began in the late eighteenth century with the Industrial Revolution in England and then the French Revolution. Until about 1815, these economic and political revolutions were separate, involving different countries and activities and proceeding at very different paces. After peace returned in 1815, the situation changed. Economic and political changes tended to fuse, reinforcing each other and bringing about what historian Eric Hobsbawm has incisively called the **dual revolution.** For instance, the growth of the industrial middle class encouraged the drive for representative government, and the demands of the French sans-culottes in 1793 and 1794 inspired many socialist thinkers. Gathering strength, the dual revolution rushed on to alter completely first Europe and then the rest of the world. Much of world history in the past two centuries can be seen as the progressive unfolding of the dual revolution.

The dual revolution posed a tremendous intellectual challenge. The meanings of the economic, political, and social changes that were occurring, as well as the ways they would be shaped by human action, were anything but clear. These changes fascinated observers and stimulated the growth of new ideas and powerful ideologies. The most important of these ideological forces were revitalized conservatism and three ideologies of change—liberalism, nationalism, and socialism. All played critical roles in the political and social battles of the era and the great popular upheaval that eventually swept across Europe in the revolutions of 1848.

The Peace Settlement

How did the victorious allies fashion a general peace settlement, and how did Metternich uphold a conservative European order?

The eventual triumph of revolutionary economic and political forces was by no means certain as the Napoleonic era ended. Quite the contrary. The conservative, aristocratic monarchies of Russia, Prussia, Austria, and Great Britain—the Quadruple Alliance—had finally defeated France and reaffirmed their determination to hold France in line. But many other international questions were outstanding, and the allies agreed to meet at the **Congress of Vienna** to fashion a general peace settlement.

Most people felt a profound longing for peace. The great challenge for political leaders in 1814 was to construct a settlement that would last and not sow the seeds of another war. Their efforts were largely successful and contributed to a century unmarred by destructive, generalized war (see Map 23.1).

The European Balance of Power

The allied powers were concerned first and foremost with the defeated enemy, France. Agreeing to the restoration of the Bourbon dynasty (see page 560), the allies were quite lenient toward France after Napoleon's abdication. The first Peace of Paris gave to France the boundaries it possessed in 1792, which were larger than those of 1789, and France did not have to pay any war reparations. Thus the victorious powers did not foment a spirit of injustice and revenge in the defeated country.

When the four allies of the Quadruple Alliance (plus a representative of the restored monarchy in France) met together at the Congress of Vienna, they also agreed to raise a number of formidable barriers against renewed French aggression. Above all, Prussia received considerably more territory on France's eastern border so as to stand as the "sentinel on the Rhine" against France. In these ways, the Quadruple Alliance combined leniency toward France with strong defensive measures.

In their moderation toward France, the allies were motivated by self-interest and traditional ideas about the balance of power. To Klemens von Metternich (**MET-uhr-nik**) and Robert Castlereagh (**KAS-uhl-rey**), the foreign ministers of Austria and Great Britain, respectively, as well as their French counterpart, Charles Talleyrand, the balance of power meant an international equilibrium that would discourage aggression by any combination of states or, worse, the domination of Europe by any single state.

The Great Powers—Austria, Britain, Prussia, Russia, and France—used the balance of power to settle their own dangerous disputes at the Congress of Vienna. There was general agreement among the victors that each of them should receive compensation in the form of territory for their successful struggle against the French. Great Britain had already won colonies and strategic outposts during the long wars. Metternich's Austria gave up territories in Belgium and

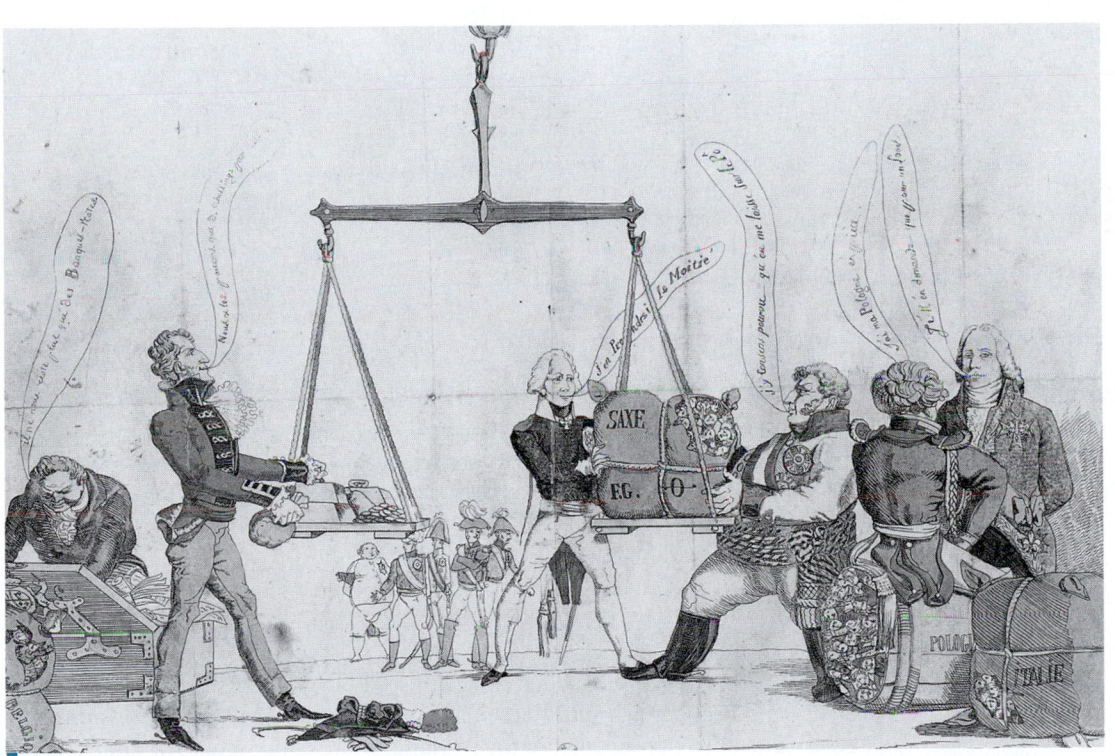

Adjusting the Balance
The Englishman on the left uses his money to counterbalance the people that the Prussian and the fat Metternich are gaining in Saxony and Italy. Alexander I sits happily on his prize, Poland. This cartoon captures the essence of how most people thought about balance-of-power diplomacy at the Congress of Vienna. (Bibliothèque nationale de France)

Map legend:
- Kingdom of Prussia
- Austrian Empire
- Boundary of German Confederation

MAPPING THE PAST

MAP 23.1 Europe in 1815

Europe's leaders re-established a balance of political power after the defeat of Napoleon. Prussia gained territory on the Rhine and in Saxony, consolidating its position as a Great Power. Austria gained the Italian provinces of Lombardy and Venetia as well as Galicia and land along the Adriatic Sea. In 1815 Europe contained many different states, but international politics was dominated by the five Great Powers (or six, if one includes the Ottoman Empire). Trace the political boundaries of each Great Power, and compare their geographical strengths and weaknesses. **[1]** In which directions might the different Great Powers seek to expand further and gain more people and territory? **[2]** At what points might these states then come into conflict with one another?

southern Germany but expanded greatly elsewhere, taking the rich provinces of Venetia and Lombardy in northern Italy as well as former Polish possessions and new lands on the eastern coast of the Adriatic. More contentious was the push for greater territory by Russia and Prussia. When France, Austria, and Great Britain allied against these central European powers, Russia accepted a small Polish kingdom, and Prussia took only part of Saxony (see Map 23.1). This compromise was very much within the framework of balance-of-power ideology.

Following Napoleon's escape from Elba and his final defeat at Waterloo, a second Peace of Paris was convened. Again the Quadruple Alliance was relatively moderate toward France, and the previously agreed-upon balance of power was left intact. The members of the Quadruple Alliance and France also agreed to meet periodically to discuss their common interests and to consider appropriate measures for the maintenance of peace in Europe. This agreement marked the beginning of the European "congress system," which lasted long into the nineteenth century and settled many international crises through international conferences and balance-of-power diplomacy.

Intervention and Repression

There was also a domestic political side to the re-establishment of peace. Within their own countries, the leaders of the victorious states were much less flexible. In 1815 under Metternich's leadership, Austria, Prussia, and Russia were determined to uphold a conservative European order. Thus they embarked on a crusade against the ideas and politics of the dual revolution. This crusade lasted until 1848. The first step was the **Holy Alliance,** formed by Austria, Prussia, and Russia in September 1815. First proposed by Russia's Alexander I, the alliance soon became a symbol of the repression of liberal and revolutionary movements all over Europe.

In 1820 revolutionaries succeeded in forcing the monarchs of Spain and the southern Italian kingdom of the Two Sicilies to grant liberal constitutions. Metternich was horrified: revolution was rising once again. Calling a conference at Troppau in Austria under the provisions of the Quadruple Alliance, he and Alexander I proclaimed the principle of active intervention to maintain all autocratic regimes whenever they were threatened. Austrian forces then marched into Naples in 1821 and restored Ferdinand I to the throne of the Two Sicilies, while French armies likewise restored the Spanish regime.

In the following years, Metternich continued to battle against liberal political change. Sometimes he could do little, as in the case of the new Latin American republics that broke away from Spain. Nor could he undo the dynastic changes of 1830 and 1831 in France and Belgium. Nonetheless, until 1848 Metternich's system proved quite effective in central Europe, where his power was the greatest.

Metternich's policies dominated not only Austria and the Italian peninsula but also the entire German Confederation, which the peace settlement of Vienna had called into being. The confederation was composed of thirty-eight independent German states, including Prussia and Austria (see Map 23.1). These states met in complicated assemblies dominated by Austria, with Prussia a willing junior partner in the execution of repressive measures.

Through this German Confederation, Metternich had the infamous **Carlsbad Decrees** issued in 1819. These decrees required the thirty-eight German member states to root out subversive ideas in their universities and newspapers. The decrees also established a permanent committee with spies and informers to investigate and punish any liberal or radical organizations.

In his efforts to hold back liberalism, Metternich was supported by the Russian Empire and, to a lesser extent, by the Ottoman Empire. Bitter enemies and often at war with each other, these far-flung empires also shared several basic characteristics. Both the Russian and Ottoman empires were absolutist states with powerful armies and long traditions of expansion and conquest. Both were multinational empires made up of many peoples, languages, and religions, but in each case most of the ruling elite came from the dominant ethnic group—the Orthodox Christian

Holy Alliance An alliance formed by Austria, Russia, and Prussia in September of 1815 that became a symbol of the repression of liberal and revolutionary movements all over Europe.

Carlsbad Decrees Issued in 1819, these decrees required the thirty-eight German member states to root out subversive ideas in their universities and newspapers.

Russians centered in central and northern Russia, and the Muslim Ottoman Turks of Anatolia (much of modern Turkey). After 1815, both multinational, absolutist states worked to preserve their respective traditional, conservative orders. Only in the middle of the nineteenth century did each in turn experience a profound crisis and embark on a program of fundamental reform and modernization, as we shall see in Chapter 25.

Radical Ideas and Early Socialism

What were the basic tenets of liberalism, nationalism, and socialism, and what groups were most attracted to these ideologies?

In the years following the peace settlement of 1815 intellectuals and social observers sought to understand the revolutionary changes that had occurred and were still taking place. These efforts led to ideas that still motivate people throughout the world.

Almost all of these basic ideas were radical. In one way or another, they rejected conservatism, with its stress on tradition, a hereditary monarchy, a strong and privileged landowning aristocracy, and an official church. Instead, they developed and refined alternative visions—alternative ideologies—and tried to convince society to act on them. With time, they were very successful.

liberalism The principal ideas of this movement were equality and liberty; liberals demanded representative government and equality before the law as well as individual freedoms such as freedom of the press, freedom of speech, freedom of assembly, and freedom from arbitrary arrest.

Liberalism

The principal ideas of **liberalism**—liberty and equality—were by no means defeated in 1815. First realized successfully in the American Revolution and then achieved in part in the French Revolution, this political and social philosophy continued to pose a radical challenge to revived conservatism. Liberalism demanded representative government as opposed to autocratic monarchy, equality before the law as opposed to legally separate classes. The idea of liberty also meant specific individual freedoms: freedom of the press, freedom of speech, freedom of assembly, and freedom from arbitrary arrest. In Europe only France with Louis XVIII's Constitutional Charter and Great Britain with its Parliament and historic rights of English men and women had realized much of the liberal program in 1815. Even in those countries, liberalism had not fully succeeded.

laissez faire A doctrine of economic liberalism that believes in unrestricted private enterprise and no government interference in the economy.

Liberalism was also aligned with the doctrine of **laissez faire** (**lay-say FAIR**), which called for unrestricted private enterprise and no government interference in the economy. (This form of liberalism is often called "classical liberalism" in the United States in order to distinguish it sharply from modern American liberalism, which usually favors more government programs to meet social needs and to regulate the economy.)

As we have seen (Chapter 19), Adam Smith posited the idea of a free economy in opposition to mercantilism, in which the government placed major restrictions on trade. Smith argued that freely competitive private enterprise would give all citizens a fair and equal opportunity to do what they did best and would result in greater income for everyone, not just the rich.

In early-nineteenth-century Britain, economic liberalism was embraced most enthusiastically by business groups and thus became a doctrine associated with business interests. Businessmen used the doctrine to defend their right to do as they wished in their factories. Labor unions were outlawed because they supposedly restricted free competition and the individual's "right to work."

Liberal political ideals in the early nineteenth century also became more closely associated with narrow class interests. Liberals favored representative government, but they generally wanted property qualifications attached to the right to vote. In practice, this meant limiting the vote to well-to-do aristocratic landowners, substantial businessmen, and successful members of the professions. Workers and peasants, as well as the lower middle class of shopkeepers, clerks, and artisans, did not own the necessary property and thus could not vote.

As liberalism became increasingly identified with the middle class after 1815, some intellectuals and foes of conservatism felt that liberalism did not go nearly far enough. Inspired by memories of the French Revolution and the example of the young American republic, they called for universal voting rights, at least for males, and for democracy. These democratic republicans were more radical than the liberals, and they were more willing than most liberals to endorse violent upheaval to achieve goals. All of this meant that liberals and radical, democratic republicans could join forces against conservatives only up to a point.

> **nationalism** The idea that each people had its own genius and its own *cultural* unity, which was self-evident, manifesting itself especially in a common language, history, and territory.

Nationalism

With immediate origins in the French Revolution and the Napoleonic wars, **nationalism** was based on the idea that each people had its own genius and its own *cultural* unity. For nationalists this cultural unity was basically self-evident, manifesting itself especially in a common language, history, and territory. In fact, in the early nineteenth century such cultural unity was more a dream than a reality. Within each ethnic grouping only an elite spoke a standardized written language. Local dialects abounded, and peasants from nearby villages often failed to understand each other. As for historical memory, it divided the inhabitants of the different German or Italian states as much as it unified them. Moreover, a variety of ethnic groups shared the territory of most states.

Despite these basic realities, sooner or later European nationalists usually sought to turn the cultural unity that they perceived into a *political* reality. They sought to make the territory of each people coincide with well-defined boundaries in an independent nation-state. This political goal was what made nationalism so explosive in central and eastern Europe after 1815, when there were either too few states (Austria, Russia, and the Ottoman Empire) or too many (the Italian peninsula and the German Confederation) and when different peoples overlapped and intermingled.

Of fundamental importance in the rise of nationalism was the push to use a standardized national language in order to facilitate communication in an increasingly complex industrial and urban society. As the entire population was educated in the national language, at least a superficial cultural unity took root. Citizens might also be brought together with emotionally charged symbols and ceremonies, such as independence holidays and patriotic parades. On such fleeting occasions the imagined nation of spiritual equals might celebrate its most hallowed traditions, which were often recent

Building German Nationalism

As popular upheaval in France spread to central Europe in March 1848, Germans from the solid middle classes came together in Frankfurt to draft a constitution for a new united Germany. This woodcut commemorates the solemn procession of delegates entering Saint Paul's Cathedral in Frankfurt, where the delegates would have their deliberations. Festivals, celebrations, and parades helped create a feeling of belonging to a large unseen community, a nation binding millions of strangers together. (akg-images)

inventions.[1] Liberals and nationalists agreed that the benefits of self-government would be possible only if the people were united by common traditions that transcended local interests and even class differences.

Early nationalists usually believed that every nation, like every citizen, had the right to exist in freedom and to develop its character and spirit. They were confident that a symphony of nations would promote the harmony and ultimate unity of all peoples. The great Italian patriot Guiseppe Mazzini (1805–1872) believed that "in laboring according to the true principles of our country we are laboring for Humanity." Thus the liberty of the individual and the love of a free nation overlapped greatly in the early nineteenth century.

Yet early nationalists also stressed the differences among peoples and they developed a strong sense of "we" and "they." To this "we-they" outlook, it was all too easy for nationalists to add two highly volatile ingredients: a sense of national mission and a sense of national superiority. Even the French historian Jules Michelet (**zhul meesh-uh-LEY**), so alive to the national aspirations of other peoples, could not help speaking in 1846 of the "superiority of France"; the principles espoused in the French Revolution had made France the "salvation of mankind." (See the feature "Individuals in Society: Jules Michelet" on page 608.)

Russian and German nationalists had a very different opinion of France. In the narratives they constructed, the French often seemed oppressive, as the Russians did to the Poles and as the Germans did to the Czechs. (See the feature "Listening to the Past: Speaking for the Czech Nation" on pages 615–616.) Thus "they" often emerged as the enemy.

socialism A backlash against the emergence of individualism and the fragmentation of society, and a move toward cooperation and a sense of community; the key ideas were economic planning, greater economic equality, and state regulation of property.

French Utopian Socialism

Socialism, the new radical doctrine after 1815, began in France, despite the fact that France lagged far behind Great Britain in developing modern industry. Early French socialist thinkers were acutely aware that the political revolution in France, the rise of laissez faire, and the emergence of modern industry in Britain were transforming society. They were disturbed because they saw these developments as fomenting selfish individualism and splitting the community into isolated fragments. There was, they believed, an urgent need for a further reorganization of society to establish cooperation and a new sense of community.

Early French socialists believed in economic planning. Inspired by the emergency measures of 1793 and 1794 in France, they argued that the government should rationally organize the economy and not depend on destructive competition to do the job. Early socialists also shared an intense desire to help the poor, and they preached that the rich and the poor should be more nearly equal economically. Finally, socialists believed that private property should be strictly regulated by the government or that it should be abolished and replaced by state or community ownership. Planning, greater economic equality, and state regulation of property—these were the key ideas of early French socialism and of all socialism since.

One of the most influential early socialist thinkers was a nobleman, Count Henri de Saint-Simon (**on-REE duh san-see-MAWN**) (1760–1825). Saint-Simon optimistically proclaimed the tremendous possibilities of industrial development: "The age of gold is before us!" The key to progress was a social organization that required the parasites—the court, the aristocracy, lawyers, and churchmen—to surrender power to the doers—the leading scientists, engineers, and industrialists. The doers would guide the economy forward by undertaking vast public works projects and establishing investment banks. Saint-Simon also stressed that every social institution ought to have as its main goal improved conditions for the poor.

The journalist Louis Blanc (1811–1882) urged workers to agitate for universal voting rights and to take control of the state peacefully. Blanc believed that the state should set up government-backed workshops and factories to guarantee full employment. The right to work had to become as sacred as any other right.

Of great importance, the message of French utopian socialists interacted with the experiences of French urban workers. Workers cherished the memory of the radical phase of the French Revolution, and they became violently opposed to laissez-faire laws that denied workers the right to organize. Developing a sense of class in the process, workers favored collective action and government intervention in economic life. Thus the aspirations of workers and utopian theorists reinforced each other, and a genuine socialist movement emerged in Paris in the 1830s and 1840s. To Karl Marx was left the task of establishing firm foundations for modern socialism.

The Birth of Marxian Socialism

In 1848 Karl Marx (1818–1883) and Friedrich Engels (1820–1895) published *The Communist Manifesto*, which became the bible of socialism. The son of a Jewish lawyer who had converted to Christianity, the atheistic young Marx had studied philosophy at the University of Berlin before turning to journalism and economics. By the time Marx was twenty-five, he was developing his own socialist ideas.

Early French socialists often appealed to the middle class and the state to help the poor. Marx ridiculed such appeals as naive. He argued that the interests of the middle class and those of the industrial working class were inevitably opposed to each other. Indeed, according to the *Manifesto*, the "history of all previously existing society is the history of class struggles." In Marx's view, one class had always exploited the other, and with the advent of modern industry, society was split more clearly than ever before: between the middle class—the **bourgeoisie** (**boor-zwah-ZEE**) and the modern working class—the **proletariat** (**proh-li-TAIR-ee-uht**).

bourgeoisie The middle class.

proletariat The modern working class.

Just as the bourgeoisie had triumphed over the feudal aristocracy, Marx predicted that the proletariat would conquer the bourgeoisie in a violent revolution. While a tiny minority owned the means of production and grew richer, the ever-poorer proletariat was constantly growing in size and in class-consciousness. In this process, the proletariat was aided, according to Marx, by a portion of the bourgeoisie who had gone over to the proletariat and who (like Marx and Engels) "had raised themselves to the level of comprehending theoretically the historical moment." The critical moment, Marx thought, was very near. "Let the ruling classes tremble at a Communist revolution. The proletarians have nothing to lose but their chains. They have a world to win.

Karl Marx

Active in the revolution of 1848, Marx fled from Germany in 1849 and settled in London. There he wrote *Capital,* the weighty exposition of his socialist theories, and worked to organize the working class. Marx earned a modest living as a journalist, supplemented by financial support from his coauthor, Friedrich Engels. (The Granger Collection, New York)

WORKING MEN OF ALL COUNTRIES, UNITE!" So ends *The Communist Manifesto.*

Marx's debt to England was great. He was the last of the classical economists. Following David Ricardo, who had taught that labor was the source of all value, Marx went on to argue that profits were really wages stolen from the workers. Moreover, Marx incorporated Engels's charges of terrible oppression of the new class of factory workers in England; thus Marx's doctrines seemed to be based on hard facts.

Marx's theory of historical evolution was built on the philosophy of the German Georg Hegel (HEY-guhl) (1770–1831). Hegel believed that each age is characterized by a dominant set of ideas; this produces opposing ideas and eventually a new synthesis. Marx retained Hegel's view of history as a dialectic process of change but made economic relationships between classes the driving force. Marx's next idea, that it was now the bourgeoisie's turn to give way to the socialism of revolutionary workers, appeared to many the irrefutable capstone of a brilliant interpretation of humanity's long development. Thus Marx synthesized a number of early-nineteenth-century ideas to create a powerful ideology that would have a major impact on world history.

The Romantic Movement

What were the characteristics of the romantic movement, and who were some of the great romantic artists?

The early nineteenth century was a time of change in literature and other arts as well as in politics. The romantic movement was in part a revolt against the emphasis on rationality, order, and restraint that characterized the Enlightenment and the controlled style of classicism.

Forerunners of the romantic movement appeared from about 1750 on. Of these, Rousseau (see page 472)—the passionate advocate of feeling, freedom, and natural goodness—was the most influential. Romanticism then crystallized fully in the 1790s, primarily in England and Germany. The French Revolution kindled the belief that radical reconstruction was also possible in cultural and artistic life (even though many early English and German romantics became disillusioned with events in France and turned from liberalism to conservatism in politics). Romanticism gained strength until the 1840s.

romanticism A movement that a revolt against classicism and the Enlightenment, characterized by a belief in emotional exuberance, unrestrained imagination, and spontaneity in both art and personal life.

Sturm und Drang The name adopted by German early Romantics of the 1770s and 1780s who lived lives of tremendous emotional intensity; it means "Storm and Stress."

Romanticism's Tenets

Romanticism was characterized by a belief in emotional exuberance, unrestrained imagination, and spontaneity in both art and personal life. In Germany early romantics of the 1770s and 1780s called themselves the **Sturm und Drang** ("Storm and Stress"), and many romantic artists of the early nineteenth century lived lives of tremendous emotional intensity. Suicide, duels to the death, madness, and strange illnesses were not uncommon among leading romantics. Romantic artists typically led bohemian lives, wearing their hair long and uncombed in preference to powdered wigs and rejecting the materialism of refined society. Great individualists, the romantics believed the full development of one's unique human potential to be the supreme purpose in life.

Nowhere was the break with classicism more apparent than in romanticism's general conception of nature. Classicism in art was not particularly interested in nature. In the words of the eighteenth-century English author Samuel Johnson, "A blade of grass is always a blade of grass; men and women are my subjects of inquiry." The romantics, in contrast, were enchanted by nature. For some it was awesome and tempestuous, while others saw nature as a source of spiritual inspiration. As the great English landscape artist John Constable declared, "Nature is Spirit visible."

Most romantics saw the growth of modern industry as an ugly, brutal attack on their beloved nature and on the human personality. They sought escape—in the unspoiled Lake District of northern England, in exotic North Africa, in an idealized Middle Ages.

Diverse, exciting, and important, the study of history became a romantic passion. History was the key to a universe that was now perceived to be organic and dynamic, not mechanical and static as the Enlightenment thinkers had believed. Historical studies also promoted the growth of national aspirations, encouraging entire peoples to seek in the past their special destinies.

Literature

Romanticism found its distinctive voice in poetry, as the Enlightenment had in prose. Its first great poets were British: Wordsworth and Coleridge were all active by 1800, to be followed shortly by Byron, Shelley, and Keats.

A towering leader of English romanticism, William Wordsworth (1770–1850) was deeply influenced by Rousseau and the spirit of the early French Revolution. Wordsworth settled in the rural Lake District of England with his sister, Dorothy, and poet Samuel Taylor Coleridge (1772–1834). In 1798 Wordsworth and Coleridge published their *Lyrical Ballads*, which abandoned flowery classical conventions for the language of ordinary speech and endowed simple subjects with the loftiest majesty. One of the best examples of Wordsworth's romantic credo and genius is "Daffodils." After describing the joyful experience of wandering into a field of flowers, the poet reflects on the power of that single experience in the last stanza of the poem:

For oft, when on my couch I lie
In vacant or in pensive mood,
They flash upon that inward eye
Which is the bliss of solitude;
And then my heart with pleasure fills,
And dances with the daffodils.

Here indeed are simplicity and love of nature in commonplace forms that could be appreciated by everyone. Wordsworth's conception of poetry as the "spontaneous overflow of powerful feeling recollected in tranquility" is well illustrated in this stanza.

Classicism remained strong in France under Napoleon and inhibited the growth of romanticism there. In 1813 Germaine de Staël (**duh STAHL**) (1766–1817), a Franco-Swiss writer living in exile, urged the French to throw away their worn-out classical models. Her study *On Germany* (1810) extolled the spontaneity and enthusiasm of German writers and thinkers, and it had a powerful impact on the post-1815 generation in France. Between 1820 and 1850, the romantic impulse broke through in the poetry and prose of Lamartine, de Vigny, Dumas, Hugo, and Sand.

The powerful novels of Victor Hugo (1802–1885) exemplified the romantic fascination with fantastic characters, exotic historical settings, and human emotions.

The hero of Hugo's famous *Hunchback of Notre Dame* (1831) is the great cathedral's deformed bell-ringer, a "human gargoyle" overlooking the teeming life of fifteenth-century Paris. Renouncing his early conservatism, Hugo equated freedom in literature with liberty in politics and society.

Amandine Aurore Lucie Dupin (1804–1876), generally known by her pen name, George Sand, defied the narrow conventions of her time in an unending search for sexual and personal freedom. After eight years of unhappy marriage she abandoned her husband and took her two children to Paris to pursue a career as a writer. There Sand soon achieved fame, notoriety, and wealth, eventually writing over eighty novels on a variety of romantic and social themes.

In central and eastern Europe, literary romanticism and early nationalism often reinforced each other. Some romantic writers became fascinated with peasant life and transcribed the folk songs, tales, and proverbs that the cosmopolitan Enlightenment had disdained. The brothers Jacob and Wilhelm Grimm were particularly successful at rescuing German fairy tales from oblivion. In the Slavic lands, romantics played a decisive role in converting spoken peasant languages into modern written languages. The greatest of all Russian poets, Aleksander Pushkin (1799–1837), rejected eighteenth-century attempts to force Russian poetry into a classical straitjacket and used his lyric genius to mold the modern literary language.

Art and Music

France's master of the romantic style in painting was Eugène Delacroix (**OO-gene duh-la-KWAH**) (1798–1863), probably the illegitimate son of French foreign minister Talleyrand. Delacroix's dramatic, colorful depictions of the violent struggle for freedom stirred the emotions. He was also fascinated with remote and exotic subjects, whether lion hunts in Morocco or dreams of languishing, sensuous women in a sultan's harem.

In England the most notable romantic painters were Joseph M. W. Turner (1775–1851) and John Constable (1776–1837). Both were fascinated by nature, but their interpretations of it contrasted sharply, aptly symbolizing the tremendous emotional range of the romantic movement. Turner depicted nature's power and terror; wild storms and sinking ships were favorite subjects. Constable painted the idyllic and soothing countryside of unspoiled rural England.

In music, the romantic movement endured well into the late nineteenth century. Abandoning well-defined structures, the great romantic composers used a wide range of forms to create a thousand musical landscapes and evoke a host of powerful emotions. Romantic composers also transformed the small classical orchestra, tripling its size by adding wind instruments, percussion, and more brass and strings. The crashing chords evoking the surge of the masses in Chopin's "Revolutionary Etude" and the bottomless despair of the funeral march in Beethoven's Third Symphony plumbed the depths of human feeling.

This range and intensity gave music and musicians much greater prestige than in the past. Music no longer simply complemented a church service or helped a nobleman digest his dinner. Music became a sublime end in itself, most perfectly realizing the endless yearning of the soul. The unbelievable one-in-a-million performer—the great virtuoso who could transport the listener to ecstasy and hysteria—became a cultural hero. People swooned for Franz Liszt (**frahnts list**) (1811–1886), the greatest pianist of his age, as they scream for rock stars today.

The first great romantic composer is also the most famous today. Ludwig van Beethoven (**BEY-toe-vuhn**) (1770–1827) used contrasting themes and tones to

Section Review

- Romanticism's tenets included a belief in emotional expression and imagination, living life to the fullest by developing one's potential, and being captivated by nature and the study of history.

- Poetry was the language of the romantics, who used ordinary speech, simple subjects, and novels with fantastic characters, historical settings, and heightened human emotions.

- Romantic art depicted the full range of expression in nature, from power and terror to the calm and serene; in music, too, the romantic goal was to evoke a range of emotions by using contrasting themes and tones.

produce dramatic conflict and inspiring resolutions. As one contemporary admirer wrote, "Beethoven's music sets in motion the lever of fear, of awe, of horror, of suffering, and awakens just that infinite longing which is the essence of Romanticism."

Reforms and Revolutions

How after 1815 did liberal, national, and socialist forces challenge conservatism in Greece, Great Britain, and France?

While the romantic movement was developing, liberal, national, and socialist forces battered against the conservatism of 1815. In some countries, change occurred gradually and peacefully. Elsewhere, pressures built and eventually caused an explosion in 1848. Three countries—Greece, Great Britain, and France—experienced variations on this basic theme between 1815 and 1848.

National Liberation in Greece

National, liberal revolution, frustrated in Italy and Spain by conservative statesmen, succeeded first in Greece after 1815. Since the fifteenth century, the Greeks had been living under the domination of the Ottoman Turks. In spite of centuries of foreign rule, the Greeks had survived as a people, united by their language and the Greek Orthodox religion. Inspired by the general growth of nationalism and independence movements in the early nineteenth century, a rising Greek national movement took root. Under Alexander Ypsilanti (**ip-suh-LAN-tee**), a Greek patriot and a general in the Russian army, revolution broke out in 1821.

The Great Powers, particularly Metternich, were opposed to all revolution, even revolution against the Islamic Turks. They refused to back Ypsilanti and supported the Ottoman Empire. Yet for many Europeans, the Greek cause became a holy one. Educated Americans and Europeans were in love with the culture of classical Greece; Russians were stirred by the piety of their Orthodox brethren. Writers and artists, moved by the romantic impulse, responded enthusiastically to the Greek national struggle. The famous English romantic poet Lord Byron even joined the Greeks and died fighting "that Greece may yet be free."

The Greeks, though often quarreling among themselves, battled on against the Turks and hoped for the eventual support of European governments. In 1827 Great Britain, France, and Russia responded to popular demands at home and directed Turkey to accept an armistice. When the Turks refused, the navies of these three powers trapped the Turkish fleet at Navarino and destroyed it. Russia then declared another of its periodic wars of expansion against the Turks. This led to the establishment of a Russian protectorate over much of present-day Romania, which had also been under Turkish rule. Great Britain, France, and Russia finally declared Greece independent in 1830 and installed a German prince as king of the new country in 1832. In the end, the Greeks had won: a small nation had gained its independence in a heroic war of liberation against a foreign empire.

Liberal Reform in Great Britain

Eighteenth-century British society had been both flexible and remarkably stable. It was dominated by the landowning aristocracy, but that class was neither closed nor rigidly defined. Successful business and professional people could buy land and become gentlefolk, while the common people had more than the usual opportunities of the preindustrial world. Nonetheless, the British Parliament was thoroughly undemocratic.

By the 1780s there was growing interest in some kind of political reform, but the French Revolution made the British aristocracy fearful and extremely hostile to any attempts to change the status quo. Conflicts between the ruling class and laborers were sparked in 1815 with revision of the **Corn Laws.** Britain had been unable to import cheap grain from eastern Europe during the war years, leading to high prices and large profits for the landed aristocracy. With the war over, grain could be imported again, allowing the price of wheat and bread to go down and benefiting almost everyone except the aristocracy. The aristocracy, however, rammed far-reaching changes in the Corn Laws through Parliament. The new regulation prohibited the importation of foreign grain unless the price at home rose to improbable levels. Seldom has a class legislated more selfishly for its own narrow economic advantage or done more to promote a class-based view of political action.

The change in the Corn Laws, coming as it did at a time of widespread unemployment and postwar economic distress, triggered protests and demonstrations. In

Corn Laws British laws, revised in 1815, that prohibited the importation of foreign grain unless the price at home rose to improbable levels.

1817 the Tory government, which was completely controlled by the landed aristocracy, responded by temporarily suspending the traditional rights of peaceable assembly and habeas corpus. Two years later, Parliament passed the infamous Six Acts, which, among other things, placed controls on a heavily taxed press and practically eliminated all mass meetings. These acts followed an enormous but orderly protest, at Saint Peter's Fields in Manchester, that had been savagely broken up by armed cavalry. Nicknamed the **Battle of Peterloo,** in scornful reference to the British victory at Waterloo, this incident demonstrated the government's determination to repress dissenters.

As their wealth grew, the new manufacturing and commercial groups insisted on a place in the framework of political power and social prestige, and they called for many kinds of liberal reform. In the 1820s, a less frightened Tory government responded with reforms that offered better urban administration, greater economic liberalism, civil equality for Catholics, and limited imports of foreign grain. These actions encouraged the middle classes to press on for reform of Parliament so they could have a larger say in government.

The Whig Party, though led like the Tories by great aristocrats, had by tradition been more responsive to commercial and manufacturing interests. After a series of setbacks, their Reform Bill of 1832 was propelled into law by a mighty surge of popular support. The Reform Bill of 1832 moved politics in a democratic direction. It increased the power in Parliament of the House of Commons at the expense of the House of Lords. The new industrial areas of the country also gained representation in the Commons, and many old "rotten boroughs"—electoral districts that had very few voters and that the landed aristocracy had bought and sold—were eliminated. As a result of the **Reform Bill of 1832,** the number of voters increased by about 50 percent, giving about 12 percent of adult men in Britain and Ireland the right to vote. Comfortable middle-class groups in the urban population, as well as some larger-scale farmers, received the vote. Thus the pressures building in Great Britain were temporarily released. A major reform had been achieved peacefully. Continued fundamental reform within the system appeared difficult but not impossible.

The movement to grant voting rights to all men gained momentum. Hundreds of thousands of people signed gigantic petitions calling on Parliament to grant universal male suffrage, first and most seriously in 1839, again in 1842, and yet again in 1848. Parliament rejected all three petitions. In the short run, the working poor failed with their demands, but they learned a valuable lesson in mass politics.

While calling for universal male suffrage, many working-class people joined with middle-class manufacturers in the Anti–Corn Law League, founded in Manchester in 1839. The League argued that lower food prices and more jobs in industry depended on repeal of the Corn Laws. Finally, in 1846, Parliament allowed for free imports of grain when the failure of the Irish potato crop threatened famine. Thereafter the liberal doctrine of free trade became almost sacred dogma in Great Britain.

The following year, the Tories passed a bill designed to help the working classes, but in a different way. The Ten Hours Act of 1847 limited the workday for women and young people in factories to ten hours. Tory aristocrats continued to champion legislation regulating factory conditions. They were competing vigorously with the middle class for the support of the working class. This healthy competition between a still-vigorous aristocracy and a strong middle class was a crucial factor in Great Britain's peaceful evolution. The working classes could make temporary alliances with either competitor to better their own conditions.

Battle of Peterloo A protest that took place at Saint Peter's Fields in Manchester in reaction to the revision of the Corn Laws; it was broken up by armed cavalry.

Reform Bill of 1832 A major British political reform that increased the number of male voters by about 50 percent and gave political representation to new industrial areas.

The Prelude to 1848

March 1814	Russia, Prussia, Austria, and Britain form the Quadruple Alliance to defeat France.
April 1814	Napoleon abdicates.
May–June 1814	Bourbon monarchy is restored; Louis XVIII issues the Constitutional Charter providing for civil liberties and representative government.
	First Peace of Paris: allies combine leniency with a defensive posture toward France.
October 1814–June 1815	Congress of Vienna peace settlement establishes balance-of-power principle and creates the German Confederation.
February 1815	Napoleon escapes from Elba and marches on Paris.
June 1815	Napoleon defeated at the Battle of Waterloo.
September 1815	Austria, Prussia, and Russia form the Holy Alliance to repress liberal and revolutionary movements.
November 1815	Second Peace of Paris and renewal of Quadruple Alliance punish France and establish the European "congress system."
1819	In Carlsbad Decrees, Metternich imposes harsh measures throughout the German Confederation.
1820	Revolution occurs in Spain and the kingdom of the Two Sicilies.
	At the Congress of Troppau, Metternich and Alexander I of Russia proclaim the principle of intervention to maintain autocratic regimes.
1821	Austria crushes a liberal revolution in Naples and restores the Sicilian autocracy.
	Greeks revolt against the Ottoman Turks.
1823	French armies restore the Spanish regime.
1824	Reactionary Charles X succeeds Louis XVIII in France.
1830	Charles X repudiates the Constitutional Charter; insurrection and collapse of the government follow. Louis Philippe succeeds to the throne and maintains a narrowly liberal regime until 1848.
	Greece wins independence from the Ottoman Empire.
1832	Reform Bill expands British electorate and encourages the middle class.
1839	Louis Blanc publishes *Organization of Work*.
1840	Pierre Joseph Proudhon publishes *What Is Property?*
1846	Jules Michelet publishes *The People*.
1848	Karl Marx and Friedrich Engels publish *The Communist Manifesto*.

Ireland and the Great Famine

The people of Ireland did not benefit from the political competition in Britain. The great mass of the population (outside of the northern counties of Ulster, which were partly Presbyterian) were Irish Catholics, who rented their land from a tiny minority of Church of England Protestants. These landlords were content to use their power to grab as much as possible.

The result was that the condition of the Irish peasantry around 1800 was abominable. The typical peasant lived in a wretched cottage and could afford neither shoes nor stockings. Hundreds of shocking accounts describe hopeless poverty. Yet in spite of terrible conditions, population growth sped onward. The 3 million of 1725 reached 4 million in 1780 and doubled to 8 million by 1840.

The population grew so quickly for three reasons: extensive cultivation of the potato, early marriage, and exploitation of peasants by landlords. Once peasants began to cultivate potatoes in the late sixteenth century, a larger population could be supported. A single acre of land spaded and planted with potatoes could feed an Irish family of six for a year, whereas two to four acres of grain and pasture were needed to feed the same number. Needing only a big potato patch to survive, Irish men and women married early. Because landlords leased land for short periods only, peasants had no incentive to make permanent improvements or hold off on marriage until they were settled. Rural poverty was inescapable and better shared with a spouse, while dutiful children were an old person's best hope of escaping destitution.

As population and potato dependency grew, conditions became more precarious. From 1820 onward deficiencies and diseases in the potato crop became more common. In 1845 and 1846, and again in 1848 and 1851, the potato crop failed in Ireland.

The result was unmitigated disaster—the **Great Famine.** Blight attacked the young plants, the leaves withered, and the tubers rotted. Widespread starvation and mass fever epidemics followed. Yet the British government, committed to rigid laissez-faire ideology, was slow to act. When it did, its relief efforts were tragically inadequate. Moreover, the government continued to collect taxes, and landlords demanded their rents. Tenants who could not pay were evicted and their homes destroyed. Famine or no, Ireland remained the conquered jewel of foreign landowners.

The Great Famine shattered the pattern of Irish population growth. Fully 1 million emigrants fled the famine between 1845 and 1851, and at least 1.5 million died or went unborn because of the disaster. Alone among the countries of

Great Famine The result of four years of crop failure in Ireland, a country that had grown dependent on potatoes as a dietary staple.

Daniel McDonald: The Discovery of the Potato Blight

Although the leaves of diseased plants usually shriveled and died, they could also look deceptively healthy. This Irish family has dug up its potato harvest and just discovered to its horror that the blight has rotted the crop. Like thousands of Irish families, this family now faces the starvation and the mass epidemics of the Great Famine. (Delargy Centre for Irish Folklore, University College, Dublin)

Europe, Ireland experienced a declining population in the nineteenth century, from about 8 million in 1845 to 4.4 million in 1911. Ireland became a land of continuous out-migration, late marriage, and widespread celibacy.

The Great Famine also intensified anti-British feeling and promoted Irish nationalism, for the bitter memory of starvation, exile, and British inaction was burned deeply into the popular consciousness. Patriots could call on powerful collective emotions in their campaigns for land reform, home rule, and, eventually, Irish independence.

The Revolution of 1830 in France

France won a liberal constitution under Louis XVIII. His Constitutional Charter of 1814 protected the economic and social gains made by sections of the middle class and the peasantry in the French Revolution, permitted great intellectual and artistic freedom, and allowed for the creation of a parliament with upper and lower houses. Immediately after Napoleon's abortive Hundred Days, the moderate king refused the counsel of reactionary aristocrats such as his brother Charles, who wished to sweep away all the revolutionary changes and return to a bygone age of royal absolutism and aristocratic pretension. Instead, Louis appointed as his ministers moderate royalists, who sought and obtained the support of a majority of the representatives elected to the lower Chamber of Deputies.

Louis XVIII's charter was anything but democratic. Only about 100,000 of the wealthiest males out of a total population of 30 million had the right to vote for the deputies who, with the king and his ministers, made the laws of the nation. Nonetheless, the "notable people" who did vote came from very different backgrounds. There were wealthy businessmen, war profiteers, successful professionals, ex-revolutionaries, large landowners from the old aristocracy and the middle class, Bourbons, and Bonapartists.

The old aristocracy, with its pre-1789 mentality, was a minority within the voting population. It was this situation that Louis's successor, Charles X (r. 1824–1830), could not abide. Crowned in a lavish, utterly medieval, five-hour ceremony in the cathedral of Reims (**reemz**) in 1824, Charles was a true reactionary. He wanted to re-establish the old order in France. Increasingly blocked by the opposition of the deputies, Charles's government turned in 1830 to military adventure in an effort to rally French nationalism and gain popular support. A long-standing economic and diplomatic dispute with Muslim Algeria, a vassal state of the Ottoman Empire, provided the opportunity.

In June 1830, a French force of 37,000 crossed the Mediterranean, landed to the west of Algiers, and took the capital city in three short weeks. Victory seemed complete, but in 1831 Muslims from the interior revolted and waged a fearsome war until 1847, when French armies finally subdued the country. Bringing French, Spanish, and Italian settlers to Algeria and leading to the expropriation of large tracts of Muslim land, the conquest of Algeria marked the rebirth of French colonial expansion.

Emboldened by the good news from Algeria, Charles repudiated the Constitutional Charter and issued decrees stripping much of the wealthy middle class of its voting rights. He also censored the press. The immediate reaction, encouraged by journalists and lawyers, was an insurrection in the capital by printers, other artisans, and small traders. In "three glorious days," the government collapsed. Paris boiled with revolutionary excitement, and Charles fled. Then the upper middle class, which had fomented the revolt, skillfully seated Charles's cousin, Louis Philippe, duke of Orléans, on the vacant throne.

Louis Philippe (r. 1830–1848) accepted the Constitutional Charter of 1814; adopted the red, white, and blue flag of the French Revolution; and admitted that he was merely the "king of the French people." Yet the situation in France remained fundamentally unchanged. The vote was extended from 100,000 to just 170,000 citizens. The upper middle class wanted only to protect their interests and the narrowly liberal institutions of 1815. Republicans, democrats, social reformers, and the poor of Paris were bitterly disappointed. They had made a revolution, but it seemed for naught. The social and political divisions that so troubled Jules Michelet in the 1840s were clear for all to see. (See the feature "Individuals in Society: Jules Michelet.")

The Revolutions of 1848

Why in 1848 did revolution triumph briefly throughout most of Europe, and why did it fail almost completely?

In 1848 revolutionary political and social ideologies combined with a severe economic crisis to produce a vast upheaval across Europe. Only reforming Great Britain and immobile Russia escaped untouched. Governments toppled; monarchs and ministers bowed or fled. National independence, liberal-democratic constitutions, and social reform: the lofty aspirations of a generation seemed at hand. Yet in the end, the revolutions failed.

A Democratic Republic in France

The late 1840s in Europe were hard economically and tense politically. The potato famine in Ireland in 1845 and 1846 had many echoes on the continent. Bad harvests jacked up food prices and caused misery and unemployment in the cities. "Prerevolutionary" outbreaks occurred all across Europe: an abortive Polish revolution in the northern part of Austria in 1846, a civil war between radicals and conservatives in Switzerland in 1847, and an armed uprising in Naples, Italy, in January 1848. Revolution was almost universally expected, but it took revolution in Paris—once again—to turn expectations into realities.

Louis Philippe's "bourgeois monarchy" had been characterized by stubborn inaction and complacency. There was a glaring lack of social legislation, and politics was dominated by corruption and selfish special interests. With only the rich voting for deputies, many of the deputies were docile government bureaucrats.

The government's stubborn refusal to consider electoral reform heightened a sense of class injustice among middle-class shopkeepers, skilled artisans, and unskilled working people, and it eventually touched off a popular revolt in Paris. Barricades went up on the night of February 22, 1848, and by February 24 Louis Philippe had abdicated in favor of his grandson. But the common people in arms would tolerate no more monarchy. This refusal led to the proclamation of a provisional republic, headed by a ten-man executive committee and certified by cries of approval from the revolutionary crowd.

The revolutionaries immediately set about drafting a constitution for France's Second Republic. Moreover, they wanted a truly popular and democratic republic so that the common people—the peasants, the artisans, and the unskilled workers— could participate in reforming society. In practice, building such a republic meant giving the right to vote to every adult male, and this was quickly done. Revolutionary

Individuals in Society

Jules Michelet

Famous proponent of democratic nationalism and generally recognized as France's pre-eminent romantic historian, Jules Michelet (1798–1874) was born and educated in Paris, the only child in a loving family of poor printers. Largely self-taught in the family print shop in his early years, the awkward apprentice-turned-student entered the prestigious Charlemagne College in 1813 and had to repeat his first year. Then he sped forward, winning prizes, earning a professorship, and building a brilliant academic career. Yet Michelet remained true to his roots in the common people, and he drew from history a vision of a generous France that would embrace all its children and heal their social divisions.

Jules Michelet, in a portrait by Joseph Court. (Photo12.com)

The young Michelet was strongly influenced by the still largely ignored Italian philosopher Giovanni Battista Vico (1668–1744), who viewed history as the development of societies and human institutions, as opposed to the biographies of great men or the work of divine providence.

After being appointed the historical director of the National Archives after the revolution of 1830, Michelet was able to combine teaching and writing with intense research in still largely unexplored documentary collections and he presented what he believed to be the first genuine history of his country and its people. Many historians, though not Michelet himself, believe that his history of France in the Middle Ages—published between 1833 and 1844 and becoming the first six volumes in his multivolume *History of France* (1833–1867)—is his most solid, useful, and lasting accomplishment. These volumes single out his vast knowledge of the sources, his uncanny evocation of times and places, and his empathic and balanced understanding of different views and individuals. His treatment of the national revival under Joan of Arc in the fifteenth century is a famous example of his early work.

Finishing his study of the Middle Ages and shaken by his wife's death, Michelet became eager to write the history of the French Revolution as the ultimate achievement, the time the French people reached maturity and began the long-delayed liberation of mankind. Yet, confronted by growing social divisions and seeing "France sinking by hour," he tried first to write a book that would save France. Published in 1846, *The People* drew on personal experience, history, and contemporary debates, painting a vivid picture of French society and the social dislocation that afflicted all classes. Rejecting socialism as an unrealistic fantasy, Michelet pleaded instead for national unity: "One people! one country! one France! Never, never, I beg you, must we become two nations! Without unity, we perish!"* He also called for universal secular education as a way to create a unified and stable citizenry. Michelet's book was widely read and discussed.

Sickened by the failure of the revolution of 1848 and refusing to swear allegiance to Louis Napoleon, Michelet lost his government positions and turned to full-time writing. He completed his seven-volume history of the French Revolution, filled in the history of the early modern period of France with another eleven volumes, and wrote popular impressions of nature and anticlerical polemics. Michelet's later history is often criticized for being overly emotional and biased against the monarchy, the nobility, and the clergy while idealizing popular forces and revolutionary upheaval. A great individualist, Michelet was a gifted writer with a grand, heartfelt historical narrative of compassionate nationhood for a noble people.

Questions for Analysis

1. How would you describe Michelet's conception of history, and how did it evolve over time?

2. Does the study of history help solve contemporary problems? Debate this question, and defend your position.

---

* Jules Michelet, *The People*, trans. with an introduction by John P. McKay (Urbana: University of Illinois Press, 1973), p. 21.

compassion and sympathy for freedom were expressed in the freeing of all slaves in French colonies, the abolition of the death penalty, and the establishment of a ten-hour workday for Paris.

Yet there were profound differences within the revolutionary coalition in Paris. On the one hand, there were the moderate, liberal republicans of the middle class. They viewed universal male suffrage as the ultimate concession to be made to popular forces, and they strongly opposed any further radical social measures. On the other hand, there were radical republicans and hard-pressed artisans. Influenced by a generation of utopian socialists, and appalled by the poverty and misery of the urban poor, the radical republicans were committed to some kind of socialism. So were many artisans, who hated the unrestrained competition of cutthroat capitalism and who advocated a combination of strong craft unions and worker-owned businesses.

Worsening depression and rising unemployment brought these conflicting goals to the fore in 1848. Louis Blanc, who along with a worker named Albert represented the republican socialists in the provisional government, pressed for recognition of a socialist right to work. Blanc asserted that permanent government-sponsored cooperative workshops should be established for workers. Such workshops would be an alternative to capitalist employment and a decisive step toward a new, noncompetitive social order.

The moderate republicans wanted no such thing. They were willing to provide only temporary relief. The resulting compromise set up national workshops—soon to become little more than a vast program of pick-and-shovel public works—and established a special commission under Blanc to "study the question." This satisfied no one. The national workshops were, however, better than nothing. An army of desperate poor from the French provinces and even from foreign countries streamed into Paris to sign up. As the economic crisis worsened, the number enrolled in the workshops soared from 10,000 in March to 120,000 by June, and another 80,000 were trying unsuccessfully to join.

While the workshops in Paris grew, the French masses went to the election polls in late April. Voting in most cases for the first time, the people of France elected to the new Constituent Assembly about five hundred moderate republicans, three hundred monarchists, and one hundred radicals who professed various brands of socialism. One of the moderate republicans was the author of *Democracy in America*, Alexis de Tocqueville (TOHK-vil) (1805–1859), who had predicted the overthrow of Louis Philippe's government.

Tocqueville observed that the socialist movement in Paris was an anathema to France's peasants as well as to the upper and middle classes. The French peasants owned land, and according to Tocqueville, "private property had become with all those who owned it a sort of bond of fraternity."[2] Returning from Normandy to take his seat in the new Constituent Assembly, Tocqueville saw that a majority of the members were firmly committed to the republic and strongly opposed to the socialists and their artisan allies, and he shared their sentiments.

This clash of ideologies—of liberal capitalism and socialism—became a clash of classes and arms after the elections. The new government's executive committee dropped Blanc and thereafter included no representative of the Parisian working class. Fearing that their socialist hopes were about to be dashed, artisans and unskilled workers invaded the Constituent Assembly on May 15 and tried to proclaim a new revolutionary state. But the government was ready and used the middle-class National Guard to squelch this uprising. As the workshops continued to fill and grow more radical, the fearful but powerful propertied classes in the Assembly took the offensive. On June 22, the government dissolved the national workshops in Paris, giving the workers the choice of joining the army or going to workshops in the provinces.

The result was a spontaneous and violent uprising. Frustrated in attempts to create a socialist society, masses of desperate people were now losing even their life-sustaining relief. As a voice from the crowd cried out when the famous astronomer François Arago counseled patience, "Ah, Monsieur Arago, you have never been hungry!"[3] Barricades sprang up in the narrow streets of Paris, and a terrible class war began. Working people fought with the courage of utter desperation, but the government had the army and the support of peasant France. After three terrible "June Days" and the death or injury of more than ten thousand people, the republican army under General Louis Cavaignac triumphed.

The revolution in France thus ended in spectacular failure. The February coalition of the middle and working classes had in four short months become locked in mortal combat. In place of a generous democratic republic, the Constituent Assembly completed a constitution featuring a strong executive. This allowed Louis Napoleon, nephew of Napoleon Bonaparte, to win a landslide victory in the election of December 1848. The appeal of his great name as well as the desire of the propertied classes for order at any cost had produced a semi-authoritarian regime.

The Austrian Empire in 1848

Throughout central Europe, the first news of the upheaval in France evoked feverish excitement and eventually revolution. Liberals demanded written constitutions, representative government, and greater civil liberties from authoritarian regimes. When governments hesitated, popular revolts followed. Urban workers and students served as the shock troops, but they were allied with middle-class liberals and peasants. In the face of this united front, monarchs collapsed and granted almost everything. The popular revolutionary coalition, having secured great and easy victories, then broke down as it had in France. The traditional forces—the monarchy, the aristocracy, the regular army—recovered their nerve, reasserted their authority, and took back many, though not all, of the concessions. Reaction was everywhere victorious.

The revolution in the Austrian Empire began in Hungary in 1848, where nationalistic Hungarians demanded national autonomy, full civil liberties, and universal suffrage. When the monarchy in Vienna hesitated, Viennese students and workers took to the streets, and peasant disorders broke out in parts of the empire. The Habsburg emperor Ferdinand I (r. 1835–1848) capitulated and promised reforms and a liberal constitution. Metternich, who had foreseen the disruptive potential of nationalism, fled in disguise toward London. The old absolutist order seemed to be collapsing with unbelievable rapidity.

The coalition of revolutionaries was not stable, however. When the monarchy abolished serfdom as part of its promised reforms, the newly free peasants then lost interest in the political and social questions agitating the cities. Meanwhile, the coalition of urban revolutionaries broke down along class lines over the issue of socialist workshops and universal voting rights for men.

The revolutionary coalition was also weakened, and ultimately destroyed, by conflicting national aspirations. In March the Hungarian revolutionary leaders pushed through an extremely liberal, almost democratic, constitution. But the Hungarian revolutionaries also sought to transform the mosaic of provinces and peoples that was the kingdom of Hungary into a unified, centralized, Hungarian nation. To the minority groups that formed half of the population—the Croats,

Serbs, and Romanians—such unification was completely unacceptable. Each felt entitled to political autonomy and cultural independence. In a somewhat similar way, Czech nationalists based in Bohemia and the city of Prague came into conflict with German nationalists. (See the feature "Listening to the Past: Speaking for the Czech Nation" on pages 615–616.) Thus conflicting national aspirations within the Austrian Empire enabled the monarchy to play off one ethnic group against the other.

Finally, the conservative aristocratic forces regained their nerve under the rallying call of the archduchess Sophia, a Bavarian princess married to the emperor's brother. Deeply ashamed of the emperor's collapse before a "mess of students," she insisted that Ferdinand, who had no heir, abdicate in favor of her son, Francis Joseph.[4] Powerful nobles organized around Sophia in a secret conspiracy to reverse and crush the revolution.

Their first breakthrough came when the army bombarded Prague and savagely crushed a working-class revolt there on June 17. Other Austrian officials and nobles began to lead the minority nationalities of Hungary against the revolutionary government. At the end of October, the well-equipped, predominately peasant troops of the regular Austrian army attacked the student and working-class radicals in Vienna and retook the city at the cost of more than four thousand casualties. Thus the determination of the Austrian aristocracy and the loyalty of its army were the final ingredients in the triumph of reaction and the defeat of revolution.

When Francis Joseph (r. 1848–1916) was crowned emperor of Austria immediately after his eighteenth birthday in December 1848, only Hungary had yet to be brought under control. But another determined conservative, Nicholas I of Russia (r. 1825–1855), obligingly lent his iron hand. On June 6, 1849, 130,000 Russian troops poured into Hungary and subdued the country after bitter fighting. For a number of years, the Habsburgs ruled Hungary as a conquered territory.

Prussia and the Frankfurt Assembly

After Austria, Prussia was the largest and most influential German kingdom. Prior to 1848, the goal of middle-class Prussian liberals had been to transform absolutist Prussia into a liberal constitutional monarchy, which would lead the thirty-eight states of the German Confederation into a liberal, unified nation. The agitation following the fall of Louis Philippe in France encouraged Prussian liberals to press their demands. When the artisans and factory workers in Berlin exploded in March and joined temporarily with the middle-class liberals in the struggle against the monarchy, Frederick William IV (r. 1840–1861) promised to grant Prussia a liberal constitution and to merge Prussia into a new national German state that was to be created. But urban workers wanted much more and the Prussian aristocracy wanted much less than the moderate constitutional liberalism the king conceded. The workers issued a series of democratic and vaguely socialist demands that troubled their middle-class allies, and the conservative clique gathered around the king to urge counter-revolution.

As an elected Prussian Constituent Assembly met in Berlin to write a constitution for the Prussian state, a self-appointed committee of liberals from various German states began organizing for the creation of a unified German state. Meeting in Frankfurt in May, a National Assembly composed of lawyers, professors, doctors, officials, and businessmen convened to write the German federal constitution. However, their attention shifted from drafting a constitution to deciding how to respond to Denmark's claims on the provinces of Schleswig (SCHLES-wig) and Holstein, which where inhabited primarily by Germans.

Street Fighting in Frankfurt, 1848
Workers and students could tear up the cobblestones, barricade a street, and make it into a fortress. But urban revolutionaries were untrained and poorly armed. They were no match for professional soldiers led by tough officers who were sent against them after frightened rulers had recovered their nerve. (The Granger Collection, New York)

Section Review

- Jules Michelet, a romantic historian and prolific writer on the history of France, called for French unity instead of socialism and had a vision of France that would provide universal education and heal social divisions.

- King Louis Philippe ruled with the help of the wealthy and corrupt; his failure to provide social programs led to revolt and an end to monarchy in 1848, and the establishment of the Second Republic.

- The moderate republicans and the republican socialists disagreed about reforms, not going far enough for the working class, who unsuccessfully revolted in the "June Days"; the reaction replaced the generous democratic republic with Bonaparte's nephew Louis Napoleon, who consolidated power once again in the hands of the propertied elite under a semi-authoritarian regime.

- Revolution in France inspired popular revolts in the Austrian Empire in 1848 and led to reforms, but conflicting national aspirations and poor organization brought defeat to the revolutionaries by the Austrian aristocracy and its loyal army.

- At the Frankfurt Assembly, Prussian liberals demanded a constitutional monarchy but urban workers wanted more radical reforms; Prussian king Frederick William refused the constitutional crown they offered and with the help of Austria and Russia reasserted his conservative and autocratic royal authority, forcing a return to the German Confederation.

Thus delayed, the National Assembly did not complete its draft of a liberal constitution until March 1849, at which time it elected King Frederick William of Prussia emperor of the new German national state (minus Austria and Schleswig-Holstein). By early 1849, however, reaction had been successful almost everywhere. Frederick William had reasserted his royal authority, disbanded the Prussian Constituent Assembly, and granted his subjects a limited, essentially conservative constitution. Reasserting that he ruled by divine right, Frederick William contemptuously refused to accept the "crown from the gutter." Bogged down by their preoccupation with nationalist issues, the reluctant revolutionaries in Frankfurt had waited too long and acted too timidly.

When Frederick William, who really wanted to be emperor but only on his own authoritarian terms, tried to get the small monarchs of Germany to elect him emperor, Austria balked. Supported by Russia, Austria forced Prussia to renounce all of its schemes of unification in late 1850. The German Confederation was reestablished. Attempts to unite the Germans—first in a liberal national state and then in a conservative Prussian empire—had failed completely.

Chapter Review

How did the victorious allies fashion a general peace settlement, and how did Metternich uphold a conservative European order? (page 590)

In 1814 the victorious allied powers sought to restore peace and stability in Europe. Dealing moderately with France and wisely settling their own differences, the allies laid the foundations for beneficial international cooperation throughout much of the nineteenth century. Led by Metternich, the conservative powers also used intervention and repression as they sought to prevent the spread of subversive ideas and radical changes in domestic politics.

What were the basic tenets of liberalism, nationalism, and socialism, and what groups were most attracted to these ideologies? (page 594)

European thought has seldom been more powerfully creative than after 1815, and ideologies of liberalism, nationalism, and socialism all developed to challenge the existing order in this period of early industrialization and rapid population growth. The basic tenets in one way or another rejected conservatism, with its stress on tradition, hereditary monarchy and aristocracy, and an official church.

What were the characteristics of the romantic movement, and who were some of the great romantic artists? (page 598)

The romantic movement, breaking decisively with the dictates of classicism, reinforced the spirit of change and revolutionary anticipation. The romantic movement was characterized by a belief in self-expression, imagination, and spontaneity, in art as well as in personal life. Some of the artists and thinkers who embodied the romantic movement include Rousseau, Wordsworth, George Sand, Delacroix, and Chopin.

How after 1815 did liberal, national, and socialist forces challenge conservatism in Greece, Great Britain, and France? (page 601)

Inspired by modern nationalism, Greek patriots rebelled against their Turkish rulers and won national independence. In Great Britain the liberal challenge to the conservative order led to fundamental reforms, as more men gained the right to vote, high tariffs on grain were abolished, and the factory workday was reduced. Elsewhere in Europe the old order held firm, and political, economic, and social pressures kept building.

Why in 1848 did revolution triumph briefly throughout most of Europe, and why did it fail almost completely? (page 607)

In 1848 the increasing pressures exploded dramatically as they culminated in liberal and nationalistic revolutions. Monarchies panicked and crumbled as revolutionaries triumphed, first in France and then all across the continent. Yet very few revolutionary

Key Terms

dual revolution (p. 590)
Congress of Vienna (p. 590)
Holy Alliance (p. 593)
Carlsbad Decrees (p. 593)
liberalism (p. 594)
laissez faire (p. 594)
nationalism (p. 595)
socialism (p. 596)
bourgeoisie (p. 597)
proletariat (p. 597)
romanticism (p. 598)
Sturm und Drang (p. 598)
Corn Laws (p. 602)
Battle of Peterloo (p. 603)
Reform Bill of 1832 (p. 603)
Great Famine (p. 605)

goals were realized. The moderate, nationalistic middle classes were unable to consolidate their initial victories. Instead, they drew back when artisans, factory workers, and radical socialists rose up to present their own much more revolutionary demands. This retreat facilitated the efforts of dedicated aristocrats in central Europe to reassert their power. And it made possible the crushing of Parisian workers by a coalition of solid bourgeoisie and landowning peasantry in France. Thus the lofty ideals of a generation drowned in a sea of blood and disillusion. Soon tough-minded realists would take command to confront the challenges of the day.

Notes

1. This paragraph draws on the influential views of B. Anderson, *Imagined Communities: Reflections on the Origins and Spread of Nationalism*, rev. ed. (London/New York: Verso, 1991), and E. J. Hobsbawm and T. Ranger, eds., *The Invention of Tradition* (Cambridge: Cambridge University Press, 1983).
2. A. de Tocqueville, *Recollections* (New York: Columbia University Press, 1949), p. 94.
3. M. Agulhon, *1848* (Paris: Éditions du Seuil, 1973), pp. 68–69.
4. W. L. Langer, *Political and Social Upheaval, 1832–1852* (New York: Harper & Row, 1969), p. 361.

To assess your mastery of this chapter, go to **bedfordstmartins.com/mckaywestbrief**

Listening to the Past

Speaking for the Czech Nation

The creation of national consciousness and nationalism often began with a cultural revival that focused on a people's language and history. In Austria, the influential historian Frantisek Palacky (1798–1876) created a portrait of the Czechs as progressive and democratic before the Counter-Reformation and the long process of Germanization under Habsburg rule.

In the revolution of 1848, the German National Assembly in Frankfurt asked Palacky to represent the Austrian province of Czech Bohemia in its efforts to form a unified Germany. In the famous letter that follows Palacky rejected this invitation. Asserting the reality of a Czech nation and warning of both Russian and German expansionism, he proposed a "union of equals" in a radically transformed Austria. A version of Palacky's proposal was passed by Austria's constituent assembly in 1849, but the resurgent absolutist government vetoed it.

Frantisek Palacky, in a frontispiece portrait accompanying his most important work on Czech history. (Visual Connection Archive)

I am a Czech of Slav descent and with all the little I own and possess I have devoted myself wholly and forever to the service of my nation. That nation is small, it is true, but from time immemorial it has been an independen0t nation with its own character; its rulers have participated since old times in the federation of German princes, but the nation never regarded itself nor was it regarded by others throughout all the centuries, as part of the German nation. The whole union of the Czech lands first with the Holy German Empire and then with the German Confederation was always a purely dynastic one of which the Czech nation, the Czech Estates, hardly wished to know and which they hardly noticed. . . . If anyone asks that the Czech nation should now unite with the German nation, beyond this heretofore existing federation between princes, this is then a new demand which has no historical legal basis. . . . The second reason which prevents me from participating in your deliberations is the fact that . . . you . . . are . . . aiming to undermine Austria forever as an independent empire and to make its existence impossible—an empire whose preservation, integrity and consoli-dation is, and must be, a great and important matter not only for my own nation but for the whole of Europe, indeed for mankind and civilization itself. [Palacky goes on to argue that a strong Austrian empire is needed as a barrier to Russian expansion.]

But why have we seen this state, which by nature and history is destined to be the bulwark and guardian of Europe against Asiatic elements of every kind—why have we seen it in a critical moment helpless and almost unadvised in the face of the advancing storm? It is because in an unhappy blindness which has lasted for very long, Austria has not recognized the real legal and moral foundation of its existence and has denied it: the fundamental rule that all the nationalities united under its scepter should enjoy complete equality of rights and respect. The right of nations is truly a natural right; no nation on earth has the right to demand that its neighbour should sacrifice itself for its benefit, no nation obliged to deny or sacrifice itself for the good of its neighbour. Nature knows neither ruling nor subservient nations. If the union which unites several different nations is to be firm and lasting, no nation must have cause to fear that by that union it will lose any of the goods which it holds most dear; on the contrary each must have the certain hope that it will find in the central authority defense and protection against possible violations of equality by neighbours; then every nation will do its best to strengthen that central authority so that it can successfully provide the aforesaid defense.

Questions for Analysis

1. Why did Palacky refuse to participate in the German National Assembly?
2. What Enlightenment ideas does Palacky draw upon in his letter?
3. Why might an absolutist government reject Palacky's argument?

Source: Slightly adapted from Hans Kohn, *Pan-Slavism: Its Ideology and History*, pp. 65–69. Copyright © 1953 by the University of Notre Dame Press. Reprinted with permission.

CHAPTER 24

Life in the Emerging Urban Society in the Nineteenth Century

John Perry, *A Bill-poster's Fantasy* (1855), explores the endless diversity of big-city entertainment. (Dunhill Museum & Archive, 48 Jermyn Street, St. James's, London)

Chapter Preview

Taming the City
What was life like in the cities, and how did urban life change in the nineteenth century?

Rich and Poor and Those in Between
What did the emergence of urban industrial society mean for rich and poor and those in between?

The Changing Family
How did families change as they coped with the challenges and the opportunities of the developing urban civilization?

Science and Thought
What major changes in science and thought reflected and influenced the new urban society?

INDIVIDUALS IN SOCIETY: Franziska Tiburtius

IMAGES IN SOCIETY: Class and Gender Boundaries in Women's Fashion, 1850–1914

LISTENING TO THE PAST: Middle-Class Youth and Sexuality

The era of intellectual and political upheaval that culminated in the revolutions of 1848 was also an era of rapid urbanization. After 1848 Western political development veered off in a novel and uncharted direction, but the growth of towns and cities rushed forward with undiminished force. Thus Western society was urban and industrial in 1900 as surely as it had been rural and agrarian in 1800. The urbanization of society was both a result of the Industrial Revolution and a reflection of its enormous long-term impact.

Taming the City

What was life like in the cities, and how did urban life change in the nineteenth century?

The growth of industry posed enormous challenges for all members of Western society, from young factory workers confronting relentless discipline to aristocratic elites maneuvering to retain political power. As we saw in Chapter 22, the early consequences of economic transformation were mixed and far-reaching and by no means wholly negative. By 1850 at the latest, working conditions were improving and real wages were rising for the mass of the population, and they continued to do so until 1914. Thus given the poverty and uncertainty of preindustrial life, some historians maintain that the history of industrialization in the nineteenth century is probably better written in terms of increasing opportunities than in terms of greater hardships.

Critics of this relatively optimistic view of industrialization claim that it neglects the quality of life in urban areas. They stress that the new industrial towns and cities were awful places where people, especially poor people, suffered from bad housing, lack of sanitation, and a sense of hopelessness. They ask if these drawbacks did not more than cancel out higher wages and greater opportunity. An examination of the development of cities in the nineteenth century provides some answers to this complex question.

Industry and the Growth of Cities

Since the Middle Ages, European cities had been centers of government, culture, and large-scale commerce. They had also been congested, dirty, and unhealthy. People were packed together almost as tightly as possible within the city limits. Infectious disease spread with deadly speed in overcrowded cities, and in the larger towns, yearly deaths outnumbered births. Urban populations were able to maintain their numbers only because newcomers were continually arriving from rural areas.

Clearly, deplorable urban conditions did not originate with the Industrial Revolution. What the Industrial Revolution did was to amplify those conditions. The steam engine freed industrialists from dependence on water power and allowed them to build factories in any location. Cities were desirable sites because they offered better access to shipping facilities, materials and markets, and a large pool of workers. Therefore, as industry grew, there was also a rapid expansion of already overcrowded and unhealthy cities.

The challenge of the urban environment was felt first and most acutely in Great Britain. The number of people living in cities of 20,000 or more in England and Wales jumped from 1.5 million in 1801 to 6.3 million in 1851 and reached 15.6 million in 1891. Such cities accounted for 17 percent of the total English population in 1801, 35 percent as early as 1851, and fully 54 percent in 1891. Other countries duplicated the English pattern as they industrialized (see Map 24.1). An American observer was hardly exaggerating when he wrote in 1899 that "the most remarkable social phenomenon of the present century is the concentration of population in cities."[1]

As the population climbed, each town or city utilized every scrap of land to the fullest extent. Parks and open areas were almost nonexistent. Narrow houses were built wall to wall in long rows. These row houses had neither front nor back yards, and only a narrow alley in back separated one row from the next. Or buildings were built around tiny courtyards completely enclosed on all four sides. "Six, eight, and even ten occupying one room is anything but uncommon," wrote one observer in 1842.

These highly concentrated urban populations lived in extremely unsanitary and unhealthy conditions. Open drains and sewers flowed alongside or down the middle of unpaved streets. Toilet facilities were primitive in the extreme. In parts of Manchester, as many as two hundred people shared a single outhouse. Sewage often overflowed and seeped into cellar dwellings. Moreover, some courtyards in poorer neighborhoods became dunghills, collecting excrement that was sometimes sold as fertilizer.

Who or what was responsible for these awful conditions? The crucial factors were the tremendous pressure of more people and the *total* absence of public transportation. People simply had to jam themselves together if they were to be able to walk to shops and factories. Another factor was that governments, on the continent as well as in Great Britain, were slow to provide sanitary facilities and establish adequate building codes. This slow pace was probably attributable more to uncertainty about what precisely should be done than to rigid middle-class opposition to government action. Moreover, because of the sad legacy of rural housing conditions in preindustrial society, ordinary people generally took dirt and filth for granted. One English miner told an investigator, "I do not think it usual for the lasses [in the coal mines] to wash their bodies; my sisters never wash themselves." As for the men, "their legs and bodies are as black as your hat."[2]

CHRONOLOGY

ca. 1850–1870	Modernization of Paris
1850–1914	Condition of working classes improves
1854	Pasteur studies fermentation and develops pasteurization
1854–1870	Development of germ theory
1857	Flaubert, *Madame Bovary*
1859	Darwin, *On the Origin of Species*
1869	Mendeleev creates periodic table
1880–1881	Dostoevski, *The Brothers Karamazov*
1880–1913	Birthrate steadily declines in Europe
1890s	Electric streetcars introduced in Europe

Public Health and the Bacterial Revolution

Although cleanliness was not next to godliness in most people's eyes, it was becoming so for some reformers. The most famous of these was Edwin Chadwick, a commissioner charged with the administration of relief to paupers. Chadwick was a follower of radical philosopher Jeremy Bentham (1748–1832), whose approach to social problems, called **utilitarianism,** aimed for a solution that provided the "greatest good for the greatest number." Chadwick believed that unsanitary conditions led to illness and that the sickness or death of a wage earner pushed the family deeper into poverty. His goal was to ward off disease and thus poverty by cleaning up the urban environment.

Chadwick documented the "sanitary conditions of the laboring populations" in an 1842 report and argued that the excrement of communal outhouses could be dependably carried off by water through sewers at less than one-twentieth the cost of removing it by hand. The cheap iron pipes and tile drains of the industrial age would provide running water and sewerage for all sections of town, not just the wealthy ones. In 1848, with the cause strengthened by the cholera epidemic of

utilitarianism The idea of Jeremy Bentham that social policies should promote the "greatest good for the greatest number."

1800

1900

MAPPING THE PAST

MAP 24.1   European Cities of 100,000 or More, 1800 and 1900

There were more large cities in Great Britain in 1900 than in all of Europe in 1800. A careful comparison of these historical snapshots reveals key aspects of nineteenth-century urbanization. **[1]** In 1800, what common characteristics were shared by many large European cities? (For example, how many big cities were capitals and/or leading ports?) **[2]** Compare the spatial distribution of cities in 1800 with the distribution in 1900. Where and why in 1900 are many large cities concentrated in two clusters?

1846, Chadwick's report became the basis of Great Britain's first public health law, which created a national health board and gave cities broad authority to build modern sanitary systems.

The public health movement won dedicated supporters in the United States, France, and Germany from the 1840s on. Governments accepted at least limited responsibility for the health of all citizens, and their programs broke decisively with the age-old fatalism of urban populations in the face of shockingly high mortality. By the 1860s and 1870s, European cities were making real progress toward adequate water supplies and sewerage systems, city dwellers were beginning to reap the rewards of better health, and death rates began to decline (see Figure 24.1).

Still, effective control of communicable disease required an understanding of the connection between germs and disease. This was to evolve through the work of Louis Pasteur (**pa-STUR**) (1822–1895), a French chemist who began studying fermentation in 1854 at the request of brewers. Using his microscope to study the fermentation process, Pasteur found that it depended on the growth of living organisms and that the activity of these organisms could be suppressed by heating the beverage—by pasteurization. The breathtaking implication was that specific diseases were caused by specific living organisms—germs—and that those organisms could be controlled.

By 1870 the work of Pasteur and others had demonstrated the general connection between germs and disease. Next the German country doctor Robert Koch (**kawkh**) and his coworkers developed pure cultures of harmful bacteria and described their life cycles, paving the way for researchers—mainly Germans—to identify the organisms responsible for disease after disease. These discoveries led to the development of a number of effective vaccines. Medical procedures became much more effective as well when the English surgeon Joseph Lister (1827–1912) reasoned that a chemical disinfectant applied to a wound dressing would destroy airborne germs.

The evolution of **germ theory** coupled with the ever more sophisticated public health movement saved millions of lives, particularly after about 1880. Diphthe-

germ theory The idea that disease was spread through filth and not caused by it.

FIGURE 24.1 The Decline of Death Rates in England and Wales, Germany, France, and Sweden, 1840–1913

A rising standard of living, improvements in public health, and better medical knowledge all contributed to the dramatic decline of death rates in the nineteenth century.

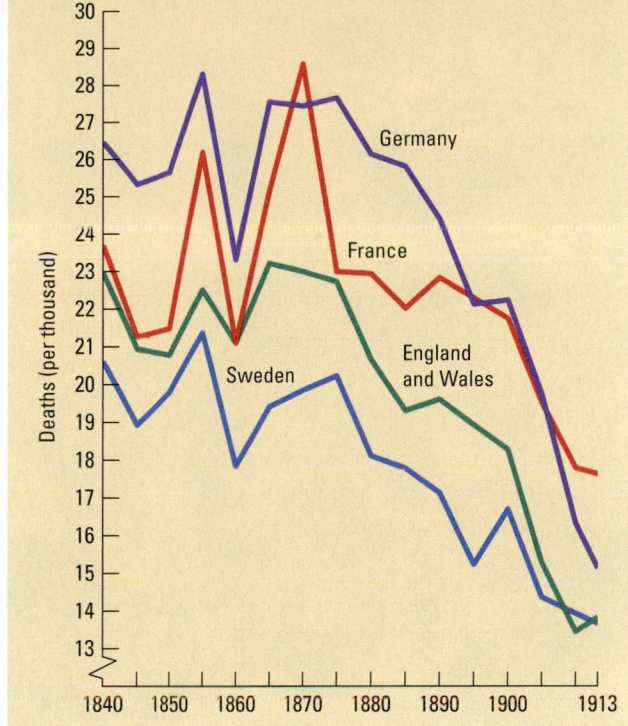

ria, typhoid, typhus, cholera, and yellow fever claimed fewer victims, and mortality rates began to decline dramatically (see Figure 24.1). By 1910 a great silent revolution had occurred: the death rates for people of all ages in urban areas were generally no higher than those for people in rural areas, and sometimes they were lower.

Urban Planning and Public Transportation More effective urban planning was one of the keys to improving the quality of urban life. France took the lead during the rule of Napoleon III (r. 1848–1870), who sought to stand above class conflict and promote the welfare of all his subjects through government action. He believed that rebuilding much of Paris would provide employment, improve living conditions, and testify to the power and glory of his empire. Under his appointee, the baron Georges Haussmann (HOUSE-muhn) (1809–1884), Paris was transformed.

Haussmann and his fellow planners proceeded on many interrelated fronts. With a bold energy that often shocked their contemporaries, they razed old buildings in order to cut broad, straight, tree-lined boulevards through the center of the city as well as in new quarters on the outskirts. These boulevards, designed in part to prevent the easy construction and defense of barricades by revolutionary crowds, permitted traffic to flow freely and afforded impressive vistas. Their creation also demolished some of the worst slums.

New streets stimulated the construction of better housing, especially for the middle classes. Small neighborhood parks and open spaces were created throughout the city, and two very large parks suitable for all kinds of holiday activities were developed—one on the wealthy west side and one on the poor east side. The city also improved its sewers, and a system of aqueducts more than doubled the city's supply of good fresh water.

The Parisian model of urban planning spread throughout Europe, particularly after 1870. In city after city, public authorities mounted a coordinated attack on many of the interrelated problems of the urban environment. They razed structures to build new boulevards, office buildings, town halls, theaters, opera houses, and museums, while also placing pipes for sewage and water underground. Zoning expropriation laws, which allowed a majority of the owners of land in a given quarter of the city to impose major street or sanitation improvements on a reluctant minority, were an important mechanism of the new urbanism.

The development of mass public transportation also contributed to better living conditions. In the 1870s, horse-drawn streetcars carried riders along the growing number of major thoroughfares. Then in the 1890s, the real revolution occurred: European countries adopted the electric streetcar.

The Urban Landscape: Madrid in 1900

This wistful painting of a Spanish square on a rainy day, by Enrique Martinez Cubells y Ruiz (1874–1917), includes a revealing commentary on public transportation. Coachmen wait atop their expensive hackney cabs for a wealthy clientele, while modern electric streetcars that carry the masses converge on the square from all directions. (Museo Municipal, Madrid/The Bridgeman Art Library)

Section Review

- Industrialization meant increasing opportunities but also greater hardships including population density, lack of public transportation, and little government oversight, resulting in unsanitary, overcrowded conditions.

- The development of germ theory and the implementation of public health laws improved sanitation in the cities and mortality rates fell dramatically.

- Beginning in France, modern urban planning included organized streets and parks, better housing, sewers and fresh water supplies, and horse-drawn and then electric streetcars.

Electric streetcars were cheaper, faster, more dependable, and more comfortable than their horse-drawn counterparts. Service improved dramatically. Millions of Europeans—workers, shoppers, schoolchildren—hopped on board during the workweek. And on weekends and holidays, streetcars carried millions on happy outings to parks and countryside, racetracks and music halls. Good mass transit helped greatly in the struggle for decent housing. While horse-drawn streetcars had allowed the middle classes to move to better housing, electric streetcars made better housing accessible to those of modest means. The still-crowded city was able to expand and become less congested.

Rich and Poor and Those in Between

What did the emergence of urban industrial society mean for rich and poor and those in between?

General improvements in health and in the urban environment had beneficial consequences for all kinds of people. Yet differences in living conditions among social classes remained gigantic.

Social Structure

How much did the almost-completed journey to an urban, industrialized world change the social framework of rich and poor and those in between? The first great change was a substantial and undeniable increase in the standard of living for the average person. The real wages of British workers, for example, which had already risen by 1850, almost doubled between 1850 and 1906. Similar increases occurred in continental countries as industrial development quickened after 1850. Ordinary people took a major step forward in the centuries-old battle against poverty, reinforcing efforts to improve many aspects of human existence.

There is another side to the income coin, however. Greater economic rewards for the average person did *not* eliminate hardship and poverty, nor did they make the wealth and income of the rich and the poor significantly more equal. In almost every advanced country around 1900, the richest 5 percent of all households in the population received 33 percent of all national income. The richest 20 percent of households received anywhere from 50 to 60 percent of all national income. Moreover, income taxes on the wealthy were light or nonexistent. Thus the gap between rich and poor remained enormous at the beginning of the twentieth century. It was probably almost as great as it had been in the age of agriculture and aristocracy before the Industrial Revolution.

The great gap between rich and poor endured, in part, because industrial and urban development made society more diverse and less unified. There developed an almost unlimited range of jobs, skills, and earnings; one group or subclass shaded off into another in a complex, confusing hierarchy. Thus the very rich and the dreadfully poor were separated from each other by a range of subclasses, each filled with individuals struggling to rise or at least to hold their own in the social order. In this atmosphere of competition and hierarchy, neither the middle classes nor the working classes acted as a unified force, counter to Marx's predictions. This social and occupational hierarchy developed enormous variations, but the age-old pattern of great economic inequality remained firmly intact.

The Middle Classes

By the beginning of the twentieth century, the diversity and range within the urban middle classes were striking. At the top stood the most successful business families from banking, industry, and large-scale commerce. As people in this upper middle class gained in income and progressively lost all traces of radicalism after the trauma of 1848, they were almost irresistibly drawn toward the aristocratic lifestyle. They purchased country places or built beach houses for weekend and summer use. They employed a staff of servants and hired private coaches and carriages to signal their rising social status.

The topmost reaches of the upper middle class tended to shade off into the old aristocracy to form a new upper class of at most 5 percent of the population. Much of the aristocracy welcomed this development. Having experienced a sharp decline in its relative income in the course of industrialization, the landed aristocracy was often delighted to trade titles, country homes, and snobbish elegance for good hard cash. Some of the best bargains were made through marriages to American heiresses. Correspondingly, wealthy aristocrats tended increasingly to exploit their agricultural and mineral resources as if they were business people. Below the wealthy upper middle class were much larger, much less wealthy, and increasingly diversified middle-class groups. Here one found the moderately successful industrialists and merchants as well as professionals in law and medicine. This was the middle middle class, solid and quite comfortable but lacking great wealth. Below it were independent shopkeepers, small traders, and tiny manufacturers—the lower middle class. Both of these traditional elements of the middle class expanded modestly in size with economic development.

As industry and technology developed, new occupations entered the middle-class sphere. Engineering, for example, emerged from the world of skilled labor as a full-fledged profession of great importance, considerable prestige, and many branches. Architects, chemists, accountants, and surveyors, to name only a few, first achieved professional standing in this period. Management of large public and private institutions also emerged as a kind of profession as governments provided more services and as very large corporations such as railroads came into being.

Industrialization also expanded and diversified the lower middle class. The number of independent, property-owning shopkeepers and small business people grew, and so did the number of white-collar employees—a mixed group of traveling salesmen, bookkeepers, store managers, and clerks who staffed the offices and branch stores of large corporations. White-collar employees were propertyless and often earned no more than the better-paid skilled or semiskilled workers did. Yet white-collar workers were fiercely committed to the middle class and to the ideal of moving up in society. In the Balkans, for example, clerks let their fingernails grow very long to distinguish themselves from people who worked with their hands. The tie, the suit, and soft, clean hands were no-less-subtle marks of class distinction than wages.

Relatively well educated but without complex technical skills, many white-collar groups aimed at achieving professional standing and solid middle-class status. Elementary school teachers largely succeeded in this effort. From being miserably paid part-time workers in the early nineteenth century, teachers rode the wave of mass education to respectable middle-class status and income. Nurses also rose from the lower ranks of unskilled labor to precarious middle-class standing. Dentistry was taken out of the hands of working-class barbers and placed in the hands of highly trained (and middle-class) professionals.

Middle-Class Culture

In spite of their diversity, the middle classes were loosely united by a certain style of life and culture. Food was the largest item in the household budget, and a well-off family might spend 10 percent of its substantial earnings on meat and fully 25 percent of its income on food and drink. The dinner party was this class's favored social occasion. A wealthy family might host eight to twelve almost every week, whereas more modest households would settle for once a month.

The middle-class wife could cope with this endless procession of meals, courses, and dishes because she had both servants and money at her disposal. Indeed, the employment of at least one full-time maid was the best single sign that a family had crossed the cultural divide separating the working classes from what some contemporary observers called the "servant-keeping classes." The greater a family's income, the greater the number of servants it employed. Food and servants together absorbed about 50 percent of income at all levels of the middle class.

Well fed and well served, the middle classes were also well housed by 1900. Many quite prosperous families chose to rent apartments, complete with tiny rooms for servants under the eaves of the top floor. By 1900 the middle classes were also quite clothes-conscious. The factory, the sewing machine, and the department store had all helped reduce the cost and expand the variety of clothing. Middle-class women were particularly attentive to the fickle dictates of fashion.

(See the feature "Images in Society: Class and Gender Boundaries in Women's Fashion, 1850–1914" on pages 626–627.)

Education was another growing expense, as middle-class parents tried to provide their children with ever more crucial advanced education. The keystones of culture and leisure were books, music, and travel. The long realistic novel, the heroics of composers Wagner and Verdi, the diligent striving of the dutiful daughter at the piano, and the packaged tour to a foreign country were all sources of middle-class pleasure.

Finally, the middle classes were loosely united by a strict code of morality. This code laid great stress on hard work, self-discipline, and personal achievement. Drunkenness and gambling were denounced as vices; sexual purity and fidelity were celebrated as virtues. Men and women who fell into crime or poverty were generally assumed to be responsible for their own downfall.

The Working Classes

About four out of five people belonged to the working classes at the turn of the century. Many members of the working classes—that is, people whose livelihoods depended on physical labor and who did not employ domestic servants—were still small landowning peasants and hired farm hands. This was especially true in eastern Europe. In western and central Europe, however, the typical worker had left the land. In Great Britain, fewer than 8 percent of the people worked in agriculture, and in rapidly industrializing Germany only 25 percent were employed in agriculture and forestry. Even in less industrialized France, fewer than 50 percent of the people depended on the land in 1900.

The urban working classes were even less unified and homogeneous than the middle classes. Not only were there divides based on skill level (see Figure 24.2),

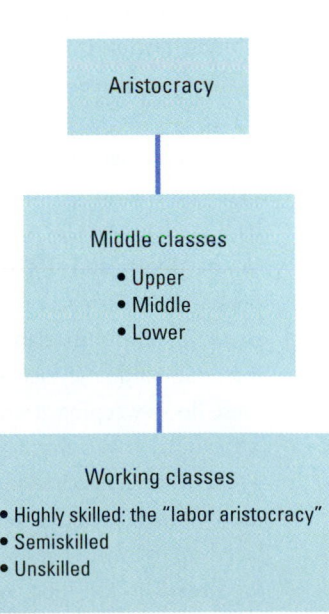

Aristocracy

Middle classes
- Upper
- Middle
- Lower

Working classes
- Highly skilled: the "labor aristocracy"
- Semiskilled
- Unskilled

FIGURE 24.2   The Urban Social Hierarchy

Images in Society

Class and Gender Boundaries in Women's Fashion, 1850–1914

Women's fashion was big business in the nineteenth century. Long the dominant industrial pursuit in human history, the production of textiles took off with the Industrial Revolution. In the later nineteenth century fashionable clothing, especially for middle-class women, became the first modern consumer industry as careful buyers snapped up the constantly changing ready-to-wear goods sold by large department stores.

In the nineteenth century, before society fragmented into many different groups expressing themselves in many dress styles, clothing patterns focused mainly on perceived differences in class and gender. The four illustrations presented here allow one to analyze the social information communicated through women's clothing. As you study these illustrations, note the principal characteristics and then try to draw out the larger implications. What does the impractical, restrictive clothing in these images reveal about society's view of women during this period? What is the significance of the emergence of alternative styles of well-groomed dress?

Most changes in women's fashion originated in Paris in the nineteenth century. Image 1 shows the attire worn by French aristocratic and wealthy middle-class women in the 1850s and 1860s. Note that these expensive dresses, flawlessly tailored by an army of skilled seamstresses, abound in elaborate embroidery, rich velvety materials, and fancy accessories. The circular spread of these floor-sweeping gowns is due to the crinoline, a slip with metal hoops that holds the skirt out on all sides. These women also are wearing the corset, the century's most characteristic women's undergarment, which was laced up tightly in back and pressed unmercifully from the breasts to the hips. What does this image tell you

about the life of these women (their work, leisure activities, and so on)?

The intriguing 1875 painting by Atkinson Grimshaw, *Summer* (Image 2), shows a middle-class interior and the evolution of women's summer fashion two decades later. The corset still binds, but crinoline hoops have given way to the bustle, a cotton fan with steel reinforcement that pushes the dress out in back and exaggerates gender differences. The elaborate costume of the wealthy elite, available in cheaper ready-to-wear versions sold through department stores and mail-order catalogues throughout Europe, had become the standard for middle-class women. Emulating the elite in

IMAGE 1 Crinoline Dresses, Paris, 1859 (ILN/Mary Evans Picture Library)

IMAGE 2 Summer Dress with Bustle, England, 1875
(Roy Miles, Esq./The Bridgeman Art Library)

IMAGE 3 Alternative Fashion, England, 1893
(© Manchester City Art Galleries)

style, conventional middle-class women shopped carefully, scouting for sales, and drew a boundary separating themselves from working-class women in their simple cotton clothes. What implications, if any, do you see this having on class distinctions?

The young middle-class Englishwoman in an 1893 photo (Image 3) has chosen a woman's tailored suit, the only major English innovation in nineteenth-century women's fashion. This "alternative dress" combines the tie, suit jacket, vest, and straw hat—all initially items of male attire—with typical feminine elements, such as the skirt and gloves. This practical, socially accepted alternative dress appealed to the growing number of women in paid employment in the 1890s. The historian Diana Crane has argued that this departure from the dominant style can be seen as a symbolic, nonverbal assertion of independence and equality with men.* Do you agree with this? If so, what was the significance of the pre-1914 turn from stifling corset to the more flexible brassiere and the mainstream embrace of loose-fitting garments, such as the 1910 dress in Image 4? Did the greater freedom of movement in clothing reflect the emerging emancipation of Western women? Or was the

coquettish femininity of these loose, flowing dresses only a repackaging of the dominant culture's sharply defined gender boundaries?

IMAGE 4 Loose-fitting Dress, France, 1910 (© Corbis)

*Diana Crane, *Fashion and Its Social Agendas: Class, Gender, and Identity in Clothing* (Chicago: University of Chicago Press, 2000), pp. 99–114.

but there were also great differences in lifestyles and cultural values. These differences contributed to a keen sense of social status and hierarchy within the working classes.

Highly skilled workers, who made up about 15 percent of the working classes, became a real **labor aristocracy.** These workers earned only about two-thirds of the income of the bottom ranks of the servant-keeping classes, but that was fully twice as much as the earnings of unskilled workers. The most "aristocratic" of the highly skilled workers were construction bosses and factory foremen, men who had risen from the ranks and were fiercely proud of their achievement. The labor aristocracy also included members of the traditional highly skilled handicraft trades that had not been mechanized or placed in factories, such as cabinetmakers, jewelers, and printers.

This group as a whole was under constant pressure. Over time, many skilled artisans such as woodcarvers and watchmakers were replaced by lower-paid semi-skilled factory workers. At the same time, new kinds of skilled workers such as shipbuilders and railway locomotive engineers entered the labor aristocracy. Thus the labor elite remained in a state of flux as individuals and whole crafts moved in and out of it.

To maintain their precarious standing, the upper working class adopted strait-laced, almost puritanical values. Like the middle classes, the labor aristocracy was strongly committed to the family and to economic improvement. Families in the upper working class saved money regularly, worried about their children's education, and valued good housing. Despite these similarities, skilled workers viewed themselves not as aspirants to the middle class but as the pacesetters and natural leaders of all the working classes. Well aware of the degradation not so far below them, they practiced self-discipline and stern morality.

The upper working class in general frowned on heavy drinking and sexual permissiveness. An organized temperance movement was strong in the countries of northern Europe. As one German labor aristocrat somberly warned, "The path to the brothel leads through the tavern" and from there quite possibly to drastic decline or total ruin for person and family.[3] Men and women of the labor aristocracy were also quick to find fault with those below them who failed to meet their standards.

Below the labor aristocracy stood semiskilled and unskilled urban workers. The enormous complexity of this sector of the world of labor is not easily summarized. Workers in the established crafts—carpenters, bricklayers, pipe fitters—stood near the top of the semiskilled hierarchy. A large number of the semiskilled were factory workers who earned highly variable but relatively good wages and whose relative importance in the labor force was increasing.

Below the semiskilled workers was a larger group of unskilled workers that included day laborers such as longshoremen, wagon-driving teamsters, teenagers, and every kind of "helper." Many of these people had real skills and performed valuable services, but they were unorganized and divided, united only by the common fate of meager earnings. The same lack of unity characterized street vendors and market people—self-employed workers who competed savagely with each other and with the established shopkeepers of the lower middle class.

Domestic servants comprised a large and steadily growing segment of the unskilled group in the nineteenth century. The great majority were women; indeed, one out of every three girls in Britain between the ages of fifteen and twenty was a domestic servant. Throughout Europe and America, a great many female domestics in the cities were recent migrants from rural areas. As in earlier times, domestic service was still hard work at low pay with limited personal independence and the danger of sexual exploitation. Nonetheless, domestic service had real attrac-

labor aristocracy The highly skilled workers who made up about 15 percent of the working classes at the turn of the twentieth century.

A School for Servants

Although domestic service was poorly paid, there was always plenty of competition for the available jobs. Schools sprang up to teach young women the manners and the household skills that employers in the "servant-keeping classes" demanded. (Corporation of London: London Metropolitan Archives)

tions for "rough country girls": higher wages than agricultural work, more varied marriage prospects, and access to a broader range of entertainment.

Many young domestics from the countryside made a successful transition to working-class wife and mother, yet they often needed to supplement the family income by working in the **sweated industries.** Like the putting-out and cottage industries of earlier times, these industries paid by the piece for work done off-site, in the home. While some women hand-decorated objects, most made clothing, especially after the advent of the sewing machine. An army of poor women accounted for the bulk of the inexpensive "ready-made" clothes displayed on department store racks and in tiny shops.

sweated industries Poorly paid handicraft production, often by married women paid by the piece and working at home.

Working-Class Leisure and Religion

While the middle classes gathered over dinner in their homes, the working classes mingled in taverns, cafés, and pubs. Working-class political activities, both moderate and radical, were also concentrated in drinking establishments. Moreover, social drinking in public places by married couples and sweethearts became an

Section Review

- The standard of living increased for the average person during the nineteenth century, but poverty still existed and income disparity remained enormous; taxes on the rich were low and the working classes were not unified.

- The middle classes had an upper middle class of business owners, a diverse middle middle class, and a lower middle class of white-collar workers and shopkeepers.

- The middle classes had some common cultural interests, including socializing at dinner parties, employing servants, wearing fashionable clothing, educating their children, and abiding by a strict moral code.

- The working class had an upper working class, or labor aristocracy, skilled workers with high moral standards who viewed themselves as leaders of the working classes; below them were the semi-skilled and unskilled workers, both highly diverse groups that were not organized.

- Social and political gatherings of the working classes took place in taverns and pubs and for the first time included women; sports and music were other favored pastimes, while church attendance declined.

accepted and widespread practice for the first time. This greater participation by women undoubtedly helped civilize the world of drink and hard liquor.

The two other leisure-time passions of the working classes were sports and music halls. A great decline in "blood sports," such as bullbaiting and cockfighting, had occurred throughout Europe by the late nineteenth century. Their place was filled by modern spectator sports, of which racing and soccer were the most popular. Men and women also frequented music halls and vaudeville theaters, the working-class counterparts of middle-class opera and classical theater. Drunkenness, sexual intercourse and pregnancy before marriage, marital difficulties, and problems with mothers-in-law were favorite themes of broad jokes and bittersweet songs.

The working poor continued to find solace and meaning in religion. Yet historians also recognize that by the last two or three decades of the nineteenth century, a considerable decline in both church attendance and church donations was occurring in most European countries. And it seems clear that this decline was greater for the urban working classes than for their rural counterparts or for the middle classes.

Why did working-class church attendance decline? Part of the reason was that the vibrant, materialistic urban environment undermined popular religious impulses, which were poorly served in the cities. Equally important, however, was the fact that throughout the nineteenth century both Catholic and Protestant churches were normally seen as conservative institutions defending social order and custom. Therefore, as the European working classes became more politically conscious, they tended to see the established (or quasi-established) "territorial church" as defending what they wished to change and as allied with their political opponents. Especially the men of the urban working classes developed vaguely antichurch attitudes, even though they remained neutral or positive toward religion. They tended to regard regular church attendance as "not our kind of thing"—not part of urban working-class culture. The pattern was different in those places where the church or synagogue had never been linked to the state and served as a focus for ethnic cohesion. Irish Catholic churches in Protestant Britain and Jewish synagogues in Russia were outstanding examples.

The Changing Family

How did families change as they coped with the challenges and the opportunities of the developing urban civilization?

Urban life wrought many fundamental changes in the family. Although much is still unknown, it seems clear that in the second half of the nineteenth century the family had stabilized considerably after the disruption of the late eighteenth and early nineteenth centuries. The home became more important for both men and women. The role of women and attitudes toward children underwent substantial change, and adolescence emerged as a distinct stage of life. These are but a few of the transformations that affected all social classes in varying degrees.

Premarital Sex and Marriage

By 1850 the ideal of romantic love had triumphed among the working classes. Couples were ever more likely to come from different, even distant, towns and to be more nearly the same age, further indicating that romantic sentiment was replacing tradition and financial considerations.

For the middle classes, however, economic considerations continued to play a major role in marriage arrangements. In France dowries and elaborate legal marriage contracts were common practice among the middle classes in the later nineteenth century, and marriage was for many families one of life's most crucial financial transactions. As in the past, this preoccupation with money led many men to marry late, after they had been established economically, and to choose women considerably younger than themselves. A young woman of the middle class found her romantic life carefully supervised by her well-meaning mother, who schemed for a proper marriage and guarded her daughter's virginity like the family's credit. After marriage, middle-class morality sternly demanded fidelity. Middle-class boys were watched, too, but not as vigilantly. By the time they reached late adolescence, they had usually attained considerable sexual experience with maids or prostitutes. (See the feature "Listening to the Past: Middle-Class Youth and Sexuality" on pages 643–644.)

In Paris alone, 155,000 women were registered as prostitutes between 1871 and 1903, and 750,000 others were suspected of prostitution in the same years. Men of all classes visited prostitutes, but the middle and upper classes supplied much of the motivating cash. Thus, though many middle-class men abided by the publicly professed code of stern puritanical morality, others indulged their appetites for prostitutes and sexual promiscuity. For many poor young women, prostitution, like domestic service, was a stage of life and not a permanent employment. They went on to marry (or live with) men of their own class and establish homes and families.

A woman's virginity before marriage was not as important to the working classes, and in urban Europe around 1900, as many as one woman in three was going to the altar an expectant mother. Unmarried young people in western, northern, and central Europe were probably engaging in just as much sexual activity as their parents and grandparents who had created the illegitimacy explosion of 1750 to 1850 (see page 514). However, the rising rate of illegitimacy was reversed in the second half of the nineteenth century: more babies were born to married mothers. What accounts for this reversal? Pregnancy led increasingly to marriage and the establishment of a two-parent household. Skipping out was less acceptable, and marriage was less of an economic challenge. Thus the urban working-class couple became more stable, and that stability strengthened the family as an institution.

Kinship Ties

Within working-class homes, ties to relatives after marriage—kinship ties—were in general much stronger than many social observers have recognized. Most newlyweds tried to live near their parents, though not in the same house. Indeed, for many married couples in later-nineteenth-century cities, ties to mothers and fathers, uncles and aunts, were more important than ties to unrelated acquaintances.

Although governments were generally providing more welfare services by 1900, many people turned to their families for help in coping with sickness, unemployment, old age, and death. Relatives were also valuable at less tragic moments. If a couple was very poor, an aged relation often moved in to cook and mind the children so that the wife could earn badly needed income outside the home. Sunday dinners were often shared, as were outgrown clothing and useful information. Often the members of a large family group all lived in the same neighborhood.

Gender Roles and Family Life

Industrialization and the growth of modern cities brought great changes to the lives of European women. These changes were particularly consequential for married women, and in the nineteenth century most women did marry.

The rigid gender roles that had developed with industrialization were firmly entrenched after 1850. Men and women occupied separate spheres: the wife as mother and homemaker, the husband as wage earner. Well-paying jobs were off-limits to women, and married women were subordinated to their husbands by law.

With all women facing discrimination in education and employment and with middle-class women suffering especially from a lack of legal rights, there is little wonder that some women rebelled and began the long-continuing fight for equality of the sexes and the rights of women. Their struggle proceeded on two main fronts. First, following in the steps of women such as Mary Wollstonecraft (see page 545), organizations founded by middle-class feminists campaigned for equal legal rights for women as well as access to higher education and professional employment. These middle-class feminists argued that unmarried women and middle-class widows with inadequate incomes simply had to have more opportunities to support themselves. Middle-class feminists also recognized that paid (as opposed to unpaid) work could relieve the monotony that some women found in their sheltered middle-class existence and put greater meaning into their lives.

In the later nineteenth century, these organizations scored some significant victories, such as the 1882 law giving English married women full property rights. More women found professional and white-collar employment, especially after about 1880. But progress was slow and hard won. For example, in Germany before 1900, women were not admitted as fully registered students at a single university, and it was virtually impossible for a woman to receive certification and practice as a lawyer or doctor. (See the feature "Individuals in Society: Franziska Tiburtius.") In the years before 1914, middle-class feminists increasingly focused their attention on political action and fought for the right to vote for women.

Women inspired by utopian and especially Marxian socialism blazed a second path. Often scorning the programs of middle-class feminists, socialist women leaders argued that the liberation of working-class women would come only with the liberation of the entire working class through revolution. In the meantime, they championed the cause of working women and won some practical improvements, especially in Germany, where the socialist movement was most effectively organized. In a general way, these different approaches to women's issues reflected the diversity of classes in urban society.

While the ideology and practice of rigidly separate spheres made women powerless outside the home, within it their power grew stronger. Among the English working classes, it was the wife who generally determined how the family's money was spent. In many families, the husband gave all his earnings to his wife to manage, whatever the law might read. She returned to him only a small allowance for carfare, beer, tobacco, and union dues. All the major domestic decisions, from the children's schooling and religious instruction to the selection of new furniture or a new apartment, were hers. Despite this power, however, a good deal of her effort was directed toward pampering her husband as he expected. In countless humble households, she saw that he had meat while she ate bread, that he relaxed by the fire while she did the dishes.

The woman's guidance of the household went hand in hand with the increased emotional importance of home and family. The home she ran was idealized as a warm shelter in a hard and impersonal urban world. For a child of the English slums in the early 1900s,

home, however poor, was the focus of all love and interests, a sure fortress against a hostile world. Songs about its beauties were ever on people's lips. "Home, sweet home," first heard in the 1870s, had become "almost a second national anthem."

Individuals in Society

Franziska Tiburtius

Why did a small number of women in the late nineteenth century brave great odds and embark on professional careers? And how did a few of those manage to reach their objectives? The career and personal reflections of Franziska Tiburtius (**tie-bur-TEE-us**), a pioneer in German medicine, suggest that talent, determination, and economic necessity were critical ingredients.*

Like many women of her time who would study and pursue professional careers, Franziska Tiburtius (1843–1927) was born into a property-owning family of modest means. The youngest of nine children on a small estate in northeastern Germany, the sensitive child wilted with a harsh governess but flowered with a caring teacher and became an excellent student.

Graduating at sixteen and needing to support herself, Tiburtius had few opportunities. A young woman from a "proper" background could work as a governess or a teacher without losing her respectability and spoiling her matrimonial prospects, but that was about it. She tried both avenues. Working for six years as a governess in a noble family and no doubt learning that poverty was often one's fate in this genteel profession, she then turned to teaching. Called home from her studies in Britain in 1871 to care for her brother, who had contracted typhus as a field doctor in the Franco-Prussian War, she found her calling. She decided to become a medical doctor.

Supported by her family, Tiburtius's decision was truly audacious. In all of Europe, only the University of Zurich in republican Switzerland accepted female students. Moreover, if it became known that she had studied medicine and failed, she would never get a job as a teacher. No parent would entrust a daughter to an "emancipated" radical who had carved up dead bodies!

Although the male students at the university sometimes harassed the women with crude pranks, Tiburtius thrived. The revolution of the microscope and the discovery of microorganisms was rocking Zurich, and she was fascinated by her studies. She became close friends with a fellow female medical student from Germany, Emilie Lehmus, with whom she would form a lifelong partnership in medicine. She did her internship with

families of cottage workers around Zurich and loved her work.

Graduating at age thirty-three in 1876, Tiburtius went to stay with her brother, a doctor in Berlin. Though well qualified to practice, she ran into pervasive discrimination. She was not even permitted to take the state medical exams and could practice only as an unregulated (and unprofessional) "natural healer." But after persistent fighting with the bureaucrats, she was able to display her diploma and practice as "Franziska Tiburtius, M.D. University of Zurich." She and Lehmus were in business.

Soon the two women realized their dream and opened a clinic, subsidized by a wealthy industrialist, for female factory workers. The clinic filled a great need and was soon treating many patients. A room with beds for extremely sick women was later expanded into a second clinic.

Franziska Tiburtius, pioneering woman physician in Berlin. (Ullstein Bilderdienst/The Granger Collection, New York)

Tiburtius and Lehmus became famous. For fifteen years, they were the only women doctors in all Berlin. An inspiration for a new generation of women, they added the wealthy to their thriving practice. But Tiburtius's clinics always concentrated on the poor, providing them with subsidized and up-to-date treatment. Talented, determined, and working with her partner, Tiburtius experienced the joys of personal achievement and useful service, joys that women and men share in equal measure.

Questions for Analysis

1. How does Franziska Tiburtius's life reflect both the challenges and the changing roles of middle-class women in the later nineteenth century?

2. In what ways was Tiburtius's career related to improvements in health in urban society and to the expansion of the professions?

*This portrait draws on Conradine Lück, *Frauen: Neun Lebensschicksale* (Reutlingen: Ensslin & Laiblin, n.d.), pp. 153–185.

Few walls in lower-working-class houses lacked "mottoes"—colored strips of paper, about nine inches wide and eighteen inches in length, attesting to domestic joys: EAST, WEST, HOME'S BEST; BLESS OUR HOME; GOD IS MASTER OF THIS HOUSE; HOME IS THE NEST WHERE ALL IS BEST.[4]

By 1900 home and family were what life was all about for millions of people of all classes.

Married couples also developed stronger emotional ties to each other. Affection and eroticism became more central to the couple after marriage. Gustave Droz (**drose**), whose bestseller *Mr., Mrs., and Baby* went through 121 editions between 1866 and 1884, saw love within marriage as the key to human happiness. Many French marriage manuals of the late 1800s stressed that women had legitimate sexual needs, such as the "right to orgasm." Perhaps the French were a bit more enlightened in these matters than other nationalities. But the rise of public socializing by couples in cafés and music halls as well as franker affection within the family suggests a more erotic, pleasurable intimate life for women throughout Western society. This, too, helped make the woman's role as mother and homemaker acceptable and even satisfying.

Child Rearing

Within the family, attitudes toward children and child rearing also shifted. As more babies survived, parents allowed themselves to form emotional attachments earlier in their children's lives. Mothers increasingly breast-fed their infants, for example, rather than paying wet nurses to do so. Breast feeding involved sacrifice—a

A Working-Class Home, 1875

Emotional ties within ordinary families grew stronger in the nineteenth century. Parents gave their children more love and better care.
(ILN/Mary Evans Picture Library)

temporary loss of freedom, if nothing else. Yet in an age when there was no good alternative to mother's milk, it saved lives. This surge of parental feeling also gave rise to a wave of specialized books on child rearing and infant hygiene, such as Droz's phenomenally successful book. Droz urged fathers to get into the act and pitied those "who do not know how to roll around on the carpet, play at being a horse and a great wolf, and undress their baby."[5]

The loving care lavished on infants was matched by greater concern for older children and adolescents. They, too, were wrapped in the strong emotional ties of a more intimate and protective family. For one thing, European couples began to limit their number of children in order to care adequately for those they had. It was evident by the end of the nineteenth century that the birthrate was declining across Europe, as Figure 24.3 shows, and it continued to do so until after World War II. The Englishwoman who married in the 1860s, for example, had an average of about six children; her daughter marrying in the 1890s had only four; and her granddaughter marrying in the 1920s had only two or possibly three.

The most important reason for this revolutionary reduction in family size, in which the comfortable and well-educated classes took the lead, was parents' desire to improve their economic and social position and that of their children. Children were no longer contributors to the family income; indeed, parents saved to provide their children with such advantages as music lessons and summer vacations and long, expensive university educations and suitable dowries. A young German skilled worker with only one child spoke for many in his class when he said, "We want to get ahead, and our daughter should have things better than my wife and sisters did."[6] Thus the growing tendency of couples in the late nineteenth century to use a variety of contraceptive methods—rhythm method, withdrawal method, and mechanical devices—certainly reflected increased concern for children.

Indeed, many parents, especially in the middle classes, probably became *too* concerned about their children, unwittingly subjecting them to an emotional pressure cooker of almost unbearable intensity. The result was that many children and especially adolescents came to feel trapped and in need of greater independence.

The rigid division of gender roles within the family contributed to feelings of tension and anxiety. It was widely believed that mother and child loved each other easily but that relations between father and child were necessarily difficult and often tragic. The father was a stranger; his world of business was far removed from the maternal world of spontaneous affection. Moreover, the father was demanding, often expecting the child to succeed where he himself had failed and making his love conditional on achievement. Little wonder that the imaginative literature of the late nineteenth century came to deal with the emotional and destructive elements of

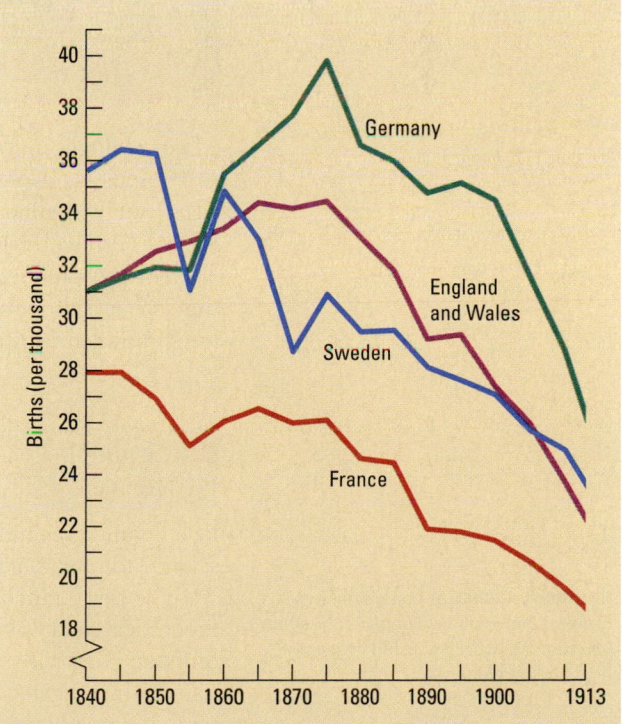

FIGURE 24.3   The Decline of Birthrates in England and Wales, Germany, France, and Sweden, 1840–1913

Women had fewer babies for a variety of reasons, including the fact that their children were increasingly less likely to die before reaching adulthood. Compare with Figure 24.1.

Section Review

- Members of the working classes now often married for love but in the middle classes marriage was still an economic arrangement, with young women carefully supervised while young men frequented prostitutes.

- Kinship ties remained important for members of a working-class family, who often lived near each other and provided needed help and care.

- Rigid gender roles led to the development of organizations that pursued women's rights.

- Within the home a woman typically had more power, managing the household's income and making domestic decisions, but her primary responsibility was still to care for her husband and family.

- Love and emotional bonding to children occurred earlier, as infant survival rates grew, and couples, for economic reasons, generally had fewer children.

- Freud blamed tension and anxiety in young adulthood on early childhood experiences, while popular literature questioned parent-child relationships; for working-class youths, escape was possible as they could find work and leave home, but for middle-class youths there was no easy escape.

thermodynamics A branch of physics built on Newton's laws of mechanics that investigated the relationship between heat and mechanical energy.

---

father-son relationships. In the Russian Feodor Dostoevski's (**dos-tuh-YEF-skee**) great novel *The Brothers Karamazov* (1880–1881), for example, four sons work knowingly or unknowingly to destroy their father. Later at the murder trial, one of the brothers claims to speak for all mankind and screams out, "Who doesn't wish his father dead?"

Sigmund Freud (**froid**) (1856–1939), the Viennese founder of psychoanalysis, formulated the most striking analysis of the explosive dynamics of the family, particularly the middle-class family in the late nineteenth century. A physician by training, Freud began his career treating mentally ill patients. He noted that the hysteria of his patients appeared to originate in bitter early-childhood experiences wherein the child had been obliged to repress strong feelings. When these painful experiences were recalled and reproduced under hypnosis or through the patient's free association of ideas, the patient could be brought to understand his or her unhappiness and eventually deal with it.

The working classes probably had more avenues of escape from such tensions than did the middle classes. Unlike their middle-class counterparts, who remained economically dependent on their families until a long education was finished or a proper marriage secured, working-class boys and girls went to work when they reached adolescence. Earning wages on their own, they could bargain with their parents for greater independence within the household by the time they were sixteen or seventeen. If they were unsuccessful, they could and did leave home to live cheaply as paying lodgers in other working-class homes. Thus the young person from the working classes broke away from the family more easily when emotional ties became oppressive. In the twentieth century, middle-class youths would follow this lead.

Science and Thought

What major changes in science and thought reflected and influenced the new urban society?

Major changes in Western science and thought accompanied the emergence of urban society. Two aspects of these complex intellectual developments stand out as especially significant. First, scientific knowledge expanded rapidly, influencing the Western worldview even more profoundly than before and spurring the creation of new products and whole industries. Second, between about the 1840s and the 1890s, European literature underwent a shift from soaring romanticism to tough-minded realism.

The Triumph of Science

The pace of scientific discoveries accelerated from the 1830s onward, stimulated by breakthroughs in industrial technology. While ordinary citizens continued to lack detailed scientific knowledge, they became convinced of the importance of science to human advancement.

The new branch of physics known as **thermodynamics** was one example of a theoretical field with roots in industry and obvious practical applications. Building on Isaac Newton's laws of mechanics and on studies of steam engines, thermodynamics investigated the relationship between heat and mechanical energy. By midcentury, physicists had formulated the fundamental laws of thermodynamics, which were then applied to mechanical engineering, chemical processes, and many other fields. The law of conservation of energy held that different forms of energy—such as heat, electricity, and magnetism—could be converted but neither created nor destroyed. Nineteenth-century thermodynamics demonstrated that the physical world was governed by firm, unchanging laws, leaving little room for either divine intervention or human will.

Chemistry and electricity were two other fields characterized by extremely rapid scientific progress. And in both fields, "science was put in the service of industry," as the influential economist Alfred Marshall (1842–1924) argued at the time.

Chemists devised ways of measuring the atomic weight of different elements, and in 1869 the Russian chemist Dmitri Mendeleev (**men-duh-LEY-uhf**) (1834–1907) codified the rules of chemistry in the periodic law and the periodic table. Chemistry was subdivided into many specialized branches, such as **organic chemistry**—the study of the compounds of carbon. Applying theoretical insights gleaned from this new field, researchers in large German chemical companies discovered ways of transforming the dirty, useless coal tar that accumulated in coke ovens into beautiful, expensive synthetic dyes for the world of fashion. The basic discoveries of Michael Faraday (**FAR-uh-dee**) (1791–1867) in electromagnetism in the 1830s and 1840s resulted in the first dynamo (generator) and opened the way for the subsequent development of the telegraph, electric motor, electric light, and electric streetcar.

organic chemistry The study of the compounds of carbon.

The successful application of scientific research in the fast-growing electrical and organic chemical industries promoted solid economic growth between 1880 and 1913 and provided a model for other industries. Systematic "R & D"—research and development—was born in the late nineteenth century.

The methods of science acquired unrivaled prestige after 1850. For many, the union of careful experiment and abstract theory was the only reliable route to truth and objective reality. The "unscientific" intuitions of poets and the revelations of saints seemed hopelessly inferior.

Social Science and Evolution

From the 1830s onward, many thinkers tried to apply the objective methods of science to the study of society. In some ways, these efforts simply perpetuated the critical thinking of the philosophes. Yet there were important differences. The new "social scientists" had access to the massive sets of numerical data that governments had begun to collect on everything from children to crime, from population to prostitution. In response, social scientists developed new statistical methods to analyze these facts "scientifically" and supposedly to test their theories. And the systems of the leading nineteenth-century social scientists were more unified, all-encompassing, and dogmatic than those of the philosophes. Marx was a prime example (see pages 597–598).

Another extremely influential system builder was French philosopher Auguste Comte (**komt**) (1798–1857), author of the six-volume *System of Positive Philosophy* (1830–1842). Comte postulated that all intellectual activity progresses through predictable stages:

> *The great fundamental law . . . is this:—that each of our leading conceptions—each branch of our knowledge—passes successively through three different theoretical conditions: the Theological, or fictitious; the Metaphysical, or abstract; and the Scientific, or positive. . . . The first is the necessary point of departure of human understanding, and the third is the fixed and definitive state. The second is merely a transition.[7]*

Satirizing Darwin's Ideas
The heated controversies over Darwin's theory of evolution also spawned innumerable jokes and cartoons. This cartoon depicts a bearded Charles Darwin and the atheistic materialist Emile Littré performing as monkeys in a circus. (Musée de la Ville de Paris, Musée Carnavalet/Archives Charmet/The Bridgeman Art Library)

positivist method Auguste Comte's discipline of sociology, which postulated that each branch of our knowledge passes successively through three different theoretical conditions; the theological, or fictitious; the metaphysical, or abstract; and the scientific, or positive.

evolution The idea, applied by thinkers in many fields, that stresses gradual change and continuous adjustment.

By way of example, Comte noted that the prevailing explanation of cosmic patterns had shifted, as knowledge of astronomy developed, from the will of God (the theological) to the will of an orderly nature (the metaphysical) to the rule of unchanging laws (the scientific). Later, this same intellectual progression took place in increasingly complex fields—physics, chemistry, and, finally, the study of society. Comte believed that by applying the scientific method, also called the **positivist method,** his new discipline of sociology would soon discover the eternal laws of human relations.

Comte's stages of knowledge exemplify the nineteenth-century fascination with the idea of **evolution** and dynamic development. Thinkers in many fields, such as the romantic historians and "scientific" Marxists, shared and applied this basic concept. In geology, Charles Lyell (LAHY-uhl) (1797–1875) effectively discredited the long-standing view that the earth's surface had been formed by short-lived cataclysms, such as biblical floods and earthquakes. Instead, Lyell posited that the earth's surface changed and continues to change over an immensely long time. The evolutionary view of biological development, first proposed by the

Greek Anaximander in the sixth century B.C.E., re-emerged in a more modern form in the work of Jean Baptiste Lamarck (luh-MAHRK) (1744–1829). Lamarck asserted that all forms of life had arisen through a long process of continuous adjustment to the environment.

Lamarck's work was flawed—he believed that the characteristics parents acquired in the course of their lives could be inherited by their children—and was not accepted, but it helped prepare the way for Charles Darwin (1809–1882), the most influential of all nineteenth-century evolutionary thinkers. Convinced by fossil evidence that he had collected and also persuaded by his friend Lyell that the earth and life on it were immensely ancient, Darwin came to doubt the general belief in a special divine creation of each species of animal. Instead, he concluded, all life had gradually evolved from a common ancestral origin in an unending "struggle for survival."

Darwin's great originality lay in suggesting precisely *how* biological evolution might have occurred. His theory is summarized in the title of his work *On the Origin of Species by the Means of Natural Selection* (1859). Decisively influenced by Thomas Malthus's (MAL-thuhs) gloomy theory that populations naturally grow faster than their food supplies (see page 572), Darwin argued that chance differences among the members of a given species help some survive while others die. Thus the variations that prove useful in the struggle for survival are selected naturally and gradually spread to the entire species through reproduction.

Darwin was hailed throughout Europe as the great scientist par excellence, the "Newton of biology," who had revealed once again the powers of objective science. Darwin's findings also reinforced the teachings of secularists such as Comte and Marx, who scornfully dismissed religious belief in favor of agnostic or atheistic materialism. In the great cities especially, religion was on the defensive. Finally, many writers applied the theory of biological evolution to human affairs. Herbert Spencer (1820–1903) saw the idea of the "survival of the fittest" at work in economic progress: the poor were the ill-fated weak; the prosperous were the chosen strong. Understandably, Spencer and other **Social Darwinists** were especially popular with the upper middle class.

Social Darwinists A group of thinkers popular with the upper middle class who saw the human race as driven forward to ever-greater specialization and progress by the unending economic struggle that would determine the survival of the fittest.

realism A literary movement that stressed the depiction of life exactly as it was.

Realism in Literature

In literature, the key themes of **realism** and naturalism emerged in the 1840s and continued to dominate Western culture and style until the 1890s. The major realist writers focused their extraordinary powers of observation on contemporary everyday life. Emphatically rejecting the romantic search for the exotic and the sublime, they energetically pursued the typical and the commonplace. Beginning with a dissection of the middle classes, from which most of them sprang, many realists eventually focused on the urban working classes, which had been neglected in imaginative literature before this time. The realists put a microscope to many unexplored and taboo subjects—sex, strikes, violence, alcoholism—and were charged by middle-class critics with sensationalism and undermining public morality.

Unlike the romantics, who had gloried in individual freedom and an unlimited universe, realists were strict determinists. Human beings, like atoms, were components of the physical world, and all human actions were caused by unalterable natural laws. Heredity and environment determined human behavior; good and evil were merely social conventions.

The realist movement began in France and was home to three of its greatest practitioners—Balzac, Flaubert, and Zola. Honoré de Balzac (BAWL-zak) (1799–1850) spent thirty years writing a vastly ambitious panorama of postrevolutionary

Manet: Emile Zola
The young novelist's sensitivity and strength of character permeate this famous portrait by the great French painter Edouard Manet. Focusing on nuances and subtle variations, Manet was at first denounced by the critics, and after Zola lost a newspaper job defending Manet they became close friends. Manet was strongly influenced by Japanese prints, seen in the background. (Erich Lessing/Art Resource, NY)

French life. Known collectively as *The Human Comedy*, this series of nearly one hundred books vividly portrays more than two thousand characters from virtually all sectors of French society. Balzac pictures urban society as grasping, amoral, and brutal, characterized by a Darwinian struggle for wealth and power.

Madame Bovary (1857), the masterpiece of Gustave Flaubert (**floh-BAIR**) (1821–1880), is far narrower in scope than Balzac's work but unparalleled in its depth and accuracy of psychological insight. The story of a frustrated middle-class housewife who has an adulterous love affair and is betrayed by her lover, *Madame Bovary* portrays the provincial middle class as petty, smug, and hypocritical.

Emile Zola (1840–1902) was most famous for his seamy, animalistic view of working-class life. Like many later realists, Zola sympathized with socialism—a sympathy evident in his overpowering novel *Germinal* (1885).

Realism quickly spread beyond France. In England, Mary Ann Evans (1819–1880), who wrote under the pen name George Eliot, brilliantly achieved a deeply felt, less sensational kind of realism. Her great novel *Middlemarch: A Study of Provincial Life* (1871–1872) examines masterfully the ways in which people are shaped by their social medium as well as their own inner strivings, conflicts, and moral choices. Thomas Hardy (1840–1928) was more in the Zola tradition. His novels, such as *Tess of the D'Urbervilles* (1891) and *The Return of the Native* (1878), depict men and women crushed by society, their own impulses, and bad luck.

The greatest Russian realist, Count Leo Tolstoy (1828–1910), combined realism in description and character development with an atypical moralizing, which came to dominate his later work. Tolstoy's greatest work is *War and Peace* (1864–1869), a monumental novel set against the historical background of Napoleon's invasion of Russia in 1812. Tolstoy went to great pains to develop his fatalistic theory of history, which regards free will as an illusion and the achievements of even the greatest leaders as only the channeling of historical necessity. Yet Tolstoy's central message is one that most of the people discussed in this chapter would have readily accepted: human love, trust, and everyday family ties are life's enduring values.

Section Review

- Scientific breakthroughs began to occur rapidly and their application to industry in the fields of physics, electrical engineering, and organic chemistry encouraged research and development to supplant the unscientific ideas of poets, philosophers, and religion.

- Social scientists studied society using scientific methods such as August Comte's positivist method.

- Charles Darwin built on Lyell's and Lamarck's ideas of evolution to propose that life on earth was immensely ancient and evolved in a slow process without the need for miraculous divine intervention.

- Herbert Spencer and other Social Darwinists applied evolution to human relations, arguing that "survival of the fittest" meant that society should accept the wealthy as the "most fit" and need not help the unsuccessful poor.

- Realism in literature branched away from the romantics and pursued middle and urban working class subjects, believing that heredity and environment were responsible for human behavior.

Chapter Review

What was life like in the cities, and how did urban life change in the nineteenth century? (page 618)

The revolution in industry had a decisive influence on the urban environment. The populations of towns and cities grew rapidly because it was economically advantageous to locate factories and offices in urban areas. This rapid growth worsened long-standing overcrowding and unhealthy living conditions and posed a frightening challenge for society. Eventually government leaders, city planners, reformers, scientists, and ordinary citizens responded. They took effective action in public health and provided themselves with other badly needed urban services. Gradually they tamed the ferocious savagery of the traditional city.

What did the emergence of urban industrial society mean for rich and poor and those in between? (page 622)

As the quality of urban life improved, the class structure became more complex and diversified than before. Urban society featured many distinct social groups, which existed in a state of constant flux and competition. The gap between rich and poor remained enormous and really quite traditional in mature urban society, although there were countless gradations between the extremes. Large numbers of poor women in particular continued to labor as workers in sweated industries, as domestic servants, and as prostitutes in order to satisfy the demands of their masters in the servant-keeping classes.

How did families change as they coped with the challenges and the opportunities of the developing urban civilization? (page 630)

Major changes in family life accompanied the more complex and diversified class system. Especially among the working classes, family life became more stable, more loving, and less mercenary. These improvements had a price, however. Gender roles for men and women became sharply defined and rigidly separate. Women especially tended to be locked into a subordinate and stereotypical role. Nonetheless, on balance, the quality of family life improved for all family members. Better, more stable family relations reinforced the benefits for the masses of higher real wages, increased social security, political participation, and education. Urban society in the late nineteenth century represented a long step forward for humanity, but it remained very unequal.

What major changes in science and thought reflected and influenced the new urban society? (page 636)

Inequality was a favorite theme of realist novelists such as Balzac and Zola. More generally, literary realism reflected Western society's growing faith in science, material progress, and evolutionary thinking. The emergence of urban, industrial civilization accelerated the secularization of the Western worldview.

Key Terms

utilitarianism (p. 619)
germ theory (p. 620)
labor aristocracy (p. 628)
sweated industries (p. 629)
thermodynamics (p. 636)
organic chemistry (p. 637)
positivist method (p. 638)
evolution (p. 638)
Social Darwinists (p. 639)
realism (p. 639)

Notes

1. A. Weber, *The Growth of Cities in the Nineteenth Century* (New York: Columbia University Press, 1899), p. 1.
2. Quoted in E. Chadwick, *Report on the Sanitary Condition of the Labouring Population of Great Britain*, ed. M. W. Flinn (Edinburgh: University of Edinburgh Press, 1965; original publication, 1842), pp. 315–316.

3. Quoted in R. P. Neuman, "The Sexual Question and Social Democracy in Imperial Germany," *Journal of Social History* 7 (Winter 1974): 276.

4. Quoted in R. Roberts, *The Classic Slum: Salford Life in the First Quarter of the Century* (Manchester, England: University of Manchester Press, 1971), p. 35.

5. Quoted in T. Zeldin, *France, 1848–1945*, vol. 1 (Oxford: Clarendon Press, 1973), p. 328.

6. Quoted in Neuman, "The Sexual Question," p. 281.

7. A. Comte, *The Positive Philosophy of Auguste Comte*, trans. H. Martineau, vol. 1 (London: J. Chapman, 1853), pp. 1–2.

To assess your mastery of this chapter, go to **bedfordstmartins.com/mckaywestbrief**

Listening to the Past

Middle-Class Youth and Sexuality

Growing up in Vienna in a prosperous Jewish family, Stephan Zweig (**zwahyg**) (1881–1942) became an influential voice calling for humanitarian values and international culture in early twentieth-century Europe. The following passage from his autobiography, The World of Yesterday (1943), offers a glimpse into late nineteenth-century attitudes toward the sexuality of young adults and Zweig's assessment of the social consequences of these attitudes.

An elegant ball for upper-class youth, with debutantes, junior officers, and vigilant chaperons watching in the background (State Russian Museum, St. Petersburg, Russia/The Bridgeman Art Library)

During the eight years of our higher schooling [beyond grade school], something had occurred which was of great importance to each one of us: we ten-year-olds had grown into virile young men of sixteen, seventeen, and eighteen, and Nature began to assert its rights. . . . It did not take us long to discover that those authorities in whom we had previously confided—school, family, and public morals—manifested an astonishing insincerity in this matter of sex. But what is more, they also demanded secrecy and reserve from us in this connection. . . .

This "social morality," which on the one hand privately presupposed the existence of sexuality and its natural course, but on the other would not recognize it openly at any price, was doubly deceitful. While it winked one eye at a young man and even encouraged him with the other "to sow his wild oats," as the kindly language of the home put it, in the case of a woman it studiously shut both eyes and acted as if it were blind. That a man could experience desires, and was permitted to experience them, was silently admitted by custom. But to admit frankly that a woman could be subject to similar desires, or that creation for its eternal purposes also required a female polarity, would have transgressed the conception of the "sanctity of womanhood." In the pre-Freudian era, therefore, the axiom was agreed upon that a female person could have no physical desires as long as they had not been awakened by man, and that, obviously, was officially permitted only in marriage. . . .

What [sexual] possibilities actually existed for a young man of the middle-class world? . . . Only a very few particularly rich young men could afford the luxury of keeping a mistress, that is, taking an apartment and paying her expenses. And only a very few fortunate young men achieved the literary ideal of love of the times—the only one which it was permitted to describe in novels—an affair with a married woman. The others helped themselves for the most part with shopgirls and waitresses, and this offered little inner satisfaction. . . . But, generally speaking, prostitution was still the foundation of the erotic life outside of marriage; in a certain sense it constituted a dark underground vault over which rose the gorgeous structure of middle-class society with its faultless, radiant façade.

We should not permit ourselves to be misled by sentimental novels or stories of that epoch. It was a bad time for youth. The young girls were hermetically locked up under the control of the family, hindered in their free bodily as well as intellectual development. The young men were forced to secrecy and reticence by a morality which fundamentally no one believed or obeyed. Unhampered, honest relationships—in other words, all that could have made youth happy and joyous according to the laws of Nature—were permitted only to the very few.

Questions for Analysis

1. According to Zweig, how did the sex lives of young middle-class women and young middle-class men differ? What accounted for these differences?

2. Was there nonetheless a basic underlying unity in the way society treated both the young men and the young women of the comfortable middle class? If so, what was that unity?

3. Zweig ends this passage with a value judgment: "It was a bad time for youth." Do you agree or disagree? Why?

Source: "Middle-Class Youth and Sexuality," from *The World of Yesterday* by Stephan Zweig, translated by Helmut Ripperger, copyright © 1943 by the Viking Press, Inc. Used by permission of Viking Penguin, a division of Penguin Group (USA) Inc., and Williams Verlag AG.

CHAPTER 25

The Age of Nationalism

1850–1914

France's Napoleon III and Empress Eugénie greet Britain's Queen Victoria and Prince Albert in a dazzling ceremony in Paris in 1855.

(The Royal Collection, © 2008 Her Majesty Queen Elizabeth II)

Chapter Preview

Napoleon III in France
How in France did Napoleon III seek to reconcile popular and conservative forces in an authoritarian nation-state?

Nation Building in Italy and Germany
How did the process of unification in Italy and Germany create conservative nation-states?

Nation Building in the United States
In what ways did the United States experience the full drama of nation building?

The Modernization of Russia and the Ottoman Empire
What steps did Russia and the Ottoman Turks take toward modernization, and how successful were they?

The Responsive National State (1871–1914)
Why after 1871 did ordinary citizens feel a growing loyalty to their governments?

Marxism and the Socialist Movement
Why did the socialist movement grow, and how revolutionary was it?

INDIVIDUALS IN SOCIETY: Theodor Herzl

LISTENING TO THE PAST: The Making of a Socialist

The revolutions of 1848 closed one era and opened another. Urban industrial society began to take a strong hold on the continent and in the young United States, as it already had in Great Britain. Internationally, the repressive peace and diplomatic stability of Metternich's time were replaced by a period of war and rapid change. In thought and culture, exuberant romanticism gave way to hardheaded realism. In the Atlantic economy, the hard years of the 1840s were followed by good times and prosperity throughout most of the 1850s and 1860s. Perhaps most important of all, Western society progressively developed, for better or worse, a new and effective organizing principle capable of coping with the many-sided challenge of the dual revolution and the emerging urban civilization. That principle was nationalism—dedication to an identification with the nation-state.

The triumph of nationalism is an enormously significant historical development that was by no means completely predictable. After all, nationalism had been a powerful force since at least 1789, but it had repeatedly failed to realize its goals, most spectacularly so in 1848. Yet by 1914 nationalism had become in one way or another an almost universal faith in Europe and in the United States, a faith that had evolved to appeal not only to predominately middle-class liberals but also to the broad masses of society. To understand this fateful evolution is the task of this chapter.

Napoleon III in France

How in France did Napoleon III seek to reconcile popular and conservative forces in an authoritarian nation-state?

The ideas of nationhood and popular sovereignty posed a fearful revolutionary threat to conservatives like Metternich. Yet from the vantage point of the twenty-first century, it is clear that nationalism wears many masks: it may be narrowly liberal or democratic and radical, as it was for Mazzini and Michelet, but it can also flourish in dictatorial states, which may be conservative, fascist, or communist. Napoleon I's France had already combined national feeling with authoritarian rule. Significantly, it was Napoleon's nephew, Louis Napoleon, who revived and extended this merger. In doing so, he provided a model for political leaders elsewhere.

The Second Republic and Louis Napoleon Although Louis Napoleon Bonaparte had played no part in French politics before 1848, he was elected president by a resounding majority. There were several reasons for his success. First, he had the great name of his uncle, whom romantics had transformed through legend from a dictator into a hero. Second, middle-class and peasant property owners wanted a tough ruler to curb the socialist agitation of workers. Third, in late 1848 Louis Napoleon had a positive "program" for France, which had been elaborated in widely circulated pamphlets before the election. He argued that the state and its leader had a sacred duty to provide jobs and stimulate the economy. Large numbers of French peasants and workers believed his claim that he would champion the interests of all classes.

Elected to a four-year term, President Louis Napoleon had to share power with a conservative National Assembly. But in 1851, after the Assembly failed to change the constitution so he could run for a second term, Louis Napoleon seized power in a coup d'état. Restoring universal male suffrage, Louis Napoleon called on the French people, as his uncle had done, to legalize his actions. They did: 92 percent voted to make him president for ten years. A year later, by the greatest electoral margin yet, the authoritarian Louis Napoleon was made emperor of the French nation.

Napoleon III's Second Empire

Louis Napoleon—now proclaimed Emperor Napoleon III—experienced both success and failure between 1852 and 1870. His greatest success was with the economy, particularly in the 1850s. His government encouraged the new investment banks and massive railroad construction that were at the heart of the Industrial Revolution on the continent. The government also fostered general economic expansion through an ambitious program of public works, which included the rebuilding of Paris to improve the urban environment (see page 621). Profits soared while unemployment declined.

Louis Napoleon aimed to garner the support of workers as well as business owners. In the 1850s he regulated pawnshops, supported credit unions, and provided better housing for the working classes. In the 1860s, he granted workers the right to form unions and the right to strike—important economic rights denied by earlier governments.

At first, political power remained in the hands of the emperor. At the same time, Napoleon III restricted but did not abolish the Assembly. Members were elected by universal male suffrage every six years, and Louis Napoleon and his government took the parliamentary elections very seriously. By persuading voters that the election of government candidates was the key to roads, tax rebates, and a thousand other benefits, Napoleon III's supporters won big victories in 1857 and 1863. Yet in the 1860s, Napoleon III encountered opposition when he attempted to reorganize Europe on the principle of nationality and gain influence and territory for France and himself in the process. Problems in Italy and the rising power of Prussia led to increasing criticism at home. With increasing effectiveness, the middle-class liberals who had always wanted a less authoritarian regime continued to denounce his rule.

Napoleon was always sensitive to the public mood. Public opinion, he once said, always wins the last victory. Thus in the 1860s, he progressively liberalized his empire. He gave the Assembly greater powers and the opposition candidates greater freedom, which they used to good advantage. In 1869 the opposition, consisting of republicans, monarchists, and liberals, polled almost 45 percent of the vote.

The next year, a sick and weary Louis Napoleon again granted France a new constitution, which combined a basically parliamentary regime with a hereditary emperor as chief of state. In a final great plebiscite on the eve of the disastrous war with Prussia, 7.5 million Frenchmen voted in favor of the new constitution, and only 1.5 million opposed it. Napoleon III's attempt to reconcile a strong national state with universal male suffrage was still evolving and was doing so in a democratic direction.

CHRONOLOGY

1852–1871	Reign of Napoleon III in France
1859–1870	Unification of Italy
1860–1900	Industrialization of Russia
1861	Freeing of Russian serfs
1861–1865	U.S. Civil War
1866	Austro-Prussian War
1870–1871	Franco-Prussian War
1870–1878	Kulturkampf, Bismarck's attack on Catholic Church
1880s	Educational reforms affect Catholic schools in France
1883	First social security laws to help workers in Germany
1905	Bloody Sunday in Russia
1908	Young Turks in Power

Section Review

- Louis Napoleon Bonaparte had several things in his favor: his name, the middle and peasant classes wanted a tough ruler, and he had a positive program for the economy.

- After his election he shared power with the National Assembly but when they would not allow him to run again, he seized power, successfully faced re-election and then took the title of emperor Napoleon III, ending the Second Republic.

- Napoleon III liberalized the Second Empire, improving the French economy through his public works program, and allowing universal male suffrage, but by the late 1860s, facing an imminent war with Prussia, his power waned in favor of the Assembly and a new constitution.

Nation Building in Italy and Germany

How did the process of unification in Italy and Germany create conservative nation-states?

Louis Napoleon's triumph in 1848 and his authoritarian rule in the 1850s provided the old ruling classes of Europe with a new model in politics. To what extent might the expanding urban middle classes and even portions of the growing working classes rally to a strong and essentially conservative national state? This was one of the great political questions in the 1850s and 1860s. In central Europe, a resounding answer came with the national unification of Italy and Germany.

Cavour and Garibaldi in Italy

Italy, which had been a collection of competing city-states during the Middle Ages and Renaissance, was reorganized at the Congress of Vienna in 1815. The rich northern provinces of Lombardy and Venetia were taken by Metternich's Austria. Sardinia and Piedmont were under the rule of an Italian monarch, and Tuscany, with its famous capital Florence, shared north-central Italy with several smaller states. Central Italy and Rome were ruled by the papacy; Naples and Sicily were ruled, as they had been for almost a hundred years, by a branch of the Bourbons. Metternich was not wrong in dismissing Italy as "a geographical expression."

Between 1815 and 1848, the goal of an Italian nation captured the imaginations of many Italians. For many, the kingdom of Sardinia-Piedmont was ideally suited to achieve the goal of national unification. Its constitution provided for a fair degree of civil liberties and real parliamentary government, with deputies elected by a limited franchise based on income. Its leaders had the diplomatic and military skills needed to unify the peninsula.

Sardinia was ruled by King Victor Emmanuel, who had appointed Count Camillo Benso di Cavour (**kah-VOOR**) to prime minister in 1850. A brilliant statesman, Cavour came from a noble family, but he had also made a substantial fortune in business before entering politics. Cavour's national goals were limited and realistic. Until 1859 he sought unity only for the states of northern and perhaps central Italy in a greatly expanded kingdom of Sardinia.

In the 1850s, Cavour worked to consolidate Sardinia as a liberal constitutional state capable of leading northern Italy. His program of highways and railroads, of civil liberties and opposition to clerical privilege, increased support for Sardinia throughout northern Italy. Yet Cavour realized that Victor Emmanuel could not drive Austria out of Lombardy and Venetia and unify northern Italy without the help of a powerful ally. Accordingly, he worked for a secret diplomatic alliance with Napoleon III against Austria.

Finally, in July 1858 Cavour succeeded and goaded Austria into attacking Sardinia in 1859. Napoleon III came to Sardinia's defense. Then, after the victory of the combined Franco-Sardinian forces, Napoleon III did a sudden about-face. Deciding it was not in his interest to have too strong a state on his southern border and criticized by French Catholics for supporting the pope's declared enemy, Napoleon III abandoned Cavour and made a compromise peace with the Austrians.

Yet Cavour's plans were salvaged by the skillful maneuvers of his allies in the moderate nationalist movement. While the war against Austria had raged in the north, nationalists in central Italy had fanned popular revolts and driven out their easily toppled princes. With the nationalists holding firm, Cavour gained Napoleon III's support by ceding Savoy and Nice to France. The people of central Italy then voted overwhelmingly to join a greatly enlarged kingdom of Sardinia-Piedmont. Cavour had achieved his original goal of a northern Italian state (see Map 25.1).

Meanwhile, in southern Italy, nationalists united under the superpatriot Giuseppe Garibaldi (juh-SEP-ee gar-uh-BAWL-dee) (1807–1882). The son of a poor sailor, Garibaldi personified the romantic, revolutionary nationalism and republicanism of Mazzini and 1848. Partly to use him and partly to get rid of him, Cavour secretly supported Garibaldi's bold plan to "liberate" the kingdom of the Two Sicilies. Landing on the shores of Sicily in May 1860, Garibaldi's guerrilla band of a thousand **Red Shirts** captured the imagination of the Sicilian peasantry. With their support, the guerrilla leader took Palermo. Then he and his men crossed to the mainland, marched triumphantly toward Naples, and prepared to attack Rome and the pope. But the wily Cavour quickly sent his forces to intercept Garibaldi.

Cavour realized that an attack on Rome would bring about war with France, and he also feared Garibaldi's radicalism and popular appeal. Thus he immediately organized a plebiscite in the conquered territories. Despite the urging of some radical supporters, the patriotic Garibaldi did not oppose Cavour, and the people

Red Shirts The guerrilla army of Giuseppe Garibaldi, who invaded Sicily in 1860 in an attempt to liberate it and won the hearts of the Sicilian peasantry.

Kingdom of Sardinia before 1859

To Kingdom of Sardinia, 1859

To Kingdom of Sardinia, 1860

To Kingdom of Italy, 1866, 1870

⭐ Major battle

▬ Boundary of Kingdom of Italy after unification

MAP 25.1 The Unification of Italy, 1859–1870

The leadership of Sardinia-Piedmont, nationalist fervor, and Garibaldi's attack on the kingdom of Two Sicilies were decisive factors in the unification of Italy.

of the south voted to join Sardinia. When Garibaldi and Victor Emmanuel rode through Naples to cheering crowds, they symbolically sealed the union of north and south, of monarch and nation-state.

Cavour had succeeded. He had controlled Garibaldi and had turned popular nationalism in a conservative direction. The new kingdom of Italy, which expanded to include Venice in 1866 and Rome in 1870, was a parliamentary monarchy under Victor Emmanuel, neither radical nor democratic. Despite political unity, only a small minority of Italian males had the right to vote. The propertied classes and the common people were divided. A great and growing social and cultural gap separated the progressive, industrializing north from the stagnant, agrarian south. The new Italy was united on paper, but profound divisions remained.

Bismarck and the Austro-Prussian War (1866)

In the aftermath of 1848, the German states were locked in a political stalemate. After Austria and Russia blocked Frederick William's attempt to unify Germany "from above," tension grew between Austria and Prussia.

At the same time, powerful economic forces were contributing to the Austro-Prussian rivalry. By the end of 1853, Austria was the only German state that had not joined the German customs union, or **Zollverein.** Middle-class and business groups in the Zollverein were enriching themselves and finding solid economic reasons to bolster their idealistic support of national unification. Prussia's leading role within the Zollverein gave it a valuable advantage in its struggle against Austria's supremacy in German political affairs.

Prussia's king William I (r. 1861–1888), who had replaced the unstable Frederick William IV, was convinced of the need for a larger army, which meant a bigger defense budget and higher taxes. His plans were opposed by parliament, however, which was in the hands of the liberal middle class. The wealthy middle class wanted society to be less, not more, militaristic. Above all, middle-class representatives wanted to establish once and for all that the parliament, not the king, had the ultimate political power and that the army was responsible to Prussia's elected representatives. King William then called on Count Otto von Bismarck to head a new ministry and defy the parliament. This was a momentous choice.

The most important figure in German history between Luther and Hitler, Otto von Bismarck (1815–1898) was a master of politics and a devoted servant of his Prussian sovereign. "One must always have two irons in the fire," he once said. He kept his options open, pursuing one policy and then another as he moved with skill and cunning toward his goal.

When the aristocratic Bismarck took office as chief minister in 1862, he made a strong but unfavorable impression. Declaring that the government would rule without parliamentary consent, Bismarck lashed out at the middle-class opposition: "The great questions of the day will not be decided by speeches and resolutions—that was the blunder of 1848 and 1849—but by blood and iron." Bismarck had the Prussian bureaucracy go right on collecting taxes, even though the parliament refused to approve the budget. Bismarck reorganized the army. And for four years, from 1862 to 1866, the voters of Prussia continued to express their opposition by sending large liberal majorities to the parliament.

Opposition at home spurred the search for success abroad. An opportunity presented itself in 1864, when the Danish king tried again, as in 1848, to bring the provinces into a more centralized Danish state against the will of the German Confederation. Prussia joined Austria in a short and successful war against Den-

Zollverein A German customs union founded in 1834 to stimulate trade and increase the revenues of member states.

mark. However, Bismarck was convinced that Austria should be expelled from German affairs so that Prussia could be in control. He knew that a war with Austria would have to be a localized one that would not provoke a mighty alliance against Prussia. By skillfully neutralizing Russia and France, he was in a position to engage in a war of his own making.

The Austro-Prussian War of 1866 lasted only seven weeks. Utilizing railroads to mass troops and the new breechloading needle gun to achieve maximum firepower, the reorganized Prussian army overran northern Germany and defeated Austria decisively at the Battle of Sadowa (**SAD-daw-vah**) in Bohemia. Anticipating Prussia's future needs, Bismarck offered Austria realistic, even generous, peace terms. Austria paid no reparations and lost no territory to Prussia, although Venetia was ceded to Italy. But the German Confederation was dissolved, and Austria agreed to withdraw from German affairs. The states north of the Main River were grouped in the new North German Confederation, led by an expanded Prussia. The mainly Catholic states of the south remained independent while forming alliances with Prussia. Bismarck's fundamental goal of Prussian expansion was being realized (see Map 25.2).

The Taming of the Parliament

In the aftermath of victory, Bismarck fashioned a federal constitution for the new North German Confederation. Each state retained its own local government, but the king of Prussia became president of the confederation, and the chancellor—Bismarck—was responsible only to the president. King and chancellor controlled the army and foreign affairs. There was also a legislature with members of the lower house elected by universal male suffrage. With this radical innovation, Bismarck opened the door to popular participation and the possibility of going over the head of the middle class directly to the people, much as Napoleon III had done in France. All the while, however, ultimate power rested in the hands of Prussia and its king and army.

Marshaling all his diplomatic skill, Bismarck reached out to parliament and asked them to pass a special indemnity bill to approve after the fact all the government's spending between 1862 and 1866. Most of the liberals jumped at the chance to cooperate. With German unity in sight, the German middle class accepted the conservative, authoritarian government that Bismarck represented. In the years before 1914, the values of the aristocratic Prussian army officer increasingly replaced those of the middle-class liberal in public esteem and set the social standard.[1]

The Franco-Prussian War (1870–1871)

The final act in the drama of German unification followed quickly. Bismarck realized that a patriotic war with France would drive the south German states into his arms. The French obligingly played their part. The apparent issue—whether a distant relative of Prussia's William I (and France's Napoleon III) might become king of Spain—was only a diplomatic pretext. By 1870 the French leaders of the Second Empire, goaded by Bismarck and alarmed by their powerful new neighbor on the Rhine, had decided on a war to teach Prussia a lesson.

As soon as war against France began in 1870, Bismarck had the wholehearted support of the south German states. With other governments standing still—Bismarck's generosity to Austria in 1866 was paying big dividends—German forces under Prussian leadership decisively defeated the main French army at Sedan on

SWEDEN

DENMARK

Baltic Sea

North Sea

SCHLESWIG

• Königsberg
• Danzig
EAST PRUSSIA

Kiel •
HOLSTEIN
• Lübeck
POMERANIA
WEST PRUSSIA

Hamburg
MECKLENBURG

RUSSIAN EMPIRE

Bremen
OLDENBURG
HANOVER

Elbe R.
BRANDENBURG

P R U S S I A

Vistula R.

• Warsaw

• Amsterdam
NETHERLANDS
• Hanover
• Berlin
POSEN

WESTPHALIA
• Essen

Warta R.

POLAND

• Antwerp

Ruhr R.

Leipzig •

Mulde R.

Oder R.

BELGIUM

• Cologne
Bonn •
RHINE PROVINCE

Weimar •
Dresden •
SAXONY

SILESIA

Sadowa
1866

• Kraków

Moselle R.

Frankfurt •

Main R.

Prague •
BOHEMIA

Olmütz •

Sedan
1870
• Luxembourg

Rhine R.

Neckar R.

• Nuremberg

Vltava R.

MORAVIA

Morava R.

Verdun •
LORRAINE
Karlsruhe •
BAVARIA
WÜRTTEMBERG

Danube R.

A U S T R I A N   E M P I R E

Nancy •
• Stuttgart

Vienna •

Strasbourg •
ALSACE
• Munich

Inn R.

Pest
Buda •

BADEN

FRANCE

SWITZERLAND
• Innsbruck

0   50   100 Km.
0   50   100 Mi.

ITALY

★ Major battle
—— German Confederation boundary, 1815–1866
—— Bismarck's German Empire, 1871

Prussia before 1866

Conquered by Prussia in Austro-Prussian War, 1866

Austrian territories excluded from North German Confederation, 1867

Joined with Prussia to form North German Confederation, 1867

South German states joining with Prussia to form German Empire, 1871

Won by Prussia in Franco-Prussian War, 1871

MAPPING THE PAST

Map 25.2   The Unification of Germany, 1866–1871

This map shows how Prussia expanded and a new German empire was created through two wars, the Austro-Prussian War of 1866 and the Franco-Prussian War of 1870–1871. It deserves careful study because it highlights how central Europe was remade and the power of Prussia-Germany was greatly increased. **[1]** What were the results of the Austro-Prussian War? Specifically, how did Prussia treat its neighbors in the north, such as Hanover and Saxony? **[2]** What losses did Austria experience in 1866? **[3]** What were the results of the Franco-Prussian War for France and for the predominately Catholic states of southern Germany, such as Bavaria and Württemberg?

September 1, 1870. Louis Napoleon himself was captured and humiliated. Three days later, French patriots in Paris proclaimed yet another French republic and vowed to continue fighting. But after five months, in January 1871, a starving Paris surrendered, and France went on to accept Bismarck's harsh peace terms. By this time, the south German states had agreed to join a new German empire.

Proclaiming the German Empire, January 1871
This commemorative painting by Anton von Werner testifies to the nationalistic intoxication in Germany after the victory over France. William I of Prussia stands on a platform surrounded by princes and generals in the famous Hall of Mirrors in the palace of Versailles, while officers from all the units around a besieged Paris cheer and salute him with uplifted swords as emperor of a unified Germany. Bismarck, like a heroic white knight, stands between king and army. (akg-images)

The victorious William I was proclaimed emperor of Germany in the Hall of Mirrors in the palace of Versailles. Europe had a nineteenth-century German "sun king." As in the 1866 constitution, the king of Prussia and his ministers had ultimate power in the new German Empire, and the lower house of the legislature was elected by universal male suffrage.

The Franco-Prussian War released an enormous surge of patriotic feeling in Germany while poisoning relations with France. Prussia had become, with fortification by the other German states, the most powerful state in Europe in less than a decade. Most Germans were enormously proud, blissfully imagining themselves the fittest and best of the European species. Semi-authoritarian nationalism and a "new conservatism," which was based on an alliance of the propertied classes and sought the active support of the working classes, had triumphed in Germany.

Nation Building in the United States

In what ways did the United States experience the full drama of nation building?

Closely linked to European developments in the nineteenth century, the United States experienced the full drama of bloody nation building. The "United" States was divided by slavery from its birth, as economic development in the young republic carried free and slaveholding states in very different directions. Northerners extended family farms westward and began building English-model factories in the Northeast. By 1850 an industrializing, urbanizing North was also building a system of canals and railroads and attracting most of the European immigrants. In the South, cotton plantations dominated the economy, producing 5 million bales a year and satisfying an apparently insatiable demand from textile mills in Europe and New England.

The rise of the cotton empire revitalized slave-based agriculture, spurred exports, and played a key role in igniting rapid U.S. economic growth. The large profits flowing from cotton also led influential Southerners to defend slavery. Even though three-quarters of all Southern white families were small farmers and owned no slaves in 1850, Southern whites developed a strong cultural identity and came to see themselves as a closely knit "we" distinct from the Northern "they." Northern whites viewed their free-labor system as being morally superior. Thus regional antagonisms intensified.

These antagonisms came to a climax after 1848 when a defeated Mexico ceded to the United States a vast area stretching from west Texas to the Pacific Ocean. Debate over the extension of slavery in this new territory caused attitudes to harden on both sides. In Abraham Lincoln's famous words, the United States was a "house divided."

Lincoln's election as president in 1860 gave Southern "fire-eaters" the chance they had been waiting for. Eventually eleven states left the Union, determined to win their own independence, and formed the Confederate States of America. When Southern troops fired on a Union fort in South Carolina's Charleston harbor, war began.

The long Civil War (1861–1865) was the bloodiest conflict in American history, but in the end the South was decisively defeated and the Union preserved. While Northern causalities were high, many people there prospered during the war years and certain dominant characteristics of American life and national culture took shape. Powerful business corporations emerged, steadfastly supported by the Republican party during and after the war. The **Homestead Act** of 1862, which gave western land to settlers, and the Thirteenth Amendment of 1865, which ended slavery, reinforced the concept of free labor taking its chances in a market economy. Finally, the triumph of the Union seemed to confirm that the nation's "manifest destiny" was indeed to straddle a continent as a great world power. Thus a new American nationalism grew out of civil war.

Homestead Act A result of the American Civil War that gave western land to settlers, reinforcing the concept of free labor in a market economy.

Section Review

- Differences between the urbanized North and the agricultural slave-owning plantations in the South led to the American Civil War.
- The factories and free market society of the North were victorious over Southern rebels in the Civil War, fostering a new American nationalism.
- The Homestead Act providing western land to settlers and the abolishment of slavery reinforced the concept of "manifest destiny," that the Union was destined to occupy the continent and become a great nation.

The Modernization of Russia and the Ottoman Empire

What steps did Russia and the Ottoman Turks take toward modernization, and how successful were they?

The Russian and the Ottoman empires also experienced profound political crises in the mid-nineteenth century. These crises were unlike those occurring in Italy and Germany, for neither Russia nor the Ottoman Empire aspired to build a single powerful state out of a jumble of principalities. Both empires were already vast multinational states, built on long traditions of military conquest and absolutist rule by elites from the dominant ethnic groups—the Russians and the Ottoman Turks. In the early nineteenth century these governing elites in both states were strongly opposed to representative government and national self-determination, and they continued to concentrate on absolutist rule and competition with other great powers.

For both states relentless power politics led to serious trouble. It became clear to the leaders of both empires that they had to embrace the process of **modernization**,

modernization The changes that enable a country to compete effectively with the leading countries at a given time.

defined narrowly and usefully as the changes that enable a country to compete effectively with the leading countries at a given time. This limited conception of modernization fits Russia after the Crimean War particularly well, and it helps explain developments in the Ottoman Empire.

The "Great Reforms"

In the 1850s, almost 90 percent of the Russian population lived on the land and industry was little developed. Agricultural techniques were backward, and serfdom was still the basic social institution. Bound to the lord on a hereditary basis, the peasant serf was little more than a slave.

Serfdom had become the great moral and political issue for the government by the 1840s. Then the Crimean War of 1853 to 1856, arising out of a dispute with France over who should protect certain Christian shrines in the Ottoman Empire, brought crisis. Because the fighting was concentrated in the Crimean peninsula on the Black Sea, Russia's transportation network of rivers and wagons failed to supply the distant Russian armies adequately. France and Great Britain, aided by Sardinia and the Ottoman Empire, inflicted a humiliating defeat on Russia.

This military defeat demonstrated that Russia had fallen behind the rapidly industrializing nations of western Europe. At the very least, Russia needed railroads, better armaments, and reorganization of the army if it was to maintain its international position. Moreover, the disastrous war had caused hardship and raised the specter of massive peasant rebellion. Reform of serfdom was imperative. Military disaster thus forced Alexander II (r. 1855–1881) and his ministers along the path of rapid social change and general modernization.

The first and greatest of the reforms was the freeing of the serfs in 1861. Human bondage was abolished forever, and the emancipated peasants received, on average, about half of the land. Yet they had to pay fairly high prices for their land, and because the land was owned collectively, each peasant village was jointly responsible for the payments of all the families in the village. Collective ownership and responsibility made it very difficult for individual peasants to improve agricultural methods or leave their villages. Thus the effects of the reform were limited.

Most of the later reforms were also halfway measures. In 1864 Alexander II established a new institution of local government, the **zemstvo** (ZEMST-voh). Russian liberals hoped that this reform would lead to an elected national parliament, but they were soon disappointed. The local zemstvo remained subordinate to the traditional bureaucracy and the local nobility. More successful was reform of the legal system, which established independent courts and equality before the law. Education and policies toward Russian Jews were also liberalized somewhat, and censorship was relaxed but not removed.

Until the twentieth century, Russia's greatest strides toward modernization were economic rather than political. Industry and transport, both so vital to the military, were transformed when the government subsidized private railway companies. The railroads enabled agricultural Russia to export grain and thus earn money for further industrialization. Industrial suburbs grew up around Moscow and St. Petersburg, and a class of modern factory workers began to take shape.

Industrial development strengthened Russia's military forces and gave rise to territorial expansion to the south and east. Imperial expansion greatly excited many ardent Russian nationalists and superpatriots, who became some of the government's most enthusiastic supporters. Industrial development also contributed mightily to the spread of Marxian thought and the transformation of the Russian revolutionary movement after 1890.

zemstvo A new institution of local government in reformed Russia, whose members were elected by a three-class system of towns, peasant villages, and noble landowners.

In 1881 Alexander II was assassinated by a small group of terrorists. The era of reform came to an abrupt end, for the new tsar (**zahr**), Alexander III (r. 1881–1894), was a determined reactionary. Nevertheless, economic modernization sped forward under Sergei Witte (**sur-GEY VIT-uh**), the tough, competent minister of finance from 1892 to 1903. Inspired by the writings of Friedrich List (see pages 575–576), Witte believed that the harsh reality of industrial backwardness was threatening Russia's power and greatness.

Therefore, under Witte's leadership the government built state-owned railroads rapidly, doubling the network to thirty-five thousand miles by the end of the century. Witte established high protective tariffs to build Russian industry, and he put the country on the gold standard of the "civilized world" in order to strengthen Russian finances.

Witte's greatest innovation was to use the West to catch up with the West. His efforts to entice Westerners to locate their factories in Russia were especially successful in southern Russia. There, in eastern Ukraine, foreign capitalists and their engineers built an enormous and very modern steel and coal industry.[2] In 1900 peasants still constituted the great majority of the population, but Russia was catching up with the industrialized West.

The Revolution of 1905

Catching up partly meant vigorous territorial expansion, for this was the age of Western imperialism. By 1903 Russia had established a sphere of influence in Chinese Manchuria and was eyeing northern Korea. When the diplomatic protests of equally imperialistic Japan were ignored, the Japanese launched a surprise attack in February 1904. After Japan scored repeated victories, Russia was forced in September 1905 to accept a humiliating defeat.

As is often the case, military disaster abroad brought political upheaval at home. The business and professional classes had long wanted a liberal, representative government. Urban factory workers had all the grievances of early industrialization and were organized in a radical and still illegal labor movement. Peasants had gained little from the era of reforms and were suffering from poverty and overpopulation. At the same time, nationalist sentiment was emerging among the empire's minorities, and subject nationalities such as the Poles and Ukrainians were calling for self-rule. With the army pinned down in Manchuria, all these currents of discontent converged in the **revolution of 1905.**

On a Sunday in January 1905, a massive crowd of workers and their families converged peacefully on the Winter Palace in St. Petersburg to present a petition to Tsar Nicholas II (1894–1917). Suddenly troops opened fire, killing and wounding hundreds. The **Bloody Sunday** massacre turned ordinary workers against the tsar and produced a wave of general indignation.

Outlawed political parties came out into the open, and by the summer of 1905 strikes, peasant uprisings, revolts among minority nationalities, and troop mutinies were sweeping the country. The revolutionary surge culminated in October 1905 in a great paralyzing general strike, which forced the government to capitulate. The tsar issued the **October Manifesto,** which granted full civil rights and promised a popularly elected **Duma** (**DOO-muh**) (parliament) with real legislative power. The manifesto split the opposition. Frightened middle-class leaders helped the government repress the uprising and survive as a constitutional monarchy.

On the eve of the opening of the first Duma in May 1906, the government issued the new constitution, the Fundamental Laws. The tsar retained great powers. The Duma, elected indirectly by universal male suffrage, and a largely appointive

revolution of 1905 A popular upheaval that overturned absolute tsarist rule and made Russia into a conservative constitutional monarchy.

Bloody Sunday A massacre of peaceful protesters at the Winter Palace in St. Petersberg in 1905 that turned ordinary workers against the tsar and produced a wave of general indignation.

October Manifesto The result of a great general strike in October 1905, it granted full civil rights and promised a popularly elected Duma (parliament) with real legislative power.

Duma The Russian parliament that opened in 1906, elected indirectly by universal male suffrage but controlled after 1907 by the tsar and the conservative classes.

upper house, could debate and pass laws, but the tsar had an absolute veto. As in Bismarck's Germany, the emperor appointed his ministers, who did not need to command a majority in the Duma.

The disappointed, predominately middle-class liberals, the largest group in the newly elected Duma, saw the Fundamental Laws as a step backwards. Efforts to cooperate with the tsar's ministers soon broke down. After months of deadlock, the tsar dismissed the Duma and rewrote the electoral law so as to increase greatly the weight of the propertied classes. When elections were held, the tsar could count on a loyal majority in the Duma. His chief minister then pushed through important agrarian reforms designed to break down collective village ownership of land and encourage the more enterprising peasants—his "wager on the strong." In 1914, Russia was partially modernized, a conservative constitutional monarchy with a peasant-based but industrializing economy.

Decline and Reform in the Ottoman Empire

The Ottoman Empire had reached its high point of development under Suleiman the Magnificent in the sixteenth century. By the eighteenth century it fell rapidly behind western Europe in science, industrial skill, and military technology. Also during the eighteenth century, Russia's powerful westernized army was able to occupy Ottoman provinces on the Danube River.

Pasha Halim Receiving Archduke Maximilian of Austria
As this painting suggests, Ottoman leaders became well versed in European languages and culture. They also mastered the game of power politics, playing one European state off against another and securing the Ottoman Empire's survival. The black servants on the right may be slaves from the Sudan. (Miramare Palace Trieste/Dagli Orti/The Art Archive)

Caught up in the Napoleonic wars and losing more territory to Russia, the Ottomans were forced in 1816 to grant Serbia local autonomy. In 1830, the Greeks won their national independence, while French armies began their long and bloody conquest of Algeria (see page 606). The Ottoman Empire was losing territory and power.

Another threat to the empire came from within, with the rise of Muhammad Ali, the Ottoman governor in Egypt. In 1831, and again in 1839, his French-trained forces occupied the Ottoman provinces of Syria and then Iraq and appeared ready to depose Sultan Mahmud II (r. 1808–1839). The Ottoman sultan survived, but only because the European powers forced Muhammad Ali to withdraw. The European powers, minus France, preferred a weak and dependent Ottoman state to a strong and revitalized Muslim entity under a dynamic leader such as Muhammad Ali.

Realizing their precarious position, liberal Ottoman statesmen launched in 1839 an era of radical reforms, which lasted with fits and starts until 1876 and culminated in a constitution and a short-lived parliament. Known as the **Tanzimat** (**TAHNZ-ee-MAT**) (literally, regulations or orders), these reforms were designed to remake the empire on a western European model. New decrees called for the equality of Muslims, Christians, and Jews before the law and a modernized administration and military. New commercial laws allowed free importation of foreign goods and permitted foreign merchants to operate freely throughout the empire. Of great importance for later developments, growing numbers among the elite and the upwardly mobile embraced Western education and accepted secular values to some extent.

Intended to bring revolutionary modernization, the Tanzimat permitted partial recovery but fell short of its goals for several reasons. First, the liberal reforms failed to halt the growth of nationalism among Christian subjects in the Balkans (see Chapter 27), which resulted in crises and defeats that undermined all reform efforts. Second, the Ottoman initiatives did not curtail the appetite of Western imperialism, which secured a stranglehold on the Ottoman economy. Finally, equality before the law for all citizens and religious communities actually increased religious disputes, which were in turn exacerbated by the relentless interference of the European powers. This development embittered relations between the religious communities, distracted the government from its reform mission, and split Muslims into secularists and religious conservatives. These Islamic conservatives became the most dependable support of Sultan Abdülhamid (**ahb-dool-hah-MEED**) (r. 1876–1909), who abandoned the model of European liberalism in his long and repressive reign.

The combination of declining international power and conservative tyranny eventually led to a powerful resurgence of the modernizing impulse among idealistic Turkish exiles in Europe and young army officers in Istanbul. These fervent patriots, the so-called **Young Turks,** seized power in the revolution of 1908, and they forced the sultan to implement reforms. Failing to stop the rising tide of anti-Ottoman nationalism in the Balkans, the Young Turks helped to prepare the way for the birth of modern secular Turkey after the defeat and collapse of the Ottoman Empire in World War I (see page 705).

Tanzimat A set of reforms that were designed to remake the Ottoman Empire on a western European model.

Young Turks Fervent patriots who seized power in the revolution of 1908 in the Ottoman Empire.

Section Review

- The Russians began to catch up with the West by modernizing, abolishing serfdom, building railroads, and attracting industry from the West, which built huge coal and steel factories.

- The rise in industrialization contributed to the spread of Marxist thought, leading to the Russian revolutionary movement.

- The Revolution of 1905 arose from defeat abroad by the Japanese and upheaval at home; when the army fired on a peaceful demonstration, revolts and strikes began and the tsar issued the October Manifesto, granting civil rights and an elected Duma (parliament).

- The Duma and the new constitution were a disappointment to the middle-class liberals because the tsar rewrote laws to secure his power and that of the propertied classes, ending collective village ownership of land and preserving the conservative constitutional monarchy with a peasant-based but industrialized economy.

- The Ottoman Empire embarked on a partially successful series of reforms, the Tanzimat, in an attempt to gain territory and power, but increasing disputes over religion and Western imperialism allowed the Young Turks to seize power in the revolution of 1908.

The Responsive National State (1871–1914)

Why after 1871 did ordinary citizens feel a growing loyalty to their governments?

For central and western Europe, the unification of Italy and Germany by "blood and iron" marked the end of a dramatic period of nation building. After 1871 the heartland of Europe was organized into strong national states. Only on the borders of Europe—in Ireland and Russia, in Austria-Hungary and the Ottoman Empire—did subject peoples still strive for political unity and independence.

General Trends

Despite some major differences between countries, European domestic politics after 1871 had in common the emergence of mass politics and growing mass loyalty toward the national state.

For good reason, ordinary people felt increasing loyalty to their governments. By 1914 most men had gained the right to vote and felt that they counted; they could influence the government to some extent. They were becoming "part of the system." Women also made some gains in their suffrage movement. By 1913

"Votes for Women!"

The long-simmering campaign for women's suffrage in England came to a rapid boil after 1903, as militants took to the streets, disrupted political meetings, and tried to storm Parliament. Manhandled by the police and often jailed, some activists responded by damaging public property and going on hunger strikes in prison. This 1908 illustration shows demonstrators giving a hero's welcome to Mary Leigh, the first suffragette imprisoned for property damage after she threw rocks through the windows of the prime minister's house. (The Art Archive)

women could vote in twelve of the western United States. In 1914 Norway gave the vote to most women. Elsewhere, the efforts of more militant feminists prepared the way for the triumph of the women's suffrage movement immediately after World War I.

As the right to vote spread, politicians and parties in national parliaments represented the people more responsively. Governments also passed laws to alleviate general problems, thereby acquiring greater legitimacy and appearing more worthy of support.

There was a manipulative aspect to building support for strong nation-states after 1871. Conservative and moderate leaders found that workers who voted socialist would rally around the flag in a diplomatic crisis or cheer when distant territory was seized in Africa or Asia (see Chapter 26). Therefore, after 1871 governing elites frequently used militaristic policies to help manage domestic conflicts, but at the expense of increasing international tensions. Some leaders fanned anti-Semitism in order to unite Christians around their party.

The German Empire

Politics in Germany after 1871 developed within the new framework of a federal union of Prussia and twenty-four smaller states. This federal government was run by a chancellor—until 1890, Bismarck—and a popularly elected lower house, called the **Reichstag** (**RIKES-tog**). Although Bismarck refused to be bound by a parliamentary majority, he tried nonetheless to maintain one. This situation gave the political parties opportunities. For most of his chancellorship Bismarck relied mainly on the National Liberals, who supported legislation useful for further economic and legal unification of the country.

Reichstag The popularly elected lower house of government of the new German Empire after 1871.

Bismarck's moves against the Catholic Church, however, gradually lost the National Liberals their parliamentary majority. Known as the **Kulturkampf** (**kool-TOOR-kahmpf**), or "struggle for civilization," Bismarck's anti-Catholic legislation was a response to Pope Pius IX's declaration of papal infallibility in 1870, which seemed to make the pope and not the government the ultimate source of authority for Catholics. Catholics throughout the country turned to the Catholic Center party, which blocked passage of national laws hostile to the church. Bismarck was forced to abandon his attack and instead court the support of the Catholic Center party, whose supporters included many small farmers in western and southern Germany. By enacting high tariffs on cheap grain from the outside the country, he won over both the Catholic Center and the Protestant Junkers, who had large landholdings in the east. With the tariffs, then, Bismark won Catholic and conservative support.

Kulturkampf A struggle for civilization, Bismarck's attack on the Catholic church resulting from Pius IX's declaration of papal infallibility in 1870.

Bismarck had been looking for a way to increase taxes, and the solution he chose was higher tariffs. Many other governments acted similarly. The 1880s and 1890s saw a widespread return to protectionism. France, in particular, established very high tariffs to protect agriculture and industry, peasants and manufacturers, from foreign competition. Thus the German government and other governments responded effectively to a major economic problem and won greater loyalty. The general rise of protectionism in this period was also an outstanding example of the dangers of self-centered nationalism: new tariffs led to international name-calling and nasty trade wars.

Like other European leaders, Bismarck feared the revolutionary language of socialism. In 1878, after two attempts on the life of William I by radicals (though not socialists), Bismarck used a carefully orchestrated national outcry to ram through the Reichstag a law that outlawed the Social Democratic party and restricted socialist meetings. However, German socialists displayed a discipline and organization worthy of the Prussian army itself. Bismarck decided to try another tack.

Bismarck's new approach was to create social programs that would win him the support of working-class people. In 1883 and 1884 the government established national sickness and accident insurance; in 1889 it established old-age pensions and retirement benefits. This national social security system, paid for through compulsory contributions by wage earners and employers as well as grants from the state, was the first of its kind anywhere. Bismarck's social security system did not wean workers from voting socialist, but it did give them a small stake in the system and protect them from some of the uncertainties of the complex urban industrial world. This enormously significant development was a product of political competition and government efforts to win popular support.

Increasingly, the great issues in German domestic politics were socialism and the Marxian Social Democratic party. In 1890 the new emperor, the young, idealistic, and unstable William II (r. 1888–1918), opposed Bismarck's attempt to renew the law outlawing the Social Democratic party. Eager to rule in his own right and to earn the support of the workers, William II forced Bismarck to resign.

Yet William II was no more successful than Bismarck in getting workers to renounce socialism. Indeed, Social Democrats won more and more seats in the Reichstag, until it became the largest single party in the Reichstag in 1912. This victory shocked aristocrats and their wealthy conservative middle-class allies, heightening the fears of an impending socialist upheaval. Yet the "revolutionary" socialists were actually becoming less radical in Germany. In the years before World War I, the German Social Democratic party broadened its base by adopting a more patriotic tone, allowing for greater military spending and imperialist expansion. German socialists concentrated instead on gradual social and political reform.

Republican France

France's progress toward a unified national state suffered in the immediate aftermath of the Franco-Prussian War (see pages 651–653). Parisians, who had bravely defended their city against Prussian forces, exploded in patriotic frustration when the National Assembly of France agreed to surrender Alsace (**al-SAS**) and Lorraine to Prussia. They proclaimed the Paris Commune in March 1871, with the goal of governing Paris without interference from the conservative French countryside. The National Assembly, led by the aging politician Adolphe Thiers (**tyer**), would hear none of it. The Assembly ordered the French army into Paris and brutally crushed the Commune. Twenty thousand people died in the fighting. As in June 1848, it was Paris against the provinces, French against French.

Out of this tragedy, France slowly formed a new national unity, achieving considerable stability before 1914. How is one to account for this? Luck played a part. Although the monarchists had gained the majority in the National Assembly, they could not find an acceptable king. Meanwhile, the middle class and people from the provinces were persuaded by Thiers's actions that the Third Republic might be moderate and socially conservative. France therefore retained the republic, though reluctantly. As President Thiers cautiously said, this was "the government which divides us least."

Another stabilizing factor was the skill and determination of the moderate republican leaders in the early years. The most famous of these was Léon Gambetta (**gam-BET-uh**), the son of an Italian grocer, a warm, easygoing, unsuccessful lawyer who had turned professional politician. By 1879 the great majority of members of both the upper and the lower houses of the National Assembly were republicans, and the Third Republic had firm foundations after almost a decade.

The moderate republicans sought to endure politically by appealing to the next generation. They worked to expand the state system of public schools, so that conservative Catholic schoolteachers were no longer the primary shapers of young minds. New laws made elementary education for girls and boys both free and compulsory. Public education served to reinforce nationalism and the value of republican government.

Although the educational reforms of the 1880s disturbed French Catholics, many of them rallied to the republic in the 1890s. The limited acceptance of the modern world by the more liberal Pope Leo XIII (1878–1903) eased tensions. The **Dreyfus affair**, however, would lead to the separation of church and state in France.

Dreyfus affair A divisive case in which Alfred Dreyfus, a Jewish captain in the French army was falsely accused and convicted of treason. The Catholic Church sided with the anti-Semites against Dreyfus; after Dreyfus was declared innocent, the French government severed all ties between the state and church.

Alfred Dreyfus, a Jewish captain in the French army, was falsely accused and convicted of treason. In 1898 and 1899, the case split France apart. On one side was the army, which had manufactured evidence against Dreyfus, joined by anti-Semites and most of the Catholic establishment. On the other side stood the civil libertarians and most of the more radical republicans.

This battle, which eventually led to Dreyfus's being declared innocent, revived republican feeling against the church. Between 1901 and 1905, the French government severed all ties to the Catholic Church. The salaries of priests and bishops were no longer paid by the government, and all churches were given to local committees of lay Catholics. Catholic schools were put on their own financially and soon lost a third of their students. In France only the growing socialist movement, with its very different and thoroughly secular ideology, stood in opposition to patriotic, republican nationalism.

Great Britain and Ireland

Britain in the late nineteenth century has often been seen as a shining example of peaceful and successful political evolution, where an effective two-party parliament skillfully guided the country from classical liberalism to full-fledged democracy with hardly a misstep. This view of Great Britain is not so much wrong as it is incomplete. The House of Commons did gradually widen the right to vote, so that by 1884 almost every adult male could participate in elections. The House of Lords, however, remained a bastion of aristocratic conservatism, ruling against labor unions and vetoing several measures passed by the Commons in the first decade of the twentieth century. The turning point came when the Lords vetoed the so-called **People's Budget**, which was designed to increase spending on social welfare services. The king threatened to create enough new peers to pass the bill, and aristocratic conservatism was forced to yield to popular democracy once and for all.

People's Budget A bill proposed after the Liberal party came to power in England in 1906, it was designed to increase spending on social welfare issues, but was vetoed in the House of Lords.

Between 1906 and 1914, extensive social welfare measures, slow to come to Great Britain, were passed in a spectacular rush. During those years, the Liberal party, inspired by the fiery Welshman David Lloyd George (1863–1945), substantially raised taxes on the rich as part of the People's Budget. This income helped the government pay for national health insurance, unemployment benefits, old-age pensions, and a host of other social measures. The state was integrating the urban masses socially as well as politically.

This record of accomplishment was only part of the story, however. On the eve of World War I, the unanswered question of Ireland brought Great Britain to the brink of civil war. The terrible Irish famine had fueled an Irish revolutionary move-

"No Home Rule"

ment. Thereafter, the English slowly granted concessions, such as the abolition of the privileges of the Anglican Church and rights for Irish peasants. Yet the question of self-rule for Ireland was divisive. Bills giving Ireland self-government failed to pass in 1886 and 1893. In 1913, however, Irish nationalists in the British Parliament were able to obtain a new home-rule bill for Ireland.

Within Ireland, the home-rule bill unleashed hostilities between north and south. The Protestants of Ulster in Northern Ireland refused to submerge themselves into Catholic Ireland and vowed to resist home rule in northern counties. By December 1913 they had raised 100,000 armed volunteers, and they were supported by much of English public opinion. Thus in 1914 the Liberals in the House of Lords introduced a compromise home-rule bill that did not apply to the northern counties. This bill, which openly betrayed promises made to Irish nationalists, was rejected, and in September the original home-rule bill was passed but simultaneously suspended for the duration of the hostilities. The momentous Irish question was then overtaken by an earth-shattering world war in August 1914.

Irish developments illustrated once again the power of national movements in the nineteenth century. Moreover, they were proof that governments could not elicit greater loyalty unless they could capture and control that elemental current of national feeling. Though Great Britain had much going for it—power, Parliament, prosperity—none of these availed in the face of the conflicting nationalisms created by Catholics and Protestants in Northern Ireland. Similarly, progressive Sweden was powerless to stop the growth of the Norwegian national movement, which culminated in Norway's breaking away from Sweden and becoming a fully independent nation in 1905. In this light, one can also see how hopeless was the case of the Ottoman Empire in Europe in the later nineteenth century. It was only a matter of time before the Serbs, Bulgarians, and Romanians would break away, and they did.

The Austro-Hungarian Empire

The dilemma of conflicting nationalisms also tore at the Austro-Hungarian Empire in the early twentieth century. In the wake of defeat in the Austro-Prussian War of 1866, a weakened Austria was forced to strike a compromise with its subjects in Hungary who had wanted independence. Through the so-called dual monarchy, the empire was divided, and the nationalistic Magyars gained virtual independence for Hungary. The two states were joined only by a shared monarch and common ministries for finance, defense, and foreign affairs.

The dual monarchy did not diffuse nationalist tensions, however. In Austria, many Germans saw their traditional dominance threatened by Czechs, Poles, and other Slavs. A particularly emotional issue in the Austrian parliament was the language used in government and elementary education at the local level. From 1900 to 1914 the parliament was so divided that ministries generally could not obtain a majority and ruled instead by decree. Even attempts to find common ground on economic issues were unsuccessful. In Hungary the Magyar nobility restricted voting to the wealthiest one-fourth of adult males, making the parliament the creature of the elite. Laws promoting the use of the Magyar (Hungarian) language in schools and government were rammed through and bitterly resented, especially by the Croatians and Romanians. While Hungarian extremists campaigned loudly for total separation from Austria, Croatian and Romanian radicals agitated for independence from Hungary. Unlike most major countries, which harnessed nationalism to strengthen the state after 1871, the Austro-Hungarian Empire was progressively weakened and destroyed by it.

Jewish Emancipation and Modern Anti-Semitism

Revolutionary changes in politics brought equally revolutionary changes in Jewish life in western and central Europe. The decisive turning point came in 1848, when Jews formed part of the revolutionary vanguard in Vienna and Berlin and the Frankfurt Assembly endorsed full rights for German Jews. In 1871 the constitution of the new German Empire consolidated the process of Jewish emancipation in central Europe. It abolished all restrictions on Jewish marriage, choice of occupation, place of residence, and property ownership. Exclusion from government employment and discrimination in social relations remained. However, according to one leading historian, by 1871 "it was widely accepted in Central Europe that the gradual disappearance of anti-Jewish prejudice was inevitable."[3]

The process of emancipation presented Jews with challenges and opportunities. Traditional Jewish occupations, such as court financial agent, village moneylender, and peddler, were undermined by free-market reforms, but careers in business, the professions, and the arts were opening to Jewish talent. By 1871 a majority of Jewish people in western and central Europe had improved their economic situation and entered the middle classes. Most Jewish people also identified strongly with their respective nation-states and with good reason saw themselves as patriotic citizens.

Vicious anti-Semitism reappeared after the stock market crash of 1873, beginning in central Europe. While Europe had a long history of anti-Semitism, this time it had modern elements. Resentment was aimed against Jewish achievement and Jewish "financial control," while fanatics claimed that the Jewish race (rather than the Jewish religion) posed a biological threat to the German people. Anti-Semitic beliefs were particularly popular among conservatives, extremist nationalists, and people who felt threatened by Jewish competition, such as small shopkeepers, officeworkers, and professionals.

Anti-Semites also created modern political parties to attack and degrade Jews. In Austrian Vienna in the early 1890s, Karl Lueger (**LEW-ay-ger**) and his "Christian socialists" won striking electoral victories, spurring Theodor Herzl to turn from German nationalism and advocate political **Zionism** and the creation of a Jewish state. (See the feature "Individuals in Society: Theodor Herzl.") Lueger, the popular mayor of Vienna from 1897 to 1910, combined fierce anti-Semitic rhetoric with municipal ownership of basic services, and he appealed especially to

Zionism A movement toward Jewish political nationhood, started by Theodor Herzl.

Individuals in Society

Theodor Herzl

In September 1897, only days after his vision and energy had called into being the First Zionist Congress in Basel, Switzerland, Theodor Herzl (1860–1904) assessed the results in his diary: "If I were to sum up the Congress in a word—which I shall take care not to publish—it would be this: At Basel I founded the Jewish state. If I said this out loud today I would be greeted by universal laughter. In five years perhaps, and certainly in fifty years, everyone will perceive it."* Herzl's buoyant optimism, which so often carried him forward, was prophetic. Leading the Zionist movement until his death at age forty-four in 1904, Herzl guided the first historic steps toward modern Jewish political nationhood and the creation of Israel in 1948.

Theodor Herzl was born in Budapest, Hungary, into an upper-middle-class, German-speaking Jewish family. When Herzl was eighteen, his family moved to Vienna, where he studied law. As a university student, he soaked up the liberal beliefs of most well-to-do Viennese Jews, who also championed the assimilation of German culture. Wrestling with his nonreligious Jewishness and his strong pro-German feeling, Herzl embraced German nationalism and joined a German dueling fraternity. There he discovered that full acceptance required openly anti-Semitic attitudes and a repudiation of all things Jewish. This Herzl could not tolerate, and he resigned. After receiving his law degree, he embarked on a literary career. In 1889 Herzl married into a wealthy Viennese Jewish family, but he and his socialite wife were mismatched and never happy together.

Herzl achieved considerable success as both a journalist and a playwright. His witty comedies focused on the bourgeoisie, including Jewish millionaires trying to live like aristocrats. Accepting many German stereotypes, Herzl sometimes depicted eastern Jews as uneducated and grasping. But as a dedicated, highly educated liberal, he mainly believed that the Jewish shortcomings he

perceived were the results of age-old persecution and would disappear through education and assimilation. Herzl also took a growing pride in Jewish steadfastness in the face of victimization and suffering. He savored memories of his early Jewish education and going with his father to the synagogue.

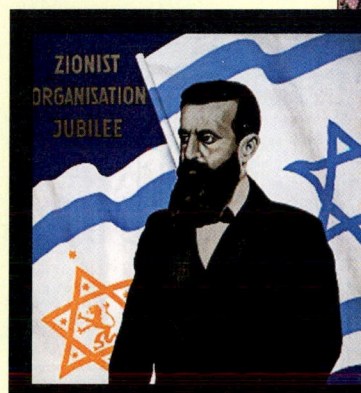

Theodor Herzl (Library of Congress)

The emergence of modern anti-Semitism shocked Herzl, as it did many acculturated Jewish Germans. Moving to Paris in 1891 as the correspondent for Vienna's leading liberal newspaper, Herzl studied politics and pondered recent historical developments. He then came to a bold conclusion, published in 1896 as *The Jewish State: An Attempt at a Modern Solution to the Jewish Question*. According to Herzl, Jewish assimilation had failed, and attempts to combat anti-Semitism would never succeed. Only by building an independent Jewish state could the Jewish people achieve dignity and renewal. As recent scholarship shows, Herzl developed his political nationalism, or Zionism, before the anti-Jewish agitation accompanying the Dreyfus affair, which only strengthened his faith in his analysis.

Generally rebuffed by skeptical Jewish elites in western and central Europe, Herzl turned for support to youthful idealists and the poor Jewish masses. He became an inspiring man of action, rallying the delegates to the annual Zionist congresses, directing the growth of the worldwide Zionist organization, and working himself to death. Herzl also understood that national consciousness required powerful emotions and symbols, such as a Jewish flag. Flags build nations, he said, because people "live and die for a flag."

Putting the Zionist vision before non-Jews and world public opinion, Herzl believed in international diplomacy and political agreements. He traveled constantly to negotiate with European rulers

*Quotes are from Theodor Herzl, *The Diaries of Theodor Herzl*, trans. and ed. with an introduction by Marvin Lowenthal (New York: Grosset & Dunlap, 1962), pp. 224, 22, xxi.

665

and top officials, seeking their support in securing territory for a Jewish state, usually in the Ottoman Empire. Aptly described by an admiring contemporary as "the first Jewish statesman since the destruction of Jerusalem," Herzl proved most successful in Britain. He paved the way for the 1917 Balfour Declaration, which solemnly pledged British support for a "Jewish homeland" in Palestine.

Questions for Analysis

1. Describe Theodor Herzl's background and early beliefs. Do you see a link between Herzl's early German nationalism and his later Zionism?

2. How did Herzl work as a leader to turn his Zionist vision into a reality?

the German-speaking lower middle class—and an unsuccessful young artist named Adolf Hitler.

Before 1914 anti-Semitism was most oppressive in eastern Europe, where Jews also suffered from terrible poverty. In the Russian empire, where there was no Jewish emancipation and 4 million of Europe's 7 million Jewish people lived in 1880, officials used anti-Semitism to channel popular discontent away from the government and onto the Jewish minority. Russian Jews were denounced as foreign exploiters who corrupted national traditions, and in 1881 through 1882 a wave of violent pogroms commenced in southern Russia. The police and the army stood aside for days while peasants looted and destroyed Jewish property. Official harassment continued in the following decades, and large numbers of Russian Jews emigrated to western Europe and the United States. About 2.75 million Jews left eastern Europe between 1881 and 1914.

Marxism and the Socialist Movement

Why did the socialist movement grow, and how revolutionary was it?

Nationalism served, for better or worse, as a new unifying principle. But what about socialism? Socialist parties, which were generally Marxian parties dedicated to an international proletarian revolution, grew rapidly in these years. Did this mean that national states had failed to gain the support of workers? Certainly, many prosperous and conservative citizens were greatly troubled by the socialist movement. And numerous historians have portrayed the years before 1914 as a time of increasing conflict between revolutionary socialism, on the one hand, and a nationalist alliance of the conservative aristocracy and the prosperous middle class, on the other.

The Socialist International

The growth of socialist parties after 1871 was phenomenal. (See the feature "Listening to the Past: The Making of a Socialist" on pages 671–672.) Neither Bismarck's antisocialist laws nor his extensive social security system checked the growth of the German Social Democratic party, which espoused the Marxian ideology. By 1912 it had millions of followers—mostly working-class people—and was the largest party in the Reichstag. Socialist parties also grew in other countries, though nowhere else with such success. In 1883 Russian exiles in Switzerland founded the Russian Social Democratic party, and various socialist parties were unified in 1905 in the French Section of the Workers International. Belgium and Austria-Hungary also had strong socialist parties.

As the name of the French party suggests, Marxian socialist parties were eventually linked together in an international organization. Marx believed that "the working men have no country," and he had urged proletarians of all nations to unite. Marx himself played an important role in founding the First International of socialists—the International Working Men's Association. Then Marx enthusiastically embraced the passionate, vaguely radical patriotism of the Paris Commune and its terrible conflict with the French National Assembly as a giant step toward socialist revolution. This impetuous action frightened many of his early supporters, especially the more moderate British labor leaders. The First International collapsed.

Yet international proletarian solidarity remained an important objective for Marxists. In 1889, as the individual parties in different countries grew stronger,

Section Review

- Ordinary people were becoming more nationalistic as they had more representation in governments; women, too, were slowly winning the right to vote, and governing elites took advantage of nationalistic sentiments using militaristic policies to manage domestic social conflicts.

- Chancellor Bismarck won popular support by imposing high tariffs on foreign grain and in an effort to take support away from the socialists, enacted the first social security system, but Emperor William II forced Bismarck to resign while the German Social Democratic party broadened its base by focusing on gradual social and political reform.

- France's mostly republican National Assembly led by Adolphe Thiers struggled to unite France and brought stabilization by expanding the state system of public schools and separating completely from the Catholic church after the Dreyfus Affair.

- Britain's House of Commons yielded to public pressure and enacted extensive social welfare measures benefiting the urban masses socially and politically, but Irish calls for home rule continued to be a problem along with Catholic-Protestant conflict in Northern Ireland.

- Conflicting nationalisms created friction as Hungarians wanted total separation from Austria while Croatians and Romanians agitated for independence from Hungary.

- German Jews won full political rights in 1848 and again in 1871, although they were still excluded from government employment and suffered from the growth of anti-Semitism in Austria, eastern Europe, and Russia.

"Greetings from the May Day Festival"
Workers participated enthusiastically in the annual one-day strike on May 1 to honor internationalist socialist solidarity, as this postcard from a happy woman visitor to her cousin suggests. Speeches, picnics, and parades were the order of the day, and workers celebrated their respectability and independent culture. Picture postcards developed with railroads and mass travel. (akg-images)

socialist leaders came together to form the Second International, which lasted until 1914. The International was only a federation of national socialist parties, but it had a great psychological impact. Every three years, delegates from the different parties met to interpret Marxian doctrines and plan coordinated action. May 1 (May Day) was declared an annual international one-day strike, a day of marches and demonstrations. A permanent executive for the International was established. Many feared and many others rejoiced in the growing power of socialism and the Second International.

Unions and Revisionism

Was socialism really radical in these years? On the whole, it was not. Indeed, as socialist parties grew, they looked more and more toward gradual change and steady improvement for the working class and less and less toward revolution. The mainstream of European socialism increasingly combined radical rhetoric with sober action.

Workers themselves were progressively less inclined to follow radical programs. There were several reasons for this. As workers gained the right to vote and to participate politically in the nation-state, they focused their attention more on elections than on revolutions. And as workers won real, tangible benefits, this furthered the process. Workers were also not immune to patriotic education and indoctrination during military service, and many responded positively to drum-beating parades and aggressive foreign policy as they loyally voted for socialists. Nor were workers a unified social group.

Perhaps most important of all, workers' standard of living rose gradually but substantially after 1850. Workers experienced gradual wage increases in most continental countries after 1850, though much less strikingly in late-developing Russia. The quality of life in urban areas improved dramatically as well. Therefore, workers tended more and more to become militantly moderate: they demanded gains, but they were less likely to take to the barricades in pursuit of them.

The growth of labor unions reinforced this trend toward moderation. In Germany, for example, unions had been denied rights and were viewed with suspicion as socialist fronts during their early years. But as German industrialization stormed ahead, almost all legal harassment of unions was eliminated, and union membership skyrocketed. Increasingly, unions in Germany focused on bread-and-butter issues—wages, hours, working conditions—rather than on the dissemination of pure socialist doctrine. Genuine collective bargaining, long opposed by socialist intellectuals as a "sellout," was officially recognized as desirable by the German Trade Union Congress in 1899. When employers proved unwilling to bargain, a series of strikes forced them to change their minds. Germany was the most industrialized, socialized, and unionized continental country by 1914.

The German trade unions and their leaders were in fact, if not in name, thoroughgoing revisionists. **Revisionism** was an effort by various socialists to update Marxian doctrines to reflect the realities of the time. Thus the socialist Edward Bernstein (**BURN-stine**) (1850–1932) argued in 1899 in his *Evolutionary Socialism* that socialists should combine with other progressive forces to win gradual evolutionary gains for workers through legislation, unions, and further economic development. These views were denounced as heresy by the German Social Democratic party and later by the entire Second International. Yet the revisionist, gradualist approach continued to gain the tacit acceptance of many German socialists, particularly in the trade unions.

Socialist parties before 1914 had clear-cut national characteristics. Russians and socialists in the Austro-Hungarian Empire tended to be the most radical. The German party talked revolution but practiced reformism, greatly influenced by its enormous trade-union movement. The French party talked revolution and tried to practice it, unrestrained by a trade-union movement that was both very weak and very radical. In England the socialist but non-Marxian Labour party, reflecting the well-established union movement, was formally committed to gradual reform. In Spain and Italy, Marxian socialism was very weak. There anarchism, seeking to smash the state rather than the bourgeoisie, dominated radical thought and action.

In short, socialist policies and doctrines varied from country to country. Socialism itself was to a large extent "nationalized" behind the imposing façade of international unity. This helps explain why when war came in 1914, almost all socialist leaders supported their governments.

revisionism An effort by various socialists to update Marxian doctrines to reflect the realities of the time.

Section Review

- The Socialist International was an organized group of socialist parties from many countries; after the First International collapsed, a Second formed in 1889, meeting every three years until 1914 to discuss Marxian doctrines and make plans, declaring each May 1 as an international one-day strike with marches and demonstrations.

- For the working class, socialism became more a means for gradual change than for revolution as they reaped the benefits of voting, union bargaining, and an increased standard of living.

- Edward Bernstein's revisionism was an attempt to make socialism less revolutionary and more gradual by combining it with legislation, unions, and economic development, but the German Social Democratic party and the Second International denounced it.

Chapter Review

How in France did Napoleon III seek to reconcile popular and conservative forces in an authoritarian nation-state? (page 646)

After 1850, Western society became nationalistic as well as urban and industrial. Conservative monarchical governments, recovering from the revolutionary trauma of 1848, learned to remodel early so as to build stronger states with greater popular support. Napoleon III in France led the way, combining authoritarian rule with economic prosperity and positive measures for the poor.

Key Terms
Red Shirts (p. 649)
Zollverein (p. 650)

(continued)

How did the process of unification in Italy and Germany create conservative nation-states? (page 648)

In Italy, Cavour joined traditional diplomacy with national revolt in the north and Garibaldi's revolutionary patriotism in the south, expanding the liberal monarchy of Sardinia-Piedmont into a conservative nation-state. Bismarck also combined traditional statecraft with national feeling to expand the power of Prussia and its king in a new German empire.

In what ways did the United States experience the full drama of nation building? (page 653)

In the mid-century years, the United States also experienced a crisis of nation building. The United States overcame sectionalism in a war that prevented an independent South and seemed to confirm America's destiny as a great world power.

What steps did Russia and the Ottoman Turks take toward modernization, and how successful were they? (page 654)

In autocratic Russia, defeat in the Crimean War led to the emancipation of the serfs, economic modernization with railroad building and industrialization, and limited political reform. The Ottoman Empire also sought to modernize to protect the state, but it was considerably less successful.

Why after 1871 did ordinary citizens feel a growing loyalty to their governments? (page 659)

Nation-states gradually enlisted widespread popular support, providing men and women with a greater sense of belonging, and giving them specific political, social, and economic improvements.

Why did the socialist movement grow, and how revolutionary was it? (page 667)

Even the growing socialist movement became increasingly national in orientation, gathering strength as a champion of working-class interests in domestic politics. Yet even though nationalism served to unite peoples, it also drove them apart—obvious not only in the United States before the Civil War and in Austria-Hungary and Ireland, but also throughout Europe. There the universal national faith, which usually reduced social tensions within states, promoted a bitter, almost Darwinian, competition between states and thus threatened the progress and unity it had helped to build, as we shall see in Chapters 26 and 27.

Notes

1. H. Schulze, *States, Nations and Nationalism: From the Middle Ages to the Present* (Oxford: Blackwell, 1994), pp. 222–223, 246–247.
2. J. McKay, *Pioneers for Profit: Foreign Entrepreneurship and Russian Industrialization, 1885–1913* (Chicago: University of Chicago Press, 1970), pp. 112–157.
3. R. Seltzer, *Jewish People, Jewish Thought: The Jewish Experience in History* (New York: Macmillan, 1980), p. 533.

To assess your mastery of this chapter, go to **bedfordstmartins.com/mckaywestbrief**

Listening to the Past

The Making of a Socialist

Nationalism and socialism appeared to be competing ideologies, but both fostered political awareness. A working person who became interested in politics and developed nationalist beliefs might well convert to socialism at a later date.

This was the case for Adelheid Popp (1869–1939), the editor of a major socialist newspaper for German working-women. Born into a desperately poor working-class family in Vienna, she was forced by her parents to quit school at age ten to begin full-time work. She struggled with low-paying piecework for years before she landed a solid factory job, as she recounts in the following selection from her widely read autobiography. She told her life story so that all working women might share her truth: "Socialism could change and strengthen others, as it did me."

1890 engraving of a meeting of workers in Berlin (Bildarchiv Preussischer Kulturbesitz/Art Resource, NY)

[At age fifteen] I was recommended to a great factory which stood in the best repute. . . . In none of the neighbouring factories were the wages so high; we were envied everywhere. . . . And even here, in this paradise, all were badly nourished. Those who stayed at the factory for the dinner hour would buy themselves for a few pennies a sausage or the leavings of a cheese shop. . . . In spite of all the diligence and economy, every one was poor, and trembled at the thought of losing her work. . . .

I did not only read novels and tales; I had begun . . . to read the classics and other good books. I also began to take an interest in public events. . . . I was not democratically inclined. I was full of enthusiasm then for emperors, and kings and highly placed personages played no small part in my fancies. . . . I bought myself a strict Catholic paper, that criticised very adversely the workers' movement, which was attracting notice. Its aim was to educate in a patriotic and religious direction. . . . I took the warmest interest in the events that occurred in the royal families, and I took the death of the Crown Prince of Austria so much to heart that I wept a whole day. . . .

Later on my mother and I lived with one of my brothers who had married. Friends came to him, among them some intelligent workmen. One of these workmen was particularly intelligent, and . . . could talk on many subjects. He was the first Social Democrat I knew. He brought me many books, and explained to me the difference between Anarchism and Socialism. I heard from him, also for the first time, what a republic was, and in spite of my former enthusiasm for royal dynasties, I also declared myself in favour of a republican form of government. I saw everything so near and so clearly, that I actually counted the weeks which must still elapse before the revolution of state and society would take place.

From this workman I received the first Social Democratic party organ. . . . I first learned from it to understand and judge of my own lot. I learned to see that all I had suffered was the result not of a divine ordinance, but of an unjust organization of society. . . .

In the factory I became another woman. . . . I told my [female] comrades all that I had read of the workers' movement. Formerly I had often told stories when they had begged me for them. But instead of narrating . . . the fate of some queen, I now held forth on oppression and exploitation. I told of accumulated wealth in the hands of a few, and introduced as a contrast the shoemakers who had no shoes and the tailors who had no clothes. On breaks I read aloud the articles in the Social Democratic paper and explained what Socialism was as far as I understood it. . . . [While I was reading] it often happened that one of the clerks passing by shook his head and said to another clerk: "The girl speaks like a man."

Questions for Analysis

1. How did Popp describe and interpret work in the factory?

2. To what extent did her socialist interpretation of factory life fit the facts she described?

3. What were Popp's political interests before she became a socialist?

4. Was this account likely to lead other working-women to socialism? Why or why not?

Source: Slightly adapted from A. Popp, *The Autobiography of a Working Woman,* trans. E. C. Harvey (Chicago: F. G. Browne, 1913), pp. 29, 34–35, 39, 66–69, 71, 74, 82–90.

CHAPTER 26

The West and the World

1815–1914

Africans in Madagascar transport a French diplomat in 1894, shortly before France annexed the island. (Snark/Art Resource, NY)

Chapter Preview

Industrialization and the World Economy
What were some of the global consequences of European industrialization between 1815 and 1914?

The Great Migration
How was massive migration an integral part of Western expansion?

Western Imperialism (1880–1914)
How and why after 1875 did European nations rush to build political empires in Africa and Asia?

Responding to Western Imperialism
What was the general pattern of non-Western responses to Western expansion, and how did India, Japan, and China meet the imperialist challenge?

INDIVIDUALS IN SOCIETY: Cecil Rhodes

LISTENING TO THE PAST: A British Woman in India

While industrialization and nationalism were transforming urban life and Western society, Western society itself was reshaping the world. At the peak of its power, the West entered the third and most dynamic phase of expansion that had begun with the Crusades and continued with the great discoveries and the rise of seaborne colonial empires. An ever-growing stream of products, people, and ideas flowed out of Europe in the nineteenth century. Hardly any corner of the globe was left untouched. The most spectacular manifestations of Western expansion came in the late nineteenth century when the leading European nations established or enlarged their far-flung political empires. The political annexation of territory in the 1880s—the "new imperialism," as it is often called by historians—was the capstone of a profound underlying economic and technological process.

Industrialization and the World Economy

What were some of the global consequences of European industrialization between 1815 and 1914?

The Industrial Revolution created, first in Great Britain and then in continental Europe and North America, a tremendously dynamic economic system. In the course of the nineteenth century, Europeans extended that system across the face of the earth through both peaceful and militaristic means. In general, they fashioned the global economic system so that the largest share of gains flowed to the West and its propertied classes.

The Rise of Global Inequality

The Industrial Revolution marked a momentous turning point in human history. It allowed those regions of the world that industrialized to increase their wealth and power enormously in comparison to those that did not. As a result, a gap between the industrializing regions (mainly Europe and North America) and the nonindustrializing or **Third World** regions (mainly Africa, Asia, and Latin America) opened up and grew steadily throughout the nineteenth century. Moreover, this pattern of uneven global development became institutionalized, or built into the structure of the world economy. Thus we evolved a "lopsided world," a world of rich lands and poor.

The enormous income disparities between developed and Third World countries (see Figure 26.1) are poignant indicators of equal disparities in food and clothing, health and education, life expectancy and general material well-being. The reason for these disparities has

Third World A term widely used by international organizations and by scholars to group the nonindustrialized nations Africa, Asia, and Latin America into a single unit.

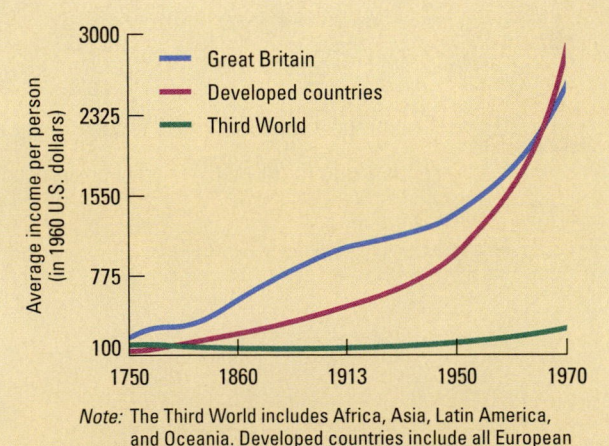

Note: The Third World includes Africa, Asia, Latin America, and Oceania. Developed countries include all European countries, Canada, the United States, and Japan.

FIGURE 26.1 The Growth of Average Income per Person in the Third World, Developed Countries, and Great Britain, 1750–1970

Growth is given in 1960 U.S. dollars and prices. (*Source:* P. Bairoch and M. Lévy-Leboyer, eds., *Disparities in Economic Development Since the Industrial Revolution.* Copyright © 1981. Reproduced with permission of Palgrave Macmillan.)

generated a great deal of debate. One school of interpretation stresses that the West used science, technology, capitalist organization, and even its critical worldview to create its wealth and greater physical well-being. Another school argues that the West used its political and economic power to steal much of its riches, continuing in the nineteenth (and twentieth) century the rapacious colonialism born of the era of expansion. These issues are complex, and there are few simple answers. It is helpful to consider them in the context of the dynamics of world trade in the nineteenth century.

1842	China cedes Hong Kong to Britain
1853	Perry "opens" Japan for trade
1863–1879	Reign of Ismail in Egypt
1867	Meiji Restoration in Japan
1869	Completion of Suez Canal
1885	Berlin Conference gives Leopold II dominion over Congo Free State; founding of Indian National Congress
1898	United States takes over Philippines
1899	Kipling, "The White Man's Burden"
1902	Conrad, *Heart of Darkness;* Hobson, *Imperialism*
1900–1903	Boxer Rebellion in China

The World Market

Trade between nations has always stimulated economic development. In the nineteenth century, an enormous increase in international commerce was directed by Europe. Great Britain took the lead in cultivating export markets for its booming industrial output. British manufacturers looked first to Europe and then around the world.

Take the case of cotton textiles. By 1820 Britain was exporting 50 percent of its production. Europe bought 50 percent of these cotton textile exports, while India bought only 6 percent. Then as European nations and the United States erected protective tariff barriers and promoted domestic industry, British cotton textile manufacturers aggressively sought and found other foreign markets in non-Western areas. By 1850 India was buying 25 percent and Europe only 16 percent of a much larger total. As a British colony, India could not raise tariffs to protect its ancient cotton textile industry, and thousands of Indian weavers lost their livelihoods.

International trade also grew as transportation systems improved. Wherever railroads were built, they drastically reduced transportation costs, opened new economic opportunities, and called forth new skills and attitudes. Much of the railroad construction undertaken in Latin America, Asia, and Africa connected seaports with inland cities and regions, as opposed to linking and developing cities and regions within a given country. Thus these railroads supported Western economic interests, facilitating the inflow and sale of Western manufactured goods and the export of local raw materials.

The power of steam revolutionized transportation by sea as well as by land. Steam power began to supplant sails on the oceans of the world in the late 1860s. Passenger and freight rates tumbled as ship design became more sophisticated, and the intercontinental shipment of low-priced raw materials became feasible. The opening of the Suez and Panama Canals shortened transport time considerably, and port facilities were also modernized to make loading and unloading cheaper, faster, and more dependable.

New communications systems directed the flow of goods across global networks. Transoceanic telegraph cables inaugurated rapid communications among the financial centers of the world. While a British tramp freighter steamed from Calcutta to New York, a broker in London was arranging by telegram for it to carry an American cargo to Australia. The same communications network conveyed world commodity prices instantaneously.

The revolution in transportation and communications encouraged European entrepreneurs to open up vast new territories around the world and develop agricultural products and raw materials there for sale in Europe. Improved transportation also enabled European ventures in Asia, Africa, and Latin America to ship not only the traditional tropical products—spices, tea, sugar, coffee—but also new raw materials for industry, such as jute, rubber, cotton, and coconut oil.

As their economies grew, Europeans began to make massive foreign investments beginning about 1840. By the outbreak of World War I in 1914, wealthy Europeans had invested more than $40 billion abroad. Great Britain, France, and Germany were the principal investing countries. Most of the capital exported did not go to European colonies or protectorates in Asia and Africa. Europeans found the most profitable opportunities for investment in construction of the railroads, ports, and utilities that were necessary for white settlers to develop the lands in such places as Australia and the Americas. Much of this investment was peaceful and mutually beneficial for lenders and borrowers. The victims were Native American Indians and Australian aborigines, who were decimated by the diseases, liquor, and weapons of an aggressively expanding Western society.

The Opening of China and Japan

While Europeans looked primarily to North America, Australia, and much of Latin America to absorb huge quantities of goods, investments, and migrants, they also hoped to penetrate the markets of Asia. In China and Japan they demonstrated their willingness to use force to remove trade barriers.

Traditional Chinese civilization was self-sufficient. For centuries China had sent more goods and inventions to Europe than it had received, and this was still the case in the early nineteenth century. Trade with Europe was carefully regulated by the Chinese imperial government—the Qing (ching), or Manchu (**man-CHOO**), Dynasty—which required all foreign merchants to live in the southern city of Canton and to buy from and sell to only the local merchant monopoly. Goods considered harmful to Chinese interests, such as opium, were forbidden.

For years the little community of foreign merchants in Canton accepted the Chinese system. By the 1820s, however, British merchants began flexing their muscles. They had found in opium a product the Chinese desired, and they wanted to stop smuggling and sell it openly. They pressured the British government to help them establish an independent British colony in China with "safe and unrestricted liberty" in trade. British merchants in Canton also enlisted the support of British manufacturers with visions of vast Chinese markets.

At the same time, the Qing government decided that the **opium trade** had to be stamped out. It was ruining the people and hurting the economy, as silver for opium was flowing to British merchants. The government began to prosecute Chinese drug dealers vigorously and in 1839 it ordered the foreign merchants to obey China's laws. The British merchants refused and were expelled, whereupon war soon broke out.

The British were able to call troops from India and used their superior sea power to occupy several coastal cities. China submitted to the Treaty of Nanking in 1842 and was forced to cede the island of Hong Kong to Britain forever, pay an indemnity of $100 million, and open up four large cities to foreign trade with low tariffs.

Thereafter the opium trade flourished, and Hong Kong developed rapidly as an Anglo-Chinese enclave. The British, joined by the French, attacked China again between 1856 and 1860, culminating in the occupation of Beijing. Another round of harsh treaties gave European merchants and missionaries greater privileges and protection and forced the Chinese to accept trade and investment on unfavorable terms for several more cities. Thus did Europeans use military aggression to open China to foreign trade and foreign ideas.

opium trade Opium was grown legally in British-occupied India and smuggled into China by means of fast ships and bribed officials; it became a destructive and ensnaring vice of the Chinese.

Britain and China at War, 1841
Britain capitalized on its overwhelming naval superiority, and this British aquatint celebrates a dramatic moment in a crucial battle near Guangzhou. Having received a direct hit from a steam-powered British ironclad, a Chinese sailing ship explodes into a wall of flame. The Chinese lost eleven ships and five hundred men in the two-hour engagement; the British suffered only minor damage. (National Maritime Museum, London)

China's neighbor Japan had decided by 1640 to seal off the country from all European influences in order to preserve traditional Japanese culture and society. When American and British whaling ships began to appear off Japanese coasts almost two hundred years later, the policy of exclusion was still in effect. An order of 1825 commanded Japanese officials to "drive away foreign vessels without second thought."[1]

Japan's refusal to share its ports complicated the provisioning of whaling ships and trading vessels in the eastern Pacific. It also thwarted the hope of trade and profit. Americans came to see it as their duty to force the Japanese to behave as a "civilized" nation.

After several unsuccessful American attempts to establish commercial relations with Japan, Commodore Matthew Perry steamed into Edo (**ED-doe**) (now Tokyo) Bay in 1853 and demanded diplomatic negotiations with the emperor. Japan entered a grave crisis. Some Japanese warriors urged resistance, but senior officials realized how defenseless their cities were against naval bombardment. Shocked and humiliated, they reluctantly signed a treaty with the United States that opened two ports and permitted trade. Over the next five years, more treaties spelled out the rights and privileges of the Western nations and their merchants in Japan. Japan was "opened."

Western Penetration of Egypt

Unlike China and Japan, nineteenth-century Egypt was attracted to European models of modernization and open to European business ventures. But it too was forced to make concessions to European powers, eventually falling under British rule.

Egypt emerged as an autonomous country in the nineteenth century under the leadership of the extraordinary Albanian-born Turkish general, Muhammad Ali (1769–1849). First appointed governor of Egypt by the Turkish sultan, Muhammad Ali set out to build his own state on the strength of a large, powerful army organized along European lines. He drafted for the first time the peasants of Egypt, and he hired French and Italian army officers to train these raw recruits and their Turkish officers. The government was also reformed, new lands were cultivated, and communications were improved. By the time of his death in 1849, Muhammad Ali had established a strong and virtually independent Egyptian state, to be ruled by his family on a hereditary basis within the Turkish empire.

Muhammad Ali's policies of modernization attracted large numbers of Europeans to the banks of the Nile. The port city of Alexandria had more than fifty thousand Europeans by 1864. Europeans served not only as army officers but also as engineers, doctors, government officials, and police officers. Others turned to trade, finance, and shipping.

khedive A prince in Egypt.

Muhammad Ali's grandson Ismail (**is-mah-EEL**) (r. 1863–1879) continued to Westernize Egypt during his rule as the country's **khedive** (**kuh-DEEV**), or prince. The large irrigation networks he promoted caused cotton production and exports to Europe to boom, and with his support the Suez Canal was completed by a French company in 1869. Cairo acquired modern boulevards and Western hotels.

As French-educated Ismail proudly declared, "My country is no longer in Africa, we now form part of Europe."[2]

Yet Ismail's projects were enormously expensive, and by 1876 Egypt owed foreign bondholders a colossal debt that it could not pay. The governments of France and Great Britain intervened to protect the European bondholders, forcing Ismail to appoint French and British commissioners to oversee Egyptian finances.

Foreign financial control evoked a violent nationalistic reaction among Egyptian religious leaders, young intellectuals, and army officers. The British pushed Ismail out and brought in his weak son, Tewfiq (r. 1879–1892), sparking anti-European riots in Alexandria. The British fleet then bombarded the city, which led to a country-wide revolt. But a British expeditionary force put down the rebellion and occupied all of Egypt.

The British said their occupation was temporary, but British armies remained in Egypt until 1956. They maintained the façade of the khedive's government as an autonomous province of the Ottoman Empire, but the khedive was a mere puppet. British rule did result in tax reforms and somewhat better conditions for peasants, while foreign bondholders received their interest and Egyptian nationalists nursed their injured pride.

British rule in Egypt provided a new model for European expansion in Africa and Asia. Such expansion was based on military force, political domination, and a self-justifying ideology of beneficial reform. This model was to predominate until 1914. Thus did Europe's Industrial Revolution lead to tremendous political as well as economic expansion throughout the world after 1880.

Section Review

- An expanding gap between industrialized countries and "Third World" non-industrializing countries developed with enormous economic disparities between them.

- Improvements in communication, such as the telegraph and transportation, including railroads and steamships, facilitated the establishment of a Western-driven global trade network, often at the expense of indigenous peoples.

- China had strict regulations for trade and when British merchants desired more favorable conditions for their opium trade, the Chinese government resisted, so Britain invaded, claiming Hong Kong and several other cities, forcing the Chinese to lift restrictions on foreign trade.

- Japan was closed to foreign trade until the Americans demanded diplomatic relations under threat of force and the Japanese reluctantly agreed to open some of their ports.

- Muhammad Ali and Ismail modernized Egypt and opened the door to foreign investors and immigrants but the expense of his projects, including the Suez Canal, put Egypt in debt and foreign commissioners took over financial control; when the Egyptians revolted the British used force to occupy Egypt until 1956.

The Great Migration

How was massive migration an integral part of Western expansion?

A poignant human drama was interwoven with economic expansion: millions of people pulled up stakes and left their ancestral lands in the course of history's greatest migration. To millions of ordinary people, for whom the opening of China and the interest on the Egyptian debt had not the slightest significance, this great movement was the central experience in the saga of Western expansion. It was, in part, because of this **great migration** that the West's impact on the world in the nineteenth century was so powerful and many-sided.

great migration A great movement of people that was the central experience in the saga of Western expansion; one reason why the West's impact on the world in the nineteenth century was so powerful and many-sided.

European Migrants

Population growth was a driving force behind European migration. The trend of falling death rates continued until the early twentieth century, mainly because of the rising standard of living but also because of improvements in medicine. Millions of country folk, seeing little available land and few opportunities, went abroad as well as to nearby cities in search of work and economic opportunity.

The United States absorbed the largest number of European migrants, but less than half of all migrants went there (see Figure 26.2). Moreover, migrants accounted for a larger proportion of the total population in Argentina, Brazil, and Canada than in the United States. The common American assumption that European migration meant migration to the United States is quite inaccurate.

Determined to maintain or improve their status, migrants were a great asset to the countries that received them. The vast majority came in the prime of life and were ready to work hard in the new land, at least for a time. Many Europeans moved but remained within Europe, settling temporarily or permanently in another European country. Jews from eastern Europe and peasants from Ireland migrated to Great Britain; Russians and Poles sought work in Germany; and Latin peoples from Spain, Portugal, and Italy entered France. Many Europeans were

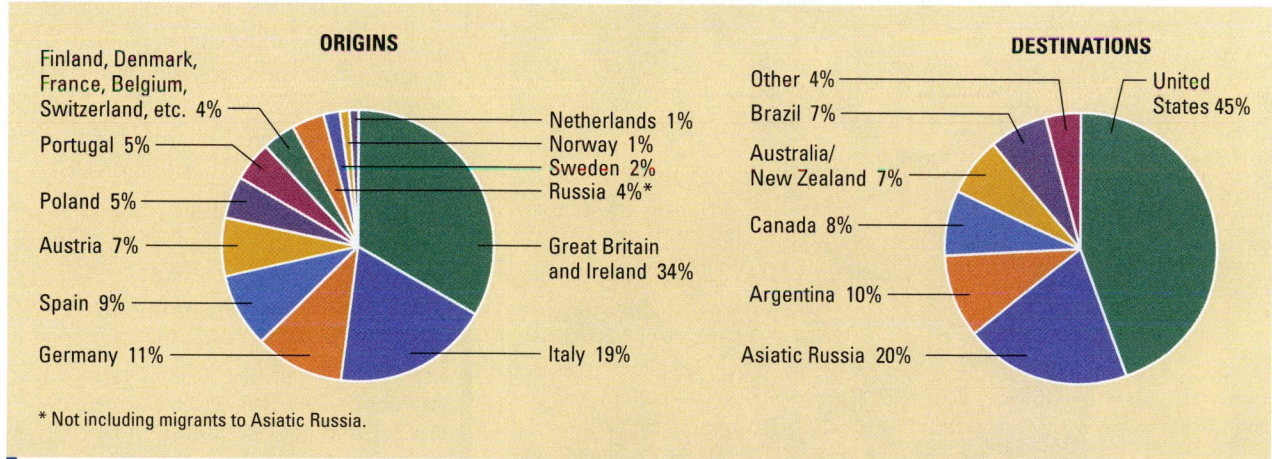

FIGURE 26.2   Origins and Destinations of European Emigrants, 1851–1960

Source: From *Impact of Western Man*, by W. Woodruff. Copyright © 1982. Reprinted by permission of University Press of America.

truly migrants as opposed to immigrants—that is, they returned home after some time abroad. One in two migrants to Argentina and probably one in three to the United States eventually returned to their native land. Once again, the possibility of buying land in the old country was of central importance.

Ties of family and friendship played a crucial role in the movement of peoples. Many people from a given province or village settled together in rural enclaves or tightly knit urban neighborhoods thousands of miles away. Very often a strong individual—a businessman, a religious leader—would blaze the way and others would follow, forming a "migration chain."

Many landless young European men and women were spurred to leave by a spirit of revolt and independence. In Sweden and in Norway, in Jewish Russia and in Italy, these young people felt frustrated by the small privileged classes, which often controlled both church and government and resisted demands for change and greater opportunity. Many a young Norwegian seconded the passionate cry of Norway's national poet, Martinius Bjørnson (**BYURN-suhn**): "Forth will I! Forth! I will be crushed and consumed if I stay."[3] Thus for many, migration was a radical way to "get out from under." Migration slowed down when the people won basic political and social reforms, such as the right to vote and social security.

Asian Migrants

Not all migration was from Europe. A substantial number of Chinese, Japanese, Indians, and Filipinos—to name only four key groups—responded to rural hardship with temporary or permanent migration. At least 3 million Asians (as opposed to more than 60 million Europeans) moved abroad before 1920. Most went as indentured laborers to work under incredibly difficult conditions on the plantations or in the gold mines of Latin America, southern Asia, Africa, California, Hawaii, and Australia. White estate owners very often used Asians to replace or supplement blacks after the suppression of the slave trade.

Such migration from Asia would undoubtedly have grown to much greater proportions if planters and mine owners in search of cheap labor had been able to hire as many Asian workers as they wished. But they could not. By the 1880s, Americans and Australians were building **great white walls**—discriminatory laws designed to keep Asians out.

great white walls Laws designed by Americans and Australians to keep Asians out.

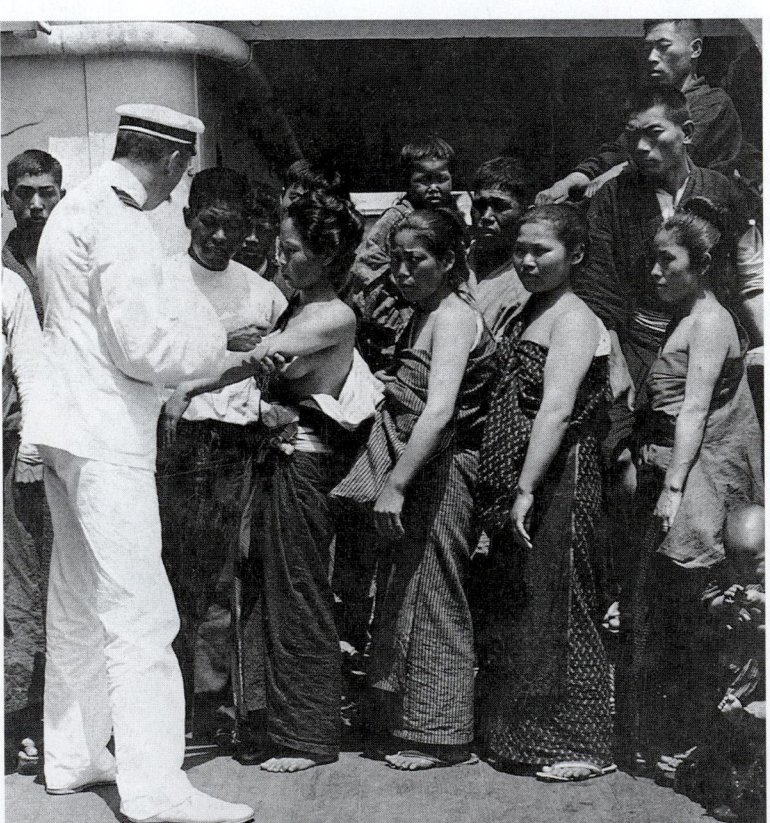

Vaccinating Migrants Bound for Hawaii, 1904
First Chinese, then Japanese, and finally Koreans and Filipinos went in large numbers across the Pacific to labor in Hawaii on American-owned sugar plantations in the late nineteenth century. The native Hawaiians had been decimated by disease, preparing the way for the annexation of Hawaii by the United States in 1898. (Corbis)

A crucial factor in the migrations before 1914 was, therefore, the general policy of "whites only" in the open lands of possible permanent settlement. This, too, was part of Western dominance in the increasingly lopsided world. Largely successful in monopolizing the best overseas opportunities, Europeans and people of European ancestry reaped the main benefits from the great migration. By 1913 people in Australia, Canada, and the United States all had higher average incomes than people in Great Britain, still Europe's wealthiest nation.

Western Imperialism (1880–1914)

How and why after 1875 did European nations rush to build political empires in Africa and Asia?

The expansion of Western society reached its apex between about 1880 and 1914. In those years, the leading European nations not only continued to send massive streams of migrants, money, and manufactured goods around the world, but also rushed to create or enlarge vast *political* empires abroad. This political empire building contrasted sharply with the economic penetration of non-Western territories between 1816 and 1880, which had left a China or a Japan "opened" but politically independent. By contrast, the empires of the late nineteenth century recalled the old European colonial empires of the seventeenth and eighteenth centuries and led contemporaries to speak of the **new imperialism.**

Characterized by a frantic rush to plant the flag over as many people and as much territory as possible, the new imperialism had momentous consequences. It resulted in new tensions among competing European states, and it led to wars and rumors of war with non-European powers. The new imperialism was aimed primarily at Africa and Asia and subjugated millions under European rule.

The Scramble for Africa

The most spectacular manifestation of the new imperialism was the scramble for Africa. As late as 1880, European nations controlled only 10 percent of the African continent (see inset, Map 26.1). Between 1880 and 1900, the situation changed drastically. Britain, France, Germany, and Italy raced one another for African possessions (see Map 26.1). By 1900 nearly the whole continent had been carved up and placed under European rule: only Ethiopia in northeast Africa, which repulsed Italian invaders, and Liberia on the West African coast, which had been settled by freed slaves from the United States, remained independent. In the years before 1914, the European powers tightened their control and established colonial governments to rule their gigantic empires.

The situation in South Africa had a different final outcome. The British had taken possession of the Dutch settlements at Cape Town during the wars with Napoleon I. The descendents of Dutch settlers, known as Boers (bores) or **Afrikaners** (**af-rih-KAHN-uhrs**), moved north and settled the regions later known as the Orange Free State and the Transvaal (**trans-VAHL**), proclaiming their political independence. Then in the early 1890s, Cecil Rhodes led the British farther north, establishing protectorates over Bechuanaland (**bech-oo-AH-nuh-land**) (now Botswana) and Rhodesia (**roh-DEE-zhuh**) (now Zimbabwe and Zambia).

Trying unsuccessfully to undermine the stubborn Afrikaners in the Transvaal, where English-speaking capitalists like Rhodes were developing fabulously rich gold mines, the British conquered their white rivals in the bloody South African

Section Review

- Population growth and the search for better economic and social opportunities drove European migration, which slowed when these conditions improved in the home country.

- Migrants were an asset to the receiving countries as they worked hard and often arrived with family and friends forming a "migration chain," all settling in the same neighborhoods or in specific areas.

- Asian migrants went to work most often as indentured laborers in awful conditions after the suppression of the slave trade, but laws allowing only whites to settle permanently limited their numbers.

new imperialism The drive to create vast political empires abroad, recalling the old European colonial empires of the seventeenth and eighteenth centuries and contrasting with the economic penetration of non-Western territories between 1816 and 1880.

Afrikaners Descendants of the Dutch in the Cape Colony.

Madeira Is.
(Portugal)

Canary Is.
(Spain)

SPANISH MOROCCO
Tangier
Casablanca
MOROCCO
IFNI
RIO DE ORO
Algiers
TUNISIA
Tripoli
Cyrene

Mediterranean Sea

ALGERIA
LIBYA
EGYPT
Cairo
Aswan

S A H A R A

ARABIA

FRENCH WEST AFRICA

Senegal R.
Niger R.
L. Chad

GAMBIA
PORTUGUESE GUINEA
SIERRA LEONE
LIBERIA
IVORY COAST
GOLD COAST
TOGOLAND
S. NIGERIA
NORTHERN NIGERIA
KAMERUN
Fernando Po (Spain)
SPANISH GUINEA
São Tomé (Portugal)

ANGLO-EGYPTIAN SUDAN
Omdurman
Khartoum
Fashoda
Adowa
ERITREA
FRENCH SOMALILAND
BRITISH SOMALILAND
ETHIOPIA
ITALIAN SOMALILAND

Nile R.
Blue Nile R.
White Nile R.

Red Sea

FRENCH EQUATORIAL AFRICA
Uele R.
Congo R.

BELGIAN CONGO

UGANDA
L. Victoria
BRITISH EAST AFRICA
Mombasa
Zanzibar (Gr. Br.)

CABINDA

ATLANTIC OCEAN

GERMAN EAST AFRICA
L. Tanganyika

INDIAN OCEAN

ANGOLA
NORTHERN RHODESIA
Zambezi R.
L. Nyasa
NYASALAND
SOUTHERN RHODESIA
MOZAMBIQUE
GERMAN SOUTHWEST AFRICA
BECHUANALAND
TRANSVAAL
SWAZILAND
ORANGE FREE STATE
Isandhlwana
BASUTOLAND
NATAL
UNION OF SOUTH AFRICA
Cape Town

MADAGASCAR

Tropic of Cancer
20°N
0° Equator
20°S
Tropic of Capricorn

COLONIAL PRESENCE IN AFRICA, 1878

ALGERIA
EGYPT
SENEGAL
SAHARA
Nile R.
Niger R.
Congo R.
CAPE COLONY

20°N
0°
20°S

20°W 0° 20°E 40°E

0   800 Km.
0   800 Mi.

0   400   800 Km.
0   400   800 Mi.

British
French
German
Italian
Portuguese
Belgian
Spanish
Independent African states

MAPPING THE PAST

MAP 26.1   The Partition of Africa

The European powers carved up Africa after 1880 and built vast political empires. European states also seized territory in Asia in the nineteenth century, although some Asian states and peoples managed to maintain their political independence, as may be seen on Map 26.2, page 686. The late nineteenth century was the peak of European imperialism. Compare the patterns of European imperialism in Africa and Asia, using this map and Map 26.2. **[1]** What European countries were leading imperialist states in both Africa and Asia, and what lands did they hold? **[2]** What countries in Africa and Asia maintained their political independence? **[3]** From an imperialist perspective, what in 1914 did the United States and Japan, two very different countries, have in common in Africa and Asia?

War (1899–1902). In 1910 their territories were united in a new Union of South Africa, established—unlike any other territory in Africa—as a largely "self-governing" colony. This enabled the defeated Afrikaners to use their numerical superiority over the British settlers to gradually take political power, as even the most educated nonwhites lost the right to vote outside the Cape Colony. (See the feature "Individuals in Society: Cecil Rhodes.")

In the complexity of the European seizure of Africa, certain events and individuals stand out. Of enormous importance was the British occupation of Egypt in 1882, which established the new model of formal political control. There was also the role of Leopold II of Belgium (r. 1865–1909), an energetic, strong-willed monarch with a lust for empire. "Steam and electricity have annihilated distance, and all the non-appropriated lands on the surface of the globe can become the field of our operations and of our success,"[4] he had exclaimed in 1861. Leopold ignited a gold rush mentality after sending the part-time explorer Henry M. Stanley to plant his flag in the Congo. The French rushed to stake their claim in the region, and the race for territory was on.

The leaders of Europe met at the **Berlin conference** in 1884 and 1885 to agree on some basic rules for this new and dangerous game of imperialist competition in sub-Saharan Africa. The conference established the principle that European claims to African territory had to rest on "effective occupation" in order to be recognized by other states. The conference recognized Leopold's personal rule over a neutral Congo free state and agreed to work to stop slavery and the slave trade in Africa.

Bismarck, who saw little value in colonies, had a change of stance when Germans clamored for a stake in Africa. In 1884 and 1885, Germany established protectorates over a number of small African kingdoms and tribes in Togo, Cameroons, southwest Africa, and, later, East Africa. In acquiring colonies, Bismarck worked with France's Jules Ferry against the British. With Bismarck's tacit approval, the French pressed southward from Algeria, eastward from their old forts on the Senegal coast, and northward from their protectorate on the Congo River.

Meanwhile, the British began enlarging their West African enclaves and impatiently pushing northward from the Cape Colony and westward from Zanzibar. Their attempt to move southward from Egypt was blocked by Muslim forces in the Sudan in 1885. A decade later, another British force, under General Horatio H. Kitchener (KICH-uh-ner), moved cautiously and more successfully up the Nile River, building

Berlin conference A meeting of European leaders held in 1884 and 1885 in order to lay down some basic rules for imperialist competition in sub-Saharan Africa; they established the principle that European claims to African territory had to rest on effective occupation in order to be recognized by other states.

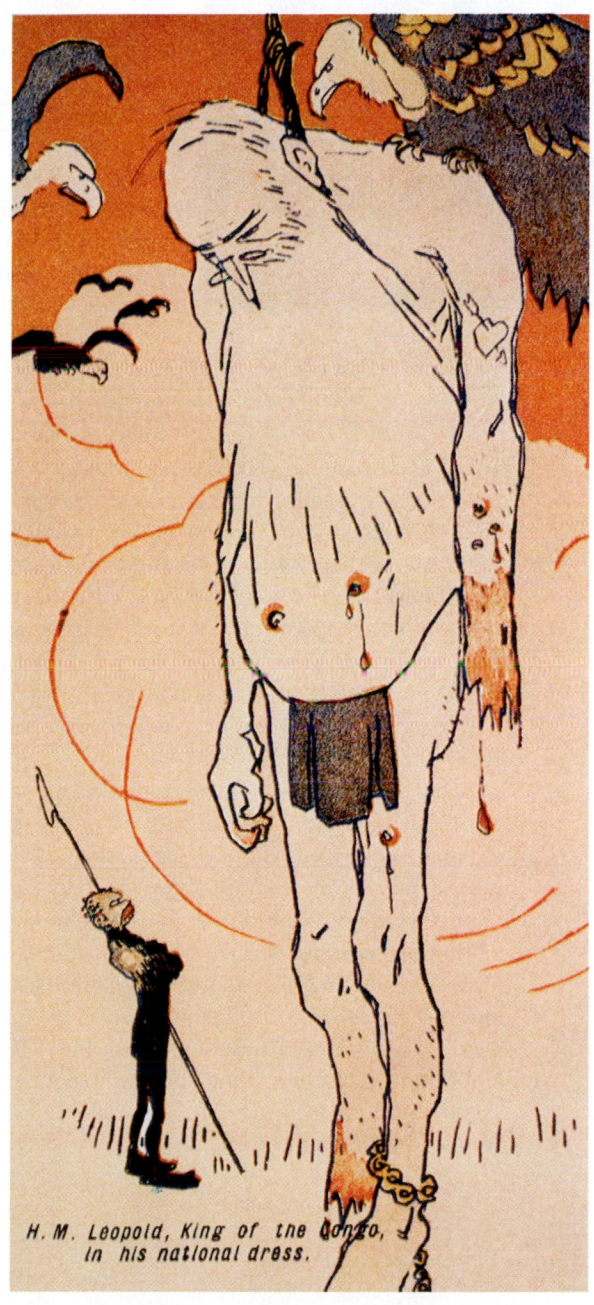

H. M. Leopold, King of the Congo, in his national dress.

European Imperialism at its Worst

This 1908 English cartoon, "Leopold, King of the Congo, in his native dress," focuses on the barbaric practice of cutting off the hands and feet of Africans who refused to gather as much rubber as Leopold's company demanded. In 1908 an international human rights campaign forced the Belgian king to cede his personal fief to the Belgian state. (The Granger Collection, New York)

Individuals in Society

Cecil Rhodes

Cecil Rhodes (1853–1902) epitomized the dynamism and the ruthlessness of the new imperialism. He built a corporate monopoly, claimed vast tracts in Africa, and established the famous Rhodes scholarships to develop colonial (and American) leaders who would love and strengthen the British Empire. But to Africans, he left a bitter legacy.

Rhodes came from a large middle-class family and at seventeen went to southern Africa to seek his fortune. He soon turned to diamonds, newly discovered at Kimberley, picked good partners, and was wealthy by 1876. But Rhodes, often called a dreamer, wanted more. He entered Oxford University, while returning periodically to Africa, and his musings crystallized in a belief in progress through racial competition and territorial expansion. "I contend," he wrote, "that we [English] are the finest race in the world and the more of the world we inhabit the better it is for the human race."[*]

Cecil Rhodes, after crushing the last African revolt in Rhodesia in 1896. (Brown Brothers)

Rhodes's belief in British expansion never wavered. In 1880 he formed the De Beers Mining Company, and by 1888 his firm monopolized southern Africa's diamond production and earned fabulous profits. Rhodes also entered the Cape Colony's legislature and became the all-powerful prime minister from 1890 to 1896. His main objective was to dominate the Afrikaner republics and to impose British rule on as much land as possible beyond their northern borders. Working through a state-approved private company financed in part by De Beers, Rhodes's agents forced and cajoled African kings to accept British "protection," then put down rebellions with Maxim machine guns. Britain thus obtained a great swath of empire on the cheap.

But Rhodes, like many high achievers obsessed with power and personal aggrandizement, went too far. He backed, and then in 1896 failed to call back, a failed invasion of the Transvaal, which was designed to topple the Dutch-speaking republic. Repudiated by top British leaders who had encouraged his plan, Rhodes had to resign as prime minister. In declining health, he continued to agitate against the Afrikaner republics. He died at age forty-nine as the South African War (1899–1902) ended.

In accounting for Rhodes's remarkable but flawed achievements, both sympathetic and critical biographers stress his imposing size, enormous energy, and powerful personality. His ideas were commonplace, but he believed in them passionately, and he could persuade and inspire others to follow his lead. Rhodes the idealist was nonetheless a born negotiator, a crafty dealmaker who believed that everyone could be had for a price. According to his best biographer, Rhodes's homosexuality—discreet, partially repressed, and undeniable—was also "a major component of his magnetism and his success."[†] Never comfortable with women, he loved male companionship. He drew together a "band of brothers," both gay and straight, to share in the pursuit of power.

Rhodes cared nothing for the rights of blacks. Ever a combination of visionary and opportunist, he looked forward to an eventual reconciliation of Afrikaners and British in a united white front. Therefore, as prime minister of the Cape Colony, he broke with the colony's liberal tradition and supported Afrikaner demands to reduce drastically the number of black voters and limit black freedoms. This helped lay the foundation for the Union of South Africa's brutal policy of racial segregation known as *apartheid* after 1948.

Questions for Analysis

1. How did Rhodes relate to Afrikaners and to black Africans? How do you account for the differences and the similarities?
2. In what ways does Rhodes's career throw additional light on the debate over the causes of the new imperialism?

[*]Robert Rotberg, *The Founder: Cecil Rhodes and the Pursuit of Power* (New York: Oxford University Press, 1988), p. 150.

[†]Ibid., p. 408.

a railroad to supply arms and reinforcements as it went. Finally, in 1898 these British troops met their foe at Omdurman (**om-door-MAHN**) (see Map 26.1), where Muslim tribesmen armed with spears charged time and time again, only to be cut down by the recently invented machine gun. In the end, eleven thousand brave Muslim tribesmen lay dead, while only twenty-eight Britons had been killed.

Continuing up the Nile after the Battle of Omdurman, Kitchener's armies found that a small French force had beaten them to the village of Fashoda (**fuh-SHOH-duh**). The result was a serious diplomatic crisis and even the threat of war. Eventually, wracked by the Dreyfus affair (see page 662) and unwilling to fight, France backed down and withdrew its forces, allowing the British to take over.

The British conquest of Sudan exemplifies the general process of empire building in Africa. The fate of the Muslim force at Omdurman was eventually inflicted on all native peoples who resisted European rule: they were blown away by vastly superior armaments. But however much the European powers squabbled for territory and privilege around the world, they always had the sense to stop short of actually fighting each other. Imperial ambitions were not worth a great European war.

Imperialism in Asia

Although the sudden division of Africa was more spectacular, Europeans also extended their political control in Asia. In 1815 the Dutch ruled little more than the island of Java in the East Indies. Thereafter they gradually brought almost all of the three-thousand-mile archipelago under their political authority, although they had to grant some territory to Britain and Germany. In the critical decade of the 1880s, the French under the leadership of Jules Ferry took Indochina. The Russians expanded to the south in the Caucasus and to the east in Central Asia and China's outlying provinces. India, Japan, and China also experienced a profound imperialist impact (see Map 26.2).

The United States's great conquest was the Philippines, taken from Spain in 1898 after the Spanish-American War. When it quickly became clear that the United States had no intention of granting independence, Philippine patriots rose in revolt and were suppressed only after long, bitter fighting. Some Americans protested the taking of the Philippines, but to no avail. Thus another great Western power joined the imperialist ranks in Asia.

Causes of the New Imperialism

Many factors contributed to the late-nineteenth-century rush for territory and empire, among them economics, nationalism, ideology, military technology, and the ambitions of individuals. While these reasons do not constitute a defense of imperialism, they are helpful in understanding what drove it.

Economic motives were a factor in the new imperialism, especially in the British Empire. By the late 1870s, Great Britain was losing its early lead in industrialization and facing increasingly tough competition from France, Germany, and the United States. When continental powers began to grab territory in the 1880s, the British followed suit immediately. They feared that France and Germany would seal off their empires with high tariffs and restrictions and that potential markets would be lost forever. In actuality, however, the overall economic gains of the new imperialism proved quite limited before 1914. The new colonies were simply too poor to buy much, and they offered few immediately profitable investments.

Colonies also seemed important for political and diplomatic reasons. For instance, the British occupation of Egypt was motivated in part by the desire to

MAP 26.2 Asia in 1914

India remained under British rule, while China precariously preserved its political independence. The Dutch empire in modern-day Indonesia was old, but French control of Indochina was a product of the new imperialism.

Territories held by
Western powers

Russian Empire

Japan and its territories

Great Britain

Independent Asian states

France

Ottoman Empire

Netherlands

United States

Major railroads

PACIFIC OCEAN

JAPANESE EMPIRE

Sea of Okhotsk

Sakhalin

Karafuto (1905)

SIBERIA

AMUR DISTRICT (1858)

Khabarovsk (1858)

Vladivostok (1860)

MANCHURIA

Harbin

JEHOL

Shenyang (Mukden)

KOREA (1905, 1910)

Lüshun (Port Arthur) (Japan 1905)

Weihai (Gr. Br. 1898)

Sea of Japan

Ryuku Is. (Jap.)

East China Sea

Formosa (1895)

RUSSIAN EMPIRE

Chita

Irkutsk

Lake Baikal

INNER MONGOLIA

OUTER MONGOLIA (Russian influence, 1912)

Beijing

Tianjin

Nanjing

Shanghai (Gr. Br. 1842)

Wuhan

Fuzhou

Xiamen (Gr. Br. 1842)

Jiaozhou (Ger. 1898)

SINKIANG

C H I N A

Yangzi R.

Huang He R.

Chongqing

Kunming

Guangzhou (Gr. Br. 1842)

Macao (Port. 1557)

Hong Kong (France 1898)

Zhanjiang (1898)

Hainan

South China Sea

Philippine Is. (U.S. 1898)

Manila

New Guinea

DUTCH EAST INDIES

Timor (Neth.) (Portugal 1859)

Celebes

BRITISH NORTH BORNEO (1888)

SARAWAK (1888)

Borneo

Java (1619)

Batavia

Sumatra

Singapore (Gr. Br. 1819)

MALAY STATES (1874, 1909)

SIAM

Bangkok

FRENCH INDOCHINA (1859, 1907)

Saigon

Haiphong

Hanoi

TIBET

HIMALAYA MTS.

BHUTAN

NEPAL

BURMA (1852, 1885)

Rangoon

Andaman Is. (Gr. Br.)

Bay of Bengal

Calcutta

KASHMIR (1846)

PUNJAB

Delhi

Ganges R.

I N D I A

Madras

Pondicherry (Fr.)

Karikal (Fr.)

Yanaon (Fr.)

Ceylon

AFGHANISTAN

Indus R.

BALUCHISTAN (1883)

BRITISH SPHERE (1907)

Karachi

Diu (Port.)

Bombay

Goa (Port.)

Arabian Sea

INDIAN OCEAN

Andizhan (1871)

Samarkand (1868)

Bukhara

Tashkent (1864)

Merv (1884)

Kushka

Ashkhabad (1881)

Lake Balkash

Krasnovodsk

Kazalinsk

Orenburg

Omsk

Samara

Aral Sea

Trans-Siberian Railway

R U S S I A N   E M P I R E

Moscow

St. Petersburg

Helsinki

Riga

Warsaw

Brest-Litovsk

Kiev

Volga R.

Dnieper R.

Danube R.

Baku

Batum (1878)

Kars (1878)

Tehran

RUSSIAN SPHERE (1907)

PERSIA

Baghdad

Caspian Sea

Black Sea

Constantinople

Angora

OTTOMAN EMPIRE

Damascus

Beirut

Medina

ARABIA

OMAN (1891)

HADRAMAUT (1888)

WEST ADEN (1903)

KUWAIT (1899)

Persian Gulf

Red Sea

Mediterranean Sea

Nile R.

A F R I C A

N

0   500   1,000 Mi.

0   500   1,000 Km.

safeguard the Suez Canal. Far-flung possessions guaranteed ever-growing navies the safe havens and the dependable coaling stations they needed in times of crisis or war.

Imperialism also served European rulers who were dealing with social tensions and political conflicts at home. The tabloid press whipped up feelings of patriotism over foreign triumphs, while leaders stressed that colonies benefited workers as well as capitalists by providing cheap raw materials for industry. In short, conservative leaders used imperialism to justify the status quo and their hold on power.

European leaders were themselves pressured to acquire colonies by special-interest groups. Shipping companies wanted lucrative subsidies. White settlers demanded more land and greater protection. Missionaries and humanitarians wanted to spread religion and stop the slave trade. Military men and colonial officials, whose role has often been overlooked, foresaw rapid advancement and high-paid positions in growing empires. The actions of such groups pushed the course of empire forward.

Many Westerners were convinced that colonies were essential to achieving greatness. "There has never been a great power without great colonies," wrote one French publicist in 1877. "Every virile people has established colonial power," echoed the famous nationalist historian of Germany, Heinrich von Treitschke (**HAHYN-rikh fuhn TRAHYCH-kuh**). "All great nations in the fullness of their strength have desired to set their mark upon barbarian lands and those who fail to participate in this great rivalry will play a pitiable role in time to come."[5]

As Treitschke's statement suggests, Social Darwinism and racist doctrines also fostered imperialist expansion. As one prominent English economist argued, the "strongest nation has always been conquering the weaker . . . and the strongest tend to be best." In the words of another, "The path of progress is strewn with the wreck . . . of inferior races." Thus imperialism was justified as the inevitable triumph of the superior European race.

Convinced of their moral and intellectual superiority, Europeans also came to believe that they should "civilize" nonwhite peoples. According to this view, nonwhites would eventually receive the benefits of modern economies, cities, advanced medicine, and higher standards of living. In time, they might be ready for self-government and Western democracy. Thus the French spoke of their sacred "civilizing mission." In 1899 Rudyard Kipling (1865–1936), who wrote masterfully of Anglo-Indian life and was perhaps the most influential British writer of the 1890s, exhorted Europeans (and Americans in the United States) to unselfish service in distant lands:

> Take up the White Man's Burden—
> Send forth the best ye breed—
> Go bind your sons to exile
> To serve your captives' need,
> To wait in heavy harness,
> On fluttered folk and wild—
> Your new-caught, sullen peoples
> Half-devil and half-child.[6]

Many Americans also accepted the ideology of the **white man's burden.** It was an important factor in the decision to rule, rather than liberate, the Philippines after the Spanish-American War. Like their European counterparts, these Americans sincerely believed that their civilization had reached unprecedented heights and that they had unique benefits to bestow on all "less advanced" peoples. Another argument was that imperial government protected natives from tribal warfare as well as cruder forms of exploitation by white settlers and business people.

white man's burden The idea that Europeans could and should civilize more primitive, nonwhite peoples and that nonwhites would eventually receive the benefits of modern economies, cities, advanced medicine, and higher standards of living.

Peace and stability under European control also facilitated the spread of Christianity. In Africa, Catholic and Protestant missionaries competed with Islam south of the Sahara, seeking converts and building schools to spread the Gospel. Many Africans' first real contact with whites was in mission schools. Some peoples, such as the Ibo in Nigeria, became highly Christianized.

Such occasional successes in black Africa contrasted with the general failure of missionary efforts in India, China, and the Islamic world. There Christians often preached in vain to peoples with ancient, complex religious beliefs. Yet the number of Christian believers around the world did increase substantially in the nineteenth century, and missionary groups kept trying. Unfortunately, "many missionaries had drunk at the well of European racism," and this probably prevented them from doing better.[7]

Critics of Imperialism

Not all Westerners were convinced of the value of imperialism. The radical English economist J. A. Hobson (1858–1940), in his *Imperialism*, contended that the rush to acquire colonies was due to the need of the rich to find outlets for their surplus capital. Yet, Hobson argued, imperial possessions did not pay off economically for the country as a whole. Moreover, Hobson argued that the quest for empire diverted popular attention away from domestic reform and the need to reduce the great gap between rich and poor. Most people, however, did not believe Hobson's economic argument and believed instead that imperialism profited the homeland.

Hobson and many other critics struck home, however, with their moral condemnation of whites imperiously ruling nonwhites. They rebelled against crude Social Darwinian thought: "Blessed are the strong, for they shall prey on the weak."[8] Kipling and his kind were lampooned as racist bullies whose rule rested on brutality, racial contempt, and the Maxim machine gun. In the novel *Heart of Darkness*, Joseph Conrad (1857–1924) castigated the "pure selfishness" of Europeans in "civilizing" Africa and dramatized how both whites and nonwhites are destroyed in the process. Henry Labouchère, a member of Parliament and prominent spokesman for this position, mocked Kipling's famous poem:

> Pile on the Brown Man's burden!
> And if ye rouse his hate,
> Meet his old-fashioned reasons
> With Maxims up to date,
> With shells and Dum-Dum bullets
> A hundred times plain
> The Brown Man's loss must never
> Imply the White Man's gain.[9]

Critics charged Europeans with applying a degrading double standard and failing to live up to their own noble ideals. At home Europeans had won or were winning representative government, individual liberties, and a certain equality of opportunity. In their empires, Europeans imposed military dictatorships on Africans and Asians; forced them to work involuntarily, almost like slaves; and discriminated against them shamelessly. Europeans who denounced the imperialist tide provided colonial peoples with a Western ideology of liberation.

Section Review

- The struggle between Dutch settlers (Afrikaners) and the British for control of South Africa led to a bloody South African war, resulting in a self-governing colony with the more numerous Afrikaners gaining political dominance, disenfranchising nonwhites.

- European leaders met at the Berlin conference (1884–1885) to set rules for the imperialistic competition for African territory, agreeing on "effective occupation" as the basis for European control of Africa.

- Asia also fell to imperialist Westerners, the Dutch occupying Indonesia, the French taking Indochina, the Russians expanding into the Caucasus, Central Asia, and China, and the United States taking over the Philippines.

- Causes of the new imperialism were: economic, as imperialistic countries feared they would lose markets; political, as leaders promoted nationalism to cover social and political tensions at home; and ideological, with social Darwinism and racist doctrines fueling the "superior" European need to "civilize" nonwhite peoples and for Christian missionaries to convert them.

- Dissenters toward European imperialism, such as J. A. Hobson, denounced its diverting attention away from domestic reform and condemned its false morality, charging that civil liberties won at home were not practiced in colonies.

Responding to Western Imperialism

What was the general pattern of non-Western responses to Western expansion, and how did India, Japan, and China meet the imperialist challenge?

To peoples in Africa and Asia, Western expansion represented a profoundly disruptive assault. Everywhere it threatened traditional ruling classes, traditional economies, and traditional ways of life. Christian missionaries and European secular ideologies challenged established beliefs and values. Non-Western peoples experienced a crisis of identity, one made all the more painful by the power and arrogance of the white intruders.

The Pattern of Response

Generally, the initial response of African and Asian rulers to aggressive Western expansion was to try to drive the unwelcome foreigners away. When that proved impossible, conquered peoples responded in a variety of ways. At one end of the spectrum were "traditionalists," who concentrated on preserving their cultural traditions at all costs. "Westernizers" or "modernizers" stood at the other, and many shades of opinion rested in between. Both before and after European domination, the struggle among these groups was often intense. With time, however, the modernizers usually prevailed.

When the power of both the traditionalists and the modernizers was thoroughly shattered by superior force, the great majority of Asians and Africans accepted imperial rule. Political participation in non-Western lands was historically limited to small elites, and the masses were used to doing what their rulers told them. Nevertheless, support for European rule was shallow and weak. Thus the conforming masses followed with greater or lesser enthusiasm a few determined personalities who came to oppose the Europeans. Such leaders always arose, both when Europeans ruled directly and when they manipulated native governments.

Those individuals who would lead the fight against imperialism found in the Western world the ideologies and justification for their protest. They discovered liberalism, with its credo of civil liberty and political self-determination. Above all, they found themselves attracted to modern nationalism, which asserted that every people had the right to control its own destiny. After 1917 anti-imperialist revolt would find another weapon in Lenin's version of Marxian socialism. Thus the anti-imperialist search for dignity drew strength from Western thought and culture, as is apparent in the development of three major Asian countries—India, Japan, and China.

Empire in India

India was the jewel of the British Empire, and no colonial area experienced a more profound British impact. Unlike Japan and China, which maintained a real or precarious independence, and unlike African territories, which were annexed by Europeans only at the end of the nineteenth century, India was ruled more or less absolutely by Britain for a very long time.

Arriving in India on the heels of the Portuguese in the seventeenth century, the British East India Company had conquered the last independent native state by 1848. In the **Great Rebellion** of 1857 and 1858, people throughout northern

Great Rebellion The 1857 and 1858 insurrection by Muslim and Hindu mercenaries in the British army that spread throughout northern and central India before finally being crushed, primarily by loyal native troops from southern India. Britain thereafter ruled India directly.

and central India tried to drive the British out, but the rebellion was crushed, primarily by native troops from southern India. Thereafter the British Parliament in London ruled India directly, with white administrators in India carrying out their orders. Many British shared the sentiments of Lord Kitchener in justifying British hegemony:

> *It is this consciousness of the inherent superiority of the European which has won for us India. However well educated and clever a native may be, and however brave he may prove himself, I believe that no rank we can bestow on him would cause him to be considered an equal of the British officer.*[10]

British women played an important part in the imperial enterprise, especially after the opening of the Suez Canal in 1869 made it much easier for civil servants and businessmen to bring their wives and children with them to India. These British families tended to live in their own separate communities, where they occu-

Imperial Complexities in India
Britain permitted many native princes to continue their rule, if they accepted British domination. This photo shows a road-building project designed to facilitate famine relief in a southern native state. Officials of the local Muslim prince and their British "advisers" watch over workers drawn from the Hindu majority. (Nizam's Good Works Project–Famine Relief: Road Building, Aurangabad 1895–1902, from Judith Mara Gutman, *Through Indian Eyes.* Courtesy, Private Collection)

pied large houses with well-shaded porches, handsome lawns, and a multitude of servants. It was the wife's responsibility to direct their households and servants with the same self-confident authoritarianism that characterized British political rule in India. (See the feature "Listening to the Past: A British Woman in India" on pages 696–697.)

With British men and women sharing a sense of mission as well as strong feelings of racial and cultural superiority, the British established a modern system of progressive secondary education in which all instruction was in English. Thus through education and government service, the British offered some Indians opportunities for both economic and social advancement. High-caste Hindus, particularly quick to respond, emerged as skillful intermediaries between the British rulers and the Indian people, and soon they formed a new elite profoundly influenced by Western thought and culture.

This new bureaucratic elite played a crucial role in modern economic development, which was a second result of British rule. Irrigation projects for agriculture, the world's third-largest railroad network for good communications, and large tea and jute plantations geared to the world economy were all developed. Unfortunately, the lot of the Indian masses improved little, for the increase in production was eaten up by population increase.

Finally, with a well-educated, English-speaking Indian bureaucracy and modern communications, the British created a unified, powerful state. They placed under the same general system of law and administration the vanquished kingdoms of the entire subcontinent—groups that had fought each other for centuries and had been repeatedly conquered by Muslim and Mongol invaders.

In spite of these achievements, the decisive reaction to European rule was the rise of nationalism among the Indian elite. No matter how anglicized and necessary a member of the educated classes became, he or she could never become the white ruler's equal. The top jobs, the best clubs, the modern hotels, and even certain railroad compartments were sealed off to brown-skinned Indians. The peasant masses might accept such inequality as the latest version of age-old oppression, but the well-educated, English-speaking elite eventually could not. For the elite, racial discrimination meant bitter injustice. It flagrantly contradicted those cherished Western concepts of human rights and equality. Moreover, it was based on dictatorship, no matter how benign.

By 1885, when educated Indians came together to found the predominately Hindu Indian National Congress, demands were increasing for the equality and self-government that Britain had already granted white-settler colonies, such as Canada and Australia. By 1907, emboldened in part by Japan's success (see the next section), the radicals in the Indian National Congress were calling for complete independence. Even the moderates were demanding home rule for India through an elected parliament. Although there were sharp divisions between Hindus and Muslims, Indians were finding an answer to the foreign challenge. The common heritage of British rule and Western ideals, along with the reform and revitalization of the Hindu religion, had created a genuine movement for national independence.

The Example of Japan

When Commodore Matthew Perry arrived in Japan in 1853 with his crude but effective gunboat diplomacy, Japan was a complex feudal society. At the top stood a figurehead emperor, but real power was in the hands of a hereditary military governor, the **shogun** (SHOH-guhn). With the help of a warrior nobility known as

shogun The hereditary governor in feudal Japan.

samurai (**SAH-muh-rye**), the shogun governed an unindustrialized country of peasants and city dwellers.

When foreign diplomats and merchants began to settle in Yokohama (**yoh-kuh-HAH-muh**), radical samurai reacted with a wave of antiforeign terrorism and antigovernment assassinations between 1858 and 1863. The imperialist response was swift. An allied fleet of American, British, Dutch, and French warships demolished key forts, further weakening the power and prestige of the shogun's government. Then in 1867, a coalition led by patriotic samurai seized control of the government and restored the political power of the emperor. This was the Meiji (**MAY-jee**) Restoration, a great turning point in Japanese development.

The immediate, all-important goal of the new government was to meet the foreign threat. The battle cry of the Meiji reformers was "Enrich the state and strengthen the armed forces." Yet how were these tasks to be done? In a remarkable about-face, the leaders of Meiji Japan dropped their antiforeign attacks and initiated a series of measures to reform Japan along modern lines. In the broadest sense, the Meiji leaders tried to harness the power inherent in Europe's dual revolution in order to protect their country and catch up with the West.

In 1871 the new leaders abolished the old feudal structure and declared social equality. They decreed freedom of movement in a country where traveling abroad had been a most serious crime. They created a free, competitive, government-stimulated economy. Japan began to build railroads and modern factories. Thus the new generation adopted many principles of a free, liberal society, and, as in Europe, such freedom resulted in a tremendously creative release of human energy.

Yet the overriding concern of Japan's political leadership was always a powerful state, and to achieve this, more than liberalism was borrowed from the West. A powerful modern navy was created, and the army was completely reorganized along European lines, so that an army of draftees and a professional officer corps replaced the aristocratic samurai warriors. Japan also adapted skillfully the West's science and modern technology, particularly in industry, medicine, and education. Many Japanese were encouraged to study abroad, and the government paid large salaries to attract foreign experts. These experts were always carefully controlled, however, and replaced by trained Japanese as soon as possible.

By 1890, the new state was firmly established. Following the model of the German Empire, Japan established an authoritarian constitution and rejected democracy. The power of the emperor and his ministers was vast; that of the legislature, limited.

Japan successfully copied the imperialism of Western society. Expansion not only proved that Japan was

The Rapid Modernization of the Japanese Army
This woodcut from about 1870 shows Japanese soldiers outfitted in Western uniforms and marching in Western formation. Japanese reformers, impressed by Prussian discipline and success on the battlefield, looked to Germany for their military models. (Ryogoku Tsuneo Tamba Collection/Laurie Platt Winfrey)

strong; it also cemented the nation together in a great mission. Having "opened" Korea with the gunboat diplomacy of imperialism in 1876, Japan decisively defeated China in a war over Korea in 1894 and 1895 and took Formosa (modern-day Taiwan). In the next years, Japan competed aggressively with the leading European powers for influence and territory in China, particularly Manchuria (man-CHOOR-ee-uh). There Japanese and Russian imperialism met and collided. In 1904 Japan attacked Russia without warning, and after a bloody war, Japan emerged with a valuable foothold in China. By 1910, with the annexation of Korea, Japan had become a major imperialist power.

Toward Revolution in China

In 1860 the two-hundred-year-old Qing Dynasty in China appeared on the verge of collapse. Efforts to repel foreigners had failed, and rebellion and chaos wracked the country. Yet the government made a surprising comeback that lasted more than thirty years. Loyal scholar-statesmen and generals quelled disturbances such as the great Tai Ping (tie-PING) rebellion, while the empress dowager Tzu Hsi (TSOO SHEE) revitalized the bureaucracy with some help from European advisers. Foreign aggression also lessened during this period, for the Europeans had obtained their primary goal of commercial and diplomatic relations.

The Qing Dynasty moved again toward collapse in the wake of the Sino-Japanese War of 1894 to 1895, which had revealed China's helplessness in the face of aggression. European powers seized the opportunity to grab concessions and protectorates in China. At the high point of this rush in 1898, it appeared that the European powers might actually divide China among themselves, as they had recently divided Africa. Probably only the jealousy each nation felt toward its imperialist competitors saved China from partition, although the U.S. Open Door policy, which opposed formal annexation of Chinese territory, may have helped tip the balance. In any event, the tempo of foreign encroachment greatly accelerated after 1894.

So, too, did the intensity and radicalism of the Chinese reaction. Like the leaders of the Meiji Restoration, some modernizers saw salvation in Western institutions. In 1898 the government launched a desperate **hundred days of reform** in an attempt to meet the foreign challenge. More radical reformers, such as the revolutionary Sun Yat-sen (**soon yot-SEN**) (1866–1925), who came from the peasantry and was educated in Hawaii by Christian missionaries, sought to overthrow the dynasty altogether and establish a republic.

On the other side, some traditionalists turned back toward ancient practices, political conservatism, and fanatical hatred of the "foreign devils." "Protect the country, destroy the foreigner" was their simple motto. In the agony of defeat and unwanted reforms, secret societies such as the Boxers rebelled. In northeastern China, more than two hundred foreign missionaries and several thousand Chinese Christians were killed. Once again the imperialist response was swift and harsh. Peking was occupied and plundered by foreign armies. A heavy indemnity was imposed.

The years after the Boxer Rebellion (1900–1903) were ever more troubled. Anarchy and foreign influence spread as the power and prestige of the Qing Dynasty declined still further. Antiforeign, antigovernment revolutionary groups agitated and plotted. Finally in 1912, a spontaneous uprising toppled the Qing Dynasty. After thousands of years of emperors and empires, a loose coalition of revolutionaries proclaimed a Western-style republic and called for an elected parliament. The transformation of China under the impact of expanding Western society entered a new phase, and the end was not in sight.

hundred days of reform A series of Western-style reforms launched in 1898 by the Chinese government in an attempt to meet the foreign challenge.

Section Review

- Natives initially met Western expansion militarily to get rid of the white invaders, but when that failed, a variety of responses ensued, from struggles to maintain "traditionalist" culture to "modernists" who assimilated Western culture within their own.

- Support for European rule was generally weak, allowing native anti-imperialist leaders to use Western ideas of nationalism to inspire the masses to revolt.

- In British-ruled India, native Indians, no matter how educated, were only second class, leading to the formation of the Indian National Congress that began to call for complete independence or at least home rule through an elected parliament.

- Japan met the imperialist threat with counterforce, restoring the emperor and completely reorganizing their nation along the Western lines of a competitive, free, liberal society; they revamped the army and navy while retaining an authoritarian constitution and competing with the West for territory and influence in China.

- The Qing Dynasty struggled to maintain control of China in a climate of rebellion, chaos, and threats on all sides from foreign imperialists, but after the failed Boxer rebellion, another uprising in 1912 finally ended the empire, calling for a republic and an elected Western-style parliament.

Chapter Review

What were some of the global consequences of European industrialization between 1815 and 1914? (page 674)

In the nineteenth century, the industrializing West entered the third and most dynamic phase of its centuries-old expansion into non-Western lands. In so doing, Western nations promoted a prodigious growth of world trade, forced reluctant countries such as China and Japan into the globalizing economy, and profitably subordinated many lands to their own economic interests.

How was massive migration an integral part of Western expansion? (page 679)

In response to population pressures at home and economic opportunities abroad, Western nations also sent forth millions of emigrants to the sparsely populated areas of European settlement in North and South America, Australia, and Asiatic Russia. Migration from Asia was much more limited, mainly because European settlers raised high barriers against Asian immigrants.

How and why after 1875 did European nations rush to build political empires in Africa and Asia? (page 681)

After 1875, Western countries grabbed vast political empires in Africa and rushed to establish political influence in Asia. The reasons for this culminating surge were many, but the economic thrust of robust industrial capitalism, an ever-growing lead in technology, and the competitive pressures of European nationalism were particularly important.

What was the general pattern of non-Western responses to Western expansion, and how did India, Japan, and China meet the imperialist challenge? (page 689)

Western expansion had far-reaching consequences. The world became in many ways a single unit, as European expansion diffused the ideas and techniques of a highly developed civilization. Yet the West relied on force to conquer and rule, and it treated non-Western peoples as racial inferiors. Thus non-Western elites, often armed with Western doctrines, responded gradually but effectively to the Western challenge. In India, a well-educated English-speaking elite rejected racial discrimination, and in 1885 it launched the Indian National Congress, which was calling for complete independence by 1907. In Japan, the Meiji reformers reorganized the society, promoted modernization, and embraced imperialism. In China, less successful at reform, a popular uprising deposed the emperor in 1912 and established a republic. By 1914 non-Western elites in all three countries were engaged in a national, anti-imperialist struggle for dignity, genuine independence, and modernization.

Key Terms

Third World (p. 674)
opium trade (p. 676)
khedive (p. 678)
great migration (p. 679)
great white walls (p. 680)
new imperialism (p. 681)
Afrikaners (p. 681)
Berlin conference (p. 683)
white man's burden (p. 687)
Great Rebellion (p. 689)
shogun (p. 691)
samurai (p. 692)
hundred days of reform (p. 693)

Notes

1. Quoted in J. W. Hall, *Japan, from Prehistory to Modern Times* (New York: Delacorte Press, 1970), p. 250.
2. Quoted in Earl of Cromer, *Modern Egypt* (London, 1911), p. 48.
3. Quoted in T. Blegen, *Norwegian Migration to America*, vol. 2 (Northfield, Minn.: Norwegian-American Historical Association, 1940), p. 468.
4. Quoted in W. L. Langer, *European Alliances and Alignments, 1871–1890* (New York: Vintage Books, 1931), p. 290.

5. Quoted in G. H. Nadel and P. Curtis, eds., *Imperialism and Colonialism* (New York: Macmillan, 1964), p. 94.

6. Rudyard Kipling, *The Five Nations* (London, 1903).

7. E. H. Berman, "African Responses to Christian Mission Education," *African Studies Review* 17 (1974): 530.

8. Quoted in W. L. Langer, *The Diplomacy of Imperialism*, 2d ed. (New York: Alfred A. Knopf, 1951), p. 88.

9. "The Brown Man's Burden," by Henry Labouchère, 1899. Quoted in Ellis, *The Social History of the Machine Gun* (New York: Pantheon Books, 1975), pp. 99–100.

10. Quoted in K. M. Panikkar, *Asia and Western Dominance: A Survey of the Vasco da Gama Epoch of Asian History* (London: George Allen & Unwin, 1959), p. 116.

To assess your mastery of this chapter, go to **bedfordstmartins.com/mckaywestbrief**

Listening to the Past

A British Woman in India

Guides for housekeeping became popular in Europe in the nineteenth century as middle-class women funneled great energy into their homes. A British woman in India probably consulted The Complete Indian Housekeeper and Cook by Flora Annie Steel and Grace Gardiner, a bestseller published in 1888 and frequently updated.

The following passage focuses on how the British mistress should manage her Indian servants, and along with practical suggestions it lays bare some basic attitudes and assumptions of Europeans in colonial settings.

An English lady attended by her Indian servants.
(Stapleton Collection, UK/The Bridgeman Art Library)

Easy, however, as the actual housekeeping is in India, the personal attention of the mistress is quite as much needed here as at home. The Indian servant, it is true, learns more readily, and is guiltless of the sniffiness with which Mary Jane [the servant in England] receives suggestions, but a few days of absence or neglect on the part of the mistress, results in the servants falling into their old habits with the inherited conservatism of dirt. This is, of course, disheartening, but it has to be faced as a necessary condition of life, until a few generations of training shall have started the Indian servant on a new inheritance of habit. It must never be forgotten that at present those mistresses who aim at anything beyond keeping a good table are in the minority, and that pioneering is always arduous work.

The first duty of a mistress is, of course, to be able to give intelligible orders to her servants; therefore it is necessary she should learn to speak Hindustani. . . .

The next duty is obviously to insist on her orders being carried out. And here we come to the burning question: "How is this to be done?" Certainly, there is at present very little to which we can appeal in the average Indian servant, but then, until it is implanted by training, there is very little sense of duty in a child; yet in some well-regulated nurseries obedience is a foregone conclusion. The secret lies in making rules, and *keeping to them.* The Indian servant is a child in everything save age, and should be treated as a child; that is to say, kindly, but with the greatest firmness. The laws of the household should be those of the Medes and Persians, and first faults should never go unpunished. By overlooking a first offence, we lose the only opportunity we have of preventing it becoming a habit.

But it will be asked, How are we to punish our servants when we have no hold either on their minds or bodies? . . .

In their own experience the authors have found a system of rewards and punishments perfectly easy of attainment. One of them has for years adopted the plan of engaging her servants at so much a month—the lowest rate at which such servant is obtainable—and so much extra as *buksheesh* (buk-SHEESH) [a bonus], conditional on good service. For instance, a *khitmutgâr* (KID-muht-gahr) [male table servant] is engaged permanently on Rs. 9 a month, but the additional rupee which makes the wage up to that usually demanded by good servants is a fluctuating assessment! . . . That plan has never been objected to, and . . . the household quite enters into the spirit of the idea, infinitely preferring it to volcanic eruptions of fault-finding. . . .

We do not wish to advocate an unholy haughtiness; but an Indian household can no more be governed peacefully, without dignity and prestige, than an Indian Empire. For instance, if the mistress wishes to teach the cook a new dish, let her give the order for everything, down to charcoal, to be ready at a given time, and the cook in attendance; and let her do nothing herself that the servants can do, if only for this reason, that the only way of teaching is to *see* things done, not to let others see *you* do them.

Questions for Analysis

1. What challenges does the British housekeeper face in India? How, according to Steel and Gardiner, should she meet them?

2. In what ways do the authors' comments and housekeeping policies reflect the attitudes of European imperialism?

Source: F. A. Steel and G. Gardiner, *The Complete Indian Housekeeper and Cook* (London: William Heinemann, 1902), chap. 1. Reprinted in L. DiCaprio and M. Wiesner, eds., *Lives and Voices: Sources in European Women's History* (Boston: Houghton Mifflin, 2001), pp. 323–328.

CHAPTER 27

The Great Break: War and Revolution

1914–1919

Chapter Preview

The First World War
What caused the Great War, and why did it have such revolutionary consequences?

The Home Front
What was the impact of total war on civilian populations?

The Russian Revolution
Why did World War I bring socialist revolution in Russia?

The Peace Settlement
How did the Allies fashion a peace settlement, and why was it unsuccessful?

INDIVIDUALS IN SOCIETY: Vera Brittain

LISTENING TO THE PAST: Arab Political Aspirations in 1919

French soldiers in the trenches man a machine gun, the weapon that killed so many, in this chilling work by Christopher Nevinson. (© Tate, London/Art Resource, NY)

I n the summer of 1914, the nations of Europe went willingly to war. They believed they had no other choice. Moreover, both peoples and governments confidently expected a short war leading to a decisive victory. Such a war, they believed, would "clear the air," and European society would be able to go on as before.

These expectations were almost totally mistaken. The First World War was long, indecisive, and tremendously destructive. To the shell-shocked generation of survivors, it was known simply as the Great War: the war of unprecedented scope and intensity. From today's perspective, it is clear that the First World War marked a great break in the course of modern Western history. World War I was a revolutionary conflict of gigantic proportions.

The First World War

What caused the Great War, and why did it have such revolutionary consequences?

The First World War was extremely long and destructive because it involved all the Great Powers and because it quickly degenerated into a senseless military stalemate. Like evenly matched boxers in a championship bout, the two sides tried to wear each other down. But there was no referee to call a draw, only the blind hammering of a life-or-death struggle.

The Bismarckian System of Alliances

In ten short years, from 1862 to 1871, Prussia-Germany had risen to become the most powerful nation in Europe, opening a new era in international relations. Yet, as Bismarck never tired of repeating after his victory over France in 1871, Germany was a "satisfied" power. Within Europe, Germany had no territorial ambitions and wanted only peace.

But how was peace to be preserved? Bismarck's first concern was to keep an embittered France from gaining military allies. His second concern was the threat to peace posed from the east, from Austria-Hungary and from Russia. Those two enormous multinational empires had many conflicting interests, particularly in southeastern Europe where the strength of the Ottoman Empire was ebbing fast. There was a real threat that Germany might be dragged into a great war between the two rival empires. Bismarck's solution was a system of alliances to restrain both Russia and Austria-Hungary, to prevent conflict between them, and to isolate France.

A first step was the creation in 1873 of the conservative **Three Emperors' League,** which linked the monarchs of Prussia-Germany, Austria-Hungary, and Russia in an alliance against radical movements. In 1877 and 1878, when Russia's victories in a war with the Ottoman Empire threatened the balance of Austrian and Russian interests in the Balkans and the balance of British and Russian interests in the entire Middle East, Bismarck played the role of sincere peacemaker. But his balancing efforts at the Congress of Berlin in 1878 infuriated Russian nationalists, and this led Bismarck to conclude a defensive military alliance with Austria against Russia in 1879. This alliance lasted until 1918 and the end of World War I. Motivated by tensions with France, Italy joined Germany and Austria in 1882, thereby forming what became known as the Triple Alliance.

Three Emperors' League A conservative alliance that linked the monarchs of Austria-Hungary, Germany, and Russia against radical movements.

Bismarck also maintained good relations with Britain, while encouraging France in Africa but keeping France isolated in Europe. While he was not able to maintain an alliance with Russia, he was able to substitute an agreement by which both states promised neutrality if the other was attacked. In sum, Bismarck's accomplishments in foreign policy after 1871 were great. For almost a generation, he maintained German leadership in international affairs, and he worked successfully for peace by managing conflicts and by restraining Austria-Hungary and Russia with defensive alliances.

The Rival Blocs

In 1890 the young, impetuous Emperor William II dismissed Bismarck, in part because of the chancellor's friendly policy toward Russia since the 1870s. William then adamantly refused to renew the neutrality agreement with Russia, prompting France to seize the chance to gain a powerful new ally. The alliance of France and Russia was to remain in effect as long as the Triple Alliance of Austria, Germany, and Italy existed. As a result, continental Europe was dangerously divided into two rival blocs.

Great Britain's foreign policy became increasingly crucial. Long content with "splendid isolation" and no permanent alliances, Britain after 1891 was the only uncommitted Great Power. Could Britain afford to remain isolated, or would it feel compelled to take sides? Many Germans and some Britons felt that a "natural alliance" of shared ancestry united the Germanic and Anglo-Saxon peoples. However, the generally good relations that had prevailed between Prussia and Great Britain ever since the mid-eighteenth century gave way to commercial and naval rivalries.

Above all, Germany's decision in 1900 to expand greatly its battle fleet posed a challenge to Britain's long-standing naval supremacy. This decision coincided with the hard-fought South African War (1899–1902) between the British and the tiny Dutch republics of southern Africa, a war of British imperialism that was widely denounced in the European press. Thus British leaders prudently set about shoring up their exposed position with alliances and agreements.

Britain improved its often-strained relations with the United States and in 1902 concluded a formal alliance with Japan. Britain then responded favorably to the advances of France's skillful foreign minister, Théophile Delcassé (**tey-aw-FEEL del-ka-SEY**), who wanted better relations with Britain and was willing to accept British rule in Egypt in return for British support of French plans to dominate Morocco. The resulting Anglo-French Entente of 1904 settled all outstanding colonial disputes between Britain and France.

Germany's leaders foolishly decided to test the strength of the entente by insisting in 1905 on an international conference on the whole Moroccan question. But Germany's crude bullying forced France and Britain closer together, and the conference left Germany empty-handed and isolated (except for Austria-Hungary).

The result of the Moroccan crisis was something of a diplomatic revolution. Britain, France, Russia, and even the United States began to see Germany as a potential threat, a would-be intimidator that might seek to dominate all Europe. At the same time, German leaders began to see sinister plots to "encircle" Germany and block its development as a world power.

Germany's decision to add a large, enormously expensive fleet of big-gun battleships to its already expanding navy also heightened tensions after 1907. Again the British saw it as a challenge to their power, and they resented having to invest in a competing fleet. Unscrupulous journalists and special-interest groups in both countries also fanned hostilities with talk of economic warfare between the trade giants. In 1909 the mass-circulation London *Daily Mail* hysterically informed its readers that "Germany is deliberately preparing to destroy the British Empire."[1] By then Britain was psychologically, if not officially, in the Franco-Russian camp.

The Outbreak of War

In the early years of the twentieth century, nationalism was destroying the Ottoman Empire in Europe and threatening to break up the Austro-Hungarian Empire. War in the Balkans seemed inevitable.

In 1875 widespread nationalist rebellion resulted in the partial division of Ottoman Turkish possessions in Europe. Serbia and Romania won independence, and a part of Bulgaria won local autonomy, but Austria-Hungary obtained the right to "occupy and administer" Bosnia and Herzegovina (her-tsuh-goh-VEE-nuh), and the Ottoman Empire retained important Balkan holdings (see Map 27.1).

By 1903, however, nationalism in southeastern Europe was on the rise once again. Serbia led the way, hoping to expand its territories at the expense of Austria-Hungary and the Ottoman Empire. The Serbs looked to

1912	First Balkan War
1914	Assassination of Archduke Francis Ferdinand
1914–1918	World War I
1915	Italy and Bulgaria enter World War I
1916	German males between seventeen and sixty required to work only for war effort; Rasputin murdered
1916–1918	Growth of antiwar movement throughout Europe
1917	Russian Revolution
1918–1920	Great Civil War in Russia
1919	Treaty of Versailles

German Warships Under Full Steam

As these impressive ships engaged in battle exercises in 1907 suggest, Germany did succeed in building a large modern navy. But Britain was equally determined to maintain its naval superiority, and the spiraling arms race helped poison relations between the two countries. (Bibliothèque des Arts Décoratifs/Archives Charmet/The Bridgeman Art Library)

MAP 27.1   The Balkans After the Congress of Berlin, 1878
The Ottoman Empire suffered large territorial losses but remained a power in the Balkans.

MAP 27.2   The Balkans in 1914
Ethnic boundaries did not follow political boundaries, and Serbian national aspirations threatened Austria-Hungary.

Slavic Russia for support of their national aspirations. To block Serbian expansion and to take advantage of Russia's weakness after the revolution of 1905, Austria in 1908 formally annexed Bosnia and Herzegovina, with their large Serbian, Croatian, and Muslim populations. The kingdom of Serbia erupted in rage but could do nothing without Russian support.

Then, in 1912, in the First Balkan War, Serbia joined Greece and Bulgaria to attack the Ottoman Empire and then quarreled with Bulgaria over the spoils of victory—a dispute that led in 1913 to the Second Balkan War. Austria intervened in 1913 and forced Serbia to give up Albania. After centuries, nationalism had finally destroyed the Ottoman Empire in Europe (see Map 27.2). This sudden but long-awaited event elated the Balkan nationalists and dismayed the leaders of multinational Austria-Hungary. The former hoped and the latter feared that Austria might be broken apart next.

Within this tense context, Archduke Francis Ferdinand, heir to the Austrian and Hungarian thrones, and his wife, Sophie, were assassinated by Serbian revolutionaries living in Bosnia on June 28, 1914, during a state visit to the Bosnian capital of Sarajevo (**sar-uh-YEY-voh**). After some hesitation, the leaders of Austria-Hungary concluded that Serbia was implicated and had to be severely punished once and for all. On July 23 Austria-Hungary presented Serbia with an unconditional ultimatum. The Serbian government had forty-eight hours in which to agree to demands that would amount to ceding control of the Serbian state. When Serbia replied moderately but evasively, Austria began to mobilize and then declared war on Serbia on July 28. Thus a desperate multinational Austria-Hungary deliberately chose war in a last-ditch attempt to stem the rising tide of hostile nationalism within its borders. The Third Balkan War had begun.

Of prime importance in Austria-Hungary's fateful decision was Germany's unconditional support. Germany's leaders realized that a resurgent Russia (and therefore France) would probably enter the war in support of Serbia, but they hoped that Great Britain would remain neutral.

In fact, the diplomatic situation was already out of control. Military plans and timetables began to dictate policy. Russia, a vast country, would require much longer to mobilize its armies than Germany and Austria-Hungary. All the complicated mobilization plans of the Russian general staff had assumed a war with both Austria and Germany: Russia could not mobilize against Austria-Hungary alone. Therefore, on July 29 Tsar Nicholas II ordered full mobilization and in effect declared general war.

The German general staff had also assumed a two-front war, and following its plans meant striking France as well as Russia. France was to be knocked out first with a lightning attack through neutral Belgium before turning on Russia. So on August 3 German armies attacked Belgium, whose neutrality had been solemnly guaranteed in 1839 by all the great states including Prussia. In the face of this act of aggression, Great Britain joined the **Triple Entente** (**on-TONT**) with France and Russia and declared war on Germany the following day. The First World War had begun.

"Never Forget!"

This 1915 French poster with its passionate headline dramatizes Germany's brutal invasion of Belgium in 1914. Neutral Belgium is personified as a traumatized mother, assaulted and ravished by savage outlaws. The "rape of Belgium" featured prominently—and effectively—in anti-German propaganda. (Mary Evans Picture Library)

| **Stalemate and Slaughter** | When the Germans invaded Belgium in August 1914, everyone believed that their side would secure a swift victory: "The boys will be home by Christmas." But |

German forces had been slowed by Belgian and British troops near the Franco-Belgian border, and by the end of August they were still making their way to Paris.

On September 6 the French attacked a gap in the German line at the Battle of the Marne. For three days, France threw everything into the attack. At one point, the French government desperately requisitioned all the taxis of Paris to rush reserves to the troops at the front. Finally, the Germans fell back. Paris and France had been saved (see Map 27.3 on page 706).

Soon, with the armies stalled, both sides began to dig trenches to protect themselves from machine-gun fire. By November 1914, an unbroken line of trenches extended from the Belgian ports through northern France, past the fortress of Verdun, and on to the Swiss frontier. Stalemate and slaughter followed. The defenders on both sides dug in behind rows of trenches, mines, and barbed wire. For days and even weeks, ceaseless shelling by heavy artillery supposedly "softened up" the enemy in a given area (and also signaled the coming attack). Then young draftees

Triple Entente The alliance of Great Britain, France, and Russia in the First World War.

The Tragic Absurdity of Trench Warfare

Soldiers charge across a scarred battlefield and overrun an enemy trench. The dead defender on the right will fire no more. But this is only another futile charge that will yield much blood and little land. A whole generation is being decimated by the slaughter. (By courtesy of the Trustees of the Imperial War Museum)

trench warfare A type of fighting behind rows of trenches, mines, and barbed wire; the cost in lives was staggering and the gains in territory minimal.

and their junior officers went "over the top" of the trenches in frontal attacks on the enemy's line.

The cost in lives of this **trench warfare** was staggering, the gains in territory minuscule. The massive French and British offensives during 1915 never gained more than 3 miles of blood-soaked earth from the enemy. In the Battle of the Somme in the summer of 1916, the British and French gained an insignificant 125 square miles at the cost of 600,000 dead or wounded, while the Germans lost 500,000 men. In that same year the unsuccessful German campaign against Verdun cost 700,000 lives on both sides. British poet Siegfried Sassoon (1886–1967) wrote of the Somme offensive, "I am staring at a sunlit picture of Hell."

The year 1917 was equally terrible. The hero of Erich Remarque's (ri-MAHRK) great novel *All Quiet on the Western Front* (1929) describes one attack:

> We see men living with their skulls blown open; we see soldiers run with their two feet cut off. . . . Still the little piece of convulsed earth in which we lie is held. We have yielded no more than a few hundred yards of it as a prize to the enemy. But on every yard there lies a dead man.

Such was war on the western front.

Trench warfare shattered an entire generation of young men. Millions who could have provided political creativity and leadership after the war were forever missing. Moreover, those who lived through the slaughter were maimed, shell-shocked, embittered, and profoundly disillusioned. The young soldiers went to war believing in the world of their leaders and elders—the pre-1914 world of order, progress, and patriotism. Then, in Remarque's words, the "first bombardment showed us our mistake, and under it the world as they had taught it to us broke in pieces."

The Widening War

On the eastern front, soldiers were spared trench warfare but the costs were equally high. The "Russian steamroller" immediately moved into eastern Germany but was badly damaged at the Battles of Tannenberg and the Masurian (**mah-ZOOR-ee-an**) Lakes in August and September 1914. Thereafter, Russia never threatened Germany again. On the Austrian front, armies seesawed back and forth, suffering enormous losses. Austro-Hungarian armies were repulsed twice by Serbia in bitter fighting. The Russians advanced on Austria's northwestern border in 1914, but Austro-Hungarian and German armies forced the Russians to retreat deep into their own territory in the eastern campaign of 1915. A staggering 2.5 million Russians were killed, wounded, or taken prisoner that year.

The war widened as previously neutral countries joined the fighting (see Map 27.3). Italy, once allied with Austria and Germany, joined the Triple Entente of Great Britain, France, and Russia in return for promises of Austrian territory. In October 1914 the Ottoman Empire joined with Austria and Germany, by then known as the Central Powers. The following September Bulgaria decided to follow the Ottoman Empire's lead in order to settle old scores with Serbia. The Balkans, with the exception of Greece, came to be occupied by the Central Powers. The entry of the Ottoman Turks carried the war into the Middle East. Heavy fighting between the Ottomans and the Russians saw battle lines seesawing back and forth and enveloping the Armenians, who lived on both sides of the border and had experienced brutal repression by the Turks in 1909. When in 1915 some Armenians welcomed Russian armies as liberators, the Ottoman government ordered a genocidal mass deportation of its Armenian citizens from their homeland. A million Armenians died from murder, starvation, and disease during World War I. In 1915 British forces tried to take the Dardanelles (**dahr-den-ELZ**) and Constantinople from the Ottomans but were badly defeated.

The British were more successful at inciting the Arabs to revolt against the Ottoman Turks. They bargained with the foremost Arab leader, Hussein ibn-Ali (**hoo-SEYN IB-uhn ah-LEE**) (1856–1931), who managed in 1915 to win vague British commitments for an independent Arab kingdom. Thus in 1916 Hussein revolted against the Turks, proclaiming himself king of the Arabs. He joined forces with the British under T. E. Lawrence, who in 1917 led Arab tribesmen and Indian soldiers in a highly successful guerrilla war against the Turks on the Arabian peninsula.

Similar victories were eventually scored in the Ottoman province of Iraq. Britain occupied the southern Iraqi city of Basra in 1914 and captured Baghdad (**BAG-dad**) in 1917. In September 1918 British armies and their Arab allies rolled into Syria. This offensive culminated in the triumphal entry of Hussein's son Faisal (**FIE-suhl**) into Damascus. Throughout Syria and Iraq there was wild Arab rejoicing. Many patriots expected a large, unified Arab nation-state to rise from the dust of the Ottoman collapse.

MAP 27.3 The First World War in Europe

Trench warfare on the western front was concentrated in Belgium and northern France, while the war in the east encompassed an enormous territory.

The Armenian Atrocities

When in 1915 some Armenians welcomed Russian armies as liberators after years of persecution, the Ottoman government ordered a genocidal mass deportation of its Armenian citizens from their homeland in the empire's eastern provinces. This photo, taken in Kharpert in 1915 by a German businessman from his hotel window, shows Turkish guards marching Armenian men off to a prison, where they will be tortured to death. A million Armenians died from murder, starvation, and disease during World War I. (Courtesy of the Armenian Library and Museum of America [ALMA], Watertown, MA)

As world war engulfed and revolutionized the Middle East, it also spread to some parts of East Asia and Africa. Instead of revolting as the Germans hoped, the colonial subjects of the British and French generally supported their foreign masters, providing crucial supplies and fighting in Europe and the Ottoman Empire. They also helped local British and French commanders seize Germany's colonies around the globe.

The Japanese, allied in Asia with the British since 1902, similarly used the war to grab German outposts in the Pacific Ocean and on the Chinese mainland, infuriating Chinese patriots and heightening long-standing tensions between China and Japan. More than a million Africans and Asians served in the various armies of the warring powers; more than double that number served as porters to carry equipment. The French, facing a shortage of young men, made especially heavy use of colonial troops.

In April 1917 the United States declared war on Germany, another crucial development in the expanding conflict. American intervention grew out of the war at sea, sympathy for the Triple Entente, and the increasing desperation of total war. At the beginning of the war, Britain and France had established a total naval blockade to strangle the Central Powers. No neutral ship was permitted to sail to

Lusitania The British passenger liner sunk by a German submarine that claimed 1,000 lives.

Section Review

- German chancellor Bismarck maintained peace in Europe by managing a balance-of-power system with the other European powers, forming first the Three Emperors' League with Austria-Hungary and Russia, and then the Triple Alliance with Italy and Austria.

- German emperor William II dismissed Bismarck, refused to renew neutrality with Russia, and, after arguing with France and Britain over Morocco, isolated himself and Austria-Hungary while Britain, formerly neutral, found itself siding with France and Russia.

- Nationalist problems in eastern Europe caused the decline of the Ottoman Empire and Serbian revolutionaries assassinated the heir to the Austrian throne, causing Austria to declare war on Serbia; confusion over military mobilization plans led Russia to declare general war, Germany overran Belgium to attack France, and Great Britain joined France and Russia to form the Triple Entente.

- The German offensive to take Paris ended as a stalemate with the Germans facing the French and British in horrific trench warfare that led to huge losses on both sides for little ground gained, resulting in disillusioned, maimed, and bitter soldiers.

- The war widened to include Italy with the Triple Entente and the Ottomans with the Central Powers, which opened fighting in the Middle East; the colonies generally supported their masters, Japan allied with the British, and finally the United States joined the Triple Entente in response to German submarine warfare.

total war In each country during the First World War, a government of national unity that began to plan and control economic and social life in order to make the greatest possible military effort.

Germany with any cargo. In early 1915 Germany retaliated with a counter-blockade using the murderously effective submarine, a new weapon that violated traditional niceties of fair warning under international law. In May 1915 a German submarine sank the British passenger liner **Lusitania,** claiming more than 1,000 lives, among them 139 Americans. President Woodrow Wilson protested vigorously. Germany was forced to relax its submarine warfare for almost two years; the alternative was almost certain war with the United States.

Early in 1917, the German military command—confident that improved submarines could starve Britain into submission before the United States could come to its rescue—resumed unrestricted submarine warfare. Like the invasion of Belgium, this was a reckless gamble. "German submarine warfare against commerce," President Wilson had told a sympathetic Congress and people, "is a warfare against mankind." Thus the last uncommitted great nation, as fresh and enthusiastic as Europe had been in 1914, entered the world war in April 1917, almost three years after it began. Eventually the United States was to tip the balance in favor of the Triple Entente and its allies.

The Home Front

What was the impact of total war on civilian populations?

Before looking at the last year of the Great War, let us turn our attention to the people on the home front. They were tremendously involved in the titanic struggle. War's impact on them was no less massive than on the men crouched in the trenches.

Mobilizing for Total War

In August 1914, most people greeted the outbreak of hostilities enthusiastically. In every country, the masses believed that their nation was in the right and defending itself from aggression. With the exception of a few extreme left-wingers, even socialists supported the war. Everywhere the support of the masses and working class contributed to national unity and an energetic war effort.

By mid-October generals and politicians had begun to realize that more than patriotism would be needed to win the war, whose end was not in sight. In each country, a government of national unity began to plan and control economic and social life in order to wage **total war.** Free-market capitalism was abandoned, at least "for the duration." Instead, government planning boards established priorities and decided what was to be produced and consumed.

Rationing, price and wage controls, and even restrictions on workers' freedom of movement were imposed by government. Only through such regimentation could a country make the greatest possible military effort. Thus, though there were national variations, the great nations all moved toward planned economies commanded by the established political leadership. However awful the war was, the ability of governments to manage and control highly complicated economies strengthened the cause of socialism. With the First World War, state socialism became for the first time a realistic economic blueprint rather than a utopian program.

The social impact of total war was no less profound than the economic impact, though again there were important national variations. The millions of men at the front and the insatiable needs of the military created a tremendous demand for

Waging Total War
A British war plant strains to meet the insatiable demand for trench-smashing heavy artillery shells. Quite typically, many of these defense workers are women. (By courtesy of the Trustees of the Imperial War Museum, neg. #Q30011)

workers. Jobs were available for everyone. This situation—seldom, if ever, seen before 1914—brought about momentous changes.

One such change was greater power and prestige for labor unions. Having proved their loyalty in August 1914, labor unions cooperated with war governments on work rules, wages, and production schedules in return for real participation in important decisions. This entry of labor leaders and unions into policymaking councils paralleled the entry of socialist leaders into the war governments.

The role of women changed dramatically. In every country, large numbers of women left home and domestic service to work in industry, transportation, and offices. Moreover, women became highly visible—not only as munitions workers but as bank tellers, mail carriers, even police officers. Women also served as nurses and doctors at the front. (See the feature "Individuals in Society: Vera Brittain.") In general, the war greatly expanded the range of women's activities and changed attitudes toward women. As a direct result of women's many-sided war effort, Britain, Germany, and Austria granted women the right to vote immediately after the war. Women also showed a growing spirit of independence during the war, as they started to bob their hair, shorten their skirts, and smoke in public.

War promoted greater social equality, blurring class distinctions and lessening the gap between rich and poor. This blurring was most apparent in Great Britain, where wartime hardship was never extreme. In fact, the bottom third of the population generally lived *better* than they ever had, for the poorest gained most from the severe shortage of labor. In continental countries, greater equality was reflected in full employment, rationing according to physical needs, and a sharing of hardships. There, too, society became more uniform and more egalitarian, in spite of some war profiteering.

Individuals in Society

Vera Brittain

Although the Great War upended millions of lives, it struck Europe's young people with the greatest force. For Vera Brittain (1893–1970), as for so many in her generation, the war became life's defining experience, which she captured forever in her famous autobiography, *Testament of Youth* (1933).

Brittain grew up in a wealthy business family in northern England, bristling at small-town conventions and discrimination against women. Very close to her brother Edward, two years her junior, Brittain read voraciously and dreamed of being a successful writer. Finishing boarding school and beating down her father's objections, she prepared for Oxford's rigorous entry exams and won a scholarship to its women's college. Brittain also fell in love with Roland Leighton (**LEYT-un**), an equally brilliant student from a literary family and her brother's best friend. All three, along with two more close friends, Victor Richardson and Geoffrey Thurlow, confidently prepared to enter Oxford in late 1914.

Vera Brittain, marked forever by her wartime experiences. (Vera Brittain Archive, William Ready Division of Archives and Research Collections, McMaster University Library)

When war suddenly approached in July 1914, Brittain shared with millions of Europeans a thrilling surge of patriotic support for her government, a pro-war enthusiasm she later played down in her published writings. She wrote in her diary that her "great fear" was that England would declare its neutrality and commit the "grossest treachery" toward France.* She seconded Roland's decision to enlist, agreeing with her sweetheart's glamorous view of war as "very ennobling and very beautiful." Later, exchanging anxious letters in 1915 with Roland in France, Vera began to see the conflict in personal, human terms. She wondered if any victory or defeat could be worth Roland's life.

Struggling to quell her doubts, Brittain redoubled her commitment to England's cause and volunteered as an army nurse. For the next three years she served with distinction in military hospitals in London, Malta, and

northern France, repeatedly torn between the vision of noble sacrifice and the reality of human tragedy. She lost her sexual inhibitions caring for mangled male bodies, and she longed to consummate her love with Roland. Awaiting his return on leave on Christmas Day in 1915, she was greeted instead with a telegram: Roland had been killed two days before.

Roland's death was the first of the devastating blows that eventually overwhelmed Brittain's idealistic patriotism. In 1917, first Geoffrey and then Victor died from gruesome wounds. In early 1918, as the last great German offensive covered the floors of her war-zone hospital with maimed and dying German prisoners, the bone-weary Vera felt a common humanity and saw only more victims. A few weeks later brother Edward—her last hope—died in action. When the war ended, she was, she said, a "complete automaton," with "my deepest emotions paralyzed if not dead."

Returning to Oxford and finishing her studies, Brittain gradually recovered. She formed a deep, restorative friendship with another talented woman writer, Winifred Holtby, published novels and articles, and became a leader in the feminist campaign for gender equality. She also married and had children. But her wartime memories were always there. Finally, Brittain succeeded in coming to grips with them in *Testament of Youth*, her powerful antiwar autobiography. The unflinching narrative spoke to the experiences of an entire generation and became a runaway bestseller. Above all, perhaps, Brittain captured the ambivalent, contradictory character of the war, when millions of young people found excitement, courage, and common purpose but succeeded only in destroying their lives with their superhuman efforts and futile sacrifices. Becoming ever more committed to pacifism, Brittain opposed England's entry into World War II.

Questions for Analysis

1. What were Brittain's initial feelings toward the war? How did they change as the conflict continued? Why did they change?

2. Why did Brittain volunteer as a nurse, as many women did? Judging from her account, how might wartime nursing have influenced women of her generation?

3. In portraying the ambivalent, contradictory character of World War I for Europe's youth, was Brittain describing the character of all modern warfare?

*Quoted in the excellent study by P. Berry and M. Bostridge, *Vera Brittain: A Life* (London: Virago Press, 2001), p. 59; additional quotes are from pp. 80 and 136. This work is highly recommended.

Growing Political Tensions

During the first two years of war, most soldiers and civilians supported their governments. Belief in a just cause, patriotic nationalism, the planned economy, and a sharing of burdens united peoples behind their various national leaders.

Each government employed rigorous censorship to control public opinion, and each used both crude and subtle propaganda to maintain popular support. German propaganda hysterically pictured black soldiers from France's African empire raping German women, while German atrocities in Belgium and elsewhere were ceaselessly recounted and exaggerated by the French and British. Patriotic posters and slogans, slanted news, and biased editorials inflamed national hatreds and helped sustain superhuman efforts. However, by the spring of 1916, people were beginning to crack under the strain of total war. Strikes and protest marches over inadequate food began to flare up on every home front.

Soldiers' morale also began to decline. Italian troops mutinied. Numerous French units refused to fight after the disastrous French offensive of May 1917. Only tough military justice for leaders and a tacit agreement with the troops that there would be no more grand offensives enabled the new general in chief, Henri Philippe Pétain (**pey-TAN**), to restore order. A rising tide of war-weariness and defeatism also swept France's civilian population before Georges Clemenceau (**zhorzh cluh-mon-SO**) emerged as a ruthless and effective wartime leader in November 1917. Clemenceau (1841–1929) established a virtual dictatorship, pouncing on strikers and jailing without trial journalists and politicians who dared to suggest a compromise peace with Germany.

The strains were worse for the Central Powers. In October 1916, the chief minister of Austria was assassinated by a young socialist crying, "Down with Absolutism! We want peace!"[2] The following month, when feeble old Emperor Francis Joseph died, a symbol of unity disappeared. In spite of absolute censorship, political dissatisfaction and conflicts among nationalities grew. In April 1917, Austria's chief minister summed up the situation in the gloomiest possible terms. The country and army were exhausted. Another winter of war would bring revolution and disintegration. Both Czech and Yugoslav leaders demanded autonomous democratic states for their peoples. The British blockade kept tightening; people were starving.

The strain of total war was also evident in Germany. In the winter of 1916 to 1917, Germany's military position appeared increasingly desperate. The social conflict of prewar Germany re-emerged, and revolutionary agitation and strikes by war-weary workers occurred in early 1917. Thus militaristic Germany, like its ally Austria-Hungary (and its enemy France), was beginning to crack in 1917. Yet it was Russia that collapsed first and saved the Central Powers—for a time.

Section Review

- Almost all governments fostered national unity by implementing "total war" using temporary socialist measures, rationing, and price and wage controls.

- Wartime conditions improved worker conditions, strengthened women's roles in the labor market, and promoted greater social equality, strengthening the cause of socialism.

- Popular support for the war remained strong during the first years through propaganda, media censorship, and patriotism, but as the war dragged on, inadequate food inflamed public sentiment, and strikes and protests began.

- The war fronts on all sides began to decline as well, with soldiers exhausted and morale low; people were starving and social conflict became evident in Italy, France, Germany, Austria-Hungary, and in Russia, which collapsed first.

The Russian Revolution

Why did World War I bring socialist revolution in Russia?

The Russian Revolution of 1917 was one of modern history's most momentous events. Directly related to the growing tensions of World War I, it had a significance far beyond the wartime agonies of a single European nation. The Russian Revolution opened a new era. For some, it was Marx's socialist vision come true; for others, it was the triumph of dictatorship. To all, it presented a radically new prototype of state and society.

The Fall of Imperial Russia

Like its allies and its enemies, Russia embraced war with patriotic enthusiasm in 1914. Crowds rallied around Tsar Nicholas II (r. 1894–1917) as he took an oath never to make peace as long as the enemy stood on Russian soil. Conservatives anticipated expansion in the Balkans, while liberals and most socialists believed alliance with Britain and France would bring democratic reforms. For a moment, Russia was united.

The Russian war machine was underprepared, however, and mobilized less effectively for total war than the other warring nations. Its supplies of shells and ammunition were quickly depleted, and substantial numbers of soldiers were expected to find the rifles they needed on the battlefield among the dead. There were 2 million Russian casualties in 1915 alone.

The great problem was leadership. A kindly, slightly stupid man, Nicholas failed to form a close partnership with his citizens in order to fight the war more effectively. He came to rely instead on the old bureaucratic apparatus, distrusting the moderate Duma (the parliament), rejecting popular involvement, and resisting calls to share power.

As a result, the Duma, the educated middle classes, and the masses became increasingly critical of the tsar's leadership. In September 1915 parties ranging from conservative to moderate socialist formed the Progressive bloc, which called for a completely new government responsible to the Duma instead of the tsar. In answer, Nicholas temporarily adjourned the Duma and announced that he was traveling to the front in order to lead and rally Russia's armies.

His departure was a fatal turning point. With the tsar in the field with the troops, control of the government fell to the empress, Tsarina Alexandra. Nicholas's wife was a strong-willed woman with a hatred of parliaments. Having constantly urged her husband to rule absolutely, Alexandra tried to do so herself in his absence. She seated and unseated the top ministers. Her most trusted adviser was "our Friend Grigori," an uneducated Siberian preacher who was appropriately nicknamed "Rasputin" (ra-SPYOO-tin)—the "Degenerate." Rasputin's extraordinary influence rested on his seeming ability to stop the bleeding of Alexis, Alexandra's fifth child and heir to the throne, who suffered from the rare blood disease hemophilia.

In a desperate attempt to right the situation and end unfounded rumors that Rasputin was the empress's lover, three members of the high aristocracy murdered Rasputin in December 1916. The empress went into semipermanent shock. Food shortages in the cities worsened; morale declined. On March 8, women calling for bread in Petrograd (formerly St. Petersburg) started riots, which spontaneously spread to the factories and then elsewhere throughout the city. From the front, the tsar ordered troops to restore order, but discipline broke down, and the soldiers joined the revolutionary crowd. The Duma responded by declaring a provisional government on March 12, 1917. Three days later, Nicholas abdicated.

The Provisional Government

The March revolution was the result of an unplanned uprising of hungry, angry people in the capital, but it was joyfully accepted throughout the country. Patriots rejoiced at the prospect of a more determined and effective war effort, while workers happily anticipated better wages and more food. All classes and political parties called for liberty and democracy. They were not disappointed. After generations of arbitrary authoritarianism, the provisional government quickly established equality before the law; freedom of religion, speech, and assembly; the right of unions to organize and strike; and the rest of the classic liberal program.

The reorganized government formed in May 1917 made the patriotic socialist Alexander Kerensky (**kuh-REN-skee**) its prime minister in July. For Kerensky and other moderate socialists, the continuation of war was still the all-important national duty. Human suffering and war-weariness grew, sapping the limited strength of the provisional government.

From its first day, the provisional government had to share power with a formidable rival—the **Petrograd Soviet** (or council) of Workers' and Soldiers' Deputies. Modeled on the revolutionary soviets of 1905, the Petrograd Soviet was a huge, fluctuating mass meeting of two thousand to three thousand workers, soldiers, and socialist intellectuals. Seeing itself as a true grassroots revolutionary democracy, this counter- or half-government suspiciously watched the provisional government and issued its own radical orders, further weakening the provisional government. Its **Army Order No. 1** stripped officers of their authority and placed power in the hands of elected committees of common soldiers. Designed primarily to protect the revolution from some counter-revolutionary Bonaparte on horseback, the order instead led to a total collapse of army discipline.

Meanwhile, masses of peasant soldiers began "voting with their feet," to use Lenin's graphic phrase. That is, they began returning to their villages to help their families get a share of the land, which peasants were simply seizing as they settled old scores in a great agrarian upheaval. All across the country, liberty was turning into anarchy in the summer of 1917. It was an unparalleled opportunity for the most radical and most talented of Russia's many socialist leaders, Vladimir Ilyich Lenin (**VLAD-uh-meer IL-yich LEN-in**) (1870–1924).

Petrograd Soviet A huge, fluctuating mass meeting of 2,000 to 3,000 workers, soldiers, and socialist intellectuals, modeled on the revolutionary soviets of 1905.

Army Order No. 1 A radical order of the Petrograd Soviet that stripped officers of their authority and placed power in the hands of elected committees of common soldiers.

Lenin and the Bolshevik Revolution

From his youth, Lenin's whole life had been dedicated to the cause of revolution. Born into the middle class, Lenin became an implacable enemy of imperial Russia when his older brother was executed for plotting to kill the tsar in 1887. Exiled to Siberia for three years for his own revolutionary activity, Lenin continued the intense study of Marxian doctrines that he had begun as a law student. After his release, he joined fellow socialists in western Europe and developed his own revolutionary interpretations of the body of Marxian thought.

Three interrelated ideas were central for Lenin. First, he stressed that capitalism could be destroyed only by violent revolution and denounced all revisionist theories of a peaceful evolution to socialism. Lenin's second, more original, idea was that a socialist revolution was possible even in non-industrial countries like Russia if an underclass was exploited. Lenin also believed that at a given moment revolution was determined more by human leadership than by vast historical laws. Thus was born his third basic idea: the necessity of a highly disciplined workers' party, strictly controlled by a dedicated elite of intellectuals and full-time revolutionaries like Lenin himself. An opposing camp of Russian Marxists wanted a more democratic party with mass membership. Lenin's camp was called the **Bolsheviks** (**BOHL-shuh-viks**), or "majority group." While his majority did not hold, he kept the fine-sounding name and developed the party he wanted: tough, disciplined, revolutionary.

Unlike most other socialists, Lenin did not rally round the national flag in 1914. Observing events from neutral Switzerland, he saw the war as a product of imperialistic rivalries and as a marvelous opportunity for class war and socialist upheaval. Hoping that Lenin would undermine the Russian war effort, the German government provided him with safe passage across Germany and back into Russia after the March revolution.

Bolsheviks Meaning "majority group," the name for Lenin's camp of the Russian party of Marxian socialism.

Arriving triumphantly in Petrograd on April 3, Lenin attacked at once. He had no intentions to cooperate with the "bourgeois" provisional government, instead declaring a radical program: "All power to the soviets"; "All land to the peasants"; "Stop the war now." But an attempt by the Bolsheviks to seize power in July collapsed, and Lenin fled and went into hiding. He was charged with being a German agent, and indeed he and the Bolsheviks were getting money from Germany.[3] But no matter. Intrigue between Kerensky and his commander in chief, General Lavr Kornilov, resulted in Kornilov's leading a feeble attack against the provisional government in September. In the face of this rightist "counter-revolutionary" threat, the Bolsheviks were rearmed and redeemed. Kornilov's forces disintegrated, but Kerensky lost all credit with the army, the only force that might have saved him and democratic government in Russia.

Trotsky and the Seizure of Power

By October the Bolsheviks had gained a fragile majority in the Petrograd Soviet by appealing very effectively to its workers and soldiers. It was now Lenin's supporter Leon Trotsky (TROT-skee) (1879–1940), a spellbinding revolutionary orator and independent radical Marxist, who brilliantly executed the Bolshevik seizure of power.

Trotsky convinced the Petrograd Soviet that it was at risk and needed to make him the leader of a special military-revolutionary committee. Then, on the night of November 6, militants from Trotsky's committee joined with trusty Bolshevik soldiers to seize government buildings and pounce on members of the provisional government. Then they went on to the congress of soviets. There a Bolshevik majority declared that all power had passed to the soviets and named Lenin head of the new government.

The Bolsheviks came to power for three key reasons. First, by late 1917 democracy had given way to anarchy: power was there for those who would take it. Second, in Lenin and Trotsky the Bolsheviks had an utterly determined and truly superior leadership, which both the tsarist government and the provisional government lacked. Third, in 1917 the Bolsheviks succeeded in appealing to many soldiers and urban workers, people who were exhausted by war and eager for socialism. With time, many workers would become bitterly disappointed, but for the moment they had good reason to believe that they had won what they wanted.

Dictatorship and Civil War

History is full of short-lived coups and unsuccessful revolutions. The truly monumental accomplishment of Lenin, Trotsky, and the rest of the Bolsheviks was not taking power but keeping it. In the next four years, the Bolsheviks went on to conquer the chaos they had helped create, and they began to build their kind of dictatorial socialist society. The conspirators became conquerors. How was this done?

Lenin had the genius to profit from developments over which he and the Bolsheviks had no control. Thus Lenin's first law, which supposedly gave land to the peasants, actually merely approved what peasants were already doing. Urban workers' great demand in November was direct control of individual factories by local workers' committees. This, too, Lenin ratified with a decree in November.

Lenin also acknowledged that Russia had lost the war with Germany and that the only realistic goal was peace. He was able to convince the majority of the Central Committee to accept Germany's demand that the Soviet government give up all its western territories. Poles, Finns, Lithuanians, and other non-Russians inhabited these areas—lands that had been conquered by the tsars over three centuries. With the Treaty of Brest-Litovsk (**brest lih-TOFSK**) in March 1918, Lenin had escaped the certain disaster of continued war and could pursue his goal of absolute political power for the Bolsheviks—now renamed Communists—within Russia.

In November 1917, the Bolsheviks had promised that a freely elected **Constituent Assembly** would draw up a new constitution. But free elections produced a stunning setback for the Bolsheviks, and Bolshevik soldiers acting under Lenin's orders permanently disbanded the Assembly after its first day. Thus even before the peace with Germany, Lenin was forming a one-party government.

The destruction of the democratically elected Constituent Assembly helped feed the flames of civil war. The officers of the old army took the lead in organizing the so-called White opposition to the Bolsheviks in southern Russia, Ukraine, Siberia, and west of Petrograd. The Whites came from many social groups and were united only by their hatred of the Bolsheviks—the Reds.

By the summer of 1918, fully eighteen self-proclaimed regional governments—several of which represented minority nationalities—were competing with Lenin's Bolsheviks in Moscow. By the end of the year, White armies were on the attack. In October 1919, it appeared they might triumph, as they closed in on Lenin's government from three sides. Yet they did not. By the spring of 1920, the White armies had been almost completely defeated, and the Bolshevik Red Army had retaken Belorussia and Ukraine. The following year, the Communists also reconquered the independent nationalist governments of the Caucasus. The civil war was over; Lenin had won.

Lenin and the Bolsheviks won for several reasons. Strategically, they controlled the center, while the Whites were always on the fringes and disunited. Moreover, the poorly defined political program of the Whites was vaguely conservative, and it did not unite all the foes of the Bolsheviks under a progressive, democratic banner. Most important, the divided Whites were no match for Trotsky's Red Army. Manned through a draft and severely disciplined by former tsarist officers, the Red Army was a superior fighting force. Through **war communism,** resources were marshaled from civilians to keep the army supplied. Civil opposition to the Bolsheviks was silenced by the **Cheka** (**CHE-kah**), a new incarnation of the tsarist secret police.

Together, the Russian Revolution and the Bolshevik triumph were one of the reasons the First World War was such a great turning point in modern history. A radically new government, based on socialism and one-party dictatorship, came to power in a great European state, maintained power, and eagerly encouraged worldwide revolution. Although halfhearted constitutional monarchy in Russia was undoubtedly headed for some kind of political crisis before 1914, it is hard to

Lenin Rallies Worker and Soldier Delegates
At a midnight meeting of the Petrograd Soviet, the Bolsheviks rise up and seize power on November 6, 1917. This painting from the 1940s idealizes Lenin, but his great talents as a revolutionary leader are undeniable. In this re-creation Stalin, who actually played only a small role in the uprising, is standing behind Lenin, already his trusty right-hand man. (Sovfoto)

Constituent Assembly A freely elected assembly promised by the Bolsheviks, but permanently disbanded within one day under Lenin's orders after the Bolsheviks won less than one-fourth of the elected delegates.

war communism The application of the total war concept to a civil conflict, the Bolsheviks seized grain from peasants, introduced rationing, nationalized all banks and industry, and required everyone to work.

Cheka The re-established tsarist secret police, which hunted down and executed thousands of real or suspected foes, sowing fear and silencing opposition.

imagine the triumph of the most radical proponents of change and reform except in a situation of total collapse. That was precisely what happened to Russia in the First World War.

The Peace Settlement

How did the Allies fashion a peace settlement, and why was it unsuccessful?

In the spring of 1918, the combined forces of the United States, Great Britain, and France decisively defeated Germany. The guns of world war finally fell silent. Then as civil war spread in Russia and as chaos engulfed much of eastern Europe, the victorious Western Allies came together in Paris to establish a lasting peace.

Expectations were high; optimism was almost unlimited. Nevertheless, the hopes of peoples and politicians were soon disappointed, for the peace settlement of 1919 turned out to be a failure. Rather than creating conditions for peace, it sowed the seeds of another war. Surely this was the ultimate tragedy of the Great War, a war that directly and indirectly cost $332 billion and left 10 million dead and another 20 million wounded.

The End of the War

Victory over revolutionary Russia boosted sagging German morale, and in the spring of 1918 the Germans launched their last major attack against France under the command of General Erich Ludendorff (**LOOD-n-dawrf**). For a time, German armies pushed forward, coming within thirty-five miles of Paris. But Ludendorff's exhausted, overextended forces never broke through. They were decisively stopped in July at the second Battle of the Marne, where 140,000 fresh American soldiers saw action. Adding 2 million men in arms to the war effort by August, the late but massive American intervention decisively tipped the scales in favor of Allied victory.

By September British, French, and American armies were advancing steadily on all fronts, and a panicky General Ludendorff realized that Germany had lost the war. Yet he insolently insisted that moderate politicians shoulder the shame of defeat, and on October 4 the emperor formed a new, more liberal German government to sue for peace.

As negotiations over an armistice dragged on, an angry and frustrated German people finally rose up. On November 3, sailors in Kiel (**keel**) mutinied, and throughout northern Germany soldiers and workers began to establish revolutionary councils on the Russian soviet model. The same day, Austria-Hungary surrendered to the Allies and began breaking apart. Revolution broke out in Germany, and masses of workers demonstrated for peace in Berlin. With army discipline collapsing, the emperor abdicated and fled to Holland. Moderate socialist leaders in Berlin proclaimed a German republic on November 9 and simultaneously agreed to tough Allied terms of surrender. The armistice went into effect on November 11, 1918. The war was over.

Revolution in Germany

Military defeat brought political revolution to Germany and Austria-Hungary, as it had to Russia. In Austria-Hungary the revolution was primarily nationalistic and republican in character. Having started the war to preserve an antinationalistic dynastic state, the Habsburg empire had perished in the attempt. In its place, independent Austrian, Hungarian, and Czechoslovakian republics were proclaimed, while a greatly expanded Serbian monarchy united the South Slavs and took the name Yugoslavia.

In Germany, the empire was replaced by the Weimar Republic, which was composed largely of Social Democrats and the Catholic party. The German Revolution of November 1918 resembled the Russian Revolution of March 1917. In both cases, a genuine popular uprising welled up from below, toppled an authoritarian monarchy, and brought the establishment of a liberal provisional republic. In both countries, liberals and moderate socialists took control of the central government, while workers' and soldiers' councils formed a counter-government. In Germany, however, the moderate socialists and their liberal allies won, and the Lenin-like radical revolutionaries in the councils lost.

The Treaty of Versailles

The peace conference opened in Paris in January 1919 with seventy delegates representing twenty-seven victorious nations. There were great expectations. A young British diplomat later wrote that the victors "were journeying to Paris . . . to found a new order in Europe. We were preparing not Peace only, but Eternal Peace."[4] This general optimism and idealism had been greatly strengthened by President Wilson's January 1918 peace proposal, the Fourteen Points, which stressed national self-determination and the rights of small countries.

The real powers at the conference were the United States, Great Britain, and France. Germany was not allowed to participate; Russia was locked in civil war; and Italy's role was limited. Almost immediately the three great Allies began to quarrel. President Wilson passionately believed that only a permanent international organization could protect member states from aggression and avert future wars, and he insisted that the creation of a **League of Nations** come first on the agenda. Wilson had his way, although Lloyd George of Great Britain and especially Clemenceau of France were unenthusiastic. They were primarily concerned with punishing Germany.

Playing on British nationalism, David Lloyd George had already won a smashing electoral victory as prime minister in December on the popular platform of making Germany pay for the war. As Kipling summed up the general British feeling at the end of the war, the Germans were "a people with the heart of beasts."[5]

France's Georges Clemenceau, "the Tiger" who had broken wartime defeatism and led his country to victory, wholeheartedly agreed. Like most French people, Clemenceau wanted old-fashioned revenge as well as lasting security for France. This, he believed, required the creation of a buffer state between France and Germany, the permanent demilitarization of Germany, and vast German reparations. Clemenceau's demands seemed vindictive to Wilson and Lloyd George, violating morality and the principle of national self-determination. By April the countries attending the conference were deadlocked on the German question, and Wilson packed his bags to go home.

In the end, Clemenceau agreed to a compromise. He gave up the French demand for a Rhineland buffer state in return for Wilson and Lloyd George's promise that their countries would come to France's aid in the event of a German attack. Thus Clemenceau appeared to win his goal of French security, as Wilson had won his of a permanent international organization. The Allies moved quickly to finish the settlement, believing that any adjustments would later be possible within the dual framework of a strong Western alliance and the League of Nations (see Map 27.4).

League of Nations A permanent international organization established during the peace conference in Paris in January 1919, designed to protect member states from aggression and avert future wars.

Legend:

Boundaries of German, Russian, and Austro-Hungarian Empires in 1914

Areas lost by Austro-Hungarian Empire

Areas lost by Russian Empire

Areas lost by German Empire

Areas lost by Bulgaria

Demilitarized Zones

Boundaries of 1926

MAPPING THE PAST

MAP 27.4 Shattered Empires and Territorial Changes After World War I

The Great War brought tremendous changes in eastern Europe. New nations and new boundaries were established, generally on the principle of national self-determination. A dangerous power vacuum was created by the new, usually small states established between Germany and Soviet Russia. **[1]** Identify the boundaries of Germany, Austria-Hungary, and Russia in 1914, and note carefully the changes caused by the war. **[2]** What territory did Germany lose, and why did France, Poland, and even Denmark receive it? Why was Austria sometimes called a head without a body in the 1920s? **[3]** What new independent states (excluding disputed Bessarabia) were formed from the old Russian Empire, and what nationalities lived in these states?

The **Treaty of Versailles** between the Allies and Germany was the key to the settlement, and the terms were not unreasonable as a first step toward re-establishing international order. Had Germany won, it seems certain that France and Belgium would have been treated with greater severity, as Russia had been at Brest-Litovsk. Germany's colonies were given to France, Britain, and Japan as League of Nations mandates. Germany's territorial losses within Europe were minor, thanks to Wilson. Alsace-Lorraine (**AL-sas-law-REYN**) was returned to France. Parts of Germany inhabited primarily by Poles were ceded to the new Polish state, in keeping with the principle of national self-determination. Germany had to limit its army to 100,000 men and agree to build no military fortifications in the Rhineland.

More harshly, the Allies declared that Germany (with Austria) was responsible for the war and had therefore to pay reparations equal to all civilian damages caused by the war. This unfortunate and much-criticized clause expressed inescapable popular demands for German blood, but the actual figure was not set, and there was the clear possibility that reparations might be set at a reasonable level in the future when tempers had cooled.

When presented with the treaty, the German government protested vigorously. But there was no alternative, especially considering that Germany was still starving because the Allies had not yet lifted their naval blockade. On June 28, 1919, German representatives of the ruling moderate Social Democrats and the Catholic party signed the treaty in the Sun King's Hall of Mirrors at Versailles, where Bismarck's empire had been joyously proclaimed almost fifty years before.

Separate peace treaties were concluded with the other defeated European powers—Austria, Hungary, and Bulgaria. For the most part, these treaties merely ratified the existing situation in east-central Europe following the breakup of the Austro-Hungarian Empire. Like Austria, Hungary was a particularly big loser, as its "captive" nationalities (and some interspersed Hungarians) were ceded to Romania, Czechoslovakia, Poland, and Yugoslavia.

Treaty of Versailles The treaty by which Germany's army was limited to 100,000 men and Germany was declared responsible for the war and had therefore to pay reparations equal to all civilian damages caused by the war.

The Peace Settlement in the Middle East

Although Allied leaders at Versailles focused mainly on European questions, they also imposed a political settlement on what had been the Ottoman Empire. This settlement brought radical changes to the Middle East, and it became very controversial. Basically, the Ottoman Empire was broken up, Britain and France expanded their power and influence in the Middle East, and Arab nationalists felt cheated and betrayed.

The British government had encouraged the wartime Arab revolt against the Ottoman Turks (see page 705) and had even made vague promises of an independent Arab kingdom. However, when the fighting stopped, the British and the French chose instead to honor secret wartime agreements to divide and rule the Ottoman lands. Arab nationalists were also angered by the **Balfour Declaration** of November 1917, named after the British foreign secretary. It announced that Britain favored a "National Home for the Jewish People" in Palestine, but without prejudicing the civil and religious rights of the non-Jewish communities already living in Palestine. The "National Home for the Jewish People" implied to the Arabs—and to the Zionist Jews as well—the establishment of some kind of Jewish state that would be incompatible with rule by the majority Arab population.

The Arab leader Hussein ibn-Ali sent his son Faisal (1885–1933) to the Versailles Peace Conference with the goal of securing Arab independence. Although President Wilson wanted to give the Arab case serious consideration, the British and the French were determined to rule Syria, Iraq, Transjordan, and Palestine as

Balfour Declaration A 1917 British statement that declared British support of a "National Home for the Jewish People" in Palestine.

Prince Faisal at the Versailles Peace Conference, 1919

Standing in front, Faisal is supported by his allies and black slave. Nur-as-Said, an officer in the Ottoman army who joined the Arab revolt, is second from the left, and the British officer T. E. Lawrence—popularly known as Lawrence of Arabia—is fourth from the left in back. Faisal failed to win political independence for the Arabs, as the British backed away from the vague promises they had made during the war. (Courtesy of the Trustees of the Imperial War Museum, neg. #Q55581)

League of Nations mandates, and they confirmed only the independence of Hussein's kingdom of Hejaz along the western coast of contemporary Saudi Arabia. In response Arab nationalists met in Damascus to call for political independence. (See the feature "Listening to the Past: Arab Political Aspirations in 1919" on pages 724–725.) Brushing aside Arab opposition, the British mandate in Palestine formally incorporated the Balfour Declaration and its commitment to a Jewish national home. When Faisal returned to Syria, his followers repudiated the agreement he had reluctantly accepted. In March 1920 they met as the Syrian National Congress and proclaimed Syria independent, with Faisal as king. A similar congress declared Iraq an independent kingdom.

Western reaction to events in Syria and Iraq was swift and decisive. A French army stationed in Lebanon attacked Syria, taking Damascus in July 1920. Faisal fled, and the French took over. Meanwhile, the British put down an uprising in Iraq with bloody fighting and established effective control there. Western imperialism, in the form of League of Nations mandates, appeared to have replaced Ottoman rule in the Arab Middle East. The Allies laid claim to the Turkish heartland as well. Great Britain and France occupied parts of modern-day Turkey, and Italy and Greece also claimed shares. There was a sizable Greek minority in western Turkey, and Greek nationalists wanted to build a modern Greek empire modeled on long-dead Christian Byzantium. In 1919 Greek armies carried by British ships landed on the Turkish coast at Smyrna (**SMUR-nuh**) and advanced unopposed into the interior. Turkey seemed finished.

But Turkey revived under the leadership of Mustafa Kemal (**MOOS-tah-fah kuh-MAHL**) (1881–1938), later known as Atatürk (**AT-uh-turk**) ("father of the Turks"). Kemal was a military man who had directed the successful defense of the Dardanelles against British attack. Watching the Allies' aggression and the sultan's cowardice after the armistice, in early 1919 he moved to central Turkey and gradu-ally unified the Turkish resistance. After a year of defeat in battle, they won a great victory in central Turkey, and the Greeks and their British allies sued for peace. The Treaty of Lausanne (loh-ZAN) (1923) recognized the territorial integrity of a truly independent Turkey. Turkey lost only its former Arab provinces.

Mustafa Kemal, a nationalist without religious faith, believed that Turkey should modernize and secularize along Western lines. He established a republic, had himself elected president, and created a one-party system—partly inspired by the Bolshevik example—in order to transform his country. Profoundly influenced by the example of western Europe, Mustafa Kemal set out to limit the place of religion and religious leaders in daily affairs. He decreed a revolutionary separa-tion of church and state, promulgated law codes inspired by European models, and established a secular public school system. Women received rights that they never had before. By the time of his death in 1938, Mustafa Kemal had imple-mented successfully much of his revolutionary program. He had moved Turkey much closer to Europe, foretelling current efforts by Turkey to join the European Union as a full-fledged member.

American Rejection of the Versailles Treaty

The rapidly concluded Versailles Treaty of early 1919 was not perfect, but within the context of war-shattered Europe it was an acceptable beginning. The principle of national self-determination, which had played such a large role in starting the war, served as an organizing framework. Germany had been punished but not dismembered. A new world organization complemented a traditional defensive alliance of sat-isfied powers. The serious remaining problems could be worked out in the future. Moreover, Allied leaders had seen speed as essential for an-other reason: they detested Lenin and feared that his Bolshevik Revolu-tion might spread. They realized that their best answer to Lenin's unending calls for worldwide upheaval was peace and tranquillity for war-weary peoples.

There were, however, two great, interrelated obstacles to such peace: Germany and the United States. Plagued by communist uprisings, reac-tionary plots, and popular disillusionment with losing the war, Germany's moderate socialists and their liberal and Catholic supporters faced an enormous challenge. Like French republicans after 1871, they needed time (and luck) if they were to establish firmly a peaceful and democratic republic. Progress in this direction required understanding but firm treat-ment of Germany by the victorious Western Allies, particularly by the United States.

However, the United States Senate and, to a lesser extent, the Ameri-can people, rejected Wilson's handiwork. Republican senators led by Henry Cabot Lodge refused to ratify the Treaty of Versailles without changes in the articles creating the League of Nations. Lodge and others believed that this requirement gave away Congress's constitutional right to declare war. Moreover, the Senate refused to ratify Wilson's treaties forming a defensive alliance with France and Great Britain. Wilson, in failing health, refused to compromise.

The Wilson-Lodge fiasco and the newfound gospel of isolationism represented a tragic and cowardly renunciation of America's responsibil-ity. Using America's action as an excuse, Great Britain, too, refused to ratify its defensive alliance with France. Bitterly betrayed by its allies, France stood alone. Very shortly France was to take actions against Germany that would feed the fires of German resentment and seriously undermine democratic forces in the new republic. The great hopes of early 1919 had turned to ashes by the end of the year. The Western alliance had collapsed, and a grandiose plan for permanent peace had given way to a fragile truce. For this and for what came later, the United States must share a large part of the guilt.

Chapter Review

What caused the Great War, and why did it have such revolutionary consequences? (page 699)

World War I had truly revolutionary consequences because, first and foremost, it was a war of committed peoples. In France, Britain, and Germany in particular, governments drew on genuine popular support. This support reflected in part the diplomatic origins of the war, which citizens saw as growing out of an unwanted crisis in the Balkans and an inflexible alliance system of opposing blocs. More importantly, popular support reflected the way western European society had been unified under the nationalist banner in the later nineteenth century, despite the fears that the growing socialist movement aroused in conservatives.

What was the impact of total war on civilian populations? (page 708)

The relentlessness of total war helps explain why so many died, why so many were crippled physically and psychologically, and why Western civilization would in so many ways never be the same again. More concretely, the war swept away monarchs and multinational empires. National self-determination apparently triumphed across Europe, not only in Austria-Hungary but also in many of Russia's western borderlands. Except in Ireland and parts of Soviet Russia and the Arab Middle East, the revolutionary dream of national unity, born of the French Revolution, had finally come true.

Why did World War I bring socialist revolution in Russia? (page 711)

Two other revolutions were products of the war. In Russia the Bolsheviks established a radical regime, smashed existing capitalist institutions, and stayed in power with a new kind of authoritarian rule. Whether the new Russian regime was truly Marxian or socialist was questionable, but it indisputably posed a powerful, ongoing revolutionary challenge to Europe and its colonial empires.

More subtle but quite universal in its impact was an administrative revolution. This revolution, born of the need to mobilize entire societies and economies for total war, greatly increased the power of government. Freewheeling market capitalism and a well-integrated world economy were among the many casualties of the administrative revolution, and greater social equality was everywhere one of its results. Thus even in European countries where a communist takeover never came close to occurring, society still experienced a great revolution.

Key Terms

Three Emperors' League (p. 699)
Triple Entente (p. 703)
trench warfare (p. 704)
Lusitania (p. 708)
total war (p. 708)
Petrograd Soviet (p. 713)
Army Order No. 1 (p. 713)
Bolsheviks (p. 713)
Constituent Assembly (p. 715)
war communism (p. 715)
Cheka (p. 715)
League of Nations (p. 717)
Treaty of Versailles (p. 719)
Balfour Declaration (p. 719)

How did the Allies fashion a peace settlement, and why was it unsuccessful? (page 716)

Finally, the "war to end war" did not bring peace—only a fragile truce. In the West, the Allies failed to maintain their wartime solidarity. Germany remained unrepentant and would soon have more grievances to nurse. Moreover, the victory of national self-determination in eastern Europe created small, weak states and thus a power vacuum between a still-powerful Germany and a potentially mighty communist Russia. A vast area lay open to military aggression from two sides.

Notes

1. Quoted in J. Remak, *The Origins of World War I* (New York: Holt, Rinehart & Winston, 1967), p. 84.
2. Quoted in R. O. Paxton, *Europe in the Twentieth Century* (New York: Harcourt Brace Jovanovich, 1975), p. 109.
3. A. B. Ulam, *The Bolsheviks* (New York: Collier Books, 1968), p. 349.
4. H. Nicolson, *Peacemaking 1919* (New York: Grosset & Dunlap Universal Library, 1965), pp. 8, 31–32.
5. Quoted ibid., p. 24.

To assess your mastery of this chapter, go to **bedfordstmartins.com/mckaywestbrief**

Listening to the Past

Arab Political Aspirations in 1919

Great Britain and France had agreed to divide up the Arab lands, and the British also had made conflicting promises to Arab and Jewish nationalists. However, President Wilson insisted at Versailles that the right of self-determination should be applied to the conquered Ottoman territories, and he sent an American commission of inquiry to Syria, even though the British and French refused to participate. The commission canvassed political views throughout greater Syria, and its long report with many documents reflected public opinion in the region in 1919.

To present their view to the Americans, Arab nationalists from present-day Syria, Lebanon, Israel, and Jordan came together in Damascus as the General Syrian Congress, and they passed the following resolution on July 2, 1919.

We the undersigned members of the General Syrian Congress, meeting in Damascus on Wednesday, July 2nd, 1919, . . . provided with credentials and authorizations by the inhabitants of our various districts, Moslems, Christians, and Jews, have agreed upon the following statement of the desires of the people of the country who have elected us to present them to the American Section of the International Commission; the fifth article was passed by a very large majority; all the other articles were accepted unanimously.

1. We ask absolutely complete political independence for Syria within these boundaries. [Describes the area including the present-day states of Syria, Lebanon, Israel, and Jordan.]

2. We ask that the Government of this Syrian country should be a democratic civil constitutional Monarchy on broad decentralization principles, safeguarding the rights of minorities, and that the King be the Emir Faisal, who carried on a glorious struggle in the cause of our liberation and merited our full confidence and entire reliance. . . .

6. We do not acknowledge any right claimed by the French Government in any part whatever of our Syrian country and refuse that she should assist us or have a hand in our country under any circumstances and in any place.

7. We oppose the pretensions of the Zionists to create a Jewish commonwealth in the southern part of Syria, known as Palestine, and oppose Zionist migration to any part of our country; for we do not acknowledge their title but consider them a grave peril to our people from the national, economical, and political points of view. Our Jewish compatriots shall enjoy our common rights and assume the common responsibilities.

8. We ask that there should be no separation of the southern part of Syria, known as Palestine,

Palestinian Arabs protest against large-scale Jewish migration into Palestine.
(Roger-Viollet/Getty Images)

724

nor of the littoral western zone, which includes Lebanon, from the Syrian country. We desire that the unity of the country should be guaranteed against partition under whatever circumstances.

9. We ask complete independence for emancipated Mesopotamia [today's Iraq] and that there should be no economical barriers between the two countries. . . .

The noble principles enunciated by President Wilson strengthen our confidence that our desires emanating from the depths of our hearts, shall be the decisive factor in determining our future; and that President Wilson and the free American people will be our supporters for the realization of our hopes, thereby proving their sincerity and noble sympathy with the aspiration of the weaker nations in general and our Arab people in particular.

We also have the fullest confidence that the Peace Conference will realize that we would not have risen against the Turks, with whom we had participated in all civil, political, and representative privileges, but for their violation of our national rights, and so will grant us our desires in full in order that our political rights may not be less after the war than they were before, since we have shed so much blood in the cause of our liberty and independence.

We request to be allowed to send a delegation to represent us at the Peace Conference to defend our rights and secure the realization of our aspirations.

Questions for Analysis

1. What kind of state did the delegates want?

2. Did the delegates view their "Jewish compatriots" and the Zionists in different ways? Why?

3. How did the delegates appeal to American sympathies?

Source: "Resolution of the General Syrian Congress at Damascus, 2 July 1919," from the King-Crane Commission Report, in *Foreign Relations of the United States: Paris Peace Conference*, 1919, 12: 780–781.

CHAPTER 28

The Age of Anxiety

ca. 1900–1940

Chapter Preview

Modernism and the Crisis of Western Thought
In what ways did new and disturbing ideas in philosophy, physics, psychology, and the arts reflect the general crisis in Western thought?

Movies and Radio
In what ways did movies and radio become mainstays of popular culture?

The Search for Peace and Political Stability
How did the democratic leaders of the 1920s deal with deep-seated instability and try to establish real peace and prosperity?

The Great Depression (1929–1939)
What caused the Great Depression, and how did the Western democracies respond to this challenge?

INDIVIDUALS IN SOCIETY: Gustav Stresemann

IMAGES IN SOCIETY: Pablo Picasso and Modern Art

LISTENING TO THE PAST: Life on the Dole in Great Britain

This detail of George Grosz's *Draussen und Drinnen* (Outside and Inside) captures the uncertainty and anxiety of the 1920s. (akg-images/ Art@Estate of George Grosz/Licensed by VAGA, New York, NY)

726

With the end of the terrible trauma of total war, most people hoped that once again life would make sense in the familiar prewar terms of peace, prosperity, and progress. These hopes were in vain. The Great Break—the First World War and the Russian Revolution—had mangled too many things beyond repair. Life would no longer fit neatly into the old molds.

Instead, great numbers of men and women felt themselves increasingly adrift in a strange, uncertain, and uncontrollable world. They saw themselves living in an age of anxiety, an age of continual crisis (this age lasted until at least the early 1950s). In almost every area of human experience, people went searching for ways to put meaning back into life.

Modernism and the Crisis of Western Thought

In what ways did new and disturbing ideas in philosophy, physics, psychology, and the arts reflect the general crisis in Western thought?

Before 1914 most people still believed in the Enlightenment ideals of progress, reason, and the rights of the individual. Yet a small band of serious thinkers and creative writers had been attacking these well-worn optimistic ideas since the 1880s. These critics rejected the general faith in progress and the power of the rational human mind. An expanding chorus of thinkers echoed and enlarged their views after the experience of history's most destructive war—a war that suggested to many that human beings were a pack of violent, irrational animals quite capable of tearing the individual and his or her rights to shreds. Disorientation and pessimism were particularly acute in the 1930s, when the rapid rise of harsh dictatorships and the Great Depression transformed old certainties into bitter illusions, as we shall see in Chapter 29.

In the midst of economic, political, and social disruptions, the French poet and critic Paul Valéry (**va-ley-REE**) (1871–1945) saw the "cruelly injured mind," besieged by doubts and suffering from anxieties. This was the general intellectual crisis of the twentieth century, which touched almost every field of thought. The implications of new ideas and discoveries in philosophy, physics, psychology, and the arts played a central role in this crisis, disturbing "thinking people" everywhere.

Modern Philosophy

The work of the nineteenth-century German philosopher Friedrich Nietzsche (**NEE-chee**) (1844–1900) laid the foundation for the twentieth-century rejection of Enlightenment ideals. His first great work in 1872 argued that ever since classical Athens, the West had overemphasized rationality and stifled the passion and animal instinct that drive human activity and true creativity. Nietzsche went on to question all values. He claimed that Christianity embodied a "slave morality" that glorified weakness, envy, and mediocrity. In Nietzsche's most famous line, a wise fool proclaims that "God is dead," dead because he has been murdered by lackadaisical modern Christians who no longer really believe in him. Nietzsche viewed the pillars of conventional morality—reason, democracy, progress, respectability—as outworn social and psychological constructs whose influence was suffocating self-realization and excellence.

Nietzsche painted a dark world, foreshadowing perhaps his loss of sanity in 1889. The West was in decline; false values had triumphed. The only hope for the individual was to accept the meaninglessness of human existence and then make that very meaninglessness a source of self-defined personal integrity and hence liberation. Little read during his active years, Nietzsche attracted growing attention in the early twentieth century, especially from German radicals who found inspiration in Nietzsche's ferocious assault on the conventions of pre-1914 imperial Germany. Subsequent generations have each discovered new Nietzsches, and his influence remains enormous to this day.

This growing dissatisfaction with established ideas before 1914 was apparent in other important thinkers. In the 1890s, French philosophy professor Henri Bergson (1859–1941) convinced many young people through his writing that immediate experience and intuition were as important as rational and scientific thinking for understanding reality. Indeed, according to Bergson, a religious experience or a mystical poem could be more meaningful than a scientific law or a mathematical equation.

The First World War accelerated the revolt against established certainties in philosophy, but that revolt went in two very different directions. In English-speaking countries, the main development was the acceptance of logical empiricism (or logical positivism) in university circles. In continental countries, the primary development in philosophy was existentialism.

Logical empiricism was truly revolutionary. This outlook began primarily with the Austrian philosopher Ludwig Wittgenstein (**VIT-guhn-shtine**) (1889–1951), who later immigrated to England, where he trained numerous disciples. Wittgenstein argued that the traditional concerns of philosophy—God, freedom, morality, and so on—are quite literally senseless, a great waste of time, for statements about them can be neither tested by scientific experiments nor demonstrated by the logic of mathematics. Statements about such matters reflect only the personal preferences of a given individual. As Wittgenstein put it in the famous last sentence of his work, "Of what one cannot speak, of that one must keep silent." People could no longer look to philosophy for answers to the great questions of life.

Another direction in philosophy, **existentialism,** argued that philosophy was necessary to understand the truth of the human condition. Most existential thinkers in the twentieth century did not believe a supreme being had established humanity's fundamental nature and given life meaning. In the words of the famous French existentialist, Jean-Paul Sartre (**zhahn-pawl sahrt**) (1905–1980), "existence precedes essence." The existentialist thinker sees the world without a caring God or an underlying order. In the face of a world without God, only the actions of individuals can give life meaning. Individuals must become "engaged" and choose their own actions courageously and consistently and in full awareness of their inescapable responsibility for their own behavior. In the end, existentialists argued, human beings can overcome life's absurdity.

Not all twentieth-century philosophers rejected the possibility of God, however. Sometimes described as Christian existentialists because they shared the loneliness and despair of atheistic existentialists, they stressed the human being's sinful nature, the need for faith, and the mystery of God's forgiveness. The revival of fundamental Christian belief after World War I was fed by the rediscovery of the work of nineteenth-century Danish religious philosopher Søren Kierkegaard (**KEER-ki-gahrd**) (1813–1855), whose ideas became extremely influential. Having rejected formalistic religion, Kierkegaard had eventually resolved his personal anguish over his imperfect nature by making a total religious commitment to a remote and majestic God.

Similar ideas were brilliantly developed by Swiss Protestant theologian Karl Barth (1886–1968), whose many influential writings after 1920 sought to re-create

logical empiricism A revolt against established certainties in philosophy that rejected most of the concerns of traditional philosophy, from the existence of God to the meaning of happiness, as nonsense and hot air.

existentialism A highly diverse and even contradictory system of thought that was loosely united in a courageous search for moral values in a world of terror and uncertainty.

the religious intensity of the Reformation. Barth urged people to accept God's word and the supernatural revelation of Jesus Christ with awe, trust, and obedience. Lowly mortals should not expect to "reason out" God and his ways. Among Catholics, the leading existential thinker was Gabriel Marcel (mahr-SEL) (1887–1973), who found in the Catholic Church an answer to what he called the postwar "broken world." Catholicism and religious belief provided the hope, humanity, honesty, and piety for which he hungered.

After 1914 religion became much more relevant and meaningful to intellectuals than it had been before the war. In addition to Barth and Marcel, many other illustrious individuals turned to religion between about 1920 and 1950. Poets T. S. Eliot and W. H. Auden, novelists Evelyn Waugh (waw) and Aldous Huxley, historian Arnold Toynbee (TOIN-bee), Oxford professor C. S. Lewis, psychoanalyst Karl Stern, physicist Max Planck (plahngk), and philosopher Cyril Joad were all either converted to religion or attracted to it for the first time. Religion, often of a despairing, existential variety, was one meaningful answer to terror and anxiety. In the words of a famous Roman Catholic convert, English novelist Graham Greene, "One began to believe in heaven because one believed in hell."[1]

The New Physics

Ever since the scientific revolution of the seventeenth century, progressive minds believed that science, unlike religion and philosophical speculation, was based on hard facts and controlled experiments. Science seemed to have achieved an unerring and almost complete picture of reality. Unchanging natural laws seemed to determine physical processes and permit useful solutions to more and more problems. All this was comforting, especially to people who were no longer committed to traditional religious beliefs. And all this was challenged by the new physics.

The work of Polish-born physicist Marie Curie (KYOOR-ee) (1867–1934) and German physicist Max Planck (1858–1947) called into question the old view of atoms as the stable, basic building blocks of nature, with a different kind of unbreakable atom for each of the ninety-two chemical elements. In 1905 the German-Jewish genius Albert Einstein (AHYN-stine) (1879–1955) went further than Curie and Planck in undermining Newtonian physics. His famous theory of special relativity postulated that time and space are relative to the viewpoint of the observer and that only the speed of light is constant for all frames of reference in the universe. The closed framework of Newtonian physics was quite limited compared to that of Einsteinian physics, which unified an apparently infinite universe with the incredibly small, fast-moving subatomic world. Moreover, Einstein's theory stated clearly that matter and energy are interchangeable and that even a particle of matter contains enormous levels of potential energy.

The 1920s opened the "heroic age of physics," in the apt words of one of its leading pioneers, Ernest Rutherford (1871–1937). Breakthrough followed breakthrough. In 1919 Rutherford showed that the atom could be split. By 1944 seven

1919	Treaty of Versailles; Freudian psychology gains popular attention; Keynes, *Economic Consequences of the Peace;* Rutherford splits the atom
1920s	Existentialism gains prominence
1920s–1930s	Dadaism and surrealism (artistic movements)
1922	Eliot, *The Waste Land;* Joyce, *Ulysses;* Woolf, *Jacob's Room;* Wittgenstein writes on logical empiricism
1923	French and Belgian armies occupy the Ruhr
1924	Dawes Plan
1925	Berg's opera *Wozzeck* first performed; Kafka, *The Trial*
1926	Germany joins League of Nations
1927	Heisenberg's principle of uncertainty
1928	Kellogg-Briand Pact
1929	Faulkner, *The Sound and the Fury*
1929–1939	Great Depression
1930	Van der Rohe becomes director of Bauhaus
1932	Franklin Roosevelt elected U.S. president
1934	Riefenstahl's documentary film *The Triumph of the Will*
1935	Creation of WPA as part of New Deal
1936	Formation of Popular Front in France

subatomic particles had been identi-fied, of which the most important was the **neutron** (NOO-tron). The neutron's capacity to pass through other atoms al-lowed for even more intense experimen-tal bombardment of matter, leading to chain reactions of unbelievable force. This was the road to the atomic bomb.

Although few nonscientists under-stood this revolution in physics, the im-plications of the new theories and discoveries, as presented by newspapers and popular writers, were disturbing to millions of men and women in the 1920s and 1930s. The new universe was strange and troubling. It lacked any absolute ob-jective reality. Everything was "relative," that is, dependent on the observer's frame of reference. Moreover, the universe was uncertain and undetermined, without stable building blocks. In 1927 German physicist Werner Heisenberg (VER-nuhr HI-zuhn-burg) (1901–1976) formulated

neutron The most important of the subatomic particles because its capacity to pass through other atoms allowed for intense experimental bombardment of matter, leading to chain reactions of unbelievable force.

the "principle of uncertainty," which postulates that because it is impossible to know the position and speed of an individual electron, it is therefore impossible to predict its behavior. Instead of Newton's dependable, rational laws, there seemed to be only tendencies and probabilities in an extraordinarily complex and uncer-tain universe.

Freudian Psychology

While physics presented an unpredictable universe, the findings and speculations of leading psychologist Sigmund Freud (see page 636) suggested that human behavior was basically irrational.

According to Freud, the key to understanding the mind is the primitive, irrational unconscious, which he called the **id**. The unconscious is driven by sexual, aggres-sive, and pleasure-seeking desires and is locked in a constant battle with the other parts of the mind: the rationalizing conscious, the **ego**, which mediates what a person *can* do; and ingrained moral values (the **superego**), which specify what a person *should* do. Human behavior is a product of a fragile compromise between instinctual drives and the controls of rational thinking and moral values. Since the

id, ego, and superego Freudian terms to describe human behavior, which Freud saw as basically irrational.

instinctual drives are extremely powerful, the ever-present danger for individuals and whole societies is that unacknowledged drives will overwhelm the control mechanisms in a violent, distorted way. Yet Freud also agreed with Nietzsche that the mechanisms of rational thinking and traditional moral values can be too strong. They can repress sexual desires too effectively, crippling individuals and entire peoples with guilt and neurotic fears.

Freudian psychology and clinical psychiatry had become an international movement by 1910, but only after 1918 did they receive popular attention, especially in the Protestant countries of northern Europe and in the United States. Many opponents and even some enthusiasts interpreted Freud as saying that the first requirement for mental health is an uninhibited sex life. Thus after the First World War, the popular interpretation of Freud reflected and encouraged growing sexual experimentation, particularly among middle-class women. For more serious students, the psychology of Freud and his followers drastically undermined the old, easy optimism about the rational and progressive nature of the human mind.

The Modern Novel

Freud's ideas about the complexity and irrationality of the human mind found expression in the **stream-of-consciousness technique** of modern novelists. In *Jacob's Room* (1922), Virginia Woolf (1882–1941) created a novel made up of a series of internal monologues, in which a character's ideas and emotions from different periods of time bubble up as randomly as from a patient on a psychoanalyst's couch. William Faulkner (1897–1962), perhaps America's greatest twentieth-century novelist, used the same technique in *The Sound and the Fury* (1929), much of whose intense drama is confusedly seen through the eyes of an idiot. The most famous stream-of-consciousness novel—and surely the most disturbing novel of its generation—is *Ulysses* (1922), in which Irish novelist James Joyce (1882–1941) weaves an extended ironic parallel between his ordinary hero's aimless wanderings through the streets and pubs of Dublin and the heroic adventures of Homer's Ulysses on his way home from Troy. Abandoning conventional grammar and blending foreign words, puns, bits of knowledge, and scraps of memory together in bewildering confusion, the language of *Ulysses* mirrors the riddle of everyday life.

As creative writers turned their attention from society to the individual and from realism to psychological relativity, they rejected the idea of progress. Some even described "anti-utopias," nightmare visions of things to come. Franz Kafka's (1883–1924) novels and stories, such as *The Trial* (1925) and

stream-of-consciousness technique
A literary technique, used by Virginia Woolf, James Joyce, and others, that used interior monologue to explore the human psyche.

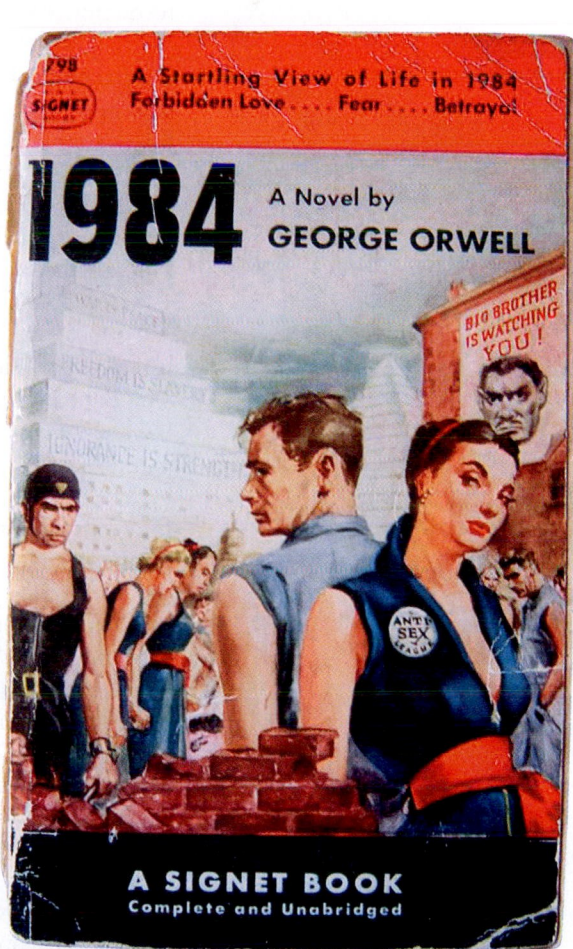

1984

This intriguing cover for an early edition of Orwell's brilliant novel hints at the tragic love affair between Winston and Julia. Considered a crime in Orwell's totalitarian dictatorship of the future, the love affair leads to the couple's arrest, torture, and betrayal. No one can escape the scrutiny of Big Brother and the Thought Police. (Signet Books/New American Library, 1949, cover illustration, James Avati. Private Collection)

The Castle (1926), portray helpless individuals crushed by inexplicably hostile forces. The German-Jewish Kafka died young, at forty-one, and so did not see the world of his nightmares materialize in the Nazi state.

Englishman George Orwell (1903–1950), however, had seen both that reality and its Stalinist counterpart by 1949, when he wrote perhaps the ultimate in anti-utopian literature: *1984*. Orwell set the action in the future, in 1984. Big Brother—the dictator—and his totalitarian state use a new kind of language, sophisticated technology, and psychological terror to strip a weak individual of his last shred of human dignity. The supremely self-confident chief of the Thought Police tells the tortured, broken, and framed Winston Smith, "If you want a picture of the future, imagine a boot stamping on a human face—forever."[2] A phenomenal bestseller, *1984* spoke to millions of people in the closing years of the age of anxiety.

Modernism in Art and Design

Like the scientists and writers who were partaking of the same culture, visual artists rejected old forms and old values. Modernism in art and music meant constant experimentation and a search for new kinds of expression. And though many people find the numerous and varied modern visions of the arts strange, disturbing, and even ugly, the first half of the twentieth century, so dismal in many respects, will probably stand as one of Western civilization's great artistic eras.

Modernism in the arts was loosely unified by a revolution in architecture. This revolution intended nothing less than a transformation of the physical framework of urban society according to a new principle: **functionalism.** Buildings, like industrial products, should be useful and "functional"—that is, they should serve, as well as possible, the purpose for which they were made. Moreover, they had to throw away useless ornamentation and find beauty and aesthetic pleasure in the clean lines of practical constructions and efficient machinery. Franco-Swiss genius Le Corbusier (**luh cor-booz-YEH**) (1887–1965) insisted that "a house is a machine for living in."[3] Featuring low lines, open interiors, and mass-produced building materials, the work of American architect Frank Lloyd Wright (1869–1959) embodied the modernist aesthetic.

In post-war Germany, Walter Gropius (**GROH-pee-uhs**) (1883–1969) established a new kind of interdisciplinary art school, called the **Bauhaus** (**BOU-hous**). The Bauhaus brought together many leading modern architects, designers, and theatrical innovators to work as a team, combining the study of fine art, such as painting and sculpture, with the study of applied art in the crafts of printing, weaving, and furniture making. Throughout the 1920s, the Bauhaus, with its stress on functionalism and good design for everyday life, attracted enthusiastic students from all over the world. It had a great and continuing impact.

In painting, the early twentieth century saw a move away from representing reality to an interest in the arrangement of color, line, and form as an end in itself. (See the feature "Images in Society: Pablo Picasso and Modern Art" on pages 734–735.) Another concern was to express a complicated psychological view of reality as well as an overwhelming emotional intensity. "The observer," said Russian-born Wassily Kandinsky (**VAS-uh-lee kan-DIN-skee**) (1866–1944), "must learn to look at [my] pictures . . . as form and color combinations . . . as a representation of mood and not as a representation of *objects*."[4] On the eve of the First World War, extreme expressionism and abstract painting were developing rapidly not only in Paris but also in Russia and Germany. Modern art had become international.

In the 1920s and 1930s, the artistic movements of the prewar years were extended and consolidated. The most notable new developments were dadaism

functionalism The principle that buildings, like industrial products, should serve as well as possible the purpose for which they were made.

Bauhaus A German interdisciplinary school of fine and applied arts that brought together many leading modern architects, designers, and theatrical innovators.

Walter Gropius: The Fagus Shoe Factory, 1911
The factory's sleek exterior is inspired by the revolutionary principles of functionalism. The striking glass façade creates a feeling of lightness and eliminates the traditional separation between interior and exterior. The glass façade also provides workers with healthy, natural light—a practical, "functional" concern. (Vanni/Art Resource, NY)

(**DAH-dah-izm**) and surrealism. **Dadaism** attacked all accepted standards of art and behavior, delighting in outrageous conduct. Its name is deliberately nonsensical. A famous example of dadaism is a reproduction of Leonardo da Vinci's *Mona Lisa* in which the famous woman with the mysterious smile sports a mustache and is ridiculed with an obscene inscription. After 1924 many dadaists were attracted to surrealism, which became very influential in art in the late 1920s and 1930s. Surrealists painted a fantastic world of wild dreams and complex symbols, where watches melted and giant metronomes beat time in precisely drawn but impossible alien landscapes. Refusing to depict ordinary visual reality, surrealist painters made powerful statements about the age of anxiety.

Dadaism An artistic movement of the 1920s and 1930s that attacked all accepted standards of art and behavior and delighted in outrageous conduct.

Modern Music

Developments in modern music were strikingly parallel to those in painting. Composers, too, were attracted by the emotional intensity of expressionism. The ballet *The Rite of Spring* by Igor Stravinsky (**struh-VIN-skee**) (1882–1971) practically caused a riot when it was first performed in Paris, in 1913, by Sergei Diaghilev's (**dee-AH-guh-lef**) famous Russian dance company. The combination of pulsating, dissonant rhythms from the orchestra pit and an earthy representation of lovemaking by the dancers on the stage seemed a shocking, almost pornographic enactment of a primitive fertility rite.

Images in Society

Pablo Picasso and Modern Art

Pablo Picasso (**pi-KAH-soh**) (1881–1973) was probably the most significant artist of the early twentieth century. For more than seventy years, he personified the individuality, freedom, and revolutionary creativity of the modern artist.

Born at Málaga in southern Spain, Picasso quickly demonstrated a precocious talent. At nineteen he headed for Paris, Europe's art capital. Suffering from poverty and falling into depression, he painted the weak and the poor in somber blue and purple tones. These pessimistic paintings of Picasso's "Blue Period" (1901–1904) are masterpieces in the tradition of Spanish realism.

Yet the young Picasso soon sought a new visual reality. In 1907 his arduous struggle to create a new style resulted in *Les Demoiselles d'Avignon* (**dem-wuh-ZEL duh-a-vee-NYAWN**) (Image 1), a painting originating in memories of a brothel scene in Barcelona. This work was considered a revolutionary upheaval in art. Since the Renaissance, artists had been expected to follow established rules, seeing objects in an orderly perspective from a single viewpoint and creating "beauty" and unified human forms. Do the faces of the central figures in this work conform to these rules? Regard the figures on either side, who were painted later. Notice how the light fails to combine with the shadow to create bodies

with continuous, three-dimensional contours. The figures appear broken into large, flat planes with heads that are twisted, fractured dislocations. Do you see the magical violence of a pictorial breakthrough or a grotesque, ugly departure?

Picasso extended his revolutionary experiments, and after 1910 he was joined by others. A critic called the new school cubism because these artists used many geometric forms in intersecting planes. Objects, viewed from many shifting viewpoints, often emerged as purely abstract designs.

Three Musicians (Image 2), painted in 1921, represents mature cubism. Many people believe that it marks the culmination of Picasso's cubist style. What similarities and differences do you see between this picture and Image 1? Notice the limited number of viewpoints, with the white clown,

IMAGE 1 Les Demoiselles d'Avignon (1907).

the harlequin, the monk, their instruments, and the table in front cut up into rectangular shapes and reassembled in recognizable form on a shallow series of planes. What is the effect of the bright primary colors and the harmonious, decorative order? Picasso had been making the sets for Sergei Diaghilev's famous Russian dance company in Paris, and these three jagged figures from traditional Italian comedy seem to convey the atmosphere of the theater and the dissonant, syncopated rhythm of modern music. Picasso always drew back from pure abstraction because he began with real objects and used models.

IMAGE 2 Three Musicians (1921). (Digital image © The Museum of Modern Art/ Licensed by Scala/Art Resource, NY/© 2004 Estate of Pablo Picasso/Artists Rights Society [ARS], New York)

Picasso's passionate involvement in his times infuses his immense painting *Guernica* (Image 3), often considered his greatest work. Painted for the Spanish pavilion at the Paris International Exhibition in 1937, this mural, with its mournful white, black, and blue colors, was inspired by the Spanish civil war and the deadly terror bombing of Guernica by fascist planes in a single night. In this complex work, a shrieking woman falls from a burning house on the far right. On the left, a woman holds a dead child, while toward the center are fragments of a warrior and a screaming horse pierced by a spear. Do cubist techniques heighten the effect? Picasso also draws on the surrealist aspect of the modernist revolution in this painting.

IMAGE 3 Guernica (1937). (Bridgeman-Giraudon/Art Resource, NY/© 2004 Estate of Pablo Picasso/Artists Rights Society [ARS], New York)

After the experience of the First World War, when irrationality and violence seemed to pervade the human experience, expressionism in opera and ballet flourished. One of the most famous and powerful examples was the opera *Wozzeck*, by Alban Berg (1885–1935), first performed in Berlin in 1925. Blending a half-sung, half-spoken kind of dialogue with harsh, atonal music, *Wozzeck* is a gruesome tale of a soldier driven by Kafka-like inner terrors to murder his mistress.

Some composers turned their backs on long-established musical conventions. As abstract painters arranged lines and color but did not draw identifiable objects, so modern composers arranged sounds without creating recognizable harmonies. Led by Viennese composer Arnold Schönberg (**SHON-burg**) (1874–1951), they abandoned traditional harmony and tonality. The musical notes in a given piece were no longer united and organized by a key; instead they were independent and unrelated. Schönberg's twelve-tone music of the 1920s arranged all twelve notes of the scale in an abstract, mathematical pattern, or "tone row." This pattern, which sounded like no pattern at all to the ordinary listener, could be detected only by a highly trained eye studying the musical score.

Movies and Radio

In what ways did movies and radio become mainstays of popular culture?

Until after World War II at the earliest, these revolutionary changes in art and music appealed mainly to a minority of "highbrows" and not to the general public. That public was primarily and enthusiastically wrapped up in movies and radio.

Moving pictures were first shown as a popular novelty in naughty peepshows—"What the Butler Saw"—and penny arcades in the 1890s, especially in Paris. But on the eve of the First World War, filmmakers were capable of producing full-length feature films such as the Italian *Quo Vadis* (**kwo VAH-dis**) and the American *Birth of a Nation*. During the First World War, the United States became the dominant force in the rapidly expanding silent-film industry. Charlie Chaplin (1889–1978), an Englishman working in Hollywood, was unquestionably the king of the "silver screen" in the 1920s. In his enormously popular role as the lonely Little Tramp, complete with baggy trousers, battered derby, and an awkward, shuffling walk, Chaplin symbolized the "gay spirit of laughter in a cruel, crazy world."[5] Chaplin also demonstrated that in the hands of a genius, the new medium could combine mass entertainment and artistic accomplishment.

The early 1920s were also the great age of German films. Protected and developed during the war, the large German studios excelled in bizarre expressionist dramas, beginning with *The Cabinet of Dr. Caligari* in 1919. Unfortunately, their period of creativity was short-lived. By 1926 American money was drawing the leading German talents to Hollywood and consolidating America's international domination.

Whether foreign or domestic, motion pictures became the main entertainment of the masses until after the Second World War. In Great Britain one in every four adults went to the movies twice a week in the late 1930s, and two in five went at least once a week. The greatest appeal of motion pictures was that they offered ordinary people a temporary escape from the hard realities of everyday life. The appeal of escapist entertainment was especially strong during the Great Depression. Millions flocked to musical comedies featuring glittering stars such as Ginger Rogers and Fred Astaire and to the fanciful cartoons of Mickey Mouse and his friends.

The Great Dictator

In 1940 the renowned actor and director Charlie Chaplin abandoned the Little Tramp role to satirize the "great dictator," Adolf Hitler. Chaplin had strong political views and made a number of films with political themes as the escapist fare of the Great Depression gave way to the reality of the Second World War. (The Museum of Modern Art/Film Stills Archive)

Radio became technically possible at the turn of the century, but only in 1920 were the first major public broadcasts of special events made in Great Britain and the United States. Lord Northcliffe, who had pioneered in journalism with the inexpensive, mass-circulation *Daily Mail,* sponsored a broadcast of "only one artist . . . the world's very best, the soprano Nellie Melba."[6] Singing from London, Melba was heard simultaneously all over Europe on June 16, 1920. This historic event captured the public's imagination. The meteoric career of radio was launched.

Every major country quickly established national broadcasting networks. In the United States such networks were privately owned and financed by advertising. In Great Britain Parliament set up an independent, public corporation, the British Broadcasting Corporation (BBC), supported by licensing fees. Elsewhere in Europe the typical pattern was direct control by the government.

Radio was also well suited for political propaganda. Dictators such as Mussolini and Hitler controlled the airwaves and could reach enormous national audiences with their frequent, dramatic speeches. In democratic countries, politicians such as President Franklin Roosevelt and Prime Minister Stanley Baldwin effectively used informal "fireside chats" to bolster their support.

Motion pictures also became powerful tools of indoctrination. Lenin himself encouraged the development of Soviet film making, and the communist view of Russian history was presented in a series of epic films, the most famous of which were directed by Sergei Eisenstein (1898–1948).

In Germany Hitler turned to a young and immensely talented woman film maker, Leni Riefenstahl (**REE-fuhn-shtahl**) (1902–2003), for a masterpiece of documentary propaganda, *The Triumph of the Will,* based on the Nazi party rally at Nuremberg in 1934. Riefenstahl combined stunning aerial photography, joyful crowds welcoming Hitler, and mass processions of young Nazi fanatics. Her film was a brilliant and all-too-powerful documentary of Germany's "Nazi rebirth." The new media of mass culture were potentially dangerous instruments of political manipulation.

Section Review

- The revolution in the arts moved the masses in the new fields of movies and radio.

- The king of the silent film era was Charlie Chaplin, who combined humor and ingenuity to entertain, providing a way to escape the hardships of everyday life.

- Radio also took off as an inexpensive means of mass entertainment and, with movies, became a tool for political propaganda.

The Search for Peace and Political Stability

How did the democratic leaders of the 1920s deal with deep-seated instability and try to establish real peace and prosperity?

As established patterns of thought and culture were challenged and mangled by the ferocious impact of World War I, so also was the political fabric stretched and torn by the consequences of the great conflict. The Versailles settlement had established a shaky truce, not a solid peace. Thus national leaders faced a gigantic task as they struggled with uncertainty and sought to create a stable international order within the general context of intellectual crisis and revolutionary artistic experimentation.

The pursuit of real and lasting peace proved difficult for many reasons. Germany hated the Treaty of Versailles. France was fearful and isolated. Britain was undependable, and the United States had turned its back on European problems. Eastern Europe was in ferment, and no one could predict the future of communist Russia. Moreover, the international economic situation was poor and greatly complicated by war debts and disrupted patterns of trade. Yet for a time, from 1925 to late 1929, it appeared that peace and stability were within reach. When the subsequent collapse of the 1930s mocked these hopes and brought the rise of brutal dictators, the disillusionment of liberals in the democracies was intensified.

Germany and the Western Powers

Germany was the key to lasting peace. Yet to Germans, the Treaty of Versailles represented a harsh, dictated peace, to be revised or repudiated as soon as possible. The treaty had neither broken nor reduced Germany, which was potentially still the strongest country in Europe. It was too harsh for a peace of reconciliation, too soft for a peace of conquest.

Moreover, with ominous implications for the future, France and Great Britain did not agree about how to treat Germany. French politicians believed that massive reparations from Germany were a vital economic necessity, as they had to shoulder the major burden of reconstruction while also repaying war debts to the United States. Many French leaders saw strict implementation of all provisions of the Treaty of Versailles as France's best chance at curbing Germany's power and ensuring France's security.

The British, however, wanted Germany to regain its economic strength so that it would again become a major market for British goods. Indeed, many English people agreed with the analysis of the young English economist John Maynard Keynes (**cainz**) (1883–1946), who argued that if Germany was impoverished by war reparations and other economic measures, all of Europe would suffer. The British were also suspicious of the fact that France had the largest army in Europe and was making alliances with the newly formed states of eastern Europe. In 1921 France signed a mutual defense pact with Poland and associated itself closely with the so-called Little Entente, an alliance that joined Czechoslovakia, Romania, and Yugoslavia against defeated and bitter Hungary.

While French and British leaders drifted in different directions, the Allied reparations commission completed its work. In April 1921, it announced that Germany had to pay the enormous sum of 132 billion gold marks ($33 billion) in annual installments of 2.5 billion gold marks. Facing possible occupation of more of its territory (Versailles already authorized France to occupy the Rhineland), the young German republic—generally known as the Weimar Republic—made its first payment in 1921. Then in 1922, wracked by rapid inflation and political assassinations and motivated by hostility and arrogance as well, the Weimar Republic announced its inability to pay more. It proposed a moratorium on reparations for three years, with the clear implication that thereafter reparations would be either drastically reduced or eliminated entirely.

Led by their tough-minded prime minister, Raymond Poincaré (**pwan-ka-REY**) (1860–1934), the French decided they had to either call Germany's bluff or see the entire peace settlement dissolve. So, despite strong British protests, in early January

1923, armies of France and its ally Belgium moved out of the Rhineland and began to occupy the Ruhr (roor) district, the heartland of industrial Germany, creating the most serious international crisis of the 1920s. If forcible collection proved impossible, France would use occupation to paralyze Germany and force it to accept the Treaty of Versailles. Strengthened by a wave of patriotism, the German government ordered the people of the Ruhr to stop working and start passively resisting the French occupation. The coal mines and steel mills of the Ruhr grew silent, leaving 10 percent of Germany's total population in need of relief. The French answer to passive resistance was to seal off the Ruhr and the entire Rhineland from the rest of Germany, letting in only enough food to prevent starvation.

By the summer of 1923, France and Germany were engaged in a great test of wills. French armies could not collect reparations from striking workers at gunpoint. But French occupation was indeed paralyzing Germany and its economy and had turned rapid German inflation into runaway inflation. Faced with the need to support the striking Ruhr workers and their employers, the German government began to print money to pay its bills. Prices soared. People went to the store with a big bag of paper money; they returned home with a handful of groceries. German money rapidly lost all value.

Runaway inflation brought about a social revolution. The accumulated savings of many retired and middle-class people were wiped out. Catastrophic inflation cruelly mocked the old middle-class virtues of thrift, caution, and self-reliance. Many Germans felt betrayed. They hated and blamed the Western governments, their own government, big business, the Jews, the workers, and the communists for their misfortune. They were psychologically prepared to follow radical leaders in a crisis.

In August 1923, a new leader in Germany was able to diffuse the situation. Gustav Stresemann (**GOOS-tahf SHTREY-zuh-mahn**) (1878–1929) called off passive resistance in the Ruhr and agreed in principle to pay reparations but asked for a re-examination of Germany's ability to pay. (See the feature "Individuals in Society: Gustav Stresemann.") Poincaré accepted, recognizing that continued confrontation was a destructive, no-win situation. The British, and even the Americans, were willing to help. The first step was a reasonable agreement on the reparations question.

Hope in Foreign Affairs (1924–1929)

The reparations commission appointed an international committee of financial experts headed by American banker Charles G. Dawes to re-examine reparations from a broad perspective. The resulting **Dawes Plan** (1924) was accepted by France, Germany, and Britain. Germany's yearly reparations were reduced and depended on the level of German economic prosperity. Germany would also receive large loans from the United States to promote German recovery. In short, Germany would get private loans from the United States and pay reparations to France and Britain, thus enabling those countries to repay the large sums they owed the United States.

This circular flow of international payments was complicated and risky, but for a while it worked. The German republic experienced a spectacular economic recovery. With prosperity and large, continual inflows of American capital, Germany easily paid about $1.3 billion in reparations in 1927 and 1928, enabling France and Britain to pay the United States. In this way the Americans belatedly played a part in the general economic settlement that, though far from ideal, facilitated the worldwide recovery of the late 1920s.

Dawes Plan The product of the reparations commission headed by Charles G. Dawes that was accepted by Germany, France, and Britain, and reduced Germany's yearly reparations, made payment dependant on German economic prosperity, and granted Germany large loans from the United States to promote recovery.

Individuals in Society

Gustav Stresemann

The German foreign minister Gustav Stresemann (1878–1929) is a controversial historical figure. Hailed by many as a hero of peace, he was denounced as a traitor by radical German nationalists and then by Hitler's Nazis. After World War II, revisionist historians stressed Stresemann's persistent nationalism and cast doubt on his peaceful intentions. Weimar Germany's most renowned leader is a fascinating example of the restless quest for convincing historical interpretation.

Stresemann's origins were modest. His parents were Berlin innkeepers and retailers of bottled beer, and only Gustav of their five children was able to attend high school. Attracted first to literature and history, Stresemann later turned to economics, earned a doctoral degree, and quickly reached the top as a manager and director of German trade associations. A highly intelligent extrovert with a knack for negotiation, Stresemann entered the Reichstag in 1907 as a business-oriented liberal and nationalist. When World War I erupted, he believed, like most Germans, that Germany had acted defensively and was not at fault. He emerged as a strident nationalist and urged German annexation of conquered foreign territories. Germany's collapse in defeat and revolution devastated Stresemann. He seemed a prime candidate for the hateful extremism of the far right.

Yet although Stresemann opposed the Treaty of Versailles as an unjust and unrealistic imposition, he turned back toward the center. He accepted the new Weimar Republic and played a growing role in the Reichstag as the leader of his own small probusiness party. His hour came in the Ruhr crisis, when French and Belgian troops occupied the district. Named chancellor in August 1923, he called off passive resistance and began talks with the French. His government also quelled communist uprisings; put down rebellions in Bavaria, including Hitler's attempted coup; and ended runaway inflation with a new currency. Stresemann fought to preserve German unity, and he succeeded.

Foreign Minister Gustav Stresemann of Germany *(right)* leaves a meeting with Aristide Briand, his French counterpart. (Corbis)

Voted out as chancellor in November 1923, Stresemann remained as foreign minister in every government until his death in 1929. Proclaiming a policy of peace and agreeing to pay reparations, he achieved his greatest triumph in the Locarno agreements of 1925 (see page 741). But the interlocking guarantees of existing French and German borders (and the related agreements to resolve peacefully all disputes with Poland and Czechoslovakia) did not lead the French to make any further concessions that might have disarmed Stresemann's extremist foes. Working himself to death, he made little additional progress in achieving international reconciliation and sovereign equality for Germany.

Stresemann was no fuzzy pacifist. Historians debunking his "legend" are right in seeing an enduring love of nation in his defense of German interests. But Stresemann, like his French counterpart Aristide Briand, was a statesman of goodwill who wanted peace through mutually advantageous compromise. A realist trained by business and politics in the art of the possible, Stresemann also reasoned that Germany had to be a satisfied and equal partner if peace was to be secure. His unwillingness to guarantee Germany's eastern borders (see Map 27.4 on page 718), which is often criticized, reflects his conviction that keeping some Germans under Polish and Czechoslovak rule created a ticking time bomb in Europe. Stresemann was no less convinced that war on Poland would almost certainly re-create the Allied coalition that had crushed Germany in 1918.* His insistence on the necessity of peace in the east as well as the west was prophetic. Hitler's 1939 invasion of Poland resulted in an even mightier coalition that almost annihilated Germany in 1945.

Questions for Analysis

1. What did Gustav Stresemann do to promote reconciliation in Europe? How did his policy toward France differ from that toward Poland and Czechoslovakia?

2. What is your interpretation of Stresemann? Does he arouse your sympathy or your suspicion and hostility? Why?

---

* Robert Grathwol, "Stresemann: Reflections on His Foreign Policy," *Journal of Modern History* 45 (March 1973): 52–70.

This economic settlement was matched by a political settlement. In 1925 the leaders of Europe signed a number of agreements at Locarno, Switzerland. Germany and France solemnly pledged to accept their common border, and both Britain and Italy agreed to fight either France or Germany if one invaded the other. Stresemann also agreed to settle boundary disputes with Poland and Czechoslovakia by peaceful means, and France promised those countries military aid if Germany attacked them. For years, a "spirit of Locarno" gave Europeans a sense of growing security and stability in international affairs.

Other developments also strengthened hopes. In 1926 Germany joined the League of Nations, where Stresemann continued his "peace offensive." In 1928 fifteen countries signed the Kellogg-Briand Pact, initiated by French prime minister Aristide Briand and U.S. secretary of state Frank B. Kellogg. This multinational pact "condemned and renounced war as an instrument of national policy." The signing states agreed to settle international disputes peacefully. Often seen as idealistic nonsense because it made no provisions for action in case war actually occurred, the pact was still a positive step. It fostered the cautious optimism of the late 1920s and also encouraged the hope that the United States would accept its responsibilities as a great world power and contribute to European stability.

Hope in Democratic Government

Domestic politics also offered reason to hope. During the occupation of the Ruhr and the great inflation, republican government in Germany had appeared on the verge of collapse. In 1923 communists momentarily entered provincial governments, and in November an obscure nobody named Adolf Hitler leaped onto a table in a beer hall in Munich and proclaimed a "national socialist revolution." But Hitler's plot to seize control of the government was poorly organized and easily crushed, and Hitler was sentenced to prison, where he outlined his theories and program in his book *Mein Kampf* (**mine kompf**) (My Struggle). Throughout the 1920s, Hitler's National Socialist Party attracted support only from a few fanatical anti-Semites, ultranationalists, and disgruntled ex-servicemen. In 1928 his party had an insignificant twelve seats in the Reichstag. Indeed, after 1923 democracy seemed to take root in Weimar Germany. A new currency was established, the economy boomed, and elections were held regularly.

Mein Kampf A book written by Adolf Hitler, in which he outlines his theories and program for a national socialist revolution.

There were, however, sharp political divisions in the country, with nationalists and monarchists on the right and newly formed Communist Party members on the left. The working classes were divided politically, but a majority supported the moderate socialist Social Democrats.

The situation in France had numerous similarities to that in Germany. Communists and Socialists battled for the support of the workers. After 1924 the democratically elected government rested mainly in the hands of coalitions of moderates, and business interests were well represented. France's great accomplishment was rapid rebuilding of its war-torn northern region. The expense of this undertaking led, however, to a large deficit and substantial inflation, which reached a crisis point in early 1926. The government restored confidence in the economy by slashing spending and raising taxes, and good times prevailed until 1930. France also became a locus of cultural energy, attracting artists and writers from all over the world. As writer Gertrude Stein (**stine**) (1874–1946), a leader of the large colony of American expatriates living in Paris, later recalled, "Paris was where the twentieth century was."[7]

Britain, too, faced challenges after 1920. The wartime trend toward greater social equality continued, however, helping maintain social harmony. Many of

American Jazz in Paris

This woodcut from a 1928 French book on cafés and nightclubs suggests how black musicians took Europe by storm, although the blacks are represented stereotypically. One French critic concluded that American blacks had attained a "pre-eminent" place in music since the war, "for they have impressed the entire world with their vibrating or melancholy rhythms." (akg-images)

Section Review

- Conflicts remained over how to treat Germany after the Treaty of Versailles; Germans thought it was too harsh, the French wanted to enforce it fully to curb Germany's power, while the British wanted Germany to regain its strength and become an important market for British goods.

- The Allied reparations commission left Germany with an enormous sum that it could not repay and led to a stalemate, with France occupying Germany in the Ruhr district until Gustav Stresemann was able to call in the British and the Americans for help in reassessing the debt.

- The Dawes Plan allowed Germany to get private loans from the United States to pay reparations to France and Britain, who then repaid their own war debt to the United States; politically all agreed to settle international disputes peacefully.

- In Germany, democracy seemed to be taking root, but division remained with nationalists and monarchists on the right and communists and socialists on the left; in France the communists and the socialists battled for support of the workers while culture thrived.

- In Great Britain, the moderate "revisionist" socialism of the Labour party led the country gradually toward socialism while Catholic Ireland finally gained full autonomy in 1922 after a bitter guerrilla war.

Britain's best markets had been lost during the war, and companies laid off massive numbers of workers in response. Yet the state provided unemployment benefits of equal size to all those without jobs and supplemented those payments with subsidized housing, medical aid, and increased old-age pensions. These and other measures kept living standards from seriously declining, defused class tensions, and pointed the way toward the welfare state Britain established after World War II. Relative social harmony was accompanied by the rise of the Labour party as a determined champion of the working classes and of greater social equality. Committed to the kind of moderate, "revisionist" socialism that had emerged before World War I (see pages 668–669), the Labour Party replaced the Liberal Party as the main opposition to the Conservatives. The new prominence of the Labour Party reflected the decline of old liberal ideals of competitive capitalism, limited government control, and individual responsibility. In 1924 and 1929, the Labour Party under Ramsay MacDonald (1866–1937) governed the country with the support of the smaller Liberal Party. Yet Labour moved toward socialism gradually and democratically, so that the middle classes were not overly frightened as the working classes won new benefits.

The Conservatives under Stanley Baldwin (1867–1947) showed the same compromising spirit on social issues. The last line of Baldwin's greatest speech in March 1925 summarized his international and domestic programs: "Give us peace in our time, O Lord." In spite of such conflicts as the 1926 strike by hard-pressed coal miners, which ended in an unsuccessful general strike, social unrest in Britain was limited in the 1920s and in the 1930s as well. In 1922 Britain granted southern, Catholic Ireland full autonomy after a bitter guerrilla war, thereby removing another source of prewar friction. Thus developments in both international relations and the domestic politics of the leading democracies gave cause for optimism in the late 1920s.

The Great Depression (1929–1939)

What caused the Great Depression, and how did the Western democracies respond to this challenge?

Like the Great War, the **Great Depression** must be spelled with capital letters. Economic depression was nothing new. Depressions occurred throughout the nineteenth century with predictable regularity, as they recur in the form of recessions and slumps to this day. What was new about this depression was its severity and duration. It struck the entire world with ever-greater intensity from 1929 to 1933, and recovery was uneven and slow. Only with the Second World War did the depression disappear in much of the world.

The social and political consequences of prolonged economic collapse were enormous. Mass unemployment and failing farms made insecurity a reality for millions of ordinary people, who looked in desperation for leaders who would "do something."

Great Depression A world wide economic depression from 1929 through 1933, unique in its severity and duration and with slow and uneven recovery.

The Economic Crisis

There is no agreement among historians and economists about why the Great Depression was so deep and lasted so long. Thus it is best to trace the course of the great collapse before trying to identify what caused it.

The Great Depression was triggered by developments in the United States that culminated in the stock market crash of 1929. The American economy had prospered in the late 1920s, but there was a serious imbalance between "real" investment and stock market speculation. Thus net investment—in factories, farms, equipment, and the like—actually fell from $3.5 billion in 1925 to $3.2 billion in 1929. In the same years, as money flooded into stocks, the value of shares traded on the exchanges soared from $27 billion to $87 billion. Although it was not clear to people at the time, a crash was inevitable.

The American stock market boom was built on borrowed money. Many wealthy investors, speculators, and people of modest means had bought stocks by paying only a small fraction of the total purchase price and borrowing the remainder from their stockbrokers. Such buying "on margin" was extremely dangerous. When prices started falling, the hard-pressed margin buyers either had to put up more money, which was often impossible, or sell their shares to pay off their brokers. Thus thousands of people started selling all at once. The result was a financial panic. Countless investors and speculators were wiped out in a matter of days or weeks.

The financial panic in the United States triggered a worldwide financial crisis. Throughout the 1920s, American bankers and investors had lent large amounts of capital to many countries. Many of these loans were short-term, and once panic broke, New York bankers began recalling them. Gold reserves thus began to flow out of European countries, particularly Germany and Austria, toward the United States. It became very hard for European business people to borrow money, and the panicky public began to withdraw its savings from the banks. These banking problems eventually led to the crash of the largest bank in Austria in 1931 and then to general financial chaos. The recall of private loans by American bankers also accelerated the collapse in world prices, as business people around the world dumped industrial goods and agricultural commodities in a frantic attempt to get cash to pay what they owed.

The financial crisis led to a general crisis of production: between 1929 and 1933, world output of goods fell by an estimated 38 percent. As this happened, each country turned inward and tried to go it alone. More than twenty nations, including Britain and the United States, went off the gold standard in order to price their goods more attractively in foreign markets, with no real advantage gained. Similarly, country after country followed the example of the United States when in 1930 it raised protective tariffs to their highest levels ever and tried to seal off shrinking national markets for American producers only. Within this context of fragmented and destructive economic nationalism, recovery finally began in 1933.

Although opinions differ, two factors probably best explain the relentless slide to the bottom from 1929 to early 1933. First, no country came forward to coordinate a response to the international economic situation. Second, almost every country suffered from poor national economic policy. Governments generally cut their budgets and reduced spending when they should have run large deficits in an attempt to stimulate their economies. After World War II, such a "counter-cyclical policy," advocated by John Maynard Keynes, became a well-established weapon against downturn and depression. But in the 1930s, Keynes's prescription was generally dismissed.

Mass Unemployment

The financial crisis led to cuts in production, and in turn workers all across Europe and the United States lost their jobs and had little money to buy goods (see Map 28.1). Along with economic effects, mass unemployment posed a great social problem. Poverty increased dramatically, although in most countries unemployed workers generally received some kind of meager unemployment benefits or public aid that prevented starvation. (See the feature "Listening to the Past: Life on the Dole in Great Britain" on pages 750–751.) Homes and ways of life were disrupted in millions of personal tragedies. Young people postponed marriages, and birthrates fell sharply. There was an increase in suicide and mental illness. Poverty or the threat of poverty became a grinding reality. Only strong government action could deal with mass unemployment, a social powder keg preparing to explode.

The New Deal in the United States

Of all the major industrial countries, only Germany was harder hit by the Great Depression, or reacted more radically to it, than the United States (see Chapter 29). Depression was so traumatic in the United States because the "Roaring Twenties" had been a period of great optimism. The Great Depression and the response to it marked a major turning point in American history.

MAPPING THE PAST

MAP 28.1   The Great Depression in the United States, Britain, and Europe

These maps show that unemployment was high almost everywhere, but that national and regional differences were also substantial. With this in mind: **[1]** In the United States, what in 1934 were the main channels of migration for workers? **[2]** In Britain, locate the areas with the highest levels of unemployment, which were generally dependent on traditional basic industries such as steel, coal, and textiles. What large area has the lowest unemployment? Why? **[3]** Which European countries in 1932 had the highest rate of unemployment, usually considered a good indicator of the level of economic hardship?

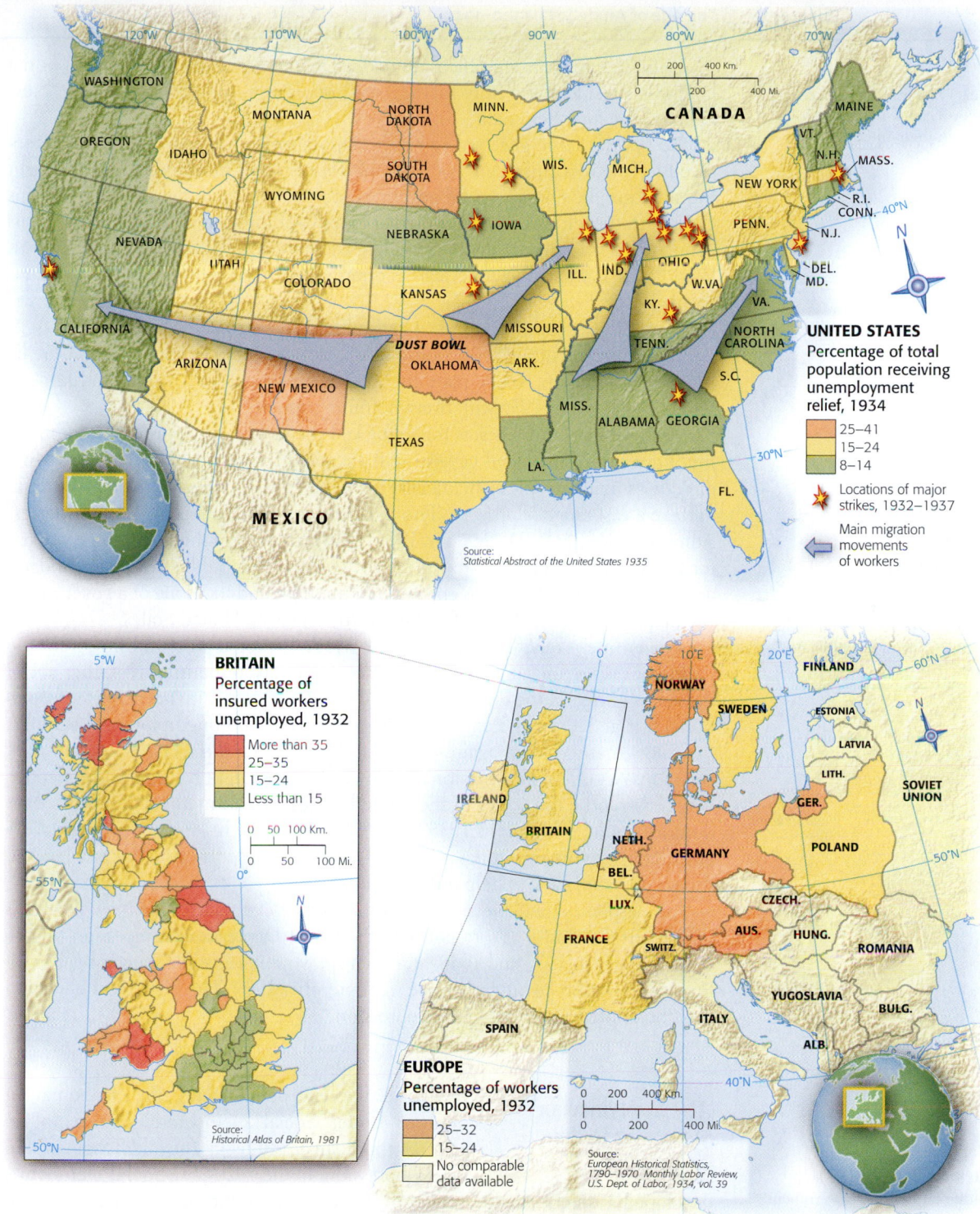

UNITED STATES
Percentage of total population receiving unemployment relief, 1934

- 25–41
- 15–24
- 8–14
- ★ Locations of major strikes, 1932–1937
- ← Main migration movements of workers

Source:
Statistical Abstract of the United States 1935

BRITAIN
Percentage of insured workers unemployed, 1932

- More than 35
- 25–35
- 15–24
- Less than 15

Source:
Historical Atlas of Britain, 1981

EUROPE
Percentage of workers unemployed, 1932

- 25–32
- 15–24
- No comparable data available

Source:
*European Historical Statistics,
1790–1970 Monthly Labor Review,
U.S. Dept. of Labor, 1934, vol. 39*

President Herbert Hoover (1895–1972) and his administration initially reacted to the stock market crash and economic decline with hope for recovery and limited action. But when the full force of the financial crisis struck Europe in the summer of 1931 and boomeranged back to the United States, people's worst fears became reality. Banks failed; unemployment soared. Between 1929 and 1932, industrial production fell by about 50 percent.

New Deal Franklin Delano Roosevelt's plan to reform capitalism through forceful government intervention in the economy.

In these tragic circumstances, Franklin Delano Roosevelt (1882–1945) won a landslide presidential victory in 1932 with grand but vague promises of a "**New Deal** for the forgotten man."

Roosevelt's basic goal was to reform capitalism in order to preserve it. Roosevelt rejected socialism and government ownership of industry in 1933. To right the situation, he chose forceful government intervention in the economy. In this choice, Roosevelt was flexible, pragmatic, and willing to experiment. He and his "brain trust" of advisers adopted policies echoing the American experience in World War I, when the American economy had been thoroughly planned and regulated.

Innovative programs promoted agricultural recovery, a top priority. The Agricultural Adjustment Act of 1933 also aimed at raising prices and farm income by limiting production. These planning measures worked for a while, and farmers repaid Roosevelt in 1936 with overwhelming support.

Roosevelt and his advisers then attacked the key problem of mass unemployment directly. The federal government accepted the responsibility of employing directly as many people as financially possible. New agencies were created to undertake a vast range of projects. The most famous of these was the Works Progress Administration, or **WPA**, set up in 1935. One-fifth of the entire labor force worked for the WPA at some point in the 1930s, constructing public buildings, bridges, and highways. The WPA was enormously popular, and the hope of a government job helped check the threat of social revolution in the United States.

WPA The Works Progress Administration, set up in 1935. The most famous of Roosevelt's New Deal programs, it employed one-fifth of the entire labor force at some point in the 1930s, constructing public buildings, bridges, and highways.

Government relief programs like the WPA marked a profound shift from the traditional stress on family support and community responsibility. Other social measures aimed in the same direction. In 1935 the government established a national Social Security system, with old-age pensions and unemployment benefits, to protect many workers against some of life's uncertainties. The National Labor Relations Act of 1935 gave union organizers the green light by declaring collective bargaining to be the policy of the United States. Union membership more than doubled, from 4 million in 1935 to 9 million in 1940. In general, between 1935 and 1938 government rulings and social reforms chipped away at the privileges of the wealthy and tried to help ordinary people.

Yet despite undeniable accomplishments in social reform, the New Deal was only partly successful as a response to the Great Depression. A recession hit the United States in 1937 and 1938, and unemployment was still a staggering 10 million when war broke out in Europe in September 1939. The New Deal never did pull the United States out of the depression.

The Scandinavian Response to the Depression

Of all the Western democracies, the Scandinavian countries under Social Democratic leadership responded most successfully to the challenge of the Great Depression. In the 1920s, the **Social Democrats** developed a unique kind of socialism. Flexible and nonrevolutionary, Scandinavian socialism grew out of a strong tradition of cooperative action in peasant communities. Labor leaders and capitalists had also been inclined to work together.

Social Democrats A flexible and nonrevolutionary socialist government in Scandinavia that grew out of a strong tradition of cooperative community action. In the 1920s, it passed important social reform legislation for both peasants and workers, gained practical administrative experience, and developed a unique kind of socialism.

When the economic crisis struck in 1929, socialist governments in Scandinavia built on this pattern of cooperative social action. Sweden in particular pioneered in the use of large-scale deficits to finance public works and thereby maintain production and employment. Scandinavian governments also increased social welfare benefits, from old-age pensions and unemployment insurance to subsidized housing and maternity allowances. All this spending required a large

Oslo Breakfast

Scandinavian socialism championed cooperation and practical welfare measures, playing down strident rhetoric and theories of class conflict. The Oslo Breakfast exemplified the Scandinavian approach. It provided every schoolchild in the Norwegian capital with a good breakfast free of charge. (Courtesy, Directorate for Health and Social Affairs, Oslo)

bureaucracy and high taxes, first on the rich and then on practically everyone. Yet both private and cooperative enterprise thrived, as did democracy. Some observers saw Scandinavia's welfare socialism as an appealing "middle way" between sick capitalism and cruel communism or fascism.

Recovery and Reform in Britain and France

In Britain, MacDonald's Labour government and then, after 1931, the Conservative-dominated coalition government followed orthodox economic theory. The budget was balanced, but unemployed workers received barely enough welfare to live. Yet the economy recovered considerably after 1932 and even improved somewhat on the 1920s economy, quite the opposite of the situation in the United States and France.

This good but by no means brilliant performance reflected the gradual reorientation of the British economy toward the domestic market. New industries, such as automobiles and electrical appliances, grew in response to British home demand. Moreover, low interest rates encouraged a housing boom. These developments encouraged Britain to look inward and avoid unpleasant foreign questions.

Because France was relatively less industrialized and more isolated from the world economy, the Great Depression came late. But once the depression hit France, it was long-lived. Economic stagnation both reflected and heightened an ongoing political crisis. There was no stability in government. As before 1914, the French parliament was made up of many political parties, which could never cooperate for very long. The difference this time was that the vital center of moderate republicanism was sapped from both sides. New Fascist-type organizations agitated against parliamentary democracy and looked to Mussolini's Italy and Hitler's Germany for inspiration (see Chapter 29). At the same time, the Communist party

Popular Front A New Deal–inspired party in France led by Leon Blum that encouraged the union movement and launched a far-reaching program of social reform, complete with paid vacations and a forty-hour workweek.

Section Review

- The economic crisis that began with the crash of the American stock market in 1929 spread across the world as American bankers recalled their loans, collapsing the world market and decreasing the output of goods; countries attempted to recover by raising tariffs and going off the gold standard.

- Cuts in production caused mass unemployment and a widespread social crisis as the poor received little government aid.

- In the United States, Franklin Roosevelt reformed capitalism through the forceful government intervention of the New Deal, enacting programs to boost agriculture and employment rates, setting up a Social Security system, and allowing collective bargaining.

- The Social Democrats in Scandinavia responded most successfully to the depression by using large-scale deficits to fund public works and increasing social welfare benefits, taxing the wealthy first and then almost everyone.

- Britain weathered the depression and recovered as new automobile and electrical appliance industries grew along with a housing boom; France, on the other hand, was caught in a political crossfire between political parties and the strength of the Popular Front, unable to pull the country out of crisis.

and many workers opposed to the existing system were looking to Stalin's Russia for guidance.

Frightened by the growing strength of the fascists at home and abroad, the Communists, the Socialists, and the Radicals formed an alliance—the **Popular Front**—for the national elections of May 1936. Their clear victory reflected the trend toward polarization. The number of Communists in the parliament jumped dramatically, while the Socialists, led by Léon Blum, became the strongest party in France. The really quite moderate Radicals slipped badly, and the conservatives lost ground to the semifascists.

In the next few months, Blum's Popular Front government made the first and only real attempt to deal with France's social and economic problems. Inspired by Roosevelt's New Deal, the Popular Front encouraged the union movement and launched a far-reaching program of social reform, complete with paid vacations and a forty-hour workweek. Popular with workers and the lower middle class, these measures were quickly sabotaged by rapid inflation and cries of revolution from fascists and frightened conservatives. Wealthy people sneaked their money out of the country, labor unrest grew, and France entered a severe financial crisis. Blum was forced to announce a "breathing spell" in social reform.

The fires of political dissension were also fanned by civil war in Spain. Communists demanded that France support the Spanish republicans, while many French conservatives would gladly have joined Hitler and Mussolini in aiding the attack of Spanish fascists. Extremism grew, and France itself was within sight of civil war. Blum was forced to resign in June 1937, and the Popular Front quickly collapsed. An anxious and divided France drifted aimlessly once again, preoccupied by Hitler and German rearmament.

Chapter Review

In what ways did new and disturbing ideas in philosophy, physics, psychology, and the arts reflect the general crisis in Western thought? (page 727)

After the First World War, Western intellectual life underwent a general crisis marked by pessimism, uncertainty, and fascination with irrational forces. Philosophers, building on the prewar writings of Nietzsche, rejected the traditional philosophical questions, focusing instead on the rules of language or an existential morality. Einstein's theories reordered the universe and overturned Newtonian physics; Freudian psychology privileged the power of the irrational in human thought. Ceaseless experimentation and rejection of old forms characterized literature, painting, and music. In short, almost every field of Western thought and art experienced revolutionary change.

In what ways did movies and radio become mainstays of popular culture? (page 736)

Motion pictures and radio provided entertainment and relaxation for the masses. They were enormously popular, offering escape from the hard realities of everyday life. Dictatorial governments used the new media for political propaganda.

Key Terms

logical empiricism (p. 728)

existentialism (p. 728)

neutron (p. 730)

id, ego, and superego (p. 730)

stream-of-consciousness technique (p. 731)

functionalism (p. 732)

Bauhaus (p. 732)

Dadaism (p. 733)

Dawes Plan (p. 739)

Mein Kampf (p. 741)

Great Depression (p. 743)

How did the democratic leaders of the 1920s deal with deep-seated instability and try to establish real peace and prosperity? (page 737)

The Treaty of Versailles left defeated Germany and the victorious Allies bitterly divided. The question of Germany reparations soon led to political stalemate, French occupation of Germany's Ruhr district, runaway German inflation, and the prospect of a general European collapse. In 1923, courageous new leaders turned to compromise. Led by Stresemann in Germany and Briand in France and backed by Great Britain and the United States, the new leaders worked out a complicated financial and political settlement that led to economic recovery and fragile political stability. Germany boomed, France rebuilt its war-ravaged areas, and Britain's Labour Party expanded social services.

What caused the Great Depression, and how did the Western democracies respond to this challenge? (page 743)

The Great Depression grew out of the fragile international financial system and the speculative boom in the U.S. stock market in the 1920s. The stock market crash in 1929 shattered international banking and triggered a disastrous downward spiral in prices and production, bringing massive unemployment to millions of workers. Turning inward to cope with the economic crisis and the related social problems, the Western democracies responded with relief measures, extended unemployment benefits, labor reforms, and social concern. These measures eased distress and prevented revolutions in the leading nations, but with significant exception of the Scandinavian countries the Western democracies failed to restore prosperity, eliminate high unemployment, and prevent widespread disillusionment. The old liberal ideals of individual rights and responsibilities, elected government, and economic freedom declined and appeared outmoded to many citizens. And in many countries of central and eastern Europe, these ideas were abandoned completely, as we shall see in the next chapter.

New Deal (p. 746)
WPA (p. 746)
Social Democrats (p. 746)
Popular Front (p. 748)

Notes

1. G. Greene, *Another Mexico* (New York: Viking Press, 1939), p. 3.
2. G. Orwell, *1984* (New York: New American Library, 1950), p. 220.
3. C. E. Jeanneret-Gris (Le Corbusier), *Towards a New Architecture* (London: J. Rodker, 1931), p. 15.
4. Quoted in A. H. Barr, Jr., *What Is Modern Painting?*, 9th ed. (New York: Museum of Modern Art, 1966), p. 25.
5. R. Graves and A. Hodge, *The Long Week End: A Social History of Great Britain, 1918–1939* (New York: Macmillan, 1941), p. 131.
6. Quoted in A. Briggs, *The Birth of Broadcasting*, vol. 1 (London: Oxford University Press, 1961), p. 47.
7. Quoted in R. J. Sontag, *A Broken World, 1919–1939* (New York: Harper & Row, 1971), p. 129.

To assess your mastery of this chapter, go to **bedfordstmartins.com/mckaywestbrief**

Listening to the Past

Life on the Dole in Great Britain

*P*eriodic surges in unemployment were an old story in capitalist economies, but the long-term joblessness of millions in the Great Depression was something new and unexpected. In Britain especially, where the depression followed a weak postwar recovery, large numbers suffered involuntary idleness for years at a time. Whole families lived "on the dole," the weekly welfare benefits paid by the government.

One of the most insightful accounts of unemployed workers was written by the British journalist and novelist George Orwell (1903–1950), who studied the conditions in northern England and wrote The Road to Wigan Pier (1937).

Poster used in the election campaign of 1931, when unemployment rose to a new record high. (Conservative Research Department/ The Bridgeman Art Library)

When people live on the dole for years at a time they grow used to it, and drawing the dole, though it remains unpleasant, ceases to be shameful. Thus the old, independent, workhouse-fearing tradition is undermined. . . .

So you have whole populations settling down, as it were, to a lifetime of the P.A.C. . . . Take, for instance, the fact that the working class think nothing of getting married on the dole. . . . Life is still fairly normal, more normal than one really has the right to expect. Families are impoverished, but the family-system has not broken up. The people are in effect living a reduced version of their former lives. Instead of raging against their destiny they have made things tolerable by lowering their standards.

But they don't necessarily lower their standards by cutting out luxuries and concentrating on necessities; more often it is the other way about—the more natural way, if you come to think of it. Hence the fact that in a decade of unparalleled depression, the consumption of all cheap luxuries has increased. The two things that have probably made the greatest difference of all are the movies and the mass-production of cheap smart clothes since the war. The youth who leaves school at fourteen and gets a blind-alley job is out of work at twenty, probably for life; but for two pounds ten on the hire-purchase system he can buy himself a suit which, for a little while and at a little distance, looks as though it had been tailored in Savile Row. The girl can look like a fashion plate at an even lower price. . . . You can stand on the street corner, indulging in a private daydream of yourself as Clark Gable or Greta Garbo, which compensates you for a great deal. . . .

Trade since the war has had to adjust itself to meet the demands of underpaid, underfed people, with the result that a luxury is nowadays almost always cheaper than a necessity. One pair of plain solid shoes costs as much as two ultra-smart pairs. . . . And above all there is gambling, the cheapest of all luxuries. Even people on the verge of starvation can buy a few days' hope ("Something to live for," as they call it) by having a penny on a sweepstake. . . . Twenty million people are underfed but literally everyone in England has access to a radio. What we have lost in food we have gained in electricity. Whole sections of the working class who have been plundered of all they really need are being compensated, in part, by cheap luxuries which mitigate the surface of life.

Do you consider all this desirable? No, I don't. But it may be that the psychological adjustment which the working class are visibly making is the best they could make in the circumstances. They have neither turned revolutionary nor lost their self-respect; merely they have kept their tempers and settled down to make the best of things on a fish-and-chip standard. The alternative would be God knows what continued agonies of despair; or it might be attempted insurrections which, in a strongly governed country like England, could only lead to futile massacres and a régime of savage repression.

Questions for Analysis

1. What were the consequences of long-term unemployment for English workers? Were some of the consequences surprising?

2. Judging from Orwell's description, did radical revolution seem likely in England in the Great Depression? Why?

Source: Excerpts from Chapter V in *The Road to Wigan Pier* by George Orwell, copyright © 1958 and renewed 1986 by the Estate of Sonia B. Orwell. Reprinted by permission of Houghton Mifflin Harcourt Publishing Company.

CHAPTER 29

Dictatorships and the Second World War

1919–1945

Chapter Preview

Stalin's Soviet Union
How did Stalin and the Communist Party build a modern totalitarian state in the Soviet Union?

Mussolini and Fascism in Italy
How did Mussolini's dictatorship come to power and govern in Italy?

Hitler and Nazism in Germany
How did Hitler gain power, what policies did totalitarian Nazi Germany pursue, and why did they lead to World War II?

The Second World War
How did Germany and Japan create enormous empires that were defeated by the Allies—Britain, the Soviet Union, and the United States?

INDIVIDUALS IN SOCIETY: Primo Levi

LISTENING TO THE PAST: Stalin Justifies the Five-Year Plan

Hugo Jager's photograph of a crowd of enthusiastic Hitler supporters. (Time Life Pictures/Getty Images)

The period following the First World War also saw the rise of political dictatorships. On the eve of the Second World War, liberal democratic governments were surviving only in Great Britain, France, the Low Countries, the Scandinavian nations, and Switzerland. Elsewhere in Europe, various kinds of "strongmen" ruled. Dictatorship seemed the wave of the future. Thus the intellectual and economic crisis discussed in Chapter 28 and the rise of dictatorship to be considered in this chapter were interrelated elements in the general crisis of European civilization.

The key development in the era of dictatorship was the rise of a particularly ruthless and dynamic tyranny. This new kind of tyranny reached its full realization in the Soviet Union and Nazi Germany in the 1930s. Stalin and Hitler mobilized their peoples for enormous undertakings and ruled with unprecedented severity. Both made an unprecedented "total claim" on the belief and behavior of their respective citizens, as a noted scholar has recently concluded.[1] While Stalin's aggression was directed within his state, Hitler wanted greater territory as well as the eradication of entire peoples whom he despised. His moves against Germany's neighbors sparked another great war that divided the world into two opposing forces and introduced new methods of mass destruction. Historians continue to ponder what led an entire society to rally behind a leader whose name has become synonymous with human evil. The question remains vital as state-sponsored atrocities and acts of genocide continue to plague our world.

Stalin's Soviet Union

How did Stalin and the Communist Party build a modern totalitarian state in the Soviet Union?

Lenin's harshest critics claim that he established the basic outlines of a modern totalitarian dictatorship after the Bolshevik Revolution and during the Russian civil war. If this is so, then Joseph Stalin (1879–1953) certainly finished the job. A master of political infighting, Stalin cautiously consolidated his power and eliminated his enemies in the mid-1920s. Then in 1928, as undisputed leader of the ruling Communist Party, he launched the first **five-year plan**—the "revolution from above," as he so aptly termed it.

five-year plan A plan launched by Stalin in 1928 and termed the "revolution from above," the ultimate goal of which was to generate new attitudes, new loyalties, and a new socialist humanity.

The five-year plans marked the beginning of a renewed attempt to mobilize and transform Soviet society along socialist lines. They were achieved through propaganda, enormous sacrifice by the people, and the concentration of all power in party hands. Thus the Soviet Union in the 1930s became a dynamic, modern totalitarian state.

From Lenin to Stalin

By spring 1921, Lenin and the Bolsheviks had won the civil war, but they ruled a shattered and devastated land. Many farms were in ruins, and food supplies were exhausted. In southern Russia, drought combined with the ravages of war to produce the worst famine in generations. Industrial production also broke down completely. The Bolsheviks had destroyed the economy as well as their foes.

Lenin's solution was to change course. In March 1921, he announced the **New Economic Policy (NEP)**, which re-established limited economic freedom in an attempt to rebuild agriculture and industry. Peasant producers were permitted

New Economic Policy (NEP) Lenin's 1921 policy to re-establish limited economic freedom in an attempt to rebuild agriculture and industry in the face of economic disintegration.

to sell their surpluses in free markets, and private traders and small handicraft manufacturers were allowed to reappear. Heavy industry, railroads, and banks, however, remained wholly nationalized.

The NEP represented a deal with the only force capable of overturning the government—the peasant majority. Economically, it brought rapid recovery. In 1926 industrial output surpassed the level of 1913, and Soviet peasants were producing almost as much grain as before the war.

As the economy recovered and the government partially relaxed its censorship and repression, an intense struggle for power began in the inner circles of the Communist Party, for Lenin had left no chosen successor when he died in 1924. The principal contenders were the stolid Stalin and the flamboyant Trotsky.

Joseph Stalin, born Joseph Dzhugashvili (**joo-guhsh-VEE-lee**), was a good organizer but a poor speaker and writer, with no experience outside of Russia. Leon Trotsky, an inspiring leader who had planned the 1917 takeover (see page 714) and then created the victorious Red Army, appeared to have all the advantages. Yet it was Stalin who succeeded Lenin. Stalin won because he was more effective at gaining the all-important support of the party, the only genuine source of power in the one-party state. Rising to general secretary of the party's Central Committee just before Lenin's first stroke in 1922, Stalin used his office to win friends and allies with jobs and promises.

The practical Stalin also won because he appeared better able to relate Marxian teaching to Soviet realities in the 1920s. Stalin developed a theory of "socialism in one country" that was more appealing to the majority of communists than Trotsky's doctrine of "permanent revolution." Stalin argued that the Russian-dominated Soviet Union had the ability to build socialism on its own. Trotsky maintained that socialism in the Soviet Union could succeed only if revolution occurred quickly throughout Europe. To many Russian communists, Trotsky's views seemed to sell their country short and to promise risky conflicts with capitalist countries.

With cunning skill, Stalin gradually achieved supreme power between 1922 and 1927. His final triumph came at the party congress of December 1927, which condemned all "deviation from the general party line" formulated by Stalin. The dictator and his followers were then ready to launch the revolution from above— the real revolution for millions of ordinary citizens.

The Five-Year Plans

The party congress of 1927, which ratified Stalin's consolidation of power, marked the end of the NEP. In its place Stalin rolled out the first in a series of five-year plans designed to catch up with the industrialized west and bring the country closer to having a true socialist economy. Building on planning models developed by Soviet economists in the 1920s, the first five-year plan had staggering economic objectives. In just five years, total industrial output was to increase by 250 percent. Heavy industry, the preferred sector, was to grow even faster. Agricultural production was slated to increase by 150 percent, and one-fifth of the peasants in the Soviet Union were scheduled to give up their private plots and join socialist collective farms. By 1930 economic and social change was sweeping the country. (See the feature "Listening to the Past: Stalin Justifies the Five-Year Plan" on pages 779–780.)

A major aspect of the second revolution was **collectivization**—the forcible consolidation of individual peasant farms into large, state-controlled enterprises. Beginning in 1929, peasants all over the Soviet Union were ordered to give up their land and animals and become members of collective farms, although they continued to live in their own homes. As for the **kulaks** (**COO-lox**), the better-off peas-

collectivization The forcible consolidation of individual peasant farms into large, state-controlled enterprises.

kulaks The better-off peasants who were stripped of land and livestock under Stalin and were generally not permitted to join the collective farms; many of them starved or were deported to forced-labor camps for "re-education."

ants, Stalin instructed party workers to "liquidate them as a class." Stripped of land and livestock, the kulaks were generally not even permitted to join the collective farms. Many starved or were deported to forced-labor camps for "re-education."

Since almost all peasants were in fact poor, the term *kulak* soon meant any peasant who opposed the new system. Whole villages were often attacked. One conscience-stricken colonel in the secret police confessed to a foreign journalist,

> I am an old Bolshevik. I worked in the underground against the Tsar and then I fought in the Civil War. Did I do all that in order that I should now surround villages with machine guns and order my men to fire indiscriminately into crowds of peasants? Oh, no, no![2]

Forced collectivization of the peasants led to economic and human disaster. Peasants, who had wanted to own their own land for centuries, slaughtered their animals and burned their crops in protest. Between 1929 and 1933, the number of horses, cattle, sheep, and goats in the Soviet Union fell by at least half. Nor were the state-controlled collective farms more productive. The output of grain barely increased between 1928 and 1938. Collectivized agriculture was unable to make any substantial financial contribution to Soviet industrial development in the first five-year plan.

The human dimension of the tragedy was absolutely staggering. As one leading historian writes in outrage, "The number dying in Stalin's war against the peasants was higher than the total deaths of all the countries in World War I." Yet, he notes, in Stalin's war only one side was armed and the other side bore almost all the casualties, many of whom were women, children, and the old.[3]

The Communists won the battle to collectivize farms, but their victory did not bring them the agricultural gains they had expected. Peasants fought back with indirect daily opposition until the government agreed to limit a family's labor on the state-run farms and gave them the right to cultivate tiny family plots. In 1938 these family plots grew 22 percent of all Soviet agricultural produce on only 4 percent of all cultivated land.

The industrial side of the five-year plans was more successful—indeed, quite spectacular. Soviet industry produced about four times as much in 1937 as it had in 1928. No other major country had ever achieved such rapid industrial growth. Heavy industry led the way; consumer industry grew quite slowly. A new heavy industrial complex was built almost from scratch in western Siberia. Industrial growth also went hand in hand with urban development, and more than 25 million people migrated to cities during the 1930s.

The great industrialization drive, concentrated between 1928 and 1937, was an awe-inspiring achievement purchased at enormous sacrifice. The money for investment in dozens of new factories was collected from the people by means of heavy, hidden sales taxes. The workers for the new factories were assigned by the government, which could force people to move to any job anywhere in the country. When factory managers needed more hands, they called on their counterparts on

CHRONOLOGY

1921	New Economic Policy (NEP) in U.S.S.R.
1922	Mussolini seizes power in Italy
1924–1929	Buildup of Nazi Party in Germany
1927	Stalin comes to power in U.S.S.R.
1928	Stalin's first five-year plan
1929	Lateran Agreement; start of collectivization in Soviet Union
1931	Japan invades Manchuria
1929–1939	Great Depression
1932–1933	Famine in Ukraine
1933	Hitler appointed chancellor in Germany; Nazis begin to control intellectual life and blacklist authors
1935	Mussolini invades Ethiopia; Hitler announces German rearmament
1936	Start of great purges under Stalin; German armies move into Rhineland; civil war begins in Spain
1938	Germany annexes Austria and Sudetenland
1939	Germany occupies Czech lands; Germany invades Poland; Britain and France declare war on Germany
1941	SS stops Jewish emigration from Europe; Germany invades Soviet Union; bombing of Pearl Harbor; U.S. enters war
1941–1945	Six million Jews killed in death camps
1944	Allied invasion at Normandy
1945	Germany surrenders; atomic bombs dropped on Japan; end of war

Life in a Forced-Labor Camp
This rare photo from about 1933 shows the reality of deported peasants and other political prisoners building the Stalin–White Sea Canal in far northern Russia, with their bare hands and under the most dehumanizing conditions. In books and plays Stalin's followers praised the project as a model for the regeneration of "reactionaries" and "kulak exploiters" through the joys of socialist work. (David King Collection)

the collective farms, who sent them millions of "unneeded" peasants over the years. Individuals, meanwhile, could not move without the permission of the police.

Life and Culture in Soviet Society

The aim of Stalin's five-year plans was to create a new society as well as a stronger economy and army. Once everything was owned by the state, the Stalinists believed, a utopian brotherhood of individuals with socialist values would inevitably emerge. The society that the Stalinists created, whose broad outlines existed into the mid-1980s, was far from utopian. It had both good and bad aspects.

Because consumption was reduced to pay for investment, there was no improvement in the average standard of living. Indeed, wages could buy significantly less than they had before the revolution. The masses of people lived primarily on black bread and wore old, shabby clothing. There were constant shortages in the stores, although very heavily taxed vodka was always readily available. A shortage of housing was a particularly serious problem. Millions were moving into the cities, but the government built few new apartments. A relatively lucky family received one room for all its members and shared both a kitchen and a toilet with others on the floor.

Life was hard but by no means hopeless. Idealism and ideology had real appeal for many communists, who saw themselves heroically building the world's first socialist society while capitalism crumbled in a worldwide depression and degenerated into fascism in the West. This optimistic belief in the future of the Soviet Union also attracted many disillusioned Westerners to communism in the 1930s.

On a more practical level, Soviet workers did receive some important social benefits, such as old-age pensions, free medical services, free education, and day-care centers for children. Unemployment was almost unknown. Finally, there was the possibility of personal advancement.

The keys to improving one's position were specialized skills and technical education. Rapid industrialization required massive numbers of trained experts, such as skilled workers, engineers, and plant managers. Thus the Stalinist state broke with the egalitarian policies of the 1920s and dangled high salaries and many special privileges before its growing technical and managerial elite. This elite joined with the political and artistic elites in a new upper class of the rich and powerful. The Stalinist state gave women access to higher education and the ranks of the better-paid specialists in industry and science. Medicine practically became a woman's profession. By 1950, 75 percent of all doctors in the Soviet Union were women. Women were expected to toil in factories and in heavy construction as the equals of men as well. The massive mobilization of women was a striking characteristic of the Soviet state.

Popular culture became a vehicle of the state, as newspapers, films, and radio broadcasts endlessly recounted socialist achievements and capitalist plots. Whereas the 1920s had seen considerable experimentation in modern art and theater, intellectuals were ordered by Stalin to become "engineers of human minds." It became increasingly important for the successful writer and artist to glorify Russian nationalism. Russian history was rewritten so that early tsars such as Ivan the Terrible and Peter the Great became worthy forerunners of the greatest Russian leader of all—Stalin.

Stalin seldom appeared in public, but his presence was everywhere—in portraits, statues, books, and quotations from his "sacred" writings. Although the government persecuted religion and turned churches into "museums of atheism," the state had both an earthly religion and a high priest: Marxism-Leninism and Joseph Stalin.

"Let's All Get to Work, Comrades!"

Art in the Stalinist era generally followed the official doctrine of socialist realism, representing objects in a literal style and celebrating Soviet achievements. Characteristically, this poster glorifies the working class, women's equality (in hard labor at least), mammoth factories, and the Communist Party (represented by the hammer and sickle by the woman's foot). Assailed by propaganda, Soviet citizens often found refuge in personal relations and deep friendships. (From *Art of the October Revolution,* Mikhail Guerman [Leningrad: Aurora Publishers.] Permission, Professor Guerman, Department of Education, St. Petersburg State University)

Stalinist Terror and the Great Purges

In the mid-1930s, the great effort to engineer a socialist state culminated in ruthless police terror and a massive purging of the Communist Party. The party and government elite publicly supported Stalin's initiatives, but in private there was grumbling. At a small gathering in November 1932, even Stalin's wife complained bitterly about the misery of the people and the horrible famine in Ukraine. Stalin showered her with insults, and she died that same night, apparently by her own hand. In late 1934, Stalin's number-two man, Sergei Kirov (**KEER-awf**), was mysteriously murdered. Although Stalin himself probably ordered Kirov's murder, he used the incident to launch a reign of terror.

Section Review

- After Lenin's death, Stalin and Trotsky vied for control of the Soviet Union, but Stalin won out due to his connections within the Communist Party; he then set out to launch his revolution from above.

- The five-year plans set up by Stalin began with collectivization of agriculture, forcing peasants to give up ownership of land and animals by force, with disastrous results and enormous casualties in purges of any who dissented; growth of heavy industry and urban development were more successful.

- Although the average Soviet citizen lived in crowded conditions and food shortages were common, many had high, idealistic hopes for communism and received educational, medical, and pension benefits and enjoyed career advancement within a gender-equal workplace, while the state-controlled media espoused the wonders of socialism, vilified capitalism, and glorified Russian nationalism.

- In an effort to reorganize a socialist state, Stalin ordered purges of the Communist Party by the secret police with public show trials and confessions, sending millions to labor camps, prisons, or execution, replacing them with new party members who would serve the party and Stalin faithfully.

In August 1936, sixteen prominent Old Bolsheviks confessed to all manner of plots against Stalin in spectacular public trials in Moscow. Then in 1937 the secret police arrested a mass of lesser party officials and newer members, also torturing them and extracting more confessions for more show trials. In addition to the party faithful, union officials, managers, intellectuals, army officers, and countless ordinary citizens were struck down. In all, at least 8 million people were probably arrested, and millions of these were executed or never returned from prisons and forced-labor camps.

Stalin and the remaining party leadership recruited 1.5 million new members to take the place of those purged. Thus more than half of all Communist Party members in 1941 had joined since the purges. Often the upwardly mobile sons (and daughters) of workers, they had usually studied in the new technical schools, and they soon proved capable of managing the government and large-scale production. A product of the great purges, this new generation of Stalin-formed communists would serve the leader effectively until his death in 1953, and they would govern the Soviet Union until the early 1980s.

Stalin's mass purges remain baffling, for almost all historians believe that those purged posed no threat and confessed to crimes they had not committed. Certainly the highly publicized purges sent a warning to the people: no one was secure, and everyone had to serve the party and its leader with redoubled devotion. Some Western scholars have also argued that the terror reflected a fully developed totalitarian state, which must always be fighting real or imaginary enemies.

The long-standing Western interpretation that puts the blame for the great purges on Stalin, which became very popular in Russia after the fall of communism, has nevertheless been challenged. Some historians argue that Stalin's fears were exaggerated but real. Moreover, these fears and suspicions were shared by many in the party and in the general population. Bombarded with ideology and political slogans, the population responded energetically to Stalin's directives. Investigations and trials snowballed into a mass hysteria, a new witch-hunt that claimed millions of victims.[4] In short, in this view of the 1930s, a deluded Stalin found large numbers of willing collaborators for crime as well as for achievement.

Mussolini and Fascism in Italy

How did Mussolini's dictatorship come to power and govern in Italy?

Mussolini, like Stalin, began as a revolutionary socialist, but in his rise to power he found it necessary to turn against the working class and seek the support of conservatives. Mussolini's fascist party was the first to establish a dictatorship in western Europe. Yet few scholars today would argue that Mussolini succeeded in establishing a totalitarian state that completely reshaped and dominated the economic, social, intellectual, and cultural aspects of people's lives. Membership in the Fascist Party was more a sign of an Italian's respectability than a commitment to radical change, and the fascist experiment was relatively short-lived.

The Seizure of Power   In the early twentieth century, Italy was a liberal state with civil rights and a constitutional monarchy. On the eve of the First World War, the parliamentary regime finally granted universal male suffrage, and Italy appeared to be moving toward democracy. But there were serious tensions. Many Italians were more attached to their villages and local interests than to the national state. Relations between church and state were often strained. Class differences were also extreme, and a powerful revolutionary socialist movement had developed.

The war worsened the political situation. Having fought on the side of the Allies almost exclusively for purposes of territorial expansion, the parliamentary government bitterly disappointed Italian nationalists with Italy's modest gains at Versailles. Workers and peasants also felt cheated: to win their support during the war, the government had promised social and land reform, which it did not deliver.

The Russian Revolution inspired and energized Italy's revolutionary socialist movement. The Socialist Party quickly lined up with the Bolsheviks, and radical workers and peasants began occupying factories and seizing land in 1920. These actions scared and mobilized the property-owning classes. Moreover, after the war the pope lifted his ban on participation by Catholics in Italian politics, and a strong Catholic Party quickly emerged. Thus by 1921 revolutionary socialists, antiliberal conservatives, and frightened property owners were all opposed— though for different reasons—to the liberal parliamentary government.

Into these crosscurrents of unrest and fear stepped the blustering, bullying Benito Mussolini (**buh-NEE-toh moos-uh-LEE-nee**) (1883–1945). Son of a village schoolteacher and a poor blacksmith, Mussolini began his political career as a Socialist Party leader and radical newspaper editor before World War I. In 1914, powerfully influenced by antidemocratic cults of violent action, the young Mussolini urged that Italy join the Allies, a stand for which he was expelled from the Italian Socialist Party. Later Mussolini fought at the front and was wounded in

Hitler and Mussolini in Italy, May 1938
At first Mussolini distrusted Hitler, but Mussolini's conquest of Ethiopia in 1936 and Hitler's occupation of the Rhineland brought the two dictators together in a close alliance. State visits by Mussolini to Berlin in 1937 and by Hitler to Rome in 1938 included gigantic military reviews, which were filmed to impress the whole world. Uniformed Italian fascists accompany this motorcade. (Time Life Pictures/Getty Images)

fascists The members of a movement characterized by extreme, often expansionist nationalism, an antisocialism aimed at destroying working-class movements, alliances with powerful capitalists and landowners, a dynamic and violent leader, and glorification of war and the military.

Black Shirts A private army under Mussolini that destroyed socialist newspapers, union halls, and Socialist Party headquarters, eventually pushing Socialists out of the city governments of Northern Italy.

1917. Returning home, he began organizing bitter war veterans like himself into a band of **fascists**—from the Italian word for "a union of forces."

At first Mussolini's program was too similar to that of the well-organized Socialist Party, and it failed to rally people behind him. When Mussolini saw that his verbal assaults on rival Socialists won him growing support from conservatives and the frightened middle classes, he shifted gears in 1920. He and his growing private army of **Black Shirts** began to use brute force against the socialists. Typically, a band of fascist toughs would roar off in trucks at night and swoop down on a few isolated organizers, beating them up and force-feeding them almost deadly doses of castor oil. Few people were killed, but socialist newspapers, union halls, and local Socialist Party headquarters were destroyed. Mussolini convinced his followers that they were not just opposing the "Reds" but also making a real revolution of their own.

His next step was to position himself publicly as the champion of order and property against the socialists and the ineffectual liberal parliamentary government. Striking a conservative note in his speeches and gaining the sympathetic neutrality of army leaders, Mussolini demanded the resignation of the existing government and his own appointment by the king. In October 1922, to force matters, a large group of fascists marched on Rome. The threat worked. Victor Emmanuel III (r. 1900–1946), who had no love for the old liberal politicians, asked Mussolini to form a new cabinet. He was immediately granted dictatorial authority for one year by the king and the parliament.

The Regime in Action

Once in power, Mussolini and his ministers changed the election laws so that the party that won the most votes was given two-thirds of the representatives in the parliament. This change allowed the Fascist Party and its allies to win an overwhelming majority in 1924. Shortly thereafter, five of Mussolini's thugs kidnapped and murdered Giacomo Matteotti (JAH-kaw-moh mat-te-AWT-tee), the leader of the Socialists in the parliament. In the face of this outrage, the opposition demanded that Mussolini's armed squads be dissolved and all violence be banned.

Although Mussolini may or may not have ordered Matteotti's murder, he stood at the crossroads of a severe political crisis. After some hesitation, he charged forward. Declaring his desire to "make the nation Fascist," he imposed a series of repressive measures. Freedom of the press was abolished, elections were fixed, and the government ruled by decree. Mussolini arrested his political opponents, disbanded all independent labor unions, and put dedicated Fascists in control of Italy's schools. Moreover, he created a fascist youth movement, fascist labor unions, and many other fascist organizations. Mussolini trumpeted his goal in a famous slogan of 1926: "Everything in the state, nothing outside the state, nothing against the state." By the end of that year, Italy was a one-party dictatorship under Mussolini's unquestioned leadership.

Mussolini, however, never destroyed the old power structure, as the Communists did in the Soviet Union, or succeeded in dominating it, as the Nazis did in Germany. Interested primarily in personal power, Mussolini was content to compromise with the old conservative classes that controlled the army, the economy, and the state. He controlled and propagandized labor but left big business to regulate itself, profitably and securely. There was no land reform.

Lateran Agreement A 1929 agreement that recognized the Vatican as a tiny independent state, with Mussolini agreeing to give the church heavy financial support. In turn, the pope expressed his satisfaction and urged Italians to support Mussolini's government.

Mussolini also drew increasing support from the Catholic Church. In the **Lateran** (LAT-er-uhn) **Agreement** of 1929, he recognized the Vatican as a tiny independent state, and he agreed to give the church heavy financial support. The pope expressed his satisfaction and urged Italians to support Mussolini's government.

Mussolini's conservative values are evident in his treatment of women. Rather than encouraging women to participate in the building of a new society, he abolished divorce and told women to stay at home and produce children. In 1938 women were limited by law to a maximum of 10 percent of the better-paying jobs in industry and government.

Mussolini's fascist Italy was repressive and undemocratic, and he insisted on the spectacle of mass obedience in rallies and salutes. Yet in spite of his posing, his fascist Italy was never really totalitarian. Indeed, he allowed Victor Emmanuel III to remain king, and it was Victor Emmanuel who dismissed him as leader after his own party refused further support of his war policy in 1943.

Hitler and Nazism in Germany

How did Hitler gain power, what policies did totalitarian Nazi Germany pursue, and why did they lead to World War II?

The most frightening dictatorship developed in Germany. There the Nazi movement, which was a form of fascism, smashed or took over most independent organizations, mobilized the economy, and violently persecuted the Jewish population. Thus Nazism asserted an unlimited claim over German society and proclaimed the ultimate power of its endlessly aggressive leader—Adolf Hitler. Truly totalitarian in its aspirations, the dynamism of Hitler and the Nazi elite was ultimately directed to war, territorial expansion, and racial aggression.

Hitler's Road to Power

Nazism grew out of many complex developments, of which the most influential were extreme nationalism and racism. These two ideas captured the mind of the young Hitler, and it was he who dominated Nazism for as long as it lasted.

The child of a customs official, Adolf Hitler (1889–1945) spent his youth in small towns in Austria. He dropped out of high school at age fourteen following the death of his father and eventually left home for Vienna, where he became deeply impressed by the mayor, Karl Lueger (1844–1910). From Lueger and others, Hitler absorbed virulent anti-Semitism, racism, and hatred of Slavs. He developed an unshakable belief in the crudest, most exaggerated distortions of the Darwinian theory of survival, the superiority of Germanic races, and the inevitability of racial conflict. Anti-Semitism and racism became Hitler's most passionate convictions, his explanation for everything. The Jews, he claimed, directed an international conspiracy of finance capitalism and Marxian socialism against German culture, German unity, and the German race. Hitler's belief was totally irrational, but he never doubted it.

Hitler served as a dispatch carrier in the First World War, finding that the struggle and disciple of war gave life meaning. Crushed by Germany's defeat, he joined a tiny extremist group in Munich called the German Workers' Party, and by 1921 he had gained absolute control of this small but growing party. He was already a master of mass propaganda and political showmanship. His most effective tool was the mass rally, where he often worked his audience into a frenzy with

Section Review

- Disappointment with Italy's modest gains at Versailles and increasing socialist agitation in Italy created conditions that allowed Mussolini to gain power using his private army, the Black Shirts, to terrorize the socialists and to force his way into government.

- Mussolini had the election laws changed so that the Fascist Party controlled the parliament, and he had the leader of the Socialist Party murdered, causing outrage and demands that he dissolve his armed squads.

- Mussolini responded by arresting his opponents, implementing fascist organizations, and winning the support of the Catholic church while leaving the old power structure alone and letting big business regulate itself.

- Fascists abolished divorce and told women to stay at home and have children, legally limiting women to a maximum of 10 percent of the better-paying jobs.

Nazism A movement born of extreme nationalism and racism and dominated by Adolf Hitler for as long as it lasted.

wild, demagogic attacks on the Versailles treaty, the Jews, Marxists, the war profiteers, and Germany's Weimar Republic.

Membership in Hitler's party multiplied tenfold after early 1922. In late 1923, the Weimar Republic seemed on the verge of collapse, and Hitler, inspired by Mussolini's recent easy victory, decided on an armed uprising in Munich. Despite the failure of the poorly organized plot and Hitler's arrest, Nazism had been born.

Hitler concluded from his unsuccessful revolt that he had to undermine, rather than overthrow, the government and come to power legally through electoral competition. He forced his more violent supporters to accept his new strategy. He also used his brief prison term to dictate his autobiography, *Mein Kampf*. There he expounded on his basic themes: "race," with a stress on anti-Semitism; "living space," with a sweeping vision of war and conquered territory; and the leader-dictator, or **Führer** (**FYUR-rer**), with unlimited, arbitrary power.

Führer A leader-dictator with unlimited, arbitrary power, this name was bestowed upon Adolf Hitler.

In the years of prosperity and relative stability between 1924 and 1929, Hitler concentrated on building his National Socialist German Workers' Party, or Nazi Party. While his party boasted 100,000 loyal followers by 1928, it received only 2.6 percent of the vote in the general elections. The Great Depression, shattering economic prosperity from 1929 on, presented Hitler with a new opportunity to gain votes. Chancellor (chief minister) Heinrich Brüning (**BREW-ning**) and President von Hindenburg inadvertently intensified the economic collapse with their economic measures, convincing many that the country's republican leaders were stupid. Never very interested in economics before, Hitler began promising German voters economic as well as political and international salvation.

Above all, Hitler rejected free-market capitalism and advocated government programs to bring recovery. Seized by panic as bankruptcies increased, unemployment soared, and the Communists made dramatic election gains, great numbers of middle- and lower-middle-class people "voted their pocketbooks"[5] and deserted the conservative and moderate parties for the Nazis. By 1932 the Nazis had became the largest party in the Reichstag.

The appeal to pocketbook interests was particularly effective in the early 1930s because Hitler appeared more mainstream, playing down his anti-Jewish hatred and racist nationalism. A master of propaganda, he had written in *Mein Kampf* that the masses were driven by fanaticism and not by knowledge. To arouse such hysterical fanaticism, he believed that all propaganda had to be limited to a few simple, endlessly repeated slogans. But now when he harangued vast audiences with wild oratory and simple slogans, he featured "national rebirth" and the "crimes" of the Versailles treaty. And many uncertain individuals, surrounded by thousands of enthralled listeners, found a sense of belonging as well as hope for better times.

Reaching a National Audience

This poster ad promotes the VE-301 receiver, "the world's cheapest radio," and claims that "All Germany listens to the Führer on the people's receiver." Constantly broadcasting official views and attitudes, the state-controlled media also put the Nazis' favorite entertainment—gigantic mass meetings that climaxed with Hitler's violent theatrical speeches—on an invisible stage for millions. (Bundesarchiv Koblenz Plak 003-022-025)

Hitler and the Nazis also appealed strongly to German youth. Indeed, in some ways the Nazi movement was a mass movement of young Germans. Hitler himself was only forty in 1929, and he and most of his top aides were much younger than other leading German politicians. "National Socialism is the organized will of the youth," proclaimed the official Nazi slogan. National recovery, exciting and rapid change, and personal advancement were the appeals of Nazism to millions of German youths.

Disunity on the left was another factor in Hitler's rise to power. The Communists refused to cooperate with the Social Democrats, even though the two parties together outnumbered the Nazis in the Reichstag, even after the elections of 1932. The Communists saw themselves as eventual victors, believing that a communist revolution would follow in the aftermath of Hitler's eventual destruction.

Finally, Hitler excelled in the dirty, backroom politics of the decaying Weimar Republic. That, in fact, brought him to power. In complicated infighting in 1932, he cleverly succeeded in gaining additional support from key people in the army and big business, who thought Hitler would advance their interests. When Hitler demanded the role of chancellor, those in power reasoned that with nine solid conservatives as ministers and only two other National Socialists, he could be controlled. On January 30, 1933, Adolf Hitler, leader of the largest party in Germany, was legally appointed chancellor by Hindenburg.

The Nazi State and Society

Hitler moved rapidly to gain total control of Germany. Continuing to maintain legal appearances, he immediately called for new elections. In the midst of a violent electoral campaign, the Reichstag building was partly destroyed by fire, and Hitler blamed the Communists. Fearing further violence, President Hindenburg agreed to emergency acts that practically abolished freedom of speech and assembly as well as most personal liberties. The Nazis in the Reichstag then gave Hitler absolute power for four years when they pushed through the so-called **Enabling Act** on March 23, 1933. President Hindenburg died the next year, and Hitler consolidated president and chancellor in the role of Führer.

Germany soon became a one-party state. Only the Nazi Party was legal. The Reichstag was jokingly referred to as the most expensive glee club in the country, for its only function was to sing hymns of praise to the Führer. Hitler and the Nazis took over the government bureaucracy intact, installing many Nazis in top positions. At the same time, they created a series of overlapping Nazi Party organizations responsible solely to Hitler.

As research in recent years shows, the resulting system of dual government was riddled with rivalries, contradictions, and inefficiencies. Thus the Nazi state was sloppy and often disorganized, lacking the all-encompassing unity that its propagandists claimed. Yet this fractured system suited Hitler and his purposes. He could play the established bureaucracy against his private, personal "party government" and maintain his freedom of action. Hitler could concentrate on general principles and the big decisions, which he always made.

In the economic sphere, strikes were outlawed, and independent labor unions and professional organizations were replaced by Nazi associations. Publishing houses were put under Nazi control, and universities and writers were quickly brought into line. Democratic, socialist, and Jewish literature was blacklisted; banned books were burned in public squares. Modern art and architecture were ruthlessly prohibited. Life became violently anti-intellectual. By 1934 a brutal dictatorship characterized by frightening dynamism and obedience to Hitler was already largely in place.

Enabling Act An act pushed through the Reichstag by the Nazis that gave Hitler absolute dictatorial power for four years.

Only the army retained independence, and Hitler moved brutally and skill-fully to establish his control there, too. The Nazi storm troopers (the SA), the quasi-military band of 3 million toughs in brown shirts who had fought commu-nists and beaten up Jews before the Nazis took power, expected top positions in the army and even talked of a "second revolution" against capitalism. Hitler decided that the SA leaders had to be eliminated. Needing to preserve good relations with the army as well as with big business, he struck on the night of June 30, 1934. Hitler's elite personal guard—the SS—arrested and shot without trial roughly a thousand SA leaders and assorted political enemies. Shortly thereafter army lead-ers swore a binding oath of "unquestioning obedience . . . to the Leader of the German State and People, Adolf Hitler." The SS grew rapidly. Under its methodi-cal, inhuman leader, Heinrich Himmler (1900–1945), the SS joined with the political police, the Gestapo, to expand its network of special courts and concen-tration camps. Nobody was safe.

From the beginning, Jews were a special object of Nazi persecution, although Slavs, Roma (Gypsies), Jehovah's Witnesses, Communists, and homosexuals were also targets. By the end of 1934, most Jewish lawyers, doctors, professors, civil ser-vants, and musicians had lost their jobs and the right to practice their professions. In 1935 the infamous Nuremberg Laws deprived Jews of all rights of citizenship. By 1938 roughly 150,000 of Germany's half a million Jews had emigrated, sacrific-ing almost all their property in order to leave Germany.

In late 1938, the attack on the Jews accelerated. In a well-organized wave of violence, known to history as "Kristallnacht," mobs smashed windows, looted shops, and destroyed homes and synagogues. German Jews were then rounded up and made to pay for the damage. Another 150,000 Jews fled Germany. Some Germans privately opposed these outrages, but most went along or looked the other way.

Hitler's Popularity

Hitler had promised the masses economic recovery—"work and bread"—and he delivered. Breaking with Brüning's do-nothing policies, Hitler launched a large public works program to help pull Germany out of the depression. Work began on superhighways, offices, gigantic sports stadiums, and public housing, and then shifted in 1936 toward rearmament and preparation for war. As a result of these policies (and plain good luck), unemployment dropped steadily and the standard of living for the average employed worker increased moderately. The profits of business rose sharply. For millions of people, economic recovery was tangible evi-dence that Nazi promises were more than show and propaganda.

Millions of modest middle-class and lower-middle-class people *felt* that Ger-many was becoming more open and equal, as Nazi propagandists constantly claimed. But quantitative studies show that the well-educated classes held on to most of their advantages and that only a modest social leveling occurred in the Nazi years. It is significant that the Nazis shared with the Italian fascists the stereo-typic view of women as housewives and mothers. Only under the relentless pres-sure of war did they reluctantly mobilize large numbers of German women for work in offices and factories.

Not all Germans supported Hitler, however, and a number of German groups actively resisted him after 1933. Tens of thousands of political enemies were im-prisoned, and thousands were executed. But opponents of the Nazis pursued vari-ous goals, and they were never unified, a fact that helps account for their ultimate lack of success. In the first years of Hitler's rule, the principal resisters were the communists and the socialists in the trade unions. But the expansion of the SS system of terror after 1935 smashed most of these leftists. A second group of opponents arose in the Catholic and Protestant churches. However, their efforts were directed primarily at preserving genuine religious life, not at overthrowing Hitler. Finally in 1938 (and again from 1942 to 1944), some high-ranking army officers, who feared the consequences of Hitler's reckless aggression, plotted against him, unsuccessfully.

Aggression and Appeasement (1933–1939)

Although economic recovery and somewhat greater opportunity for social advancement won Hitler support, they were only byproducts of the Nazi regime. The guiding and unique concepts of Nazism remained space and race—the territorial expansion of the superior German race. As we shall see, German expansion was facilitated by the uncertain and divided Western democracies, which tried to appease Hitler to avoid war.

Hitler realized that his aggressive policies had to be carefully camouflaged at first, for Germany's army was limited by the Treaty of Versailles to only one hundred thousand men. As he told a group of army commanders in February 1933, the early stages of his policy of "conquest of new living space in the East and its ruthless Germanization" had serious dangers. If France had real leaders, Hitler said, it would "not give us time but attack us, presumably with its eastern satellites."[6] Thus, Hitler loudly proclaimed his peaceful intentions, while signaling otherwise by withdrawing from the League of Nations.

Following this action, Hitler sought to incorporate independent Austria into a greater Germany. But a worried Mussolini threatened to fight, and Hitler backed down. When in March 1935 Hitler repudiated the Treaty of Versailles by establishing a general military draft and declaring Germany's right to rearm, other countries appeared to understand the danger. With France taking the lead, Italy and Great Britain protested strongly and warned against future aggressive actions.

Yet the emerging united front against Hitler quickly collapsed. Of crucial importance, Britain adopted a policy of **appeasement**, granting Hitler everything he could reasonably want (and more) in order to avoid another horrific war. The first step was an Anglo-German naval agreement in June 1935 that broke Germany's isolation. The second step came in March 1936 when Hitler suddenly marched his armies into the demilitarized Rhineland, brazenly violating the Treaties of Versailles and Locarno. This was the last good chance to stop the Nazis, but an uncertain France would not move without British support, and Britain refused to act (Map 29.1).

As the Great Powers stood on the sidelines, Hitler found allies in Italy and Japan. He supported their wars of aggression—Italy against Ethiopia and Japan against China—and they agreed to join the Axis alliance.

The fascist leaders of Germany and Italy came to the aid of another fascist power in the Spanish civil war (1936–1939). Their support eventually helped General Francisco Franco's fascist movement defeat republican Spain. Only the Soviet Union offered official support for the Spanish government, as public opinion in Britain and especially in France was hopelessly divided on the Spanish question.

In late 1937 Hitler moved forward with plans to crush Austria and Czechoslovakia at the earliest possible moment as the first step in his long-contemplated drive to the east. Threatening invasion, he forced the Austrian chancellor in March 1938 to put local Nazis in control of the government. The next day, German armies moved in unopposed, and Austria became part of Greater Germany (see Map 29.1).

appeasement The British policy toward Germany prior to World War II that aimed at granting Hitler whatever he wanted, including western Czechoslovakia, in order to avoid war.

MAP 29.1   The Growth of Nazi Germany, 1933–1939

Until March 1939, Hitler brought ethnic Germans into the Nazi state; then he turned on the Slavic peoples he had always hated. He stripped Czechoslovakia of its independence and prepared for an attack on Poland in September 1939.

Simultaneously, Hitler began demanding that the pro-Nazi, German-speaking minority of western Czechoslovakia—the Sudetenland—be turned over to Germany. Yet democratic Czechoslovakia was prepared to resist, and it counted on France, its ally since 1924, and the Soviet Union, France's ally. War appeared inevitable, but appeasement triumphed again. In September 1938, Britain's prime minister Chamberlain flew to Germany three times in fourteen days. In these negotiations, to which the U.S.S.R. (Union of Soviet Socialist Republics) was deliberately not invited, Chamberlain and the French agreed with Hitler that the Sudetenland should be ceded to Germany immediately. Returning to London from the Munich Conference, Chamberlain told cheering crowds that he had secured "peace with honor . . . peace for our time." Sold out by the Western powers, Czechoslovakia gave in.

Appeasement confirmed Hitler's belief that the Western democracies were weak and unwilling to fight. He accelerated his eastern expansion, moving into the remaining Czech lands in March 1939. The Western public now recognized Hitler's moves as acts of aggression since he was seizing Czechs and Slovaks as captive peoples. Thus when Hitler used the question of German minorities in Danzig as a pretext to claim Poland, a suddenly militant Chamberlain declared that Britain and France would fight if Hitler attacked his eastern neighbor. Hitler did not take Chamberlain's warning seriously, but he was concerned about the possible response from Poland's Soviet neighbor.

In a stunning about-face, Hitler and Stalin signed a ten-year Nazi-Soviet non-aggression pact in August 1939. Each dictator promised to remain neutral if the other became involved in war. In secret they agreed to divide eastern Europe into German and Soviet zones, "in the event of a political territorial reorganization." The nonaggression pact itself was enough to make Britain and France cry treachery, for they, too, had been negotiating with Stalin. But Stalin had remained distrustful of Western intentions, and Hitler had offered immediate territorial gain.

For Hitler, everything was set. He told his generals on the day of the nonaggression pact, "My only fear is that at the last moment some dirty dog will come up with a mediation plan." On September 1, 1939, German armies and warplanes smashed into Poland from three sides. Two days later, Britain and France, finally true to their word, declared war on Germany. The Second World War had begun.

The Second World War

How did Germany and Japan create enormous empires that were defeated by the Allies—Britain, the Soviet Union, and the United States?

War broke out in both western and eastern Europe because Hitler's ambitions were essentially unlimited. On both war fronts, Nazi soldiers scored enormous successes until late 1942, establishing a vast empire of death and destruction. Hitler's victories increased tensions in Asia between Japan and the United States and prompted Japan to attack the United States and overrun much of Southeast Asia. Yet reckless aggression by Germany and Japan also raised a mighty coalition determined to smash the aggressors. Led by Britain, the United States, and the Soviet Union, the Grand Alliance—to use Winston Churchill's favorite name for it—functioned quite effectively in military terms. Thus the Nazi and Japanese empires proved short-lived.

Hitler's Empire (1939–1942)

Using planes, tanks, and trucks in the first example of a **blitzkrieg** (BLITS-kreeg), or "lightning war," Hitler's armies crushed Poland in four weeks. While the Soviet Union quickly took its part of the booty—the eastern half of Poland and the independent Baltic states of Lithuania, Estonia, and Latvia—French and British armies dug in in the west. They expected another war of attrition and economic blockade.

In spring 1940, the lightning war struck again. After occupying Denmark, Norway, and Holland, German motorized columns broke through southern Belgium, split the Franco-British forces, and trapped the entire British army on the beaches of Dunkirk. By heroic efforts, the British withdrew their troops but not their equipment.

blitzkrieg A "lightning war" that used planes, tanks, and trucks; Hitler first used this method to crush Poland in four weeks.

London, 1940

Hitler believed that his relentless terror bombing of London—the "blitz"—could break the will of the British people. He was wrong. The blitz caused enormous destruction, but Londoners went about their business with courage and calm determination, as this unforgettable image of a milkman in the rubble suggests. (Corbis)

France was taken by the Nazis. Aging marshal Henri-Philippe Pétain formed a new French government—the so-called Vichy (**VISH-ee**) government—to accept defeat, and German armies occupied most of France. By July 1940, Hitler ruled practically all of western continental Europe; Italy was an ally, and the Soviet Union and Spain were friendly neutrals. Only Britain, led by the uncompromising Winston Churchill (1874–1965), remained unconquered.

Germany sought to gain control of the air, the necessary first step toward an amphibious invasion of Britain. In the Battle of Britain, up to a thousand German planes attacked British airfields and key factories in a single day, dueling with British defenders high in the skies. Losses were heavy on both sides. Then in September Hitler angrily turned from military objectives to indiscriminate bombing of British cities in an attempt to break British morale. British aircraft factories increased production, and the heavily bombed people of London defiantly dug in. In September and October 1940, Britain was beating Germany three to one in the air war. There was no possibility of an immediate German invasion of Britain.

Turning from Britain and moving into the Balkans by April 1941, Hitler now allowed his lifetime obsession with a vast eastern European empire for the "master race" to dictate policy. In June 1941, German armies suddenly attacked the Soviet Union along a vast front (see Map 29.2, p. 774). By October, Leningrad (St. Petersburg) was practically surrounded, Moscow was besieged, and most of Ukraine had been conquered. But the Soviets did not collapse, and when a severe winter struck German armies outfitted in summer uniforms, the invaders were stopped.

Stalled in Russia, Hitler ruled over a vast European empire stretching from the outskirts of Moscow to the English Channel. Hitler, the Nazi leadership, and the loyal German army were positioned to greatly accelerate construction of their "New Order" in Europe, and they continued their efforts until their final collapse in 1945. In doing so, they showed what Nazi victory would have meant.

Hitler's **New Order** was based firmly on racial imperialism, the guiding principle of Nazi **totalitarianism.** Within this New Order, the Nordic peoples—the Dutch, Norwegians, and Danes—received preferential treatment, for they were racially related to the master race, the Germans. The French, an "inferior" Latin people, occupied a middle position. All the occupied territories of western and northern Europe were exploited with increasing intensity. Material shortages and both mental and physical suffering afflicted millions of people.

Slavs in the conquered territories to the east were treated with harsh hatred as "subhumans." At the height of his success in 1941 and 1942, Hitler set the tone. He painted for his intimate circle the fantastic vision of a vast eastern colonial empire where Poles, Ukrainians, and Russians would be enslaved and forced to die out, while Germanic peasants resettled the resulting abandoned lands. But he needed countless helpers and many ambitious initiators to turn his dreams into reality. These accomplices came forth.

Himmler and the elite corps of SS volunteers shared Hitler's ideology of barbarous racial imperialism, and they rarely wavered in their efforts to realize his goals.[7] Supported (or condoned) by military commanders and German policemen in the occupied territories, the SS corps pressed relentlessly to implement the program of destruction and to create a "mass settlement space" for Germans. Many Poles, Communists, Roma, and Jehovah's Witnesses were murdered in cold blood.

The Holocaust

Nazi racism culminated in the **Holocaust,** the systematic, state-sponsored effort to annihilate all the Jews of Europe. After the fall of Warsaw, the Nazis stepped up their expulsion campaign and began deporting all German Jews to occupied Poland. There they and Jews from all over Europe were concentrated in ghettos, compelled to wear the Jewish star, and turned into slave laborers.

In 1941, following the invasion of the Soviet Union, the large-scale "extermination" of Jews began. On the Russian front, Himmler's special SS killing squads and also regular army units forced Soviet Jews to dig giant pits, which became mass graves as the victims were lined up on the edge and cut down by machine guns. Then in late 1941, Hitler and the Nazi leadership, in some still-debated combination, ordered the SS to stop all Jewish emigration from Europe and speeded up planning for mass murder. As one German diplomat put it, "The Jewish Question must be resolved in the course of the war, for only so can it be solved without a worldwide outcry."[8] The "final solution of the Jewish question"—the murder of every single Jew—had begun. Jews were systematically arrested, packed like cattle onto freight trains, and dispatched to extermination camps. Many Jews could hardly imagine the enormity of the crime that lay before them.

Arriving at their destination, small numbers of Jews were sent to nearby slave labor camps, where they were starved and systematically worked to death. But most of the victims were moved immediately to the death camps, where they were taken by force or deception to "shower rooms" that were actually gas chambers. These gas chambers, first perfected in the quiet, efficient execution of seventy

New Order Hitler's program based on the guiding principle of racial imperialism, which gave preferential treatment to the Nordic peoples while the French, an "inferior" Latin people, occupied a middle position. Slavs in the conquered territories to the east were treated harshly, as "subhumans."

totalitarianism A dictatorship that exercises unprecedented control over the masses and seeks to mobilize them for action.

Holocaust The systematic effort of the Nazi state to exterminate all European Jews, which resulted in the murder of six million Jews.

Prelude to Murder

This photo captures the terrible inhumanity of Nazi racism and the Holocaust. Frightened and bewildered families from the soon-to-be-destroyed Warsaw Ghetto are being forced out of their homes by German soldiers for deportation to concentration camps. There they face murder in the gas chambers. (Hulton Archive/Getty Images)

thousand mentally ill Germans between 1938 and 1941, permitted rapid, hideous, and thoroughly bureaucratized mass murder. For fifteen to twenty minutes came the terrible screams and gasping sobs of men, women, and children choking to death on poison gas. Then, only silence. Special camp workers quickly yanked the victims' gold teeth from their jaws, and the bodies were then cremated or sometimes boiled for oil to make soap. At Auschwitz-Birkenau (**OUSH-vits beer-ken-OW**), the most infamous of the Nazi death factories, as many as twelve thousand human beings were slaughtered each day. The extermination of European Jews was the ultimate monstrosity of Nazi racism and racial imperialism. By 1945, 6 million Jews had been murdered. (See the feature "Individuals in Society: Primo Levi.")

Who was responsible for this terrible crime? An earlier generation of historians usually laid most of the guilt on Hitler and the Nazi leadership. Ordinary Germans had little knowledge of the extermination camps, it was argued, and those who cooperated had no alternative given the brutality of Nazi terror and totalitarian control. But in recent years, many studies have revealed a much broader participation of German people in the Holocaust and popular indifference (or worse) to the fate of the Jews.

The reasons for the active participation or complacency of Germans and others in the Holocaust are debated. The American historian Daniel Goldhagen has made the provocative claim that the extreme anti-Semitism of "ordinary Germans" led them to respond to Hitler and to become his "willing executioners" in World War II.[9] Yet in most occupied countries, local non-German officials also cooperated in the arrest and deportation of Jews to a large extent. As in Germany, only a

Individuals in Society

Primo Levi

Most Jews deported to Auschwitz were murdered as soon as they arrived, but the Nazis made some prisoners into slave laborers and a few of these survived. Primo Levi (1919–1987), an Italian Jew, became one of the most influential witnesses to the Holocaust and its death camps.

Like much of Italy's small Jewish community, Levi's family belonged to the urban professional classes. The young Primo graduated in 1941 from the University of Turin with highest honors in chemistry. But since 1938, when Italy introduced racial laws, he had faced growing discrimination, and two years after graduation he joined the antifascist resistance movement. Quickly captured, he was deported to Auschwitz with 650 Italian Jews in February 1944. Stone-faced SS men picked only ninety-six men and twenty-nine women to work in their respective labor camps. Primo was one of them.

Nothing prepared Levi for what he encountered. The Jewish prisoners were kicked, punched, stripped, branded with tattoos, crammed into huts, and worked unmercifully. Hoping for some sign of prisoner solidarity in this terrible environment, Levi found only a desperate struggle of each against all and enormous status differences among prisoners. Many stunned and bewildered newcomers, beaten and demoralized by their bosses—the most privileged prisoners—simply collapsed and died. Others struggled to secure their own privileges, however small, because food rations and working conditions were so abominable that ordinary Jewish prisoners perished in two to three months.

Sensitive and noncombative, Levi found himself sinking into oblivion. But instead of joining the mass of the "drowned," he became one of the "saved"—a complicated surprise with moral implications that he would ponder all his life. As Levi explained in *Survival in Auschwitz* (1947), the usual road to salvation in the camps was some kind of collaboration with German power.* Savage German criminals were released from prison to become brutal camp guards; non-Jewish political prisoners competed for jobs entitling them to better conditions, and, especially troubling for Levi, a small number of Jewish men plotted and struggled for the power of life

and death over other Jewish prisoners. Though not one of these Jewish bosses, Levi believed that he himself, like almost all survivors, had entered the "gray zone" of moral compromise. Only a very few superior individuals, "the stuff of saints and martyrs," survived the death camps without shifting their moral stance.

For Levi, compromise and salvation came from his profession. Interviewed by a German technocrat for the camp's synthetic rubber program, Levi performed brilliantly in scientific German and savored his triumph as a Jew over Nazi racism. Work in the warm camp laboratory offered Levi opportunities to pilfer equipment that could then be traded for food and necessities with other prisoners. Levi also gained critical support from three saintly prisoners, who refused to do wicked and hateful acts. And he counted "luck" as essential for his survival: in the camp infirmary with scarlet fever in February 1945 as advancing Russian armies prepared to liberate the camp, Levi was not evacuated by the Nazis and shot to death like most Jewish prisoners.

Primo Levi, who never stopped thinking, writing, and speaking about the Holocaust. (Giansanti/Corbis Sygma)

After the war Primo Levi was forever haunted by the nightmare that the Holocaust would be ignored or forgotten. Always ashamed that so many people whom he considered better than himself had perished, he wrote and lectured tirelessly to preserve the memory of Jewish victims and guilty Nazis. Wanting the world to understand the Jewish genocide in all its complexity so that never again would people tolerate such atrocities, he grappled tirelessly with his vision of individual choice and moral compromise in a hell designed to make the victims collaborate and persecute each other.

Questions for Analysis

1. Describe Levi's experience at Auschwitz. How did camp prisoners treat each other? Why?
2. What does Levi mean by the "gray zone"? How is this concept central to his thinking?
3. Will a vivid historical memory of the Holocaust help to prevent future genocide?

---

* Primo Levi, *Survival in Auschwitz: The Nazi Assault on Humanity*, rev. ed. 1958 (London: Collier Books, 1961), pp. 79–84, and *The Drowned and the Saved* (New York: Summit Books, 1988). These powerful testimonies are highly recommended.

few exceptional bystanders did not turn a blind eye. Thus some scholars have concluded that the key for most Germans (and most people in occupied countries) was that they felt no personal responsibility for Jews and therefore were not prepared to help them. This meant that many individuals, conditioned by Nazi racist propaganda but also influenced by peer pressure and brutalizing wartime violence, were psychologically prepared to join the SS ideologues and perpetrate ever-greater crimes. They were ready to plumb the depths of evil and to spiral downward from mistreatment to arrest to mass murder.

Japan's Empire in Asia

By late 1938, 1.5 million Japanese troops were bogged down in China, holding a great swath of territory but unable to defeat the Nationalists and the Communists (see Map 29.3). Nor had Japan succeeded in building a large, self-sufficient Asian economic zone, for it still depended on oil and scrap metal from the Netherlands East Indies and the United States. Thus Japanese leaders followed events in Europe closely, looking for alliances and actions that might improve their position in Asia. At home they gave free reign to the anti-Western ultranationalism that had risen in the 1920s and 1930s. In speeches, schools, and newspapers ultranationalists proclaimed Japan's liberating mission in Asia, glorified the warrior virtues of honor and sacrifice, and demanded absolute devotion to the semidivine emperor.

The outbreak of war in Europe in 1939 and Hitler's early victories opened up opportunities for the Japanese in Southeast Asia, where European empires appeared vulnerable. Expanding the war in China, the Japanese also pressured the Dutch to surrender control of the Netherlands East Indies and its rich oil fields, but Dutch colonial officials, backed by the British and the Americans, refused. The United States had repeatedly condemned Japanese aggression in China, and it now feared that embattled Britain would collapse if it lost the support of its Asian colonies.

Japan's invasion of southern Indochina in July 1941 further worsened relations with the United States. President Franklin Roosevelt demanded that Japan withdraw from China, and they refused. The United States responded by cutting off the sale of U.S. oil to Japan and thereby reducing Japan's oil supplies by 90 percent. Japanese leaders believed increasingly that war with the United States was inevitable, for Japan's battle fleet would run out of fuel in eighteen months, and its industry would be crippled. After much debate, Japanese leaders decided to launch a surprise attack on the United States. They hoped to cripple their Pacific rival, gain time to build a defensible Asian empire while getting oil from Indonesia, and eventually win an ill-defined compromise peace.

The Japanese attack on the U.S. naval base at Pearl Harbor in the Hawaiian Islands was a complete surprise but a limited success. On December 7, 1941, the Japanese sank or crippled every American battleship, but by chance all the all-important American aircraft carriers were at sea and escaped unharmed. More important, Pearl Harbor united Americans in a spirit of anger and revenge.

Hitler immediately declared war on the United States. Simultaneously, Japanese armies successfully attacked European and American colonies in Southeast Asia. Japanese armies were small (because most soldiers remained in China), but they were well trained, highly motivated, and very successful. By May 1942 Japan held a vast empire in Southeast Asia and the western Pacific (see Map 29.3, p. 776).

The Grand Alliance

Facing war across both the Pacific and the Atlantic, the United States agreed with its allies Great Britain and the Soviet Union on a policy of **Europe first.** Only after Hitler was defeated would the Allies turn toward the Pacific for an all-out attack on Japan, the lesser threat. The Allies agreed to wage war until the "unconditional surrender" of both Germany and Japan.

The military resources of the Grand Alliance were awesome. The strengths of the United States were its mighty industry, its large population, and its national unity. Gearing up rapidly for all-out war in 1942, the United States acquired a unique capacity to wage global war. In 1943 it outproduced not only Germany, Italy, and Japan but also all of the rest of the world combined.

Britain continued to make a great contribution as well. The British economy was totally and effectively mobilized, and the sharing of burdens through rationing and heavy taxes on war profits maintained social harmony. By early 1943 the Americans and the British were combining small aircraft carriers with radar-guided bombers to rid the Atlantic of German submarines. Britain, the impregnable floating fortress, became a gigantic frontline staging area for the decisive blow to the heart of Germany.

As for the Soviet Union, so great was its strength that it might well have defeated Germany without Western help. In the face of the German advance, whole factories and populations were successfully evacuated to eastern Russia and Siberia. There war production was reorganized and expanded, and the Red Army was increasingly well supplied and well led. Above all, Stalin drew on the massive support and heroic determination of the Soviet people, especially those in the central Russian heartland. Broad-based Russian nationalism, as opposed to narrow communist ideology, became the powerful unifying force in what the Soviet people appropriately called the "Great Patriotic War of the Fatherland."

Finally, the United States, Britain, and the Soviet Union had the resources of much of the world at their command. They were also aided by a growing resistance movement against the Nazis throughout Europe, even in Germany. After the Soviet Union was invaded in June 1941, communists throughout Europe took the lead in the underground resistance, joined by a growing number of patriots, Christians, and agents sent by governments-in-exile in London.

Europe first   The Allied policy to defeat Hitler in Europe before turning their attack on Japan.

The War in Europe (1942–1945)

Barely halted at the gates of Moscow and Leningrad in 1941, the Germans renewed their offensive against the Soviet Union in July 1942, driving toward the southern city of Stalingrad and occupying most of the city in a month of incredibly savage house-to-house fighting.

Then, in November 1942, Soviet armies counterattacked. They rolled over Romanian and Italian troops to the north and south of Stalingrad, quickly closing the trap and surrounding the entire German Sixth Army of 300,000 men. The surrounded Germans were systematically destroyed, until by the end of January 1943 only 123,000 soldiers were left to surrender. Hitler, who had refused to allow a retreat, had suffered a catastrophic defeat. In summer 1943, the larger, better-equipped Soviet armies took the offensive and began moving forward (Map 29.2).

Not yet prepared to attack Germany directly through France, the Western Allies saw heavy fighting in North Africa from 1940 onward. In May 1942, combined German and Italian armies were finally defeated by British forces only seventy miles from Alexandria at the Battle of El Alamein (**al-uh-MAYN**). Almost immediately thereafter, an Anglo-American force landed in Morocco and Algeria. These

MAPPING THE PAST

MAP 29.2   World War II in Europe

The map shows the extent of Hitler's empire before the Battle of Stalingrad in late 1942 and the subsequent advances of the Allies until Germany surrendered on May 7, 1945. This map, combined with Map 29.1 on page 766, can be used to trace the rise and fall of the Nazi empire over time. **[1]** First, using Map 29.1 on page 766, what was the first country to be conquered by Hitler (and divided with the Soviet Union)? **[2]** Second, locate Germany's advance and retreat on the Russian front at different dates: December 1941, November 1942, Spring 1944, and February 1945. Locate the position of British and American forces on the battlefield at similar points in time, and then compare the respective Russian and British-American positions. What implications might the battle lines on February 1945 have for the postwar settlement in Europe?

Legend:
- Hitler's Greater Germany
- Allied with Germany
- Occupied by Germany and its allies
- Grand Alliance
- Neutral nations
- ★ Major battle

French possessions, which were under the control of Pétain's Vichy government, quickly went over to the side of the Allies.

Having driven the Axis powers from North Africa by spring 1943, Allied forces maintained the initiative by invading Sicily and then mainland Italy. Mussolini was deposed by a war-weary people, and the new Italian government publicly accepted unconditional surrender in September 1943. Italy, it seemed, was liberated. Yet German commandos rescued Mussolini in a daring raid and put him at the head of a puppet government. German armies seized Rome and all of northern Italy. Fighting continued in Italy.

Indeed, bitter fighting continued in Europe for almost two years. Germany, less fully mobilized for war than Britain in 1941, applied itself to total war in 1942 and enlisted millions of German women and millions of prisoners of war and slave laborers from all across occupied Europe in that effort. Between early 1942 and July 1944, German war production actually tripled in spite of heavy bombing by the British and American air forces. German resistance against Hitler also failed. After an unsuccessful attempt on Hitler's life in July 1944, SS fanatics brutally liquidated thousands of Germans. Terrorized at home and frightened by the prospect of unconditional surrender, the Germans fought on with suicidal stoicism.

On June 6, 1944, American and British forces under General Dwight Eisenhower landed on the beaches of Normandy, France, in history's greatest naval invasion. In a hundred dramatic days, more than 2 million men and almost half a million vehicles pushed inland and broke through German lines. Rejecting proposals to strike straight at Berlin in a massive attack, Eisenhower moved forward cautiously on a broad front. Not until March 1945 did American troops cross the Rhine and enter Germany.

The Soviets, who had been advancing steadily since July 1943, reached the outskirts of Warsaw by August 1944. For the next six months, they moved southward into Romania, Hungary, and Yugoslavia. In January 1945, the Red Army again moved westward through Poland, and on April 26 it met American forces on the Elbe River. The Allies had closed their vise on Nazi Germany and overrun Europe. As Soviet forces fought their way into Berlin, Hitler committed suicide in his bunker, and on May 7 the remaining German commanders capitulated.

The War in the Pacific (1942–1945)

In Asia, as gigantic armies clashed in Europe, the greatest naval battles in history decided the fate of warring nations (see Map 29.3). First, in the Battle of the Coral Sea in May 1942, an American carrier force fought its Japanese counterpart to a draw, thereby stopping the Japanese advance on Port Moresby and relieving Australia from the threat of invasion. This engagement was followed in June 1942 by the Battle of Midway, in which American carrier-based pilots sank all four of the attacking Japanese aircraft carriers and established overall naval equality with Japan in the Pacific. In August 1942 American marines attacked and took Guadalcanal in the Solomon Islands in heavy fighting.

Hampered by the policy of "Europe first," the United States gradually won control of the sea and air as it geared up massive production of aircraft carriers, submarines, and fighter planes. By 1943 the United States was producing one hundred thousand aircraft a year, almost twice as many as Japan produced in the entire war. In July 1943 the Americans and their Australian allies opened an "island hopping" campaign toward Japan. Pounding Japanese forces on a given island with saturation bombing, American army and marine units would then hit the beaches with rifles and flame throwers and secure victory in hand-to-hand

MAP 29.3   World War II in the Pacific

Japanese forces overran an enormous amount of territory in 1942, which the Allies slowly recaptured in a long, bitter struggle. As this map shows, Japan still held a large Asian empire in August 1945, when the unprecedented devastation of atomic warfare suddenly forced it to surrender.

combat. Many islands were bypassed, and their Japanese defenders were blockaded and left to starve.

The war in the Pacific was extremely brutal—a "war without mercy," in the words of a leading American scholar—and atrocities were committed on both sides.[10] Knowing of Japanese atrocities in China and the Philippines, the U.S. Marines and Army troops seldom took Japanese prisoners after the Battle of Guadalcanal, killing even those rare Japanese soldiers who offered to surrender. A product of spiraling violence, mutual hatred, and dehumanizing racial stereotypes, the war without mercy intensified as it moved toward Japan.

In June 1944 giant U.S. bombers began a relentless bombing campaign that intensified steadily until the end of the war. In October 1944, as Allied advances in the Pacific paralleled those in Europe, American forces won a great victory in the four-day Battle of Leyte (**LEY-tee**) Gulf, the greatest battle in naval history, with 282 ships involved. The Japanese navy was practically finished.

In spite of all their defeats, Japanese troops continued to fight with enormous courage and determination. Indeed, the bloodiest battles of the Pacific war took place on Iwo Jima in February 1945 and on Okinawa (**oh-kee-NAH-wah**) in June 1945. American commanders believed the conquest of Japan might cost a million American casualties and claim 10 to 20 million Japanese lives. In fact, Japan was almost helpless, its industry and dense, fragile wooden cities largely destroyed by incendiary bombing and uncontrollable hurricanes of fire. Yet the Japanese seemed determined to fight on, ever ready to die for a hopeless cause.

On August 6 and 9, 1945, the United States dropped atomic bombs on Hiroshima (**heer-oh-SHEE-muh**) and Nagasaki (**nah-gah-SAH-kee**) in Japan. Mass bombing of cities and civilians, one of the terrible new practices of World War II, had ended in the final nightmare—unprecedented human destruction in a single blinding flash. On August 14, 1945, the Japanese announced their surrender. The Second World War, which had claimed the lives of more than 50 million soldiers and civilians, was over.

Section Review

- The Germans used a blitzkrieg to crush Poland and most of western continental Europe except Britain, turning next to the Soviet Union, where they gained vast amounts of territory; their aim was to have Germanic peoples occupy and populate the conquered territories, enslaving and eliminating the "inferior" races there.

- Hitler's ultimate horror was his goal of racial imperialism, including the deportations to concentration camps and slave labor camps, culminating in the outright mass murder of millions of Jews and other "undesirables" in the Holocaust.

- Japan tried to expand into Southeast Asia, angering the United States, who cut off the sale of oil to Japan, which responded with a surprise attack on Pearl Harbor in Hawaii and European and American colonies in Southeast Asia, sparking Hitler's declaration of war against the United States.

- The Allied powers agreed to liberate Europe first and then to take on Japan in the Pacific; they effectively mobilized for war, with the United States out-producing every other country while Britain and the Soviet Union also fielded well-organized war machines.

- The Germans pursued their attack on the Soviet Union but suffered defeat while the Soviets went on the offensive, and with the western Allies, closed the noose, surrounding and finally entering Germany where Hitler committed suicide and the remaining Germans surrendered.

- The brutal war in the Pacific, a "war without mercy," involved an Allied "island hopping" campaign on the way to Japan; intense fighting pressed Japan to the limit, but the United States dealt the final catastrophic blow by dropping two atomic bombs to end the war.

Chapter Review

How did Stalin and the Communist Party build a modern totalitarian state in the Soviet Union? (page 753)

The crafty Stalin consolidated his power in the 1920s, and in 1928 he launched the five-year plans. In doing so, Stalin's Soviet Union asserted a total claim on the lives of its citizens. It posed ambitious goals in the form of rapid state-directed industrialization and savage collectivization of agriculture. And it found enthusiastic supporters who believed that Stalin and the Communist Party were building their kind of socialism and a new socialist personality at home. Relentless propaganda and the great purges reinforced the Party's claims of unlimited control of its citizens.

How did Mussolini's dictatorship come to power and govern in Italy? (page 758)

Mussolini began as a socialist but he turned to the right when he received growing support from conservatives. Coming to power with the king's help, Mussolini proclaimed the revolutionary, "totalitarian" character of his one-party rule. In fact, Mussolini's government retained many elements of conservative authoritarianism, such as compromising with the Catholic Church and keeping women in traditional roles.

Key Terms

five-year plan (p. 753)
New Economic Policy (NEP) (p. 753)
collectivization (p. 754)
kulaks (p. 754)
fascists (p. 760)
Black Shirts (p. 760)
Lateran Agreement (p. 760)
Nazism (p. 761)
Führer (p. 762)
Enabling Act (p. 763)

(continued)

How did Hitler gain power, what policies did totalitarian Nazi Germany pursue, and why did they lead to World War II? (page 761)

Failing to overthrow the government in 1923 in an attempted coup, Hitler came to power legally in 1933 by promising voters national renewal and economic recovery from the Great Depression. His policies appeared to help the economy and he quickly established a one-party totalitarian regime with ambitious goals and widespread popular support. But whereas Stalin concentrated on building socialism at home, Hitler and the Nazi elite aimed at unlimited territorial and racial aggression on behalf of a master race. He proceeded gradually at first, and Britain and France sought to "appease" Hitler with various diplomatic concessions. Only Hitler's unprovoked attack on Poland in 1939 brought a military response from Britain and France and the beginning of World War II.

How did Germany and Japan create enormous empires that were defeated by the Allies—Britain, the Soviet Union, and the United States? (page 767)

Nazi racism and unlimited aggression made war inevitable, first with the western European democracies, then with hated eastern neighbors, and finally with the United States. Joined by Japan after Pearl Harbor, Hitler's forces overran much of western and eastern Europe, annihilated millions of Jews, and plunged Europe into the ultimate nightmare. But unlimited aggression unwittingly forged a mighty coalition led by Britain, the Soviet Union, and the United States. This Grand Alliance held together and smashed the racist Nazi empire and its leader. The United States also destroyed Japan's vast, overextended empire in the Pacific, thus bringing to a close history's most destructive war.

appeasement (p. 765)
blitzkrieg (p. 767)
New Order (p. 769)
totalitarianism (p. 769)
Holocaust (p. 769)
Europe first (p. 773)

Notes

1. I. Kershaw, *The Nazi Dictatorship: Problems and Perspectives of Interpretation*, 2d ed. (London: Edward Arnold, 1989), p. 34.
2. Quoted in I. Deutscher, *Stalin: A Political Biography*, 2d ed. (New York: Oxford University Press, 1967), p. 325.
3. R. Conquest, *The Harvest of Sorrow: Soviet Collectivization and the Terror-Famine* (New York: Oxford University Press, 1986), pp. 4, 303.
4. R. Thurston, *Life and Terror in Stalin's Russia, 1934–1941* (New Haven, Conn.: Yale University Press, 1996), esp. pp. 16–106; also Malia, *The Soviet Tragedy*, pp. 227–270.
5. W. Brustein, *The Logic of Evil: The Social Origins of the Nazi Party, 1925–1933* (New Haven, Conn.: Yale University Press, 1996), pp. 52, 182.
6. Quoted in K. D. Bracher, *The German Dictatorship: The Origins, Structure and Effects of National Socialism* (New York: Praeger, 1970), p. 289.
7. R. Allen, *The Business of Genocide: The SS, Slave Labor, and the Concentration Camps* (Chapel Hill: University of North Carolina Press, 2002), pp. 270–285.
8. Quoted in M. Marrus, *The Holocaust in History* (Hanover, N.H.: University Press of New England, 1987), p. 28.
9. D. Goldhagen, *Hitler's Willing Executioners: Ordinary Germans and the Holocaust* (New York: Vintage Books, 1997).
10. J. Dower, *War Without Mercy: Race and Power in the Pacific War* (New York: Pantheon, 1986).

To assess your mastery of this chapter, go to **bedfordstmartins.com/mckaywestbrief**

Listening to the Past

Stalin Justifies the Five-Year Plan

On February 4, 1931, Joseph Stalin delivered the following address, entitled "No Slowdown in Tempo!," to the First Conference of Soviet Industrial Managers. Published the following day in Pravda, the newspaper of the Communist Party, and widely publicized at home and abroad, Stalin's speech sought to rally the people and generate support for the party's program. His address captures the spirit of Soviet public discourse in the early 1930s.

It is sometimes asked whether it is not possible to slow down the tempo somewhat, to put a check on the movement. No, comrades, it is not possible! The tempo must not be reduced! On the contrary, we must increase it as much as is within our powers and possibilities. This is dictated to us by our obligations to the workers and peasants of the U.S.S.R. This is dictated to us by our obligations to the working class of the whole world.

To slacken the tempo would mean falling behind. And those who fall behind get beaten. But we do not want to be beaten. No, we refuse to be beaten! One feature of the history of old Russia was the continual beatings she suffered because of her backwardness. She was beaten by the Mongol khans, . . . the Turkish beys, . . . and the Japanese barons. All beat her—because of her backwardness, cultural backwardness, political backwardness, industrial backwardness, agricultural backwardness. They beat her because to do so was profitable and could be done with impunity. . . . Such is the law of the exploiters—to beat the backward and the weak. It is the jungle law of capitalism. You are backward, you are weak—therefore you are wrong; hence you can be beaten and enslaved. You are mighty—therefore you are right; hence we must be wary of you.

That is why we must no longer lag behind. . . .

But we have yet other, more serious and more important, obligations. They are our obligations to the world proletariat. . . . We must march forward in such a way that the working class of the whole

"Our program is realistic," Stalin proclaims on this poster, "because it is you and me working together." (David King Collection)

world, looking at us, may say: There you have my advanced detachment, my shock brigade, my working-class state power, my fatherland; they are engaged on their cause, *our* cause, and they are working well; let us support them against the capitalists and promote the cause of the world revolution. Must we not justify the hopes of the world's working class, must we not fulfill our obligations to them? Yes, we must if we do not want to utterly disgrace ourselves.

Such are our obligations, internal and international.

As you see, they dictate to us a Bolshevik tempo of development.

I will not say that we have accomplished nothing in regard to management of production during these years. In fact, we have accomplished a good deal. . . . But we could have accomplished still more if we had tried during this period really to master production, the technique of production, the financial and economic side of it. . . .

It is said that it is hard to master technique. That is not true! There are no fortresses that Bolsheviks cannot capture. We have solved a number of most difficult problems. We have overthrown capitalism. We have assumed power. We have built up a huge socialist industry. We have transferred the middle peasants on the path of socialism. We have already accomplished what is most important from the point of view of construction. What remains to be done is not so much: to study technique, to master science. And when we have done that we shall develop a tempo of which we dare not even dream at present.

And we shall do it if we really want to.

Questions for Analysis

1. What reasons does Stalin give to justify an unrelenting "Bolshevik" tempo of industrial and social change? In the light of history, which reason seems most convincing? Why?

2. Imagine that the year is 1931 and you are a Soviet student reading Stalin's speech. Would Stalin's determination inspire you, frighten you, or leave you cold? Why?

3. Some historians argue that Soviet socialism was a kind of utopianism—that zealots believed that the economy, the society, and even human beings could be completely remade and perfected. What utopian elements do you see in Stalin's declaration?

Source: From Joseph Stalin, "No Slowdown in Tempo!" *Pravda,* February 5, 1931.

CHAPTER 30

Cold War Conflicts and Social Transformations

1945–1985

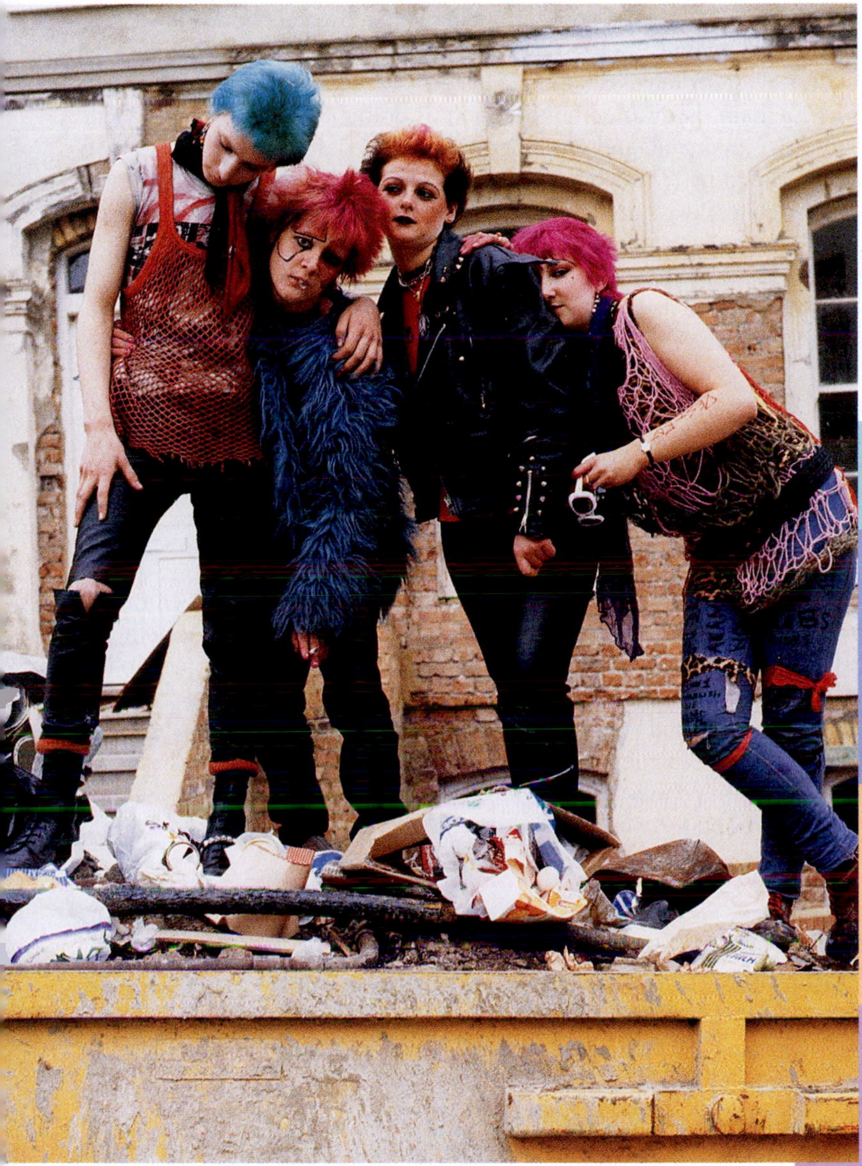

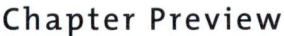

The youth revolution. London, ca. 1980. (Anthea Sieveking/Wellcome Images)

Chapter Preview

The Division of Europe
What were the causes of the cold war?

The Western Renaissance (1945–1968)
Why did western Europe recover so successfully? How did colonial peoples win political independence and American blacks triumph in the civil rights movement?

Soviet Eastern Europe (1945–1968)
What was the pattern of postwar rebuilding and development in the Soviet Union and communist eastern Europe?

Postwar Social Transformations (1945–1968)
How did changing patterns in technology, class relations, women's work, and youth culture bring major social transformations?

Conflict and Challenge in the Late Cold War (1968–1985)
What were the key aspects of political conflict, economic stagnation, and the feminist movement in the late cold war?

INDIVIDUALS IN SOCIETY: Margaret Thatcher

LISTENING TO THE PAST: A Feminist Critique of Marriage

The total defeat of the Nazis and their allies in 1945 laid the basis for one of Western civilization's most remarkable recoveries, as Europe dug itself out from under the rubble and fashioned a great renaissance. Yet there was also a tragic setback. The Grand Alliance against Hitler gave way to an apparently endless cold war in which tension between East and West threatened world peace.

In the late 1960s and early 1970s, three major changes marked the end of the era of postwar Western renaissance. First, as cold war competition again turned very hot in Vietnam, postwar certainties such as domestic political stability and social harmony evaporated, and several countries experienced major crises. Second, the astonishing postwar economic advance came to a halt, and this had serious social consequences. Third, new roles for women after World War II led to a powerful "second wave" of feminist thought and action in the 1970s, resulting in major changes for women and gender relations. Thus the long cold war created an underlying unity for the years 1945–1985, but the first half of the cold war era was quite different from the second.

The Division of Europe
What were the causes of the cold war?

In 1945 triumphant American and Russian soldiers came together and embraced on the banks of the Elbe River in the heart of vanquished Germany. At home, in the United States and in the Soviet Union, the soldiers' loved ones erupted in joyous celebration. Yet victory was flawed. The Allies could not cooperate politically in peacemaking. Motivated by different goals and hounded by misunderstandings, the United States and the Soviet Union soon found themselves at loggerheads. By the end of 1947, Europe was rigidly divided. It was West versus East in a cold war that was waged around the world for forty years.

The Origins of the Cold War

The most powerful allies in the wartime coalition—the Soviet Union and the United States—began to quarrel almost as soon as the threat of Nazi Germany disappeared. This hostility between the Eastern and Western superpowers was the sad but logical outgrowth of military developments, wartime agreements, and long-standing political and ideological differences.

In the early phases of the Second World War, the Americans and the British chose to avoid discussing with Stalin the shape of the eventual peace settlement. They feared that hard bargaining would encourage Stalin to consider making a separate peace with Hitler. They focused instead on the policy of unconditional surrender to solidify the alliance.

By late 1943, discussion about the shape of the postwar world could no longer be postponed. The conference that Stalin, Roosevelt, and Churchill held in the Iranian capital of Teheran in November 1943 thus proved of crucial importance in determining subsequent events. There, the **Big Three** searched for the appropriate military strategy to crush Germany. Roosevelt chose to meet Stalin's wartime demands whenever possible and so supported Stalin's plan for an American-British frontal assault through France. This strategy meant that the Soviet and the American-British armies would come together in defeated Germany along a north-

Big Three Russia, the United States, and England.

south line and that only Soviet troops would liberate eastern Europe. Thus the basic shape of postwar Europe was emerging even as the fighting continued.

When the Big Three met again in February 1945 at Yalta on the Black Sea in southern Russia, advancing Soviet armies were within a hundred miles of Berlin. The Red Army had occupied not only Poland but also Bulgaria, Romania, Hungary, part of Yugoslavia, and much of Czechoslovakia. The temporarily stalled American-British forces had yet to cross the Rhine into Germany. Moreover, the United States was far from defeating Japan. In short, the Soviet Union's position was strong and America's weak.

It was agreed at Yalta that Germany would be divided into zones of occupation and would pay heavy reparations to the Soviet Union. At American insistence, Stalin agreed to declare war on Japan after Germany was defeated. An ambiguous compromise was reached on Poland and eastern Europe: their governments were to be freely elected but pro-Russian.

The Yalta compromise over eastern Europe broke down almost immediately. Even before the Yalta Conference, Bulgaria and Poland were controlled by communists who arrived home with the Red Army. Elsewhere in eastern Europe, pro-Soviet "coalition" governments of several parties were formed, but the key ministerial posts were reserved for Moscow-trained communists.

At the postwar Potsdam Conference of July 1945, differences over eastern Europe finally surged to the fore. The new American president, Harry Truman, demanded immediate free elections throughout eastern Europe. Stalin refused point-blank. "A freely elected government in any of these East European countries would be anti-Soviet," he admitted simply, "and that we cannot allow."[1]

Here, then, is the key to the much-debated origins of the cold war. American ideals, pumped up by the crusade against Hitler, and American politics, heavily influenced by millions of voters from eastern Europe, demanded free elections in Soviet-occupied eastern Europe. Stalin, who

The Big Three

In 1945 a triumphant Winston Churchill, an ailing Franklin Roosevelt, and a determined Joseph Stalin met at Yalta in southern Russia to plan for peace. Cooperation soon gave way to bitter hostility. (Franklin Delano Roosevelt Library)

had lived through two enormously destructive German invasions, wanted absolute military security in relation to Germany and its potential Eastern allies. Suspicious by nature, he believed that only communist states could be truly dependable allies, and he realized that free elections would result in independent and possibly hostile governments on his western border. Moreover, by the middle of 1945, there was no way short of war that the United States could control political developments in eastern Europe, and war was out of the question. Stalin was bound to have his way.

West Versus East

The American response to Stalin's refusal to allow elections was to "get tough." In May 1945, Truman abruptly cut off all aid to the U.S.S.R. In October he declared that the United States would never recognize any government established by force against the free will of its people. In March 1946, former British prime minister Churchill ominously informed an American audience that an "iron curtain" had fallen across the continent, dividing Germany and all of Europe into two antagonistic camps. Emotional, moralistic denunciations of Stalin and communist Russia emerged as part of American political life. Yet the United States also responded to the popular desire to "bring the boys home" and demobilized its troops with great speed. Some historians have argued that American leaders believed that the atomic bomb gave the United States all the power it needed, but "getting tough" really meant "talking tough."

Stalin's agents quickly reheated what they viewed as the "ideological struggle against capitalist imperialism." The large, well-organized Communist Parties of France and Italy obediently started to uncover "American plots" to take over Europe and challenged their own governments with violent criticisms and large strikes. The Soviet Union also put pressure on Iran, Turkey, and Greece, while a bitter civil war raged in China. By the spring of 1947, it appeared to many Americans that Stalin was determined to export communism by subversion throughout Europe and around the world.

The United States responded to this challenge with the Truman Doctrine, which was aimed at "containing" communism to areas already occupied by the Red Army and supporting governments facing a communist threat. To begin, Truman asked Congress for military aid to Greece and Turkey, countries that Britain, weakened by war and financially overextended, could no longer protect. Then, in June, Secretary of State George C. Marshall offered Europe economic aid—the **Marshall Plan**—to help it rebuild.

Stalin refused Marshall Plan assistance for all of eastern Europe and attempted unsuccessfully to add West Berlin to the Soviet bloc. In 1949, intent on containment, the United States formed an anti-Soviet military alliance of Western governments: the North Atlantic Treaty Organization, or **NATO**. Stalin countered by tightening his hold on his satellites, later united in the Warsaw Pact. Europe was divided into two hostile blocs and the bitter **cold war** was begun (see Map 30.1, page 786).

In late 1949, the communists triumphed in China, which many Americans perceived as new evidence of a powerful worldwide communist conspiracy. When the Russian-backed communist army of North Korea invaded South Korea in 1950, President Truman acted swiftly. American-led United Nations forces under General Douglas MacArthur intervened. The bitter, bloody contest seesawed back and forth, but President Truman rejected General MacArthur's call to attack China and fired him instead. In 1953 a fragile truce was negotiated, and the fight-

Marshall Plan Secretary of State George C. Marshall's plan of economic aid to Europe to help it rebuild, which Stalin refused for all of eastern Europe.

NATO The North Atlantic Treaty Organization, an anti-Soviet military alliance of Western governments.

cold war The long period after World War II during which Europe and the United States were divided between East and West into two hostile military alliances and the tension threatened world peace.

ing stopped. Thus the United States extended its policy of containment to Asia but drew back from an attack on communist China and possible nuclear war.

The Western Renaissance (1945–1968)

Why did western Europe recover so successfully? How did colonial peoples win political independence and American blacks triumph in the civil rights movement?

As the cold war divided Europe into two blocs, the future appeared bleak on both sides of the iron curtain. European economic conditions were the worst in generations, and the overseas empires of western Europe were crumbling in the face of nationalism in Asia and Africa. Yet in less than a generation, western Europe and the United States achieved unprecedented economic prosperity and social transformation. It was an amazing rebirth—a true renaissance.

The Postwar Challenge

After the war, the people of western Europe faced severe shortages and hardships. Suffering was most intense in defeated Germany. The major territorial change of the war had moved the Soviet Union's border far to the west. Poland was in turn compensated for this loss to the Soviets with land taken from Germany. To solidify these changes in boundaries, 13 million Germans were driven from their homes and forced to resettle in a greatly reduced Germany. The Russians were also seizing factories and equipment as reparations in their zone, even tearing up railroad tracks and sending the rails to the Soviet Union.

In 1945 and 1946, conditions were not much better in the Western zones, for the Western allies also treated the German population with severity at first. Countless Germans sold prized possessions to American soldiers to buy food. By the spring of 1947, Germany was on the verge of total collapse and threatening to drag down the rest of Europe. Yet the seeds of recovery were also planted, for the people had had enough of old ideas, and new leaders were coming to the fore to guide these aspirations for change. In Italy, France, and the Federal Republic of Germany (as Western Germany was officially known), the **Christian Democrats** and Catholic Party offered strong leaders. They steadfastly rejected authoritarianism and narrow nationalism and placed their faith in democracy and cooperation. The socialists and the communists, active in the resistance against Hitler, also emerged from the war with increased power and prestige, especially in France and Italy. They, too, provided fresh leadership and pushed for social change and economic reform. In the immediate postwar years, welfare measures such as family allowances, health insurance, and increased public housing were enacted throughout continental Europe. Britain followed the same trend, as the newly elected socialist Labour Party established a "welfare state." Many British industries were nationalized, and the government provided free medical service. Thus all across Europe, social reform complemented political transformation, creating solid foundations for a great European renaissance.

Massive economic aid and ongoing military protection from the United States was also essential to rebuilding Europe. As Marshall Plan aid poured in, the battered economies of western Europe began to turn the corner in 1948. The outbreak of the Korean War in 1950 further stimulated economic activity, and Europe entered a period of rapid economic progress that lasted into the late 1960s. Never

Section Review

- Stalin and the Western Allies could not agree on a post-war settlement: Stalin argued for communist states in eastern Europe as dependable allies and the west pushed for free elections; Stalin, in a stronger position militarily, got his way.

- The Americans responded by cutting off aid to the U.S.S.R., issuing the Truman Doctrine to "contain" communism; negative propaganda was pursued by both sides; the United States formed the anti-Soviet military alliance, NATO, while Stalin formed the Warsaw pact, dividing Europe into two hostile zones, initiating the cold war.

- When China fell to the communists and North Korea attacked South Korea, the United States defended the Truman Doctrine by sending troops to intervene in Korea, but held short of invading China.

Christian Democrats Progressive Catholics and revitalized Catholic political parties that became influential after the Second World War.

Participants in the Marshall Plan

$ Member of NATO,* formed in 1949

Member of COMECON,** formed in 1949, and the Warsaw Pact, organized in 1955

Member of the European Common Market, formed in 1958

● Iron Curtain

* North Atlantic Treaty Organization
** Council for Mutual Economic Assistance

400 Mi.

400 Km.

200

200

UNION OF SOVIET SOCIALIST REPUBLICS

Exploded first atomic bomb, 1949

Caspian Sea

Volga R.

Don R.

Dnieper R.

● Moscow

40E

60N

40N

40E

20E

Black Sea

Truman Doctrine, 1947
Joined NATO, 1952

● Ankara

TURKEY

CYPRUS ● Nicosia

Truman Doctrine, 1947
Joined NATO, 1952
Joined Common Market, 1981

● Athens

GREECE $

Bucharest ●

ROMANIA

BULGARIA

Danube R.

Sofia ●

Communist coup, 1948
U.S.S.R. invasion, 1968

Warsaw ●

POLAND

CZECHOSLOVAKIA

Prague ●

Budapest ●

HUNGARY

Belgrade ●

YUGOSLAVIA

Tito-Stalin schism, 1948

Tiranë ●
ALBANIA

Revolution, 1956

Left COMECON, 1961
Withdrew from WP, 1968

Berlin blockade, 1948–1949

○ East Berlin

West Berlin ●

EAST GERMANY

FINLAND

● Helsinki

Stockholm ●

SWEDEN $

Baltic Sea

Copenhagen ●

Oslo ●

NORWAY $

DENMARK $

Joined Common Market, 1973

Vienna ●

Joined NATO, 1955

AUSTRIA $

Zones of occupation ended, 1955

Bern ●
SWITZ. $

Rome ●

ITALY $

Corsica

Sardinia

Sicily

U.S. loan of $3.5 billion, 1946
Exploded first atomic bomb, 1952
Joined Common Market, 1973

Amsterdam ●
NETHERLANDS

Bonn ●
WEST GERMANY

Brussels ●
BELGIUM **LUX.** $

Paris ●

Exploded first atomic bomb, 1960
Withdrew from NATO, 1966

FRANCE

UNITED KINGDOM $

London ●

IRELAND $ ● Dublin

Joined Common Market, 1973

North Sea

Mediterranean Sea

Balearic Is.

Joined Common Market, 1986

SPAIN

Madrid ●

Joined NATO, 1982
Joined Common Market, 1986

PORTUGAL

Lisbon ●

ATLANTIC OCEAN

N

Arctic Circle

ICELAND $

Reykjavík ●

20W

0

MAPPING THE PAST

MAP 30.1   European Alliance Systems, 1949–1989

After the cold war divided Europe into two hostile military alliances, six western European countries formed the Common Market in 1957. The Common Market grew later to include most of western Europe. The communist states organized their own economic association—COMECON. **[1]** Identify the countries that were the original members of the Common Market. What do they have in common? **[2]** Identify the members of COMECON. What communist country or countries did not join COMECON? Why? **[3]** Which non-allied nations had joined the Common Market by 1989?

before had the European economy grown so fast. In most countries, there were many people ready to work hard for low wages and the hope of a better future. Moreover, although many consumer products had been invented or perfected since the late 1920s, few Europeans had been able to buy them. In 1945 the electric refrigerator, the washing machine, and the automobile were rare luxuries. There was a great potential demand, which the economic system moved to satisfy. Finally, western European nations abandoned protectionism and gradually created a large unified market known as the **Common Market** (see Map 30.1). This historic action, which certainly stimulated the economy, was part of a larger search for European unity.

Common Market The European Economic Community, created by six western European nations in 1957 as part of a larger search for European unity.

The development of the Common Market fired imaginations and encouraged hopes of rapid progress toward political as well as economic union. In the 1960s, however, these hopes were frustrated by a resurgence of more traditional nationalism. France took the lead. Mired in a bitter colonial war in Algeria, the French turned in 1958 to General de Gaulle (**duh GOHL**), who established the Fifth Republic and ruled as its president until 1969. Charles de Gaulle (1890–1970) was at heart a romantic nationalist, and he viewed the United States as the main threat to genuine French (and European) independence. He withdrew all French military forces from the "American-controlled" NATO, developed France's own nuclear weapons, and vetoed the scheduled advent of majority rule within the Common Market. Thus throughout the 1960s, the Common Market thrived economically but remained a union of sovereign states.

Decolonization in East Asia

In the postwar era, Europe's long-standing overseas expansion was dramatically reversed. Future generations will almost certainly see this rolling back of Western expansion as one of world history's great turning points.

The most basic cause of imperial collapse—what Europeans called **decolonization**—was the rising demand of Asian and African peoples for national self-determination, racial equality, and personal dignity. This demand spread from intellectuals to the masses in nearly every colonial territory after the First World War. As a result, colonial empires had already been shaken by 1939, and the way was prepared for the eventual triumph of independence movements.

decolonization The reversal of Europe's overseas expansion caused by the rising demand of Asian and African peoples for national self-determination, racial equality, and personal dignity.

European empires had been based on an enormous power differential between the rulers and the ruled, a difference that had greatly declined after western Europe was battered by war. In addition, strong nationalist movements continued to develop under the Japanese occupation of European colonies in Southeast Asia. With their political power and moral authority in tatters in 1945, many Europeans had little taste for bloody colonial wars and wanted to concentrate on rebuilding at home.

Gandhi Arrives in Delhi, October 1939
A small and frail man, Gandhi possessed enormous courage and determination. His campaign of nonviolent resistance to British rule inspired the Indian masses and nurtured national identity and self-confidence. Here he arrives for talks with the British viceroy after the outbreak of World War II. (Corbis)

India, Britain's oldest, largest, and most lucrative nonwhite possession, played a key role in decolonization. Nationalist opposition to British rule coalesced after the First World War under the leadership of British-educated lawyer Mohandas "Mahatma" Gandhi (**GAHN-dee**) (1869–1948), one of the twentieth century's most significant and influential figures. In the 1920s and 1930s Gandhi built a mass movement preaching nonviolent "noncooperation" with the British. In 1935 the British agreed to a new constitution that was practically a blueprint for independence. When the Labour party came to power in Great Britain in 1945, it was ready to relinquish sovereignty.

If Indian nationalism drew on Western parliamentary liberalism, Chinese nationalism developed and triumphed in the framework of Marxist-Leninist ideology. In the turbulent early 1920s, a broad alliance of nationalist forces within the Soviet-supported Guomindang (Kuomintang) (**kwoh-min-TANG**), or National People's party, was dedicated to unifying China and abolishing European concessions. But in 1927 Chiang Kai-shek (**chang kie-SHEK**) (1887–1975), successor to Sun Yat-sen (see page 693) and leader of the Guomindang, broke with his more radical communist allies, headed by Mao Zedong (Mao Tse-tung) (**maow dzuh-DONG**), and tried to destroy them.

In the civil war that ensued, Mao's Soviet-backed forces defeated Chiang's American-backed forces, with the crucial support of the Chinese peasantry. Chiang's nationalists withdrew to the island of Taiwan in 1949. Mao (1893–1976) and the communists united China's 550 million inhabitants in a strong centralized state, expelled foreigners, and began building a new society along Soviet lines, collectivizing the peasants and implementing five-year plans to expand heavy industry.

Most Asian countries followed the pattern of either India or China. In 1946 the Philippines achieved independence peacefully from the United States. Britain quickly granted Sri Lanka (Ceylon) and Burma independence in 1948. However, Indonesian nationalists had to beat off attempts by the Dutch to reconquer the Dutch East Indies before Indonesia emerged in 1949 as a sovereign state.

The French also tried their best to re-establish colonial rule in Indochina, but despite American aid, they were defeated in 1954 by forces under the communist and nationalist guerrilla leader Ho Chi Minh (**hoh chee min**) (1890–1969), who was supported by the Soviet Union and China. But Indochina was not unified, and two independent Vietnamese states came into being, which led to civil war and subsequent intervention by the United States (see pages 800–801).

Decolonization in the Middle East and Africa

In the Middle East, the movement toward political independence continued after World War II. In 1944 the French gave up their League of Nations mandates in Syria and Lebanon. In British-mandated Palestine, where after 1918 the British government established a Jewish homeland alongside the Arab population, violence and terrorism mounted on both sides. In 1947 the frustrated British decided to leave Palestine, and the United Nations then voted in a nonbinding resolution to divide Palestine into two states—one Arab and one Jewish, which became Israel. The Jews accepted the plan but the Arabs did not, and in 1948 they attacked the Jewish state as soon as it was proclaimed. The Israelis drove off the invaders and conquered more territory, as roughly 900,000 Arabs fled or were expelled. Holocaust survivors from Europe streamed into Israel, as Theodor Herzl's (**HER-tsuhl**) Zionist dream came true (see page 665). The next fifty years saw four more wars between the Israelis and the Arab states and innumerable clashes between the Israelis and the Palestinians.

The Arab defeat in 1948 triggered a powerful nationalist revolution in Egypt in 1952, where a young army officer named Gamal Abdel Nasser (**gah-MAHL AHB-dal NAH-suhr**) (1918–1970) drove out the pro-Western king. In 1956 Nasser abruptly nationalized the foreign-owned Suez Canal Company, the last symbol and substance of Western power in the Middle East. Infuriated, the British and the French, along with the Israelis, invaded Egypt. This was, however, the dying gasp of traditional imperial power: the Americans joined with the Soviets to force the British, French, and Israelis to withdraw. Nasser and anti-Western Egyptian nationalism triumphed.

The failure of Britain and France to unseat Nasser in 1956 encouraged Arab nationalists in Algeria. Although they met tough resistance from the country's large French population, the Algerians won their independence in 1962. South of the Sahara, decolonization proceeded with little or no bloodshed. Beginning in 1957, Britain's colonies achieved independence and then entered a very loose association with Britain as members of the British Commonwealth of Nations. In 1958 the clever de Gaulle offered the leaders of French black Africa the choice of a total break with France or immediate independence within a kind of French commonwealth. All but one of the new states chose association with France. In exchange for aid from France, the African countries granted the French access to untapped markets for their industrial goods, raw materials for their factories, outlets for profitable investment, and good temporary jobs for their engineers and teachers. The British acted somewhat similarly.

As a result, western European countries actually managed to increase their economic and cultural ties with their former African colonies in the 1960s and 1970s. Above all, they used the lure of special trading privileges and heavy investment in French- and English-language education to enhance a powerful Western presence in the new African states. This situation led a variety of leaders and scholars to charge that western Europe (and the United States) had imposed a system of neocolonialism on the former colonies. According to this view, **neocolonialism** was a system designed to perpetuate Western economic domination and undermine the promise of political independence, thereby extending to Africa (and much of Asia) the economic subordination that the United States had established in Latin America in the nineteenth century. At the very least, enduring influence in sub-Saharan Africa testified to western Europe's resurgent economic and political power in international relations.

neocolonialism A system designed to perpetuate Western economic domination and undermine the promise of political independence, thereby extending to Africa (and much of Asia) the economic subordination that the United States had established in Latin America in the nineteenth century.

America's Civil Rights Revolution

The Second World War cured the depression in the United States and brought about an economic boom. In the postwar years, America experienced a genuine social revolution. The civil rights movement threw off a deeply entrenched system of segregation, discrimination, and repression of African Americans. As civil rights leader Martin Luther King, Jr. (1929–1968), told the white power structure, "We will not hate you, but we will not obey your evil laws."[2] Through civil disobedience and court challenges, separate schools and facilities for African Americans were deemed illegal, as were job discrimination and obstacles to voting

The March on Washington, August 1963
The march marked a dramatic climax in the civil rights struggle. More than 200,000 people gathered at the Lincoln Memorial to hear the young Martin Luther King, Jr., deliver his greatest address, the "I have a dream" speech. (Time Life Pictures/Getty Images)

rights. By the 1970s, substantial numbers of blacks had been elected to public and private office throughout the southern states, a sign of dramatic changes in American race relations.

President Lyndon Johnson (1908–1973) also declared "unconditional war on poverty," and Congress and the administration created a host of antipoverty programs intended to aid all poor Americans and bring greater economic equality. Thus the United States promoted in the mid-1960s the kind of fundamental social reform that western Europe had embraced immediately after the Second World War. The United States became more of a welfare state, as government spending for social benefits rose dramatically and approached European levels.

Soviet Eastern Europe (1945–1968)

What was the pattern of postwar rebuilding and development in the Soviet Union and communist eastern Europe?

While western Europe surged ahead economically after the Second World War and increased its political power as American influence in Europe gradually waned, eastern Europe followed a different path. The Soviet Union first tightened its grip on the "liberated" nations of eastern Europe under Stalin and then refused to let go. Thus postwar economic recovery in eastern Europe proceeded along Soviet lines, and political and social developments were strongly influenced by changes in the Soviet Union.

Stalin's Last Years (1945–1953)

The "Great Patriotic War of the Fatherland" had fostered Russian nationalism and had unified the Russian people under their leaders. Having made a heroic war effort, many people hoped in 1945 that a grateful party and government would grant greater freedom and democracy. Such hopes were soon crushed.

Stalin's new foreign foe in the West provided an excuse for re-establishing a harsh dictatorship. Many returning soldiers and ordinary citizens were purged in 1945 and 1946, as Stalin revived the terrible forced-labor camps of the 1930s. Artists who did not promote anti-Western ideology were denounced, and Soviet Jews were accused of being pro-Western and antisocialist.

Five-year plans were reintroduced to cope with the enormous task of economic reconstruction. Once again, heavy industry and the military were given top priority, and consumer goods, housing, and collectivized agriculture were neglected. Everyday life was very hard. In short, it was the 1930s all over again in the Soviet Union, although police terror was less intense.

Stalin's prime postwar innovation was to export the Stalinist system to the countries of eastern Europe. One-party states were established by 1948 and the middle class was stripped of its possessions. Forced industrialization lurched forward, and the collectivization of agriculture began.

Only Josip Broz Tito (**TEE-toh**) (1892–1980), the resistance leader and Communist chief of Yugoslavia, was able to resist Soviet domination successfully. Tito stood up to Stalin in 1948, and since there was no Russian army in Yugoslavia, he got away with it. Yugoslavia prospered as a multiethnic state until it began to break apart in the 1980s. Tito's proclamation of independence infuriated Stalin. Elsewhere Stalin sought obedient leaders and purged those who had the potential to challenge him.

Sergei Eisenstein: Ivan the Terrible

Eisenstein's final masterpiece—one of the greatest films ever—was filmed during the Second World War and released in two parts in 1946. In this chilling scene, the crafty paranoid tyrant, who has saved Russia from foreign invaders, invites the unsuspecting Prince Vladimir to a midnight revel that will lead to his murder. The increasingly demonic Ivan seemed to resemble Stalin, and Eisenstein was censored and purged. (David King Collection)

de-Stalinization The liberalization of the post-Stalin Soviet Union, led by reformer Nikita Khrushchev.

Reform and De-Stalinization (1953–1964)

By the time of Stalin's death in 1953, it was apparent that support for the system was eroding and reforms were needed. However, the Communist leadership was badly split on the extent of changes needed. Conservatives wanted to make as few changes as possible. Reformers, who were led by Nikita Khrushchev (**KROOSH-chof**), argued for major innovations. Khrushchev (1894–1971), who had joined the party as an uneducated coal miner in 1918 and risen to a high-level position in the 1930s, emerged as the new ruler in 1955.

To strengthen his position and that of his fellow reformers within the party, Khrushchev launched an all-out attack on Stalin and his crimes at a closed session of the Twentieth Party Congress in 1956. In gory detail, he described to the startled Communist delegates how Stalin had tortured and murdered thousands of loyal Communists, how he had trusted Hitler completely and bungled the country's defense, and how he had "supported the glorification of his own person with all conceivable methods." Khrushchev's "secret speech" was read at Communist Party meetings held throughout the country, and it strengthened the reform movement.

The liberalization—or **de-Stalinization,** as it was called in the West—of the Soviet Union was genuine. While the Communist Party maintained its monopoly on political power, Khrushchev brought in new members with new ideas. Some resources were shifted from heavy industry and the military toward consumer goods and agriculture, and Stalinist controls over workers were relaxed. The Soviet Union's very low standard of living finally began to improve and continued to rise substantially throughout the booming 1960s.

De-Stalinization created great ferment among writers and intellectuals who hungered for cultural freedom. The writer Aleksandr Solzhenitsyn (**sol-zhuh-NEET-sin**) (b. 1918) created a sensation when his *One Day in the Life of Ivan Denisovich* was published in the Soviet Union in 1962. Solzhenitsyn's novel portrays in grim detail life in a Stalinist concentration camp—a life to which Solzhenitsyn himself had been unjustly condemned—and is a damning indictment of the Stalinist past.

Khrushchev also de-Stalinized Soviet foreign policy. "Peaceful coexistence" with capitalism was possible, he argued, and great wars were not inevitable.

Khrushchev even made concessions, agreeing in 1955 to real independence for a neutral Austria after ten long years of Allied occupation. Thus there was considerable relaxation of cold war tensions between 1955 and 1957. At the same time, Khrushchev began wooing the new nations of Asia and Africa—even if they were not communist—with promises and aid.

De-Stalinization stimulated rebelliousness in the eastern European satellites. Poland took the lead in 1956, when extensive rioting brought a new government that managed to win greater autonomy. In Hungary, revolution brought tragic results. Soviet troops were forced out and a new liberal communist leader was made chief in October 1956. But after the new government promised free elections and renounced Hungary's military alliance with Moscow, the Russian leaders ordered an invasion and crushed the national and democratic revolution. Fighting was bitter until the end, for the Hungarians hoped that the United States would come to their aid. When this did not occur, most people in eastern Europe concluded that their only hope was to strive for small domestic gains while following Russia obediently in foreign affairs.

The End of Reform

By late 1962, opposition in party circles to Khrushchev's policies was strong, and in 1964 Leonid Brezhnev (**BREZH-nef**) (1906–1982) took control. Under Brezhnev, the Soviet Union began a period of stagnation and limited "re-Stalinization." The basic reason for this development was that Khrushchev's communist colleagues saw de-Stalinization as a dangerous threat to the dictatorial authority of the party.

Another reason for conservative opposition was that Khrushchev's policy toward the West was erratic and ultimately unsuccessful. In 1958 he ordered the Western allies to evacuate West Berlin within six months. In response, the allies reaffirmed their unity in West Berlin, and Khrushchev backed down. Then in 1961, as relations with communist China deteriorated dramatically, Khrushchev ordered the East Germans to build a wall between East and West Berlin, thereby sealing off West Berlin in clear violation of existing access agreements between the Great Powers. The recently elected U.S. president, John F. Kennedy, acquiesced to the construction of the Berlin Wall. Emboldened and seeing a chance to change the balance of military power decisively, Khrushchev ordered missiles with nuclear warheads installed in Fidel Castro's communist Cuba in 1962. President Kennedy countered with a naval blockade of Cuba. After a tense diplomatic crisis, Khrushchev agreed to remove the Soviet missiles in return for American pledges not to disturb Castro's regime. Khrushchev looked like a bumbling buffoon; his influence, already slipping, declined rapidly after the Cuban fiasco.

When Brezhnev and his supporters took over, they launched a massive arms buildup to counter American nuclear superiority. Yet Brezhnev and company avoided direct confrontation with the United States. They were, however, willing to act as aggressor against any Soviet bloc country moving toward liberalization. The 1968 invasion of Czechoslovakia exemplified the **Brezhnev Doctrine** regarding the Soviet Union's right to intervene in any socialist country whenever they saw the need.

In January 1968, the reform elements in the Czechoslovak Communist Party had gained a majority and voted out the long-time Stalinist leader in favor of Alexander Dubček (**DOOB-chek**) (1921–1992), whose new government aimed to build what they called "socialism with a human face." Local decision making by trade unions, managers, and consumers replaced rigid bureaucratic planning, and censorship was relaxed. Hardliners in Poland and East Germany were afraid that

Brezhnev Doctrine The doctrine created by Leonid Brezhnev and exemplified by the Soviet invasion of Czechoslovakia in 1968, according to which the Soviet Union had the right to intervene in any socialist country whenever it saw the need.

The Invasion of Czechoslovakia
Armed with Czechoslovakian flags, courageous Czechs in downtown Prague try to stop a Soviet tank and repel the invasion and occupation of their country by the Soviet Union and its eastern European allies. This dramatic confrontation marked a high point, because the Czechs and the Slovaks realized that military resistance would be suicidal. (AP/Wide World Photos)

the reform movement would spread and push them out of power, while Moscow feared that a liberalized Czechoslovakia would eventually be drawn to neutrality or even to the democratic West. Thus the Eastern bloc countries launched a concerted campaign of intimidation against the Czechoslovak leaders, and in August 1968, 500,000 Russian and allied eastern European troops suddenly occupied Czechoslovakia. The arrested leaders surrendered to Soviet demands, and the reform program was abandoned.

The 1968 invasion of Czechoslovakia was the crucial event of the Brezhnev era, which really lasted beyond the aging leader's death in 1982 until the emergence in 1985 of Mikhail Gorbachev (**GORE-beh-chof**). The invasion demonstrated the determination of the ruling elite to maintain the status quo throughout the Soviet bloc. Only in the 1980s, with Poland taking the lead, would a strong current of reform and opposition develop again to challenge Communist Party rule.

The Soviet Union to 1985

Determined to maintain firm control of eastern Europe, Soviet leaders set the example at home. There was a certain **re-Stalinization** of the U.S.S.R., but now dictatorship was collective rather than personal, and coercion replaced terror. This compromise seemed to suit the leaders and a majority of the people.

re-Stalinization An attempt by Soviet leaders to maintain firm control of eastern Europe.

A slowly rising standard of living for ordinary people contributed to the apparent stability in the Soviet Union, although long food lines and innumerable shortages persisted. Ambitious individuals had a tremendous incentive to do as the state wished in order to gain access to special, well-stocked stores, to attend special schools, and to travel abroad.

The strength of the government was expressed in the re-Stalinization of culture and art. Acts of open nonconformity and public protest were often punished by blacklisting, leaving the dissident unable to find a decent job. More determined protesters were quietly imprisoned, while celebrated nonconformists such as Aleksandr Solzhenitsyn were permanently expelled from the country.

Eliminating the worst aspects of Stalin's dictatorship strengthened the regime, and almost all Western experts concluded that rule by a self-perpetuating Communist Party elite in the Soviet Union appeared to be quite solid in the 1970s and early 1980s. Yet Soviet life was changing profoundly in the Brezhnev era, laying the groundwork for the revolution to come under Gorbachev. The urban population grew rapidly in the 1960s and 1970s, and these city dwellers were better educated and more sophisticated than the peasants of earlier generations. Many of them were highly trained scientists, managers, and specialists. Educated people read, discussed, and formed definite ideas on important issues, many of which could be approached and debated in "nonpolitical" terms. Developing ideas on such questions as environmental pollution and urban transportation, educated urban people increasingly saw themselves as worthy of having a voice in society's decisions, even its political decisions.

Postwar Social Transformations (1945–1968)

How did changing patterns in technology, class relations, women's work, and youth culture bring major social transformations?

During the postwar period, the patterns of everyday life and the structure of Western society were changing along with the economy and politics. New inventions and technologies profoundly affected human existence. The structure of women's lives changed dramatically. An international youth culture took shape and rose to challenge established lifestyles and even governments.

Science and Technology

With the advent of the Second World War, most leading university scientists went to work on top-secret government projects. British scientists, for example, developed radar to detect enemy aircraft, which was key to Britain's victory in the battle for air supremacy in 1940. The air war also greatly stimulated the development of jet aircraft and spurred further research on electronic computers, which calculated the complex mathematical relationships between fast-moving planes and anti-aircraft shells to increase the likelihood of a hit. However, it was the atomic bomb, the product of three years of intensive research, that showed the world both the awesome power and the heavy moral responsibilities of modern science.

The spectacular results of directed research during World War II inspired a new model for science—**Big Science.** By combining theoretical work with sophisticated engineering in a large organization, Big Science could attack extremely difficult problems, from better products for consumers to new and improved

Section Review

- Stalin's post-war programs were harsh, building up industry and the military at the expense of consumer goods, housing, and agriculture; in eastern Europe, Soviet-backed countries, with the exception of Yugoslavia, set up similar programs.

- Stalin's successor Khrushchev brought to light the horrors of Stalin's regime and began de-Stalinizing the country, bringing reforms that improved the standard of living; he also relaxed Soviet foreign policy, albeit erratically, easing cold war tensions.

- Khrushchev's successor Brezhnev went back to a Stalinist type of rule, ending reform and implementing strict control of Eastern bloc countries, putting down a progressive new government in Czechoslovakia in 1968 and launching an arms buildup to counter American superiority.

- The Soviet dictatorship was collective and domestic conditions improved, but personal advancement was based on loyalty to the party, which punished dissenters, although an increasingly educated public began to gain interest in influencing political decisions.

Big Science   The combination of theoretical work with sophisticated engineering in a large organization to create improved consumer products and military weapons.

weapons for the military. Big Science was extremely expensive, requiring large-scale financing from governments and large corporations.

Populous, victorious, and wealthy, the United States took the lead in Big Science after World War II. Between 1945 and 1965, spending on scientific research and development in the United States grew five times as fast as the national income, and by 1965 such spending took 3 percent of all U.S. income. It was generally accepted that government should finance science heavily in both the "capitalist" United States and the "socialist" Soviet Union. In both countries a large portion of all postwar scientific research went for "defense." New weapons such as rockets, nuclear submarines, and spy satellites demanded breakthroughs no less remarkable than those of radar and the first atomic bomb. Sophisticated science, lavish government spending, and military needs all came together in the space race of the 1960s. In 1957 the Soviets put a satellite in orbit, and in 1961 they sent the world's first cosmonaut circling the globe. The United States raced to catch up with the Soviets and landed a crewed spacecraft on the moon in 1969. Four more moon landings followed by 1972.

The rise of Big Science and of close ties between science and technology greatly altered the lives of scientists. The scientific community grew much larger than ever before. There were about four times as many scientists in Europe and North America in 1975 as in 1945. With increased specialization, modern scientists and technologists normally had to work as members of a team, typically in large bureaucratic organizations. There the individual was very often a small cog in a great machine. Modern science also became highly, even brutally, competitive. James Watson, who worked with Francis Crick to discover the structure of DNA, exemplified the competitive spirit in his race to crack the molecule of heredity before another research team. With so many thousands of like-minded researchers in the wealthy countries of the world, scientific and technical knowledge rushed forward in the postwar era.

The Changing Class Structure   Scientists and engineers were not the only people to experience a transformation of the workplace in the postwar years. For both the middle and lower classes, the new economy brought new opportunities for making and spending money.

A new breed of managers and experts replaced traditional property owners as the leaders of the middle class. Well paid and highly trained, often with backgrounds in engineering or accounting, these experts increasingly came from all social classes, even the working class. The ability to serve the needs of a big organization largely replaced inherited property and family connections in determining an individual's social position. This new middle class was more open, democratic, and insecure than the old propertied middle class. At the same time, the middle class grew massively and became harder to define.

The lower classes were also transformed, as many people abandoned the traditional, rooted life of the farm for a more mobile urban existence. Meanwhile, the number of factory jobs ceased to expand and began to decline, and the remaining industrial workers became better educated and more specialized. Job opportunities for white-collar and service employees grew rapidly.

European governments were reducing class tensions with a series of social security reforms. Many of these reforms—such as increased unemployment benefits and more extensive old-age pensions—simply strengthened social security measures first pioneered in Bismarck's Germany before the First World War (see page 661). Other programs were new, like comprehensive national health systems directed by the state. Most countries introduced family allowances—direct government grants to parents to help them raise their children. Most European governments also gave maternity grants and built inexpensive public housing. These and other social reforms provided a humane floor of well-being. Reforms also promoted greater equality because they were paid for in part by higher taxes on the rich.

The rising standard of living and the availability of credit made consumer goods such as washing machines, refrigerators, vacuum cleaners, radios, TVs, and even automobiles more accessible to workers. With the expansion of social security safeguards for hard times and old age, ordinary people were increasingly willing to take on debt. This change had far-reaching consequences.

Leisure and recreation occupied an important place in consumer societies. The most astonishing leisure-time development was the blossoming of mass travel and tourism. With month-long paid vacations required by law in most European countries and widespread automobile ownership, beaches and ski resorts came within the reach of the middle class and much of the working class. By the late 1960s, packaged tours with cheap group flights and bargain hotel accommodations had made even distant lands easily accessible. Truly, consumerism had come of age.

Consumers on the Move

In the early postwar years the Italians had their motor scooters and the French their motorbikes. This ad promises young people that "sooner or later" they will have a "Velo," and it subtly assures housewives that the bike is safe. In small towns and villages the slow-moving motorbike could be a godsend for errands and daily shopping.   (Roger Perrin/The Bridgeman Art Library)

New Roles for Women

The postwar era saw significant transformations in the lives of women, preparing the way for the success of a new generation of feminist thinkers and a militant women's movement in the 1970s and 1980s (see pages 802–803). Building on trends that had developed with the Industrial Revolution, this period was one of early marriage, early childbearing, and small family size in wealthy urban areas. By the early 1970s, about half of Western women were having their last baby by the age of twenty-six or twenty-seven. When the youngest child trooped off to kindergarten, the average mother had more than forty years of life in front of her.

This was a momentous change. Throughout history male-dominated society insisted on defining most women as mothers or potential mothers, and motherhood was very demanding. In the postwar years, however, motherhood no longer absorbed the energies of a lifetime, and more and more married women looked for new roles in the world of work outside the family (see Figure 30.1).

Three major forces helped women searching for jobs. First, the economy boomed from about 1950 to 1973 and created a strong demand for labor. Second, the economy continued its gradual shift away from the old, male-dominated heavy industries, such as coal, steel, and shipbuilding, to the more dynamic, "white-collar" service industries, such as government, education, trade, and health care. Some women had always worked in these service fields. Third, young Western women shared fully in the postwar education revolution and could take advantage of the growing need for office workers and well-trained professionals. Thus more and more married women became full-time and part-time wage earners.

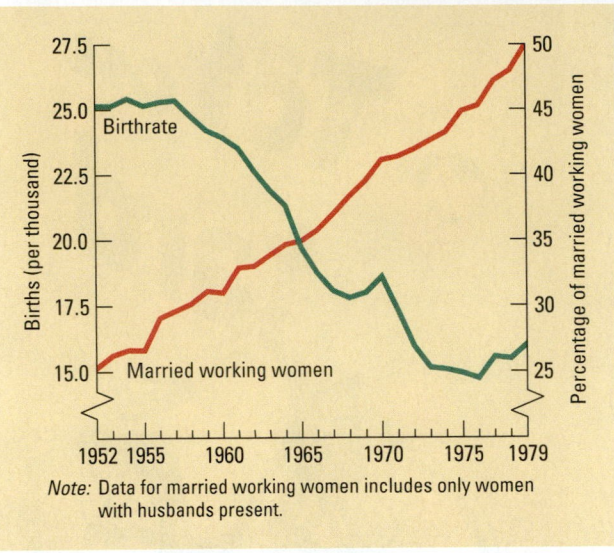

Note: Data for married working women includes only women with husbands present.

FIGURE 30.1   The Decline of the Birthrate and the Increase of Married Working Women in the United States, 1952–1979

The challenge of working away from home encouraged American wives to prefer fewer children and helped lower the birthrate.

The trend went the furthest in communist eastern Europe, where women accounted for almost half of all employed persons. In noncommunist western Europe and North America, there was a good deal of variation, with the percentage of married women in the workforce rising from a range of roughly 20 to 25 percent in 1950 to a range of 40 to 70 percent in the early 1980s.

Married women entering (or re-entering) the labor force faced widespread, long-established discrimination in pay, advancement, and occupational choice in comparison to men. Moreover, many women could find only part-time work. As the divorce rate rose in the 1960s, part-time work, with its low pay and scanty benefits, meant poverty for many women with teenage children. Finally, in the best of circumstances, married working women still carried most of the child-raising and housekeeping responsibilities. A reason for many to accept part-time employment, this gendered imbalance meant an exhausting "double day"—on the job and at home—for the full-time worker.

The injustices that married women encountered as wage earners contributed greatly to the subsequent movement for women's equality and emancipation. A young unmarried woman of a hundred years ago was more likely to accept such problems as temporary nuisances because she looked forward to marriage and motherhood for fulfillment. In the postwar era, a married wage earner in her thirties gradually developed a very different perspective. She saw employment as a permanent condition within which she, like her male counterpart, sought not only income but also psychological satisfaction. Sexism and discrimination in the workplace—and in the home—grew loathsome and evoked the sense of injustice that drives revolutions and reforms. When powerful voices arose to challenge the system, they found widespread support among working women.

Youth and the Counterculture

The "baby boom" generation born after World War II developed a distinctive and very international youth culture, which eventually became a "counterculture" of social rebellion.

Young people in the United States took the lead. By the late 1950s the "beat" movement was stoking the fires of revolt in selected urban enclaves, such as the Near North Side of Chicago. There the young (and the not-so-young) fashioned a highly publicized subculture that blended radical politics, unbridled personal experimentation (with drugs and communal living, for example), and new artistic styles. This subculture quickly spread to major American and western European cities. In the words of folksinger Bob Dylan, "the times they are a'changing."[3]

Certainly the sexual behavior of young people appeared to change dramatically in the 1960s and into the 1970s. More young people engaged in sexual intercourse, and they did so at an earlier age, in part because the discovery of safe and effective contraceptive pills could eliminate the risk of unwanted pregnancy. Perhaps even more significant was the growing tendency of young unmarried people to live together in a separate household on a semipermanent basis, demonstrating in effect that the long-standing monopoly of married couples on legitimate sexual unions was dead.

Several factors contributed to the emergence of the international youth culture in the 1960s. First, mass communications and youth travel linked countries and continents together. Second, the postwar baby boom meant that young people became an unusually large part of the population and could therefore exercise exceptional influence on society as a whole. Third, postwar prosperity and greater equality gave young people more purchasing power than ever before. This enabled them to set their own trends and patterns of consumption, which fostered generational loyalty. Finally, prosperity meant that good jobs were readily available, and employers might be more willing to hire unconventional young people. The youth culture practically fused with the counterculture in opposition to the established order in the late 1960s. Student protesters saw the materialistic West as hopelessly rotten but believed that better societies were being built in the newly independent countries of Asia and Africa. Thus the Vietnam War was perceived by young radicals as an immoral and imperialistic war against a small and heroic people. As the war intensified, so did worldwide student opposition to it.

Student protests in western Europe were also a response to the negative consequences of the rapid expansion of higher education. Classes were badly overcrowded and competition for grades became intense. Moreover, although more practical areas of study were gradually added, many students felt that they were not getting the kind of education they needed for jobs in the modern world. At the same time, some reflective students feared that universities would soon do nothing but turn out docile technocrats both to stock and to serve "the establishment."

Student Rebellion in Paris
These rock-throwing students in the Latin Quarter of Paris are trying to force education reforms and even to topple de Gaulle's government. Throughout May 1968 students clashed repeatedly with France's tough riot police in bloody street fighting. De Gaulle remained in power, but a major reform of French education did follow. (Bruno Barbey/Magnum Photos)

The many tensions within the exploding university population came to a head in the late 1960s and early 1970s, most famously in France in May 1968. Students occupied buildings and took over the University of Paris, which led to violent clashes with police. In defiance of union officials, many workers across France joined the protest by going on strike. It seemed certain that President de Gaulle's Fifth Republic would collapse.

In fact, de Gaulle stiffened, like an old-fashioned irate father. He moved troops toward Paris and called for new elections. The masses of France, fearing an eventual communist takeover, voted overwhelmingly for de Gaulle's party and a return to law and order. Workers went back to work, and the mini-revolution collapsed. Yet within a year de Gaulle resigned. Growing out of the counterculture and youthful idealism, the student rebellion of 1968 signaled the end of an era and the return of unrest and uncertainty in the 1970s and early 1980s.

Conflict and Challenge in the Late Cold War (1968–1985)

What were the key aspects of political conflict, economic stagnation, and the feminist movement in the late cold war?

The Vietnam War also marked the beginning of a new era of challenges and uncertainties in the late 1960s. The war and its aftermath divided the people of the United States, shook the ideology of containment, and weakened the Western alliance. A second challenge affecting the whole world appeared when the great postwar economic boom came to a close in 1973, opening a long period of economic stagnation, widespread unemployment, and social dislocation. The era also saw the birth of new liberation movements, including the women's movement for gender equality.

The United States and Vietnam

President Johnson wanted his legacy to be as the champion of civil rights and the leader of the "war on poverty." Instead, his presidency is better known for having drafted thousands of young American men for a foreign war that divided the nation.

American involvement in Vietnam was primarily a product of the cold war and the policy of containing the spread of communism. As western Europe began to revive and China established a communist government in 1949, efforts to contain communism shifted to Asia. The bloody Korean War (1950–1953) ended in stalemate, but the United States did succeed in preventing a communist victory in South Korea. After the Vietnamese won their independence from France in 1954, the United States refused to sign the Geneva Accords that temporarily divided Vietnam into two zones pending national unification by means of free elections. (Ho Chi Minh led a socialist state in the northern zone.) When the anticommunist South Vietnamese government declined to hold elections, President Eisenhower supported it with military aid. President Kennedy greatly increased the number of American "military advisers" in South Vietnam to sixteen thousand.

After winning the 1964 election on a peace platform, President Johnson greatly expanded the American role in the Vietnam conflict. The United States gave South Vietnam massive military aid, American forces in the South gradually grew to half a million men, and the United States bombed North Vietnam with ever-greater intensity.

The undeclared war in Vietnam, fought nightly on American television, eventually divided the nation. In October 1965, student protesters joined forces with old-line socialists, New Left intellectuals, and pacifists in antiwar demonstrations in fifty American cities. By 1967 a growing number of critics denounced the war as a criminal intrusion into a complex and distant civil war. Criticism reached a crescendo in January 1968, after the Tet Offensive, the first comprehensive attack by the Vietcong on major cities in South Vietnam. Although the Vietcong suffered heavy losses, the Tet Offensive signaled that the war was not close to ending, as Washington had claimed. President Johnson called for negotiations with North Vietnam and announced that he would not stand for re-election.

The new president, Richard Nixon (1913–1994), promised "peace with honor." In his second term in office, Nixon and Secretary of State Henry Kissinger finally reached a peace agreement with North Vietnam. The 1973 agreement allowed American forces, which had been withdrawing since 1971, to complete their withdrawal, and the United States reserved the right to resume bombing if the accords were broken. Fighting declined markedly in South Vietnam, where the South Vietnamese army appeared to hold its own against the Vietcong. But in early 1974, when North Vietnam launched a general invasion against South Vietnamese armies, the United States Congress refused to permit a military response. At this point Nixon had resigned as a result of the **Watergate** scandal, in which he and others were exposed in lies about the illegal break-in of the Democratic Party headquarters. The belated fall of South Vietnam in the wake of Watergate shook America's postwar confidence and left the country divided and uncertain about its proper role in world affairs.

End Bad Breath.

Seymour Chwast: End Bad Breath

Antiwar messages came in every shape and form as opposition to the Vietnam War heated up. This vibrant poster assumes, quite reasonably, that the American viewer is steeped in the popular culture of the mass media. It ridicules American military involvement with a sarcastic parody of familiar television commercials. (Courtesy, Seymore Chwast/PushPin Group)

Watergate   The scandal in which Nixon's assistants broke into the Democratic Party headquarters in July 1972 and the administration attempted to cover it up.

détente   The progressive relaxation of cold war tensions.

Détente or Cold War?

One alternative to the badly damaged policy of containing communism was the policy of **détente** (dey-TAHNT), or the easing of cold war tensions. Thus while the cold war continued to define superpower relations between the Soviet Union and the United States, West Germany took a major step toward genuine peace in Europe.

West German leader Willy Brandt (1913–1992) aimed at nothing less than a comprehensive peace settlement for central Europe and the two German states established after 1945. Winning the chancellorship in 1969, Brandt negotiated treaties with the Soviet Union, Poland, and Czechoslovakia that formally accepted existing state boundaries in return for a mutual renunciation of force or the threat of force. Using the imaginative formula of "two German states within one German nation," Brandt's government also broke decisively with the past policy of refusing to recognize the legitimacy of East Germany and entered into direct relations with that state. He aimed for modest practical improvements rather than reunification, which at that point was inconceivable.

The policy of détente reached its high point when all European nations (except Albania), the United States, Canada, and the Soviet Union signed the Final Act of the Helsinki Conference in 1975. The thirty-five nations participating agreed that Europe's existing political frontiers could not be changed by force. They also solemnly accepted numerous provisions guaranteeing the human rights and political freedoms of their citizens.

Hopes for détente in international relations gradually faded in the later 1970s. Many Americans became convinced that the Soviet Union was steadily building up its military might and pushing for political gains and revolutions in Africa, Asia, and Latin America. The Soviet invasion of Afghanistan in December 1979, which was designed to save an increasingly unpopular Marxist regime, was especially alarming. Fearing that the oil-rich states of the Persian Gulf would be next, Americans looked to the Atlantic alliance to thwart communist expansion and hold Brezhnev to the human rights provisions of the Helsinki Agreement.

President Jimmy Carter (b. 1924), elected in 1976, tried to lead the Atlantic alliance beyond verbal condemnation and urged economic sanctions against the Soviet Union. Yet only Great Britain among the European allies supported the American initiative. The alliance showed the same lack of concerted action when the Solidarity movement rose in Poland. Some observers concluded that the alliance had lost the will to think and act decisively in dealing with the Soviet bloc.

The Atlantic alliance endured, however. The U.S. military buildup launched by Carter in his last years in office was greatly accelerated by President Ronald Reagan (1911–2004), who referred to the Soviet Union as the "evil empire." Increasing defense spending enormously, the Reagan administration concentrated on nuclear arms and an expanded navy as keys to American power in the post-Vietnam age.

A broad swing in the pendulum toward greater conservatism in the 1980s gave Reagan invaluable allies in western Europe. In Great Britain, Margaret Thatcher worked well with Reagan and was a forceful advocate for a revitalized Atlantic alliance. In West Germany, Helmut Kohl worked with the United States to coordinate military and political policy toward the Soviet bloc. In maintaining the alliance, the Western nations gave indirect support to ongoing efforts to liberalize authoritarian communist eastern Europe.

The Women's Movement

The 1970s marked the birth of a broad-based feminist movement devoted to securing genuine gender equality and promoting the general interests of women. Three basic reasons accounted for this major development. First, ongoing changes in underlying patterns of motherhood and paid work created novel conditions and new demands (see pages 797–798). Second, a vanguard of feminist intellectuals articulated a powerful critique of gender relations, which stimulated many women to rethink their assumptions and challenge the status quo. Third, taking a lesson from the civil rights movement in the United States and worldwide student protest against the Vietnam War, dissatisfied individuals recognized that they had to band together if they were to influence politics and secure fundamental reforms.

One of the most influential written works produced by this new feminist wave was *The Second Sex* (1949) by the French writer and philosopher Simone de Beauvoir (1908–1986). Beauvoir analyzed the position of women within the framework of existential thought (see pages 728–729). She argued that women had almost always been trapped by particularly inflexible and limiting conditions. (See the feature "Listening to the Past: A Feminist Critique of Marriage" on pages 808–809.) Only by courageously embracing her freedom could a woman escape the role of the inferior "other." Drawing on history, philosophy, psychology, biology, and literature, Beauvoir's massive investigation inspired a generation of female intellectuals.

Celebrating Women's History

Judy Chicago's multimedia creation *The Dinner Party* features thirty-nine handcrafted placemats and ceramic plates, each embellished with a painted motif associated with the woman being honored. Begun in 1974 and completed in 1978 with the participation of more than one hundred women, *The Dinner Party* was intended to represent the "historic struggle of women to participate in all the aspects of society." It attracted enormous crowds. (© Judy Chicago, 1979/Artists Rights Society [ARS], New York)

One such woman was the American writer and organizer Betty Friedan (**fri-DAN**) (1921–2006). In *The Feminine Mystique* (1963), Friedan concluded that many well-educated women shared her growing dissatisfaction with a life devoted to the service of husbands and children. According to Friedan, women faced a crisis of identity because they were not permitted to become mature adults and genuine human beings. In short, women faced what feminists would soon call *sexism*, a pervasive social problem that required drastic reforms.

Friedan took the lead in 1966 in founding the National Organization for Women (NOW) to press for women's rights. NOW flourished, growing from seven hundred members in 1967 to forty thousand in 1974. Many other women's organizations took root in Europe and the United States. Throughout the 1970s, a proliferation of publications, conferences, and institutions devoted to women's issues reinforced the emerging international movement.

This movement generally shared the common strategy of pushing for new statutes in the workplace: laws against discrimination, "equal pay for equal work," and supportive measures such as maternal leave and affordable day care. In addition, the movement concentrated on gender and family questions, including the right to divorce (in some Catholic countries), legalized abortion, the needs of single mothers, and protection from rape and physical violence. In almost every country, the effort to decriminalize abortion served as a catalyst in mobilizing an effective, self-conscious women's movement (and in creating an opposition to it, as in the United States). The sharply focused women's movement of the 1970s was successful in winning new rights for women. Subsequently, the movement became more diffuse, a victim of both its successes and the resurgence of an antifeminist opposition.

The accomplishments of the women's movement encouraged mobilization by many other groups. Gay men and lesbian women pressed their own demands, organizing politically and calling for an end to legal discrimination and social harassment. People with physical disabilities joined together to promote their interests. Thus many subordinate groups challenged the dominant majorities, and the expansion and redefinition of human liberty—one of the great themes of modern Western and world history—continued.

Society in a Time of Economic Uncertainty

The 1970s and early 1980s witnessed the worst economic decline since the Great Depression. The great postwar boom had been fueled by cheap oil from the Middle East, which permitted energy-intensive industries—automobiles, chemicals,

OPEC The Arab-led Organization of Petroleum Exporting Countries.

and electric power—to expand rapidly and lead other sectors of the economy forward. By 1971 the Arab-led Organization of Petroleum Exporting Countries (**OPEC**) was no longer satisfied to see the price of oil decline as the price of manufactured goods rose, and they presented a united front against the oil companies. When OPEC declared an embargo on oil shipments to the United States, during the fourth Arab-Israeli war in October 1973, oil prices quadrupled within the year. Governments, industry, and individuals had no other choice than to deal piecemeal with the so-called oil shock—a "shock" that turned out to be an earthquake.

The energy-intensive industries that had driven the economy upward in the 1950s and 1960s now dragged it down. Unemployment rose; productivity and living standards declined. By 1976 a modest recovery was in progress. But when a fundamentalist Islamic revolution struck Iran and oil production collapsed in that country, the price of crude oil doubled in 1979 and the world economy succumbed to its second oil shock. Unemployment and inflation rose dramatically before another uneven recovery began in 1982. In 1985 the unemployment rate in western Europe rose to its highest level since the Great Depression. Nineteen million people were unemployed.

Throughout the 1970s and 1980s, anxious observers, recalling the disastrous consequences of the Great Depression, worried that the Common Market would disintegrate in the face of severe economic dislocation and that economic nationalism would halt steps toward European unity. Yet the Common Market—now officially known as the European Economic Community—continued to attract new members. In 1973 Denmark and Iceland, in addition to Britain, finally joined. Greece joined in 1981, and Portugal and Spain entered in 1986. The nations of the European Economic Community also cooperated more closely in international undertakings, and the movement toward unity for western Europe stayed alive.

As a consequence of the economic stagnation of the 1970s and early 1980s, optimism gave way to pessimism; romantic utopianism yielded to sober realism. This drastic change in mood—a complete surprise only to those who had never studied history—affected states, institutions, and individuals in countless ways.

Governments responded with social programs to prevent mass suffering and degradation. Indeed, government spending increased sharply in most countries during the 1970s and early 1980s. In all countries, however, people were much more willing to see their governments increase spending than raise taxes. This imbalance contributed to the rapid growth of budget deficits, national debts, and inflation. By the late 1970s, a powerful reaction against government's ever-increasing role had set in, however, and Western governments were gradually forced to introduce austerity measures to slow the growth of public spending and the welfare state.

This conservative backlash helped bring Margaret Thatcher (b. 1925) to power in Britain in 1979. Thatcher was determined to scale back the role of government in Britain, and in the 1980s—the "Thatcher years"—she pushed through a series of controversial "free market" policies that transformed postwar Britain. In one of its most popular actions, Thatcher's Conservative government encouraged low- and moderate-income renters in state-owned housing projects to buy their apartments at rock-bottom prices. This initiative, part of Thatcher's broader privatization campaign, created a whole new class of property owners, thereby eroding the electoral base of Britain's socialist Labour Party. (See the feature "Individuals in Society: Margaret Thatcher.")

President Ronald Reagan's success in the United States was more limited. With widespread support, Reagan in 1981 pushed through major cuts in income taxes all across the board. But Reagan and Congress failed to cut government spending, which increased as a percentage of national income in the course of his

Individuals in Society

Margaret Thatcher

Margaret Thatcher (b. 1925), the first woman elected to lead a major European state, stands as one of the most significant leaders of the late twentieth century. The controversial "Iron Lady" attacked socialism, promoted capitalism, and changed the face of modern Britain.

Born Margaret Roberts in a small city in southeastern England, her father was a small shopkeeper who instilled in his daughter the classic lower-middle-class virtues—hard work, personal responsibility, and practical education. A scholarship student at a local girls school, she entered Oxford in 1943 to study chemistry but soon found that politics was her passion. Elected president of the student Conservatives, she ran in 1950 for Parliament in a solidly Labour district to gain experience. Articulate and attractive, she also gained the attention of Denis Thatcher, a wealthy businessman who drove her to campaign appearances in his Jaguar. Married a year later, the new Mrs. Thatcher abandoned chemistry, went to law school, gave birth to twins, and practiced as a tax attorney. In 1959, she returned to politics and won a seat in the Conservative triumph.

For the next fifteen years Mrs. Thatcher served in Parliament and held various ministerial posts when the Conservatives governed. In 1974, as the economy soured and the Conservatives lost two close elections, a rebellious Margaret Thatcher adroitly ran for the leadership position of the Conservative Party and won. In the 1979 election, as the Labour government faced rampant inflation and crippling strikes, Mrs. Thatcher promised to reduce union power, lower taxes, and promote free markets. Attracting swing votes from skilled workers, she won and became prime minister.

A self-described "conviction politician," Thatcher rejected postwar Keynesian efforts to manage the economy, arguing that governments had created inflation by printing too much money. Thus her government reduced the supply of money and credit, and it refused to retreat as interest rates and unemployment soared. Her popularity plummeted. But Thatcher was saved by good luck—and courage. In 1982, the generals ruling Argentina suddenly seized the Falkland Islands off the Argentine coast, the home of 1,800 British citizens. Ever a staunch nationalist, Thatcher detached a naval armada that recaptured the Falklands without a hitch. Britain loved Thatcher's determination, and the "Iron Lady" was reelected in 1983.

Thatcher's second term was the high point of her success and influence. Her whole hearted commitment to privatization changed the face of British industry. More than fifty state-owned companies, ranging from the state telephone monopoly to the nationalized steel trust, were sold to private investors. Small investors were offered shares at bargain prices to promote "people's capitalism." Thatcher also curbed the power of British labor unions with various laws and actions. Most spectacularly, when in 1984 the once mighty coal miners rejected more mine closings and doggedly struck for a year, Thatcher stood firm and beat them. This outcome had a profound psychological impact on the public.

Elected again in 1987, Thatcher became increasingly stubborn, overconfident, and uncaring. Working well with her ideological soul mate, U.S. president Ronald Reagan, she opposed greater political and economic unity within the European Community. This, coupled with an unpopular effort to assert financial control over city governments, proved her undoing. In 1990, as in 1974, party stalwarts suddenly revolted and elected a new Conservative leader. Raised to the peerage by Queen Elizabeth II, the new Lady Thatcher then sat in the largely ceremonial House of Lords. The transformational changes of the Thatcher years endured, consolidated by her Conservative successor and largely accepted by the "New Labour" prime minister, the moderate Tony Blair.

Margaret Thatcher as prime minister. (AP Images/Staff-Caulkin)

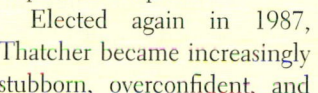

Questions for Analysis

1. Why did Margaret Thatcher want to change Britain, and how did she do it?
2. Historians have often debated whether great leaders determine the course of history, or whether they only ride successfully the major forces of their time. Which view of history is supported by Thatcher's achievements? Why?

Section Review

- The United States backed the anti-communist South Vietnamese militarily, gradually expanding the American presence in Vietnam until protests at home led to a peace agreement with North Vietnam and fighting subsided, but when the North invaded the South, the United States did not respond and the South fell to the communists.

- The Helsinki conference gave hope that political and human rights for European countries was ensured, but the Soviets invaded Afghanistan and the United States revitalized NATO to contain the Soviet "evil empire."

- Feminist leaders founded the National Organization for Women, pressing for an end to sexual discrimination, giving strength to other subordinate group movements such as gays and lesbians, but also creating an anti-feminist movement, mostly angered by the abortion issue.

- Economic decline and a sharp rise in unemployment followed increasing oil prices; governments responded by increasing social welfare programs and going into debt; the new austerity sparked a trend toward environmentalism and health consciousness.

presidency. Reagan's massive military buildup was partly responsible, but spending on social programs also grew rapidly as more people needed unemployment and welfare benefits. Thus the budget deficit soared and the U.S. government debt tripled in a decade.

Individuals felt the impact of austerity at an early date, for unlike governments, they could not pay their bills by printing money and going ever further into debt. The energy crisis of the 1970s forced them to re-examine not only their fuel bills but also the whole pattern of self-indulgent materialism in the postwar years. A growing number of experts and citizens concluded that the world was running out of resources and decried wasteful industrial practices and environmental pollution. In West Germany young activists known as the Greens in 1979 founded a political party to fight for environmental causes. The German Green movement elected some national and local representatives, and similar parties developed throughout Europe as environmentalism became a leading societal concern.

Another consequence of austerity in both Europe and North America was a self-improvement movement that focused on strict diet and exercise routines as a means to longevity. In addition, men and women were encouraged to postpone marriage until they had put their careers on a firm foundation, so the age of marriage rose sharply for both sexes in many Western countries. Indeed, career planning became important to a generation faced with the very real threat of unemployment or "underemployment" in a dead-end job.

Harder times also help explain why ever more women entered or remained in the workforce after they did marry. Although attitudes related to personal fulfillment were one reason for the continuing increase—especially for well-educated, upper-middle-class women—many wives in poor and middle-class families simply had to work outside the home because of economic necessity. As in preindustrial Europe, the wife's earnings provided the margin of survival for millions of hard-pressed families.

Chapter Review

What were the causes of the cold war? (page 782)

The Cold War grew out of the way World War II was fought in Europe. American and British forces met Stalin's armies in the middle of Germany and central Europe, so that the war-torn continent was already divided militarily in 1945. Extremely suspicious of the West and well aware that democratic governments in eastern Europe would be opposed to the Soviet Union, Stalin gradually established dependent Communist dictatorships in eastern Europe to ensure the security of the Soviet Union. Stalin's action in Eastern Europe, together with bitter disagreements between the wartime allies over the treatment of Germany, then led to a spiraling ideological confrontation between East and West. The Cold War match-up in Europe was institutionalized and extended to Asia, Africa, and Latin America for a long generation.

Why did western Europe recover so successfully? How did colonial peoples win political independence and American blacks triumph in the civil rights movement? (page 785)

Western Europe's success was due to a combination of political recovery, fundamental social changes, and unprecedented economic expansion. Political recovery included the establishment of democratic governments, the NATO alliance for military security, and the movement toward European unity. A whole series of social reforms provided

Key Terms

Big Three (p. 782)

Marshall Plan (p. 784)

NATO (p. 784)

cold war (p. 784)

Christian Democrats (p. 785)

Common Market (p. 787)

decolonization (p. 787)

neocolonialism (p. 790)

de-Stalinization (p. 792)

Brezhnev Doctrine (p. 793)

re-Stalinization (p. 794)

Big Science (p. 795)

Watergate (p. 801)

the citizens of the welfare state with national health systems, family allowances, paid vacations, and shorter workweeks. In about 1950 economic growth took off for a generation, fueled by Marshall Plan aid, a consumer revolution, and the liberal trade policies of the new Common Market. The transition from imperialism to decolonization proceeded rapidly, surprisingly smoothly, and without serious damage to western Europe. American blacks won victories in the struggle for civil rights because of their courageous determination and the inspired leadership of Martin Luther King, Jr.

détente (p. 801)
OPEC (p. 804)

What was the pattern of postwar rebuilding and development in the Soviet Union and communist eastern Europe? (page 791)

Postwar developments in the Soviet Union and communist eastern Europe displayed both similarities to and differences from developments in western Europe and North America. Perhaps the biggest difference was that Stalin imposed harsh one-party rule in the lands occupied by his armies, which led to the bitter cold war. Stalin also reimposed rigid central planning in the Soviet Union after the war and made satellite countries follow his lead. Nevertheless, the Soviet Union became less dictatorial under Khrushchev, and the standard of living in the Soviet Union improved markedly in the 1950s and 1960s.

How did changing patterns in technology, class relations, women's work, and youth culture bring major social transformations? (page 795)

In the years after 1945 pure science combined with applied technology to achieve remarkable success. The triumphs of applied science contributed not only to economic expansion but also to a more fluid, less antagonistic class structure, in which specialized education was the high road to advancement for men and women. Married women entered the labor force in growing numbers. The growing prosperity of the postwar era gave young people confidence and money, spurring the development of a distinct youth culture in the 1960s.

What were the key aspects of political conflict, economic stagnation, and the feminist movement in the late cold war? (page 800)

In the late 1960s and early 1970s, Europe and North America entered a time of crisis and rapid change. Many nations, from France to Czechoslovakia to the United States, experienced major political difficulties, as cold war conflicts and ideological battles divided peoples and shook governments. Beginning with the oil shocks of the 1970s, severe economic problems added to the turmoil and brought real hardship to millions of people. Yet in western Europe and North America, the welfare system held firm, and both democracy and the movement toward European unity successfully passed through the storm. The women's movement mobilized effectively and won expanded rights in the best tradition of Western civilization. Finally, efforts to achieve détente in central Europe while still maintaining a strong Atlantic alliance met some success. This modest progress helped lay the foundations for the sudden end of the cold war and the opening of a new era.

Notes

1. Quoted in N. Graebner, *Cold War Diplomacy, 1945–1960* (Princeton, N.J.: Van Nostrand, 1962), p. 17.
2. Quoted in S. E. Morison et al., *A Concise History of the American Republic* (New York: Oxford University Press, 1977), p. 697.
3. Quoted in N. Cantor, *Twentieth-Century Culture: Modernism to Deconstruction* (New York: Peter Lang, 1988), p. 252.

To assess your mastery of this chapter, go to **bedfordstmartins.com/mckaywestbrief**

Listening to the Past

A Feminist Critique of Marriage

The existentialist writer Simone de Beauvoir (1908–1986) turned increasingly to feminist concerns after World War II. Her most influential work was The Second Sex *(1949), a massive declaration of independence for contemporary women. Beauvoir argued that men had generally used education and social conditioning to create a dependent "other," a negative nonman who was not permitted to grow and strive for freedom.*

Marriage—on men's terms—was part of this unjust and undesirable process. Beauvoir's conclusion that some couples could establish free and equal unions was based in part on her experience with philosopher Jean-Paul Sartre, Beauvoir's encouraging companion and sometime lover.

Simone de Beauvoir as a teacher in 1947, when she was writing *The Second Sex.* (Hulton-Deutsch Collection/Corbis)

In domestic work, with or without the aid of servants, woman makes her home her own, finds social justification, and provides herself with an occupation, an activity, that deals usefully and satisfyingly with material objects—shining stoves, fresh, clean clothes, bright copper, polished furniture—but provides no escape from immanence and little affirmation of individuality. . . . Few tasks are more like the torture of Sisyphus than housework, with its endless repetition: the clean becomes soiled, the soiled is made clean, over and over, day after day. The housewife wears herself out marking time: she makes nothing, simply perpetuates the present. She never senses conquest of a positive Good, but rather indefinite struggle against negative Evil. . . . Washing, ironing, sweeping, ferreting out rolls of lint from under wardrobes—all this halting of decay is also the denial of life; for time simultaneously creates and destroys, and only its negative aspect concerns the housekeeper. . . .

Thus woman's work within the home gives her no autonomy; it is not directly useful to society, it does not open out on the future, it produces nothing. It takes on meaning and dignity only as it is linked with existent beings who reach out beyond themselves, transcend themselves, toward society in production and action. That is, far from freeing

the matron, her occupation makes her dependent upon husband and children; she is justified through them; but in their lives she is only an inessential intermediary. . . .

The tragedy of marriage is not that it fails to assure woman the promised happiness—there is no such thing as assurance in regard to happiness—but that it mutilates her; it dooms her to repetition and routine. The first twenty years of woman's life are extraordinarily rich, as we have seen; she discovers the world and her destiny. At twenty or thereabouts mistress of a home, bound permanently to a man, a child in her arms, she stands with her life virtually finished forever. Real activities, real work, are the prerogative of her man: she has mere things to occupy her which are sometimes tiring but never fully satisfying. . . .

Marriage should be a combining of two whole, independent existences, not a retreat, an annexation, a flight, a remedy. . . . The couple should not be regarded as a unit, a closed cell; rather each individual should be integrated as such in society at large, where each (whether male or female) could flourish without aid; then attachments could be formed in pure generosity with another individual equally adapted to the group, attachments that would be founded upon the acknowledgment that both are free. This balanced couple is not a utopian fancy: such couples do exist, sometimes even within the frame of marriage, most often outside it. Some mates are united by a strong sexual love that leaves them free in their friendships and in their work; others are held together by a friendship that does not preclude sexual liberty; more rare are those who are at once lovers and friends but do not seek in each other their sole reasons for living. Many nuances are possible in the relations between a man and a woman: in comradeship, pleasure, trust, fondness, co-operation, and love, they can be for each other the most abundant source of joy, richness, and power available to human beings.

Questions for Analysis

1. Do you agree with Beauvoir's assertion that domestic work is neither creative nor fully satisfying? How is domestic work depicted in current popular culture?

2. What was Beauvoir's solution to the situation she described? Was her solution desirable? Realistic?

3. What have you learned about the history of women that supports or challenges Beauvoir's analysis? Include developments since World War II and your own reflections.

Source: The Second Sex by Simone de Beauvoir, translated by H. M. Parshley, copyright © 1952 and renewed 1980 by Alfred A. Knopf, a division of Random House, Inc. Used by permission of Alfred A. Knopf, a division of Random House, Inc.

CHAPTER 31

Revolution, Rebuilding, and New Challenges

1985 to the Present

Chapter Preview

The Collapse of Communism in Eastern Europe and the Soviet Union
How did Mikhail Gorbachev try to revitalize communism in the Soviet Union? What were the radical consequences of his policies?

Building a New Europe in the 1990s
How, in the 1990s, did the different parts of a reunifying Europe meet the challenges of postcommunist reconstruction, resurgent nationalism, and economic union?

New Challenges in the Twenty-first Century
Why did the prospect of population decline, the reality of large-scale immigration, and concern for human rights emerge as critical issues in contemporary Europe?

The West and the Islamic World
How and why did relations between the West and the Islamic world deteriorate dramatically in the early twenty-first century?

INDIVIDUALS IN SOCIETY: Tariq Ramadan

LISTENING TO THE PAST: The French Riots: Will They Change Anything?

Italians protesting government economic policies gather in front of the Roman Coliseum during a nationwide strike in October 2003.

(Philippe Desmazes/AFP/Getty Images)

810

In the late twentieth century, massive changes swept through eastern Europe and opened a new era in human history. In the 1980s a broad movement to transform the communist system took root in Poland, and efforts to reform and revitalize the communist system in the Soviet Union snowballed out of control. In 1989 revolutions swept away communist rule throughout the entire Soviet bloc. The cold war came to a spectacular end, West Germany absorbed East Germany, and the Soviet Union broke into fifteen independent countries. Thus after forty years of cold war division, Europe regained an underlying unity, as faith in democratic government and some kind of market economy became the common European creed. In 1991 hopes for peaceful democratic progress throughout Europe were almost universal.

The post–cold war years saw the realization of some of these hopes, but the new era brought its own problems and tragedies. The cold war division of Europe had kept a lid on ethnic conflicts and nationalism, which suddenly burst into the open and led to a disastrous civil war in the former Yugoslavia. Moreover, most western European economies were plagued by high unemployment and were struggling to adapt to the global economy. In eastern Europe, the process of rebuilding shattered societies was more difficult than optimists had envisioned in 1991, and in western Europe, the road toward greater unity and eastward expansion proved bumpy. Nevertheless, the will to undo the cold war division prevailed, and in 2004 eight former communist countries as well as the islands of Cyprus and Malta joined the European Union—a historic achievement.

The twenty-first century brought a growing awareness of a new set of fundamental challenges, which were related to the prospect of population decline, the reality of large-scale immigration, and the promotion of human rights. These challenges promise to preoccupy Western society for years to come.

More dramatically, the old, often contentious question of relations with the Islamic world suddenly reemerged as a critical issue after the attack on New York's World Trade Center and the Pentagon in 2001. Although the West united in a quick response against al Qaeda (**al-KIGHduh**) and the Taliban in Afghanistan, the subsequent war in Iraq divided western Europe and threatened the future of Western cooperation in world affairs. The war in Iraq also complicated the ongoing integration of Europe's rapidly growing Muslim population.

The Collapse of Communism in Eastern Europe and the Soviet Union

How did Mikhail Gorbachev try to revitalize communism in the Soviet Union? What were the radical consequences of his policies?

Following the 1968 invasion of Czechoslovakia (pages 793–794), the Soviet Union repeatedly demonstrated that it was determined to uphold its rule throughout eastern Europe. Periodic efforts to achieve fundamental political change were doomed to failure sooner or later—or so it seemed to most Western experts into the mid-1980s.

And then Mikhail Gorbachev burst on the scene. The new Soviet leader opened an era of reform that was as sweeping as it was unexpected. His reforms rapidly transformed Soviet culture and politics, and they drastically reduced cold war tensions. But communism, which Gorbachev wanted so desperately to revitalize in order to save it, continued to decline as a functioning system throughout the Soviet bloc. In 1989 Gorbachev's plan to reform communism snowballed out of control. A series of largely peaceful revolutions swept across eastern Europe, overturning existing communist regimes and ending the communists' monopoly of power.

The revolutions of 1989 had momentous consequences. First, the countries of eastern and western Europe were no longer separate, and a new European Union slowly emerged. Second, an anticommunist revolution swept through the Soviet Union, which broke into a large Russia and fourteen other independent states. Third, West Germany quickly absorbed its East German rival and emerged as the most influential country in Europe. Finally, the long cold war came to an abrupt end, and the United States suddenly stood as the world's only superpower.

Gorbachev's Reforms in the Soviet Union

Fundamental change in Russian history has often come in short, intensive spurts, which contrast vividly with long periods of immobility. The era of reform launched by Mikhail Gorbachev in 1985 was one such decisive transformation. Gorbachev's initiatives brought political and cultural liberalization to the Soviet Union, and they then permitted democracy and national self-determination to triumph spectacularly in the old satellite empire and eventually in the Soviet Union itself, although this was certainly not Gorbachev's original intention.

As we have seen, the Soviet Union's Communist Party elite seemed secure in the early 1980s as far as any challenge from below was concerned. The long-established system of administrative controls continued to stretch downward from the central ministries and state committees to provincial cities, and from there to factories, neighborhoods, and villages. At each level of this massive state bureaucracy, the overlapping hierarchy of the Communist Party, with its 17.5 million members, continued to manage every aspect of national life. Yet the massive state and party bureaucracy was a mixed blessing. It safeguarded the elite, but it promoted apathy in the masses. Therefore, when the ailing Brezhnev finally died in 1982, his successor Yuri Andropov (**YOOR-ee an-DROH-pawf**) (1914–1984) tried to invigorate the system. Relatively little came of these efforts, but they combined with a sharply worsening economic situation to set the stage for the emergence in 1985 of Mikhail Gorbachev (b. 1931), the most vigorous Soviet leader in a generation.

Gorbachev believed in communism, but he realized it was failing to keep up with Western capitalism and technology. This was eroding the Soviet Union's status as a superpower.

Mikhail Gorbachev

In his acceptance speech before the Supreme Soviet (the U.S.S.R.'s parliament), newly elected president Mikhail Gorbachev vowed to assume "all responsibility" for the success or failure of perestroika. Previous parliaments were no more than tools of the Communist party, but this one actively debated and even opposed some government programs. (Vlastimir Shone/Gamma Presse/EYEDEA)

Thus Gorbachev (and his wife, Raisa, a professor of Marxist-Leninist thought) wanted to save the Soviet system by revitalizing it with fundamental reforms. In his first year in office, Gorbachev attacked corruption and incompetence in the bureaucracy, and alcoholism and drunkenness in Soviet society. He consolidated his power and elaborated his ambitious reform program.

The first set of reform policies was designed to transform and restructure the economy, in order to provide for the real needs of the Soviet population. To accomplish this economic "restructuring," or **perestroika** (per-ih-STROY-kuh), Gorbachev and his supporters permitted an easing of government price controls on some goods, more independence for state enterprises, and the setting up of profit-seeking private cooperatives to provide personal services for consumers. While these reforms produced a few improvements, the economy stalled at an intermediate point between central planning and free-market mechanisms. By late 1988, widespread shortages threatened the entire reform program.

Gorbachev's bold and far-reaching campaign "to tell it like it is" was much more successful. Very popular in a country where censorship, dull uniformity, and outright lies had long characterized public discourse, the newfound "openness," or **glasnost** (GLAZ-nost), of the government and the media marked an astonishing break with the past. Long-banned writers sold millions of copies of their works in new editions, while denunciations of Stalin and his terror became standard fare in plays and movies. Thus initial openness in government pronouncements quickly went much further than Gorbachev intended and led to something approaching free speech and free expression, a veritable cultural revolution.

Democratization was the third element of reform. Beginning as an attack on corruption in the Communist Party, it led to the first free elections in the Soviet Union since 1917. Gorbachev and the party remained in control, but a minority of critical independents was elected in April 1989 to a revitalized Congress of People's Deputies. Millions of Soviets then watched the new congress for hours on television as Gorbachev and his ministers saw their proposals debated and even rejected. The result was a new political culture at odds with the Communist Party's monopoly of power and control.

The Soviet leader also brought "new political thinking" to the field of foreign affairs. He withdrew Soviet troops from Afghanistan and pledged to respect the political choices of the peoples of eastern Europe, repudiating the Brezhnev Doctrine. Of enormous importance, he sought to halt the arms race with the United

CHRONOLOGY

1985	Glasnost leads to greater freedom of speech and expression in the Soviet Union
1985–	Decline in birthrate in industrialized nations continues
1986	Single European Act lays groundwork for single currency
August 1989	Solidarity gains power in Poland
November 1989	Collapse of the Berlin Wall
November–December 1989	Velvet Revolution ends communism in Czechoslovakia
October 1990	Reunification of Germany
1990–1991	First war with Iraq
July 1991	Failed coup against Gorbachev in Russia
November–December 1991	Dissolution of the Soviet Union
1991	Maastricht treaty sets financial criteria for European monetary union
1991–2000	Resurgence of nationalism and ethnic conflict in eastern Europe
1991–2001	Civil war in Yugoslavia
1992–1997	"Shock therapy" in Russia causes decline of the economy
1993	Creation of the European Union; growth of illegal immigration in Europe
1998–	Growing support for global human rights in Europe
1999	Russian economy booms
2000	Controversy over Muslim headscarves in French schools begins
September 2001	Terrorist attack on the United States
2001	War in Afghanistan
January 2002	New euro currency goes into effect in the European Union
2003	Second war with Iraq begins
2004	Ten new states join European Union

perestroika Economic restructuring and reform implemented by Gorbachev that permitted an easing of government price controls on some goods, more independence for state enterprises, and the setting up of profit-seeking private cooperatives to provide personal services for consumers.

glasnost Openness, part of Gorbachev's campaign to tell it like it is, marked a break from the past; long-banned writers sold millions of copies of their works, and denunciations of Stalin and his terror were standard public discourse.

States and convinced President Ronald Reagan of his sincerity. In December 1987, the two leaders agreed in a Washington summit to eliminate all land-based intermediate-range missiles in Europe, setting the stage for more arms reductions. Both leaders saw the opportunity to ease the strains on their national budgets that the arms race had created.

The Revolutions of 1989

Gorbachev's reforms interacted with a resurgence of popular protest in the Soviet Union's satellite empire. Developments in Poland were the most striking and significant.

Poland had been an unruly satellite from the beginning. Stalin said that introducing communism to Poland was like putting a saddle on a cow. As a result of widespread riots in 1956, Polish Communists dropped their efforts to impose Soviet-style collectivization on the peasants and to break the Roman Catholic Church. Yet they were determined to plan the economy, with poor results. Even the booming 1960s saw little economic improvement.

In 1970 Poland's working class rose again in angry protest. A new Communist leader came to power, and he wagered that massive inflows of Western capital and technology, especially from rich and now-friendly West Germany (see pages 801–802), could produce a Polish "economic miracle." Instead, bureaucratic incompetence and the first oil shock in 1973 put the economy into a nosedive. Then the real Polish miracle occurred: Cardinal Karol Wojtyla (**KAH-rol voy-TIL-ah**), archbishop of Cracow, was elected pope in 1978. The following year, now as Pope John Paul II, he returned from Rome and electrified the Polish nation with talk of the "inalienable rights of man." The economic crisis became a moral and spiritual crisis as well.

In August 1980, the sixteen thousand workers at the gigantic Lenin Shipyards in Gdansk (gdahynsk) (formerly known as Danzig) laid down their tools and occupied the plant. As other workers joined "in solidarity," the strikers advanced revolutionary demands, including the right to form free trade unions, freedom of speech, release of political prisoners, and economic reforms.

Led by Lenin Shipyards electrician Lech Walesa (**leck wah-LENS-ah**) (b. 1943), the workers proceeded to organize their free and democratic trade union. They called it **Solidarity.** Joined by intellectuals and supported by the Catholic Church, Solidarity became the union of a nation. By March 1981, it had 9.5 million union members. Yet as the economic situation worsened and some members of Solidarity became more radical, the Polish Communist leadership shrewdly denounced Solidarity for promoting economic collapse and provoking the Soviet Union. In December 1981, Communist leader General Wojciech Jaruzelski (**VOI-chekh yah-roo-ZEL-skee**) suddenly struck, proclaiming martial law, arresting Solidarity's leaders, and "saving" the nation.

Although it was driven underground, Solidarity maintained its organization and continued to voice the aspirations of the Polish masses after 1981. Part of the reason for the union's survival was the government's unwillingness (and probably its inability) to impose full-scale terror. Moreover, millions of Poles decided to continue acting as if they were free, even though they were not. Cultural and intellectual life remained extremely vigorous as the faltering Polish economy continued to deteriorate. Thus popular support for outlawed Solidarity remained strong under martial law in the 1980s, preparing the way for the union's political rebirth during the Gorbachev era at the end of the decade.

Solidarity Led by Lech Walesa, this group of workers in Poland organized their free and democratic trade union and quickly became the union of a nation with a full-time staff of 40,000 and 9.5 million union members by March 1981.

Lech Walesa and Solidarity
An inspiration for fellow workers at the Lenin Shipyards in the dramatic and successful strike against the Communist bosses in August 1980, Walesa played a key role in Solidarity before and after it was outlawed. Speaking here to old comrades at the Lenin Shipyards after Solidarity was again legalized in 1988, Walesa personified an enduring opposition to Communist rule in eastern Europe. (G. Merrillon/Gamma Presse/EYEDEA)

In early 1989, on the brink of economic collapse and political stalemate, Poland became the first eastern European country to experience revolution. Solidarity skillfully pressured Poland's frustrated Communist leaders into legalizing Solidarity and declaring that a large minority of representatives to the Polish parliament would be chosen by free elections in June 1989. Still guaranteed a parliamentary majority and expecting to win many of the contested seats, the Communists believed that the status quo could be maintained.

Instead the Communists were roundly defeated. Solidarity mobilized the country and won most of the contested seats in an overwhelming victory. Moreover, many angry voters crossed off the names of unopposed party candidates, so that the Communist Party failed to win the majority its leaders had anticipated. Solidarity members jubilantly entered the Polish parliament, and a dangerous stalemate quickly developed. But Solidarity's gifted leader Lech Walesa adroitly obtained a majority as two minor procommunist parties that had been part of the coalition government after World War II now joined forces with Walesa. In August 1989, the editor of Solidarity's weekly newspaper was sworn in as Poland's new noncommunist leader.

In its first year and a half, the new Solidarity government eliminated the hated secret police, the Communist ministers in the government, and finally Jaruzelski himself, but it did so step by step in order to avoid confrontation with the army or the Soviet Union. However, in economic affairs, the Solidarity-led government was radical from the beginning. It applied **shock therapy** designed to make a clean

shock therapy The Solidarity-led government's radical take on economic affairs that were designed to make a clean break with state planning and move to market mechanisms and private property.

break with state planning and move quickly to market mechanisms and private property. Thus the Solidarity government abolished controls on many prices on January 1, 1990, and reformed the monetary system with a "big bang."

Hungary followed Poland. Hungary's Communist Party boss, János Kádár (**KAH-dahr**), had permitted liberalization of the rigid planned economy after the 1956 uprising in exchange for political obedience and continued Communist control. In May 1988, in an effort to retain power by granting modest political concessions, the party replaced Kádár with a reform communist. But opposition groups rejected piecemeal progress, and in the summer of 1989 the Hungarian Communist Party agreed to hold free elections in early 1990. Welcoming Western investment and moving rapidly toward multiparty democracy, Hungary's Communists now enjoyed considerable popular support, and they believed, quite mistakenly it turned out, that they could defeat the opposition in the upcoming elections. In an effort to strengthen their support at home and also put pressure on East Germany's hard-line Communist regime, the Hungarians opened their border to East Germans and tore down the barbed-wire "iron curtain" with Austria. Thus tens of thousands of dissatisfied East German "vacationers" began pouring into Hungary, crossed into Austria as refugees, and continued on to immediate resettlement in thriving West Germany.

The flight of East Germans led to the rapid growth of a homegrown protest movement in East Germany. Intellectuals, environmentalists, and Protestant ministers took the lead, organizing huge candlelight demonstrations and arguing that a democratic but still socialist East Germany was both possible and desirable. These "stayers" failed to convince the "leavers," however, who continued to flee the country en masse. In a desperate attempt to stabilize the situation, the East German government opened the Berlin Wall in November 1989, and people danced for joy atop that grim symbol of the prison state. East Germany's aging Communist leaders were swept aside, and a reform government took power and scheduled free elections. In March 1990, the East German **Alliance for Germany,** which was closely tied to Kohl's West German Christian Democrats, won almost 50 percent of the votes in an East German parliamentary election. The Alliance for Germany quickly negotiated an economic union on favorable terms with Chancellor Kohl.

Finally, in the summer of 1990, the crucial international aspect of German unification was successfully resolved. In a historic agreement signed by Gorbachev and Kohl in July 1990, Germany solemnly affirmed its peaceful intentions and pledged never to develop nuclear, biological, or chemical weapons. In October 1990, East Germany merged into West Germany, forming henceforth a single nation under the West German laws and constitution.

In Czechoslovakia, communism died in December 1989 in only ten days. This so-called **Velvet Revolution** grew out of popular demonstrations led by students, intellectuals, and a dissident playwright turned moral revolutionary named Václav Havel (**VAH-slav HAH-vel**). The protesters practically took control of the streets and forced the Communists into a power-sharing arrangement, which quickly resulted in the resignation of the Communist government. As 1989 ended, the Czechoslovakian assembly elected Havel president.

Only in Romania was revolution violent and bloody. There, ironfisted Communist dictator Nicolae Ceauşescu (**chow-CHES-ku**) (1918–1989) had long combined Stalinist brutality with stubborn independence from Moscow. Faced with mass protests in December, Ceauşescu, alone among eastern European bosses, ordered his ruthless security forces to slaughter thousands, thereby sparking a classic armed uprising. After Ceauşescu's forces were defeated, the tyrant and his wife

Alliance for Germany A political party that was set up in East Germany, calling for the unification of East and West Germany, which they felt would lead to an economic bonanza in East Germany. In March 1990 they won almost 50 percent of the votes in the East German parliamentary election, thereby beating out the Socialist party.

Velvet Revolution The moment when communism died in 1989 with an ousting of Communist bosses in only ten days; it grew out of popular demonstrations led by students, intellectuals, and a dissident playwright.

The Fall of the Berlin Wall
The sudden opening of the Berlin Wall in November 1989 dramatized the spectacular collapse of communism throughout eastern Europe. Built by the Soviet leader Nikita Khrushchev in 1961, the hated barrier had stopped the flow of refugees from East Germany to West Germany. (Patrick Piel/Gamma Presse/EYEDEA)

were captured and executed by a military court. A coalition government emerged from the fighting, although the legacy of Ceauşescu's oppression left a very troubled country.

The breakdown of barriers between western and eastern Europe, with the peaceful reunification of Germany as a key element, led to agreements liquidating the cold war. In November 1990, delegates from twenty-two European countries joined those from the United States and the Soviet Union in Paris and agreed to a scaling down of all their armed forces. The delegates also solemnly affirmed that all existing borders in Europe—from unified Germany to the newly independent Baltic republics—were legal and valid. The **Paris Accord** was for all practical purposes a general peace treaty, bringing an end to World War II and the cold war.

In the months that followed, the United States and the Soviet Union agreed to scrap a significant portion of their nuclear weapons. In September 1991, the leaders of both countries canceled the around-the-clock alert status for bombers outfitted with atomic bombs. For the first time in four decades, Soviet and American nuclear weapons were no longer standing ready to destroy capitalism, communism, and life itself.

Paris Accord A general peace treaty that brought an end to World War II and the cold war that followed; it called for a scaling down of all armed forces and the acceptance of all existing borders as legal and valid.

The Disintegration of the Soviet Union

As 1990 began, revolutionary changes had triumphed in all but two eastern European states—tiny Albania and the vast Soviet Union. The great question now became whether reform communism would give way to a popular anticommunist revolution.

The elections of February 1990 provided the first indication that reform communism would not survive. As in the eastern European satellites, democrats and anticommunists won clear majorities in the leading cities of the Russian Federation. Moreover, in Lithuania the people elected an uncompromising nationalist as president, and the newly chosen parliament declared Lithuania an independent state. Gorbachev responded by placing an economic embargo on Lithuania, but he refused to use the army to crush the separatist government. The result was a tense political stalemate, which undermined popular support for Gorbachev. Separating himself further from Communist hard-liners, Gorbachev asked Soviet citizens to ratify a new constitution, which formally abolished the Communist Party's monopoly of political power and expanded the Power of the Congress of People's Deputies. Retaining his post as party secretary, Gorbachev convinced a majority of deputies to elect him president of the Soviet Union.

Gorbachev's eroding power and his unwillingness to risk a universal suffrage election for the presidency strengthened his great rival, Boris Yeltsin (1931–2007). A radical reform communist who had been purged by party conservatives in 1987, Yeltsin embraced the democratic movement, and in May 1990 he was elected leader of the Russian Federation's parliament. He boldly announced that Russia would put its interests first and declare its independence from the Soviet Union. Gorbachev tried to save the Soviet Union with a new treaty that would link the member republics in a looser, freely accepted confederation, but six of the fifteen Soviet republics rejected Gorbachev's pleas.

Opposed by democrats and nationalists, Gorbachev was also challenged again by the Communist old guard. A gang of hard-liners kidnapped a vacationing Gorbachev and his family in the Caucasus and tried to seize the Soviet government in August 1991. But the attempted coup collapsed in the face of massive popular resistance, which rallied around Yeltsin. As the world watched spellbound on television, Yeltsin defiantly denounced the hard-liners from atop a stalled tank in central Moscow and declared the "rebirth of Russia." The army supported Yeltsin, and Gorbachev returned to power as head of the Soviet Union.

The leaders of the coup wanted to preserve Communist power, state ownership, and the multinational Soviet Union, but they succeeded only in destroying all three. An anticommunist revolution swept the Russian Federation as Yeltsin and his supporters outlawed the Communist Party and confiscated its property. Locked in a personal and political duel with Gorbachev, Yeltsin and his democratic allies declared Russia independent and withdrew from the Soviet Union. All the other Soviet republics also left. The Soviet Union—and Gorbachev's job—ceased to exist on December 25, 1991 (see Map 31.1). The independent republics of the old Soviet Union then established a loose confederation, the Commonwealth of Independent States, which played only a minor role in the 1990s.

The Gulf War of 1991

As the Soviet Union collapsed, losing both the will and the means to intervene in global conflicts, the United States emerged rather suddenly as the world's only surviving superpower. In 1991 the United States used its military superiority to chal-

MAP 31.1   Russia and the Successor States

After the attempt in August 1991 to depose Gorbachev failed, an anticommunist revolution swept the Soviet Union. Led by Russia and Boris Yeltsin, the republics that formed the Soviet Union declared their sovereignty and independence. Eleven of the fifteen republics then formed a loose confederation called the Commonwealth of Independent States, but the integrated economy of the Soviet Union dissolved into separate national economies, each with its own goals and policies.

lenge Iraq's August 1990 invasion and annexation of its oil-rich southern neighbor, Kuwait.

Reacting vigorously to free Kuwait, the United States mobilized the U.N. Security Council, which in August 1990 imposed a strict naval blockade on Iraq. Receiving the support of some Arab states, as well as of Great Britain and France, the United States also landed 500,000 American soldiers in Saudi Arabia near the border of Kuwait. When the defiant Iraqi leader Saddam Hussein (**sah-DAHM who-SANE**) (1937–2006) refused to withdraw from Kuwait, the Security Council authorized the U.S.-led military coalition to attack Iraq. The American army and air force then smashed Iraqi forces in a lightning-quick desert campaign, although the United States stopped short of toppling Saddam because it feared a sudden disintegration of Iraq.

The defeat of Iraqi armies in the Gulf War demonstrated the awesome power of the U.S. military, rebuilt and revitalized by the spending and patriotism of the 1980s. Little wonder that in the flush of yet another victory, the first President Bush spoke of a **"new world order,"** an order that would apparently feature the

"new world order" President George H. W. Bush's vision after the U.S. defeat of Iraqi armies in the Gulf War that would feature the United States and a cooperative United Nations working together to impose peace and stability throughout the world.

Section Review

- Gorbachev attempted to save communism through perestroika (restructuring), easing government control of economic markets; glasnost (openness), easing censorship of the media; democratization, allowing free elections; and by easing foreign policy and the arms race with the United States.

- Poland experienced a revolution led by the Solidarity movement that won free elections and control of the government, defeating the communists, eliminating the secret police, and abolishing state controls.

- Hungary followed Poland in its bid for free elections, ousting the communists and opening the border for East Germans to leave, which promoted protests, the fall of the Berlin Wall, and the rejoining of East and West Germany.

- Czechoslovakia's Velvet Revolution ended communism there; only in Romania was revolution accompanied by fighting, as Eastern European countries joined the West at the Paris Accord, ending the cold war.

- Political unrest plagued the Soviet Union, with Gorbachev trying to save reformed communism while Yeltsin declared independence for the Russian Federation along with the other Soviet republics, forming a loose confederation, the Commonwealth of Independent States.

- The United States challenged Iraq's invasion of Kuwait in 1991 and then, authorized by the United Nations' Security Council, attacked and defeated Iraqi forces in a quick desert campaign.

United States and a cooperative United Nations working together to impose stability throughout the world.

Building a New Europe in the 1990s

How, in the 1990s, did the different parts of a reunifying Europe meet the challenges of postcommunist reconstruction, resurgent nationalism, and economic union?

The fall of communism, the end of the cold war, and the collapse of the Soviet Union opened a new era in European and world history. The dimensions and significance of this new era, opening suddenly and unexpectedly, are subject to debate. We are so close to what is going on that we lack vital perspective. Yet the historian must take a stand.

First, we shall focus on three of the most important trends: the pressure on national economies increasingly caught up in global capitalism; the defense of social achievements under attack; and a resurgence of nationalism and ethnic conflict. Second, with these common themes providing an organizational framework, we shall examine the course of development in the three overlapping but still distinct regions of contemporary Europe. These are Russia and the western states of the old Soviet Union, previously communist eastern Europe, and western Europe.

Common Patterns and Problems

The end of the cold war and the disintegration of the Soviet Union ended the division of Europe into two opposing camps with two different political and economic systems. Thus, although Europe in the 1990s was a collage of diverse peoples, the entire continent shared an underlying network of common developments and challenges (see Map 31.2).

Of critical importance, in economic affairs European leaders embraced, or at least accepted, a large part of the neoliberal, free-market vision of capitalist development. Postcommunist governments in eastern Europe freed prices, turned state enterprises over to private owners, and sought to move toward strong currencies and balanced budgets. In western Europe, new free-market initiatives produced changes in western Europe's still-dominant welfare capitalism, which featured government intervention, high taxes, and high levels of social benefits.

Two factors were particularly important in accounting for this ongoing shift from welfare state activism to tough-minded capitalism. First, western Europeans

MAPPING THE PAST

MAP 31.2   Contemporary Europe

No longer divided by ideological competition and the cold war, today's Europe features a large number of independent states. Several of these states were previously part of the Soviet Union and Yugoslavia, both of which broke into many different countries. Czechoslovakia also divided on ethnic lines, while a reunited Germany emerged, once again, as the dominant nation in central Europe. **[1]** Which countries shown here were previously part of the Soviet Union? **[2]** Which countries were part of Yugoslavia? **[3]** Where did the old "iron curtain" run? (See Map 30.1, page 786, if necessary.)

looked to the stronger U.S. economy and borrowed the practices and ideologies instituted there and in Great Britain in the 1980s (see page 804). Second, eastern Europeans wanting to compete in the global economy were compelled to follow the rules of Western governments, multinational corporations, and international financial organizations such as the International Monetary Fund (IMF). These rules called for the free movement of capital and goods and services, as well as low inflation and limited government deficits.

The ongoing computer and electronics revolution strengthened the move toward a global economy. The computer revolution reduced the costs of distance, speeding up communications and helping businesses tap cheaper labor overseas. Reducing the friction of distance made threats of moving factories abroad ring true and helped hold down wages at home.

Globalization, the emergence of a freer global economy, probably did speed up world economic growth as enthusiasts invariably claimed, but it also had powerful and quite negative social consequences. Millions of ordinary citizens in western Europe believed that global capitalism and freer markets were undermining hard-won social achievements. As in the United States and Great Britain in the 1980s, the public in other countries generally associated globalization with the increased unemployment that accompanied corporate downsizing, the efforts to reduce the power of labor unions, and, above all, government plans to reduce social benefits. The reaction was particularly intense in France and Germany, where unions remained strong and socialists championed a minimum of change in social policies.

Indeed, the broad movement toward neoliberal global development sparked a powerful counterattack as the 1990s ended. Critics insisted that globalization hurt the world's poor, because multinational corporations destroyed local industries and paid pitiful wages, and because international financial organizations demanded harsh balanced budgets and deep cuts in government social programs. These attacks shook global neoliberalism, but it remained dominant.

In politics, European countries embraced genuine electoral competition, with elected presidents and legislatures and the outward manifestations of representative liberal governments. With some notable exceptions, such as discrimination against Roma (Gypsies), countries also guaranteed basic civil liberties. Thus, for the first time since before the French Revolution, almost all of Europe followed the same general political model of liberal democracy, although with variations.

globalization The emergence of a freer global economy; it also refers to the exchange of cultural, political, and religious ideas throughout the world.

Recasting Russia

Politics and economics were closely intertwined in Russia after the attempted Communist coup in 1991 and the dissolution of the Soviet Union. President Boris Yeltsin and his economic ministers listened to those Western advisers who argued that private economies were always best and opted in January 1992 for breakneck liberalization. Their "shock therapy" freed prices on 90 percent of all Russian goods, with the exception of bread, vodka, oil, and public transportation. The government also launched a rapid privatization of industry and turned thousands of factories and mines over to new private companies. Each citizen received a voucher worth 10,000 rubles (about $22) to buy stock in private companies, but control of the privatized companies usually remained in the hands of the old bosses—the managers and government officials from the communist era.

President Yeltsin and his economic reformers believed that shock therapy would revive production and bring prosperity after a brief period of hardship. The results of the reforms were in fact quite different. Prices increased 250 percent on the very first day, and they kept on soaring, increasing twenty-six times in the course of 1992. At the same time, Russian production fell a staggering 20 percent. Nor did the situation stabilize quickly. Throughout 1995 rapid but gradually slowing inflation raged, and output continued to fall. Only in 1997 did the economy stop declining, before crashing yet again in 1998 in the wake of Asia's financial crisis.

Runaway inflation and poorly executed privatization brought a profound social revolution to Russia. A new capitalist elite acquired great wealth and power, while large numbers of people fell into abject poverty, and the majority struggled in the midst of decline to make ends meet.

Rapid economic decline in 1992 and 1993 and rising popular dissatisfaction encouraged a majority of communists, nationalists, and populists in the Russian parliament to oppose Yeltsin and his coalition of democratic reformers and big-business interests. The erratic, increasingly hard-drinking Yeltsin would accept no compromise and insisted on a strong presidential system. Winning in April 1993 the support of 58 percent of the population in a referendum on his proposed constitution, Yeltsin then brought in tanks to crush a parliamentary mutiny in October 1993 and literally blew away the opposition. Subsequently, Yeltsin consolidated his power, and in 1996 he used his big-business cronies in the media to win an impressive come-from-behind victory. But effective representative government failed to develop, and many Russians came to equate "democracy" with the corruption, poverty, and national decline they experienced throughout the 1990s.

This widespread disillusionment set the stage for the "managed democracy" of Vladimir Putin (**VLAD-ih-mir POO-tin**), first elected president as Yeltsin's chosen successor in 2000 and re-elected in a landslide in March 2004. An officer in the secret police in the communist era, Putin maintained relatively free markets in the economic sphere but gradually re-established semi-authoritarian political rule. Aided greatly by high prices for oil, Russia's most important export, this combination worked well and seemed to suit most Russians. In 2007, the Russian economy had been growing rapidly for eight years, the Russian middle class was expanding, and the elected parliament supported Putin overwhelmingly. Proponents of liberal democracy were in retreat, while conservative Russian intellectuals were on the offensive, arguing that free markets and capitalism required strong political rule to control corruption and prevent chaos. Historians saw a reassertion of Russia's long authoritarian tradition. In March 2008 Putin's ally and hand-picked successor, Dmitry Medvedev, was elected president in a landslide.

Putin's forceful, competent image in world affairs also soothed the country's injured pride and symbolized its national resurgence. Nor did the government permit any negative television reports on the civil war in Chechnya (**CHECH-nee-ah**), the tiny republic of one million Muslims on Russia's southern border, which in 1991 had declared its independence from the Russian Federation (see Map 31.1). The savage conflict in Chechnya continued, largely unreported, with numerous atrocities on both sides.

Progress in Eastern Europe

Developments in eastern Europe shared important similarities with those in Russia, as many of the problems were the same. Thus the postcommunist states of the former satellite empire worked to replace state planning and socialism with market mechanisms and private property. Western-style electoral politics also took hold, and as in Russia, these politics were marked by intense battles between presidents and parliaments and by weak political parties. The social consequences of these revolutionary changes were similar to those in Russia. Ordinary citizens and the elderly were once again the big losers, while the young and the ex-Communists were the big winners. Inequalities between richer and poorer regions also increased. Capital cities such as Warsaw, Prague, and Budapest concentrated wealth, power, and opportunity as never before, while provincial centers stagnated and old industrial areas declined. Crime and gangsterism increased in the streets and in the executive suites.

Yet the 1990s saw more than a difficult transition, with high social costs, to market economies and freely elected governments in eastern Europe. Many citizens had never fully accepted communism, which they equated with Russian imperialism and the loss of national independence. The joyous crowds that toppled communist regimes in 1989 believed that they were liberating the nation as well as the individual. Thus communism died and nationalism was reborn.

The surge of nationalism in eastern Europe recalled a similar surge of state creation after World War I. Then, too, authoritarian multinational empires had come crashing down in defeat and revolution. Then, too, nationalities with long histories and rich cultures had drawn upon ideologies of popular sovereignty and national self-determination to throw off foreign rule and found new democratic states.

The response to this opportunity in the former communist countries was quite varied in the 1990s, but most observers agreed that Poland, the Czech Republic, and Hungary were the most successful (see Map 31.2, page 821). Each of these three countries met the critical challenge of economic reconstruction more successfully than Russia, and each could claim to be the economic leader in eastern Europe, depending on the criteria selected. The reasons for these successes included considerable experience with limited market reforms before 1989, flexibility and lack of dogmatism in government policy, and an enthusiastic embrace of capitalism by a new entrepreneurial class. In the first five years of reform, Poland created twice as many new businesses as Russia, with a total population only one-fourth as large.

The three northern countries in the former Soviet bloc also did far better than Russia in creating new civic institutions, legal systems, and independent broadcasting networks that reinforced political freedom and national revival. Lech Walesa in Poland and Václav Havel in Czechoslovakia were elected presidents of their countries and proved as remarkable in power as in opposition. After Czechoslovakia's "Velvet Revolution" in 1989, Havel and the Czech parliament accepted a "velvet divorce" in 1993 when Slovakian nationalists wanted to break off and form their own state. All three northern countries managed to control national and ethnic tensions that might have destroyed their postcommunist reconstruction.

Above all, and in sharp contrast to Russia, the popular goal of "rejoining the West" reinforced political moderation and compromise. Seeing themselves as heirs to medieval Christendom and liberal democratic values of the 1920s, Poles, Hungarians, and Czechs hoped to find security in NATO membership and economic prosperity in western Europe's ever-tighter **European Union** (the former Common Market or EEC, see page 787). Membership required many proofs of character and stability, however. Providing these proofs and endorsed by the Clinton administration, Poland, Hungary, and the Czech Republic were accepted into the NATO alliance in 1997. Gaining admission to the European Union (EU) proved more difficult, because candidates also had to accept and be ready to apply all the rules and regulations that the EU had developed since 1956—an awesome task.

Romania and Bulgaria were the eastern European laggards in the postcommunist transition. Western traditions were much weaker there, and both countries were much poorer than neighbors to the north. In 1993 Bulgaria and Romania had per capita national incomes of $1,140, in contrast to Hungary ($3,830) and

European Union The new name as of 1993 for the European Community.

the Czech Republic ($2,710). Although Romania and Bulgaria eventually made progress in the late 1990s, full membership for both countries in either NATO or the EU still lay far in the future.

Tragedy in Yugoslavia

The great postcommunist tragedy was Yugoslavia, which under Josip Tito had been a federation of republics and regions under strict communist rule. Yugoslavia had the most ethnically diverse population of Europe (see Map 31.3), and the different ethnic groups held historic grievances against one another. After Tito's death in 1980, power passed increasingly to the sister republics. Tensions among the republics mounted throughout the decade as they desired greater autonomy.

The revolutions of 1989 accelerated the breakup of Yugoslavia. Serbian president Slobodan Milosevic (**SLOH-buh-dain muh-LOH-suh-vich**) (1941–2006) pushed to unite all Serbs, including those living outside the existing borders of Serbia, into a "greater Serbia." The republics of Slovenia, Croatia, Bosnia-Herzegovina, and Macedonia rejected this idea while advocating for separation. In June 1991 Slovenia and Croatia declared their independence from Yugoslavia.

MAP 31.3   The Ethnic Composition of Yugoslavia, 1991

Yugoslavia had the most ethnically diverse population in eastern Europe. The Republic of Croatia had substantial Serbian and Muslim minorities. Bosnia-Herzegovina had large Muslim, Serbian, and Croatian populations, none of which had a majority. In June 1991, Serbia's brutal effort to seize territory and unite all Serbs in a single state brought a tragic civil war.

Milosevic, who controlled the Yugoslavian army and intended to maintain a united Yugoslavia under Serbian domination, sent forces to the break-off republics. Slovenia repulsed this attack, but Milosevic's armies managed to take about 30 percent of Croatia.

In 1992 the conflict spread to Bosnia-Herzegovina, which was home to Catholic Croats, Orthodox Serbs, and Muslim Slavs. When the republic voted for independence, the Serbian minority rebelled. They shared the goal of their military ally Milosevic—a "greater Serbia" composed of all Serbian-held lands. The resulting civil war between the three ethnic groups unleashed ruthless brutality, with murder, rape, destruction, and the herding of refugees into concentration camps. In 1994, the Muslims and Croats called a truce and formed an alliance. The turning point came in July 1995, when Bosnian Serbs overran Srebrenica—a Muslim city previously declared a United Nations "safe area"—and killed several thousand civilians. World outrage prompted NATO to bomb Bosnian Serb military targets intensively, and the Croatian army drove all the Serbs from Croatia. In November 1995, President Bill Clinton helped the warring sides agree to a complicated accord dividing the country between the Serbs and Muslim-Croats. Troops from NATO countries patrolled Bosnia to try to keep the peace.

Violence then flared in Kosovo, a province within Serbia that was stripped of self-rule by Milosevic in 1989. Most Kosovars were Muslim ethnic Albanians. In early 1998, frustrated Kosovar militants formed the **Kosovo Liberation Army (KLA)** to fight for independence. Serbian repression of the Kosovars increased, and in 1998 Serbian forces attacked both KLA guerrillas and unarmed villagers, displacing 250,000 people within Kosovo. By January 1999, the Western powers, led by the United States, were threatening Milosevic with heavy air raids if he did not withdraw Serbian armies from Kosovo and accept self-government (but not independence) for Kosovo. Milosevic refused, and in March 1999 NATO began bombing Yugoslavia (now reduced to Serbia and Montenegro). Serbian paramilitary forces responded by driving about 780,000 Kosovars into exile. NATO redoubled its highly destructive bombing campaign, which eventually forced Milosevic to withdraw and allowed the joyous Kosovars to regain their homeland. The impoverished Serbs eventually voted the still-defiant Milosevic out of office, and in July 2001 a new pro-Western Serbian government turned him over to the war crimes tribunal in the Netherlands. Milosevic died while standing trial for crimes against humanity.

Kosovo Liberation Army (KLA)
Formed in 1998 by frustrated Kosovar militants who sought to fight for their independence.

Unity and Identity in Western Europe

The movement toward a European identity that transcended destructive national rivalries was revitalized in the 1980s and 1990s as European leaders put forth new proposals for economic and political unity. Implementing a 1986 agreement, the European Union went to a single market in 1993 through which labor, capital, services, and goods could travel freely. The next step, a monetary union and single currency, the euro, went into effect on January 1, 2002, after more than a decade of planning and debate. Then on May 1, 2004, the European Union added 70 million people and expanded to include 455 million citizens in twenty-five different countries. The largest newcomer by far was Poland, followed in descending size by the Czech Republic, Hungary, Slovenia, Slovakia, Estonia, Lithuania, Latvia, Malta, and Cyprus.

In June 2004, more than two years after charging a special commission to write "a new constitution for European citizens," the leaders of the European Union reached agreement on the final document. Above all, the new constitution, with

Turkey's Struggle for EU Membership
Turkish elites and the general population want to "join Europe," but the road to EU membership is proving long and difficult. The EU has required Turkey to make many constitutional reforms and give greater autonomy to Turkish Kurds. Yet the Turks face ever more demands, and many now believe that the real roadblock is Europe's anti-Muslim feeling. (CartoonStock Limited)

almost 350 articles, established a single rulebook to replace the complex network of treaties concluded by the member states since the 1957 creation of the European Economic Community. The EU constitution created a president, a foreign minister, and a voting system weighted to reflect the number of people in the different states. The result of intense debate and many compromises, the constitution moved toward a more centralized federal system in several fields, but each state retained veto power in the most sensitive areas, such as taxation, social policy, and foreign affairs. In order for the constitution to take effect, each and every EU country needed to ratify it.

Nine countries, led by Germany, Italy, and seven east European members, soon ratified the constitution by parliamentary action, while seven states planned to go beyond the political elites and let the voters decide. The referendum campaigns were noisy and contentious, as generally well-informed citizens debated whether the new constitution surrendered too much national sovereignty to an emerging central European government in Brussels. British voters were considered most likely to vote no, but both the French and the Dutch beat them to it, rejecting the new constitution by clear majorities. Nationalist fears about losing sovereignty were matched by fears that an unwieldy European Union would grow to include Ukraine, Georgia, and Muslim Turkey—countries with cultures and histories that were very different from those in western Europe. Thus the long postwar march toward ever-greater European unity stopped,

Section Review

- Most European countries adopted free-market capitalism but as neoliberal global development emerged, critics argued that it hurt the poor and undermined social welfare programs.

- Yeltsin's rapid privatization of industry was successful only for the new elite, while the masses struggled; Putin re-established semi-authoritarian rule while maintaining free markets and managed some economic recovery and a resurgence of nationalism.

- Poland, Hungary, and the Czech Republic were able to make the transition from communism to capitalism and regain prosperity far better than Russia, Romania, or Bulgaria due to their leadership, flexibility, and ability to control ethnic and national tensions.

- Ethnic tensions within Yugoslavia led to civil war, with the Serbian president Milosevic pushing for a "greater Serbia" and other republics wanting independence, before NATO intervened and replaced Milosevic with a pro-Western Serbian government.

- The European Union reworked itself and expanded to include more countries, redrafting its constitution, although not all countries ratified it because they feared losing their national sovereignty.

or at least stalled, and the European Union concentrated on fully integrating the new eastern European members and redrafting the constitution.

New Challenges in the Twenty-first Century

Why did the prospect of population decline, the reality of large-scale immigration, and concern for human rights emerge as critical issues in contemporary Europe?

baby bust Falling European birthrates at the opening to the twenty-first century, that seemed to promise a shrinking and aging population in the future.

As the twenty-first century opened, European society faced new uncertainties. Of great significance, Europe continued to experience a remarkable **baby bust,** as birthrates fell to levels that seemed to promise a shrinking and aging population in the future. At the same time, the peaceful, wealthy European Union attracted rapidly growing numbers of refugees and illegal immigrants from the former Soviet Union, the Middle East, Africa, and Asia. The unexpected arrival of so many newcomers raised many perplexing questions and prompted serious thinking about European identity, Europe's humanitarian mission, and its place in the world.

The Prospect of Population Decline

Population is still growing rapidly in many poor countries, but this is not the case in the world's industrialized nations. In 2000 women in developed countries had only 1.6 children on average; only in the United States did women have, almost exactly, the 2.1 children necessary to maintain a stable population. In European countries, where women had been steadily having fewer babies since the 1950s, national fertility rates ranged from 1.2 to 1.8 children per woman.

If the current baby bust continues, the long-term consequences could be dramatic, though hardly predictable. At the least, Europe's population would decline and age. Projections for Germany are illustrative. Total German population, barring much greater immigration, would gradually decline from 82 million in 2001 to only 62 million around 2050. The number of people of working age would drop by a third, and almost half of the population would be over sixty. Social security taxes paid by the shrinking labor force would need to soar for the skyrocketing costs of pensions and health care for seniors to be met—a recipe for generational tension and conflict.

Why, in time of peace, were birthrates falling? Certainly the uneven, uninspiring European economic conditions of the 1980s and much of the 1990s played some role. But in our view, the ongoing impact of careers for married women and the related drive for gender equality remained the decisive factors in the long-term decline of postwar birthrates. Research showed that European women (and men) in their twenties, thirties, and early forties still wanted to have two or even three children—about the same number as their parents had wanted. But unlike their parents, young couples did not realize their ideal family size. Many women postponed the birth of their first child into their thirties in order to finish their education and establish themselves in their careers. Then, finding that raising even one child was more difficult and time-consuming than anticipated, new mothers tended to postpone and eventually forgo a second child. This was especially true of professional women.

By 2005 some population experts believed that European women were no longer postponing having children. At the least, birthrates appeared to have stabilized. Moreover, the frightening implications of dramatic population decline had emerged as a major public issue. Opinion leaders, politicians, and the media started to press the case for more support for families with children.

The Growth of Immigration

While the European birthrates declined in the 1990s, population numbers got a push from the surge in immigration. The collapse of communism in the East and savage civil wars in Yugoslavia sent hundreds of thousands of refugees fleeing westward. Equally brutal conflicts in Afghanistan, Iraq, Somalia, and Rwanda—to name only four countries—brought thousands more from Asia and Africa. Illegal immigration into the European Union also exploded, rising from an estimated 50,000 people in 1993 to perhaps 500,000 a decade later. This movement exceeded the estimated 300,000 unauthorized foreigners entering the United States each year.

In the early twenty-first century, many migrants still applied for political asylum and refugee status, but most were eventually rejected and classified as illegal job-seekers. Certainly, greater economic opportunities exerted a powerful pull. Germans earned on average five times more than neighboring Poles, who in turn earned much more than people farther east and in North Africa.

Illegal immigration also soared because powerful criminal gangs turned to "people smuggling" for big, low-risk profits. A large portion of the illegal immigrants were young women from eastern Europe, especially Russia and Ukraine. Often lured by criminals promising jobs as maids or waitresses and sometimes simply kidnapped and sold like slaves from hand to hand for a few thousand

Illegal Immigrants from Eritrea

Italian police have just rescued these young immigrants from an overloaded boat off the coast of Italy. Fleeing civil war and desperate for work, the immigrants are weary because of the long and dangerous voyage from Libya. Every year thousands of illegal immigrants try to reach Italy and Spain from North Africa. Many are found dead on the shoreline. (Mimi Mollica/Corbis)

dollars, these women were smuggled into the most prosperous parts of central Europe and into the European Union and forced into prostitution or slavery.

Illegal immigration generated intense discussion and controversy in western Europe. A majority opposed the newcomers, who were accused of taking jobs from the unemployed and somehow undermining national unity. The idea that cultural and ethnic diversity could be a force for vitality and creativity ran counter to deep-seated beliefs. Concern about illegal migration in general often fused with fears of Muslim immigrants and Muslim residents who had grown up in Europe. As busy mosques came to outnumber dying churches in parts of some European cities, rightist politicians especially tried to exploit widespread doubts that immigrant populations from Muslim countries would ever assimilate to the different national cultures. These doubts increased after the attack on New York's World Trade Center, as we shall see later in the chapter.

An articulate minority challenged the anti-immigrant campaign and its racist overtones. They argued that Europe badly needed newcomers—preferably talented newcomers—to limit the impending population decline and provide valuable technical skills. European leaders also focused on improved policing of EU borders and tougher common procedures to combat people smuggling and punish international crime. Above all, growing illegal immigration pushed Europeans to examine the whys of this dramatic human movement and to consider how it related to Europe's proper role in world affairs.

Promoting Human Rights

The tide of refugees and illegal job-seekers, the ethnic violence of Yugoslavia, and western Europe's relative prosperity were some of the factors prompting European visionaries to seek a leadership role in promoting human rights.

In practical terms, western Europe's evolving human rights mission meant, first of all, humanitarian interventions to stop civil wars and to prevent tyrannical governments from slaughtering their own people. Thus the European Union joined with the United States to intervene militarily to stop the killing in Bosnia, Kosovo, and Macedonia and to protect the rights of embattled minorities. The states of the EU also vigorously supported U.N.-sponsored conferences and treaties that sought to verify the compliance of anti–germ warfare conventions, outlawed the use of hideously destructive land mines, and established a new international court to prosecute war criminals.

Europeans also pushed for broader definitions of individual rights. Abolishing the death penalty in the European Union, for example, they condemned its continued use in China, the United States, Saudi Arabia, and some other countries as inhumane and uncivilized. Rights for Europeans in their personal relations also continued to expand. In the pacesetting Netherlands, for example, a growing network of laws gave prostitutes (legally recognized since 1917) pensions and full workers' rights and legalized gay and lesbian marriages, the smoking of pot in licensed coffee shops, and assisted suicide (euthanasia) for the terminally ill.

As the twenty-first century opened, western Europeans also pushed as best they could to extend their broad-based concept of social and economic rights to the world's poor countries. For example, Europe's moderate social democrats combined with human rights campaigners in 2001 to help African governments secure drastic price cuts from the big international drug companies on the drug cocktails needed to combat Africa's AIDS crisis. Strong advocates of greater social equality and state-funded health care, European socialists embraced morality as a basis for action and the global expansion of human rights as a primary goal.

Section Review

- Population growth continues in many poor countries but is declining in the industrialized nations, most likely because of the impact of education and careers for women who delay first births as they face the expense and difficulty of managing a career and family.

- Immigration rates soared as refugees fleeing civil war and poverty sought refuge in the European Union, but conflicts over illegal immigration pushed Europeans to debate and plan their role in this human dilemma.

- Europeans led the way in promoting human rights around the world by agreeing to humanitarian intervention in civil wars, ending the use of land mines and germ warfare, opening an international court, broadening individual rights, and offering help to African nations for the AIDS crisis.

The West and the Islamic World

How and why did relations between the West and the Islamic world deteriorate dramatically in the early twenty-first century?

A hundred years from now, when historians assess developments in the early twenty-first century, they will almost certainly highlight the dramatic deterioration in the long, rich, up-and-down relationship between the West and the Islamic world. They will examine the reasons that the peaceful conclusion of the cold war and the joyful reunification of a divided continent gave way to spectacular terrorist attacks, Western invasions of Muslim countries, and new concern about Muslims living in the West. Unfortunately, we lack the perspective and the full range of source materials that future historians will have at their disposal. Yet we are deeply involved in this momentous historical drama, and we must try to find insight and understanding.

The al-Qaeda Attack of September 11, 2001

On the morning of September 11, 2001, two hijacked passenger planes from Boston crashed into and destroyed the World Trade Center towers in New York City. Shortly thereafter a third plane crashed into the Pentagon, and a fourth, believed to be headed for Washington, crashed into a field in rural Pennsylvania. These terrorist attacks took the lives of more than three thousand people from many countries.

The United States, led by President George W. Bush, launched a military campaign to destroy the perpetrators of the crime—Osama bin Laden's al-Qaeda network of terrorists and Afghanistan's reactionary Muslim government, the Taliban. With the support of an international coalition, the United States joined its tremendous airpower with the faltering Northern Alliance in Afghanistan, which had been fighting the Taliban for years. In mid-November the Taliban collapsed, and Afghan opposition leaders and United Nations mediators worked out plans for a new broad-based government. The hunt for bin Laden, however, was unsuccessful.

The use of terrorist tactics by organized groups against governments has its roots in the early twentieth century. Beginning in the 1920s and peaking in the 1960s, many nationalist movements used terrorism in their battles to achieve political independence and decolonization. This was the case in several new states, including Algeria, Cyprus, Ireland, Israel, and Yemen.[1] In the Vietnam War era, a second wave of terrorism saw some far-left supporters of the communist Vietcong, such as the American Weathermen, the German Red Army Faction, and the Italian Red Brigade, practicing "revolutionary terror." They added airplane hijacking to the earlier tactics of bombings, assassinations, and kidnappings. More than one hundred passenger planes a year were hijacked in the 1970s, as terrorists used civilian hostages to achieve the release of fellow terrorists or other demands. Some terrorists trained in the facilities of the PLO (the Palestine Liberation Organization) operated international networks and targeted Israel and U.S. installations abroad. This second wave receded in the 1980s as painstaking police work and international cooperation defeated these "revolutionaries" in country after country.

Scholars of the contemporary wave of terrorism have avoided the media's tendency to focus almost exclusively on extreme Islamic fundamentalism as the motivation for attacks. They have noted that recent deadly attacks had been committed by terrorists inspired by several religious faiths and religious sects and

al-Qaeda A terrorist organization led by Osama bin Laden that is committed to jihadist revolution in Muslim countries, violently anti-Western, and responsible for the September 11, 2001, attack on New York's World Trade Center.

New York, September 11, 2001
Pedestrians race for safety as the World Trade Center towers collapse after being hit by jet airliners.
Al-Qaeda terrorists with box cutters hijacked four aircraft and used three of them as suicide missiles
to perpetrate their unthinkable crime. Heroic passengers on the fourth plane realized what was
happening and forced their hijackers to crash in a field. (AP Images/Suzanne Plunkett)

were by no means limited to Islamic extremists.[2] Instead they trace the terrorists'
roots to political conflicts and civil wars.

In the case of Osama bin Laden and al-Qaeda members, two stages stand out.
First, bin Laden and like-minded "holy warriors" developed terrorist skills and a
fanatical Islamic puritanism over years of fighting against the Soviet Union and
local communists in Afghanistan. They also developed a hatred of most existing
Arab governments, which they viewed as corrupt, un-Islamic, and unresponsive to
the needs of ordinary Muslims. The objects of their hostility included Egypt, Iraq,
and bin Laden's native country, Saudi Arabia. Second, when al-Qaeda members
returned home from Afghanistan and began to organize, they were usually jailed
or forced into exile, often in tolerant Europe. There they blamed the United States
for being the supporter and corrupter of existing Arab governments, and they
organized murderous plots against the United States—a despised proxy for the
Arab rulers they could not reach.

The War in Iraq

Unfortunately, Western unity in Afghanistan soon
turned into bitter quarreling and international crisis
over the prospect of war with Iraq. Many in the Bush
administration believed that the United States could create a democratic, pro-
American Iraq, an Iraq that would transform the Middle East, make peace with
Israel, and ensure access to the world's second-largest oil reserves. They publicly

argued that Saddam Hussein was still developing weapons of mass destruction in flagrant disregard of his promise to end all such programs following the first war with Iraq, in 1991.

Iraq declared that it had destroyed all prohibited weapons, and it allowed United Nations weapons inspectors to return to the country. As 2003 opened, the inspectors operated freely in Iraq and found no weapons of mass destruction. However, the United States and Britain said Iraq was hiding prohibited weapons, moved armies to the Middle East, and lobbied for a new United Nations resolution authorizing immediate military action against Iraq. France, Russia, China, Germany, and a majority of the smaller states argued for continued weapons inspections. Western governments became bitterly divided, and the Security Council deadlocked and failed to act.

In March 2003 the United States and Britain invaded Iraq from bases in Kuwait and quickly toppled Saddam's dictatorship. The allies found no weapons of mass destruction, which raised many questions about a prewar manipulation of intelligence data.

American efforts to establish a stable, pro-American Iraq proved difficult if not impossible. Poor postwar planning and management by President Bush, Defense Secretary Donald Rumsfeld, and other top aides was one factor, but there were others. Modern Iraq, a creation of Western imperialism after World War I (see page 720), is a fragile state with three distinct groups: non-Arab Kurds, and Sunnis and Shi'ites—Arab Muslims who were forever divided by a great schism in the seventh century. Saddam's dictatorship preached Arab and Iraqi nationalism, but it relied heavily on the Sunni minority—20 percent of the population—and repressed the Shi'ites, who made up 60 percent of the population. Jailed or ousted from their positions by American forces for having supported Saddam, top Sunnis quickly turned against the occupation, rallied their supporters, and launched an armed insurgency. By late 2004, radical Sunnis and al-Qaeda converts were

The Golden Mosque of Samara: Before and After
Built to commemorate two of Shi'ite Islam's most revered saints, the Golden Mosque drew countless Shi'ite pilgrims. Then, on June 13, 2006, insurgents dressed as Iraqi policemen entered the mosque, overwhelmed the guards, and detonated two bombs that collapsed the golden dome and destroyed the mosque. Sectarian conflict exploded. (A second terrorist bombing in June 2007 leveled the two minarets seen on the right.) (AP Images/Khalid Mohammed, Hameed Rasheed)

slipping into Iraq, where they directed horrendous suicide bombings at American soldiers, Iraqi security forces, and defenseless Shi'ite civilians.

Believing in democracy and representative institutions, the Americans restored Iraqi sovereignty in July 2004, formed a provisional government, and held relatively free national elections in January 2005. Boycotted by the Sunnis, these elections brought the Shi'ite majority to power and marked the high point of Iraqi and American hopes for security and a gradual reconciliation with the Sunni population. Instead, Sunni fighters and jihadist (ji-HAHD-ist) extremists stepped up their deadly campaign. Then, in February 2005 in a carefully planned operation, they blew up the beautiful Golden Mosque of Samarra, one of the most sacred shrines of Shi'ite Islam. This outrage touched off violent retaliation. Shi'ite militias became death squads, killing Sunnis and driving them from their homes. By 2006 a deadly sectarian conflict had taken hold of Baghdad. American solders, loyally continuing to do their duty, were increasingly caught in the crossfire.

In 2007, in the face of widespread American opposition to the war, President Bush ordered more troops to Iraq in an attempt to quell the growing chaos. American commanders on the ground succeeded in forming a critical alliance with some Sunni tribal leaders, who accepted American money and arms and agreed to fight against rather than for the al-Qaeda–led Sunni extremists. As 2008 opened, the military situation in some Sunni provinces and in Baghdad had improved, but Iraq was still very far from peace, stable government, and American withdrawal.

The West and Its Muslim Citizens

After the attacks of September 11, the people of the United States braced for further terrorist acts. But instead Europe was next to receive the extremists' blows. In May 2004 Moroccan Muslims living in Spain exploded bombs planted on morning trains for Madrid and killed 252 commuters. A year later a similar attack was carried out in London by British citizens of Pakistani descent, young men who had grown up in Britain. The brutal murder of filmmaker Theo van Gogh (van GOH) by a young Dutch Muslim avenging van Gogh's satirical depiction of Muhammad seemed to illustrate the depths of Muslim intolerance.

These spectacular attacks and lesser actions by Islamic militants led a shrill chorus to warn that Europe's rapidly growing Muslim population threatened the West's entire Enlightenment tradition of freedom of thought, representative government, toleration, separation of church and state, and, more recently, equal rights for women and gays. Muslim clerics were believed to turn their followers into anti-Western radicals, and even those who urged assimilation were viewed with suspicion. (See the feature "Individuals in Society: Tariq Ramadan.") And time was on the side of Euro-Islam. Europe's Muslim population, estimated at 15 million in 2006, appeared likely to double to 30 million by 2025, and it would increase rapidly thereafter as the percentage of non-Muslim Europeans plummeted because of their baby bust.

Admitting that Islamic extremism could pose a serious challenge, many mainstream observers focused instead on the problem of immigrant integration. Whereas the first generation of Muslim immigrants had found jobs as unskilled workers in Europe's great postwar boom, many Muslims of the second and third generations were finding themselves locked out of work in their adopted countries. This argument was strengthened by widespread rioting in France in November 2005 that saw hundreds of young second- and third-generation Muslim men torch automobiles night after night in Paris suburbs and large cities. (See the feature "Listening to the Past: The French Riots: Will They Change Anything?" on pages

Individuals in Society

Tariq Ramadan

Religious teacher, activist professor, and media star, Tariq Ramadan (b. 1962), is Europe's most famous Muslim intellectual. He is also a controversial figure, praised by many as a moderate bridge-builder and denounced by others as an Islamic militant in clever disguise.

Born in Switzerland of Egyptian ancestry, Ramadan is the grandson of Hassan al-Banna, the charismatic founder of the powerful Muslim Brotherhood. Al-Banna fought to reshape Arab nationalism within a framework of Islamic religious orthodoxy and anti-British terrorism until he himself was assassinated in 1949. Growing up in Geneva, where his father sought refuge in 1954 after Nasser's anti-Islamic crackdown in Egypt, the young Tariq attended mainstream public schools, played soccer, and absorbed a wide-ranging Islamic heritage. For example, growing up fluent in French and Arabic, he learned English mainly from listening to Pakistani Muslims discuss issues with his father, who represented the Muslim Brotherhood and its ideology in Europe.

Ramadan studied philosophy and French literature as an undergraduate at the University of Geneva, and he then earned a doctorate in Arabic and Islamic Studies. Marrying a Swiss woman who converted to Islam, Ramadan moved his family to Cairo in 1991 to study Islamic law and philosophy. It proved to be a pivotal experience. Eagerly anticipating the return to his Muslim roots, Ramadan gradually realized that only in Europe did he feel truly "at home." In his personal experience he found his message: that Western Muslims should feel equally "at home" and that they should participate fully as active citizens in their adopted countries.

In developing his message, Ramadan left the classroom and focused on creating non-scholarly books, audio cassettes that sell in the tens of thousands, and media events. Slim and elegant in well-tailored suits and open collars, Ramadan is a brilliant speaker. His public lectures in French and English draw hundreds of Muslims (and curious non-Muslims).

Ramadan argues that Western Muslims basically live in security, have fundamental legal rights, and can freely practice their religion. He notes that Muslims in the West are often more secure than are believers in the Muslim world, where governments are frequently repressive and arbitrary. According to Ramadan, Islamic teaching requires Western Muslims to obey Western laws, although in rare cases they may need to plead "conscientious objection" and disobey on religious grounds. Becoming full citizens and refusing to live in parallel as the foreign Other, Muslims should work with non-Muslims on matters of common concern, such as mutual respect, better schools, and economic justice.[*] Ramadan is most effective with second- or third-generation college graduates. He urges them to think for themselves and distinguish the sacred revelation of Islam from the nonessential cultural aspects that their parents brought from African and Asian villages.

Tariq Ramadan.
(AP Images/Keystone/
Salvatore Di Nolfi)

With growing fame has come growing controversy. In 2004, preparing to take up a professorship in the United States, he was denied an entry visa on the grounds that he had contributed to a Palestinian charity with ties to terrorists. Defenders disputed the facts and charged that his criticism of Israeli policies and the invasion of Iraq were the real reasons. Ramadan's critics also claim that he says different things to different groups: hard-edged criticism of the West found on tapes for Muslims belies the reasoned moderation of his books. Some critics also argue that his recent condemnation of Western capitalism and globalization is an opportunistic attempt to win favor with European leftists, and does not reflect a self-proclaimed Islamic passion for justice. Yet, on balance, Ramadan's reputation remains intact.[†] An innovative bridge-builder, he symbolizes the growing importance of Europe's Muslim citizens.

Questions for Analysis

1. What is Ramadan's message to Western Muslims? How did he reach his conclusions?
2. Do you think Ramadan's ideas are realistic? Why?

[*]See, especially, Tariq Ramadan, *Western Muslims and the Future of Islam* (Oxford: Oxford University Press, 2004).
[†]See Ian Buruma, *The New York Times Magazine*, February 4, 2007.

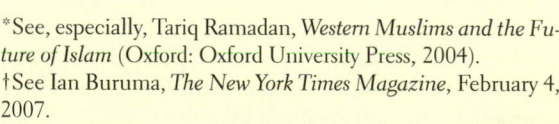

Section Review

- The terrorist attacks on the United States on September 11, 2001, motivated by al-Qaeda's hatred of Arab governments supported by the West, inspired a U.S. military campaign against Osama bin Laden's al-Qaeda network and Afghanistan's Muslim government, the Taliban.

- The United States and Britain invaded Iraq without United Nations sanction under the pretense of finding weapons of mass destruction, which they failed to find, and in their attempt at setting up a pro-Western government, touched off a civil war between opposing Muslim groups, with American soldiers caught in the middle.

- Discrimination and fear of Muslims increased as the war in Iraq waged, while Muslim immigrant populations in Europe grew and complained of unfair treatment; acceptance of European Muslims is the way to mutual understanding and the prevention of future violence.

838–839.) The rioters complained bitterly of very high unemployment, systematic discrimination, and exclusion. Religious ideology appeared almost nonexistent in their thinking. Studies sparked by the rioting in France found poor, alienated Muslims in unwholesome ghettos throughout western Europe.

Finally, as Europe has become more secular, western Europeans have tended to find all traditional religious belief irrational and out-of-date. The renowned French scholar Olivier Roy argues that Europe must recognize that Islam is now a European religion and a vital part of European life. This recognition, he argues, will open the way to eventual full acceptance of European Muslims in both political and cultural terms. It will head off the resentment that can drive Europe's Muslim believers to separatism and acts of terror.

Chapter Review

How did Mikhail Gorbachev try to revitalize communism in the Soviet Union? What were the radical consequences of his policies? (page 811)

Gorbachev was an idealist who wanted to reform communism in order to save it. His initiatives sought to restructure the stagnant economy, provide accurate information, have meaningful elections, and improve relations with the West. When he refused to use Soviet armies in eastern Europe, the peoples of the satellite nations revolted. Led by Solidarity in Poland, they overturned communist rule in the spectacular, peaceful revolutions of 1989. The democratic movement then triumphed in the Soviet Union, East Germany was reunited with West Germany, and the cold war ended. Emerging as the only superpower, the United States defeated Iraq in the first Gulf war.

How, in the 1990s, did the different parts of a reunifying Europe meet the challenges of postcommunist reconstruction, resurgent nationalism, and economic union? (page 820)

In the 1990s, post–cold war Europe grappled with neoliberal market economies, welfare systems under continuing attack, and globalization. Post-communist reconstruction in Russia was less successful than it was in the newly independent countries of eastern Europe. The former Yugoslavia, tragically destroyed by resurgent ethnic nationalism and civil war, was the glaring exception. Eastern Europe's rebuilding and its determination to "rejoin Europe" stimulated the long postwar movement toward European unity, and the newly named European Union expanded to include almost all of Europe west of Russia, Ukraine, and the Caucasus. This expansion was the shining achievement of the post–cold war era.

Key Terms

perestroika (p. 813)

glasnost (p. 813)

Solidarity (p. 814)

shock therapy (p. 815)

Alliance for Germany (p. 816)

Velvet Revolution (p. 816)

Paris Accord (p. 817)

"new world order" (p. 819)

globalization (p. 822)

European Union (p. 824)

Kosovo Liberation Army (KLA) (p. 826)

baby bust (p. 828)

al-Qaeda (p. 831)

> Why did the prospect of population decline, the reality of large-scale immigration, and concern for human rights emerge as critical issues in contemporary Europe? (page 828)

The failure of Europeans to reproduce themselves posed a multitude of serious long-term problems related to pensions, health care, and social vitality. Immigrants fleeing civil war and poverty in Africa and Asia offered a possible solution to Europe's "baby bust," but most Europeans were not prepared to accept large numbers of illegal immigrants from very different cultures. Forced to examine their consciences, Europeans concentrated on promoting human rights around the world, agreeing to humanitarian intervention in civil wars, promoting international courts of justice, and offering help to African nations for the AIDS crisis.

> How and why did relations between the West and the Islamic world deteriorate dramatically in the early twenty-first century? (page 831)

The most disturbing development in the early twenty-first century was the renewed hostility between the West and the Islamic world, which was marked indelibly by the al-Qaeda attack of 2001, the American campaign to punish Afghanistan, and the American and British invasion of Iraq. The Anglo-American occupation of Iraq began as a confident effort to remake Iraq (and the Arab world) along Western lines, but early optimism quickly faded. American soldiers in Iraq ran up against a potent combination of Arab nationalism, Islamic extremism, and sectarian conflict between Sunnis, Shi'ites, and Kurds. In western Europe, war in the Middle East encouraged shrill cries about an ominous Muslin threat from immigrants living in western Europe, but a thoughtful consideration of Tariq Ramadan and his audience suggests that these fears were greatly exaggerated.

Notes

1. D. Rappaport, "The Fourth Wave: September 11 in the History of Terrorism," *Current History*, December 2001, pp. 419–424.
2. Ibid.

To assess your mastery of this chapter, go to **bedfordstmartins.com/mckaywestbrief**

Listening to the Past

The French Riots: Will They Change Anything?

In late November 2005, young Muslim males rioted for several nights in the suburbs of Paris and other French cities. Intensely reported, this explosion of car-burning and arson ignited controversy and debate throughout France and across Europe. What caused the riots? What could, what should, be done? How did the conditions of second- and third-generation Muslims in France compare with conditions of Muslims in other Western countries? One penetrating commentary, aimed at an American audience and reprinted here, came from William Pfaff, a noted author and political columnist with many years of European experience.

French police face off with young rioters, silhouetted against the frames of burning automobiles. (Reuters/Corbis)

The rioting in France's ghetto suburbs is a phenomenon of futility—but a revelation nonetheless. It has no ideology and no purpose other than to make a statement of distress and anger. It is beyond politics. It broke out spontaneously and spread in the same way, communicated by televised example, ratified by the huge attention it won from the press and television and the politicians, none of whom had any idea what to do. . . .

[The rioters'] grandfathers came to France, mostly from North Africa, to do the hard labor in France's industrial reconstruction after the Second World War. Their fathers saw the work gradually dry up as Europe's economies slowed, following the first oil shock in the early 1970s. After that came unemployment. The unemployment rate in the zones where there has been the most violence is nearly 40 percent and among young people it is higher. Many of the young men in these places have never been offered a job. When they applied, their names often excluded them.

Their grandfathers were hard-working men. Their fathers saw their manhood undermined by unemployment. These young men are doomed to be boys. They often take their frustration out on their sisters and girlfriends, who are more likely to have done well in school and found jobs—and frequently a new life—outside the ghetto. . . .

The Muslim mothers and wives of the French ghetto are often confined in the home. Drugs are big business in the American ghetto; they are not that big in France. The crimes of the French ghetto are robbery and shoplifting, stealing mobile phones, stealing cars for joyrides, burning them afterward to eliminate fingerprints, or burning cars just for the hell of it, as well as robbing middle-class students in the city and making trouble on suburban trains, looking for excitement.

Religion is important . . . in the French ghetto, it provides the shell that protects against the France that excludes Muslims. To the European Muslim, it seems that all of the powerful in the world are in collusion to exclude Muslims—or are at war with them. The war in Iraq, on television, is the constant backdrop to Muslim life in Europe. There are itinerant imams who can put the young ghetto Muslim on the road to danger and adventure in Afghanistan, Pakistan, Iraq—or elsewhere. There are plenty more who preach a still deeper ghettoization: a retreat inside Islamic fundamentalism, totally shutting out a diabolized secular world.

One would think there would be a revolutionary potential in these ghettos, vulnerability to a mobilizing ideology. This seems not to be so. We may be living in a religious age, but it is not one at political ideology. In any case, it is difficult to imagine how the marginalized, thirteen- to twenty-three-year-old children of the Muslim immigration could change France other than by what they are doing, which is to demonstrate that the French model of assimilating immigrants as citizens, and not as members of religious or ethnic groups, has failed for them. It has failed because it has not seriously been tried.

The ghettoization of immigrant youth in France is the consequence of negligence. It has been as bad as the ghettoization through political correctness of Muslims in Britain and the Netherlands, where many people who thought of themselves as enlightened said that assimilation efforts were acts of cultural aggression. The immigrant in France is told that he or she is a citizen just like everyone else, with all the rights and privileges of citizenship—including the right to be unemployed.

Questions for Analysis

1. Describe the situation of young Muslims in France. What elements of their situation strike you most forcefully? Why?

2. France has maintained that, since all citizens are equal, they should all be treated the same way. Why has this policy failed for French Muslims? What alternatives would you suggest? Why?

Source: William Pfaff, "The French Riots: Will They Change Anything?" Reprinted with permission from *The New York Review of Books*, December 15, 2005, pp. 88–89.

Index